W9-CTW-249

Contemporary
Literary Criticism

Guide to Gale Literary Criticism Series

For criticism on	Consult these Gale series
Authors now living or who died after December 31, 1959	*CONTEMPORARY LITERARY CRITICISM (CLC)*
Authors who died between 1900 and 1959	*TWENTIETH-CENTURY LITERARY CRITICISM (TCLC)*
Authors who died between 1800 and 1899	*NINETEENTH-CENTURY LITERATURE CRITICISM (NCLC)*
Authors who died between 1400 and 1799	*LITERATURE CRITICISM FROM 1400 TO 1800 (LC)* *SHAKESPEAREAN CRITICISM (SC)*
Authors who died before 1400	*CLASSICAL AND MEDIEVAL LITERATURE CRITICISM (CMLC)*
Black writers of the past two hundred years	*BLACK LITERATURE CRITICISM (BLC) AND BLACK LITERATURE CRITICISM SUPPLEMENT (BLCS)*
Authors of books for children and young adults	*CHILDREN'S LITERATURE REVIEW (CLR)*
Dramatists	*DRAMA CRITICISM (DC)*
Hispanic writers of the late nineteenth and twentieth centuries	*HISPANIC LITERATURE CRITICISM (HLC)*
Native North American writers and orators of the eighteenth, nineteenth, and twentieth centuries	*NATIVE NORTH AMERICAN LITERATURE (NNAL)*
Poets	*POETRY CRITICISM (PC)*
Short story writers	*SHORT STORY CRITICISM (SSC)*
Major authors from the Renaissance to the present	*WORLD LITERATURE CRITICISM, 1500 TO THE PRESENT (WLC)*
Major authors and works from the Bible to the present	*WORLD LITERATURE CRITICISM SUPPLEMENT (WLCS)*

ISSN 0091-3421

Volume 115

Contemporary Literary Criticism

Excerpts from Criticism of the Works
of Today's Novelists, Poets, Playwrights,
Short Story Writers, Scriptwriters, and
Other Creative Writers

Jeffrey W. Hunter
Timothy J. White
EDITORS

Tim Akers
Pamela S. Dear
Catherine V. Donaldson
Daniel Jones
John D. Jorgenson
Jerry Moore
Deborah A. Schmitt
Polly Vedder
Thomas Wiloch
Kathleen Wilson
ASSOCIATE EDITORS

The Gale Group

DETROIT • SAN FRANCISCO • LONDON • BOSTON • WOODBRIDGE, CT

STAFF

Jeffrey W. Hunter. Timothy J. White, *Editors*

Tim Akers, Pamela S. Dear, Catherine V. Donaldson, Daniel Jones, John D. Jorgenson, Jerry Moore,
Deborah A. Schmitt, Polly Vedder, Thomas Wiloch, and Kathleen Wilson, *Associate Editors*

Tracy Arnold-Chapman, Jay Daniel, Linda Quigley,
Paul Serralheiro, and Lynn Spampinato, *Contributing Editors*

Kimberly F. Smilay, *Permissions Specialist*
Steve Cusack, and Kelly Quin, *Permissions Associates*
Sandy Gore, *Permissions Assistant*

Victoria B. Cariappa, *Research Manager*
Julia C. Daniel, Tamara C. Nott, Michele P. Pica, Tracie A. Richardson,
Norma Sawaya, and Cheryl L. Warnock. *Research Associates*
Laura C. Bissey, Alfred A. Gardner I, and Sean R. Smith, *Research Assistants*

Mary Beth Trimper, *Production Director*
Deborah L. Milliken, and Cindy Range, *Production Assistants*

Barbara J. Yarrow, *Graphic Services Manager*
Sherrell Hobbs, *Macintosh Artist*
Randy Bassett, *Image Database Supervisor*
Robert Duncan and Mikal Ansari, *Scanner Operators*
Pamela Reed, *Imaging Coordinator*

Library of Congress Catalog Card Number 76-46132
ISBN 0-7876-3190-6
ISSN 0091-3421

Printed in the United States of America
10 9 8 7 6 5 4 3 2 1

Contents

Preface vii

Acknowledgments xi

Preface

A Comprehensive Information Source
on Contemporary Literature

Named "one of the twenty-five most distinguished reference titles published during the past twenty-five years" by *Reference Quarterly*, the *Contemporary Literary Criticism (CLC)* series provides readers with critical commentary and general information on more than 2,000 authors now living or who died after December 31, 1959. Previous to the publication of the first volume of *CLC* in 1973, there was no ongoing digest monitoring scholarly and popular sources of critical opinion and explication of modern literature. *CLC,* therefore, has fulfilled an essential need, particularly since the complexity and variety of contemporary literature makes the function of criticism especially important to today's reader.

Scope of the Series

CLC presents significant passages from published criticism of works by creative writers. Since many of the authors covered by *CLC* inspire continual critical commentary, writers are often represented in more than one volume. There is, of course, no duplication of reprinted criticism.

Authors are selected for inclusion for a variety of reasons, among them the publication or dramatic production of a critically acclaimed new work, the reception of a major literary award, revival of interest in past writings, or the adaptation of a literary work to film or television.

Attention is also given to several other groups of writers—authors of considerable public interest—about whose work criticism is often difficult to locate. These include mystery and science fiction writers, literary and social critics, foreign writers, and authors who represent particular ethnic groups.

Format of the Book

Each *CLC* volume contains individual essays and reviews taken from hundreds of book review periodicals, general magazines, scholarly journals, monographs, and books. Entries include critical evaluations spanning from the beginning of an author's career to the most current commentary. Interviews, feature articles, and other published writings that offer insight into the author's works are also presented. Students, teachers, librarians, and researchers will find that the generous critical and biographical material in *CLC* provides them with vital information required to write a term paper, analyze a poem, or lead a book discussion group. In addition, complete bibliographical citations note the original source and all of the information necessary for a term paper footnote or bibliography.

Features

A *CLC* author entry consists of the following elements:

- The **Author Heading** cites the author's name in the form under which the author has most commonly published, followed by birth date, and death date when applicable. Uncertainty as to a birth or death date is indicated by a question mark.

- A **Portrait** of the author is included when available.

- A brief **Biographical and Critical Introduction** to the author and his or her work precedes the criticism. The first line of the introduction provides the author's full name, pseudonyms (if applicable), nationality, and a listing of genres in which the author has written. To provide users with easier access to information, the biographical and critical essay included in each author entry is divided into four categories: "Introduction," "Biographical Information," "Major Works," and "Critical Reception." The introductions to single-work entries—entries that focus on well known and frequently studied books, short stories, and poems—are similarly organized to quickly provide readers with information on the plot and major characters of the work being discussed, its major themes, and its critical reception. Previous volumes of *CLC* in which the author has been featured are also listed in the introduction.

- A list of **Principal Works** notes the most important writings by the author. When foreign-language works have been translated into English, the English-language version of the title follows in brackets.

- The **Criticism** represents various kinds of critical writing, ranging in form from the brief review to the scholarly exegesis. Essays are selected by the editors to reflect the spectrum of opinion about a specific work or about an author's literary career in general. The critical and biographical materials are presented chronologically, adding a useful perspective to the entry. All titles by the author featured in the entry are printed in boldface type, which enables the reader to easily identify the works being discussed. Publication information (such as publisher names and book prices) and parenthetical numerical references (such as footnotes or page and line references to specific editions of a work) have been deleted at the editor's discretion to provide smoother reading of the text.

- Critical essays are prefaced by **Explanatory Notes** as an additional aid to readers. These notes may provide several types of valuable information, including: the reputation of the critic, the importance of the work of criticism, the commentator's approach to the author's work, the purpose of the criticism, and changes in critical trends regarding the author.

- A complete **Bibliographical Citation** designed to help the user find the original essay or book precedes each critical piece.

- Whenever possible, a recent **Author Interview** accompanies each entry.

- A concise **Further Reading** section appears at the end of entries on authors for whom a significant amount of criticism exists in addition to the pieces reprinted in *CLC*. Each citation in this section is accompanied by a descriptive annotation describing the content of that article. Materials included in this section are grouped under various headings (e.g., Biography, Bibliography, Criticism, and Interviews) to aid users in their search for additional information. Cross-references to other useful sources published by The Gale Group in which the author has appeared are also included: *Authors in the News, Black Writers, Children's Literature Review, Contemporary Authors, Dictionary of Literary Biography, DISCovering Authors, Drama Criticism, Hispanic Literature Criticism, Hispanic Writers, Native North American Literature, Poetry Criticism, Something about the Author, Short Story Criticism, Contemporary Authors Autobiography Series,* and *Something about the Author Autobiography Series.*

Other Features

CLC also includes the following features:

- An **Acknowledgments** section lists the copyright holders who have granted permission to reprint material in this volume of *CLC*. It does not, however, list every book or periodical reprinted or consulted during the preparation of the volume.

- Each new volume of *CLC* includes a **Cumulative Topic Index,** which lists all literary topics treated in *CLC, NCLC, TCLC,* and *LC 1400-1800.*

- A **Cumulative Author Index** lists all the authors who have appeared in the various literary criticism series published by The Gale Group, with cross-references to Gale's biographical and autobiographical series. A full listing of the series referenced there appears on the first page of the indexes of this volume. Readers will welcome this cumulated author index as a useful tool for locating an author within the various series. The index, which lists birth and death dates when available, will be particularly valuable for those authors who are identified with a certain period but whose death dates cause them to be placed in another, or for those authors whose careers span two periods. For example, Ernest Hemingway is found in *CLC,* yet F. Scott Fitzgerald, a writer often associated with him, is found in *Twentieth-Century Literary Criticism.*

- A **Cumulative Nationality Index** alphabetically lists all authors featured in *CLC* by nationality, followed by numbers corresponding to the volumes in which the authors appear.

- An alphabetical **Title Index** accompanies each volume of *CLC*. Listings are followed by the author's name and the corresponding page numbers where the titles are discussed. English translations of foreign titles and variations of titles are cross-referenced to the title under which a work was originally published. Titles of novels, novellas, dramas, films, record albums, and poetry, short story, and essay collections are printed in italics, while all individual poems, short stories, essays, and songs are printed in roman type within quotation marks; when published separately (e.g., T. S. Eliot's poem *The Waste Land),* the titles of long poems are printed in italics.

- In response to numerous suggestions from librarians, Gale has also produced a **Special Paperbound Edition** of the *CLC* title index. This annual cumulation, which alphabetically lists all titles reviewed in the series, is available to all customers. Additional copies of the index are available upon request. Librarians and patrons will welcome this separate index: it saves shelf space, is easy to use, and is recyclable upon receipt of the next edition.

Citing *Contemporary Literary Criticism*

When writing papers, students who quote directly from any volume in the Literary Criticism Series may use the following general forms to footnote reprinted criticism. The first example pertains to material drawn from periodicals, the second to material reprinted in books:

[1]Alfred Cismaru, "Making the Best of It," *The New Republic,* 207, No. 24, (December 7, 1992), 30, 32; excerpted and reprinted in *Contemporary Literary Criticism,* Vol. 85, ed. Christopher Giroux (Detroit: Gale, 1995), pp. 73-4.

[2]Yvor Winters, *The Post-Symbolist Methods* (Allen Swallow, 1967); excerpted and reprinted in *Contemporary Literary Criticism,* Vol. 85, ed. Christopher Giroux (Detroit: Gale, 1995), pp. 223-26.

Suggestions Are Welcome

The editors hope that readers will find *CLC* a useful reference tool and welcome comments about the work. Send comments and suggestions to: Editors, *Contemporary Literary Criticism,* The Gale Group, 27500 Drake Rd., Farmington Hills, MI 48333-3535.

Acknowledgments

The editors wish to thank the copyright holders of the criticism included in this volume and the permissions managers of many book and magazine publishing companies for assisting us in securing reproduction rights. We are also grateful to the staffs of the Detroit Public Library, the Library of Congress, the University of Detroit Mercy Library, Wayne State University Purdy/Kresge Library Complex, and the University of Michigan Libraries for making their resources available to us. Following is a list of the copyright holders who have granted us permission to reproduce material in this volume of CLC. Every effort has been made to trace copyright, but if omissions have been made, please let us know.

COPYRIGHTED MATERIAL IN *CLC*, VOLUME 115, WAS REPRODUCED FROM THE FOLLOWING PERIODICALS:

The American Book Review, v.10, May-June, 1988; v. 17, February-March, 1996. © 1988, 1996 by The American Book Review. Both reproduced by permission.—*American Studies*, v. 30, Spring, 1989 for "Lake Wobegon: Mythical Place and the American Imagination" by Stephen Wilbers. Copyright © Mid-American Studies Association, 1989. Reproduced by permission of the publisher and the author.—*Belles Lettres: A Review of Books by Women,* v. 5, Spring, 1990; v.8, Fall, 1992; v. 9, Spring, 1994. All reproduced by permission.—*Black American Literature Forum,* v. 21, Winter, 1987 for "Amiri Baraka on Directing" by Sandra G. Shannon. Copyright © 1987 Indiana State University. Reproduced by permission of Indiana State University and the author.—*The Canadian Fiction Magazine,* n. 47, 1983. Copyright © 1983 by *The Canadian Fiction Magazine*. Reproduced by permission of the author.—*Canadian Literature,* n. 132, Spring, 1992 for "Eyre and Anglos" by Gary Boire. Reproduced by permission of the author—*The Centennial Review,* v. 31, Fall, 1987 for "The Distance Between Gopher Prairie and Lake Wobegon: Sinclair Lewis and Garrison Keillor on the Small Town Experience" by John E. Miller. © 1987 by *The Centennial Review*. Reproduced by permission of the publisher and the author.—*The Christian Science Monitor,* v. 86, January 26, 1994. © 1994 The Christian Science Monitor Publishing Society. All rights reserved. Reproduced by permission from *The Christian Science Monitor.—The Classical Journal,* v. 39, March, 1996. Reproduced by permission of the publisher.—*Colby Library Quarterly,* v. 24, September, 1988. Reproduced by permission of the publisher.—*Colby Quarterly,* v. 32, June, 1996. Reproduced by permission.—*Commonweal,* v. CI, January, 3 1975; v. 119, April 10, 1992. Copyright © 1975, 1992 by the Commonweal Publishing Co. Both reproduced by permission of Commonweal foundation.—*Comparative Drama,* v. VII, Fall, 1973. © copyright 1973, by the Editors of Comparative Drama. Reproduced by permission—*Contemporary Literature,* v. 34, Summer, 1993; v. 35, Spring, 1994. © 1993, 1994 by the Board of Regents of the University of Wisconsin. Both reproduced by permission of The University of Wisconsin Press.— *Critique,* v. XI, 1969. Copyright © by the 1969 Helen Dwight Reid Educational Foundation. Reproduced with permission of the Helen Dwight Reid Educational Foundation, published by Heldref Publications, 1319 18th Street, NW, Washington, DC 20036-1802.—*Critique: Studies in Contemporary Fiction,* v. XXXIV, Fall, 1992. Copyright © 1992 by the Helen Dwight Reid Educational Foundation. Reproduced with permission of the Helen Dwight Reid Educational Foundation, published by Heldref Publications, 119 18th Street, N. W., Washington, DC 20036-1802.—*Critique: Studies in Modern Fiction,* v. XXIV, Spring, 1983;v. 26,Fall, 1984. Copyright © 1983, 1984 by the Helen Dwight Reid Educational Foundation. Both reproduced with permission of the Helen Dwight Reid Educational Foundation, published by Heldref Publications, 1319 18th Street, NW, Washington, DC 20036-1802.—*Denver Quarterly,* v. 20, Fall, 1985 for "'Into the Bladelike Arms of God': The Quest for Meaning Through Symbolic Language in Thoreau and Annie Dillard" by Mary Davidson McConahay. Copyright © 1985 by the University of Denver. Reproduced by permission of the publisher.—*English Journal,* v. 78, December, 1989 for "Fellow Rebels: Annie Dillard and Maxine Hong Kingston" by Joan Bischoff. Copyright © 1989 by the National Council of Teachers of English. Reproduced by permission of the publisher and the author.—*English Studies in Canada,* v. 21, June, 1995 for "Producing Visability for Lesbians: Nicole Brossard's Quantum Poetics" by Barbara Godard. © Association of Canadian University Teachers of English 1995. Reproduced by permission of the publisher and the author.—*Essays on Canadian Writing,* n. 7/8, Fall,1977; n. 61, Spring, 1997. © 1977, 1997 by Essays on Canadian Writing Ltd. Both reproduced by permission.—*Essays in Literature,* v. XIX, Spring, 1992. Copyright 1992 by Western Illinois University. Reproduced by permission.—*The*

Amiri Baraka

1934-

(Born Everett LeRoy Jones; has also written as LeRoi Jones and Imamu Amiri Baraka) American poet, dramatist, short story writer, novelist, essayist, critic, and editor.

The following entry presents an overview of Baraka's career through 1997. For further information on his life and works, see *CLC,* Volumes 1, 2, 3, 5, 10, 14, and 33.

INTRODUCTION

A seminal figure in the development of contemporary black literature, Baraka is a controversial writer. His career has encompassed the Beat movement, black nationalism, and the tenets of Marxist-Leninist philosophy, and his verse is imbued with such concerns as cultural alienation, racial tension and conflict, and the necessity for social change through revolutionary means. According to some scholars, he succeeded James Baldwin and Richard Wright as one of the most prolific and persistent critics of post-World War II America. Having rejected Western values, Baraka endeavors to create art with a firm didactic purpose: to forge a viable art form that reflects the true values of the African-American community and of oppressed peoples throughout the world.

Biographical Information

Born in 1934 as Everett LeRoy Jones in Newark, New Jersey, Baraka spent his early childhood creating comic strips and writing science fiction. At school Baraka excelled in his studies, graduating from high school at the age of fifteen. He enrolled in Howard University in 1952 and just before beginning his first year, started spelling his name LeRoi. At Howard, Baraka studied with such noted black scholars as E. Franklin Frazier, Nathan A. Scott, Jr., and Sterling A. Brown who is regarded as the patriarch of African-American literary critics. Despite these exceptional teachers, Baraka found Howard University stifling and flunked out in 1954. He then joined the United States Air Force. In 1957, after being dishonorably discharged, he moved to New York's Greenwich Village and became part of the Beat movement. That same year he married Hettie Roberta Cohen and together they founded *Yugen,* a magazine forum for Beat poetry. During the next few years, he also established himself as a music critic, writing about jazz for *downbeat, Metronome,* and the *Jazz Review.* Baraka first received critical acclaim as a poet, for his collection *Preface to a Twenty Volume Suicide Note. . . . ,* which was published in 1961. In 1960, Baraka was invited to Cuba by the New York chapter of the Fair Play for Cuba Committee. Baraka began to make it his life's work to incorporate his political, social, and spiritual beliefs into his writing. No longer content with art for art's sake, Baraka would use poetry and drama to teach people, opening their eyes to reality as he saw it. Following the murder of Black Muslim leader Malcolm X in 1965, Baraka divorced his white, Jewish wife and moved to Harlem. He dissociated from white people and dedicated himself to creating works that were inspired by and spoke to the African-American community. This same year, he founded the Black Arts Repertory Theatre/School in Harlem. He married Sylvia Robinson (she later changed her name to Amina Baraka), a black woman, in 1966. Around this time, Baraka's hatred of whites peaked. When a white woman asked him what whites could do to help blacks, he retorted, "You can help by dying. You are a cancer." In 1968 he converted to Islam and changed his name to Imamu Amiri Baraka, meaning "blessed spiritual leader." In 1974, in another radical shift, Baraka dropped the spiritual title of Imamu and declared himself an adherent of Marxist-Leninist thought. Rejecting Black Nationalism as racist in its implications, he now advocated socialism as a viable solution to the problems in America. He also repudiated his past anti-Semitic and anti-white statements. He concluded: "Nationalism, so-called, when it says 'all non-blacks are our enemies,' is sickness or criminality, in fact a form of fascism." In the fall of 1979, he joined the Africana Studies Department at State University of New York at Stony Brook as a teacher of creative writing. In 1979, as reported by William J. Harris in his 1985 retrospective study of Baraka and his work, "[Baraka] was arrested after two policemen allegedly attempted to intercede in a dispute between him and his wife over the price of children's shoes." While serving his sentence at a Harlem halfway house, Baraka wrote *The Autobiography of LeRoi Jones* (1984). Since then he has written "Why's/Wise" (1985), an epic poem; *The Music: Reflections on Jazz and Blues* (1987) with his wife Amina Baraka; and "Reflections" (1988), a poem published in the periodical *Black Scholar*.

Major Works

A sense of rebellion is the one consistent theme throughout Baraka's canon. Following the Beats' abandonment of traditional poetic structure and adopting their free use of slang, Baraka earned praise and respect as a poet with his first volume of poetry, *Preface to a Twenty Volume Suicide Note. . . .* This volume reflects the influence of "Howl" author Allen Ginsberg's poetry and Charles Olson's projective verse theory, which rejects closed, traditional forms in favor of what Olson termed "composition by field." In this collection, Baraka satirizes various aspects of post-World War II popular culture, particularly the heroic cowboys and comic book superheroes. The majority of the poems, however, discuss concerns typical of the bohemian milieu Baraka identified with, including themes of dislocation and detachment from mainstream society. Also in 1961, Baraka published *Cuba Libre,* an essay describing his trip to Cuba to join in the anniversary celebration of Fidel Castro's first revolutionary attempt. During this period of Baraka's metamorphosis from literary bohemian to black nationalist, he published some of his best-known works, including an analysis of contemporary black music, *Blues People. . . . Negro Music in White America* (1963), and a second volume of poetry, *The Dead Lecturer* (1964). Although Baraka wrote a number of plays during this period, *Dutchman* (1964) is widely considered his masterpiece. The play received the Obie Award for best Off-Broadway play and brought Baraka to the attention of the American public. Involving a conflict between a black middle-class college student and a flirtatious white woman, *Dutchman* is said to mark the emergence of Baraka's heightened racial awareness. *The Slave* (1964) also demonstrates the philosophical change Baraka was undergoing. This play revolves around a black revolutionary leader who confronts his ex-wife and her husband, both of whom are white. Another 1964 drama, *The Toilet,* concerned a white homosexual boy who is beaten up by a gang of black boys.

After Baraka severed all of his ties with white people and culture, his writings, with increasingly violent overtones, called for blacks to unite and establish their own nation. Experimenting with ritual forms in his drama, he penned *Slave Ship* (1967), a recreation of the wretched circumstances experienced by enslaved Africans during their passage to America. Other works written during Baraka's black nationalist period are *The System of Dante's Hell* (1965), his only novel, and *Tales* (1967), a collection of short stories. After Baraka aligned himself with the socialist philosophy, his works began to call for a working-class revolt against the bourgeoisie. Baraka's works in this vein include *Hard Facts: Excerpts* (1975), a volume of poetry that includes several poems which accuse well-known black artists and activists of self-promotion—disguised as nationalism—at the expense of working class African Americans. Baraka's dramas since 1974, including *S-1* (1978), *The Motion of History* (1978), and *The Sidney Poet Heroical* (1979), reflect his commitments to Marxist-Leninist-Maoist thought and Communism. *S-1* and *The Motion of History* are reminiscent of the agit-prop dramas of the 1930s, particularly in their appeals to working-class solidarity and in their suggestion that working class revolution is society's only hope.

Critical Reception

Baraka's first volume of poetry, *Preface to a Twenty Volume Suicide Note. . . .,* met with general approval for its unconventional style and language. Critics would later observe that this is the only work of Baraka's that is "free from ethnic torment." *Dutchman,* Baraka's most widely studied and well received work, was acknowledged by Norman Mailer as "the best play in America." While some critics praised *Dutchman* for its "power," "freshness," and "deadly wit," others expressed outrage at its language, what they perceived as its perpetuation of interracial hostility, and its portrayal of whites. Baraka's next plays, *The Slave* and *The Toilet,* also met with mixed reviews. The latter play was described by one reviewer as an "obscene, scatological, bloody confrontation of the races in a school lavatory." Critic C. W. E. Bigsby called it "a barely stageable homosexual fantasy in which the setting is a urinal and the theme of the sexual nature of violence and the degradation of the white world." After becoming a vocal proponent of socialism, Baraka has been faulted for polemicism. In his study, Harris observed that assessment of Baraka has fallen into two general camps: "The white response . . . has been either silence or anger—and, in a few cases, sadness. . . . One general complaint is that Baraka has forsaken art for politics. . . . Another common accusation holds that Baraka used to be a good poet before he became a virulent racist. The reaction to Baraka in most of the black world has been very different from that in the white. In the black world Baraka is a famous artist. He is regarded as a father by the younger generation of poets; he is quoted in the streets—a fame almost never claimed by an American poet. . . ." Many critics maintain that audiences bristle at Baraka's depictions of "white America," because he mirrors the ugly and hideous facets of American society.

PRINCIPAL WORKS

*A Good Girl Is Hard to Find (drama) 1958

*Cuba Libre (essay) 1961

*Dante (drama) 1961; also produced as *The Eighth Ditch,* 1964

*Preface to a Twenty Volume Suicide Note. . . . (poetry) 1961

*Blues People: Negro Music in White America (essay) 1963

*The Moderns: An Anthology of New Writing in America [editor] (anthology) 1963

*The Baptism (drama) 1964

*The Dead Lecturer: Poems (poetry) 1964

*Dutchman (drama) 1964

*The Slave (drama) 1964

*The Toilet (drama) 1964

*Experimental Death Unit #1 (drama) 1965

*J-E-L-L-O (drama) 1965

*The System of Dante's Hell (novel) 1965

*A Black Mass (drama) 1966

*Home: Social Essays (essays) 1966

Baptism (drama) 1966

Black Art (poetry) 1967

Black Music (essay) 1967

Madheart: A Morality Play (drama) 1967

Slave Ship: A Historical Pageant (drama) 1967

Tales (short stories) 1967

Black Spring (screenplay) 1968

Home on the Range (drama) 1968

Police (drama) 1968

Black Magic: Sabotage, Target Study, Black Art; Collected Poetry, 1961-1967 (poetry) 1969

Bloodrites (drama) 1970

It's Nation Time (poetry) 1970

Junkies Are Full of SHHH . . . (drama) 1970

A Fable (screenplay) 1971

Raise, Race, Rays, Raze: Essays since 1965 (essays) 1971

Strategy and Tactics of a Pan-African Nationalist Party (essay) 1971

Supercoon (screenplay) 1971

Spirit Reach (poetry) 1972

Afrikan Revolution (poetry) 1973

A Recent Killing (drama) 1973

Hard Facts: Excerpts (poetry) 1975

Sidnee Poet Heroical or If In Danger of Suit, The Kid Poet Heroical (drama) 1975

Three Books by Imamu Amiri Baraka (LeRoi Jones): The System of Dante's Hell, Tales, The Dead Lecturer (novel, short stories, and poetry) 1975

S-1 (drama) 1976

America More or Less (musical) 1976

The Motion of History (drama) 1977

AM/TRAK (poetry) 1979

Selected Plays and Prose of Amiri Baraka/LeRoi Jones (dramas and prose) 1979

Selected Poetry of Amiri Baraka/LeRoi Jones (poetry) 1979

The Sidnee Poet Heroical: In 29 Scenes (drama) 1979

Spring Song (poetry) 1979

What Was the Relationship of the Lone Ranger to the Means of Production?: A Play in One Act (drama) 1979

"Confessions of a Former Anti-Semite" (essay) 1980; published in periodical *Village Voice*

In the Tradition: For Black Arthur Blythe (poetry) 1980

Boy and Tarzan Appear in a Clearing! (drama) 1981

"Sounding" (poetry) 1982; published in periodical *Black American Literature Forum*

The Autobiography of LeRoi Jones (autobiography) 1984

Daggers and Javelins: Essays, 1974-79 (essays) 1984

"Wailers" (poem) 1985; published in periodical *Callaloo*

"Why's/Wise" (poem) 1985; published in periodical *Southern Review*

The Music: Reflections on Jazz and Blues [with Amina Baraka] (essay) 1987

"Reflections" (poem) 1988; published in periodical *Black Scholar*

Wise, Why's, Y'z (poetry) 1995

Transbluency: The Selected Poems of Amiri Baraka/LeRoi Jones (1961-1995) (poetry) 1996

*Published under the name LeRoi Jones.

CRITICISM

Amiri Baraka (as LeRoi Jones) with David Ossman (interview date 1963)

SOURCE: An interview in *The Sullen Art: Interviews by David Ossman with Modern American Poets,* Corinth Books, 1963, pp. 77-81.

[*In the following interview, Baraka discusses his magazine,* Yugen, *his poetry, and his various literary influences.*]

Jones published only two more issues of *Yugen* after his interview was recorded early in 1960. Since then, he has co-edited **The Floating Bear** and has seen Corinth's publication of his first book of poems, **Preface to a Twenty Volume Suicide Note,** in association with his own Totem Press. Morrow has scheduled his study, **Blues, Black & White America** and Grove will do his **System of Dante's Inferno.** He continues working on prose, plays and on poems for a second collection.

[*Ossman:*] *Yours seems to be one of the three or four "clique" magazines around today, in that it publishes a fairly restricted group of so-called "beat," "San Francisco" and New York writers. Why do you publish this group—this "stable" of writers?*

[Baraka:] Well, it does seem to fall that way. But for a long time Dr. Williams couldn't get into the *Hudson Review,* and several other mature, older poets like Kenneth Patchen were never admitted there or in magazines like the *Partisan Review* or *Sewanee.* If those editors had a literary point of view in excluding their work, then I feel I have as much right, certainly, to base my choice on my literary taste. If it seems like a coterie—well, it turns out to be that way. There are other reasons—but that's the simplest explanation, actually.

The writers that I publish are really not all "beat" or "San Francisco" or "New York." There are various people who could also fit into other groups—for instance, the people who went to Black Mountain College—and others not affiliated with any real group. But they have some kind of affinity with the other so-called groups—their writing fits into a certain kind of broad category.

Many of the same names appear regularly in Yugen, Big Table, Evergreen. . .

It's a little different though. Most of the people that, say, Paul Carroll prints, he wouldn't have printed if it hadn't been for a magazine like *Yugen.* And *Evergreen Review,* to a great extent, has picked up on things that I've done already and that have appeared in magazines like the *Black Mountain Review* and *Neon.* They pick them up. As a matter of fact, in Paul Carroll's case, I know of at least two poets who appear in his magazine only because of various things he saw in *Yugen* and in an essay I wrote. He said he picked up some things in that essay that enabled him to understand or become more sympathetic with certain people's work.

I'd like to have your thoughts on a kind of contemporary writing that could be illustrated by Frank O'Hara's "Personal Poem" in Yugen 6. *In it he describes his thoughts before and after having lunch with one "LeRoi." With its highly and specifically personal references it seems to be more an anecdote of interest to future scholars than something partaking of the heightened qualities of a more traditional poetic nature. What is the validity in this kind of writing?*

I didn't especially think that there was any charted-out area in which the poetic sensibility had to function to make a poem. I thought that anything—anything you could grab—

was fit material to write a poem on. That's the way I think about it. Anything in your life, anything you know about or see or understand, you could write a poem about if you're moved to do it. I'm certain that if they have to footnote what the House of Seagrams was in his poem, or who the LeRoi, was, that will only be of interest to academicians and people doing Master's theses. Anybody who is concerned with the *poem* will get it on an emotional level—or they won't get it at all. Certainly, if I didn't like it, I wouldn't go through any book to look up those names with the hope that I would feel moved once I knew where the building was or who LeRoi was. I don't think that means anything at all. I don't think that has anything to do with the *poem,* actually. What the poem means, its function, doesn't have to do with those names—that's just part of it. It doesn't seem to me to be the same kind of stupidity that's found when you have to go to Jessie Weston's book to find out what a whole section of *The Wasteland* means. The House of Seagrams is certainly less obscure than certain Celtic rites. And I don't see what makes it any less valid because it's a casual kind of reference or that it comes out of a person's life, rather than, say, from his academic life.

I'd say that if a poem, as a whole poem, works, then it's a good poem. . .

Right. . .

You once wrote that, "MY POETRY is whatever I think I am. I make a poetry with what I feel is useful and can be saved out of all the garbage of our lives." Would you like to develop that a little more fully?

Well, it's part of what you mentioned about "traditional" poetic areas. I believe that the poet—someone with a tempered sensibility—is able, or should be able to take almost any piece of matter, idea, or whatever, and convert it if he can, into something really beautiful. I don't mean "beautiful" the way Bernard Berenson means it—but into something moving, at least.

And I don't think that there are any kind of standard ideas or sentiments or emotions or anything that have to be in a poem. A poem can be made up of anything so long as it is well made. It can be made up out of any feeling. And if I tried to cut anything out of my life—if there was something in my life that I couldn't talk about . . . it seems monstrous that you can tell almost anything about your life except those things that are most intimate or mean the most to you. That seems a severe paradox.

You've mentioned your influences as including Lorca, Creeley and Olson. What from Lorca—a surrealist approach?

Yes, that, but at the time I got hold of Lorca, I was very much influenced by Eliot, and reading Lorca helped to bring me out of my "Eliot Period" and break that shell—not so much *Poet in New York,* which is the more surreal verse, but the early *Gypsy Ballads*—that kind of feeling and exoticism.

What about the Black Mountain people, and Williams?

From Williams, mostly how to write in my own language—how to write the way I *speak* rather than the way I *think* a poem ought to be written—to write just the way it comes to me, in my own speech, utilizing the rhythms of speech rather than any kind of metrical concept. To talk verse. Spoken verse. From Pound, the same concepts that went into the Imagist's poetry—the idea of the image and what an image ought to be. I learned, probably, about verse from Pound—how a poem should be made, what a poem ought to *look* like—some little inkling. And from Williams, I guess, how to get it out in my own language.

Is there a middle ground between natural speech and formal metrics?

Oh, yes. I don't mean that I write poems completely the way I'm talking now, although I'm certain that a great deal of my natural voice rhythm dominates the line. For instance, my breathing—when I have to stop to inhale or exhale—dictates where I have to break the line in most cases. Sometimes I can bring the line out longer to effect—you learn certain tricks, departures from a set method. But mostly it's the *rhythms* of speech that I utilize, trying to get closer to the way I sound *peculiarly,* as opposed to somebody else.

Does your being a Negro influence the speech patterns—or anything else, for that matter, in your writing?

It could hardly help it. There are certain influences on me, as a Negro person, that certainly wouldn't apply to a poet like Allen Ginsberg. I couldn't have written that poem "Kaddish," for instance. And I'm sure he couldn't write certain things that have to deal with, say, Southern Baptist church rhythms. Everything applies—everything in your life. Sociologically, there are different influences, different things that I've seen, that I know, that Allen or no one knows.

I asked that because I don't find in your work the sense of "being a Negro" that occurs, say, in the poetry of Langston Hughes. . . .

That may be part of, like they say, his "stance." You have to set up a certain area in which you're going to stand and write your poems, whether you do it consciously or not. There has to be that stance. He is a Negro. It doesn't lessen my feeling of being a Negro—it's just that that's not the way I write poetry. I'm fully conscious all the time that I am an American Negro, because it's part of my life. But I know also that if I want to say, "I see a bus full of people," I don't have to say, "I am a Negro seeing a bus full of people." I would deal with it when it has to do directly with the poem, and not as a kind of broad generalization that doesn't have much to do with a lot of young writers today who are Negroes. (Although I don't know that many.) It's always been a separate section of writing that wasn't quite up to the level of the other writing. There were certain definite sociological reasons for it before the Civil War or in the early part of the 20th century, or even in the 30's, but it's a new generation now, and people are beset by other kinds of ideas that don't have much to do with sociology, *per se.*

I'm always aware, in anything I say, of the "sociological configuration"—what it *means* sociologically. But it doesn't have anything to do with what I'm writing at the time.

Ralph Ellison (review date 6 February 1964)

SOURCE: "Blues People," in *The Collected Essays of Ralph Ellison,* edited and with an introduction by John F. Callahan, The Modern Library, 1995, pp. 278-87.

[*In the following review, which originally appeared in* The New York Review *on February 6, 1964, Ellison points to both positive and negative aspects of* Blues People.]

In his introduction to **Blues People** LeRoi Jones advises us to approach the work as

> . . . a strictly theoretical endeavor. Theoretical, in that none of the questions it poses can be said to have been answered definitely or for all time (sic!), etc. In fact, the whole book proposes more questions than it will answer. The only questions it will properly move to answer have, I think, been answered already within the patterns of American life. We need only give these patterns serious scrutiny and draw certain permissible conclusions.

It is a useful warning and one hopes that it will be regarded by those jazz publicists who have the quite irresponsible habit of sweeping up any novel pronouncement written about jazz and slapping it upon the first available record liner as the latest insight into the mysteries of American Negro expression.

Jones would take his subject seriously—as the best of jazz critics have always done—and he himself should be so taken. He has attempted to place the blues within the context of a total culture and to see this native art form through the disciplines of sociology, anthropology and (though he seriously underrates its importance in the creating of a viable theory) history, and he spells out explicitly his assumptions concerning the relation between the blues, the people who created them and the larger American culture. Although I find several of his assumptions questionable, this is valuable in itself. It would be well if all jazz critics did likewise; not only would it expose those who have no business in the field, but it would sharpen the thinking of the few who have something enlightening to contribute. *Blues People,* like much that is written by Negro Americans at the present moment, takes on an inevitable resonance from the Freedom Movement, but it is in itself characterized by a straining for a note of militancy which is, to say the least, distracting. Its introductory mood of scholarly analysis frequently shatters into a dissonance of accusation, and one gets the impression that while Jones wants to perform a crucial task which he feels *someone* should take on—as indeed someone should—he is frustrated by the restraint demanded of the critical pen and would like to pick up a club.

> **Blues People, like much that is written by Negro Americans at the present moment, takes on an inevitable resonance from the Freedom Movement, but it is in itself characterized by a straining for a note of militancy which is, to say the least, distracting.**
>
> —*Ralph Ellison*

Perhaps this explains why Jones, who is also a poet and editor of a poetry magazine, gives little attention to the blues as lyric, as a form of poetry. He appears to be attracted to the blues for what he believes they tell us of the sociology of Negro American identity and attitude. Thus, after beginning with the circumstances in which he sees their origin, he considers the ultimate values of American society:

> The Negro as slave is one thing. The Negro as American is quite another. But the *path* the slave took to "citizenship" is what I want to look at. And I make my analogy through the slave citizen's music—through the music that is most closely associated with him: blues and a later, but parallel, development, jazz. And it seems to me that if the Negro represents, or is symbolic of, something in and about the nature of American culture, this certainly should be revealed by his characteristic music. . . . I am saying that if the music of the Negro in America, in all its permutations, is subjected to a socio-anthropological as well as musical scrutiny, something about the essential nature of the Negro's existence in this country ought to be revealed, as

well as something about the essential nature of this country, i.e., society as a whole. . . .

The tremendous burden of sociology which Jones would place upon this body of music is enough to give even the blues the blues. At one point he tells us that "the one peculiar reference to the drastic change in the Negro from slavery to 'citizenship' is in his music." And later with more precision, he states:

> . . . The point I want to make most evident here is that I cite the beginning of the blues as one beginning of American Negroes. Or, let me say, the reaction and subsequent relation of the Negro's experience in this country in *his* English is one beginning of the Negro's conscious appearance on the American scene.

No one could quarrel with Mr. Jones's stress upon beginnings. In 1833, two hundred and fourteen years after the first Africans were brought to these shores as slaves, a certain Mrs. Lydia Maria Child, a leading member of the American Anti-Slavery Society, published a paper entitled: *An Appeal in Favor of that Class of Americans Called Africans.* I am uncertain to what extent it actually reveals Mrs. Child's ideas concerning the complex relationship between time, place, cultural and/or national identity and race, but her title sounds like a fine bit of contemporary ironic *signifying*—"signifying" here meaning, in the unwritten dictionary of American Negro usage, "rhetorical understatements." It tells us much of the thinking of her opposition, and it reminds us that as late as the 1890s, a time when Negro composers, singers, dancers and comedians dominated the American musical stage, popular Negro songs (including James Weldon Johnson's "Under the Bamboo Tree," now immortalized by T. S. Eliot) were commonly referred to as "Ethiopian Airs."

Perhaps more than any other people, Americans have been locked in a deadly struggle with time, with history. We've fled the past and trained ourselves to suppress, if not forget, troublesome details of the national memory, and a great part of our optimism, like our progress, has been bought at the cost of ignoring the processes through which we've arrived at any given moment in our national existence. We've fought continuously with one another over who and what we are, and, with the exception of the Negro, over who and what is American. Jones is aware of this and, although he embarrasses his own argument, his emphasis is to the point.

For it would seem that while Negroes have been undergoing a process of "Americanization" from a time preceding the birth of this nation—including the fusing of their bloodlines with other non-African strains—there has persisted a stubborn confusion as to their American identity. Somehow it was assumed that the Negroes, of all the diverse American peoples, would remain unaffected by the climate, the weather, the political circumstances—from which not even slaves were exempt—the social structures, the national manners, the modes of production and the tides of the market, the national ideals, the conflicts of values, the rising and falling of national morale, or the complex give and take of acculturalization which was undergone by all others who found their existence within American democracy. This confusion still persists, and it is Mr. Jones's concern with it which gives **Blues People** a claim upon our attention.

Mr. Jones sees the American Negro as the product of a series of transformations, starting with the enslaved African, who became Afro-American slave, who became the American slave, who became, in turn, the highly qualified "citizen" whom we know today. The slave began by regarding himself as enslaved African during the time when he still spoke his native language or remembered it, practiced such aspects of his native religion as were possible and expressed himself musically in modes which were essentially African. These cultural traits became transmuted as the African lost consciousness of his African background, and his music, religion, language and speech gradually became that of the American Negro. His sacred music became the spirituals, his work songs and dance music became the blues and primitive jazz, and his religion became a form of Afro-American Christianity. With the end of slavery Jones sees the development of jazz and the blues as results of the more varied forms of experience made available to the freedman. By the twentieth century the blues divided and became, on the one hand, a professionalized form of entertainment, while remaining, on the other, a form of folklore.

By which I suppose he means that some Negroes remained in the country and sang a crude form of the blues, while others went to the city, became more sophisticated, and paid to hear Ma Rainey, Bessie or some of the other Smith girls sing them in night clubs or theaters. Jones gets this mixed up with ideas of social class—middle-class Negroes, whatever that term actually means, and light-skinned Negroes, or those Negroes corrupted by what Jones calls "White" culture—preferring the "classic" blues, and black, uncorrupted, country Negroes preferring "country blues."

For as with his music, so with the Negro. As Negroes became "middle class" they rejected their tradition and themselves; ". . . they wanted any self which the mainstream dictated, and the mainstream *always* dictated. And this black middle class, in turn, tried always to dictate that self, or this image of a whiter Negro, to the poorer, blacker Negroes."

One would get the impression that there was a rigid correlation between color, education, income and the Negro's preference in music. But what are we to say of a white-skinned Negro with brown freckles who owns sixteen oil wells sunk in a piece of Texas land once farmed by his ex-slave parents who were a blue-eyed, white-skinned, red-headed (kinky) Negro woman from Virginia and a blue-gummed, black-skinned, curly-haired Negro male from Mississippi, and who not only sang bass in a Holy Roller church, played the market and voted Republican, but collected blues recordings and was a walking depository of blues tradition? Jones's theory no more allows for the existence of such a Negro than it allows for himself, but that "concord of sensibilities" which has been defined as the meaning of culture allows for much more variety than Jones would admit.

Much the same could be said of Jones's treatment of the jazz during the thirties, when he claims its broader acceptance (i.e., its economic success as entertainment) led to a dilution, to the loss of much of its "black" character which caused a certain group of rebellious Negro musicians to create the "anti-mainstream" jazz style called bebop.

Jones sees bop as a conscious gesture of separatism, ignoring the fact that the creators of the style were seeking, whatever their musical intentions—and they were the least political of men—a fresh form of entertainment which would allow them their fair share of the entertainment market, which had been dominated by whites during the swing era. And although the boppers were reacting, at least in part, to the high artistic achievement of Armstrong, Hawkins, Basie and Ellington (all Negroes, all masters of the blues-jazz tradition), Jones sees their music as a recognition of his contention "that when you are black in a society where black is an extreme liability [it] is one thing, but to understand that it is the society which is lacking and is impossibly deformed because of this lack, and not *yourself*, isolates you even more from that society."

Perhaps. But today nothing succeeds like rebellion (which Jones as a "beat" poet should know), and while a few boppers went to Europe to escape, or became Muslims, others took the usual tours for the State Department. Whether this makes *them* "middle class" in Jones's eyes I can't say, but his assertions—which are fine as personal statement—are not in keeping with the facts; his theory flounders before that complex of human motives which makes human history, and which is so characteristic of the American Negro.

Read as a record of an earnest young man's attempt to come to grips with his predicament as Negro American during a most turbulent period of our history, **Blues People** may be worth the reader's time. Taken as a theory of American Negro culture, it can only contribute more confusion than clarity. For Jones has stumbled over that ironic obstacle which lies in the path of any who would fashion a theory of American Negro culture while ignoring the intricate network of connections which binds Negroes to the larger society. To do so is to attempt delicate brain surgery with a switchblade. And it is possible that any viable theory of Negro American culture obligates us to fashion a more adequate theory of American culture as a whole. The heel bone is, after all, connected through its various linkages to the head bone. Attempt a serious evaluation of our national morality, and up jumps the so-called Negro problem. Attempt to discuss jazz as a hermetic expression of Negro sensibility, and immediately we must consider what the "mainstream" of American music really is.

Here political categories are apt to confuse, for while Negro slaves were socially, politically and economically separate (but only in a special sense even here), they were, in a cultural sense, much closer than Jones's theory allows him to admit.

"A slave," writes Jones, "cannot be a man." But what, one might ask, of those moments when he feels his metabolism aroused by the rising of the sap in spring? What of his identity among other slaves? With his wife? And isn't it closer to the truth that far from considering themselves only in terms of that abstraction, "a slave," the enslaved really though of themselves as *men* who had been unjustly enslaved? And isn't the true answer to Mr. Jones's question, "What are you going to be when you grow up?" not, as he gives it, "a slave" but most probably a coachman, a teamster, a cook, the best damned steward on the Mississippi, the best jockey in Kentucky, a butler, a farmer, a stud, or, hopefully, a free man! Slavery was a most vicious system, and those who endured and survived it a tough people, but it was *not* (and this is important for Negroes to remember for the sake of their own sense of who and what their grandparents were) a state of absolute repression.

A slave was, to the extent that he was a *musician,* one who expressed himself in music, a man who realized himself in the world of sound. Thus, while he might stand in awe before the superior technical ability of a white musician, and while he was forced to recognize a superior social status, he would never feel awed before the music which the technique of the white musician made available. His attitude as "musician" would lead him to seek to possess the music expressed through the technique, but until he could do so he would hum, whistle, sing or play the tunes to the best of his ability on any available instrument. And it was, indeed, out of the tension between desire and ability that the techniques of jazz emerged. This was likewise true of American Negro choral singing. For this, no literary explanation, no cultural analyses, no political slogans—indeed, not even a high degree of social or political freedom—was required. For the art—the blues, the spirituals, the jazz, the dance—was what we had in place of freedom.

Technique was then, as today, the key to creative freedom,

but before this came a will toward expression. Thus, Jones's theory to the contrary, Negro musicians have never, as a group, felt alienated from any music sounded within their hearing, and it is my theory that it would be impossible to pinpoint the time when they were not shaping what Jones calls the mainstream of American music. Indeed, what group of musicians has made more of the sound of the American experience? Nor am I confining my statement to the sound of the slave experience, but am saying that the most authoritative rendering of America in music is that of American Negroes.

For as I see it, from the days of their introduction into the colonies, Negroes have taken, with the ruthlessness of those without articulate investments in cultural styles, whatever they could of European music, making of it that which would, when blended with the cultural tendencies inherited from Africa, express their own sense of life, while rejecting the rest. Perhaps this is only another way of saying that whatever the degree of injustice and inequality sustained by the slaves, American culture was, even before the official founding of the nation, pluralistic, and it was the African's origin in cultures in which art was highly functional which gave him an edge in shaping the music and dance of this nation.

The question of social and cultural snobbery is important here. The effectiveness of Negro music and dance is first recorded in the journals and letters of travelers but it is important to remember that they saw and understood only that which they were prepared to accept. Thus a Negro dancing a courtly dance appeared comic from the outside simply because the dancer was a slave. But to the Negro dancing it— and there is ample evidence that he danced it well— burlesque or satire might have been the point, which might have been difficult for a white observer to even imagine. During the 1870s Lafcadio Hearn reports that the best singers of Irish songs, in Irish dialect, were Negro dockworkers in Cincinnati, and advertisements from slavery days described escaped slaves who spoke in Scottish dialect. The master artisans of the South were slaves, and white Americans have been walking Negro walks, talking Negro-flavored talk (and prizing it when spoken by Southern belles), dancing Negro dances and singing Negro melodies far too long to talk of a "mainstream" of American culture to which they're alien.

Jones attempts to impose an ideology upon this cultural complexity, and this might be useful if he knew enough of the related subjects to make it interesting. But his version of the blues lacks a sense of the excitement and surprise of men living in the world—of enslaved and politically weak men successfully imposing their values upon a powerful society through song and dance.

The blues speak to us simultaneously of the tragic and comic aspects of the human condition, and they express a profound sense of life shared by many Negro Americans precisely because their lives have combined these modes. This has been the heritage of a people who for hundreds of years could not celebrate birth or dignify death, and whose need to live despite the dehumanizing pressures of slavery developed an endless capacity for laughing at their painful experiences. This is a group experience shared by many Negroes, and any effective study of the blues would treat them first as poetry and as ritual. Jones makes a distinction between classic and country blues, the one being entertainment and the other folklore. But the distinction is false. Classic blues were both entertainment *and* a form of folklore. When they were sung professionally in theaters, they were entertainment; when danced to in the form of recordings or used as a means of transmitting the traditional verses and their wisdom, they were folklore. There are levels of time and function involved here, and the blues which might be used in one place as entertainment (as gospel music is now being used in night clubs and on theater stages) might be put to a ritual use in another. Bessie Smith might have been a "blues queen" to society at large, but within the tighter Negro community where the blues were part of a total way of life, and a major expression of an attitude toward life, she was a priestess, a celebrant who affirmed the values of the group and man's ability to deal with chaos.

It is unfortunate that Jones thought it necessary to ignore the aesthetic nature of the blues in order to make his ideological point, for he might have come much closer had he considered the blues not as politics but as art. This would have still required the disciplines of anthropology and sociology, but as practiced by Constance Rourke, who was well aware of how much of American cultural expression is Negro. And he could learn much from the Cambridge School's discoveries of the connection between poetry, drama and ritual as a means of analyzing how the blues function in their proper environment. Simple taste should have led Jones to Stanley Edgar Hyman's work on the blues instead of Paul Oliver's sadly misdirected effort.

For the blues are not primarily concerned with civil rights or obvious political protest; they are an art form and thus a transcendence of those conditions created within the Negro community by the denial of social justice. As such they are one of the techniques through which Negroes have survived and kept their courage during that long period when many whites assumed, as some still assume, that they were afraid.

Much has been made of the fact that *Blues People* is one of the few books by a Negro to treat the subject. Unfortunately for those who expect that Negroes would have a special insight into this mysterious art, this is not enough. Here, too, the critical intelligence must perform the difficult task which only it can perform.

Amiri Baraka with D. H. Melhem (interview date Fall 1982)

SOURCE: "Amiri Baraka: Revolutionary Traditions," in *Heroism in the New Black Poetry: Introductions and Interviews,* University Press of Kentucky, 1990, pp. 215-63.

[In the following interview, conducted in 1982 by D. H. Melhem and Michael Bezdek, Baraka discusses a variety of topics including his upbringing, his work, and his views on art and politics.]

Since the early 1960s, the figure to be reckoned with in Black political life and art has been Amiri Baraka. Controversial, responsive to changing social ambience, he has articulated the riotous "language of the unheard" (to invoke Martin Luther King's definition once again) within a vernacular and a new idiom of radical solutions. A founder of the Black Arts Movement of the sixties, he propounded a view that was, as the late Larry Neal put it, "radically opposed to any concept of the artist that alienates him from his community . . . the Black Arts Movement believes that your ethics and your aesthetics are one." Baraka's impact has been such that as early as 1973, Donald B. Gibson placed him among "major influences on black poetry: (1) the Harlem Renaissance of the twenties; (2) the protest writing of the thirties as reflected in the work of Richard Wright; (3) the beat movement of the fifties; (4) the life and work of a single poet, Amiri Baraka."

Amiri Baraka was born Everett Leroy Jones in Newark, New Jersey, on October 7, 1934, to Anna Lois and Coyote (Coyt) Leroy Jones. His mother, a social worker, had been a student at Fisk University; her father, Tom Russ, had owned businesses, helped found a Baptist church, and endured persecution in Alabama by envious white businessmen who three times burned down his establishments before he moved his family to Newark. Although he died when his grandson was eleven, Russ remained a significant figure for the poet. Baraka's father, a man of independent thought, taught his son the importance of self-defense.

Coyt Jones's grandmother had been noted for her storytelling, especially about the era of slavery, and Baraka—recognized as a prodigy by his parents—was encouraged in his ability to make speeches before he was old enough for school. His dynamic competence as a public speaker and reader began in those early days.

After a year's unhappy encounter with Rutgers, Baraka attended Howard University, where as LeRoi Jones, he studied with Sterling A. Brown and Nathan Scott. Shortly before his twentieth birthday, he left Howard to enter the air force, which he refers to as the "error farce," serving two years, mainly in Puerto Rico and Germany. In 1958 he and Hettie

Cohen, a Jewish writer, were married in a Buddhist temple on Manhattan's Upper West Side. Two daughters, Kellie Elisabeth and Lisa Victoria Chapman, were born to the couple. Baraka and his wife collaborated on publishing *Yugen,* an important literary magazine (later, with Diane di Prima, he edited *Floating Bear*). Since their divorce, Hettie Jones has remained active on the New York literary scene.

In the sixties Baraka wrote poetry and jazz reviews, and began writing plays with **The Eighth Ditch** (which is part of his 1965 novel, **The System of Dante's Hell**) and **Dutchman.** Turning to Black Nationalism, deeply affected by the murder of Malcolm X in February 1965, he left Greenwich Village for Harlem where, in the previous year, he had already founded the Black Arts Repertory Theatre/School (BART/S). In 1966 he was united with Amina Baraka (née Sylvia Robinson) in a Yoruba wedding ceremony. Formerly a painter, dancer, and actress, Amina is a strong poet in her own right and coedited with him **Confirmation: An Anthology of African American Women** (1983), in which several of her poems appear (Brooks, Sanchez, and Cortez are also among the forty-nine Black women writers represented). A woman of deep political convictions, Amina shares her husband's world view and directs the New Ark Afrikan Free School, which originated in Spirit House, the community cultural center that he had organized in the 1960s. Her children with Baraka are Obalaji Malik Ali, Ras Jua Al Aziz, Shani Isis Makeda, Amiri Seku Musa, and Ahi Mwenge.

Throughout the sixties Baraka steadily gained respect for his work in jazz history, particularly **Blues People;** in poetry, with books including **Preface to a Twenty Volume Suicide Note** and **Black Magic;** in drama, with **Dutchman,** which won an "Obie" for the best off-Broadway play of 1964, and **The Slave,** which won the drama prize at the first World Festival of Negro Arts in Dakar, Senegal (1966); and in fiction with **The System of Dante's Hell** and **Tales.** Recognized as a political and cultural leader, he was welcomed tumultuously at the Second Fisk University Writers' Conference in 1967. In the Newark riots later that year, he encountered a different sort of tumult when he was nearly beaten to death by police [an event which is recollected in Baraka's **Autobiography.**]

Home, a collection of his essays from 1960 through 1965, shows the development of Baraka's early thought. "After 1966," he says, "my work became self-consciously spiritual." In this period, he wrote **Spirit Reach** (1972). Richly experimental, mimetic of instruments, its "Preachments" contribute to a moving poetic document of spiritual striving.

In 1974, as chairman of the Congress of Afrikan Peoples (CAP), which split off into the Revolutionary Communist League, the poet attended the Sixth Pan-African Congress at Dar es Salaam. The assembly marked a deepening schism

among Black intellectuals: some clinging to Nationalism; others, like Baraka, embracing the new wave of socialism. Ten years later, on the occasion of the writer's fiftieth birthday, Woodie King, Jr., asked, "What is it about Baraka that calls us to attention? I believe it is his daring." In his candid *Autobiography,* Baraka, using a Mao-invoking metaphor, writes of his "long march to better understanding" (p. 325). For him, change is the constant present and presence, the quintessential fact of existence and growth. He dares to grow and chafes at being held back by his own former positions, whether they were error or insight. The anti-Semitism that marred some of his early poetry, for example, plagued him for years after he disavowed the sentiments. Even his **"Confessions of a Former Anti-Semite"** failed to remove the stigma. It persisted mainly because of his view of Zionism as nationalism and therefore incompatible with his late Marxist/Leninist/Maoist international stance. "People are always catching you where you were," he says. One recalls the hero of Brooks's "Boy Breaking Glass," who cries, "Nobody knew where I was and now I am no longer there." While many have known where Baraka was at a particular moment, they could not seize his protean reality, because he was always both of his time and ahead of it, struggling, in a Hegelian labor, to achieve a further level of synthesis.

As artist, Baraka wants "more than anything, to chart this change within myself. This constant mutability in the face of the changing world." And yet it is the reality of his changeless core that generates his vision. William J. Harris views him as a Manichaean and a vatic poet in the line of Whitman, Pound, Patchen, and Ginsberg. In quest of philosophical truth, Baraka has turned to a variety of religious and political faiths. A serious artist, he has absorbed classical and modern literature and contributes uniquely to art that is experimentally alive to its social and political content. He uses music and multimedia to further the accessibility and impact of his works, in order to convey to the people his messages of strength, resistance, and political instruction. Like a great dancer (or skater), he risks all with bold leaps and turns, as evidenced by his play **The Motion of History** and **Money: A Jazz Opera,** neither of whom quite comes off theatrically, and **The Sidney Poet Heroical,** which does. His work has moved from concern with self and schools of white poetry to replacement of that Black self in a national and world community, at the same time developing an experimental Black art rooted in traditions of language, music, and religious and secular rhetoric.

Harris gives a solid interpretation of Baraka's methodology, which converts white aesthetics to Black aesthetic purposes: "Amiri Baraka's entire career is characterized by transformations of avant-garde poetics into ethnic poetics, of white liberal politics into black nationalist and Marxist politics, of jazz forms into literary forms . . . I call Baraka's method of transformation the Jazz Aesthetic Process, a procedure that uses jazz variations as paradigms for the conversion of white poetic and social ideas into black ones." Harris gives appropriate credit to Henry Louis Gates, Jr. (who, in turn, acknowledges Roger D. Abrahams) in perceiving that the process is one of suggesting structure by dissemblance, a form of "signifying," and that "repeating a form and then inverting it through a process of variation" is the essence of the jazz aesthetic. Baraka's own explanation of how he turned the Black Sambo minstrel image into the fear-inspiring Uncle Sambo revolutionary patches worn by Walker Vessel's Black army, in *The Slave,* exemplifies the process.

Because over the years Baraka has become a recognizable part of American popular multiculture, familiarity makes him appear less threatening than was once the case. As professor (since (1979) and director (since 1986) of Africana Studies at the State University of New York at Stony Brook, and recently as visiting professor at Rutgers University, he may even tempt us to think of him as nearly an "establishment' figure (one can hear him chortle), though of a unique variety, to be sure. But he is ever Baraka: his mind, ranging freely, remains unfettered. His integrity as an artist and his ready polemics are partly witnessed by the history of some of his essays in *Daggers and Javelins,* pieces commissioned and paid for by such publications as the *New York Times, Black Enterprise* magazine, the *Village Voice,* and *Playboy* (Japan) and then not published—or, in journalistic parlance, "killed." Their survival and subsequent publication recall the mighty words of labor organizer Joe Hill in Alfred Hayes's ballad: "I never died, said he."

Dedicated to promulgating his views, Baraka has let nothing, not even enforced weekends on Rikers Island or teaching commitments, ever prevent him from writing, publishing, and participating in functions and causes he deems worthy. Among other activities, he continues to participate generously in Black writer's conferences. At the Medgar Evers Second National Black Writers' Conference in March 1988 he discussed destructive stereotypes about Black writing (such as maintaining that it doesn't exist, that American writing is white, and that Blacks fixate on the subject of slavery) and called for the mass infusion of Black literature into school curricula. At the Langston Hughes Festival in New York the following November he presented a paper titled **"Langston, McKay, and Du Bois: The Contradictions of Art and Politics During the Harlem Renaissance."**

Baraka's stature in American letters was further evident on two occasions honoring Black writers. At James Baldwin's funeral "celebration" on December 8, 1987, at the Cathedral Church of Saint John the Divine in New York, where tributes were given by Baldwin's friends Maya Angelou and Toni Morrison and by the ambassador of France, Baraka—also a close friend—served as honorary pallbearer and delivered a memorable eulogy: "Jimmy was God's black

Revolutionary mouth," he said, "if there is a God, and revolution his righteous natural expression and elegant song the deepest and most fundamental commonplace of being alive." The eulogy was printed by Baldwin's family as part of the memorial program.

On February 11, 1988, Baraka participated in the public television literary series *Voices and Visions,* in its tribute to Langston Hughes. Baraka regards Richard Wright, W. E. B. Du Bois, and Hughes as the three most eminent authors of the Harlem Renaissance. His appreciation of both Hughes and Baldwin has as much to do with music as with message. His kinship with their knowledge, esteem, and application of Black music has been demonstrated by his own major writings on blues and jazz; he is vitally concerned with the relation of music to Black culture as a whole, the revolutionary impulse it expresses and the cultural tradition it embodies. Currently, his weekly music and poetry series, "Kimako's Blues People," named after his late sister and codirected with his wife Amina, continues to project his vision of art merged with politics and to support the creative struggle of Black artists.

Baraka's deep concern with tradition is part of a pervasive concern among Black intellectuals with identifying and codifying an existing tradition. In addition to Black music, literature, and religious and secular oratory, slave narratives are also being perceived as "central to American culture." The development of literary theory and the establishment of canons—begun with the prodigious work of W. E. B. Du Bois and the Harlem renaissance writers; carried forward by Baraka, the late Larry Neal, and the legacies of Hoyt W. Fuller and George E. Kent—continue apace, along with emphases that range from poststructuralism to feminism.

Underlying or overt, the concern with tradition and traditions (also evident in the other poets discussed here) counterpoints both political and aesthetic radicalism, and it locates unequivocally in Baraka's major poem *In the Tradition* (1982), which he has both published and recorded (with music). Dedicating it to "Black Arthur Blythe," the alto saxophonist (whose 1979 record album lent the poem its title), Baraka calls it "a poem about African American history . . . a cultural history and political history." If a single work could sum him up "at a certain point," he says, it would probably be that poem. It incorporates his spirit, his energy, his musicality, all that he ever learned about and contributed to the visual and aural elements of modern poetry. As Joe Weislmann points out (like Darwin Turner speaking of Madhubuti; see Chapter 3 above), "Baraka's recent work lives fully only in performance, yet rarely do Baraka's critics take that into account." A stirring reader, he frequently shares the stage with Amina, herself a dynamic performer.

The recent poetry seems to be gaining power through its

depth and expansion. While it supports the range of his concerns—**"Soundings,"** a passionate outcry against war; **"Wailers,"** a poem for Larry Neal and Bob Marley that is essentially a tribute to Black music (it has been reprinted in **"The Music"**); and **"Why's/Wise,"** which, Baraka notes in introducing a published fragment, is a long poem about "African American (American) History," recalling his earlier description of "In the Tradition"—two new aspects bear mention. First, the poet seems to be adapting his earlier connection to Olson and the Projectivists within the framework of Black culture. In his preface to **"Why's/Wise,"** the poet mentions "the tradition of the Griots," but also includes Melvin B. Tolson's *Libretto for the Republic of Liberia,* William Carlos Williams's *Paterson,* Charles Olson's *Maximus Poems* (one could also cite Ezra Pound's *Cantos* here) as antecedents, "in that it tries to tell the history/life like an ongoing-offcoming Tale" (*Southern Review,* 801). In the poem, which is still in progress, Baraka celebrates heroes (and excoriates real and putative villains) from all aspects of Black life. Utilizing the full vocabulary of his artistic development, he is seen by one critic as "moving forward in the world armed with both curiosity and wisdom."

Baraka's new book, *The Music,* clearly locates in its very title his focus for present and future. It is Black music that has provided the lens, the cohesion, and the communication he has been pursuing as he "investigates the sun." This anthology of recent work, of Amina's poetry and his own poetry, essays, and "anti-nuclear jazz musical," reveals a second and relatively new emphasis: Baraka as a poet/musician of praise—a lover of **"The Music"** (by which Black music is understood) and the family of Black musicians who create and interpret it, and a lover of his own family, itself consanguine within it. Witness his poet and prose tributes to great artists of jazz and blues, his instrumental articulations (he defines poetry as "speech musicked"), his remark that "Amina's poetry is itself child of the music, as Jazz is Blues'," and the poem to his sons, **"Obalaji as drummer, Ras as Poet,"** in which he affirms: "and when the music goes through me I swear I imagine all kinds / of things. A world without pain, a world of beauty, for / instance." A Black Family man who remains lyrical with hope, he is a formidable champion of the cultural contribution of African American music and fierce defender against **"The Great Music Robbery,"** the plundering of its resources by whites (328-32; cf. Gwendolyn Brooks, "Gottschalk and the Grande Tarantelle," Interview, Chapter 1).

Baraka's appraisal of Malcolm X may well serve as his own epitome: "A whole swirl of turnarounds hurricaned from him. The world was going through changes, and that world was in us too. We had to reevaluate all we knew. There were lives in us anyway filled with dynamite. We had a blackness to us, to be sure. It was always in us, we had but to claim it. And it claimed us."

To travel through the sprawling Black area of Newark is to be drawn into the nexus of Baraka's urgent rage: acres of slums, sullen in July—one imagines their bleakness in December. It is the Tuesday morning of our interview [conducted on July 21, 1981; the last question was posed to Baraka on November 24, 1988 at the Langston Hughes Festival at the City College of New York and is included in the text as an appropriate conclusion to the interview]. My cab drives on and on, through a city still partly burned out since the 1967 riots, until we come to a section of attractive private houses. And then: the red, rambling, Victorian-style brick house of Amiri Baraka. A tree, its trunk curving like a snarl, explodes into an umbrella of green to the left of the entrance walk.

Inside: Baraka, wearing a red T-shirt imprinted in black with a picture of the late Bob Marley. Inside: clean lines, beige walls; a fireplace with African art objects; an ample, beige sectional sofa. On the coffee table: Langston Hughes, *The Ways of White Folks.* Baraka speaks briefly with a telephone repairman after showing me to the living room.

Mike Bezdek, a pleasant southerner on assignment from the Associated Press to report on illustrious Newark citizens, is seated on the sofa when I enter. I had not expected a second interviewer. Baraka joins us. He is budgeting his time, trying to do two things in the space of one, aware of the days slipping past until October 16 when he will be sentenced, wondering aloud whether he might be "taken off" in prison. He explains that he has been speaking to the telephone repairman, who has just left. "Every time I have to go to court, the phone is fouling up. You get a recording saying the phone is disconnected." He sits before us, flecks of gray in his hair and beard, poised yet intense as he mentions a "hit list" he will discuss in the interview, a list on which his name appears.

How does one live with fear and maintain sanity? Baraka's secret may be his productivity. During the interview he refers to a play, a jazz opera, a book of essays, a book of autobiographical essays, and an anthology to be co-edited with his wife—all works at various stages of completion and all subsequently produced or published.

The interview lasts approximately two hours. The poet speaks rapidly, but without haste, with seriousness and occasional humor, his manner forthright. The house is filled at times with sounds of activity from invisible children; no one invades the scene or interrupts the conversation. Baraka is to travel in the afternoon. Even though we are only one in a continuous series of commitments, he is relaxed. I am reminded of him at the New School, where I was first struck by his patience and quick intelligence as a teacher, his use of a socratic method, his description of "art for art's sake" as art created for the bourgeoisie. Once again I have the sense of constant reassessment or revaluation, of the very process of thought to which we are being admitted.

INTERVIEW WITH AMIRI BARAKA

[*D. H. Melhem:*] *As a child, it seems you were regarded by your family as a prodigy. Did anyone at home or at school directly encourage you to write?*

[Baraka:] In school I took a writing course as a senior in high school, before that in grammar school. When I was in elementary school I did a comic strip in seventh grade for a little seventh grade newspaper that we had, and I contributed cartoons for that. I didn't start really to get a sense of writing until high school.

[*Melhem:*] *That comic strip you did, would you say that showed the influence of the radio and so forth—the comedians, mysteries, and dramas that dominated radio at the time? Would you say that the radio influenced your turn to drama?*

Well, I think the radio was probably the biggest influence on me—radio and movies. I was always really an avid radio listener. Every day, after the playground, I'd listen to all the adventure stories. I think they'd start coming on about five-fifteen, Hop Harrigan and Captain Midnight—

[*Mike Bezdek:*] *The Shadow.*

Yes, that was on Sundays.

[*Bezdek:*] *That was one of your most widely publicized early poems—*

Right.

[*Bezdek:*] *—about the Shadow.*

Yes. All of those were. I guess what television is probably to little kids now, radio was to us then.

[*Melhem:*] *Is the Green Lantern the Green Hornet?*

No. The Green Lantern was actually a comic strip character, and he had a ring, and he used to take this ring and he'd sort of, I guess, recharge it at the end of each one of his bouts with crime. Then he had this little poem that he would recite, "In darkest day, in darkest night / No evil shall escape my sight." [*Laughter*] Something like that. And I always identified with that.

[*Melhem:*] *Your paternal great-grandmother was an accomplished storyteller. You have an exuberant relationship with words per se, as well as a remarkably fertile imagination.*

Would you say that your great-grandmother's talent influenced you in both respects, the lexical and the imaginative?

I can't really be sure. I know that those stories were always fascinating. She would tell those stories out of the *Arabian Nights*—they were stories that I came to know later as the stories from the *Arabian Nights*—only in her own, unique, kind of way. But I think the whole language thing is the thing from the streets, really, from the playground, finding out that using words was as useful as being able to use your hands in some situations.

[*Bezdek:*] *Was this in Newark?*

Yes.

[*Melhem:*] *Would you say that joy in words is part of a Black cultural—*

Yes.

[*Melhem:*] *—predilection?*

Yes, certainly the whole oral aspect of the culture, the fact of being kept out of formal replication just reinforces the oral quality. The fact that you couldn't just come off the farm and be a writer, you know, on the plantation and have access to the formal arts. It reinforces the kind of normally oral tradition of most people in the world. I think in saying that the African American people, because of being blocked in one area—it just reinforces that oral kind of tradition.

[*Melhem:*] *Your identification with leadership seems to have begun early, with the independence and ego strength shown by both your parents, and your admiration for and closeness to your heroic maternal grandfather, Tom Russ, whom you refer to as "an American pioneer" in your dedication to* Dutchman *and* The Slave. *Would you couple his loss, when you were eleven, with the death of Malcolm X in 1965, as deeply significant events for you, influencing and even changing your life?*

Well, I don't know. See, the Malcolm thing was much more conscious, much more of a conscious commitment and seeing somebody you consciously had seen as important, killed. My grandfather was such a personal loss. I think the loss begins early when he got hurt. He got hit in the head with a street light they said fell off the pole and crippled him, which is still a wild kind of coincidence. But I think the loss begins there, because the kind of prestige he had in the community and the awe that I hold him in was at that point, you know, sharply kind of—just weakened, because he then became a paralyzed person who couldn't move, who had to sit in a wheelchair. That sort of eliminated a lot of the kind of heroic projection that I had around him. And then his death was kind of—anticlimax.

[*Melhem:*] *Was he in a wheelchair long?*

Well, I guess the last few years of his life, about three years he lived after that, three or four years.

[*Bezdek:*] *What did he do?*

He was a storekeeper; he was a politician; he was in Black Republican politics. He lost his store in the Depression, and they gave him a political patronage job, which is very ironic. He was the night watchman I the election machine factory [*chuckling*], in the election machine warehouse where they kept the election machines. He was the night watchman in there, so we used to go over there in the evenings and sit around the election machines, protecting democracy, or something. [*Laughter*]

[*Melhem:*] *More recently, do you consider Lu Hsun an important example for you of the writer as revolutionary?*

Oh, yes. Absolutely. Yes, absolutely. I think that it's a pity that his works are not known more widely in this country. But he's a very, very skilled short story writer and an acid essayist—

[*Melhem:*] *Like "A Madman's Diary"*—

Yes.

[*Melhem:*] *—a great story.*

Yes. I have a book coming out in the fall, a book of essays, and I took the title from him. The title is ***Daggers and Javelins,*** and that's what he used to call his essays. He had some "dagger" essays, which were short and swift, and then he had some javelin essays, for long-distance [*laughs*] elimination.

[*Melhem:*] *Who's publishing that?*

Greenwood. Academic Press. *Essays, 1975-1979.* [Later published by Morrow.]

[*Bezdek:*] *Speaking of academic life, you were well-known way back in the fifties. Do you have some trouble getting university positions? I seem to remember hearing that. Did that not further your anger, especially your home state where, for God knows what reason—*

Yes, yes. Well, in New Jersey, I applied to Rutgers, Newark, about three or four years in a row. Then I applied to Rutgers, New Brunswick; Rutgers in Livingston, a couple of times; then Princeton; Essex county College— I've ap-

plied to all of these schools around here with the exception, I guess, of Seton Hall Upsala. But all the rest of the major schools I applied to. I know people inside these schools, and they tell me what's going on. They tell me, you know, in Newark Rutgers the English department says they will not have you. The head of the English department, a guy named Henry Christian, maintains that he will die first—

[*Bezdek:*] *Where is that?*

Newark Rutgers.

[*Bezdek:*] *And why?*

I think it's basically because my work in New Jersey has been—most people know it principally as political. And so it's different if you have a political professor who is essentially a professor and is political in that sense. But when you have somebody who people identify primarily as a political activist and only secondarily as a writer—a lot of these people around New Jersey and especially in Newark, they think of me primarily as a political activist. In terms of writing and stuff like that, they don't know a thing about that. [*Laughs*]

[*Bezdek:*] *Uh-huh.*

So it's like you want to hire a militant to be on the faculty. They don't want to do that. The fact that I can get jobs and go teach at Yale and George Washington, Columbia, you know, is lost on them. So that's essentially where it still is.

[*Bezdek:*] *Has that ever entered your writing? Have you ever written about that?*

What—the Rutgers thing?

[*Bezdek:*] *About New Jersey, specifically?*

I mentioned that I a couple of essays that I've done recently, in the last three years. I've mentioned that specifically in about three essays. One that Rutgers is supposed to be publishing in a collection called—you remember they had a conference on urban literature, something like that, a couple of years ago? They have a collection of those essays coming out in the fall, and one of those essays talks about Rutgers being a racist institution, and so forth and so on. And then I wrote about it in a couple of other essays, specifically about having applied and being turned down; having been sent a ditto sheet back, not even an answer—one of those purple ditto sheets from Rutgers. [*Laughs*] And all kinds of stuff like that. But I think it's par for the course. I don't see it as being weird, given the situation in New Jersey, specifically in Newark, the kind of intense political confrontation we went through, that I was involved with and identified with.

You can see what their point is. I mean, it's so backward. Obviously, most people in the country look at it as extremely backward, you know, what goes on. I have yet to get even a grant from the State Council on the Arts in New Jersey, you understand? That kind of—refusal to identify me as anything but a political figure, a political militant that they don't want to deal with. Which is very interesting.

[*Bezdek:*] *Do we have any native sons who are more well known than you? I don't—*

I don't know—not in that particular field, I would think.

[*Bezdek:*] *I read about you for the first time in Alabama* [*Laughs*] *and if they know about your poetry down there, my God—*

I don't think so. There are a great many well-known writers from New Jersey. Strangely enough, some of the best-known American poets are from New Jersey. Walt Whitman—

[*Bezdek:*] *Carlos—*

Yes, William Carlos Williams, Allen Ginsberg—

[*Bezdek:*] *He's from New Jersey?*

Yes. They're all from New Jersey. New Jersey has a particular, weird soil that turns out poets. Yes. But Ginsberg was born in Newark. He was raised, of course, in Paterson. William Carlos Williams lived most of his life in Paterson. Walt Whitman lived most of his life in Camden. So there's something in New Jersey that promotes poetry.

[*Melhem:*] *I just want to go back to the childhood for a moment.*

Yes.

[*Melhem:*] *There's a great deal of pain—inflicted and endured—in your work. As an adult, you observed discrimination in the army and suffered beatings by police during the Newark riots of 1967. Did you experience any comparable cruelty or discrimination from whites, Blacks, or anyone else when you were a child or an adolescent?*

Well, see, interestingly enough, I'm writing this book now for Wyndham Press, which is a spinoff of Simon & Schuster, and it's memoirs. That's what they wanted, I don't know why. I'm writing all about the youth part now, and I will put there one of the first incidences that I recognized—God knows what happened that I *don't* recognize—was when we went to the Bronx Zoo. Students—they took us to the Bronx Zoo, and I was sort of lagging along at the end, the group had sort of passed through and I was still in the elephant house.

There was this white guy clearing the place up, so I go over to him; I said, "Gee, mister, how can you stand it?—you know, the elephant house stinks!" and he says, "Well, I don't worry about that. I live in Harlem," he says. And you know I was about nine, and I knew what he meant. I couldn't really get down and argue with him or anything like that, but it went right through me, and I knew what he meant. And I began then to be much more aware of—you know. And I think we lived close to the Italian community when I was in my middle—what is it, nine, ten, eleven, twelve?—and, you know, there were always incidents.

[*Melhem:*] *Well,* **The System of Dante's Hell** *and* **Tales** *are poeticized autobiographical—*

Yes.

[*Melhem:*] *—works. Would you say that they're complementary? Would you consider* **Tales** *as, perhaps, an epilogue to* System?

I'd say that there are certainly parallels, things focusing on the same things in a slightly different way. The things that I try to do in the Dante book I really wasn't even aware of, in a sense. I was just trying to stop writing like other people. And it's interesting that years later I read where Aime Cesaire did the same thing to get away from French Symbolist poetry. He says, "I'm going to stop writing poetry. I'm just going to write prose." And so then he turns up *Return to my Native Land.* But that's what I did when I started—I was tired of writing poetry like Robert Creeley and Charles Olson, you know, in principle. And so I said, "I'm going to do something that's going to very consciously break away." And so I just tried to just write spontaneously and without any kind of literary usage. Some critics say that's pretty obvious. [*Laughs*]

[*Melhem:*] *They are unique. It really was a break.*

Yes. But I tried to get away from just literary—from "literature." Then I think what happened was that I was permitted to find my own voice, and once I thought I had it near the end of that book; then I sort of calmed down and began to write more recognizable narrative.

[*Melhem:*] *In* **"Heroes Are Gang Leaders,"** *the protagonist, sitting in a hospital bed, notes that "the concerns are still heroism." Does that show early interest in that whole theme?*

Yes. Oh, yes. You see, what has always intrigued me, and I've talked to my wife a lot about this, that they taught us to love heroes, and specifically in my youth, when the United States was not quite as bloody as it is now, I mean, in its pursuits all over the world, they were able to project the straight-ahead type heroes. Our heroes were people like Robin Hood, Errol Flynn as Robin Hood—you know, "take from the rich and give to the poor"—that was a clear, you know—[*Laughs*]

[*Melhem:*] [Laughing] *That was a good idea.*

And so you really begin to be animated by those ideas in a real way; then later on you find out that it's all a lie. They don't really mean for you to believe that. But I internalized, certainly, a lot of—

[*Melhem:*] *Is that* [**"Heroes"**] *an autobiographical story?*

That story? Generally so. I think writers always lie about something—

[*Melhem:*] *That took place in a hospital.*

Yes—I think in taking autobiographical cores, writers always see parallel things that they blow up and other things that they leave out. [*Chuckles*] You know, it's never exactly, but it's generally so.

> **. . . I think in taking autobiographical cores, writers always see parallel things that they blow up and other things that they leave out . . . You know, it's never exactly, but it's generally so.**
> —*Amiri Baraka*

[*Bezdek:*] *Do you have friends still around Newark from when you were a child?*

Oh yes, yes. That's really the best part of being in this town. That's one of the reasons that I remain here. I do have friends that go all the way back to childhood, early childhood.

[*Bezdek:*] *Do you have certain difficulties sometimes with your prominence with some of them? Do they have a hard time with that?*

No. I think most of the people I know take it for what it is—you know, "It's a friend of mine." We get on pretty well. There's always some weird people. I know for instance I've gone to school with most people, probably with more people than [*laughing*] most people—then you find they went to school with you. You got a graduating class of three thousand! [*Chuckling sound*] But aside from that, most people, I think, a lot of people feel good by what you do, because they know that it's part of them, that it's actually been made public, you know. They feel, "Hey, I know him, and how he

says some things that other people are interested in, and part of me is in that."

[*Bezdek:*] *It's important for your work, I would imagine, to keep in touch with people in the city, all kinds of people. I know Baldwin had some trouble—he's sometimes considered by certain Blacks to be a little bit of an elitist. Some say he's lost a little bit of touch.*

Well, I guess maybe what they mean is he doesn't—you know, Jimmy goes back and forth to Europe; he stays in Europe a lot of the time. But interestingly enough, when we had that conference on urban literature, they were doing a movie, some English filmmakers were doing a movie on him, and because we were together, they asked me to show him around to see Newark, since I lived here. I took him to the Scudder Homes, which is about the worst project in Newark, and I think what most impressed Jimmy—first of all, when we came here, there was almost nobody on the street. Inside of five minutes there must have been three hundred people on the street, because they had camera equipment, and stuff like that. And I think what impressed him most was some of the young people, teenage types and young adults, saying, "How you doing, Mr. Baldwin? I read your last book." And so on and so on and so on and so on, showing how people never really, once they know you and identify you—that they do try to keep track of you, you see, and you might not think so. You might think that you disappeared from sight. But I think that's important to remember, that you never do disappear from sight. There are some people who always measure certain things in the world by what you're doing. I think it's a very important idea.

[*Bezdek:*] *Who is your preferred audience? Who would you like to meet on the street and have him say, "Hey I just read your latest essay"?*

Well, I'd say the great majority of working people in this country. Certainly I'm closer to Black people, for the obvious reason of American segregation, you know, we've grown up in our own communities. And it's very very gratifying for some working person, some black working—some person that you know goes to work every day, you know what I mean, in some factory or on some assembly line, but any kind of working person, let's say, whatever their nationality, that's the most gratifying to me. When somebody you know who's a real person, who's in the real world, dealing with the real world, has taken some time, has put some space in their life for what you're saying, that's really gratifying—much more than college professors or students, or people you know whose job it is, in the intellectual world. I mean, some guy who makes cars all his life, and says, "Hey, I read that book you wrote and I really liked it."

[*Melhem:*] *Now this is your current target audience, but*

would you say that in the past you had a different audience you were writing for?

Well, I'd say this: I think that my early days of writing—I think I wanted to reach everybody, but obviously, my concerns were not broad enough. I think when I was a Nationalist, obviously, I then wanted to focus strictly on Black people. But I think now, the difference between, say, myself as a young writer, when I really was just talking to anybody who would listen but my concerns were narrow—now I try to broaden my concerns to make that voice broad enough to touch different people's lives. Now obviously I'm speaking as a Black person, and any person has got to speak from their own experience and where they are, but I think it's a—you desire communication with most people at a level that they can deal with it, use it.

[*Melhem:*] *Did you start writing poetry when you were in the army?*

I started writing poetry I guess in college. I started writing Elizabethan poetry, like [*laughs*] Sir John Suckling, Philip Sidney, people like that.

[*Bezdek:*] *Which college was that?*

Howard University.

[*Bezdek:*] *Did you go there first?*

No. I went to Newark Rutgers, when it was an all-white school. [*Laughs*]

[*Bezdek:*] *What about Columbia?*

That was later. That was much later. No, when I first came out of high school, I went to Newark Rutgers. I had scholarships to a lot of places, strangely enough. But I chose Newark Rutgers for some reason, I guess because it was in Newark, it was close, but I hated it once I got there. So I got out of there.

[*Melhem:*] *Do you still consider yourself basically a poet?*

Yes. Sure. Fundamentally a poet and, you know, a political activist. But you see, I've always liked to write other things. I mean, I think—well, I always wrote essays, even when I first started writing poetry; a little while after that I started writing essay reviews, jazz reviews, first. I started writing plays about '63 and, you know, my work had gotten more and more dramatic. In the poetry there were people always talking. [*Laughs*] Suddenly in the poem I would have a conversation between two people, and it gradually worked itself into—**The System of Dante's Hell** had plays in it.

[*Melhem:*] *"The Eighth Ditch"*—

Yes. I think that I developed the dramatic thing, and I liked that, because I think it's a much more ambitious thing to try and put people on the stage and make believe it's the real world or *some* real world, anyway.

[*Melhem:*] *Your writing seems as visual as it is aural. How early were you interested in painting? And do you still paint?*

Well, I took drawing lessons when I was a kid. I guess my mother was one of those middle-class women who was trying to put you in these different places. But I think it helps, because it gives you some kind of attention to things as other than just random, boring kind of life. You then see, oh, there's such a thing as music. I took trumpet lessons. I took drum lessons. I took art lessons. She used to have me singing and dancing with my sister on the stage. And then when I got into the service, I painted, because I met a friend of mine down there, William White, who became a painter, who was a painter, a very good painter. He died of drugs, unfortunately. But then that stimulated me to want to paint. And then I got back to New York. I made a decision as to whether I want to paint or do I want to write. I decided it was easier to write. In painting you had to go through too many changes.

[*Bezdek:*] *How many brothers and sisters do you have?*

One.

[*Bezdek:*] *One?*

Girl—

[*Bezdek:*] *One sister?*

Yes.

[*Bezdek:*] *Does she live around here?*

She lives in New York, New York City.

[*Bezdek:*] *And then, your folks—are they still living?*

Yes. My mother and father. They're still living in Newark. They're both retired now.

[*Melhem:*] *There is often a fluid sense for me of exchange between your plays and your poetry and prose. Do you see them as distinct genres, or would you say your poetry is now being absorbed into your drama and prose?*

Oh, I see them as distinct in terms of certain formal considerations, but I think my view has always been that poetry is the fundamental concern. If you're interested in words, then fundamentally you have to be a poet. I think that might be some poet chauvinism, but I think that fundamentally if you're really interested in words, then you will be a poet, because it seems to me that's the concern with words even before they become words, you know, sounds. And then I think that you have to utilize the poetic as much as you can in all the forms, because the poetic to me is just an intense sense of language, an intense concern with language; you know, rhythm, sound connote like "high speech," I call it. I think that you have to be concerned with that, whether you write a novel or a play or an essay. Lu Hsum said that he liked essays because in essays he could do anything. He could have a little poem; he could have a little novelistic bit of fiction, you know, but within the essay form. And so he could make that essay anything he wanted, but at the same time be talking in an expository kind of form about clearly identifiable reality.

[*Bezdek:*] *If you had—it's impossible to do, but what would be a typical poem? What would be a poem that you would say, "That's what I'm all about"? More than some of the others mean? I know all—*

Mine?

[*Bezdek:*] *Yes.*

I guess you always tend to want to uphold [*laughs*] your most recent works. I guess a poem I wrote recently called **"In the Tradition,"** which is a long poem, a poem about African American history. It's a cultural history and political history. I think that would be, if I could say it was something that sums you up at a certain point, I would say probably that poem.

[*Melhem:*] *Where does that appear?*

It was published in the Greenfield Review, and then it was— I read it with music last year at Soundscape. It's coming out on a record called New Music, New Poetry, with David Murray and Stephen McCall. In fact, I got the test pressing today, so it should be out momentarily.

[*Melhem:*] *Is your departure from lyricism, basically—although you still are writing poems, but you seem to be turning towards satire and the historical pageant—would you say that it is simply a function of the genre? It's not that you're consciously rejecting lyricism as a mode?*

No. I've always had that, the lyrical thing, if you mean—to me, the highly personal song, which is what I've given up on, the lyric poems. On the one hand, I've always told my students you can't write lyric poems too long, only when

you're a kid, because in those [*laughs*] you know, "I hurt, I feel, I love, I want"—after a while it gets to be—[*laughter*] kind of old, you know what I mean. [*Laughs*] So I try to—I think I do—maintain a connection with the lyrical urge, a sense of the self in the world, sensitive to it. But at the same time, that satirical thing that you perceive has always been present in my work, even from the first book that I put out, the poetry. There's edged in there, you know, the kind of satire and irony. And I think that's been a kind of characteristic of my view of things, even as a little boy, hearing these various dudes I know in this town talk about how I used to be when I was a kid. It was really the same thing. They were just subjected to the same kind of satire and irony, though, in speech, back and forth, back and forth, and that's why I always had to learn to run fast, because [*laughing*] you'd say certain things to people you didn't know would provoke them to such an extent. You had to get in the wind. But that has always been there, a kind of seeing, for instance, negative things in a very ironical and satirical way and really making them funny, with a bitter kind of humor. I think that's always been my way to a certain extent, and I mean I've suffered for that, God knows, in school and college, the service. If you make some comment to a sergeant or a lieutenant [*chuckles*], they wouldn't particularly like it. But I think that's always been there.

[*Bezdek:*] *Do you think you're mellowing now? I don't mean—*

No, I understand what you mean. I think in some ways, probably. But I don't think so. People still seem to think not. I mean in terms of reactions to various things that people— you know, they don't want to publish this, they don't want to publish that, so it seems like mellowing but it's still objectionable in a lot of quarters.

[*Bezdek:*] *I mean do you think you're still perceived as a militant, angry, or—*

I think in some quarters, obviously, because those people will not give you an inch. Obviously, a writer who's been around as long as I have is supposed to be able to make a living from magazine articles, those kinds of things, you know what I mean. A regularly published book a year—you're supposed to be able to make it. But I can't. And the only explanation of that is that the content still disturbs people. They still want to wrestle with you about your conception of reality. So it makes it difficult. I think the mellowing, if anything, has been, perhaps, a greater kind of understanding of certain things. For instance, I thought that revolution would be immediate, at one point. And I don't think that's so much mellowing but deepening your understanding to find that that's not reality, that it's not an event, that it's a process, and you have to be aware of that process, help speed that process up, but not get so frustrated that it doesn't come about, that you actually drive yourself crazy.

[*Melhem:*] *Do you think that any degree of revolutionary change can come through the polls or legislation?*

. . . I think that my early days of writing—I think I wanted to reach everybody, but obviously, my concerns were not broad enough. I think when I was a Nationalist, obviously, I then wanted to focus strictly on Black people. But I think now, the difference between, say, myself as a young writer, when I really was just talking to anybody who would listen but my concerns were narrow—now I try to broaden my concerns to make that voice broad enough to touch different people's lives.
—*Amiri Baraka*

Well, let's say this. To me, the use of electoral politics is only a tactic. I mean I think it does have to be utilized, because I think if you don't utilize it, you will find yourself in a position where you're backed up against the ovens, you know, and then the only thing you can do is fight for your life, I mean quite literally. Like people are talking about now they want to repeal the Voting rights Act. They came on with an editorial on Channel 11, WPIX, "Repeal the Voting rights Act." Now if you sit still and say, well, we can't fight against that, because finally, voting is not going to change monopoly capitalism—and it's not. I don't think, in the end, anything other than short of armed revolution will change this system of monopoly capitalism and end racism and women's oppression. But for you to sit quietly and let them wipe out the Voting Rights Act is just bizarre. For you not to fight for every kind of democratic right, inch by inch—you know what I mean, like they say, fight for every inch—is mad. It's like, I was very critical of a lot of people on the Left in the recent election, because their line was "Carter and Reagan are exactly the same." Well, look, they represent the same class, but there are different sectors of that class, and they are not identical, you see, as you now found out. Here's a man now talking about getting rid of Social Security—you can't say that's the *same* as Jimmy Carter. So I think that those kinds of sweeping, Leftist, ultrarevolutionary statements serve to do nothing but fog up the reality that you have to fight for every inch. Yes, you have to utilize voting. Absolutely you have to utilize it. People died in the South to get the right to vote, and then you're going to tell people, "Don't vote. It doesn't mean anything." That's bizarre. The question is, what *does* it mean? It has a limited and specific meaning, but it has to be utilized.

[*Melhem:*] *Do you see any progress at all, in Newark or elsewhere, since the sixties?*

Well, yes, sure. There's been general progress. I think we're in a period now when they're trying to eliminate that, and you'll find that in this particular kind of society, that's what happens all the time. For instance, in the 1860s, a period of revolution, the Civil War—the Civil War was a democratic revolution: It eliminated slavery; it changed the Constitution to guarantee democratic rights, equality, you know, not only for black people but poor whites, which is always a well-kept secret. But by the 1870s, 1880s, that had been almost eliminated. By that time, you had laws on the books now ensuring the inequality that had been fought in the 1860s. The same thing now: 1960s people struggled for affirmative action. Man comes along in the seventies and tch-tch—one signature, the Bakke decision [*whistles*]. Get rid of it. And the stuff that Reagan is doing now, to me, is the same that happened in the 1870s and 1880s, now in the 1970s, the 1980s, the same kind of attempt to eliminate what gain, what inch of gain was made.

[*Bezdek:*] *Now there's talk—I don't know if it's some sociologist at Harvard or some place like that recently, in one of these vague generalizations about America, but he said that we are on the brink in some cities, I think Newark was one of them, with a permanent underclass of people, you know, who forever will be shackled to the situation. Do you think that that's—*

Well, I think that as far as the present economy, that would have to be true, but since, if we understand reality, we know nothing stays the same. Things are not static. There is going to be motion; it's either going to be upward or downward. Then you know that those people are not going to stand for that, and the only thing you're doing then is preparing for some kind of broad, urban unrest. I mean, this Heritage Foundation has already advised Reagan to abandon the cities—don't give any aid to the cities, talking about the Northeast, in particular—abandon those cities, leave them, and the Midwest, the New Yorks, and the Detroits, and the Chicagos, and the Clevelands, and the Phillies, and Pittsburgh, abandon those cities, head for the Sun Belt. And then now, you see, even in this pseudopopular culture that they manufacture—there's a movie called *Escape from New York*, which actually now would turn New York into Alcatraz—

[*Melhem:*] [*Laughing*] *I find that insulting.*

Well, if you see who's in there, locked up in there, you would really find that insulting: Blacks, Latinos, Asians, homosexuals, aggressive women, punk rockers. [*Laughs*] They're the ones who are locked up.

[*Melhem:*] *I wanted to ask you something about that. In*

terms of your current position, your article in the Village Voice, *"Confessions of a Former Anti-Semite"*—

—which is not my title.

[*Melhem:*] *Oh, it wasn't? What was your title?*

My title was "A Personal View of Anti-semitism." That's our friend [David] Schneiderman, who was the editor. That's his idea of something that would sell papers. What apparently it did.

[*Melhem:*] *Okay. Well, in that article, you equate Zionism with white racism as "reactionary." Would you now add Black Nationalism to that list?*

Well, I say this. To me, all nationalism, finally, taken to any extreme, has got to be oppressive to the people who are not in that nationality. You understand what I mean? If it's taken to the extreme, any nationalism has got to be exclusive and has got to say, "Us, yes; you, no." I mean, that's the nature of nationalism. But you have to make a distinction between, say, people who are oppressed as a nationality, who are fighting national liberation struggles. I think in terms of Zionism, the difference is this: that previous to the Second World War, Jews generally were not interested in Zionism, what Chaim Weizmann and, you know, the other dude put forward. Generally it was like some right-wing intellectuals, some right-wing nationalist intellectuals. Once the British got hold of that, the Balfour Declaration, in which then it's made a part of British foreign policy to settle Jews in a Palestinian homeland, you know, obviously to look over the oil interests—that changes into an instrument of imperialist policy. Now, a certain sector of the Jewish population becomes interested in Zionism as a result of the Holocaust, for obvious reasons, for obvious reasons. Once you knock off seven million people, then, if there's somebody saying, "Look, you got to get out of here, that's the reason, you got to get out of here," then that's going to become attractive.

But I do not believe that Zionism is the general ideology of Jews in the world. I think the great contributions that Jews have made in the world have been much more advanced than a narrow nationalism, and I think obviously what [Menachim] Begin and Company are doing now, it just isolates the State of Israel from the world. I think more and more people will come to see, and especially Jews, that the state of Israel and Jews are two separate entities. And I think that it's a great cover story for somebody who may jump on Israel, for you to say you're attacking Jews generally, and you have to shut up. But I don't think that's going to work. It's very interesting, for instance, to see a lot of Palestinian Jews, now, organizations. It's an incredible thing, but I think of course in New York, when you've got a stronghold of world Zionist organization, it's very hard for you to say things like that

without people beating you to death as being anti-Jewish, which has been my fate. Even that article I wrote, which was an attempt to set the record straight, you know, was hacked up so unmercifully. It made you wonder just what they wanted to present. I mean, at the end it seemed like they wanted to present you as an anti-Semite, even though I volunteered to write the article.

[*Melhem:*] *You're talking about the editing of that article?*

Oh, yes, yes, oh yes. You see, what I did—

[*Melhem:*] *The "Confession," with Jewish people I've spoken to, was not received as any kind of apology.*

Oh, no. Well, the thing on Zionism, the minute you jump on Zionism, you're going to get it back, no matter what you say. You see, what was removed, to me, was critical, because I did a whole history of anti-Semitism. Essentially, it's an ideological justification for fundamentally economic and political oppression. Anti-Semitism rises, you know, in the struggle between the Greeks and Jews in the Middle East, and the Romans and the Jews, and basically then in the Middle Ages as an attempt to keep economic superiority. Economic attack is what it justifies: "These people are Christ-killers. Let's take their money." You know, it's like the Japanese you've put in a concentration camp: "These people are our enemies; let's get their truck farms. Let's get their truck farms; these people are our enemies." You know what I mean. There's always an ideological justification for some economic and political shenanigans. That's what it essentially is. No matter that you might have some people down the road who really believe it, like you might have some Klansmen walking around who really believe such and such a thing is true, when actually, what's happening is you've got some landowners who are not going to let Black people, for instance, have democracy down there because it means they're not going to control that land. They're not going to control the U.S. Senate or the colonies anymore. You always have people who walk around, who believe stuff on one level; but you also have the people who are putting that out, who are gaining from that. That's the real significance of that.

[*Melhem:*] *I'd like to ask you about your thinking on homosexuality and also on the women's movement. Even as late as* **The Sidney Poet Heroical,** *which was published in '79, you refer to gay men as "faggots,", referring in a derogatory way. Has your thinking changed with the movement for gay rights? Would you say—*

Well, I say this—

[*Melhem:*] *—there's a certain parallel in, you know, the raising of your consciousness in thinking about those things?*

Well, in a certain way. You see, first of all, I say this. The use of the term "faggot," although obviously it's derived from homosexuality, from homosexuals, was not meant in the Black community simply as "homosexual." It meant, essentially, a weak person, you know, somebody who could not do what they were supposed to do. That's what it really meant.

[*Melhem:*] *You're saying you absorbed this.*

Oh, sure. So that, a lot of times, calling people "faggots" did not mean specifically that it had to do with homosexuality. It had to do with the question of weakness, although obviously it is taken from that, and as such still is a kind of what would you call it—attack.

[*Melhem:*] *Yes, attack.*

Yes, attack. I don't think I believe in any gratuitous attacks on homosexuals as such. I've tried to stop saying that, calling people "faggots," even though, still I would say when the majority of Black people say "faggot," they're not talking about homosexuals. You might say, "Reagan is a faggot"; I mean, you're not talking about him being a homosexual [*laughs*]; you're talking about him being a weak, jive person. But I think it does come from the denigration of homosexuality, and I think that, as I said, gratuitous attacks on homosexuals have to be opposed. We do have to oppose any kind of attempt to limit homosexuals' democratic rights, because when they're doing that, they're coming for *us*. You know, attack homosexuals' democratic rights—it's really coming for everybody's democratic rights, but at the same time, I believe this: that homosexuality is a minority issue, except in the way that I just mentioned, where it can be connected up to everybody's democratic rights. I think that living in L.A. or New York or San Francisco, one might tend to think that it's much more of a mass issue than it is. But the majority of people are not interested in homosexuality; they don't care anything about it. I think this: if you were to raise up as a mass question, "Do you want this homosexual to teach your children?" I think that, in the main, is going to be negative. I think most people are going to say, like, negative.

[*Melhem:*] *But how do you feel?*

Well, I think this. The question is, if a homosexual is teaching my child in a way that I can see is beneficial to the child, it doesn't matter to me. You see what I'm saying? But obviously I don't want the child to be taught homosexuality, and I don't want the child to *be* a homosexual. I don't want that to be raised up as a positive thing, because I do believe that homosexuality is a social aberration. I do believe it's a social aberration, and I think it's a product of class society, essentially. I do not believe that homosexuality, by and large,

is going to help human beings to make progress. But I do not believe that homosexuals need to be attacked.

[*Melhem:*] *So your thinking is somewhat modified, but not—*

Oh, yes. It's modified in the sense that I think that just loose-mouthed calling people "faggots" is out of the question. I mean, even when some of my best friends—that sounds really corny, and it is—but see, even when some of my best friends—that sounds really corny, and it is—but see, even when some of my best friends were homosexuals, I still called people "faggots," and I didn't mean *them*. [*Laughs*] It meant something else. But I think that that question of dealing with homosexuals and understanding that you cannot attack these people's democratic rights—they cannot be subjected to any gratuitous attacks—does not, in any way, justify homosexuality, because I don't think I can justify it in that sense.

[*Melhem:*] *What about women's rights? Women don't seem to come off very well in your work, except, at best, in a passive—*

Um-hum.

[*Melhem:*] *Has your consciousness been raised at all in connection with the Feminist Movement?*

Probably, but I don't think the Feminist Movement per se; but I think the whole struggle for women's rights—the Feminist Movement is part of that; it's certainly in there. I would agree with you that until the last four or five years, works on women or about women have either been missing or, as you say, largely passive. In the last four or five years there has been some kind of significant change. I would attribute that to my wife, principally.

[*Bezdek:*] *What is her name?*

Amina, A-m-i-n-a. And to the whole question of—you see, when people like, for instance, Michele Wallace come off talking about it in that book that *Ms.* magazine wants to push to give a kind of a feminist interpretation of Black Liberation—that's completely off the wall, because what it does is it attacks Black women again. Because if you think that because you weren't there, that the Black women in the Movement just went for that, just passively said, "Oh, yes, we must go and deal with these male chauvinists," well, you saddle your thinking, because our whole history of women's participation in the Black Liberation Movement of the sixties, from my own knowledge of it, was constantly marked by women fighting against the male chauvinism of people like myself, you know, and a great many other people. So that for somebody to come and make it seem that "Yes, you know, the problem with the Black Liberation Movement is male chauvinism, and none of these black women knew it" is like the height of an attack, and the only person who could do that is somebody who didn't know, who wasn't there. But talk to the people who were in the Movement, who knew, and who know, and had to go through that, and had to be subjected to that, while people like Michele Wallace were off in some private school in Paris. It's ludicrous, because they actually had to be subjected to that and fight against that and have their lives crippled by that, and then somebody comes along and says, "Well, you know what the problem was."

[*Bezdek:*] *What do you remember about Newark in 1967, the riots—just immediately, what comes to mind?*

Well, the fires; seeing U.S. Army military weapons in a city that was supposed to be in America. I mean, you look up and see tanks, and soldiers fully armed; then you want to know where you are—this must not be America, because this is what they did in Vietnam or Korea. But then people, the police checking people's ID. . . . I was arrested the first night of the thing and I was locked up through the period of the worst kind of burning and fighting. But the police came up into my house, which is the Spirit House on Stirling Street. My wife and child—young child was in there, oldest son— were in there, and they were on the third floor, I think, and then the National Guard and the cops came in on the first floor, destroying stuff, turning stuff over, breaking up things. They never went up to the third floor; they didn't think anybody was there. And, you know, bullets through the windows, and stuff like that.

[*Bezdek:*] *What were the circumstances of your being arrested?*

Well, we were driving around looking at it, what was going on. A couple of friends and I were riding around the Central Ward—you know, I lived there at the time—looking at what was happening. Picked up a couple of people, took them to the hospital, things like that, and then we stayed out too late afterward. People had cleared off the streets and we were coming down the street, and we were stopped by about twenty cops, I don't know. They pulled us out of the car and they started beating us. They split my head open, knocked my teeth out, I mean I couldn't see, I mean my face was so covered with blood I thought I was going to die, you know; there just was blood everywhere, I couldn't even see. But the people in the window were screaming, there were black people up there who kept screaming, kept screaming—that's what cooled it out. Otherwise, I was finished. When you feel the blood in your face, you can feel it warm in your face, and you can't even see for the blood; it's in your mouth, your eyes—

[*Melhem:*] [*Softly*] *And then you could have been killed.*

Oh, yes. That was understood. That was understood, you know. Oh, that was it. I mean, that was really where they were going to take us off. But, after that, they charged us with possession of weapons, which was the first trial we lost, and then we got another trial because the judge was obviously out of his mind. He reads a poem and sentences. He reads one of my poems as a reason to sentence me. I knew that was out, even if he wouldn't do anything, I said this guy's a nut. As if the poem was the reason to—it was a poem about rebellion that had been written just before the [Black] rebellion. And so that was—I got a retrial and it was thrown out. It took about two years, three years.

[*Bezdek:*] *Have you ever served time?*

No. I've never served any; I've been in jail a lot but I never—except for a couple of days.

[*Bezdek:*] *I mean, you've never been, like, sentenced, like this thing coming up.*

Well, even when I was sentenced to three years, no parole, for this gun thing—

[*Bezdek:*] *This thing?*

No. The thing in '67. I was sentenced to three years, but I didn't—I served about three or four days and got out on appeal. And I had done a couple of days before that. This time I did about four days and was discharged. But that's about the most time I've ever done.

[*Bezdek:*] *What do you think of this ninety days coming up, if that goes down?*

Well, that stuff is so wild that it's very hard to consistently take it seriously, but now we've been at it two and a half years; they've been on us for two and a half years.

[*Bezdek:*] *This case?*

Yes. From '79, June of '79.

[*Bezdek:*] *You mean this incident with the argument? Is that it?*

Yes. June '79. So, apparently they're serious they're going to lock me up. Why they will get so much satisfaction in locking me up for ninety days is something that needs to be looked into. I mean, they've had two years of court costs, five days of grand jury hearings for a resisting-arrest charge. You're wondering, "Why, why would you spend so much money when you're talking about the need to cut the budget?" Our boy William Butz just got sentenced to thirty days for a $96,000 tax evasion. [*Laughs*] What is it in this "resisting arrest"? But really, it's a form of intimidation—not only for me, but I think they want to intimidate, generally, people. They want the people to know, "Look. This is what we do." And then there's also the possibility that they're going to do something to you in the prison. You could never be sure of that. Especially with this hit list that's circulating. We just published this hit list of cultural workers and artists. Two people who work for the government leaked this out to a publisher—not a publisher, to a producer, and somebody in his office leaked it to me. And I've been trying to leak it to various people. We published it in our newspaper [*Unity*]; I've read it on the radio; I've sent it to different newspapers. Interestingly, one of the people who was on the hit list died last week—Harry Chapin, the folksinger.

[*Melhem:*] *He was on that?*

Yes, he was on there. He got this mysterious accident—somebody hit him from behind. That is so spooky that I think that I'm going to reopen that whole thing. I've got a copy of it upstairs; I'll show it to you. But there are about twenty people on it, who they say have to be, you know, done something to—people like Pete Seeger, Bread and Puppet Theatre—

[*Bezdek:*] *Where did the list come from?*

[*Melhem:*] *Are you on that list?*

It was supposed to be leaked from a government—two people working in a government agency, who were cultural workers working in a government agency, and said these people would have two things going: blacklist, which is to make it difficult for these people to get their works out; and a hit list, that is, certain people within this list need to be done away with. And it talks about arranging accidents for some of them, and a couple of them who have already disappeared, a guy named Dan Silver, a guy who made films in El Salvador. Then there were a lot of people who do political theater, who are cultural activists, things like that. When that Harry Chapin thing happened, really, my eyes shot right open. Jesus Christ!

[*Melhem:*] *Are you on either list?*

Yes. Oh, yes.

[*Melhem:*] *You're on both lists?*

Yes, I'm on that list. They put them together. The ones that are supposed to be killed have asterisks by them. [*Laughs*] Chapin was supposed to be—they said they were going to do something to remove him, something like that.

[*Bezdek:*] *Do you know what agency it came from?*

No. They didn't say. It was a letter, with a list attached to it. The letter said that "we are two people who work for a government agency, whose business it is to set up a blacklist on the following artists and also remove the ones that are listed on there." So we published it. Like I said, I broadcast it over the radio. I've sent it to a couple of big publications, but they haven't done anything with it. Recently, I just sent it back out, saying, "Well, look, since this Chapin thing, you can at least raise that up; you know, you might be able to sell a few papers." Because I believe that's the only thing that would really cool that out; to a certain extent, it's publicity.

[*Bezdek:*] *Yes, sure.*

Even if it turned out to be a hoax. Obviously, generally we know such things exist. I've got two thousand pages from the FBI that I had a lawyer get through the Freedom of Information Act, but now they're getting ready to close that loophole.

[*Melhem:*] *This list was published before Chapin's—*

Yes. I'm sure. Published a couple of weeks before Chapin died.

[*Melhem:*] *That's scary.*

Oh, yes. It was published in June.

[*Melhem:*] *That should really be investigated.*

Yes. So we're going to try to get some more publicity on that.

[*Melhem:*] *In moving from Kawida to Marxist-Leninist-Maoism, did you have any strong influences on your transition before the Sixth Pan-African Congress in 1974?*

Influences to change to Marxism?

[*Melhem:*] *Yes. And people, thinkers—*

Yes. A lot of changes. First of all, I think my own experience in terms of dealing in this town with electoral politics; seeing a Black middle class benefit from those electoral politics and no changes for the majority. So I began to understand what "classes" and "class struggle" was about, you know, from my own experience. Meeting Black Marxists in different united fronts I belonged to, like the African Liberation Support Committee; beginning to see and talk to people who are on the Left; finding out that a lot of people that I admired who were African revolutionaries were really anti-imperialists and Marxists. They were not talking "hate white," as I was at the time, people like Amilcar Cabral in

Guinea-Bissau; Nkrumah in Ghana; Samora Machel in Mozambique; the Pan-African Congress in South Africa— people like that. Beginning to see that, hey, there was a whole different view by Black activists around the world. And I think those are the things. I had read Mao, but I would always come to excise the part about communism, where he would talk about he was a communist, and stuff. [*Laughs*] You know, censor that part and try to read the rest of it, which was, of course, bizarre. And so then I decided that I was fooling myself, and I should go ahead and investigate and find out what was happening, and I did. I mean it was in a lot of ways a painful experience, in a lot of ways. Organization nationally split in half. We had a large organization in some sixteen, seventeen cities, and then split in half.

[*Melhem:*] *Which organization?*

That was the Congress of Afrikan Peoples. But I thought that it was necessary, and I still do think it is necessary and important.

[*Melhem:*] *The deep concern of your leadership is with "unity and struggle." Whom are you seeking to unite?*

Well, the great majority of people in this country—in fact, the great majority of people in the world—who have the same general enemies. I think the great majority of people in this country are objective allies; they're fighting against the same class of people: I think the six-tenths of one percent of the people that actually own the land, that actually own CBS and NBC and ABC, that actually own Standard Oil and Exxon, I mean those of us who have been taught to think like them, I mean the six-tenths of one percent that actually own that, the rulers. I think a great many other people, let's say, 90 percent of the people—there's another 9 percent that will die with that six-tenths of one percent. But I think 90 percent of the people in this country can unite, and I think eventually they will. Everybody comes to it in different ways. You have some very deep problems in this country with that unity. Obviously, the whole history of slavery and chauvinism in this country makes that very difficult. But I don't think it's impossible.

[*Melhem:*] *In looking toward unity, what about coalition on the Left? I mean the breach between Soviet-oriented communism, scorned as "Red Squad Functionaries" in your play S-1, and Mao-oriented communism, expressed by the "Revolutionary People's Union" in that? Do you see any possibility of a coalition?*

Well, you see, no, because I think that if you look at the world with the view that I have, the view I guess best expressed by the "Theory of Three Worlds" of Mao Tse-tung, in my view, the United States and the Soviet Union are two imperialist super-powers, and while obviously a lot of people

in the Communist Party U.S.A. are just—don't understand what's happening, are dupes, the people in the leadership there act as a kind of fifth column of the Soviet Union in the United States, and even make it difficult to struggle against U.S. imperialism; they make it more difficult to struggle against U.S. imperialism, even though it seems that they're struggling against it. And I say they make it more difficult because they are always putting out this line that reforms are the answer, that reforms are the end. They're even telling people that no, you can get socialism through the election machines—that's like somebody selling dope, you know. You're not going to get socialism; you're not going to elect the people's control of the wealth anywhere in the world; I mean, Chile should have taught us that for all times. It was a legally elected socialist government in a modern, industrial country. What is it now? A fascist state. So I think the question is, if you've got people representing a superpower, imperialist country, whether it's the U.S. or the Soviet Union, then you can't make a coalition with it.

[*Bezdek:*] *When you were young, did you ever talk politics with your parents? Your father, say, a Republican—you must have had a hard time with that.*

No, no. My *grand*father was Republican. My father has always been a Democrat. My father says he voted for the man, not the party, whatever that meant. But he tended to be a Democrat. I think he was a Roosevelt man. Now, I don't know where he's at, but I would think that he's generally a Democrat-leaning person. But my grandfather was a Republican, obviously, even up until Wendell Willkie. We used to have Willkie buttons around the house. And, you know, my father was a Democrat, so there would be some tension in that. But I talked politics to them or raised up political issues, and we'd agree and disagree. I think for one thing, though, both my father and mother were radicalized *somewhat* by the '67 rebellion, and I think when my father, especially when he saw what they had done to me, it snapped him out, because he had been much more conservative before then. But I think that when he saw that they had tried to kill me, he knew that whatever I was doing, it wasn't that bad. I think it really snapped him out. And then he came to the court and saw the kind of obvious racism. It's one thing to see it abstractly, but when you see that it's your child they're doing these things to, that probably would light you up.

[*Bezdek:*] *Were you a fighter as a child, or were you more, as you mentioned earlier, a wordsmith? I mean you would say things—*

Really, when I had to fight it was because there was no other way out. [*Laughs*] But no, words became weapons for me a long time ago, and my physical prowess was in speed. If you couldn't talk your way out of it, then you had to decamp, change landscapes rapidly. But then when I got into the service was when I really started actually having to fight all the time. I'd never wanted to or even found it necessary to get into fisticuffs, but then I got into the air force and I really had to, first because of that kind of overt racism which I could not *stand*. It's one thing to see the Klan in the newspaper, but to have somebody call you a name, it always just set me on fire, and that's when I came in contact with that. Then I actually started to roll around on the ground with people, and I really had not done much of that before—especially when I didn't feel I could win, anyway. [*Laughter*] But in the service, though, I found that, always coming up with that.

[*Bezdek:*] *Did you grow up in the Central Ward?*

Yes.

[*Bezdek:*] *You mentioned Italian, so you must have been near the North Ward.*

West Ward, near the North Ward, yes, right by Central Avenue. I grew up, my early days, right in the Central Ward, Barclay Street, Boston Street, and then later on, Central Avenue, back over to the Central Ward, Belmont Avenue.

[*Bezdek:*] *What high school did you go to?*

Barringer; it's in the North Ward. At the time, there were very few Blacks in it.

[*Bezdek:*] *And how many children do you have?*

Five by the present marriage, two by a previous marriage.

[*Bezdek:*] *Five by the present; two by a previous.*

Um-hum.

[*Melhem:*] *You're including the two children that are in Manhattan, before—*

No. She has two by a previous marriage.

[*Melhem:*] *Oh—so there are seven?*

In the house?

[*Melhem:*] *Yes.*

Well, there are six in the house. One of them is not here; one of them is actually on vacation somewhere, and the other lives elsewhere. There usually are six kids here.

[*Melhem:*] *Three were in a play, weren't they—**S-1**—I saw three names—*

Yes. That's right.

[*Melhem:*] *—"Baraka." Are they interested in the theater?*

I think so. Well, let me see, one of them, the oldest boy, plays the drums; he's a very good drummer. The next boy—I don't know if he's interested in drama; I think he wants to be a writer. The little girl is always reading poetry aloud, so I think she wants to be an actress.

[*Melhem:*] *Um-hum.*

She's always proclaiming these poems, so she might want to act.

[*Melhem:*] *Do you act?*

No, no [*Laughs*] My mother was always putting me in different little things, skits, but I never did any serious adult acting.

[*Melhem:*] *I was wondering about the responses of Black writers. Intellectuals, to your views. How receptive have they been to your view on these political aspects?*

Well, I think you'll find that there's a kind of class struggle raging among Black intellectuals like everywhere else, and I think that the people are divided around the lines they take. I think there are more and more people who are much less hostile, say, to Marxism than they were in '74, '75. In '74 and '75 people were calling us all kinds of bad words, you know, "traitors," I remember at the Sixth Pan-African Congress this woman actually went to the foreign minister, weeping, saying stuff that I had said and this other guy, Owusu Sadaukai, had said; that we were really betraying Black people. And I mean I thought that was kind of extraordinary. There is still, of course, a lot of sentiment in the Black community, but I think there's much less hostility to Marxist ideas.

[*Melhem:*] *I just want to ask you a couple of more things on [Charles] Olson.*

Um-hum.

[*Melhem:*] *Olson's theories of Projectivism and "composition by field" still seem alive and well in your work. Apart from your progress toward a Black aesthetic and the Marxist approach of your recent work, would you say that Olson remains your most useful poetic influence?*

Well, no. I think my most useful poetic influence is Langston Hughes. Charles Olson was important to me at one time, and I think the most importance that he had was that within the kind of aesthetic that I was actually involved in, he provided a kind of opening for the ideas that I saw, and then I said, Well, wow! A lot of the things that I think and want to do, he's actually expressing these things. You see? Because I was drawn to certain white poets, like Allen Ginsberg, even before Olson. I was drawn to them because they legitimized things that I wanted to do and that I felt. When I came up against the *New Yorker* magazine poets and the *Hudson Review* and *Partisan Review* poets, they made me weep, because I really didn't want to write like that; I really didn't think I could write that; I mean, it was dull, it was dead. The things that I wanted to write, I didn't think could even be called "poetry" by their standards, you know—so that was very depressing and discouraging. But then when I got to New York and discovered, wow! Somebody like Allen, who was talking about, you know, the "nigger streets" and junkies and all kinds of things that I could see and I could identify with, then I said, yeah, that's closer to what I want to do. And then when I saw Olson's statement, he was saying, actually, that this old dead poetry that people have been writing is exactly that, exactly what you thought it was: old, dead poetry. Then it actually just encouraged me, because I had thought these things anyway. It's like somebody saying something that you've got bubbling around in your head, and then they come out with it, and it legitimizes what you're dong; it encourages you.

[*Bezdek:*] *What about [Jack] Kerouac—him, too, as part of—*

Well, in a way. But Ginsberg always was more important to me, I guess being a poet. Because Allen is an intellectual; Kerouac was not much of an intellectual; he was more of a—

[*Bezdek:*] *Street wise—*

—yes, kind of person. I think you could see that when his later views became so backward, because he was never really rooted in investigation of ideas. It was more like reacting to things, spontaneous, which, because it was so open and free in terms of its form, was positive. Because there was no deep investigation into the history of ideas, then the form could be undermined by the content.

[*Melhem:*] *Ginsberg said, "First thought, best thought." Do you agree with that?*

No. [*Laughs*] Obviously.

[*Melhem:*] *Do you revise it all?*

Yes. So does he.

[*Melhem:*] *In all genres—*

Yes.

[*Melhem:*] *—in all genres, poetry and prose?*

Yes, sure. So does he—so what? [*Laughs*]

[*Melhem:*] *I don't know whether he'll admit it, though.*

Oh, I don't see why not. I say this: what he means is that you get to a point where at one point in the fifties people were then showing you just—poems—"I worked on this poem *twenty years!*" Really. There's so much more in people's normal perception that's worth being exposed to. But to tell somebody you're working on something—getting a word changed for twenty years is not really impressive anymore. It becomes like some prescription for—a mummy farm.

[*Melhem:*] *So then you're somewhere in between* le mot juste—*Flaubert's* le mot juste—*and "if I write it, it's a poem."*

Oh yes, sure. I don't believe in "absolute spontaneity is always the best." No. Absolutely not. That's why you have certain levels of understanding. You know, there is perception where you do perceive a thing, and sometimes that perception can hold. But then you bring your rational mind to bear on it, and sometimes you have to modify that, or sometimes you see a way that you can make a thing stronger, and that helps. And then a lot of times you find out, whoa! You're way off base; you might come back to something a few years later and say, "Oh, Jesus—did I say that? Oh, get that out of there." And that's obvious.

I don't like to . . . pretend that I never thought those things—somebody says, "Well, look, you had these backward ideas on such and such a date"—and then sneak around and cross them out. No. I think the point is to say, "Yeah. Well, that's true. But, hopefully, the later work has changed and shows some kind of growth and development." But I don't think you can hide your tracks. And that's kind of—

[*Bezdek:*] *When is your birthday?*

October 7, 1934.

[*Bezdek:*] *So you're coming up for—*

Forty-seven. Forty-eight? [*Laughs*]

[*Melhem:*] *A young man.*

[*Bezdek:*] *Well, you'll be forty-seven—*

Yes.

[*Bezdek:*] *I don't want to say that too loudly in case your son was around and it was a secret he wasn't supposed to—*

Oh, no! [*Chuckling*] He asked me that the other day.

[*Melhem:*] *There's an abundance of punning in your work, and you'll recall Olson's saying, "Pun is rime" in his "Projective Verse" essay?*

Yes. Right.

[*Melhem:*] *Did he to any extent spark that interest in punning?*

No. That's a street thing.

[*Melhem:*] *That's just a street thing.*

Oh, yes. The pun—the rhyme and the pun are really part of the Black oral tradition. I think they're part of everybody's oral tradition—the whole first, what you'd call "delicious accident," and then a much more rational juxtaposition of sounds and things. But that always, I think, goes back to the oral tradition, the pun.

[*Melhem:*] *The use of the word* Negro, *the pun "Knee-grow," and "New Ark" —these are your inventions?*

"Knee-grow" is: "New Ark" is the original name of the town. People resist that.

[*Bezdek:*] *That's what it's called in Delaware.*

Yes. If you look on the charter, it's two words, "New Ark," and obviously, it's a biblical reference, but when he started to use it, then people resisted it because it was identified with us, I mean, the backward people in this town. But that's the real name. And it's interesting that southern Blacks always say that to this day; you know, they keep saying, "New Ark."

[*Bezdek:*] *The town in Delaware is spelled the same way, and they all call it "New Ark."*

Yes, that's interesting. That's obviously the name. And I think the southern Blacks probably say that because they're probably going back to an older English, too, that's "New Ark."

[*Bezdek:*] *Actually Newark lately has become a sort of— when the guy on the train announces it—"Nerk"* [laughing], *it becomes the one syllable—*

It's not even there—

[*Bezdek:*] *"Nerk!"*

I know. That's another kind of speech.

[*Bezdek:*] *Speaking of speeches, can you—I'm sure your answer to this is "yes"—you can go out there and talk jive, right? You can go down to the corner and—you don't talk—*

Black English.

[*Bezdek:*] *Not only Black English. I mean you just—I don't really mean Black English; I mean, just guys-on-the-corner sort of talk. I don't know what the name is, but—*

Sure.

[*Bezdek:*] *I mean, you don't talk the way you're doing now.*

No, not altogether. But I think I've always had a reputation in this town—

[*Bezdek:*] *If I could borrow one of them at—*

No, I've always had a reputation in this town for talking "funny." [*General laughter*] Obviously, I do speak more like these people around here speak. I've always had a reputation of sounding funny and so on. I know people—about the way I used to say "motherfucker," they'd say, "I don't want you to call me that because you say it too nasty. [*Laughter*] Because you pronounce— you say 'mother'—you know what mean? That is really *ugly* when you say it like that." [*Laughter*] But no, I tend to sound more like the people out there, I would imagine. But it be hard to get all your training out of it. [*Laughs*]

[*Melhem:*] *Would you say the Dozens were an influence in the frequency of direct insult in your work? Like* **Hard Facts,** *would you say the Dozens—*

Oh, sure.

[*Melhem:*] *Did you do the Dozens as a child?*

Oh, sure.

[*Melhem:*] *Did you play it as a rhyming game?*

Both, both rhyming and unrhymed, oh, yes. And I think that was my real introduction to the strength and use of poetry. Because by it you cold actually keep people off you; with poetry you could make them leave you alone. I mean if you couldn't fight, if you could really use those words like that, they would get away from you, because they didn't want to be called twenty-five different kinds of motherfuckers in twenty-five seconds, you know? So they would leave you alone. And then it did become very conscious to me. Yes, speech can be as effective, almost, as your fist. But that was my real introduction to the uses of poetry.

[*Melhem:*] *So that was very young.*

Oh, yes. Oh, sure. But they used to have some people—still do, obviously—walking around, going for hours, rhyming, rhyming, rhyming, rhyming, rhyming, you know, top speed.

[*Melhem:*] *Yes.*

Just a whole flow of insults.

[*Melhem:*] *In some of your recent work, do you use what Stephen Henderson refers to as "virtuoso free-rhyme"?*

Um-hum.

[*Melhem:*] *Rhymes within a long sentence with lots of different rhymes strung—*

Yes. I have much more respect for rhyme, now. I've always used internal rhyme like that, because I felt that was, you know, slick, to do it like that; but I have much more respect for end rhyme, too. And it's like the old story about how, as you get older, you discover how wise your parents were [*laughing*]. I've grown to love Langston Hughes's poetry more now, because I want to use rhyme more. I begin to see then the strengths of that in ways I couldn't see when I was just dismissing rhyme completely. Obviously, rhyme can become a very dead weight in any kind of language. The kind of unrhymed verse that academic poets write is probably as deadly as rhyme. So—[*Laughs*]

[*Melhem:*] *Yes. Well, in connection with that, apart from the critically important work you've done in writing* **Blues People** *and* **Black Music,** *you seem to be using music and musicians increasingly in your poetry and drama, the Advanced Workers, which is your musical group, specifically. Would you say there's a connection between the interest in music and the interest in rhyme? And what, specifically, is the function of the music?*

Well, the music, to me, is two things, but it's one thing first. The music, first of all, is poetry. I mean, to me, fundamentally, poetry is a combination. Poetry is a musical form, just like blues. I think blues is a verse form, but it's a musical form, too. You see what I mean? And to me, poetry has to be that, and at the same time, verse, but it has to be a musical form. I mean it doesn't exist as poetry unless it's musical, you know, "musicked speech," high speech. And I think that my own interest in poetry comes from the kind of love that I've always had for music, basically. I played trumpet when I was a kid, and I wrote this poem called **"I Would Have Been a Trumpet Player If I Hadn't Gone to College."** And essentially, that had something to do with it, because once I left this town and went away to school, I stopped playing the trumpet. I never lost my love for mu-

sic. I began to listen to it, of course, to study it—I studied it informally with Sterling Brown. At Howard he had classes for a lot of us in the dormitory in the evenings, and he'd teach us about the blues and early forms of jazz.

> **The music . . . first of all, is poetry . . . .**
> **Poetry is a musical form, just like blues. I**
> **think blues is a verse form, but it's a**
> **musical form, too . . . . And to me, poetry**
> **has to be that, and at the same time, verse,**
> **but it has to be a musical form.**
> **—*Amiri Baraka***

[*Melhem:*] *You had some fine teachers there; you had Nathan Scott, too.*

Yes, Nathan Scott, right. He taught me Dante. That's where I got my interest in Dante. It wasn't even because I understood it, you know. He was so enthusiastic about it—

[*Melhem:*] *Was it a course—*

—I said, "Jesus, this must be good!" [*Laughs*]

[*Melhem:*] *It was a course in Dante?*

No. It was a survey course in Western literature. We got all the biggies, everybody we were supposed to get, in that one-year survey course. And when he came to Dante, he was so in love with it. And now I understand why—because he was religious. I didn't know that. He was a Reverend—something like that. He was a Doctor of Divinity, as well as a Ph.D.

[*Melhem:*] *In your adaptation of a Black aesthetic to Marxist, agit-prop aesthetics, you seem to be seeking new forms for the new content: for example, your historical pageants,* **Slave Ship** *and* **The Motion of History,** *and your satire,* **The Sidney Poet Heroical,** *in which you musically adapt a classical, Greek-style chorus. Apart from your self-criticism of* **The Sidney Poet** *as "petit bourgeois cultural nationalism," are you satisfied with these works? How do you feel about* **S-1?** *. . .*

The Sidney Poet. No, I'm satisfied with that as a work of a certain period; it said certain things. I think it still has some kind of general uses. It got Sidney Poitier mad at me, though, so I don't know—there was a negative feedback to it. But as far as **S-1** is concerned and **The Motion of History,** I would like to see them done again. I directed both of them, you know; I had this thing of directing my works, at least one a year, every other year, when I could. I took the moneys that I had, whatever money I could borrow, and I would do some performances of the play, because I couldn't get any producers. Since this police harassment two years ago, I haven't been able to do that, and as a matter of fact, that interrupted the production of **The Lone Ranger** that was being done, which I was producing at that time, because I had to use all the money for the court thing, you see, so I didn't have any extra money to use for the production. I would like to see **S-1** done again; I would like to see **The Motion of History** done again. I think particularly **S-1** is relevant during these Reagan times, because what that was about was the attempt to bring fascism to the United States, and I think that's a very, very relevant play, now. I would like to get somebody who would produce it and direct it.

[*Melhem:*] *Was* [*Bertolt*] *Brecht an influence?*

Brecht has been an influence, I'd say, in the last few years. In the last few years, certainly, this whole educational theater, in that sense, the "theater of instruction" is important to me, and a lot of the technical innovations. The jazz opera [*Money*] that I wrote a couple of years ago that we're going to do parts of the end of the year at La Mama, I think is closer to, say, Brecht than cold, traditional opera.

[*Melhem:*] *And the use of scene—one scene after another?*

Yes. Well, certainly in the way I tried to direct **The Motion of History.** That was influenced by Brecht's wanting to use signs, you know, those kinds of things. I've always been, I think, interested in using audiovisuals along with the theater. In the play that we're doing in the fall, called **Boy and Tarzan Appear in a Clearing!**—they're going to do that at the Henry Street in October. That uses a lot of video, television, and film at the same time. I'm interested in expanding the theater, using technological advances of society in general.

[*Melhem:*] *Which of your works would you say has given you the most satisfaction, so far?*

Always the most recent one [*laughter*], when you see it produced—although I've done some bad productions myself. I think it's always gratifying to be able to see the most recent thing, the last thing that I've done, so I'm looking forward to the two things we're doing this fall and winter.

[*Melhem:*] *You have a cinematographic technique in your later works.*

Yes.

[*Melhem:*] *Who would you say has influenced you there—* [*Sergei*] *Eisenstein?*

Movies generally. Movies generally. I think Eisenstein intellectually, if I look at his theories on the dialectics of im-

age. I think it would be impossible for anybody who makes film, whether they know it or not, to say they haven't been influenced by Eisenstein. The question of montage is impossible without Eisenstein, whether they know it or not. But then, I've been influenced by all the moviemakers that I've seen. I'm a moviegoer. I've always been a moviegoer. It always insults me when people try to say that movies somehow are some kind of inferior art form. I can never understand that. That always seems to me the most bizarre thing in the world to say.

[*Melhem:*] *You said you would prefer a less sentimental ending for* **The Toilet.**

Yes.

[*Melhem:*] *Although you don't turn your back on that time of your creative life.*

No. That ending was tacked on, that's what I meant, first of all. When I wrote it, I wrote it straight through and I tacked this ending on. The way it ended was first with the guy just left there, in the toilet, and then I tacked it on I guess as some kind of attempt to show some kind of, you know, reconciliation, or something like that. And I think that's where I was at that time.

[*Melhem:*] *Is there any other work you feel that way about, that you would like to redo or revise?*

[*Emphatically*] oh, yes Shhhhh! [*Laughter*] Different things I see, the different reasons. Some, I might. But most, I won't, because, like I said, I don't want to cover up my tracks, you know what I mean? You should at least show where you've been, so people can understand how you got to where you are, and what have you.

[*Melhem:*] *Okay . . . . What advice do you have for beginning writers, white, Black, or otherwise?*

Um-hum. Well, I say this, what I tell my writing students: The only thing that helps you—I'm not going to say the only thing—I say the main thing that will help you learn to write is to write. That's the first step. That's the most important, is to write. The second thing is to read. Now those two things are very important, writing and reading. Of course the other thing, analysis, is observation, observation of everybody and everything: all classes of people and their relationship with each other; their ideas, how they contrast, how they be similar. And I say that the other thing is that for any serious writer in the United States, regardless of nationality, it's going to be difficult to get published. And so they better also learn how to run a mimeograph machine; photo-offset machine [*laughter*], learn how to bind and staple and how to put out their own works; and I would say, it's best you start putting out your own work. Don't wait to be discovered—

[*Melhem:*] *Yes, right.*

—because for most people that's going to be a myth.

[*Melhem:*] *Of desire.*

Yes, exactly. It's going to be a myth. You're going to have to do it yourself. Even if you're later discovered, it's best to start.

[*Melhem:*] *Do you have any advice for contemporary American writers, Black or white or any other?*

Those things, and I think it's important that they be very, very aware of what is happening in society. Because I don't think your work can either be viewed, nor is it obtained, in isolation from society; and especially in this period now that we're moving rapidly to the right, it's very important. The rise of censorship, for instance—these kinds of wild things. I'm especially gratified to see this American Writers' Congress that they're going to have in the fall, that the *Nation* magazine is sponsoring, Victor Navasky. It's going to be, I think, a three- or four-day writers' congress at the Roosevelt Hotel in October; I'm supposed to be on one of the panels. I think that's a very important thing.

[*Melhem:*] *Okay. What are your current or future projects?*

Well, like I said, this play ***Boy and Tarzan*** is going to be done in October. Then this jazz opera that we're going to do in workshop, that we're really going to try to raise money for; we're going to try to raise money to produce it. So those are two things in drama. I have a book of essays that's going to be published in the fall; I told you about ***Daggers and Javelins.*** And then I've got some other projects that are on the back burner, unfortunately. Oh, another important project is my wife and I are doing an anthology of Black women writers—

[*Melhem:*] *Oh!*

—that Morrow has just accepted. And so we'll be doing that. In the next couple of weeks we're going to start on that.

[*Melhem:*] *Are there any misconceptions—about yourself or your work—that you want cleared up?*

[*Laughing*] Oh, ho-ho!

[*Melhem:*] [*Laughing*] *I mean, any* outstanding *misconceptions.*

I can't, I can't. No. Except that people are always catching you where you were.

[*Melhem:*] *This is the last question. What role do your foresee for Black poets in the 1990s, and whom do you think they should address?*

That's a good question in this sense. I expect the same role from them that they have had—the same role that Margaret Walker had, the same role that Langston [Hughes] had, the same role that [Claude] McKay had. That is, intellectual leadership, you understand, commitment and struggle. But we must always learn from each other's lives. And in terms of the audience, the audience is all of the people, the majority of the people.

Henry Louis Gates Jr. (review date 11 March 1984)

SOURCE: "Several Lives, Several Voices," in *New York Times Book Review,* March 11, 1984, pp. 11-12.

[*In the following review, Gates outlines* The Autobiography of LeRoi Jones.]

When I first met his father, Coyette Leroy Jones, I was shocked by his striking resemblance to his son. Amiri Baraka locates his first identity through this resemblance to his father: "That I was short and skinny with big eyes and looked just like my father. These were the most indelible. My earliest identity." If that's true then for much of a half-century, it is fair to say, he has been running away from that very identity.

LeRoi Jones predicted as much, even as early as 1964 when he wrote in **"The Liar":** "When they say, 'It is Roi / who is dead?' I wonder / who they will mean?" Anyone else who had hoped that his autobiography would at last answer this rhetorical question will be disappointed. What emerges here is not a unified, coherent pattern of a life, but reconstructions of a series of lives or selves, the lives of LeRoi Amiri Baraka Jones.

LeRoi Jones/Amiri Baraka is, without question, one of the most prolific Afro-American authors. In addition to his autobiography, he has published books of poetry, a novel and a collection of short stories, five books of essays, two books analyzing black music, 24 plays and four anthologies—all in the last 23 years. He has been a most mutable political figure as well, trading worn-out ideologies for new ones when circumstances decree, and, as he puts it, transforming his metaphorical colors from brown to yellow, white and black.

Perhaps not since [Gertrude] Stein's *Autobiography of Alice B. Toklas* have we had an autobiography so ironically titled. Mr. Baraka anticipated this "multiple self" in **"The Liar"** (1964):

> Publicly redefining
> each change in my soul, as if I had predicted
> them,
> and profited, biblically, even tho
> their chanting weight,
> erased familiarity
> from my face.

He might have added "publicly renaming myself and my ideologies," as well, as his extended metamorphosis took him from a "brown" Newark to a "yellow" Howard (where he flunked out) to a "white" Air Force to his "white" life as a Greenwich Village poet and editor, married to a white woman and father of two girls, to the crazy Wild West days of the raucous Black Arts Repertory Theater in Harlem, then over to Newark to marriage with Sylvia Wilson (Amina Baraka), the mother of five more children, and to his much vaunted black cultural nationalism, and, most recently, to polka-dotted Marxism, which he is still struggling to master.

At each crucial ideological transformation, he assigned himself another name. Christened Everett Leroy Jones, brown Leroy from Newark became the black Village bohemian LeRoi, who is turn became the blacker Ameer Barakat (the Blessed Prince), who in turn became Imamu (poet/priest) Amiri Baraka, the blackest Leroy of all. With each new name came a change in his style of writing.
—*Henry Louis Gates Jr.*

At each crucial ideological transformation, he assigned himself another name. Christened Everett Leroy Jones, brown Leroy from Newark became the black Village bohemian LeRoi, who is turn became the blacker Ameer Barakat (the Blessed Prince), who in turn became Imamu (poet/priest) Amiri Baraka, the blackest Leroy of all. With each new name came a change in his style of writing. We can "frame" these changes of diction with two extreme examples, taken from the extremes of his career. In his first book of poems (written in Greenwich Village), we read:

> but this also
> is part of my charm.
> A maudlin nostalgia

that comes on
like terrible thoughts about death.
How dumb to be sentimental about anything
To call it love
& cry pathetically
into the long black handkerchief
of the years.

Compare these typically "modernist" lines of alienation with his more recent play, *What Was the Relationship of the Lone Ranger to the Means of Production?* (1978):

MASKED MAN: You have a stake in this system.

REG: What system?

MASKED MAN: The free enterprise system! You're free. You can do anything, go anywhere, because you live in a free society . . . you can't have this much freedom in a totalitarian country like—

DONNA: Crown Heights, South Bronx, Newark, Lower East Side, for instance.

From alienated modernist to agitprop is a long way to tumble in 17 years. From imitating Yeats, Eliot, Pound, Williams and Charles Olson, when he was the Jackie Robinson of Greenwich Village, Mr. Baraka descended into the Heart of Blackness (keeping Pound's fascism and Eliot's Anglo-Catholicism turned inside out), only to graduate to agitprop. It is this radical shift in diction that forces me to question his latest mask as a Marxist, even if I believe the move to have been inevitable.

In which voice does he narrate his story? Each of Mr. Baraka's lives has its own flavor of language, its own distinct style. He draws upon style as a correlative of his changing spots; reading his book is like listening to albums by Coleman Hawkins, Charlie Parker, James Brown, then late John Coltrane, a remarkable stylistic achievement. It is the serial lives depicted here, however, and the acts of betrayal that connect them, that make this autobiography problematical indeed.

"The world has changed so much since my youth," Mr. Baraka tells us early on, "And I want, more than anything, to chart this change within myself." He recreates his childhood with a lyricism largely absent from his writing since *The Dead Lecturer* (1964). We hear of his childhood friends, "long-headed colored Norman" and "Eddie, of the tilted old smelly house." Joe Louis and F.D.R., we learn, were young Leroy's "maximum heroes," just as we learn what it meant to experience the rituals of watching games played by teams of Negro National League in "those bright lost summers," engulfed in a "a garment of feeling," a "collective black aura that can only be duplicated with black conversation or music." Only occasionally does he interrupt this lyrical re-creation of youth to preach to us about "the open barn door of monopoly capitalism" or to tell us what "Mao points out," too soon after he has re-created a 1930's or 1940's colored world more movingly than has any novelist.

Life at Howard was "a blinding yellow," where class-as-color (or as grade of hair) reigned supreme—"the rumble of crazy Negro yellow crazy." Yet Howard was also where Sterling Brown and Nathan Scott taught him music and literature. Mr. Brown's classes were "the high point of my 'formal' education," while Mr. Scott's "preaching about Dante" was "like some minister pushing us toward Christ." Howard, finally, was failing grades, expulsion, and a tearful retreat home to Newark, then to the Air Force.

LeRoi Jones read and wrote his way through the Air Force, imbibing "the New Criticism and the word freaks and the Southern Agrarians," along with *Accent,* the *Hudson, Partisan* and *Kenyon Reviews,* and just about all of the canonical Western writers. It was here, he tells us in moving prose, that he learned to dream the life of the mind, "a life of ideas, and, above all, Art." It was his eclectic pursuit of words that led to his undesirable discharge for being a "Communist"— all because he had received rejection letters from a magazine published by the Congress for Cultural Freedom!

Life in the Village was a series of affairs with white women and intimate friendships with just about anybody in the Beat world of the Village, where LeRoi Jones and his first wife published poetry journals and turned their home into a veritable salon. LeRoi was the "noble savage in the buttermilk," the ink spot on a vast white table cloth, "the one colored guy." But not even Mr. Baraka's urge to purge the "white" forms of his early poetry and his life can mask the sheer energy and joy that these rich decadent years in the Village gave him. His account reads like a blissful trip through an intellectual Disney World, where at last he mastered the forms of literature and became a principal within the American avant-garde. These pages are full of brilliant analyses of poetic forms, from Whitman and Williams and Pound and Apollinaire and the Surrealists to "the Jewish Apocalyptic," Black Mountain, and the New York schools. This long chapter is marred only by the cold ambiguity with which he recalls his first marriage and its dissolution. "My parents took it in stride," he tells us of the marriage. "There was not even any eye rolling or excessive questioning. (Such is the disposition and tenor of the oppressed, they are so in love with democracy!)" When it was over it was over: "In a minute or so, I was gone. Seeking revolution!"

A trip to Cuba in 1960, writings about black music (reviews, liner notes, and *Blues People* in 1963), the success of *Dutchman* (1964), a growing identification with Malcolm X, and,

finally, Malcolm's murder in February 1965, took him uptown, to Harlem as the head of The Black Arts Repertory Theater and School, in full retreat from his white life and wife. "Arriving full up in the place of blackness, to save myself and to save the black world," he writes ironically, now that he has repudiated this phase of his political life. His escapades in Harlem read like Tom Wolfe's "Mau-Mauing the Flack Catchers," and I am still not yet certain which version I prefer. Mr. Baraka describes his life at this point as that of "a fanatical patriot." "The middle-class native intellectual," he continues, "having out integrated the most integrated, now plunges headlong back into what he perceives as blackest, native-est."

Uptown, he was running from his white friends and white influences, but most of all from his guilt, not for leaving his family but for marrying a white woman in the first place: "I was guilty for having lived downtown for so long with a white wife." Life in the Black Arts, he tells us, was "very messy" and "confused."

"Home," the long penultimate chapter, means Newark and the blackness of blackness, where between late 1965 and the early 1970's, as Imamu Amiri Baraka, he tried to purge himself of "my individualism and randomness, my Western, white addictions, my Negro intellectualism," to find "that dark brown feeling that is always connected with black and blues." Judging as a Marxist, Mr. Baraka can write that "I, so long whited out, now frantically claiming a 'blackness' that in many ways was bogus, a kind of black bohemianism. . . .Hey, all that . . . was yellow, very very yellow." Perhaps all this was more "yellow" than he intends.

Mr. Baraka offers a remarkably detailed account of his cultural nationalist years in Newark, where he masterfully ran the first successful mayoral campaign of Kenneth A. Gibson (now called "our fat stupid mayor"). He began the Committee for Unified New Ark, was brutally, beaten by the police in the 1967 riots and directed the formation of the highly influential Congress of Afrikan Peoples. This section of the book will be scrutinized as avidly by his black compatriots as his Village years will be read by his white friends. So, too, will his critique of the black nationalist movement and its fantasy of "a never-never land of Africa," a movement, he tells us, that failed because it lacked "the scientific exegesis of the state," because it was "feudalistic," "male chauvinistic," and "metaphysical." He might have added anti-Semitic and racist as well.

Mr. Baraka pronounces nationalism's death as happening in May, 1974, at a conference at Howard, where the black Marxist left defeated Stokely Carmichael and company, providing Mr. Baraka with "a point of departure, a jumping-off place, and I was ready to jump." And jump he has: "When the people of the world united to bring this giant oppressor to its knees we would be part of that contingent . . . chosen by the accident of history to cut this thing's head off and send it rolling through the streets of North America." The text ends with his "final" transformation into a Marxist-Leninist.

"All these words," Mr. Baraka tells us, "are only to be learned from," just two paragraphs after he writes that "in 1970, my wife Amina and I . . . paid down on a big square fortress of a stucco house which I painted red and trimmed in black, and when the seasons allow the trees to come out, the tableau is like a not quite subtle black nationalist flag."

Mr. Baraka still has a lot of accounting to do, despite the length, density and lyricism of his narrative. He is cursed, if I may, in a peculiar, unenviable way: Whereas most of us can experience identity crises in splendid, if painful, isolation, he consistently builds a program or a movement around his. Few of us, thank goodness, are able to institutionalize our hang-ups, our "changes." One must wonder at the costs of those who, at any given phase, have been his true believers. He is largely silent about his responsibilities to the people who trusted him. Perhaps the almost defensive, if not apologetic, tone generated by his proliferation of facts and events is directed at those readers who shared these worlds with him, those who will still feel betrayed.

And what *does* this autobiography teach us about LeRoi Amiri Baraka Jones? He hopes that it teaches us "that struggle and defeat finally are useful if our heads are harder, our grasp of reality firmer. I think they are." I remain unconvinced. If the "black bohemianism" of his (white) life in the Village and his progressively "blacker" lives in Harlem and Newark have been replaced by a stable and loving family life and a tenured professorship, Mr. Baraka has yet to convince me that his "Marxism" is any more sophisticated than any of his other political theories. He will never convince "the close reader" until he discards the cant and rhetoric of undigested Marxist discourse. In the end, we cannot take Mr. Baraka at his word, because his language betrays him. He has failed, thus far, to make Marx his, to escape the confusion of jargon for "scientific analysis." Until he does so, he will remain as he was at the beginning of his journey, "A renegade / behind the mask. And even / the mask, a renegade / disguise Black skin. . ." (**"A Poem for Willie Best,"** 1964).

Amiri Baraka with Sandra G. Shannon (interview date Winter 1987)

SOURCE: "Amiri Baraka on Directing," in *Black American Literature Forum,* Vol. 21, No. 4, Winter, 1987, pp. 425-33.

[*In the following interview, Baraka discusses his work as a director and his views on directing.*]

Amiri Baraka is an artist of the 1960s' political scene still hard at work in the 1980s. Playwright, poet, political activist, Marxist, anti-Semitic, anti-feminist have all been used to label him, yet a less controversial label is often ignored—director. Most noted for his plays **Dutchman** and **The Slave,** Baraka has done some of his own directing and collaborated with directors such as Gilbert Moses, Jerry Benjamin, Jim Malette, Edward Parone, Ernie McClintock, Irving Vincent, and Leo Garen in staging his Revolutionary Theater of the 1960s' Black Arts and Civil Rights movements.

In a recent interview at his office at the State University of New York at Stony Brook, where he is Director of Africana Studies, Baraka discussed several of his 1960s' plays from a director's perspective. Undoubtedly, he has been both impressed and skeptical about how his works have fared in the hands of other directors. What follows is a revelation of Baraka's own vision as director.

[*Shannon:*] *The questions that I'd like to ask you today are specifically oriented toward directing. My first question is this: I see that you have directed several of your own sixties' plays. What motivated you to want to direct your own works?*

[Baraka:] Well, because directing was something that I hadn't done, but I always had a great appreciation for directing. Also, I thought that I could give the work an added kind of accuracy in terms of the interpretation. I like to direct actually. Directing is more work than people might think.

Does directing, for you, involve everything—such as teaching the actors how to convey a particular point in your works, incorporating music. . .?

Well, I think that first it has to do with helping the actors understand the play and to understand the characters because I think that if they don't understand what the play is about and what all of the characters are about . . . in particular, they've got to have some insight into their own characters. But they've got to know the whole play. They've got to know all the relationships, the history of the characters. Like a life situation, they have to know it like that and be in tune with it.

How is the fact that they know the play portrayed in the way they act? How can you tell they know the play?

Well, because their motivations ring true. What they do seems real or justifiable or legitimized in some kind of way. They have to understand the play, and I think too often you see people just sort of sleepwalking through a play or going through these kinds of formal blocking moves stage left and downstage right, and you don't see any acting going on. You see mostly people being placed on different parts of the stage.

So you're saying that a certain amount of what they portray comes from within?

Yeah. There has to be an understanding. To me, it's like a piece of music. You can't play it if you don't understand it. Or if you can't read the notes and it's a written piece of music, you're in trouble. I think you have to know the composer's intentions, what feelings the composer was trying to transmit. The same thing with the play—you have to know what the playwright was trying to say.

What directors have you worked with?

Well, I've liked quite a few people's directing, but the director that I've liked best has been Gil Moses, who did **Slave Ship.** To me, he's one of the most intelligent and innovative directors that I've known. But I've had some other good directors. At the Black Arts, we had a guy named Jim Campbell—very good director. He's now a principal of an elementary school.

What do you think makes a good director?

Understanding the play and being able to put that in dramatic terms—to transpose it from literary terms to dramatic terms, which sometimes calls for things that the playwright has not seen that are obvious from the interpretation.

Do directors consult you? Do you feel it necessary that they consult you, or do you just leave them alone?

I usually leave them alone, but I think good directors always want to know what the playwright thinks, even if they don't agree with him. There are a lot of good directors around now, for example, the guy who's directing this play of mine at NYU named George Ferrinks. He's a white director. He's a good director. He's Hungarian. He understands texts, and he can improvise. Glenda Dickerson, a black woman who is out here with us at Stony Brook, is an excellent director.

What makes your job as a director easier?

Well, what makes it easier is if you have all of the resources to translate a play from literature into drama and into theater without a hassle. And the principal of those resources is actors—people who are intelligent. You've got some who are intelligent; you've got some who are sort of mediocre; and you've got some whom you shouldn't get stuck with under any circumstances.

To what extent do you get involved in the music which becomes part of the play?

See, music has ideas in it. People think that it's only if they hear lyrics that ideas are being communicated. That's not true. There are ideas in the music—what the composer wants to say, what he feels, what kind of emotional parallel music conjures up. There are all kinds of ideas and thoughts and feelings, of course, in music. And so the music, to me, is an added dramatic dimension—as narrator, as actor. Music, to me, is as much alive as the actors. It has as much importance.

So the concept, then, that you tried to get from the use of Sun Ra or, say, Albert Ayler was a certain disorderliness, unpredictability, anti-establishment feeling?

With Sun Ra, I wanted the feeling of some kind of otherworldly wisdom or dimension, which changes sometimes to fear, terror, contemplation of the laboratory, contemplation of what wisdom and knowledge really are. With Ayler, it was the kind of power and force that he has which is so striking when you hear him live. I've used him when I've wanted improvisation added to the text; in other words, let the musician look at the play and improvise. I've done that a few times. But I think that's interesting because the play is as much a generator of emotions as any other kind of thing. And if you have a musician improvising off the emotions he gets from the play, then it creates a kind of improvised life of the play at the same time that you have a kind of stated life of the play.

How do you deal with such production limitations as space and budget?

Well, you just have to do other things. You have to do things that don't require space, and you have to do things that are cheap. That's been my story all of my life—all of my theatrical life. There were a couple of times I thought I was going to have some money. We were supposed to do a jazz opera in the Paris opera and the Berlin opera, and the Americans got to the French to cancel it. They were going to spend a million and a half francs on it.

Oh really! What did the Americans say?

They said it was an anti-American play.

Your 1960s' plays leave much room for the creative director—for example, **Black Mass.** *I listened to the album. I read the play. But I cannot understand how the beast is portrayed on stage. Do you settle for a facsimile of the hideous creature, or do you expect some other rigid interpretation?*

How is it interpreted on the stage? I guess you could say

that it is up to the imagination of the director. But what we did was take grease paint and paint all over the guy, and we had a red mask, which was turned into a tail like a dinosaur's tail. That was Ben Caldwell's design. I thought that it was something with room for improvisation.

In **The Slave,** *what stage props did you suggest to depict the surrounding race wars and the ultimate bombing of Easley's home?*

The sound was going on throughout the play.

Was that an album or a sound track?

It was taped. Largely war sounds—shots, bombs—and, near the end of the play, it gets closer and closer and closer, and then there is the very final scene where they're up close with near hits, near misses, and direct hits. Then we actually had to use the kind of explosion techniques that you use in theater: smudge pots, a soft ceiling with plaster up in it that you could release, a blackout, turning chairs and stuff over, pulling down false walls—simple stage techniques. It was gradually a kind of closing in of war sounds.

Did you ever use colors to capture a particular effect? To what extent were colors involved? For example, if you would like to portray fire, did you just splatter orange and red?

You mean real fire and burning?

Yes.

Well, again, we used different kinds of pots and things for fire—things that can actually burn. And sometimes to get a fire effect, we used lights. But we usually used pots that were turned on, usually electrically. The stage manager or the lighting person would handle that. It was a simple process, although those kinds of things can be dangerous.

In **Experimental Death Unit #1,** *your stage notes call for "a white man's head still dripping blood." Can you explain how this was translated to the stage?*

There was a friend of mine, a white painter, who made an exact facsimile of the actor's head out of papier-mâché, and it was so life-like that it actually created a kind of sensation. A guy named Dominique Capobianco molded papier-mâché face masks. He's an artist at Rutgers. He made papier-mâché heads that were exactly like the actors'. We had a special kind of dramatic effect that we used wherein the actors who were supposed to be beheaded would twist their heads down in their chests and pull up some kind of jackets we had. And they would fall so they were upstage and you couldn't see their heads, and then the guy who was cutting them off would look like he'd cut one off and he had

the head already inside his coat. When he'd cut like that, you couldn't see the head struck and then he'd go down and his body would cover the dead man's body and he'd take the head out from under his coat and then come up with the head.

Ingenious!

Well, theater people think of these things. When you get theater people and you've got a project, you discuss it. That's why set designers, prop people, lighting people—these people are key to directors. No theater production is a one-person operation. That's absurd. Some of the technical aspects of these things I wouldn't begin to be able to put together. I could just say, "I think it should be like this," and that would be the way it was done. You've got people who know the theater. That's why, in really doing heavyweight theater, you've got to have some skilled people with you to really bring it off.

I can imagine **Slave Ship** *called for a lot of ingenuity.*

Yeah. That's why I say Gil Moses, to me, . . . I directed *Slave Ship* first in Newark at the Spirit House, and that was like. . . I mean we had on-and-off lights: "Click, click." It was nothing but the first floor of a house that I had torn the walls of down. We had almost nothing at all to work with. But when Gil took it on and when he used his imagination and the kind of technical resources that were available to us at the Brooklyn Academy, which were quite a bit, we were really able to do something good.

In 1967 you directed **Great Goodness of Life: A Coon Show** *at the Spirit House in Newark. Can you recall how you portrayed Attorney Breck? "A bald-headed smiling house slave in a wrinkled dirty tuxedo crawls across the stage; he has a wire attached to his back leading off-stage. A huge key in the side of his head. We hear the motors 'animating,' his body groaning like tremendous weights. He grins, and slobbers, turning his head slowly from side to side. He grins. He makes little quivering noises."*

Well, we were pretty faithful to that. Actually, we had . . . who played that? L. Earl Jay played that, I think, when we did it in New York. Are you talking about the wires and the big key in his head and stuff like that? Well, we made a hat like a hairpiece or something like that. Anyway, it sat up on his head and had a big key in it that whirled around—the key actually whirled around. It sort of fit over his head like a strap on top of his head. In other words, the key was the cap, and he put the cap on and then the key was attached to it on one side. It was like a rod coming down, off the cap and then the key stuck out of the rod. In the rod was the kind of mechanism that turned the key. And it was a key that you actually did wind up, and it was spring-loaded so that when you wound it up—when the attorney pushed the starter that he had on—it actually would turn: "Ch-ch-ch." It would look like the little toy soldiers or little robots that you see for kids.

Returning to your means of adapting to various limitations, at any time did your street plays **Arm Yourself, Or Harm Yourself** *and* **Police** *encounter obstacles because of uncertain conditions due to temporary settings?*

Yeah. Real police came into this loft where we were rehearsing. They had told us something about we weren't supposed to read poetry down in the cellar in Newark. There was some controversy around that, but, in those days, the Newark police were the worst on the planet. That was one of the reasons that we were so quick to get a black mayor. That was the only kind of respite that we got from the Negroes that had been running the city. They did cool out the police, and they couldn't have stayed in there if they hadn't because the people had demonstrated in 1967 what they would do. Police ran up in my rehearsal and actually took a script out of my hand. We were rehearsing and police came in there. That's the kind of harassment outside in the street. We had to do plays, and we were never quite sure how we would be greeted by the powers that be—the police, etc. One time we did *Junkies Are Full of Shhh . . .* and a woman started beating the junky—started beating the dope pusher like she thought it was really happening. She started whipping Yusef Iman's butt. We had to pull her off him. She was going to beat him up. I guess her child had gotten involved in drugs. It's always uncertain outside.

Several prominent actors showed up in your early plays. Can you talk about the contributions of, say, Barbara Teer or Al Freeman?

Well, Barbara did *Experimental Death Unit #1,* and as it turned out, the guy who was directing it first was a nut. I mean, he was absolutely a maniac and he and Barbara got to talking and he slapped her.

You're talking about Tom Hackensack?

Right. He slapped her face, and then I had to take over the direction. I thought she did a very very good job myself. That was one of the plays that I directed both downtown and up at the Black Arts. I think it came off all right. We did it at this benefit down at the Saint Mark's Theater, and we had the resources and stuff. I thought it was a good experience. There were a lot of things I learned directing then. Now, interestingly enough, Barbara—when we first started working—said there was no such thing as Black Theater. She said theater was theater. We used to stand out there and argue—she and this guy named McBeth, who later got to be head of the Lafayette. They were both opposed to the concept of Black Theater. They said it didn't exist. They said it was just

theater. Later on, it is interesting that they came to understand the fact that there is such a thing as Black Theater and that they have gotten a great deal of success in Black Theater. Barbara is a good actress and a very capable director.

I don't know what she is doing now with the National Black Theater. But that was something that we called for in the 1968 Black Power Conference—a National Black Theater. The Negro Ensemble is the Negro Ensemble. But we need a theater that can encompass, coast to coast, the best actors, the best directors, the best playwrights, the best set designers, the best musicians who would tour the country and play to our people all over the country. That's what we need definitely.

I noticed that your wife was a member of the cast of **Black Mass.** *To what extent has she helped in shaping and developing your 1960s' plays?*

Well, my wife certainly has a great deal of influence on me—I guess just like everybody else's wife or husband has on them. We had just met some months before that. I was making a movie which never got seen by anybody except the FBI. They have records of this movie that we made and the images in it, and nobody has ever seen it. It's fantastic.

Did they confiscate it?

No. They were just watching when we made it. We didn't know it, but when I got the Freedom of Information Act papers, they had listed it in there. They saw us shooting out in the yard, and I had nooses hanging off the trees and people in KKK costumes marching. We had met not long before the time of **Black Mass,** and I think that it was subsequent to **Black Mass** that we began to see each other. But she has been a very strong influence upon me in terms of . . . you know, a lot of times you bounce concepts off people whether you know it or not. People do shape your concepts. In a lot of my earlier plays, the black woman is not dealt with well at all. And I think that she has been very very forceful in terms of trying to make me understand that, which I hope I have understood, and just generally in terms of helping me to give some weighty attention to black people's real problems rather than the problems of one sector of the black middle class, which, I think, is another one of my tendencies—to make my problems everybody's problems or my own kinds of concepts sort of automatically all black people's. So, I think she's helped clarify—to the extent that it can be called clarified—that thing. It's a continuing influence obviously. We work together. She was in the Spirit House Movers when it first began. Then the organization that we put together got in the way of that, and she wasn't in the Movers later on. Now we are working together with this group called Blue Ark that we have. We do poetry and we work usually with three musicians, and she's a part of that and hopefully we are going to do some more dramatic work together.

How were the changes in your ideology—that is, from nationalist to Marxist—reflected on stage?

I had a big falling out with the woman who played Lula when I directed **Dutchman** in Newark when I first came back to Newark in 1966. This white woman—I can't think of her name—she said something that I didn't like, and I said, "Well, you know. I don't even like white people. I don't even know why I'm standing here arguing with you." That kind of stupid stuff. Certainly, during my post-nationalist phase, I would not be involved in some kind of crazy stuff like that. I mean, when you just crack people over the head because you get angry with them, and then you take them out the worst way you can. I don't think I would do that. It was the nationalism certainly that fueled that kind of approach. I guess people can tell you stories about that. I used to do a lot of that.

I think the most important change has been in terms of the content of the plays—the line, the political line, the ideological line that comes out of the plays. I think that is the real critical change—from plays that pretty much focus on kicking white folks' asses and getting them off ours to trying to find a way to bring in the more complex reality that we live, which obviously is full of white supremacy, racism, and exploitation, with black people being on the bottom of the heap. But I think that what that is really is what I try to talk about: how it got to be the way that it is, and, I guess, what we can do about it—and that we can survive it.

Douglas A. Ramsey (review date 29 March 1987)

SOURCE: A review of *The Music: Reflections on Jazz and Blues,* in *Los Angeles Times Book Review,* March 29, 1987, p. 6.

[*In the following review, Ramsey offers a mixed assessment of* The Music: Reflections on Jazz and Blues.]

When Amiri Baraka listens to music, he hears things that might escape us if we could not depend upon him to point them out with his eloquent insistence, indignation and anger. He hears political oppression, capitalist exploitation, racist duplicity and class struggle. The beauty in the works of the great jazz masters comes to him transformed through Marxist-Leninist dialectic into ideology and sociology. That may seem a grim and joyless route to music appreciation, but Baraka has been following it for more than a quarter of a century in poetry, plays, essays, reviews and album liner notes.

[*The Music: Reflections on Jazz and Blues*] is made up of work from each of those categories. It has the brilliance of Baraka at his analytical best, with musical and extra-musical considerations in balance, as in his essay on Miles Davis. It also has him at his polemical worst, as in this passage, from a piece about the drummer Max Roach on commercial exploitation of innovations by the great creative giants of black music: "And each time, the same corporations that had got over exploiting the African's tragic willingness to sell off pieces of weself [sic] to anybody who had the necessary trinketry, these same villains would reappear to scoop out the insides of our hearts and sell them for super profits and then convince us that the scooped-out portions of ourselves existed as such because we had never been whole, never, we had only and always at any time in anybody's history been simply *Niggers.*"

> [*The Music: Reflections on Jazz and Blues*]
> **... has the brilliance of Baraka at his
> analytical best, with musical and extra-
> musical considerations in balance, as in his
> essay on Miles Davis.**
>   *—Douglas A. Ramsey*

When his spleen is less exercised, Baraka is capable of educating with great clarity and a sense of history: "Jazz incorporates blues, not just as a specific form, but as a cultural insistence, a feeling-matrix, a tonal memory. Blues is the national consciousness of jazz—its truthfulness in a lie world, its insistence that it is itself, its identification as the life expression of a specific people, the African-American nation. So that at its strongest and most intense and indeed most advanced, jazz expresses the highest consciousness of that people itself, combining its own history, as folk form and expression, with its more highly developed industrial environment, North America. Without blues, as interior animation, jazz has no history, no memory. The *funkiness* is the people's lives in North America as slaves, as an oppressed nation, as workers and artists of a particular nationality."

Baraka is largely correct when he writes that . . . "if non-African-American who played the music had not played it, it would not change the essential history of African-American music." Yet, that position would be strengthened, not weakened, were he willing to allow more than a crumb of recognition of major white jazzmen. His attempt to downplay the influence of Bill Evans is made ludicrous by the inconvenient fact that Evans, a white man, was the last great mainstream jazz piano innovator in a line of stylistic development that runs from Earl Hines through Fats Waller, Teddy Wilson and Bud Powell to Evans.

Baraka is helpful in explaining how the current jazz avant-garde was born and why he believes social, cultural and commercial conditions have always made necessary the creation of a next avant-garde movement.

He writes about poetry as a form of speech and music, an understanding that is helpful in dealing with his own poetry, which makes up about half of this book. (At the beginning of the volume, there is also a short selection of poems by Mrs. Baraka.) His poems are full of rhythms and subliminal meanings that cannot possibly be grasped by a silent reading. At its least self-conscious, Baraka's poetry has a surprising stateliness, as in the love poem, **"For Sylvia or Amina (Ballad Air & Fire)."** When it attempts to reproduce musical sounds . . . "uuuudeeeelyah uudeeeelyall/ yaboom rabbababab. . ." it encounters difficulties that have plagued poetry at least as far back as Vachel Lindsay. Baraka evaluates music based on its quotient of authentic funkiness, that he convincingly traces to its source in the blues. It is apparently impossible for him to consider music without passing judgment on its makers' presumed political and racial convictions and intentions.

For the reader who is interested simply in learning about the music and who does not go all the way with Baraka on racism, imperialism and exploitation, his political message can be a barricade. His answer to this objection is that you can't have all of one without all of the other, "Your aesthetic is created by your deepest politics, whether you are *consciously* making political choices as such or not. In other words, what you think of as 'hip' is essentially a political choice."

Years ago, I heard the great bassist Eugene Wright talking backstage at a Dave Brubeck concert with a group of younger musicians. Art Blakey, Horace Silver and Sonny Rollins were on their minds, and funky music was under discussion. "Absorb it, feel it," Wright told his admirers. "Then get past that funk thing, man, and *all* of music will open up to you."

Baraka has never been able to get past that funk thing, and he may well believe that a musician like Eugene Wright, by expanding his musical aesthetic to encompass more than the social and political, has sold out to . . . "the corporations that . . . scoop out the insides of our hearts and sell them for super profits. . . ." But that is not Eugene Wright's problem. Or mine. Or yours. It is Amiri Baraka's.

Barry Wallenstein (review date February-March 1996)

SOURCE: A review of *Transbluency: The Selected Poems of Amiri Baraka/LeRoi Jones (1961-1995),* in *American Book Review,* Vol. 17, No. 3, February-March, 1996, pp. 7, 30.

[*In the following review, Wallenstein provides a positive assessment of* Transbluency.]

Deeply political, Amiri Baraka writes poems that have bothered many, reflecting as they do his dream of revolution, where the social orders will be recast, the races realigned. Much of his work is topical, written for the moment, and, as with agitprop verse, it's run the danger of becoming an historical footnote. Perhaps to consciously counter this eventuality, Baraka has placed musicality at the center of his efforts as a poet. He has often stated his aesthetic or purpose: "The poetry I want to write is oral by tradition, mass aimed as its fundamental functional motive."

Paul Vangelisti, the editor of *Transbluency,* divides the selected poetry into three periods, the Beat, Black Nationalism, and, finally, Third World Socialism. Baraka's "lyrical realism" is a stylistic constant, and his "political avant-garde[ism]" is the impulse that holds the work together. Almost from the beginning, the poetry is infused with the poet's emotional conflict between his racial culture and his self-recognition as an educated black man having come of age within a white culture. He copes with this dichotomy in a variety of ways, from expressions of rage to poses of cool detachment. In his best, most moving work, the "positions" are felt as coming not from the hardened heart or the fixed idea, but from the mind in flux, jockeying for a take on the particular situation at hand.

Marsilio Press deserves praise for bringing out this *Selected Poems,* an ample presentation from ten books. After the success of his first two books, *Preface to a Twenty Volume Suicide Note* (1961) and *The Dead Lecturer* (1964, the year of the *Dutchman*), came *Black Magic* (1969) itself a collection of three revolutionary books, *Sabotage, Target Study,* and *Black Art,* some of the most influential publications of the Black Arts Movement.

This book marked his nationalist phase, a period he'd look back on, not many years later, as "reactionary." However, passages abound that transcend the taint of narrow practicality. The first poem, **"Three Modes of History and Culture,"** concludes:

I think about a time when I will be relaxed
When flames and non-specific passion wear
    themselves
away. And my eyes and hands and mind can turn
and soften, and my songs will be softer
and lightly weight the air.

Similarly, when he says in **"Gatsby's Theory of Aesthet-**

ics" that "Poetry aims at difficult meanings," he is speaking about his personal response and understanding of the objective world: "I write poetry in order to feel, and that, finally, sensually, all the terms of my life. I write poetry to investigate my self, and my meaning and meanings." These are words of the artist superseding the polemicist.

Although **Black Magic** makes pronouncements and develops ideas about black nationalism, one finds further examples where poetry reaches inward: "I am real, and I can't say who / I am. Ask me if I know, I'll say / yes. I might say no. Still ask. / I'm Everett LeRoi Jones, 30 yrs old. / A black nigger in the universe. / A long breath singer, / wouldbe dancer, strong from years of fantasy, / and study."

Ultimately, he would like to be viewed as one speaking less for himself than the larger group his poems are intended for. One could imagine the following lines being issued from a soap box, an incendiary pulpit, or a hate rally. This is from **"Black Art"**:

> We want poems
> like fists beating niggers out of Jocks
> or dagger poems in the slimy bellies
> of the owner-jews. Black poems to
> smear on girdlemamma mulatto bitches
> whose brains are red jelly stuck
> between 'lizabeth taylor's toes. Stinking
> Whores! We want 'poems that kill.'

The poem ends: "We want a black poem. And a / Black World. / Let the world be a Black Poem / And Let All Black People Speak This Poem / Silently / or LOUD." One might imagine a deeply sensitive man, one steeped in modernist literature, Kafka and so forth, finding a tormented comfort away from the subjective quarrels of the struggling self, comfort behind the "we" of his people's painful history and daily oppressions. By the early '70s he'd moved from the nationalist sentiments and strategies of **Black Magic** to the Marxist-Leninist investigations of **Hard Facts** (1972), where he still sees art, as did Vallejo, Aragon, and Aimé Césaire, as "a weapon of revolution."

Concurrent with Baraka's political/racial passions has been his commitment to jazz as a liberating force, as a balm and inspiration. Not only do his poems refer to music, players and songs, but the language and urban landscape of the poetry clearly have a jazz feel. He came of age during the bop revolution of the late 1940s and was involved in performing his poetry in jazz clubs and coffee houses. An exemplar of the Beat counterculture, Baraka's aesthetic includes emphasis on spontaneity, improvised structure, and the use of argot, and "natural" speech. Along with everything else wild and untethered, such as line breaks, punctuation, diction, and so forth.

In the 1960s Baraka wrote for *Downbeat* magazine and published two important books on jazz, **Blues People** (1963) and **Black Music** (1968). In his **Autobiography** (1984) he remembers: "Art Williams . . . also had poetry readings (at the Cellar) and I even read there myself one evening with a poet . . . Yusef Rahman. Yusef's poetry was a revelation to me. He was like Bird in his approach to poetry, seeming to scat and spit rapid-fire lines of eight notes at top speed. It was definitely speech musicked." His phrase is an updating of Emily Dickinson's famous definition of poetry as "language musically employed." Baraka has strengthened this emphasis throughout his career. "[We] were drenched in black music and wanted our poetry to *be* black music. Not only that, we wanted that poetry to be armed with the spirit of black revolution."

From the 1979 book, *Poetry for the Advanced,* is a good example of Baraka's jazz inspired poetry, **"Pres Spoke in a Language"** (dedicated to Lester Young): "Pres / had a language / and a life, like, / all his own, / but in the teeming whole of us he lived / tooting on his sideways horn." The poem evokes other classic players, "Bird's feathers / Trane's sinewy tracks / the slickster walking through the crowd / surviving on a terrifying wit / it's the jungle the jungle the jungle / we living in." At the end of this lyrical, controlled meditation on jazz and survival, Baraka reaches out to include his readers: "Save all that comrades, we need it."

More recent books go all out with Baraka's involvement in jazz. **In the Tradition** (1982), dedicated to "Black Arthur Blythe," the great alto player and exemplar of free jazz, is a long poem celebrating the heritage of black music. Lists of tunes are arranged along with jazz artists and political figures mixed in. It's an amazing performance piece that Baraka has chanted or half-sung around the world. **"Speech #38,"** from **Wise, Why's, Y'z** (1995), is an example of Baraka's sound poetry and the sound is pure jazz. It opens, "OoBlahDee / Ooolyacoo / Bloomdido / OoBopShabam / Perdido Klackto-/ Veestedene / Salt Peanuts oroonie / McVouty / rebop," and continues for two pages that way.

In **The Selected Poems,** there are many poems that do not touch racial issues and do not make use of jazz idiom, but still demonstrate Baraka's individual voice. For instance, there are the **"Crow Jane"** poems from **The Dead Lecturer,** rich in literary reference, and then there is the opening of the famous **"Black Dada Nihilismus."** It begins with a quiet prayer-like sound; "Against what light / is false what breath / sucked, for deadness." Soon oblique references to violent revolution sweep in. Sartre is referred to before "Plastique, we / do not have, only thin heroic blades. / The razor. Our flail against them, why / you carry knives." Finally in the infamous second section, after signaling "A cult of death," he calls forth "black dada / Nihilismus. Rape the white girls. Rape / their fathers. Cut the mothers' throats. / Black dada

Nihilismus, choke my friends / in their bedrooms. . . ." The poem moves to elegy as it offers a list of black heroes who have absorbed the violence of racism and for whom suffering and resistance have been identical: Willie Best, Du Bois—"The Black buckaroos / For Jack Johnson . . . billie holiday." But the end complicates even hatred; placed in an open parenthesis are the troubling words: "(May a lost god . . . save us / against the murders we intend / against his lost white children. . .)."

Viewing Baraka's work through a selected poem is a trip that inspires smiles (not always the comfortable kind) and admiration for qualities beyond the jazzy rhythms and the rage. There is restraint, sudden detachment, and technical control, often not noticed or mentioned in deference to the legend of poet as improvisor, poet as spontaneous bard. In **"Balboa, The Entertainer,"** Baraka says: "Let my poems be a graph / of me." His is a complex graph, defying simple conclusions. His first book, **Preface to a Twenty Volume Suicide Note** has not yet been followed by the note, nor is the Preface finished.

Sandra G. Shannon (essay date March 1996)

SOURCE: "Manipulating Myth, Magic, and Legend: Amiri Baraka's *Black Mass*," in *CLA Journal*, Vol. 39, March, 1996, pp. 357-68.

[*In the following essay, Shannon illustrates how Baraka drew upon myths, traditional symbols, popular literature, and established institutions in* Black Mass.]

The assassination of Malcolm X on February 21, 1965, profoundly affected Amiri Baraka and gave fuel to his developing nationalist position. What resulted was a more focused appeal to the cultural consciousness of exclusively African-American audiences and a need for an experimental theatre. Inspired by the martyred Malcolm X, Baraka abandoned the restraints of self-defeating naturalistic themes and featured instead the uncompromising African-American hero; he satirized the racist aspects of popular white culture and, in so doing, sought to reverse the brain-washing trend among members of his African-American audiences; he parodied repressive African-American status symbols and institutions; and, above all, he exposed African-American viewers to positive images of themselves using the very same tokens of their oppression. This is perhaps nowhere more evident than in his 1965 play *Black Mass,* written while he was based at the Black Arts Theater School in Harlem.

The play, which uses the Nation of Islam's myth of the origin of the white species as a story line, represents an eclectic array of techniques served up to African-American

viewers as propaganda for cultural nationalism. The plot is as follows: Jacoub, an African-American magician, works in his laboratory at creating a mutant human being in order to "bring something into space that was never there." Although cautioned by the other magicians, Jacoub creates a repulsive creature, which, for all intents and purposes, is a mutation of a member of the white race. Determined to make something useful of his creation, Jacoub tries to teach it "civilized" behavior. Unfortunately, the creature breaks free of its restraints, bites one of the three females involved and ultimately transforms her into a feminine version of the same mutation. Ultimately the two creatures join in killing the magicians and remaining women. Afterward they "howl and hop, and then, turning to the audience, their mouths drooling and making obscene gestures, they move out into the audience."

> ... [Baraka] satirized the racist aspects of popular white culture and, in so doing, sought to reverse the brain-washing trend among members of his African-American audiences; he parodied repressive African-American status symbols and institutions; and, above all, he exposed African-American viewers to positive images of themselves using the very same tokens of their oppression. This is perhaps nowhere more evident than in his 1965 play *Black Mass,* written while he was based at the Black Arts Theater School in Harlem.
> —*Sandra G. Shannon*

It is important to note that *Black Mass* is based upon the principal myth on which the Islamic religion was founded— the myth of Yacub, "the big-headed scientist." So popular was Islam within African-American urban communities of the mid-sixties that Baraka could justly assume that the majority of African Americans in the audience would readily comprehend his many imitated references to the Yacub story. Robert Allen, author of *Black Awakening in Capitalist America,* notes that the Black Muslim religion had "a membership estimated in the early 1960's between sixty-five thousand and one hundred thousand. Their temples are found in practically every major city." Islam offered African Americans of the 1960s, just as it does today, an alternate philosophy to the devastating emotions caused by oppression. It promotes individual worth while focusing upon separate identity and self-sufficiency. Thus, it attracted a large following.

Baraka's use of myth is not coincidental. Myths, by virtue of their universal persuasiveness, often exist alongside scientifically proven truths and are sometimes indistinguishable.

Moreover, the validity of their premise defies disproof because they often are the products of an oral rather than written tradition; thus, the inability to discount the truth of numerous myths has contributed greatly to their longevity and validity. With the Yacub myth as its framework, *Black Mass* had a better-than-average chance of being regarded by its viewers as the fictional reenactment of the actual history of African Americans. As such, Baraka is able to gain acceptance of his updated version of the Muslim myth for the more current concern of African-American cultural consciousness. In *Black Mass,* therefore, Baraka redirects the truth of the original myth toward the specific needs of the Black Arts Movement.

Within the mythical context of an African setting are the African-American magicians. For the African-American viewer who is more than likely saturated with Western interpretations of Africa, magicians in a supposed African context inevitably conjure up expectations of a masked and painted voodoo witch doctor performing convulsive, ritual dances while summoning supernatural assistance via charms and unintelligible incantations. Quite unlike the unsophisticated practices of the witch doctor, however, Jacoub conducts his experiments with all the trappings of a modern scientist, complete with laboratory and its familiar equipment.

In the opening scene, Jacoub "is bent over a mortar, and is jamming a pestle into it, watching very closely." Ironically, as a magician—especially an African-American magician—Jacoub already possesses the power to create for the *good* of his people; instead, he confines himself to the laboratory environment and labors in an exacting cerebral science to create an alien being. In essence, he is no better than the witchdoctor, whose practices are at least part of his culture. Even though Jacoub is endowed with the means by which to avoid the trial and error of scientific methods, he prefers to follow them rather than resort to magic. In *Black Mass* Baraka uses the Muslim myth of Yacub (Jacoub), the wayward scientist, to show his African-American audience that their identity cannot be secure as long as it is subjected to the contagion of "the white thing."

The informing Muslim myth of *Black Mass* yields two interpretations, both of which are instructional: one explicitly addresses the African-American artist or creator; the other is implicitly relevant to the immediate sensibilities of lay African-American viewers. Nevertheless, for both artists and lay viewers, the play appears to have an easily recognizable moral much like that of the medieval morality play. Its lesson, simply translated, equals, "One who misdirects his talents toward creating for the sake of creation sins and will be duly punished." Upon closer examination, however, the play echoes many real concerns outside its fictional boundaries.

The same philosophy of the play's moral represents Baraka's staunch belief in the social utilitarianism of art and the sanctity of the artist's words. In his 1963 essay, **"Brief Reflection on Two Hot Shots,"** in which he lambastes James Baldwin and South African writer Peter Abrahams, he argues,

> We need not call to each other through the flames if we have nothing to say, or are merely diminishing the history of the world with descriptions of it that will show we are intelligent. Intelligence is only valuable when it is contained naturally in the matter we present as a result of the act [of writing . . . of feeling]. A writer is committed to what is real and not to the sanctity of his own FEELINGS.

Via *Black Mass* Baraka advocates an artistic alliance among all African-American artists to use their talents in both praising and raising the level of pride in African-American communities. In accordance with the collaboration of African-American artistic talents, which the Black Arts Movement urged, the play's message is an omen for African-American artists who overlook their social responsibility by creating art for amusement or purely capitalistic gain.

For the audience of lay African-American viewers who may have had little, if any, artistic inclination, *Black Mass* also offers a disturbing view of the psychology of self-hatred. In this sense, the play, far from being one-dimensional, invites one to wonder just what it is which compels Jacoub, a black man, to create a creature who is a foiled attempt to copy characteristics which—even though he does not understand them—he deems worthy of imitation. Not coincidentally, the words of Jacoub's creature identify it as being an imitation of a white creation gone awry: "I white. White. White." Jacoub's preference for "the white thing" shows not only the uselessness of his magical art but also an obsessive urge to mimic something alien to his own culture. [In his 1968 work, *Soul On Ice*] Eldridge Cleaver offers an interesting assessment of the kind of self-hatred which consumes Jacoub:

> Self-hatred takes many forms; sometimes it can be detected by no one, not by the keenest observer, not by the self-hater himself, not by his most intimate friends. Ethnic self-hate is even more difficult to detect. But in American Negroes, this ethnic self-hatred often takes the bizarre form of a racial death wish, with many and elusive manifestations.

Thus, in bypassing the untapped resources of his own culture, Jacoub admits his inferiority and worthlessness and consequently proves his dislike for himself and other African Americans by creating a homicidal monster. Cleaver, therefore, concludes that the "myth of the creation of the white race, called 'Yacub's History,' is an inversion of the racial death wish of American Negroes."

In the context of the particularly prevalent social oppression which African Americans faced during the mid-sixties' staging of **Black Mass,** however, the racial self-hatred which the play suggests seems to be more of a symptom than a cause: "Art does not create sickness, it reflects or demonstrates sickness that already exists." In this sense, the remedy offered by proponents of the Black Arts Movement sought to blot out the source of the malignant ailment by turning from Western models as frames of reference and establishing new black concepts of cultural and moral beauty. As long as Western influence remained suppressed, racial self-hatred was less likely to thrive.

Because of its mythical references to Africa, **Black Mass** has been rightfully called Baraka's "most important play." This is particularly true as Africa's undeniable influence facilitates Baraka's efforts to transport his audience's cultural consciousness from America's hostile environment to the pastoral serenity of Africa. The mythical African context provides the viewer with only hints of the play's locale through subtle references, such as the magician's attire: "They are dressed in long, exquisite robes on with skull cap, one with fez, one with African hat"; their obvious un-American names: Nasafi, Tanzil, Jacoub, Rulalie, Olabumi, and Tiila; their regard for the unique ethnic identity of their art: "These are the beauties of creation. / Holding a large bowl aloft. It glows softly gold in the dim light. / The beauties and strength of our blackness, of our black arts"; and vestiges of their means of communication: "Signs in Arabic and Swahili on the wall, Strange drawings, diagrams of weird machines."

Unlike Marcus Garvey, who in the 1920s advocated that African Americans actually return to Africa, Baraka merely calls for a metaphorical return of his people to their pastoral serenity.
—*Sandra G. Shannon*

Unlike Marcus Garvey, who in the 1920s advocated that African Americans actually return to Africa, Baraka merely calls for a metaphorical return of his people to their pastoral serenity. This return to the source brings with it a self-confidence born of a freedom from mimicking other standards of art or mores. Africa, then, serves as the new frame of reference, especially suitable for the nationalist cause. Neal notes in his contribution to the *Black American Reference Book,* "Among black Americans today, the nationalist impulse gives rise to romantic longing for the pastoral innocence of the African past. Increasingly writers and art-

ists are turning to the folk culture for inspiration and new formal ideas.

The term "black magic" is such a slippery one that it often lends itself to a variety of interpretations. Yet Baraka's particular use of it in **Black Mass** points to his earlier arguments against the industrious though isolated art of Abrahams and Baldwin. [In his 1980 book, *Amiri Baraka*] Lloyd Brown eloquently sums up the role of magic in African-American literature:

> It [magic] is both an ethnic and aesthetic power, attacking rationalistic systems in the culture as tools of economic and racial exploitation, and rejecting overly formalistic approaches to art. The idea of magic in both ethnic and aesthetic terms is therefore intrinsically bound up with the experience of transformation: self-hatred is replaced by ethnic pride and art-for-art's sake gives way to art as responsive and committed design. Magic, the very essence of "irrationality" and disorder, in rationalistic terms, is now the symbol of a new, rebellious antirationalism.

Black magic, too, can be perceived as a weapon. It allows African Americans to conceptualize the power of transformation and, more importantly, to realize that they possess that power.

The Black Muslim myth further allows Baraka to propagate the idea of diseased Western influences by creating a sort of allegory drawn from various popular Western legends, such as *Frankenstein, Dr. Faustus, Dracula, Tarzan,* and *Pandora's Box.* What is evidenced by all of these influences is the playwright's attempt to draw from the audience's reservoir of Western icons to insure some kind of affinity with the new African-American consciousness which the play promotes. In addition to the broader Muslim myth in which the play is set, references to images promoted by fiction and the screen are more assured of striking chords of familiarity within viewers. Hence, this new consciousness does not represent a radical departure from Western images which extends toward a redefined African-American consciousness.

It should come as no surprise that the concept of the Beast in **Black Mass** initially evolves as a result of Baraka's close alignment with many of Elijah Muhammad's ideas about Western white male domination over the African-American male. In his *Autobiography of Malcom X,* Malcolm frequently claims that "the white man is the devil" and that "the black man had great fine, sensitive civilizations before the white man was out of the caves." Evident from the context of Baraka's Beast is the Islamic view that whites—like the way Satan and his army were depicted in heaven—were initially rabble-rousers among members of Islamic heaven. According to world history as Elijah Muhammad interprets it [in his 1965 *Message to the Black Man*], once these whites were discovered, however,

> [they] were punished by being deprived of divine guidance, for 2,000 years which brought them almost into the family of wild beasts—going upon all fours; eating raw and unseasoned, uncooked food; living in caves and tree tops, climbing and jumping from one tree to the other.

Apparently, Baraka's depiction of the Beast from the context of Islamic history is a strategy which draws learned responses from among members of his African-American audience, most of whom knew the Muslim credo. First, the Beast introduces ominous typological parallels to the beast of the Book of Revelations; thus, these parallels, as seen in the prophetic premise of *Black Mass,* suggest equally gloomy predictions for African Americans who favor white creations. Second, the actual appearance of the Beast and its subsequent role in the didactic drama allow viewers to focus upon the exemplum of the Beast as a tangible product of "art for art's sake."

Several Western influences assume seemingly lesser roles in the multiple strategies which Baraka employs for depicting the Beast. For example, Mary Shelley's *Frankenstein* provides a suitably familiar plot which allows Baraka to elaborate upon Elijah Muhammad's philosophy, with few alterations. Several of the novel's stock qualities figure prominently: the obsessed scientist who gives life to a hideous being; the innocent creature doomed to a life of isolation because of its physical distortions; and the creature's ultimate destruction of its creator. Although Baraka utilizes these particular aspects of Shelley's novel, he deviates, especially in his portrayal of the Beast. The creature that was put together by Dr. Frankenstein is given to compassion and kindness. Baraka's nameless Beast, though carved from Shelley's mold, is the antithesis of her warm, human-like protagonist: Instead of the refined diction of Shelley's version, Baraka's Beast is barely intelligible, capable only of reiterating one phrase: "I white. White. White. White." Instead of empathy which the readers are able to experience through first-person narration, viewers only see the Beast's physical repulsiveness and thus are more likely to have a one-dimensional view of it.

The Faustian legend is also identifiable in *Black Mass,* yet it is doubtful that Baraka's intended audiences could identify it as an influence nor, for that matter, did they need it to comprehend the basic truths of Baraka's morality play unfolding before them. The plot of Christopher Marlowe's dramatized version of the legendary Dr. Faustus involves an overly ambitious Renaissance man who sells his soul to gain the magical powers of necromancy. To be sure, each of the

unemployed, poverty-stricken, and disillusioned blacks who witnessed the play could easily identify with this level of high-stakes bartering needed to merely survive in America.

The Faustian legend is also identifiable in *Black Mass,* yet it is doubtful that Baraka's intended audiences could identify it as an influence nor, for that matter, did they need it to comprehend the basic truths of Baraka's morality play unfolding before them.
—*Sandra G. Shannon*

Another Western legend evident in *Black Mass,* which, more than likely, immediately jogs the consciences of African-American viewers, is that of Dracula. Versions of the legend have appeared in so many aspects of American cultures that it is very easily recognizable. The Gothic tale of the highly contagious vampire whose bite transforms its prey into one of the same is suggested when the Beast bites Tilla:

> The woman stumbles toward Jacoub, her face draining of color. Her voice grows coarse, she screams, covering herself with her robes. She emerges, slowly, from within the folds of the garment, her entire body shuddering, and beginning to do small hop the beast did. Suddenly she throws back the robes, and she is white, or white blotches streak her face and hair. She laughs and weeps in deadly cross between white and black. Her words have turned to grunts, and she moves like an animal robot.

In his use of the Dracula legend, Baraka likens the influence that the dominant white culture has over blacks who embrace assimilation to the ghastly interdependence between a bloodthirsty vampire and its unwitting prey. These highly suggestive images become especially evident when the white beast bites one of the female characters and "infects" her with his whiteness. Baraka also shows, however, through the victim's incomplete transformation from black to white that the effects of assimilation for blacks is never absolute. Unfortunately for Tilla, these remnants become evident when she "laughs and weeps in deadly cross between white and black." No matter how much they claim whiteness, they will always be black and will always be regarded by whites and other blacks as such. For African Americans who have abandoned their culture in favor of another, their awkwardness is multiplied by "the widespread use of cosmetics to bleach the black out of one's skin . . . and nose thinning and lip-clipping operations." What results is a similar mutation.

Implications of Edgar Rice Burrough's legendary creation Tarzan are also intertwined throughout Baraka's *Black Mass.*

Enjoying immense popularity in the United States, the edenic version of the white man of the jungle was catapulted by the visual media to a symbol of American culture, much like today's Rambo image. Just as Dracula is an easily recognizable prototype for the African-American audience, so too is Tarzan.

Baraka's inversion of the Tarzan legend is particularly relevant to his concept of wasted or misdirected knowledge. In the original legend, Jane insists upon instructing Tarzan in etiquette and proper speech, though he obviously has no need of either in his jungle home. Similarly, in **Black Mass,** Jacoub insists that the Beast be taught: "We will teach this thing the world of humanity. And we will benefit by its inhuman. . . ." He proceeds to educate the creature using a patronizing manner similar to Jane's.

Amiri Baraka's **Black Mass** incorporates principles from yet another western myth—*Pandora's Box.* The basic storyline of this Greek myth and universally popular tale involves a woman who is entrusted with a box containing all the ills that could plague mankind. Not able to resist temptation and against the counsel of others, she eventually opens the box and lets loose a myriad of evil forces. In particular, **Black Mass** follows three sections of the myth's structure: the prophesy, the disobedience, and the prophetic fruition. In this sense, the unleashing of evil upon the world is a result of Jacoub's disobedience to the prophetic entreaties of his associates, and the prophetic fruition occurs as the Beast eventually escapes out into the audience of the theater. The influence of the *Pandora's Box* myth is especially evident in the comments of Tanzil ("You have turned loose absolute evil") and in the appended words of the final detached Narrator:

> And so, Brothers and Sisters, these beasts are still loose in the world. Still they spit their hideous cries. There are beasts in our world, Brothers and Sisters. There are beasts in our world. Let us find them and slay them. Let us lock them in their caves.

Baraka's recurrent tendency to juxtapose opposites in order to create absurd images is prevalent in Jacoub's determination to teach a creature that Baraka has so grossly caricatured that the act appears laughable. Just as he parodies the science and magic which Jacoub initially misuses in creating the Beast, in this instance, he underscores the futility of knowledge which does no more than ricochet off the Beast.

Mel Gussow, who reviewed the 1972 production of **Black Mass** at a Baraka Festival in New York, notes, in particular, the play's offensive story line: "Black man creates white man—definitely not in his own image—and then ridicules him. A portentous ritual suddenly turns into a clown show, a notion that seemed to delight the almost all-black audience

opening night." Clearly the white critic was offended by what he perceived as the play's condescension toward the white race. Yet apparently Baraka had staged a play in which the ends justify the means. That is, he harnesses the general popularity and acceptance of the Islamic myth, makes several alterations, and produces a humorous, though disturbing, statement about the African-American's ritual practice of imitating white America.

George Piggford (essay date Spring 1997)

SOURCE: "Looking into Black Skulls: Amiri Baraka's *Dutchman* and the Psychology of Race," in *Modern Drama,* Vol. XL, No. I, Spring, 1997, pp. 74-82.

[*In the following essay, Piggford explores Baraka's psychological analysis of black American men in* Dutchman.]

Houston A. Baker, Jr. has rightly observed [in *The Journey Back: Issues in Black Literature and Criticism,* 1980] that "the radical chic denizens of Bohemia [and] the casual liberals of the academy" have never recognized LeRoi Jones's/Amiri Baraka's achievement as a playwright and a poet because his "brilliantly projected conception of black as country—a separate and progressive nation with values antithetical to those of white America—stands in marked contrast to the ideas set forth by Baldwin, Wright, Ellison, and others in the fifties." That is, according to the integrationist politics that continue to dominate discussions of race in the United States, what we might in the 1990s call the "African-American problem" is indeed seen as the *African-American's problem* to examine and solve, not the white's. Baraka's Black Power political agenda, which perceives the United States as a society at least as black as it is white, a country built on "oppression and destruction," stands in marked contrast to the general integrationist bent of American racial politics. The call to revolutionary action inscribed into his drama demands a rethinking of both the American social system and the ways that it is typically examined in the generally liberal critical discourses of the predominantly white academy.

Baraka's one-act play **Dutchman** (1964) amply illustrates the persistence of racial tension in the United States in the 1960s and represents an emerging militant attitude on the part of American blacks, and on the part of black American playwrights. According to Samuel A. Hay [in *African/American Theatre: A Historical and Critical Analysis,* 1994], the African American Protest Drama of W. E. B. Du Bois, which viewed theatre as an integrationist "political weapon," was transformed by Baraka into the separatist Black Revolutionary Theatre of the 1960s, which "no longer represented appeals to share power," but depicted "seizures of power."

Baraka himself has claimed that his play is an early example of "The Revolutionary Theatre," a theatre, like Artaud's "theatre of cruelty," that "should force change; it should be change" [Baraka, *Home: Social Essays*]. Baraka continues:

> The Revolutionary Theatre must EXPOSE! Show up the insides of these humans, look into black skulls. White men will cower before this theatre because it hates them. Because they themselves have been trained to hate. The Revolutionary Theatre must hate them for hating. For presuming with their technology to deny the supremacy of the Spirit. They will all die because of this.

Baraka's strong words point emphatically toward the end of this theatre: a revolutionary change in social structures. The idea that theatrical performance should attempt to force social change was initially articulated by Antonin Artaud in *The Theatre and Its Double:* "our present social state is iniquitous and should be destroyed. If this is a fact for the theater to be pre-occupied with, it is even more a matter for machine guns." Theatrical groups such as Julian Beck and Judith Malina's Living Theatre, founded in 1951, attempted to put Artaud's theories into practice. For the directors and performers of the Living Theatre: "Life, revolution, and theatre are three words for the same thing: an unconditional NO to the present society" [Julian Beck, quoted by Theodore Shank, in *American Alternative Theater*, 1982]. The Black Revolutionary Theatre represents an attempt to racialize the Artaudian "theatre of cruelty" by instigating its audience to act in revolutionary and violent ways to overthrow the white-dominated American social order.

For Baraka, the theatre of which *Dutchman* is an example is centrally political; it will ultimately lead to the (at least) symbolic death of the white race. It is also, however, a psychological study, though one that exposes the limitations of the psychoanalytic process. As Samuel Hay states it, "Black Revolutionary drama deconstructed both Outer Life *and* Inner Life." In *Dutchman,* Baraka attempts to psychoanalyze the black male in America, typified by the character Clay; his technique is meant to lay bare the social forces that make black men into neurotic subjects. His cure for their neurosis is race revolution and mass murder.

Frantz Fanon, in *Black Skin, White Masks,* extols the power of *language* rather than political activism to solve what he terms the "color problem," suggesting that this problem exists primarily in language itself: "From all sides dozens and hundreds of pages assail me and try to impose their wills on me. But a single line would be enough. Supply a single answer and the color problem would be stripped of all its importance." Fanon implies in this passage that if language is transformed—if the answer to this "problem" is found—the issue of race will simply disappear. This assumption is based on Fanon's naïve trust in the Freudian psychoanalytic method. Freudian psychoanalysis asserts that one can solve psychological problems through language in a similar way, by making unconscious desires conscious through therapy. The surfacing of a psychological disorder in the conscious mind of the patient through the linguistic give-and-take of psychotherapy should, according to Freud, cure the disorder. He makes this clear in *Dora:* "the practical aim of . . . treatment is to remove all possible symptoms and to replace them by *conscious thoughts*" (emphasis mine).

Fanon's approach to the "color problem" reproduces Freud's method within a sociological frame: "I believe that only a psychoanalytical interpretation of the black problem can lay bare the anomalies of affect that are responsible for the structure of the complex." By applying the psychoanalytic process to the black man as an idea, Fanon hopes to "destroy" the "massive psychoexistential complex" that underlies "the juxtaposition of the white and black races . . . . *by analyzing it*" (emphasis mine). Like Freud, Fanon assumes that by making this "psychoexistential complex" conscious, he will eradicate it. *Dutchman* as historical text demonstrates that Fanon's solution was overly optimistic: the problems associated with black and white race relations did not evaporate in the decade between the publication *Peau Noire, Masques Blancs,* and the first performance of Baraka's play; indeed, they had multiplied and intensified. Baraka's text explores the psychology of race in the United States by looking "into black skulls," and is in this way similar to a Freudian case study like *Dora. Further,* it provides a thematization of the ways that race, gender, and sexuality are constructed in American social consciousness.

However, Baraka, unlike Fanon, does not attempt to understand the "color problem" in order to solve it through a psychoanalytic sleight-of-hand; rather, his exposition of the situation of blacks in American culture is geared to an ultimate destruction of that culture: "The Revolutionary Theatre, which is now peopled with victims, will soon begin to be peopled with new kinds of heroes . . . . [T]hese will be new men, new heroes, and their enemies most of you who are reading this" [Baraka, *Home: Social Essays*]. *Dutchman*'s Clay is presented as an example of the "victims" that people Revolutionary Theatre; he is identifiable as a Faustian anti-hero rather than a hero. But Baraka's intentions are clear: Clay, characterized primarily by his repressed desires to rape and murder whites, is martyred for the black revolutionary cause.

It is within the gothic, dreamlike atmosphere of *Dutchman* that the text's anti-hero, Clay, moves from a state of repression to one of acceptance of his unconscious desires. Indeed, the play encourages its black audience members to do likewise and warns its white viewers that the revolution is coming. Though he eventually expresses his desire to "[m]urder,"

Clay refuses to act on this impulse—indeed, it is Lula, the white villainess of the play, who will murder him. Clay dies at Lula's hands, then, as a self-aware but impotent and castrated subject. Lula functions in **Dutchman** as both Clay's mother and his demonic psychotherapist by bringing Clay's repressed desires to the surface of his consciousness. Through her verbal taunting she eventually peers into Clay's "black skull" and finds his murderous unconscious impulses.

A dutchman, "the theatrical term meaning a strip of cloth used to hid[e] the crack between the seams of flats, or, in a more general sense, a contrivance used to hide a defect of some kind"[Robert L. Tener, "Role Playing as a Dutchman," *Studies in Black Literature,* Vol. 3, No. 3, 1972], connotes something impermanently and fragilely held together that provides the illusion of solidity and permanence. The title **Dutchman** can be understood in this way as a metaphor for "the meretricious facade of civility" [George Ralph, "Jones's *Dutchman,*" *The Explicator,* Vol. 43, No. 2, 1985] utilized by Clay both in his dress and his language to hide his murderous inner desires. It is this façade that Lula relentlessly strips away, as a psychoanalytic therapist might, attempting to access Clay's unconscious by getting behind "whatever surface his unconscious happens to be presenting to his notice at that moment," by asking him leading questions about his innermost thoughts. Towards the end of scene one, Lula informs Clay, "You're a murderer, Clay, and you know it," and, anticipating his denial, continues, "You know goddamn well what I mean." The still-repressed Clay uncertainly responds to this accusation with a questioning "I do?" Lula's pronouncement of Clay's desire to murder whites is based on the assumption that all black men are secretly murderers, and she successfully proves this theory by bringing out the potential murderer in Clay. This is Clay's innermost "defect," the secret buried in his unconscious mind.

Though Lula suggests that Clay is "too serious to be psychoanalyzed," her comment can only be read as ironic, for she proceeds to psychoanalyze him successfully. As Sherley Anne Williams has correctly observed [in "The Search for Identity in Baraka's *Dutchman,*" in *Imamu Amiri Baraka (Leroi Jones): A Collection of Critical Essays,* edited by Kimberley W. Benston, 1978], "Lula . . . control[s] the situation. *She* picks Clay up. *She* encourages him. And it is she who goads him into revealing things which must have been carefully hidden deep in the most secret places of his heart." When Lula makes her diagnosis, when she reveals Clay's inner self to him, he resists coming to terms with his own murderous "pumping black heart":

> LULA [. . .] Clay, you got to break out. Don't just
> sit there dying the way they want you to die. Get
> up.

> CLAY Oh, sit the fuck down. [. . .] Sit down,
> goddamn it.

> LULA [. . .] Screw yourself, Uncle Tom. Thomas
> Woolly-head. [. . .]

> CLAY Lula! Lula! [. . .] Lula . . . you dumb bitch.
> Why don't you stop it?

But she eventually goads him into disclosing his "neurosis":

> LULA You're afraid of white people. And your fa-
> ther was. Uncle Tom Big Lip!

> CLAY [. . .] Now shut up and let me talk. Shit, you
> don't have any sense, Lula, nor feelings either. I
> could murder you now. [. . .] It takes no great ef-
> fort. [. . .] Just let me bleed you, you loud whore
> [. . . .] A whole people of neurotics, struggling to
> keep from being sane. And the only thing that
> would cure the neurosis would be your murder.
> Simple as that. I mean if I murdered you, then other
> white people would begin to understand me. You
> understand? No. [. . .] Murder. Just murder! Would
> make us all sane.

Clay's insanity, according to his newly discovered understanding of it, is a by-product of the neurotic, *white* culture which insists that he hide his inner feelings while it goads him into revealing them. His neurosis is simply the neurosis endemic to being a black man in American culture. Immediately after making this discovery, he imagines a utopic space where this neurosis would be eliminated in the act of black revenge for his "castration" at the hands of whites.

But even after revealing his inner nature, Clay embraces the essential repressiveness of his social and cultural situation: "Ahhh. Shit. But who needs it? I'd rather be a fool. Insane." Unlike a Freudian case study, and unlike Fanon's approach, Baraka's text does not provide a cure for the "color problem" through an understanding of it. Though Fanon's "single answer" to the "color problem" is articulated by Clay—and that answer is "murder"—the problem is not eliminated. For Baraka, a public expression of this answer is a necessary first step but it is not—as Fanon wrongly assumed—the revolution itself. Even Freud acknowledges that the efficacy of psychoanalysis is limited by "the patient's own will and understanding," and it is Clay's own desire to remain an "Uncle Tom" that forecloses the possibility of his becoming an actual murderer, at least for the moment.

But by goading Clay into revealing his unconscious wishes, Lula has produced a self-conscious potential murderer, one who might pose a threat to white society sometime in the future. She has pointed out to Clay his hidden identity: he is a middle-class black, which she identifies with the insulting label "Uncle Tom"; simultaneously, he is a potential revolutionary who wants to murder her. As Louis Phillips explains [in "LeRoi Jones and Contemporary Black Drama," in *The Black American Writer,* edited by C. W. E. Bigsby, vol. II, *Poetry and Drama,* 1969], "Lula mocks Clay and accuses him of being an Uncle Tom . . . whereas Clay would like to see himself as a black revolutionary. The truth, however, is that he is neither one nor the other, and, hence, feels a real lack of identity." This lack, or space internal conflict, can be understood metaphorically in Freudian terms as evidence of Clay's "castration" by white society, represented ultimately by Lula's murder of Clay with a suspiciously phallic knife. Indeed, Lula indicates clearly to Clay that their entire dialogue is about Clay's status as a man:

> LULA [. . .] we'll sit and talk endlessly, endlessly.
>
> CLAY About what?
>
> LULA About what? About your manhood, what do you think? What do you think we've been talking about all this time?
>
> CLAY Well, I didn't know it was that. That's for sure. Every other thing in the world but that.

Numerous critics have pointed to Clay's "emasculated life" and have discussed his "castration" at the hands of Lula. Lula's power over Clay is based on what seems to be her uncanny knowledge of him, but when Clay says to her, "Hey, you still haven't told me how you know so much about me," Lula responds, "I told you I didn't know anything about *you* . . . you're a well-known type." **Dutchman,** therefore, adheres to the pattern of a Freudian case study, in which the neurosis of a particular individual typifies a general kind of neurosis that can be treated following the methods of a particular case.

It is possible to understand Lula and Clay both as lovers and as mother and son, suggesting that the themes of black revenge and incest are crucial to Baraka's play. According to Diane Weisgram [in "LeRoi Jones' *Dutchman:* Inter-racial Ritual of Sexual Violence," *American Imago,* Vol. 29, No. 3, 1972], "Clay and Lula are the primordial parents fused in a violent sexual encounter; and in keeping with the fluid identifications of primal scene fantasies, they are also mother and son. Clay's expulsion from the car [after his murder] suggests an image of violent birth. This situation places the two characters in a position of incestuous seduction. The text raises the issue of incest when Lula tells Clay: "You tried to make it with your sister when you were ten. [. . .] But I succeeded a few weeks ago." Not only does this statement suggest "an unconscious incestuous union" between Clay and Lula, but also it places Lula securely in the phallic position

in their relationship. After all, Lula is the one who "made it," a phrase used for both for Clay's failed attempt and implicitly for Lula's successful attempt to penetrate Clay's sister.

In order to prepare Clay for his death/birth at the end of the text, Lula—playing her part of white phallic mother—even teaches him his proper lines, his proper role, as a mother would instruct her son. But she teaches him the exact words he should use to commence a seduction of her:

> LULA [. . .] Now you say to me, "Lula, Lula, why don't you go to this party with me tonight?" It's your turn, and let those be your lines.
>
> CLAY Lula, why don't you go to this party with me tonight, Huh?
>
> LULA Say my name twice before you ask, and no huh's.
>
> CLAY Lula, Lula, why don't you go to this party with me tonight?

This interaction generally parallels what Freud has termed "parental seduction"; Lula, the mother/lover, attempts to seduce Clay the son/lover, though her seduction will not lead to sexual union but to her murder of Clay. This seduction scene, with its overtones of miscegenation, suggests what has traditionally been perceived as the horrifying possibility of an incestuous union between races; Baraka here explores the horror of the sexual aspect of the politics of integration.

According to Baraka, in **"American Sexual Reference: Black Male,"** "white women become men-things, a weird combination, sucking the male juices to build a navel orange, which is themselves" [*Home: Social Essays*]. White women are forced to play this vampiric role because white men have become castrated and feminine: "[m]ost American white men are trained to be fags," an identification he associates with powerlessness, femaleness, and therefore castration [*Home: Social Essays*]. This identification exists at odds with Baraka's more conflicted understanding of homosexuality in his play **The Toilet,** which was running off Broadway at the same time as **Dutchman.** In that text, the mutual homosexual desire between a black student gang leader, Foots, and a white student, Karolis, is treated with complexity and sympathy. After Foots' gang beats up Karolis for sending Foots a "love letter" (though it may have been Foots himself who sent the note), Foots, alone with Karolis, "*kneels before the body, weeping and cradling the head in his arms.*"

In **"American Sexual Reference,"** however, Baraka's simplistic (and often misogynistic and homophobic) discussion of the gender/race system reinscribes binaristic constructions of male/female, white/black, heterosexual/homosexual. Baraka strives to invert these binaries; he does not challenge the overarching binaristic system which privileges one (albeit arbitrary) category over another.

Further, Baraka associates the mutilation of genitals that often accompanied the lynching of black men with an attempt to "remove the threat of the black man asserting [his] manness" [**Home: Social Essays**], that is, the threat of black men raping white women, the revenge of black Americans for the horrifying oppressions of slavery. "[White] America," he asserts, "has always tried to . . . make [the black man] swallow his manhood" [**Home: Social Essays**]. White women, Baraka claims, are both repulsed by and sexually attracted to black men. The feelings of black men are mutual: "[f]or the black man, acquisition of a white woman always signified some special power the black man had managed to obtain . . . within white society" [**Home: Social Essays**]. Fanon associates this power with the "whitening" of the black man:

> Out of the blackest part of my soul . . . surges this desire to be suddenly *white.*

> I wish to be acknowledged not as *black* but as *white.*

> Now . . . who but a white woman can do this for me? By loving me she proves that I am worthy of white love. I am loved like a white man.

For Baraka, as for Fanon, the relationship between black men and white women can be contextualized in terms of seduction. Understood in this way, however, the seduction between Lula and Clay must be in some sense mutual.

One way to make sense of the relationship between Lula and Clay in **Dutchman** is found in a reading of the text as an internal conflict. Certainly the "dreamlike" quality of the text noted above supports a reading of the play as a representation of an identity crisis experienced within Clay's psyche. Traditional Freudian readings tend to interpret Baraka's play as "a play which exemplifies the function of the id, and . . . its so-called 'absurdity' and 'obscenity' are reflections of its function" [George R. Adams, "Black Militant Drama," *American Imago,* Vol. 28, No. 2, 1971]. From this perspective, Lula and Clay become manifestations of Clay's split self. **Dutchman** raises the possibility that Lula was a hidden aspect of Clay's own "black skull," an intrinsic part of Clay's own psyche. Lula is both separate from and a part of Clay, much as white and black America are both distinct and inseparable. Lula can be understood in this text as what bell hooks [in "Representing Whiteness in the Black Imagination," in *Cultural Studies,* 1992] has discussed as "the representation of whiteness as terrorizing" in the consciousness of black Americans. Understood in this way, Baraka's play

suggests that the terror of whiteness must be removed from black skulls before it can be removed from society through political action.

This reading is supported by Julia Kristeva's re-theorizing of Freud's notion of parental seduction. According to Kristeva [in "Place Names," in *Desire in Language: A Semiotic Approach to Literature and Art,* 1980], this seduction happens only in the realm of the imaginary, as a result of an individual's repressed wish *to have been seduced* by his parent: "We thus come to the shaping of this image of the child-parent, the seducing child, a child always already older, born into the world with compound drives, erogenous zones, and even genital desires." This understanding of parental seduction can be associated metaphorically with Baraka's notion of the relationship between white women and black men. Black men want both to murder and to seduce their phallic mothers, the white women who are made "men-things" by American society. But for Kristeva this desire exists primarily within an individual psyche: "through the seduction myth, [the child] sees itself as being attached by drive . . . to this object of love [its phallic mother]." This mother is, however, simply an idea generated in the mind of the "child"; she is a "type" rather than a "real" individual.

The dumb show presented before the dialogue begins in **Dutchman** supports the plausibility of this reading:

> *The man [Clay] looks idly up, until he sees a woman's face staring at him through the window; when it realizes that the man has noticed the face, it begins very premeditatedly to smile. The man smiles too, for a moment, without a trace of self-consciousness. Almost an instinctive though undesirable response. Then a kind of awkwardness or embarrassment sets in, and the man makes to look away, is further embarrassed, so he brings back his eyes to where the face was, but by now [. . .] the face would seem to be left behind.*

This scene parallels a Lacanian/Kristevan "mirror stage," where "the Same sees itself altered through the well-known opening that constitutes it as a representation, sign, and death." In this reading, Lula becomes a "return of the repressed," a re-enactment of a primal scene in which the subjectivity of Clay takes on identity through the perception of an other—in this case his own internalized terror of whiteness—within his own imagination. Importantly, this entire exchange occurs in the mise-en-scène of the play, rather than in its relatively naturalistic dialogue.

If **Dutchman** can be understood as an internal conflict, a dream, it is a dream in which the binaries black and white, male and female, become contextualized in the individual psyche of one person. Blackness signifies in this text virtue and naïveté; whiteness vice and disingenuousness. Maleness signifies castration, and femaleness phallic power. The text inverts the typical significations of the tropes of whiteness and blackness in white American culture. The relationship of these significations to the themes of incest and parricide, particularly patricide, is made clear by Clay:

> CLAY [. . .] tell this to your father, who's probably the kind of man who needs to know at once. So he can plan ahead. Tell him not to preach so much rationalism and cold logic to these niggers. Let them alone.[. . .] Don't make the mistake, through some irresponsible surge of Christian charity, of talking too much about the advantages of Western rationalism, or the great intellectual legacy of the white man, or maybe they'll begin to listen. And then, maybe one day, you'll find they actually do understand exactly what you are talking about, all these fantasy people.[. . .] And on that day, as sure as shit, when you really believe you can 'accept' them into your fold, as half-white trustees late of the subject peoples.[. . .] They'll murder you, and have very rational explanations. Very much like your own. They'll cut your throats, and drag you to the edge of your cities so the flesh can fall away from your bones, in sanitary isolation.

Clay's desires are clear: he wants to murder the white father. The character Clay, himself a castrated, "half-white trustee," here reveals a vision of race revolution which will lead to an inversion of the dominant structure of power. First he will purge the internalized whiteness from his own psyche (the seductive phallic mother, in Kristeva's terms), then murder the white father who controls the social structures of racial domination.

Clay's apocalyptic vision also evokes the hellish atmosphere of Baraka's novel ***The System of Dante's Hell,*** his exploration of a particularly middle-class black nightmare. While the representation of an anti-hero like Clay is a necessary step in the history of black Revolutionary Theatre, Baraka's attitude towards this neurotic black is expressed in his contemporaneous novel: "I put The Heretics in the deepest part of hell, though Dante had them spared, on higher ground. It is heresy against one's own sources, running in terror, from one's deepest responses and insights . . . that I see as basest evil." ***Dutchman,*** then, examines the "skull" of a repressed middle-class black in order to expose the horror of his daily life, his personal hell as it were. It also functions as a warning—both to "heretical" blacks like Clay who help support the nightmare of black oppression through inaction and to whites—that *the revolution is coming*. By exposing the horror of race relations in America through the psychological case study ***Dutchman,*** Baraka both diagnoses the problem

in American society—white dominance—and prescribes his cure: race revolution and murder.

Carla J. McDonough (essay date 1997)

SOURCE: "Amiri Baraka: Angry Young Men," in *Staging Masculinity: Male Identity in Contemporary American Drama,* McFarland & Company, 1997, pp. 30-2.

[*In the following excerpt from her* Staging Masculinity, *McDonough studies Baraka's treatment of black manhood in his works.*]

While [Eugene] O'Neill, [Arthur] Miller, and [Tennessee] Williams were produced chiefly on the main stages of Broadway, the avant-garde, off-Broadway plays of Amiri Baraka (LeRoi Jones), which were often written within and for the Black Revolutionary theater, became a powerful voice for issues of race within American culture, an issue that is at the heart of American identity. His confrontational style of theater is at the forefront of the 1960s off-off-Broadway movement that cultivated Shepard and opened the way for . . . other dramatists. . . . Baraka's theater, however, is distinctly masculine in its orientation, as Michele Wallace's *Black Macho and the Myth of the Superwoman* has so vividly and controversially demonstrated. Wallace argues that, like many other leaders of the Black Power movement, Baraka's fight for black power and black liberation in his plays and essays is focused chiefly on black manhood. Referring to Baraka's essay **"American Sexual Reference: Black Male,"** which opens with the statement "Most American white men are trained to be fags" [***Home: Social Essays,*** 1966], Wallace shows that "according to Jones the struggle of black against white was the purity of primitivism against the corruption of technology, the noble savage against the pervert bureaucrats, the super macho against the fags." Baraka's equation of white men with "fags" is clearly intended to be the worst insult he can think to throw at another man, a concept based on homophobia, which Wallace also critiques. This homophobia has traditionally been a key to maintaining and protecting the dominance of a certain type of heterosexual masculinity, as is apparent, for instance, in *Streetcar Named Desire.*

Though many critics may have been taken aback by Wallace's critique that demonstrates how the African American fight for power was collapsed by its male leaders into the black man's fight for his manhood, Baraka himself has indicated that ***Dutchman*** is first and foremost about black masculinity. In **"LeRoi Jones Talking"** he wrote:

> ***Dutchman*** is about the difficulty of becoming a man in America. It is very difficult, to be sure, if

you are black, but I think it is now much harder to become one if you are white. In fact, you will find very few white American males with the slightest knowledge of what manhood involves. They are too busy running the world or running from it.

[The first half of this] highly provocative statement regarding white males . . . begs for attention now.

True to Baraka's statement above, perhaps no other play within the American theatrical canon illustrates more vividly the dilemma that results from being black and male in America, a country that insists that its men enact an assertive and powerful masculinity at the same time that it crushes and even kills black men who attempt to do so. The issue of enacting gendered behavior, of gender as performance, is as crucial to this play as it is to *Streetcar*. The audience of **Dutchman** is encouraged to view Clay's actions—his masculinity—as a *performance* he has chosen to enact. Lula calls Clay a well-known "type," and Clay later admits to being so out of choice. When pushed by Lula's insults to take a stand for himself, Clay tells her:

> If I'm a middle-class fake white man . . . let me be.
> And let me be in the way I want. I'll rip your lousy
> breasts off! Let me be who I feel like being. Uncle
> Tom. Thomas. Whoever. It's none of your business.
> You don't know anything except what's there for
> you to see. An act. Lies. Device. Not the pure heart,
> the pumping black heart.

This self-knowledge seems to be the ultimate cause of Clay's murder. Clay is acting the part of a "middle-class fake white man," and warns Lula that he does so "to keep myself from cutting all your throats." He reveals to Lula that although he pretends to be an "Uncle Tom" he is actually hiding or repressing his anger and hatred, and it is this anger that Lula wants revealed so that she will have a reason, or an excuse, to kill him. As long as he plays the Uncle Tom "type" (as does the conductor whom Lula ignores at the end of the play) without acknowledging his performance, he is no threat to the system, but Clay both enacts a demure exterior as a defensive measure *and* remains aware of "the pure heart, the pumping black heart" within him. Subsequently, he is considered to be dangerous to the white patriarchal system, ironically represented (in a more vivid way than we saw in *The Hairy Ape*) by a white *woman*. Clay's "danger," as his final speech indicates, is that he might at any moment choose to perform his role differently.

Clay's self-knowledge is somewhat akin to that of Blanche, who performs a role created for her by the white patriarchy of her Southern culture, at the same time knowing it is a role. Although it is not always comfortable for her, though it is often even hypocritical, that performance is also necessary

for survival, something that Blanche understands. Like Clay, it is her self-knowledge that destroys her because she cannot reconcile the performance with the reality, although Stanley manages to do so for himself by simply not acknowledging his performance as anything but reality. In a certain way, Blanche and Clay both expose the danger and dilemmas of self-knowledge if the self does not fit into neatly, predefined social categories. In Stanley's world, there is no place for Blanche because she does not fit into only one of the "appropriate" roles he envisions for women: wife, mother, or whore. In Lula's world, there is no place for Clay because he resists neat dichotomies: he is neither a white man nor an Uncle Tom.

Clay's emphasis on his performance reveals, however, the extent to which performance is necessary to his survival. In proving that his performance is a way to mask his rage, Clay's references are to professional entertainers from the black community, notably Bessie Smith and Charlie Parker, who he claims also mask their rage behind their performances. The professional "performance" of music or poetry, Clay argues, is simply channellings of the rage that all blacks, all the "blues people," actually feel towards whites. Clay, Baraka's version of the average black man, is presented as playing the same game as the professional performer, what Richard Majors and Janet Mancini Billson refer to in *Cool Pose: The Dilemmas of Black Manhood in America* as a "relentless performance . . . in a theater that is seldom dark." To "pass" through a white world that refuses to acknowledge a black man's right to existence and chooses to see him as a threat, he must disguise himself in a manner that will be perceived by his white viewers as nonthreatening. This image of the mask appears often in plays by African Americans that treat the difficulty of finding and knowing one's identity in a culture that seeks to take away that identity.

In addition to the theme of masculine identity that Baraka details, **Dutchman** provides an influential style of theater for presenting this issue. The violence and rage of his male characters, while overtly motivated by racial injustice, are covertly reflecting a confusion regarding gender identity that is apparent in the rage and violence among the men in the plays of [Sam] Shepard, [David] Mamet, [David] Rabe, and, to a lesser extent, [August] Wilson. Violence and aggression are associated with masculinity not only by these playwrights, but by sociological definitions of masculinity. . . . Baraka's theater is an angry theater, his men are bitter and defensive, threatened and imperilled, but fighting back. We . . . see similar characteristics among men in [other] plays . . . , indicating that certain gender issues are at the heart of the anger and violence that are so often exhibited by male characters in contemporary plays by both black and white men in America.

The vagaries, the fracturings, the insecurities of male identity are all present within plays by O'Neill, Williams, Miller, and Baraka, who serve as sometimes direct, sometimes shadowy influences on the leading male playwrights of the next generation. Although all of the playwrights . . . indicate that they see their plays as encompassing a wide canvas of American experience (the family, business, war, the frontier), consistently within the plays of all four dramatists, that canvas shrinks as the American myths or subjects they treat reveal themselves to be gendered as male. The plays . . . reveal, at times unintentionally, the "invisible" or "unspeakable" idea that masculinity is often as disempowering for the men who seek to enact it as it is empowering. This disempowerment explains in part the defensiveness and even paranoia that plagues so many male characters. Masculinity, manliness and manhood, far from comprising a stable, monolithic construct, become fractured and insecure in these plays, yet masculinity is also the territory over which these playwrights and their characters fiercely fight for mastery.

FURTHER READING

Criticism

Andrews, W. D. E. "The Marxist Theater of Amiri Baraka." *Comparative Drama* 18 (Summer 1984): 137-60.
    Examines how Baraka's Marxist ideology is reflected in his plays.

Bone, Robert. "Action and Reaction." *New York Times Book Review* (8 May 1966): 3.
    A negative assessment of *Home: Social Essays.*

Casimer, Louis J., Jr. "*Dutchman:* The Price of Culture Is a Lie." In *The Binding of Proteus,* edited by Marjorie W. McCune, Tucker Orbison, and Philip M. Withim, pp. 298-310. Lewisburg: Bucknell University Press, 1980.
    Studies the treatment of myth and ritual in *Dutchman.*

Coles, Robert. "More Exiles." In *Times of Surrender: Selected Essays,* pp. 151-53. Iowa City: University of Iowa Press, 1988.
    A mixed assessment of *Blues People.*

Dieke, Ikenna. "Sadeanism: Baraka, Sexuality, and The Perverse Imagination in *The System of Dante's Hell.*" *Black American Literature Forum* 19, No. 4 (Winter 1985): 163-66.
    Explores the influence of the works of the Marquis de Sade on Baraka's works.

Van Duyn, Mona. "The Poet as Novelist." *Poetry* 109, No. 5 (February 1967): 338-39.
    Illustrates the lyrical aspects in *The System of Dante's Hell.*

Wilson, John. "The New Jazzmen." *New York Times Book Review* (17 March 1968): 46.
    A positive review of *Black Music.*

Additional coverage of Baraka's life and career is contained in the following sources published by Gale: *Black Literature Criticism; Black Writers,* Vol. 2; *Concise Dictionary of American Literary Biography 1941-1968; Contemporary Authors,* Vols. 21-24R; *Contemporary Authors Bibliographic Series,* Vol. 3; *Contemporary Authors New Revision Series,* Vols. 27, 38, and 61; *Dictionary of Literary Biography,* Vols. 5, 7, 16, and 38; *Dictionary of Literary Biography Documentary Series,* Vol. 8; *DISCovering Authors; DISCovering Authors: Canadian; DISCovering Authors Modules: Most-Studied, Multicultural, Poets,* and *Popular Fiction and Genre Authors; Drama Criticism,* Vol. 6; *Major Twentieth Century Writers; Poetry Criticism,* Vol. 4; and *World Literature Criticism Supplement.*

Donald Barthelme
1931-1989

(Also wrote under the pseudonym of Lily McNeil) American short story writer, novelist, essayist, and author of books for children.

The following entry presents an overview of criticism on Barthelme's works through 1997. For further information on his life and works, see *CLC*, Volumes 1, 2, 3, 5, 6, 8, 13, 23, 46, and 59.

INTRODUCTION

A preeminent writer of experimental fiction, Barthelme created humorous and often unsettling stories by juxtaposing incongruous elements of contemporary language and culture. His prose has been described as a verbal collage in which words are intended to function as objects and are intentionally stripped of meaning by their unlikely combinations. Barthelme's writing is characterized by the absence of traditional plot and character development, disjointed syntax and dialogue, parodies of jargon and cliché, and a humor, according to Thomas M. Leitch, that arises "from a contrast between outrageous premises and deadpan presentation." His work contains allusions to literature, philosophy, art, film, and popular culture, and considers such themes as the ability of language to express thought and emotion, the function of art and the role of the artist in society, the complications of sexuality, the frailty and transience of human relationships, and the fragmentary nature of reality.

Biographical Information

Barthelme was born in Philadelphia, Pennsylvania, and raised in Houston, Texas, where his father became established as an innovative architect. While sharing his father's respect for visual art and architecture, Barthelme developed a strong interest in literature. After serving as editor for a literary journal published by the University of Texas, and as a journalist and a museum director, Barthelme traveled to New York City in the early 1960s where he edited *Location,* a short-lived arts and literary journal. During a great portion of his life, Barthelme made his home in Greenwich Village, often strolling around the area, observing the goings-on and finding material he could rework in his fiction.

Major Works

Barthelme's first stories appeared in literary periodicals dur-

ing the early 1960s. In these works, many of which were first published in the *New Yorker* and subsequently collected in *Come Back, Dr. Caligari* (1964), *Unspeakable Practices, Unnatural Acts* (1968), *City Life* (1971), and *Sadness* (1972), Barthelme incorporates advertising slogans, comic-book captions, catalogue descriptions, and jacket blurbs from records and books into a style that features verbal puns, non sequiturs, and fractured dialogue and narrative. Barthelme's first novel, *Snow White* (1967), is a darkly comic and erotic parody of the popular fairy tale. It is set in contemporary Greenwich Village, and the title character is an attractive yet unsatisfied young woman who shares an apartment with seven men. Composed largely of fragmented episodes in which undistinguishable characters attempt to express themselves in jargonistic and often nonsensical speech, *Snow White* has commonly been interpreted as an examination of the failure of language and the inability of literature to transcend or transform contemporary reality. In his second novel, *The Dead Father,* a surrealistic, mock-epic account of the Dead Father's journey to his grave and his burial by his son and a cast of disreputable characters, Barthelme weaves mythological, biblical, and literary allusions to create a story, according to Hilton Kramer, that lends "a sense of mystery and complexity and a certain decorative appeal to what . . . is actually a rather simple fantasy of filial revenge." In his third novel, *Paradise* (1986), Barthelme uses spare, formalistic prose marked by both a sense of playfulness and sorrow to relate the story of Simon, a fifty-three-year-old architect recently separated from his wife and teenage daughter, who is sharing his New York City flat with three women. The accounts of Simon's exotic and often erotic experiences with his housemates are interspersed with sections of revealing dialogue involving Simon and what appears to be either his psychologist or his alter ego. In addition to his works for adults, Barthelme authored a children's book, *The Slightly Irregular Fire Engine: or, The Hithering Thithering Djinn* (1971), which received the National Book Award for children's literature. *Sixty Stories* (1981) contains a selection of his short fiction as well as miscellaneous prose pieces and an excerpt from *The Dead Father.* Barthelme also adapted his novel *Snow White* and seven stories from *Great Days* for the stage.

Critical Reception

The unconventional nature of Barthelme's work has provoked extensive critical debate. His detractors perceive in his work a destructive impulse to subvert language and culture and an emphasis on despair and irrationalism. These critics claim that he offers no remedies for the ills of contemporary life that he documents and that he refuses to convey order, firm values, and meaning. On the other hand, Barthelme enjoyed widespread critical acclaim during his lifetime and was particularly praised as a stylist who offered vital and regenerative qualities to literature. Several critics have commended him as an insightful satirist who exposed pretentious ideas and purported to answer life's mysteries. Of his numerous works, *Come Back, Dr. Caligari; Unspeakable Practices, Unnatural Acts; City Life;* and *Sadness* contain some of Barthelme's best-known and most highly praised stories. Although some critics expressed concern over the monotonous tone and the apparent meaninglessness of many of the pieces, most praised Barthelme's inventiveness and technical skill. Some critics faulted *Overnight to Many Distant Cities* (1983) for Barthelme's idiosyncratic use of literary devices, but others noted the presence of hope in many of the pieces as well as an uncharacteristic willingness by Barthelme to confront and reflect emotions. *The Dead Father* is often considered one of Barthelme's most sustained and cohesive narrative works. William Peden has stated: "Beneath the clowning and the cutting-and-pasting and the ransacking of archives, Barthelme is a conventional moralist, alternately attracted, amused, and appalled by what he sees as the sickness of his times, by its dullness and insipidity, by its indifference to art and things of the imagination, by its affronts to individual life and dignity."

PRINCIPAL WORKS

Come Back, Dr. Caligari (short stories) 1964
Snow White (novel) 1967; first published in the *New Yorker*
Unspeakable Practices, Unnatural Acts (short stories) 1968
City Life (short stories) 1970
The Slightly Irregular Fire Engine: or, The Hithering Thithering Djinn (juvenilia) 1971
Sadness (short stories) 1972
The Dead Father (novel) 1975
Great Days (short stories) 1979
Sixty Stories (short stories) 1981
Overnight to Many Distant Cities (short stories) 1983
Paradise (novel) 1986
Forty Stories (short stories) 1987
The Teachings of Don B.: The Satires, Parodies, Fables, Illustrated Stories, and Plays of Donald Barthelme (satire, fables, short stories, and dramas) 1992

CRITICISM

Peter J. Longleigh, Jr. (essay date 1969)

SOURCE: "Donald Barthelme's *Snow White,*" in *Critique,* Vol. II, No. 3, 1969, pp. 30-4.

[*In the following essay, Longleigh provides an analysis of Barthelme's treatment of the title character as an anti-heroine in* Snow White.]

As an archetypal heroine (counterpart of the anti-hero, as defined in recent criticism), Donald Barthelme's title character in **Snow White** is a significant example of the play of light and darkness at the heart of modern value systems. Very important is an analytic penetration into this character, for she may stand for each of us, time and flesh being like all things relative. She is a character of flux and stasis, a semi-virginal anti-heroine who is in the end revirginized in a daring apotheosis. In her we are at the nexus of the tumultuous symbolic Other, as in the last chapters of *Moby-Dick,* or the dream symbolism of *The Tempest.* Indeed, one begins to understand in the work of the seven (sic) little men, as they wash buildings, that the underside of Snow White is Soot Black. This is, perhaps, one of the first ambiguous paradoxes of the book. For instance, the group narrator (cleverly evidencing certain traits) says:

> "Then we were out to wash the buildings. Clean buildings to fill your eyes with sunlight, and your heart with the idea that man is perfectable. Also they are good places to look at girls from, those high, swaying wooden platforms."

Notice the teasing duality of motive. One recalls the skeptical analyses of cause-and-effect not only in Wittgenstein's lectures at Cambridge in 1938, but also Hume's *Enquiries,* as well as in his better-known *Treatise.* Why, after all, do we act?

Donald Barthelme invites much insightful interplay of idea and dialogue. The more one brings to this tale, as one takes away, too.

Indeed, like other modernists, Barthelme aspires to pure intuition, unsullied by the older incumbrances. To get to the higher realities, one must now dispense with the lower conveniences. One must take the Kierkegaardian leap into Faith which transcends the ethical and aesthetic art forms of past eras. The result may seem to some of the more uninitiated, strange; but a true *artiste* knows that, epiphany-wise, he may have to wait for fit audience though few. Barthelme's fictions invite what may be the ultimate in reading and criticism: a peering into the deeper abysses of the feminine which might evade the more conventional verbal forms. One might describe it as a kind of Kierkegaardian *dread* on the verge of an Aristotelian *catharsis.*

Motive and emotion are also inter-twined in this tale of social criticism and psychology. We learn that "BILL IS TIRED OF SNOW WHITE NOW. BUT HE CANNOT TELL HER." This is a sentiment that rings true. Faced with a similar dilemma, anybody would linger on the threshold. One would not go to the shower. One would hope she will catch on.

But the female psychology, acidly etched by Barthelme, is different. Confronted with the silent language of the male, Snow White shouts: "OH I WISH THERE WERE SOME WORDS IN THE WORLD THAT WERE NOT THE WORDS I ALWAYS HEAR." Barthelme raises linguistic and epistemological questions with little effort. Language and knowledge seem the *topoi,* as it were, of the book, for Barthelme seems to transcend orderliness, passing into an almost mystical fire of obscurity, summed up in that further remark of the cumulative narrator who speaks for "we": "BUT ALSO PAY ATTENTION TO THE BUILDINGS, GRAY AND NOBLE IN THEIR FALSE ARCHITECTURE AND CLADDING. . . . *HEIGH-HO.*" We must attend to the grace and humor of the book; also to its structure and cladding, its form, its elaboration of themes—even its denial for form! After all, as we know, when nothing is significant, everything is significant, even the denial of that statement, in the existential dimension of human anguish. A study of the mono-mythic perceptions in the novel might be fruitful.

The philosophical theme of the novel is suggested variously. First in the romantic, pathetic, so poignant cry: "'BUT WHOM AM I TO LOVE?' SNOW WHITE ASKED HESI-TANTLY. BECAUSE SHE ALREADY LOVED US, IN A WAY, BUT IT WASN'T ENOUGH. STILL, SHE WAS SLIGHTLY ASHAMED." Who to love! Barthelme is a novelist in the great tradition of the heart-rending query. That remarkable speech just quoted introduces the underside of love which is shame. The beautiful and the ugly, strange and familiar, under and over: all are part of the great Unity Barthelme hauntingly depicts in his stories and in this novel which positively approaches the unspeakable. (Compare the negative approach in the novels of Samuel Beckett.)

Notice that the anti-heroine is named "Snow White." Yet she writes "a dirty poem four pages long." That a Snow White woman could write a four-page dirty poem was, needless to say, unthinkable during the Victorian epoch; and the myth of pure woman is exploded in this vibrantly styled novel. That Snow White *would not let the little men read the dirty poem* is a further insight into the feminine mystique. Barthelme's anti-heroine is the epitome. Why wouldn't she let them look at it? We are never told; but the motive is obvious. The poem was her ace in the hole, too much for the little men. Snow White exclaims: "I AM TIRED OF BEING JUST A HOUSEWIFE." This is the trauma of so many women in our time. The inner emasculation leads to outer protest; but notice that the outward protest is spoken silently—a stunning insight. In this novel, modern psychology, philosophy, and linguistics interact in a setting which Barthelme calls "This ball of half-truths, the earth."

Social criticism has, of course, been grist for the novel's mill ever since its inception. Consider the form and function of *Don Quixote,* the thought and theme of *Tom Jones,* the significance and sorrow of *Great Expectations,* the depth and desperation of *Crime and Punishment,* and the colorful insights of James Baldwin. Half-truths are the stuff human wisdom is made of. That the earth is a "ball of half-truths" is itself a half-truth. But to purge the half-truth is to *complete* the half-truth, giving it its essential nature via an enthymeme of the Absurd.

Having questioned profundities such as language, love, and the duties of a housewife, Snow White drops her hair out the window as she asks the ultimate question: "WHICH PRINCE?" thus raising the philosophical problem of verification. She utters this question while "brushing her teeth." The oral fixation is, of course, of utmost import. (An artist *selects* details like that.)

But before we go further into the psychological analysis of the anti-heroine in flux and stasis, we must consider the overall narrator, so that we understand the tale, continuum-wise. The plural narrator is, frankly, an embodiment of the universal unconscious, presented in the particularized form of seven little men, prototypes of the seven types of racio-universal unconsciousness. In the middle distance, the fictional shading becomes enchanting, as the Sisyphus-like labor of the narrators, cleaning buildings that grow always dingy in the expanding waste-land civilization, indicates the importance of ritual cleansing. Often the libidinal sector of the unconscious symbolism comes to the fore, as in Snow White's hanging her hair out of the window. The darker impulses of her collective unconscious are symbolized by the blackness of her hair. One might mention Harry Levin's *The Power of Blackness*; but more important is our realization that she hangs her HAIR out at the window, and that blackness grows from the HEAD of Snow White. Thus from the rational part springs the symbol of the libidinous part. Yet her skin is snow white. SNOW, mark you! If we examine the color symbolism of the novel in this light, we notice that as Snow White melts, the colors grey, as black of hair and white of skin start to merge into what T. S. Eliot called an "objective correlative."

Reviewing *Ulysses,* Eliot insighted that "In using the myth, in manipulating a continuous parallel between contemporaneity and antiquity, Mr. Joyce is pursuing a method which others must pursue after him." And now magnificently Mr. Barthelme has selected his controlling myth, underpinning the contemporary tale with this great archetypal vision, like a figure in the carpet, or rug.

The mythic import of beauty (Snow White) versus the beast (Jane), of the One finding happiness with the Many, and of that life being transcended when finally another One (the Prince) unites the implicit divisiveness of the Seven, as One coalesces with One. The number symbolism paradoxically *mounts* as the numbers themselves grow *less.* This upward trend is suggested early in the tale by the little men's cry of "HEIGH-HO"!

The Prince is thus a Christ Figure: by waking Snow-White-Eve, he promises redemption (i.e Love), giving the Little Men (Mankind!) a hope for a better tomorrow. So Eve becomes Mary, and is taken to his castle by the Christ-Prince who may or may not also be a Fisher King. Notice that Barthelme has many scenes laid in the shower, superbly introducing the water symbolism.

One of the burning issues in the book is whether or not Snow White has a Castration Complex. The issue is never discussed in the novel, of course. Barthelme uses images, rather than abstractions. Notice that Snow White lives in a world of men. She seems incapable of renunciation and ideal-formation which might resolve her conflicts over the female component in her overall makeup. Secondary Narcissism is the logical outcome. Thus we see that Snow White is having sublimated homosexual relations with the little men.

If we undertake retrospective analysis, we suddenly recognize the similarity of Barthelme's vision to that of Sophocles, who also dealt with profound psychological states. For indeed, though Oedipus goes blind, Barthelme makes Snow White visible. And though in *Oedipus at Colonus* the hero is reported to have gone underground (compare Ralph Ellsion's *Invisible Man*), in *Snow White* the anti-heroine is subsumed into the heavens, revirginized. What could be a more compelling end?

Neil Schmitz (essay date Fall 1971)

SOURCE: "Donald Barthelme and the Emergence of Modern Satire," in *The Minnesota Review,* No. 1, Fall, 1971, pp. 109-18.

[*In the following essay, Schmitz examines Barthelme's satirical treatment of language in his works.*]

"Oh God comma I abhor self-consciousness," declares the narrator of "Title" in John Barth's *Lost in the Funhouse.* "I despise what we have come to; I loathe our loathsome loathing, our place our time our situation, our loathsome art, this ditto necessary story." Still another narrator, the teller of "Life-Story," punches his way irately through the convolute form of his text and plucks the reader into complicity. "The reader! You, dogged, uninsultable, print-oriented bastard, it's you I'm addressing, who else, from inside this monstrous fiction. You've read me this far, then? Even this far? For what discreditable motive?" There is unhappily no violence in the accusation. The voyeur peering intently into the fiction simply discovers another voyeur glaring back at him. The shameful act in which both are caught is the jaded experience of a decadent literature, an old domesticated habit that keeps them from the pleasures of tennis and love. Barth's narrators are not lost in deep Dostoyevskian wells of self-consciousness, they are enmeshed in the process of composition, entangled in their syntax, and thus their voices seem curiously dehumanized. There is no person apart from the writer writing, no drama apart from the question (constantly posed) of whether the writing is valid. It is Literature, not the villainy of the self, that stalks Barth through *Lost in the Funhouse*—the spectre of stale familiarity, this "ditto necessary story." The language of fiction has become its rhetoric, certain words in certain places. Narrative unfolds through cranking turns of predictable plots and is invariably inlaid with indicative motifs and symbolic patterns. It is not in a private funhouse that the modern writer engages his reader but in a public museum, a museum in which even the most blasphemous screams are swallowed up by the echoes of former obscenities uttered decades and periods past. Roland Barthes has written eloquently about this institution in *Writing Degree Zero,* the "ritual language" of the "great traditional writing."

Other writers have thought they could exorcise this sacred writing only by dislocating it. They have therefore undermined literary language, they have ceaselessly exploded the ever-renewed husk of cliches, of habits, of the formal past of the writer; in a chaos of forms and a wilderness of words they hoped they would achieve an object wholly delivered of History, and find again the freshness of a pristine state of language. But such upheavals end up by leaving their own tracks and creating their own laws. The threat of becoming a Fine Art is a fate which hangs over any language not based exclusively on the speech of society. In a perpetual flight from a disorderly syntax, the disintegration of language can only lead to the silence of writing.

It is the issue of this silence, a silence Barth interminably invokes in *Lost in the Funhouse,* that Donald Barthelme has made one of the central comic themes in his fiction. "Oh I wish there were some words in the world that were not the words I always hear," Snow White complains in Barthelme's satiric version of the fairy tale. And there is Edgar, the hapless fabulist of **"The Dolt"** who has twice failed the National Writers' Examination and with whom Barthelme sympathizes. "I myself have this problem. Endings are elusive, middles are nowhere to be found, but worst of all is to begin, to begin, to begin." Although the fly-leaf on the jacket of *City Life,* his most recent anthology of fiction, ominously announces that "he is working on a novel," Barthelme has consistently treated the novel as an artifact, a fossilized object. In **Come Back, Dr. Caligari** there is a formulary *roman de societé* with all the interstitial packing removed, the connective tissue gone. **"Will You Tell Me?"** moves through two generations in several pages. Barthelme's primary tense is the present. Edgar's problem in **"The Dolt"** is not just with his attempt to render the alien experience of the Blazacian *conte*; it has to do also with his inability to grasp the preterit. The eight-foot son who bursts into the apartment clad in a serape woven of transistor radios, each tuned into a different station, thrusts back the immediate Edgar has sought fruitlessly to abandon. The emptiness of the novel and the irrelevance of traditional writing is a given in Barthelme's fiction. The writing schools and correspondence courses in which so many of his characters are futilely enrolled, Snow White's droll transcript from Beaver College, and Tolstoy as artifact in **"At the Tolstoy Museum,"** variously record that declaration. **"At the Tolstoy Museum"** is filled with visual puns that underscore the historicity of Tolstoy, his status as a specimen, the antiquarian nature of the novel. An engraving of the Anna-Vronsky pavilion depicts the coldly formalistic temple of the novel with the architect's intersecting lines concentering on Vronsky holding Anna in a climactic swoon—creatures caught on the grid of plot, a spider-web of diverse themes. The embodiment of the nineteenth-century novelist, Tolstoy is an overwhelming iconic presence: "some thirty thousand pictures" of him line the walls of the museum which is multitudinously chambered according to

genre. In brief, he is the enshrined *maître* of college courses on the novel, but his meaning is ambiguous (his outline that of a distant mountain range), and Barthelme concludes his tour in a state of diffidence. Is the novel dead? a Barthelmian interrogator asks in **"The Explanation,"** and the Barthelmian respondent replies, yes. But that is not the primary issue in **"The Explanation,"** it is an aside. The central problem is technology, the machine and warm-blooded humanity. As an occasion, the death of the novel barely impinges on the problems of living in the modern world. It is only Snow White out of Beaver College, well-rounded in her fatuous egocentrism, who agonizes about silence, who moves in a state of anesthesia through a prolix world of brilliant objects and provocative events.

> **Barthelme's language is richly (and ironically) idiomatic. The words and phrases that spill in tumult through his prose are drawn not just from the diction of the literary modernist but erupt as well from the contemporary socio-political lexicon, the codes employed by the mass media, and from all the articulating objects with which the individual surrounds himself.**
> **—*Neil Schmitz***

Barthelme, then, has chosen a mode of writing that enables him to escape the labyrinth in which Barth finds himself enclosed. His language is richly (and ironically) idiomatic. The words and phrases that spill in tumult through his prose are drawn not just from the diction of the literary modernist but erupt as well from the contemporary socio-political lexicon, the codes employed by the mass media, and from all the articulating objects with which the individual surrounds himself. As Richard Schickel has helpfully suggested, the structural principle of Barthelme's fiction is collage. History (as it is forming) pours into this fiction. Barthelme does not arrest and decipher the flow of words and things by straining them through the serial development of traditional narration, forcing them into categories and linear progression, the structure of deliberating thought. They have, as it were, their own specific gravities. They are found, not created, and in their contrast and/or cohesion yield manifold meaning. The narrator in Barthelme's fiction is typically attentive to the *thisness* of the world. If he lapses into revery or meditation, his attention is invariably brought back to the whirl of phenomena about him, by the pull of the object, whether a girl's thigh or an issue of *Newsweek.* "Strings of language extend in every direction to bind the world into a rushing ribald whole," Barthelme writes in **"The Indian Uprising."**

By displacing the value of linear structure, Barthelme necessarily dislocates the centrality of characterization. There are no densely conceived protagonists in his fiction, no Burlingames or Jacob Horners caught in endless copulatory talk with Ebenezer Cookes or Joe Morgans, describing the split self, the brink of nonbeing. It is the quality of situations, not points of view, that Barthelme presents. The names of his characters are often whimsical or simply letters. Anonymous and ephemeral, they exhibit themselves through their language, and they speak generally an urbanized post-baccalaureate jargon. It is what they have read, which books and magazines, and what they have seen, which movies and exhibitions, that defines their posture in the world. If Barthelme wishes to convict a character, he does not enter the closet of the individual's consciousness, but rather catches him downstairs *in the act* of speaking and choosing, packaging his experience in clichés. The stories dealing with Edward and Pia in *Unspeakable Practices, Unnatural Acts,* stories in which Barthelme reverses the priorities of narrative selection, are exemplary. Disjunctive stacks of abrupt sentences methodically record the random movement and banal talk of the two deracinated lovers. What is customarily left out of such romances is here scrupulously presented. It is the dramatic that is sardonically cramped within the text. "Edward felt sick. He had been reading *Time* and *Newsweek.* It was Thursday. Pia said to Edward that he was the only person she had ever loved for this long. 'How long is it?' Edward asked. It was seven months. Edward cashed a check at American Express. The girl gave him green-and-blue Scandinavian money. Edward was pleased." In **"Robert Kennedy Saved from Drowning,"** which appears in the same volume, Barthelme again, but with much greater concentration, brings dead prose into contact with live flesh. The journalistic profile which seeks to humanize the great man by revealing the trivial and the intimate succeeds only in declaring the one-dimensional enormity of the figure's self-consciousness, an ego that has rigorously stylized behavior into a series of gestures. Yet this same Kennedy, master of the stock response, humorlessly quotes Poulet at the end of the piece, Poulet on the Marivaudian man "born anew" in each instant of experience, constantly "*overtaken* by events." It is a scathing picture of the human surface.

For all the brevity of his pieces and the slenderness of his volumes, Barthelme thus seems more prolific than Barth who has produced gargantuan tomes—prolific in the sense of his engagement, his interests and topics. Where Barth appears confined in an interior monologue, Barthelme seems to be dancing in the phenomenal world, to have commenced a turn from the current metafictional modes of writing toward the "living languages" that emanate from the world moving in time outside the province of literary tradition. "Before his eyes," Barthes observes of the modern writer, "the world of society now exists as a veritable Nature, and this Nature speaks, elaborating living languages from which the writer

is excluded: on the contrary, History puts in his hands a decorative and compromising instrument, a writing inherited from a previous and different History, for which he is not responsible and yet which is the only one he can use." What one finds in *Lost in the Funhouse* is the weight of the compromised instrument, Alexandrian ingenuity. "It is an exasperating fact," Richard Poirier complains in *The Performing Self,* "that it takes such a lot of time, a part of one's life, to discover in some of the most demanding of contemporary literature that its creators are as anxious to turn you off as to turn you on, that they want to show not the decisiveness but rather the triviality of literary structuring." Indeed Barth's experimentation, his attempt to free himself from the coils of the Novel, has tended to be typographical, print-oriented. His professed movement back toward the oral tradition has moved him past Lenny Bruce and Mark Twain into ingeniously academic versions of the Homeric tales. In "The Menelaiad" we are still clenched by the teller, a teller obsessed with the telling, immured in his artifice. "Fiction for Print, Tape, Live Voice" is the subtitle of *Lost in the Funhouse,* but the transference causes no qualitative change in the substance of the language. The voice remains cerebral and literary, whether seen or heard.

Yet if Barthelme's innovative strategies—the summary abandonment of plot, his dismissal of traditional forms and ironic embrace of the "world of society" in all its flux and waste—have managed to release him from the masochistic circularity of *Lost in the Funhouse,* the question of what his revised form and renovated language achieves, apart from stylistic liberation, remains. In the early stories collected in *Come Back, Dr. Caligari,* for example, the sophistication of Barthelme's irony often seems spent on slight themes, his use of the surrealistic fable little more than stylistic legerdemain, verbal slapstick. It is only in the later volume, *Unspeakable Practices, Unnatural Acts,* and in *Snow White,* where Barthelme begins to deal with the problems of defining a linguistic and philosophical perspective, that his style and an emergent satiric vision converge, words and things coalescing to form the "rushing ribald whole" of the brilliantly conceived collage, **"The Indian Uprising."** "All this," Gertrude Stein wrote of a carafe in *Tender Buttons,* "and not ordinary, not unordered in not resembling." In **"The Indian Uprising"** Barthelme seems to have mastered in his own way the sense of that earlier experiment in attending to objects. Only here the separations of space that enabled Gertrude Stein to go calmly from roast beef to malachite, unravelling the word-chains latent in them, have vanished; everything is intensely politicized, charged with "unordered" meanings that paradoxically resemble.

Simply put, **"The Indian Uprising"** is a manifestation, the cruelest of Happenings. With the insane coolness of a TV commentator, Barthelme's narrator renders a Vietnamized world lurching toward an apocalypse by juxtaposing in quick flashes all its profuse objects, events and language, bringing them into collisions which reveal in wreckage their historical sources, their contemporary analogies. "Red men in waves like people scattering in a square startled by something tragic or a sudden, loud noise accumulated against the barricades we had made of window dummies, silk, thoughtfully planned job descriptions (including scales for the orderly progress of other colors), wine in demijohns, and robes." The passage begins by evoking the famous St. Petersburg photograph of the massacre through which the nineteenth century poured its failure into the twentieth. Yet it is not Russians who flee within the venerable frame but Comanches (or Algerians or South Vietnamese), and we are ostensibly in New York or Philadelphia except that all the streets and squares have been renamed: Boulevard Mark Clark, Rue Chester Nimitz, Patton Place, Skinny Wainwright Square. "Do you know Fauré's 'Dolly'?" a character asks, leading his quotidien life amidst the violence, this phantasmagoria of a student revolt, race riot and exemplary revolution. The images and the dialogue are saturated with signification (both comic and terrifying) and our apprehension of them is at once immediate and complex. Barthelme continues: "I analyzed the composition of the barricade nearest me and found two ashtrays, ceramic, one dark brown and one dark brown with an orange blur at the lip." He then enumerates the other articles stacked there: bottles of wine and sherry, "a hollow-core door in birch veneer on black wrought-iron legs," blankets and pillows, corkscrews and can openers, "a woven straw basket," ceramic plates and cups, "a yellow-and-purple poster; a Yugoslavian carved flute, wood, dark brown; and other items." In brief, the emptied insides of shopping plazas, import stores and middle class apartments.

The "woven straw basket" wedged into the barricade, grotesque in its jarred familiarity, describes distance, not essence. It exists with the pregnant solitude of Jasper Johns' flag or Andy Warhol's cans of soups, neutral and amodal, yet profoundly socio-political. In Antonioni's *Zabriskie Point* these objects, the same objects strewn throughout Barthelme's fiction, do a ballet at the end of the film and are by far the most interesting characters in the movie. Stacked in piles, the garbage of a trashed civilization, they are in **"The Indian Uprising"** the only constant and veritable things to be noted. Which side are you on? the narrator cries after a friend at one point in the piece, and the question is left hanging. There are no sides, the loyalties of class and race have become confused, ideological politics do not exist, a Hobbesian jungle thrives in the streets. It is only the enduring junk that clarifies **"The Indian Uprising,"** looming in those barricades like horrid totem poles.

Like Alexander Pope in *The Rape of the Lock* (which **Snow White** resembles in technique and theme), Barthelme disorganizes the familiar by inserting it into an imposing frame-

work and reveals with stunning clarity the substance of its value. The careful recording of Snow White's courses in the liberal arts at Beaver College is similar to Pope's "Puffs, powders, patches, Bibles, billetdoux." Both styles are crowded with nouns, with catalogues, with mock-inflations of the banal. In Barthelme's case, however, the discernment is genially democratic. The hems and haws of discourse, both written and spoken, are given their due. One of the dwarfs in **Snow White,** the manufacturer of plastic buffalo humps, compares his product to the parenthetical fill stuffed into syntax. "It's that we want to be on the leading edge of this trash phenomenon, the everted sphere of the future, and that's why we pay particular attention, too, to those aspects of language that may be seen as a model of the trash phenomenon." The iconic dime-store basket and the stereotypical expression are similarly situated in Barthelme's prose. They are before us, as though screened, discretely filling the space of our attention, and in motion, not from *A* to *B,* but instant, seized first by the eye and only latterly designated and grouped. If Barth is the teller who shapes our mental reconstruction of an experience, building line by line, event by event, thought by thought, Barthelme is the *cinéaste* addressing the eye, investing our field of vision.

In short, Barthelme plunges us into a Bachelardian sphere of experience, a luminous phenomenological world in which the objects of everyday life (and those disposable units of speech) are all charged with significance, and yet it is a world that does not glow with Bachelard's humanism. The characters in Barthelme's fiction inhabit this minefield of meaning with little sense of its potent nature.

> Then Snow White cleaned the gas range. She removed the pans beneath the burners and grates and washed them thoroughly in hot suds. Then she rinsed them in clear water and dried them with paper towels. Using washing soda and a stiff brush, she cleansed the burners, paying particular attention to the gas orifices, through which the gas flows. She cleaned out the ports with a hairpin, rinsed them thoroughly and dried them with paper towels. Then she returned the drip tray, the burners and grates to their proper positions and lit each burner to make sure it was working. Then she washed the insides of the broiler compartment with a cloth wrung out in the warm suds, with just a bit of ammonia to help cut the grease.

Barthelme goes on, meticulously following the movement and the object until the stove is done and Snow White moves on to "piano care." In *The Poetics of Space,* Bachelard's housewife (decidedly not a Barthelmian "horsewife") becomes a poetic shaman doing the same job Snow White mechanically executes.

The minute we apply a glimmer of consciousness to a mechanical gesture, or practice phenemonology while polishing a piece of old furniture, we sense new impressions come into being beneath this familiar domestic duty. For consciousness rejuvenates everything, giving a quality of beginning to the most everyday actions. It even dominates memory. How wonderful it is to really become once more the inventor of a mechanical action! And so, when a poet rubs a piece of furniture—even vicariously—when he puts a little fragrant wax on his table with the woolen cloth that lends warmth to everything he touches, he creates a new object; he increases the object's human dignity; he registers this object officially as a member of the human household.

In *Snow White* it is the satirist who rubs the object. Through the reverberative friction of diverse languages (in **"The Report"** the jargons of a hardware man and a software man, technician and humanist, are brilliantly contrasted) and the disjunctive tension between narcotized consciousness and the explosive object, Barthelme establishes the method of his satire. Jane's letter to Mr. Quistgaard in *Snow White,* a name she has plucked at random from the telephone book, epitomizes Barthelme's relationship to his reader, a relationship he has examined with increasing seriousness. Jane warns Quistgaard of a "threatening situation."

> You and I, Mr. Quistgaard, are not in the same universe of discourse. You may not have been aware of it previously, but the fact of the matter is, that we are not. We exist in different universes of discourse. Now it may have appeared to you, prior to your receipt of this letter, that the universe of discourse in which you existed, and puttered about, was in all ways adequate and satisfactory. It may never have crossed your mind to think that other universes of discourse from your own existed, with people in them, discoursing. You may have, in a commonsense way, regarded your own u. of d. as a plenum, filled to the brim with discourse. You may have felt that what already existed was a sufficiency. People like you often do. That is certainly one way of regarding it, if fat self-satisfied complacency is your aim. But I say unto you, Mr. Quistgaard, that even a plenum can leak.

Yet given the detonation of Mr. Quistgaard's u. of d., what is the full import of Jane's cunning note? Clearly the "threatening situation" is the possibility of Mr. Quistgaard's liberation, his sudden awareness of new and strange horizons. But on the other hand, Mr. Quistgaard could as easily be delivered over to the nausea of experiencing the absurd, of seeing words and things crazily fly apart. If the satirist explodes one's familiar universe of discourse, his prosaic sanity, does

he then reconstitute another more ample universe simply by endowing his reader with an ironic attitude toward all structures of vision and speech? The emergent anomie that Pope cursed in the awful figure of Dulness fills Barthelme with the same horror; in *Snow White* it is *blague,* but where Pope had Augustan verities to sustain his malice toward the eighteenth-century version of the "trash phenomenon," Barthelme has none. Jane is not a particularly desirable character. In an early fable, **"A Shower of Gold,"** the protagonist, a minor artist beset by the commercialism of his age, finally advises: "Don't be reconciled. Turn off your television sets . . . cash in your life insurance, indulge in a mindless optimism." Then, somewhat plaintively, he asks: "How can you be alienated without first having been connected?" It is a hard question. What is left of Shakespearian or Augustan or Wordsworthian Nature? The artist will imagine it.

In *Snow White* Barthelme's sense of his art is strikingly more complex, though the irrepressible levity remains. Near the end of the book there appears in boldface isolated on the page an aphorism: "ANATHEMATIZATION OF THE WORLD IS NOT AN ADEQUATE RESPONSE TO THE WORLD." Yet the world Snow White inhabits is rigorously anathematized. Barthelme does not emerge from the novella encouraging his readers, like Norman O. Brown at the anti-climactic end of *Life Against Death,* to practice a little more phenomenology, a little more other-awareness to go along with the self-awareness. *Snow White* ends with the unbroken continuance of stupidity straggling forward. Barthelme manifests Snow White's attenuated consciousness forcefully, rebukes it with the unassailable dignity of shower-curtains and yellow pajamas, but he has less success with the pervading issue of good and evil in the novella. The translation of the fairy tale into mock-fairy tale subtly reverses the moral sides. It is Jane and Hogo de Bergerac, villainess and villain, who are finally sympathetic, who cut through the tedious *angst* of the Dwarfs and Snow White's indulgent *ennui* with the acidic simplicity of their desires, the "vileness" of their realism. An aging and cynical brute, Hogo is fundamentally a well-integrated Hobbesian who proceeds on the assumption that in this life, this war of desires, it is every man for himself. Jane has the moral clarity of a Borgia. So Barthelme leaves it. Paul, the sophomoric prince, drinks the poison intended for Snow White, dies and is buried. Life goes on, a suffocating urban life. Alternatives are shut like doors at the conclusion. Hogo joins the firm owned and operated by the Seven Dwarfs. "The moment I inject discourse from my u. of d. into your u. of d.," Jane writes to Mr. Quistgaard, "the yourness of yours is diluted. The more I inject, the more you dilute. Soon you will be presiding over an empty plenum, or rather, since that is a contradiction in terms, over a former plenum, in terms of yourness." Since Jane's u. of d. is itself intolerable, the triumph if Pyrrhic. The aphoism, ANATHEMATIZATION OF THE WORLD IS NOT AN AD-

EQUATE RESPONSE TO THE WORLD, thus exists as a frail thesis.

Barthelme returns to this problem, the negativity of his satire, in *City Life,* his most recent volume. **"Kierkegaard Unfair to Schlegel"** begins with a Barthelmian respondent explaining to an interrogator how he annihilated a situation, his discomfort in a rented house filled with games and recreational devices, by subjecting the "shuffleboard sticks, the barbells, balls of all kinds" to an ironic perception. Taking as his text Kierkegaard's *The Concept of Irony,* the respondent then confronts himself in this performance. Irony explodes the object, he relates, deprives it of its reality and leaves a space in which the ironist establishes his subjective freedom. Yet the tonic of that freedom leads the ironist to direct his irony against the whole of existence and he then tumbles into estrangement and poetry. The poetic work (Schlegel's *Lucinde*) fills the void the ironist has created by destroying the historical actuality with a "higher actuality," the realm of imaginative truth. "But what is wanted," the respondent continues, paraphrasing Kierkegaard, "is not a victory over the world but a reconciliation." Barthelme whirls through this gloss, but his grasp is firm—firmly paradoxical. Kierkegaard, it is argued, belabors Schlegel from a narrow viewpoint, taking up *Lucinde* only because it is didactic. He neglects or overlooks its "objecthood." Yet the defense of Schlegel, it soon appears, is a screen behind which the respondent seeks ironically to annihilate Kierkegaard and therein he impales himself on Kierkegaard's point. The discourse of the satirist invariably shatters the object and the new actuality he creates is at best "a comment upon a former actuality rather than a new actuality." What remains is an emptied plenum, a zero.

Yet the "objecthood" of **"Kierkegaard Unfair to Schlegel"** also remains. Barthelme's meditation on the destructive nature of irony is framed by manifestations: the girl on the train, the round of her thigh appearing and the humorous evocation of desire, and then again another girl caressing her breasts, a trip to Central Park, a remembered dream, dinner and conversation, a touching anecdote about the suffering of Louis Pasteur. Irony distinguishes, ascertains value, does not destroy. The ironist who believes he has the "magical power" to make objects cringe and disappear puts himself within the pale of his irony. The paraphrase of Kierkegaard is rammed home in short hard sentences, but its declarative intellectuality is subsumed fore and aft by the variegated plenum of experience, by the constant stream of relationship to things, speech, people and art. It is this consciousness, always slipping away from the fixed locus of the abstract, this plastic consciousness which attends so uniquely and diversely to the world, that Barthelme ultimately celebrates. For it is the discourse of that attuned consciousness that is at once his subject and his morality. There is no place where one can break into "The Sentence," since this Barthelmian sentence has properly no beginning or end. It is "aiming for the bottom," Barthelme tells us, but where the bottom of the page is, this page or some other page, no one knows, and so it simply proceeds, simply *is,* enjoys being, goes forward engaging itself and the world outside it. It reminds us, Barthelme suggests, that "the sentence itself is a man-made object, not the one we wanted of course, but still a construction of man, a structure to be treasured for its weakness, as opposed to the strength of stones". It also reminds us that even as the *blague* and the "brain damage" of contemporary life seem everywhere, "brain damage covering everything like an unbreakable lease," the imagination, artificer of the best sentences, continues to pose its choices: to be or not to be. The Phantom of the Opera, offered a "normal" life through plastic surgery and psychological rehabilitation, will decline.

Donald Barthelme with Larry McCaffery (interview date 1982)

SOURCE: "An interview with Donald Barthelme," in *Partisan Review,* Vol. 49, No. 2, 1982, pp. 184-93.

[*In the following interview, Barthelme discusses his life, his literary influences, his views on language and literature, and his works.*]

[*McCaffery:*] *You've published two novels, but most of your work has been in short fiction.*

[Barthelme:] Novels take me a long time; short fiction provides a kind of immediate gratification—the relationship of sketches to battle paintings. Over a period of years I can have a dozen bad ideas for novels, some of which I actually invest a certain amount of time in. Some of these false starts yield short pieces; most don't. The first story in *Sadness*—**"La Critique de la Vie Quotidienne"**—is salvage.

Do stories typically begin for you by landing on you, like the dog in **"Falling Dog"**?

Well, for about four days I've been writing what amounts to nonsense. And then suddenly I come across an interesting sentence—or at least interesting to me: "It is not clear that Arthur Byte was wearing his black corduroy suit when he set fire to the Yale Art and Architecture Building in the spring of 1968." I don't know what follows from this sentence; I'm hoping it may develop into something. I did know someone who was at Yale teaching in the architecture department at the time of that notorious fire; I'm not sure if the date was 1968, I'd have to check. I don't believe they ever found out who set it; I certainly have no idea. But I'm positing a someone and hoping that tragic additional material may accumulate around that sentence.

At the end of your story **"Sentence,"** *your narrator says that the sentence is "a structure to be treasured for its weaknesses, as opposed to the strength of stones." Am I right in assuming that one of the things that interests you most about the sentence as an object is precisely its "treasured weaknesses"?*

I look for a particular kind of sentence, perhaps more often the awkward than the beautiful. A back-broken sentence is interesting. Any sentence that begins with the phrase, "It is not clear that . . . ," is clearly clumsy, but preparing itself for greatness of a kind. It's a way of backing into a story—of getting past the reader's hard-won armor. Then a process of accretion occurs, like barnacles growing on a wreck or a rock. I'd rather have a wreck than a ship that sails. Things attach themselves to wrecks; strange fish find your wreck or rock to be a good feeding ground. After a while you've got a situation with possibilities.

Have you ever studied philosophy of language in any kind of systematic way?

I look for a particular kind of sentence, perhaps more often the awkward than the beautiful. A back-broken sentence is interesting.
—Donald Barthelme

No. I spent two years in the Army in the middle of my undergraduate days at Houston. When I came back to the university, which must have been about 1955, there was a new man—Maurice Natanson—teaching a course titled "Sociology and Literature" that sounded good. I enrolled, and he talked about Kafka and Kleist and George Herbert Mead. I wasn't a particularly acute or productive student of philosophy, but in that and subsequent classes, I got acquainted with people Mauri was interested in: Husserl, Heidegger, Kierkegaard, Sartre, and company.

You were originally interested in journalism, weren't you?

It seemed clear that the way to become a writer was to go to work for a newspaper, as Hemingway had done—then, if you were lucky, you might write fiction. I don't think anybody believes that anymore. But I went to work for a newspaper while I was still a sophomore and went back to the newspaper when I got out of the Army. I was really very happy there—thought I was in high cotton.

By the late fifties, when you became editor of the Forum,

you were obviously already interested a great deal in parody and satire as literary forms. What so attracted you to this type of writing?

People like S. J. Perelman and E. B. White—people who could do certain amazing things in prose. Perelman was the first true American surrealist—ranking with the best in the world surrealist movement—and West was another. Also, Wolcott Gibbs—all those *New Yorker* writers. And Hemingway as parodist, like in *The Torrents of Spring*.

Somewhere along the line you got involved as a director of an art museum. How did that come about?

A peculiar happenstance. I was entrusted with a small museum for a couple of years—the Contemporary Arts Museum in Houston. They had just lost the director, didn't have a prospect, and I'd been on the board. They asked me to fill in temporarily, which I did for a while, and then they made me director—probably more fun than anything I've done before or since. For two years I mounted shows and developed programs in music, theater, and film. In consequence, I met Harold Rosenberg in 1962. At that time Harold had in mind starting a new magazine, which he and Thomas B. Hess would edit. They needed someone to be the managing editor—that is, someone to put out the magazine—and they hired me.

This was the now-legendary magazine, Location?

Yes. It was meant to be not just an art magazine, but an art-and-literary magazine. We were able to publish some wonderful material—some early Gass, some of John Ashbery's work, Kenneth Koch's stuff. It was supposed to be a quarterly, but in fact we published only two issues. Tom and Harold were not worried about putting the magazine out on time and certainly never put any pressure on me. We waited until we had enough decent stuff for a good issue. That experience was a great pleasure—listening to Tom and Harold talk. But getting back to the museum, it was a very small place. My responsibility was to put some good shows together, mildly didactic, modestly informative. So I had to study quite a lot very fast to be able to do this—to make intelligent or useful shows. Luckily, I've always gotten along well with painters and sculptors, mostly by virtue of not asking the wrong questions of them.

It's been my experience that asking a painter what his work "means" is considered to be in bad taste. This seems to hold true for writers as well.

It's a separate study, "How to manifest intelligent sympathy while not saying very much." The early sixties were, as you know, an explosive period in American art, and I learned on the job, nervously. Just being in the studio teaches you something. I'll give you an example: when we were doing *Location* I went over to Rauschenberg's studio on lower Broadway with Rudy Burkhardt, the photographer, to take some pictures. Rauschenberg was doing silk-screen pieces, and the tonality of these things was gray—very, very gray. I looked out the windows and they were dirty, very much the tonality of the pictures. So I asked Rudy to get some shots of the windows, and we ran one of them with the paintings. They were very much New York lower Broadway windows. A footnote.

Your narrator in **"See the Moon?"** *comments enviously at one point about the "fantastic metaphysical advantage" possessed by painters. What is he referring to?*

The physicality of the medium—there's a physicality of color, of an object present before the spectator, which painters don't have to project by means of words. I can peel the label off that bottle of beer you're drinking and glue it to the canvas and it's there. This sort of thing is of course what Dos Passos did in the Newsreels, what Joyce did in various ways. I suppose the theater has the possibility of doing this in the most immediate way. I'm on the stage, and I suddenly climb down into the pit and kick you in the knee. That's not like writing about kicking you in the knee, it's not like painting you being kicked in the knee, because you have a pain in the knee. This sounds a bit aggressive, forgive me.

Another aspect of painting that seems relevant to your fiction is the surrealist practice of juxtaposing two elements— different sorts of language—for certain kinds of effects in fiction or poetry.

It's a principle of construction. This can be terribly easy and can become cheapo surrealism, mechanically linking contradictions. Take Duchamp's phrase, in reference to *The Bride and the Bachelors,* that the Bride "warmly refuses" her suitors. The phrase is very nice, but you can see how it could become a formula.

How do you avoid falling into this trap in your own work?

I think you stare at the sentence for a long time. The better elements are retained, and the worse fall out of the manuscript.

There is a tendency in the painting of this century to explore itself, its own medium—the nature of paint, colors, shapes, and lines, rather than attempting to reproduce or comment on something outside itself. This tendency seems relevant not only to your work, but also to that of several other important writers of the past fifteen years. Is this a fair analogy?

It is. I also think that painting—in the sixties but especially in the seventies—really pioneered for us all the things that it is not necessary to do. Under the aegis of exploring itself, exploring its own means or the medium, painting really did a lot of dumb things that showed poets and prose writers what might usefully not be done. I'm thinking mostly of conceptual art, which seems to me a bit sterile. Concrete poetry is an example of something that is, for me, not very nourishing, though it can be said to be explorative in the way that a lot of conceptual art is explorative. I can see why in some sense it had to be done. But perhaps not twice.

What about some of the "New-New-Novelists" in France— Pinget, Sollers, Baudry, LeClezio? They seem to be trying to push fiction to the same limits of abstraction that conceptual artists have pushed toward.

Of a work like Butor's *Mobile,* after a time there's nothing more you can say than "I like it" or "I don't like it"—the stupidest of comments. A more refined version is "I know this is good, but I still don't like it." And I think that this is a fair comment. There are more *récherché* examples of this kind of thing. *Triquarterly* did an issue a while back, entitled "In the Wake of the Wake," featuring several gallant Frenchmen whose work I'd seen in scattered places. The emphasis was towards "pure abstraction." For me this is a problem since they get further and further away from the common reader. I understand the impulse—towards the condition of music—but as a common reader I demand that this be done in masterly fashion or not at all. Mallarmé is perhaps the extreme, along with Gertrude Stein. I admire them both. But I don't have any great enthusiasm for fiction about fiction. Critics, of course, have been searching for a term that would describe fiction after the great period of modernism— "postmodernism," "metafiction," "surfiction," and "superfiction." The last two are terrible. I suppose "postmodernism" is the least ugly and most descriptive.

What do you think about Philip Roth's famous suggestion back in the early sixties that reality was outstripping fiction's ability to amaze us?

I do think something happened in fiction about that time but I'd locate it differently. I think writers got past being intimidated by Joyce. Maybe the reality that Roth was talking about was instrumental in this recognition, but I think people realized that one didn't have to repeat Joyce (if that were even possible), but could use aspects of his achievement.

One of your most evident abilities is your gift at mimicking a wide range of styles, jargons, and lingoes. Where do these voices come from?

I listen to people talk, and I read. I doubt that there has ever been more jargon and cant of various professions and semiprofessions than there is today. I remember being amazed when I was in basic training, which was back in the early fifties, that people could make sentences in which the word *fucking* was used three times or even five times.

How did your relationship with the New Yorker *begin?*

I sent them something in the mail and they accepted it. Agented probably by a nine-cent stamp. Also, once in a while when I was low on cash I'd write something for certain strange magazines—the names I don't even remember. Names like *Dasher* and *Thug.* I do remember picking up five hundred bucks or something per piece. I did that a few times. Kind of gory, or even Gorey, fiction.

Have any of these things ever resurfaced?

No. Nor shall they ever.

It wasn't long before the New Yorker *began publishing a story of yours almost every month. You didn't develop a specific understanding with them about regularly accepting your work?*

I had moved to New York to work with Tom and Harold doing *Location,* and since I was only working half-time on the magazine, I had more time to write fiction. I had and have what they call a first-reading agreement.

Have you had a specific editor working with you at the New Yorker?

Yes, Roger Angell.

Do your stories usually require much in the way of editing?

Roger makes very few changes. If he and the magazine don't like a piece that I've written, they'll turn it down. The magazine sometimes turns down a piece I don't think should be turned down—but what else can I think? Roger is a wonderful editor, and if he objects to something in a story, he's probably right. He's very sensitive about the editing process, which makes it a pleasure.

Do you see yourself working out of some kind of New Yorker *tradition?*

The magazine in recent years has been very catholic. Anybody who publishes Singer, Merwin, Lem, Updike, Borges, and Marquez has got to be said to be various in terms of taste. Plus Grace Paley and Susan Sontag and Ann Beattie, and who knows who else.

I've noticed that in your last few books you seem to have dropped the interest in typographical or graphic play that was so evident in **City Life** *and* **Guilty Pleasures.** *What got you interested in this sort of thing in the first place?*

I think I was trying to be a painter, in some small way. Probably a yearning for something not properly the domain of writers. Maybe I was distracted by the things painters can do. I had an ambition toward something that maybe fiction can't do—an immediate impact—a beautifully realized whole that can be taken in at a glance and yet still be studied for a long time. Flannery O'Connor says, very sourly, very wittily, that she doesn't like anything that looks funny on the page. I know what she's talking about, but on the other hand, I'm intrigued by things that look funny on the page. But then there was the flood of concrete poetry, which devalued looking funny on the page.

I recall a comment of yours that you not only enjoyed doing layout work but that you could cheerfully become a typographer. Did you do all your own visual work?

They're mostly very simple collages, Ernst rather than Schwitters.

Have you tried your own hand at drawing?

Can't draw a lick.

At the end of the title story in **City Life,** *Ramona comments about life's invitations "down many muddy roads" that she accepted: "What was the alternative?" I find a similar passivity in many of your characters—an inability to change their lot. Does this tendency spring from a personal sense of resignation about things or are you trying to suggest something more fundamental about modern man's relationship to the world?*

The quotation you mention possibly has more to do with the great world than with me. In writing about the two girls in **"City Life"** who come to the city, I noticed that their choices, which seem to be infinite, are not so open-ended. I don't think this spirit of resignation, as you call it, has to do with any personal passivity; it's more a sociological observation. One attempts to write about the way contemporary life is lived by most people. In a more reportorial fiction, one would of necessity seek out more "active" protagonists—the mode requires it, in order to make the book or story work. In a mixed mode, some reportage and some play (which also makes its own observations), you might be relieved of this restriction. Contemporary life engenders, even enforces, passivity, as does television. Have you ever tried to reason with a Convenience Card money machine? Asked for napkin rings in an Amtrak snack-bar car? Of course you don't. Still, the horizon of memory enters in, you attempt to register change, the color of this moment as opposed to the past or what you know of it.

In **The Dead Father,** *you deal with the notion that we're* *all dragging around behind us the corpses of our fathers, as well as the past in general.*

Worse: dragging these *ahead* of us. I have several younger brothers, among them my brother Frederick, who is also a writer. After **The Dead Father** came out, he telephoned and said, "I'm working on a new novel." I said, "What's it called?" and he said, "*The Dead Brother.*"

Was "A Manual for Sons" originally conceived as being a part of the novel? It seems like a marvellous set piece.

Originally it was distributed throughout the book as a kind of seasoning, but in time it became clear that it should be one long section. My German publisher, Siegfried Unseld, said rather sternly to me one evening, "Isn't this a digression?" I said, "Yes, it is." He was absolutely right, in technical terms.

In **The Dead Father,** *and more recently in* **Great Days,** *you strip the narrative almost completely of the old-fashioned means of story development. In fact, by the time we get to the stories in* **Great Days,** *what we find are simply voices interacting with one another.*

In **The Dead Father,** there are four or five passages in which the two principal women talk to each other, or talk *against* each other, or over each other's heads, or between each other's legs—passages which were possible because there is a fairly strong narrative line surrounding them. It's questionable whether such things can be made to fly without the support of a controlling narrative.

Was Beckett an influence in this recent form of experimentation?

Beckett has been a great influence, which I think is clear. But the effort is not to write like Beckett. You can't do Beckett all over again anymore than you can do Joyce again. That would waste everyone's time.

Have you ever tried writing poetry, as such?

No, too difficult. I can't do it. A very tough discipline, to be attempted by saints or Villons.

We've talked about the influence of painting on your work. What about the cinema?

I was bombarded with film from, let us say, my sixth year right up to yesterday, when I saw Wiseman's *Basic Training.* There has to have been an effect, including the effect of teaching me what waste is. As with painting, film has shown us what not to pursue. The movies provide a whole set of stock situations, emotions, and responses that can be

played against. They inflect contemporary language, and one uses this.

Your fiction has often drawn materials from the realm of pop culture—Snow White, Batman, the Phantom of the Opera, King Kong, and so forth. What do you find useful in this kind of material?

Relatively few of my stories have to do with pop culture, a very small percentage, really. What's attractive about this kind of thing is the given—you have to do very little establishing, and can get right to the variations. The usefulness of the Snow White story is that everybody knows it, and it can be played against. The presence of the seven men made possible a "we" narration that offered some tactical opportunities—there's a sort of generalized narrator, a group spokesman who could be any one of the seven. Every small change in the story is momentous when everybody knows the story backwards; possibly I wasn't as bold in making these changes as I should have been.

It's very obvious in **Snow White**—*and in nearly all your fiction—that you distrust the impulse to "go beneath the surface" of your characters and events.*

If you mean doing psychological studies of some kind, no, I'm not so interested. "Going beneath the surface" has all sorts of positive-sounding associations, as if you were a Cousteau of the heart. I'm not sure there isn't just as much to be seen if you remain a student of the surfaces.

What function do the lists that appear in your work serve?

Litanies, incantations, have a certain richness per se. They also provide stability in what is often a volatile environment, something to tie onto, like an almanac or a telephone book. And discoveries—a list of meter maids in any given city will give you a Glory Hercules.

Who are some of the contemporary writers you find most interesting?

Along with the South Americans, who everyone agrees are doing very well, I think the Germans: Peter Handke, Max Frisch, certainly Grass, Thomas Bernhard, who did *Correction.* I think the Americans are doing very well. The French perhaps less so.

Raymond Federman says that while Samuel Beckett had devised a means of taking the world away from the contemporary writer, Garcia Marquez has shown writers a way to reconnect themselves with the world.

I don't agree with Ray that that's what Beckett has done; the Marquez portion of the comment seems more appropriate. I think they've both opened things up, in different ways. Marquez provided an answer to the question of what was possible after Beckett—not the only answer, but a large and significant one. Robert Coover, among American writers, seems to be doing something parallel, with good results.

Do you feel that New York City has helped shape your sensibility over the years?

I think my sensibility was pretty well put together before I came here. Although I've now lived here close to twenty years, I've also lived in other places in the meantime—Copenhagen for a year, Paris, Tokyo. I like cities. But this is a tiny corner of New York, very like a real *village* village. Once I was walking down Seventh Avenue with Hans Magnus Enzensberger, we'd just finished lunch, and we bumped into my daughter, who was then about eight. I introduced them, and she went home and told her mother she'd just met Hans Christian Andersen. And in a way she had.

Do you see any changes having taken place in your approach to writing over the past twenty years?

Certainly fewer jokes, perhaps fewer words.

Jochen Achilles (essay date Spring 1982)

SOURCE: "Donald Barthelme's Aesthetic of Inversion: Caligari's Come-Back as Caligari's Leave-Taking," in *The Journal of Narrative Technique,* Vol. 12, No. 2, Spring, 1982, pp. 105-20.

[*In the following essay, Achilles traces Barthelme's use of elements from the German film* Das Cabinet des Dr. Caligari *in his works, examines various other themes employed by Barthelme, and notes some sources from which the author has extracted ideas for his writings.*]

At first glance the title of Donald Barthelme's first collection of short stories, **Come Back, Dr. Caligari,** appears somewhat enigmatic—even menacing if considered outside the context of the meeting of the Toledo Medical Society described in Barthelme's **"Up, Aloft in the Air,"** Where Dr. Caligari meets such other worthies as Dr. Scholl, Dr. Mabuse and Dr. Melmoth. Caligari makes his original appearance in *Das Cabinet des Dr. Caligari* (1920), one of the earliest German horror films and now a famous paradigm of the genre. In several respects this film can be regarded as a paradigm of important aspects of Barthelme's fiction too. In his seminal study of the German Film, *From Caligari to Hitler* (1947), Siegfried Kracauer gives an interpretation of *Das Cabinet des Dr. Caligari* that emphasizes features that are also recognizable in Barthelme's prose. [It is not unlikely

that Barthelme's reference to Dr. Caligari is influenced not only by the film, but also by Siegfried Kracauer's book. Barthelme's interest in the history and styles of the film becomes manifest in several of his stories. Yet it is not the intention of this essay to trace such potential influences. This article tries, rather, to demonstrate that modifications of structural features central to *Das Cabinet des Dr. Caligari* recur in Barthelme's works and it tries to describe the nature of these modifications.]

I

The film's reality is as used up and second-hand as the "trash phenomenon" Barthelme keeps depicting and satirizing in all its aspects. During the course of the film Dr. Caligari, a psychiatrist who uses one of his patients as a medium and who leads this patient through hypnosis into a series of heinous crimes, models himself on an eighteenth century Italian showman and murderer of the same name. He had read about this obscure Italian in an old tome later discovered among his belongings, and it is in light of this discovery that Caligari's atrocious deeds reveal themselves as attempts to reenact and to verify a report of past events.

A number of Barthelme's stories and both his novels reveal ironic variations of various models, too. Many of these are provided by film. In **"Hiding Man"** the narrator continually reflects on his own experiences in terms of scenes from the numerous horror films he has seen. In **"Me and Miss Mandible"** the overgrown narrator's female classmates try to make up for their lack of experience with the other sex by a voracious consumption of magazine reports on the love life of movie stars. This precocious approach to sex leads to the adoption of these prefabricated patterns as standards of behavior. In **"The Indian Uprising"** scenes from a film and from real life merge and in **"The Captured Woman"** the title figure insists that the events she is involved in are part of a film. **"A Film"** is a satire on film production and **"L'Lapse"** is a parodic imitation of a film script by Michelangelo Antonioni.

Barthelme's "nostalgia for the terms of the fairy tale," which finds expression in **"The Glass Mountain," "Departures," "The Dragon,"** and most prominently in *Snow White,* as well as his reliance on traditional and popular myths in **"The Joker's Greatest Triumph," "A Shower of Gold," "The Party,"** and *The Dead Father* are further indications of the derivative quality of his works. **"The Phantom of the Opera's Friend," "Daumier,"** and **"The Question Party"** are in part founded on literary sources; **"Kierkegaard Unfair to Schlegel"** is based on a philosophical one. Even the medium of Barthelme's art, his language, brims with linguistic patterns derived from all sorts of jargons and resounds with the hollowness of standardized phraseology.

In addition to the preoccupation with exemplars of behavior and expression, *Das Cabinet des Dr. Caligari* and Barthelme's oeuvre share an ambivalent attitude towards these exemplars. The film expresses this ambivalence by embedding the story proper, the unmasking of the renowned psychiatrist Caligari as an insane murderer, in a framing story which inverts the film's message. The framing story presents Francis, the 'central intelligence' of the story proper who discloses Caligari's secret machinations, as the raving inmate of Caligari's lunatic asylum. Francis's revelations of Caligari's crimes turn out to be nothing but so many symptoms of his mental illness, which Caligari gladly promises to cure. As Caligari's crimes take place in Francis's imagination only, Francis's version of the case, the denunciation of illegitimate authority, is transformed into Caligari's final vindication and into the glorification of authority as such.

Kracauer elucidates the political implication of this basic ambiguity. He sees the relation between Caligari and his medium as an analogy of the relation between authoritarian political leaders and a passive and pliable population ready to be hypnotized. The condemnation of such leadership as irrational and tyrannical, which is implied in Francis's version of the story, is undermined by its presentation as frantic babbling. The film, produced in the pre-fascist era, wavers between the warning against the unthinking adherence to leaders whose charisma seems only to veil thinly their morally rotten core and the fear of the chaos that may ensue if all leadership is abolished. On the one hand, Caligari may be seen as "a premonition of Hitler"; on the other hand, the film suggests that the total absence of any authorities and ordering forces may entail anarchy and chaos. The "seemingly unavoidable alternative of tyranny or chaos" stands at the very heart of *Das Cabinet des Dr. Caligari.*

In a wider sense, this alternative stands in the center of Barthelme's writing too. Barthelme continually probes into the justifiability not only of political authority but also of all kinds of metaphysical, ethical and aesthetic values. He thereby exposes the contemporary dilemma of the pervasive need for guide lines and normative concepts on the one hand and of their questionable legitimacy on the other. Like one of the characters in his story **"The Leap"** Barthelme, too, is an "incorrigibly double-minded man". This instability finds expression in his technique of inversion, which establishes one version of an event or situation only to undercut it immediately. Several modes of this technique are distinguishable in Barthelme's oeuvre.

II

The most obvious of these modes is the reversal of life-roles—e.g., the inversion of the parent-child-relationship including grotesque contortions of bodily size that are vaguely reminiscent of Swift's Gulliver and Carroll's Alice. The re-

versal of life roles also occurs in the shape of the wholesale rejection of and desperate flight from the life one has led and the institutions and events that have molded it. Consider the title figure of Barthelme's first collected story **"Florence Green Is 81,"** who has lived through the fascist era which *Das Cabinet des Dr. Caligari* foreshadows, and who wants to escape her and her generation's history. She wishes to go somewhere where Quemoy, Matsu and Berlin do not represent focuses of political tension, where Lake Hurst and Buchenwald are not names connected with destruction and death, where novels do not glorify unquestioning submission to military authorities as the narrator's novel, *The Children's Army,* seems to do. In short Florence Green wants to go "somewhere where everything is different."

Burligame, the narrator and protagonist of **"Hiding Man,"** actually goes. The story, set in a cinema while the science-fiction shocker "Attack of the Puppet People" is on show, is a parable of the hardship and even violence a rearrangement of one's life may involve. Burligame tries to hide from his clerical education and its hypocritical moral standards, but he has to learn that the only effective way to rid himself of his obsessions is not to run away from them, but to destroy them. It dawns on him that there is a connection between his religious past and his fascination by horror films. Both religion and horror films supply, whether sacred or demoniacal, variants of authority one has to sacrifice one's identity to. Selfhood can only be restored by unrelenting opposition to such authorities and by the destruction of the hierarchical structures they are based on. Burligame defeats his fellow moviegoer and persecutor, the negro Bane-Hipkiss, who turns out to be a white episcopal envoy in disguise, just as humankind defeats the Puppet People in the film they have both been watching. He shakes off the yoke of his guilt-ridden past, of a morality which he had very early begun to regard as false but which for a very long time still had a grip on him. Thus he changes his life-role completely and acquires a new self-confidence. But his actions still unconsciously and perhaps unavoidably follow the pattern of the film described in the story. It is hardly possible to become entirely independent.

In **"Me and Miss Mandible,"** the idea to relive one's life is transformed into a literal fact. Joseph, a thirty-five-year-old ex-soldier and ex-claims adjuster for an insurance company finds himself back in sixth form. He is reduced to the social status of an eleven-year-old schoolboy although he retains his former intellectual and sexual capacity. As in the previous story, inversion also works on several levels in **"Me and Miss Mandible."** Not only does Joseph revert to child status, but his teacher, Miss Mandible, also appears to him like a child. On the other hand, one of his infant classmates reminds him "of the wife I had in my former role." This confusion of roles and blurring of distinctions is an indication of Joseph's ability to see through the artificiality of such roles and distinctions: "The distinction between children and adults, while probably useful for some purposes, is at bottom a specious one, I feel. There are only individual egos, crazy for love." Joseph's re-education does not lead to the desired heightened adaptability to the rules he was not able to follow in his former life-role, but rather to an increasing awareness of the arbitrariness of these rules. Joseph begins to understand that the social patterns of school education, army, insurance company, and marriage have no validation beyond their sheer existence and self-perpetuation. There is no substantial moral reason not to ignore these patterns except the pragmatic consideration that one is punished for the refusal to fulfill one's role within them. Joseph cannot accept this. He cannot bring himself to confuse "authority with life itself" any more. He breaks the rules once again when he begins an illicit love affair with his teacher that leads to his expulsion from the school and, one must assume, from the orderly conventional life this school prepares for.

Contrary to Caligari's example, Florence Green, Burligame, and Joseph refuse to model themselves on the patterns that seem to have engulfed them. Instead, they try to break away from those patterns and to reorganize their lives autonomously. Contrary to the reactionary use of inversion in *Das Cabinet des Dr. Caligari,* which rehabilitates Caligari and re-establishes his authority, the technique of inversion functions in an emancipatory manner in Barthelme's writing as it forms the turning point from dependence on conventional norms to freedom. In other words, Barthelme inverts the function inversion has in *Das Cabinet des Dr. Caligari.*

In two later stories and in his second novel, *The Dead Father* (1975), Barthelme concentrates on a particular variant of the reversal of life-roles, the inversion of the father-child relationship that manifests itself in the dwindling power of the fathers, the increasing independence of the children, and grotesque distortions of bodily size. In **"A Picture History of the War,"** Kellerman "runs through the park at noon with his naked father slung under one arm". In vain does the father endlessly reminisce about the battles he claims to have fought as a general from antiquity down to World War II. He has to relinquish forever his position as a military leader and, like Joseph, finds himself "folded into a schoolchild's desk, sitting in the front row" with his own son as his condescending teacher.

One of the three strands of plot in **"Views of My Father Weeping"** resumes this reduction of a father figure to the status of a little boy who plays with his water pistol, crayons, and dolls. The other two strands emphasize the difficulties involved in dispossessing a father of his paternal prerogatives. One of the two finds the narrator, who desperately tries not to feel guilty, in submission before a groundlessly weeping father figure. The third one analyzes the narrator's vain attempts to clarify the circumstances of his father's death. All three together give ample proof of the contradictory emotions involved in a son's relation to his father. The narrator cannot refrain from trying to find out who is responsible for his father's fatal accident, although (or even because) he once tried to shoot him himself. As an appropriate expression of the narrator's wavering between rivalry and sympathy, compassion, guilt and hate, the story ends with an "Etc.", which is indicative of the ongoing struggle between the admiration for authorities and the urge to overthrow them.

In *The Dead Father* Barthelme brings this struggle to an end. The Dead Father's absurdly huge size, symbolic of his former might, is of no avail against his children's conspiracy to change the *status quo.* His son Thomas retrieves his hitherto repressed oedipal feelings of murderous hatred and gradually divests the Dead Father of his insignia until he is finally as helpless as a child again. Not his biological death, but the dissolution of his fatherly power is the aim of the expedition that organizes the novel's plot. The burial of the Dead Father at the end of the book is an image of the achievement of what "A Manual for Sons," which Thomas and Julie read with interest, recommends: "*Fatherhood can be, if not conquered, at least 'turned down' in this generation—by the combined efforts of all of us together.*" In **"A Picture History of the War"** Kellerman's father had appeared as the universal embodiment of military leadership through his participation in so many historical battles, but in this novel the Dead Father has emerged as the incarnation of patriarchal dominion from Jahwe and Laios down to present political leaders by manifold biblical, mythological and literary references. The dissolution of fatherhood advocated in *The Dead Father* therefore appears as a signal for the general decomposition of authorities and hierarchies.

"At the Tolstoy Museum" demonstrates that Barthelme's antiauthoritarian criticism does not spare literary father figures. The literally oppressing outline of the museum, which "suggests that it is about to fall on you", is mockingly described as an architectural expression of Tolstoy's overpowering "moral authority." The impression conveyed by the many Tolstoy portraits that line the walls of the museum, furthermore, is much like "committing a small crime and being discovered at it by your father." These awe-inspiring aspects of the museum are lost on the narrator. They cannot induce him to pay homage to Tolstoy's genius. He attempts, instead, to push Tolstoy from his pedestal. Both the title of the Tolstoy article he quotes, "'Who Should Teach Whom to Write, We the Peasant Children or the Peasant Children Us?,'" and the Tolstoy story he reads about the three hermits who teach a bishop that there are more ways to heaven than the one sanctioned by the Church again illustrate the relativity of norms and values. They are restatements of Joseph's persistent and wondering question in **"Me and Miss Mandible,"** "Who decides?" As in **"Views of My Fa-**

ther Weeping," the insight into the unjustifiability of authority is again accompanied by weeping, depression, and sadness.

What is new in **"At the Tolstoy Museum"** is the fact that the standards thus questioned are aesthetic as well as moral and metaphysical. Although Tolstoy is primarily presented as a moral authority, he is obviously a literary one too, and, if only by implication, the story raises the question whether a contemporary writer can find artistic models for his own work in the museum of world literature. It also raises another even more complicated string of interrelated questions: Does a writer not unavoidably make a claim to authority if he presents well-made stories to his readers? Does he not willy-nilly establish a variant of the parent-child or teacher-pupil relationship with his readers for the simple reason that he actively shapes and the reader only passively receives what he has to say? Given the one-way communication between writer and reader and given the anti-authoritarian intentions of the writer, how are the two reconcilable?

III

Barthelme tries to answer both questions, and thus his works assume a self-reflective quality. The first question concerning models for one's own writing receives a predictably negative answer. This answer consists in the revocation of artistic options Barthelme practices in many works. Comparable to Eliot and Joyce in this respect, furthermore, Barthelme considers myths and fairy tales as elements that may furnish otherwise amorphous tales with structural coherence. But contrary to these modernist mythotherapists, Barthelme unavoidably demonstrates the obsolescence and invalidity of such mythical or legendary patterns.

In Barthelme's first novel, **Snow White** (1967), all of the three fairy tale motifs the novel is founded upon prove abortive. Behind Paul's miserable outward appearance no heroic prince conceals himself as in the fairy tale of the Frog Prince. Therefore Snow White comments disappointedly: "Paul is frog. He is frog through and through . . . . *pure frog.*" By letting her hair hang out of the window Snow White attempts to overcome her isolation from more impressive men than the seven dwarfs who "only add up to the equivalent of about two *real men.*" But this conscious imitation of the Rapunzel motif does not lead to the desired result. She has to acknowledge that the world is not "civilized enough to supply the correct ending to the story." The Snow White plot of the novel ends accordingly. The prince figure is killed by a poisoned drink originally meant for Snow White herself. The novel thus revokes the conciliatory solutions of its fairy tale sources. It has turned against itself the principle of retraction by which it has been dominated from Snow White's complaint about the used-upness of words or her poem on loss or Paul's palinode "to retract everything" to the disso-

lution of semantic references and syntactic structures or even to the suspension of all judgments and explanations.

The revocation of the hope for happiness fairy tales engender recurs in several short stories. On top of **"The Glass Mountain"** the narrator does not find "the beautiful enchanted symbol" (*City Life*) he is in search of in order to leave behind permanently the shabby urban scene he has climbed up from. What he does find is "only a beautiful princess" devoid of the magic and the "layers of meaning" that used to supply fairy tales with the power to transcend reality. With resignation, he throws the princess down from the glass mountain back into the streets crowded with jeering people, cars, faeces and cut-down trees, the remnants of the enchanted forest. One of the episodes in **"Departures"** departs from its own fabulous quality and offers this negation at the end: "This is not really how it went. I am fantasizing" (*Sadness*). **"The Dragon"** in *Guilty Pleasures* similarly suffers from suicidal tendencies caused by the feeling of his own meaninglessness which has not left him since the thirteenth century. The only remedy contemporary society has to offer him is the status of "endangered species."

Not only do mythical and legendary models prove inapplicable to contemporary reality since the historical conditions of their validity cannot be reproduced, the position of the artist as such is also in danger of becoming untenable as society tends to occupy and to integrate every artistic vantage-ground which used to allow its criticism. In **"A Shower of Gold"** the painter and sculptor Hank Peterson discovers that TV-shows are now premised on the absurdity of human existence, a diagnosis of life that not so very long ago used to belong to the exclusive qualms of esoteric circles. In addition, Peterson's barber lectures him on existentialist philosophy and rounds his speech off by an extremely pessimistic quotation from Pascal. To Peterson's edification, this quotation is again thrown at him a little later by one of three California girls who have by chance managed to gain access to his loft. These episodes put together, Peterson finds himself cornered by a society that seems to have decided to absorb the most radical judgments on human nature as matters of course.

The upshot is that Peterson's position as artist is subjected to an ironic inversion. If in former times the philistine was despised by the cultural elite, it is now the artist who is almost bullied into apologizing for not being sufficiently interested in absurdity by Miss Arbor, the talkmaster of the TV-show he wishes to participate in for financial reasons. The limits of this avantgarde consciousness turned mass consciousness only come in sight when it interferes with economic or political interests as in the case of Peterson's dealer Jean-Claude who, for the sake of better saleability, wishes to saw one of Peterson's pictures in two and in the case of the President and his men who, for obscure reasons, actually do destroy the sculpture Peterson is working on and most of his studio equipment into the bargain. These limits also come in sight when Peterson's TV-speech against alienation appears so subversive to the program officials that they desperately try to turn him off. The truth the artist Peterson hesitatingly and uncertainly gropes after proves strong enough in the end to penetrate the cocksure pseudo-radicalism of TV-society.

In **"Engineer-Private Paul Klee Misplaces an Aircraft between Milbertshofen and Cambrai, March 1916"** reality not only absorbs art as in **"A Shower of Gold,"** but it actually becomes a work of art. Both Klee and the members of the Secret Police who watch over his actions fear official reprimands because one of the three aeroplanes Klee is responsible for has disappeared unnoticed. With "his painter's skill which resembles not a little that of the forger" Klee manipulates the manifest and the Secret Police manipulate their report so that the third aeroplane appears to have never existed. In analogy to the production of a work of art, they produce the reality they desire and thus give one more proof of the fictional nature of reality, which has been exposed by many postmodern writers from Borges and Nabokov to Barth and Sukenick. Ironically, the same "painter's skill" that creates the delusion others take for reality also preserves the truth of the matter: out of sheer aesthetic curiosity Klee spontaneously draws a sketch of the flatcar and the loose wrapping from which the aircraft disappeared.

The inversion of the mimetic relation between art and reality is complete in **"A Shower of Gold"** and **"Engineer-Private Paul Klee."** On the one hand reality appears either as a hysterical performance by the Theatre of the Absurd or as the delusive product of an artistic imagination directed by highly subjective interests. On the other hand Peterson's desperate confession and Klee's disinterested sketch remain as artistic residues of a reality that is what it seems. Reality turns into an imitation of stock artistic styles and techniques, whereas only an art that is uncontaminated by social convention and personal interests is able to retain a sense of what is real.

The poetological parable **"And Then"** suggests in a different manner that art must not be deprived of its spontaneity and autonomy. At the beginning of the story, the narrator's problem seems to be strictly poetological. Similar to Edgar, the writer-to-be in **"The Dolt,"** he is unable to finish the anecdote he is trying to tell his visitor. A link is missing in the sequence of events. His reflections on how to go on with his anecdote gradually acquaint the reader with the narrative situation. The apparent poetological problem of how to give coherence to an anecdote reveals itself as depending upon a far less abstract personal problem. By means of the anecdote the narrator wants to convince his visitor, a police sergeant who happens to have married the narrator's mother

and who has arrived with two colleagues and his newly wed wife to take away the narrator's harpsichord, to leave him the harpsichord and to annul his marriage. The narrator's real problem consists in his belief that it is possible to reach these ends by literary means, that a story can be invented which will solve his difficulties for him:

> I wondered . . . what kind of 'and then' I could contrive which might satisfy all the particulars of the case, which might redeliver to me my mother, retain to me my harpsichord, and rid me of these others, in their uniforms.

It is characteristic of Barthelme that all the narrator can think of as a continuation of his anecdote is a children's story, which, of course, furthers his ends as little as any other sequel that he might contrive.

Beyond the rejection of mythical and legendary patterns as structural models for contemporary story-telling in *Snow White,* **"The Glass Mountain," "Departures,"** and **"The Dragon"** and beyond the inversion of the relation between art and reality in **"A Shower of Gold"** and **"Engineer-Private Paul Klee,"** Barthelme denies the possibility of changing or even influencing reality by artistic means in **"And Them."** In this story, the shift from its poetological to its existential aspect drastically demonstrates that the power of the story-teller ends precisely where his story ends. By means of the stimulation of a narrator-listener situation within the story, Barthelme reminds his readers that what he confronts them with are only stories. This obviously refers back to the questions raised in connection with the discussion of **"At the Tolstoy Museum,"** i.e. the question of the authority stories can claim for themselves on the strength of being works of art and the concomitant question of their appropriate reception.

IV

The structure of Barthelme's writing discourages any attempt to extrapolate political, moral or aesthetic judgments from it. Barthelme's position as a writer is as far removed as possible from that of the seer. He does not want his readers to accept his works submissively as sources of wisdom. He rather forces the reader to think for himself. Barthelme's stories emancipate the reader from the authority he consciously or unconsciously attributes to the text he is reading. In other words, Barthelme directs his anti-authoritarian impulse against his own writing.

He does so by means of the two most prominent and most frequently analyzed features of his works, his pervasive irony and his disruptive technique of collage and fragmentation that make it impossible for the reader both to take at face value what he reads and to smoothly imbibe the stories' contents without interruption. He does so, too, by less conspicuous sudden shifts of perspective that produce totally different valuations of identical situations. They recall the shift from Francis's to Caligari's point of view in *Das Cabinet des Dr. Caligari* that changes the meaning of the film completely. In **"And Then"** the transference of the narrator's problem from the poetological to the existential level changes the story's meaning quite similarly. Variations of this technique are noticeable in several other stories.

"Kierkegaard Unfair to Schlegel," the second story in *City Life* (1970) that is based on the interview pattern of a sequence of questions and answers, begins with the description of a scene in a railway compartment that bursts with subdued erotic potential. Precisely at the point when the reader's mind begins to wallow in sexual fantasies that anticipate the continuation of the very slowly developing situation, the promising narrative is interrupted by the questioner's comment: "That's a very common fantasy." This remark explains the initially puzzling first sentence of the story: "I use the girl on the train a lot." The luscious episode reveals itself as nothing but one of its narrator's strategies to overcome his sexual tensions. The reader's disappointed expectations teach him not to confide too easily in the veracity of what is presented him. The reader implied in **"Kierkegaard Unfair to Schlegel"** is the suspicious reader.

In **"Daumier"** changes of perspective are psychologically motivated, too. The story consists of episodes from the life of Daumier and two "self-transplants" that he constructs in order to pacify his insatiable self. These surrogates seem to exist independently of him. An interesting identity problem arises when emotions of the original self intermingle with those of one of the surrogates: "I then noticed that I had become rather fond—fond to a fault—of a person in the life of my surrogate. . . . I began to wonder how I could get her out of his life and into my own." When he has achieved this transference and has thus secured a new female companion for his authentic self, his insatiability is miraculously, though only temporarily, cured. For the time being Daumier does not need his surrogates any more, but he knows that his happiness will not last. Therefore he carefully wraps them up and stores them away in a drawer together with the other members of the scenarios his transplants were involved in.

In **"Daumier"** the desire to change one's life-role is not treated as seriously as in some of Barthelme's earlier stories. The roles of musketeer, westerner and debonair optimist Daumier's surrogates take pains to fulfill are too ridiculous or fantastic not to be seen through as cliches at first glance. They are Daumier's pastime, a distraction, not a serious alternative. **"Daumier"** is a surrealist comment on the inescapability of self-stylization that the reader can appreciate because he is carefully initiated into Daumier's

schizoid way of maintaining his psychic stability. Changing levels of reality and shifts of perspective in the different episodes do not take the reader by surprise as they do in **"Kierkegaard Unfair to Schlegel."**

"Daumier" is a surrealist comment on the inescapability of self-stylization that the reader can appreciate because he is carefully initiated into Daumier's schizoid way of maintaining his psychic stability.
—*Jochen Achilles*

A more puzzling situation again arises in **"The Phantom of the Opera's Friend,"** a first person narration by the title figure about his vain attempts to impel his friend to give up his phantom existence and to begin a normal life. Suddenly, half way through the story, the perspective changes to third person and the reader is informed that "Gaston Leroux was tired of writing *The Phantom of the Opera*." Leroux prefers to postpone finishing *The Phantom of the Opera* and decides to begin a new work instead. After this interlude, the first person narration is resumed as if nothing had happened.

What has happened resembles Francis's detection of the volume on the original eighteenth century Italian magician Caligari among his psychiatrist's books. Barthelme's story reveals its source, the novel *Le Fantome de l'Opera* (1910) by the French author of psychological romances and detective stories Gaston Leroux. The unexpected and abrupt changes of focus from the situation of the phantom to that of its original creator and back again heighten the reader's awareness that what he reads is dependent upon several mediators. The interdependence of their perspectives remind him of the relativity of each individual perspective, of the unattainability of objective presentation and of the probability that a story has been told before. This function of multiperspectivity is diametrically opposed to its use in *Das Cabinet des Dr. Caligari*. The manner in which Francis's and Caligari's mutually exclusive views are presented force the reader to reject the one as false and to accept the other as true. The authority of one perspective is played out against the other, whereas in **"The Phantom of the Opera's Friend"** absolute claims to truth are generally undermined.

Like **"Kierkegaard Unfair to Schlegel"** and **"And Then,"** **"What to Do Next"** simulates a narrator-listener situation. A person who apparently needs advice is recommended by an authoritative voice to lose himself "in the song of the instructions, in the precise, detailed balm of having had solved . . . that most difficult of problems, what to do next". The instructions lecture him on all aspects of his life until they finally absorb him:

"We have therefore decided to make you *a part of the instructions themselves*—something other people must complete, or go through, before they reach their individual niches, or thrones, or whatever kind of plateau makes them, at least for the time being, happy."

This changes the communicative situation significantly. As the addressee turns into a part of the address, he quits the field for the reader who suddenly realizes that he belongs to the "other people" the instructions appeal to, i.e., that he is their real addressee. Yet it is precisely this identification with the situation of being lectured on what to do next which discloses to the reader the repressive nature of the situation. Is the reader to become part of the instructions, too? This would mean that he, too, is ready to submit to any authoritative voice that chooses to give him directions and that he, too, decides to become a model of self-sacrifice. Inversely this means that he has to react like Burligame in **"Hiding Man"** if he wants to retain his selfhood. He has to reject instructions from outside and to instruct himself. By the sudden shift from figural to reader perspective the story reveals its hidden meaning, which amounts to a revocation of what it pretends to provide—advice on how to live.

"The Discovery," another story in *Amateurs* (1976), exploits the discrepancy between figural and reader perspective in a less complex manner but with a similar result. The discoveries the characters in the story and the readers of the story make are diametrically opposed. The discovery of the characters consists in their consensus on the dullness of one of them, whereas the reader has a quite contrary impression. It is the character who is unanimously pronounced dull who passes the only mildly funny and intelligent remark in the whole story. By the endless repetition of trite remarks and stock phrases all the others go into an orgy of dullness without even noticing it.

In **"What to Do Next"** and **"The Discovery"** Barthelme again employs shifts of perspective not to establish authority but to subvert it. He teaches the reader that he has every reason to confront with distrust what is presented to him as authoritative and/or authorial truths.

V

Barthelme's aesthetic of inversion, the reversal of life roles, the revocation of artistic options and the relativity of perspectives, is prefigured by the derivative nature of events and the changes of perspective in *Das Cabinet des Dr. Caligari*. But Barthelme does not simply imitate this film as Caligari copies his Italian forerunner. He applies the technique of inversion he takes over from the film to the film's own message and thus denounces the authoritarian principle the film

vindicates. In Barthelme's fiction Caligari only comes back to take his leave for good.

The question remains why he comes back at all. The other side of the coin of Barthelme's wholesale dismissal of authorities and his total rejection of models of behavior and expression is disorientation and incoherence. Although Barthelme does not seem to believe in the possibility either of validating the legendary and mythical structures that underlie his fiction or of justifying the numerous father figures who populate it, his art would come to nothing were it not for these structures and figures. Barthelme depends upon the "trash phenomenon" not because he wants to transfigure it in the way *Das Cabinet des Dr. Caligari* whitewashes Caligari, but simply "because it's all there is".

In **"Nothing: A Preliminary Account"** Barthelme explains the epistemological implications of this situation. He points out that the aim of apprehending nothingness and the only means there is to reach this aim are mutually exclusive. All one can do to approach nothing is to make a list of what nothing is not. In other words, a list of everything. If the list were complete, nothing would remain. But obviously it is impossible to achieve this:

> And even if we were able, with much labor, to exhaust the possibilities, get it all *inscribed,* name everything nothing is not, down to the last rogue atom, the one that rolled behind the door, and had thoughtfully included ourselves, the makers of the list, on the list—the list itself would remain. Who's got a match?

This dilemma adequately describes the dilemma of Barthelme's own fiction. The story betrays its poetological significance if it is seen as another manifestation of Barthelme's aesthetic of inversion. Contrary to the search for nothing in **"Nothing: A Preliminary Account"** Barthelme is, like the dwarfs in *Snow White* and the angels in **"On Angels,"** in search of a new principle. But all the cultural, social, and historical phenomena he examines in the course of this search prove deceptive and false. There are not substantial moral authorities or structural patterns on which life and art can be built. All that is found is trash. The search for something proves as hopeless as the search for nothing and yet it is the only task Barthelme regards as worth his while. Precisely because it is insoluble "the task will remain always before us, like a meaning for our lives." Each individual story is only **"A Preliminary Account"** of this search for authority resulting in the negation of authority.

Robert A. Morace (essay date Fall 1984)

SOURCE: "Donald Barthelme's *Snow White:* The Novel, the

Critics, and the Culture," in *Critique,* Vol. 26, No. 1, Fall, 1984, pp. 1-10.

[In the following essay, Morace analyzes Snow White *as a work of experimental fiction.]*

Delight in formal experimentation is one characteristic of much of our contemporary American fiction. Another, either explicit in the choice of subject matter or implicit in the narrative treatment, is the scornful criticism of the popular culture and its audience. While the former has received considerable attention from critics, the latter has more often been cited as a given than discussed in any detail. Perhaps the reason for this reticence lies not so much with the critics as with the writers themselves, who prefer to deride the popular culture rather than to analyze it or their basic assumptions about it. In the peremptory words of William Gass, "This muck cripples consciousness" [*Fiction and the Figures of Life,* Nonpareil Books, 1978]. Gass, appropriately, is presently writing a novel he hopes will be so good no one will publish it. Other writers associated with the new fiction, such as Jerzy Kosinski, attack the mass culture reductively, while still others, Robert Coover and Ishmael Reed for example, resort to caricature (not without good reason). Kurt Vonnegut is both more sympathetic and, in his way, more analytic. But the most important exception to the general rule is, I believe, Donald Barthelme, especially in his curious little novel *Snow White.*

The very unconventionality of this oddly mimetic book has obscured for many readers the degree to which it serves as a remarkably detailed, and in some ways even melancholy, critique of the reductive linguistic democracy of the contemporary American mass culture. To those already disposed towards innovative fiction, *Snow White*'s being "stylistically appropriate" [Jack Shadoian, "Notes on Donald Barthelme's *Snow White*," *Western Humanities Review,* Winter, 1970] and "a remarkably entertaining performance" [Albert J. Guerard, "Notes on the rhetoric of anti-realistic fiction," *Triquarterly,* Spring, 1974] are sufficient to ensure its worth. To those who wonder where-have-all-the-Tolstoys-gone, *Snow White* is merely slick and self-indulgent. Neither view does justice to the complexity, as distinct from the technical proficiency, of Barthelme's writing, which at least to some readers is very clearly the work of a "conventional moralist". More to the point, when Tony Tanner compared Barthelme's fiction to the Watts Towers in Los Angeles, he in effect set the stage for what has emerged as the single most important question for readers of *Snow White:* to what extent is the novel a surrender to the contemporary culture or a criticism of it? For the more tradition-minded reader, the answer is simple. According to John Gardner, Barthelme "reflects his doubting and anxious age because he is, himself, an extreme example of it," one whose only advice is "better to be disillusioned than deluded." Gerald Graff goes a step

further. Although in his ambivalent and even contradictory remarks on the novel, Graff does admit that Barthelme's style parodies empty language—language as gesture rather than language as communication—and acknowledges that *Snow White* is "finally a form of cultural statement," he criticizes what he considers the author's "irreverent stance toward his work" and "the novel's inability to transcend the solipsism of subjectivity and language. . . ." In sum, the novel does not entirely succeed in playing the "adversary role" prescribed by Graff because Barthelme "lacks a sufficient sense of objective reality" and therefore does not fully resolve what Graff identifies as "the writer's problem": "to find a standpoint from which to represent the diffuse, intransigent material of contemporary experience without surrendering critical perspective to it."

> **When Tony Tanner compared Barthelme's fiction to the Watts Towers in Los Angeles, he in effect set the stage for what has emerged as the single most important question for readers of *Snow White:* to what extent is the novel a surrender to the contemporary culture or a criticism of it?**
> **—Robert A. Morace**

The tendency to read *Snow White* as a sign of an ethically bankrupt age rather than as a critique of it culminates in Christopher Lasch's controversial study, *The Culture of Narcissism.* Those characteristics Lasch associates with pathological narcissism—"dependence on the vicarious warmth provided by others combined with a fear of dependence, a sense of inner emptiness, boundless repressed rage, and unsatisfied oral cravings . . . pseudo self-insight, calculating seductiveness, nervous self-deprecatory humor . . . intense fear of old age and death, altered sense of time, fascination with celebrity, fear of competition, decline of the play spirit, deteriorating relations between men and women"—these are the same characteristics noticeable throughout *Snow White,* as Lasch himself acknowledges. In what ways then has Barthelme failed? In Lasch's view, Barthelme's perfunctory ironic humor and refusal to present himself as an authority evidence the fact that he "waives the right to be taken seriously." Moreover, Lasch charges, in their fiction Barthelme, Vonnegut, and other innovative contemporary writers have abdicated their responsibility to provide psychologically and socially useful fantasies for their readers, readers who then turn to the escapist fantasies of the popular culture, which, Lasch says, are not only not psychologically useful but also socially dangerous in that they tend to increase the individual's dissatisfaction without suggesting to him viable ways to improve his condition.

In order to understand just how mistaken is the view held

by Gardner, Graff, and Lasch, it is necessary to examine the specific ways in which Barthelme analyzes in his novel the language used in today's society. For the most part, however, Barthelme's supporters have been as quick as Gardner or Lasch to deny the presence of *any* content, ethical or otherwise, in Barthelme's work. Ronald Sukenick, for example, views Barthelme as the exemplar of the non-representational, improvisational, opaque "Bossa Nova" fiction that, according to Sukenick, began sweeping the country in the late 1960s. By opacity, Sukenick means that the fiction and the experience of reading the fiction exist solely "in and for" themselves; moreover, "opacity implies that we should direct our attention to the surface of the work, and such techniques as graphics and typographical variation, in calling the reader's attention to the technological reality of the book, are useful in keeping his mind on that surface instead of undermining it with profundities." Although Barthelme does draw the reader's attention to the surface of *Snow White,* he does so chiefly in order to show the ways in which language and explanations mediate between self and experience and to make clear that the result of this mediation, in the contemporary culture at least, is the cheapening or perversion of words, experiences, values, and people. Unlike his surface-loving characters, Barthelme penetrates his novel's various surfaces—of character, of clichéd language, of printed page—in order to expose the melancholy absence of any deeper, humanizing meaning (the very "profundities" Sukenick wishes to exclude). It is the dwarfs, not their author, who love books that require them to do nothing more than read, or experience, the words printed on the page, the way a jaded traveler reads the print on a timetable. Barthelme dives beneath these surfaces—not so deeply as Melville perhaps, or at least not in the same ways—in order to expose the plastic (no longer pasteboard) mask of dwarf language and culture. Thus, to call Barthelme a "very bossanova writer," as Sukenick does, or an "action writer" whose aim, according to Jerome Klinkowitz [in *The Practice of Fiction in America: Writers from Hawthorne to the Present*], is "to create a *new* work, which exists as an object in space, not in discursive commentary on the linear elements that form it," only serves to emphasize the significant formal innovativeness of the fiction at the expense of what Gardner would term its "moral" content. More importantly, Sukenick's formulation invites and indeed almost makes plausible the misguided criticism of Graff and Lasch, who argue for a literature in which the author presents this "moral" content to the reader directly, perhaps (considering Graff's praise of *Mr. Sammler's Planet*) even didactically.

A few reviewers and critics have managed to avoid this either/or approach to Barthelme's disconcerting little novel and have made at least passing mention of his critique of the language of the contemporary culture, but only one, William Stott [in "Donald Barthelme and the Death of Fiction," *Pros-*

pects: An Annual of American Cultural Studies], has attempted to define its specific nature. Stott persuasively argues that Barthelme's "stories are about what happens to fiction in a non-fiction world [a world in which "the facts of life" are supplied primarily by non-fiction], or—to put it another way—what happens to private values when all facts are treated as public." What happens is that private values can no longer be maintained because they have been supplemented by "non-fiction's public definitions." One effect of this cultural change is the perversion of private expression, and another is the devaluation of significant historical acts.

The method of radical devaluation noted by Stott is at the heart of Barthelme's critique of American mass culture in *Snow White.* The method is decidedly not "genially democratic," as one sympathetic critic has claimed [Neil Schmitz, "Donald Barthelme and the Emergence of Modern Satire," *Minnesota Review,* Vol. 1, 1972]. Rather, it is precisely the reverse of what Pearl Bell finds so abhorrent in his fiction. Bell flatly asserts that Barthelme's stories do

> not pretend to any ideas, comic or otherwise, about the "trash phenomenon"—the steadily mounting detritus of words and things that forms Barthelme's image of American life—but are composed of the trash itself. . . . What could be more perfectly expressive of contempt for the ordering intellect, for the authority of culture, for any discriminatory distinctions between the multitudinous and the valuable—if all men are equal, all things are also equal—than a writer whose works consist almost entirely, or so he likes to claim, of the raw sewage of spontaneous expression.

To a degree it is true that "Barthelme operates by a law of equivalence according to which nothing is intrinsically more interesting than anything else," as Gerald Graff has claimed, but this method is a criticism of, not, as Graff and Lasch have charged, a surrender to, the contemporary culture. What we find in *Snow White* is, in fact, Barthelme's tracing of that leveling tendency which Tocqueville recognized as a danger inherent in a democracy. The purposely anonymous society sketched in the novel (one can hardly say "depicted") is characterized not merely by a reductive political equality but more importantly by a radical and insidious democratization of language—a linguistic democracy in which any word can be substituted for any other word, in which all utterances are equally empty gestures produced as if just so many plastic buffalo humps, and in which the hollowness of the mass culture is reflected in the hollowness of the characters' language and in the general "failure of the imagination" of a culture given entirely over to the mindless consumption of ideas as well as goods. Such a world Donald Barthelme neither surrenders to nor endorses.

Snow White is, among other things, a one hundred-and-eighty-page verbal vaudeville show (itself a kind of theatrical collage) in which the form of the jokes often constitutes the author's critique of dwarf culture. In all speech, says Dan, one of Snow White's seven dwarf lovers, there is always "some other word that would do as well, . . . or maybe a number of them." Promiscuous as the novel's characters may be, it is their linguistic promiscuity which titillates the reader. Incongruities abound, obscure and archaic words appear as often as contemporary slang, and literally anything can be obscene: consider Snow White's sexually loaded plea for "more perturbation!" and the "pornographic pastry" which, alas, is not "poignant." And, of course, just the reverse can happen: a "cathouse" mentioned several times turns out to be a house for cats. Similarly, anything can be a dead metaphor. Characters are frequently "left sucking the mop" or finding "the red meat on the rug." One character becomes "a sack of timidities"; others worship "the almighty penny." Filled with a dread induced in part by introductory courses in philosophy and psychology, they have no difficulty coming up with such existential aphorisms as "The *Inmitten*-ness of the *Lumpwelt* is a turning toward misery."

"Give me the odd linguistic trip, stutter and fall, and I will be content," says dwarf Bill; and early in the story Snow White laments, "Oh I wish there were some words in the world that were not the words I always hear." Both complaints are, in one sense at least, foolish, as Barthelme's fantastically inventive word-play makes clear. Whether such crippled imaginations as theirs can successfully struggle against the usurping, homogenizing culture which dwarfs them and make the Barthelmean leap of language is, however, more than just a little suspect. The Snow White who, apparently not having taken a course in modern poetry at Beaver College, has never before heard the expression "murder and create" is nonetheless writing "a dirty great poem" about "loss." Given the would-be poet's lack of both a tradition and an individual talent, the reader may find "the President's war on poetry" a rather gratuitous undertaking. The dwarfs have certainly already surrendered, as the mixing of metaphors in the following passage attests:

> Of course we had hoped that he [Paul] would take up his sword as part of the Presidents war on poetry. The time is ripe for that. The root causes of poetry have been studied and studied. And now that we know that pockets of poetry still exist in our great country, especially in the large urban centers, we ought to be able to wash it out totally in one generation, if we put our backs into it.

In addition to the swords, wars, ripenings, roots, pockets, and washings, the speaker's moribund recitation of political jargon and his unknowing allusions evidence Barthelme's critical stance towards the culture's junk heap approach to language and history, the debased contemporary version of Ruskin's storehouse.

Freed at last and entirely from that retrospection flailed by Emerson in *Nature,* that trash civilization in *Snow White* is marked not by the Emersonian injunction "Build therefore your own world" but instead by the inability to discriminate as to either words or values. The dwarfs ponder the *bon mots* of Apollinaire and LaGuardia with equal deliberation, and Snow White lavishes equal attention on the cleaning of the books, oven, and piano (in that order) and includes in her catch-all list of princes the historical Pericles, the contemporary Charlie, the literary Hal, the comic-strip Valiant, and the Madison Avenue Matchabelli. The omnivorous dwarfs read novels aloud and in their entirety, even the "outer part where the author is praised and the price quoted," while the prince-figure Paul is torn between acting heroically and eating a "duck-with-blue-cheese sandwich." Worse yet is the narrator's unconscious and incongruous juxtaposition of the emotional and the anatomical in this passage: "At the horror show Hubert put his hand in Snow White's lap. A shy and tentative gesture. She let it lay there. It was warm there; that is where the vulva is." Such are the fruits of what Barthelme's narrator calls "the democratization of education" and Christopher Lasch terms "the mindless eclecticism" of today's brand of higher education. This radical and entirely reductive equality is applied not merely to words, including names, but to people as well who, as a result, are often confused with and reduced to the level of objects, future trash, as in the novel's opening sentence, which begins, "She is a tall dark beauty containing a great many beauty spots . . ." Even when, on rare occasions, Snow White becomes uncomfortable with this kind of language, she is only able to substitute one form of it for another. Looking at herself in a mirror, she decides to

> take stock. These breasts, my own, still stand delicately away from the trunk, as they are supposed to do. And the trunk itself is not unappealing. In fact *trunk* is a rather mean word for the main part of this assemblage of felicities. The cream-of-wheat belly! The stunning arse, in the rococo mirror! And then the especially good legs, including the important knees. I have nothing but praise for this delicious assortment.

Unwilling to be a cadaverous "trunk," Snow White prefers to think of herself, unwittingly of course, as a hot breakfast cereal and a Whitman's sampler.

Another way in which language is used by these unreflective consumers is as a means of deflecting from problems at hand. Just as most of the characters turn to drinking at one point or another, all of them turn to language as a means of escape. Troubled by their deteriorating relationship with

Snow White, the dwarfs busy themselves with a description of a room's interior decor; Edward transforms their problem into a sermon on the "horsewife," and Dan decides it is not really Snow White that troubles them but the red towel she wears. The best and funniest example of deflection is the dwarfs' "situation report":

> "She still sits there in the window, dangling down her long black hair black as ebony. The crowds have thinned somewhat. Our letters have been returned unopened. The shower curtain initiative has not produced notable results. She is, I would say, aware of it, but has not reacted either positively or negatively. We have asked an expert in to assess it as to timbre, pitch, mood and key. He should be here tomorrow. To make sure we have the *right sort* of shower curtain. We have returned the red towels to Bloomingdale's." At this point everybody looked at Dan, who vomited. "Bill's yellow crêpe-paper pajamas have been taken away from him and burned. He ruined that night for all of us, you know that." At this point everybody looked at Bill who was absent. He was tending the vats. "Bill's new brown monkscloth pajamas, made for him by Paul, should be here next month. The grade of pork ears we are using in the Baby Ding Sam Dew is not capable of meeting U.S. Govt. standards, or indeed, any standards. Our man in Hong Kong assures us however that the next shipment will be superior. Sales nationwide are brisk, brisk, brisk. Texas Instruments is down four points. Control data is up four points. The pound is weakening. The cow is calving. The cactus wants watering. The new building is abuilding with leases covering 45 percent of the rentable space already in hand. The weather tomorrow, fair and warmer."

The comic deflection evident in this passage serves a serious purpose. Like the questionnaire Barthelme inserts into his novel, the purpose of which is not, as Christopher Lesch believes, "to demolish the reader's confidence in the author," the situation report suggests the extent to which the Age of Journalism that Kierkegaard predicted a century and a half ago has come to pass: the age of quick information (not wisdom) and skimmed surfaces. Small wonder that the dwarfs find in digression so effective a means of evading the problem Snow White poses and of achieving the promise of better days to come. Barthelme's reader is delighted, but at the same time dismayed and provoked, by the ludicrous literal-mindedness of the characters in the situation report and, for example, the "interrupted screw" and "bat theory of child-raising" passages. This same journalistic literal-mindedness leads to the explanatory overkill evident on virtually every page of the novel, including the first. There the reader is told not only of Snow White's "many beauty spots" but also, in the driest, most mechanically repetitive language possible, *where* these beauty spots appear, and just in case the reader sill has not gotten the picture, the narrator appends that picture, a diagram showing the position, "more or less," of each of the spots. Such explanations are similar to the reading preferences of the dwarfs, who like

> books that have a lot of *dreck* in them, matter which presents itself as not wholly relevant (or indeed, at all relevant) but which, carefully attended to, can supply a kind of "sense" of what is going on. This "sense" is not to be obtained by reading between the lines (for there is nothing there, in those white spaces) but by reading the lines themselves—looking at them and so arriving at a feeling not of satisfaction exactly, that is too much to expect, but of having "completed" them.

Both the reading and the explanations take time, fill up time, thus creating the illusion of completeness and understanding. And too they resemble those empty, usually verbal gestures sprinkled throughout the story: seasoning for Barthelme's readers but more of the word-bog for his dwarfish characters who are at once the victims and the perpetrators of such linguistic absurdities as Jane's signing her threatening letter to Mr. Quistgaard "Yours *faithfully*" or a conversation in which "somebody had said something we hadn't heard. . . . Then Bill said something. . . . Other people said other things. . . . But Bill had something else to say." With conversations such as these can Vonnegut's verbal shrug, "so it goes," be far away?

"I just don't like your world," says Snow White at one point, " a world in which such things can happen." Just what these "things" may be Snow White never makes clear, or perhaps never can make clear, given that increase int he "blanketing effect of ordinary language" which parallels an increase in the "trash phenomenon" in Snow White's world. The triumph of this "blanketing effect" will restore the dwarfs to their longed-for state of "equanimity for all" and will put an end to Snow White's complaint: "Oh why does fate give us alternatives to annoy and frustrate ourselves with?" But it will do so only at a price: the loss of their linguistic and (thinking of Orwell's equation) political freedom, including the freedom to choose the *extra*ordinary possibilities of language rather than accept the blanketed language of dwarf culture. The triumph of the blanketing effect will result in a society even more tasteless and unprincely than the one found in the novel where it is believed that "It must be all right if it is ordinary," a society already deafened by amplified but meaningless sound and inundated by trash, a society of over-heating "electric wastebaskets" and "the democratization of education," a society where the individual (or what remains of the individual) is subjected to public scrutiny, where "vatricide" is the "crime of crimes" and blanketing the song of songs, and where there is heard the novels' melancholy refrain, "the problem remained."

"Language," George Steiner has noted [in *After Babel*], "is the main instrument of man's refusal to accept the world as it is." The ultimate linguistic democracy of **Snow White,** however, is characterized not by any such active refusal but instead by passive acceptance, indiscriminate consumption, and echolalia ("I have not been able to imagine anything better," says Snow White; "*I have not been able to imagine anything better*" reads the next sentence). The result is indeed a "failure of imagination" or, more specifically, a sadly reductive democracy in which all words, things, or people, emotions, and values are finally equal—that is to say, equally worthless, equally insignificant and interchangeable, equally dehumanized and dehumanizing. Such "muck" does indeed cripple consciousness. Much to his credit, Donald Barthelme does not turn away from the contemporary mass culture, nor does he scornfully and condescendingly belittle it. As one aphoristic chapter near the very end of the novel warns, "ANATHEMIZATION OF THE WORLD IS NOT AN ADEQUATE RESPONSE TO THE WORLD." For the characters in the novel, this means the uncritical acceptance ("Heigh Ho") of their situation. For Barthelme it means something quite different. **Snow White** is not a book "crippled by the absence of a subject," as Morris Dickstein has said [in *Gates of Eden: American Culture in the Sixties*], but instead a fiction that is very much about a crippled culture, a book that uses parody and various innovative techniques to analyze the texture of contemporary life. The character who admits, "But to say what I have said, gentlemen, is to say nothing at all," speaks for himself and his dwarfish kind but not at all for his author, whose purpose is to clarify the relationship between the state of the society and state of its language. Clearly and inventively, Donald Barthelme's novel suggests that in a dwarf culture of plastic buffalo humps, religious sciences, hair initiatives, unemployed princes, "hurlments," attractively packaged jars of Chinese baby food, *dreck* and *blague,* one well-aimed joke is worth considerably more than a thousand words from the collective mouth of Bill, Dan, Edward, Hubert, Henry, and Clem.

Lance Olsen (essay date November 1986)

SOURCE: "Linguistic Pratfalls in Barthelme," in *South Atlantic Review,* Vol. 51, No. 4, November, 1986, pp. 69-77.

[*In the following essay, Olsen illustrates how Barthelme transforms elements of physical comedy into linguistic humor in his works.*]

Why does language subvert me, subvert my senior-

ity, my medals, my oldness, whenever it gets a chance? What does language have against me—me that has been good to it, respecting its little peculiarities and nicilosities, for sixty years.

Donald Barthelme (*Unspeakable Practices*)

A critical commonplace: absurdity, parody, irony, burlesque, farce, satire, and so on abound at the stratum of events in Donald Barthelme's projects. In **"The Joker's Greatest Triumph,"** a spoof on our superchic cartoonish consumer society, for instance, Batman is stunned and finally unmasked while his friend—or perhaps lover?—Fredric Brown looks on horrified, and Robin, who is supposed to be away at Andover doing poorly in French, swoops out of the Gotham City sky in a backup Batplane (this society has two of *everything*) as a kind of comic book *deus ex machina*; conscious again, our superhero undertakes a textual analysis of the arch villain by paraphrasing Mark Schorer's biography of Sinclair Lewis.

Another critical commonplace: often the fantastic mislocation of events in Barthelme's fictions is overshadowed by the discourse that shapes it. In fact, it is not infrequently that nothing much happens in his works. Two people sit in an underground missile silo and watch each other in **"Game."** A doctor contemplates his best friend's wife while spinning on a piano stool in **"Alice."** A ludicrous lyrical philosopher contemplates Sartrean absence for four pages in **"Nothing: A Preliminary Account."** And since the middle of the last decade Barthelme has constituted his pieces more and more out of pure dialogue devoid of traditional tags that let us know who is speaking, and where, and why, thereby undercutting what Robbe-Grillet has somewhat misleadingly dubbed the Balzacian mode of fiction. Barthelme's pieces point to themselves as artificial and deliberate modes of discourse, flag their self-reflexivity, and to this extent participate in what has come for better or worse to be known as postmodernism, along with works by writers such as Handke in Germany, Calvino in Italy, Butor in France, Cabrera Infante in Latin America, and Gaddis in the United States. According to Norman Holland, in the works of those writers, "the arts take as their subject matter the relationship between the work of art and its artist or between the work of art and its audience. It is as though we changed the subject matter of our arts from something behind the canvas to the canvas itself and now to the space between the canvas and us." Interest, then, no longer falls on the modern and premodern quest for a transcendental signified, some ultimate realm of truth, some eventual coherence, some *over there* that in the end helps define, articulate, unify, and make intelligible the *here.* Rather, interest falls on the signifier and its relationship both to the writer and reader. Interest falls on the linguistic game in the texts, the lexical play on the page.

What is *not* a critical commonplace, and what so far has not received any critical attention, is that such verbal frolic in Barthelme's projects carries with it affinities to the cinematic slapstick of Chaplin, Laurel and Hardy, Keaton, and so on. [Though I should not want to suggest a simple cause-and-effect relationship between Barthelme's film interests and his fiction, I should point out that Barthelme is well acquainted with the knockabout falls and fastspeed chases that were the mainstay of comic films from 1912 onward. As a child growing up in Texas, he attended movies habitually. As the editor of *Cougar,* the college newpaper at the University of Houston, he often reviewed films from 1950 to 1951. When he turned reporter for the *Houston Post,* he reviewed a wide range of cultural events, including cinematic ones. And since the mid-sixties he has turned out a number of essays on the current cinema for the *New Yorker.* He has also acknowledged the profound effect film has had on contemporary consciousness, hence suggesting link between film and fiction generally. He has argued that, just as modern painters had to reinvent painting because of the discovery of photography, so contemporary writers have had to reinvent writing because of the discovery of film—both, I assume, because of the new subject matter and the fragmentary, short-scened, high-paced, surface-oriented form.] But what is important here is that the situational has transfigured into the discursive. That is, sight-gags have metamorphosed into language-gags. Barthelme takes the dislocation that is, according to Kant, Schopenhauer, Freud, Bergson, and others, at the core of comedy, plucks it out of the domain of events and plugs it into the domain of discourse. He presents the reader with the knockabout falls and futile chases of a language trying to remain on its own two feet and catch up with some kind of steady, clear meaning. His language wears outrageously ill-fitting words that bump and thump over themselves, ineffectually pursuing a center, careering off cliffs of significance into ridiculousness. As a result, a brand of linguistic illegality arises. The dogma of lexical and tonal consistency collapses. Verbal banana peels undermine the self-confident syntax of an earlier mode of writing and slip up the tidy control every sentence once wanted over itself.

To accomplish this, Barthelme often plays around with what the structuralists and Barthelme himself in *Snow White* call "universes of discourse"—areas of vocabulary that refer to specific spheres of experience in a unique way. Rather than interesting himself in consistent universes of discourse, as did to some extent moderns such as Thomas Mann, Proust, and Conrad, and the so-called realists such as Flaubert, George Eliot, and Tolstoy, Barthelme concerns himself with stylistic deformity and the inherent incongruities of language it assumes. Thus he sets up one sector of vocabulary (thereby generating certain reader expectations about the linguistic unit's level of usage, social register, inflection, and so on) only immediately to insert another or several others (thereby shattering those expecta-

tions). Consequently, the original sector of vocabulary takes a dive.

By this point it is probably time for some examples—and they occur at all linguistic strata from the sentence to the text as a whole. To begin small and subtle, an instance from one of Barthelme's bestknown and frequently anthologized fictions, **"The Glass Mountain":** "The sidewalks were full of dogshit in brilliant colors: ocher, burnt umber, Mars yellow, sienna, viridian, ivory black, rose madder". The verbal *splat*! takes place as the text brings together the word "dogshit" (from the universe of discourse of street talk) with the lyrical and precise list of "brilliant colors" (from the lexical field of the eloquent artist). The prosaic with its two hard syllables topples the poetic with its exquisite cluster of diverse and pleasingly smooth sounds: *o*-cher, *bur*-nt, *um*-ber, *Mars yel-low, si-en-na, viri*-dian, i-*vory bla*-ck, *rose ma*-dder. Soon it becomes apparent that the sentence is not about the description of *feces,* but about the *description* of feces. In other words, it is a sentence about sentences, about writing, about creating art, just as the story as a whole, where the poetic of the fairy-tale genre slips on the prosaic of corpse piles, drug addicts shooting up in doorways, endlessly unfulfilled desire, is about the artist's climb toward a transcendental signified and the final realization that reaching such an absolute is never "plausible, not at all, not for a moment."

A more pronounced pratfall occurs in **"Alice,"** the internal record of an obstetrician's longing for his best friend's wife: "I want to fornicate with Alice but it is a doomed project fornicating with Alice there are obstacles impediments preclusions estoppels I will exhaust them for you what a gas cruel deprivements SECTION SEVEN moral ambiguities SECTION NINETEEN Alice's thighs are like SECTION TWENTY-ONE." This is a Beckettian "sentence," reminiscent of those in *How It Is*—and Barthelme is always nodding in the Irishman's direction—a clump of words whose pacing is jagged and clunky. Because of its lack of punctuation, it is in its very structure a sentence prone to trip over its own feet, "a doomed project." On top of this, it destroys any momentum it may have gained by switching universes of discourse three-fourths of the way through. Words like "fornicate," "project," "impediments," "preclusions," and "estoppels" are from the linguistic field of law. They possess an exact and unemotional charge. But as the sentence turns into the homestretch, it hits a linguistic banana peel, a unit from another universe. "What a gas" overthrows the authority of the first three-fourths of the sentence and sends it into a messy skid where it does a comic softshoe between the language of desire and legalese: "cruel" / "deprivements"; "Alice's thighs are like" / "SECTION TWENTY-ONE." Incongruity wells up as the dogma of the litigious factual tone—another kind of absolutism—skids on the perplexity of longing.

The same sort of interplay takes place at the level of paragraph and even passage, as in the following from *The Dead Father:*

> The Dead Father was slaying, in a grove of music and musicians. First he slew a harpist and then a performer upon the serpent and also a banger upon the rattle and also a blower of the Persian trumpet and one upon the Indian trumpet and one upon the Hebrew trumpet and one upon the Roman trumpet and one upon the Chinese trumpet of copper-covered wood. . . . and during a rest period he slew four buzzers and a shawmist and one blower upon the water jar. . . . and then whanging his sword this way and that the Dead Father slew a cittern plucker . . . and two score of finger cymbal clinkers . . . and a sansa pusher and a manipulator of the guilded ball.
>
> The Dead Father resting with his two hands on the hilt of his sword, which was planted in the red and steaming earth.
>
> My anger, he said proudly.
>
> Then the Dead Father sheathing his sword pulled from his trousers his ancient prick and pissed upon the dead artists, severally and together, to the best of his ability—four minutes, or one pint.

At the outset the tone of the passage is biblical. The repetition of the "he slew" and "upon the" formula echoes the universe of epic catalogues. "Hilt of his sword," "planted in the red and steaming earth," "my anger, he said," "sheathing his sword," and "severally and together" all cue the reader to expect more elevated language of heroic legend whose center is a figure of imposing stature. But long before the end of the first passage a hint ("whanging," "clinkers") appears that the conventional contract between reader and writer may be tenuous at best. And, of course, verbal slapstick sounds through loud and clear with the introduction of "prick," "pissed," and "four minutes, or one pint"—all from the universe of contemporary slang. The verbal planes shift, teeter, and tumble. Just as one of the impulses of the text as a whole is to subvert traditional notions of the quest and romance by implanting them with anachronisms, characters that are difficult to distinguish, structures from painting, theater, cartoons, and so forth, the language of the text subverts traditional notions of the quest and romance by implanting them with a plethora of lexical fields that refuse the gravity of such traditional ideal visions. The only real quest here seems to be for different forms of linguistic frolic, different ways of making language career off the cliff.

A second instance of how this slapstick of language works at the level of passage comes from **"A Shower of Gold"** (*Sixty Stories*), the story of Peterson, a sculptor who lives in a hyper-educated age and who decides to go on a television program called "Who Am I?" to earn some extra money. Here his barber and lay analyst, Kitchen, talks about Peterson's relationship to the President, who has just burst into the sculptor's apartment and beaten him up:

> "It's essentially a kind of I-Thou relationship, if you know what I mean. You got to handle it with full awareness of its implications. In the end one experiences only oneself, Nietzsche said. When you're angry with the President, what you experience is self-as-angry-with-the-President. When things are okay between you and him, what you experience is self-as-swinging-with-the-President. Well and good. But . . . you want the relationship to be such that what you experience is the-President-as-swinging-with-you. You want his reality, get it? So that you can break out of the hell of solipsism. How about a little more off the sides?"

Peterson's is the story about how television has become *the* contemporary art form—a form that slams us with thousands of information bits every evening, all popularized and anesthetized, so that in the end our consciousness is shaped by them. In this way, the above passage becomes a microcosm of the text. A number of lexical fields struggle and stumble over each other: psychology ("handle it," "full awareness of the implications"), philosophy ("I-Thou relationship," "one experiences only oneself," "hell of solipsism"), breezy hip American ("a kind of," "if you know what I mean," "you got to," "things are okay," "self-as-swinging-with-the-President," "well and good"), and even the language of barbershops ("a little more off the sides"). Freud, Buber, Sartre, and Nietzsche slide on the banana peel of a hip haircutter. The languages of psychology and philosophy are reduced to the level of psychobabble of the jazz musician and the barber (or is it the other way around?).

Both of Barthelme's novels, **Snow White** and **The Dead Father,** generate the same kind of discursive clash. Only this time it not only occurs at the strata of sentence and passage, but at that of the text as a whole. Both projects are collage novels, texts constructed as fragments. And the essence of fragmentary form is mutilation—a sign of impossibility, jammed expectations, narrative incongruity. And mutilation is the essence of the postmodern, a mode of consciousness whose basic impulse is to dismantle and deconstruct. For this reason, it is interesting to note that Barthelme, like Kafka, Borges, Robbe-Grillet, Cortázar, and a great number of other postmodern writers, finds it inconceivable to produce extended unified fictions that through their structure try to persuade us that our lives are parts of an interlocking, beautifully sculpted whole. Kafka, in many ways the father of what has come to be called the postmodern, could not complete any of the novels he began. Borges turns out short stories exclusively. The scant length of Robbe-Grillet's works is achieved only through frequent repetition of a few scenes. Cortázar writes a book called *Hopscotch* whose small parts one can literally shuffle around as one chooses. And Barthelme fashions short short "stories" and defaced "novels."

In **Snow White** the reader comes upon a multitude of lexical fields bumbling into each other. The discursive universes of social science, philosophy, business, technology, politics, academics, and advertising misstep on those of comic books, television cartoons, hip lingo, film, songs, and fairy-tales. And in addition to most of these, **The Dead Father** includes those from medicine, engineering, the thesaurus, the Bible, cliché, the logician, mathematics, Lucky's speech in *Waiting for Godot,* romance, epic, and the "how-to" manual. Just as Snow White *à la* Barthelme finds it impossible to devise a steady and coherent identity for herself since for her existence is an uninterpretable and inadequate script, so the text finds it impossible to commit to a steady and coherent genre or language. The same is true of the Dead Father who has so many identities that in the end he has none. He is both alive and dead, both mythic and comic, an omnipresent authority and a dismembered god, omnipotent and finally impotent, Orpheus, Zeus, Prometheus, Oedipus, Lear, the Fisher King, and on and on. Again, his personality is that of the text itself; both struggle for a pure literary identity only to be bulldozed into rubble.

Such examples serve to raise the next question: so what? What does the presence of all this discursive slapstick *do* in the projects we have been examining? First, it cuts language loose from its moorings. Words themselves fall under erasure. This marks the moment of radical skepticism in Western culture that Jacques Derrida points to when language itself is "invaded by the universal problematic; that [moment] in which, in absence of a center or origin, everything became discourse. . . . when everything became a system where the central signified, the original or transcendental signified, is never absolutely present outside a system of differences. The absence of the transcendental signified extends the domain and interplay of signification *ad infinitum.*" In other words, language turns relative. Unfixed, it drifts among a multiplicity of "meanings." Any attempt at a stable linguistic "significance" decomposes into an infinite freeplay that refuses truth. Barthelme's pieces realize, as does the narrator of **"Me and Miss Mandible,"** that "signs are signs, and some of them are lies". And since one does not know which are not lies, it follows that, as Peterson in **"A Shower of Gold"** knows, "possibilities . . . proliferate and escalate all around us." Hence the reader is asked to become partial prevaricator of the texts he reads, asked to frolic in a freeplay where, as Snow White knows, "my nourishment is refined from the ongoing circus of the mind

in motion. Give me the odd linguistic trip, stutter and fall, and I will be content."

Moreover, the existence of discursive slapstick in the texts does not only interrogate our notions of language. It also interrogates that to which the words try to point—our culture. With respect to this Leonard Lutwack in his discussion of the form of the novel [in "Mixed and Uniform Prose Styles in the Novel," in *Theory of the Novel*] distinguishes between two modes of presentation in fiction: uniform style and mixed style. Texts employing the former—Lutwack cites *Pamela* and *The Ambassadors* as examples—signal the presence of a writer's conviction (after all, our narrative strategies always register our metaphysical strategies) about a single, unambiguous coherent view of reality. Lutwack writes: "A uniform style is assimilative in that it helps to create under a single aspect of language a single vision of the multiplicity of reality; it is a bond between author and reader, insuring that no different adjustment to language and viewpoint will be demanded from the reader than that established at the outset." On the other hand, texts that employ a mixed style—*Moby Dick, Tristram Shandy, Gravity's Rainbow,* and Barthelme's pieces, for instance—signal the presence of a writer's *lack* of conviction about a single, unambiguous, coherent view of reality. Indeed, it may signal a writer who *revels* in refusing a compensatory and stable vision. It may revel in multiplicity. Again, Lutwack: "A mixture of styles has the effect of making the reader pass through a succession of contradictory and ambiguous attitudes; it offers no sure stylistic norm by which the reader may orient himself permanently to the fiction and to the point of view of the author." In other words, not only the vocabularies but the value systems they signify are shown to be both viable and arbitrary. The presentation of mixed-style projects—particularly those where the mix occurs at the level of the sentence—thereby becomes a mode of decenterment, demystification, detotalization, delegitimation.

By employing it, Barthelme enters into the mode of consciousness that Nabokov, Pynchon, Beckett, and other postmodern writers whose projects refuse centrism, total intelligibility, closure, and absolute "significance" inhabit; theirs is an impulse to go around "deconstructing dreams like nobody's business". They represent, on the one hand, the negative drive toward disruptions of human systems, of Cartesian reason, of humanist art and all it exemplifies. They are suspicious of our belief in the shared speech, the shared values and the shared perception that, we would like to believe, form our culture, but which are in fact fictions that exist, as the narrator of **"Me and Miss Mandible"** points out, only as part of the "debris of our civilization" and the "vast junkyard" of our planet. At the same time, however, and equally if paradoxically as important, they represent a positive drive that disorients the law of mimesis, affirms touchingly, wittily, and wonderfully the power of the human imagination, and leaves us in a state of eternal weightlessness where nothing will ever be in its final place.

Caryn James (review date 25 October 1987)

SOURCE: A review of *Forty Stories,* in *The New York Times Book Review,* October 25, 1987, pp. 14-15.

[*In the following review, James offers a positive appraisal of* Forty Stories.]

In one of the best, most typical Donald Barthelme stories, a show is staged in an abandoned *palazzo.* Among descriptions of performing grave robbers, tax evaders and trapeze artists, one sentence jumps out like a crucial clue to this volume of **Forty Stories.** "Some things appear to be wonders in the beginning, but when you become familiar with them, are not wonderful at all," worries the narrator of **"The Flight of Pigeons From the Palace."** Versions of that fear may haunt the reader of this selection from nearly 20 years as well: How will Mr. Barthelme's iconoclastic stories hold up after he has shattered the icons of character and plot? Will reading these now-familiar, fantastic tales resemble an adult's visit to the circus, where the magician's tricks are far less wondrous than they once seemed?

The comforting rediscovery to be found in **Forty Stories** is that Mr. Barthelme was always more than a first-rate circus performer. Even in stories from the 1970's (more than half of this collection), he is not content to stand on his head so we can see the world differently. His funny, ludicrous tales follow the emotional logic of a dream, and as he tells them no slice-of-life could seem more substantial. St. Anthony moves to a middle-class suburb; a genius uses "a green Sears toolbox" as a briefcase. In daylight, on the printed page, these cockeyed scenarios evoke nervous laughter, for dreams too often reveal the distilled, uncensored truth. Gossips say St. Anthony put his hand on a young woman's knee. The genius "is a drunk."

In creating these strange conjunction Mr. Barthelme does not play nonsense games, and does not force his imagination to mold neat little symbols. His stories have substance because he locates his characters—from unnamed narrators, to a generic "play-wright" to Paul Klee and Goethe—in the precise place where the weight of history intrudes on the present where desire meets imagination. That is the spot where they live, and often it is a place Mr. Barthelme must invent. He is especially fond of made-up museums.

In **"The Educational Experience,"** students are guided through exhibits that include a bird's lung and a gas turbine. The teacher-narrator describes the tour: "The students looked

at each other with secret smiles. Rotten of them to conceal their feelings . . . The invitation to indulge in emotion at the expense of rational analysis already constitutes a political act, as per our phoncon of 11/9/75. We came to a booth where the lessons of 1914 were taught. There were some wild strawberries there, in the pool of blood, and someone was playing the piano, softly, in the pool of blood, and the Fisher King was fishing, hopelessly, in the pool of blood. The pool is a popular meeting place for younger people but we aren't younger anymore so we hurried on." As the narrator's brusqueness swiftly gives way to lyricism, we are pulled toward the forbidden, politicized emotion.

"At the Tolstoy Museum," certainly among Mr. Barthelme's finest stories, is a comic and touching romp that starts by emphasizing the sentimental pull of the past and ends by stating the confusion of the present. "At the Tolstoy Museum we sat and wept. Paper streamers came out of our eyes," the narrator begins. "The guards at the Tolstoy Museum carry buckets in which there are stacks of clean white pocket handkerchiefs. . . . Even the bare title of a Tolstoy work, with its burden of love, can induce weeping." Mr. Barthelme succesfully weaves illustrations into the story; we can see this museum. Identical portraits of Tolstoy look out at us from facing pages, but in one of them a tiny figure of Napolean stares up at the giant face. A woman faints in a man's arms in an architectural drawing of "The Anna-Vronsky Pavilion." Still, the "burden of love" Tolstoy's words carry is a thorny problem, and at the story's end the narrator isn't sure whether he's glad Tolstoy existed or not.

Mr. Barthelme's most resonant stories end with such unresolved questions, or with images that will not allow themselves to be explained. **"Visitors"** is a rather conventional work about a man named Bishop. He stays up all night looking after his daughter, who is ill, and thinking about a failed love affair. Suddenly, the story ends with an image that distills questions about how we love and get on with life. From his window, Bishop often sees the "two old ladies" in the apartment behind his "having breakfast by candlelight. He can never figure out whether they are terminally romantic or whether, rather, they're trying to save electricity." Who are these women? What are they to one another, and how do they live? They are haunting figures precisely because Mr. Barthelme will not say; but like his strongest characters they live in a moment of heightened reality, containing the extremes of endless romance and penny-pinching practicality (both of which are probably terminal).

The creeping realism in **"Visitors"** marks it as a work from the 80's. It is, in fact, one of seven stories taken from Mr. Barthelme's 1983 volume, **Overnight to Many Distant Cities.** Nine more of the **Forty Stories** have not appeared in collections. Most of these fairly recent works are of a piece with Mr. Barthelme's 1986 novel, **Paradise,** which anchors its hero's sexual fantasies in the fairly mundane reality of his family life and work. **"Construction"** is a deft meditation by a businessman confused about "the long-range plan," and the mystery of a colleague named Helen; next to Mr. Barthelme's at his ambiguous best, though, the story feels too pat when the narrator comes out and asks, "Why am I doing this?" The most memorable recent work is still the least realistic. **"Bluebeard,"** for example, is a gleeful retelling of the legend. Set in 1910, the story piles reversal on reversal until the tormented wife enters Bluebeard's secret chamber and faints "with rage and disappointment" at the silly vision—it involves Coco Chanel—only Donald Barthelme could have imagined.

Collections such as **Forty Stories** are, of course, uneven by nature. Many of the best Barthelme works were included in **Sixty Stories** in 1981. And a few tales in the new volume show Mr. Barthelme at his most glib. **"Porcupines at the University"** is a mere cartoon, dated by its references to the Sonny and Cher show. By contrast, though, it reveals how very well almost all these stories have aged.

Forty Stories also suggests why Mr. Barthelme cannot be easily classified. His playful fiction does not deeply resemble the extravagant work of John Barth or Robert Coover; at his most realistic, he's a far cry from John Updike; and he is much more than the fractured flip side of minimalism. Donald Barthelme is the author who discovers small, bizarre conjunctions that make enormous sense and offers them in a voice that remains uniquely rewarding and often sounds ageless.

Patrick O'Donnell (essay date 1992)

SOURCE: "Living Arrangements: On Donald Barthelme's *Paradise*," in *Critical Essays on Donald Barthelme*, edited by Richard F. Patteson, G. K. Hall, 1992, pp. 208-16.

[*In the following essay, O'Donnell illustrates how Barthelme comments on various aspects of contemporary life and society in* Paradise.]

> Shall our blood fail? Or shall it come to be
> The blood of paradise? And shall the earth
> Seem all of paradise that we shall know?
> The sky will be much friendlier then than now,
> A part of labor and a part of pain,
> And next in glory to enduring love,
> Not this dividing and indifferent blue.
>
> —Wallace Stevens, "Sunday Morning"

Donald Barthelme's third novel, *Paradise* (1986), is, perhaps, his least-read and most disregarded work. Poorly received by many reviewers, it appears to be Barthelme's failed attempt to write in a more traditional novelistic mode. Even at that, its status as a novel remains questionable, as it is, conceivably, a patchwork of more recognizably Barthelmean short fictions (such as the exchanges between the protagonist, Simon, and his physician scattered throughout *Paradise,* and collated in the story **"Basil from Her Garden"** previously published in the *New Yorker*) cobbled together to form a series of interrelated vignettes of uneven intensity and quality. In *Paradise,* there is, ostensibly, a more conventional narrative situation than can be found in *Snow White* or *The Dead Father.* Here, those familiar bourgeois subjects of the traditional novel—middle age, adultery, marriage, and domesticity—are at issue, and the autobiographical elements of the novel are foregrounded (Simon is a Philadelphia architect; he has experienced a failed marriage and is recently divorced; he is taking a sabbatical from marriage in Manhattan) while its fabulistic qualities are largely confined to Simon's dreams. And while the major events of *Paradise* may arise from the projection of a male fantasy (three beautiful young women, looking for a temporary residence, move in with Simon for eight months), there is such a lack of causality in this "utopian" vision as to intimate the careless, unmotivated, ironic "realism" we associate with Woody Allen's representations of contemporary heterosexuality. The "paradise" of Simon's *ménage à quatre* is as ordinary as one could imagine, as the novel consists largely of whimsical, everyday conversations between Simon and the women, scenes of cooking, concerns about housecleaning, and so on. Yet, despite its somewhat unexpected nature, this ignored novel reflects upon certain formal issues that rejoin Barthelme's important, characteristic concern with "living arrangements" in postmodern society—a concern that reveals his profound skepticism regarding the permanence of human relations matched by a desire for order and continuity in an environment where order and repression are equals.

As these preliminary comments indicate, *Paradise* may be regarded as a compilation of Barthelmean forms (the "Q and A" dialogue, the minimally absurdist dream, vignettes of domesticity cast within the fantasy framework of one man living with three beautiful women) that problematizes "form" itself, converting it into one of the novel's primary subjects. Charles Molesworth has commented that the "typical" Barthelme protagonist "values form over substance, but he is also often defeated by his inability to deal properly with form"; this condition, Molesworth argues, arises from a "longing for the fugitive" that signals "an existential ethos, an awareness that all human desire for permanency remains condemned to frustration, and that to institutionalize means to destroy, though *not* to do so is to face the same result."

In *Paradise,* Simon's trade, on the one hand, and his current "lifestyle," on the other—which involves both the extrapolation and undermining of male fantasy—places him solidly in the middle of the dilemma Molesworth describes. As an architect, Simon values structure, repetition, symmetry, yet as "a tattered coat upon a stick," he recognizes that the preservation of form which architecture represents is analogous to the mummification of life, to death. Trapped within an entropic body ("Getting old, Simon. Not so limber, dear friend, time for the bone factory? The little blue van. Your hands are covered with pepperoni. Your knees predict your face. Your back stabs you, on the left side, twice a day. The belly's been discussed. The soul's shrinking to a microdot. We're ordering your rocking chair, size 42"), Simon has "settled for being a competent, sometimes inventive architect with a tragic sense of brick." For him, the resistant medium of his art assumes tragic form because of its permanence—a form that will "stand" (unlike the body) the mock the transitoriness of human corporeality, but one that does not "live."

The paradox of his occupation bespeaks the paradox of his life, where the cyclical and formal features of existence—often perceived as the guarantors of continuance and renewal—have become, in their "institutionalization,"the signs of paralysis and advancing death. Marriage, Simon says, is an "architectural problem": "If we could live in separate houses, and visit each other when we felt particularly gay," as if gaiety could be "housed" in any manner. Jazz, his favorite kind of music and, here, as throughout Barthelme's fiction, representing the grafting of improvisation and spontaneity to mercurial form, is important to Simon both because of its rich singularity (in individual musicians) and its historicity or genealogy as a national resource:

> He's listening to one of his three radios, this one a brutish black Proton with an outboard second speaker. The announcer is talking about drummers. "Cozy Cole comes straight out of Chick Webb," he says. Simon nods in agreement. "Big Sid Catlett. Zutty Singleton, Dave Tough. To go even further back, Baby Dodds. All this before we get to Krupa and Buddy Rich." Simon taxes his memory in an attempt to extract from it the names of ten additional drummers. Louis Bellson. Shelly Manne. Panama Francis. Jo Jones, of course. Kenny Clarke. Elvin Jones. Barrett Deems. Mel Lewis, Charlie Persip. Joe Morello. Next, twenty bass players. Our nation is rich in talent, he thinks.

Simon notes that individual architectural styles, when periodized, can be easily incorporated into larger cycles of fashion and design: "[The glass block] had been popular in the 30s, considered a design cliché in the 40s, 50s, 60s, and 70s, and presented itself again in the 80s, fresh as new

dung." In each of these instances—marriage, jazz, architecture—Simon maintains an ironic attachment to form or structure—house, genealogy, architectural material. He seems to recognize that the phenomenological "content" of these forms—the gaiety of human relationships; the noise of jazz; the transparency of glass blocks—can only be manifested through some kind of formal arrangement or contextualization, but at the same time, he detests their reduction into mere cliché or formula when they are institutionalized, historicized. In the end, it may be "history" that Simon implicitly fears, or at least that sense of history that reveals itself when one has lived long enough: history as mere repetition where, in the domestic sphere (*the* realm of Barthelme's fiction), routine patterns of habit, form, and convention are all that survive in the long run. Yet, to reassert the paradox, this is a kind of history that Simon also desires, as his avid pursuit of jazz genealogies and naming would suggest—a history of successions, styles, and orders that can be labeled, variously, as "paternal" or "authorial."

In some sense, *Paradise* is the portrayal of a projected alternative to this paradoxical condition: it is fantasy given shape and substance, but the "materials" of the male fantasy that *Paradise* engages suborns its teleology, which includes bringing desire into the realm of domestic order and, thereby, potentially ensuring its continuance and renewal. For Simon and the three women he temporarily lives with (Anne, Dore, and Veronica), there is a kind of rough symmetry to the network of relationships they create as they casually establish the domestic rituals of cooking, conversing, intercourse. In the novel, the trio of women take on a number of stereotyped roles, in a sense, tripling the quantity of the fantasy and "perfecting" it: three mistresses, three graces, three wives. At first, to Simon, it seems (as the women put it to him) like "hog heaven," or the best of both worlds: both guilt-free sexuality and the opportunity to experience the multiplicity of desire, and the calming ordinariness of household order. Indeed, the melding of the libidinous and the symmetrical, desire and domesticity, is so pervasive in Simon's view that his descriptions of his roommates' eroticism often take on, in their variety, the qualities of repetition and banality we usually associate with the quotidian, not the exotic: "White underwear with golden skin. Acres and acres of it. Was it golden? Conventionally described as golden. The color of white birch stained with polyurethane.... Dressed women, half-dressed women, quarter-dressed women"; or,

> Dore is brusque upon awakening, Anne cheerful as a zinnia. Veronica frequently comes to the breakfast table ... pale with enthusiasm, for *Lobengrin* or oyster mushrooms or Pierre Trudeau. They're so lovely that his head whips around when one of them enters the room, exactly in the way one notices a strange woman in the crowd and can't avoid, can't

physically avoid, loud and outrageous staring. My senses are being systematically dérégled, he thinks, forgive me, Rimbaud. Dore is relatively tall, Anne not so tall (but they are all tall), Veronica again the middle term. Breasts waver and dip and sway from side to side under t-shirts with messages so much of the moment that Simon doesn't understand a tenth of them . . .

In this portrayal of breakfast in paradise, the erotic is made symmetrical and sensuality made routine, banal, as contemporary commonplaces—incomprehensible to Simon because of "the generation gap"—mark for him both the women's voluptuousness and his own advancing age.

This conception of a male utopia, in essence, exists as a recapitulation of those orders and anxieties that, implicitly, and however temporarily, should have been transcended and subsumed in the figuration of paradise. When a major component of this male erotic fantasy—the multiple combinations and exchangeability of female sexual partners—is viewed for its repetitions and symmetries, when sensuality reminds Simon of his own anachronicity, then "paradise" must be regarded as a desire for order over desire, even if that architecture has the consequence of "instituting" fantasy. In other terms, the true end of male desire which *Paradise* reveals is not the entropy of libidinous expression but design, pattern, "author"-ity.

The "Q and A" conversations between Simon and his physician—conversations between men largely focused on the female subjects of "paradise"—and Simon's fairly ordinary dreams, reveal most clearly the lineaments of his provisional Eden. Alan Wilde (reading "Basil From Her Garden") has characterized the conversations, where "Q" is the physician and "A" is Simon, in this manner: "For Q transcendence implies an ordering of the world (as well as a removal from it), a ridding it . . . of everything that makes life uneven, unpredictable and recalcitrant, whereas for A it is a matter of coming to terms with guilt, anxiety, and thoughts of inadequacy *in the world,* as it is and as it offers itself to consciousness." However true this may be of the positions taken by Q and A at a certain point in the dialogue, as often happens in Barthelme's Socratic conversations, the interlocutors often exchange positions so that the different views exchanged by Simon and the physician, taken together, articulate the paradox of Simon's dilemma, which, again, is the authorial desire to give form to fantasy or to the world "as it offers itself to consciousness."

In their penultimate conversation, Q spins out a fantasy in which he imagines he is "in Pest Control." He visualizes himself in an immaculate outfit meticulously fumigating the house of "a young wife in jeans and a pink flannel shirt worn outside the jeans." In explicit detail, he imagines the orderly furnishings of the house and his role in maintaining its cleanliness. Finally, "the young wife escorts me to the door, and, in parting, pins a silver medal on my chest and kisses me on both cheeks. Pest Control!" If, as is often the case in Barthelme's stories, Q and A can be seen to make up the self-questioning aspects of a single identity—"a central speaking voice or subject, with a weak sense of identity, constantly seeking refuge in fantasy, word-play or self-pity, endlessly playing games of delusion which barely conceal a terror of failure, loss and disintegration"—then Q's Pest Control fantasy can stand as an extreme version of Simon's obsession with domestic order, even in the midst of paradise. What constitutes this order? Fastidious attention to detail and the arrangement of physical objects in the world ("I do the study, spraying behing the master's heavy desk on which there is an open copy of the *Columbia Encyclopedia,* he's been looking up the Seven Years War, 1756-63, yellow highlighting there, and behind the fortyfive inch RCA television"); ritualistic movement through space ("I point the nozzle of the hose at the baseboards and begin to spray. I spray alongside the refrigerator, alongside the gas range, under the sink, and behind the kitchen table. Next, I move to the bathrooms, pumping and spraying"); logical supposition based upon empirical evidence ("Finally I spray the laundry room with its big white washer and dryer, and behind the folding table stacked with sheets and towels already folded. Who folds? I surmise that she folds. Unless one of the older children, pressed into service. In my experience they are unlikely to fold. Maybe the au pair"). Simon longs for the Newtonian world of the eighteenth-century rationalist, but as this vision and his dreams suggest, this is an order which both "includes" a barely repressed version of a clichéd male sexual fantasy ("pumping and spraying"; "a young wife"), along with the implicit forcefulness or violence that seems to inevitably accompany it ("The master bedroom requires just touches, like perfume behind the ears, short bursts in her closet which must avoid the two dozen pair of shoes there and in his closet which contains six to eight long guns in canvas cases").

In his dreams, Simon reiterates the dialectic of control and disorder, cleanliness and pestilence in situations where the "irrationality" of personal assault and the outbreak of violence form continual threats to the installments of dream and dreamer. After the women have left him (the novel is cast in the mode of recollection), Simon begins to dream

with new intensity. He dreamed that he was a slave on a leper island, required to clean the latrines and pile up dirty-white shell for the roads, wheelbarrow after wheelbarrowful, then rake the shell smooth and jump up and down on it until it was packed solid. The lepers did not allow him to wear shoes, only white athletic socks, and he had a difficult time finding a pair that matched. The leper, a man who seemed to be named Al, embraced him repeatedly and tried repeatedly to spit in his mouth.

In this ironic "nightmare," Simon is a comic Sisyphus condemned to sanitize (make sane?) a world of physical decrepitude, and to be continually confronted with the passion and violence of that world's chief embodiment. Simon confesses to Q that he seems to be suffering from an abnormally distended succession of nightmares, most of which seems to involve his inability to put his clothes on correctly or (as in the dream of the leper island) to find his socks. He often has more than one dream a night and recalls them as seemingly unrelated scenes or vignettes: "In the first dream he was grabbed by three or four cops for firing a chrome .45 randomly in the street. . . . In the second dream he awoke sitting on a lounge in a hotel lobby wearing pants and shoes but bare-chested. . . . He couldn't find a shirt. His mother came out of a closet and asked him to be a little quieter." In such dreams, where maintaining control is the central issue, Simon negotiates the "logic" of the anxieties that beset him, which is also the logic he uses in projecting "paradise." Living in a world where random or planned violence threatens to burst forth, and where Simon fears his bodily erosion, literally, loss of command over bodily functions (intimated by dreams about his inability to clothe himself), the solution—to project a daytime vision where domestic order and eros commingle, the wild energy and gaiety of the latter harnessed to the comforting rituals and institutions of the former—seems self-evident.

Yet what Simon's seemingly casual, unplanned living arrangements exclude or repress, and what his dreams clearly suggest is that the ends of "paradise"—the forestalling of the dissolution of (male) corporeal identity, the maintenance of rational order and control over one's "space," the fantasy of eternal potency—include the means of violence. Like all of Barthelme's fiction, *Paradise* is humorous, ironic, parodic; yet there is a strong undertow of violence in the novel that gives it a more "sociological" dimension, especially in its depictions of violence toward or the abuse of women. Dore bears a scar from a knife wound administered by a former husband who cut her in the act of "'explaining himself.'" For unknown reasons, a complete stranger—a Vietnam veteran—walks up to Veronica in a market and slaps her; moreover, Anne reveals to Simon that Veronica "got knocked around a lot as a kind," a series of events Veronica herself typifies: "'He used a rolled up newspaper . . . what you'd use on a dog. Only he put his back into it, when I was twelve and thirteen and fourteen.'" At one point, Simon witnesses two men beating up a female cop. Simon recounts, or projects, other scenes of violence amidst his recollections of paradise: his wife's Caesarean ("The doctor's name was Zernike and he had a pair of large dull-steel forceps inside the birth canal and was grappling for purchase. The instrument looked to Simon, who knew something of the weight and force of

tools, capable of shattering the baby's head in an instant"); his own imagined vulnerability with the women ("Q: These women spread out before you like lotus blossoms. . . . A: More like anthills. Splendid, stinging anthills. . . . Q: The ants are plunging toothpicks into your scrotum, as it were. As they withdraw the toothpicks, little pieces of flesh like shreds of ground beef adhere to the toothpicks. A: Very much like that. How did you know?"). In all of these instances except the last (which is the projection, not the realization of an anxiety) the enforcers or victims of what might be termed "male cultural institutions" are behind the violence: fathers, husbands, ex-soldiers, and doctors seem to be responsible for the inflictions of force upon female subjects in *Paradise.*

Perhaps it might be argued, as Simon implicitly argues to himself, that he offers the three women a safe, if temporary, haven from a violent, hostile "reality"; in return, they offer him erotic renewal and good conversation. But as I have suggested, the very installment of "paradise"—its formation—rests upon the sanitizing or repression of those elements of force, violence, or culturally perceived eroticism that are part of its constitution, and which, fended off, return in dream and recollection. What is forestalled in paradise?

> Simon was a way-station, a bed-and-breakfast, a youth hostel, a staging area, a C-141 with the jumpers of the 82nd Airborne lined up at the door. There was no place in the world for these women that he loved, no good place. They could join the underemployed half-crazed demi-poor, or they could be wives, those were the choices. The universities offered another path but one they were not likely to take. The universities were something Simon believed in (of course! he was a beneficiary) but there was among the women an animus toward the process that would probably never be overcome, not only inpatience but a real loathing, whose source he did not really understand.

These beautiful, tall, "perfect" women are the products of desire, and their choices are limited to marginalization or institutionalization within the very cultural organizations (marriage, the university) that either articulate them as "permanent," domestic objects of desire or, as Simon realizes in the case of the university, are intimately linked to the militarism that is simply the most highly organized form of violence that has threatened them in other male cultural institutions: "Simon had opposed the Vietnam War in all possible ways short of self-immolation but could not deny that it was a war constructed by people who had labored through *Psychology I, II, III,* and *IV* and *Main Currents of Western Thought.*" Simon's paradise is no haven at all from this bleak future for, as we have seen, it reproduces the women as the locus of cultural order, on the one hand, and organized eroticism (i.e., prostitution) on the other. Nor is it a haven for

Simon himself, however joyful and gay its separate banalized moments, since the events that take place within paradise serve as a constant reminder of his mortality, the artificial (domesticated, structured) and, thus, impermanent form of his own identity. As in the case with architecture, Simon's paradise is ultimately an agonized quest for permanent form using imperfect, time-bound, culture-bound and culturally constrained materials.

In *Paradise,* Barthelme reveals most fully his acknowledgment that the modernist aesthetic quest for form matched with the attempt to maintain the identity of the artist is inflected with certain social and political consequences that comply with prevailing orders. Indeed, much of his fiction is an attempt to break down or break up the connection between form and identity that conservative modernism assumed to be innocent of these consequences. In *Paradise,* we see that he confronts the two dominating impulses of the modern (and, since he is careful to identify it in terms of gender in this novel, male) psyche: rational singularity of form and erotic multiplicity. These impulses can only be "managed" through banalization or force threatening to become violent, specifically in *Paradise,* violence toward women largely promulgated through social agency. Here, the preservation of male identity or the defense against anxieties about its dissolution seems to demand the continuance of the status quo disguised as erotic festival, vacation from marriage. In *Paradise,* what might be nostalgically termed man's individual freedom is played out within the confinements of the institutional orders that dictate both the nature of desire and legitimate its often violent deployments. As Vincent Pecora has argued, the autonomous self in modernist narrative, seeking absolute freedom from all social and cultural orders, ends up reduplicating them as part of "the nature of identity": "the discourse of the autonomous individual . . . is historically made possible by the reifications of consciousness produced in a capitalist market economy; but the unerring tendency of that discourse, even in its self-critical attempts to break through the mystifications circumscribing it, is a reproduction within consciousness of the division and organization of economic life that only increases its susceptibility to manipulation and control by monopolistic or authoritarian administration." Thus Simon, in his recounting, naively reinstitutes domestic order in the household even as he indulges in the fantasy of sexual freedom in a realm dominated, if only numerically, by women. As much as Barthelme's *oeuvre* resists and critiques this state of affairs, it also—in its fascination with material productions, its concern with the breakdown or continuance of identity, and its paradoxically continuous use and deconstruction of received generic forms—partakes of it.

Paradise, then, stands as Barthelme's most extensive reflection on the state of art and the artist in postmodern culture. It is a book about mortality: not one that, as do the lines from

Stevens' "Sunday Morning," celebrate the permanent impermanence of life as our only parousia, but one that limns the conditions of our mortal existence as historical beings. The artist seeks to escape these conditions, but his art remakes them, even, and especially, when it comes to utopias. Barthelme's distinctly antiutopian sky is not indifferent—for that would be to attribute to it something beyond ourselves—but it is a dividing blue, in that, for him, what occurs "down here" is of our own doing, the extension of our own desire for order and control. With characteristic irony, he asks in *Paradise,* "but what else could we do, given our models of heaven"?

James Marcus (review date 6 December 1992)

SOURCE: A review of *The Teachings of Don B.,* in *The New York Times Book Review,* December 6, 1992, p. 30.

[*In the following review, Marcus offers a commendatory assessment of* The Teachings of Don B.]

At a glance, this collection of material by Donald Barthelme—who died of cancer in 1989, at the age of 58—might be mistaken for a bit of valedictory barrel-scraping. In fact, it's nothing of the kind.

Culled from a variety of sources, including his signed and unsigned contributions to *The New Yorker,* the pieces in *The Teachings of Don B."* (most of which have never' previously been collected) offer a superb cross section of what Thomas Pynchon, in his live introduction, calls *Barthelmismo.* The author's straight parodies—of Michelangelo Antonioni, or Carlos Castaneda or Bret Easton Ellis—are expert and amusing. Yet Barthelme's art was pre-eminently one of surprises, darting from satire to lyricism to poker-faced banality in a single paragraph, and the most effective pieces here keep jumping genres in midstream.

"The Angry Young Man," for instance, begins as a satirical profile of the British Literary Rebel, late 1950's model, complete with "brown corduroy pants, black turtleneck sweater, work shoes, coonskin cap, glass of porter in right hand." Soon, however, it segues into a meditation on the ineffectual nature of anger itself: "As your gaze is fixed upon something immediately in front of you—the object of your anger, for example—history makes a slight, almost imperceptible slither: or shudder, in a direction of its own choice. The distinguishing mark of this direction is that it is not the one that you had anticipated." As in much of Barthelme's work, comedy is undergirded with resignation.

A similar quick change takes place in **"Swallowing."** The piece opens with a denunciation of American politics in the early 1970's: "The American people have swallowed a lot in the last four years. . . . We have swallowed electric bugs, laundered money, quite a handsome amount of grain moving about in mysterious ways, a war more shameful than can be imagined, much else."

After a paragraph, however, Barthelme swerves into a shaggy dog story about a 4,000-pound Gouda cheese at the New York World's Fair. Recounting a jurisdictional squabble over who would dispose of "the enormous *fromage*," the author provides a delicious parody of political rhetoric. And surely no one has hit upon a more peculiar objective correlative for our national indigestion of the Watergate era.

But here and there, despite the efforts of the book's editor, Kim Herzinger, Barthelme nods. In the three plays that make up the last 100 pages of the book (**"The Friends of the Family," "The Conservatory"** and **"Snow White"**), his quicksilver shifts in tone and diction can sometimes fall flat. Taken as a whole, though, *The Teachings of Don B.* is a small education in laughter, melancholy and the English language.

Michael Zeitlin (essay date Summer 1993)

SOURCE: "Father-Murder and Father-Rescue: The Post-Freudian Allegories of Donald Barthelme," in *Contemporary Literature*, Vol. 34, No. 2, Summer, 1993, pp. 182-203.

[*In the following essay, Zeitlin studies the role of psychoanalysis and Freudian theory in Barthelme's works.*]

Here is another absurd dream about a dead father.

Sigmund Freud, *The Interpretation of Dreams*

For a good many of his critics Donald Barthelme represents American postmodernism at its formally self-conscious and experimental best. There is no reason to deny Barthelme's brilliance as an inventor of forms, but I believe we insufficiently appreciate the nature and scope of his achievement insofar as we continue to stress technique over substance, structure over content, signifiers over signifieds, language "itself" over the materials—texts, ideas, realities—it represents and transforms. In the prevailing discussions of Barthelme the valorization of form and technique entails the virtual annulment of "content" and "meaning" as usable concepts of literary analysis. As Jerome Klinkowitz has provocatively put it recently, in Barthelme "signs (and not meanings) are what are read." An associated and equally widespread critical notion about Barthelme's discourse is that, lacking a central meaning or stable subject, Barthelme's characteristic tale forms itself out of the fragments and junk of our

contemporary civilization—"the refuse of our culture, our post-Gutenberg heap"—whose random components are pasted together in a manner akin to dadaist collage. The meaning of the apparently contingent arrangement of figures, if bewildering in its peculiar manifestation, is all too clear in its overall import: such narrative disorder must be taken as signifying a predominating cultural disorder and hence, in the memorable words of Walter Benjamin, "a crisis in perception itself". Since contemporary existence is bereft of large-scale spiritual and metaphorical coherence, Barthelme's stories appropriately have no traditional beginnings, middles, or ends; they make no conventionally logical transitions between events and, in being irreducible or untotalizable, refrain from giving us a sentimental or fraudulently coherent picture of the world. Hence the foregrounding of Barthelme's technique and his most quoted dictum, "Fragments are the only forms I trust" (**"See the Moon?"**). Or as one early critic explained, "We perceive in fragments, live in fragments, are no doubt dying by fragments; should we not, then, write in fragments, emphasizing thereby the strange disjunctions, the even stranger juxtapositions, that are part of the everyday experience of modern life?"

> **A widespread critical notion about Barthelme's discourse is that, lacking a central meaning or stable subject, Barthelme's characteristic tale forms itself out of the fragments and junk of our contemporary civilization. . . .**
> —*Michael Zeitlin*

Of course we've encountered this kind of argument before, but if in refracting "the immense panorama of futility and anarchy" Barthelme's narratives imply a potent critique of "contemporary history", the characteristic critical gesture turns from assessing the substance of that critique toward valorizing form and experimentation, and so toward celebrating, as Barthelme's greatest achievement, the production of a prodigious readerly vertigo. In the words of Maurice Couturier and Régis Durand, "All [of Barthelme's linguistic] devices stagger our imagination, baffle our intelligence, and eventually induce us to evolve our private interpretation, no matter how extravagant it may be, to escape the tension and embarrassment". Any private interpretation, however, must fall—fortunately, for these critics—into the Slough of Indeterminacy, despite the positivistic aspirations of even the most sophisticated and scientific of semiotic analyses: "the prime lesson that can be drawn from this linguistic analysis, which emulates Barthelme's own research, is that language has a life of its own *which no amount of scientific investigation can ever hope to describe or comprehend*" (Couturier and Durand; emphasis added). That is to say, if Barthelme's "appealing nonsense . . . flouts all our learned discourses [and] cannot be reduced to tame structures," then "indeterminacy," "undecidability," and other celebrated variations on the "endless freeplay of signification" must hold unchallenged sway over the world of Barthelme criticism, dissolving in the ubiquitous metatheme of "writing itself" any interpretive project interested in grasping a further meaning out of the sequence of printed signifiers on the page. As Charles Molesworth has articulated the predominating view of Barthelme's art:

> We can easily enough identify Barthelme as a writer of metafiction . . . as one who writes less obviously about the traditional subjects—love, fame, death— than about the conventions of writing itself.
>
> . . . . .
>
> There is little overt sense that Barthelme wants to engage psychological or social questions of great import in a manner of high seriousness.
>
> . . . . .
>
> For Barthelme the highest success is not if the story strikes us as true, but rather if it shows us how it works.

The overall purpose of my discussion here, then, is to probe for ways of moving beyond the prevailing insistence on "formal questions" as the only ones worth asking about Barthelme's fiction; to see whether we can acknowledge— even celebrate—the "structural function" of the sign without suppressing its power of representing the kinds of social and psychological realities that one encounters in a narrative like *The Dead Father*; and to locate Barthelme's narrative experiments with reference to a literary and cultural context that promises to illuminate the organizational principles inherent in the apparent disorder of his literary surfaces.

I take as one among many possible starting points the following premise: that as a highly self-conscious and sophisticated postmodernist, Donald Barthelme not only knew about Freud but read many of his major texts; that through a process of absorption, assimilation, and transfiguration, psychoanalysis came to take up a central presence in Barthelme's narrative discourse; and that there were important personal as well as artistic reasons (if the distinction is an intelligible one in Barthelme's case) for his interest in psychoanalysis. If the premise is true, then as a strict matter of literary criticism and cultural history, a decent if not detailed familiarity with psychoanalytic texts is indispensable to an understanding of the essential ideas, purposes, and strategies of Barthelme's cardinal narratives. That is to say, one of my

goals in this essay, borrowing the words of Fredric Jameson (and hyperbole aside), is

> to enlarge the conception of the literary text itself, so that its . . . psychoanalytic . . . and social resonances might become audible (and describable) *within* that experience of literary language and aesthetic form to which I remain committed. (The stereotypical characterization of such enlargement as *reductive* remains a never-ending source of hilarity).

To proceed then: In **"Views of My Father Weeping," "Robert Kennedy Saved from Drowning,"** and *The Dead Father,* Barthelme rereads and rewrites some central narratives of classical psychoanalysis as they appear in the writings of Sigmund Freud and his psychoanalyst contemporary, Karl Abraham. In Barthelme, in other words, postmodern must also mean post-Freudian; identifiable "thought structures," "phantasies," "wish-creations," and typical patterns, as they are isolated and defined in the classical psychoanalytic literature, guide Barthelme to the kind of personal and intertextual material with which he works, influence his modes of wit and humor, and frame the narrative problems that generate that remarkable variety of experimental solutions to which the critics have rightly pointed. Appreciating Barthelme's revisionary project opens the way to seeing his fragmentary discourse as less a refraction of postmodern disarray than as an effect of a more or less disguised and intensely polemical dialogue with modernism's foremost "cartographers of the mind" and theorists of the father-son relation—fathers and sons are Barthelme's flood subject, after all.

"Views of My Father Weeping": Barthelme/Freud/Abraham

Jerome Klinkowitz has observantly noted that **"Views of My Father Weeping"** "puts Barthelme straight on the road to *The Dead Father,*" but reading this tale within the context of psychoanalysis it unmistakably draws upon, I reject the notion that with the opening two sentences of the short story Barthelme "starts with a fresh slate in a realm of writerly action never yet inscribed." In one of its major aspects, Barthelme's story is a deliberate fictional recasting of Karl Abraham's classic psychoanalytic essay "Father-Murder and Father-Rescue in the Fantasies of Neurotics" (1922), which is itself a psychoanalytic elaboration of the Oedipus myth as it occurs in Sophocles and then, decisively, in Freud. **"Views of My Father Weeping,"** that is to say, is an intertextual discourse par excellence, announcing its troubled affiliation with Abraham's essay in its opening gambit:

> An aristocrat was riding down the street in his carriage. He ran over my father. . . .
>
> I stood in the square where my father was killed and

asked people passing by if they had seen, or knew of anyone who had seen, the incident. At the same time I felt the effort was wasted. Even if I found the man whose carriage had *done the job,* what would I say to him? "You killed my father." "Yes," the aristocrat would say, "but he ran right in under the legs of the horses. My man tried to stop but it happened too quickly. There was nothing anyone could do." Then perhaps he would offer me a purse full of money.

(emphasis added)

This is a splendidly ironical amplification and reversal of the fantasy (or "wish-creation") as described in Abraham's essay:

> In the fantasy I have in mind the patient imagines he is walking along a street. He unexpectedly sees coming towards him at a terrific pace a carriage in which is sitting the king (or another highly placed personage). He instantly seizes the horses by the reins and brings the carriage to a standstill, thus saving the king from the risk of death.

In *Oedipus the King,* of course, the son kills the father:

> Making my way toward this triple crossroad I began to see a herald, then a brace of colts drawing a wagon, and mounted on the bench . . . a man, just as you've described him, coming face-to-face, and the one in the lead and the old man himself were about to thrust me off the road—brute force—and the one shouldering me aside, the driver, I strike him in anger!—and the old man, watching me coming up along his wheels—he brings down his prod, two prongs straight at my head! I paid him back with interest! Short work, by god—with one blow of the staff in this right hand I knock him out of his high seat, roll him out of the wagon, sprawling head-long—I killed them all—every mother's son!

(ellipsis in original)

In Abraham's report, the son rescues the father; however, Abraham furnishes us with a standard piece of psychoanalytic logic with which to link the two narratives: "Freud pointed out that the tendency to rescue the father is chiefly the expression of an impulse of defiance on the son's part"; and where there is defiance, the way is opened to the most heinous of "unspeakable practices, unnatural acts" (the title, of course, of Barthelme's 1968 short story collection), namely parricide, "the principal and primal crime of humanity as well as of the individual" (Freud, "Dostoevsky and Parricide"). Where in Abraham the father is rescued, that rescue is a screen for a darker impulse which, "inadmissible to consciousness," is disguised and transfigured into its opposite: only thus can it "evade the censorship" and press its way into the light. As a highly charged symbolic "complex" of emotions and ideas, "the rescue," when subjected to the ineluctable hermeneutic impulse of Freudian psychoanalysis, can be made to reveal the original parricidal impulse it screens within itself.

With such standard psychoanalytic logic in mind, let's turn to Barthelme's revision. Here the son (the central subject of the "My" of the title, that is, the narrator, dreamer, witness—let's call him "Oedipus"—who in Abraham's narrative is the prototype of the figure who rushes forth to seize the reins of the runaway horses) suddenly and without explanation becomes the *father* who is run over by "an aristocrat" with whom the son seeks but never achieves rapprochement, or more: as he muses at the outset, "perhaps he will offer me a purse full of money"; or, as the logic of the story shows, fusing family romance into the structure of the unfolding oedipal fantasy, perhaps he has a beautiful daughter whom he'll invite me to marry (when he arrives at the aristocrat's abode he finds "a dark-haired, beautiful girl, quite young, who said nothing and looked at no one"); or, continuing to paraphrase the barely disguised "underthoughts" of the narrative, perhaps he will acknowledge me as his son and love me.

Since contemporary existence is bereft of large-scale spiritual and metaphorical coherence, Barthelme's stories appropriately have no traditional beginnings, middles, or ends; they make no conventionally logical transitions between events and, in being irreducible or untotalizable, refrain from giving us a sentimental or fraudulently coherent picture of the world.
—Michael Zeitlin

At first glance, one might be tempted simply to view Barthelme's revision—or should we say condensation and displacement—of Abraham's narrative as his way of refusing the blandishments of the always already established Freudian oedipal fantasy. Indeed at that level it works as a notably transgressive and parodic gesture of narrative self-assertion. But if we believe there is something more at play here (for in Barthelme it is invariably wrong to assume that there are no large-scale patterns of thought which draw into conceptual coherence the complex display of the signifiers), we need to enter more fully into the game of interpretation. We must attempt "a construction."

Let us note, then, that Barthelme's revision begins by undoing Abraham's strategy of displacement and reversal, returning us to the archaic and proscribed impulse of *Oedipus the King* which "lies beneath" the manifest screen of the pseudorescue as reported in Abraham. But there is a crucial difference between Barthelme's version and the one whose genealogy connects Sophocles, Freud, and Abraham: in the originary version, the figure "Oedipus" rushes toward the carriage with the intention of murdering (or rescuing) and *succeeds* in that action; in Barthelme's revision, the running figure who would "seize the horses by the reins" *is himself run over and killed*; moreover, that figure is no longer the son (as the structure of the scene would demand) but *the father*. How, in other words, did the father become displaced out of his seat in the carriage to be killed in the son's place?

Clearly, with this radical displacement and audacious reversal we are still in the "constellation of the Oedipus dream", whose intention, the killing of the father, is, if anything, intensified. But so too is the problem of agency: where in the prior version the son is unmistakably responsible for the crime, Barthelme's sleight-of-hand revision has covered the son's role in a fog of unknowing. No simple *exchange* of positions appears to have taken place, for the son is not in the driver's seat of the carriage where we might expect to find him; instead he is only a passive, *after-the-fact* witness to the crime. Despite this normally airtight alibi, he still bears some mysterious sense of guilt, for he lets slip the telltale clue: "I had been notified by the police, who came to my room and fetched me to the scene of the accident." Naturally, as Barthelme surely intends, "the police" may be taken as a standard form of the "projection" of what psychoanalysis calls the "proscriptive agency." In taking up residence in the individual psyche, that agency is more commonly designated as the superego, the force which observes, judges, and punishes the self and, in so doing, reinforces what the conversationalists in Barthelme's brilliant tale **"Daumier"** call "a deep and abiding sense of personal worthlessness."

The son, as it were, is guilty "by definition." But the problem at the level of the tale's plot is still why the son would feel guilty if he was not "directly" involved in what is generally being described as an "accident" but which he himself treats as a terrible "crime." A clue from Freud may be helpful in this regard: "It is a matter of indifference who actually committed the crime; psychology is only concerned to know who desired it emotionally and who welcomed it when it was done" (Freud, "Dostoevsky"). Certainly, once arrived at "the scene," the son takes a rather keen interest in what he finds: "I bent over my father, whose chest was crushed, and laid my cheek against his. His cheek was cold. I smelled no liquor but blood from his mouth stained the collar of my coat." The focus of the problem must accordingly shift, then, to the question of who it was who was "driving" (literally, symbolically, emotionally, imaginatively, and so forth) the chariot. And indeed the tale is structured, in one

of its principal narrative vectors, which runs in a linear and progressive fashion, as the tracking down of a mystery. The son, like Nathaniel Hawthorne's young Robin Molineux, sets out in search of his (would-be) kinsman, a "highly placed personage" who not only lies behind some strange and mysterious crime but will also be subjected to a terrible public debasement (in Barthelme's tale the drunken, deranged, and pathetic father is the aristocrat's inevitable psychical counterpart). And like young Molineux's, the son's "subject of inquiry" leads inexorably towards a rude confrontation with his own unsuspected complicity in the patriarch's undoing. What is more difficult to understand, however, is the son's motivation in **"Views of My Father Weeping"** for undertaking his quest toward the revelation of what must be a terrible secret, the identity of the one responsible for the father's death. That secret once revealed, will the son want to avenge the killing? Establish his affiliation with the one who "did the job"? Rescue the aristocrat from the rage of the demented father? Kill the aristocrat himself in a repetition of the founding crime of the narrative? Marry into the family? And so on. (Remember, quoting Emily Dickinson, "This was a dream," and so we need to alter radically any sense of psychical temporality and causality that might reduce "the subject's history to a linear determinism envisaging nothing but the action of the past upon the present".)

It is this psychic tangle of contradictory and coexisting impulses that finds its "objective correlative" in the disturbances of the tale's narrative structure, in all the ways in which that would-be steady and linear progress toward the discovery of a secret is radically disrupted by a succession of fragmentary and absurd views of weeping and pathetic fathers. With respect to that perennial "Barthelme problem," the apparent disorganization of his literary "surfaces," let us immediately grant the conspicuous fact that those surfaces seldom unfold in a purely regular (chronological or otherwise) order. Rather, one encounters a persistent interference with the narrative's progressive flow, not only by means of "flashbacks," "fantasies," and subjective "countercurrents" of imagery (such shameless metaphors and anthropomorphisms tend to remain remarkably relevant), but also through spatial divisions (the notorious fragments) and an achronological arrangement of the blocks of narrative themselves. Within these blocks there are also rapid shifts of attention and frequent ellipses, substantial gaps in narrative continuity which must signify something beyond simply themselves. The point would not necessarily be to naturalize such phenomena as the effects of some particular character's "repression," let alone as the disfunctioning of the author's fragmented or schizoid psyche, but to recognize the analogy of the dreamwork according to which *the narrative as a whole* appears to behave. In the imaginative "work" of narrative discourse, the disruption of surfaces is an effect of "the evasion of the censorship"; it is also a signature of the impact of guilt and repression on the sequence of memory and on the construction and reconstruction of what is remembered. To borrow a line from Jacques Lacan, in Barthelme's narrative discourse "the amnesia of repression is one of the most lively forms of memory." That is to say, Barthelme's "experimentation in narrative structure" is fully a part of what psychoanalysis would call the emotional "deep material" of the story, suggesting a historically specific (that is, Freudian and modernist) conception of the modes and structures of fantasy, memory, and repression that problematize the coherent telling of any psychosexual history, psychological allegory, or postmodernist refraction and amplification of such traditional narrative forms. If Barthelme then gives us a *postmodernist mimesis* of "modernist" repression, the formally self-conscious and parodic terms with which he does so are fully responsive to the dramatic, psychological, and intertextual contexts of his narrative.

Klinkowitz is therefore acutely observant when he notes that Barthelme's narratives tend to bring about a "shift of both writerly and readerly energy from the depth of meaning to the surface of signification." But I think he misreads the import of that phenomenon when he concludes that "the surface of signification" is the place to which Barthelme wants us to confine our attention, or further, that the surface "indeed is where the business of being human takes place." Take as an example this crucial passage from the story:

> I remember once we were out on the ranch shooting peccadillos (result of a meeting, on the plains of the West, of the collared peccary and the ninebanded armadillo). My father shot and missed. He wept. This weeping resembles that weeping.

Critics of Klinkowitz's persuasion, interested in the way in which the text "shift[s] . . . attention from thought to words" or "transfer[s] . . . attention from the depths of meaning to the texture of surface," will naturally be drawn to the linguistic play of the passage. But clearly, in the context of the story, that play is a kind of diversionary tactic ("see how playful, clever, and postmodern I'm being") transferring our attention away from the underlying parricidal theme which one may infer from the undisguised "content" of the passage, that is, the father's humiliation. The meaning of that humiliation comes closer to "the real story," one which is "beneath the surface" only in the sense that its thematic, ideational, and symbolic complexities are precisely what the conspicuous play on "peccadillo" attempts to divert our attention away from. If Barthelme sometimes "ask[s] his readers to look away from the previously central concerns of character and plot in order to sense the more subtle aspects of his art," those subtle aspects of his art do not prevent its central obsessive concerns from existing, and so from demanding our closest attention. In fact, this might be identified as a cardinal principle of his art, or at least precisely its point: the shifting of attention away from "central concerns" is a

gambit, a ruse, and a deflection; it is also a manifest invitation to reverse the trend of the narrative's centrifugal force, and so to read from the sign on the surface to the ruling ideas "beneath" it—the conceptual and intertextual organizational principles that structure the disposition of the signifiers throughout the narrative as a whole. When in the presence of the literary act of condensation and displacement, it is best to recognize it for the "defense" that it is and attempt to undo, imaginatively, its effects: one might then be taken to a place where an equally important part of "the real business of being human takes place."

Having made this polemical excursion, we are now in a better position to return to the narrative's "code of action" and follow its complex, devious, though inexorable path to the lair of "the aristocrat." As we have already noted, that path is bestrewn with multiple, fragmentary, and pathetic images of weeping fathers, and so the picture of a fundamental ambivalence emerges more clearly. On the one hand there is the aristocrat, Abraham's "highly placed personage," the exalted figure out of Freudian family romance ("A count! I had selected a man of very high rank indeed to put my question to" ["**Views**"]) whose idealization may be read as a defense against latent or repressed hostile impulses. On the other hand there is his lowly "real life" counterpart, the sheer frequency of whose reiteration in the narrative is an index of the intensity of that hostility. No aristocrat, king, or prince, the son's father appears in the narrative as a mailman, insurance salesman, child, and fool, as a weeping and pathetic figure exposed again and again in scenes of humiliation, feminization, failure:

> I entered the shop and made inquiries. "It was your father, eh? He was bloody clumsy if you ask me. . . . If your father hadn't been drunk—."
>
> . . . . .
>
> He is fatherly. The gray in the head. The puff in the face. The droop in the shoulders. The flab on the gut. Tears falling. Tears falling. Tears falling. Tears falling. More tears.
>
> . . . . .
>
> My father has written on the white wall with his crayons.
>
> . . . . .
>
> My father is looking at himself in a mirror. He is wearing a large hat (straw) on which there are a number of blue and yellow plastic jonquils. He says: "How do I look?"

Suffused by a tone of derision and ridicule, the immoderate and exaggerated features of these passages are at the heart of the psychoanalytic notion of "the absurd," which in the process of imaginative unfolding (be it dream or artistic production) is an effect of the censorship as it contends with irrepressible thoughts of a disrespectful kind. In **"Views of My Father Weeping,"** the debasement of the father is in this sense an act of imagination preparatory to his more complete undoing at the level of "plot," which may be taken as indicating the realm of "motility" or the "place" where imaginary impulses are "acted out." If "ambivalence . . . prepares us for the possibility of the father being subjected to a debasement", then debasement leads to the possibility of the father's murder, the ruling fantasy which presses into its service the narrative's general modes of derision and violence. One hardly needs a carriage—in Barthelme, death and mortification of the patriarch are simply inevitable effects of narrative discourse itself:

> He was dragged, you know. The carriage dragged him about forty feet.

>   . . . . .

> The heavy wheels of the carriage passed over him (I felt two quite distinct thumps), his body caught upon a projection under the boot, and he was dragged some forty feet, over the cobblestones. . . . nor could any human agency have stopped them.

Despite this last disclaimer we may still feel impelled to pin the "accident" on some one person, preferably someone as much like the son as possible but sufficiently different so as to be in no danger of being taken literally for the son himself. Barthelme accomplishes the necessary doubling with a neat trick of plot. A little girl to whom the son had given some candy now for five crowns gives him a crucial piece of information to help him in his search: "The coachman's name is Lars Bang." The sounding of the strange name conjures up an uncanny effect: "When I heard this name, which in its sound and appearance is rude, vulgar, not unlike my own name, I was seized with repugnance." Bang is a figure, in other words, who comes to us, perhaps directly, from the pages of Edgar Allan Poe's "William Wilson," where "repugnance" is also an effect of one part of the self's horrible recognition of its vulgar, "low class" other half. The son, in other words, *has been there in the driver's seat all along:* it was he, Lars Bang, the doppelgänger as Self, whose negotiation of the carriage actually "did the job."

But if we feel we have "solved" the mystery we are again thwarted, for even Lars Bang seems to have a convincing alibi, so complex, tenacious, and devious are the mechanisms of the son's defenses. In Bang's oral account of "the accident" one encounters a steady and inexorable displacement of blame from any active intention, purpose, or responsibility. Listening to his exculpatory discourse, one is surely meant to be alert to the signatures of "unconscious agency" and thus to the obvious fraudulence and bad faith of his alibi:

> we found ourselves set upon by an elderly man, thoroughly drunk, who flung himself at my lead pair and began cutting at their legs with a switch, in the most vicious manner imaginable. . . . At this renewed attack the horses, frightened out of their wits, *jerked the reins from my hands,* and ran headlong over your father, who fell beneath their hooves.

> The heavy wheels of the carriage passed over him (I felt two quite distinct thumps), his body caught upon a projection under the boot, and he was dragged some forty feet, over the cobblestones. *I was attempting, with all my might, merely to hang on to the box, for, having taken the bit between their teeth, the horses were in no mood to tarry; nor could any human agency have stopped them.* We flew down the street . . .

(emphasis added; second ellipsis Barthelme's)

The emphasis on the passive quality of his role takes us into the domain of the self's internal foreign territory, the place where blind, murderous force is disowned and denied even as it has its day in the realm of motility. As Freud wrote in *The Interpretation of Dreams,* "when conscious purposive ideas are abandoned, concealed purposive ideas assume control of the current of ideas" and thus of the action. Besides, as Barthelme knew if Lars Bang didn't, scape-goating the horses is an old and transparent psychoanalytic ploy:

> The ego's relation to the id might be compared with that of a rider to his horse. The horse supplies the locomotive energy, while the rider has the privilege of deciding on the goal and of guiding the powerful animal's movement. But only too often there arises between the ego and the id the not precisely ideal situation of the rider being obliged to guide the horse along the path by which it itself wants to go.

To sum up, in Barthelme's intensification of the ultimately fatal import inherent in Abraham's "wish-creation," he completes a prior narrative that, in the words of Harold Bloom [in *The Anxiety of Influence: A Theory of Poetry*], "failed to go far enough." He does so by going back to the latent Sophoclean significance which, inherent in Abraham's report, enters **"Views of My Father Weeping"** like an eruption of the archaic into the ironically self-conscious but still dark and troubled heart of American postmodernism. But by completing that modernist narrative, Barthelme clearly has succeeded only in raising the stakes of the dangerous game of "father-murder and father-rescue," not, of course, in winning it. Yes, "the father" has been run over, but from the *position* reserved for the *son* within the structure of the prototypical oedipal scene; that is, in this narrative of simultaneous, contradictory, and yet also complementary investments of "subject positions" within a psychical structure, the son runs out to "save" the father but is murdered by him instead. Or, transferring that dramatized relation to the narrative's mimesis of a "psychic level" of experience, the son kills the father in fantasy but is left to be ravaged forevermore by guilty dreams—or views—of weeping and pathetic fathers (the last world of the story is "etc."). After all, who is this dead and weeping father but the father-in-the-son, the imago of the father whom the son loves, hates, fears, and wishes to become but also not to become himself. Barthelme's version of the myth, then, is darker even than Sophocles': Barthelme's son is denied his oedipal victory, dying the thousand deaths of remorse before he gets anywhere close to Jocasta or to solving the mystery of the roots of his own existence.

Robert Kennedy Saved/The Dead Father Bulldozed

A second major example of what may be placed under the sign of "psychoanalytic intertextuality" indicates just how pervasive and deep-going in Barthelme's art is the complex of ideas involving the rescue/murder of the father. **"Robert Kennedy Saved from Drowning,"** Freud's essay, "A Special Type of Object Choice Made by Men" (1910), and *The Dead Father* illustrate the dialectical relation of the theme and press into bold, self-conscious articulation the shaping narrative forces which in **"Views of My Father Weeping"** remain latent though no less purposive and consequential in their effects. **"Robert Kennedy Saved from Drowning"** ends with a scene of striking oneiric intensity:

K. Saved from Drowning

K. in the water. His flat black hat, his black cape, his sword are on the shore. He retains his mask. His hands beat the surface of the water which tears and rips about him. The white foam, the green depths. I throw a line, the coils leaping out over the surface of the water. He has missed it. No, it appears that he has it. His right hand (sword arm) grasps the line that I have thrown him. I am on the bank, the rope wound round my waist, braced against a rock. K. now has both hands on the line. I pull him out of the water. He stands now on the bank, gasping.

"Thank you."

Barthelme's *explication de texte* may be found in his masterwork, his manual for sons, *The Dead Father:*

On the rescue of fathers. . . .

. . . When you have rescued a father from whatever terrible threat menaces him, then you feel, for a moment, that you are the father and he is not. For a moment. This is the only moment in your life you will feel this way.

Here Barthelme is following and reiterating the original Freudian explication of the rescue fantasy: "All [the son's] instincts, those of tenderness, gratitude, lustfulness, defiance and independence, find satisfaction in the single wish *to be his own father*". Freud's explanation is worth quoting at greater length:

It is as though the boy's defiance were to make him say: "I want nothing from my father; I will give him back all I have cost him." He then forms the phantasy of *rescuing his father from danger and saving his life*; in this way he puts his account square with him. This phantasy is commonly enough displaced on to the emperor, king or some other great man; after being thus distorted it becomes admissible to consciousness, and may even be made use of by creative writers. In its application to a boy's father it is the defiant meaning in the idea of rescuing which is by far the most important.

The Dead Father makes clear the defiant meaning at the root of the rescue fantasy. Indeed the entire book is structured as an ambiguous rescue/murder of the father: a band of sons and a couple of daughters are dragging the dead father, who is attached to a cable, across a barren, elemental (or is it simply cardboard?) landscape, in the direction of the Golden Fleece (or is it simply a deep pit in the ground and a view of a raised skirt at the end?). The Dead Father is dead, we are told, because "We *want* the Dead Father to be dead. We sit with tears in our eyes wanting the Dead Father to be dead." But the Dead Father is dead only "in a sense": he is a human being, a granite monument, a gigantic "super-male with horns, tail, and a big penis snake" (as Freud might describe the Great Father Serpent); a strange, majestic, awe-inspiring object; a pathetic, dangerous, infantile, and paralytic old man; a figure who comes apart; a voice that takes up residence inside one's head. But in all of his manifestations he must be defeated, displaced, gotten beyond. With Freud we should conclude that "the insistence with which [*The Dead Father*] exhibited its absurdities could only be taken as indicating the presence in the dream-thoughts of a particularly embittered and passionate polemic". In the classical Freudian dynamic model, absurdity implies the activity of a vigilant censorship on the watch to repress derisive (or parricidal) dream thoughts. The signs of the struggle emerge as the immoderate and exaggerated features of the dream production. But in the imaginative process of Barthelme's *The Dead Father,* the censorship fails again and again, for the principle of corpse-baiting is built into the very structure of Barthelme's fictional vision, where it becomes the principal form of narrative action: the Dead Father is berated, tied up, teased, tortured, hacked, rudely addressed. In Barthelme's hyperbolic construction of the dead father, the "particularly embittered and passionate polemic" may be taken as generating those warping effects which, as we have seen in **"Views of My Father Weeping,"** emerge as narrative "absurdity" and its various modes of derision.

What is it about the Dead Father that invites so much animus? A silly question.

> Can you tell us . . . what that hussar had done? The one we saw hanged by the neck from the tree back down the road a bit.

> Disobeyed a ukase, said the Dead Father. I forget which ukase.

> Oh, said Thomas.

> Nobody disobeys a ukase of mine, said the Dead Father. He chuckled.

> Smug, isn't he, said Julie.

> A bit smug, said Thomas.

> A bit, the Dead Father said.

With the Dead Father in his wrath we recognize "a great narcissist" who "regards any interference as an act of *lèse majesté*" in response to which he demands "(like the Draconian code) that any such crime shall receive the one form of punishment which admits of no degrees".

Hence, presumably, the importance of the fool's cap in Barthelme, which hardly conceals the signatures of the father's discipline and the son's resentment:

> Thomas pulled an orange fool's cap tipped with silver bells from his knapsack.

> To think that I have worn this abomination, or its mate, since I was sixteen.

> Sixteen to sixty-five, so says the law, said the Dead Father. . . .

> And had I been caught out-of-doors without it, my ears cut off, said Thomas. What a notion. What an imagination. . . . But remember there was a time

when he was slicing people's ears off with a wood chisel. Two-inch blade.

However, it is well to be reminded by Ernst Kris that

> When we laugh at the fool, we never forget that in his comic fancy dress, with bladder and cap, he still carries crown and scepter, symbols of kingship. And is it not possible that the freedom exploited by the fool is a direct inheritance from the omnipotence of his demonic predecessor?

With "His orange tights, orange boots, silver belt buckle with rubies, white Sabatini shirt. His clear and true gold-rimmed spectacles," Barthelme's Thomas, the Dead Father's son, is the archetype of the fool as parricide: we mustn't forget that he ends up with the Dead Father's watch, belt buckle, sword, passport, and power and presides at his funeral.

But does he ever free himself of the remorse, self-doubt, and other residual effects of the father's power? The father has taken up permanent residence in the son's soul, intertwining himself with the son's own most intimate definition of self. In Freud's darkest musings on the subject, the superego is guilt-producing, sadistic, obscene, and savage, the pure agency of the death instinct. Barthelme's version is characteristically more clinical, philosophical, resigned:

> you must deal with the memory of a father. Often that memory is more potent than the living presence of a father, is an inner voice commanding, haranguing, yes-ing and no-ing—a binary code, yes no yes no yes no yes no, governing your every, your slightest movement, mental or physical. At what point do you become yourself? Never, wholly, you are always partly him. That privileged position in your inner ear is his last "perk" and no father has ever passed it by.

Hence the need for the fantasy, allowing a temporary and symbolic victory over an indomitable adversary, even if, in turn, that victory generates the soul-killing and son-directed waves of remorse. Is there, then, any way out of this vicious circle? Better let Barthelme, who has thought longer and deeper on these issues than any American writer since Hawthorne, give the glimmer of hope:

> Patricide is a bad idea, first because it is contrary to law and custom and second because it proves, beyond a doubt, that the father's every fluted accusation against you was correct: you are a thoroughly bad individual, a patricide!—a member of a class of persons universally ill-regarded. It is all right to feel this hot emotion, but not to act upon it. And it is not necessary. It is not necessary to slay your fa-

ther, time will slay him, that is a virtual certainty. Your true task lies elsewhere.

Carl D. Malmgren (essay date 1995)

SOURCE: "Exhumation: *The Dead Father,*" in *Narrative Turns and Minor Genres in Postmodernism,* edited by Theo D'haen and Hans Bertens, Rodopi, 1995, pp. 25-40.

[*In the following essay, Malmgren presents a detailed, thorough examination of* The Dead Father.]

PRETEXT: Our presentation consists of two kinds of commentaries:

> LECT: Readings—descriptive, analytic, interpretive—of the Barthelmean corpus and the Barthelmean text.

> IDIOLECT: Countertexts, in which Barthelme is unfair to Malmgren.

The autopsy itself unfolds in three stages, each with several reading operations, as follows:

I. The Barthelmean Corpus

     1. Impure Text
     2. Collage
     3. Fragments

II. The Corpse of *The Dead Father:* Partial Anatomy

     4. The Body
     5. Blazon
     6. The Mute Text

III. The Dead Father: Identifying the Corpse

     7. Examining the Corpse
     8. Mythification
     9. Overdetermination
    10. Totalization
    11. Totalization Revisited
    12. Resurrection: The Live Father

I myself have these problems. Endings are elusive, middles are nowhere to be found, but worst of all is to begin, to begin, to begin.

                       —Barthelme, **"The Dolt"**

I. *The Barthelmean Corpus: Overview (See **Dead Father**)*
A. LECT 1. Impure Texts

For matters of classification, heuristic rather than absolute, we can distinguish between two tendencies or inclinations in postmodern fiction, based upon the criterion of inclusion or exclusion. The exclusive postmodern text turns hermetically inward, brooding obsessively on its own processes and strategies. For it narrativity is a curse of self-consciousness; the writer, as Barth notes in *Lost in the Funhouse,* is "committed to the pen for life." This fiction sees the separation between Art and Life as irreconcilable. It aspires to the condition of silence, longs for textual suicide, but is forced to go on, spinning out texts for nothing. The inclusive, or "impure," postmodern text, on the other hand, turns itself outward towards Life and gleefully appropriates the discourses in which it finds itself situated. Using techniques of collage, paste-up, and parody, this text undertakes the "murdering" of competing texts. The impure text celebrates, and even adds to, the din created by culture. The Barthelmean corpus is, for the most part, "impure." What we see only intermittently operative in **The Dead Father** is the dominant feature in his other work—the attempt, through structure, typography, parody, and graphics, to appropriate various "universes of discourse" (**Snow White**) in order to open art to life, to locate the text in something outside itself. This form of postmodernism is not necessarily hostile toward bourgeois and popular culture; it tends to collaborate with its environment. At the same time, the principle of inclusion allows the impure text to pre-empt, subvert, or co-opt the discourses it incorporates. The impulse to assemble, synthesize, or appropriate should thus be seen as a defense mechanism against the proliferation of language systems, information, cultural noise. Borrowing from Barth's *Giles Goat-Boy,* we can say that Barthelme attempts to EAT culture and language before they EAT him. This might be termed the carnivorization of discourse.

> **Barthelme is reported to have said that collage is the "central principle" of twentieth-century art. Collage is a basic strategy of impure art, at once a way of replicating the feel of twentieth-century experience and a way of dealing with the tension between Art and Life.**
>   **—Carl D. Malmgren**

LECT 2: Collage

In an early interview, Barthelme is reported to have said that collage is the "central principle" of twentieth-century art. Collage is a basic strategy of impure art, at once a way of replicating the feel of twentieth-century experience and a way of dealing with the tension between Art and Life. According to Harold Rosenberg, collage is both a child of technology and a form born of reservations about the absolute separation of Art from Life; collage, he says, "appropriates the external world;" the object in collage straddles two realms, suspended, as it were, between its extratextual reality and its formal location within an artistic whole. These observations apply to the Barthelmean collage. We might, however, distinguish between modernist and postmodernist collage in terms of their epistemological assumptions. Modernist collage is informed by a metaphysic of totality:

> For the modernists collage is a way of getting at the true meaning of reality; the depth of it; it is an implicit statement about the inadequacy of linear approaches to the human situation. . . . Underneath the modernists' rejection of linearity, however, there is the belief that what *seems* fragmented is indeed imbued with a higher cohesiveness invisible to the distracted modern man. Collage in modernist fiction, in other words, is a tribute to the higher order of reality and as such there is in modernist art the faith that the surface fragments can be reconstituted into a total whole.

Modernist collage juxtaposes heterogeneous "bits" of reality in order to capture the shape of the twentieth-century— its texture, its centrifugality—and at the same time to circumscribe a trace of a totality (as in Dos Passos's *USA*). Postmodernist collage is much less ambitious; it dispenses with any such metaphysical baggage. The surface reality is not informed—charged with depth, quizzicality, the possibility of reconstitution. What Robbe-Grillet asserts about the world obtains for the collage: it is "neither significant nor absurd. It *is*, quite simply." For the modernists collage is a means to an end; for the postmodernists it is both means and end. As Ronald Sukenick says in *98.6*, "Interruption. Discontinuity. Imperfection. It can't be helped. . . . This novel is based on The Mosaic Law the law of mosaics or how to deal with parts in the absence of wholes."

IDIOLECT 1: Barthelme, interview in *The New Fiction*

Klinkowitz: In Richard Schickel's *New York Times Magazine* piece last year, you were reported as saying that "The principle of collage is the central principle of all art in the twentieth century in all media." Would you care to expand and perhaps tell me how it specifically applies to fiction?

Barthelme: I was probably wrong . . .

LECT 3: Fragments

A character in an early Barthelmean text says "Fragments are the only form I trust." Some critics, assuming this to be

an essential tenet of Barthelme's aesthetic, have taken him to task for it:

> "Fragments are the only forms I trust." This from a writer of arguable genius, whose works reflect the anxiety he himself must feel, in book after book, that his brain is all fragments. . . . But. There is a point at which Wilde's remark comes horribly true, that life will imitate art. And who then is in charge, who believed himself cleverly impotent, who supposed he had abandoned all conscious design?
>
> —Joyce Carol Oates

To an extent, especially as regards certain short fictions such as **"Views of My Father Weeping,"** fragmentation and its syntactic equivalent, parataxis, are basic Barthelmean strategies, ways of subverting conscious design, of resisting totalization. Together they work to undermine teleology and continuity. In *The Dead Father* we can see these principles at work especially in the dialogues of Julie and Emma where we are forced to "look at the parts separately," to "get an exploded view." It should be noted that Barthelmean fragments frequently consist of the flotsam and jetsam of exploded language systems, of linguistic trash. By using linguistic refuse as his collagistic unit and incorporating it undigested, in discrete fragments, Barthelme in effect "trashes" his collage, placing himself "on the leading edge of this trash phenomenon".

IDIOLECT 2: News Release, from *The New Fiction*

WRITER CONFESSES THAT HE NO LONGER TRUSTS FRAGMENTS
. . . . .
Trust 'Misplaced,' Author Declares
. . . . .
DISCUSSED DECISION WITH DAUGHTER, SIX
. . . . .
Will Seek 'Wholes' in Future, He Says
. . . . .
CLOSING TIME IN GARDENS OF WEST WILL BE EXTENDED, SCRIVENER STATES
. . . . .

New York, June 24 (A&P)—Donald Barthelme, 41-year-old writer and well-known fragmentist, said today that he no longer trusted fragments. He added that although he had once been "very fond" of fragments, he had found them to be "finally untrustworthy."

The author, looking tense and drawn after what was described as "considerable thought," made his dramatic late-night announcement at a Sixth Avenue laundromat press conference, from which the press was excluded.

Sources close to the soap machine said, however, that the agonizing reappraisal, which took place before their eyes, required only four minutes.

"Fragments fall apart a lot," Barthelme said. Use of antelope blood as a bonding agent had not proved. . .

II. *The Corpse of* **The Dead Father:** *Partial Anatomy*

LECT 4: The Body

Much of the above does not seem to apply to **The Dead Father,** which is for the most part novelistic, with distinct and individuated characters rendered in transparent language; identifiable, if surrealistic, topoi; a univocal, if laconic, narration; and, most important, an irreversible and teleological plot. The novel tends to unravel, however, if we look at its elements carefully. The plot, for example, is open to divergent, and conflicting, categorizations, depending upon the characters' perspectives. From the point of view of the Dead Father, the company is embarked upon the most traditional of actions—a Quest for an Object of Desire, the Golden Fleece. The Fleece signifies rebirth for the Dead Father: "When I douse myself in its great yellow electricity," he says, "then I will be revivified." The company, on the other hand, is undertaking an anti-Quest; its goal is to get rid of an Object of Loathing. For Thomas and the others the journey can only end in the ultimate act of dispossession, Death. Rebirth and Death; Quest and Anti-Quest: the plot effectively cancels itself out. The master trope for the macrotext is thus chiasmus (just as it is for the microtext: "Dead, but still with us, still with us but dead"). Chiasmus derives from the Greek lette *chi* or *X* and signifies a figure which has been marked by that letter. **The Dead Father,** of course, is just such a textual figure, insofar as it culminates in a crossing-out, an elimination. The eponymous hero of the novel, the Dead Father, is literally a marked man; the overview of the march designates him with an *x*. Indeed, his very name enacts a figural chiasmus. His basic attributes, as he frequently reminds the troupe, are creating ("fathering") and destroying ("slaying"). The Dead Father thus occupies the empty site where that which creates is slain. And it's hardly necessary to remark that *X* marks the spot where one digs a hole in order to cover/discover/uncover an Object of Value. The plot and characterization of the text are thus tainted with cross-purposes; a known entity is converted into an unknown quantity (an *X*). The same can finally be said of the discourse of the text, which alternates between two extremes, noise and silence, the one shown to be a simple transform of the other, the two together creating cacography.

LECT 5: The Blazon

One aspect of the noisy text is the blazon. We borrow the term from Roland Barthes who uses it in *S/Z* to refer to a device of the classic or realist text—the inventory, or the attempt to "capture" a predicate (Barthes uses the example of Beauty) through a systematic and exhaustive enumeration of its parts, attributes, characteristics. The blazon tries to capture "reality" in the lists of language, in a network of linguistic nets (just as Melville tries to catch a whale in the whaling chapters of *Moby Dick*). In **The Dead Father** Barthelme supplies the reader with a number of blazons: the inventory of the musicians and animals slain by the Dead Father; the inventory of the progeny from the Dead Father's affair with Tulla; the inventory of the types of fathers. Barthes argues that "as a genre, the blazon expresses the belief that a complete inventory can produce a total body, as if the extremity of enumeration could devise a new category, that of totality." But Barthelme's lists are hardly classical: "First he slew a snowshoe rabbit cleaving it in twain with a single blow and then he slew a spiny anteater and then he slew two rusty numbats and then whirling the great blade round and round his head he slew a wallaby and a lemur and a trio of oukaris and a spider monkey and a common squid." Here, in the noisy text, the inventory is over-totalized; there is an information overload. The list draws attention to itself as simply that, a device; what is (em)bodied here is not reality but discourse itself, its infinite lexicon, its noisiness. Related to this device is Barthelme's treatment of the telling detail, the bit of superfluous information that in the classic text serves to reinforce the mimetic contract. The telling detail, Barthes claims, gives the "effect of the real" ("l'effet de reel"), linking the fiction to reality and validating the text. In the noisy text, the significant detail is blatantly overdone (e.g., "Small gifts to the children: a power motor, a Blendor"). It is so incredible, so incongruous, that it serves to countersignify; the material becomes simply the lexical. The detail's incongruity, its implausibility, its excess, subvert the reality effect, rupturing the continuity between fictional and real worlds.

LECT 6: The Mute Text

In order to subvert its novelistic identity, **The Dead Father** takes the basic elements of fiction—description, narration, dialogue—and transforms them, essentially by so impoverishing them, minimalizing them, as to impart to them an empty, automatic, formulaic, banal quality. The code of description becomes a silent list of lonely nouns: "The countryside. Flowers. Creeping snowberry. The road with dust. The sweat popping from little sweat glands. The line of the cable." The narration is similarly muted: "Edmund claims the first dance. No that is for the Dead father. Happiness of the Dead Father." Can the omniscience of the last enunciation be any more laconic, any more muted? Dialogue in the mute text invariably reverts to cliché ("Till the cows come home, said the Dead Father, so much are we on each others' wavelengths") or becomes mere babble. The dialogues of Emma and Julie typify this process. Barthelme has referred to them as "collections of non sequiturs, intended . . . to provide a kind of counter-narration to the main narration." They represent a form of countercommunication—prattle, chatter—a kind of noise, interfering with the narrative transmission. They are "printed circuits reprinting themselves," meant to leave the reader with "a boiled brain and a burnt one." Together all the minimalistic features of the text, in their muteness, serve paradoxically a noise function. It is, the text tells us, a "matter of paring down to a supportable minimum," but that minimum disrupts narrative continuity and momentum. The minimalized features act as narrative static, create a blanketing effect, serving at last to blank the text's blank.

III. *The Dead Father: Identifying the Corpse*

LECT 7: Examining the Corpse

The key figure here, the one to be exhumed if only so that we can finally lay him to rest, is of course the eponymous hero—he who, as the text frequently reminds us, has been "at work ceaselessly night and day for the good of all." At a generalized level we can say that he represents any hegemonic belief system—at one time or another he comes to embody all the systems of authority that Western culture has enshrined: God, King, Reason, History, State. In psychoanalytic terms he is the very source of that which creates and structures reality, the parent/father. His is the voice of religion, as when he delivers the "tongue-lashing" of the Biblical patriarch. His is the voice of science, as when he gives a speech to the men ("Quite extraordinary, said Emma, what did it mean? Thank you, said the Dead Father. It meant I made a speech"). He incorporates machine technology in his multi-purpose wooden leg. He enacts laws, issues ukases, and, when he is offended, dispenses punishment: "I award punishment. Punishment is a thing I am good at." Fathers are also teachers; they "teach much that is of value. Much that is not."

LECT 8: Mythific(a)tion

Certainly the most obvious level of signification for the Dead Father, in terms of overcoding, is the mythic. At first Julie thinks Thomas has an exaggerated view of the Dead Father's stature, but she soon changes her mind. "I apologize for saying you were perpetuating myths," Julie says to him. "I am beginning to come round to your opinion." The Dead Father occupies a plethora of positions in the mythological pantheon, including those of:

1. the Christian God the Father, Christ (doubting Thomas, Luke his steward).

2. the Hellenic Zeus, because of his anthropomorphic incarnation, his volatile temper, and his shape-shifting (turning into a haircut to seduce Tulla); also Orpheus, because of his journey to the Underworld and his eventual dismemberment.

3. a Norse god, because of the "twilight of the gods" motif.

4. the Indian Great Father Serpent ("I like him, said the Dead Father").

5. the Medieval Dying God/Fisher King

6. a Vegetation Deity, because he is the "one who keeps the corn popping from the fine green fields."

7. the Freudian Primal Father, against whom the sons rebel.

We might add to this list specific mythic narremes, such as the quest for the golden fleece, the seduction accomplished via metamorphosis, the descent to the underworld, the ritual of dismemberment, and the consumption of one's offspring ("And the worst was their blue jeans, my meals course after course of improperly laundered blue jeans, T-shirts, saris, Thom McAns. I suppose I could have hired someone to peel them for me first"). In many of these mythic echoes and parallels (not to mention literary antecedents such as Anchises and Lear), the Dead Father represents the ritualized god who must be dismembered and sacrificed but who retains authority and creates morality, culture, society.

LECT 9: Overdetermination

The weight, the pressure, the force that these mythic parallels exert is dissipated, perhaps even annihilated, at the local level by the way in which they are parodied or undercut in the act of being presented. The irony of the discourse deflates the mythic intention, converting kings into pretenders. Clearly Barthelme is not using myth in the same way that Eliot claimed Joyce was, "as a way of controlling, of ordering, of giving a shape and a significance to the immense panorama of futility and anarchy which is contemporary history." At the global level of the macrotext we can say that the system of mythical references is overdetermined. Christine Brooke-Rose defines overdetermination in literature as follows:

> A code is over-determined when its information (narrative, ironic, hermeneutic, symbolic, etc.) is too clear, overencoded, recurring beyond purely informational need. The reader is then in one sense also over-encoded, and does in fact sometimes appear in the text, dramatized, like an extra character: the "Dear Reader." But in another sense he is treated

as a kind of fool who has to be told everything, a subcritical (*hypo-crite*) reader.

The Dead Father as mythic father archetype is so systematically over-determined and thoroughly thematized that this reading subverts itself by being too easy, too available, ultimately banal. By being oversaid, it "goes without saying." Such a reading is not only parodied and subverted by the irony of the discourse, it is also so overcoded as to be hypocritical, beneath understanding.

LECT 10: Totalization

All of the features and readings I have discussed up to this point share a common ground—a resistance to totalization. The discourse of *The Dead Father* refuses to contain or circumscribe its fictional world within sustained and stable structures of signifieds. The postmodernist text presupposes the world to be chaotic and contingent and, in a kind of "cheerful nihilism", abandons the notion of totalization, of supplying a univocal, coherent, comprehensive "take" on that world. Postmodernist fiction is content to project a field of signifiers that float freely or cancel each other out. A case in point in *The Dead Father* is the signifier 23. There are twenty-three characters in the troupe, twenty-three chapters in the novel, twenty-three sections in "The Manual for Sons," twenty-three types of fathers (including the dead father). The number seems loaded with significance but finally fails to signify; it is simply a prime number, indivisible, without factors. Similarly the reader is invited to see Emma (M-A) as a mother figure but cannot really make anything of the equation. In other places the text turns on itself, acting out a semantic textermination: "[the Dead Father] controls what Thomas is thinking, what Thomas has always thought, what Thomas will ever think, with exceptions." In this world both anxiety and signification are free-floating, and we find ourselves lost in the funhouse of the signifier.

LECT 11: Totalization Revisited

And yet this Barthelmean text is finally so readily recuperable, so available to "translation," so easily naturalized and domesticated that it risks becoming that modernist *bête noire,* allegory. In one of Barthelme's short stories, **"Nothing: A Preliminary Account,"** a character responds to his project, the task of defining nothing, in the following way: "How joyous, the notion that, try as we may, we cannot do other than fail and fail absolutely, and the task will remain always before us, like a meaning for our lives." *The Dead Father* draws us onward and upward to a place where we can give it a proper name; it forces us to undertake the Sisyphean task before us, like a meaning for our lives. Interpretation crowds interpretation, as the Dead Father becomes omnisignificant.

We see in his lineaments, for example, the literary tradition in whose shadow Barthelme writes, with respect to whom he suffers no small anxiety of influence—those masters of meaning, the great modernists. There are several places at which the text invites this particular interpretive move. The Dead Father embodies the drive for meaning: "You take my meaning. We had no choice." And yet he resists final naming, preferring the teasing pleasure of ambiguity: "Having it both ways is a thing I like"; "Has it both ways does he? In this as in everything." The Dead Father is literally and figuratively a Yeatsian marmoreal "monument of its own magnificence": "Fathers are like blocks of marble, giant cubes, highly polished, with veins and seams, placed squarely in your path. They block your path. They cannot be climbed over, neither can they be slithered past. They are the 'past.'" Indeed, the penultimate chapter transforms the Dead Father into the biggest block of them all, a reincarnation of Joyce's Wakian Allfather, that blockhead AndI, obsessed with the sense of an ending and the sound of pitterpatter. In this chapter sound and sense conflate as pitterpatter becomes Pitterpatter: he who pits the pater.

Again and again, the novel invites this kind of totalized reading. The Dead Father seems finally connected to our innate need to discover meaning; he is the motor that drives our meaning-making machinery. We hear his voice as "the shudder of an enormous machine which is humanity tirelessly undertaking to create meaning without which it would no longer be human". His gender accentuates for us the "masculine profile of metaphysical hegemony". Moving to a higher level of generalization, we can say that the "father is the embodiment of all forces and desires which require of persons and cultures alike to *totalize* experience". He is the personification of order and coherence, the avatar of totalizing passion, the meaning we seek and the control we seek to escape. He is always already dead but still with us, still with us but dead, and even a dead father is dangerous.

Fatherhood is thus not only one of those metanarratives which serve to legitimate knowledge and culture, it is the very source—the wellspring, the engine—of such narratives. Given the postmodern "incredulity toward metanarratives", and at the same time the inescapability of the metanarrative drive, there remains but one solution, which the "Manual for Sons" spells out for us: "Your true task, as a son, is to reproduce every one of the enormities touched upon in this manual, but in an attenuated form. You must become your father, but a paler, weaker version of him. . . . *Fatherhood can be, if not conquered, at least 'turned down' in this generation*—by the combined efforts of all of us together." Turning down fatherhood—putting it to bed, reducing its volume (muting its phonocentrism), refusing to dance with it, repudiating it—in this way we can serve as the Manual's author's namesakes and begin to scatter the pater.

IDIOLECT 3: Barthelme, *Snow White*

This sense is not to be obtained by reading between the lines (for there is nothing there, in those white spaces) but by reading the lines themselves—looking at them and so arriving at a feeling not of satisfaction exactly, that is too much to expect, but of having read them, of having "completed" them.

LECT 12: Resurrection: The Live Father

Naming is a way of exerting power. As Toni Morrison remarks in *Beloved,* the power of naming belongs to the master, and the act of naming represents an assertion of mastery. By naming the significations of *The Dead Father,* by identifying its thematic strings, we convert it into an object of knowledge—something to be owned, commanded, commandeered. Knowledge of the text means power over it. Knowing the text, we have mastered the text; we have made it our property by giving it our properties. In so doing, however, we have inevitably succumbed to the text's logic; we have assumed patriarchal privilege, we have slipped into the role of the father. The text informs us that "the key idea, in fatherhood, is 'responsibility,'" and, almost unwittingly, we have played the part of responsible critics. All the more reason then that we remind ourselves that getting rid of the Dead Father must needs be a "rehearsal," something which we must do over and over again, playfully, in order to get it right. For there lurks within each of us our own dead father, and in this postmodern moment he is dead but still with us, still with us but dead.

IDIOLECT 4: Barthelme, "Brain Damage"

Some people feel that you should tell the truth, but those people are impious and wrong, and if you listen to what they say, you will be tragically unhappy all your life.

Kirkus Reviews **(review date 1 June 1997)**

SOURCE: A review of *Not-Knowing: The Essays and Interviews of Donald Barthelme,* in *Kirkus Reviews,* June 1, 1997, pp. 843-44.

[*The following is a negative assessment of* Not-Knowing: The Essays and Interviews of Donald Barthelme.]

What Thomas Pynchon called "Barthelmismo" is somewhat lacking in [*Not-Knowing: The Essays and Interviews of Donald Barthelme*] the second posthumous collection edited by Herzinger of Barthelme's miscellaneous writings, which here includes film and book reviews, art catalog essays, and *New Yorker* pieces.

"Barthelme Takes On Task of Almost Deciphering His Fiction" ran the *New York Times* headline when Barthelme delivered a lecture for New York University's Writer at Work series. That headline could equally well describe many of these abbreviated critical pieces and not wholly forthcoming interviews. The often-reprinted **"Not-Knowing"** (1982) is a spirited, idiosyncratic analysis of creativity—the search for an adequate rendering of the world's "messiness"—as well as a playful, sometimes self-parodying literary performance piece. The essay contains a short "letter to a literary critic" expressing condolences on the demise of Postmodernism, which Barthelme recycled into an unsigned piece for his favorite publication, the *New Yorker.* Barthelme's many other pieces for the magazine waver lamely between its characteristic wryness and his own fabulist flair, though there is one happy, humorous piece that purports to answer a *Writer's Digest* questionnaire about his drinking habits. Barthelme also tried his hand at film criticism for the *New Yorker* in 1979, but his reviews of Truffaut, Herzog, and Bertolucci are surprisingly heavy going, as are his writings on abstract expressionists and contemporary architecture. Editor Herzinger (English/Univ. of Southern Mississippi) has also included a number of interviews with Barthelme, of widely varying quality. The longest interview, a radio serial chat from 1975-76, seems dated and pretentious (e.g.: "I would not say that *Snow White* predicts the Manson case"); the most stimulating is actually the transcript of a 1975 symposium with his peers William Gass, Grace Paley, and Walker Percy.

Though John Barth calls this a "booksworth of encores" in his introduction, many of the pieces seem to be merely magazine outtakes and literary b-sides.

FURTHER READING

Criticism

Evans, Walter. "Comanches and Civilization in Donald Barthelme's 'The Indian Uprising.'" *Arizona Quarterly* 42, No. 1 (Spring 1986): 45-52.
  Provides an analysis of the short story "The Indian Uprising."

Meisel, Perry. "Mapping Barthelme's 'Paraguay.'" In *Fragments: Incompletion and Discontinuity,* pp. 129-38, guest editor, Lawrence D. Kritzman, and general editor, Jeanine Parisier Plottel, New York: New York Literary Forum, 1981.
  Examines the short story "Paraguay."

Robertson, Mary. "Postmodern Realism: Discourse As Antihero in Donald Barthelme's 'Brain Damage.'" In *Critical Essays on Donald Barthelme,* pp. 124-39, edited by Richard F. Patteson, New York: G. K. Hall and Co., 1992.
  Studies the connection between technique and meaning in Barthelme's works.

Stevick, Philip. "Ridiculous Words." *The Gettysburg Review* 3, No. 4 (Autumn 1990): 738-43.
  Surveys Barthelme's particular method of using language to create comic fiction.

Trussler, Michael. "Metamorphosis and Possession: An Investigation into the Interchapters of *Overnight to Many Distant Cities.*" *Critical Essays on Donald Barthelme,* pp. 196-207, edited by Richard F. Patteson, New York: G. K. Hall and Co., 1992.
  Explains how the stories in *Overnight to Many Distant Cities* defy "possession by the reader."

Upton, Lee. "Failed Artists in Donald Barthelme's *Sixty Stories.*" *Critique* 26, No. 1 (Fall 1984): 11-17.
  Delineates the theme of the failed artist within the narratives collected in *Sixty Stories.*

Additional coverage of Barthelme's life and career is contained in the following sources published by Gale: *Contemporary Authors,* Vols. 21-24R, and 129; *Contemporary Authors New Revision Series,* Vols. 20, and 58; *DISCovering Authors Modules: Novelists; Dictionary of Literary Biography,* Vol. 2; *Dictionary of Literary Biography Yearbook,* 1980, 1989; *Major Twentieth Century Writers; Something about the Author,* Vols. 7, and 62; and *Short Story Criticism,* Vol. 2.

Nicole Brossard
1943-

French Canadian poet, novelist, playwright, and essayist.

The following entry presents an overview of Brossard's life and career through 1997.

INTRODUCTION

Nicole Brossard played a pivotal role in the development of a postmodern literary movement in Quebec which focused on gender and language. As co-founder of the avant-garde periodical *La Barre du Jour* and the feminist collective *Les Têtes de Pioche,* Brossard helped to create a dialogue in Quebec poetics which affected a generation of writers. Eventually Brossard gained an international reputation as a feminist theorist as her works were translated into English, German, Italian, and Spanish.

Biographical Information

Born in Montreal, Brossard attended several different schools, including the University of Montreal. In 1965, she published her first group of poems in *Trois*—a collection of poetry which also featured Michel Beaulieu and Micheline de Jordy. That same year she co-founded *La Barre du Jour,* a literary journal devoted to the fusion of social and political analysis and the creative process. She taught from 1969 to 1971 before devoting herself to writing full time. Brossard's published work includes poetry, novels, and essays on feminist and literary theory. In 1976, she co-founded the radical feminist newspaper *Les Têtes de Pioche.* In 1991 she received the Athanase-David Prize of Quebec for her body of work.

Major Works

Brossard's career has had three distinct phases. In the 1960s she attempted to overcome the tendency in Quebec nationalist poetry to portray women as a mere representation of the land. The main focus of her poetry was similar to that of other 1960s writers in Quebec: portraying the country and its spatial features. However, Brossard took a new approach by using the human body and physiological features to map out history. She used language as a tool to explore new dimensions of being. In her poems, Brossard disrupted traditional rules of language, including syntax and French gender rules. In the 1970s, the second phase of her career, Brossard continued to write poetry, but also began experimenting with the novel. Her *Un livre* (1970; *A Book*) examines the construction of characters and plot as surface constructions ac-

cessible only through the acts of reading and writing. To Brossard, literature does not need to represent reality, but takes on a life of its own. Asserting that writing is research, therefore a hypothesis-generating act, not a reality-representing one, Brossard combines fiction and theory in her poetry and novels. She believes in the power of language to liberate the individual and to restructure social institutions. *Le Centre Blanc* (1978) is characteristic of the poetry of this period, with syntactical subversion and a lack of traditional grammatical order. The third phase of her career tackles issues of sexual difference. The focus of Brossard's work has increasingly narrowed to the topics of feminist and lesbian politics. *L'Amèr* (1977; *These Our Mothers*) is both a search for new language and an exploration of the responsibilities of motherhood. This work, in conjunction with *Le Sens apparent* (1980; *Surface of Sense*) and *Amantes* (1980; *Lovhers*), attempts to overcome patriarchal censorship and celebrate a lesbian utopia. *Amantes* is a collection of poetry dealing with lesbian love and the emotion of thought. *Picture Theory* (1982) reworks these ideas in a complex theoretical way. By developing combinations of meanings, the reader must engage in the creation of the text. *Le Désert*

Mauve (1987; *The Mauve Desert*) takes up the issue of translation of language, and how translation is an act of transformation.

Critical Reception

Some reviewers of Brossard's work complain that it is too complicated and difficult to understand. Critics assert that the intellectual nature and difficulty of Brossard's work makes it elitist and inaccessible to the masses. Marguerite Anderson admits that "while reading Nicole Brossard is invigorating, it is not easy." Much of the discussion surrounding Brossard's work centers on her theories of politics and literature. Louise H. Forsyth states that "Brossard writes with the assumption that both the personal and the poetic are political." Many reviewers point out Brossard's unique subversion of traditional syntax and narrative technique. Whether in complete agreement with her politics or her approach, most reviewers agree with Brossard's contributions to the literature of Quebec. Forsyth asserts Brossard's importance, saying, "Her works and activities have served to redefine Quebec letters and culture so effectively that her voice and the voices of many other women speaking and writing autonomously out of women-centered space are being heard and heeded."

PRINCIPAL WORKS

Mordre en sa chair [*To Bite the Flesh*] (poetry) 1966
L'Echo bouge beau (poetry) 1968
Suite logique (poetry) 1970
Un Livre [*A Book*] (novel) 1970
Sold-out, étreinte/illustration [*Turn of a Pang*] (novel) 1973
Mécanique jongleuse [*Daydream Mechanics*] (poetry) 1973
French Kiss: étreinte-exploration (novel) 1974
La Partie pour le tout (poetry) 1975
La Nef des sorcières [with Marie-Claire Blais, Marthe Blackburn, Luce Guilbeault, France Theoret, Odette Gagnon, and Pol Pelletier; *A Clash of Symbols*] (plays) 1976
L'Amèr; ou, le chapitre effrité [*These Our Mothers, or The Distintegrating Chapter*] (novel) 1977
Le Centre blanc: poèmes 1965-1975 (poetry) 1978
D'Arc de cycle la derive (poetry) 1979
Amantes [*Lovhers*] (poetry) 1980
Le Sens apparent [*Surface of Sense*] (novel) 1980
Picture Theory (novel) 1982
Double Impression: poèmes et textes 1967-1984 (poetry) 1984
Journal intime, ou, Voilà donc un manusrit (novel) 1984
L'Aviva (poetry) 1985

Domaine d'écriture (poetry) 1985
La Lettre aérienne [*The Aerial Letter*] (essays) 1985
Le Désert Mauve [*Mauve Desert*] (novel) 1987
Installations (poetry) 1989
A Tout regard (poetry) 1989
Typhon gru (poetry) 1990
Langues obscures [*Obscure Tongues*] (poetry) 1992
Green Night of Labyrinth Park (poetry) 1993
Baroque d'aube [*Baroque Dawn*] (novel) 1995

CRITICISM

Caroline Bayard (essay date Fall 1977)

SOURCE: "Subversion Is the Order of the Day," in *Essays on Canadian Writing,* Nos. 7/8, Fall, 1977, pp. 17-25.

[*In the following essay, Bayard compares Brossard's earlier work to her later writing, tracing her growth as a writer.*]

It has been said about Québécois writers that they start writing earlier and produce more than their English Canadian or European counterparts, as if the inner pressures and the cultural motivations which sustain them are intensely productive. Whether or not this generalization is valid, it holds true for Nicole Brossard. In 1965, when she was 22, her first volume of poetry, **Aube à la saison,** was published, and in that same year she founded *La Barre du Jour;* and her next, **Mordre en sa chair,** came out the following year.

It is surprising to examine these early works today in the light of her later, more daring, and complex avant-garde experiments, for they seem bent upon a different quest, less looped into their own linguistic movements and more interested in mapping out their spatial territory, their "appartenance".

This term, from *appartenir* or to belong to, to be owned by, to be possessed by, is essential to an understanding of the middle 50's and early 60's in Quebec. The poetic output from this period is constantly preoccupied with embodying a country and its spatial features. In his long poem *Arbres,* Paul-Marie Lapointe not only enumerates all the trees of Quebec but through them affirms a specific space, the specific features of the land. Jean-Louis Major refers to this process in the following way:

> En un sens, le verbe dire est premier, mais par un autre biais il a—avec toutes les fonctions qui s'y apparentent—valeur de naissance et de fondation; dans la poésie québécoise, la parole participe d'ailleurs à la structure sémantique de la naissance.

It has been said more particularly of Gaston Miron and Paul Chamberland that their poetry at that time was "La recherche ardente d'un mode d'habiter" and that they had to assume the ownership of their land by naming it, by giving linguistic weight to its physical features.

It has been said about Québécois writers that they start writing earlier and produce more than their English Canadian or European counterparts, as if the inner pressures and the cultural motivations which sustain them are intensely productive. Whether or not this generalization is valid, it holds true for Nicole Brossard.
—*Caroline Bayard*

This need to describe a territory in order to define it, this hunger for a word which is capable of giving flesh to the Québécois genesis, is still present in Brossard's first two volumes. It does not have the rage of Paul Chamberland's *Génèses* or the passionate minuteness of Paul-Marie Lapointe's *Arbres.* Clearly, this territory has already been charted by other explorers. Brossard knows that she comes after them, that she cannot duplicate their achievements. Thus there is no plea for a passionate assertion of space-time structures in her lines. Instead, what she sets out to map in 1966 is not Quebec's territory but the human body. "les yeux collent à la peau . . . / ou étire le ventre de l'angoisse; / il fait brume à la moëlle du coeur; / le feu blanchit l'épiderme." History or time takes on physiological features, it is made flesh, given corporeal pleasure, pain, veins, blood, hair and muscles: "tout demain a des ciselures sur la peau." Thus it is not surprising to see her look for a face, a human face, when she needs a mirror for the world:

> sur miroir insolite de visage
> saltimbanque et planète
> mosaïque de sensations
> à perte de vue découpée

or to observe the way she refers to her belly as a place for the day to sink:

> il croule   en mon ventre
> ce jour pendu à sa racine

The uninitiated reader whose eye jumps from these poems to her more complex, illogical, semantically and grammatically ambiguous constructions in *La Partie pour le tout* will be puzzled. The key to a perceptive reading of Brossard's latest writings is to be found in a number of articles published in *La Barre du Jour* between 1968 and 1970, as well

as in a manifesto which came out in *La Presse* in 1970. These writings illuminate the ideological and esthetic milieu out of which Brossard comes.

In the view of Francois Charron and Roger Des Roches, the changes in contemporary literature arise from their denunciation of the text as a mirror, as a reflection of the objective world. What they advocate, instead, is that full recognition be given to the text-matter, to its phonemes, linguistic components, sounds and signs. The vital components of the literary text, as they see it, are the linguistic tensions among its visual, graphic and sonic elements, and the way these are resolved. Charron and Des Roches envision these changes as the struggle of materialistic philosophy against idealism, a productive-transformativeprocess which does not sublimate the poetic act or reduce the text to what they call "un simple reportage . . . la description d'un match".

Therefore her poetry, as in *Le Centre blanc,* and her novels, in *French Kiss,* do not have to reproduce or reconstruct reality as we know it; they grow and exist on their own, each sentence organically growing and feeding the next, one word, or even one phoneme, calling for another.

The reader who enjoys poetry but does not find the arid lands of theory attractive will probably be puzzled by a first reading of *Le Centre blanc.* Two main factors may arouse uneasiness. First of all, the syntactical foundations of this text have exploded into disconnected units. Verb, predicate, article, adverb—each element has been displaced, or misplaced, and even an obstinate reader, tempted to re-establish this order, will fail to do so. There is no grammatically sound order; her lines are all the more beguiling in that they invite error by first making us expect a poetic but syntactically safe structure:

> romprou la tension très difficile de savoir,
> ailleurs qu'en ses muscles ceux-ci tendus,
> à l'extrême force puisque modification
> l'ordre des contraintes n'étante plus le même
> l'équilibre perdu toute concentration cependant vibrante la tension ou quand l'attention est soutenue plusiers fois systématique dans une seule tentative l'attention portée versdans énonçant l'intelligence de chaque chacun

Conjunctions and adverbs linking clauses are missing, or when present, are used in such a way as to make them look obsolete. All punctuation has been banished; the reader becomes a prey to great uncertainties as the visual necessity to discern logical clusters of words becomes too pressing.

This shaken syntax produces a variety of possible word-clusters, henceforth a range of possible meanings. Quite simply, the semantic direction of this text is closely dependent upon the number of units one chooses to permit in a given clause, upon the way the eye uses blanks or ignores them.

The tense rectangular paragraphs in *Le Centre blanc* are a labyrinth full of holes, blanks, thick word-clusters which take the reader close to the edge of meaning while losing him in a syntactical maze out of which no Ariadne's tricks can free him. Discomfort arises not so much from the negation of old expectations as from the constant illusion that some meaning will emerge. And, as the eye is led from trap to trap, it becomes apparent that this is the only finality of the text: to lure us and to abandon us. The reader's uneasiness may take him in two opposite directions. He may find that such discontinuity demands too much of a leap, or he may accept the game with its alternatives, its illogical patterns. Similar alternatives emerge from her novels. *French Kiss* is particularly illustrative of this new fiction which buries characters, their psychology, and their tensions in order to explore the fine movements of their muscles, the smell of their pores, the texture of their hair. The novel's focus is upon objects, sensations, and the way they hit the eye or start chain reactions of varying orders and intensities in all five senses. But the narrative flow also turns in upon itself:

> Le bleu du ciel, topographie, courbe d'arc-en-ciel. Le bleu du ciel tautologique et obsédant (pluriel: bleu/ciel).

or

> Le décor est à abolir
> Parchemin, on n'oserait / D / écrire: réanimer à la occasion que l'on provoque. Narrateur / détonateur. On m'entend venir de loin, délire conique, on me voit venir en pelisse de louve, prête comme une narratrice à bondir sur tout sujet, toute bonbance.

There are in fact two narrators somewhat at odds with each other here: the "narrator/detonator", an obvious intruder who mocks writing by showing us its mechanisms—stratagems, artifices, nuts and bolts; and the "neutral receptor", a resounding board for all the sensations crowding the text. Narrator no. 1 exerts censorial control over no. 2, but it is difficult to assess how much or when. As we are being taken from street to room to bed to ceiling, the inevitability of this narrative wandering is as absolute as it is arbitrary. Yet we never actually know what the other possibilities are, or would have been. All we know is that no. 1 is energized by syntactical rules:

> Chevauche la syntaxe. Ça m'incite et dicte une suite très matinale encore à cette heure-ci qu'il est long le pont à traverser.

Even he feels betrayed and/or manipulated by a huge reservoir of obscure forces behind him:

> Les yeux se dérobent. Une tradition, une lecture, des ancêtres dont aucun narrateur ne peut être certain.

More often than not he is the great manipulator, the magician who stops the other's (no. 2) tricks. As the text verges on the erotic, he moves in and promptly stops all proceedings:

> On pourrait jouer aux échecs, aux dames, au no, au domino [. . . .] faire l'amour. [. . . .] Camomille, j'ai très envie de caresser tes seins. Rideau fictif.

> Derrière la fiction, le miroir, le verre et le tain, Camomille et Lucy comme projection holographique, visages tridimentionnels sur le rideau, l'écran qui révèle le plaisir et ne le cache point comme un pan d'ombre, une circonstance irrecevable.

Brossard has said of *French Kiss* that it offered her the opportunity to let her imagination and her senses go unfettered, that anything could be said, played with, thrown on the white page, and experimented with. Even more than syntactical rules it is the false order of fictions which is broken here: what the eye sees, the tongue narrates. Logic and inner coherence have been dispersed to the four winds of narrative subversion. The narrator is as unreliable as his syntax.

> **L'Amèr is not only an act of courage about an era of experience which had to be poetically explored, it is also an attempt to reconcile the irreconcilable poles of political commitment and esthetic statement.**
> **—Caroline Bayard**

With the poetry in *Mécanique jongleuse* and *La Partie pour le tout,* she stylistically remains on the offensive. Syntax, grammar, lay-out, punctuation, spelling, omissions, all concur, to different degrees, to upset the rules and give us a provocative text, lashed by blanks and typographical variations, ambiguous hyphens, brackets and parentheses.

Although referentiality is reduced to a minimum in these texts, there are nevertheless sexual images, the erotic metaphors which Brossard weaves through her precarious syntactical scaffoldings. Literary eroticism becomes a linguistic tension between the sign on the page and sexual satisfaction.

If there are dialectically opposed movements, each still re-

veals itself as game-like, playful, gratuitous, intensely enjoyable exercises.

> l'épiderme une grammaire gratuite
> de silence toile d'impressions de
> représentation
> feu: l'artifice un parcours
> de derme s'en détache les voyelles
> illustrent
> les éponges douces sur l'épi beau

There is a complicity, but also an ironic sense of defiance,
between the two movements, as if they were almost bent on
similar ends and yet wanted to destroy each other at the same
time:

> la vague retracée surface lubrifiante dénude son
> corps pendant
> qu'elle remue sur vos hanches endoréiques sans
> qu'il soit de
> comparaison mais de sous-entendu

Stylistic figures and sexual movements occasionally—but
only occasionally—become one:

> percevant du domaine textuel
>   l'engageante
> surface
> est-ce transparence ou plutôt écran
> et trace de mauve et d'humide désir
>   jouxtant
> là au centre et cerne de moi
> ETREINDRE
> alors que dure en la démemce
> ce connaître éprouvé vacillant
> avance et s'étend presque comme jailli
>   le blanc de toi

This new writing tolls the death of the old humanism, as
Brossard's pre-1975 writings show; but this death takes on
new significance in the light of her growth as a feminist
writer. For if new writing has no social responsibility, how
are we to read Brossard's latest yet unpublished work
L'Amèr? Neither her two novels **Sold-out** or **French Kiss**
or her later volumes of poetry **Méconique jongleuse** and **La
Partie pour le tout** allows a challenge of her formalistic positions through ideological necessity or social responsibility. **L'Amèr** deals with both the theory of writing and a
woman's daily experience. The conflicts here are raw: they
brutally expose the contradictions between a search for a new
language and the responsibilities of motherhood. One finds
in **L'Amèr** the need for a linguistic exploration as well as a
brutal awakening to pain, guilt and fear:

> j'écris, ma fille a la fièvre

si je continuais d'écrire elle pourrait en mourir.

Brossard practises little or no censorship here. The fears, the
anger, the ugly frustrations, the guilt-patterns which underline a mother and child relationship are all left bare for other
women's eyes to see and recognize—if they have the courage to do so. **L'Amèr** is, according to Brossard's own words,
"une fiction du privé" where she opens all the taboos—
sexual love between women, "les mères enlacées" and the
hidden truths, that of the milk turned sour in women's
breasts, "le lait est vert, il a sûri".

But **L'Amèr** is not only an act of courage about an era of
experience which had to be poetically explored, it is also
an attempt to reconcile the irreconcilable poles of political
commitment and esthetic statement. Brossard does not want
to give up her new awareness of herself as a feminist and a
mother, any more than she rejects the quest for a new idiom,
fresh, unfettered and frightening. She does not envision the
praxis of political work as destructive of poetic intuitions
for, as she says in **L'Amèr,** "ce qui devient réalité politique
est influencé par le fictif". The role of fiction is to continue
shaking the pillars of the old order, as liberation goes through
the destruction of syntax and phallocentrism. One's own militancy is to be witnessed not only on picket lines and women's
collectives but also on the page, squarely facing the print
and phonemes yet to be born.

Nicole Brossard with *Canadian Fiction Magazine* (interview date 1983)

SOURCE: "Interview with Nicole Brossard on Picture
Theory," in *Canadian Fiction Magazine,* No. 47, 1983, pp.
122-35.

[*In the following interview, Brossard discusses the form and
major themes of her novel* Picture Theory, *and its relationship to her other work.*]

[*Canadian Fiction Magazine:*] *Firstly, why did you return
to an English expression by an Austrian writer, Wittgenstein,
in a Québecois novel that deals with language?*

[Brossard:] In **Amantes,** I had already used the expression
"Picture theory" for its intriguing, aesthetic qualities, if I may
use those terms. It's an expression that fascinated, seduced
me. On the one hand because of the word "picture," and on
the other because of the word "theory." Little by little I got
to know the works of Wittgenstein. So "Picture theory" could
be rendered by "picture of reality" or "painting of reality."
I don't think the word "theory" can be translated by the same
word in French, not in that expression anyway. I was intrigued and probably got my first inspiration after reading:

"one can not express reality, one can only show it." That's why I wrote in the last chapter: "Language is a spectacle of what we can not imagine as such." The only way I could express the spectacle of the unthinkable was by the grammatical intervention of the feminine plural. I am inspired by the works of Wittgenstein in much the same way as by the works of Barthes, among others. So much reading has stimulated my research, my examination of language and its fictitious reality. For instance, I am interested in tautology and its relation to sense and nonsense, and I intend to work on that among other things as a follow-up to the paper I presented at the conference on "The emergence of culture in the feminine," as well as on the reading of the works of Gertrude Stein, which function according to that principle. Wittgenstein is important as a stimulus support, but so is the idea of the hologram, which applied to writing prompts me to want to explore a word, an idea, a concept in order to grasp all its dimensions. Just as I have to explore my own subjectivity.

In the whole of your works, however, this is still an important innovation: for the first time, you haven't invented it all yourself. That brings us back to the intertextuality of the title, which may be metonymical in relation to the workings of your text. One could also emphasize the fact that Wittgenstein didn't choose the titles of any of his books.

But when you talk of borrowing, you mustn't forget that **French Kiss** is a ready-made expression, as are **Un livre, Sold-out,** and **Suite logique.**

Let us move on to the two quotations you use as an epigraph to your novel. The quotation from Wittgenstein in a literal translation might read: "What can be said, can only be said by means of the sentence, and so nothing necessary to the comprehension of all the sentences, can be said." Does this imply a failure of language?

Not a failure; to quote again from Wittgenstein: "The world is everything that happens." One could also say: the sentence is everything that happens. And that surely links up with what I was saying about "Picture theory"—one can not express, one can only show. I would even add: one can not express, one can only write. In that sense it is necessary for the understanding of the word "show." I've continually been playing with enigmas, of which the first and greatest is: how to make a woman appear, how to "show" her through whom anything can happen. This is doubtless why the idea of the hologram is so important in this book: for what is a hologram if not a visibly fictitious reality? And that is the question I asked myself to see if I wasn't, in my turn, going to make another woman appear fictitious. When I want to make a woman appear real. But still, I wasn't able to remove all the images that I had around the hologram and it may well be that without these images, I would not have been able to

portray in words her through whom anything can happen. I wanted, at all costs, to avoid repeating that the first woman is a mother. Am I answering the question?

Yes, in as far as you say you want to "show." But this sentence is very striking at the beginning of the book. It is difficult to integrate with the rest. For the moment, there is still a barrier.

The sentences follow one another and each one creates the whole of the plan by showing the other sentences and being shown by them. Could one understand the whole plan if one expressed it in a single sentence as plan? Each sentence is part of the plan and makes the last chapter, which is the hologram, plausible. The whole book is structured so as to arrive at the writing of this *Hologramme*. To me, **Picture Theory** is a novel that I wrote with the feeling of having a three-dimensional consciousness, that is, at a certain point, especially in chapter 4 and even throughout the writing of the text, I had the feeling that for the first time I was experiencing the aerial vision that I've already talked about in other works. I was seeing immediately the semantic, syntactic, grammatical and acoustic effect. At the time of writing this novel I had the feeling of an absolutely extraordinary synthesis. This synthesis was accompanied by an enigma, a feeling of strangeness, just as there is a feeling of strangeness when one sees a hologram. It is "obvious," one sees the object, one knows how the image is produced, but one can't get rid of the feeling of total illusion. Effect, feeling, or emotion cause the resurgence of the enigma or the strangeness that I felt throughout the writing of **Picture Theory,** while still having the most acute sense of synthesis and precision. I hope the novel will be read as I wrote it, in a continuous to and fro between the pages.

*In that sense **Picture** would be like the illustration paving the way by various means to finally arrive at a definition, a "showing" so that this woman manages, as the last sentence of your book puts it: "in the total illusion of abundance to claim to be perfectly readable."*

Yes, but at the same time these are not stages in the sense that "because I know A I will know B, because I know B I will know C." It is quite complex: these are not explanatory or demonstrative markers that work in any linear way (although in certain details or fragments there is some linearness which dissolves completely at the end of the last chapter). I think we have to talk in terms of sentences rather than in terms of stages or milestones. *In the term of a sentence* keeping in mind both the singular and the plural of "term," could also have been the title of **Picture Theory.**

Can one say that the repetition and metaphorical use of definitions in the novel have created a sort of hologram, the por-

trait of this woman one is trying to show, in a fictitious relationship, of course?

I would hope so. I try to portray this woman by considering all subjectivities as well as my own. The choice of one word over another serves to define or to image the logic of the text. For instance, when I say that Sarah Stein is listening to a recording of Schumann. I had at first written Schubert, but logic demanded Schumann because of the sound "shoe" and "man" since the expression *the heel of man* appears often in the text. It is the text itself that structures its system of images and meaning.

There is also a sort of repetition, a "logical series" in the constant presence of the city. How is this expressed in the novel?

> **To me, *Picture Theory* is a novel that I wrote with the feeling of having a three-dimensional consciousness, that is, at a certain point . . . I had the feeling that for the first time I was experiencing the aerial vision that I've already talked about in other works.**
> **—*Nicole Brossard***

The word city actually has two meanings: *the place,* and that links up with the feeling one has of life amid the noises and the bodies, the feeling of the place, a sort of cultural sensuality; and then, of course, the city as the *business centre,* which evokes the institutions. The first chapter, entitled *L'Ordinaire,* introduces the city by describing it in, and through the concept of darkness (for instance: the subway, the elevator, the black-out of New York, the bars, the entrance halls of the Hotel), the blackness here being associated with the patriarchy, not in contrast to white, but as the absence of light. In the second chapter, which in fact becomes Book One, one enters into the light, supported by a vocabulary heavy in the symbolist tradition: forest, water, sea, angel, helmet, etc. The city, then, is especially evident in *L'Ordinaire,* but it appears again in chapter 4, *La Pensée.* Here I am concerned with two things: the city where the writing is taking place (Montreal) and the writing table. The author returns to her writing table and the city is born in the fiction as it develops. *Un livre* and *French Kiss* both had similar chapters dealing with the city. I have the impression that with *Picture theory* (this is what I felt while I was writing) I have produced a synthesis of all the novels I have written. A synthesis of what is working plurally within me.

Where does the first sentence come from: "I am exercising my faculties of synthesis"? It echoes **le Sens apparent,** **Amantes** *and* **L'Amèr.** *The last sentence of* **L'Amèr** *here becomes concrete.*

We mustn't leave out *Un livre,* because I believe that everything I consent to as well as everything I reject at a textual level is expressed in condensed form in this book.

In this novel the city is more than just a force—there are also privileged places where privileged things happen. Often a kind of homosexuality is connoted. It is striking that the more the characters are in a fringe area inside the city, the more the women-sentences seem free and light—on the island, south of Cape Cod for example. Things are less rushed, less "blacked-out" than in New York. Even at the level of the writing—when the women are around the table one feels a certain freedom in the style and wonders why this is not the case in New York?

The city-centre is homo-ideological, the city is homo-sexist; the island is utopian, the island is the place of replenishment. But what interests me in the city as well as on the island is that people are thinking. That is why, in all my books, novels anyway, there is always a table. A writing table and/or a restaurant table where people are engaged in discussions while eating, drinking, smoking. Inside, outside around a table. In my work there is always a table and a street. Basically, the places mentioned in the city are almost always mentioned in reference to my view of writing, my desire to write, or to an actualization of the writing. For example, the third chapter is set on an island, but one can also say that the heart of the chapter is set around the table when the five women come together for their meals. The island is a privileged place because it recalls utopia and because the imaginary world proceeds both from the utopia and from the books the women brought with them to the island. As far as the writing is concerned, the city demands elliptical writing—one doesn't want to see everything and one can't see everything given the number of stimuli. On the island, time works differently, and the writing reflects this by its fluidity.

Isn't there some danger of isolation in a mythical or utopian spot, which is more or less what the desert island is, the setting of the emotion in the third chapter? Isn't emotion always somewhere on the fringe?

The male imagination lacks the ability to conceive that women together could re-invent the world (ideas, emotion, sexuality, creativity, games). This inability rubs off on the female imagination. The island, the utopian spot, thus becomes a challenge for the imagination, for writing. Emotion becomes civilization: one reads, one thinks, one discusses, one writes, one exchanges. The emotion doesn't go in circles, it does have consequences. Utopia is not a dream, it is an emotion.

Don't you feel you could be criticized for not having seen the emotion in New York?

I don't see how. But one could say: "Isn't there a contradiction: you put the women together and you express emotion, and then return a little later in chapter 4 to say that you know little about emotion?" That's true, but in chapter 4 emotion has taken another meaning; it concerns the individual, the narrator, the woman who is writing and who certainly wouldn't be were she not emotion itself. What interests her in emotion is the idea of emotion, the process of emotion. She gives up the emotion of the spoken word in order to write. If she didn't the writing would not be emotion. As for suffering, which she also claims to know little about, this must be seen as a strategic lie that refers us once again to the writing. I know that for many women suffering is at the root of their writing; for me, writing is at the root of writing. That can be neither shown nor is it said.

It must have been impossible to use a setting other than this isolated island for the conversation, the creation of the text, the words and the language, for the emotional creation as well as the definitions (all this filtered by a woman's vision) so that women might isolate themselves to rediscover themselves, to reformulate themselves, in women concepts.

I think this is a reference to what one calls privileged places where privileged people are gathered with whom one can go the farthest distance possible in discussions, thoughts, insofar as one accepts critical and exploratory work. To me, it is clear that women can only be thought by themselves. They must, therefore, avoid anything that acts as a parasite on their thought. Woman's work is produced in chapter 1 when Florence Derive gives her lecture, but immediately there are distractions. Someone says: "Yes, but men. . . ." There are always interruptions. Discussion does take place, but you can not follow your train of thought. The island, on the other hand, is the place where thought can expand, where time and mental space become other. I say on the island, but I must add "around the table, on the island."

But the real work of research on women and on writing is carried out on this island where the five women meet up, where there is an elaboration, women's words that are neither blocked nor stopped.

Yes, and when the women leave the big house, they are immediately overwhelmed by sexist songs, by the need to negotiate, to deal with the patriarchy; they are caught up again by this atmosphere. Even on the boat, on their arrival, there is a flash: the old reflex, they turn around. They don't just turn toward the flash, but toward the man who is taking the picture. There are all these reminders of the patriarchy. The only place they can really become explorers is around the table on their own. When an anecdote filters in, it is inter-

rupted. For instance, when Oriana tells the story of her life, twelve or fifteen sentences suffice, because for each sentence one can guess the rest.

The concept of abstraction recurs very often in this novel. Perhaps we should talk about it. One particular sentence refers to the relation between emotion and abstraction: "At the source of every emotion, is an abstraction. . . ." And this ends with: "Abstraction is a solution." One thus starts off from an abstraction, which gives rise to an emotion, only to realize that at the end one is returning to the abstraction. Could you elaborate on that?

The word abstraction works just like the title "Picture theory." As a seductive word, a vital enigma. It is linked to the notion of theory, which is also often seen as an abstraction. I see nothing abstract in an abstraction insofar as it is the result of a feeling, an intuition, or an emotion. It is always the result of what appears in the subjectivity of the person who is expressing himself. Abstraction is transcended subjectivity. Once it has been expressed, it becomes the source of emotion because the mystery is resurfacing. Because along the way one forgets one's subjective course. Abstraction is thought-compelling because it is "strangely" familiar. In a word it tells the truth without one really remembering the why. To be afraid of abstraction would be like being afraid of life itself.

One doesn't have all the pieces; one has lost (in the sense of abstracted) some along the way. One only has a conceptualized sign that has lost its subjective embodiment, and given rise to the abstraction. . . .

Little by little, one abstracts the essential from things and from beings. One concentrates on the abstraction becoming motivation and primary motive. In that sense one has lost nothing, but rather eliminated the detailed anecdotes and retained only the idea. This is not easy, but it is exhilarating. That is partly what I mean when I talk of aerial vision and aerial letter. This is something vertiginous, but bedazzling.

*Might this word "abstraction" not be the new link with the other books? One suddenly finds this word in the centre, the concrete origin of l'Hologramme. And the hologram one could find at the level of the analysis already in **French Kiss**, or by allusion in the other texts. In some settings the omnipresence of abstraction as a positive plan, in the general sense, would be something to be avoided. In **Picture Theory** abstraction is automatically linked to utopia (and once again the meaning of the word utopia is altered in relation to utopia in general, whether one sees it as the utopia of the counter-culture or as the origin of utopia). This is where strangely enough the woman appears to exist between abstraction and utopia. And here is a new link with abstraction, a word that is strictly taboo even among intel-*

lectuals, and a notion of utopia which engenders a definite emotion specific to women in the course of organizing themselves.

I think it is new because here the word is "shown," written. It has its own radiation. I must say this was essential to my plan. For from the real, from reality—for example in the white scene, which is a love scene—I absolutely had to abstract the essential or the light, the aura produced by the two lovers. That is why I end the chapter saying: "we had become vital abstractions." It is only when these women have become abstractions that they can be everything, complete. They can be angels, light, the four elements, etc. I can say that textually, without this scene, I would not have been able to portray "her through whom anything can happen," the woman who "makes contact." In relation to her, the mother is a symbolical by product. Some day one should try to understand why abstraction is so striking to the imagination. I feel that there is something mythical there.

We must talk about integrality and origin, which may have been seen as a passage toward difference.

The notion of completeness and integrity appears in **Picture Theory** (the woman who appears is complete, inalterable). In **Picture Theory** there is theoretical work on this question, but it is self-actualized through the fiction. At the origin of words is Man's subjectivity, and as far as we have learned to consume words, we have consumed them with their root. We are now in the process of uprooting ourselves from the subjectivity/objectivity of Man to take root in our own subjectivity that transforms reality. Women have to be at the root of the meaning they give to life, to their lives. **Picture Theory** is the pleasure of writing, but it is also the question about origin that troubles Claire Derive and the narrator M. V. considerably. In fact, it is the origin of meaning. By what means can one get to the origin of meaning? For life to have a meaning, for life to be accessible by being readable, for it not to be the constant effect of contradiction. To put *an end* to ambiguity. And that brings us back to the question of sense and nonsense, back to tautology. At the beginning of this novel there is a fundamental question: will the patriarchy take place again? How can we make the word *woman* be at the root and generate general and specific meaning, be the driving force behind all the reading of all the realities, and plausible at the same time? I would place the turning-point in **Skin Screen Utopia** when I make this woman appear. I say that this time Claire Derive will speak *without an accent* to make her through whom anything can happen, appear. I end book 4 with "skin the tongue goes to the brain." For finally this woman has become readable, completely. She has become plausible, readable insofar as she is the creation of a feminine (mine and others) and a feminist subjectivity. She is accessible in the philosophical sense of the word: she can actually become her through whom anything can hap-

pen. She can generate abstraction, emotion, vitality, energy, "truth." One can never be complete without first being radically curious about meaning. For women the question of meaning is fundamental because it links with the question of their onto-symbolical existence. For a man, *to be or not to be* is an incidental phrase because man exists. I would even say he over-exists, he pre-exists through God. For a woman, *to be* is the question. Thus the fusion of the root and integrality gives the verb to be.

Might there not be another side to concrete abstraction in the dichotomy between an intertextuality with Joyce and the relation with perfectly readable sentences? Usually Joyce is the author who is furthest removed from perfect readability. Might there not be a new synthesis that draws a picture, a new "picture theory"? The reference to Joyce is surprising: why choose Finnegan's Wake *if not for the complexity of this novel, a reference to its different styles?*

The reference is there. It is like an obsession with a final examination of form and expression, and again also of sense and non-sense. How far can one go with the whole and with detail? One can do almost anything with words. I also thought of Gauvreau; everything retraced as being plausible, letter by letter one can retrace a subjectivity. There is even sense in the nonsense when there is an existential stake. When there is no stake, there are "clownish cats sadly." Writing, when one doesn't think of abandoning it, and I have no intention of that, is its own beginning and end. But an obsession with size must accompany it, an obsession doubtlessly nourished by a who am I in the language that speaks to me internally—by this I don't mean the mother tongue, but a figurative language, so figurative that to live with it, I have to abstract its essential. For Joyce it is Ireland, for me it is Woman. In answer to the question who I am in this language: I am all or nothing. That is why writing exhausts itself at everything, and ends by touching the untouchable body of the language, the grammar. Intertextuality is the memory of the sweat of writing. The sweat that "take pains."

Could one describe this novel as being baroque? One of the characteristics of the baroque is, after all, mobility, changing perspectives.

I couldn't use that term in my plan; it is not one of the dimensions that I am aware of in **Picture Theory.** I always imagine a great lack of precision in the baroque because of this change in perspective. Whereas with perspective in thought and writing, one always maintains a sense of precision of the image one observes or even of the image one thinks. In an analysis one may see some correspondence with the baroque; but in practice and within the circuit of my imagination the baroque did not serve as an inspiration.

But in the repetition, the plurality, the varying angles, in the question of anamorphosis, one could see the appearance of the woman as a sort of angle. It is interesting that an author doesn't always see all the ways his work can be read. Your resistance to the word baroque is interesting. It is a corpus or an idea from which all women have been removed: there are no famous women architects of the baroque. Perhaps because the baroque is quite near madness, and women, afraid of being surcharged with madness, did not "embark" on the idea of the baroque, while the men do it casually.

I see the baroque as a great exuberance of form and relief. When one works with the hologram, it is the feeling of relief, and not the relief as such, that predominates. It is a game of virtual and real images. Simply the fact of thinking in terms of the hologram and the laser (coherent light) places us in a different relationship with reality, and with forms, which transforms our impression of the world, the knowledge, the learning, the illusion of the world. In terms of energy, this is simple and produces new perspectives and, especially, new dimensions. When one talks about mobility, it would be preferable to use the expression chromatic fringe, that is, the blur of the chromatic fringe. All the references are linked to light, also to scientific dimensions, to work on the use of energy. I think we must be careful not to connote the novel feelings of the 20th and the 21st centuries with other feelings, products of a totally different observation of the body in space, of the eye and consequently of the imagination.

From the perspective of this light, wouldn't the Scène blanche *be a libidinous bond, a privileged place?*

It is a privileged place that appears in quite an unexpected way. Someone goes to look for a book, and one doesn't know if it is a scene from the book or the white scene on the rug with the arbitrary date May 16. It is a love scene where little of the action is seen or consummated—although I say the opposite in presenting it—a relatively novel scene in our everyday life. It is a love scene, but above all a scene of this light which gives life and completeness, which makes each one of the two women become whole. One witnesses the appearance of the mother, the mirror; one explores nature, the city-centre, the cities through their filled libraries, life, death. One experiences energy in its most concrete, most scientific, most materialized form. It was a desire for synthesis where the whole of life would be given. Everything is concentrated here. These words meant nothing as long as I wasn't writing the text. There again is cliché whose meaning is turned around: it can be a hand that directly touches the breast or the clothing or the genitals. It isn't necessary that this happen very gently to contrast with the cliché of brutality. Anything can happen. There is something else that accompanies this scene: the idea, the abstraction, the concept, everything we experience in real or abstract terms.

Could the Scène blanche *be the origin?*

Exactly. It is the spiritual birth, which, at that point, can only be expressed by poetry and which, although apart, is all-pervasive. It is a scene of concentration, of meditation, expressions that I use in **Amantes.**

The scene appears sporadically, especially in the chapter **L'Ordinaire,** *and acts as an important counterpoint allowing the utopia of* **Skin Screen Utopia** *to come to light, a counterpoint taken up again in the whole, but this time as a hope of* l'Hologramme *come true.*

This scene does in fact haunt the whole book. In the first chapter it is already there, almost announced, then it becomes more concrete. Then it is put aside a little, but it actually nourishes the whole text to arrive at myself—writing, to give birth to this woman—not as a mother but as a writer, in a relation to words, in their organization. She can be born, can exist, can take her whole place.

Could this be le Centre blanc *of poetry? In the story it would become a* Scène blanche?

It is true that **le Centre blanc** is the first collection I wrote, in the belief that in writing one could express the essential. That one could really say the ultimate about life, that poetry could satisfy the expression of that energy. In **Scène blanche** it is basically the same process that makes me want to express the essential. Here it occurs between two women and will create words as a result, will give rise to other words which will make this woman appear, at the same time abstract, real, fictitious, concrete and carnal. It is fundamentally the same principle. Just now I said it was the same obsession that gave rise to **Un livre,** and to the inserts in **French Kiss** and in **Sold-Out.** I think the **Scène blanche** comes from the same search for the essential, the energy of the subject as in **le Centre blanc.** The same person did write the two texts.

There is something almost subliminal about the story (almost in the perverse sense used in advertising) that treats the women's issue in a new way, and by superimposition, by images like those in the hologram, actually makes us believe in the existence of this utopian testimony about the necessary existence of women in history.

That is a very perverse question. It is true that the word "subliminal" has been very important. The question has been there throughout the text. But what does it mean? It means that one has perceived something as a truth and that suddenly one has lost track of what was true (the working of the hologram). However, instead of being in front of us, this truth is in our heads. It has been recorded. I am sure that in the writing of this text, the subliminal is at work. It works especially by the repetition and the appearance of words like "abstraction" (sometimes where they are not expected) and by the linking of words like "emotion," "feeling," "idea," "concept," then by a sort of geographical environment of words like "the city," "the water," "the desert," "the mountain," and finally by a certain number of references to "heel," to "helmet," etc. All that is at work. But every time it reappears, it does so in a meaningful way, so that one can not help but recall that "it's been here before." Even if one feels one has forgotten, it crosses the different levels of consciousness.

Like the word **Skin Screen,** *which has a vast range of meaning. The* screen *can be a net, a veil; it can hide, it can unveil, it can allow something to pass, to escape, etc. The order of the subliminal certainly enters in that sense.*

I even say that "when you have a room of your own, you can still screen a corner of the room." I have a room of my own, but not in order to unveil everything; it is also in order to have a screen and I need to cross it, to attract Michèle Vallée ("I knew that the screen behind her would be lowered"). There again it is a question of virtual and real images, or of images to be guessed or suspected. The *screen* of the skin is also very important. The skin is a screen filled with images which provide sensations.

In advertising, the subliminal sets out to convince. Isn't this aspect dealt with in the most "subliminal" way in **Picture Theory?** *This seems to be a new aspect in relation to the theoretical aspect expressed in* **l'Amèr.**

That is why I could not call this book theoretical fiction as I did *l'Amèr.* **Picture Theory** is a book that prepares for theory. I think that all fictional writing works with the subliminal, whatever its quality or its mediocrity. When I say, for instance, "one word rather than another at the speed of light," it reflects the subliminal trait of thought and of writing. That also explains the terror we have of losing our manuscripts. Every writer is himself the "victim" of the subliminal in his texts. It is true to say that the subliminal is at work—I would even draw attention to it by virtue of the fact that this process reflects what in me tries to rise onto the screen of my thought. The chapter of the *Hologramme* is in a certain way the visual moment when the image finally stays fixed on the retina long enough to no longer be an illusion. "Shown," it is perfectly readable. The whole of **Picture Theory** is the story of the implementation of this image, in other words, everything was written so that I might capture a clear image of her through whom anything can happen. An image that is clear, complete, three-dimensional, inalterable.

The work of writing is thus done in transparent strata and this produces the movement of reading (which refers back to the working of the hologram). How then, can one find in this book the markers that indicate the other works? Does **Picture Theory** *function as a condensation of the thought processes of writing and of feminism?*

Yes, I think it is a synthesis of my method of writing from a feminist consciousness, from lesbian emotion and thought that open into essay and poetry. When I look at **Picture Theory,** I realize that the first chapter could have been a page from **Un livre.** The second, although it is different from **Amantes,** could be the moment of **Amantes;** but it works differently. It goes beyond sensuality, beyond sexuality, it joins **le Centre blanc** in the way we already discussed. It moves on into a transcendent, even philosophical dimension. The third chapter is what appears in **Sold-Out, French Kiss** and **le Sens apparent,** in other words, there is always this attempt to write a chapter with a subject-verb-complement as in the inserts of **Sold-Out** and **French Kiss,** or in the fluid writing of **Sens apparent.** It is the temptation of the always disputed, always diverted story. I very seldom consent to the subject-verb-complement or to the anecdote. I have played on the present and the imperfect tenses which create quite a different relationship between very fluid sentences. I played on a certain number of clichés like "the obscure clarity." Chapter 4 is in my usual style. Chapter 5 is quite novel in terms of breathing and rhythm. This is a synthesis which in a different way could nourish the books yet to come. I am thinking of an essay on modernity, on writing, on feminism and lesbianism, on the imaginary, aerial vision, the hologram, light, etc. On tautology also. **Picture Theory** is obsessed with the poem, and I have the impression that this word will probably actualize other writing. **Picture Theory** is a loose novel that examines many dimensions, that is concerned with writing, the women's issues, the ontological existence of women. Strange as it may seem—I have, after all, been talking about it for some time—**Picture Theory** remains an enigma for me. I know and I don't know *what* wrote this book. In that sense I think it will be a tool in writing the essay I am planning.

Marthe Rosenfeld (essay date 1985)

SOURCE: "The Development of a Lesbian Sensibility in the Work of Jovette Marchessault and Nicole Brossard," in *Traditionalism, Nationalism, and Feminism: Women Writers of Quebec,* edited by Paula Gilbert Lewis, Greenwood Press, 1985, pp. 227-39.

[*In the following essay, Rosenfeld compares the "great contributions [of Nicole Brossard and Jovette Marchessault] to the development of a lesbian sensibility in the literature of Quebec."*]

Until the rise of the women's liberation movement, lesbianism as a theme had no real existence in the history of literature. From the age of Sappho in the sixth century B.C. to the beginnings of a lesbian culture in the Paris of the early twentieth century, a silence of two thousand five hundred years bears witness to the long war which the patriarchy waged against lesbianism. In Quebec the literary expression of lesbian love would be censored for an even longer period of time due to the misogyny of the Catholic Church and the sexism of the State. In this essay, I shall try to answer the following questions: Does a relationship exist between lesbianism as a way of life and as a form of writing? What audiences are the lesbian books of Jovette Marchessault and Nicole Brossard addressing? Are the experimentations of Brossard and Marchessault affecting the contemporary literature of Quebec?

Jovette Marchessault is a self-taught person. Born in Montreal in 1938, she is of mixed ancestry, having both French and Indian forbears. Although she describes her early childhood as a time of joy and growth, she experienced despair at the age of five after her impoverished family had moved from the country to the slums of Montreal. She left school as an adolescent, worked for many years in factories, and continued to learn at night by borrowing books from the public library. Having come of age during the dark and bigoted Duplessis era, Jovette Marchessault felt isolated as a lesbian. Indeed her main reason for wishing to become a writer was to break the silence. But years would pass before she would finally overcome the self-censorship which society imposes on its outcasts.

Since Jovette Marchessault came out as a lesbian only in 1979, she could not openly express her chosen way of life in the early seventies when she first wrote *Comme une enfant de la terre*. This book, however, clearly foreshadows the themes and sensibility which will ripen and bloom in her later works. Even at this early stage of the author's career, the lesbian spirit shines through the heroine's total identification with other amazons of Quebec.

Having eschewed woman's traditional roles of marriage and motherhood, Jovette Marchessault sought to express her feelings and her goals. She wanted, above all, to expand her horizons through readings and travel. With Francine, an old friend, the female protagonist of this work leaves her home in April on a sumptuous journey through North America. But the object of the voyage is neither sightseeing nor pleasure; rather, it is an amazon's quest for the promised land in which women can live in harmony with each other and with their natural surroundings. Similarly, during her nonstop journey from Quebec to Mexico, the young female warrior discovers new relationships between words and culture, between language and her amazonian identity. To Francine, her traveling companion, she expresses her faith in the power of words: "Les mots," she tells her, "m'apparaissent comme des escaliers en spirale qui aboutissent à une porte. Qui s'ouvre!"

Jovette Marchessault would continue to write five more years before discovering those particular words that communicate the spirit of a lesbian culture.

Between 1976 and 1977, while the author was writing *La Mère des herbes,* her most explicitly autobiographical novel, she brought out some of the factors which prompted her to become a lesbian and a feminist. Having grown up in a predominantly female setting, the protagonist felt drawn at an early age to the women and girls who inhabited the world of her youth. She loved the Pépin sisters and the happiness which the latter built after the death of their tyrannical father. She also admired the schoolgirls who worked collectively during the summer to write a play. Unlike the prosaic males in charge of the scenery, the young girls used their imagination to express in beautiful language their feminist vision of the past. The protagonist's feelings of love toward women go back, however, to the close relationships which existed between grandmother and grandchild, between mother and daughter. Both women helped one another to raise the child in a warm and caring atmosphere; both of them spoke to her about their work in the store or the factory. It was the grandmother's system of values, however, her empathy with the living creatures of nature, and her rebellion against all forms of oppression, which later would give the protagonist/Marchessault the insight as well as the courage to fight against the patriarchy. With its marvelous descriptions of the mother spirit in plant, beast, and grotto, *La Mère des herbes* may be interpreted as a mythopoetical evocation of the ancestral goddess culture. Indeed, the beautiful images which illuminate this autobiographical novel bring out the closeness of the protagonist/Marchessault to her natural environment as well as her gynocentric vision of the world:

> En visite dans la terre, sous la terre, nous sommes une somme inouïe de possible, tout est possible à l'embryon qui descend dans la mine pour se mettre au monde dans son rayon d'élection, s'installer dans le ventre de sa mère retrouvée et s'en extraire ainsi qu'une pépite d'or après un temps raisonnable de mûrissement, d'incubation.

Written two years after *La Mère des herbes, Tryptique lesbien* is Jovette Marchessault's most openly lesbian text. Through the use of myth and allegory, this book illustrates the long history of patriarchal violence against women. Indeed, a major theme of the first panel of the work, "Chronique lesbienne du moyen-âge québécois," is the lesbian heroine's journey from the dark ages of religious bigotry to the bright and joyous realm of a woman-centered culture. Appearing now as a real person, now as a legendary character, the child protagonist of this section is both a prophet who foretells the coming of a new feminist era and a fighter against the heterosexual ideology of male supremacy. Thus, Jovette Marchessault shows the immense grief which the female protagonist experiences as an adolescent when her beloved cousin leaves her for the sake of a man.

"Les Vaches de nuit" begins appropriately with the radical critique of a culture that robs women of their sexuality and freedom. But the mythical mother cow and her daughter remember a pre-patriarchal world, and this remembrance stimulates them to travel at night far from the daily drudgery. As mother and daughter leave the old kitchen behind, they begin to experience long-forgotten feelings of closeness towards one another. Having joined their sister mammals in a region of jubilation and desire, the mother is now able to initiate her daughter to the mysteries of lesbian love in a way that would have been taboo under the patriarchy.

Similarly "Les Faiseuses d'anges," the last panel of *Tryptique lesbien,* portrays a mother who is both a midwife and a goddess. Indeed the abortionist appears as a revolutionary figure, one who defies the norms of the heterosexist culture, and as a healer who helps her sisters to break the cycle of the ever-increasing family, the endless toil, the self-sacrifice. Mother and daughter give birth metaphorically, to their new identities as women making conscious choices for personal freedom and for the quality of life on this planet.

By using analogies, myths, and symbols from a feminist perspective, Jovette Marchessault here tries, as in her earlier texts, to show the courage, the capacity for love, the solidarity of women. But the writer's growing militancy has given her an immediate awareness of the difficulties of expressing herself in a language molded predominantly by men. Writing now as a lesbian, Jovette Marchessault can proudly ignore the sexist rule which has legislated the priority of the masculine over the feminine in French grammar. The pronouns, "ils" and "elles," for example, refer in this text either to men only or to female creatures exclusively. Instead of being complementary to masculine third persons, absorbed in the dominant language, feminine third persons are, in addition, strongly present in *Tryptique lesbien.* Other ways of interfering with the rules of the inherited language include such techniques as the fracturing of the autobiographical "I" which in turn represents a variety of female types (the independent girl-child, the rebellious adolescent, the prostitute, the separatist) and the periodic repetition of the "nous" form to emphasize, for example, the author's identification with the other lesbians who resisted the indoctrination of a hateful Catholic upbringing:

> En ce temps-là du moyen-âge québécois, toutes les petites lesbiennes tiraient la langue et bavaient sur le plancher ou sur les images du petit catéchisme. Dès la fête des rois mages, ils avaient décidé de nous faire subir un entraînement intensif. Nous

> étions les fétiches de l'année, têtes de cochon, anneau d'or dans le groin, les monstres! Du planifié! Du prémédité! Du déchaîné! Jusqu'à l'épuisement complet de cette résistance qui n'en finissait pas de résister.

But Jovette Marchessault's rebellion against the patriarchal language transcends issues of grammar and stylistics. In order to express her rage against a culture which has severed women from their bodies, from the memory of their foremothers, from themselves, Marchessault had to unmask the taboos and the apparent logic of the dominant language as hypocritical veneers which hide the confusion and the pain of the oppressed. Ignoring the double standard of taste which has influenced literary critics to scoff at women writers for using words that would be accepted in texts written by men, Marchessault attaches strong particles such as "Super mâle" and "sperme" to the most exalted religious figures. The following passage is one example of a blasphemous description of the sacred and sadistic ceremonies of Christianity which rape the mind and spirit of the young lesbians: "A genoux les petites filles! C'est l'heure exquise de la fellation divine. A genoux! Ouvrez la bouche! Grande! Plus grande encore! Recevez la giclée de sperme du grand mâle eucharistique."

To subvert the traditional bourgeois language of its facade of rationality, the author also experiments with the sound of words, the analogous formation of idioms, the emergence of the absurd. In fact, the power of the phonetic language to shape new perceptions is illustrated at the beginning of *Tryptique lesbien* when the young lesbian's discovery of the choke of a car produces a linguistic illumination. The words, "choke" and "chum," become so closely associated in her mind that a new truth dawns on her: the boyfriend is a strangler; heterosexual relationships are a trap. Similarly, the author's play on the sound and rhythm of idioms succeeds in communicating feelings of anger which might never surface in a purely rational discourse. The following passage describes men harassing young girls at the end of the school day: "Ils montent à l'assaut, les mâles, l'air hagard, leurs dents en tremblent, la salive dans la poussière de la genèse, à l'assaut, à la pinçade, à la rigolade, à la renverse." Even more powerful than these word games are the passages in *Tryptique lesbien* which seem to arise from the subconscious. For example, when the lesbian is first confronted with the oppression of the working-class women of Quebec as prisoners in their own homes, as mothers of numerous children, as unwitting agents of the patriarchy, she cries out: "Cannibales, arrêtez le bal!" Strange and dreamlike, this seemingly absurd little sentence expresses the chaos and the intensity of feelings as they are actually experienced.

In order to communicate women's true perceptions of reality, Marchessault felt the need to go even further: to reexamine the words, the very terms which shape our, thinking and which mirror the prevailing attitudes of the class in power. Thus, while the word "fête" means public rejoicing to the dominant culture, the same term conveys notions of pain and sacrifice to the lesbian protagonist: "[Q]uand ils disaient: 'Fête,' moi j'entendais autre chose! J'entendais l'hiver du sang sur la Terre des hommes." These semantic differences account for the author's desire to create other expressions and to give new meanings to a vocabulary which is incapable of expressing the feelings of minorities. In *Tryptique lesbien,* for instance, the words "rue" and "trottoir" come to mean the territories or gender roles in which the patriarchal culture imprisons both women and men. Likewise, the word "relique," which evoked the remains of a saint, now symbolizes the suffering and the appropriation of female bodies under patriarchal law. Other recurring expressions in *Tryptique,* such as "la Terre du sacrifice permanent," "le troupeau des ténèbres," and "l'ordre-des-castrants," are suggestive of women's bondage in the world of the fathers.

Brossard's ability to reconcile her lesbian/ feminist perceptiveness with her original interest in new writing accounts for the depth of feeling which emanates from a book such as *L'Amèr.*
                    —*Marthe Rosenfeld*

These syntactic and lexical experimentations would not have changed the medium of expression sufficiently, however, to transport us into a female space had not Jovette Marchessault also rejected the lifeless and univocal discourse of the mainstream. The deep feelings which she brings to her text are not watered down by the necessities of an antiquated narrative form. On the contrary, thoughts and emotions succeed one another so swiftly that the words, liberated from the restrictions of pause and period, go beyond the traditional sentence with its main and subordinate clauses, its finished character, its closed appearance. In the following passage, heart-gripping regrets over the lost childhood of the young lesbians produce the uninterrupted flow of a new language:

> Je vous dis qu'ils nous ont volé notre temps quotidien.

> Notre précieux temps de tous les jours pour jouer dehors, dedans, dans la verdure de la tendresse mutuelle. Notre temps à nous autres, temps de feu, de passion dans le velours rouge des bercements d'extase, des embrassements du corps.

Boundless and flowing, this new language is like a large river. The energy that emanates from this text helps to break down the old order, to challenge the powers that be. As a matter of fact, these passages with their rhythmical patterns, their pulse, their movement suggest, better than any specific ideas, the world of female creatures, the Utopia in which mother and daughter, memory and insight, struggle and sisterhood are brought together:

> Le lait coule! Le lait gicle! Le lait coule à flot! Beauté, beauté, bonté blanche. Le lait neige! Le lait goutte, le lait odore! Le lait poudre! Le lait rafale! Le lait ouragane! Le lait nuage, le lait est maculé d'images!

The exuberant language of "Les Vaches de nuit" has become a paradigm for the liberation of all women.

While Jovette Marchessault began to write in her thirties, and while she struggled for a long time to develop a style that would convey her lesbian/feminist vision of the world, Nicole Brossard revealed a passion for the modernistic expression of thought from the very outset of her literary career in the 1960s. By the mid-1970s, however, her personal life began to change dramatically. She read, in rapid succession, Simone de Beauvoir, Kate Millett, and Ti-Grace Atkinson, gave birth to a daughter, and fell in love with another woman. Although Brossard had always shared Quebec's aspirations for sovereignty and independence, her feminist consciousness and her quest for a non-patriarchal language also led her, during this same period of time, to turn away from the phallocentric vocabulary of the nationalist writers. In 1976, as a co-founder of *Les Têtes de Pioche,* she became politically active, penning incisive articles, many of which unmasked the oppressiveness of the heterosexual ideology. In ***L'Amèr, Le Sens apparent,*** and ***Amantes,*** she takes the reader on a long journey from the hell of patriarchal censorship to the glorious vision of a lesbian Utopia.

Brossard's ability to reconcile her lesbian/feminist perceptiveness with her original interest in new writing accounts for the depth of feeling which emanates from a book such as ***L'Amèr.*** This work deals with both the theory of writing and a woman's daily experience of her fragmentation as the lesbian mother of a young child. The narrator's anger over the erasure of the female self enables her to reveal the frightful conflict between her yearning for autonomy and her painful awakening to the endless responsibilities of motherhood. ***L'Amèr*** begins, appropriately, with words of defiance: "C'est le combat." The woman's struggle to free herself from this millennial bondage is a violent one. Although she loves her daughter, she totally rejects society's image of the mother as a paragon of virtue, a selfless drudge, a breeder and nurturer of children. While woman has been preoccupied with the survival of the young, man has appropriated to himself the symbolic order, the indispensable tool of language—hence his ideological control over the silent one, the stranger, the other. To take this language back, woman must challenge all of society, including its principal means of perpetuating itself: discourse. This questioning of the traditional language looms as a vital interrogation, a challenge which deals with the root causes of female oppression.

In *L'Amèr,* Brossard brings to light the arbitrariness of French grammar, and she shows in what way it has limited woman's self-expression. For example, the narrator, in the park with her young daughter, is unable to speak with the other mothers, the patriarchal mothers, devoted to men. Not only opposite attitudes towards life, but also language hampers communication: "Tout gravite autour d'une grammaire insensée." The narrator of *L'Amèr* condemns this senseless grammar as a symbolic system which has institutionalized the subordination of feminine persons to masculine persons. While Jovette Marchessault circumvented this grammatical sexism by refusing to describe mixed groups in *Tryptique lesbien,* Brossard takes the issue a step further, for she recommends a genderless tongue. Speaking to a woman friend, the narrator of *L'Amèr* thus expresses her wish: "[M]ais je te veux immense et chaude du corps saches nos énergies autrement que dans ton ventre mais des yeux. Asexu( ) ou peut-être invariable." The ending of the adjective has disappeared, just as gender will disappear in a society of equals.

Rebelling against the traditional idea of woman's subordination to the species and yearning to assert her own individuality, the narrator of *L'Amèr* writes: "J'ai tué le ventre et fait éclater la mer." But like Marchessault, Brossard comes up against the limitations of a vocabulary which has been contaminated by centuries of patriarchal rule. As an enthusiastic proponent of modernism, however, Brossard is the more innovative writer. Not only does she play with the meaning and the sound of words as Marchessault has done in *Tryptique lesbien,* she experiments also in *L'Amèr* with syntax and orthography. This method of interfering with the traditional language appears, for instance, in the changing physiognomy of the word "mère," a term full of ambiguities. Having acquired an *A,* the A of Alpha, the beginning of all things, and having lost its powerless, mute *e, L'Amèr* symbolizes a woman whose creativity and assertiveness enable her to assume her identity as "fille-mère-lesbienne," the desirable mother, the autonomous person whose energy circulates among women. When written in two words, *L'A Mèr* connotes a radical questioning of female reproduction, the absence of the mother. Spelled with a final *e, l'Amère* acquires the bitterness of female dependency, while yet in another context *la mer* signifies the sea, powerful and uncontrollable, the very antithesis of domesticated motherhood. A text which reduces the gap between fiction, theory, and reality, this book marks the end of an old order and promises a new beginning. It announces the coming of another world, of a non-patriarchal space in which women will relate to one another as independent creatures of desire and strength.

While *L'Amèr* transmits glimpses of lesbian love, *Le Sens apparent* tells the story of a deep friendship between Adrienne, Gertrude, Yolande, and the narrator, four women writers, who meet in restaurants and cafés traveling to and from New York and Montreal. Unlike the nameless character of *L'Amèr* who must first destroy the myth of woman's "biological destiny" before she can begin to write, however, the authors in *Le Sens apparent* possess the artistry, the leisure, and the love to support each other in their creative projects. As a matter of fact, one of the major themes of this novel is the narrator's protracted search for an amazon language: "Le temps tel que décrit par les amazones contemporaines."

The narrator's dual aim—to evoke the spirit of the island of Lesbos and to discover new forms of writing—accounts for the twofold character of the book itself. On the one hand a series of poems celebrates the relation between two lesbian writers; on the other hand a feminist manifesto recalls the long history of women's oppression and identifies the qualities that will enable them to recreate, through their writing, the greatness of their amazonian past. This quest for a lesbian literature is of the utmost importance not only because of the millennia of erasure and censorship, but also because the limited concept of reality in patriarchal societies compels women to seek their own reality in the realm of fiction. In *Le Sens apparent* Brossard tries to reclaim words and forms in order to call an oppressive order into question and to produce a new environment for the women writers who circulate in the twilight zone between fiction and reality. Eschewing the photographic portrayal of everyday life as a two-dimensional and linear narrative that perpetuates an obsolete vision of the world, Brossard now writes in an open-ended and circular manner. The book ends as it began with the narrator reflecting on love and on the text itself: "J'avais pensé follement le grand amour car je voulais à tout prix écrire un livre. . . . J'avais pensé follement le grand amour car je voulais à tout prix écrire un livre de manière à ne pas exagérer cette folle tentation, ce fol incident qui parcourt l'échine à mon insu et qui me fait écrire *toutes ces choses.* . . ."

While *Le Sens apparent* shows women exploring together the relationship between fiction and reality, *Amantes,* as a lesbian continent, illustrates the link which exists between female eroticism and the development of a new form of writing. Divided into five parts by means of black and gray pages, illustrated with photographs of the modern world, and printed with a variety of types—capital letter, small letter, italics—this book immediately challenges the unidirectional character of patriarchal systems of thought. The vision of a rotating space and of a circular time in *Amantes,* however, is connected not only to the artist's search for new forms, but also to her lesbian passion which enables her to invent a version of reality outside of patriarchal censorship. That is why physical love between women, as a path leading to wholeness and integrity, forms the major theme of this volume of poetry. While the heterosexual view of woman's otherness leads to the erosion of the female self, erotic relationships between lesbians are conducive to the rediscovery of a new and multidimensional language.

Nowhere in Brossard's work is the rapport between lesbianism on the one hand and language on the other hand more evident than in *Amantes,* for the large number of grammatical feminines, in this book, constitutes a potent visual reminder of the separatist nature of this continent. Moreover, the recurrence of the "nous" form, plural and collective, expresses, as it does in *Tryptique lesbien,* the solidarity of a world of lesbians. But while Marchessault obeys the grammatical rules, Brossard does not hesitate to transgress them, omitting parts of the sentence, disrupting the subject-predicate sequence, altering punctuation and gender:

> ma continent, je veux parler l'effet
> radical de la lumière au grand jour
> aujourd'hui, je t'ai serrée de près,
> aimée de toute civilisation, de toute
> texture, de toute géométrie et de braise,
> délirantes, comme on écrit: et
> mon corps est ravi

Amantes, Brossard's most avant-garde work, not only describes the touching, the embraces, the physical union of the lovers; it also brings out the omnipresence of words. Implicit in these pages is the existence of the subtle relationship which exists between Sapphic love and the writer's ability to create a new space or territory where lesbian women can be together. One of Brossard's principal methods for suggesting such an environment is the verbal spiral. Repeating the same words at intervals, but in so doing advancing a step each time, Brossard's twirling is related to her lesbian concept of love. The first spiral shows the lovers sharing the meaning of their nocturnal dreams:

> la nuit décline ses relais. explorer:
> l'ultime intime ailleurs
>
> la tête tourne, enlaçons le détail de notre science,
> nouées
> (l'ultime intime ailleurs). . . .

The second spiral brings out in a rhythmical flow of words the joy of yielding to temptation:

> j'ai succombé à toutes les visions
> séduite, surface, série et sérieuse
>
> j'ai succombé à la vision claire

> des végétations et des événements
> matinales, . . .
>
> j'ai succombé à l'écho, au retour,
> à la répétition. *au commencement*
> *des verièbres* était la durée
> une réplique essentielle à tout instant
> dans la joie que j'ai de toi, . . .

In the third spiral, we see the connection between the texture of the words and the taste of a kiss:

> et nous imaginons de nou-
> velles moeurs avec ces bouches mêmes qui savent
> tenir un
> discours, les nôtres au goût des mots au goût du
> baiser. . . .
>
> les faits sont tels que le project du texte et le
> texte
> de projet s'accomplissent au goût des mots, au
> goût du
> baiser, je sais que tu m'es réelle / alors

A subversive style which breaks the monotony of traditional and linear writing, the spiral signifies openness, continuity and the perpetuation of life. In the words of Brossard: "'[The spiral is] a very dynamic form . . . which is related to lesbian sensibility.'"

Jovette Marchessault and Nicole Brossard, two lesbian/feminist writers of Quebec, have had the courage to explore the world of their dreams and to translate their experience into language. What distinguishes these two authors is their emotional honesty combined with their quest for a non-sexist idiom —fresh, daring, and uninhibited. Refusing the very thought of male domination, these women-identified-women are not afraid of venturing into the unknown, of taking chances with new modes of writing and new forms.

A careful reading of *Tryptique lesbien* and particularly of *Amantes* shows that there is a rapport between lesbianism, as a rediscovery of woman's desire, and writing outside of the heterosexual hegemony. As lesbian/feminists, Jovette Marchessault and Nicole Brossard address themselves primarily to women; as innovators, questioning the very nature of fiction, they are beginning to change the character of literature in Quebec. In spite of the differences between these two writers—Brossard, an enthusiast of the big city, is urbane and modernistic; Marchessault, a devotee of the land, is an adherent of the earth goddesses, a friend of the mammals—both of these authors have undoubtedly made great contributions to the development of a lesbian sensibility in the literature of Quebec.

Marguerite Andersen (review date January 1987)

SOURCE: "Women of Skin and Thought," in *The Women's Review of Books,* Vol. IV, No. 4, January, 1987, p. 16.

[In the following review, Andersen discusses the feminist aims of Brossard's French Kiss *and* Lovhers.*]*

Nicole Brossard is one of the leading writers of Quebec. From a feminist literary viewpoint she is probably the most important one: she is an innovative writer who is also a radical feminist. Questioning established cultural patterns and systems, her texts—prose, poetry, theory and often a *mélange* of the three—have since the seventies been showing Quebec writers the way to modernity. Brossard's writing is literary theory as well as political statement; it promotes and uses almost exclusively women's images, symbols, language and experiences. Her aim is to place woman in the center—of society, culture and politics.

Brossard has written more than twenty books since 1965. Several have already been translated; now, these two recent and excellent translations, and a forthcoming translation of **La lettre aérienne,** to be published by the Toronto Women's Press, will help anglophone readers make the more thorough acquaintance of this avant-garde feminist from Quebec.

In Brossard's poetic prose, writing perpetually resists two elements which threaten, like parasites, to invade the text. One is reality, whether dull or exciting, the other is traditional fiction with its plots, its intriguing characters and/or objects. From the struggle against these tempters, which takes place within each sentence, emerges the text: condensed and at the same time exuberant, lucid and essential, textual essence, an energizing fluid, a literary super-fuel.

While reading Nicole Brossard is invigorating, it is not easy. I had to read every book of hers three, four, five times in order to comprehend the words, the pages and their meaning, and to arrive at an understanding—which nevertheless remains very personal. For Brossard's books demand that every reader grasp in her own way, through her personal sensitivity, her individual emotion and reflection—in short, with her *différence*—the multispiralled work. I can only speak of *my* reading(s) of Brossard's prose, readings always animated by the desire to see what is not evident, to decipher the innumerable secrets of the work in which Brossard inscribes women's existence and growth.

In *A Book,* the first of her novels, Brossard says that "evidences are not literary matter." Her writing does not include the already seen, heard, observed, understood, said, written. Brossard demands of herself a different *écriture.* Differently real, differently fictive. A variant. Deviant. In **French Kiss,** for example, she chooses "to brandish suspended meanings."

She rides astride syntax, shifts vowels, dilates syllables, breeds analogies, takes stabs at civil narrative, cuts out "trite intrigues." Her writing feeds on "zigs and zags and detours," the letters of her words fornicate before settling on the pages of her books.

Quebec history, women's history, women's lives, their loving and their thinking are the canvas onto which these texts are woven. In the case of **French Kiss,** which takes place in Montreal, the translator has added "occasional unobtrusive aids" which will help the reader to understand the east-west (francophone-anglophone) opposition in the city, as well as the frequent allusions to Quebec history and literature. **Lovhers** is a later text, written after Brossard had come to know American feminism, after she and Luce Guilbeault had made the documentary **Some American Feminists** in 1976. This was a time when American feminism was perceived as much more radical than Canadian, Quebec and French feminisms. Maybe it was for that reason that **Lovhers** takes place mainly in New York's Barbizon Hotel for Women, where

> . . . the girls of the Barbizon
> in the narrow beds of America
> have invented with their lips
> a vital form of power
> to stretch out side by side
> without parallel and: fusion.

In **Lovhers,** text is body and body is woman, writing is bending over the paper and the "lovher" and begins with the declaration of love, is love. Brossard's texts exalt women and their creative powers. She joyously overturns such negative symbols as the castrating abyss, the devouring mother, woman as sinner. In her writing we see a euphemization of the female body, of belly, vulva, breasts and lips. Her women are intelligent, playful, productive, imaginative, creative all at once. They are women of skin and thought (*peau et pensée*), of their own will and voluptuousness (*volonté et volupté*), women no longer isolated, ignorant, ignored, lobotomized by patriarchy. They are free, free to create a network of women strengthened by a common drive, a common desire to reinvent the world. A utopian desire, yes, but one that generates pleasure, certitude, hope, thought, dream and emotion. **Lovhers** can be contrasted with that other recent Canadian novel, Margaret Atwood's *The Handmaid's Tale,* which is equally visionary but icily frightening. Indeed, in *The Handmaid's Tale* and **Lovhers,** dystopia and utopia, Canadian literature has captured the polarities of women's image of the future.

French Kiss, first published in 1974, still reflects the sixties and early seventies. It tells of five individuals' attempts to live outside social constraints. Resistance fighters in the urban labyrinth of Montreal, a city which terrifies and fascinates them, Marielle, Alexander, George, Lucy and

Camomille question everything in their search for "the perfect (total) usage of their bodies, viscera, epidermises." In the five years they spend together, before police intervention puts an end to their communal adventure, they achieve relative harmony: "At least we managed to communicate among ourselves all the fragments of knowledge and wisdom each of us had access to from our own enquiry and experience. We were awareness and communication."

Because of the role played by men in *French Kiss,* it seems less radically feminist than *Lovhers.* Yet it celebrates the energy of women. The narrator of the story is a woman who creates a new language, a *nouvelle écriture,* mixing blood and ink, life and writing, and who, above all, fits a filter into the story in order to "sift out static and clumps of cartilaginous words"—patriarchalsyntax, vocabulary, linearity—"the language-power which controls." The text she produces is like the daily bread that women have baked for so long; blackening a page is compared to toasting a slice of bread. Writing is woman's work and woman does away with the old dualism of body and mind. In the process, women meet each other: ". . . on Camomille's lips a kiss, rather chaste. Nibbled lips. Pain/relaxation. Pleasure, lips licked, left wet. I slip through the slot the text provides . . ."

Lovhers (first published in 1980 as *Amantes*) brings us into the center of Nicole Brossard's writing. We penetrate into the open yet secret mandala of women's existence. The title of the book announces a celebration of lesbian love and, as the combining of conventionally opposite ideas is one of the dominant features of Brossard's writing, that celebration is reflective as well as exuberant, bringing together all the polarities of female being. We read of lesbian rejoicing and rejoicing over text. For the lovhers, loving, reading and writing are simultaneous and equally important. Reading and delirium (*lire et délire*) are interconnected, sensual pleasure and intellectual discourse are punctuated by kisses.

The New York Barbizon Hotel for Women witnesses the lovhers' encounter, at once intellectual and sensual. Real yet vertiginously symbolic, this space is both mathematical figure and luxuriant dream in which the four lovhers invent a new beginning for women. Without shame the body moves from the private to the political; female excess rejoices in the emotional as well and as much as the cerebral.

A mandala is a circle of complex design, often enclosed by a square. It is a symbol of outer space as well as an image of the world. It is also a shrine for divine powers. In *Lovhers,* the Barbizon rises like a clitoris on the map of New York. (I must say I prefer the French edition of the book, not only because of the language—I myself usually write in French—but also because it is illustrated with photographs of the New York skyline, making the geometric design of the mandala more visible.) In this rectangular building Brossard assembles the circle of four lovhers, cardinal points of her intimate universe.

The sacred space of the mandala houses an exemplary figure: Woman. (How lucky we are in French to have the word *femme* which does not include the word "man.") The symbol by which she is represented in *Lovhers* is her mouth. In *French Kiss* mouths already ventured "blindly towards each other, allowing each to lose itself inside the other's geography." Lips gaped "like hungry traps inviting flies into the ink, there to sleep and sleep some more while I get back to the text and Camomille's lips." But in *French Kiss* men are still present, are still lovers. In *Lovhers* they do not exist. Here woman is the divinity, characterized by the mouth, a mouth which Brossard juxtaposes to the vulva.

I read *Lovhers* as a modern illustration of the long-forgotten, almost erased, myth of Baubo. In the myth, Baubo (who was either Persephone's or Demeter's nursemaid) managed to make Demeter smile again after the abduction of Persephone by lifting her gown and exposing her vulva. The Baubo figure was worshipped during the festivities of the thesmophoria, a women's festival which included lesbian activities. Men were excluded from this festival, one of the most important of ancient Greece. (Did you hear about it in school? I didn't.)

Far from being one of the curious obscenities of mythology, the Baubo story emphasizes the possibility of solidarity among women and celebrates women's pride. In *Lovhers* women exult in their reunion. They find in each other what Demeter found in Baubo's gesture: friendship, intimacy, pleasure and strength.

In this book, all activities are double. Celebration is exuberant at the same as it is thoughtful meditation. While writing, the narrator of *Lovhers* never stops reading other women's texts. Mouths are places for words as well as kisses, an "orgasm is like a process leading / to the integral: end of fragments / in the fertile progress of lovhers." Lovhers can conceive anything:

> woman is coming showing the tip of a breast
> as though to signal the beginning of a cycle,
> if nobody moves in this instant, everything
> can vertigo to become virtual.

Lovhers speaks of woman's journey towards the luminous center of female intimacy and inscribes in it the word "mouth" which is at once lips, tongue, language and vulva. *Parole de femme,* voluptuous orgasm, utopia, this is what happens in the shameless orgy in the mandala of the Barbizon where the forces of women converge. This location, this happy island, exists outside the patriarchal world. Here in the "sleep/wake" of women, the future is present, everything is open, accessible, mind and body are no longer separated, are satisfied. Harmony consists of "the voice of a thousand spectacles in us." The moon rises while a thousand women meet in the intimacy of their desire, to know pleasure and pride. Thanks to Brossard, we are finally stripped of our "shameful parts" (*parties honteuses*) and our feeble minds; we come into possession of our bodies, our thinking, all of our imagination, able to express ourselves without inhibition.

Is utopia dangerously unrealistic? Brossard does not think so. On the contrary, she believes that we cannot live without its challenge. According to her, men have been unable to imagine that a sisterhood of women could reinvent the world, its ideas, emotion, sexuality, creativity, play. This lack in man's imagination has, of course, marred the female imagination. Brossard asks us to accept the challenge of imagining the island of utopia as an island for women only. For those who, like me, find man's world insufferably dangerous, Brossard's utopian island can be something like a clearinghouse for the mind, maybe even a pleasure-house, a dream instead of a nightmare; fleeting, yes, but absolutely essential.

Barbara Godard (review date May-June 1988)

SOURCE: "Feminism and Postmodernism," in *American Book Review*, Vol. 10, No. 2, May-June, 1988, pp. 8, 20.

[*In the following review, Godard discusses Nicole Brossard's* Le Désert mauve *and Gail Scott's* Heroine *and asserts that "It will be hard for [other writers] to surpass the brilliance of the writing of Gail Scott and Nicole Brossard in their critiques of representation and of narrative."*]

Especially in Quebec, feminists have played an important role in theorizing postmodernism through their intervention as editors of the prominent periodicals *La nouvelle barre du jour* and *Spirale,* of which Nicole Brossard and Gail Scott were founding coeditors, respectively. The feminist editor of *Island* and *Periodics,* Daphne Marlatt, fulfilled a similar, if less lauded, function in English-Canadian writing. Feminism in these milieux has been seen as the salient feature of postmodernism through its deconstruction of binary oppositions and its critique of the master narratives of Western culture, indeed its critique of all narratives and all totalizing theories.

The publication of new fictions by two of the leading feminists and postmodernist writers of francophone and anglophone Canada, *Le désert mauve* by Nicole Brossard and *Heroine* by Gail Scott, reminds us once again of the pertinency of this linking of these discourses of critique. Indeed, the back cover of *Le désert mauve* specifically heralds the work as a postmodern novel, while the imprint of Coach House—centre of English-Canadian postmodern publishing—fulfills the same signalling function for *Heroine.* Other ties are forged through the feminist-postmodernist connection. The dialogue between anglophone and francophone feminists in Canada and Quebec has been the only point of contact between these two literatures. It has stimulated the most innovative writing of the last decade and, with the impressive roster of young women whose first books are appearing on the appropriate small press lists this year, promises to do so for several more years.

For a number of years Brossard and Scott have participated in a theory discussion group along with other prominent feminist writers: Louky Bersianik, Louise Cotnoir, Louise Dupré, Daphne Marlatt, France Théoret, and Betsy Warland. Through their talks, theoretical articles and texts, this discussion has been shared with an audience stretching across the continent. Both Brossard and Scott have already published texts announcing their resistance to the line, to any party line, but especially to the line of narrative. With its insistence on temporality as causality, so grammars of minimal narratives instruct us, narrative employment is entrapment. The narrative line catches readers, making them accept as inevitable and hence as natural that which is constructed, fabular. With their focus on the endings of marriage or death, the plots of fictional narrative—especially the "heroine's plot," as Ellen Moers has called it, the marriage plot of the realist novel—are deadly traps for the independent feminist reader and writer. She must resist the line.

Brossard's writing, writing as research, in her words, is a writing of resistance. In *L'Amèr, où le chapitre effrité* (*These Our Mothers: Or the Disintegrating Chapter*), she developed a theory of sexual difference as relational difference, deconstructed the master fictions through which the reality of women's lives has been constructed, and disrupted the line. Chapters disintegrate as the text circles around five discrete moments: "Strategic wound or suspended meaning"—"combat." "Fiction begins suspended mobile between words and the body's likeness to this *our* devouring and devoured mother." In this suspension, the sentence is also disrupted, syntax abandoned. Brossard works on language, deconstructing its gendered plot(ting) and opening multiple new meanings through her work on the material signifier. In *Spare Parts,* Gail Scott focuses on short narrative sequences which are further broken up in resistance to the line when individual sentences or paragraphs fly off in new directions, as in the surrealist *cadavre exquis.* Such syntactic and narrative discontinuity is reinforced by an exploration of the fragmented female body. The excessive and detached parts are both grammatical and corporeal, the title of the collection foregrounding the ruling metaphor of this phase of feminist exploration of language and meaning.

In their new books, Brossard and Scott extend their resistance in new directions, particularly into the problematics of the referent in the creation of the "reality effect." Both risk the line in what are exciting new ways for each writer. Scott's *Heroine* is the most important feminist fiction yet to emerge in English Canada and in its short life has already attracted enthusiastic audiences. Part of the pleasure for the reader lies in the possibility for nostalgic reminiscence on the left-wing political and intellectual scenes of the seventies, which the narrator evokes in bits and pieces of exceptionally vivid detail while she negotiates a rite of passage, trying to make sense of her life and orient herself in a new direction. The narrative remains in suspense, however, between the rhythm of Marxist political action, legacy of the open love affair with a left-wing leader where passion has died, and the shadowy promise of feminist sorority held out by a friend, Marie, who urges the narrator to participate in demonstrations in support of abortion. Nostalgia is a trap, though. Memory is purely fictive, a world-being called "Sepia," with whom the narrator engages in monologue.

The temptation to empathize with the character is further undermined by the narrative framing. The narrator is seated in a bath in a rooming house trying to plan out a novel, struggling with the difficulty of creating a positive heroine in a context where symbolically women do not exist. Through its meditation on the negative image of women—"she looks instinctively for her own reflection in a store window. But it's too dark to see clearly"—the fiction offers a critique of representation intertwined with a critique of patriarchal domination of the symbolic. The mimetic element in the novel is undercut by the processual hermeneutic of the narrator's self-reflexive discussion of her difficulties of writing, of the problem of gaining enough distance from her character. Maybe this would be easier if she got out of the bath, she wonders.

But it is also undercut by the blurring of levels of narrative which occurs. The only dialogue the narrator has in the text is with her heroine, a confounding of fiction and reality in the narrated text which foregrounds and defamiliarizes the tendency for the reader to enter into dialogue with the fictional narrator. The constructed and aleatory aspects of the narrative are also laid bare through two other narrative devices, the grey woman who inexplicably appears on the Montreal street to both narrator and heroine and the black tourist whose bird's eye view through the telescope on the top of Mount Royal panning the cityscape is the opening scene of the novel. His progress through the city provides the frame for each chapter. But the black tourist has no story to tell, does not engage with the characters, remains an inexplicable figure undermining our attempts to effect closure and make sense of the narrative. Closure is resisted also in the parodic reworking of the heroine's plot which lays bare its grammar: the heroine does not choose a marriage partner, but is chosen. Even more passive is the heroine of

Scott's novel within a novel, who is the epitome of negativity. Needless to say, *Heroine* is an ironic title.

Although the past is fictive and the future unrepresentable, the present of narration is ludic. Scott's prose is as densely textured as a poem, indeed like a poem it echoes and reechoes, structured not around the temporal sequence of clauses but around repeated segments which allow the work to take shape in the mind's ear. This clashes with the emphasis on detailed visual imagery which creates the scintillating surfaces of the novel. Everything is illusion. In the same way the extraordinarily rich symbolic imagery clashes with negativity to create further paradoxes which disrupt linear logic. Such a novel, needless to say, does not end. The final section, entitled "Play It Again, S," invites us to think associatively through this collage. It breaks off, after a list of sentences stating what she thinks or she does, in midsentence with the word "She-."

Scott's fiction also disrupts linguistic norms with its mixture of English and French. This is a feature of *Le désert mauve* as well, though, in keeping with its setting in Nevada, Spanish is thrown in too. But in Brossard's novel, the question of the multiple possible signifiers for a single referent is not just a question of realistic effect. In this novel about a translator it is at the heart of the matter, the inevitable slipperiness of language. For Brossard, translation has become a trope for difference, for the continual suspension or deferral of meaning which is the work of the critical text, the fiction/theory she writes. Writing as re/writing, always already written. The text is also a sequel to Brossard's experiences both of being translated and as a translator, a mode of re/writing she has recently become engaged in as she and Daphne Marlatt have translated each other's work (*Mauve* and *Characters/Jeu de lettres*). Subsequently Brossard began experiments in self-translation in which she repeated the process of composition, rather than doubling the referent, as is the usual model for translation practice. In *L'Aviva,* emotion is first voiced and heard, then "translated" into works and acted upon in textual pleasure. Subsequently, in a second moment, this emotion is translated into a second text through a process of sound association and play on words which effect a transformation in the material signifier like the reverberations and mimicry of the echo. "La peau de décrire un instant" becomes "l'eau qui décrit car c'est lent." In fact, this is an extension of Brossard's habitual process of composition in the surrealist mode, linking chains of auditory association rather than making imagistic connections.

Le désert mauve is divided into four sections. The first is composed of a book, "Le désert mauve," purportedly by Laure Angstelle, published by Editions de l'Arroyo, a book which we learn has been discovered by Maude Laures in a secondhand bookstore in Montreal and which she decides to translate. The second and longest section, "Un livre à traduire", relates the process of "transformance" as Maude Laures works on the text in preparation for translating it. In turn divided into sections—places and objects, characters, scenes and dimensions—Maude's text breaks the first narrative down into its component parts, offering descriptive detail to produce the "reality effect." Simultaneously, it explores the process of translation, the mysterious connection that leads a translator to extend her life through the pages of a book written by another woman. The immersion of translator in the writer's world is complete, suggests Brossard, so that the translator engages in a process of rewriting, confronting the necessity for betraying the language in order to maintain the fiction. To the old adage of the translator's inevitable treason, Brossard counters with writing as doubling or difference. Writing is doubling or not(h)ing.

The final section, a book titled "Mauve l'horizon," translated by Maude Laures and published by Editions de l'Angle, demonstrates that drift at work. This section repeats the first section. As is the case with the titles, the "translated" text uses almost the same words, substituting synonyms or reworking sentence division. "Je filais la lumière" becomes "Je tissais la lumière," for example. But repetition is always difference: there is only the simulacrum, words repeating other words already written.

Another type of translation or transposition is introduced into the book to form a fourth part folded within the second section. As she grapples with Laure's narrative, Maude works through the story of the tall man in images. A series of five photographs is positioned at the centre of the book, framed within photographs of the front and back of a file folder which bear the handwritten inscription "L'homme long." In this way, as in the anamorphic photograph of the author which graced the cover of her diary, *Journal intime,* Brossard offers a critique of the representative features of art. Photography, which is the most mimetic of the arts, is here shown to be self-referential: the link between image and referent is blurry. The whole question of original and reproduction becomes preposterous, moreover, in face of the intertwining of the two texts, "original" and "translated," within Brossard's novel. Here, as in her earlier fiction, it is the fiction which makes us real. Significant in this regard is the meditation on "reality" in Maudes "Un livre à traduire." In this section, Maude attempts to "isolate reality," that is, to "insulate" it like a self-contained room in which she can give herself up to the "most concrete mental adventures in the company of Laure Angstelle and her characters." But reality, Maude observes, is "what we find through an incalculable return of things imaged." While "reality counts," we tend to plunge into it "naturally," thinking it to be a valid category. Reality, however, must be constructed through words. She will condense reality so that it can be felt on her skin: "La réalité serait tout à fait palpable, concrète, dense.

Les couleurs seraient précises, les mots utiles, univoques" (Reality will be quite palpable, concrete, dense. The colours will be exact, the words useful, univocal). "Vraisemblance," likeness, is defined by Maude as that appearance which is upheld by the will to be. Brossard's self-reflexive fiction about these processes of doubling or re/writing develops her perennial concerns through the metaphor of translation. In doing so, it resists the temptation to repeat earlier work and offers new challenges to the reader through her consideration of all writing as translation and her experiments in homolinguistic translation.

To herald these two new fictions as the most outstanding works of the year, as one is tempted to do, is premature, perhaps in light of the forthcoming publications promised by major avant-garde women writers. . . . It will be hard for them to surpass the brilliance of the writing of Gail Scott and Nicole Brossard in their critiques of representation and of narrative.

Louise H. Forsyth (review date Autumn-Winter 1989)

SOURCE: A review of *Lovhers* and *Le Désert mauve,* in *Canadian Literature,* Nos. 122-123, Autumn-Winter, 1989, pp. 190-93.

[*In the following review, Forsyth states that in Brossard's* Lovhers *and* Le Désert mauve *she "writes with the assumption that both the personal and the poetic are political."*]

Nicole Brossard published *Amantes* in 1980. Except for *D'arcs de cycle la dérive,* a limited edition poem and engraving, this was her first book of poetry following the publication of the retrospective *Le Centre blanc* in 1978. She was widely recognized by then as the major radical feminist and post-modern writer in Quebec. *Amantes* continues the experimental direction Brossard had established in her poetry, while also marking a fresh stage in her theoretical development. A set of love poems written for another woman, *Amantes* is richly erotic in language and theme. Along with the prose work *Le sens apparent,* it indicates the direction Brossard was to take in her writing through the 1980's.

Brossard makes use of unexpected interfaces in traditional literary genres to work out, in language that is sparse, condensed and rigorously precise, her compelling vision of women choosing to occupy all dimensions of space on their own terms by beginning at the vital centre. Therefore, the novel *Picture Theory* picked up in narrative form major images and expressions from *Amantes.* In doing so the novel further opened thematic perspectives, particularly those related to the complex bonds which form in all areas among women who express their love for women. Brossard's latest prose work *Le Désert mauve,* a challenging novel in language and form, is both a lyrical celebration of women's love for girls and women and an urgent quest for vital truths which have not yet found form in the traditions of dominant culture. It is a matter of making a different kind of sense.

Brossard makes use of unexpected interfaces in traditional literary genres to work out, in language that is sparse, condensed and rigorously precise, her compelling vision of women choosing to occupy all dimensions of space on their own terms by beginning at the vital centre.
—Louise H. Forsyth

The language of love between women has broad connotations in Brossard's work. Always present is the sensual pleasure of being fully awake to one's body, its emotions and sensations, along with the further joy of shared ecstasy. Concrete images evoking relations of intimacy abound. Intense emotional experience is accompanied by intellectual awareness, a sense of self and a sense of the other: knowing who one is—as a fully integrated individual—and where one is, asking questions about what each particular situation means. By virtue of its special nature, lesbian love serves as a metaphor for women's radical transformation: "orgasm like a process leading to the integral." The experience of sensual fulfillment is never detached in Brossard's work from themes of language. Love known is love expressed. The taste of lips is inseparable from the taste of words, however hard the right ones are to find. To know love is to speak, read and write. Love brings production of texts where women reclaim submerged memory, imagine new forms, envision futures and utopias, emerge into the reality of a social and cultural landscape congenial to their experience and knowledge. Lesbian love poetry and fiction in the radically revolutionary writing of Nicole Brossard offer perception of unknown universes whirling within and flowing through other unknown universes, ranging from the most personally intimate to the most lost in space.

Brossard writes with the assumption that both the personal and the poetic are political. *Lovhers* and *Le Désert mauve* explore important ramifications of the inseparability of these areas. Both books contain characters who write, read and appreciate the texts of others: words have unlimited power to move the imagination. The title of the first section of *Lovhers* is "(4): Lovhers/Write." The book's theme and structure is established by the figure 4, in whose graphic form one can see the spiral so central to Brossard's vision. The number 4 suggests wholeness and cyclical completion

in its association with such notions as four primordial elements, four seasons, four compass points. Such is the nature of the full love between the women, for whom the number 4 could also suggest the look of complicity and passion between them, two lucid eyes gazing into two lucid eyes: $2 + 2 = 4$. "The Vision" in which the passion grows intense and which then opens onto women's autonomous space contains four parts: *Vertigo, Spiral, Sleep, Excess,* each of which in turn contains four parts. The title "Lovhers/ Write" establishes from the start the inseparable relationship between lesbian love and writing, for the delirium of love between women means a dynamic sense of identity: "integral presence," gives "the body back intelligence" and brings the energy to assault conventional constructs of reality, particularly as they serve the blind interests of power in the modern city. Erotic images insist upon the excitement of meeting at new intersections. As the two lovers arouse each other, through their bodies as well as their texts, as new questions form out of the difference between the women, and as words and voices of other women are quoted, they grow "igneous" and their rapture is enhanced. Its relevance is broadened; its nature as exciting process is emphasized; primordial memory surges forth, and images of what might be socially and culturally for women swell like a passion from the sea: "we can conceive anything."

As ardour intensifies in *Lovhers* to the point of vertigo and excess, new states of consciousness are reached. *Lovhers* and readers feel themselves "slip gently into the continent of women." Succumbing to the temptation of women in love they move through the looking glass to "pass through / take shape and choose [themselves]," to explore their "ultimate intimate elsewhere." Brossard uses her fragmented language to evoke the experience, not describe it. Word play suggests the intense emotion surpassing words, "with a tongue that has visions," leaving the reader to move herself in the openings among the words and images. Barbara Godard's translation conveys the richness of this poetic experience admirably, for her English text has almost as rich evocative powers as the French original. It is a shame, however, that *Lovhers* does not contain the drawing and photographs which so enhance *Amantes.*

In the final section, "My Continent," the *lovhers,* moving in "the spatial era of women," claim their geographical, conceptual and cultural space; they have been brought into the world by their love, their awareness, their language and the exchange of their experience. The result is dazzling, with the poet's voice stating in the end that her "body is enraptured."

The search for new modes of being in space is also the subject of *Le Désert mauve,* where indescribable and unlimited possibilities appear in the desert, the novel's dominant metaphor. The same anger found in *Lovhers,* against patriarchal institutions responsible for the torture of women and the re-

pression of their experience, is expressed with particular ve-
hemence in this novel. Also stressed, both thematically and
structurally, is the importance of women writing, women
reading texts written by women, women "translating,"
whether in their own language or another, so their active involvement in the text gives it the extra shot of energy needed
to ensure it circulates in society and works its transformational and generative magic.

Le Désert mauve is the story of a tale. It begins with the
text of a short novel written by a certain Laure Angstelle,
"Le Désert mauve." A copy of this novel within the novel
was found in a second-hand shop in Montreal by another
character, Maude Laures, who, strangely fascinated by its
mysterious author and its tantalizing characters and events,
decided to translate it. The final part of *Le Désert mauve* is
the second book, her "translated" version of the first:
"Mauve, l'horizon." Between these two books is the long
central section in which the "translator" uses her imaginative and spiritual powers during the process of working
through the meaning of the book and its various elements
as she prepares to find her own language and perspective
on the tale. She gives free rein to her own inventiveness and
no doubt winds up thinking what neither the characters nor
the first author thought—such is the joy of shared experience and free expression. It is this process, this creative work
with words, this active reflection on the questions raised by
the book's fiction, which represent the major element of the
novel's action. There is lots of room left for the reader to
enter into the action by imagining and telling her own version of the enigmatic events.

The three variations on Mélanie's story establish the anec-
dotal subject of *Le Désert mauve.* Fifteen-year-old Mélanie
lives in the Arizona desert at her mother's motel, a place of
empty images and social ritual. The essential danger inherent in such superficiality becomes clear in the end. Driving
her mother's Meteor at breakneck speed across the desert,
Mélanie is a centre of awareness and ardent energy seeking
knowledge, yearning to push back horizons in order to discover the mode whereby she might pass as an integral
woman into human society. Her mother's lesbian lover has
helped her learn to read and to discover "la splendeur du
mauve" of the desert. The story traces the steps of Mélanie's
initiation in her urgent thirst to retain her freedom while
bringing myriad hidden riches into the light. Unfortunately
the initiation brings knowledge not only of the desert but also
of the sordid reality of human society.

Each chapter of Mélanie's story is interwoven with a chapter containing the faceless, nameless "homme long," who
haunts the motel and the novel in mysterious association with
threatened violence and explosion. The modified form of his
name in "Mauve, l'horizon," "l'hom'oblong," suggests a
negative force imprisoning the dawn, the richest moment in

the desert for Mélanie. "L'homme long" or "l'hom'oblong,"
a scholar who feels only contempt for humanity, seems to
be one of those who are an absolute threat to the desert and
all it means, as they impose their sterile formulas—their so-
called knowledge—on it, bringing the destruction of atomic
blasts. In the end of both fictional novels, the woman who
offers knowledge and passion to Mélanie, while confirming
the legitimacy of her quest, is shot while dancing in
Mélanie's arms, presumably by "l'homme long." The meaning of this cruel death is not explained, although it suggests
that mankind's reality, spreading dangerously to destroy life
everywhere even into the vast and powerful desert, has absolutely no room for women's dynamic energy and vision.
Above all, the inexorable mechanics of this hollow reality
cannot tolerate the lucid gaze and the free expression of
those who have truly known the desert, its mauve and fluid
treasures. Blindly, anonymously, unemotionally, the social
machine crushes and exterminates free spirits.

Despite the final destructive act which marks the end of
Mélanie's quest, Brossard's novel is not a tale of defeat,
since the story is told and retold by women who read each
other's texts, translate them, imagine and invent them in different ways. The story told by Laure Angstelle about
Mélanie does not lie forgotten. Its message is transported
across space and time by Maude Laures, who enters actively
into the creative process, finds the necessary words, brings
the story to a new community. The act of translating is the
act of transforming dangerous language patterns and old
mind sets, building new community. Barbara Godard expresses well this particularly rich notion of translation as a
collective process of transforming and bringing forth meaning in her Preface to *Lovhers* when she describes translation as: "a conglomerate, not a unitary, structure . . . a
practice of reading/writing and, as such, the historical adventure of a subject," while the translator is "an active participant in the creation of meaning." Translation, inspired by
ecstasy, is thereby a richly poetic and profoundly subversive
practice.

Christian Bok (essay date 1991)

SOURCE: "i, a mother / i am other: *L'Amèr* and the Matter
of *Mater,*" in *Studies in Canadian Literature,* Vol. 16, No.
2, 1991, pp. 17-38.

[*In the following essay, Bok asserts that in Brossard's
L'Amèr, she "disarms phallogocentric language, disarms
such words as 'mother' and 'woman' and 'figure' so that
they can no longer be used as masculine weapons."*]

Nicole Brossard calls *L'Amèr* a book of combat, and indeed
the (s)wordplay begins with the title—one word that suggests

three: *la mère* (the mother), *la mer* (the sea), and *l'amer* (the bitter). The English translation **These Our Mothers** by Barbara Godard cleverly sustains this tripartite pun through elision: these our mothers, the sea our mother, and the sour mothers. Such paranomasia recalls *The Newly Born Woman* by French feminists Hélène Cixous and Catherine Clément, a text whose title in French also suggests a phonetic conflation of signifiers: *la jeune nèe* (the newly born woman), *là je n'est* (there the first-person subject does not exist), and *là je une nais* (there an origin of a feminine subject). Within both texts, the (s)wordplay in the title immediately announces the feminist attempt to undercut, to parry, to disarm, the hegemony of phallogocentric signification. The word "title" has more than one meaning: a title not only represents the proper name for a text, but also signifies a univocal right to authority over property. Titles entitle books to be appropriated by author(itie)s for the purpose of expressing an apparently stable position within discourse; however, the title of Brossard's text disrupts this stability through a linguistic self-consciousness that reveals the signifier's persistent tendency to evade the univocity of the proper name. Brossard's title does not lend itself to an economy of monosemic restrictions, but gives itself away to an economy of polysemic excess. The title in effect prepares the reader for the text's own violent attempt to destabilize any fixed, authoritative relationship of exchange between writer and reader.

(S)wordplay is violent, but this violence is always an act of self-defense. The defender, by virtue of her sex, cannot avoid participating in the duel of discourse without surrendering her life to the opponent, the master, a man skilled in the use of his weaponry, "language"—weaponry that the defender is always forced to employ, albeit according to her own style of combat. The battle is staged within the for(u)m of the book, an are(n)a where violence erupts at the level of both form and content. The syntactical fragmentation of the text parallels the deconstructive activity of the depicted narrator, who explicitly juxtaposes an act of violence with an act of writing: *"[j]'ai tué le ventre et je l'écris"*—"I have murdered the womb and I am writing it. The violence of the narrator is directed self-reflexively at both her uterus and her text, but this attack is not a spectacle of self-mutilation— the kind of masochistic spectacle that, according to Clément in *The Newly Born Woman,* typifies the experience of the hysteric, who reifies her suffering by repeatedly attacking herself instead of her male audience in order to sustain the voyeuristic attention of men. While Brossard's narrator attacks her opponent by miming an assault upon her own body and upon the body of her text, this attack is not designed to reaffirm the inevitability of either feminine suffering or feminine speechlessness (as the attack does in the case of the hysteric); on the contrary, the violence of the narrator symbolizes the irrevocable rejection of such inarticulate pain. Her attack does not result in the impotent aphasia of hyste-

ria; instead, the death of her womb, of her "[a]nonymous matrix," is correlated with the birth of her writing, of her "polysemous dream."

Brossard's text sets out to dramatize what Jacques Derrida in *Of Grammatology* might call "the unity of violence and writing"—the notion that "writing cannot be thought outside of the horizon of intersubjective violence": in short, language is the site of struggle, of hierarchies both established and dismantled. Brossard's text demonstrates that women have been the historical victims of language and that this victimization is enacted through the very words that women have traditionally spoken: such oppression appears to be embodied, for example, in the uterine terminology deployed by Brossard's text. The Latin word for "womb," *matrix,* is derived from the Latin word for "mother," *mater;* however, any biogenetic connotations to the word *matrix* have been virtually lost over time due to the advent of technical discourses that have appropriated the word *matrix* for the purposes of defining specific types of mathematical arrays, circuit diagrams, and chemical substrates, all of which are associated with what Brossard in *L'Amér* calls *le laboratoir,* a masculinized space forbidden to women. Moreover, the French word for "womb," *le ventre,* is a masculine noun, whose homophony with the word *vendre,* "to sell," suggests not only man's appropriation of the female anatomy, but also man's subsequent prostitution of it. Claude Lévi-Strauss in *The Elementary Structures of Kinship* points out that the history of sociocultural law begins with exogamy, the exchange of women—an exchange coeval with language, the exchange of words. Luce Irigaray in *This Sex Which Is Not One* goes on to observe that both systems of exchange occur only amongst men in, what she calls, an "hom(m)o-sexual monopoly," a monopoly that not only denies women any control over such exchanges, but also places the female body under erasure so that it may be subsequently transformed into a sign invested with the value of a (re)productive commodity. Women who participate in this hom(m)o-sexual economy are, according to Irigaray, rendered *indifférentes,* undifferentiated, in that they have no right to their own sexual identity, only to masculine definitions of it.

Femininity is merely fabricated by men through language, through the symbolic order, and is then reiterated by women, especially by mothers, who remain unwittingly complicit in this patriarchal project:

> Mothers are essential to its (re)production[. . . .] Their responsibility is to maintain the social order without intervening so as to change it. Their products are legal tender in that order, moreover, only if they are marked with the name of the father, only if they are recognized within his law: that is, only insofar as they are appropriated by him.

Brossard's narrator retraces this theoretical framework poetically by pointing out that such appropriation always implies an arbitrary declaration of ownership, a linguistic act of violence performed upon the body—an act reserved only for the male: "[h]e took possession of the child as of a word in the dictionary" writes the narrator, who denounces "[p]atriarchal mothers able only to initiate their daughters to a man"—mothers who willingly participate in what Irigaray calls *"la mascarade,"* a false femininity that permits the mother to experience desire only as it is prescribed by the desires of the father. Brossard's narrator emphasizes that "[e]very distinction which already takes away her body and her senses [. . .] by force of words keeps her at the other end, exiled, brought forth from him, aborted." The killing of the womb by the narrator therefore becomes the dominant metaphor for the killing of an inauthentic self, one whose reproductive function has been historically subject to masculine control.

Brossard's text demonstrates that linguistic activity has always been intimately connected with man's oppression of woman and that any attempt to do violence to such oppression necessarily entails an attempt to do violence to discourse: "[t]he biological mother isn't killed without a simultaneous explosion of fiction, ideology, utterance." The exclusion of woman from any condition of reproductive autonomy is directly correlated with her exclusion from any condition of discursive independence: she is acknowledged as a subject only insofar as she is subject to a male, who relegates her to the function of a mere mother, an exploited childbearer, a woman "motherhoodwinked" and then written off as a pretext for hom(m)o-sexual relationships among men. Independent exchanges conducted solely among women are, according to Irigaray, always repressed within this hom(m)o-sexual economy because such female relationships, particularly acts of lesbianism, necessarily imply a woman's rejection of her own commodification, and this rejection requires that men reappropriate the lesbian experience by interpreting it as a pathological, masculine behaviour. Women are forbidden to relate independently to each other, to indulge in "free association," so to speak; consequently, there exists a linguistic void between patriarchal mothers, a void that Brossard's narrator describes as "the domestic silence" and "the senseless grammar." Irigaray proposes that, in order to disrupt this masculine monopoly on exchange, a woman must reject *la mascarade* of imposed exogamy, of imposed language, in order to adopt an aesthetic of endogamous excess, an aesthetic that allows women to interact with each other, both physically and discursively, outside the restrictive scrutiny of masculine authority.

Brossard's text certainly embodies this aesthetic manifesto and demonstrates that, while phallogocentric ideology enforces an established schism between a woman's body and a woman's language, placing both under masculine control, a lesbian experience can defy this control by imbricating the poetic and the erotic. Writing within such an aesthetic paradigm becomes for Brossard's narrator: "[a]n exercise in deconditioning that leads me to acknowledge my own legitimacy"—"[t]he means by which every woman tries to exist, to be illegitimate no more." With this utterance, Brossard's narrator violates the univocity of phallogocentric signification by blurring the definitions for "legitimate" and "illegitimate." The word "legitimacy," derived from the Latin word for "law," *lex,* signifies both the state of being born into wedlock and the state of being accordant with legal regulations. These two states of being are synonymous with respect to women: to be involved in either state is to undergo the feminine version of bastardization, to be placed in an alienating, familial structure that is illegitimate in the sense that it is both spurious and false, misrepresenting sexual difference while denying women the possibility of any intercourse with each other: "[t]o submit to the father (in body) or representation [. . .] brings every woman back to her illegitimacy." Brossard elaborates her point in a 1981 *Broadsides* interview: "[t]he fact of not existing for a man is the worst thing that can happen to him"; "[b]ut that is just what men have insisted about women, that they don't exist"; "[w]e need to legitimate our own existence". Paradoxically, legitimacy for the illegitimate women lies in committing a crime, in killing the womb, in literally breaking the letter of the law.

Brossard's text uses syntactical fragmentation, disrupted sentences and textual lacunae, "[s]harp words, full of gaps," in order to stage this criminal activity allegorically: after all, the word "sentence" is not only a linguistic term for a syntagmatic chain that obeys grammatical rules, but also a legal term for a judgement that prescribes a time of punishing imprisonment. Brossard's narrator tries to break out of this linguistic prison, the sentence, in order to resuscitate the original, erotic connotations of the word "sentence," a signifier derived from the Latin verb *sentire,* "to feel." The text disobeys syntactic rules, in part through its apparent abuse of punctuation: the period, for example, does not consistently break up the text into discrete, syntactic units, each having a predicate structure; instead, the period frequently breaks up the text into fragments determined more by the rhythm of speech than by the meaning of words. The period is in this way transformed from a masculine indicator of resolute completion to a feminine indicator of rhythmic suspension: "period" in fact intricates within its own definition both the processes of the written text and the processes of the feminine body. Such a breaking of grammatical law does not result in mere senselessness, however, but expands the established parameters that restrict discourse to a utilitarian function: the transmission of univocal meaning.

When Brossard's narrator writes that, "[i]f it weren't lesbian, this text would make no sense at all," she acknowledges that within the hom(m)o-sexual monopoly her text must appear relatively unintelligible since it violates the predominant standard of phallogocentric exchange against which all discourse is judged—the phallus, the law of the father, with its formulaic production of fixed meaning. Brossard's text, however, subscribes to an altogether different system of exchange, a system that concentrates more upon the material corporeality of writing than upon the efficient production of meaning. Steve McCaffery in *North of Intention* defines meaning as profit earned through the exchange of language's material elements, the graphemic, the phonetic, the gesticulative, all of which must be expended, withdrawn, dematerialized, in order for meaning to be foregrounded. McCaffery borrows the terminology of George Bataille in order to distinguish between a "restricted economy" and a "general economy," the former maximizing meaning's production at the expense of language's materiality, the latter maximizing language's materiality at the expense of meaning's production. Within the restricted economy, the message is more important than the medium; within the general economy, the medium is itself the message, albeit one that may appear incomprehensible. Michelle H. Richman in *Reading Georges Bataille* points out that the restricted economy sustains itself by asserting a monologic relationship between signifier and signified, by insisting that each word has no more than one signification. Whereas the restricted economy privileges content over form, referentiality over non-referentiality, intentionality over non-intentionality, monosemy over polysemy, the general economy disrupts such hierarchization through an excess expenditure of linguistic material.

Brossard's text demonstrates that phallogocentricity exemplifies the operation of a restricted economy because masculine discourses valourize the monosemic, referential function of language: just as women are reduced to objects of utilitarian value, so also is language reduced to the status of an exogamic commodity—exogamic, in the sense that language must mediate reference to an extra-linguistic domain rather than disperse reference across an intra-linguistic domain. Brossard in **"Corps d'Energie/Rituels d'Ecriture"** responds to the restricted economy of phallogocentricity by resorting to four "rituals," among them "the ritual of sliding," a ritual that emphasizes the materiality of language—a ritual that "consists [. . .] in concentrating sufficiently long on words (their sonority, their orthography, their usual sense, their potential polysemy, their etymology) in order to seize all the nuance and potentiality, to do this until the forces that work in us stage a scene that is absolutely unpredictable." Auto-referential violence in **L'Amèr** may therefore be seen to represent an endogamous activity that challenges not only female commodification, but also linguistic commodification. Brossard's text participates in the general economy by drawing particular attention to the material corporeality of the words written upon the page: what the narrator variously calls the "[d]omesticated symbol," the "calligraphic alpha-

bet of [. . .] childhood," the "acid [that] has begun to soak into the paper of the book." Within the context of the restricted economy, the lesbian text does not simply make a nuisance of itself, but comes to make a new sense of its self.

Brossard's text demonstrates that any attempt to preserve the body of woman from phallogocentric exploitation implies that the materials of language must also be preserved from such exploitation. The word "material" recurs frequently within the text since the etymological derivation for the word "material" is also the Latin word for "mother," *mater.* Irigaray in *The Speculum of the Other Woman* points out that this historical synonymy between matter and *mater* stems directly from the platonic insistence that materiality, like maternity, represents nothing more than passive receptivity to an essentially masculine power. Women and language, like all forms of matter, have been traditionally represented as the amorphous substrate that awaits definition by men. Within the terminology of **L'Amèr,** women have become "avide de mots"—translated "av(o)id for words": women are "a void" in that they are infinitely receptive to a language extrinsic to their gender; they are "a void" in that they are completely empty of any language intrinsic to their gender; and they are "avid" in that they are eager to obtain independent access to a linguistic alternative. Brossard's narrator suggests that such an alternative lies in the creation of a purely feminine, linguistic space that preserves both the body of woman and the materiality of language from phallogocentric exploitation—"a clandestine space where every law is subordinate to the imaginary," a space that exceeds the parameters of the restricted economy's symbolic order. Brossard explains in the *Broadsides* interview:

> Things can happen in your body, in your skin, but as long as you cannot create a satisfactory syntactic environment for words of emotion you can be devoured by them. You can vanish in a sea of silence or disintegrate in a patriarchal society. For me to use words is not only a matter of expressing myself, but also a way to produce a new territory, a new space, a new environment for my body as a skin able to transform and be transformed by language.

Brossard's text places itself in explicit opposition to materialism, to the unchecked appropriation of mat(t)er, and points toward a new materialism, toward the unexploitive celebration of mat(t)er. "Materialism is," in either case, "reached only by the symbolic route"; language in effect provides the for(u)m for the political agenda.

Brossard's text opens this new, generic space for feminine speech, in part by disrupting the generic categories that already exist within the restricted economy. Brossard in the *Broadsides* interview describes her text as *"une fiction théoretique,"* a conflation of two, historically antagonistic, genres: the philosophical and the literary. Frederic Jameson in "Magical Narratives" points out that a genre is a species of social code, a prescribed literary structure that attempts with varying degrees of success to impose interpretive parameters upon the reader, to devise a formula for the automatic exclusion of all but one response to a given literary utterance. Genre is therefore merely another manifestation of the restricted economy's desire for authoritative meaning. Brossard's text, however, defies the monosemic imperialism of genre in order to produce a new, elusive "genre" that makes a virtue of polysemic rebellion. Brossard's text intersplices fragments of domestic biography with fragments of academic explication and, in doing so, undermines generic convention and rhetorical coherency, both of which have traditionally ensured the conveyance of monosemic expression: "[a]ll convention subjugated, it's delirious to approach matter like a conversation dispersing the institution." Within **L'Amèr,** the French word for "delirious," *délirant* is used in a context that suggests the neologistic verb *délire,* "to unread"; consequently, Brossard's delirious attack upon generic convention implies an act of unreading, of deconstruction, that may at first appear essentially hysterical to a reader accustomed to a purely referential discourse; nevertheless, the subversion of genre is intentionally political. Brossard's narrator writes that "the extent to which the gap between fiction and theory is reduced, the ideological field is eaten up"; the relentless disintegration of generic boundaries implies a directly proportional disintegration of phallogocentric mastery.

Daphne Marlatt in "Theorizing Fiction Theory" observes that "fiction theory" is "a corrective lens which helps us see *through* the [. . .] fictions which have [. . .] constructed the very 'nature' of woman," but "this is not to say that fiction theory is busy constructing a new ideology, a new 'line,'" for being "suspicious of correct lines [. . .], it enters a field where the 'seer' not only writes it like she sees it but says where she is seeing from—and with whom (now) and for whom (soon to be)." Brossard in **The Aerial Letter** declares: "I must enunciate everything, articulate an inexpressible attitude, one that wants to remake reality endlessly, in order not to founder in its fictive version nor be submerged in sociological anecdote." Brossard's transgression of generic boundaries is correlated with her attempt to destabilize any fixed, monologic division between lived experience and aesthetic representation:

> [W]hen I was writing **L'Amér,** I felt that I had to move reality into fiction because patriarchal reality made no sense and was useless to me. I also had the impression [. . .] that my fictions were reality [. . .] and that from there I could start a theoretical work.

Brossard's disruption of the reified differences between fiction and reality recalls a similar disruption made by Monique Wittig in *The Lesbian Body:*

> Our reality is the fictional as it is socially accepted[. . . .] [W]e possess an entire fiction into which we project ourselves and which is already a possible reality. It is our fiction that validates us.

Brossard and Wittig attempt to expose the masculine fiction of reality so as to reaffirm the feminine reality of fiction: this attempt to use her "fiction" to undermine his "reality," to invert the epistemological hierarchy traditionally maintained between the two terms, parallels the attempt of both writers to examine critically the categorical distinctions between art and life, the poetic and the erotic, text and body. The lesbian aesthetic in effect appears to regard the schism between the *poetic* (the body of the text) and the *erotic* (the text of the body) as codified, as essentially generic in structure, and therefore subject to a kind of literary hybridization: text and body can be synthesized so that they become metonymous extensions of each other, become what Brossard's narrator might call a "cortex," a word that suggests not only the biomaterial foundation of consciousness, but also a vascular membrane, like a sheet of either skin or paper, through which biogenetic exchanges can occur; moreover, the word "cortex" also suggests a pun on *corps/texte*— literally, a body language, an expressive form resistant to the violent abstraction of masculine discourse.

Brossard's narrator attempts to defend the female "cortex" from masculine violence, particularly the violence of the male eye that objectifies woman in order to reaffirm the predominance of male subjectivity. Brossard's narrator in the section entitled "The State of Difference" points out that the schism established by the eye between subject and object provides one of the foundations for the structure of sexual differentiation:

> I chose to speak first about his look. Because this is where the perception of difference begins. In this way difference is confirmed and nourished. Science of looking: observation. Exact use of difference: control and mastery of that which is under observation.

This schism between subject and object, between male and female, sustains itself through language, since words are a medium of exchange, a phallogocentric substitute for the direct, physical contact that initially obtains between mother and child. Brossard's narrator points out that, whereas the early relationship with the mother is characterized by both the tactile and the unspoken, the later relationship with the father is characterized by the visual and the spoken; maternal relationships maintain closeness, while paternal relationships maintain distance: "to know him, I need my eyes, I must speak to him": "[h]e won't let himself be touched." Brossard's narrator points out that entry into language requires that the daughter be divorced from the constant touch of the mother in order to submit to the gaze of the father: "[M]y hand pushing back my mother's body, my mouth parted to organize myself like him[. . . .] Under his eyes. Then to align myself at his side." Brossard's text in effect reiterates the psychoanalysis of Jacques Lacan, who argues that the child experiencing the "Imaginary" during the pre-Oedipal phase of development identifies itself completely with its mother and thus cannot conceptualize either difference or absence; the eventual entry of the child into the "Symbolic," a position of subjectivity within language, occurs during the advent of the Oedipal crisis when the father forbids access to the body of the mother and thus forces the child to repress any continuing experience of the "Imaginary" in order to assume a distinct identity: the entry of the child into language in effect requires submission to the law of the father, to phallogocentricity. Linguistic initiation for the female child entails entry into a subject position already defined in advance by masculine authority. Language establishes the difference between mother and father, male and female, but in the words of Brossard's narrator: "[h]is difference is transformed into *systematic* power", and "[f]rom this point he secures for himself control of the differences." His vision of the world in effect becomes her version of the world.

Brossard in *The Aerial Letter* observes that "[t]he image of woman is a foreign body in the eye of man," and she argues that women must refuse to submit to this paternal scopophilia in order to maintain a paradigm that privileges touch over sight. Brossard explains in the *Broadsides* interview:

> What is working most in [the] lesbian sensibility is skin. The skin provides the thought and the thought affects the whole surface of the body. It is through the skin that you catch and transmit energy. The skin is tactile memory. It protects your interiority, your integrity. Your skin works like a synthesizer, transmitting words, emotions, and ideas[. . . .] Imagination is travelling through our skin, all of its surface. A woman's skin sliding on a woman's skin creates a slipperiness in the meaning of words and makes a new version of reality and fiction possible.

Brossard in *The Aerial Letter* emphasizes that "[t]he imagination travels through the skin," that "[s]kin is energy," and that "[s]kin reflects its origins": "*touching* [. . .] impresses upon each skin cell that it must work at the emotion of living." Touch, unlike sight, closes the gap between people, between words, and so disrupts a scopophilic system of differentiation. This feminine emphasis upon touch informs the very notion of *une fiction théoretique:* the word "theory" is derived from the Greek word *theorien,* "to see," and con-

notes an epistemology based upon the visual; the word "fiction," however, is derived from the Latin word *fingere,* "to shape with the hands," and connotes an epistemology based upon the tactile. Brossard's conflation of genres may therefore be seen as an attempt to produce a theoretical discourse that incorporates touch as its fundamental episteme: a "[f]ictional theory" in which "words will have served only in the ultimate embrace."

Brossard in *L'Amèr* goes on to deconstruct the male gaze most explicitly in the section entitled "Act of the Eye"—a section divided into two parts: the first corresponding to the position of the "eye," the surveying subject; the second part corresponding to the position of the "figure," the surveyed object. The first section's running title begins as "Act of the Eye" and acquires an extra, lexical fragment with each subsequent page until the title ends as "The Violent Act of the Eye on Enamoured Purple Infiltrates Enraptured Unfolding *Her.*" The form of this running title parallels its content: the full title describes metaphorically the project that the eye of the reader must undertake when plotting the gradual expansion of the title across its ten pages. The running title is structured as a progressively unveiled secret, what Roland Barthes in *S/Z* might call an "hermeneutic sentence," a syntagmatic enigma, whose solution is divulged suspensefully during a series of interruptions or delays. The structure of the title parallels the structure of a striptease: just as the voyeur watches the woman disrobe herself progressively until her naked body is revealed, so also does the reader watch the title unfold itself progressively until its full message is laid bare. Within a scopophilic paradigm, the materiality of both body and text (intersecting at the italicized *"Her"* in the title) become objectified sources of satisfaction for a voyeuristic appetite; however, Brossard's text undermines the satisfaction of the voyeur, the reader, by overloading the voyeur with textual enigmas that resist reduction to complete solutions and singular perspectives. The first section of "Act of the Eye" is in fact structurally panoptical. Barbara Godard in "*L'Amèr* or the Exploding Chapter" points out that Brossard's narrator multiplies perspectives by allowing other female writers to make a statement in their own voice about the various operations of the eye: such a "communal feminist text," according to Godard, "denounces the economics of proprietorship on which authorship is based" and instead valourizes an economics of both cooperation and sharing, an economics that emphasizes a plurality of viewpoints. Brossard's narrator in "Act of the Eye" does not submit to the male gaze, but goes on to disrupt it by exploring visual sensation polyvalently, by assuming the vantage point of several kinds of gaze: the darting eye that resists fixing its glance upon a single object of desire; the closed eye that temporarily suspends the gaze in favour of inner meditation; the tearful eye that blurs distinctions between perceived objects; the amorous eye that in the tradition of courtly love establishes a primary bond between lovers; the voyeuristic eye that facilitates the violent objectification of women; the specular eye that sees its own evolving identity reflected in others; the clairvoyant eye that permits a multifaceted perspective of time and space; the staring eye that views the world blankly; the vigilant eye that maintains a close watch upon its own operations; and the transformed eye that represents a chrysalis giving birth to a new consciousness.

The second section of "Act of the Eye" has a series of titles that represent variations upon the word "figure," a word in which body and text again intersect, since "figure" signifies both a feminine physique and a textual trope. The word "figure" suggests that what women have historically regarded as the reality of their own bodies is in fact no more than a metaphorical phantasm conditioned by the male gaze. John Berger in *Ways of Seeing* writes:

> A woman must continually watch herself. She is almost continually accompanied by her own image of herself[. . . .] And so she comes to consider the *surveyor* and the *surveyed* within her as the two constituent yet always distinct elements of her identity as a woman[. . . .] Her own sense of being in herself is supplanted by a sense of being appreciated as herself by another.

Women are socialized to accept as natural, as realistic, the male perception of their bodies; however, the second section of "Act of the Eye," disrupts this socialization and traces the future evolution of the female body from a "realistic figure," static and recognizable, "the most submissive there is," to a "free figure," dynamic and unrecognizable. Such a free figure eludes sight; she "breaks the contract binding her to figuration"; she disfigures figuration so that such figuration cannot disfigure her. Brossard's narrator resists being reduced to the kind of image both depicted on the cover of *L'Amèr* and contemplated in the segment entitled "The Figurine"—an image of the Venus of Willendorf, a terra cotta statue of a woman, whose lack of both eyes and mouth, a lack offset by the contrasting exaggeration of her breasts and belly, represents for the narrator a blind, speechless female imprisoned within a primitive mythology of maternal fecundity. Brossard's text tries to escape the imprisonment of reproduction by suggesting an alternative textuality that endows women with discursive autonomy.

Brossard's writing stresses that any attempt made by women to disrupt a restricted economy based upon exogamic exchange requires that women participate both physically and discursively in a general economy based upon endogamous exchange. Brossard's narrator argues that "[i]t is while caressing the body of another woman over its entire living surface that she kills the mother" and that, "if she wants to survive, a woman must assert herself in reality and become recognized as symbolic mother: incestuous in power, but in-

accessible sexually for reproduction." The narrator's denunciation of patriarchal mothers as nothing more than "maternal clowns" and "filles du roi" heralds the lesbian celebration of metaphorical "daughter mothers" who obliterate patriarchal forms of differentiation, mothers who "experience bliss in the ultimate intercourse like two signifiers and metamorphose so mutually that they contain a single meaning"— mothers for whom the *jouissance* of body and the *jouissance* of language are no longer disjoined. The very term "daughter mother" suggests a metaphorical fusion of the female child with the female parent, a fusion reminiscent of a pre-Oedipal psychology. Brossard's term "daughter mother" also suggests a mother who can be her own daughter, a woman who can "engender" herself so to speak, and thus remain free from masculine definitions of the feminine. Moreover, Brossard's term suggests an exclusively female economy, a purely matrilineal heritage "without intermediary without interruption," a heritage effaced by the historical valourization of masculine primogeniture. The "daughter mother" thus corresponds with not only the pre-Oedipal fusion of mother and child, but also implies a form of maternity that must have existed before the reproductive commodification of mothers by fathers.

Brossard's narrator attempts to revive this maternal origin forgotten by masculine history: in the section entitled "The Vegetation," she undergoes a figurative, evolutionary retrogression in order to move from culture to nature, from the city to the jungle, from the "civilized" world of masculinity to the "uncivilized" world of femininity—from the conscious mind that represses to the unconscious mind that is repressed. This attempt to return to a prehistoric epoch unconditioned by patriarchal civilization parallels the attempt to. return to a childhood psychology unconditioned by patriarchal feminization—a return seen to be necessary for acquiring discursive autonomy:

> None of what appears in front of me could be nourished or even in a state of being if I didn't break in from the margin where *I have plunged within myself* not the woman but the little girl the mutilated girl resisting *the* woman.

Such an assertion recalls the narrator's earlier description of herself as an infant touching the mouth of her mother, an act that represents an erotic allegory for the narrator's archaeological endeavour:

> I open her mouth with thumb and index finger. The struggle begins in silence. The search. I part her lips[. . . .] I have to see for my own ends. She lets me do it, I don't threaten any part of her true identity yet. She's my m ther, she knows it and I am supposed to know it just as well. Her mouth like an

essential and vital egg, ambiguous. In the beginning. AAAAA.

The signifier "m ther" in the English text is the translation of the signifier "m're" in the French text, and within both cases the form of the signifier concretizes its content: the erasure of the first vowel does violence to the word by rendering the word unpronounceable, thus suggesting that this maternal, pre-linguistic figure cannot be incorporated into a phallogocentric signifying practice without suffering distortion. The originary "m ther" resists being definitively articulated and thus appears linguistically transcendent, ineffable; however, this feminine ineffability differs in character from the masculine ineffability of God, the originary father. God is the Word, the first signifier, monosemic and transcendental, inaccessible to phallogocentric discourse, yet nevertheless subtending it; the archaic mother, on the other hand, is not so much a signifier as the material precondition for signification: in the beginning is not so much the word as "the fictional character of the first A," the "dream of the letter in the beginning," "the a the acme the ancient('s) course"—in other words, the "AAAAA," a spontaneous, primal cry, devoid of meaning and thus pregnant with a potential multiplicity of meanings. Whereas God is understood as a site of monosemic transcendence that ensures the semantic closure of the signifying system, the archaic mother is understood as a site of polysemic transcendence that ensures the semantic aperture of the signifying system. Whereas God is understood as a self-present identity; the archaic mother is: "Amazon. Her identity is not single."

Abby Wettan Kleinbaum in *The War Against the Amazons* observes that, historically, the image of the Amazon does not serve to glorify woman; instead, the Amazon has been used by "male authors, artists, and political leaders to enhance their own perception of themselves as historically significant."

Patriarchy has portrayed the Amazons as a matriarchal society, whose ritual of initiation requires that a woman emulate the male physique by cutting off one of her breasts in order to wield a longbow more comfortably: the stories about the inevitable defeat of such militant women, such masculine pretenders, serves only to certify for men the preeminence of an authentic masculinity. Brossard's text revises the terms of reference for this myth so that the myth might conform more closely to a lesbian aesthetic that regards the Amazon as a connotation for a feminist utopia, a utopia of purely independent women who do not wish to imitate men so much as resist their influence.

Self-inflicted mastectomy in this lesbian context becomes a metaphorical act that parallels the self-inflicted hysterectomy performed by Brossard's narrator: both acts of violence symbolize the rejection of maternal subservience to patriarchy,

not a reification of such patriarchy. Just as Brossard's narrator wishes to discard the burden of her womb, her "backpack," so also does she wish "[t]o set our breasts ablaze," to "[s]our milk," so that "breasts will no longer smother anybody," no longer make women subservient to a nurturing function; moreover, just as the loss of the breast permits the Amazon to use a masculine weapon more effectively against men, so also does the loss of the uterus permit Brossard's narrator to deploy a phallogocentric language more effectively against its masters: whereas such violence in the phallic myth is portrayed as an aggressive act, such violence in the lesbian myth is portrayed as a defensive act.

Monique Wittig and Sande Zeig in *Lesbian Peoples* in fact define the word "Amazon" by relating a pagan myth of origins, in which an edenic age declines with the advent of motherhood:

> [W]ith the settlement of the first cities, many companion lovers disrupted the original harmony and called themselves mothers[. . . .] [A]mazon meant, for them, daughter, eternal child, she who does not assume her destiny. Amazons were banished from the cities of the mothers. [Amazons] became [. . .] violent [. . .] and fought to defend harmony. For them the ancient name [. . .] had retained its full meaning.

Wittig and Zeig use this narrative to suggest that the status of the Amazon corresponds to the status of Eve before the Fall, before receiving the divine punishment of childbirth. Within Brossard's text, the Amazon is a militant "daughter mother," who yearns to reclaim a feminine history suppressed by patriarchy; however, the dichotomy between the Amazonian and the maternal is not so sharply demarcated as it is in the case of Wittig and Zeig, since Brossard's narrator is herself a mother of a daughter—albeit a lesbian mother who rejects any form of patriarchal indoctrination. Moreover, the narrator's heterosexual sister calls to mind Amazonian imagery by virtue of her breast cancer and subsequent mastectomy; within this case, Brossard's narrator realize that both the "daughter mother" and the patriarchal mother suffer disfiguration under patriarchy—although in qualitatively different ways, the former kind of mother "[a]mputating oneself", the latter kind of mother "[a]mputated." Whereas the "daughter mother" represents a "woman surgeon" who actively excises from her body the masculine influence that debilitates her, the patriarchal mother represents a "white bride" who passively relinquishes her body to the masculine influence that debilitates her. Brossard's narrator responds to the suffering of patriarchal mothers, a suffering for which they are not entirely responsible, by trying ultimately to inscribe herself "in the practice of a surgery sympathetic to [. . .] differences."

Such Amazonian imagery may at first glance appear to be a problematic iconography for a feminist aesthetic since the very militancy of the Amazon suggests overtones of masculine combativeness: after all, the classical legend depicts Amazons kidnapping men, appropriating their masculine reproductive function in order to sustain a female society. Cixous in *The Newly Born Woman* addresses this potential problem by pointing out that Amazons do not kill, but capture men alive, only to liberate them again:

> Amazons don't make war for reasons that men understand[. . . .] The Amazons go around gathering men[. . . .] Defeating, yes, but in order to espouse. It is the invention of a union that is the opposite of rape[. . . .] Although the Amazons have broken off from the masculine world and created another State, they are in the minority[. . . .] And to get what they want from the others, they still must come and conquer, snatch it away; they have to venture onto the other side in an exchange where the terms are still dictated by masculine law, by men's behavior and their codes. For a free woman, there can be no relationship with men other than war[. . . .] To be an Amazon is to [. . .] repeat the act that proves or symbolizes that she is not captive or submissive to a man[. . . .] He dominates to destroy. She dominates to not be dominated; she dominates the dominator to destroy the space of domination.

According to Cixous, Amazonian violence is self-reflexive; it is paradoxically a violence needed to destroy the necessity of violence. The violence in the form of Brossard's text may therefore be seen as an Amazonian allegory for the feminine entry into a masculine territory, where the narrator must do violence to the violence of discourse in order to obliterate violence and invigorate language.

The violence in the form of Brossard's text may be seen as an Amazonian allegory for the feminine entry into a masculine territory, where the narrator must do violence to the violence of discourse in order to obliterate violence and invigorate language.
—*Christian Bok*

When Brossard's narrator says that, "[c]aught in the whirlpool, the wave, the dread, the pallor, I write," she points out that to express herself within a lesbian aesthetic is not without risks: "[t]o write I am a woman is heavy with consequences," possibly because it may inadvertently repeat a masculine project by opening the way to what Lola Lemire Tostevin in "Reading After the (Writing) Fact calls

"vulvalogo-centricity," the displacement of the law of the father with a new law of the mother. Brossard's narrator writes that "[t]he sisterhood of women is the ultimate test of human solidarity laying itself open to another beginning of delusions of grandeur"—but while the narrator worries whether or not her book is going to be "the product of a fever or of a major exercise in survival," her text demonstrates that she does not wish to repeat the masculine, oppositional structures of difference, but wishes instead to disrupt these differences in order to free women from masculine conditioning:

> I am working so that the convulsive habit of initiating girls to the male as in a contemporary practice of lobotomy will be lost. I want to see *in fact* the form of women organizing in the trajectory of the species.

Brossard does not reaffirm feminine suffering, but rejects such ineffectual pain: *"Je sais que pour beaucoup de femmes la souffrance est l'origine de l'écriture; pour moi, l'écriture est à l'origine de l'écriture";* to Brossard, feminine writing disrupts the masculine "practice of lobotomy" by disrupting discourse, by refusing an economy of exogamic exchange while simultaneously embracing an economy of endogamic exchange: she protects both body and text from a purely utilitarian function by celebrating their materiality instead of exploiting it, and she posits a way of knowing that does not merely restrict itself to metaphors of sight, but incorporates the entire body in its epistemology. Brossard disarms phallogocentric language, disarms such words as "mother" and "woman" and "figure" so that they can no longer be used as masculine weapons: after all, words such as these harm others.

Marthe Rosenfeld (essay date 1993)

SOURCE: "Modernity and Lesbian Identity in the Later Works of Nicole Brossard," in *Sexual Practice/Textual Theory: Lesbian Cultural Criticism*, edited by Susan J. Wolfe and Julia Penelope, Blackwell, 1993, pp. 199-207.

[*In the following essay, Rosenfeld discusses Brossard's* Amantes *and* Picture Theory *to show that "Nicole Brossard's postmodernism is linked inextricably to her lesbian-feminist vision of the world."*]

Although there is no unique style that characterizes the work of all lesbian writers, it is not surprising that Nicole Brossard, the most famous lesbian poet of contemporary Quebec, should also be "resolutely modern" in her textual practice. A writer who seeks to convey a way of life that runs counter to the norms and values of the dominant culture is likely also to challenge the institutions that perpetuate those norms: the literary canon and the language of tradition. In an informative book entitled *Les mots et les femmes,* Marina Yaguello emphasizes the priority of the masculine over the feminine gender in French grammar; she demonstrates moreover how French words in the course of history have acquired meanings that convey negative images of women. Brossard's early awareness that language, as a system of communication, transmits the cultural codes of a society accounts for her faith in the transformative power of experimental writing even in the early 1970s, when the liberation of Quebec still aroused her deepest feelings. Not until the middle of that decade, when the author had chosen to identify as a feminist and as a lesbian, did she move beyond the theories of "new writing" to struggle with other women against the sexism and restrictiveness of the official language. Indeed it is this quest for a medium of expression outside of the mainstream that elucidates the intersection between Brossard's lesbian-feminist identity and her postmodernism.

Because the meanings of words such as "modernism," "modernity" and "postmodernism" change according to the culture in which they are defined, a brief history of these movements from a francophone perspective might be in order here. Since *modernité* grew out of modernism, there is no visible demarcation line that separates these two periods from each other.

In early twentieth-century France, a shift in attitude toward the arts began to manifest itself. Apollinaire, with his unusual poetry, epitomized this new spirit and its rejection of art's mimetic approach to nature. Similarly, by reducing all shapes to their geometric components, experimental painters such as Braque and Picasso transformed the concepts of space and of the human figure. Cubism with its multiplicity of perspectives also influenced the younger generation of poets to avoid ordinary descriptions. Instead of reproducing exterior reality, they juxtaposed images without regard to logic and thus communicated the rapidity of the modern age. In 1916 the Dadaists, expressing the utter confusion of a world at war, cast systematic doubt on everything except chance. A few years after the end of the hostilities, the surrealists, having overcome the initial nihilism of Dada, tried to revitalize the language, impoverished by the mediocre fiction of that period. Attentive to their stream of thought, the surrealists would give free play to the association of words whose unusual combinations could explode in a brilliant image. With its free-flowing imagery and its minimum of preconceived ideas, surrealism increased the autonomy of the readers as interpreters of poetry.

The novel, however, with a few exceptions, continued to stagnate. In 1932 Nathalie Sarraute began to jot down the minute inner movements, the impulses, the conflicting sentiments which bump against each other on the threshold of consciousness in *L'Ere du soupçon.* By illuminating the profusion of sensations that often accompany, follow, or precede a dialogue, Sarraute invited her readers to experience for themselves the inner dramas of her anonymous people. But the preoccupation of the author of *Tropisms* with the subterranean movements that form an integral part of everyone's existence made it necessary for her to challenge the traditional novel with its individualized characters, its linear plots, its chronological time. Thanks to her lonely experimentations, Sarraute became a pioneer of the *nouveau roman.*

In the novels of Robbe-Grillet, objects, passions and different versions of the same event are presented to the reader through the eyes of a narrator whose vision is both limited and fragmented. Unlike the surrealists, who sought to attain a higher form of reality by fusing the states of dream and of wakefulness, the new novelists, in true postmodern fashion, insisted on the purely fictional character of their work. Similarly, in *Writing Degree Zero,* Roland Barthes underscored the self-reflective nature of postmodern writing. In a world divided by factionalism, conflicts, and strife, "alienated writing" would seek its own self-transcendence, its own peculiarities, sounds, and functions, just as the *nouveau roman* had no other reality outside of its own narrative.

It was in the 1960s that the ideas of postmodernism gained ground in Quebec, precisely at the time of its cultural revolution, a period often referred to as *La Révolution Tranquille.* Given Brossard's early adherence to the principles of modernity, it is not surprising that *Un livre,* her first novel, should read like an archetype of the *nouveau roman* in Quebec. For, unlike many other Quebec novels of that period, which dealt with the land, the snow, the ever-increasing family, this book questioned the relationship between fiction and reality, between words and meanings, between the printed lines and the blank spaces. But the more the text turned inward, the more the female narrator vanished from the scene.

In this essay I plan to show the relation between Brossard's identity as a lesbian and her formalist approach to writing in two of her later works: in *Amantes,* translated as *Lovhers,* and in *Picture Theory.* From that time onward Brossard was able to distill her experience as a lesbian in such a way that her words communicate not only her personal desire but the essence of sapphic love.

An avant-garde composition consisting of poems and prose passages, *Amantes* deals with the lovemaking of four lesbians who are staying at the Barbizon Hotel for women and who learn to articulate their feelings as well as their thoughts by associating with their own kind. To evoke the atmosphere of this female space, Brossard experiments with both form and typography. Divided into five parts by means of black and gray pages, illustrated with photographs of the New York skyline, and printed with a variety of types—capital letters, small letters, italics, blank spaces—this book immediately challenges our reading habits as well as the unidirectional character of patriarchal systems of thought. Similarly, the traditional concept of literature as a succession of masterpieces created in isolation by individual geniuses has given way to a more communal vision of literary creation. That is why numerous quotations from other lesbian writers—Adrienne Rich, Monique Wittig, Louky Bersianik—embellish *Amantes.*

> **By showing how the subversive love between two women is related to their quest for a new language, Brossard also brings out the connection between lesbianism and postmodernism.**
> **—*Marthe Rosenfeld***

By showing how the subversive love between two women is related to their quest for a new language, Brossard also brings out the connection between lesbianism and postmodernism. Unlike traditional literature, whose texts refer for the most part to an objective reality, the words of *Amantes* create their own mental space. In fact what characterizes the writing of this book is the breaking up of the sentence with its subject, verb, predicate sequence into word-clusters, units that are no longer attached to one another by conjunctions, adverbs or punctuation:

> concentrées dans l'île amoureuses
> *picture theory* / juillet la mer
> dire l'intention des langues

If the reader tries in vain to restore the grammatical order, it is because postmodern writing rejects the determinism that underlies the traditional narrative form. To express an open-ended reality, one that mirrors the dreams, hopes, and desires of women-loving women, the lesbian writer must also redefine all the words that have been contaminated by centuries of patriarchal ideology.

For example, the concept of memory, to which Brossard devotes a section entitled MA MEMOIRE D'(AMOUR), is a word that needed to be reexamined because the official memory, by ignoring or maligning women, has separated us from each other and from our past. Consequently Brossard links the nostalgic quest for our history to the physical love between women. Moreover, unlike the word that has been restricted in the dictionaries of the dominant culture to mean "remembrance of past events," memory in the work of Brossard also connotes the arrival of a bright future, a Utopian future which helps women to live in the present:

> la nuit venue lorsque de mèche
> nos fronts se souviennent des plus belles
> délinquances, on bouge un peu la main
> pour que s'ouvre sous nos yeux
> la mémoire agile des filles de l'utopie
> se déplaçant en italique
> ou en une fresque vers toutes les issues

Likewise, in order to describe the pleasure of lesbianism without resorting to heterosexual language, Brossard found it necessary to alter the definition of the word *skin.* Unlike the dominant sexuality with its emphasis on penile penetration, lesbian loving has no single sensual center. Disproving the image of superficiality that the mainstream culture has given to the expression "only skin deep," Brossard illustrates how "a woman's skin sliding on a woman's skin creates a slipperiness in the meaning of words and makes a new version of reality and fiction possible." In *Amantes,* the knowledge derived from sensations of taste and touch enables the lesbian lovers to rediscover a multidimensional language.

If Brossard found it necessary as a lesbian writer to question grammatical structures and dictionaries, as a devotee of *modernité* she felt the need to reject traditional writing with its linear time and its binary system of opposition: man/woman, culture/nature, activity/passivity, intellect/feeling. It is precisely the author's rebellion against these manifestations of the "straight" mentality that accounts for the paramount importance of the spiral in her work from *L'Amèr* onward. This shape, which appears in everything from seashells to nebulas, from the flight of birds to the movement of planets and stars, enables the female writer to explore new analogies, new rhythms, a new way of relating with the world and of being. In postmodern texts by women each spiral repeats the same words but in so doing adds another element to the previous notation, thus advancing the turn of the coil every time. For example, the following spiral of *Amantes* brings out in a rhythmical flow of words the joy of yielding to temptation:

> j'ai succombé à toutes les visions
> séduite, surface, série et sérieuse
>
> j'ai succombé à la vision claire
> des végétations et des événements
> matinales, . . .
>
> j'ai succombé à l'écho, au retour,
> à la répétition. *au commencement*
> *des vertèbres* était la durée
> une réplique essentielle à tout instant
> dans la joie que j'ai de toi, . . .

Another spiral of that book makes the connection between the texture of the words and the taste of a kiss:

. . . et nous imaginons de nouvelles moeurs avec ces
bouches mêmes qui savent tenir un discours, les
nôtres au goût des mots au goût du baiser . . .

les faits sont tels que le projet du texte et le texte
de projet s'accomplissent au goût des mots, au goût
du baiser. je sais que tu m'es réelle / alors

A synthesis of all of Brossard's previous books, *Picture Theory* resumes some of the major themes of *Amantes,* but it delves more deeply than the love poems into the issue of lesbianism and writing. One of the reasons why Brossard insists so vehemently on this question is her belief that women's literary expression is of paramount importance because it can change the world. However, in order to achieve this transformation, lesbians should be at the origin of the meaning they give to their lives. For the capacity to name and redefine the world depends largely on our place in the language. Since the French idiom, with its unequal gender structure, mirrors the heterosexist appropriation of the class of women by the class of men, Brossard chose lesbianism not only because she passionately loves people of her own sex, but because she seeks to alter the language.

Written from a lesbian-feminist perspective, *Picture Theory* beckons the reader to travel through five different areas of artistic creation, the five chapters that constitute the book. "L'Ordinaire" introduces us to the characters of the novel as well as to its spiral composition. "La Perspective" evokes the relationship between the female narrator and Claire Dérive, her lover. The third chapter, entitled "L'Emotion," underscores the sense of well-being that characterizes feminist utopias, especially when Amazons show solidarity with one another in pursuit of common goals. "La Pensée," the most important chapter in the book, announces the arrival of a sister poet, a contemporary Sappho whose genius will enable her to reshape the language. In the last chapter, this dreamlike image of the poet comes into clear focus; she is emulated by other women, for she can interact with them by means of the hologram that helps to illuminate aspects of the associative memory and of other thought processes.

In an interview with the lesbian-feminist journal *Vlasta* published five years ago, Brossard emphasized the significance of expressing one's personal truth. But the difficulty of articulating our intimate thoughts in patriarchal societies accounts for the importance the author attaches to the solidarity of women. It is not surprising therefore that the female characters of *Picture Theory* acquire their sense of self by living together one summer in a communal setting. Breathing the sea air of a holiday resort on the New England coast, they discuss their youth, the stilted images of women in mainstream films, the danger of confusing "father time" and the time of Amazon friendships. ". . . Nous sommes cinq au lever du soleil à . . . voir éperdument la mer, prononçant

d'une manière atonale des phrases complètes et abstraites liant la vie et la parole dans l'heure horizontale." The frequent use of the feminine plural indicates not only that the women are pooling their energies but also that they challenge one another to communicate their ideas, ideas which will give them a new sense of being in the culture: "Je disais . . ." noted the lesbian narrator ". . . qu'un témoignage utopique de notre part pouvait stimuler en nous une qualité d'émotion propice à notre insertion dans l'histoire."

When preceded by the definite article, the word *histoire* often denotes that branch of learning which relates and analyzes the "important events" of the life of a people. However, since meanings, values, and notions of reality have been shaped by centuries of patriarchal cultures, women as a class have been excluded from this narrative. While certain francophone feminists seek to inscribe a female presence into the language by using such terms as *hystoire, écrivaine, auteure,* Brossard tends to redefine existing words and thus to produce a form of writing that breaks the continuity of patriarchal culture. As our experiences and perceptions have no credibility in that culture, the attempt to translate into words those "fictions" that are our realities becomes a utopian venture. In Brossard's *Picture Theory,* the utopian quest arouses a quality of emotion conducive to women's insertion into history, that word having acquired the dual meaning of a female presence here and now as well as in the future.

But if women can become part of history by means of their communal efforts, it is lesbianism that enables them to express their own view of the world in new and modernistic terms. One of the ways in which the author links the themes of sapphic love and language is through the world of the senses. Surface/skin, in *Amantes,* constitutes an avenue of approach to sensuous and verbal knowledge. In *Picture Theory,* however, the vast expanse of touching is explored to attain the body of the beloved as well as the art of writing: "sa main me touchait comme une raison / écrire allait devenir un souci permanent." If Michèle Vallée, the narrator, and her lover, Claire Dérive, choose words for their sound and their evocative power rather than for their meaning, it is because they do not wish to see their poetry retrieved by existing cultural institutions:

je reprenais les sons
autour de sa bouche, les liaisons
presque sans accent la fièvre sonore

Although *Amantes* and *Picture Theory* both link lesbian sexuality to language and to literature, it is the latter book that brings together lesbian poetry and postmodernism. In the arts this quest for new forms is related to the concept of abstraction. To accelerate her progress toward that goal, the narrator of *Picture Theory* uses a vocabulary rich in the symbolist tradition: forest, water, sea, angel, helmet. The following poem, for example, conjures up a scene of freshness that is at once lesbian and abstract:

> Claire Dérive est entrée dans la forêt
> et les songes emportée par la vision
> du temps qui s'écoule entre ses lèvres
> elle entend la pluie qui danse sur son casque
> elle traverse la forêt ruisselante
> et déterminée comme l'est sa bouche
> Claire Dérive est dans la rosée
> l'horizon, allongée entre mes cuisses

Exposed at the end of the second chapter to "l'abstraction vitale," the lesbian lovers have become symbolic characters, mythical figures who announce the coming of a poetess: "her through whom anything can happen."

The arrival for the first time in history of a female subject in the language is evoked in different ways: plays on words, scene shifts without transition, travels back and forth between Paris, Montreal, and Curaçao. But more important than these signs of modernity in announcing the advent of the female poet who "makes contact" is the spiral, a form that Brossard relates to lesbian sensibility. In *Picture Theory,* as in *Amantes,* phrases and analogous sentences build on each other to form an ever-widening curve, a spiral that challenges the linear structure of traditional fiction even as it favors the development of the texts' lesbian-feminist themes. "C'est elle," writes the narrator of *Picture Theory* as she envisions the coming of the female author, "il faudrait la voir venir, virtuelle à l'infini," "je la vois venir," "je la vois venir les femmes synchrones au matin chaque fois plus nombreuse," "je la vois venir dans l'angle lorsque la phrase se divise en deux." Similarly the repetition of the phrase "peau la langue monte au cerveau" takes on the quality of a chant, a recitative which also announces the arrival of her who generates meaning in words. Indeed the issue of woman's position in the language looms so large that the spiral now moves in a centripetal manner toward that focal point.

The utopian quest is a major theme linking *Picture Theory* to *Amantes.* These two works point to a reimagined space where lesbians live in harmony with each other. Moreover, both novels illustrate the paramount importance of language as a means of expressing female-centered societies. In her transformation of Wittgenstein's picture theory, Brossard has shown how lesbianism challenges the limitations of a philosophy that views the concepts of language and of picture as synonymous terms. Instead of being captive in a two-dimensional model of reality, the lesbians in Brossard discover words while making love, and the radiance that emanates from this lovemaking, like a laser beam, alters the picture into a holographic three-dimensional image.

In *Amantes* as well as in *Picture Theory,* Brossard develops a polyvalence of meaning, a new form of writing that communicates the intensity of lesbian relationships as well as the momentous significance of female subjectivity in the language that has excluded women and lesbians as agents of thought and action. Rooted in the present and looking toward the future, Nicole Brossard's postmodernism is linked inextricably to her lesbian-feminist vision of the world.

Alice A. Parker (review date Spring 1994)

SOURCE: "The Enigma of Writing," in *Belles Lettres,* Vol. 9, No. 3, Spring, 1994, pp. 6-7, 9.

[*In the following review, Parker argues that Brossard's* Picture Theory *and* Mauve Desert *"are fine samples of how Brossard integrates the language of current scientific theories and technological advances into an intuitive, utopian vision of a more just future for women, lesbians, and other marginalized groups."*]

Thanks to two fairly recent translations, American readers have access to major works of prose fiction by one of Québec's most provocative writers, Nicole Brossard. *Picture Theory,* a complex, challenging, exuberant, and erotic response to Joyce and Wittgenstein, and *Mauve Desert,* the first text Brossard is willing to call postmodern, are fine samples of how Brossard integrates the language of current scientific theories and technological advances into an intuitive, utopian vision of a more just future for women, lesbians, and other marginalized groups.

Brossard is an acknowledged leader among those writers whose experimental practices are usually categorized by the term "modernity"; she is also a spokeswoman for the feminist community. Like Adrienne Rich, Brossard received early recognition for the formal expertise of her poetry, and has since won many awards, including the prestigious Prix David for the ensemble of her work, now totalling more than 30 volumes. In addition to poetry, fiction, and theory, of which the most important collection is *The Aerial Letter,* Brossard cofounded the experimental literary journal *La Barre du Jour* and the feminist *Les Tetes de Pioche,* and has collaborated on film and theater projects.

In *Picture Theory,* her most ambitious work, Brossard explores figures that suggest the indeterminacy and multidimensionality of quantum physics and laser optics, light, vertigo, the spiral, cortex (corps-texte), the hologram, and the horizon. *Picture Theory* raises epistemological questions in a "desire to unravel the great patriarchal enigma," setting language adrift in an effort to capture the "subliminal" or "generic" woman. Brossard uses holography to figure "mental space for a contemporary vision," working with "potential" forms to "conquer reality, makes it plausible."

As a modernist, Brossard is insistently urban(e): her native Montréal figures in her work as a site of writing and renewal. In *Picture Theory* she invents "border crossers, radical city dwellers": at their vacation retreat on a coastal island, five "synchronous women" pool their instinctual, artistic, and intellectual resources to "modify the horizon," using "the science of energy." Always transgressive in her thinking and in her writing, Brossard forces her readers to ask hard questions, to negotiate with her the paths between fiction and reality.

The death of Brossard's father in 1982 occasioned an uncharacteristic anguish over her writing. Brossard wrote poetry and pondered translation—issues raised by the dual-language, postcolonial context of Québec, by Brossard's work with her translators, and by her collaboration with Daphne Marlatt. Eventually, *Mauve Desert* resulted, representing the "postmodern condition," set in the hyperreal and unforgiving southwestern landscape with its bombs and fragile motels, where no window frames the blinding play of light.

Like Escher's hand drawing itself drawing, the text is a self-translation. The hyped-up young narrator criss-crosses the desert at breakneck speed in her mother's Meteor, trying to understand, to "bend reality toward the light," while the translator tries to slip between the words. Translation, like writing, opens up a quantum field of inquiry into words, syntax, grammar, and the production of meaning. *Mauve Desert* thus focuses on the processes whereby we transform our thoughts and feelings into words, in essence how a writer creates a work of prose fiction, using translation to allegorize writing and reading (interpretation).

Like the heroine of *Mauve Desert,* Brossard was a philosopher at 15: "Very young, I was already crying over humanity. With every new year I could see it dissolving in hope and in violence." With other writers and artists of a generation that came to consciousness in Quebec during the Quiet Revolution of the early 1960s, Brossard rejected the conservative values of the French Canadian tradition, which was based on nostalgia for a mythic agrarian past and obeisance to the Catholic Church. For women this meant compulsory procreation and subservience to patriarchal directives.

The problem for Brossard was how to reinvent (rewrite) a life to correspond to values that, by the mid-1970s, positioned her (as a woman, a feminist, and a lesbian) in direct opposition to the major discourses of the culture. She "would have to venture, body and soul, into a semantic field strewn with countless mines, some already exploded in the form of everyday sexism, others, even more terrifying, the buried

mines of misogyny." Along with the terror came a surge of energy, a communal sense of urgency shared with women of many backgrounds, and a perception that "normal" heterosexual lives now seemed incongruous or even surreal.

For the last decade and a half, Brossard's project has been to design a subject-status for the woman writer who must operate in a male-centered communication system. Thus, she invents what she calls "rituals of presence in the language." A guiding spirit of a generation determined to be "resolutely modern," Brossard's unconventional praxis has stood her in good stead as she addresses the problems of creating a space in language—the inherited system of codes and symbols—for the desire of women. Beginning with *These Our Mothers or The Exploding Chapter* she has created texts that are radical in their approach to gender and sexuality while continuing to deconstruct literary conventions. The next two volumes in her lesbian trilogy, *Lovhers* and *Surfaces of Meaning,* continue to attack phallogocentrism and refurbish the imagination. Not only does the chapter on motherhood explode, but so do syntax, grammar, and even words, each of which must be examined for its accretion of patriarchal values and the desire projected by a male libidinal economy.

Brossard's fiction foregrounds writing and bookmaking, playing with typography, problematizing narrative conventions, interfacing visual images, creating books within books. She investigates "surfaces of meaning," black marks on the white page, sometimes figured as skin or screen. Her "virtual" texts resemble holographic images, with narrative elements continuously displaced. The utopian energy that fuels her work has its source in the lesbian body. Relieved of gravity (in both senses) the island/continent of lesbian desire has "aerial roots." With modernist writers Gertrude Stein and Djuna Barnes as models, she combines a formalist approach with a feminist consciousness, working always "in the light of a woman's gaze." The result is a "writing in the feminine" that blends poetry, theory, and fiction, exploding generic boundaries. Such writing also taps into an erotic substratum that is necessarily creative despite the nightmares, despite a symbolic code that forces women to stutter, and despite the daily violence of women's lives. Brossard believes that anything can happen in writing; it can dismantle the lies, the violence, and lead us out of silence. To intervene through writing is to create an alternate reality. Writing, like reading, is exciting, a privileged act because it permits us to modify our relationship to the world. As a spiritual event, Brossard writes in *Mauve Desert,* writing helps us "bend the light toward reality."

Nicole Brossard with Lynne Huffer (interview date 1995)

SOURCE: "An Interview with Nicole Brossard: Montreal, October 1993," in *Yale French Studies,* No. 87, 1995, pp. 115-21.

[In the following interview, Brossard discusses her relationship with feminism and fiction.]

[Huffer:] I would like to begin by talking about your work both as a writer and a feminist. Since the 1970s you have been a part of the feminist movement as a poet, novelist, editor, essayist. Could you put the history of these various activities in a contemporary context?

[Brossard:] The poet, the novelist, and the feminist are still very active. I am still trying to answer questions about what it means to be a contemporary subject in a civilization about to shift into another dimension. Very early on, I said that I saw myself as an explorer in language and that I was writing to comprehend the society in which I live and the civilization to which I belong. Actually, understanding what goes on means trying to process the double-time in which I feel I am living: on the one hand, a historical linear time-space with familiar patriarchal scenarios such as war, rape, and violence; on the other, a polysemic, polymorphic, polymoral time where the speed and volume of information erase depth of meaning, where science proposes itself as an alternative to nature, where reality and fiction manage exaequo to offer proof of our ordeals and of the most dreadful fantasies.

While scientific information and images of violence multiply to the point that ethics becomes a polymorphic version of virtual behaviors, I am still Nicole Brossard, born in Montreal, with a sense of the history of Quebec and of belonging in that French part of the North American continent. I am still the writer who cannot let go of the idea that literature is subversion, transgression, and vision. I am still the feminist who thinks women have been and are still marginalized by the patriarchal system. I am still the lesbian who enjoys the way desire shapes itself among women of *paroles.*

The radical feminist does not wish to repeat questions and answers she has given in her previous texts. I can only rewrite my obsession for language and for the enigma of creative writing. I also know that desire is definitely a key word for any kind of creative process and that collective dreaming is at the core of any political involvement. I also have in mind that keeping the focus on women's present and future is the most challenging feat.

Let's come back to the subject of writing. Could you talk about your thoughts on fiction, in its etymological sense, as a sort of ruse or lie that transforms reality?

Yes, I have often said "in reality there is no fiction." The

dictionary associates fiction with faking, dissimulation, and lying. Fiction has always been opposed to reality, as being the fruit of our imagination, as if our imagination came out of the blue. We do not construct fiction differently from the way we construct our relation to reality. In other words, we behave (in terms of patterns) in fiction the way we do in reality. Fiction is not only about story-telling, it is also about the logic of the stories each person initiates in language. By logic I mean the coherence of a universe we construct with such materials as sensations, emotions, memory, knowledge, and beliefs which are at work subterraneously within our usual practice of language which is speech. Part of that logic comes along with the literary tradition we belong to, as well as from the language we use. Part of it is idiosyncratic. It is by becoming a feminist that I was forced to question the words fiction and reality. For it seemed to me that what women were experiencing was discarded into "you are making things up," fictions or lies. One can only think about the rejection into fiction of revelations about incest, rape, and so on. Sexual practice other than plain heterosexual penetration was also seen as fictive, "unbelievable." On the other hand, men's fictions about women always came out as being "true." I think that for a long time the word fiction was an underground territory for what society did not want to admit as being part of the real. Fiction is the hidden face of the unavowable as well as of the unexplainable. I think that by telling their reality, by bearing witness to their experiences, women have narrowed the territory of fiction, of lies about them. It seems now that reality, science, and fiction have proved equal in representing the unbelievable. What is fiction now that "reality shows"—those dramatizations of real stories about serial killers—provide all the details we wanted to know about sex, violence, and injustice? What is fiction when, through technology, a grandmother can bear and give birth to her daughter's child? Nevertheless, I see fiction as an open space for desire to figure out the narrative of all those permutations we are capable of in order to give meaning to our lives.

*In discussing theory and fiction in **Aerial Letter,** you say: "It is precisely where there is a referential illusion that theoretically women traverse the opaque reality of language and* le sujet fabuleux *we contain becomes operative." What is the relationship between fiction and this "fabular subject"?*

Le sujet fabuleux is constructed in fiction because it can only be developed in the unpredictable part of the narrative; where words and thoughts derive, blossoming with unexpected ramifications, and henceforth initiating threads of meaning that help us to protect the positive image each woman intuits of herself. This image is the fabular subject, but in a patriarchal society the image is seen subliminally. Writing and the referential illusion that it creates allow time to retrace and to focus on the positive image. It is through Man's fiction that we have become fiction; let us exit fiction via fiction. When you pass through written language there is more of an opportunity to deal with the symbolic or to make the symbolic act for you, to be able to question or to skirt around the given course of what seems to be the universal patriarchal symbolic order. Even by using the word "fabular," something already shapes itself into a proposition. Things (meaning, images, a sense of truth) happen in writing that would never happen otherwise. I will probably write all my life because the act of writing allows for an encounter with unusual images, unexpected thoughts; a new world is opened each time.

I started to read about holography and was totally taken by some of the vocabulary relating to it: real image, virtual image, reflection, wave length, holographic brain. Also by the fact that all the information about the image is contained in every fragment of the holographic plate. I related that information to the fact that sentences might also contain the whole of what is at stake in a novel.

—Nicole Brossard

Can you talk about the image of the hologram that is so important to your work?

I have always been interested in everything that has to do with the eye and the gaze. When I first saw a hologram, in New York in 1979, I was absolutely fascinated by it. I started to read about holography and was totally taken by some of the vocabulary relating to it: real image, virtual image, reflection, wave length, holographic brain. Also by the fact that all the information about the image is contained in every fragment of the holographic plate. I related that information to the fact that sentences might also contain the whole of what is at stake in a novel. For me, the hologram became the perfect metaphor to project the intuitive synthesis that I had in mind of a woman who could be real, virtual, and symbolic. By symbolic I mean she who, by being other than the mother symbol, could alter the course of meaning, values, and patterns of relationship. The hologram is tied to the idea that somehow we women have to invent our own idea of woman in order to enjoy being a woman and to proceed as a creative subject in language. I often say that if each woman could project the best that she senses in herself onto other women, we would already have accomplished a lot. I, for example, have a tendency to project onto other women the image that they are writers, straightforward speakers, and so forth. With the metaphor of the hologram I was able to integrate reality (women characters living in Montreal, New York), fiction (construction of a space for them to exist beyond their status as characters), and utopia (projection of the

desire for the female symbolic). There is utopia, celebration, and projection of a positive image of women in my books. I know that in the United States there is a debate about essentialism. I think feminists should be grateful to those feminist and lesbian writers who are criticized for being essentialist. Thanks to them, the feminist movement has developed beyond the issues of equality and equity into an important cultural and social movement. Fiction, particularly innovative fiction by lesbian writers and philosophers, was the site of an overflow that allowed energy to circulate among women, and that also permitted feminist discourse to open up questions beyond the ones raised in the nineteenth century. Without celebration, desire, radical statements, and lesbian desire, feminism could have been left in the hands of liberal lawyers, lobbyists, or civil servants.

So you're suggesting that essentialism is a necessary risk.

Absolutely. Somehow, I think there is a great deal of confusion between an essentialism that would refer to biological determinism and essentialism as the projection of a mythic space freed of inferiorizing patriarchal images. Usually the accusers associate mythic essentialism, which in fact is an ontological creation, with the biological one. This confusion is not only misleading but dull.

*Perhaps we can come back to what you were saying about projection—this new intervention of woman—and, in particular, a woman's gaze. In **Aerial Letter** you say that you write "with a woman's gaze upon you," and you continue: "A woman's gaze means: who knows how to read."*

Man's gaze—the father's gaze—certainly legitimates a woman writer; it might even inspire her to excellence, as long as the writing stays within the boundaries of patriarchal meaning. It can even allow her to challenge literary tradition, or to write pornographic texts; she can try, if she so choose, to compete with Henry Miller or the Marquis de Sade. But in regard to disobedience to phallocentrism, Man's gaze has proven to censure and silence women. It promises to retaliate.

I believe that a woman's gaze is the only one that can legitimate and challenge a woman writer to go beyond the description of her social experience. The gaze of the other woman is vital because it induces recognition, complicity, and possibly desire. The gaze between women breaks the line, the fluidity of a system where men and women are trained to direct their eyes on the capital M of man because we are thought to believe that M is humanity.

In "The Textured Angle of Desire," I remark on just how difficult it is to keep focusing on women, and that lesbian love is one of the elements that allows us to maintain this focus. It is difficult to keep the focus on women as a subject of interest, recognition, and desire because of our marginalization. She who chooses to live on the margins (by identifying herself as a feminist or a lesbian), but this time in full control of her choice, gives herself a chance to keep the focus.

For me, the loss of the gaze of the other woman is also related to the difficulty feminists have in reproducing themselves from one generation to another. In other words, losing the gaze and the focus, we always skip a generation of feminists.

I find the idea of a woman's gaze very difficult to conceptualize, to the extent that the gaze itself is part of the constitution of masculine knowledge and desire. There is a philosophical relationship between the gaze and comprehension, between the gaze and amorous desire. All of this is based on the eye.

It is true that the gaze itself is part of the constitution of masculine knowledge and desire. If you are not a voyeur, the gaze means that you are introducing yourself in another space which is not your own, but which can eventually become part of your world or yourself.

The woman's gaze is meaningful because it works at filling the gap between women. What women see between them is as important as what they see of each other and in one another. The back and forth of the gaze between women (writer and reader) textures the space between them and to me that creates a social semantico-imaginative environment where meaning can be debated. I am amazed how difficult it seems for women playwrights to create dialogue between women outside of the mother-daughter relationship. Most of the time, female characters will interact through monologues. Is it because of a feminist ethic that won't allow for power relations or hierarchical roles among women? The woman's gaze acknowledges the reality of the other woman. It makes her visible, present. I believe that it actualizes she who has more than a story to tell. By that I mean she who can play with me as well as with words.

In concluding, I would like us to go back to an idea we started with: the importance of the place from where one writes. In **Aerial Letter** *you talk about urbanity, and, more precisely, of "urban radicals," urban women who write and publish. Do you feel that there is still a* Québecois *specificity to this radical urbanity?*

It is strange, but I have always felt that speaking and writing about Montreal is making a statement about being a North American of French descent. It is also a way of valuing our own literature. For a long time in our literature, the city was associated with sin, depravation, a place where you lose your soul. So for someone of my generation, I guess it

is easy to associate radicalism with the city. Somehow the city seems to organize a metaphoric network that integrates delinquency, belonging, movement, excitement, and excess. In a recent text, I was saying that I am an urban woman on the graffiti side of the wall, on the sleepless side of night, on the free side of speech, on the side of writing where the skin is a fervent collector of dawns. I am from the city; I've always lived there; and I love the city and the freedom it allows even if it is dangerous for women. So I'm an urban radical. It's also a metaphor for me to say: I am a girl in combat in the city of men.

The fabular subject again?

I guess so. Certainly one aspect of the fabular subject. *Urbaine radicale, sujet fabuleux, ma continent* are probably noticeable as expressions not only for the meaning they suggest but also for their linguistic fabric, a semantic mix which creates its own aura of resonance. But to come back to *la fille en combat dans la cité,* I guess she is the product of a choice that I make which is to stay in the *polis* in order to confront patriarchal meaning instead of retiring to the mythic island of the Amazons, whose subtext to me is peace and harmony, while the subject for *la cité* is the law (not harmony), the written word (not the song), and constant change. The mythic island is in me, in books, and in the women with whom I surround myself.

I am a woman of the here and now, fascinated with the virtual that exists in the human species. But have we women been damaged by men's way of ordering the world and proving their "humanity"? Because I want all the energy and creativity that women are capable of, I will stay in the city so the law can be changed. Of course, there is that possibility that the law will be changed into something else only when we are done with the written word, which is definitely a partner to patriarchy and history—history being the trajec*story* of desire. I guess it is difficult for me to stay on the island because I am a woman of the written word, nonetheless aware of the metaphoric network that comes along with it: individualism, and an endless process of desire and hope that often comes out as an excess or a quest for the absolute. For me, staying in the city means to be alert, vigilant, in order to discriminate between propositions for a future and procedures that would lead to catastrophe.

I think we now understand how the double constraint, the double-bind that women experience in a sexist, misogynist, and phallocentric society works. We now know that this double-bind immobilizes, demobilizes women.

What you're saying reminds me of Monique Wittig's Le Corps lesbien [The Lesbian Body] *where she also talks about this island separated from the continent, the "dark continent" of the patriarchal order. But it is not about find-*

ing the island and remaining there calmly and peacefully. What really remains is the tension between the island and the continent.

The tension which is desire is creative, the tension of debate is also creative. I want women's creativity to sparkle throughout the city, in the university, on the radio, in books, in films.

I now feel that besides the creative tension of being *une fille en combat dans la cité,* there is also another tension which is the one I referred to in the beginning of this interview: a double-time where the sensation of the slowness of the act of writing and the sensation of speeding among images (virtual, fractal, or numeric) mix in such a way that the writer wonders with a sudden disquietude to what world she belongs; if she is drifting away from the shore or heading back toward the idea of a future, another shore.

Barbara Godard (review date June 1995)

SOURCE: "Producing Visibility for Lesbians: Nicole Brossard's Quantum Poetics," in *English Studies in Canada,* Vol. 21, No. 2, June, 1995, pp. 125-37.

[*In the following essay, Godard discusses Brossard's use of quantum theory in her discussion of visualization and lesbian politics in* Picture Theory.]

Vision, passion, reading, a mathematics of the imaginary—these key terms from the opening stanzas of "The Vision" section in Nicole Brossard's long poem *Lovhers* interweave the formal and thematic concerns more fully developed in her 1982 fiction, *Picture Theory.* The epigraph to the hologram version of the text, written in the future anterior of 2002 and presented as the final section of *Picture Theory,* includes in the list of titles produced by the same author "*Faire exister ce qui existe,* essai, Éditions de l'Hexagone 1992." This frames Brossard's concern with the affective as well as the cognitive and sensory networks of meaning production as a question of *making* visible, producing visibility, or outing. I use the term "outing" deliberately here to underline the fact that Brossard's concern with visualization in reading is connected to a lesbian politics. The poetics developed in *Picture Theory* is explicitly a theory of reading as research and aims to effect (and theorize—which literally means to be-hold or visualize—) a shift in perspective or parallax, a reframing, that would put in what is usually left out and expose out as the very heart of within—lesbians as desiring subjects. This project is advanced also by shifting the boundaries in reading to make the reader aware of manipulating a concrete textual object, not effacing it in the quest for meaning. In this, the text expands on what is

always already (t)here, though visible only to some. To this end, *Picture Theory* deploys a number of different strategies of ostension, some verbal, some visual.

The critical gesture that initiates the parallax—a quantum leap—is a woman desiring to read another woman's book, a narrative thread that turns on the polysemy of the French term "delire," which means contradictorily both "delirious" and "about reading" or "to unread." This production of meaning is figured in *Picture Theory* as the "white scene" of May 16 between the narrator and Claire Dérive (light adrift/derivative),the "love scene" that works its way through the section "The Perspective" and is distinguished by its unspeakability, as silence, whiteness, and transparency. The visuality of this drift of pure light is subsequently materialized as the "white page" in the section "Skin Screen" where Michelle Vallée, the character of the fiction within the fiction, is the focalizer for a meditation on the "screen of selection" through which language and a rhythm are instantiated to produce a simulation of sensation (pain) and, subsequently, of emotion. These are concretized as the white page on which the reader projects images to make sense:

> C'était donc cela qu'elle cherchait au coeur de la lettre aerienne, cela cette phosphorescence dans la nuit comme une permanence féminine prenant relief dans la pierre. L'image est floue. Les mots lapidaires. Le sense trouble. Toute la réalité se condense en abstraction. Se dédouble, floue encore, une succession d'images visiblement de femmes (sans ordre chronologique) tridimensionnelle, font une proposition+ SCREAM-SKIN-SCREEN . . . SKIMMING THROUGH A NOVEL, me promener fièvreusement dans les rues de Montréal.

So that's what she was seeking in the heart of the aerial letter, that phosphorescence in the night like a permanent feminine presence taking on relief in stone. The image is fluid. Words lapidary. Sense troubled. All reality is condensed in abstraction. Doubled fluid still, a succession of images visibly of women (without chronological order) three-dimensional, make a proposition.+ SCREAM-SKIN-SCREEN . . . SKIMMING THROUGH A NOVEL, me promener fièvreusement dans les rues de Montréal.

A footnote at the bottom of the page informs the reader that, according to Wittgenstein, "A Proposition is a Picture of Reality." Wittgenstein continues, pointing out the difference between a predicative logic that names, defines, ontologically, and a propositional logic that shows forth from a particular combination of elements or scale of relations: "The proposition is a model of the reality as we think it is." "The proposition can only say *how* a thing is not *what* it is" and it does this by "show[ing] its sense." The critical question is what something *does,* not what it is, what relations or effects are set in play. Ontologizing truth claims are not framed in a propositional logic. Brossard quotes Wittgenstein in an epigraph to **Picture Theory:** "What can be said can only be said by means of a sentence, and so nothing that is necessary for the understanding of all sentences can be said." Translated into linguistic terms, this logic asserts a demonstrative or performative rather than nominal function. Shifts between French and English in this section demonstrate the ways in which meaning depends, as Wittgenstein puts it, on which language game one is in. Framing, perspective is the significant element. For language(s) is a filter that allows some things but not "everything" to be articulated. Bodily sensations—pain, pleasure—are some of the things filtered out of ordinary language. These are what Brossard seeks to im/press on language, especially the bundle of sensory signifiers activated in lesbian love. Her concern is with bodies and attachments, affective and effective in relation to images, with the desiring production of mental images.

The text plays with the white scene foregrounding it as the scene of reading as well as the scene of lesbian love. All reading by implication entails an investment (cathexis or transference?). Meanings are hence partial in both senses of the term. As the white page, the scene signifies the materiality of reading where the reader manipulates black marks on a white page. It continues Brossard's earlier textual practice of playing with typefaces and framing devices that simultaneously function as, and metacritically comment on, the use of typography to produce boundaries delimiting inside/outside in order to focus the reader's attention on different parts of a text with varying intensities. As blank space, the white scene also offers itself as virtuality, screen of potentiality for projection where the reader can make what she will of the text. Her co-creative powers working to produce textual drift are thus inscribed at the very centre of the text, making and unmaking meaning at the same time.

In this figure of the white scene that is simultaneously material and abstract, pure light and the ineffable, Brossard takes on the history of the figuration of the feminine as vanishing point in western philosophical discourse to refigure this absence as a question of perspective, an angle of vision. As she writes: "Writing is making oneself visible. To show all sorts of forms and experiences. To impose upon the gaze of the other before he gets a chance to." While the patriarchal tradition of the west has focused on death and the feminine as the unspeakable horror, as site of both absence and transcendence, the gap across which meaning is made as theological moment of closure or matricide, Brossard, in company with other feminist theorists such as Cixous and Irigaray, reads this hollow through a different frame of desire as a space of potentiality, of virtuality, as a space of becomings. This is writing/reading as research, as Brossard

has termed it in **"E muet mutant"** (silent "e" changing), a mutation brought about by a change in intellectual paradigms from biology to cybernetics, a movement from red to white, from the blood and body to the synapses and neo-cortex (corps-texte, the body as text or sign system). "Our keys of information and practice no longer open the same desires and anticipations." This movement involves an encounter with the radically other, an outpouring that is a reversible movement in recognition of the other that I might be in another language (game): "Être traduite, c'est être enquêtée . . . dans sa façon même de penser dans une langue, de même que dans la façon dont nous sommes pensées par une langue. C'est avoir à s'interroger sur cette autre que je pourrais être si je pensais en anglais, en italien, ou en toute autre langue."

Like Cixous, Brossard could claim to be writing "from," writing from something given by the other, from the body, writing "away from . . . death our double mother." This is an attempt to go beyond the law of the Father, the sacrificial social contract into which women are bound in western society predicated on elimination of her (perceived) threat to the authority of the gaze, the sight and death of a woman (Orphic version), or loss of sight and death caused by a woman (Oedipal version). In both mythemes, the connection of Woman to vision and her requisite erasure en route to truth and subjectivity, produces for women the tragedy of exclusion, of being heterogeneous or excess to society. Invisibility is a problem especially for the lesbian who is also collapsed into homosociality. For this is the maternal space, territory of the "imaginary mother" described by Kristeva, only symbolic space accorded Woman in philosophic and psychoanalytic discourse, one of "christic sublimination" in which the feminine is completely absorbed in the maternal function and becomes an abstraction, leaving the body for the soul and fusion with the Ideal. The mother is "the absolute because primeval seat of the impossible—of the excluded, the outside-of-meaning, the abject," as Kristeva summarizes the negative sublime.

This exclusion is the legacy of the Hegelian and idealist dialectic in which a sensory signifier is sublated in an ideal signified and meaning is produced through a synthesis that effects a substitution based on the privileging of presence. Even the Lacanian reversal of this move to make castration a contract of truth by focusing on endless substitution of affects, substitution in which the subject and object are both present and absent, persists in mapping the phallus as indivisible and hence perpetuates its identity function over a gendered opposition of masculine/present, feminine/absent. Metaphor is the figure that best performs this kind of substitution that is grounded in a binary logic of either/or, present/absent. It performs on the level of the signifier the work of appropriation and specularization effected by the *Aufhebung* in the order of subjectivity, desire, knowledge. Such a hermeneutics of aletheia advances a singular truth by forecluding difference(s). The narrative contract of subject-desires-object epitomized in the romance model, participates in this same economy of mastery wherein the subject (masculine) pursues and overcomes the object (feminine) in a closure as effacement. Even psychoanalytic anamnesis, concerned with fixing the affective element of substitution, works through screen memories to disengage an absent bundle of affects or signifiers from the first relations with the maternal in order to acknowledge loss and castration and to *separate* from her body into language and representation. Here the feminine is eclipsed along with the erasure of materiality in an instance of re-covery by synthesis that is simultaneously a covering-up or rendering invisible in what is an "interiorizing idealization."

Brossard does not explicitly challenge this philosophic legacy in elaborating her hermeneutics of making visible or recombination that offers different versions of truth. Rather she cites the legacy and reworks it, hollowing it out to transform a culture of death into one of life. By focusing on processes, not entities, Brossard avoids a new ontology and changes the models of knowing and identity. Instead of separation of mind and body in internalization that institutes the separation of knowing subject from object of knowledge, she works for greater expansion by showing the attachment of mind to body. In what she calls the "fervent relay," they are contingently related through the image that sets up lines of desire, engendering relations of effective and affective movement. Most explicitly she cites the western tradition as she rewrites the great modernist books of the night, Joyce's *Finnegan's Wake* and Djuna Barnes's *Nightwood,* to transform them into pure light. "Patriarchal machine for making the blues," she calls them. She does this by working from death, working from quotations and fragments of these texts of death, which she rewrites in a new context—displacement through repetition—as a strategy of modulation, working upon the signifier to make it vibrate and resonate in a different web or network of signification with a different intensity, with a different energy. Joyce's Bloomsday is enlightened in the amorous white scene of May 16th: indeed, his Dublin is invoked as the site of a "mutilated voice" just before the scene. As a golden helmeted woman, Claire Dérive traverses Barnes's nightworld of crossed lovers into the pages of a poetry sequence where the virtual subject and object (two women) embrace:

> i uttered some words whose invisibility
> on the skin of cheeks i signed
> a time of Utopian arrest. i had
> against my body abstract the sensation of the body
> of Claire Dérive and i declared my feelings.

> *I was energy without end, the sensation of the*
> *idea, i*
> *was a woman touched by the appearance of a rose*

> *in*
> *Utopia's expression. i was this morning of May*
> *16th,*
> *with Claire Dérive, exposed to vital abstraction.*

Claire, as clarity and transparency, "the wave . . . the space the memory," is pure energy changing the angle of vision. As image, she sets bodies in movement, slipping endlessly through meanings, allowing us to see what the system cannot bring us to say. "Encircling the intention for the brilliant burst of things and feeling. . . . I am moving forward, she said to herself. . . . Using language and the dictionary to go beyond. . . ." The fictive writer does this by working through potentialities, superimposing rather than excluding. She shows forth, she brings to the surface of the skin and the screen of culture what its ordinary perception and language have not been able to see or display. The white scene of absence is also the skin/screen of textual surface, the medium of inscription for the production of a palimpsest. Surface effects. Embodied effects. For Brossard's work is regulated not by an oppositional logic, but by a quantum logic in which contradictions coexist as virtualities. Consequently, the scenes of reading in *Picture Theory* involve both the book as virtual object and the material object, a "fold of continuous paper" where may be found the trace of the city that brings e-motion.

The operative term in this multiplying of screens is "with": *Picture Theory* is a musing with/against Joyce, Barnes, Stein, Wittgenstein, and others to display/displace them in a practice of the fragment and of repetition. The "narrative" of *Picture Theory* is no quest for an absent woman, but a conjuring with the traces of women in other narratives inserted into *Picture Theory* as quotation and topoi to make it a story of reading and writing, of selection and reworking, where fragments are repeated in a series of different "takes" through a different filter. Emotion and politics both tint the lenses. Brossard frames this through the fictive writer M. V.:

> Sometimes, emotion was in this body which has a predilection for and cultivates sensations a sort of spatial equation that excites M. V. to the pitch. Seen from this angle, the screen was becoming a lithophany of changing appearance and M. V. had to begin breathing again to describe the impression she was feeling when the word *emotion* was written mechanically to follow through on the *idea,* sort of prerequisite, the idea in order to remember there exist dissimulated networks.

The selection of one's subject of reading turns one into an author of the reading. Yet one is reciprocally read by the text in a dynamic interaction. Following the "white scene," this process of self-portraiture is described as "kaleidoscopic":

"'senseless' work on the sense of meaning to the point of exhaustion or, until a breach of law is committed." The breach is Brossard's focus: she follows a trace until an opening is made which shifts the frames and undoes the boundaries or limits to produce something different. This work of repetition, of building up a fiction through different takes or perspectives, is Brossard's method of interrupting the figurations of the feminine as spectral woman. The effect of repetition, which is a reading or an interpretation of an Other woman, is to force attention to the textuality of linking, of doubling, as an action or performance in language and to open up other possibilities in the venerable story of "Love [as] homesickness." Brossard writes of this as the "serial circulation of spatial gestures." Relational points of desire and becoming, images work as movement. Images are a way of thinking a trajectory from body to body. The image is, in Brossard's words, "une ressource vitale qui forme des propositions complexes à partir d'éléments simples et isolés. Chaque fois qu'une image relaie le désir, cette image pense avec une vigueur insoupçonnée la dérive du sens. C'est ainsi que les images pénètrent à notre insu la matière solide de nos idées." Narrative, a system for ordering relations, becomes a modality/model for repetition or change over/as time. The logical conjunctions operative in a temporal image are subordinate to a movement image that represents time indirectly as a succession of frames or takes, a virtual becoming, not a simultaneity, a potentiality that calls into question the notion of "truth" because of its ability to break through boundaries and effect metamorphoses.

Though the superposition of divergent sign systems in the palimpsest, codes are set aslant one another in what functions as an "intensive system," telescoping signifiers, multiplying or ramifying their resonance to infinity, proliferating new ambiguities and branching out in many "heterogeneous series." The discontinuity and diagonal encounter of these complex sign systems produce displacement at the heart of "reading" a text that sets up surface events, lines of flight. Such "sorties" draw attention to the work of mediating images, of apprehending "reality," foreground the way in which a shift in the angle of viewing produces a different "take" on "reality." Such work of repetition and intensification sets up a disequilibrium that functions as an active force of deformation and recombination within social protocols of representation, reorganizing within a regime of signs the networks of signifiers and so instituting transformations of the language acts that allocate subjects and signs their positions in an order of social obligations within specific relations of law and desire. In this way are introduced lines of variation, of potential metamorphoses, a dispersion of points of "subjective" observation throughout images of movement. "L'image glisse étonnante re/source qui n'en finit plus de glisser entre les sens cherchant l'angle des pensées." Through such lines of escape may be ordered a virtual woman.

On the "skin/screen" in successive sections ("Skin Screen," "Skin Screen Two," "Skin Screen Utopia") are displayed the sensations, the emotions, and the ideas of M. V. Through this overlapping Brossard points to the inseparability of sensations and ideas. New sensations or sights, new "visions," arise "*after the text.*" In the third of these sections, focusing on possible world or Utopian theory, the mimetic contract grounded in substitution is supplemented by the concept of a virtual woman born in the letter who will carry the fiction forward, "push[ing] death away." This is the vital "thinking woman" who, with her idea of making another woman through whom everything might happen, "imagine[s] an abstract woman who would slip into my text." She would not be invented in fiction but fiction would be the "precise term," the modality in which she would "loom into view." "[T]his woman participant in words, must be seen coming, virtual to infinity, form-elle in every dimension of understanding, method and memory." "Writing is always virtual," she underlines, but it has effects, bodily and political, actualized through reading: "artifice of fiction on the shelves of a suburban municipal library. It was book after book of sentiment stuck to the tongue (the body follows when in winter the curious tongue adventures onto metal." "All reality condenses into abstraction. Doubles, splits, swindles, difficult reference." The difficulties of reference and mimesis are those that have been produced by the "haunting memory of Man" through the "semantic line" and the net of "patriarchal subjectivity." To intercept these "effects of the real" that are taken for reality, to shift signifying systems, to organize them around another network contiguous with the female body, requires work on the virtual, in/as fiction to produce different figurations that will transform the real. This is the task of reading as unreading as the five women on the island demonstrate:

> All night long exploring in broad daylight the dictionary, the context in which ideas were formed then renewed, identical and machine gun for repetition in our mouths beginning with the worst, *a* of deprivation. Studious girls, we will divert the course of fiction, dragging with us words turn and turn about, igneous spiral, picture theory.

This may also be considered, in Brossard's phrase, the work of a mathematics of the imaginary, to develop different models and modalities, pictures of different scales of relations among elements, that will permit the actualization of this virtual woman in a process of reading. Reality will be figured (thought/lived) in another way.

Brossard's main trope for virtual reality is the hologram, the title she gives to the final section of *Picture Theory,* a repetition and reworking of all the other sections, one, moreover, that through its explicit quotation of earlier sections of the text, of groups of phonemes repeated in many variations throughout, draws attention to the text's organization as a combinatory. It is through the concept of the hologram as combinatory, both in its ability to produce a three-dimensional simulation of an image, consisting of many fragments, each holding the entire image, in its mathematical formulation, and as light, most specifically the laser beam, that Brossard introduces theoretical models from contemporary physics to conceptualize accounts of (re)combination and transformation. In this, she demonstrates Wittgenstein's theory of picture reality. The "picture is a model of reality" in that it is a "scale" applied to reality whose specific combination of elements or "form of representation" can only be shown forth not represented. "The picture consists in the fact that its elements are combined with one another in a definite way." "The proposition shows its sense. The proposition shows how things stand if it is true." The particular "scale" or relation of elements Brossard shows forth in the hologram is the Uncertainly principle of Quantum theory, that is the wave/particle theory of light.

Quantum physics changes our understanding of relationships. Movement is no longer the mechanical, sequential and return patterns ruled by cause and effect of classical physics but, at the level of sub-atomic particles, is random, spontaneous, discontinuous movement, reversible and synchronous across time. If Newton asked how can anything ever happen, quantum theorists ask how can anything ever be. Reality is not fixed actualities that can be known but rather the probabilities of all the various actualities that might be known. Quantum moves are made through probability waves that are temporary feelers put out toward stability, a trying out all possible new positions as if throwing out imaginary scenarios. These are "virtual transitions" that become real transitions under specific conditions. Among the many possible mutations only one gets actualized in a particular instance of interference. None of the potentials is lost, however. Intervention is crucial here. For the particular way we observe quantum reality partly determines what we see. The quantum universe is a participatory one in which whatever we call reality is revealed to us only through an active construction in which we participate. That is not to say that we create reality, rather we evoke and give concrete form to one of many possibilities to produce truth within a situation.

This is demonstrable for what we know as light, which quantum physics has shown to exist indeterminately in two contradictory modes as wave motions on a surface and as disturbed particles in a high energy field of dynamic flux. Both are necessary, in that each supplies a kind of information the other lacks, but only one mode is available at a given time, according to Heisenberg's Uncertainty Principle. Which one depends on the kind of filter or measuring system set in place as Schrödinger demonstrated. The cat to be observed exists in a superimposed state of total potentiali-

ties, both alive and dead simultaneously. In the moment in which a researcher observes the cat, however, only one of those potentialities is actualized. What this experiment demonstrates is the role of observation or intervention in moulding "reality." Observed systems have an associated wave function that is the coherent superposition of all the possible results of an interaction between the observed system and a measuring system. The development in time of this coherent superposition of possibilities is expressed in Schrödinger's wave equation, which is used to calculate the form of this coherent superposition of possibilities called a wave function at this particular time. This gives a probability function different from, though calculated from, a wave function. Quantum theory cannot predict events, only probabilities. In this, quantum theory is based on a non-Aristotelian logic in which a statement can be either true or false or merely possible. In such a logic, the fixed point of vision and perspective taken up outside the space observed of Euclidean geometry would be replaced by a topological geometry of the Mobius strip in which apparently opposing sides are formed from a single, continuous surface.

Such models of interactive moulding of reality through an observation/intervention from a specific point under particular conditions—here those of a woman reading another woman's book—are introduced metonymically in *Picture Theory* through the hologram. In the hologram, a three-dimensional optical illusion produced by a parallax or leap between potentialities effected by a laser beam of light, is active as a superposition of wave functions such as described in Schrödinger's equation. Holography or writing is transformed in the whiteout of the scene of production/seduction where desire, time, memory "flow as information in optical fibre" into the "Hologram," a combinatory through which a potential woman is modelled: "At the ultimate equation I would loom into view." "[S]he had come to the point in full fiction abundant(ly) to re/cite herself perfectly readable." "Today a white light made them real." The hologram is like the Wittgenstein "picture" a "model of reality," not a record of the object but a light wave or event.

For Brossard, the hologram is the "superposition" of multiple images from successive exposures, an overlapping, a trope of intertextuality, of the interaction of discourses, of the intermingling of bodies. The hologram is metonymic in that each part can produce the entire image. This reconstitution results in a "virtual" image, the record of the process of illumination by the laser beam. The hologram displays its transformation of (f)act: a woman's voice pierces the screen of skin and like the laser beam piercing the optical encoding, reconstructs or actualizes a "virtual" image. The illusion of the hologram functions like Wittgenstein's understanding of picture as fact in displaying the logic of relations, but does so not iconically but by performing it. The hologram is a model of text as event, mapping specific relations of energy.

The particular relations are those of combinations or "junctional structures" working in intertextual networks through protocols of self-referral and rehearsal in sets of recursive functions. In the splitting of the laser beam are "interference patterns," especially "neighbourhood interactions" or "superpositions," activated in a process of repetition and produced through a set of filters or screens as waves of light.

Textual function, like brain function, takes the form of "superposition." The excitation of a single optic nerve—of a single verbal fragment—affects the discharge rate of neighbouring units and creates interferences. The neighbourhood interaction of waves is described as the convolution of one wave with another and accounted for by equations called "convolutional integrals." The interaction of many convolutional integrals, when configurations of excitation converge from several sources, produces interference patterns. Such interference effects may also be described by equations based on Fourier transformations. This transformation is a parallax or sudden shift in perspective to explain something from another point of view. The transformation produced in this case is a shift in space/time where the time of a signal is transformed into the space of a signal. The transformation is produced by means of an integral, or the sum of a function—that is, of a transformation to be made, of a potential transformation. Fourier's transformational function is a function in the sense of the differential equation in calculus. A mathematical curve joins an infinity of discrete points in a passage toward a limit it never reaches. This is the operation of folding or "le pli," an unfolding to infinity. It is also an infolding of infinity: each segment of the curve contains, in potentiality, an infinite number of other functions and each point on the curve is divisible into an infinity of other points—each of which in turn belongs to yet another infinite set of potential functions. Folding is a serial process linking an infinity of discrete elements into an endless curve.

The curve and the fold, two terms repeated in the combinatory that is *Picture Theory.* Brossard is interested in this fiction as mathematics of the imaginary not only in mapping all the curve potentials for systems, but also in mapping changing local minima, that is, locating points where jumps are made across unstable pathways between one unstable state and another. For jumps are the moments when rapid or revolutionary change may take place. In *Picture Theory,* this point of inflection producing disequilibrium and a movement to a new state is the work of memory stimulated by a woman's desire to read another woman's book, memory engaged in the repetition and recontextualization of signs in the performance of reading, such repetition related to potentia, to energy. The leap in mental process is doubled by a shift in affective relations between women to effect a transformation in the gendered ordering of social and discursive formations, a revolutionary potential figured by a discontinuous curve. The potential for different organization of relations is figured in *Picture Theory.* This awaits the intervention of a reader to actualize them under specific constraints.

In that it establishes an unfinalizable system, *Picture Theory* frames its truth claims in a general performative theory of discourse where what is at stake in an utterance is not an opposition between truth and falsehood but varying degrees of felicity in performance, the degree to which they carry out what they promise, the richness of that promise. What the performative stages is the risk of loss, the gap between potential and act. This figure of incompletion sets in play the condition generating the principle of repetition, the condition of beginning again and again, the necessity of going beyond loss. The utterance functions not as a fulfillment of an absence but as a process, an event, in an enunciating instance that exposes the place and energy of the subject. Language is a complex network of turns and counterturns setting in play a reign of effects and affects. In this regime of meaning production, reading is posited in the subjunctive as a potential intervention in some unfinalizable time. Reading here is a performance, a beginning again and again—anaphora, not metaphor. There is no carrying across into meaning, but becomings ever overcoming the inevitable failure of such closure in the heart of a promise.

Brossard moves the figuration of the feminine from excess read out to excess reading in. The woman reader is chance intervention that destabilizes the equilibrium of first and second, subject and object, present and absent, and so calls into the question the logic of either/or, displacing it with the logic of the combinatory, of the series, given over to expansion, to proliferation, to potentiality. Although there is a possibility for setting the system careening wildly in all directions, at any one point in the relay only one possibility will be actualized at a time. It matters that it is a woman reading *Picture Theory,* more specifically that it is a lesbian reading, because the network of relations between body, signs, images produced in the work of reading will be inflected by her singular desire and energy. For, as Brossard has shown, what we do is inflected by who we are. The kind of image produced on the screen on which the beam of light or meaning is captured will differ depending on the energy of the receiving body. Ignitability, fluidity, provisionality, are all open to the play of chance. In the realm of quantum forces, energy is measured not in terms of depth and intention, but by degrees of pleasure/satisfaction to corporealized effects and affects. This work of relating the vibrations of the uncertain with the certain body is a "fabulous mathematics," matter for writing like "the entire surface of my skin." "Surfaces of reading," Brossard terms this concern with literature as action or event, distinguished from representation where the "economy of the mirror" circulates. Writing on that surface in "d'une surface," she summarizes: "Les mots étaient en action. . . . le texte attira mon attention." Reading words for surface effects is to intervene with all one's affects in a relay of images, to inflect them in a particular order of relations that opens up certain possibilities to be actualized in some future reading. No longer condemned to exile, the reading woman will make herself visible through her "creative wandering" from image to image, actualizing lesbian desire.

Lynne Huffer (essay date 1996)

SOURCE: "From Lesbos to Montreal: Nicole Brossard's Urban Fictions," in *Yale French Studies,* No. 90, 1996, pp. 95-114.

[*In the following essay, Huffer asserts that "Brossard's* oeuvre *distinguishes itself from an entire Sapphic tradition of lesbian writing by demystifying nostalgia rather than celebrating it.*"]

Helen, my grandmother, is one hundred-and-one years old. Having never remarried since her husband died over thirty-five years ago, she dines and plays bridge with the other elderly residents of the group facility where she lives in Toledo, Ohio. It's funny how women endure. Like a lesbian enclave, the place is virtually without men. I think of this as some strange connection between us, a certain similarity between her home and mine, but one that will never be spoken. My grandmother will never know about me, unless, perhaps, she reads these lines. She will never know about the woman, my mother, who married her son, and who later came out as a lesbian, long before I did, when the going was rough and the stakes were high. Now, among the aunts and uncles and distant cousins, some know about us and whisper discreetly. Others, to be fair, are sympathetic. A few embrace us. But when you become a lesbian, you automatically get written out of someone's history. There is no branch there, for mother and daughter and the women we love, on the precious family tree.

Sometimes details, like trees and cousins, can bring you through detours to the heart of a matter. In one branch of the family we recently discovered the captain of a ship: a distant cousin, I believe. Not long ago my uncle found this cousin's log-book in my grandmother's safe. The travel log, dated 1811, recorded his movements, his thoughts, the food he ate, the weather he encountered, as he crossed the Atlantic. When my uncle sat down and plotted out the ship's course from Dublin to New York he found, not surprisingly, that sailing ships never travel in straight lines. Although journeying from east to west, most days the boat traveled northeast to southwest or southeast to northwest. Some days it sailed backwards or scarcely changed its position at all. It

moved erratically, like the lightning flare of a heart, pumping, flashing across an EKG monitor.

After more than a century of life, my grandmother's heart is still beating. I would like her rhythm to be recorded, just as the zigzagging motion of a ship was given pulse and flare again through my uncle's diligent tracings. But there are other journeys within those lines: the hidden lives that will not be recorded on my uncle's map or the family tree. These are the journeys I want to record.

We can conceive of a life lived, like we can a journey, as a game of connect-the-dots. Moments in experience, like points on a map, can be linked to reveal a pattern. The result is a network of beginnings, destinations, and bridges that only make sense when they are plotted against other visible cultural patterns. So, if meanings assemble like flags on a map or letters on a page, how might a cartographer of the invisible proceed? In particular, how might a cartographer of lesbian history and culture plot the unrecorded movements of lesbian lives?

Let's look again at Winterson's parable about the Greek letter. She gives us a recipe for writing and reading the hidden life: one part milk, one part coal-dust sprinkled, of course, by someone who knows what she's doing. Reading Winterson's description of the coded letter, I want the "life flaring up" to be subversive, lesbian, refusing invisibility and silence. But is it? Is lesbian writing like a secret message written in milk and made visible by those who know better? I can see it now:

> Lesbian #1: Ah hah! Look what I found! An ancient letter!
>
> Lesbian #2: Yeah, and it's sticky! I think I'll sprinkle it with coal-dust! What do you think?
>
> Lesbian #1: Go for it, babe. I have a good feeling about this one . . .
>
> Lesbian #2: Hmmm, let's see. . . . Yep, just as I suspected! A message from Sappho . . .
>
> Lesbian #1: It takes one to know one . . .

Is secret communication the way of liberation? It's true that oppression forces people to be creative in finding alternative forms of expression. But, *pace* Cixous, I cringe at the thought of snapping a cartridge filled with milk into my fountain pen. I'd rather work at changing the conditions of our lives: we all deserve a pen, lots of paper, and a lifetime supply of ink. Besides, these days coal-dust is hard to come by.

Still, I'm attracted to cultural myths, like the Sapphic one, about hushed secrets finding voice. Some days, for example, I dream of sailing away, like a good lesbian, to Lesbos. I'd bring my mother along, and together we'd plot our course back through some other history, some other time, to an alternative family origin. Gathering like sibyls to read the crumpled leaves strewn beneath the family tree, we'd map shapes and scenes of passion from the censored thoughts and silent scribblings lying there like unmailed letters. Casting off, we'd say goodbye to patriarchy and oppression:

> farewell black continent of misery and suffering farewell ancient cities we are embarking for the shining radiant isles for the green Cytheras for the dark and gilded Lesbos.

Of course, this kind of escapist vision in which I sometimes indulge is hardly new, as a whole lesbian separatist tradition can attest, to say nothing of a long line of lesbian and nonlesbian writers who celebrate some version of a Sapphic heritage. Leaving the continent for the island is a frequently plotted route for those who find in Lesbos a symbol of political and cultural origins. As Judy Grahn puts it:

> Sappho wrote to us from (this) island . . . to those of us holding Sappho in our mind's eye as *the* historic example both of Lesbianism and of Lesbian poetry, everything she represents lies on an island.

If, for Grahn and others, Sappho is *the* historic example of lesbian life and lesbian writing, the move from the continent to the island is hardly surprising. However, isn't this pilgrimage to a Greek Island another version of the secret milk-writing described by Winterson? Isn't this just a lesbian form of nostalgia? Finding a lost island is like finding the lost lines of a letter: both function to constitute an exclusive community around the revelation of a secret. Again, we can ask this question: is this hidden, insular, coded communication the way of liberation? Do lesbians just need to get back to the island, to the source of our desire, to the milky place of our Sapphic mother?

If we answer, "no! that's not it," and "no, again, that's still not it!" the problem becomes: so now what? If we agree that "every journey conceals another journey within its lines," how do we trace that other journey without falling into the nostalgic trap of coded letters and secret islands? How do we map invisibility and silence? What is revealed, and what disappears in that mapping? The question is complex, as Adrienne Rich reminds us in her poem "Cartographies of Silence":

> Silence can be a plan
> rigorously executed
>
> the blueprint to a life

> It is a presence
> it has a history a form
>
> Do not confuse it
> with any kind of absence

History and form go together: a game of connect-the-dots. Just as bits of family history are brought to light as a branch on a verdant tree, so too a certain version of lesbian history can assemble itself into a deceptively singular shape—a Greek letter, an island—that gives it cultural meaning. To ignore the island and the sticky letter would be to do what Rich warns us not to do: to erase the blueprint, to confuse silence with absence. But to remain stuck there isn't the answer either. Most crucially, many lesbians will never find their way with that milky map. What do Sappho, Lesbos, and Greek culture represent, for example, for a lesbian of African descent? For the native people of North America? Indeed, the plotting of that journey back to ancient Greece not only fails to acknowledge other histories and other maps, but it has effaced the paths and cultural symbols through which those stories can be traced. Liberation means more than making maps from silence and giving shape to the invisible. What flares up as a flag on the map, and what is erased by that marker?

Rich's poem suggests that lesbian writing, like silence, has a history and a form, but its shape is dynamic, multilayered, and changing. Here I'm reminded of my uncle's discovery: sailing ships never travel in straight lines. Recording "the unrecorded" can only be an erratic and complex undertaking; like history itself, lesbian lives might be seen as layers of journeys superimposed on a map thick with time. Lesbian writing cannot be a straight shot home to some Sapphic paradise: check the turn of the compass needle and watch the change of sails as the ship shifts direction to find the wind. There it is: another "path not taken," another "forgotten angle."

"Every journey conceals another journey within its lines": grandmothers hide log-books and ships and sailors; lesbian daughters hide lesbian mothers; continents hide islands; silence hides the blueprint to a life, someone writing. Like every journey, every writing conceals another writing: behind Homer lies Sappho; behind Proust lies Colette; behind France and its literary canon lie Sénégal and Senghor, Martinique and Césaire, Guadeloupe and Condé, Québec and Hébert. Conversely, writing, flaring up, can make other writings disappear, just as new cities can violently efface old ones, as the conquest of continents makes abundantly clear. The flight of sailors into the uncharted azure may be the stuff of poems as well as family lore, but those expansive journeys are hardly innocent: pouf! and there goes a city, a civilization, an island. I remember the light through the window, splashing the table, taking shape at the heart of writing. . . .

After my conversation with Nicole Brossard, I met up with my friend Serene. We were there in Montreal and we loved the image of girls in the city with diaphanous wings and combat boots: "an urban radical," "a *fairy* in combat in the city of men." This translation of Brossard's metaphor was a mistake on my part, I was later to learn. She had said "*fille* en combat," not "*fée* en combat." Oh well, I thought, French is a language that is never mastered. I was embarrassed by my linguistic ineptitude; but to be honest, I was also . . . disappointed. I have to admit, I still want them to be fairies: urban fairies, in combat, in the city of men, "in this dark adored adorned gehenna."

So I've been looking for a place for my fairy to live, and I think I've found it, right here in the city, in the pages of Brossard's **French Kiss.** As in kissing, so in speaking: it's never certain where those lips and swirling tongues will take you. Her lips pronounced *fille* and I heard *fée,* a fairy in "a forest smelling pungently of brick, cool green forest painted on a wall of brick." I remember Brossard saying: "if each woman could project the best that she senses in herself onto other women, we would already have accomplished a lot." So that's how I became an urban fairy, projected by her, coming out into a forest painted cool and green. I was still myself, but I was also just a bit more than myself: braver, slightly larger, more expansive.

She was a sight to behold, this urban fairy I became, unfolding beyond the mirror Brossard was holding. She belonged to another dimension: magnified and armed to the hilt, not with milk and parchment, but with spray paint, a wand, and wings to take her spiralling up and down those walls. What a dyke! I perceived her clearly, moving "under the surface with wing-like texture to confront reality," writing her aerial letter for all to see.

Graffiti-writing fairies may seem a long way off from secret letters and sailing ships, to say nothing of my grandmother in Toledo, Ohio. I can't help but see the connections, though: family trees become urban forests, coal-sprinkled letters become graffiti-marked walls. How do we remember and record what is lost? Who is writing, and who is reading?

I'm still moving through the glass that Brossard holds before me: there, beneath the surface, where wings and wand turn to arc and spiral, people stand on platforms waiting for the trains to come. Their daily travels across the city reveal the writing on the walls, the places beneath the surface where meanings appear, like fairies coming out into an urban forest.

Which realities do we remember and choose to record? Brossard has written: "I am an urban woman on the graffiti side of the wall, on the sleepless side of night, on the free side of speech, on the side of writing where the skin is a fer-

vent collector of dawns." And she continues: "I guess it is difficult for me to stay on the island because I am a woman of the written word." I keep imagining her, like my urban fairy, finding her home among the paint-scribbled walls of the city.

In leaving the island behind, Brossard's urban radical also leaves behind the milk-writers and coal-dust-readers whose privilege allows them to construct for themselves an exclusionary world difficult to access, one that begins and ends with Greek culture. Unlike that private world of coded letters, Brossard's work should be imagined as "publicly fiction," kaleidoscopic layers of graffiti that illuminate an opening space of lesbian writing. Further, this contrast between Brossard's public urban fictions and a private Sapphic island represents more than just a difference in decor or geographical predilections. Unlike Brossard's Montreal, Lesbos functions symbolically both as a utopian escape and as a space of origins. In that sense, Brossard's *oeuvre* distinguishes itself from an entire Sapphic tradition of lesbian writing by demystifying nostalgia rather than celebrating it. In fact, most of Brossard's writing, in one way or another, uncovers and subverts the nostalgic structures through which a concept of origins is produced.

What is a nostalgic structure, and how is it connected to lesbians, maps, and origins? A nostalgic structure is a system of thought that begins with the idea of return, from the Greek *nostos:* "the return home." This movement of return takes many different forms, depending on who is thinking nostalgically and what the context of that thinking might be. Most crucially, while the Greeks with their *nostos* might hold out the promise that, yes, you can return whence you came, nostalgia happens because you can't go home again. What looked like home is an illusion of home, the mirage of a content that disguises a blank.

Let's look at the way feminist theory analyzes gender and patriarchy in the context of a nostalgic structure. In addition to producing economic, sexual, social, and cultural forms of male domination, patriarchy also privileges men over women as thinkers, knowers, and speakers. That unequal dyad of man over woman produces a logic of analogous pairings such as thought over body and spirit over matter. Because women bear children, in a male-dominated system women are symbolically reduced to their corporeal, material form as reproductive bodies. As a result, to be a woman is, symbolically, to be a mother.

The privileging of man over woman as a thinking subject connects the logic of gender described above with the search for origins that lies at the heart of a nostalgic structure. Because thought involves a quest for knowledge, thinking is an activity of seeking that is motivated by desire. As patriarchy's privileged seeker of knowledge, man must construct an other-to-be-known as the object of his desire. And since gender inequality creates man as subject and woman as object and silent other, the object of man's search becomes, metaphorically, the lost mother. As a result, this form of nostalgia becomes a dominant structure of thought in a system that privileges men over women.

However, man's nostalgic quest is a sham because the son can never return to the mother; in fact, patriarchy *requires* the repeated failure of the son to unite with his lost other. By repeatedly missing her, the son sustains himself as an endlessly desiring subject. In this way, the object of desire—the ever-disappearing woman-as-mother—guarantees the existence of the subject of that desire—the ever-questing son. Man thus comes to exist by differentiating himself from that which he is not: the blank space, the unreachable mother, his silent and invisible other.

Feminist theory shows how a nostalgic structure works to perpetuate patriarchal oppression, but nostalgia also functions *within* oppressed groups struggling for liberation. For example, some feminist critics have noted the nostalgic structure underlying the desire to retrieve a lost canon of literary foremothers to counter the male-dominated tradition. Similarly, scholars in African-American studies have pointed to a nostalgic longing for "mother Africa" among African-Americans struggling in the context of a white racist culture. Finally, the Sapphic myth highlights the lesbian nostalgia for a Greek source of woman-loving art and culture that would challenge traditional heterosexist models.

While nostalgia has been harnessed for both oppressive and liberatory aims, the structure underlying nostalgic thinking ultimately reinforces a conservative social system. Because nostalgia requires the construction of a blank space, a lost origin to be rediscovered and claimed, it necessarily produces a dynamic of inequality in the opposition between a desiring subject and an invisible other. Further, in a nostalgic structure, an immutable lost past functions as a blueprint for the future, cutting off any possibility for uncertainty, difference, or fundamental change. Because nostalgia is necessarily static and unchanging in its attempt to retrieve a lost utopian space, its structure upholds the status quo.

Focusing on the workings of nostalgia allows me to map Brossard's journey as a lesbian writer in relation to the concept of an originary blank space and, ultimately, to ask political questions about the subversive potential of her writing. From her earliest days as a poet, Brossard has rejected the nostalgic thinking that constructs an empty origin as the lost object of the poet's desire. As Karen Gould points out, for Brossard and others at the avant-garde journal *La barre du jour* during the late 1960s, "to be modern meant to 'look lucidly into the hole' and to refuse to fill it, rejecting the lure of myth, ideology, and nostalgia." Brossard's early work

explores the space of that unfilled hole by inscribing, within literature, literature's own dissolution. Confronted with a blank origin that refuses to hold a content, the poetic subject disappears into the movement of the work itself; both subject and object disappear, and all that remains is the pure desire that brings the work into being.

By the mid-1980s, Brossard's critique of nostalgic thinking had moved from fundamentally aesthetic questions to more explicitly political concerns related to her identity as a woman and as a feminist. Commenting on the influence of Blanchot, on his concept of neutrality, and on the notion of literature as a subjectless space of dissolution, Brossard explains this shift in her thinking:

> Blanchot was very important to me. What was involved in the question of neutrality was the white space, which was linked to the question of ecstasy, to the present, the place where the "I" is dispersed to make room for the science of being, its contemplation. Neutrality also meant putting a halt to lyricism and to romanticism, to inspiration, in the ways in which I of course understood these words. Needless to say, neutrality was undoubtedly a fine displacement allowing me to forget that I was a woman, that is to say that I belonged to that category of non-thinkers. Feminist consciousness would de-neutralize me.

Just as Brossard found she could no longer forget she was a woman, so too the identity politics of writing as a lesbian became increasingly important. That recognition gives birth to the "girl in combat in the city," the "urban radical," and the "fabular subject." Brossard rejects the structure of origins that produces "woman" and, in so doing, also questions the nostalgic thinking that produces Lesbos as home of the True Lesbian. As Brossard puts it in reference to the girl in combat in the city:

> She is the product of a choice that I make which is to stay in the *polis* in order to confront patriarchal meaning instead of retiring to the mythic island of the Amazons, whose subtext to me is peace and harmony, while the subject for *la cité* is the law (not harmony), the written word (not the song), and constant change. The mythic island is in me, in books, and in the women with whom I surround myself.

So while Brossard's "urban radical" doesn't explicitly reject Lesbos and Sappho as empowering cultural symbols, she isn't about to catch the next boat to lesbian paradise either. "I am a woman of the here and now," she says. Brossard begins where she finds herself: in Montreal, on the North American continent, in the material world. That world is plagued with misery and pain, *"the silence of bodies elon-*

gated by hunger, fire, dogs, the bite of densities of torture" (Brossard's italics); but, that same world also offers hope, possibility, and the creative desire that brings an affirmation of life, "like the ultimate vitality and wisdom."

Brossard not only anchors herself in a city, on a continent, and in a world heavy with the baggage of history and tradition; through her writing she continually creates another city, another continent, and another world as well. Grounded in the reality of the everyday, Brossard's project is also visionary, virtual, aerial. "I am a woman of the here and now, fascinated with the virtual that exists in the species." Thus, while she grounds herself in her own identity—"I am still Nicole Brossard, born in Montreal, with a sense of the history of Quebec and of belonging in that French part of the North American continent"—she also creates the virtual figure of *"MA continent,"* an intuitive dream of a lesbian body as light, lucidity, and transformation. But even in that projection of an opening lesbian space—"(mâ) it's a space / an hypothesis"—the lesbian continent is still grounded in the gravity and the weight of the everyday world:

> *my continent woman* of all the spaces
> cortex and flood: a sense of gravity
> *bringing me into the world*

Similarly, in **French Kiss,** the protagonists are both anchored in Montreal and, to a large extent, part of an infinitely layered, virtual Montreal, "glowing volatile in darkness" among the "illuminated cities issued from the method of writing." Like the characteristically Brossardian hologram, the surface of the city contains other pictures, exposes deeper three-dimensional realities within itself. The city contains the multiplicity of the memories of its inhabitants:

> Memory makes itself plural, essential, like the vertigo that foreshadows an aerial vision. . . . I thus come to imagine myself hologram, real, virtual, three-dimensional in the imperative of coherent light.

Just as a three-dimensional image allows multiple surfaces to appear, so too memory can become plural, synchronic, holographic. One reality doesn't replace the other; rather, they coexist: Homer and Sappho; the French and British empires and the province of Quebec; the lives of Montreal and those of Caughnawaga.

"What's left for our story is to break up and be lost. Caughnawaga's underbrush. *Expenditure* for a sign." Holographic writing reveals not only the virtual possibilities of future stories and future paths, but also uncovers the breakup and loss of stories that form the fabric of past identities and histories. In the holographic image, both memory and possible futures are pluralized. This Brossardian logic of the

hologram exposes a political aspect of nostalgic origin myths. The nostalgic gesture—to create an empty originary place and give it a content—falsely and imperialistically starts from the premise that the space for that content was in fact empty to begin with.

On the surface, the hologram may seem similar to the nostalgic myth. When the holographic picture comes into focus, something flares up but something else slips out of sight, just as the identity of the nostalgic son makes the mother disappear. However, unlike the complementary parts—subject and object, son and mother—of a nostalgic structure, every part of a holographic plate also contains an image of the whole; thus each fragment contains what is real, already there, or in the background, as well as what is virtual, possible, and waiting to be seen. When something flares up and something else disappears, that shift occurs because of a change in focus. So unlike the binary logic of presence and absence underlying the nostalgic gesture, the hologram allows for a synthesis of the multiple layers of realities and fictions contained within it.

Let's take the urban radical again as an example. Grounded in the city, she is a potential victim of rape, injustice, discrimination, and violence. But she is also, simultaneously, projected toward the realm of invented possibilities: another mythic figure, she is the lucid lesbian, *"ma continent femme,"* coming into expression. Similarly, the city she inhabits and reconfigures is not just the reality of modern-day Montreal. The urban landscape that appears is a present-day Montreal thick with histories to be uncovered and, simultaneously, a virtual Montreal to be imagined and created. Brossard's metaphor of holographic writing points to the layered meanings, like the textured surfaces of graffiti on city walls, inscribed in the trace of pen on paper: that trace is both the mark that says "someone was here" and, at the same time, the opening path toward an "unrecorded thought" waiting to be imagined, waiting to be written.

How can the grounding mark and the virtual path coexist *in writing?* Comparing writing to holograms, Brossard imagines that "sentences," like holographic fragments, "might also contain the whole of what is at stake in a novel." So what *is* at stake in Brossard's writing? Again, to begin with, what is at stake for *me* (I want to say *us,* but my friend Carla won't let me) is the undoing of nostalgic structures. This core of Brossard's work can be examined not just conceptually, but also, more fundamentally, in the particular textured surfaces of the writing itself. In nostalgic writing, when something flares up something else is covered over; when the Greek letter is sprinkled with coal-dust, the blank of its milky origin disappears. In contrast, Brossard's holographic metaphor suggests that a single sentence of her writing would contain, simultaneously: first, the visible lines of the original letter; second, the lines in between, in their manifestation both as milk and coal; and, third, a plurality of other lines tracing other lives lived and other potential lives. It would open up multiple origins and multiple futures. It would invite inclusive communities of readers and writers instead of shutting out all but an educated, Eurocentric elite. So the question remains: does she pull it off? And if so, what does this have to do with lesbian writing?

To begin answering these questions, let's take Montreal in **French Kiss** as an example: "What's left for our story is to break up and be lost. Caughnawaga's underbrush. *Expenditure* for a sign." The final page of **French Kiss** suggests that writing requires an "expenditure": "*expenditure* for a sign." That expenditure of writing both uncovers a reality by naming what is there and, at the same time, creates a layered vision of a past and future city. But in addition to naming and creating a fictional reality called Montreal, the expenditure of writing also produces a reserve, an excess called Caughnawaga that the name "Montreal" cannot contain:

> Leaving the city, now, by Route 2, heading for the Mercier Bridge. Its rusty old steel and worn white lines. Out of line. The blackness of the blue. The river and the Caughnawaga *Reserve.* [Brossard's emphasis]

So how does Caughnawaga function as the excess and reserve of the writing of Montreal in **French Kiss?** On a historical level, when Brossard alludes to Caughnawaga, she exposes the "reserve" of native peoples on which a "North American of French descent" identity depends. When that identity was "founded" in 1535 with Jacques Cartier's arrival at the Saint Lawrence River, the blank space on which that founding was inscribed, in fact, wasn't blank at all. Someone was already there:

> Montreal surface and totems: "And in the middest of those fieldes is the sayd citie of Hochelaga, placed neere, and as it were ioyed to a great mountaine that is tilled round about, very fertill, on the toppe of which you may see very farre."

Brossard's quotation of Cartier's journal exposes a deeper reality beneath the surface of Montreal. Hochelaga was the city Cartier "discovered" when he traveled up the river in search of a mythical land of gold and jewels called the Kingdom of Saguenay. Standing at the site of modern-day Montreal, Hochelaga was home to over a thousand people who were part of an extensive group of tribes known as the Saint Lawrence Iroquoians. What we know of the Hochelagans comes from Cartier's notebooks and the speculations of scholars who have gathered evidence and unearthed artifacts, thereby mapping their own versions of the history of the Saint Lawrence valley. Most agree that Hochelaga was probably a walled city, that its inhabitants lived and worked in longhouses, and that they subsisted primarily on the planting and harvesting of corn. The arrival of the French most likely drew them into the economy of the fur trade, as it did other native tribes such as the Algonquin, the Montagnais, the Mahican, the Abenaki, the Sokoki, and the Iroquois. Exactly what happened to Hochelaga after the beginning of the European invasion in the sixteenth century will probably never be known with certainty. But by the turn of seventeenth century, the Hochelagans had disappeared.

So "what's left . . . for our story," for history? What's left is Montreal and Caughnawaga: a French-founded city, and a space outside it designated for the descendants of the native people who survived that founding. What's left for the writing of reality and fiction is the break-up, loss, and symbolic reconstruction of lives lived, of "villages scrambled in the ink of history." In the nostalgic model, the map of French history and culture needs the blank page of its writing: Hochelaga "disappears" and French history moves on. Nostalgic memory would therefore found Montreal on an originary blank, an empty space to be conquered and inscribed with a French identity. In contrast, Brossard's holographic, graffiti memory exposes the real and symbolic violence that produces the illusion of that originary blank. Reading **French Kiss** is like deciphering the many coats of scrawl that collect as graffiti on subway walls. That graffiti becomes holographic: layers of paint simultaneously come into focus as the many faces of Montreal-Hochelaga. To ignore those layers is to repeat the violence that both replaced Hochelaga with Montreal, and produced the "reserve" called Caughnawaga. "For your whole life," Brossard writes, "you will remember the graffiti in the subway, my only daughter." That uniquely Brossardian graffiti contains the "frescoes, multiple in the prism" that trace the invisible: mapping, as Rich puts it, "the blueprint to a life."

Does Brossard succeed in dismantling the logic of presence and absence at the heart of nostalgia and writing? I would like to think of her work as another kind of lesbian writing that is not just *by* a lesbian or *about* lesbians, but which explores the very processes through which people and their stories are made invisible. Such a writing would think about Hochelagans as well as lesbians; and it would tell a story, as in **French Kiss,** not just of woman-loving tongues swirling in mouths, but also of the genocidal "kiss" of death that is the legacy of the map-makers, fur-trappers, conquerors, and colonizers of this planet. In addition, such a writing would not just replace one story with another, but would restructure the very logic of replacement, reconfiguring the relation between the writing subject and the reserve on which the writing depends. In that sense, this other kind of "lesbian" writing might come to name a thick, holographic, urban poetry in which reality, fiction, and utopia would coexist.

But what would it look like, exactly? Ah, there she would be: "The generic body would become the expression of woman and woman would have wings above all, she'd make (a) sign." Yes, she might disappear for a while, but then I would see her, my urban fairy, tracing spirals of graffiti up and down the walls. A holographic projection—"woman and woman would have wings above all"—there she (and I) would be:

> Plunged into the centre of the city, I would dream of raising my eyes. FEMME SKIN TRAJECTOIRE. *Donna lesbiana* dome of knowledge and helix, already I'd have entered into a spiral and my being of air aerial urban would reproduce itself in the glass city like an origin.

There she, and I, would be. We would find each other through the words in their reading, and there we would be: "being of air aerial urban," reproducing ourselves "*like* an origin," but already changing, spiralling elsewhere.

This reading can only happen, at least for me, in the form of a conditional: it would tell a story . . . and it would look like this . . . and there, can't you see? we (or perhaps just I) would be. . . . That conditional reading, like the hologram, is always there, waiting to be read, waiting to flare up like a flag on a map. But beyond that conditional, more explicitly political questions remain.

What does Brossard's writing say or do for lesbian politics? How does her urban radical work for feminism? Where is the link between the memory of Hochelaga and the contemporary struggles of native peoples in North America? Does the writing itself function as the kind of public fiction that the theory proclaims? Indeed, one of the most commonly heard complaints about Brossard's writing is that it is opaque and inaccessible, that it speaks to an audience of educated elites who share a common practice and way of thinking. Who is reading her, and to whom is she writing? Do her complex urban fictions really speak like graffiti on a subway wall?

What *is* at stake in her writing? Perhaps that question, more than any other, contains the seeds of my impatience at the difficulty of Brossard's writing. We all live in one world, but privilege allows some of us to choose a room of our own from among many possible worlds. Brossard lives in an urban room filled with fractals, holograms, and virtual realities. And I know that she from her room, as I from mine, wants the world to heal. But who among us can hear her? Some of us need narrative and the prose of preachers, not translucent letters in a metaphorical cyberspace. To be sure, I deeply respect and admire Brossard's holographic writings. But I long for stories that my mother and grandmother might hear.

"And now," says Winterson, stepping out from the wings backstage, "swarming over the earth with our tiny insect bodies and putting up flags and building houses, it seems that all the journeys are done." Alas, we long for stories, but it seems that there are no more earthly places to travel. The world is mapped: there are no more journeys and no more stories to tell. "Not so," I hear, and it's Winterson speaking again. But it could just as easily be Brossard, saying, "Not so! Not so! See, here's another layer of graffiti, another aerial letter!" Okay, I think, so let's look again.

Something's happening beneath the surface, waiting to be noted and marked. It could be my mother, proud, with her lover, on a wide leafy branch of the family tree. It could be my grandmother's century-old heart, beating to the rhythm of my cousin's ship, or measuring time across my uncle's chart. It could be other rhythms and other lives uncovered, stories whose lines on my particular map might only be obvious to me. Who knows what patterns I'll end up tracing? Who knows what I'll end up saying?

More important, who knows what *we'll* choose to say and do? As Brossard puts it, "*I* speak to an *I* to ensure the permanence of the *we*. If I don't take on that which says *we* in *me,* the essence of what I am will have no longevity but the time of one life, mine, and that's too short for us" (translation modified). I think Brossard is one of those cartographers of an invisible *I* who speaks from the heart of an invisible *we.* The line of that *we* runs parallel with mine, for a moment, perhaps, but it also stretches away behind and before me. Of course, we have to constantly ask the question: who are *we?* For Brossard that asking is part of the struggle. Nothing is given from the start, especially not the origin of an identity. The *we* can only find itself in the effort and the struggle of the searching.

In that sense Brossard is a map-maker, working for liberation, who can help us pull ourselves together and find our way when we're lost in the forest or adrift at sea. And if it's true that all the journeys aren't done, perhaps it's also true that new maps and new discoveries don't have to efface old ones. "Round and flat," Winterson says, "only a very little has been discovered." So perhaps Brossard can help us to make different maps and different journeys "toward the idea of a future, another shore." And perhaps that future will bring healing to the places erased in violence, uncovering sedimented histories and shifting forms in the spaces on the map where there was never absence, just a "rigorously executed" silence.

Kimberly Verwaayen (essay date Spring 1997)

SOURCE: "Region/Body: In? Of? And? Or? (Alter/Native)

Separatism in the Politics of Nicole Brossard," in *Essays on Canadian Writing,* No. 61, Spring, 1997, pp. 1-16.

[In the following essay, Verwaayen discusses the role of separatism in the politics set forth by Brossard in her writing.]

"What kind of message is this?" was one feminist response during a CBC round table (aired on "Prime Time Magazine" in prereferendum October 1995) in reaction to propagandist remarks made by Lucien Bouchard in a recent "yes"-side campaign linking reproduction and the sovereignty project in Quebec. While Bouchard's alienating comments exemplify a centuries-old validation of women through their reproductive function, their assigned use-value in Western tradition, my purpose here is to trace how the patriarchal impetus of the Quebec separatist movement circumscribes feminist aims and to suggest, through the movement from the regional to the international in the fiction of Nicole Brossard, the incompatibility of feminist and Quebec nationalism as discursive constructions. While both separatist and feminist ideologies are interested in issues of sameness and difference, of language/shared cultural experience/history, Brossard's evolving awareness of the incompatibility in definition of the "us/them" dichotomy can be traced throughout her oeuvre, in which physical place (Quebec) becomes supplanted, displaced, by the international feminist body as site for political resistance. For Brossard, ultimately, the linguistic signifier "separatism" spirals into an "other" direction, signalling a process not toward an autonomous, segregated discursive region identified as Quebec but toward an independently cooperative, transnational community of women, a lesbian separatism.

The factious relationship between feminist and sovereigntist interests in 1970s Quebec was not a natural, not an essential, one. It would be a form of imperialism itself to suggest that women inherently cannot engage in political activism as both feminists and nationalists: to argue that women must choose, as Trinh T. Minh-ha says, between ethnicity and womanhood is to participate in the patriarchal system of "dualistic reasoning and its age-old divide-and-conquer tactics." In fact, for many early female separatists, the nationalist movement—with its distrust of the status quo and its discourse of decolonization—seemed to be a forum through which women could challenge their double marginalization as Québécoise; they shared with the male population, as Paula Gilbert Lewis contends, feelings of impotency, inferiority, and alienation (a colonized existence) under the economic and linguistic dominance of English Canada and the powerful hegemony of the Catholic Church. But the 1970 FLF(Q) slogan, "Pas de libération du Québec sans libération des femmes," already signified the tension between feminist and nationalist discourses in Quebec, since the freedom of women was not inherent in the vision of a free Quebec.

Certainly a patriarchal impetus is locatable in some of the major separatist texts of the era, reflecting the kinds of patriarchal inscription exploded in Brossard's oeuvre. In the mid-1960s, texts such as Claude Jasmin's *Pleure pas, Germaine* and Jacques Ferron's *La Nuit* portrayed women, like the *romans de terre* before them, as representations of the earth, of the mother, as *terre Québec,* as interchangeable entities of imprinted function. In perhaps the most acclaimed separatist text of the era, Hubert Aquin's *Prochaine épisode,* the narrator's mistress, K., blends indistinguishably into the picture of Venus the first time the protagonist sees her, and throughout the text her identity is mysteriously conflated with that of H. de Heutz's treacherous blonde. (Repeated emphasis on the colour of [both?] women's hair imprints the suggestion of connection. Also, the reiterated wordplay in the original, "ma blonde," used to identify K., suggests that possession/definition is linked to attribute, to woman's objectification in the male gaze.) Furthermore, K. stands as a metaphor for Quebec, *la terre* that is "le pays qui te ressemble, mon vrai pays natal et secret. . . ." Aquin posits K.'s body in geographically physical terms—but K. is like Quebec not because both are colonized but because of a centuries-old identification (the lay of the land) in which the text seems complicit: "Sur ton lit de sables calcaires et sur tes muqueuses alpestres, je descends à toute allure, je m'étends comme une nappe phréatique, j'occupe tout; je pénètre, *terroriste absolu,* dans tous les pores de ton lac parlé . . ." (emphasis added). The text does not seem to explode this violent deposing of woman, her colonization, but to engage in it to serve its nationalist proclivities: "Les noms impurs de nos villes redisent l'infinie conquête que j'ai réapprise en te conquérant, mon amour. . . . Ton pays natal m'engendre révolutionnaire: sur ton étendue lyrique, je me couche et je vis."

It was in fact this phallocratic law of the father under which the nationalist movement, like patriarchy generally, was largely impelled that induced many female nationalists to distinguish between their oppression as Québécois(es) and as women, to choose to break from the Marxist-Leninist groups that identified the women's movement as secondary to the liberation of working classes and the creation of a sovereign Quebec. As Claude Lizé has said, "les femmes ont compris qu'elles ne pourraient pas participer à la 'joute oratoire' sans renoncer à leur propre discours."

Such difference/*différence* experienced by women in the movement is articulated early in Brossard's fiction, if authorially absent from her theory. Brossard has stated in an interview her collective involvement with Roger Soublière: "nous avons lu *Parti Pris* et nous avons compris. Il n'y avait pas à discuter: les positions critiques de cette revue ajoutées à notre expérience quotidienne du Québec . . . achevèrent de transformer notre impatience en un naturel contestaire." Engaged in the political struggles of Quebec, she shared the goal of the *Parti Pris* (the journal-organ of the nationalist movement that she helped to found)—that of an independent and socialist Quebec liberated from the political influence of the Catholic Church. Yet in her earliest novel, *Un livre,* published in 1970, the sexist blindsiding of women in the separatist movement is already manifest in the book's tension between patriarchal nationalism and feminist impulses, a tension not yet theoretically evident in the rhetoric she espoused. In an interview, Brossard has said that *"Un livre* a été écrit à l'époque où j'avais des préoccupations politiques en rapport avec toute la question nationale, alors que **French Kiss** est arrivé à un moment où j'étais imbibée ... d'informations que touchaient la biologie, l'écologie, le corps [la féminisme]...." The fairly facile split between feminist and nationalist proclivities espoused here is not borne out in the fiction. Although *Un livre* evinces solidarity with the nationalist movement, a vision of political collectivity imaged throughout in the interchangeability of the text's male and female actors, this interchangeability is exploded by the text. It is not a neutral but a politically loaded representation: the text begs attention to the minutia, invites interpretation of its gaps and interstices, its system of signs in small letters:

> Lire O. R., c'est aussi lire Dominique et Mathieu car tous trois s'inscrivent identiques dans le livre.... La lecture ... de O. R., Dominique et Mathieu doit être envisagée comme une démarche essentiellement ludique: l'ocil répond aux moindres stimulations AVIS.... Lire: ou faire le tri dans la masse noire des mots.... O. R., assise par terre, jambes croisées, un livres sur les genoux. Un livre qu'elle ne lit pas. Mais qu'elle touche. Dominique et Mathieu, l'un devant l'autre, penchés sur un damier de go, impatients de créer chacun pour soit l'espace vainqueur.

The particulars enumerated are not gratuitous ("l'oeil répond aux moindres stimulations"): the characters are not identical. O. R. is scripted differently from the men around her (all are vaguely identified with the FLQ) despite the text's literal assertion *other*wise; she is excluded from the male competition, from the male quest for product. The men are "anxious" not in the pleasure, the ecstasy of the *jeu,* but in the single desire to master the game; her activity, however, is not end-goal oriented. She delays/defers even the pleasurable act of reading in the process of touching the book.

The women are further unlike the male separatists in the group since O. R. and Dominique C. are scripted, whereas the others are not, in silence; O. R. "n'a rien à dire et c'est Dominique qui parle." Again, although the text tries to suggest on an open level the notion that all the five "variables" in the text are anonymously similar, it is only the women, O. R. and Dominique C., who are identified by initial, by

the truncation of a proper name. (The male Dominique needs no other identifying mark.) O. R. identifies her lack of a name with her exclusion from the male realm, the symbolic: "O. R.: initiales. Des lettres à l'origine d'un nom que personne jusqu'ici n'a prononcé." Nameless, she is ever in the service of her use-value: "Garder l'anonymat: être la personne qui écrit au nom de plusieurs autres." Her body is commodified, a unit of exchange, manipulated by Dominique as payment to Mathieu for his debts without her consent.

Thus, for O. R., as for Dominique C., the glass must always be empty—there is little room for female freedom in a movement in which many of the male leaders remain patriarchs, in which women's autonomy is not implied in e*man*cipated discourse. Rarely unfettered, the women are caught instead in the specular vision of the same (this is the explosion of the representation of the indistinguishability of identities represented in the text), which negates difference reflected back against itself: "Dominique la regarde et ne se souvient de rien. La devine dans la distance: une jeune femme parmi les autres." Woman is invisible in the male gaze except as the same (an inferior model of the same, o.r. as conflations of an other, *a nothing to see*) in a male-dominated movement. That it is only woman who is equated with the subaltern other is evident in the power relations that constitute the text: O. R. is Dominique's visible "cible," the object of his desire, his control: "D'une seule main Dominique couche O. R. à ses côtés. Violemment pourquoi? Parce que selon les règles d'un vieux jeu." Dominique is part of a collective movement organizing for sociopolitical change—but clearly the imperial patriarchy that he seeks to overthrow will be replaced, simply, by a more nationalist (sovereign) one. The conquest here challenged by Brossard is that of the female body, its history of exploitation, abuse, colonization, by men.

Yet the text offers space beyond such containment: O. R.'s desires exceed the command of Dominique's hand. O. R. is liberated from his control of her body, from the societal inscription of its market value, when naked and free on the balcony. Liberated in her nudity, freed from society's clothing/coding of her body, her celebration becomes "le *scandale* de la liberté" (emphasis added); her act is scandalous because it is transgressive. Phallocratic law cannot read such female *jouissance* except in signs of denigration. Yet when she/her body is decried "Trop belle, laide, vulgaire, putain," the narrative voice intervenes, overwrites the paternal ownership of meaning in language, for "Etrangement les mots s'accumulent mais ne font guère que s'accumuler." Sings in the phallocratic system can only accrue hollowly upon each other because O. R. exceeds the phatic, swells beyond the conventional agreement/conspiracy between patriarchal society and language: "[elle] vit déjà autre chose. Dominique le sait." Even her shadow (woman's image often mistaken for her self and overwritten by the male gaze into the dream of the same) is, ultimately, "étrangère au regard de Dominique qui entrouve les paupières." She is not the same, she exceeds the same: there is "quelque chose de plus dans le regard de O. R." There is, suggests the text, an ever-increasing "plus" in women's vision, a comprehension of the scripted lack juxtaposed with a growing awareness of plenitude. Thus, in *Un livre,* already in 1970, the tension between male interests in the nationalist cause and women's role and subjugation by men in the movement is being interrogated, and revolutionary fervour for an independent Quebec is slowly—but surely—yielding presence to feminist concerns:

> O. R. troublée parce qu'il s'est agi pendant toute la soirée des autres à travers elle. Parce qu'elle fait partie d'une collectivité qui crève, lentement, le ventre offert. O. R. et Dominique C. partageant leur révolte. *Qui s' apaise.* Se confond doucement aux caresses qu'elles s'échangent du bout des doigts, de la langue. (emphasis added)

Similar to *Un livre,* Brossard's second work of fiction, *Sold-out* (published in 1973 and translated into English as *Turn of a Pang* three years later), ostensibly treats a political commitment to Quebec nationalism in its interrogation of federal control over provincial affairs in its dual treatment of the 1943 conscription crisis and the 1970 invocation of the War Measures Act. As in the earlier novel, there is an articulation of male and female collectivity, a conflation of identities united in a general cause, for the text represents itself as "une histoire de je tu il nous et autres pluriels . . . dans le microcosme québécois; toutes les phases de la destruction d'ils d'elles. . . . Se poursuivent le temps de l'animation collective, les inscriptions." Bodies are "mâle et / ou femelle," again an indistinguishable blur. But here, too, the narrative contradicts itself. The masses are not uniform:

> Ce qui frappe et déferle déborde la limite effrayant plus que miroir et la révision qu'il impose à l'oeil vision lutte *dedans* le mur reflétant graduellement image aperçue dans le cadre ovale /quel secret? / on y voit bien d'autres choses mais que les foules ne se ressemblent pas toutes pan toute quand elles produisent des événements HISTORIQUES (hiéroglyphes quand on y songe sur quelle surface? à déterminer en cours de cheminement (les surfaces s'imposent tout autant que les compas qui les pénètrent)).

In *Sold-out,* the surfaces carved, the sites of inscription, are the texts of women's bodies, phallically overwritten, used/ abused in the market exchange, scars that need to be read and interpreted. The textual graffiti is a writing on the wall for women:

> ailleurs que sur le mur cela se dessine au pinceau large entamant la bouche de l'homme politique
>
> LE QUÉBEC AUX QUÉBÉCOIS
> sue l'oeil TRAÎTRE, entre les dents, le I phallique
> Indépendance retroussant (une impression) le noir
> de la moustache fraîchement peinturée.

That the liberation sought "le Québec aux québécois" is a phallically constructed independence as spelled out in the writing on the wall.

For Brossard, to break the code, to shatter the phallocentric law of the same, gender interests must supersede those of Quebec culture and language in the development of her fiction. Whereas separatists work for the preservation of the French language (a sensitivity to language, cultural identity, collective autonomy born out of the English conquest of Quebec in 1769), feminists struggle against the even older oppressive power of this language and attempt to alter this language into new rather than preserved forms. As Luce Irigaray has queried, "Si nous continuons à nous parler le même langage, nous allons reproduire la même histoire." For Brossard, too, language must be r/evolutionized: "comment la femme qui utilise quotidiennement les mots (comédienne, journaliste, écrivain(e), professeur(e)), peut-elle utiliser un language qui, phallocratique, jour au départ contre elle?" As Bill Ashcroft, Gareth Griffiths, and Helen Tiffin contend, control over language is one of the main features of imperial oppression: "Language becomes the medium through which a hierarchical structure of power is perpetuated, and the medium through which conceptions of 'truth,' 'order,' and 'reality' become established. Such power is rejected in the emergence of an effective post-colonial voice." Marginalized voices must wrest language and writing—with its "signification of authority"—from the dominant culture. "Nous n'avons d'autre repère que nous. Nous sommes entourées de signes qui invalident notre présence," says Lorna Myher (My/her) in *Le Désert mauve.* Such silence must be shattered, silent *e* shouted forward: "Il faut que j'apprenne à parler," says one of Brossard's voices; "S'il ne consent, toute ma vie je l'attendrai ce mot de lui. Il parlera à ma place. Toute une vie."

So Brossard breaks the code of silence in order to challenge the hegemony of male discourse; her (de)constructive strategies attempt to out*man*oeuvre language, its relegation of women to death, the *e muet mutant* to explode the breach (birth) between sign and object. In *L'Amèr ou le chapître effrité,* the signifier "l'amèr" (*la mére, amére, la mer, l'aimer*), for example, suspends the monoreferential in its endless freeplay of meanings: mother, bitter, sea, (to) love. For Brossard,

> When a woman invests a word with all her anger,

energy, determination, imagination, this word crashes violently into the same word, the one invested with masculine experience. The shock that follows has the effect of making the word burst: certain words lose a letter, others see their letters reform in a different order.

What she wants is writing at degree zero, an *écriture blanche* emptied into new significations, for "language does not know anything about women—or we should say, rather, that it only knows the clamorous lies that generations' of misogynous, sexist phallocrats have repeated to it. In fact, we know that patriarchal language discredits, marginalizes, constitutes the feminine as inferior. . . ." Brossard, however, develops women's desire in language: she places tongue in women's mouths, a sexual/textual French kiss.

This is, for Brossard, the link between textuality and corporeality: the body speaks forth from its ruptured excess, from the space of its traditional erasure. The only access to the symbolic that phallocentrism has historically allowed women is by absence, proxy, exchanged body (real estate), to (re)produce only as mother and to be muffled/muzzled otherwise: "l'homme s'est assuré par là mainmise sur tous les modes de production énergétiques du corps féminin (cerveau, utérus, vagin, bras, jambes, bouche, langue). Dans la mesure où il est fragmenté, le corps de la femme, la femme, ne peut entamer la vision globale de l'homme." But the body bodies forth, overwrites the scarred female cortext (cortext as sign disperses through the notions *corps* and *texte*—the body is written in/by language); it becomes the site of political and textual resistance, an other coding to phallocentric inscription. Brossard's work is reactionary, revolutionary; it produces, rather than reproduces, by writing against traditional literary forms and by challenging the representational systems of society (where the representable is male). Plurality, polyvocality, of women's sexual morphology (always already coded in language) breaks the phallocratic law of the same, for *woman has sex organs more or less everywhere.* To represent this proliferation, this body spiralling, Brossard plays with the gyre as configuration of the mobility and multiplicity, indeterminacy, of the lesbian text; the multiple female body (of the text), its doubleness, deferral, multiple female intertexts, the convulsions of the circle, of the gyre, disrupt the univocal, phallic patrilinearity of patriarchal writing. Ellipses and parentheses like multiple genitalia flower to confound the phallacies of the paternal text, to dissociate the alter/native from the unifying authority of the phallus: "Mais le corps a ses raisons, le mien, sa peau lesbienne, sa place dans un contexte historique, son aire et son contenu politique. Sous mes yeux, les lignes s'arrondissent: linéarité et fragments de linéarité (vous savez les ruptures) se transforment en spirale."

Multiple women's voices also delegitimize monologic ori-

gin in male discourse (Brossard's polyphony is a *rêve polysémique,* a border crossing of textual blank spaces across which touch women's bodies and regard[e]s). For the nationalist movement, solidarity must be internal, not international (the history of Quebec is one of subjection to three imperialisms, French, English, and American, which separatist discourse endeavours to resist), but Brossard's writing exceeds boundaries demarcated by a measurable physical space or territorialization. The textual inscription of her feminism, as for Quebec feminism generally, owes much, as critics have shown, to a cross-fertilization of three distinct cultural perspectives: Québécois, French, and American. Solidarity is bound not by place but by body: territory is that of the imaginary suffused by female subjectivity and feminist consciousness. For Brossard, American feminism is a desirable influence: "le discours des femmes américaines, des féministes m'est extrêmement important, celui de Millet, de Firestone, de Rita May Brown, de Ti-Grace Atkinson. Je me sens beaucoup plus, au niveau des discours d'exploration théoriques, près d'elles." There is sameness in difference not (simply) because "us" is distinct from "them" but because "us" is itself a diverse and polysemous group: "Les écritures de femmes me stimulent énormément parce qu'elles sont aussi très variées, que ce soit celle de France Théoret ou de Virginia Woolf, celle de Wittig ou de Stein." Epigrams in *L'Amèr* from Luce Irigaray, Virginia Woolf, Mary Barnes, Monique Wittig, Sande Zeig, Anaïs Nin, and Flora Tristan, among others (many, but not all, lesbian women), and Sappho, Gertrude Stein, Djuna Barnes, Adrienne Rich, Mary Daly, Monique Wittig, Isabel Millee, Viviane Forrester, and others in *La Lettre aérienne,* establish an international community of women, and these allusions build a shared language and a shared tradition of struggle beyond territorial borders.

Yet there is a distinct and desired physical space in Brossard's writing, though it remains one that serves her international poetics: it is city place, the *polis.* Brossard's protagonists are, as M. Jean Anderson notes, explicitly urban; the bustle of a metropolitan centre "talks back" to the discourse of *la terre,* which has constituted the site of a protectionist and paternalist French Canadian history, the space and the state of mind once mythologized as integral to the survival of Quebec as a separate identity, to the survival of *la race française,* and often imaged as the mother. With the cultural upheaval in the early 1960s and 1970s, and the break-with-the-past mentality of post-World War II urbanization in the province, new nationalist ideology desired to break from agrarian (and Catholic) values, to appropriate for Québécois interests the commercial centres then dominated by anglophone business. But for Brossard, control must be wrested back from patriarchy generally. Her argument is not an economic one for separatist progress but an engagement in the economy of transnational feminism. Her heroines reject the rural Quebec for Montreal, New York, or Florence:

Adrienne's story "aurait pu tout aussi bien se passer à Montréal" as in New York. It is the theoretical concept of city, fluid in space, imaged and accessed by women everywhere, rather than an identifiable geographical locale, that is the locus in Brossard's writing.

Certainly "Where is here?" is a different question for women than for men. The "here" that Brossard seeks/speaks in her desire is a feminist utopia, positing women desiring themselves, embracing other women, a choice, an alter/native, rather than the dream of the same. For Brossard, lesbianism subverts the paternal order; like Alice going through the looking glass, she has crossed through (her opening, a birth) to the other side, where things are topsy turvy, no longer reflected back the same:

> La différence a prise. S'installe comme lui dans ma vie. M'englobe comme un territoire. Sa différence s'est transformée en pouvoir *systématique*. Il s'assure dès lors du contrôle des différences.
>
> *Modifiant ma fonction, je me transforme. Travaille le creux du ventre: curetage. Le dérèglement, cataclysme des formes.* (emphasis added)

Brossard, as a lesbian, murders the womb, the site of woman's silence, the locus of her use-value, again to engender productivity rather than reproductivity:"*J'ai tué le ventre et je l'écris.*" Sexually, textually, lesbianism constitutes for Brossard "le seul relais plausible pour me sortir du ventre de ma mére patriarcale. . . . Traverser le symbole alors que j'écris. Une pratique de déconditionnement qui m'amène à reconnaître ma propre légitimité. Ce par quoi toute femme tente d'exister: ne plus être illégitime." To write the lesbian text is to create women's own locus of desire outside the matter of the womb.

This is radical feminism. Patriarchy as a dominantly male colonizer must be subverted, *written out* in the creative act: "On ne peut inscrire *femmes entre elles* sans avoir à mesurer l'ampleur de cette petite expression:'se passer d'un homme,' sans se heurter à la lecture du mur patriarcal sur lequel sont inscrites toutes les lois qui nous séparent de nous-même, qui nous isolent des autres femmes." Ultimately for Brossard, the political "separatism" for which she contends is one that "stresses separation from all aspects of male culture so that women can concentrate on themselves and other women and create their own subjectivity." Her vision is of a new, transnational world order whose trajectory spirals ever outward in its embracing of women: "La solidarité des femmes est la dernière épreuve de solidarité humaine . . ."; "je travaille à ce que se perde la convulsive habitude d'initier

les filles au mâle comme une pratique courante de lobotomie. Je veux *en effet* voir s'organiser la forme des femmes dans la trajectoire de l'espèce." Concerns for women's place in language and history thus supersede those of Québécois nationalism, in which the identities of the collectivity, *les Québécois,* are signed (linguistic hegemony) in the masculine; for women to engage in any political struggle constructed as antagonistic toward or as resistant to feminism is to remain Québécois (rather than Québécoises), to participate in the code that defines women synonymously with men. This is the in/definition, the in/difference, of patriarchally constructed nationalism (which interpolates the same)—neo(patriarchal) imperialism of *maîtres chez nous*—that Brossard, one might say, will over*turn* (with a pang?) in the fluid feminist body, everywhere: *mettre, m'être, chez toutes.*

FURTHER READING

Criticism

Anthony, Elizabeth. Review of *Mauve Desert,* by Nicole Brossard. *Books in Canada* XIX, No. 8 (November 1990): 47.

> Asserts that the reader is "frequently enriched by [Brossard's] gambles [in *Mauve Desert*]; at times, however, her philosophical abstractions so dematerialize the real that we lose the necessary obstruction and grounding of objects' provident solidity."

Baehler, Aline. "Traversée du Désert." *Canadian Literature,* No. 132 (Spring 1992): 177-79.

> Reviews Brossard's *A tout regard* in French.

Bishop, Neil B. "Installations." *Canadian Literature,* No. 135 (Winter 1992): 158-60.

> Regards Brossard's collection of poems, *Installations,* as "a joy."

Diehl-Jones, Charlene. "The Dance of Reading." *Books in Canada* XXII, No. 5 (Summer 1993): 38-40.

> Remarks that in Brossard's *Green Night of Labyrinth Park* "there are moments of great loveliness."

Tilley, Jane. "Found Again." *Canadian Literature,* Nos. 138/139 (Fall/Winter 1993): 166-67.

> Asserts the importance of *Anthologie de la poésie des femmes au Québec,* edited by Brossard and Lisette Girouard, to the canon of poetry in Quebec.

Additional coverage of Brossard's life and career is contained in the following sources published by Gale: *Contemporary Authors*, Vol. 122; *Contemporary Authors Autobiography Series*, Vol. 16; and *Dictionary of Literary Biography*, Vol. 53.

Annie Dillard
1945-

American essayist, poet, nonfiction writer, autobiographer, and novelist.

The following entry presents an overview of Dillard's career through 1996. For further information on her life and works, see *CLC,* Volumes 9 and 60.

INTRODUCTION

Dillard is a Pulitzer Prize-winning author best known for her transcendental philosophy and naturalist writings in *Pilgrim at Tinker Creek* (1974). Her works of fiction and nonfiction explore issues such as the role of the self within the universe, the relationship between beauty and horror, the nature of God, and the art of writing. She is considered one of the most influential and unorthodox American environmental writers.

Biographical Information

Dillard was born on April 30, 1945 in Pittsburgh, Pennsylvania to Frank and Pam (Lambert) Doak. The oldest of three girls, Dillard grew up rebelling against her parents and exploring the issues about which she would later write. In her autobiography, *An American Childhood* (1987), she reveals that the teachings at Shadyside Presbyterian Church, the expectations of her middle-class environment, and her explorations of the area parks filled her thinking. In 1967 she graduated from Hollins College with a B.A. in English and a year later she completed a master of arts degree. She married Richard Dillard in 1964, whom she later divorced. In 1980 she married writer Gary Clevidence with whom she shares one daughter and two stepchildren. In 1988, again divorced, Dillard married Robert D. Richardson Jr., a professor and writer. Throughout the late 1970s and 1980s, Dillard taught creative writing at a number of American universities, including Western Washington State University and Wesleyan University. In addition to winning the Pulitzer Prize for general nonfiction for *Pilgrim at Tinker Creek,* she has won the New York Presswomen's Award for Excellence in 1975, the Washington State Governor's Award for Literature in 1978, and the Catholic Book Club Campion Medal in 1994. She has also receive several grants, including one from the National Endowment for the Arts, and a Guggenheim fellowship.

Major Works

Throughout her literary career, Dillard has worked in many genres. She began in 1974 with a collection of poetry en-

titled *Tickets for a Prayer Wheel* and returned to poetry with *Mornings Like This* (1995), a collection of experimental poetry based on the writings of others. Her most famous works are her nonfiction, naturalist, spiritual writings such as *Pilgrim at Tinker Creek, Holy the Firm* (1977) and *Teaching a Stone to Talk* (1982). Styled in response to Henry David Thoreau's *Walden, Pilgrim at Tinker's Creek* follows the progression of seasons in Roanoke Valley, chronicling the evolution of the observer's consciousness through meditations on life in the woods. In highly personal essays replete with scientific facts, Dillard recounts her expeditions into the forest, relating both horror at scenes of predatory violence and joy at the beauty of natural wonders. From these observations, Dillard creates a cosmology, using her observations as a metaphor for the universal nature of self and the relationship of self with God and the universe. At the heart of all three of the naturalist writings is a concern with the meaning of existence and other spiritual matters. Set on Puget Sound, *Holy the Firm* is a journal of her struggle to come to terms with senseless suffering. *Teaching a Stone to Talk* consists of fourteen essays that continue to develop her philosophy, which posits that people need to discover metaphysical truth in familiar objects. Dillard's other primary interest has been in the act of writing and creating. She has published three collections of essays on literary criticism and writing: *Living by Fiction* (1982), *Encounters with Chinese Writers* (1984) and *The Writing Life* (1989). In these works she explains her own need to write, considers the role of literature in society, and attempts to stimulate writers to be fully committed to their art. In addition, Dillard has also written a fictional historic epic, set in eighteenth-century Washington state, entitled *The Living* (1992), and her autobiography, *An American Childhood* which chronicles her youth in Pittsburgh.

Critical Reception

Dillard's writing has consistently received strong positive reviews by critics. Scholars praise Dillard's unique voice, and her use of poetic language to merge philosophy with her observations of the natural world. James S. Torrens observes, "Dillard's writing is often poetic, pursuing knowledge through metaphor and analogy, yet compact and far from florid." Dorothy Parker states, "[Dillard] is a fanatical marvelously percipient observer; and she has the poet's inner eye." However, Dillard's propensity for finding meaning, if not order, in her observations of the natural world has sparked debate. Margaret Loewan Reimer argues that Dillard's unorthodox writing style in *Pilgrim at Tinker Creek* results in confusion about the genre of the book, and debate over what criteria should be used to evaluate it. Reimer and other critics such as Mary Davidson McConahay and William J. Scheik praise Dillard's ability to find larger meaning in specific small events she observes in the natural world around her, to find universal metaphors for the self. However, Elaine Tietjen argues, "Other scholars have noted Dillard's unusual focus on the particular as a path toward the universal. In fact, this focus also limited her." Although some critics called Dillard's essays on literary criticism amateurish, most scholars agree that her work is thought-provoking, insightful and enthusiastic, drawing from her own experiences and passion for writing. Dillard earned similar praise for her novel *The Living*. However, in the genre of poetry Dillard has not found overwhelming success. Her first poetry collection, *Tickets for a Prayer Wheel,* earned very little notice, although the reviews were favorable. Her poems in *Mornings Like This* garnered little approval. Elizabeth Lund says that at her most successful, Dillard produces "near-misses" and John Haines suggests that the lines which she borrows from an eclectic range of prose writings may be more powerful in their original sources.

PRINCIPAL WORKS

Pilgrim at Tinker Creek (nonfiction) 1974

Tickets for a Prayer Wheel (poetry) 1974
Holy the Firm (nonfiction) 1978
Living by Fiction (essays) 1982
Teaching a Stone to Talk: Expeditions and Encounters (essays) 1982
Encounters with Chinese Writers (essays) 1984
An American Childhood (autobiography) 1987
The Writing Life (essays) 1989
The Living (novel) 1992
Mornings Like This: Found Poems (poetry) 1995

CRITICISM

Margaret Loewen Reimer (essay date Spring 1983)

SOURCE: "The Dialectical Vision of Annie Dillard's *Pilgrim at Tinker Creek,*" in *Critique,* Vol. XXIV, No. 3, Spring, 1983, pp. 182-91.

[*In the essay below, Reimer argues that Dillard employs a dual dialectic in* Pilgrim at Tinker Creek, *first between nature and religion, then between beauty and horror.*]

When **Pilgrim at Tinker Creek** appeared in 1974, reviewers agreed that it was a highly unusual treatise on nature. The work obviously exerted a peculiar power, for reviewers were either rhapsodic in their praise or passionate in their indignation. Neither side, however, was quite sure in what tradition or genre the book belonged, or in what context to evaluate the author's rather disconcerting conclusions about the natural world. That is where the matter has stayed. A bibliographical search some five years later turned up no articles on the book besides the initial reviews. Although the book has gone through twelve printings in two editions, the critics have been silent.

Why? Perhaps the book falls between several categories or disciplines—the scientists relegate the work to the religious; the religious view the book as an aberration of scientific investigation. Indeed, the subtitle, "A mystical excursion into the natural world," hints at the paradox and incongruity which characterize the book. **Pilgrim at Tinker Creek** appears to be a scientific study overlaid with spiritual contemplation, an examination of natural phenomena which leads the author to an encounter with the Divine. This fervent observer is an unusual empiricist and a still more unusual mystic.

In this book, Annie Dillard sets forth her dialectical vision of the world. The first level of that dialectic is the tension between the material and the spiritual, the natural and the transcendent, but another dialectic is at work within this framework: the prevailing contradiction between the beauty and the horror within the natural world. These two extremes define existence as Dillard observes it and form the focus of her work. In the first paragraph of the book, the author lays out the basic dialectic:

> And some mornings I'd wake in daylight to find my body covered with paw prints in blood; I looked as though I'd been painted with roses. . . . We wake, if we ever wake at all, to mystery, rumors of death, beauty, violence.

Since Dillard pursues her investigation of the beauty and the horror primarily in religious terms—within the language and framework of religion, both Christian and non-Christian, we shall here set her vision against traditional, orthodox religious categories (in the broadest sense of those terms) in order to analyze it.

Among Dillard's influences, both religious and literary, are certain American writers who have developed their visions of the world within the American Puritan heritage. One of the writers who was most adept at drawing metaphysical conclusions from the natural world was Herman Melville. He was able, as one introduction to his writings states, "to set the metaphysical thunderbolt side by side with factual discussion or commonplace realism." Melville's eyes saw mainly the darkness and the horror, a legacy, perhaps, of the darker side of New England Puritanism. Annie Dillard's vision of the world includes the sinister side although her conclusions stem more from a horror at the seeming mindlessness of nature's design than from a deeply pervasive sense of evil.

> It is the fixed that horrifies us, the fixed that assails us with the tremendous force of its mindlessness. . . . The fixed is the world without fire—dead flint, dead tinder, and nowhere a spark. It is motion without direction, force without power, the aimless procession of caterpillars round the rim of a vase, and I hate it because at any moment I myself might step to that charmed and glistening thread.

In Dillard's vision, Moby Dick is reduced to a mindless insect.

Most reviewers of **Pilgrim at Tinker Creek** see Dillard as having some kind of link with American transcendentalism. One states it most unequivocally when he says: "In essence her view is plain old-fashioned optimistic American transcendentalism, ornamented though it may be with examples from quantum physics and bio-chemistry." Another also places her in the tradition of Henry Thoreau and Ralph Waldo Emerson but goes on to make a distinction. Dillard, he says, turns things back on themselves to ask what kind of world this really is, and what kind of minds we must have

that they (the world and our minds) respond the way they do to each other. Even another reviewer calls the book a "kind of gutsy Walden."

Other critics are uncomfortable with identifying Dillard's work too closely with the transcendentalists. Most reviewers have not quite known what to make of her strange views. One calls Dillard's writing an "exuberant mingling" of all the different ways of writing about nature, using nature as the "source of an intoxicating personal dream grown to rhapsodic proportion." Another thinks the book is quite contemporary because it is interested in pure sensation, in simple perception divorced from preconceptions and categories. These imprecise observations are not very helpful in placing Dillard within a literary-religious tradition. Significantly, she rarely quotes from any of her predecessors, focusing her attention almost completely on the observations of scientists and biblical writers. In her attitude to nature, however, Dillard seems to echo some of the views of her transcendentalist forebears. Like Emerson and Thoreau, Dillard watches the details of her natural environment with a sense of amazement and is overwhelmed with the lessons which nature can teach. One has only to "see," to observe natural phenomena in order to learn the wisdom which they offer.

"I've been thinking about seeing," says Dillard. In her discussion about seeing she observes: "But there is another kind of seeing that involves a letting go. When I see this way I sway transfixed and emptied." This statement is an echo of Emerson who states in his essay "Nature": "I become a transparent eyeball; I am nothing; I see all; the currents of the Universal Being circulate through me." Dillard, in her chapter on seeing, goes on to qualify her exuberance and the tone changes: "If we are blinded by darkness, we are also blinded by light. When too much light falls on everything, a special terror results." There can be too much seeing. "I reel in confusion; I don't understand what I see." At this point all meaning flees and the writer faces the opposite of seeing: "I turn from the window. I'm blind as a bat, sensing only from every direction the echo of my own thin cries." The vision of the transcendentalists is only a fond remembrance at this point of a world which seemed to promise more clarity than Dillard can find.

Emerson's philosophy rests on the orderliness, the unity, and the progress of the natural world and man within it—whatever horror may exist is horror because of man's limited understanding of it: "We must trust the perfection of the creation so far as to believe that whatever curiosity the order of things has awakened in our minds, the order of things can satisfy." Dillard cannot long sustain that vision; her delight and wonder quickly change into horror and disgust and then back again to delight. Her experiences lead her to see both the unity and the diversity, the order and the chaos, the uplifting and the destructive.

Dillard does share with transcendentalism a notion that "every natural fact is a symbol of some spiritual fact." She, too, is compelled to see the hand of the Creator behind every living thing, to recall the religious wisdom of the ages as she observes a tree, but her concentration focuses on the minute, the tiniest particle of creation and moves to the universal. She is more the scientist contemplating the atom than the idealist beginning with a conviction about the unity of all things.

> Idealism . . . beholds the whole circle of persons and things . . . as one vast picture which God paints on the instant eternity for the contemplation of the soul. Therefore the soul holds itself off from a too trivial and microscopic study of the universal tablet. It respects the end too much to immerse itself in the means.

Dillard also differs from Emerson in her suspicion that "God absconded" with the sense of his creation and left a gulf between creator and creation. That God's spirit moves through every living thing and sustains the universe within a divine plan is not obvious to her. She can never state with Emerson's certainty that "In the woods, we return to reason and faith." She may be closer in this respect to the Deists who affirmed an inscrutable deity who had left a great gulf between himself and his creation.

Although Dillard shares certain attitudes about the natural world with the transcendentalists, she draws more tentative and contradictory conclusions. Her preoccupation is more personal, less inclined to make final statements about the human and social order.
—*Margaret Loewen Reimer*

Although Dillard shares certain attitudes about the natural world with the transcendentalists, she draws more tentative and contradictory conclusions. Her preoccupation is more personal, less inclined to make final statements about the human and social order. Her conclusions are highly personal—in a sense, she is the only person in her world, and her judgments are based entirely on her observations, except for the substantiation she seeks from other writers.

What, then, are the specifics of this "private" vision which Dillard outlines in her book? Her view of the world centers on two contrasting images: one is the image of "the tree with lights in it"; the other is the frog sucked out by the waterbug.

> Then one day I was walking along Tinker Creek thinking of nothing at all and I saw the tree with the lights in it. I saw the backyard cedar where the mourning doves roost charged and transfigured, each cell buzzing with flame. . . . The vision comes and goes, mostly goes, but I live for it, for the moment when the mountains open and a new light roars in spate through the crack, and the mountains slam.

> He was a very small frog with wide, dull eyes. And just as I looked at him, he slowly crumpled and began to sag. The spirit vanished from his eyes as if snuffed. His skin emptied and drooped . . . it was a monstrous and terrifying thing. I gaped bewildered, appalled. An oval shadow hung in the water behind the drained frog; then the shadow glided away. The frog skin bag started to sink.

Around these two central visions are clustered all the other phenomena which Dillard observes. Her experience of the natural world ranges from the wildly beautiful experiences which lead to ecstasy to the repulsive, terrifying sights which result in nightmares. Observation of the natural world can yield two opposite conclusions, says Dillard. These two opposites she holds in constant tension throughout the book.

The two sides of her vision are best illustrated in the chapters "Intricacy" and "Fecundity." "Intricacy" celebrates the "extravagance of minutiae."

> This is the truth of the pervading intricacy of the world's detail: the creation is not a study, a roughed-in sketch; it is supremely, meticulously created, created abundantly, extravagantly, and in fine.

Anything is dared in this mass of forms—"the creator loves pizzazz." What this means for Dillard is that "there is the possibility for beauty here, a beauty inexhaustible in its complexity, which opens to my knock, . . . which trains me to the wild and extravagant nature of the spirit I seek."

Amidst such celebration of the excessive profusion comes a note of misgiving: "The wonder is—given the errant nature of freedom and the burgeoning of texture in time—the wonder is that all the forms are not monsters, that there is beauty at all." Really, she concludes, anything can happen in such a world.

In "Fecundity" Dillard expands her misgivings into a portrait of intricacy gone awry. The world has become a nightmare: "I don't know what it is about fecundity that so appalls. I suppose it is the teeming evidence that birth and growth, which we value, are ubiquitous and blind, that life itself is so astonishingly cheap, that nature is as careless as it is bountiful, and that with extravagance goes a crushing waste that will one day include our own cheap lives." Endless repetition and mindless procreation reduce life to "a universal chomp." In this world mothers eat their offspring; children devour their parents, and insects gobble up their mates. "What kind of world is this, anyway?" she asks in amazement. "Are we dealing in life, or in death?"

In this chapter Dillard becomes explicit about her two-edged vision.

> The picture of fecundity and its excesses and of the pressures of growth and its accidents is of course no different from the picture I painted before of the world as an intricate texture of a bizarre variety of forms. Only now the shadows are deeper. Extravagance takes on a sinister, wasted air, and exuberance blithers.... I saw how freedom grew the beauties and the horrors from the same live branch.

Dillard's style of writing itself constantly reflects this dialectical vision. In winter, she says, "I come in to come out" as she reads about and analyzes her experiences. As she walks in the snow, "the dark is overhead and the light at my feet" in opposition to the natural order of things. About knowledge she says, "We know now for sure that there is no knowing." This sudden shift in perspective is also reflected in the sudden change of mood. As Eudora Welty wryly observes, Dillard's shifts of mood are rather disconcerting—one time we feel like we are reading letters from camp when the moment before we were deep in the Book of Leviticus. The sudden injections of humor are also examples of the sudden juxtapositions of mood and thought: "My fingers were stiff and red with cold, and my nose ran. I had forgotten the law of the Wild, which is, 'Carry Kleenex'."

Dillard describes herself as a "pilgrim" on a "mystical excursion." Her house is an anchor hold; she is the anchorite. In the first three pages she uses the word "mystery" five times. Her goal is expressed as the desire to "lose herself" in her contemplation of the world, to empty herself in order to experience the present and regain her innocence (Chapter 6). Dillard's journey in this book is the journey of the religious mystic, and the work is full of religious references. Dillard constantly makes the leap from observation of natural phenomena to religious interpretation of the phenomena. Her exegesis of the fish as the symbol of spirit and holiness is an obvious illustration. Besides the many straightforward religious allusions, however, Dillard weaves some subtler shades into the overall scheme. Why a chapter, all of a sudden, about the flood during the summer solstice? Is it merely an interesting aside or is she hearkening back to the great flood which once swept the world? She does not say. She envisions herself as "a sacrifice bound with cords to the horns of the world's rock altar" and ends the book at the winter solstice with "the waters of separation." At the end, the mystic has been purified; she has been "into the gaps" and has seen the works of God, both glorious and terrifying. She has been baptized both into the world—united with it—and separated from it by achieving a certain transcendence over it. She has eaten the world.

Dillard's theology, always dialectical, contains both the conventional language of religious mysticism as well as more macabre elements of religious experience. A critic has put a finger on this latter aspect of Dillard's thought by comparing the book to a celebration of the eucharist and says the eucharist is unusual because the author both ordains the ritual and receives the sacrament—she is both priest and supplicant, going further to note that the scars left by the tomcat become the author's stigmata.

In a description of her role, Dillard says: "I am the arrow shaft, carved along my length by unexpected lights and gashes from the very sky, and this book is the straying trail of blood." At these points the ecstasy and solitary anguish of the mystical experience converge. One receives overtones of primitive religious rites and the suffering of the tortured anchorite who is seeking the ultimate: "Sometimes I ride a bucking faith while one hand grips and the other flails the air, and like any daredevil I gouge with my heels for blood, for a wilder ride, for more." In her frenzy for experience, Dillard tempts the snake and imagines being attacked by a swarm of locusts. Such fervor probably also explains her fascination with Eskimos who keep reappearing in the book as people of her highest esteem. To her, the Eskimo represents the edge of civilization, the people who encounter life at its most primitive level. Only the Eskimo might survive the suffocating "prayer tunnel" which brings an excruciating death, and Dillard likens this experience to the religious hermit sitting in his cell. The yearning for the edge of experience, almost a wish for death, characterizes the dark side of Dillard's mysticism, but this same passion, this same intensity, allows her to experience the light.

Throughout the book, Dillard affirms the existence of a creator, but what kind of a creator does she imagine? She wonders if the world was created in jest or whether it is "the brainchild of a deranged manic-depressive with limitless capital." Later on she says, "For if God is in one sense the igniter, a fireball that spins over the ground of continents, God is also in another sense the destroyer, lightning, blind power, impartial as the atmosphere." Again, her vision includes both sides of possibility. In one of the most chilling passages in the book, she speculates:

> Could it be that if I climbed the dome of heaven
> and scrabbled and clutched at the beautiful cloth till
> I loaded my fists with a wrinkle to pull, that the
> mask would rip away to reveal a toothless old ugly,
> eyes glazed with delight?

Her conclusion is, finally, that there is no knowing. God is hidden from us. We see, but we cannot understand. The creator "loves pizzaz" on the one hand and creates in "solemn incomprehensible earnest" on the other. His creation can be seen through one eye as "supremely, meticulously created," and through the other eye as "a mindless stutter." The author can only accept what she observes and continue to make her way. Even as she is bound as a sacrifice on the world's altar, "waiting for worms," the moment of understanding, of reality, reappears, and she can go on again. Life can only be accepted as a mystery: "The Lord God of gods, he knoweth."

Looking more closely at Dillard's religious vision, one is struck by an unusual quality. In some ways her attitude is an inversion of conventional religious and philosophical truths. She seems to turn certain beliefs on their heads, so to speak, and views them from a perspective entirely opposite to the accustomed one. The mystic, for example, desires to move from the material world to the spiritual, from the particular to the universal, from the self to God. The mystic strives to leave self, to become "empty" in order to experience the divine. Dillard, who casts herself in the role of the mystic, also strives to become "transfixed and empty," but her attention is focused always on the most minute detail, the most particular of objects—"I never ask why of a vulture or shark, but I ask why of almost every insect I see." Almost as though she desires to become lost in the particular instead of the universal, she explicitly asserts her conviction about the value of "particularity":

> That Christ's incarnation occurred improbably, ridiculously, at such-and-such a time, into such-and-such a place, is referred to—with great sincerity even among believers—as "the scandal of particularity." Well, the "scandal of particularity" is the only world that I, in particular, know. What use has eternity for light? We're all up to our necks in this particular scandal.

In the contemplation of the particular, then, Dillard experiences the divine, but in doing so, she seems almost to become lost in the "lower world" instead of the "higher." Her gaze is concentrated on Tinker Creek, and there she searches for God. She laments the legacy from evolution which separates human beings not only from the creator, but from fellow creatures. By "fellow creatures" she means the animal world and appears to lament that separation more than her separation from fellow human beings: "Adam seems sometimes an afterthought in Eden"; in an inversion of the old philosophical question she asks, "What if I fell in a forest: would a tree hear?" Convinced that Dillard yearns for the purity of animal existence, one critic states that Dillard finds human self-consciousness the "curse of mankind" because it "prevents us from attaining to the purity of animal exist-

ence, absorbed in greater reality." The book, from this view, is dangerous and subversive because of its atavistic and essentially passive views.

Although the critic overstates the case, Dillard realizes the danger of her intense involvement but feels that she saves herself by bringing her own humanity to that world. She also saves herself by interpreting her experiences in human, religious terms, thus bringing the particular and the universal, if not together, at least a bit closer to each other. In her attempt to define the nature of her mysticism, Dillard again demonstrates the paradoxical nature of her thinking. Although she desires to transcend her present self-consciousness and recover her innocence, she wants, at the same time, to remain fully conscious and observant.

> What I call innocence is the spirit's unself-conscious state at any moment of pure devotion to any object. It is at once a receptiveness and total concentration. One needn't be, shouldn't be, reduced to a puppy.

She sees and interprets her world in a highly conscious fashion: "Seeing is of course very much a matter of verbalization. Unless I call my attention to what passes before my eyes, I simply won't see it." Later she says the opposite: "And the second I verbalize this awareness in my brain, I cease to see the mountain or feel the puppy."

What lies at the heart of *Pilgrim at Tinker Creek* is a basic theological problem: How do we explain evil in the world? Dillard tackles this question in theological terms based on her empirical observations of nature. "Creation itself was the fall," she states, implying again the distance between God and the creation. In seeing evil in this fallen world, Dillard stands in a very orthodox Christian tradition, but her conclusions (or lack of them) are far from the traditional Christian answers. Christian theology, broadly speaking, looks at the horror, the chaos, and concludes that hope can be sought only outside the created order—redemption comes from outside and gives hope for a better world, a transformed world. Dillard makes no such claim. Even though she feels the need to affirm a creator, she sees no hope of redemption—she can only "wait and stalk" and continue to wonder.

Another critic puts it rather well: "Here is not only a habitat of cruelty and 'the waste of pain' but the savage and magnificent world of the Old Testament, presided over by a passionate Jehovah, with no Messiah in sight." The creator is there but has not yet been revealed. "Our God shall come," she quotes from an Advent Psalm, "and shall not keep silence; there shall go before him a consuming fire, and a mighty tempest shall be stirred up round about him." The only moments of revelation thus far, for Dillard, have come from the natural world. Nature, or more specifically, the creek, is the mediator in her world. "The creek is the one great giver," she says. "It is, by definition, Christmas, the incarnation." Salvation must come from the natural order, but Dillard is not quite sure how.

On the first page of her book, Dillard introduces her religious questions:

> And some mornings I'd wake in daylight to find my body covered with paw prints in blood; I looked as though I'd been painted with roses. . . . What blood was this, and what roses? It could have been the rose of union, the blood of murder, or the rose of beauty bare and the blood of some unspeakable sacrifice or birth. The sign on my body could have been an emblem or a stain, the keys to the kingdom or the mark of Cain. I never knew. I never knew as I washed, and the blood streaked, faded, and finally disappeared, whether I'd purified myself or ruined the blood sign of the Passover. We wake, if we ever wake at all, to mystery, rumors of death, beauty, violence.

At the end of the book Annie Dillard still has not found the answers to those questions. The purpose of creation and the workings of the creator are still shrouded in mystery.

The final chapter of the book sums up in marvelously inspired prose the lessons which Dillard has learned from her "mystical excursion." She has experienced a deep encounter with the beautiful and the evil and, like Job, has hurled her questions and misgivings at the creator. Although no answers come, it is enough for her that she has been touched and purified by her encounter. She has seen the sign. Given the gift of acute sight, she has dared to look at both sides and to accept them both at the same time.

The power of Dillard's vision arises from her strength to maintain the contradictions within a single vision. The dialectic remains and is accepted without flinching. This book is a profound realization of the author's ability to articulate that vision and, in the face of uncertainty, to move out on a wave of ecstasy.

Mary Davidson McConahay (essay date Fall 1985)

SOURCE: "'Into the Bladelike Arms of God:' The Quest for Meaning through Symbolic Language in Thoreau and Annie Dillard," in *Denver Quarterly*, Vol. 20, No. 2, Fall, 1985, pp. 103-16.

[*In the following essay, McConahay compares Henry David Thoreau's* Walden *to Dillard's* Pilgrim at Tinker Creek, *noting that both writers focus on self in their efforts to explain the universe.*]

> I went to the woods because I wished to live deliberately, to front only the essential facts of life, and see if I could not learn what it had to teach, and not, when I came to die, discover that I had not lived.
>
> Thoreau, *Walden*

> I propose to keep here what Thoreau called "a meteorological journal of the mind," telling some tales and describing some of the sights of this rather tamed valley, and exploring, in fear and trembling, some of the unmapped dim reaches and unholy fastnesses to which those tales and sights so dizzingly lead.
>
> Dillard, ***Pilgrim at Tinker Creek***

Many American writers are uncomfortable with the nonfiction genre. In her 1953 essay "Memoirs, Conversations and Diaries," Elizabeth Hardwick suggests that "the fear of outrageous vanity, of presuming to offer simply one's own ideas and moods, speaking in one's natural voice, which may appear—any number of transgressive adjectives are exact: boastful, presumptive, narcissistic, indulgent," makes writers eschew the first-person non-fiction narrative voice. Annie Dillard herself asks: "Precisely where does journalism or memoir become literature? . . .Formerly the novel was junk entertainment; if you wanted to write significant literature— if you wanted to do art or make an object from idea—you wrote nonfiction. We now think of nonfiction as sincere and artless." However, in her metaphysical exploration ***Pilgrim At Tinker Creek,*** Dillard markedly disavows her own expertise and relies instead on her intuition as "seer" or "observer" to interpret the meaning of human experience. Likewise, Thoreau assumes a similar stance in relating his own wilderness experiment at Walden Pond, even though throughout the work he seems to address his readers, along with the rest of humanity (those of us who lead "lives of quiet desperation") in a rather condescending tone: "If I seem to boast more than is becoming, my excuse is that I brag for humanity rather than for myself; and my shortcomings and inconsistencies do not affect the truth of my statement.

Although the genre uses a deceptively spontaneous tone, a rather off-handed conversational case of expression, the constrictions of the first-person narrative are nonetheless stringent. We are well aware of Thoreau's laborious revisions in achieving the final published version of *Walden*. Although, as Leo Marx reveals in his appraisal of Thoreau's narrative persona, "the hero of *Walden* is a model of self-sufficiency, untroubled by guilt or anxiety or worldly ambition," who "lives out the fantasy of an indefinitely protracted adolescence," we know that Thoreau structured his account after the fact, as it were, to produce an organic literary and philosophical whole. Similarly, Dillard waxes rhapsodic in many early passages of **Pilgrim** as she reveals her own experience of nature. Nevertheless, after having been "nourished by the search within the manifold glories of nature, Dillard straight forwardly admits: "You're writing consciously, off of hundreds of index cards, often distorting the literal truth to achieve an artistic one." While the ideas intrinsic to metaphysical self-exploration germinate from objective observation of the workings of the natural world, in Thoreau's case the writer "begins with things as they are and then proceeds to celebrate them in language that adds meaning to their substance and translates what is fleeting to the level of permanent truth." Thus, the search for self-discovery blends inexorably with one's experience in the natural world.

Thoreau states at the outset that one of his primary aims in undertaking the Walden Pond experiment was to earn his living "by the labor of [his] hands only" (*Walden*), and he hastens to add a justification of the written work as a response to "very particular inquiries made by my townsmen concerning my mode of life." For her part, Dillard seems remarkably unconcerned about such questions, and ignores mundane matters, making few comments justifying her rationale for the journey into solitude.

For each writer, first-hand examination of Nature's mysterious ways is of paramount importance, and both Thoreau and Dillard thrive on the minute observations which only solitude can permit. In meeting Nature head-on, beyond the realm of human society, each writer arrives at an interpretation of the human experience which enables him/her to return to life with an altered, motivating perspective. The insights which Nature provides enable the writer to go back to society rejuvenated and enlightened, better able to cope with a world which had been previously untenable.

The role or position of the naturalist/writer is of extreme importance. What we encounter is actually an artist/catalyst rather than an autobiographer; thus, in the genre, it is essential that we *believe* the writer—that is, that we have faith in his revelations, that we see what he has seen through his writing. The aim of the naturalist/philosopher appears to be less a demonstration of the writer's individual expertise or a factual account of a wilderness experience than a summons to share a similar experience of self through the literary work. The writer encourages his reader to adopt whatever part of the work may be necessary to assist him in making his own discoveries of self. Anhorn suggests that Thoreau "uses his own experiences and revelations as examples of how anyone can derive from himself the authority for his own existence and actions. He is a 'parable maker' and a 'shepherd' of men who teaches his readers to make a religion not of Thoreau, but of himself." Dillard, also, acts as a summoner

in concentrating her focus on the landscape, the minutiae of the creek-world, and diverting the reader's focus from herself. So it is that while we learn next to nothing about Annie Dillard the woman, we approximate her experience. Each writer insists that the human perception of nature around him depends upon an existential commitment to awareness. Thoreau urges: "We must learn to reawaken and keep ourselves awake, not by mechanical aids, but by an infinite expectation of the dawn, which does not forsake us in our soundest sleep" (*Walden*). Dillard repeats Thoreau's message: "To anticipate, not the sunrise and the dawn merely, but, if possible, Nature herself! . . .It is true, I never assisted the sun materially in his rising, but, doubt not, it was of the last importance only to be present at it" (**Pilgrim**). ". . .Beauty and grace are performed whether or not we will or sense them. The least we can do is try to be there" (**Pilgrim**). In order for this revelation to materialize, then, the traditional American "journey into the wilderness" is an inevitable mission.

We readers are not the only ones to recognize the undeniable philosophical parallel between Dillard and Thoreau. Dillard herself repeats passages from Thoreau in **Pilgrim,** and appropriates themes, direction and symbols from her transcendental mentor. Even the shape of the work, the cyclical form of the journey through a calendar year, the focus on sense impressions, and the isolation of the writer could be superimposed on Thoreau's work. The fascinating fact emerges that Thoreau himself seemed to know that a kindred voice would follow his own. It is as though he anticipated his own literary descendant:

> Sometimes, on Sundays I heard the bells . . . when the wind was favorable, a faint, sweet, and as it were, natural melody, worth importing into the wilderness. At a sufficient distance over the woods this sound acquires a certain vibratory hum, as if the pine needles in their horizon were the strings of a harp which it swept . . . There came to me in this case a melody which the air had strained, and which had conversed with every leaf and needle of the wood, that portion of the sound which the elements had taken up and modulated and echoed from vale to vale. The echo is, to some extent, *an original sound,* and therein is the magic and charm of it. It is not merely a repetition of what was worth repeating in the bell. (*Walden*)

Dillard *is* Thoreau's bell, at once the echo who translates his message and the "original sound" who forms a new one. "I walk out," she says, "I see something, some event that would otherwise have been utterly missed and lost; or something sees me, some enormous power brushes me with its clean wing, and I resound like a beaten bell" (**Pilgrim**). "I was still ringing. I had been my whole life a bell, and never knew it until at that moment I was lifted and struck" (***Pilgrim***). She compares her voice to that of a "cast iron bell hung from the arch of my rib cage; when I stirred it rang, or it tolled, a long syllable pulsing ripples up my lungs and down the gritty sap inside my bones, and I couldn't make it out; I felt the voiced vowel like a sigh or a note but I couldn't catch the consonant that shaped it into sense" (***Pilgrim***). It is this symbolic identity that makes Dillard so multidimensional, at once a contemporary oracle and a literary anachronism.

Even more important than Thoreau's experiment in simple living at Walden Pond and Dillard's scientific observations at Tinker Creek are the writers' experimentations with utilizing a central symbol as a universal metaphor for the self. Thoreau's choice of Walden Pond ("earth's eye, looking into which the beholder measures the depth of his own nature"; "a mirror which no stone can crack"; "a great crystal on the surface of the earth"; "the landscape's most beautiful feature"; "a perfect forest mirror") as the site for his retreat assumes direct symbolic meaning. He approaches the pond as he does his inmost self, and finds reflected in its lucid depths truths deep within him. The pond, a body of water with no apparent inlet or outlet, symbolizes the encapsulation of the self, the transcendent identity which Thoreau was convinced he would—given the circumstances of solitude—discover. Walden Pond is Thoreau's "still point at the center of the turning world." Dillard's choice of place as symbol is no less purposeful, although she is stimulated to awareness not by the transfixing gaze of a pond but by the actual movement of Tinker Creek itself on its never-ending journey in the cyclical pattern of Nature. "I had thought to live by the side of the creek in order to shape my life to its free flow," she writes (***Pilgrim***). She returns from the creek "exhilarated or becalmed, but always changed, alive" (***Pilgrim***). Both writers present their symbols as idealized loci which provide the necessary setting for self-discovery. Thoreau tells us:

> Walden is a perfect forest mirror, set round with stones as precious to my eye as if fewer or rarer. Nothing so fair, so pure, and at the same time so large, as a lake, perchance, lies on the surface of the earth. Sky water. It needs no fence. Nations come and go without defiling it. It is a mirror which no stone can crack, whose quicksilver will never wear off, whose gilding Nature continually repairs; no storms, no dust can dim its surface ever fresh;— a mirror in which all impurity presented to it sinks, swept and dusted by the sun's hazy brush . . . which retains no breath that is breathed on it, but sends its own to float as clouds high above its surface, and be reflected in its bosom still. (*Walden*)

while Dillard explains her awareness of her surroundings thus:

> I think of this house clamped to the side of Tinker Creek as an anchor hold. It holds me at anchor to the rock bottom of the creek itself and it keeps me steadied in the current as a sea anchor does, facing the stream of light pouring down. It's a good place to live; there's a lot to think about. The creeks— Tinker and Carvin's—are an active mystery, fresh every minute. (***Pilgrim***)

Whether in flow or in stasis, water symbolizes the inscrutable natural universe that exists as an intermediary between the elements of land and air. The pond and creek assume the totality of the human experience and return it, purified as it were, by a sort of sacramental healing process. In his description of the changeable color of Walden Pond, Thoreau writes: "Lying between the earth and the heavens, it partakes of the color of both" (*Walden*), implying that the pond represents not just its own aqueous element, but it provides insight to the other elements through its reflective power. The truth the pond tells, then, is not a static, immovable verity at all, despite its self-contained nature. Instead, it shimmers and ripples, providing an ever-new vision to the attentive Thoreau. Dillard sees Tinker Creek as the physical emblem of movement and growth which becomes so central to her being. "The creek is the mediator, benevolent, impartial, subsuming my shabbiest evils and dissolving them, transforming them into live moles, and shiners, and sycamore leaves. It is a place even my faithlessness hasn't offended; it still flashes for me, now and tomorrow" (***Pilgrim***).

As symbols, the pond and the creek must necessarily reverberate beyond the confines of the individual self into realms of generalization which expand their immediate meaning. The extended metaphor Thoreau constructs reinforces the meaning of symbol itself: "What I have observed of the pond is no less true in ethics. It is the law of average. Such a rule of the two diameters not only guides us toward the sun in the system and the heart in man, but draws lines through the length and breadth of the aggregate of a man's particular daily behaviors and waves of life into his coves and inlets, and where they intersect will be the height or depth of his character" (*Walden*). Likewise, Dillard embraces the creek as symbol: "I wonder whether what I see and seem to understand about nature is merely one of the accidents of freedom, repeated by chance before my eyes, or whether it has any counterpart in the worlds beyond Tinker Creek" (***Pilgrim***). Like the proverbial concentric circles issuing from a stone tossed into calm water, the symbolic inferences produced by the central images of pond and creek extend meaning beyond the shoreline and the bank of the writer's experiences. While at once providing calm and solace for their residents, both symbols uplift and transport them from self-awareness to higher planes of cosmic awareness. "The creek rests the eye, a haven, a breast; the two steep banks vault from the creek like wings" (***Pilgrim***). For both writers this metaphysical transformation becomes translated into a religious mode of expression which is suggested in Thoreau and explicit in Dillard. The symbols come to reflect not merely the transcendent nature of man, but ultimately the perfect nature of God. Those who behold Walden Pond experience an "activated natural-spiritual nature" and confront their true nature, their soul, their Godlike image, which is purified by the pond. Dillard approaches the creek with a reverence born of spiritual communion with the Creator. "My God, I look at the creek. It is the answer to Merton's prayer 'Give us time!' It never stops. . . . The creek is the One Great Giver. It is, by definition, Christmas, the incarnation" (*Pilgrim*). At this juncture we are confronted with Thoreau and Dillard as symbolist writers, as participants in the tradition of language-exploration. Thus we turn to an examination of how each writer views the "problem of language," its boundless potential, and its ability to produce meaning through paradox.

Dillard . . . comes to voice her praise after enduring an excruciatingly painful observation of a Nature which is *not* benevolent in the least, which destroys, which repeatedly exhibits its grotesque mode of operation.
—*Mary Davidson McConahay*

An obvious contrast between Thoreau's works and those of Annie Dillard might suggest that Thoreau's unquestionable transcendental philosophy allowed him a simpler scope of vision in observing the workings of Nature. His comments on the beauty, simplicity, and efficiency of Nature grow saccharine, perhaps, as a result of his certain optimism. He praises the Creator whose wondrous works make man gape in awe. Dillard, on the other hand, comes to voice her praise after enduring an excruciatingly painful observation of a Nature which is *not* benevolent in the least, which destroys, which repeatedly exhibits its grotesque mode of operation. The paradox, for Dillard, seems clear—if, indeed, the meaning of paradox can ever denote clarity. By embracing the grotesque aspect of Nature which instinctively repels us as an element of the non-static totality of life, of the created universe, and by seeing ourselves as part and parcel of this flux ("The terms are clear: if you want to live, you have to die; you cannot have mountains and creeks without space, and space is a beauty married to a blind man." [*Pilgrim*]), we can actually come to affirm the power of the Creator. "Everything, everything is whole and a parcel of everything else. I myself am falling down, slowly, or slowly lifting up."

A close reading of *Walden* reveals Thoreau's own doubts about the universal goodness of God. Just as Dillard hesitates: "I have been thinking that the landscape of the intri-cate world that I have painted is inaccurate and lopsided. It is too optimistic" (*Pilgrim*). Thoreau offers an uncharacteristic confrontation with the dark underside of the creative process:

> We are cheered when we observe the vulture feeding on the carrion which disgusts and disheartens us and deriving health and strength from the repast . . . I love to see that Nature is so rife with life that myriads can be afforded to be sacrificed and suffered to prey on one another; that tender organizations can be so serenely squashed out of existence like pulp . . . The impression made on a wise man is that of universal innocence. Poison is not poisonous after all, nor are any wounds fatal. Compassion is a very untenable ground. (*Walden*)

So the paradox is faced by both writers, and critics who label either one as purely optimistic or existentially naive ignore this aspect. However, since Thoreau appears unwilling to develop the paradox, it is worthwhile to return to Dillard's self-imposed metaphor of the bell, the resounding echo which provides overtones of meaning to the original tone or message. As she confronts the utter depravity of nature halfway through *Pilgrim* and faces the senseless victimization of the child Julie Norwich, Dillard's alter ego in *Holy the Firm,* the writer must either find a means of interpreting the horrible along with the exhilarating aspects of life or give up. She reaches a point of crisis similar to the horrors faced by Melville, and although she does not rail against Thoreauvian or Emersonian optimism, we suspect she finds their unquestioning acceptance of Nature's destructive element frustrating. She voices her deepest doubts, and balances between a forced rationalism and a hopeless desperation: "I suppose it is the teeming evidence that birth and growth, which we value, are ubiquitous and blind, that life itself is so astonishingly cheap, that nature is as careless as it is bountiful, and that with extravagance goes a crushing waste that will one day include our own cheap lives" (*Pilgrim*). No doubt it is at this point that Dillard takes issue with Thoreau's chapter ("Economy") which describes the simple needs of the animals and the satisfaction man would experience if he could only approximate these basic requirements of life. Thus she is forced, paradoxically, to discover meaning in the grotesque, to pursue that which unhinges her perception of the beauty of nature. She poses this paradox: "Do we need more victims to remind us that we're all victims? Is this some sort of parade for which a conquering army shines up its terrible guns and rolls them up and down the streets for the people to see?" (*Holy*). Grumbach interprets Dillard's despair: "The maniac (God) seems to be in charge of the bitter and pied world of nature she describes at such length, with such precision, and so lovingly—a world that exists side-by-side with Thoreau's benign and God-directed beauty." For Dillard, the collision with the grotesque becomes an issue of unending existential proportions. "What do we think of the created universe, spanning an unthinkable void with an unthinkable profusion of forms? . . . Or what do we think of nothingness, those sickening reaches of time in either direction?" (*Pilgrim*).

Suddenly, through the medium of language, Dillard experiences a revelation akin to that of Thoreau atop Mount Katahdin. In viewing humanity as such a minute portion of the complexity of all creation, she admits: "It could be that our faithlessness is a cowering cowardice born of our very smallness, a massive failure of imagination" (*Pilgrim*). When she comes to accept her own role in the dynamic "hurdy-gurdy of time" (*Holy*), the paradox of the grotesque can be transformed into affirmation. Perhaps Dillard recalls the suggestion of Thomas Merton: "Decision begins with the acceptance of one's own finiteness, one's own limitation, in fact, one's own nothingness. But when one's own nothingness is seen as a matter of personal choice, of free acceptance, and not as part of the vast, formless void of the anonymous mass, it acquires a name, a presence, a voice, an option in the actions of the real world." Dillard admits that natural phenomena are not in any real sense necessary per se to the world or to its creator. "Nor am I. The creation in the first place, being itself, is the only necessity, for which I would die, and I shall" (*Pilgrim*). The catalyst for Dillard's arrival at this point of self-realization is the operation of language itself, for "seeing is of course very much a matter of verbalization" (*Pilgrim*). For Dillard, the ability to see steadily and unflinchingly is the same as the ability to order.

At first, Dillard fears that resolution is impossible, and she doubts, as does Thoreau, the ability of language to produce any sort of transferable meaning—that is, meaning which will reach beyond individual interpretation. In her introduction to her collection of critical essays **Living By Fiction,** Dillard poses the following questions: "Is the search for meaning among the high heaps of the meaningless a fool's game? Is it art's game? What is (gasp) the relationship between the world and the mind? Is knowledge possible? Do we ever discover meaning, or do we always make it up?" She continues: "Knowledge is impossible. We are precisely nowhere, sinking on an entirely imaginary ice floe, into entirely imaginary seas themselves adrift" (*Holy*). The paradox, of course, is that resolution comes only *through language,* which is itself suggestive and imprecise. Thoreau feared the inadequacy of language to express his ideas, but felt instinctively that the writer could transcend this barrier. "A written word is the choicest of relics. It is something at once more intimate with us and more universal than any other work of art. It is the work of art nearest to life itself" (*Walden*). Yet Thoreau questions his own ability to convey essential meaning. "I fear chiefly lest my expression not be *extravagant* enough, may not wander enough beyond the narrow limits of my daily experience, so as to be adequate to the truth of which I have been convinced; . . . the volatile truth of our words should continually betray the inadequacy of the residual statement. Their truth is instantly *translated*; its literal monument alone remains" (*Walden*). Ultimately, Dillard and Thoreau must invest all their hope in the innate power of language, however weighted with subjective referents and elusive symbols it may be, which alone enables man to interpret the totality of human experience. It is, quite literally, the only tool we have. Thus, instead of turning from the ambiguity of language in frustration, Dillard comes to realize that although language cannot signify things as they are, because none of us knows things as they are, a writer's language "does an airtight job of signifying his *perceptions* of things as they are" (*Living*).

Symbols, then, as constructs of language, can be at once "personalized" by individual perception and "shared" because they spring from agreed-upon conventions of meaning (*Living*). Paradoxically, they are formed *from* language and yet they almost simultaneously escape definition *through* language. As we confront the presence of symbols in *Walden* and ***Pilgrim at Tinker Creek,*** we begin to realize the explosive potential of symbolic meaning itself. "Language is weighted with referents. It is like a beam of light on Venus. The writer, unlike the painter, sculptor, or composer, cannot form his ideas of order directly in his materials; for as soon as he writes the least noun, the whole world starts pouring onto his page . . ." "There is no such thing as a *mere* symbol. When you climb to the higher levels of abstraction, symbols, those enormous, translucent planets, are all there is. They are at once your only tools of knowledge and that knowledge's only object" (*Living*). Through affirmation of this paradox, Dillard admits that we must dedicate ourselves to continual reinterpretation of symbols if meaning through language can ever be achieved. ***Pilgrim at Tinker Creek*** stands not as a repetition of Thoreau's in *Walden* but as a symbolic extension of the work. Dillard's sense of order relies on this "unique cognitive property of symbol: there is no boundary, and probably no difference, between symbol and the realm it comes to mean" (*Living*).

William J. Scheick (essay date 1985)

SOURCE: "Annie Dillard: Narrative Fringe," in *Contemporary American Women Writers: Narrative Strategies,* edited by Catherine Rainwater and William J. Scheick, University Press of Kentucky, 1985, pp. 51-63.

[*In the essay below, Scheick discusses the narrative structure of Dillard's works and the junctions she creates between elements in her narrative.*]

We wake, if we ever wake at all, to mystery," says Annie Dillard at the beginning of *Pilgrim at Tinker Creek* (1974). This remark is a thesis statement, not only for *Pilgrim at Tinker Creek* but also for Dillard's *Tickets for a Prayer Wheel* (1974), *Holy the Firm* (1977), and *Teaching a Stone to Talk* (1982). So inscrutable is this mystery of creation, Dillard explains, that the best one can do in life is to "discover at least *where* it is that we have been so startlingly set down, if we can't learn why" (*Pilgrim at Tinker Creek*): "There is nothing to be done about it, but ignore it, or see" (*Pilgrim at Tinker Creek*). Seeing is everything for Dillard: "All I want to do is stay awake, keep my head up, prop my eyes open, with toothpicks" (*Pilgrim at Tinker Creek*). In her writings, her Thoreauvian "meteorological journal[s] of the mind" (*Pilgrim at Tinker Creek*), Dillard seeks to awaken the reader to a new way of seeing, to make the reader undergo a radical change of vision tantamount to a conversion experience; "I am not making chatter," Dillard warns, "I mean to change his life" (*Pilgrim at Tinker Creek*).

This new perception in the reader is evoked by Dillard's language. Language, however, is an ambiguous instrument. On the one hand, "seeing is . . . very much a matter of verbalization" for Dillard, who says, "unless I call attention to what passes before my eyes, I simply won't see it" (*Pilgrim at Tinker Creek*). On the other hand, she notes later in her first book, "the second I verbalize this awareness in my brain, I cease to see" (*Pilgrim at Tinker Creek*). Reconciling these two remarks is not easy. In the latter comment Dillard stresses the paradox of language; language focuses on, and at the same time inadvertently veers away from, that which is seen. Language displaces the perceived object and in this sense conceals what it tries to reveal: "In order to make a world in which their ideas might be discovered, writers embody those ideas in materials solid and opaque, and thus conceal them." This ambiguous capacity of language to reveal and conceal mimics nature, which also, according to Dillard, "does reveal as well as conceal" some mystery. Especially the mystery of natural beauty appears to be a "language to which we have no key; it is the mute cipher, the cryptogram, the uncracked, unbroken code" (*Pilgrim at Tinker Creek*).

For Dillard, language is important as language, however vexing its failure to signify things as they are. The mysterious matrix between seeing and not seeing that constitutes verbalization is, for Dillard, intrinsically artful. For her the matrix of language "is a selection and abstraction from unknowable flux"; "language is itself like a work of art" insofar as "it selects, abstracts, exaggerates, and orders" (*Living by Fiction*). Implicitly artful, language achieves its highest ends for Dillard when it is directed by a writer to function within a still more encompassing artful structure designed to awaken a reader to the mystery of natural beauty. "Art is the creation of coherent contexts," Dillard says in *Living by Fiction:* "The work of art may, like a magician's

act, pretend to any degree of spontaneity, randomality, of whimsy, so long as the effect of the whole is calculated and unified" (*Living by Fiction*). In other words, just as in nature "from follows function" (*Pilgrim at Tinker Creek*), so too should form follow function in literary art, especially literary art concerning nature. Throughout her writings Dillard strives for a calculated and unified narrative manner that exemplifies the intrinsic artistry of language and of nature, a revealing and concealing manner designed to evoke in her readers a mode of seeing equivalent to her own experience of rapt concentration on the mysterious mute cipher of natural beauty.

Dillard's narrative manner creates a laminal space between verbalizing the seen (revealed surfaces) and seeing beyond what can be verbalized (concealed depths). For Dillard nature abounds with revealed surfaces and concealed depths: "nature is very much a now-you-see-it, now-you-don't affair" (*Pilgrim at Tinker Creek*). Sometimes nature's opaque surfaces become translucent, when an influx of light can give the human perceiver a sense of the depth and continuity of nature. Dillard remarks one of these occasions near the conclusion of *Pilgrim at Tinker Creek:* "A kind of northing is what I wish to accomplish, a single-minded trek toward that place where any shutter left open to the zenith at night will record the wheeling of all the sky's stars as a pattern of perfect concentric circles." At such a time nature's light intimates some unifying order—the perfect concentric circles of the stars—some underlying continuity or code at the heart (depths) of the mute cipher that is natural beauty. For most of us such moments of "enlightenment" are rare, and Dillard's wish to "stay awake" derives from her aim to "change [her reader's] life," to make her reader—like camera film on which "the moment's light prints"—more sensitive to occasions when nature's opacity transforms into translucence. Although as a part of creation we can never know the whole of which we are a part, during such moments of translucency we receive hints of an overall artistic design informing the mysterious language of natural beauty. These moments of translucency reveal the laminal edge of the particular (the temporal, the opaque surface) where it touches the universal (the eternal, the transparent depth). This laminal edge is most often detected at the margin of nature's particulars; the tops of mountains, for example, are "serrated edges . . . so thin they are translucent" and the breaking waves evince an edge of "live water and light" that is "translucent, laving, roiling with beauty" (*Pilgrim at Tinker Creek*).

Sometimes Dillard refers to this laminal edge as a *hemline* between eternity (spirit) and time (matter) in nature, "a fabric of spirit and sense so grand and subtle, so powerful in a new way, that we can only feel blindly of its hem" (*Pilgrim at Tinker Creek*). Most often Dillard refers to this edge as a *fringe*—the fringe of a bird's wing or of a fish's fin, for example. "Spirit and matter are a fringed matrix," Dillard explains; "intricacy means that there is a fluted fringe to the something that exists over against nothing, a fringe that rises and spreads, burgeoning in detail" (***Pilgrim at Tinker Creek***). This fringe demarcates where the terror (matter) and beauty (spirit) of life intersect, for "terror and a beauty insoluble are a ribband of blue woven into the fringes of garments of things both great and small" (***Pilgrim at Tinker Creek***).

The intersection of this terror and beauty is "God's Tooth" (***Holy the Firm***), where life is flayed and frayed. "All our intricate fringes, however beautiful, are really the striations of a universal and undeserved flaying" (***Pilgrim at Tinker Creek***), Dillard observes, for "the world is actual and fringed, pierced here and there, and through and through, with the toothed conditions of time and the mysterious, coiled spring of death" (***Pilgrim at Tinker Creek***): "we the living are nibbled and nibbling—not held aloft on a cloud in the air but bumbling pitted and scarred and broken through a frayed and beautiful land" (***Pilgrim at Tinker Creek***).

For Dillard this frayed laminal edge raises as many doubts as it seems to provide affirmative answers about the meaning of life. The terror of the flaying of life seems balanced by the beauty of the fraying of life. Even if Dillard cannot confidently affirm that "the frayed and nibbled fringe of the world is a tallith, a prayer shawl" (***Pilgrim at Tinker Creek***), she knows that "beauty is real" within "the intricate fringe of spirit's free incursions into time" (***Pilgrim at Tinker Creek***); that is, given the reality of the intricate beauty of nature's cryptogram, Dillard accepts life's "undeserved flaying" as a mystery within an overall artistic design in nature, within a divine artistry providing—like literary art, in Dillard's opinion—a calculated, coherent, and unified context.

For Dillard all art, literary or natural, conveys this frayed laminal fringe. For her great art is "juncture itself, the socketing of eternity into time and energy into form" (***Living by Fiction***). Great art conveys "the rim of knowledge" (***Living by Fiction***), where beauty and terror intersect. In her own art Dillard tries to depict this frayed intersection of matter and spirit, of the temporal and the eternal, of opaque surfaces and translucent depths, of terror and beauty. In her art Dillard relies on a narrative fringe, a laminal edge where the reader glimpses the rim or hemline between time and eternity.

Holy the Firm is an excellent example of this narrative technique. Like ***Pilgrim at Tinker Creek, Holy the Firm*** cues the reader to its author's technique whenever it specifically refers to the "serrate margin of time," to "the fringey edge where elements meet and realms mingle, where time and eternity spatter each other with foam." ***Holy the Firm*** also emphasizes the figure of the artist as someone who encounters the "lunatic fringe" (***Pilgrim at Tinker Creek***), someone who *sees* the intersection of matter and spirit in the world as well as in himself or herself. In Dillard's opinion, the artist spans "all the long gap with the length of his love, in flawed imitation of Christ on the cross stretched both ways unbroken and thorned. So must the work be also, in touch with, in touch with, in touch with; spanning the gap, from here to eternity" (***Holy the Firm***). In ***Holy the Firm*** Dillard achieves a narrative fringe suggesting this terrible and beautiful Christlike intersection of time and eternity.

Ostensibly ***Holy the Firm*** consists of a journal record of three days, 18-20 November, recording Dillard's thoughts about a seven-year-old girl named Julie Norwich, who on the 19th had her face severely burned and disfigured by an exploding airplane. At first the reader of ***Holy the Firm*** might anticipate a narrative governed by a linear, sequential sense of time. The narrative, however, consists of various fragments without evident transitions, a narrative collage, depriving the reader of a comfortable sense of continuity at the level of narrative surface. At one point Dillard suddenly and without transition warns the reader, who has already been having trouble detecting a temporal narrative progression in the book, that "nothing is going to happen in this book. There is only a little violence here and there in the language, at the corner where eternity clips time" (***Holy the Firm***). Referring here to a correspondence between her narrative technique (her narrative fringe) and the laminal edges (the intersections of eternity and time) glimpsed in nature, Dillard suggests that for a sense of continuity in her book one must look not at the surface of temporal details, but into the depths of their eternal significance.

In fact ***Holy the Firm*** commences with an impressionistic account of the author awakening to exigent sunlight on the morning of November 18. This event is presented as an experience of a laminal edge in nature, when eternity and time intersect, "when holiness holds forth in time" (***Holy the Firm***). In lieu of temporal sequential narration as the sun rises there is rapture, and this rapture is epitomized by the waking author's only spoken word, an inarticulate but reverent "Oh" (***Holy the Firm***). To her awakening senses, especially her sight, the day becomes ever more sharply focused until "the sky clicks securely in place over the mountains, locks around the islands, snaps slap on the bay" (***Holy the Firm***). This brief experience of translucence at the "serrate margin of time," of an illuminated depth intimating an underlying divinity—"I wake in a god" (***Holy the Firm***)—in nature, coalesces with the opaque particulars of mountains, islands, and bay clicking securely into place. Then the reader suddenly encounters without transition another narrative beginning, one of a conventional sort: "I live on northern Puget Sound, in Washington State, alone. I have a gold cat, who sleeps on my legs, named Small" (*Holy the Firm*). However much the reader might prefer this fulfillment of a conventional expectation of a narrative, he or she will not find sufficient continuity at the surface level of *Holy the Firm*; the absence of this continuity at the linear, temporal narrative level urges the reader to find it elsewhere in Dillard's book. In *Holy the Firm* continuity is intimated, just as in nature an underlying continuity is intimated. In Dillard's work this underlying continuity is suggested by her narrative fringe—moments when surface details in her account are brought to the edge of visibility, where momentarily they lose their revealed and verbalizable temporal surface opacity (their "thingness," their conventional meaning) and seem—to author and reader—to become translucent; in *Holy the Firm,* as in nature for Dillard, this translucency suggests a concealed and unverbalizable, eternal depth, where an artlike continuity and design can be faintly detected.

Consider, for instance, the islands Dillard sees from her home on northern Puget Sound. These islands are first mentioned in the opening impressionistic account of morning sunlight, and in this account the islands emerge as if from the dawn of creation: "Islands slip blue from [the god-of-day's] shoulders and glide over the water . . . [as] the sky clicks securely in place . . . [and] locks round" them (*Holy the Firm*). The islands attain increasing temporal reality until they become "unimaginably solid islands" (*Holy the Firm*). Dillard tries to draw a key to the islands seen from her window and she wishes to discover their names. But the names vary from one source to another, and Dillard eventually realizes the futility of her desire to fix each island temporally with a name, as if a name could designate the essential definition of the chunk of land it apparently identifies.

The trouble is that these islands exist, from Dillard's perspective, "at the world's rim" (*Holy the Firm*), and occasionally she receives hints that something else, perhaps other islands, exist just beyond her usual range of vision on the horizon. On November 18, for example, "a veil of air" lifts, and Dillard sees "a new island . . . the deepening of wonder, behind the blue translucence the sailor said was Salt Spring Island," an island newly seen, the name of which she has "no way of learning" (*Holy the Firm*). "The deepening of wonder": the newly seen island signifies more than another temporal solidity; it becomes a metaphoric index to a pervasive continuum within creation that evokes wonder, a continuum that includes something spiritual beyond the horizon of the phenomenological. On the horizon perceived by our reading mind's eye Dillard's image of islands transubstantiates into a metaphor for spiritual insight, even as on November 18 the actual islands before her eyes give a glimpse of their origins from within the deep continuum of eternity and time. It is a matter of seeing: "I see it! I see it all! Two islands, twelve islands, worlds, gather substance, gather the blue contours of time, and array themselves down

distance, mute and hard" (*Holy the Firm*). As perceived from the window of her room and—since "this room is a skull" (*Holy the Firm*)—from the window of her eyes, these islands indicate for Dillard that sometimes nature's temporal solid surfaces can momentarily become translucent; when this happens with the islands at the rim of the world, she gets a glimpse of the "serrate margin of time" where eternity and time intersect in a way intimating a continuity of an artlike design or purpose within creation:

> And now outside the window, deep on the horizon, a new thing appears, as if we needed a new thing. It is a new land blue beyond islands, hitherto hidden by haze and now revealed, and as dumb as the rest. I check my chart, my amateur penciled sketch of the skyline. Yes, this land is new, this spread blue spark beyond yesterday's new wrinkled line, beyond the blue veil a sailor said was Salt Spring Island. How long can this go on? But let us by all means extend the scope of our charts.

> I draw it as I seem to see it, a blue chunk fitted just so beyond islands, a wag of graphite rising just here above another anonymous line, and here meeting the slope of Salt Spring: though whether this be headland I see or heartland, or the distance-blurred bluffs of a hundred bays, I have no way of knowing, or if it be island or main. I call it Thule, O Julialand, Time's Bad News; I name it Terror, the Farthest Limb of the Day, God's Tooth.

> [*Holy the Firm*]

Just as the newly seen island gave Dillard a glimpse of the rim of the world, the "serrate margin of time," God's Tooth, where eternity and time interpenetrate, so too in the above passage does Dillard's prose, her narrative fringe, convey to the reader translucent hints of a transcendental significance to the temporal specificity of the islands she sees in Puget Sound.

When, in the foregoing long quotation, Dillard refers to the newly seen island as a "spread blue spark" she coalesces the image of the island and another image important in her management of narrative in *Holy the Firm:* the image of fire. Late in the book, in fact, she "sees" the "islands on fire," a "thousand new islands today, uncharted . . . on fire and dimming" (*Holy the Firm*). In Dillard's mystical perception all of nature burns, as if, like the burning morning described at the opening of the account, everything in nature ceaselessly emanates from the dawn of creation at the margin of time. In *Holy the Firm* Dillard develops this image of fire in her remarks concerning the attraction of moths to flames. She describes in detail the fate of a golden female moth, with a two-inch wing span, that flew into the flame of Dillard's candle. Dillard describes in succession the burning of the moth's six legs, two antennae, and various mouth parts—each fact emphasizing the physical reality of the moth. Her final description reads, "And then this moth-essence, this spectacular skeleton, began to act as a wick. She kept burning. The wax rose in the moth's body from her soaking abdomen to her thorax to the jagged hole where her head should be, and widened into flame, a saffron-yellow flame that robed her to the ground like any immolating monk. That candle had two wicks, two flames of identical height, side by side. The moth's head was fire. She burned for two hours, until I blew her out" (*Holy the Firm*). This image of the moth with a head of fire surfaces from time to time in *Holy the Firm,* but the specificity and opacity of its phenomenological surface reality as described in Dillard's introduction of the image is transformed until the image becomes a translucent emblem signifying the artist.

Dillard subtly prepares the reader for this metamorphosis of the image of the burning moth by noting that at the time of the moth's immolation she was reading James Ramsey Ullman's *The Day on Fire,* a novel about Rimbaud, who, Dillard says, "burnt out his brains in a thousand poems" (*Holy the Firm*). Like the moth's head of flame, the artist's "face is flame . . . lighting the kingdom of God for the people to see; his life goes up in the works" (*Holy the Firm*). This remark, appearing late in the book, requires the reader to perceive a deeper meaning in the apparently mundane destruction of a moth by a candle flame; it also requires the reader to interpret differently the extraordinary accident that produced Julie Norwich's burned face. Julie, the reader is told at the end of the book, is "like the moth in wax, [her] life a wick, [her] head on fire with prayer, held utterly, outside and in" (*Holy the Firm*). Julie, who looks somewhat like Dillard, has come to know the experience of the artist, the experience of Rimbaud, with his burnt-out brains, and of Dillard: "I am moth, I am light" (*Holy the Firm*). By coalescing the images of the moth, Julie, herself, and the artist, Dillard creates a narrative fringe where specific concrete, ordinary particulars of life become translucent signifiers of continuity and design, depths of meaning below phenomenological surfaces.

Dillard's images of "islands on fire," a moth's "head on fire," and a child's face on fire coalesce with her images of seraphs, saints, and nuns in *Holy the Firm.* The artist's "face is flame like a seraph's" (*Holy the Firm*), and seraphs "are aflame with love of God"; "they can sing only the first 'Holy' before the intensity of their love ignites them again and dissolves them again, perpetually, into flames" (*Holy the Firm*). In Julie's tragic accident Dillard sees an emblem of the artist's face burning like that of a seraph. Just as the moth with the burning head looks "like a hollow saint, like a flame-faced virgin gone to God" (*Holy the Firm*), so too Julie, "like the moth . . . [with her] head on fire," becomes

a nun in the service of the divinity behind nature: "You might as well be a nun" (*Holy the Firm*). A "nun lives in the fires of the spirit" (*Holy the Firm*), Dillard mentions early in the book; and such a nun is like an artist who—like the moth, Julie, and a seraph—has a face of flame, is like Dillard herself: "I'll be the nun for you. I am now" (*Holy the Firm*).

At first Dillard's image of the nun appears in a literal context. We are told that Julie once dressed Dillard's cat in a "curious habit" so that the cat "looked like a nun" (*Holy the Firm*). We have no sense yet of how this episode foreshadows what will happen to Julie; nor do we anticipate that the violence of Julie's conversion of the cat into a nun—she rammed the cat into the dress and hit it on its face—adumbrates the violence—the exploding airplane—that will hit Julie's face and convert her, metaphorically, into a nun. Later in the book these specific, opaque, temporal details become translucent when they intimate some "eternal" truth about the artist; then they intimate that some aesthetic continuity informs the design both of nature and of Dillard's work.

That Dillard's artistry reflects the underlying design of nature is also suggested by the imagery of the arch in *Holy the Firm.* In the impressionistic rendering of sunrise that commences the book we read that "today's god," objectified in the sun, "arches, cupping sky in his belly; he vaults, vaulting and spread, holding all" (*Holy the Firm*). Even at night Dillard senses this divine arch as she stands "under the ribs of Orion" (*Holy the Firm*). This macrocosmic arch is microcosmically reflected in every human being, who possesses within him or herself "buttressed vaults of . . . ribs" (*Holy the Firm*). Insects, too, exhibit this pattern when, for instance, dead moths become "arcing strips of chitin . . . like a jumble of buttresses for cathedral domes" (*Holy the Firm*). Within macrocosmic and microcosmic expressions of nature is manifested an arched place of worship.

The act of worship within vaulted and vaulting nature is itself an act of arching, of arced burning—"light arches" (*Holy the Firm*). This image of arching or arcing becomes translucent—suggestive of a deeper significance—when it coalesces with Dillard's fire and nun, or saint, imagery. In *Holy the Firm* all creation is depicted as immolated in a flaming service arching toward the divinity behind nature; all creation worships—that is, burns—in nature's church: the cathedral-like buttresses that are within each natural form besides being characteristic of nature generally. A moth with a head of fire, a little girl flamefaced, a seraph aflame with love of God—everything burns and arches as it "flutter[s] . . . in tiny arcs" (*Holy the Firm*). Even the exploding airplane, which snagged its wing on a tree, like a moth "fluttered in a tiny are" (*Holy the Firm*). All nature arches, burns, or prays with love, "vaulting . . . [with] love . . . and arcing to the realm of spirit bare" (*Holy the Firm*).

Especially the nunlike artist burns, or prays; like the moth, like Julie, like the seraph, the artist has a head of arcing flame. The artist's work archlike "span[s] the gap, from here to eternity" (*Holy the Firm*). This mystical worship, or burning, of the artist through the arcing art work, however, remains earthbound; the artist's are strives heavenward "till 'up' ends by curving back" (*Holy the Firm*): "Eternity sockets twice into time[,] and space curves" (*Holy the Firm*). Even the islands at the rim of creation, at "the fringey edges where . . . realms mingle," seem to burn, to arch, between two sockets of an eternity intimated by the blank spread of water and the spread of sky. The coalescing of the image of arcing or arching with the images of island, fire, and nuns—artists—occurs in Dillard's narrative fringe, where the temporal opacity of these images seems to become translucent—where pushed to the edge of their conventional meanings they "enlighteningly" intimate some artlike divine pattern in the depths of creation.

The image of arcing or arching, moreover, informs the narrative structure of *Holy the Firm*, which comprises three essays that record Dillard's thoughts during three successive days in November. The first day, Wednesday, is a newborn and salted day socketed into eternity. It is a day of intense worship, of prayerful arching, for the artistnun who celebrates how the god of day "sockets into everything that is, and that right holy" (*Holy the Firm*).

On Thursday, in contrast, Julie Norwich has her face burned by an exploding airplane. Thursday, the date of the second essay of *Holy the Firm*, is characterized by a downward arc, the reverse of the upward thrust of the preceding day and of the first essay in the book. On this second day Dillard descends into the dark night of the soul, where she contemplates the fact of Julie's terrible suffering. Nervous, rattled, Dillard sits by her window and chews the bones in her wrist. Since she and Julie look somewhat alike, Julie's fate seems to bear implications concerning Dillard's own fate—a bleak prospect as Dillard stares out the window at "no wind, and no hope of heaven . . . since the meanest of people show more mercy than hounding and terrorist gods" (*Holy the Firm*). Dillard confronts the "evidence of things seen: one Julie, one sorrow, one sensation bewildering the heart, and enraging the mind, and causing [Dillard] to look at the world stuff appalled. Little wonder that she chews the bones in her wrist as her doubts begin to border on severe skepticism:

> Has God a hand in this? Then it is a good hand. But has he a hand at all? Or is he a holy fire burning self-contained for power's sake alone? Then he knows himself blissfully as flame unconsuming, as all brilliance and beauty and power, and the rest of us can go hang. Then the accidental universe spins mute, obedient only to its own gross terms, meaningless, out of mind, and alone. The universe is nei-

ther contingent upon nor participant in the holy, in being itself, the real, the power play of fire. The universe is illusion merely, not one speck of it real, and we are not only its victims, falling always into or smashed by a planet slung by its sun—but also its captives, bound by the mineral-made ropes of our senses.

[*Holy the Firm*]

Julie's tragedy and Dillard's dark night of the soul position them both at the Thule-like fringe of life and of its meaning—the fringe where they are torn by God's Tooth.

Friday, the third day, recorded in the third essay of the book, is marked by a slow but certain recovery from the near despair of the preceding day. Having kept awake in order to deal with sobering thoughts through the night and through the dark night of the soul, Dillard drinks boiled coffee as morning begins to arrive. With morning comes her acceptance of the fact "that we are created, *created*, sojourners in a land we did not make, a land with no meaning of itself and no meaning we can make for it alone. Who are we to demand explanations of God?" (*Holy the Firm*). Faith arcs within her as she reaffirms that a Christlike "spanning the gap, from here to eternity" is our destiny, especially evident in the burning worship of nun-artists such as Julie and Dillard. Dillard's arcing forth reaffirms the reality of a pattern within "the one glare of holiness": "the world in spectacle perishing ever, and ever renewed" (*Holy the Firm*). The perishing, or downward are, of Thursday transforms into the renewal, or upward are, of Friday, and the third essay in *Holy the Firm* appropriately concludes with a celebration of the arrival of morning that recalls the ecstatic celebration of morning at the start of the first essay: "Mornings, when light spreads over the pastures like wings, and fans a secret color into everything, and beats the trees senseless with beauty, so that you can't tell whether the beauty is in the trees—dazzling in cells like yellow sparks or green flashing waters—or *on* them—a transfiguring silver air charged with the wings' invisible motion; mornings, you won't be able to walk for the power of it: earth's too round" (*Holy the Firm*).

> **Neither the structure of [*Holy the Firm*], with its seemingly contradictory variations in mood and its nonlinear progression of narrative, nor its style, with its many interfacing images, permits the reader any certain reliance on firmness of detail.**
> **—*William J. Scheick***

Just as the earth is round and the diurnal cycle comes round to morning, so moves the tripartite pattern of faith, doubt, and faith renewed. Faith and doubt compose a continuum similar to the juncture of eternity and time. The arcing affirmation of the opening and closing sections of *Holy the Firm* dramatizes how "eternity sockets twice into time[,] and space curves." The beginning and ending of *Holy the Firm* are socketed into eternity; they are with faith upward into eternity. The downward curve—doubt—of the middle section of the book is merely the lower half of the mystical circle, or roundness, of creation. The uppermost are of this circle, toward which the opening and closing passage of the book tend, remains veiled in mystery as are the spread sea and sky which surround the are of each island Dillard tries to map. What is important is the fact that "space curves," that the very curve of either the upward are of faith or the downward are of doubt implies circular completion. This implied circular continuum is what nature at once reveals (in the arcs we perceive) and conceals (the completed circuits we cannot see but which we intuit). For Dillard, this circular continuum combining time (the seen) and eternity (the unseen) is the origin of art—"any work of art symbolizes juncture itself, the socketing of eternity into time and energy into form" (*Living by Fiction*); this circular continuum is also the foundation of hope, for our consideration of the "world as a text . . . as a work of art . . . . absolutely requires that we posit an author for it" (*Living by Fiction*).

Where eternity and time are twice socketed in this circular reality is God's Tooth, where "holiness splinter[s] into a vessel" (*Holy the Firm*), where terror (splintering) and beauty (holiness) interface, where matter (vessel) and energy (holiness) intersect. Julie's story is an instance of "holiness splintered into a vessel" at the frayed fringe of creation. To tell Julie's story and her own story—for she and Julie are somewhat alike as nun-artists—Dillard manages a narrative structure and a narrative technique that convey a sense of this juncture of time and eternity by "expand[ing] the arc of the comprehended world" to "the rim of knowledge where language falters" (*Living by Fiction*). The narrative structure of *Holy the Firm* begins with an arc of affirmation, curves downward into doubt, and then with renewed faith arcs upward again. The total, circular configuration of this narrative structure suggests that the two upward arcs are veiled in mystery but nonetheless apparently meet in a divinity which gives meaning, purpose, and design to all of creation abiding in the lower half of this mystical circle. This narrative structure in *Holy the Firm* is reinforced by Dillard's technique of narrative fringe: moments when surface details, such as islands, flames, nuns, and arcs, in her account are brought to the edge of visibility at the rim of their conventional meaning, where momentarily they lose their revealed temporal surface opacity (their usual sense) and seem to become translucent—that is, they suggest a concealed "eternal" depth, or significance, where an artlike continuity and design in nature and in Dillard's book can be faintly detected.

Neither the structure of the book, with its seemingly contradictory variations in mood and its nonlinear progression of narrative, nor its style, with its many interfacing images, permits the reader any certain reliance on firmness of detail. The underlying firmness, or significance, of what is narrated in Dillard's book must be sought elsewhere by the reader; it must be sought in the hinted at holy depths beneath the opaque surface details made translucent in Dillard's narrative fringe. In these depths the reader glimpses "holy the firm"—an underlying continuity and design which is at once the revealed and concealed secret of nature and the revealed and concealed art of Dillard's book.

Elaine Tietjen (essay date Summer 1988)

SOURCE: "Perceptions of Nature: Annie Dillard's *Pilgrim at Tinker Creek,*" in *North Dakota Quarterly,* Vol. 56, No. 3, Summer, 1988, pp. 101-13.

[*In the essay below, Tietjen argues that Dillard focuses too much on individual experience in* Pilgrim at Tinker Creek *and misleads the reader.*]

She stared as if she were about to tell me that she dreamed last night of hanging in space above our blue planet. With her leather jacket, loose wool pants, serious hiking boots, and a collecting pouch slung over her neck, she looked the perfect image of the woodswoman I desperately wanted to become. Her cornsilk hair was lit up like a lamp. Annie Dillard sat on a ledge in a clearing, beckoning the reader to come into her woods. I held her Pulitzer Prize-winning book on my lap in the back of an old bus, headed for Canyonlands.

Pilgrim at Tinker Creek was one of three books I took into the wilderness for a semester of expeditions in the Rockies. Edward Abbey's *Desert Solitaire* and Aldo Leopold's *Sand County Almanac* both waited in my pack. Up until two weeks before, I had never heard of Dillard, but the sheer force of her image on the cover convinced me to buy her book. The cover said *Pilgrim* was "a mystical excursion into the natural world." So I read it first. I was glad the trip to Utah was a long one; I had to savor each paragraph three or four times and stare out the window at the rolling world, dumbfounded.

Dillard liked to exaggerate, I discovered, but she convinced me to believe her buoyant claims. Here was a power in language I had never heard before from a woman, or from anyone really—a freedom to be wild, deep, outrageous, exposed. Her voice was confident, striding, and then unashamedly silly. Dillard had me to herself for days.

I had enrolled in this outdoor education program to experience the "essence" of wilderness. I wanted an ultimate physical and spiritual baptism, to see if I, like Thoreau, could live deliberately. As I opened Dillard's book I was looking for a like mind and an affirmation that life meant something serious. Surrounded by sixteen fellow students who spent the bus ride comparing beer brands and former girlfriends, I wanted to talk about evolution, plant dispersal, buzzards, sunsets. We were living in alpine meadows, at the base of desert cliffs, in silent caves, on the ridgelines of Wind River peaks—and I needed to exclaim wonder with someone. Annie Dillard hit that deepest chord.

"I wish I could get hold of this country. I wish I could breathe it into my bones," I wrote with pained longing from a cramped position in a wind-whipped tent. It was the late seventies. I had grown up reading *Audubon* magazine, hiking in the Adirondacks, and attending school assemblies on Earth Day. At college I had just lived for a year in Ecology House—where I finally learned what multi-national corporations did. Wilderness was being destroyed at an alarming rate, I discovered, and few people seemed to care. Hardly anyone had even *heard* of the Congressional debate over the future of Alaska when I knocked on their doors with a petition in hand. How could human culture survive if we eliminated the very foundation of what made us human? I wanted to experience wilderness before it was too late. I was ready to devote myself to saving it.

It's no wonder that Dillard's apparent "visionary naturalism" (to quote one critic) became a kind of intellectual template for me. Dillard went into the natural world to SEE, the way children and adults blind from birth with cataracts, and given sight through a special operation, suddenly could see the world for the first time. They found it either horrifying or beautiful. Dillard wanted to see the world freshly, as if for the first time—a flat plane of "color patches" raw and real—the world unfiltered by human senses, untrammeled by human meaning.

> Peeping through my keyhole I see within the range of only about thirty percent of the light that comes from the sun; the rest is infrared and some little ultraviolet, perfectly apparent to many animals, but invisible to me. A nightmare network of ganglia, charged and firing without my knowledge, cuts and splices what I do see, editing it for my brain. Donald E. Carr points out that the sense impressions of one-celled animals are *not* edited for the brain: "This is philosophically interesting in a rather mournful way, since it means that only the simplest animals perceive the universe as it is."

Undaunted by this information, Dillard set out to observe the universe as it really is. Both scientist and poet, she wrestled with the spiritual underpinnings of each field, gathering information by the armload to sort into colorful patterns. She was an explorer and stalker, she tells us, determined to discover the meaning of life—or rather, of suffering, pain, and death, for these are the phenomena that do not make coherent sense. Dillard wanted to get below and around human perceptual limitations. She would have liked to see God in the face if she could do so without dying.

On a first reading of *Pilgrim,* I identified with Dillard's brave explorations. Life is rough, she seemed to say, and the world unfair and insane; all creatures suffer; we're all in this together. She was willing to grant that the rest of life besides us humans mattered. She quoted John Cowper Powys, who said, "We have no reason for denying to the world of plants a certain slow, dim, vague, large, leisurely semiconsciousness." Dillard added, "The patch of bluets in the grass may not be long on brains, but it might be, at least in a very small way, awake."

This writer was a keen observer, and a collector of incredible facts. Through her eyes natural history came alive for me. I was a biology student who wrote poetry; Dillard seemed to be a poet who conducted experiments on life. She waited on the bridge for hours to catch a glimpse of a muskrat. She stuffed praying mantis egg-cases in her pockets and attached them to a bush outside her window where she would be sure to see them hatch. She tried to untie a snakeskin; chased grasshoppers; shouted into the cliffs to see if the echo would disturb a bee foraging at her elbow.

All of life was worth noticing to Dillard because any piece of it could lead to revelation. The natural world, if we could only perceive it as it really is, would provide us with a door into mystery.

> Then one day I was walking along Tinker Creek thinking of nothing at all and I saw the tree with the lights in it. I saw the backyard cedar where the mourning doves roost charged and transfigured, each cell buzzing with flame. I stood on the grass with the lights in it, grass that was wholly fire, utterly focused and utterly dreamed. It was less like seeing than like being for the first time seen, knocked breathless by a powerful glance. The flood of fire abated, but I'm still spending the power. Gradually the lights went out in the cedar, the colors died, the cells unflamed and disappeared. I was still ringing. I had been my whole life a bell, and never knew it until at that moment I was lifted and struck.

This was the way I had been struck, too, I exclaimed to myself, one night in the mountains when I had perched on a rock mid-stream and stared at the stars until I could actually see the distances between them, and could feel the earth turn under me, a round speck I rode through a vast reality usually ignored. Dillard, "the arrowshaft," went purposefully in life, seeking and readying herself for such moments of revelation. It was up to us, she exhorted by example or directive, to be seekers and look for the world's meaning. She looked on faith and expected meaning to be real—on faith and on the non-rational knowledge of having seen the tree with the lights in it. Her seeking led her to eventually hold horror in one hand, beauty in the other, and to give thanks for all of it; she exits the book with her left foot saying "Glory" and her right foot "Amen": "in and out of Shadow Creek, upstream and down, exultant, in a daze, dancing, to the twin silver trumpets of praise."

I remember closing the book with reverence, breathless myself, convinced that I was parting from a soul-mate. Surely, I thought, if we were to meet, oh surely we would become the closest of friends. I could not have guessed then how wrong I was, and how young.

The following fall I returned to college for my senior year. Standing outside the English office, inspecting the schedule of new courses taped to the door, I nearly exploded with adrenaline when I read "A. Dillard." Rushing to my house, I called Dillard immediately to ask her to be my advisor for an honors project I had just that minute created. We had a long talk, at the end of which she flatly refused, having inquired why in the world I would want to write about environmental problems when "it's been done before." The encounter deflated me for weeks.

The next semester I was on the class list for Dillard's "Writing Poetry" course. It proved to be one of the most hypnotizing and frustrating I had as an undergraduate. At one point Dillard admitted that she would have called the course "Writing and Living Poetry"—"this class is really about writing as a way of life," she said. "You must turn away from the pleasure of being one of the people of the world. The mission of endeavor is more important than the pleasure of life." If we had a choice, she asked us, of going to Afghanistan or reading in the library, which should we do? I thought of her forays onto the island in Tinker Creek. I thought of her standing on the bridge over the creek one summer in a hurricane while the flood waters swirled a few inches below her feet. I thought of her longing to go "northing"—to see the caribou for herself perhaps, hear their hoof joints clicking. Of course, I thought, GO, I would go. "The library," she said.

When Dillard first walked into that classroom I had been struck by how young she looked—too young to have absorbed so much wisdom. Her hair was long and loose like many of the young women in the class. She was soft-skinned but put a hard set in her jaw when she wanted to. She liked to wear hats. She talked about softball. She liked to smoke at the head of the wide rectangular conference table around which we thirty students sat, and willingly, I forgave her. She

remained distant and private about her own life, and devoted herself to the class. She was tough, demanding: every poem came back with comments all over it. In the margins of mine she admonished me to "eschew sentimentality." By the middle of the semester I finally got the hang of her all-encompassing definition for that oft-repeated word—anything that had been done before: anything that came too easily; anything that borrowed its power from the world, instead of creating its own; anything that was too comfortable, that did not dare and plunge.

One day she asked how many of us would be writing poems ten years from now. The week before we had heard, "The people who are accomplishing things are the people sitting in their rooms missing life." Most of the hands in the room went up. She was surprised; her eyes softened a bit. "Good for you," I think she said. The look on her face was pained, pleased, worried—writing mattered too much. I think we made her day. I think we made her anxious.

Confronted each week by such declarations, I soon wondered what had happened to the woodswoman I had first met. Hadn't she stalked a coot all of one afternoon, listened to insects, attained a glorious moment while patting a puppy? Her classroom directives for a strict intellectualism did not fit the sense-based "experiential" image I had of her from the book. In an interview with Mike Major for *America* in 1978, Dillard set the record straight: ". . . people want to make you into a cult figure because of what they fancy to be your life style, when the truth is your life is literature! You're writing consciously, off of hundreds of index cards, often distorting the literal truth to achieve an artistic one . . . [People] think it happens in a dream, that you just sit on a tree stump and take dictation from some little chipmunk!"

My new role model appeared progressively more disciplined, more severe, and more driven than I would have guessed from reading *Pilgrim,* but she was no environmentalist. One day she commented that she didn't see how any of us would want to be vegetarians; it took too much time away from writing to cook that stuff. She showed no allegiance to any political causes that I could detect. Her sole cause was Meaning and Art.

We budding poets learned that our purpose was to take the whole world as material and bend it to make Art. Art objects had to cohere, with every part utterly clear and the meanings interconnected. Even if the intent was to portray the meaninglessness of the world, the artist did it "the usual way, the old way, by creating a self-relevant artistic whole," by imposing "a strict order upon chaos," wrote Dillard in *Living by Fiction,* a book she was working on while teaching our class. "In this structural unity lies integrity, and it is integrity which separates art from nonart."

Pilgrim is a non-fiction work with fiction in it. Its author sought the integrity of the very world, and so blurred her own distinction between art and nonart. One expectation behind many of her questions in this book is that life should behave coherently. Conscious observant seeking should reveal the world to be an art object itself—unified, ordered, and resplendent. But the chaotic world resists the attempt to impose order on it, presenting instead raw pain, illogical death, and suffering. Thus, the world she sees engenders Dillard's ever more determined struggle to find Reason at the foundation of life.

Artistic energy in a work is derived from the material, instructed this teacher. You need real objects in the real world to write successfully, but writing, ultimately, is *about* something abstract. For Dillard, the relationship between time and eternity stimulated her work. "I've devoted my life to trying to figure this out," she said, implying that each of us in the class should find an equally worthy goal and stick to it fiercely as a life project.

> *Pilgrim* **is a non-fiction work with fiction in it. Its author sought the integrity of the very world, and so blurred her own distinction between art and nonart.**
> **—Elaine Tietjen**

Looking so closely at eternity, Dillard was torn between beauty and horror throughout her "mystical excursion" in *Pilgrim.* The *logos* force compelled her to explore, analyze, and question the meaning of existence, and eventually to write a reasoning book. *Logos* also, necessarily, divided her from the very world she sought, while the force of *eros* compelled her toward integration. *Pilgrim* is Dillard's effort to find a balance point between reason and intuition, classification and unification. As an art work, the book rings and reverberates with its own energy—but can the inner light of mystical knowledge manifest into words on a page? *Pilgrim* records the attempt, but cannot validly represent Nature itself, for the author tips the balance in favor of *logos.* One could say, as did Kabir, a fifteenth-century poet (quoted by Lewis Hyde in *The Gift*) that ". . . all our diseases / are in the asking of these questions." Dillard remains too focused on her own idiosyncratic life projects to achieve a convincing epiphany by the end of her book. Although many readers admire her as both a naturalist and a mystic, she is primarily, fundamentally, an artist, and the core of her book is not about the whole of Nature, but only one small part—*Pilgrim* is about human beings.

Dillard immediately interprets every one of her observations in spiritual terms, in relation to human life. The "tree with the lights in it" represents spiritual revelation at its finest. The collapsed body of the frog eaten by a giant water bug becomes Dillard's refrain for suffering and insane death. The Polyphemous moth reappears again and again—it hatched in a jar in young Dillard's classroom and could not spread its beautiful wings to dry. Released an hour later, the crippled insect crawled down the school driveway at Dillard's feet. She never forgot its crumpled useless wings, and the moth crawls into her narrative in *Pilgrim* repeatedly to symbolize the part we humans play in the fabric of nature's horror. The creek—to whose side Dillard's house is clamped like an "anchor-hold"—is "continuous creation"—pure energy, flux, the rush of the future and the promise of rebirth, while the mountains hold up eternity: "Theirs is the one simple mystery of creation from nothing, of matter itself, anything at all, the given." Dillard uses all the elements of her landscapes to search for God, just as she uses the library. The natural world is itself a text. This pilgrim uses Nature as a bridge to a direct relationship with God, following a long tradition of American nature writers, it is true, but failing to free herself from her own personality in her search. Dillard did not escape her perceptual filtering systems, and in some ways, she did not try to escape them. Some danger lies in taking this work as a model for natural history or metaphysical explorations, since it offers a specifically human-centered view of reality.

Dillard actually went out into the natural world to learn about her own unwilling role in the cycles of horror. This is the darker side of Thoreau and Melville that Dillard bravely explores, but she does not go quite far enough. This road can only lead to the embrace of paradox. On a first reading, under the huge skies of the Rockies, I was convinced that Dillard had found Meaning by the end of the book, as she sways with confidence, clasping beauty and horror together in thanksgiving. Reading *Pilgrim* again, I have to wonder whether her quest had actually ended—or did the book simply need finishing? Her exultations seem forced—an intellectually conscious construction, a loud shouting to drown out the tremendous fear that still tips the balance.

Other critics have noted Dillard's unusual focus on the particular as a path toward the universal. In fact, this focus also limited her. She insisted on seeing creatures and plants as individuals with identities that are bounded by their skins or shells or coats. But this way of seeing overlooks some basic lessons of ecology. Individuals often do not matter in the network of energy exchanges as much as do whole systems. Is this necessarily a horrifying idea? Perhaps it is, if it threatens the human ego's sense of identity and autonomy. Horror here is an artifact of the drive to differentiate the world into parts. The patterns that might really be operating in the world do not carry as much weight as the chaos Dillard chose to perceive. Life ought to make sense, she asserted, the way it makes sense to *us.*

Even though revelatory experiences succeed in dissolving the ego completely, if only for a brief moment, Dillard could not maintain the vision of the tree with the lights in it. Near the end of the book, she hoists herself out of despondency by focusing on a particular maple key seed, a symbol of renewal:

> Hullo. I threw it into the wind and it flew off again, bristling with animate purpose, not like a thing dropped or windblown, pushed by the witless winds of convection currents . . . , but like a creature muscled and vigorous, or a creature spread thin to that other wind, the wind of the spirit which bloweth where it listeth, lighting, and raising up, and easing down. O maple key, I thought, I must confess I thought, o welcome, cheers.

But a little later she is gone again into the dark:

> The waters of separation, however lightly sprinkled, leave indelible stains. Did you think, before you were caught, that you needed, say, life? Do you think you will keep your life, or anything else you love? But no. Your needs are all met. But not as the world giveth. You see the needs of your own spirit met whenever you have asked, and you have learned that the outrageous guarantee holds. You see the creatures die, and you know you will die. And one day it occurs to you that you must not need life. Obviously. And then you're gone. You have finally understood that you're dealing with a maniac.

At times, Dillard's outward seeking attention led her to moments of truth. She saw the tree with the lights in it, or a monarch butterfly climbing a hill by coasting, or some other miracle of affirmation. But she never fully considered that the horrors she perceived might reflect her Self. *Logos* keeps us within the confines of our own minds, while *eros* breaks us out. Italo Calvino wrote, in *The Uses of Literature,* that "The power of modern literature lies in its willingness to give a voice to what has remained unexpressed in the social or individual unconscious: this is the gauntlet it throws down time and again. The more enlightened our houses are, the more their walls ooze ghosts. Dreams of progress and reason are haunted by nightmares."

Could it be that many of Dillard's awestruck fears in confronting the alien world of insects come from her own unresolved experiences in her unconscious? Dillard's own sorts of ghosts rise up in nearly every chapter, most frequently in the bodies of insects who do "one horrible thing after another." In her recently published memoir, *An American Childhood,* Dillard described several incidents that had enormous emotional and psychological power over her. One day

a dead, dried butterfly fell out from between the pages of a book she was reading. The wings and body crumbled to bits that slipped under her shirt and stuck to her chest. One day she returned home from summer vacation to discover a carrion beetle still alive in her insect collection box. Stuck through with a pin, it had been swimming in the air for days. The contribution she made to the crippling of the Polyphemous moth had haunted her ever since. Dillard's unusual obsession with the horrors of the alien lives of insects could be, in part, an effort to accommodate the dark side of her own psyche. Is the terror that she faces the terror of nightmares rather than a directly perceived external reality? Perhaps the darker side of God, the face he will not show us, hides a uniquely human image.

> I used to kill insects with carbon tetrachloride—cleaning fluid vapor—and pin them in cigar boxes, labeled, in neat rows. That was many years ago: I quit when one day I opened a cigar box lid and saw a carrion beetle, staked down high between its wing covers, trying to crawl, swimming on its pin. It was dancing with its own shadow, untouching, and had been for days. If I go downstairs now will I see a possum just rounding a corner, trailing its scaled pink tail? I know that one night, in just this sort of rattling wind, I will go to the kitchen for milk and find on the back of the stove a sudden stew I never fixed, bubbling, with a deer leg sticking out.

As much as Dillard insists that she focuses on the world, her witty, jerking, twisting, or joking language frequently draws attention to herself. Dillard's portrait on the cover of *Pilgrim* was not entirely out of place, since she so often serves as subject as well as author of her book. Dillard the artist brings these "horror-show" images together; Dillard the poet makes the point.

Spiritual seeking and mystical experiences have been recorded and discussed for centuries. Dillard does not have much that is new to say about revelation, although her path, that focuses on the particular and the alien, is somewhat new. Her overriding concern with structured meaning and coherent integrity leads her more easily to her ego Self than to the gate of the raw universe.

In *Living by Fiction* Dillard wonders, "Do artists discover order, or invent it? Do they discern it, or make it up?" In *Pilgrim,* the question of whether Meaning is absolute seems urgent, for our very sanity might depend on the answer. We can explain the horrors of the world either because the God that made the world is a monster and our own ordered minds are freaks, or because the horrors are themselves projections or reflections of a Mind that is a monster in an ordered universe.

Although this woods explorer poses both sides of the question in *Pilgrim,* she addresses them unequally. More ready and willing to call God a maniac and the world insane, she resists abandoning her own ego to consider that life may not Mean in the way we human beings assume it to mean. Afraid to redefine her understanding of beauty, she asks, as might each of us, "Or is beauty itself an intricately fashioned lure, the cruelest hoax of all?" She recounts an Eskimo tale in which an ugly old woman kills her beautiful daughter and skins the daughter's face to wear as a mask, so as to fool her daughter's husband into sleeping with her. "Could it be that if I climbed the dome of heaven and scrabbled and clutched at the beautiful cloth till I loaded my fists with a wrinkle to pull, that the mask would rip away to reveal a toothless old ugly, eyes glazed with delight?" To revive herself from this tug of horror Dillard again focuses on the outer "real" world:

> A wind rose, quickening; it seemed at the same instant to invade my nostrils and vibrate my gut. I stirred and lifted my head. No, I've gone through this a million times, beauty is not a hoax—how many days have I learned not to stare at the back of my hand when I could look out at the creek? Come on, I say to the creek, surprise me; and it does, with each new drop. Beauty is real. I would never deny it; the appalling thing is that I forget it. Waste and extravagance go together up and down the banks, all along the intricate fringe of spirit's free incursions into time. On either side of me the creek snared and kept the sky's distant lights, shaped them into shifting substance and bore them speckled down.

To see beauty as pure energy flung alongside time, one has to escape one's sense of self; one has to swim in the wild, free, crazy, shifting creek. Dillard cannot stay there—perhaps none of us can. But we might come closer to seeing Meaning consistently if we were to step outside of the anthropomorphic framework Dillard assumes. Her insistence that the parts of the world *fit* misleads the reader, intentionally or not, into regarding the natural world as a forum for human Idea. The world can be taken and used in our art works, but the world remains mysterious, completely autonomous from that art.

Reading *Pilgrim* again, I am still swept by Dillard's nimble language, by her wit and curiosity, by her sheer boldness to expose her fears, and by her intense driven vision. But I am also unsatisfied. Dillard's god is too profoundly human. She expects a Him of some kind, related to her in some way, operating out of rationality. I do not feel the horror she does when considering how a female dragonfly consumes its mate, for instance—I am fascinated. This precise behavior may have made the species better able to adapt. Dillard's horror

is misplaced, for if life, like all matter, is simply made of light energy, then the particular forms life takes are not as significant as the flow of energy life participates in. Creatures consume other creatures; energy changes and transforms. Quite likely, the dragonfly does not experience death in the way that we would. The dragonfly's death may not make sense on the level of the individual, but on the level of the community or the biosphere such a death may be quite beautiful. So, too, might a human death be beautiful, if it can be perceived as a transformation to another form. This idea, of course, is the ultimate challenge of faith, and the foundation of knowledge for mystics. We are all part of a pattern larger than we can ever see, more complex than we can rationally comprehend. What if the Meaning of it all— the ultimate pattern of the universe—is not discernible in human terms? What if the Meaning requires that we abandon our "human-ness" to understand it, or accept that it can never be expressed in rational words? For all her bravery, Dillard seems to resist this question, perceiving Nature as a collection of discrete parts that ought to illuminate her own life. In a world rapidly becoming dominated and destroyed by human needs and rational human meaning, it may be time to consider the human mind as the monster.

To allow for the possibility of an ultimate or absolute pattern in the universe, we should make an effort to leap outside of the limitations of rational perception. It is not simply a matter of seeing "color patches" in a flat plane. It may require us to abandon the notion of the sanctity of the "individual" above all else. Simplifying the reality of the natural world by disconnecting its interlocking parts will not lead to Truth. At her revelatory moments in *Pilgrim,* Dillard understands this, but a good deal of the book reveals her ego's attempt to come to terms with its own destruction. The ultimate pattern of the universe—whatever it may be—seems to insist on such a dissolution.

People who come to this book, as I did originally, looking for an ecology of perception, will misread *Pilgrim.* Dillard sometimes too consciously exploits the natural world for her own artistic purposes. Today, in the late eighties, we need to consider more than humanly defined identity in our efforts to seek wisdom.

Interestingly, the authors of the other two books I carried to Canyonlands offer quite different ethical views of Nature. In *Desert Solitaire,* Edward Abbey tells us he is not writing *about* the desert: "The desert is a vast world, an oceanic world, as deep in its way and complex and various as the sea. Language makes a mighty loose net with which to go fishing for simple facts, when facts are infinite. If a man knew enough he could write a whole book about the juniper tree. . . . Since you cannot get the desert into a book any more than a fisherman can haul up the sea with his nets, I have tried to create a world of words in which the desert figures more as medium than as material." Dillard uses Tinker Creek as medium also, but doesn't admit to this as clearly.

Abbey foresees that he will be criticized for dealing "too much with mere appearances, with the surface of things," and for failing "to engage and reveal the patterns of unifying relationships which form the true underlying reality of existence." To this idea he responds: "Here I must confess I know nothing whatever about true underlying reality, having never met any." Abbey shies away from calling himself a mystic. He regards the world from a biocentric point-of-view—the natural world has intrinsic value wholly apart from its relationship to us. If this desert lover had to make a choice between killing a rare wildflower or killing a man, he probably would choose the man—or so he says.

In contrast, Aldo Leopold embodies another sort of vision, one that in my mind provides a more ethically coherent framework for a perception of the true "reality" of the natural world. In *Sand County Almanac,* the former forester proposes a Land Ethic based on the value of a whole system, including human beings. "A thing is right when it tends to preserve the integrity, stability, and beauty of the biotic community. It is wrong when it tends otherwise." This is an ecocentric perspective, and it is also holistic because it does not perceive the world as composed of discrete parts. Isn't this view, in so many words, the essence of mystical wisdom also? Leopold is considered by many the founder of environmental ethics, having successfully combined the romantic tradition of nineteenth-century naturalists with the rational knowledge of twentieth-century ecological sciences.

Life cannot be divided into parts at any level really, whether cell, organism, species, population, or community. Dillard persists in seeing horror because she insists on focusing on the particular *too closely.* She divides and separates and catalogues, and seems to forget that she has reduced her field of vision, and so perceives the horror as the real, the raw stuff of the universe.

Leopold may have had a better footing in addressing the question of whether artists perceive meaning, or make it up. Dillard tried to perceive meaning based on the existence of individual, discrete egocentric lives. Leopold said: "The ordinary citizen today assumes that science knows what makes the community clock tick; the scientist is equally sure that he does not. He knows that the biotic mechanism is so complex that its workings may never be fully understood." Leopold proposed a shift in consciousness. When considering the human use of wilderness areas, he suggested that "Recreational development is a job not of building roads into lovely country, but of building receptivity into the still unlovely human mind."

At moments, Dillard succeeds in dissolving her Mind's autonomy to perceive the patterns of which she is a part. At these moments, *Pilgrim* remains a gripping book, nearly accomplishing the impossible task of transmitting in words an experience that is outside logical processes, independent of time, and impenetrable by reason. For this effort on her part, I still close the book with reverence. *Pilgrim* is not a dangerous book—*if* the reader understands that the natural world portrayed in it is more a vision of a human mind, limited, self-focused, and filtering, than of the universe. We may yet find that it is human meaning that does not make sense. We may discover that the natural world is not here as a bridge for us, that our personal journeys are part of a pattern we will never fully comprehend.

Susan M. Felch (essay date Spring 1989)

SOURCE: "Annie Dillard: Modern Physics in a Contemporary Mystic," in *Mosaic,* Vol. 22, No. 2, Spring, 1989, pp. 1-14.

[*In the following essay, Felch provides an overview of Dillard's writing and investigates how physics has shaped Dillard's cosmology.*]

"Art is my interest, mysticism my message, Christian mysticism," Annie Dillard wrote early in her career to a fellow English professor (Wymard). With such authorial support and direction, many critics have naturally concentrated their analyses on Dillard's mystical vision or Christian commitments (Dunn; Keller; Ronda; Peterson). Others have, with good warrant, considered her affinity to American transcendentalists (McConahay; McIlroy). A few have noticed her consuming concern with esthetics (Lavery; Scheick). Little attention has been paid, however, to Dillard's fascination with modern scientific theories.

In her latest book, *An American Childhood,* Dillard records a French teacher's evaluation of her as an adolescent: "Here, alas, is a child of the twentieth century." Nowhere does the mature Dillard live up to this epithet more fully than in her knowledge of both the facts and the philosophy of twentieth-century science, particularly apparent in her early and best known book, *Pilgrim at Tinker Creek* (McIlroy, "Burden").

It is tempting to describe the Dillard of *Pilgrim at Tinker Creek* as an isolated, and perhaps old-fashioned, naturalist meticulously recording observations in her neighborhood with little regard for the larger outside world. Margaret Loewen Reimer, for example, characterizes her as "the only person in her world" with "judgments . . . based entirely on her observations, except for the substantiation she seeks from other writers." Such solipsism, however, is at odds with Dillard's extensive quotations which are used not simply to substantiate her own empirical deductions, but to extend the meaning of what she sees to that which she cannot see. Because Dillard tells us so often that she is looking at nature and that she keeps her eyes propped open "with toothpicks, with trees," we tend to miss the fact that she actually spends much of her time reading books and thinking abstract thoughts, that in her reading as well as in her observations, she is a "noticer" (Lavery).

To summarize a chapter entitled "Present," she chooses not to describe a scene but to quote a subatomic physicist: "Everything that has already happened is particles, everything in the future is waves." Or again, the mystery of a crippled but undaunted Polyphemus moth lies not in what can be seen or even deduced but in the possibility that it had "in its watery heart one cell, and in that cell one special molecule, and in that molecule one hydrogen atom, and round that atom's nucleus one wild, distant electron that, split, showed a forest, swaying." And finally, describing the elusiveness of nature she says bluntly, "I find in quantum mechanics a world symbolically similar to my world at the creek," goes on for several pages to explain her understanding of indeterminacy and then concludes: "These physicists are once again mystics, as Kepler was, standing on a rarefied mountain pass, gazing transfixed into an abyss of freedom."

If much of *Pilgrim* is, as Dillard admits, a feverish gathering of facts and statistics from observations and books, her next book, *Holy the Firm,* is a more studied reflection on these facts, a reflection thoroughly informed by modern physics. Dillard is convinced that if there is one thing twentieth-century science has taught us, it is that we cannot believe our eyes. Since Einstein we have learned to assert that (contrary to our common-sense notions) matter is energy, three-dimensional space is curved and time and space are not isolated categories. It is particularly the space/time continuum which snags and baffles Dillard's imagination. If she begins talking about time, she often ends by contemplating space; or vice versa. She describes the land around her Puget Sound home as "a poured thing and time a surface film lapping and fringeing at fastness, at a hundred hollow and receding blues. . . . The actual percentage of land mass to sea in the Sound equals that of the rest of the planet: we have less *time* than we knew" (emphasis mine). Similarly, she sees the far away mountains as both bulwarks of solid space and "the last serrate margin of time."

Modern physics, however, has raised other and even more perplexing images as it has moved into the realm of the atom. Scientists developing quantum mechanics in the early decades of this century began to argue that subatomic particles did not behave according to the cause and effect rules of classical physics, that they did not, in fact, behave at all like forces and bodies in the visible world.

Dillard is convinced that if there is one thing twentieth-century science has taught us, it is that we cannot believe our eyes.
—*Susan M. Felch*

Experimenters found, for instance, that both the position and the momentum of a subatomic particle could not be simultaneously and precisely measured. Werner Heisenberg accounted for this phenomenon in the 1920s with his Uncertainty Principle. Experimenters further discovered that the observer and the observed were inextricably intertwined in subatomic experiments so that a particle was shown to have the characteristics of a wave if the experimental instruments were set up to measure a wave but the characteristics of a particle if the instruments were set up to record a particle. Heisenberg's colleague, Niels Bohr, developed the Principle of Complementarity to explain why logically incompatible models—such as the wave-like and particle-like models of subatomic events—must both be held for a complete description of quantum mechanics. The impossibility of isolating a single subatomic event for analysis encouraged scientists to speak in terms of statistical averages—probability—rather than deterministic cause and effect relationships. Eventually, the concept of action at a distance, or non-local causality, also seemed to be confirmed by experiments, particularly those conducted by J.S. Bell and Alain Aspect.

In her writings subsequent to *Pilgrim at Tinker Creek,* Dillard has explored more thoroughly the impact of these modern physical theories on literature, handling the issue discursively in *Living by Fiction* and imaginatively in *Holy the Firm.*

Living by Fiction takes up the "contemporary modern" novels of Borges, Nabokov, Beckett, Coover, Barth, Hawkes, Burroughs, Barthelme, Pynchon, Wurlitzer, Disch, Robbe-Grillet, Baumbach, Hjorstberg, O'Brien, Calvino, Landolfi, Cortazar, Puig, Canetti and Fuentes and analyzes them as the "fiction of quantum mechanics." Such fiction is not science fiction, as we are accustomed to using that term, but fiction which incorporates recent scientific thinking about reality. Narrative collage, "the shattering of narrative line" and the most typical feature of modern literature is, according to Dillard, well suited to contemporary views which no longer understand time as "a great and widening stream," but as "a flattened landscape, a land of unlinked lakes seen from the air." Similarly space "is no longer a three-dimensional 'setting'" but a "public, random, or temporary place."

Not only is time "in smithereens" and space released from

its boundaries, but both science and literature now question the traditional relationship of cause and effect, the possibility of a fixed point of view and the certainty of knowledge. If, as quantum mechanics tells us, a particle's velocity and position cannot both be known, either in practice or in principle, then the essence of the world at its subatomic heart is not simply uncertain but uncertainty. Writers thus begin to see the world as "an undirected energy . . . an infinite series of random possibilities." In this world characters, like subatomic "events," are flattened out in a sharpedged art of surfaces. They become less human simulacra, less interested in society, and more focal points for action or idea. Point of view, like characterization, is used to distance the reader from "reality" and to "emphasize the isolation of individual consciousness." Even narration itself can become optional. Such a quantum mechanics perspective allows a writer to create "a world shattered, and perhaps senseless, and certainly strange. It may emphasize the particulate nature of everything. We experience a world unhinged. Nothing temporal, spatial, perceptual, social or moral is fixed." In such a world, the relationship between the chaotic "reality" and the ordering mind becomes a dominating question.

Dillard does not resolve this relationship in *Living by Fiction.* Instead, she concludes the book with a series of questions and an apology: "Do art's complex and balanced relationships among all parts, its purpose, significance, and harmony, exist in nature? Is nature whole, like a completed thought? Is history purposeful? Is the universe of matter significant? I am sorry; I do not know."

In *Holy the Firm,* however, she provides an alternative to the contemporary modern novels she discusses in *Living by Fiction* while nevertheless incorporating many, of their techniques within a carefully controlled tripartite structure. Part One, "Newborn and Salted," begins with a briskly modern empiricism. Dillard's scientific eye clearly catalogs the world of spiders, sow bugs, moths, blackberries, snowberries, jewelweed, harlequin ducks, scoters and grebes. No romanticism obscures the fact that spiders gobble up sow bugs, or that cats kill birds, or that moths burn to death in candles. Dillard writes with a confidence in cause and effect and a firm belief in the objective reality of nature.

"The day is real," she proclaims. It is real because she sees the dawn, touches the cat, hears the click of teeth on metal sutures, makes the bed, eats the breakfast, analyzes the spider. She names the "confusion of arcing strips of chitin" moths, because "I have had some experience with the figure Moth reduced to a nub." The rock mountains and salt sea are "hard things." The islands can be categorized, for although "everyone told me a different set of names for them . . . one day a sailor came and named them all with such authority that I believed him. So I penciled an outline of the horizon on a sheet of paper and labeled the lobes: Skipjack,

Sucia, Saturna, Salt Spring, Bare Island." And so Day One, Wednesday, November 18 ends confidently. "I seem to be on a road walking, familiar with neighbors, high-handed with cattle, smelling the sea, and alone. Already, I know the names of things. I can kick a stone."

Yet even in the midst of such scientific confidence philosophic doubt intrudes. Describing the particulars of the landscape seen from her window, Dillard concludes, "You can't picture it can you? Neither can I. . . . In the Middle Ages, I read, 'the idea of a thing which a man framed for himself was always more real to him than the actual thing itself'." Later, while actually walking in the landscape rather than merely observing it from her window, she feels it to be even less real and more a product of her own imagining: "I seem to see a road; I seem to be on a road, walking. I seem to walk on a blacktop road that runs over a hill. The hill creates itself, a powerful suggestion. It creates itself, thickening with apparently solid earth and waving plants, with houses and browsing cattle, unrolling wherever my eyes go, as though my focus were a brush painting in a world. I cannot escape the illusion."

In Part Two, "God's Tooth," philosophic doubt mingles with scientific doubt. The immediate catalyst for catastrophic doubt is the crash of a small plane on Thursday, November 19, during which little Julie Norwich loses her face to a fire ball. But the event also generates widening skepticism. Even the islands so confidently categorized now seem to crop up with infinite randomness: "a new thing appears, as if we needed a new thing. It is a new land blue beyond islands, hitherto hidden by haze and now revealed, and as dumb as the rest. I check my chart, my amateur penciled sketch of the skyline. Yes, this land is new, this spread blue spark beyond yesterday's new wrinkled line, beyond the blue veil a sailor said was Salt Spring Island. How long can this go on? But let us by all means extend the scope of our charts."

The sure knowledge of the scientist/thinker is replaced by a sickening sense of randomness and chaos and illusion so that "everything I see—the water, the logwrecked beach, the farm on the hill, the bluff, the white church in the trees—looks overly distinct and shining. (What is the relationship of color to this sun, of sun to anything else?) It all looks staged. It all looks brittle and unreal, a skin of colors painted on glass, which if you prodded it with a finger would powder and fall." Dillard, in fact, wrestles with the possibility raised by modern physics that randomness and uncertainty are the essence of physical reality. If that is so, "it is the best joke there is that we are here, and fools—that we are sown into time like so much corn, that we are souls sprinkled at random like salt into time and dissolved, here, spread into matter, connected by cells right down to our feet, and those feet likely to fell us over a tree root or jam us on a stone."

Part Three, "Holy the Firm," rejects the conclusions of both traditional science and total randomness. Dillard peers through the infinite particulars to the fusion of interconnectedness, to the "one glare of holiness" where "there is nothing, no one thing, nor motion, nor time. There is only this everything. There is only this, and its bright and multiple noise."

It is possible to read the progression of *Holy the Firm* in several ways. There is naive confidence in Part One, followed by the shattering tragedy of Part Two, culminating in the mature faith of Part Three. There is traditional science naming reality in Part One, modern science promoting skepticism and randomness in Part Two, and a post-modern unified field theory in Part Three. Philosophically we have platonic forms in Part One, existential despair in Part Two and mysticism in Part Three. Yet all such neat schemes, although supportable from the text, are vaguely unsatisfying. The question of what is real and what is illusion permeates the book, even in the most confident first section. God is never rejected, even in the bleakest moments of Part Two. Questions of space and time, reality and illusion, meaning and despair are never completely answered, even in Part Three. Nor do any of these neat schemes address the central questions of the book—what does it mean to be an artist and what is the relationship between artist, art object and the world?

Holy the Firm thus joins the raging debate over the relation of language, science, art and reality, a debate which is, says Dillard, an obsession of our times. Until this century, Dillard argues in *Living by Fiction,* we thought that science at least dealt in certainties and in language which matched definitions with reality. We trusted in science which "actually and certainly connects at base with things as they are." But modern science, along with modern philosophy, modern art and much modern religion forces us to abandon such hope, for "what can we know for certain when our position in space is limited, our velocity may vary, our instruments contract as they accelerate, our observations of particles on the microlevel botch our own chance of precise data, and not only are our own senses severely limited, but many of the impulses they transmit are edited out before they ever reach the brain?" Language itself becomes only a human invention, a cognitive structure, a not entirely accurate grid through which we see the world.

Dillard recognizes that such issues engage the attention of many thinkers in the twentieth century. But she points out that while we expect philosophers (and linguists and literary critics) to be subjective, it is startling to have our scientists so pessimistic about language and knowledge: "Sir Arthur Stanley Eddington, British Astronomer Royal, said in 1927: 'The physical world is entirely abstract and without "actuality" apart from its linkage to consciousness.' It

is one thing when Berkeley says this; when a twentieth-century astronomer says this, it is a bit of another thing" (*Living*).

Dillard is quite correct in diagnosing an attitudinal change among theoretical scientists, the rejection of "a purely natural science which actually and certainly connects at base with things as they are" (*Living*). Niels Bohr argued that language could not match physical reality one for one but could only describe the experimental situation so that "we are suspended in language in such a way that we cannot say what is up and what is down. The word 'reality' is also a word, a word which we must learn to use correctly" (French & Kennedy). Our suspension in language led Bohr to state that "there is no quantum world. There is only an abstract quantum physical description. It is wrong to think that the task of physics is to find out how nature is. Physics concerns what we can *say* about nature" (French & Kennedy; emphasis mine).

Heisenberg—with one important caveat—agreed; he was firmly convinced that indeterminacy was an objective feature of nature itself. Thus he could say that "in the experiments about atomic events we have to do with things and facts, with phenomena that are just as real as any phenomena in daily life. But the atoms or the elementary particles themselves are not as real; they form a world of potentialities or possibilities rather than one of things or fact."

As Dillard knows, thinkers after Bohr and Heisenberg were quick to point out that such conceptions made it difficult to believe in the objectivity of science. Twenty years before Thomas Kuhn argued that the sciences proceed on the basis of shared paradigms whose foundational commitments are largely unexamined, Simone Weil wrote a review of Max Planck's *Introduction to Physics* for the *Cahiers du Sud.* In it she argued that science in the twentieth century had become simply a convention, the averaged opinion of a cloistered esoteric group. Planck had written that "the creator of a hypothesis has practically unlimited possibilities at his disposal. He is as little bound by the functioning of the organs of his sense as he is by that of the instruments he is using. . . . One might even say that he makes for himself whatever geometry he chooses" (qtd. in Cabaud). From these and other similar statements, Weil concluded that science was gratuitous, dependent on the scientist's inventiveness, and removed from the realm of common-sense knowledge (Cabaud).

Although Weil was critical of science for abandoning reality and truth, many subsequent thinkers have accepted the movement of science into the realm of creativity. Thus Italo Calvino writers: "Science is faced with problems not too dissimilar from those of literature. It makes patterns of the world that are immediately called in question, it swings between the inductive and the deductive methods, and it must always be on its guard lest it mistake its own linguistic conventions for objective laws."

Dillard acknowledges that the language of modern physics does not seem to correspond directly with the real world. And if language does not correspond with physical reality, if it has no objective link to the "real" world, then it becomes an end not a means, an artifact rather than a medium. For Dillard, then, this language of quantum mechanics becomes also the language of contemporary modern novelists who use words to create "a chunk in the hand . . . a self-lighted opacity, not a window and not a mirror. It is a painted sphere, not a crystal ball" (*Living*). Or as John Barth puts it, "The storyteller's trade is the manufacture of universes. . . . What he offers you is not a *Weltanschauung* but a *Welt*; not a view of the cosmos, but a cosmos itself."

In *Holy the Firm,* Dillard writes not only with an understanding of but also an appreciation for the language possibilities explored by contemporary modern novelists in their fiction of quantum mechanics. *Holy the Firm* shares with Barth's novels and other contemporary modern works a self-conscious awareness of language philosophy and the self-conscious creation of a literary artifact. Dillard observes that writers of quantum-mechanics fiction often allow the bare bones of their work to protrude. *Holy the Firm* is nearly entirely bone. The stark house ("plain as a skull") in which the author lives is a fitting analogy for that which she creates. Her recurring motifs—fire, skin, salt, cat, moth, read, are, line—are one-syllable skeletons across which is pulled only the thinnest skin of narration. Her structure is tight to the point of rigidity: three sections, three days, three flashbacks, three viewpoints on the world, all interconnected and spiraling deeper and deeper not into the world, but into the writer's mind.

Although Dillard appears to use a traditional narrative approach, describing three days consecutively and placing her flashbacks in their appropriate historical contexts (two summers ago, on Sunday, two weeks ago), in fact occurrences, conversations, visions, imaginations all jostle for attention on the same flat terrain of the book. Time, space, character, point of view, narration are fractured, the shards lying edge to edge to refract the light of her intelligent language. Descriptions of Small the cat being thrown out of the house are set back to back with a tale of Small bringing into the house a small scorched god, "fair, thin-skinned in the cat's mouth, and kicking. . . . One of his miniature hands pushes hard at her nose. He waves his thighs; he beats her face and the air with his smoking wings." The little girl who is burned in the plane crash is apparently a real seven year old with red knees and green socks, but she is also the namesake of a fourteenth-century mystic, Julian of Norwich, and the author's alter ego. Buying communion wine at the store (charge or cash?) vies with a first-person description of Christ's baptism: "He lifts

from the water. Water beads on his shoulders. I see the water in balls as heavy as planets, a billion beads of water as weighty as worlds, and he lifts them up on his back as he rises."

If her syntax is sparse, her structure rigid, her artifact scarcely a realistic representation of the world, Dillard still takes pleasure in the dense poetry of textured words: "If days are gods, then gods are dead, and artists pyrotechnic fools. Time is a hurdy-gurdy, a lampoon, and death's a bawd. We're beheaded by the nick of time. We're logrolling on a falling world, on time released from meaning and rolling loose, like one of Atalanta's golden apples, a bauble flung and forgotten, lapsed, and the gods on the lam."

Yet more often she relies on plain writing, carefully honed words which honor the world by examining it piece by piece, prose which can claim the "clarity of light" (*Living*). Thus a very simple paragraph—"There are a thousand new islands today, uncharted. They are salt stones on fire and dimming; I read by their light. Small the cat lies on my neck. In the bathroom the spider is working on yesterday's moth"—is both courteously intelligent and drenched with meaning. Nearly every word—islands, uncharted, salt, stones, fire, reading, light, cat, neck, spider, yesterday and moth—has been previously so examined, probed and layered with meaning that the paragraph takes on the form of a summary, or perhaps better, a cipher.

> **If her syntax is sparse, her structure rigid, her artifact scarcely a realistic representation of the world, Dillard still takes pleasure in the dense poetry of textured words.**
> **—*Susan M. Felch***

Yet the question remains—what does this carefully structured, beautifully written artifact mean? Why be a writer? That ultimate esthetic question—is there any meaning to art?—which is the question of *Living by Fiction* is also a recurring issue in *Holy the Firm.* And it is on this issue that *Holy the Firm* diverges from the fiction of quantum mechanics. For unlike Barth and company, Dillard does not simply aspire to create a "painted sphere" or to "manufacture a universe." Instead, as William Scheick puts it, Dillard is an artist "who sees the intersection of matter and spirit in the world as well as in . . . herself" and as such tries to unveil the "intersection of matter and spirit, of the temporal and the eternal, of opaque surfaces and translucent depths, of terror and beauty." Dillard wants to experience reality and she wants her art to connect with and illuminate the world that actually exists.

In Part One, the flashback which tells the story of the burnt moth occurs within a personal literary context: "I had hauled myself and gear up there to read, among other things, James Ramsey Ullman's *The Day on Fire,* a novel about Rimbaud that had made me want to be a writer when I was sixteen; I was hoping it would do it again." Later, teaching her students she asks, "Which of you want to give your lives and be writers?" and then adds "I tried to tell them what the choice must mean: you can't be anything else. You must go at your life with a broadax. . . . They had no idea what I was saying."

To go at her life with a broadax, Dillard moved from the civilized East to the far West: "I came here to study hard things—rock mountain and salt sea—and to temper my spirit on their edges." The experiences recorded in the book, therefore—looking at nature, thinking about the world, reflecting on Julie's tragedy, going to church, raging against God, the universe, suffering, people and cats—are all part of the process of becoming and being a writer.

Initially, she feels hollow, a mere conduit seeking to call from nature the reality of an artistic work: "There is, in short, one country, one room, one enormous window, one cat, one spider, and one person: but I am hollow. And, for now, there are the many gods of mornings and the many things to give them for their work—lungs and heart, muscle, nerve, and bone—and there is the no man's land of many things wherein they dwell, and from which I seek to call them, in work that's mine." Her unfocussed energy is expressed by a quote of a quote from another author: "Henry Miller relates that Knut Hamsun once said, in response to a questionnaire, that he wrote to kill time. This is funny in a number of ways. In a number of ways I kill myself laughing, looking out at islands."

Yet Dillard's energy does not remain unfocussed for long. Her hollow self is confronted by the tragedy of Julie Norwich's accident, a hard thing Dillard did not expect, and it works to temper not only her personal spirit but her artistic self, as well. Dillard acknowledges in the cider squeezing flashback of Part Two that she and Julie were united by the cat, Small, whom Julie had dressed to look like a nun, but especially by their similar appearances: "She saw me watching her and we exchanged a look, a very conscious and self-conscious look—because we look a bit alike and we both knew it; because she was still short and I grown."

Dillard addresses the tragedy of her small alter ego by writing; "a fool's lot," she calls it, "this sitting always at windows spoiling little blowy slips of paper and myself in the process." And writing is a fool's lot because not only must she confront the meaning of life, but the meaning of writing about life. Staring her in the face is that hard question, "Does fiction illuminate the great world itself, or only the mind of its human creator?" (*Living*). Do language and the artifacts of language—books—have any meaning?

Of course, Dillard is not alone in raising this question. As she has said in **Living by Fiction,** it is the dominant question of the twentieth century. Dillard, however, is particularly concerned to deal with the question as it is raised by the traditional "hard" sciences rather than by scholars in the humanities and "soft" sciences.

On the one hand, we have the scientists like Bohr who argue that we can speak only of the experimental situation and never of the real world itself or like Heisenberg who adds that the only thing we can posit about the real world is that it is indeterminate. On the other hand, we have Einstein who insisted to his death that such interpretations were incomplete, that nature is objective, that science can speak about reality and that some form of determinism and order underlies apparent quantum "weirdness."

David Bohm, another scientist who insists that the so-called Copenhagen interpretation represented by Bohr and Heisenberg is incomplete, has developed his own theory of implicate order which accepts indeterminacy, interdependence of experiment and experimenter and non-local causality, while retaining a realistic view of language and an objective description of nature. Bohm contends that the rejection of his ideas as the leading paradigm owes more to philosophic currents of thought than to the superiority of the Copenhagen interpretation over his own. At the Solvay Congress of 1927 Louis de Broglie proposed a theory similar to Bohm's own system. His realistic view of quantum entities argued that waves, field and particles actually existed, that their actual rather than statistical behavior could be predicted at least in principle and that scientific language could correspond with physical reality. After his ideas were severely criticized by Wolfgang Pauli, de Broglie dropped these proposals. Commenting on this fact Bohm states that

> it occurred to me that if de Broglie's ideas had won the day at the Solvay Congress of 1927, they might have become the accepted interpretation. Then if someone had come along to propose the current interpretation, one could equally well have said that, since, after all it gave no new experimental results, there would be no point in considering it seriously. In other words, I felt that the adoption of the current interpretation was a somewhat fortuitous affair, since it was affected not only by the outcome of the Solvay Conference, but also by the general positivist empiricist attitude that pervaded physics at the time.

From a different perspective, Karl Popper argues in favor of realism by showing historically that while the "Copenhagen Interpretation" is still a powerful philosophic construct, and is generally accepted as the leading paradigm in quantum mechanics, it has been surpassed scientifically both in theory and in fact. Popper, in fact, sees a "crisis in understanding" in physics which he attributes to "(a) the intrusion of subjectivism into physics; and (b) the victory of the idea that quantum theory has reached complete and final truth." From a third perspective, that of inductive logic, Mary Hesse argues that there are genuine, if incomplete, analogies between scientific models and the world.

Dillard wrestles with these conflicting assumptions about reality and its description. It is possible, she admits, that the Copenhagen interpretation and the contemporary modern novelists who fictively incorporate its dicta are correct and that language has no reference to the world. But then we have an enormous problem. If "the natural world which churned out the mind is a wreck and a chaos, like a rock slide, then the mind is a marvelous monster indeed." If order exists only in our minds, then "the only significance and value which obtain anywhere are in the mind's discernment of these fictive qualities in its own manufactured models. We create value and locate it in our monstrously overdeveloped mental self-replication, our stuttering repetitions of our brains' own order, with which we have covered the gibbering earth" (*Living*).

To such a possibility Dillard can only conclude, "This is the most dismal view—of art and of everything—I can imagine." Or, expressed more poetically—and violently—in *Holy the Firm:* "If [God] abandoned us, slashing creation loose at its base from any roots in the real; and if we in turn abandon everything—all these illusions of time and space and lives—in order to love only the real; then where are we? Thought itself is impossible, for subject can have no guaranteed connection with object, nor any object with God. Knowledge is impossible. We are precisely nowhere, sinking on an entirely imaginary ice floe, into entirely imaginary seas themselves adrift."

In contrast to this dismal view, Dillard suggests an alternative, which is similar to the ideas of Bohm and Popper. Her perspective is not a return to a one-to-one correspondence between language and reality, not an acknowledgement of language and art as transparent windows onto or even mirrors of the world, but a notion of translucence. As Scheick has pointed out, Dillard sees both in art and in nature revealed surfaces and concealed depths. In the depths is an "underlying continuity and design" which is revealed when "moments of translucency reveal the laminal edge of the particular (the temporal, the opaque surface) where it touches the universal (the eternal, the transparent depth)." Art can, if only briefly and intermittently, actually admit a diffused light: "As symbol, or as the structuring of symbols, art can render intelligible—or at least visible, at least discussible—those wilderness regions which philosophy has abandoned and those hazardous terrains which science's tools do not fit" (*Living*).

Art, particularly literature, renders the world intelligible, visible, discussible because the art object, an orderly coherent whole which can be analyzed and explored, also refers to the world. That we cannot know everything about that world does not mean that we cannot know some things. For Dillard the art object "does something quite definite: it knows and understands, and presents its knowledge and understanding" (*Living*). It is "a cognitive instrument which presents to us, in a stilled and enduring context, a model of previously unarticulated or unavailable relationships among ideas and materials. Insofar as we attend to these art objects, these epistemologically absurd and mysterious hot-air balloons, we deepen our understanding. The order which the artist devises for his fabrications is a chip off the universal order, and partakes of its being" (*Living*). Thus writing becomes for Dillard the mediating agent between genuine but hidden physical reality and meaning. It becomes, like Hesse's scientific models, a positive though not perfect analogy of the world.

To use Popper's language, the work of literature does not simply belong to World 2, the world of subjective experience, but also to Worlds 1 and 3, the worlds of physical objects and products of the human mind. It has, therefore, both objective and subjective existence, both private and community functions (Desalvo). Or as Dillard herself bluntly puts it: "I like to be aware of a book as a piece of writing, and aware of its structure as a product of mind, and yet I want to be able to see the represented world through it" (*Fashion*). Or again, "what interests me here, and elsewhere, is the possibility for a purified nonfiction narration—a kind of Chekhovian storytelling which might illuminate the actual world with a delicate light" (*Encounters*). For Dillard, the close examination of physical objects, the scientific examination of data, combines with subjective reflection to produce an apprehension of reality—an epiphany, a flash of insight, an experience, which is a product of the human mind, but not limited to that mind.

Thus in *Holy the Firm* the diffuse particulars of science, art, philosophy, reality and perception merge: "The landscape . . . is starting to utter its infinite particulars, each overlapping and lone, like a hundred hills of hounds all giving tongue. . . . Each thing in the world is translucent, even the cattle, and moving, cell by cell. . . . Everything, everything, is whole, and a parcel of everything else, I myself am falling down, slowly, or slowly lifting up. On the bay's stone shore are people among whom I float, real people, gathering of an afternoon, in the cells of whose skin stream thin colored waters in pieces which give back the general flame."

As I have already said, the question—is there meaning in

art?—is not definitely answered in *Living by Fiction.* Dillard leaves us in no doubt that she prefers the non-dismal alternative, but she does not claim absolute truth for this position. *Holy the Firm,* however, proceeds on the basis that literature does refer to the world, that it does have meaning and that the order writers discern and create reflects an actual and non-subjective order—"a chip off the universal order." The notion that art does have meaning is founded, ultimately, in God. For Dillard's God is not merely tacked on, a kind of god-of-the-gaps notion. Rather she agrees with Simone Weil that "if there is a God, it is not an insignificant fact, but something that requires a radical rethinking of *every little thing.* Your knowledge of God can't be considered as one fact among many. You have to bring all the other facts into line with the fact of God" (qtd. in Fitzgerald). The "fact of God" which particularly bears on Dillard's esthetics are the complementary notions of his transcendence and immanence.

In *Holy the Firm,* God's transcendence is affirmed by acknowledging him as creator and recognizing that God cannot or will not make the world fit our need for logical explanations. God does not exist for our rational or emotional satisfaction so that "we do need reminding, not of what God can do, but of what he cannot do, or will not, which is to catch time in its free fall and stick a nickel's worth of sense into our days. And we need reminding of what time can do, must only do; churn out enormity at random and beat it, with God's blessing, into our heads: that we are created, *created,* sojourners in a land we did not make, a land with no meaning of itself and no meaning we can make for it alone." Thus God's transcendence underlines the fragility of human existence and knowledge.

Yet God is also immanent; he has not abandoned the world. If we have the faith, we can believe that God entered time, "that he bound himself to time and its hazards and haps as a man would lash himself to a tree for love." Dillard has this faith which she affirms through her participation in the church, her quotations of the Bible, her flat statements of belief: "I know it as given that God is all good."

It is, however, not faith that Dillard explores in *Holy the Firm.* It is the facts of the world, what she terms truth and the evidence of things seen: "One Julie, one sorrow, one sensation bewildering the heart, and enraging the mind, and causing me to look at the world stuff appalled, at the blithering rock of trees in a random wind, at my hand like some gibberish sprouted, my fist opening and closing, so that I think, Have I once turned my hand in this circus, have I ever called it home?" It is in the exploration of these horrific particulars, the physical world apart from history and the Bible, that Dillard finds God immanent. She does not look for God in Christ, who "holds the tip of things fast and stretches eternity clear to the dim souls of men." She looks

for God "at the base of things, some kernel or air deep in the matrix of matter from which universe furls like a ribbon twined into time."

And there she finds Him as Holy the Firm, the unseen ground beneath the dullest level of material. Although God is hidden, the fact that he is there means that there is also reality and design and meaningful language: "Thought advances, and the world creates itself, by the gradual positing of and belief in, a series of bright ideas. Time and space are in touch with the Absolute at base. Eternity sockets twice into time and space curves, bound and bound by idea. Matter and spirit are of a piece but distinguishable; God has a stake guaranteed in all the world."

Yet the immanence of God does not result in pantheism. As Dillard says, "Pantheism is not the only meaningful reading of the natural world. One need not find a spirit in each bush and rock for these things to mean. The bush and rock may be, as it were, literary symbols" (*Living*). These literary symbols, provided by God who is both immanent and transcendent, give to humans a world which is both mysterious and knowable.

Within this given reality, this creation, then, the artist finds meaning for herself and for her work. The artist takes a humble stance, for she is not God, not Holy the Firm, not the Creator, but her work nevertheless reveals meaning for she can create linguistic artifacts which illuminate the real as long as these works are "in touch with, in touch with, in touch with; spanning the gap, from here to eternity, home."

Joan Bischoff (essay date December 1989)

SOURCE: "Fellow Rebels: Annie Dillard and Maxine Hong Kingston," in *English Journal,* Vol. 78, No. 8, December, 1889, pp. 50-67.

[*In the following essay, Bischoff compares Dillard's* American Childhood *with Maxine Hong Kingston's autobiography* The Woman Warrior, *noting that despite different backgrounds the two authors depict similar experiences.*]

For all their pseudosophisticated behavior and easy familiarity with high technology, today's high-school students continue to respond to and relish books about fictional young adults who, like themselves, struggle with generic teenage problems: rebellion against parental strictures, competition with siblings, the confines of school, fascination with and fear of the opposite sex, the looming necessity of momentous decisions about career choices and lifestyles. Traditionally, most such novels featured the adventures of young men (with the exception of the ubiquitous Nancy Drew); more recently, we have seen the skyrocketing popularity of such written-for-teens books as those of Judy Blume.

Certainly, such works have their place as leisure reading; however, the senior-high-school English instructor who seeks teachable contemporary literature that has both the virtues of writerly excellence and the popular appeal of the merely entertaining paperbacks is often left floundering in search of titles that promise to be appropriate, accessible, and well-received in the senior-high-school classroom. I'd like to suggest a pair of books published at opposite ends of the past decade that are well written, discussion-worthy, and sufficiently alike in content that they can be taught in tandem for comparative purposes as part of a contemporary-literature unit. Both books come to terms with the problems of adolescence noted above; both authors have fine literary reputations, as attested by their being named Pulitzer Prize winner (Dillard) and Pulitzer Prize runner-up (Kingston); both works offer satisfying reading challenges to students. And as an added bonus for teachers attempting to foster respect for cultural diversity in their classroom reading, the authors are women of diverse ethnic backgrounds.

Despite their cultural differences, Annie Dillard and Maxine Hong Kingston show remarkable similarities in their accounts of teenage rebellion in their respective autobiographies. Both Dillard's **American Childhood** (1987) and Kingston's *Woman Warrior: Memoirs of a Girlhood among Ghosts* (1977) relate their authors' conflicts with family and society, culminating in emotional confrontation scenes that leave the problems unresolved. In both instances, the authors' self-descriptions portray them as intense questioners of the status quo, feeling out of place in their respective worlds, biding their time until they can escape to the greater opportunities hovering tantalizingly just beyond the reaches of their neighborhoods.

For all their parents' efforts to rein them in, both Dillard and Kingston had parents who were themselves rebels. When Dillard was ten, her father "quit the firm his great-grandfather had founded a hundred years earlier . . . [and] sold his own holdings in the firm" in order to emulate his hero Mark Twain by going down the Mississippi River alone in a cabin cruiser. While Frank Doak abandoned his journey after only six weeks, he had set a memorable example for his daughter. Dillard's mother was similarly unconventional. She was witty, playing deft verbal games with duller people and, says Dillard, "collar[ing] us into her gags"; she held unpopular opinions about the McCarthy hearings and people who lived in trailer parks and the humanity of blue collar workers.

Kingston's father, too, strayed from the norm: as a young man, alone among his brothers, he chose an education rather than land as his share of the family inheritance and, after emigrating to the United States, eventually elected to send for his wife rather than return to China himself. Kingston's mother, Brave Orchid, was a strong and liberated woman for her era: she used the money sent her from America by her husband to sail alone to Canton and enroll in medical school to become a physician. She refused to share prevailing beliefs in the overwhelming powers of the supernatural, facing down a Sitting Ghost and continuing to cross a bridge on which she had once seen the smoky ghosts called Sit Dom Kuei. Although Brave Orchid tried to mold her Biggest Daughter along more conformist lines, she herself furnished a contrary illustration of fierce independence.

Both Dillard and Kingston had two sisters, and in each case the younger siblings were a contrast to them. Dillard describes Amy, three years younger than she, "Quiet. And little, and tidy, and calm, and more or less obedient," while Kingston describes her next youngest sister as being "neat while I was messy." Neither did this sister share Kingston's active imagination. Kingston relates her horror at discovering that her sister, whom she had thought of as "the person most like me in all the world," did not share her habit of "talk[ing] to people that aren't real inside your mind." Amy and her older sister shared more free-spiritedness than did the Hong sisters. However, in both families, the age gap between the youngest and oldest of the three sisters was great enough to prevent either from having much influence on the other.

Within each family, the oldest girl deliberately flouted many of her parents' injunctions. Dillard advanced from snowballing passing cars to "try[ing] to kill a streetcar by overturning it," putting stones on the tracks; she refused to take Communion and quit the church. She was fingerprinted in juvenile court after a drag-racing accident in which she injured her knees; she was suspended from school for smoking cigarettes. At home, she stayed in her own room whenever she could and "read or sulked." Dillard describes herself as being fanatical about her privacy:

> Actually, it drove me nuts when people came in my room. Mother had come in just last week. My room was getting to be quite the public arena. Pretty soon they'd put it on the streetcar routes. Why not hold the U.S. Open here?

Kingston faced additional challenges growing up in a Chinese-American household: she was constantly fighting the ingrained Chinese put-down of women. She quotes endless derogatory proverbs: "Feeding girls is feeding cowbirds": "There's no profit in raising girls. Better to raise geese than girls"; "When fishing for treasures in the flood, be careful not to pull in girls." Though her mother exhorted Kingston not to be a rebel like her father's sister, whose illegitimate pregnancy led to her suicide and the family's subsequent refusal to acknowledge she had ever lived, Kingston deliberately set out to be a "bad girl." She refused to cook; she broke dishes; she raised unlucky dust swirls while sweeping; she got into fights in junior-high school; she looked at dead slum people. When her exasperated mother would call her "bad," Kingston says, "Sometimes that made me gloat rather than cry. Isn't a bad girl almost a boy?"

Kingston refused to see her future role as that of the Chinese wife—or slave. If she couldn't be a boy, or a Fa Mu Lan, a warrior woman, she was determined to have a career. Perhaps the fervor of her rebellion was at least partially responsible for the mysterious illness she contracted: at about this time, Kingston quit battling for eighteen months, bedridden by an illness that had no perceptible symptoms and no apparent cause. Possibly the psychological conflict raging within her found manifestation in this way.

Both Dillard and Kingston rebelled against the limitations of society as represented by their school and/or community. As she grew older, Dillard says, "I wanted to bust up the Ellis School with my fists." She planned classroom insurrections:

> It was a provocative fact, which I seemed to have discovered, that we students outnumbered our teachers. Must we then huddle like sheep? . . . Lately I had been trying to inflame my friends with the implications of our greater numbers. We could pull off a riot. We could bang on the desks and shout till they let us out. Then we could go home and wait for dinner.

However, Dillard laments, "I got no takers." Looking around at the world of the girls of her school, Dillard says,

> I hated it so passionately I thought my shoulders and arms, swinging at the world, would split off from my body like loose spinning blades, and fly wild and slice everyone up. With all my heart, sometimes, I longed for the fabled Lower East Side of Manhattan, for Brooklyn, for the Bronx, where the thoughtful and feeling people in books grew up on porch stoops among seamstress intellectuals.

Dillard also was fed up with the country club, and with church. "At the country club," she says, "you often wanted to leave as soon as you had come, but there was no leaving to be had." She faulted the values of the woman who "never washed her face all summer, to preserve her tan," writhed at the predictability of "figures in a reel endlessly unreeling," who drank old-fashioneds in winter and frozen daiquiris in summer. She was equally critical of that society's religious observances:

> Nothing so inevitably blackened my heart as an

obligatory Sunday at the Shadyside Presbyterian Church: . . . the putative hypocrisy of my parents, who forced me to go, though they did not; the putative hypocrisy of the expensive men and women who did go.

In sum, says Dillard,

> I adored, I longed for, everyone on earth, especially India and Africa, and particularly everyone on the streets of Pittsburgh—all those friendly, democratic, openhearted, sensible people—and at Forbes Field, and in all the office buildings, parks, streetcars, churches, and stores, excepting only the people I knew, none of whom was up to snuff.

Kingston's schooldays were a trial for her, too, though for a different reason. Uncertain of herself and of her spoken English, Kingston says,

> During the first silent year I spoke to no one at school, did not ask before going to the lavatory, and flunked kindergarten. . . . It did not occur to me I was supposed to talk.

During those early years, she was more victim than rebel: the Japanese kids picked on her, and she and the other Chinese girls were left out of the second-grade play. By the time she got to sixth grade, however, Kingston "was arrogant with talk"; she became a straight-A student, determined to join clubs and activities and win a scholarship to college. But because of her struggles to cope successfully with the American educational system, Kingston did not aspire to overturn it, as Dillard did. Her rebellion instead was against the obstacles provided by her culture that slowed her rise to the top.

Like Dillard, Kingston disapproved of many of the customs and behaviors of her community. She resented having to lie and say she had already eaten when offered food, instead of bluntly admitting, "I'm starved. Do you have any cookies? I like chocolate chip cookies." She keenly felt the unfairness inherent in Great-Uncle's pleasure in taking her brothers out for candy and new toys while refusing to take her and her sisters because they were girls ("Maggots!"). She cringed with embarrassment when her mother made her go to the drugstore for "reparation candy" to remove the curse of a mistaken delivery of medicine to their family. She hated both the awful power of the white people ("ghosts") that forced her to be circumspect in all she said and the Chinese propensity for secrecy that prevented her from revealing to her teachers her parents' real names or birthdays or occupations. Perhaps most of all, she grew up angry at the confusing bedrock of Chinese culture: the habit of never explaining holiday observances or proper behavior patterns and the indoctrination into a bewildering mixture of truth and "talk-story" that made family history an inseparable combination of fact and make-believe.

Neither Dillard nor Kingston claims to have understood boys very well while growing up, although Dillard, who says she was "conspicuous" though not "central," had a much more active social life, beginning with dancing school at age ten and progressing to dinner dances at the Sewickley Country Club. She played football and baseball with boys when she was little; by sixteen, she had a boyfriend whom she loved "so tenderly, I thought I must transmogrify into vapor." Nevertheless, for all her appreciation of the boys' "cuteness," Dillard laments, "How little I understood them! How little I even glimpsed who they were." She imagined that they, as she, fought losing battles to avoid going to church and thus observed with disbelief their apparent devotion at prayer. She thought that the boys shared her own aspirations to do romantic and exciting things, only to discover soon thereafter that their aspirations were much more worldly: to make money, to head powerful corporations. If, deep within them, they also longed to escape the expectations of their society, Dillard reflects, "I never knew them well enough to tell."

Kingston's social experience lacked many of the parent-arranged boy-girl activities that were common in Dillard's life; as a teenager, she was hampered by having to change her naturally loud Chinese voice to one that was quiet "American-feminine," her "Chinese-feminine" pigeon-toed walk to Americanized "walking erect." Like Dillard, Kingston didn't understand boys very well; unlike Dillard, she was frightened by their mystery:

> As if it came from an atavism deeper than fear, I used to add "brother" silently to boys' names. It . . . made them less scary and as familiar and deserving of benevolence as girls.

However, says, Kingston, by such action

> I hexed myself also—no dates. I should have stood up, both arms waving, and shouted out across libraries, "Hey, you! Love me back." I had no idea, though, how to make attraction selective, how to control its direction and magnitude. If I made myself American-pretty so that the five or six Chinese boys in the class fell in love with me, everyone else—the Caucasian, Negro, and Japanese boys—would too. Sisterliness, dignified, and honorable, made much more sense.

Both Dillard and Kingston had a penchant for wandering far from their home territory, as if unconsciously searching for something before they were even able to give it a name. Dillard first "memorized the neighborhood" and by age

seven had "traveled over the known world's edge" on her bicycle. She spent years exploring the 380-acre Frick Park; she kept "push[ing] at my map's edges." Kingston was also an intrepid adventurer:

> I took my brothers and sisters to explore strange people's houses, ghost children's houses, and haunted houses blackened by fire. We explored a Mexican house and a red-headed family's house. . . . We explored the sloughs, where we found hobo nests.

By sixteen, says Dillard, "I was going to hell on a handcart . . . and I knew it and everyone around me knew it, and there it was." "I morally disapproved most things in North America," Dillard remembers, "and blamed my innocent parents for them." She convulsed with laughter over private jokes in school and volunteered too exuberantly in class; she damaged musical instruments with her wild, free playing: "I was what they called a live wire. I was shooting out sparks that were digging a pit around me, and I was sinking into that pit." She needed outlets but didn't know what they were: "I wanted to raise armies, make love to armies, conquer armies." She felt impelled to do *something,* but didn't know what to do first: "What would you do if you had fifteen minutes to live before the bomb went off?"

At this age, Dillard, like Kingston, had a voice problem, but whereas Kingston initially was too quiet, Dillard was too loud: "I couldn't lower my voice although I could see the people around me flinch." She was a turmoil of emotions: rage, anger, hatred, boredom, disdain, wildness. At various times, Dillard recalls, "I approved almost nothing," and "I despised everything and everyone about me"; "I woke every morning full of hope, and was livid with rage before break-fast." She would have done something about her condition, if only she had known what to do.

During the same time in her life, Kingston too felt anger, hatred, rage, as well as consciousness of her own faults. She wanted to take revenge on the people who had figuratively written the "chink" and "gook" words on her back, to avenge the injustices that the Communists had perpetrated on her Chinese relatives and that the American bureaucracy had dealt her parents in taking away their laundries. Had it been possible, Kingston says, she would have become an outlaw Chinese knot-maker, dedicated to tying a special complex knot that had been ruled illegal; the position seemed symbolically right for her. She browbeat herself, remembering some two hundred misdeeds she had kept secret from her mother: praying for a horse of the unlucky white color, stealing money for candy, fighting at Chinese school, envying Catholics, killing an innocent spider. Once she had pinched and hair-pulled and screamed at another Chinese girl who reminded her too much of herself in being perpetually the last chosen for her team and in being so desperately quiet (though for many more years than Kingston was). It was part of her emotional confusion that while Kingston didn't truly repent any of these actions, she nonetheless desperately wanted to be forgiven for them.

In Dillard's case, eventually she and her parents sat down together late one evening to try to resolve Mrs. Doak's despairing question, "'Dear God, what are we going to do with you?'." "We all seemed to have exhausted our options," says Dillard. "They asked me for fresh ideas, but I had none. I racked my brain, but couldn't come up with anything. The U.S. Marines didn't take sixteen-year-old girls." At this stage of her life, according to Dillard, she thought of herself as "the intelligentsia around these parts, single-handedly"; "it was beginning to strike me that Father, who knew the real world so well, got some of it wrong." She was determined that she wasn't going to marry the "right" boy; she didn't want to grow up to lead the kind of life that was expected of her. Dillard had never faced an insurmountable obstacle within what she calls "the narrow bounds of my isolationism," so she was certain that she could be and do anything that she pleased. She didn't want to be smoothed down, as her headmistress had suggested she would be, by college: "I had hopes for my rough edges. I wanted to use them as a can opener, to cut myself a hole in the world's surface, and exit through it." The alternative filled her with horror: "Would I be ground, instead, to a nub? Would they send me home, an ornament to my breed, in a jewelry bag?"

Even Dillard's friend Ellin recognized that Dillard's eyes were willfully closed to the realities of the social—and greater—worlds around them; in answer to Dillard's questions, she would often sigh and exclaim to everyone at large, "'She still doesn't get it!'" Dillard's father could only aggrievedly conclude that sometimes, as in the case when she quit the church, Dillard "was deliberately setting out to humiliate" her parents. There is no indication that she was. Rather, the portrait of Dillard that emerges is one of a bright, creative young woman who was hyperactively restless, whose "idea was to stay barely alive . . . until the time came when I could go [elsewhere]." Dillard pictures her departure from home as inevitable: books "would propel me right out of Pittsburgh altogether." Yet, Dillard says, although her "mother knew we would go [,] she encouraged us." It was simply a matter of determining for once and for all to "drive to Guatemala, drive to Alaska" instead of to the family garage. Until then, Dillard could only bide her time and whisper "the password phrase. . . 'There is a world. There is another world'." As she finished her days at Ellis School, she knew that her first stop in it would be at Hollins College.

While the confrontation scene in Dillard's book describes trembling voices and full ashtrays, its counterpart in

Kingston's book takes place at the crowded dinner table in the laundry as Kingston stands up screaming, impelling her mother to begin shouting back, her father to ignore her, and her siblings to steal away silently. In an emotional diatribe, Kingston pours out a disorganized list of grievances and declarations and private goals: she wants the mentally retarded man banished from consideration as husband material for her or her sister; she's suffered her whole lifetime over the confusions of the lies of "talk-story"; she's going to quit Chinese school and abandon the Chinese customs she thinks are stupid; she's going to go to college and become a professional instead of getting married.

Much of this resembles Dillard's youthful convictions and protestations. Like Dillard, Kingston is convinced she is intelligent: "Do you know what the Teacher Ghosts say about me? They tell me I'm smart, and I can win scholarships. I can get into colleges. I've already applied. I'm smart. I can do all kinds of things. I know how to get A's." No more than Dillard does Kingston declare herself willing to abide by her parents' ideas of a suitable marriage partner: "You think you can give us away to freaks. You better not do that, Mother." Again, like Dillard, Kingston believes she can do and be anything:

> I could be a scientist or a mathematician. . . . But I didn't say I wanted to be a mathematician either. That's what the ghosts say. I want to be a lumberjack and a newspaper reporter. . . . I'm going to chop down trees in the daytime and write about timber at night.

And as Ellin did for Dillard, Mrs. Hong has to explain to a rebellious young woman that she "doesn't get it": when Kingston protests being called ugly, her mother tells her, "That's what we're supposed to say. That's what Chinese say. We like to say the opposite."

In the "Epilogue" of her book, Dillard notes,

> Possibly because Father had loaded his boat one day and gone down the Ohio River, I confused leaving with living, and vowed that when I got my freedom, I would be the one to do both.

She suggests that with maturity she learned that one can do the second without necessarily doing the first. On the other hand, Kingston declares,

> I had to leave home in order to see the world logically, logic the new way of seeing. I learned to think that mysteries are for explanation. I enjoy the simplicity. Concrete pours out of my mouth to cover the forests with freeways and sidewalks. Give me plastics, periodical tables, t.v. dinners with veg-

etables no more complex than peas mixed with diced carrots. Shine floodlights into dark corners: no ghosts.

As a mature woman come home to visit her family, Kingston relates that she tells her mother,

> I've found some places in this country that are ghostfree. And I think I belong there, where I don't catch colds or use my hospitalization insurance. Here I'm sick so often, I can barely work. I can't help it, Mama.

For Kingston, leaving home seems to have been a necessary move in order to remain healthy and happy and balanced.

Thus, the resolutions of the books differ, but in other respects, their contents are strikingly the same. Both the young WASP and the young Oriental woman describe themselves as teenage rebels, feeling trapped within their families and their societies. Both are bright, ambitious, curious; both seek to come to terms with a world larger than that immediately known to them. By comparing the two works, one finds that Dillard's and Kingston's struggles to do this illuminate each other. And by comparing the growing-up problems of the authors with their own trials and uncertainties, student readers of Dillard and Kingston may find reassurance that their own rebellions are not singular, while they broaden their literary backgrounds through exposure to the works of two fine writers.

Suzanne Berne (review date Spring 1990)

SOURCE: "The Lonely Life," in *Belles Lettres,* Vol. 5, Spring, 1990, p. 6.

[*In the review below, Berne argues that* The Writing Life *is at its best when Dillard is less strident and relentless.*]

What happens when you've been writing seriously for years, devoting much of your life to your art, and suddenly you begin to doubt your purpose? You have two options. One is to quit writing; the other is to talk yourself out of your doubts. Reminding other writers of the value of writing is a way of reminding yourself. In *The Writing Life,* meditations on being a writer, Annie Dillard tells of the time she's spent in lonely cabins, tool sheds, and library, carrels, writing, writing, writing. "It takes years to write a book," she informs us solemnly, "between two and ten years." So why, we ask, does anyone choose to be a writer? Dillard once knew a painter, who when asked how he decided to be a painter replied, "I liked the smell of the paint," What draws a writer to writing? Sentences, she says. It is knowing and loving your own

medium so much that you're intoxicated by it, lured away from other pursuits.

But how does a writer *keep* writing? Beyond loving sentences, from where does the motivation come? Day after day year after year, there is the writer in a small room staring into a blank page or screen, trying to make something from what appears, gloatingly, to be nothing. Writing is a drudge's life. Work all day and there is still more, always more, to do. The writer, according to Dillard, "must be sufficiently excited to rouse himself to the task at hand, and not so excited he cannot sit down to it. He must have faith sufficient to impel and renew the work, yet not so much faith he fancies he is writing well when he is not." Alone in that small room, you bore yourself, praise yourself, goad yourself. Not even the smell of paint and turpentine is there to wake you.

The Writing Life begins: "When you write, you lay out a line of words. The line of words is a miner's pick, a woodcarver's gouge, a surgeon's probe. You wield it, and it digs a path you follow." These sentences introduce Dillard's examination of the drive, the destination, even the madness, behind the solitary struggle with words. These sentences also reveal what she's really up to: She wants to snatch writing out of the realm of the ephemeral and plunge it back into the physical. She wants to make the work of writing familiar, part of the world—to feel less alone as a writer herself. She wonders at one point, "Why wasn't I running a ferryboat, like sane people?"

Why else search so hard for ways to make writing's labor visual but to seem like a sane person to everybody else? "One of the few things I know about writing is this," she announces toward the end of *The Writing Life,* "spend it all, shoot it, play it, lose it, all, right away, every time." Unpredictability is an occupational hazard: one minute writing is honest labor—like a miner's or a woodcarver's work—the next it's gambling. Writing is a pocketful of change, a crap game, a poker hand. You win by risking everything you know in an attempt to discover more. "Anything you do not give freely and abundantly becomes lost to you," warns Dillard. "You open your safe and find ashes." In other words, writing doesn't last unless it's on paper. A writer keeps going because, finally, she wants to make something last.

For people looking for pointers about writing, this is no how-to handbook; it offers no hints for the beginner on developing characters, handling plot, or outlining an essay. Instead, Dillard offers exhortations to the entrenched writer. "Push it," she yells like a drill sergeant. "Examine all things intensely and relentlessly." Don't give up. Keep looking. Get it on paper.

There is no writing without an examination of the physical world. There is no sense to be made of the world without contemplation and interpretation. Yet the external world, necessary as it is, can be distracting. She tells us she once had to tape a drawing of the scene outside her window to the closed venetian blinds so she would stop looking out at life in her effort to see into it. To capture what she sees, Dillard believes she must turn toward an inward vision. "If I had possessed the skill, I would have painted directly on the blind, in meticulous colors, a *trompe l'oeil* mural view of all that the blinds hid, Instead, I wrote it."

Her attempts to inspire us are generous. There is something companionable in knowing that someone else is trying to make sense out of why we scratch words on paper. Yet there's a nagging little jeer of "so what?" running through the musings and anecdotes in this book. Shut the blinds, tape a drawing to them and what do you have? A drawing and a dark room. Behind the stories of late-night vigils at the computer screen, coffee-primed revelations, relentless examinations, *The Writing Life* is about being alone and not liking it much. As Dillard notes, "The written word is weak. Many people prefer life to it." The next moment she's off on another meditation, but the worry has slipped in.

Write and keep writing, she seems to be saying, because if you stop, if you take too deep a breath and look around at what other people are doing, you might realize that what you are doing is tinged by the ridiculous. In another moment of doubt, she admits that writers cling to "the ludicrous notion that a reasonable option for occupying yourself on the planet until your life span plays itself out is sitting in a small room for the duration, in the company of pieces of paper." At least painters have that smell of paint.

One of the pleasures of this book is its specificity. Dillard, who won a Pulitzer Prize for *Pilgrim at Tinker Creek,* a personal narrative about the mysteries of the natural world, is a collector of precise terms and proper names. We are treated to all the places she has gone to write: an island on Haro Strait in Northern Puget Sound, a library carrel in Roanoke, Virginia a pine shed on Cape Cod. We are presented with heroes, nonwriters who exhibit daring and skill and afford parallels between other jobs and writing. She gives us lots of quotations, good, inspiring quotations, the kind to print on index cards and tape above the word processor. But much of this book reads like a pep talk. The most convincing moments are when Dillard lowers her voice and something confidential creeps in. After describing yet another instance of her devotion to writing, she allows. "But the fanaticism of my twenties shocks me now. As I feared it would."

"It's all right," we want to say. It's part of writing to get sick of writing Still, perhaps if Dillard had admitted that to herself, we wouldn't have this book. She is always, no matter what her subject, a wonderful stylist. And what finally convinces us of the importance of the writing life are the wondrous sentences that she uses to describe it.

Thomas Keneally (review date 3 May 1992)

SOURCE: "Beneath the Wheels of Progress," in *New York Times,* May 3, 1992, p. 9.

[*In the following review of* The Living, *Keneally praises Dillard's style and tone.*]

Annie Dillard, a poet and essayist whose nonfiction work has won the Pulitzer Prize, has moved to fiction now with an invigorating, intricate first novel, *The Living.* Here she displays everything a person could need to know about what befell the Lummi, Skagit and Nooksack Indians between 1855 and the end of the last century; everything about European and Asian settlement in the Washington Territory in the same period; everything about tree felling, hops farming, railroad fever, land speculation, fashion, politics and education in the Bellingham Bay region in the extreme northwest corner of the United States.

At first, the reader might think that the celebration of the setting is the most important part of the book, that this is to be a hymn to the peculiar frontier passages, enthusiasms and griefs of the community of Whatcom on Bellingham Bay. Ms. Dillard so frankly cherishes her material that we are willing to forgive what, at first, seems a peremptory narrative pace. The passage of time seems so brisk, in fact, that a sort of anxiety is momentarily induced. How can the material last the narrator near to 400 pages?

For example, we are at first merely told that young Ada Fishburn has buried her 3-year-old boy child, Charley, crushed by the wagon wheels, under a lone tree on the Oregon Trail in earth thickly sown with the bones of earlier, unhappy voyagers. We are also told in a few sentences how Rooney Fishburn, Ada's husband, digging a well on their small, misty claim among the Douglas firs, asphyxiates when his shovel strikes a pocket of gas. An Englishman, a former manservant who goes to help Rooney, perishes just as instantly. The narrative moves from 1855 to 1872 in a few crammed paragraphs.

Ms. Dillard deals with an entire population as briskly as she deals with the Fishburns. Young John Ireland Sharp's entire family, parents and siblings, drown when their skiff sinks off Madrone Island near Puget Sound. "It seemed to him that his submerged family listed north and gestured towards Lummi Island every day when the sea flooded in from the Strait of Juan de Fuca. . . . They swayed like singers in a chorus under the pillars of the sea. . . . God pinned people under the sea among crabs." Again, in the style of the book, this event is bluntly announced. "It was in May that the Sharp family met with an accident; they drowned, except for John Ireland."

Not even William Kennedy's grand, roistering novel of 19th-century Albany, *Quinn's Book,* travels so headlong and produces such anxieties of pace.

The reader is quickly taught, however, to have more faith in Annie Dillard's tremendous gift for writing in a genuinely epic mode. For the action of *The Living* is cyclical, returning again and again to events, imbuing them with poignancy. The wealth of cherished detail is met in full by a wealth of cherished character. No fake suspense in Annie Dillard's writing. Instead the same incident enriches us over and over again.

Her writing has another extraordinary quality that is, in fact, the whole point of her narrative. She convinces us of, rather than simply positing, the fragility of the lives of all her people. This is, above all, why we remain fascinated for all the length of this strange and marvelous account. The indigenous crab of this foggy rainy region stands as a symbol of the tenuousness of life, the omnipresence of death. It eats the face of Lee Chin, an unhappy Chinese man tethered to a pier in a rising tide by the scholarly hermit Beal Obenchain. In turn, a crab scurries from the boots of the possibly murdered Obenchain.

Death's pincers work on the forested shore too. "Men died from trafficking in superior forces, like rivers and horses, bulls, steam saws, mill gears, quarried rock, or falling trees or rolling logs. Women died in rivers, too, and under trees and rockslides, and men took fevers, too, and fevers took men." Everywhere the tribes of the dead press in on the living and work at their memories. The widowed Minta Honer goes to meet her parents, Senator and Mrs. Green Randall, at the pier, and while she is gone two of her children are consumed in flame. Nooksack Indians must rid her of these ghosts, squeezing them from her body, starting with her shoulders, ending with her feet.

Beneath such shadows, enthusiasms flare riotously. The account begins with the Fraser River gold rush in 1858, just 18 miles away in British Columbia, and ends with the Klondike rush of 1897. Hearing of the Klondike strike, Pearl Sharp, enjoying a picnic on Madrone Island with her reclusive, bewildered husband, cries, "Let's go home, troops. Hard times is over."

Amid flux and loss, people have time to be worldly. The advice girls were given was "to marry a man from New England, for New England men treated their wives right fine. . . . And by all means arrange to become a man's sec-

ond wife, at least: the previous wife will have accomplished the back-breaking labor of improving his claim."

None of this prevents Senator Randall's second daughter, June, from marrying the apparently feckless Clare Fishburn, or prevents beautiful young Grace, who keeps house for a Seattle madam, Old Mother Damnable, from marrying Clare's intense, surly brother Glee.

> *The Living* is an August celebration of human frenzy and endurance. Her living are hectically alive, her dead recur in furious memory. And Annie Dillard, sometimes by an apparent crabwise indirection but with utter thoroughness, proves herself a fine novelist.
> —*Thomas Keneally*

Just as ill-advisedly, socialists and unionists so forget the dream of brotherhood as to expel or murder the Celestials (the Chinese), who, with the Terrestrials (the Irish), are the great railroad builders of the day.

And every time there is a rumor of Whatcom becoming a railway terminus or a center for Japanese trade, real estate booms and speculation and its attendant angel, embezzlement, seize the civic soul. People lose faith in society, ideology, brothers, spouses, God—but never their faith in a boom time. Only a few stand back from the fever: John Ireland, the disabused socialist schoolteacher, and Beal Obenchain, who lives in the millennium-old stump of a giant cedar. Having taken possession of the soul of a calf that he strangled in his boyhood, Obenchain now plans to take possession of the soul of one of his fellow citizens, a possession which has nothing to do with real estate, which is not on the temporal plane.

Ms. Dillard's tale is packed with oddity of character and incident. For oddity of character, try the Pullman conductor Tommy Cahoon, who survived being scalped by the Sioux while fishing in Wyoming. For oddity of incident, try the scene in which Eustace Honer chooses his moment to raise his concern with the Nooksack chief, Kulshan Jim, that the Indians treat their women too harshly, working them like mules. He finds that Kulshan Jim is thereby free to raise *his* concern about the way "the Bostons" treat *their* women, striking them in anger. "All the Nooksacks pitied the Boston women—pitied them! he said softly . . .—whose houses were long journeys apart, who worked alone, got hit, and died young."

What is more important than any of this, and harder to convey, is the way Annie Dillard gives weight to every detail.

The Living is an August celebration of human frenzy and endurance. Her living are hectically alive, her dead recur in furious memory. And Annie Dillard, sometimes by an apparent crabwise indirection but with utter thoroughness, proves herself a fine novelist.

Dianne Ganz (review date Fall 1992)

SOURCE: "None Abiding," in *Belles Lettres,* Vol. 8, No. 1, Fall, 1992, pp. 22-3.

[*In the following review of* The Living, *Ganz praises Dillard's ability to find meaning in ordinary settings.*]

With Annie Dillard's first novel [*The Living*], a frontier saga of life along the Puget Sound during the latter 19th century, the Pacific Northwest has been given its Willa Cather. Dillard's pioneers, like Cather's, are drawn against a powerful landscape, but instead of the bright, horizontal immensities of Cather's prairies, Dillard sets her characters down in the dark, towering Pacific rain forests, where 200-foot Douglas firs grow as "close as grass" and as "thick as buildings."

Measured against these giant trees, human beings are fragile things, and it seems the burden of Dillard's narrative, right from the start, to make the reader experience this fragility. In the opening scene, Ada Fishburn surveys this "rough edge of the world" to which she and her family have come, and repeats to herself, like a litany: "Our days on earth are as a shadow, and there is none abiding." The land has already claimed her three-year-old son, who was crushed under the wheels of their oxen train back on the Oregon Trail, and Ada has wakened to the shock of how quickly life can be erased. It's a shock the reader is wakened to repeatedly during the course of this novel, as these settlers die from "trafficking in superior forces," the women die from "fever and . . . from having babies," and their children die "as other people did, as a consequence of their bodies' material fragility."

Death throws strong shadows across these pages, but even stronger is the sense of the headlong energy, the clamor, and the din of "the living." Dillard's story covers a period of tumultuous social and ecological change. Farmers wrestle with the forest to "rid the land of this tonnage of tree." Beaches transform into coastal villages and then into bustling seaport towns. The Fraser River gold rush of 1858 and the building of the railroad draw people westward like magnets: scheming prospectors, impoverished Chinese and Irish immigrants—a bouillabaisse of racial and ethnic peoples whose eccentricities and differences haven't yet been melted down.

Most compelling is Dillard's portrayal of the region's Na-

tive Americans, the Nooksack, the Lummis, and the Skagits, without whom the settlers "would have starved to death a dozen times." The Lummis regard the settlers sympathetically, as "homeless people . . . who did not know how to behave"; they especially pity the womenfolk, "whose houses were long journeys apart, who worked alone, got hit, and died young." There are poignant scenes—the Methodist Nooksacks at a funeral singing "Shall We Gather at the River" in their own tongue, and powerful ones—a tent full of Skagit men ministering to a pioneer who has just lost her two children, only a month after also losing her husband. The medicine man moans a soft chant as the others tenderly massage Minta's body, from her forearms down to her toes, to squeeze out the ghosts.

One of the traits that readers of Dillard's previous work have most admired is the energy and attentiveness she brings to the ordinary. Here her gift for "paying attention" to mundane details gives us an imaginary world so richly furnished that it provides the reader with what Henry James called the "illusion of having lived another life." Dillard's narrator is thoroughly acquainted with the processes and paraphernalia of 19th-century frontier life; she knows how to dress bear meat, sew an astrakhan coat, fell a fir tree, and read steamship schedules. From the shape of their barns and petticoats to the shape of their speech, from their thoughts and fears to their droll frontier humor, these characters' lives are rendered with exquisite attention to detail and nuance.

Finally, paying attention emerges in Dillard's tale, not only as literary method, but also as morality. The key event involves Beal Obenchain, an intellectual hermit who lives in a cedar stump and performs calculated experiments in cruelty to assuage his loathing of life. After grotesquely murdering a Chinese laborer, he decides that murder is less rewarding than threatening death and then watching a man's gradual unraveling; in this way he possesses not merely a carcass, but his victim's very soul. For this torment he randomly chooses Ada Fishburn's eldest son, Clare, who has grown from a rambunctious boy into an upstanding citizen, given to pretension and self-importance.

Unexpectedly, Clare's forced confrontation with the certainty of death, far from shriveling his soul, instead rescues him from his shallow preoccupations. Looking at the world "as if for the last time" enables him to see it truly for the first time. His petty self-importance gives way to a realization of the solidarity of "all the living breasting into the crest of the present together . . . opening time like a path in the grass." Ironically, Beal Obenchain's threat initiates Clare into the wisdom of "memento mori," the paying attention to death that overcomes our resistance to life. At the same time, "memento mori" provides the clue to how it is that Dillard's novel, so strongly shadowed by death is, even more powerfully, a rousing celebration of "the living."

Terri Brown-Davidson (essay date April 1993)

SOURCE: "'Choosing the Given with a Fierce and Pointed Will': Annie Dillard and Risk-Taking in Contemporary Literature," in *The Hollins Critic,* Vol. XXX, No. 2, April, 1993, pp. 1-9.

[In the essay below, Brown-Davidson provides an overview of Dillard's works.]

Imagine this. You are a lectured-into-submission child, attending another dull Protestant church service with your parents. The ordinariness of your life has driven you into a repressed fury that makes your stomach knot at the meat-and-potatoes dinner you eat every Wednesday night, at the English homework (verbs-adjectives-adverbs-nouns) that always fails to engage you, at a life in which you seem to be peering through one smeared window or the next to glimpse a landscape that loses color as you age. Then you begin to paint. Secretly, at first. The bumbled efforts of any child, the too pastel watercolors you smear onto the tiny stretched canvas with your fist, the windows that open out suddenly, like pulled-apart storm shutters, onto a charged world that was whirling by without you, make you squirm on your hard little pew, but with joy, remembering how it felt to layer Red #2 onto the white as the minister leads you and the congregation in another sorry hymn. You are full, complete, whole for the first time in your miserable six years. You've discovered the essence that the two hundred adults surrounding you haven't, the euphoria in shape, color, patterning that will propel you through your days like an Arctic explorer riding a fast-moving ice floe, conscious of the danger, exhilarated and refreshed by the possibility of threat.

Let's look at that threat. It pumps up our adrenalin faster than a bee. When I was four or five, I molded sinister-looking, branchless trees from red and blue Play-do. I can still remember how it felt to hunch over that card table, slicking the slim and slimmer trees up, up, with my squeezing fingers until the trunks elongated so far they collapsed onto themselves. Those trees terrified me. I pretended that they were part of some night forest that seized the unwitting explorers I also fashioned out of clay, seized and strangled them with their trunks. But my terror was relief. I was confronting darkness in myself I hadn't yet discovered; I was wrestling with the terror of mortality and death though no one I'd ever known had, as some friend's genteel mother phrased it, "passed to the other side." Through plummeting myself up to the eyes in the mire of emotional and spiritual complexity, even at four I was beginning to understand the essence of things.

Annie Dillard, in her essays, poetry, and fiction, wrestles with the essence of things with the strength of a grizzly wrapping us in its arms. She is fierce, undaunted by the rest of the world's desire to let the world drift by in a bliss of passivity. Rather than watching the "eternal splendor" of nature, she participates in its manifold mysteries by bringing the whole of her consciousness to bear on every moment. She never looks for the sake of looking, never creates art for art's sake. Annie Dillard is one of the most fearless writers I have ever read because, like a prism filtering the greens and violets and golds of the spirit, she sees loss, suffering, ecstasy, grief, anger, betrayal, the meaning of life, the questions of life, the huge patternings of our cosmos, in every split and melting ice floe, in every tarantula that seizes a moth with its long and hairy legs. Like Blake, she possesses the ability to see a universe in a grain of sand or in a cracked kernel of corn. Reading a book as spiritually audacious as *Holy the Firm,* I can well believe that Dillard was the Pittsburgh child who set a stone under a streetcar to see it topple in her memoir, *An American Childhood,* for Dillard, even now, I think, would like to slide a stone under our passivity and see us all scramble for footing as we fall headfirst onto the slick and dangerous steel tracks of meaning, Certainly the first paragraph of this essay is a fiction, but, for many writers, I believe, it is an emotional truth, and I see Dillard in this paragraph, I see Dillard, above all, as the rebellious child in artists that keeps them furious with and enamored of the world well into their forties or, if they're lucky, until death: Annie Dillard picks a fight with the universe and means to win.

In this we, as writers, need to emulate her. For we, too, need to win. But, even more than winning, we desperately need to fight, to shake off our passivity, cast off our shallowness. Contemporary literature has lost its guts. And we are a deluded species, looking to the future for answers or to the past when we should be glancing around at what's *here.* Dillard understands this. Whether she is pondering the horrific aggressor-prey relationship that results in a frog having its innards sucked out by a giant water bug (*Pilgrim at Tinker Creek*) or the captured-for-dinner deer in an Ecuador jungle whose pain becomes, in her mind, impossible to ameliorate because its tiny vein of suffering links it to a vaster body of anguish (**"The Deer at Providencia,"** *Teaching a Stone to Talk*), what makes Annie Dillard not only a compelling writer but also, perhaps, one of the most important writers of our time is her refusal to back down from issues that matter, the spiritual, emotional, and ethical quandaries that link us to a vaster body of humanity, whether we acknowledge the relationship or not. In an era in which literature has become increasingly safe, Annie Dillard's work releases us, refreshingly, into the mind of a writer who questions nothing less than the meaning and multiple ramifications of life for us, a dying species whose future on this planet is, at best, uncertain.

Yet, this is not to suggest that Dillard's questioning leads her straight into pessimism or, concomitantly, into an admiration for or an acceptance of the "suicide story." Dillard herself asserts, in *Living by Fiction,* that "meaninglessness in art is a contradiction in terms. Meaning is contextual," and this assertion is aptly borne out by most of Dillard's essays and by the multigenerational, panoramic life-struggle in her novel, *The Living.* The creator, in her active engagement in shaping words on a page or casting a bronze sculpture or wielding a tube of paint for the most random-seeming abstract-expressionism spatters, is, through activity and process, engaged in a creation of meaning. Of course, producing gobbledegook is always a risk when attention is not paid to the seriousness of the act itself or to the product such an almost-holy engagement pulls into the world, for, as Dillard reminds us, "We judge a work on its integrity" (*Living by Fiction*). And, in fact, when randomness or faulty organization is involved, the author cannot lacquer her failings with the simple affirmation that her fragmentation reflects the fragmentation of an emotionally/ethically crumbling society; such a declaration is hypocritical in the extreme because it breaks the holiness of the act of creating art and also calls into question the integrity of the product itself, which Dillard sees as the distinguishing characteristic in producing a successful fictional work and which I, by extension, see as not only necessary for fiction but important for all contemporary literature that, like Dillard's, is erected on a wellspring of significance from which her readers can drink and drink again. Dillard wrestles with the issue on pages 26-27 of *Living by Fiction:*

> As in the realm of feeling, so in the realm of intellect. Naming your characters Aristotle and Plato is not going to make their relationship interesting unless you make it so on the page; having your character shoot himself in the end does not mean that anyone has learned anything; and setting your novel in Buchenwald does not give it moral significance. Now: may a work of art borrow meaning by being itself meaningless? May it claim therefore to have criticized society? Or to have recreated our experience? May a work claim for itself whole hunks of other people's thoughts on the flimsy grounds that the work itself, being so fragmented, typifies our experience of this century? Can a writer get away with this? I don't think so.

For Dillard, meaning itself is the issue, is what's at stake. "K-Mart Realism" holds no appeal for her; she'd rather straddle a metaphysical limb in her quest for the emotionally and spiritually significant. This "I dare myself to" attitude leads her into Roethke's "desperate leaps" or the beautiful, aggressive structures that allow her to suck the world into the now protean form I think of as the "Dillard essay." In **"An Expedition at the North Pole"** from *Teaching a Stone to Talk,* with muted humor Dillard addresses the age-old problem of the spiritual quest—what it is, how

we determine if the quest is more satisfying than the reward—through juxtaposing, in sections labeled "The Land" and "The People," journalistic narrations of real explorers' attempts to "conquer the Pole" against an account of the hilariously secular services at the Catholic church Dillard, a lapsed Protestant, began attending in her obviously mistaken search for the splendors of ritual, of Mass:

> For a year I have been attending Mass at this Catholic church. Every Sunday for a year I have run away from home and joined the circus as a dancing bear. We dancing bears have dressed ourselves in buttoned clothes; we mince around the rings on two feet. Today we are restless; we kept dropping onto our forepaws.

Contrast the metaphorical exaggeration of this passage with Dillard's primarily "pure" account of Captain Oates's search for the Pole. Though the Arctic explorers, in their lack of preparation for their expeditions, come in for Dillard's all-too-scathing examining eye, it is easy to see which "expedition" she finds less ludicrous:

> Polar explorers were chosen, as astronauts are today, from the clamoring, competitive ranks of the sturdy, skilled, and sane. Many of the British leaders, in particular, were men of astonishing personal dignity. Reading their accounts of life *in extremis,* one is struck by their unending formality toward each other. When Scott's Captain Oates sacrificed himself on the Antarctic peninsula because his ruined feet were slowing the march, he stepped outside the tent one night to freeze himself in a blizzard, saying to the others, "I am just going outside and may be some time."

Though both quests are subject, in the breadth of their aspirations, seriousness of purpose, and worthiness of spiritual goals, to Dillard's humorous scrutiny, it is clearly the polar expeditions which fare better in her estimation because of the explorers' fierceness of desire to wrest what knowledge of beauty they could from that white, bleak landscape as well as their willingness to prepare themselves for the epiphanic experience of planting their flag. Dillard believes in an earned spirituality which is the natural result of a slow accumulation of observed details, of the world drunk in its wholeness and completeness to render the *receiver* whole. Sometimes, such a transformation cannot be accomplished with a wafer; Dillard notes, in this essay, the wafer a priest handed her which "proved to be stuck to five other wafers." And sometimes vanity can prevent any poor, hapless human being from reaching his spiritual goal, that moment of epiphany or rush of lit inner joy we all aspire to as our inheritance from participation in the natural world, as in the case of the Franklin expedition, which, although it proved a "turning point in Arctic exploration," was doomed because its participants insisted on being, above all else, gentlemen, carrying a "twelve-day supply of coal for the entire projected two or three years' voyage" so they would have room to accommodate, on their ship, a "1,200 volume library," 'a hand-organ, playing fifty tunes,' china place settings for officers and men, cut-glass wine goblets, and sterling silver flatware." Few *tableaux vivànt* are as pathetic as the one Dillard revives of the Franklin expedition men carrying their "sterling silver flatware" across the ice, where it would endure longer than their uniformed skeletons. But Dillard makes the point that, although vanity killed them, the quest was all; that failure, at least initially, is an integral element in any spiritual journey, may, in fact, only propel the seeker more fiercely toward his goal.

It is this sense of the quest to which Dillard clings and which is, I believe, lacking in much contemporary literature. As Dillard herself indicates in *Living by Fiction,* "contemporary modernist writers flatten their characters by handling them at a great distance, as if with tongs." This "flatness" is, to paraphrase Dillard, the equivalent of a primarily cubistic view prevalent today in literature: time is flattened, disjointed, dislocated; points of view tend to be limited; characters are "objectified" as in a Picasso painting in which, the mistress dismantled, one is permitted to see every side; in the least satisfying instances of cubism, one never receives the cumulative effect. Certainly there is power in the cubistic approach, this flattening: no longer do we have to endure the tedium of carefully-set-up introductions, of characters so richly and unnecessarily fleshed that we know with certainty the exact location and hairiness of a particular black mole under our heroine's arm. But there are disadvantages, too. In our zeal to avoid "overwriting" or the "risk of the gratuitous," we are producing montages so spare their very angularity prevents the reader from entering the text; in our rampaging fear of the "sentimental," we are producing characters and emotions so repellingly reticent that they lead to a plethora of what I call the "Bad Day poem"; in our preoccupation with movement and pace, we have produced works so breathlessly disassociative that, in poets like April Bernard, Laura Jensen, and Michael Burkard, the unravelling of surface text has become a mission all its own, muddying those deeper benefits—insight, emotional deepening, spiritual awakening and understanding—that I believe most readers *want* to find in a work of literature.

Annie Dillard commits none of these sins. Though her imagistic leaps are as breathtaking as one could wish, they are rarely obscure and nearly always in service of text. Along with the spiritual quest explored so beautifully in *Teaching a Stone to Talk* and *Pilgrim at Tinker Creek,* the enriching power of solitude is another concern of Dillard's, the meditative conversation with self that stretches the ability of the imagination to grasp circumstance and limitation, the physi-

cal, emotional, and spiritual boundaries we must either adhere to (because nature decrees thus) or surpass because, Dillard believes, we do have free will. In *Holy the Firm,* nature's beauties become a revelatory meditative force for Dillard, who has isolated herself with a cat on an island in Puget Sound solely for the sake of questioning the nature of God, man, and existence, an undertaking which most contemporary literature, with its emphasis on the everyday emotion, the discrete autobiographical incident, and the pragmatically easy grasp of the world, would scorn. Unsurprisingly, these "beauties" Dillard unearths have much to do with a celebratory examination of suffering, decay, and death as Dillard takes us to a bathroom wake with a pile of dessicated moths:

> And the moths, the empty moths, stagger against each other, headless, in a confusion of arcing strips of chitin like peeling varnish, like a jumble of buttresses for cathedral domes, like nothing resembling moths, so that I should hesitate to call them moths, except that I have had some experience with the figure moth reduced to a nub.

These "cathedral dome" moths, which carry all the glory of man as well as nature in their decaying carcasses, exemplify the spiritual link between the inner and outer worlds we can all only experience with our single, limited bits of consciousness, but every part of that world is hallowed, and the small, physical details (the moths) have as much psychological weight for us as the "cathedral domes" into which, with one instant's perception, they can be transformed. The transforming powers of consciousness are what *Holy the Firm* is about, and the girl, Julie Norwich, who is burned in a plane crash is no less nor more a symbol of our suffering and our ability to "rise from the ashes" than that paper-pile of moth-ash itself. This suffering encompasses the richness of human existence, which is necessarily stuffed full of terror and anguish as well as joy:

> You might as well be a nun. You might as well be God's chaste bride, chased by plunderers to the high caves of solitude, to the heartless rooms empty of voices, and of warm limbs hooking your heart to the world. Look how he loves you! Are you bandaged now, or loose in a sterilized room? Wait till they hand you a mirror, if you can hold one, and know what it means. That skinlessness, that black shroud of flesh in strips on your skull, is your veil.

It is a painful fact that the burned Julie Norwich may be shunned by a society that will call her "deformed," but it is also a fact that the moth Dillard perceives as Norwich's spiritual equivalent flies into a flame where its thorax ignites, where its head burns away and dissolves as "the glowing shell of her abdomen and thorax—a fraying, partially collapsing gold tube jammed upright in the candle's round pool" burns on and on.

We are that burning tube, Dillard is convinced. Through suffering and contentment, through blankness and perception, we live on aided by the god of day. It is this god Dillard worships above all others, even, seemingly, above Christ, whom she seems to regard as an extension of the holiness that lies, like the substance Holy the Firm, at the base of the universe, "underneath salts," at "absolute zero." As Dillard indicates, "matter and spirit are of a piece but distinguishable; God has a stake guaranteed in all the world. And the universe is real and not a dream, not a manufacture of the senses; subject may know object, knowledge may proceed, and Holy the Firm is in short the philosopher's stone." It is in "subject knowing object" that subject discovers both object and itself, and the result is combustion, a spiritual flaming-up that is the highest point of consciousness, whether we call that consciousness "epiphany" or "oneness with God." But the most powerful spiritual experience, the most powerful experience of self-knowledge (gleaned from the taking-in of the object) is bestowed by pure dailiness, the god of day who surrounds us like water hugging an island, coloring our senses, our every perception, as in the extraordinary opening paragraph of **Holy the Firm:**

> Every day is a god, each day is a god, and holiness holds forth in time. I worship each god, I praise each day splintered down, splintered down and wrapped in time like a husk, a husk of many colors spreading, at dawn fast over the mountains split.

The days themselves are husks, remnants, like the moths. Yet, like the moths, for twenty-four hours they are breathing, colorful, magical, floating, packed full with the promise of insight and ordinary perception, a kernel of holiness. This god of dailiness, to Dillard's startlement, appears everywhere, even when she hears "a ruckus on the porch" and we expect her cat has killed another wren. Instead, it is "a god, scorched," that the cat has dragged in, "a perfect, very small man" with "smoking wings." Thus it is not the extraordinary but the ordinary that governs our lives; thus it is this god of the ordinary who perpetually rides, as Dillard claims, "barefoot on my shoulder, or astride it," and, in our luring-in of this magic in the ordinary, we create our spiritual selves, we turn our bodies-becoming-husks into cathedrals.

But, though we may turn them into cathedrals, we are never allowed to forget, either, the homelier joy of inhabiting the body as *home.* Dillard's two primary strengths as a writer may well be her ability to render primary this "sensuality of ontology" as well as the metaphysical surrounding our fleshly beings. In **An American Childhood,** a much "cozier" book than **Holy the Firm,** Dillard succeeds in converting what could have been a typical story of growing up in the Pittsburgh suburbs in the 1950's into her own *Bildungsroman* replete with humor, warmth, and those metaphysical flashes characteristic of her work as a whole. This memoir is not so much Dillard's portrait of the artist, however, as her portrait of herself as reader. Inspired by her father, an executive at American Standard who purchases Twain's *Life on the Mississippi* so habitually during his business trips that the Doak family (Dillard's family) ends up with dozens of copies of the book on their shelves, and by her mother, an avid baseball fan/nonconformist with a penchant for quizzing her children on spellings of difficult words as well as on the thoughtfulness of their opinions, Dillard grows up surrounded by both sisters and books and learns to discover in people and in reading the mirror of her consciousness. Even during a charged and difficult adolescence, Dillard never loses sight of this early acquired passion and transfers her avaricious appetite for the world into an appetite for the page. In stunning passage after passage, Dillard manages to recreate with a fresh sense of discovery these first intellectual yearnings and communicates well what every habitual reader might here recognize, a physical *greed* for books:

> All spring long I crawled on my pin. I was reading *General Semantics*—Alfred Korzybski's early stab at linguistics; I'd hit on it by accident, in books with the word "language" in their titles. I read Freud's standard works, which interested me at first, but they denied reason. Denying reason had gotten Rimbaud nowhere. I read without snobbery, excited and alone, wholly free in the indifference of society. I read with the pure, exhilarating greed of readers sixteen, seventeen years old; I felt I was exhuming lost continents and plundering their stores. I knocked open everything in sight—Henry Miller, Helen Keller, Hardy, Updike, and the French. The war novels kept coming out, and so did John O'Hara's. I read popular social criticism ... *The Ugly American, The Hidden Persuaders, The Status Seekers.* I thought social and political criticism were interesting, but not nearly so interesting as everything else.

It is vital to note in this passage Dillard's repeated insistence on the importance of reason, for her location of beauty in reason (a beauty which leads, inevitably and *logically,* to a striving after the metaphysical) informs all her texts. Dillard is no softheaded, solipsistic yearner after the spiritual, but a writer who apprehends the religious through the physical touchstones of this world: nature, humankind, and, especially in **An American Childhood,** her beloved books. In this respect, and in her frequent and resplendent maximalism, she resembles no writer so much as Gerard Manley Hopkins and his own densely sensual tributes to a Higher Power.

As Dillard delves ever deeper and deeper into this metaphysical aspect of her work, her books become simultaneously more privately encoded, like Wallace Stevens's "difficult" poems, and more personal. Still, the roots of *The Writing Life* are inextricably entwined in the more "public" *An American Childhood,* though *The Writing Life,* despite its surface difficulties, may be an even stronger book. In *The Writing Life* we sense Dillard the artist discovering her great subject at last, hinted at in *Holy the Firm:* the individual progress of a mind immersed in the creative process. Although most writers, succumbing to a type of prejudice that also decrees poems about paintings must be inherently imitative, might be dismissive of this subject matter regardless of the *approach,* Dillard refuses to dismiss this "dangerous" topic; Dillard, with her customary fearlessness, uncovers in this book, which is unabashedly *about* writing, exciting and provocative new territory. What might, as the product of a lesser mind, a lesser art, easily become obsessive navel-gazing is, in *The Writing Life,* profound, beautiful, and unutterably moving. As in *Holy the Firm,* we experience in *The Writing Life* a book almost without props: we feel only the presence of Dillard's purposeful mind at work surrounded by the writing "scenery" of typewriter, legal pads, a chair, a pen. What we quickly discover, though, as salient to Dillard's vision of the creative process, is that the mind makes *everything* animate. In this passage, rest assured that it is not an actual earthquake that sets this typewriter ablaze:

> I saw at once that the typewriter was erupting. The old green Smith-Corona typewriter on the table was exploding with fire and ash. . . .
>
> I pulled down the curtains. When I leaned over the typewriter, sparks burnt round holes in my shirt, and fire singed a sleeve. . . . The typewriter did not seem to be flying apart, only erupting. On my face and hands I felt the heat from the caldera. The yellow fire made a fast, roaring noise. The typewriter itself made a rumbling, grinding noise; the table pitched. Nothing seemed to require my bucket of water. The table surface was ruined, of course, but not aflame. After twenty minutes or so, the eruption subsided.
>
> That night I heard more rumblings—weak ones, even farther apart. The next day I cleaned the typewriter, table, floor, wall, and ceiling. I threw away the burnt shirt. The following day I cleaned the typewriter again—a film of lampblack still coated the caldera—and then it was over. I have had no trouble with it since. Of course, now I know it can happen.

The passage is boldly Romantic, exploits—boldly—the pathetic fallacy, and captures, with a minimum of narration, the unpredictability of the writing process itself, which, according to Dillard's philosophy, can lead an artist in minutes toward a masterpiece or, in hours, toward nothing at all. This passage, and the whole of *The Writing Life,* establishes Dillard not only as a neo-Romantic who believes, to paraphrase Keats, that if writing does not come easily it had better not come at all, but also as a neo-Platonist who senses always the realm of the ideal beyond the actual, *believes* in this realm, and experiences it through the vatic voice. This does not imply that Dillard thinks the vatic can't be invited, coaxed like a bird with crumbs daily into her writing room. Only through such patient and deliberate coaxing, Dillard asserts, can *magic* happen:

> When you write, you lay out a line of words. The line of words is a miner's pick, a wood-carver's gouge, a surgeon's probe. You wield it, and it digs a path you follow. Soon you find yourself deep in new territory. Is it a dead end, or have you located the real subject? You will know tomorrow, or this time next year.

Watching Dillard "lay out her line of words" is both exhilarating and harrowing. That she can make the creative process seem so vital is a tribute not only to her own ability as a writer but to what she *believes.* In her engagement with the passions of the mind, passions that vault inevitably up into the spiritual, there is much for us to admire, especially as inhabitants of a society that appears too frequently focused on what is numbed in us, what lies dead at our core. This is risk-taking at its finest.

And Dillard, apparently, is continuing her risk-taking with a new foray into fiction, one eagerly awaited by those of us, especially, who have admired her astute analysis of the complete "fictional universe" in *Living by Fiction. The Living* is a bold, "old-fashioned" novel, panoramic in its scope, which signifies in its 400-or-so pages that Dillard is aligning herself within this "universe" as a sprawling, rural Dickensian, one for whom maximalism is a creed and a challenge. How different she appears in this novel, which signifies her swing from the personal process-of-the-mind approach in *The Writing Life* out into a world inhabited by "others"—an imaginative act of empathy—from the minimalist and somewhat uncertain poet who was just starting to explore her literary universe in *Tickets for a Prayer Wheel.* Dillard, in a sense, has come full circle.

But in all her works, including *Tickets for a Prayer Wheel* and *The Living,* it is her ability to enter into the spiritual with the artlessness of the steers that wander into Tinker Creek that distinguishes Annie Dillard from most writers of her generation. She is never afraid of the waters closing over her head; she is never afraid of drowning in the unanswered questions the universe of necessity poses; she makes no pretense of being able to answer her own questions as she offers them. It is her willingness to investigate the difficult emotional and spiritual terrain that sets her apart from those contemporaries who would make of sex a game. of death a morbidity, of spirituality a begged question. In her opulent. Biblical prose, Dillard refuses to address the question of excess, believing that in the piling-up of rich. lovely. accurate detail lies our perception of experience. And flatness. for her. of language, character. point of view. narrative line. is never an issue: after all, if the world were flat. Columbus would have sailed off the edge—so why pretend that things are other than they are?

In *Pilgrim at Tinker Creek,* Ezekiel. Dillard reminds us. "excoriates false prophets as those who have 'not gone up into the gaps.'" These gaps are the unclaimed spiritual territory our faint hearts caution us not to investigate. These gaps contain the knowledge of ourselves and the world we would lay claim to if we dared. Annie Dillard is fearless before these gaps, for she understands that they will teach her not only how to write but also how to live. As she asserts in the essay, **"Living Like Weasels,"** from *Teaching a Stone to Talk:*

> The weasel lives in necessity and we live in choice, hating necessity and dying at last ignobly in its talons. I would like to live as I should, as the weasel lives as he should. And I suspect that for me the way is like the weasel's: open to time and death painlessly, noticing everything, remembering nothing, choosing the given with a fierce and pointed will.

Reading this passage, I can remember when I lived as I should. I can remember when I shaped my red and blue Playdo trees with the thrill and panic and joy of discovery. As I labored over my desk, as the trees strangled passersby with the ferocity of a god, I felt connected to the external world through each flash of perception that dragged me closer until the inner and outer embraced, were intertwined. Each time I write, I grow closer to living that way again.

Annie Dillard understands this. Annie Dillard understands how to live in necessity. She has gone into the gaps, and she has emerged unscathed. For us, the writers who read her now, who have been cowed or saddened by the spiritual and emotional "flatness" of our age and art, Dillard has much to impart about courage and necessity, about "choosing the given with a fierce and pointed will."

James I. McClintock (essay date 1994)

SOURCE: "'Pray without Ceasing': Annie Dillard among the Nature Writers," in *Earthly Words: Essays on Contemporary American Nature and Environmental Writers,* edited by John Cooley. University of Michigan Press, 1994, pp. 69-86.

[*In the following essay, McClintock considers Dillard's work in comparison to the genre of American environmental writing. arguing that her work is uniquely Christian in perspective.*]

"Sons and daughters of Thoreau abound in contemporary American writing," Edward Abbey writes in his introduction to *Abbey's Road* (1979), mentioning Edward Hoagland, Joseph Wood Krutch, Wendell Berry, John McPhee, Ann Zwinger, and Peter Matthiessen, as well as himself. He reserves his highest praise for Annie Dillard, who "is the true heir of the Master." The others are Thoreauvian primarily in their identification with special locales—from Central Park in Hoagland's essay to Zwinger's Rockies. Abbey's one objection to Dillard's "otherwise strong, radiant book [*A Pilgrim at Tinker Creek*] is the constant name dropping. Always of one name"—God (*Abbey's Road*). Abbey's assessment is astute, because it highlights the essential characteristics of Annie Dillard's nature writing: her writing about place, the language she uses to evoke her experiences, and her religious preoccupation and vocation. Abbey's assessment is also eccentric, because his objection to her religious preoccupation is directed at Dillard's most distinctive achievements in the nature essays of *A Pilgrim at Tinker Creek* (1974). The objection would apply also to *Holy the Firm* (1977) and *Teaching a Stone to Talk* (1982), the two other Dillard books that use nature as a touchstone for spiritual insight.

Nature writing in America has always been religious or quasireligious. All the important studies on the subgenre conclude that nature writing is "in the end concerned not only with fact but with fundamental spiritual and aesthetic truth." That is true of essays by Thoreau, John Muir, John Burroughs, Aldo Leopold, Edwin Teale, and Joseph Wood Krutch, whose works represent more than a century of American nature writing. And Edward Abbey's work is infused with spiritual impulse, as he engages "Mystery."

I suspect that Abbey's objection to Dillard's name-dropping is that her God is identifiably Judeo-Christian. That objection is understandable, because nature writers and, more broadly, conservationists, environmentalists, and students of American responses to nature have consistently held the Judeo-Christian tradition responsible for land abuse. In *A Sand County Almanac* (1949), for example, conservationist and nature essayist Aldo Leopold objected to an "Abrahamic concept of land" as commodity for technological man's use. Historian Lynn White, Jr., concluded that the root of the postwar ecological crisis is a Judeo-Christian tradition that desacralizes nature and gives man "dominion" over it. Rejecting Judeo-Christian anthrocentricity, writers have turned to spiritual alternatives. In "Lord Man: The Religion of Conservation," Steven Fox identifies many nature writers and conservationists who "embraced a variety of non-Christian religions." Typical of many, poet and environmental activist Gary Snyder embraced Zen Buddhism and drew from Native American religious spiritual practices. Others, such as Joseph Wood Krutch, rejected Christian orthodoxy at first and a stoical humanism later, to embrace, finally, a pantheism that gave Krutch the profound sense that "we are all in this together," and that thus mirrored the thought of photographer Ansel Adams, who described his spiritual perspective simply as "a vast impersonal pantheism." A pantheistic perspective fits well with the insights of modern ecological science, as is seen in Aldo Leopold's essay "Thinking Like a Mountain," an account of his "conversion" from an anthropocentric to a biocentric stance.

I had a head for religious ideas. They were the first ideas I ever encountered. They made other ideas seem mean.
                                        —Annie Dillard

Nature writing, then, has been broadly religious in the sense that Wendell Berry finds religion in the poetry he most highly values—poetry that has a "sense of the presence of mystery or divinity in the world" and "attitudes of wonder or awe or humility before the works of the creation." Such poets, like nature writers, go on what Berry calls "a secular pilgrimage," which "seeks the world of the creation, the created world in which the Creator, the formative and quickening spirit, is still immanent and at work."

Theology has always attracted Annie Dillard. As an adolescent attending a Presbyterian summer vacation bible camp, she realized: "I had a head for religious ideas. They were the first ideas I ever encountered. They made other ideas seem mean." *A Pilgrim at Tinker Creek, Holy the Firm,* and *Teaching a Stone to Talk* are saturated with religious thought, longing, and experience. Dillard is after the "pearl of great price," religious vision, which will reconcile the self—which is pulled between faith and doubt—with a nature that is often cruel and ugly, and with a God who seems as irrational as loving. She is within meditative traditions and records repeated mystical experiences. She prepares for mystical reconciliation by performing rituals that mingle conventions for encountering nature that are found in nature writing with Judeo-Christian traditions and rituals. She is an offbeat Christian who walks in nature and reads science as part of her preparation for vision.

In *Holy the Firm,* Dillard finds unsatisfactory the "accessible and universal view," mentioned by Wendell Berry and "held by (Meister) Eckhart and by many peoples in various forms, . . . that the world is immanation, that God is in the thing, and eternally present here if nowhere else." That view is "scarcely different from pantheism," she writes, because from that perspective, "Christ is redundant and all things are one." This statement sets Dillard apart from the other nature writers; her perspective is Christian.

Dillard's books are dotted with biblical allusions, and she unselfconsciously uses the word *Christ.* During the central mystical moment in *Holy the Firm,* to cite the most extended example, she is walking home from a country store with communion wine for her church when suddenly she is filled with light, "everything in the world is translucent," the bay below is "transfigured," "everything is whole, and a parcel of everything else," and she sees that "Christ is being baptized" by John. Christ "lifts from the water. Water beads on his shoulders. I see the water in balls as heavy as planets, a billion beads of water as weighty as worlds, and he lifts them up on his back as he rises." Dillard writes throughout *Holy the Firm* in imagery that evokes the opening of the book, when she wakens, looks across Puget Sound, and greets the morning:

> I wake in a god. . . . Someone is kissing me—already. . . . I open my eyes. The god lifts from the water. His head fills the bay. He is Puget Sound, the Pacific; his breast rises from pastures; his fingers are firs; islands slide wet down his shoulders. Islands slip blue from his shoulders and glide over the water, the empty, lighted water like a stage.

In fact the entire structure of *Holy the Firm* is Christian. Dillard equates the three days the book spans to Creation, the Fall, and Redemption; and the subjective framework is "the tripartite pattern of faith, doubt, and faith renewed." Robert Dunn notes that the book's three chapters parallel the "three stages of the mystic way—illumination, purgation, and union."

Pilgrim at Tinker Creek also opens with Dillard awakening to a world seen through Christian experience, even if her doubt is constant. She is, after all, an anchorite and a pilgrim, awakened in the morning to the possibility of mystery by her cat, which has left her "body covered with paw prints in blood: I looked as though I'd been painted with roses." This imagery is profoundly linked to the Judeo-Christian tradition through the Passover, on the one hand, and through Christ's redemptive blood and the rose symbolizing Mary, on the other. The central mystical experience in *Pilgrim at Tinker Creek,* the vision of "the tree with the lights in it," is a revelation of "Christ's incarnation," which Dillard accepts despite liberal theological objections to a belief that Christ's incarnation took place at a particular time and a particular place. She affirms "the scandal of particularity," because "I never saw a tree that was no tree in particular"; the tree with lights on it is, after all, a particular backyard cedar.

Though Annie Dillard sees from the standpoint of Christian orthodoxy, she is still heterodox and unconventional. Critic Margaret Reimer has shown that though "Dillard stands in the orthodox Christian tradition" in her views of evil, for example, "her conclusions (or the lack of them) are far from the traditional Christian answers." Dillard has always been uncomfortable within orthodoxy, even though, paradoxically, she is also uncomfortable outside a Christian perspective. From childhood on, she was neither quite inside nor completely outside conventional religious experience. When she went off to a Presbyterian summer bible camp where she learned she had a "head for religious ideas" and got "miles of Bible by memory," she was aware that her parents would have objected to the evangelical intensity of "the faith-filled theology . . . only half a step out of a tent." As an adolescent, she was already absorbed in the theological question that is at the center of both *Pilgrim at Tinker Creek* and *Holy the Firm*—"If the all-powerful Creator directs the world, then why all this suffering?" She had written a paper about the Book of Job, but she had also quit the Presbyterian church. Her off-tempo relation to Christianity is caught in the moment when she meets with her family's minister to tell him of her decision to quit but, at the same time, accepts from him books by C. S. Lewis, including *The Problem of Pain.* More than two decades later, she still has not found her institutional place, although she attends church. In *Teaching a Stone to Talk,* she notes that she has "overcome a fiercely anti-Catholic upbringing in order to attend Mass"; but she does so "simply and solely to escape Protestant guitars" and likens her attendance to having "run away from home and joined the circus as a dancing bear."

At times, Dillard strains to remain Christian. For instance, she rejects pantheistic immanence—that "God is in the thing," referred to above—but cannot quite accept the conventional Christian view that "emanating from God, and linked to him by Christ, the work is infinitely other than God" (*Holy the Firm*). While the concept of eminence permits a representation of Christ that allows for the salvation of "the souls of men," it leaves the rest of nature "irrelevant and nonparticipant," unreal to "time," "unknowable, an illusory, absurd, accidental, and overelaborate state"—fallen, in a word. Unwilling to accept a view that denies a sacralized, familiar natural world, Dillard entertains a view from "esoteric Christianity" that there is a substance called "Holy the Firm" that is "in touch" with both the lowest of material reality—the "salts and earths"—and the absolute. The absolute and the most ordinary aspects of nature are connected: "Matter and spirit are of a piece but distinguishable; God has a stake guaranteed in all the world" (*Holy the Firm*). Characteristically, affirmations are undercut, this time

with the anticlimactic aside that "these are only ideas" (*Holy the Firm*). For Dillard, however, there is no such thing as "only" ideas. She proves herself outside orthodoxy and beyond conventional Christianity, without abandoning Christian preoccupations, beliefs, and longings.

As Reimer has shown, Dillard's "theology is always dialectical" and contains "both the conventional language of religious mysticism as well as more macabre elements of religious experience." The dialectical tension is between "the material and the spiritual, the natural and the transcendent . . . the beauty and the horror within the natural world." I agree with Reimer's assessment that "the power of Dillard's vision arises from her strength to maintain the contradictions within a single vision." Dillard's vision is contradictory at its most extreme, and dialectical in its most powerful insights. The kinds of ritual she creates and writes about explain in large measure how she balances these unresolved contradictions within a single, unified vision. Her rituals are familiar to both religious practitioners and nature observers.

Students of myth and ritual know that worldviews, or myths, contain contradictions and unresolved mysteries that adherents live with despite doubt, and that ritual is a way both of moving toward deeper understanding and of affirming belief publicly—a way of acting, without complete knowledge. Annie Dillard seeks a vision that is the "pearl of great price," which "may be found" but "may not be sought" (*Pilgrim at Tinker Creek*), so the question becomes "how then is she to act? How is the search to be conducted?" Annie Dillard's ritual acts allow her to affirm life and God without a theological resolution of fundamental religious questions. Through these rituals, she strives for—and experiences—reconciliation between herself, a sometimes horrible—as well as beautiful—nature, and a mysterious God who, at times, seems as maniacal as loving. Fittingly, the rituals are a blend of Judeo-Christian rites in nature; they are the rituals of stalking, seeing, and dancing.

Walking, as more than exercise, has a long tradition in literature, from Plato's' walks when he formulated his dialogues, to Saint Augustine's walk on the seashore, to the walks of seventeenth-century Christian literary walkers: "The walk is an occasion and setting for revelation, for a sudden increase in their awareness of the indwelling of God in the world." Walkers are pilgrims seeking visions. As Thoreau comments in "Walking," those few who understand "the art of Walking," who "have a genius for *sauntering*," are linked with medieval pilgrims about whom children exclaimed, "'There goes a-*Sainte-Terre*,' a Saunterer, a Holy-Lander." Those who walk in Thoreau's way

> saunter toward the Holy Land, till one day the sun shall shine more brightly than ever he has done, shall perchance shine into our minds and hearts, and

light up our whole lives with a great awakening light, as warm and serene and golden as on a bankside in autumn. ("Walking")

Thoreau's imagery of light is echoed in Dillard's mystical moments, as it is in all the mystical tradition, including the Christian. John Elder writes that for inveterate walker William Wordsworth, the "Pilgrim" of "The Prelude," "walking is a process of reconciliation: it provides the dynamic unity of his life" and art. "The Prelude," for example, is a work organized in part by walking. Elder, in ways applicable to Dillard's essays, writes about walking in the works of others, such as contemporary poet A. R. Ammons. That is particularly true if we remember that Dillard's vision is dialectical. Writing about Ammons, Elder might as well be writing about Dillard: "There is no absolute unity available for existence in a physical, and thus temporal, work. Rather, going from one foot to the other, human life takes its passage through a universe of particulars"; and the major response to the relations between nature, human imagination, and spirit is "one of ambivalence: right foot, left foot."

In the chapter "Stalking" in *Pilgrim at Tinker Creek,* Dillard tells us she learned to stalk fish and muskrats, who "by their very mystery and hiddenness crystallize the quality of my summer life at the creek." Learning to stalk muskrats took "several years," until one evening, when she had "lost" herself, "lost the creek, the day, lost everything but (the creek's) amber depth," a young muskrat "appeared on top of the water, floating on its back" (*Pilgrim at Tinker Creek*). She was ecstatic. The excitement and wonder of sighting an "ordinary" muskrat through her ritual stalking is described with the language of revelation. She records her joy and surprise "at having the light come on so suddenly, and at having my consciousness returned to me all at once and bearing (a) . . . muskrat." Fearing that the encounter was a once in a lifetime experience, she stalks muskrats day and night; and at the point she sees another, she reports, with the Thoreauvian extravagance that Edward Abbey so admired, "My life changed." What Dillard calls stalking is, obviously, closer to meditating. The "*via negative,*" she says, is a form of stalking "as fruitful as actual pursuit." She waits "emptied," like "Newton under the apple tree, Buddha under the bo." Dillard reminds us that Ezekiel "excoriates" false prophets who will not go up into the gaps, and she exhorts us to "stalk the gaps," which are the cliffs on the rock where you "cower to see the back parts of God." Such stalking will reveal "more than a maple," she writes; it will reveal "a universe."

Dillard's walks around Tinker Creek in Virginia and her stalking of the muskrat reveal not merely the habits of the secretive animal, for the mystery and hiddenness she often attributes to muskrats are those she most often attributes to God. Moreover, her personal ritual of stalking is ultimately described in Christian terms: on the night her life changed

as a result of seeing the muskrat, she summarizes the nature of the stalking ritual as "Knock; seek; ask," obviously a variant of the biblical "Ask, and it shall be given to you; seek, and ye shall find; knock, and it shall be opened to you. For everyone that asketh receiveth; and he that seeketh findeth; and to him that knocketh it shall be opened." In Dillard's work the nature-writing conventions of encountering nature directly and immediately through such ordinary activities as walking while one is open to aesthetic and spiritual experience mingle and meld with Christian ritual, tradition, and experience. Ordinary experience fuses with the millennial, the temporal with the transcendent.

In *Holy the Firm* and *Teaching a Stone to Talk* Dillard is more conventional in her use of the walking ritual than in *Pilgrim at Tinker's Creek,* but she makes the same points. In *Holy the Firm,* she is deeply troubled by the terrible suffering of Julie Norwich, who is in the hospital, her face burned in a plane accident. Worrying about and questioning the Christian response to the sufferings of the innocent, Dillard, near despair, asks, "Do we really need more victims to remind us that we're all victims?" and she reminds herself that we are "sojourners in a land we did not make, a land with no meaning of itself and no meaning we can make for it alone" (*Holy the Firm*). In this state of mind, she feels unworthy to buy the communion wine she had volunteered to get, but she goes anyway. She walks home, "and I'm on the road again walking, my right hand forgetting my left. I'm out on the road again walking, and toting a backload of God." As she starts up a hill, the landscape starts "to utter its infinite particulars," and she lists particular features of the landscape about her—"blackberry brambles, white snowberries, red rose hips, gaunt and clattering broom." Soon, the particulars are alive: "mountains are raw nerves; . . . the trees, the grass . . . are living petals of mind." Finally,

walking faster and faster, weightless, I feel the wine. It sheds light in slats through my rib cage, and fills the buttressed vaults of my ribs with light pooled and buoyant. I am moth; I am light. I am prayer and I can hardly see.

At that moment, she experiences the vision that is central to the book; she beholds Christ being baptized.

The essays in *Teaching a Stone to Talk* often expand the notion of ordinary walking to larger journeys and expeditions. In **"Sojourner"** she notes that the title word appears frequently in the Old Testament and "invokes a nomadic people's sense of vagrancy, a praying people's knowledge of estrangement, a thinking people's intuition of sharp loss" (*Teaching a Stone to Talk*). Thus, she alternates, in this essay and in her writing in general, between "thinking of the planet as time" and "as a hard land of exile in which we are all sojourners." A number of the essays in *Teaching a Stone to Talk* explore the dialectic between being at home and being estranged, as she moves her setting from Tinker Creek to places as remote as the Napo River in the Ecuadorian jungle and the North Pole. In **"An Expedition to the Pole,"** she combines personal experience, history, and fantasy. The personal experience of visiting the Arctic and viewing the Arctic Sea fuses with the history of various Polar expeditions that entailed enormous suffering for ill-equipped explorers. She fantasizes that she has "quit my ship and set out on foot over the polar ice," and that she has traveled across an ice floe, where she encounters both historical personages and members of the congregation of the Catholic church she has been attending. They are all together on a spiritual quest. Her attendance at Catholic services is part of her search for "the Pole of Relative inaccessibility," or "The Absolute." She asks, "How often have I mounted this same expedition, has my absurd barque set out half-caulked for the Pole?" And she quotes Pope Gregory in seeking to define her aim: "'To attain to somewhat of the unencompassed light, by stealth'." Although Dillard emphasizes alienated experience because she is poorly and absurdly equipped for the spiritual expedition to the Pole, she ends the essay with a fantasy in which she is on the floor with the church members, "banging on a tambourine" and singing loudly. "How can any of us tone it down?" she asks, "for we are nearing the Pole." Dillard actually seeks and creates the conditions for ecstatic, mystical experience; doubt and hope are held in balance within the imaginative framework of sojourning, of exploring on foot.

Annie Dillard walks and stalks so that she can "see" in more than one sense. To see truly, she must prepare herself ritualistically, must become both innocent and informed. Dillard defines innocence as "the spirit's unselfconscious state at any moment of pure devotion to any object. It is at once receptiveness and total concentration" (*Pilgrim at Tinker Creek*). Innocence is a state she values as highly as did the romantics and Christians before her. That may be why she often identifies the stalking and seeing rituals with childhood and childhood games. "Only children keep their eyes open," she writes. She describes nature as "like one of those line drawings of a tree that are puzzles for children: Can you find hidden in the leaves a duck, a house, a boy, a bucket, a zebra, and a boot?" (*Pilgrim at Tinker Creek*). The universe is a merry-go-round, and the cost is a child's rubber duck. Dillard evokes her childhood, as well as others', and always in the service of seeing, in all senses of the word, the microcosm of Tinker Creek: "If I seek the senses and skill of children. . . I do so only, solely, and entirely that I might look well into the creek" (*Pilgrim at Tinker Creek*). A major motif of the book is, as I have already noted, the hiddenness of God as well as of nature. Childhood games are played to coax the Creator from hiding. She alludes to John Knoepfle's poem in which "'christ is red rover . . . and the children are calling / come over come over'" (*Pilgrim at Tinker Creek*).

Longing for God, she compares the banging of her will against rock with a child beating on a door and calling: "Come on out!. . . I know you're there."

That she seeks to see by entering "the spirit's unselfconscious state" through "pure devotion to any object" is one of many obvious signs that Annie Dillard is intensely aware of her absorption in meditative traditions. Her efforts to see are rewarded in the numerous mystical moments recorded in *Pilgrim at Tinker Creek, Holy the Firm*, and *Teaching a Stone to Talk.* One summer evening, when she is practicing being "an unscrupulous observer" of shiners feeding in Tinker Creek,

> something broke and something opened. I filled up like a new wineskin. I breathed an air like light; I saw a light like water. I was the lip of a fountain the creek filled forever; I was ether, the leaf in the zephyr; I was flesh-flake, feather, bone.

> (*Pilgrim at Tinker Creek*).

Because of such moments, critics have rightly seen in Dillard's mystical experiences parallels with Ralph Waldo Emerson's experiences and views recorded in "Nature." Dillard's observation that "there is [a] kind of seeing that involves a letting go [and] when I see this way I sway transfixed and emptied" is justifiably compared with Emerson's famous statement that "I became a transparent eyeball; I am nothing; I see all; the currents of the Universal Being circulate through me."

Dillard also is Emersonian in preparing herself for vision by exercising her "Understanding," by disciplining her nature experiences with scientific information and ideas. While she rightly states, "I am no scientist" (*Pilgrim at Tinker Creek*), her essays are packed with allusions to scientific reading of all sorts. Not surprisingly, those allusions fall into two, dichotomous categories. One evokes a nature that is deterministic—the insect world, in which a giant water bug sucks out the innards of a frog, "a monstrous and horrifying thing" that leaves her deeply shaken. In a more light-hearted moment, she makes the same point in a chapter about nature's horrors: "Fish gotta swim and bird [*sic*] gotta fly; insects, it seems, gotta do one horrible thing after another." The other category of scientific allusions focuses on the indeterminant nature described by twentieth-century physics. In the chapter "Stalking," Dillard has a two-page commentary on Werner Heisenberg's "Principle of Indeterminacy," and she quotes, in addition, physicists Sir Arthur Eddington and Sir James Jeans, whose views, she notes gleefully, mean that "some physicists now are a bunch of wild-eyed, raving mystics" (*Pilgrim at Tinker Creek*). To illustrate, she quotes Eddington's statement that the Principle of Indeterminacy "'leaves us with no clear distinction between the Natural and the Supernatural'."

Critics, especially Gary McIlroy and Margaret Reimer, have done very well in pointing out Dillard's response to science, especially to the Principle of Indeterminancy. Her ritual preparation for seeing, however, has depended on a broader range of science and science-related reading than has been discussed. Often her reading is specific to phenomena she observes. When she stalks the muskrat, she refers to biologist and expert on muskrats Paul Errington. She refers to biologist and science historian Howard Ensign Evans on dragonflies, limnologist Robert E. Coker on plankton movement, Rutherford Platt on trees (noting that his *The Great American Forest* is "one of the most interesting books ever written"), and so on. In Emersonian fashion, she "disciplines" her "Understanding" in preparing for visions.

Two writers important in disciplining Dillard's understanding are Frenchman Henri Fabre and American Edwin Way Teale, sources for a number of her comments on the horrors of the insect world. In her chapter "The Fixed" in *Pilgrim at Tinker Creek,* which contains some of her most pessimistic and horrific conclusions, Dillard refers frequently to turn-of-the-century Fabre. She notes that "even a hardened entomologist like F. Henri Fabre confessed to being startled witless every time" a praying mantis strikes its prey, and she quotes a long passage of his describing the macabre mantis mating ritual during which the female gnaws on her "swain" until there is just that "masculine stump" going "on with the business" (*Pilgrim at Tinker Creek*). Edwin Way Teale is the most frequently cited writer in the other dark chapter in *Pilgrim at Tinker Creek,* "Fecundity," in which nature seems primarily a matter of eating, breeding, and dying: the "universe that suckled us is a monster that does not care if we live or die. . . . It is fixed and blind, programmed to kill." She illustrates this grim, amoral natural world with examples drawn from Teale's *The Strange Lives of Familiar Insects,* which is, she exclaims, a "book I couldn't live without."

Although Dillard draws on Fabre's and Teale's writings to underscore a deterministic, amoral natural world that may be "the brainchild of a deranged manic-depressive with unlimited capital," these writers achieved their fame as popularizers of science by maintaining optimistic spiritual outlooks. Fabre never accepted Darwinian evolutionary theory and remained a devout Roman Catholic. A humble French provincial who was not accepted by the academy until very late in life, Fabre was less the laboratory scientist in a white lab coat than a living example of the persona familiar to the nature essay in general and to Annie Dillard's essay in particular—the amateur who is faithful to his local environment and who experiences awe and wonder in nature's small moments. Edwin Way Teale, who admired

Fabre and introduced the English translation of his collected essays, is also optimistic, despite his chronicles of the violent and grotesque insect world. In *Speaking for Nature,* Paul Brooks describes Teale as one of the finest "literary naturalists" since Thoreau. He adds that Teale, with others, has "opened the eyes of millions of readers . . . to a widespread feeling of kinship with the other forms of life with which we share the earth." From his *Strange Lives of Familiar Insects* to his widely read and well-regarded books on the American seasons, Teale's works reflect the affirmation and joy characteristic of American nature writers and of one side of Annie Dillard's dialectical view. The two men offered her more than scientific information.

In her intellectual preparations for reaching a state of innocence followed by mystical insight, Dillard's reading is often as much the focus of her attention as the natural object itself. Some of the more important categories in her diverse reading are theology and other religious matters (Martin Buber, Thomas Merton, Julia[n] of Norwich, and the Koran); art (DaVinci, Van Gogh, Breughel, and El Greco); adventure (Lewis and Clark, Heyerdahl, and the Franklin Polar expedition); and literature (Thoreau, Coleridge, Blake, Goethe, and Eliot). A full accounting of the interplay between her reading and her responses to nature is impractical here, but one intellectual source is crucial—the philosopher Heraclitus.

Dillard associates Heraclitus with views close to those of quantum physics, that "nature is wont to hide herself." Moreover, his perspective is akin to her dialectical vision. Dillard opens *Pilgrim at Tinker Creek* with the following epigraph from Heraclitus:

> It ever was, and is, and shall be,
> ever-living Fire, in measures being
> kindled and in measures going out.

Heraclitus was the philosopher of opposites. But they are opposites that have underlying connections; for instance, good and evil define one another. The same is true for all natural events. Though they are described and seen in terms of opposites, there is an underlying interrelatedness, a hidden connection, of which fire is the physical embodiment. The epigraph in *Pilgrim at Tinker Creek* and the pervasive fire imagery in *Holy the Firm* are signs that the intellectual aspects of Dillard's meditations prepare her for a sense of wonder no less than horrific vision. As a result, she sees not only the dead frog but also the "tree with the lights in it . . . transfigured, each cell buzzing with flame" (*Pilgrim at Tinker Creek*). It is a vision that, as Heraclitus would have predicted, comes and goes. It is a vision she lives for. In that moment, her spirit's aspirations and her own reality are confirmed. In *Holy the Firm,* the fire is the fire that attracts the moth to destruction and the fire that disfigures Julie; but it is also the light that comes into Dillard's spirit and onto her face, as onto the face of every artist, which, "like a seraph's" face, lights "the kingdom of God for the people to see." Heraclitus's imagery of forever waxing and waning fire is the perfect metaphor for her thematic dualities for good and evil, beautiful and grotesque, and repulsive and awesome—all of which coexist in God's nature.

At times, however, Dillard's ritual stalking and ritual preparations to see are undercut by nature's grotesquery. Reading, in particular, is not a sufficient stay against confusion. Dillard discovers that she can get lost in the "labyrinthine tracks of the mind," when she most needs to live in the senses: "So long as I stay in my thoughts . . . my foot slides" and "I fall" (*Pilgrim at Tinker Creek*). In a passage from *Teaching a Stone to Talk* that echoes the creekside frog episode in *Pilgrim at Tinker Creek,* Dillard encounters a resting Guernsey cow during one of her rambles but is shocked to find that it is dead. The cow's insides are gone, "her udder and belly . . . open and empty." Horrified, Dillard sees that the cow's legs had broken when a limestone sinkhole had suddenly opened under her weight (*Teaching a Stone to Talk*). Dillard is shocked and disoriented, fearing that the ground will open beneath her and she will fall unchecked. The alternative to falling, to terror, and to doubt, she writes, is to dance. Ritual dance, real or imagined, allows Dillard to quiet morbid intellectualizing, to enter into direct contact with the natural world, and to praise despite the threat of meaninglessness. Dance is her least-mentioned ritual, but it is crucial for keeping her spiritual balance.

In *Pilgrim at Tinker Creek,* falling and dancing imagery combine as Dillard seeks signs of hope but fears that the monstrous may prevail. Near the book's end, she describes herself as a "sojourner seeking signs" and remembers that Isak Dinesen, brokenhearted, had stepped into the Kenyan morning seeking a sign and had witnessed a rooster tear from its root a chameleon's tongue—the unwelcome sign again of pervasive cruelty. But Dillard's thoughts and feelings about that shocking moment in Dinesen's experience and about cruelty in nature are altered; she is once again "transfigured" as a maple key twirls down toward her on the wind. She becomes aware of that other "wind of the spirit" and thinks, "If I am a maple leaf falling, at least I can twirl." Similarly, in concluding "Sojourner" in *Teaching a Stone to Talk,* Dillard turns from "thoughts of despair" about purposelessness sensed everywhere, to thoughts about beauty, and she invites us, "with as much spirit as we can muster, [to] go out with a buck and wing." That said, she envisions nature joining in:

> The consort of musicians strikes up, and we in the chorus stir and move and start twirling our hats. A Mangrove island turns drift to dance . . . rocking over the salt sea at random, rocking day and night

and round the sun, rocking round the sun and out toward east of Hercules.

Moreover, as she has with stalking and seeing, Dillard locates the dance ritual in the tradition of Judeo-Christian ritual and mysticism. She recalls that King David "leaped and danced naked before the dark of the Lord in a barren desert," a model for herself in the face of spiritual emptiness, and a reminder to us, she says, to "make connections; let rip; and dance whenever you can." She is dancing significantly, as *A Pilgrim at Tinker Creek* ends: "I go my way and my left foot says 'Glory,' and my right foot says 'Amen' in and out of Shadow Creek, upstream and down, exultant, in a daze, dancing to the two silver trumpets of praise."

There are powerful moments in *Pilgrim at Tinker Creek* when Annie Dillard, performing her stalking, seeing, and dancing rituals, has the sudden insight that not only is she stalking but she is being stalked, not only is she seeing but she is being seen, and not only is she dancing but music is being played for her. On the dark side, God is a stalker-hunter, a destroyer, the ultimate "'archer in cover,'" whose arrows bring fear and mortality. Being seen, though, is joyful. In the central mystical moment of the book, when Dillard is taken unaware by the "tree with the lights in it," she exclaims that "it was less like seeing than like being for the first time seen, knocked breathless by a powerful glance." We do not need to be told who has seen her. And the agent of the dance is more than nature. When Dillard imagines herself spinning through the universe to stop her "sweeping fall," she notices that "Someone" pipes as "we are dancing a tarantella until the sweat pours." Having divined that she is stalked, seen as well as seeing, a dancer to "Someone's" tune, Dillard concludes that she "cannot ask for more than to be so wholly acted upon," even if by a plague of locusts, because she would willingly pay the price in discomfort to be "rapt and enwrapped" in the "real world" (*Pilgrim at Tinker Creek*). Her imagery of being acted on climaxes as the book ends in passages about ritual sacrifice that, again, combine her personal vision with the Judeo-Christian.

As Dillard debates whether corruption and beauty are equal in creation and concludes that corruption is not "beauty's very heart," she describes herself as "a sacrifice bound with cords to the horns of the world's rock altar." There she takes a deep breath and opens her eyes, seeing "worms in the horn of the altar," as "a sense of the real exults me; the cords loose; I walk on my way" (*Pilgrim at Tinker Creek*). In this mystical moment, she finds freedom in accepting the fallen world. But she needs to go beyond supplication and acceptance to praise, from "please" to "thank you." And she does. The last two chapters of *Pilgrim at Tinker Creek* focus on sacrificial rituals that Dillard must know are in the Judeo-Christian tradition, rituals of purification and thanksgiving rather than merely propitiating the gods. She concentrates on an ancient Israelite ritual, "the wave breast of thanksgiving," which is—significantly, considering Dillard's joy in being seen—"a catching [of] God's eye." The priest dresses in clean linen, comes to the altar, and is given a consecrated breastbone of a ritually slain ram, which he waves as an offering to the Lord. Dillard knows this ritual of thanksgiving works, and she ends her discussion with a phrase from Catholic liturgy: "Thanks be to God." She then calls on a second part of the ritual to acknowledge her ongoing problem with the cruel, horrible, and monstrous in nature. After the priest waves the breastbone, he "heaves" the ram's shoulder bone. Dillard interprets this to mean that after catching God's eye, one can "speak up for the creation," can protest cruelty and waste in the natural world. "Could I heave a little shred of frog shoulder at the Lord?" she muses, remembering the frog's death she had witnessed at creekside. She finally understands, though, that both the "wave" to capture God's glance and the "heave" to lodge protest are necessary for a unified ritual; "both meant a wide-eyed and keen-eyed thanks," and neither was whole without the other.

As one stalking and being stalked, seeing and being seen, dancing to someone's tune, performing rituals of sacrifice, and serving as victim of the sacrifice, Dillard places herself in a mystical relationship with both a nature and a God who are at once both concealed and revealed. She concludes with prayers of affirmation, no matter how bleak the moment's reality is. In *Teaching a Stone to Talk*, she notes that "we as a people have moved from pantheism to pan-atheism." We have desacralized nature, she says, and God no longer speaks from the whirlwind. Until "God changes his mind, until the pagan gods slip back to their hilltop groves, or until we can teach a stone to talk, all we can do with the whole inhuman array is watch it." Dillard observes: "we are here to witness.... The silence is all there is." Nevertheless, she concludes with an exhortation to prayer: "you take a step in the right direction to pray to this silence.... Pray without ceasing."

The remarkable conclusion to *Holy the Firm* is, in effect, an extended, unceasing prayer that reveals the God beyond nature who is linked with it by "holy the firm." Here the book's major thematic and artistic elements coalesce. The images of the burning moth, Julie the burned child, and Annie Dillard herself are intertwined with Puget Sound's "islands on fire" and seraphs' and the artists' faces that "can sing only the first 'Holy' before the intensity of their love ignites them again and dissolves them again, perpetually, into flames" (*Holy the Firm*). Dillard is the artist-nun, aflame with holiness. Dillard's book-prayer is "lighting the kingdom of god for the people to see" (*Holy the Firm*).

If Dillard's Christian desire to light the kingdom of God marks her apart from other nature writers, it is only a matter of degree. All non-Christian writers I have mentioned,

and many more, are fascinated with the relationships between nature, human consciousness, and "mystery." Troubled by the combined intellectual and spiritual consciousness of Newtonian and Cartesian thought, which separated spirit and matter and placed nature beneath humans in importance, by nonteleological, Darwinian natural selection, and by technological assaults on the natural environment, twentieth-century nature writers have explored alternative views. Committed to science as guide, writers as diverse as Joseph Wood Krutch, Edward Abbey, Loren Eiseley, Peter Matthiesen, Barry Lopez, and Ann Zinger have nevertheless kept as their first loyalty and touchstone direct, experiential encounters with nature. All report aesthetic and spiritual rewards for doing so. In Dillard's essays, the same persona speaks to us as from the works of other nature writers—the solitary figure in nature, moved to philosophical speculation and, finally, to awe and wonder, to self-forgetting, and to an affirmation of realities that resist modern and contemporary threats of hopelessness and despair.

Despite such affinities, however, Annie Dillard has a special voice that speaks of balancing the tension between fear and hope, between horror and celebration, through rituals of stalking, seeing, and dancing. In such rituals, she has awakened not only to mystery in nature but to mystery beyond nature. Her Christian obsessions and ritual practice culminate in prayer without cessation. "[I] resound," she writes, "like a beaten bell" (*Pilgrim at Tinker Creek*).

John Haines (review date Winter 1996)

SOURCE: Review of *Mornings Like This: Found Poems*, in *Hudson Review*, Vol. XLVIII, No. 4, Winter, 1996, pp. 663-71.

[*In the excerpt below, Haines argues that Dillard's experimentations in* Mornings Like This *raise some disturbing questions about sources.*]

When I first looked through Annie Dillard's *Mornings Like This* and read her program notes, I was ready to set the book aside as a stunt and not worth serious attention. Subsequent reading has, to an extent, modified that impression. The book is subtitled *Found Poems*. The lines, as quoted throughout, are taken from various prose texts—from an eighth grade English text, from Van Gogh's Letters, a Boy Scout Handbook, etc.—and, according to Ms. Dillard, arranged in such a way as to simulate a poem originating with a single author. In her "Author's Note" she says of the poems, "Their sentences come from the books named. I lifted them. Sometimes I dropped extra words; I never added a word." She is at least honest about her sources, in contrast to a recent perpetrator who has actually lifted whole poems from a contemporary poet, changed a word or two, and published them as his own (see Neal Bowers, "A Loss for Words, Plagiarism and Silence," *The American Scholar,* Fall 1994).

A few of her adaptations are especially effective. Among the best are those taken from the diary of a Russian naturalist, Mikhail Prishvin. Here are the last two stanzas of a poem constructed by Dillard from a walk in the woods as described by Prishvin, and to which she has given the title **"Dash It":**

> As for myself, I can only speak of what
> Made me marvel when I saw it for the first time.
> I remember my own youth when I was in love.
> I remember a puddle rippling, the insects aroused.
>
> I remember our own springtime when my lady told
>   me:
> You have taken my best. And then I remember
> How many evenings I have waited, how much
> I have been through for this one evening on earth.

These lines are indeed poetic and moving, and might perhaps be even more so in their original context. There are others of a similar nature, such as the title poem, taken from *The Countryman's Year,* by David Grayson, and on the whole the collection has in places considerable interest. Nonetheless, what she has done here arouses some concern. What does work like this say about the legitimacy of authorship? Who in this instance is the author? Who can claim to be? I worry too about the example being set, and who might be influenced to attempt to repeat it. As it stands, it is mainly an interesting experiment; in the hands of someone less resourceful and intelligent than Ms. Dillard, little more than a trick to be dismissed.

FURTHER READING

Criticism

Bradbury, Malcolm. "The Bridgeable Gap." *Times Literary Supplement,* No. 4633 (17 January 1992): 7-9.
  Compares Dillard's *Writing Life* with other works on creative writing and finds the book successful in describing writing as an activity.

Chénetier, Marc. "Tinkering, Extravagance: Thoreau, Melville, and Annie Dillard." *Critique* XXXI, No. 3 (Spring 1990): 157-72.
  Considers the different treatments of nature and morality in Henry David Thoreau's *Walden,* Herman Melville's short stories, and Dillard's *Pilgrim at Tinker Creek.*

Clark, Suzanne. "Annie Dillard: The Woman in Nature and the Subject of Nonfiction." In *Literary Nonfiction: Theory, Criticism, Pedagogy,* edited by Chris Anderson, pp. 107-24. Carbondale: Southern Illinois University Press, 1989.
  Argues that as a female nature writer, Dillard creates a distinct perspective.

Gaston, Patricia S. A Review of *The Living,* by Annie Dillard. *Southern Humanities Review* XXVII, No. 2 (Spring 1994): 198-99.
  Finds *The Living* a typical example of historical fiction.

Goldman, Stan. "Sacrifices to the Hidden God: Annie Dillard's *Pilgrim at Tinker Creek* and Leviticus." *Soundings* 74, Nos. 1-2 (Spring-Summer 1991): 195-213.
  Argues that the symbolism of sacrifice in the Bible chpater Leviticus is key to comprehending *Pilgrim at Tinker's Creek.*

Grumbach, Doris. A review of *Pilgrim at Tinker Creek,* by Annie Dillard. *New Republic* 170, No. 14 (6 April 1974): 32.
  Praises Dillard's vision of nature and God in *Pilgrim at Tinker Creek.*

Gunn, Janet Varner. "A Politics of Experience: Leila Khaled's *My People Shall Live: The Autobiography of a Revolutionary.*" In *De/Colonizing the Subject: The Politics of Gender in Women's Autobiography,* edited by Sidonie Smith and Julia Watson, pp. 65-80. Minneapolis, University of Minnesota Press, 1992.
  Uses Dillard's autobiography *An American Childhood* to make sense of Leila Khaled's autobiography.

———. "A Window of Opportunity: An Ethics of Reading Third-World Autobiography." In *Teaching and Testimony: Rigoberta Menchú and the North American Classroom,* edited by Allen Carey-Webb and Stephen Benz, pp. 271-78. Albany: State University of New York Press, 1996.
  Compares Dillard's *An American Childhood* with other forms of autobiography.

Lund, Elizabeth. "Stanzas Spun from Inspiration." *Christian Science Monitor* 87 (7 September 1995): 13.
  Argues that the poems in *Mornings Like This: Found Poems* vary in quality and have not been adequately developed.

Marget, Madeline. "Being around Words." *Commonweal* CXXIII, No. 7 (5 April 1996): 32-3.
  Compliments editors Dillard and Cort Conley for their selections in the collection of autobiographical writings *Modern American Memoirs.*

Smith, Pamela A. "The Ecotheology of Annie Dillard: A

Study in Ambivalence." *Cross Currents* 45, No. 3 (Fall 1995): 341-58.

    Argues that there are consistent theological elements in Dillard's writing.

Torrens, James S. "Of Many Things." *America* 171, No. 16 (19 November 1994): 1.

    Reviews *The Annie Dillard Reader,* praising her writ-

ing style and discussing her relationship with the Catholic Church.

Webb, Stephen H. "Nature's Spendthrift Economy: The Extravagance of God in *Pilgrim at Tinker Creek.*" *Soundings* 77, Nos. 3-4 (Fall-Winter 1994): 429-51.

    Considers the techniques Dillard employs to develop her conceptualization of God.

Additional coverage of Dillard's life and career is contained in the following sources published by Gale: *Authors and Artists for Young Adults,* Vol. 6; *Contemporary Authors,* Vols. 49-52; *Contemporary Authors New Revision Series,* Vols. 3, 43 and 62; *Dictionary of Literary Biography Yearbook, 1980; DISCovering Authors Modules: Novelists; Major Twentieth-Century Writers;* and *Something about the Author,* Vol. 10.

Brian Friel

1929-

Irish dramatist and short story writer.

The following entry provides an overview of Friel's career through 1998. For further information on his life and works, see *CLC,* Volumes 5, 42, 59.

INTRODUCTION

As part of the flourishing Irish literary movement that occurred at the turn of the century, Friel has produced drama that is clearly indigenous to Ireland. Friel's canon characterizes not only individuals but an entire people, whose hopes and disappointments play themselves out against a menacing undercurrent of violence and death. In nearly all his plays, the interplay of reality, memory, and dream suggests the spiritual flux of a people whose sense of tradition and place is frequently at war with contemporary realities. Yet even as Friel creates his cameos of Irish life, his themes acquire an elasticity stretching beyond the private lives of his characters to the unlocalized realm of the human spirit. Friel is also noted as a politically committed writer who has addressed pressing social concerns in his work, and at the same time achieved commercial and critical success.

Biographical Information

Brian Friel was born outside of Omagh, Country Tyrone, Northern Ireland in 1929. At the age of ten, he left for Londonderry with his parents, Patrick and Christina MacLoone Friel. After primary education and some time at St. Patrick's College, a seminary from which he obtained a B.A. in 1948, Friel abandoned his plans for the priesthood and attended St. Joseph's Teacher Training school in Belfast from 1949 until 1950. In 1954, he married Ann Morrison, with whom he went on to have five children. Upon graduation he taught until 1960. After the steady publication of his stories in *The New Yorker,* he began writing full-time. His early work consisted of radio plays and stories, the latter collected in two volumes: *The Saucer Of Larks* (1962) and the *Gold in the Sea* (1966). His stage plays were produced at the Abbey Theatre, famous for being home to the dramaturgical talents of William Butler Yeats, J. M. Synge and Sean O'Casey. Although Friel dismisses much of his early work, plays such as *The Enemy Within* (1962) helped to establish his reputation. Seeking training in dramaturgy and theatre arts, Friel sojourned to the United States to study at the Tyrone Guthrie Theatre in Minneapolis, Minnesota in 1963. The following year Friel completed the play that was to be his first commercial success and which would secure

his international reputation: *Philadelphia, Here I Come!* (1964). At the Helen Hayes Theatre, it played for 326 performances, the longest run for an Irish play on Broadway. A steady stream of dramatic works followed, and Friel returned to Ireland in 1973. The link between literature and politics, and between narrative and history led Friel, with Stephen Rea, to found Field Day Theatre Company, Northern Ireland, in 1980, a company that provided Irish writers with a platform for addressing pressing social and political matters. *Translations* (1980), considered by many to be his best play, was staged by Field Day. Friel has also produced several collections of short stories, *Selected Stories* (1979) and *The Diviner* (1983). His talent and contributions to his art have earned him many distinguished accolades such as the Olivier Award in 1991, a Tony Award in 1992 and honorary doctorates from several academic institutions.

Major Works

Characterized as expressions of "the human spirit asserting itself in the face of impediments" by Richard Tillinghast, Friel's plays are at times reevaluations of historical-political realities. They also demonstrate, however, a subtle knowledge and handling of psychological complexities and the medium of language itself. *Philadelphia, Here I Come!* takes place the night before Gareth O'Donnell's departure from Ireland to the promise of a new life in Philadelphia and explores the issue of emigration by delving into the inner states of its central character. Friel's greatest critical success, *Translations,* concerns itself with the political intricacies of language as a colonizing tool, but is also an exploration of the nature of language itself. *Faith Healer* (1979) focuses on the writer's work itself in telling the story of Frank Hardy in the words of different characters and from different perspectives. Critics observed in *Faith Healer* and *Translations* a move away from overt political statements into a more subtle handling of truth, in a wider, deeper sense. *Dancing at Lughnasa* (1990), another metaphorically suggestive play, explores notions of the pagan and the profane, and elaborates a revision of received colonial-rooted ideas of culture. Notably, most of Friel's plays are set in Ballybeg, a name derived from the 19th century Baile Beag, a locale that functions as a paradigmatic microcosm of Ireland—no place in particular but giving Irish concerns a local habitation and a name.

Critical Reception

Critics see language and translation as central themes in Friel's work, most clearly and artfully expressed in *Translations,* a touchstone work in the opinion of many commentators. In it one can observe the panoply of issues that appear in Friel's other works. Language is also an element that critics identify as common to the Irish dramatic tradition—from Richard Binsley Sheridan through Oscar Wilde, W. B. Yeats, and Samuel Beckett. This tradition, states Richard Tillinghast, includes plays that are known for their dialogue rather than the "inventiveness of their dramatic structure." The lack of pure dramatic flare, a flaw noted by several critics of Friel's work, is amply compensated by Friel's knack for storytelling and ability to convey an intimate understanding of his subjects. These subjects range from a post-colonial reclaiming of Irish history and identity to the relationships between individuals, often within the family. Richard Kearney asserts that one of Friel's concerns is "to explore the complex relationship between political ideology and the problematic nature of language itself." According to Marilyn Throne, Friel's expression of Irish experience and sensibilities involves "the displacement of culture," a result of colonization and its effects. These effects are felt not only in the public sphere but in private life as well.

PRINCIPAL WORKS

The Saucer of Larks (short fiction) 1962

The Enemy Within (drama) 1962
Philadelphia, Here I Come! (drama) 1964
The Gold in the Sea (short fiction) 1966
Faith Healer (drama) 1979
Selected Stories (short fiction) 1979
Translations (drama) 1980
The Diviner (short fiction) 1983
Dancing at Lughnasa (drama) 1990
Wonderful Tennessee (drama) 1993

CRITICISM

James Coakley (essay date Fall 1973)

SOURCE: "Chekov in Ireland: Brief Notes on Friel's Philadelphia," in *Comparative Drama,* Vol. VII, No. 3, Fall 1973, pp. 191-97.

[*In the following essay, Coakley draws parallels between Friel's methods and themes in* Philadelphia, Here I Come! *and the "artistic, poetic and moral" procedures of Russian author Anton Chekov.*]

Probably no recent Irish play of more than passing interest has been so largely ignored by critics as has Brian Friel's **Philadelphia, Here I Come!** A success in Dublin and New York, it enjoyed inclusion in the annual, dreary volume which grants the title of "Best" to scripts sometimes, though not always, "Good" or "Better" than most of the commercial theatre's products. But box office returns or fame in the marketplace do not necessarily guarantee recognition in the study, and the play's considerable virtues, both literary and dramatic, have gone unnoticed, perhaps overlooked in the ballyhoo surrounding "the longest running Irish play on Broadway."

Friel, of course, is no stranger to the theatre; once a teacher in the public schools of northern Ireland, he abandoned his academic career in 1960; since then he has written full time, publishing two books of short stories and eight plays, the latter produced in Ireland and America with varying success. He is a playwright, however, of note: further proof, if it be needed, that the English theatre is, essentially, an Irish creation. And he brings to the stage a remarkably sophisticated literary sensibility, a confident sense of what is theatrical, and a precise and exquisitely lyrical talent for the spoken word which are noteworthy. What I propose to do in this brief essay is discuss Friel's play in what seems to me the most profitable and useful terms: those we have come to call *Chekovian.* To relate certain of Friel's dramatic methods to those of Chekov is to illuminate, I think, the structure and effects of a substantial new Irish drama which deserves to be better known.

Philadelphia, Here I Come! is a memory play set in the country of a young man's mind. To explore that difficult terrain it avoids "big moments"; its attitudes are ironic, its emotions understated, and its dialogue painfully, though not self-consciously, introspective. Its characters are not larger than life, and unlike so many vague, imprecise examples of dramatized memories, it refuses to sentimentalize its experience; uncovers a past not burdened with guilt, but merely tinged with regret; lingers over a difficult present devoid of meaning; and looks forward to a future neither bright nor promising. Devoid of Celtic mists and windy heroics, however, the play is remarkable for the skill with which it dramatizes a common experience in a most uncommon manner. Essentially retrospective in outlook, its subject matter concerns that most Chekovian of rituals: departure or leave-taking; and its plot is simple, familiar, even banal: a young man of 25, Gareth O'Donnell, is about to leave a frustrating and dull life in a rural Irish village for the adventure promised by a job in America, a position at a Philadelphia hotel arranged for by his Aunt Lizzy, the sister of his dead mother. And like the Moscow of Chekov's famous sisters, the Philadelphia of this play's protagonist is a supposed mecca, a glorious place where wishes come true and dreams are realized. It is then upon this characteristic principle of the incongruity between reality and delusion, this clash between things as they are and things as they are believed to be that the drama rests. Subtitled a comedy, the play's action is "on the night before, and the morning of, Gar's departure for Philadelphia," circumstances old-fashioned critics might call ripe, but which Friel regards as no more than the sources of uncertainty. What he dramatizes then are not only a young man's growing pains with their attendant loss of illusions (albeit a large part of the play's concerns), but, more importantly, of how fearful and difficult it is to speak our deepest feelings, particularly to those we love. Indeed, the integrity of feelings (hence the poignant drama) Friel discovers in this most everyday of situations constitutes the play's most admirable theatrical virtue. It is in its very commonality of interests, its refusal to be original or significant that Friel's play recalls the methods of Chekov. Like him Friel balances familiar truths with the most complex of emotions and mixes banalities with the profoundest of sentiments, while he develops that most truly comic and Chekovian of attitudes: human understanding.

Following a typical Chekovian strategy, Friel sets out seeming to write a conventional play, a series of farewells in which half a dozen people arrive to say goodbye to young Gar, and then depart. Ostensibly, the action moves from event to event, a linked sequence filled with reminiscence. However, in lieu of a "plot," Friel substitutes a pattern, or string of incidents which operate only in context. Firmly threaded, however, to the forward line of movement (Gar's imminent journey to America), these incidents do not function in the action-counteraction motions of traditional drama,

but move more vertically into the obstinate, ragged, often contradictory levels of experience. Eager to recapture the flux of personality, its myriad and evanescent nature, in short, to preserve the ephemeral, Friel practices a realism neither photographic nor repertorial, nor fulsome, dull, or patronizing about its milieu or the inhabitants thereof. It is a realism no doubt better organized than life, an awareness that the slightest gesture or intonation can demonstrate the self; that there is a poetry discoverable in the kitchen, the pub, or a young man's room neither sentimental nor maudlin, but real and vital, possessed of a quiet unassuming theatricality which reveals but does not impose itself or its values upon an audience. It is realism not of representation, but one to the essence of life, an insistence that the dramatist has come not to judge, but merely to show, to make us see things as they really are. Organized upon artistic principles (what Coleridge called "organic" principles), *Philadelphia, Here I Come!* firmly and quietly insists, as does any Chekov play, that life is neither funny nor sad, but more often is both, simultaneously. Necessarily, its action is indirect, sometimes leaving the impression that it is all moods or reflections, when, in fact, it plunges deeply and tenaciously into its characters' lives in a way the linear play does not. Moreover, its rhythms are not simple, but complex, bound up in the dynamics of countless details which function contextually. This does not mean that the play is formless, a labyrinth of minuscule data and no more. On the contrary, each character who comes to say goodbye to Gar (his teacher, girlfriend, priest, or drinking pals, for example) does so in a scene bristling with subject matter. And these scenes are rituals of strict form, as each of the visitors contributes his share to an increasingly complex examination of Gar's feelings about his departure. Thus it is not the absence of plot, but its very density and richness which best describes the play's form. To be sure, its incidents are rife with details, but only those which precisely fulfill the demands of the situation in context. They are not the result of narrative or descriptive obligations, as they link, control, and integrate the mercurial associations of words, thoughts, and emotions of characters turning inward upon themselves. Within this organic form, *what* is done is not as important as *how* it is done so that, as in Chekov, method becomes a servant of manner, tone, or gesture; and action, at once indirect, oblique, and intricate concerns itself not so much with *events* in the characters' lives as with the *effects* of those events upon them. Causality, the essence of linear drama, is not welcome in the uneasy, tenuous land of this play where nothing is fixed but the multiplicity of life within the teeming brevity of the vignette.

Such a verticular structure strongly affects characterization. And here the play most closely resembles Chekovian drama, for Friel develops his characters solely in context, sketches them with a minimum of information, gives them depth and dimension, but little, if any, direction. They are simple, ordinary people who must be played plainly and sincerely. Like the characters of, say, *Uncle Vanya,* they are absorbed in trivialities, immersed in minutiae, allowing the audience to learn only in passing of important changes in their lives. It is the theatre of small-talk, dove-tailed information, gossip, or hints which signal a perfervid subtextual life. Stern moralists, to be sure, would condemn these people as failures at life, but they have done the best they can; to do less is immoral. To discuss them is to note how Friel gently and dispassionately places them upon the stage, telling us little about them directly. Slowly, cautiously, we must infer who they are, were, or might have been. None dominates; all relate to the play's major concerns, as complicated actions unravel to disclose complicated relationships. Each is searching for the meaning of life, of love; yet each is tainted, flawed, betrayed not so much by emotional inertia as by present circumstances which, for one reason or another, have denied them some kind of fulfillment, some peace with themselves. Unable to reach out to those they love, they flee a situation rather than confront it. Still, one cannot make neat lists of these characters, nor moralize about their shortcomings, dividing them into recognizable types. Scrupulously, Friel balances and intermingles them; structurally, they interrelate, providing a sense of true ensemble. Of the three women (Madge Mulhern, the O'Donnell's housekeeper, Lizzy Burton, the aunt from America, and Katie Doogan, Gar's ex-fiancee), two are childless, turning to Gar for a son they could never have, nor ever will, while the young girl is doomed to an arranged, loveless, and socially acceptable marriage. The men fare no better. There is, for example, the dour, taciturn S. B. O'Donnell, a father who is no father to a son he can never reach; fixed forever, it seems, on memories of the untimely death of a wife he admits was too young for him; a priest who dispenses nothing but aphorisms; a schoolmaster who had loved Gar's mother, had been once a poet and is now a drunk; and, finally, Gar's friends, content to remain in the village drinking, carousing, avoiding responsibilities and maturity. What rescues these people from the realm of the portentous is their complete unselfconsciousness, their inability to be no more than what they are. Like their Chekovian counterparts they are hardly aware of what has passed them by. And Friel does not present them as downtrodden souls dwelling in perpetual gloom. On the contrary, as Chekov does, he mixes humor with pathos, blending irony and compassion with an equal lack of self pity, or sentimentality. These people, then, make do, endure, and Friel knows that their struggle requires a kind of courage heroes will never know. To each of them he gives, in exemplary Chekovian fashion, a moment when their inner life surfaces to tell us not some great truth, but their truth; it is a realization neither histrionic nor spectacular, but merely and deeply profound; an awareness of what life might have been and is not. But these discoveries (or morals, if you will) are within the situation and within the characters, not superimposed by the playwright. Hence the characters

function as a Chekovian "chorus element" (to borrow Magarshack's phrase) *i.e.,* they perform a choral function, of moral judgment upon the action. "Characters," Magarshack asserts, "assume the mantle of the chorus whenever their inner life bursts through the outer shell of their everyday appearance and overflows into a torrent of words." Like Chekov, then, Friel allows his characters to stumble upon themselves, and when this occurs they move from the world of realism into the world of art, giving the play an evocative stage poetry, enlarging its scope. They become, in short, symbols of us all.

> **Organized upon artistic principles,**
> ***Philadelphia, Here I Come!* firmly and**
> **quietly insists, as does any Chekov play,**
> **that life is neither funny nor sad, but more**
> **often is both, simultaneously.**
> **—James Coakley**

Yet even as Friel builds his own version of the Chekovian play of indirect action, he introduces an important innovation of his own. In a shrewd *coup de théâtre,* he splits the character of the protagonist, using two actors to portray the public and private selves of Gar. A convention as old as the medieval theatre, recalling the notion of the divided self, it is the pivotal conceit of the play, and its use has manifold implications. First, as an immediate source of tension or interplay between the two selves, the device obviously enhances the possibilities for character delineation of Gar, as intricate strands of experience buried with the private self are released and dramatized. Unseen and unheard by the other characters, often berating, cajoling, or goading his public counterpart, the private self is both omniscient narrator and confidant, a guide to the past, an alter ego who forces the other Gar to examine what he is about to leave. And if dramatically this use of a dual protagonist enlarges our knowledge of Gar, technically, it is a godsend. The private self performs double duty: supplying the audience with necessary information, or intrusting his public self with the "facts" needed to play a scene. For the private self distanced from the action, free to move in and out of scene at will, can, as if by poetic fiat, speak the unspeakable, express the unexpressable, do or say the forbidden. Expectedly, Friel seizes upon the comedy intrinsic in these privileges. To let the private self speak his "true" feelings is to give the audience information denied the other characters; it is to create discrepancy, promote irony, and the result is laughter. On the other hand, the use of a private self has a direct effect on the play's forward movement. Frequently he will halt the action of a scene to comment on its significance; or permit a character to leave a scene in progress to step forth and reveal heretofore unsuspected thoughts and feelings. What Friel has done, of course, is combine the dramatic liberty implicit in the convention of the dual protagonist with the old-fashioned Chekovian monologue, or tirade, put to new use. Here it encourages a cinematic expressivity to the play's action, a Joycean fluidity to the expression of the character's inner lives, while they move in and out of Gar's experience. Yet this mixture, at once loose and supple, pushes on to more complicated ends. Upon this flexible structure which bends but does not break, Friel imposes a double time scheme, utilizing flashbacks which shuttle from present to past to future. So fantasy, memory, and desire merge, as remarkably sophisticated techniques support an equally sophisticated dramatic form. Time and space linger, pause, and reflect upon the important moments in Gar's life which demand to be relived. And we have the clarity of true complexity.

But if *Philadelphia, Here I Come!* follows the practices of Chekovian dramaturgy, it is also touched with Chekovian grace, an atmosphere *sui generis*. It is a comedy, to be sure, neither black nor dark, but merely and acutely aware. It looks at, accepts, and understands human limitations, insisting, as does all comedy, that people do not change, learn nothing, but somehow go on. A play of many excellences, its techniques are noteworthy, its feelings honest, but it is, in sum and tone, a play of indecision, ambiguity, uncertainty, where loneliness is omnipresent, but never mentioned; where love is hidden, denied or non-existent. And it adds up to nothing but the doubts, fears, and confusions of a young man about to leave Ireland for America. Still, this very irresolution complements a dramatic action focused on the imprecision of memory, the aches linked with desires, and the humor implicit in dreams. Neither sociological, nor psychological, it is artistic, poetic, and moral, but all in a Chekovian sense. There is a nostalgia for a non-existent past, but, more pertinently, the individual's search for love and the meaning of life. And Friel's play walks a shaky middle ground which is so very real, so very human. In its quiet, modest way *Philadelphia, Here I Come!* is a paradigm for a large part of good drama today.

Edmund J. Miner (essay date Spring 1977)

SOURCE: "Homecoming: The Theme of Disillusionment in Brian Friel's Short Stories," in *Kansas Quarterly,* Vol. 9, No. 2, Spring 1977, pp. 92-9.

[*In the following essay, Miner addresses the theme of disillusionment in Friel's "Among the Ruins" and "Foundry House" by examining the details of the characters' reevaluation of childhood from an adult perspective.*]

Brian Friel is probably best known to both Americans and Canadians for such commercially successful plays as *The Loves of Cass McGuire* and *Philadelphia, Here I Come!*

Born in County Tyrone in 1929, he spent many years, like Bryan MacMahon, his compatriot and fellow-playwright, as a school-teacher. Since 1960, however, he has devoted himself almost exclusively to a literary career. A shareholder in the Abbey Theatre, he has been prominent in the field of contemporary Irish drama; he has also, however, earned an enviable reputation as a writer of short stories, many of which have appeared in *The New Yorker*. Two collections of short stories, *The Saucer of Larks* (1956) and *The Gold in the Sea* (1966) are deeply rooted in his beloved Tyrone as well as in Donegal, where he now lives. The earlier book contains some of Friel's finest and most representative writing, in both the serious and the comic vein; not all the stories are masterpieces, but the collection as a whole is worth reading and a few individual pieces are eminently entertaining. Irish commentators have singled out **"Among the Ruins"** and **"Foundry House"** as especially memorable, and these stories serve to illustrate as well as any Brian Friel's pervasive theme of disillusionment, a subject which characterizes both his short fiction and his drama.

"Among the Ruins" is a brief recounting of a special outing which a young wife organizes to Corradinna in Donegal so that her reluctant husband may revisit his old homestead and afford his two young children the opportunity to see where their father had lived and played at their age. Neither child is actually interested—Peter prefers the seaside to a lot of ruins—but Margo forces the issue and eventually persuades her husband with the argument: "Even if it's only to see if you have lost the feel of the place." Ironically, Joe's enthusiasm increases as the trip progresses, while Margo's diminishes as a result of the children's constant bickering and her husband's obvious relish.

Despite its simplicity, this is not a story for or about children. Brian Friel expects the reader to identify immediately with Joe, who, for a sentimental day, is to relive his own childhood by the remembrance of things past that cling to his old ruined house. The hero of a nostalgic tale is usually solitary so that he may give himself up wholly and undistractedly to his memories. The violation of this canon is what makes **"Among the Ruins"** different. Joe's wife, his son Peter, and his daughter Mary are painfully present on this pilgrimage and viewing all they see by the mere light of common day in flat images, while Joe, with the double vision of then and now, revels in poignant contrasts or in mystical resemblances not noted by the others. For the day at least Joe alone views the world by stereopticon. Joe and Margo are Walter and Mrs. Mitty but in a minor mode, for Joe's trips into his fantasized past do not span such a vast valley of tears and laughter as do those of the timid little prototypal dreamer. This day is for Joe, however, one of successive disillusionments. True it is that the sight of his old home reminds him of his most vital years: chasing foxes with his dogs to the point of exhaustion, daring his sister to jump with him a veritable Mississippi of a river, rambling through a dense forest, inventorying the treasures of the old barn, glorying in the exhilarating freedom of their hideout in the garden bower. Epic days.

This romantic theme, though, is challenged by Margo's unimaginative scrutiny of facts. Beautiful golden hillocks inhabited by fairies in the moonlight of Joe's sentiment—even his grand mountains with their poetic names, Altanure, Glenmakennif, and Meenalaragan—become mere dungheaps when exposed under the harsh noon sunlight of Margo's inspection. Joe remembers that at that age he was overcome with gales of laughter by the words he and his sister Susan had made up—words like "sligalog" and "skookalook." But Margo insists upon a law-court reply to her barrister's question: "Susan and you in the bower. Once you got in there together, you laughed your heads off. And I want to know what you laughed *at*." The "infinite moments" of Joe's childhood are reduced to mere instances of childish silliness under his wife's inquisition: "'Skookalook.' What's funny about that?" And later: "Poor silly, simple Joe."

The range of the story may be limited, the mood at times curiously uneven. Even the theme of disillusionment falls occasionally below the threshold of visibility. Competing themes rear their heads now and again to produce a multiplicity which threatens—but only threatens—the unity and strength of the story. Of these competing themes the most interesting may be Proust's—that we do not correctly evaluate nor do we appreciate direct experiences, that it is only in the second-told tale of recollection that we can really understand their import. Hence Joe does not insist upon explanations. When his nostalgic activity renders him oblivious to the fact that Peter has disappeared at departure-time, he finds the boy playing at a rabbit-hole, "donging the tower" he explains. Margo may demand explanations, but Joe knows that the heart of childhood—and the funnybone—have reasons which the reasoning mind cannot begin to understand. If he did not consciously realize it before, Margo has brought it home to him this very day. "Donging the tower" takes its place, together with "sligalog" and "skookalook," in the hallowed and unapproachable recesses of the mind of childhood.

It is the same nostalgic comprehension that impels Joe to sympathize with his son on the way home when the boy is reduced to tears first by Mary, then by his mother. Is not Peter Joe himself some years earlier? And when Margo slaps the boy for calling Mary a "liar," it is significant that the father has not cast the first stone: hasn't he too behaved like that to his own sister? For Joe has learned this day that despite his enthusiastic memories of childhood, the river and the forest *have* proven to be shockingly small. Even more, he recalls now that he and Susan did not spend all their times laughing in the bower; they had fought, too, and Susan had

reported him and brought him many a punishment. Peter and Mary are Joe and Susan to the life. Strangely enough, this somewhat unsuccessful visit to ancient beloved ruins, with all the disillusionment, the squabbling of the children, and his wife's insistent and belittling cross-examination, has furnished Joe with a deeper understanding of his own young boy and girl. Reliving one's own life in one's children, Joe finds, makes for sympathetic insight.

Joe's education, encompassing but a few hours of one day, is best expressed in Brian Friel's two closing paragraphs:

> Silence filled the car. Through the mesmerism of motor, fleeing hedges, shadows flying from the headlights, three words swam into Joe's head 'Donging the tower.' What did Peter mean, he wondered dreamily, what game was he playing, donging the tower? He recalled the child's face engrossed, earnest with happiness, as he squatted on the ground by the rabbit hole. A made-up game, Joe supposed, already forgotten. He would ask him in the morning, but Peter would not know. Just out of curiosity, he would ask him, not that it mattered . . . And then a flutter of excitement stirred in him. Yes, yes, it did matter. Not the words, not the game, but the fact that he had seen his son, on the first good day of summer, busily, intently happy in solitude, donging the tower. The fact that Peter would never remember it was of no importance; it was his own possession now, his own happiness, this knowledge of a child's private joy.
>
> Then, as he turned the car into the road that led to their house, a strange, extravagant thought struck him. He must have had moments of his own like Peter's, alone, back in Corradinna, donging his own towers. And, just as surely, his own father must have stumbled on him, and must have recognized himself in his son. And his father before that, and his before that. Generations of fathers stretching back and back, all finding magic and sustenance in the brief, quickly destroyed happiness of their children. The past did have meaning. It was neither reality nor dreams, neither today's patchy oaks nor the great woods of his boyhood. It was simply continuance, life repeating itself and surviving.

There is a difference, Joe realizes, between matter and spirit. Matter has no future: homes turn to ruins, rivers become trickles, giant forests are reduced to clumps of trees. Disillusionment with material things is of little consequence. What matters is that futurity is in the ensouled child and the continuity of the race.

It is tempting, as admittedly it often is in the case of Irish plays and short stories, to interpret **"Foundry House"** in terms of the political and religious conflicts which have plagued that unfortunate nation for so many years. For some readers with a traditional sense of what constitutes a short story, **"Foundry House"** lacks, perhaps, the clash of motive against obstacle, thus offering little suspense or intense interest. As a *tableau vivant,* it may be more intelligible, but it can be argued that it is scarcely *vivant.* When submitted on one occasion to an undergraduate English class, the story was rejected as anemic with regard to character, action, and atmosphere. The story does make good sense if viewed as a sociological palimpsest sounding the depths of politics, religion, and general culture by a succession of heavily-weighted symbols. The drama then shifts from the story itself to the reader's competence to read the symbols and judge their truth. Naturally, it would take an Ulsterman's background to prepare one for this difficult task.

The situation of **"Foundry House"** is simplicity itself. Joe Brennan, a radio and television mechanic, upon his parents' deaths, applies for their house, the gate lodge to Foundry House. Mrs. Hogan, the wife of the wealthy foundry owner, for whom Joe's father had worked for half a century, is quite content to let him move into the place of his birth. Most of the story concerns a family reunion at Foundry House itself, to which Joe Brennan is invited in order to operate a tape recorder so that the Brennans' daughter, a missionary nun in Africa, may participate by means of a tape which she has mailed to her family. Like his namesake in **"Among the Ruins,"** Joe experiences in the course of the afternoon a shattering of several of his childhood illusions.

In recent years the world's news media have regaled us with tales of the Ulster class struggle between unionist and nationalist, Protestant and Catholic, and the modern equivalents of the big house feudal lord and the peasant fief, the British-supported patron and the native suppliant. Now, **"Foundry House"** does not exactly symbolize this struggle and its accompanying atrocities, but it does help to define the cultural foundation and social background from which the conflict arises. If Brian Friel had written a story of the strife itself—and even in the fifties today's animosities were bitterly present—the result would have been a slight measure of history or a piece of propaganda for grim viewing by partisan or committed readers. And undoubtedly disillusionment would have been a strong ingredient of such a portrait: do we not find O'Casey's disillusionment with 1916 and its aftermath reflected in the ironies of so many of the characters and situations of his Dublin plays? But by making all the characters of **"Foundry House"** Catholic, the author has disburdened himself of an ugly and seemingly insoluble reality and has cleared the way for the pure exercise of the story art. Here that art deals only with the common culture of the North, whether for Catholic or Protestant; it presents the tilled field

without pursuing the subsequent harvest of weeds and flowers.

The two families represent the polarized classes within Ulster itself. The Hogans are revered still as the inheritors of wealth and power in the county, a form of Catholic Ascendancy, the descendants of conquerors and entrenched greed. They have always owned the factory, the true source of their wealth, have used people like the Brennans for years, and now patronize them. Their home is desolate, except for dying oldsters. But where such Ulster diehards are decadent and dying out, the underling Celtic element, the Brennans, have a family of nine vigorous, fighting offspring. This contrast moves Mrs. Hogan to a regretful—if, indeed, not to a jealous and even insincere—utterance of praise: "I've seen them playing on the avenue. And so . . . so healthy." Here she echoes the fear of the decadent unionists, her own house decimated by emigration, palsy, and age.

"Foundry House," a shockingly inartistic name for a "big house," lays stress on the feature that distinguishes the North from the South: they are industrial, materialist, eager beavers at doing and making as contrasted with the more artistic dreamers of the South. The title also symbolizes who is possessor of privilege and patronage, who moulds life to his own pattern or will. The gatekeeping Brennans, tenants at will, are prisoners of Hogan demands. The two families know their distance from each other. When old Mrs. Hogan, in the course of the curious and pathetic reunion at Foundry House, says commandingly, "Quiet, boy," she reminds Joe Brennan of his place "Croppies, lie down."

These are the broad lines of the story's meaning, of its latent conflict, if we tend to regard Irish literature as almost invariably an expression of religious and political differences. When we start interpreting the shading of **"Foundry House"** from this viewpoint, we touch on the more sacred inhumanities of the Ulsterman, his intransigence, his silences, his taboos, his shibboleths and formulas—all indelibly preserved in mummifying juices; his mechanical ways of thinking, speaking, and acting; his aversion for talk or discussion of an open nature, his solemn taking of himself and his neighbor's rights and property for granted; his *ipse dixit* dogmatism; his constant fear in the silences that make ambushes for every conspirator; his dearth of spontaneity or modernity, committed as he is to ancient formulas of hate and intolerance.

But **"Foundry House,"** in addition to its social and political implications, is an illustration of Brian Friel's preoccupation with the theme of life's disillusionments. Joe Brennan, like the hero of **"Among the Ruins,"** has come home again only to find that his memories of childhood fall short of the reality. He is visibly frightened by the grandeur of the big house; he is even paralyzed into silence by the first visit of

Her Eminence, Mrs. Hogan, to his humble gate-house abode, with its nine unruly children. Joe is still living in a past where Foundry House, inhabited by a Heathcliff of a master, accompanied by a fearsome Great Dane, had filled him with awe and dread. As he approaches the house on the day of the reunion, the knocker displays an evil, leering face, reminiscent of Marley's apparition to the unnerved Ebenezer Scrooge. His introduction to his boyhood acquaintance, Declan Hogan, now a Jesuit, is not impressive and becomes a presage of the disillusionments in store for him in the Great Hall itself.

The passage of time has produced a general ugliness, an atmosphere of decay, even a condition of penury in the once proud Foundry House of Joe Brennan's youthful memories. Mrs. Hogan is a pitiful semblance of what she once was; Declan is a nervous, ill-at-ease caricature of a Jesuit; Sister Claire, fat and unlovely in her childhood, is shrill and artificial in her taped message; and more startlingly, Mr. Hogan, the awesome figure of bygone days, is now a stroke victim, unkempt, powerless, and incapable of even the most basic kind of communication:

> It took them five minutes to get from the door to the leather armchair beside the fire, and Joe was reminded of a baby being taught to walk. Father Declan came in first, backward, crouching slightly, his eyes on his father's feet, and his arms outstretched and beckoning 'Slow-ly Slow-ly, he said in a hypnotist's voice. 'Slow-ly, Slow-ly. Then his father appeared. First a stick, then a hand, an arm, the curve of his stomach, then the beard, yellow and untidy, then the whole man. Since his return to the gate lodge, Joe had not thought of Mr. Bernard beyond the fact that he was there. In his mind there was a twenty-year-old image that had never been adjusted, a picture which was so familiar to him that he had long ceased to look at it. But this was not the image, this giant who had grown in height and swollen in girth instead of shrinking, this huge, monolithic figure that inched its way across the faded carpet, one mechanical step after the other, in response to a word from the black, weaving figure before him. Joe looked at his face, fleshy, trembling, coloured in dead purple and grey-black, and at the eyes, wide and staring and quick with the terror of stumbling or of falling or even of missing a syllable of the instructions from the priest. 'Lift again. Lift it. Lift it. Good. Good. Now down, down. And the right, up and up and up—yes—and now down.' The old man wore an overcoat streaked down the front with food stains, and the hands, one clutching the head of the stick, the other limp and lifeless by his side, were so big they had no contour. His breathing was a succession of rapid sighs.

Joe Brennan had not been to the Great House for two decades and was ill prepared for the startling transformation. Like Joe in **"Among the Ruins,"** his homecoming has been fraught with disillusionment and the disquieting realization that in his childhood rivers and forests and mansions were oversize; now they appear undeniably undersize. There is a general ugliness that embraces not only the decaying grandeur of life associated with Foundry House, but also with the building itself. The furnishings now seem hard and decrepit: the ceilings are unwarrantably high, the marble forbiddingly black, the place itself cold and cheerless—a far cry from the crowded but cozy gatehouse with its noise of nine tumbling children and sense of life being lived. But what gives Joe some measure of assurance in his afternoon at Foundry House is his realization that, while time and events have passed the Hogans by, he, an electronic engineer, exercises a mastery in the house that once filled him with awe.

There is one sense in which the story may be viewed as a contrast between mechanism and humanism. The description of the characters deals almost solely with their physical, anatomical, and physiological qualities and motions; as moral beings they are not presented: whether they are human beings at all or the repositories of moral or religious beliefs, there is nothing. When she first induces her husband to write away to apply for the gatehouse, Rita insists on his mentioning their nine children, for 'Aren't they [the Hogans] supposed to be one of the best Catholic families in the North of Ireland?' But there is no indication of this fact in Joe's afternoon at Foundry House. Even Father Declan appears more in the guise of a male nurse going through his daily formalities than a religious priest and son possessed of spiritual consolation for his aged parents. Likewise, he is utterly oblivious to the true nature of his sister's missionary work among the African natives and the motives that inspired her to devote her life to such a cause. Joe Brennan himself finds it strange that both Hogan children have turned their backs on the potential wealth of Foundry House and left it as a mausoleum for their incompetent parents.

The Hogans, are, in fact, machines rather than living people. Sister Claire in her taped message notes that the "machines" are in need of parts: ". . . I hope you have found a good maid at last . . ." she says to her mother, and ". . . why don't you get yourself a third [dog]. . . ?" she asks her father, a man unable to rise from his bed without assistance. Actually, the tape reveals that Sister Claire does not know a thing about her parents' condition and is not in communication with them or her brother regularly enough to find out. There is a "family reunion" on this bleak Sunday afternoon, mainly to hear Sister Claire's message and presumably digest it, but the discussion of the assembled characters is almost entirely limited to the mechanics of the whole venture. The fact that Sister Claire, instead of writing her parents in pen and ink, has used a taped recording, reduces communication to a problem in mechanics, finding a tape-recorder, locating an expert who can explain it—and even Declan has to turn mechanic and run the machine despite the expert's presence—learning to use the unfamiliar buttons and knobs, and trying to find an electric power plug in a house still dependent mainly on gas. As a communication the message itself becomes completely secondary to the opportunity for a display of a mechanical device; mechanism affords Sister Claire a chance to use her violin—not for the beauty of the music which is tinny and often out of tune—but to reveal her acquaintance with the latest instrument for communication. As it turns out, Sister Claire is largely forgotten in a "reunion" that deals unconscionably with knobs, volume, power plugs, electricity, and a toneless violin, as well as a quality of voice which Joe Brennan himself mentally likens to "a teacher reading a story to a class of infants, making her voice go up and down in pretended interest." Admittedly, in these times when more and more people are using tapes to transmit family messages, it may seem harsh to denigrate Sister Claire's use of a tape, but the circumstance does appear to indicate her lack of knowledge of her parents' physical condition and the unavailability of modern contrivances at Foundry House. Nevertheless, the use of the taped message does produce one very dramatic moment: it puts a sudden end to the family reunion. At the height of the violin concert, the partially paralyzed old man realizes that it is his daughter on the tape, something that a written letter could probably not have accomplished.

> Then even as Joe watched, he suddenly levered himself upright in the chair, his face pulsating with uncontrollable emotion, the veins in his neck dilating, the mouth shaping in preparation for speech. He learned forward, half pointing toward the recorder with one huge hand.
>
> 'Claire!'
>
> The terrible cry—hoarse, breathy, almost lost in his asthmatic snortings—released father Declan and Mrs Hogan from their concentration on the tape. They ran to him as he fell back into the chair.

An hour later, without seeing any of his hosts again, Joe Brennan switches off the machine and leaves Foundry House for the last time. His greatest disillusionment of the day has not been merely the onset of age and palsy, but the reduction of Foundry House itself as the grand old mansion of his childhood. It has been a shock to learn that the drawing room is used no longer—"too large and too expensive to heat"—that the parents occupy now only the breakfast room, that they subsist on snacks, like milk and bananas, that the house is too cold for human habitation, and that the grounds are shamefully neglected. Joe Brennan, too, has spent an afternoon "among the ruins" and returns home to his inquisitive, sharp tongued wife a soberer man. But Joe keeps his illusions to himself; he has been fortunate to have visited the past in solitary. During his wife's insistent questioning, he remains loyal to his childhood memories: the house inside is "very nice", Mr Bernard is "the same as ever. Older, of course, but the same Mr. Bernard", Father Declan is "a fine man. A fine priest. Yes, very fine", "The tape was lovely. . . . They loved it, loved it. It was a lovely recording", "The breakfast room? Oh, lovely, lovely. . . . Glass handle on the door and a beautiful carpet and beautiful pictures . . . everything. Just lovely:"

> 'So that's Foundry House,' said Rita, knowing that she was going to hear no gossipy details.
>
> 'That's Foundry House,' Joe echoed. 'The same as ever no different.'
>
> She put out her cigarette and stuck the butt behind her ear.
>
> They're a great family, Rita,' he said. A great, grand family.'

And with unconscious irony Rita casually agrees with her husband's assessment.

In the stories of these two homecomings with their accompanying disillusionments—and note that neither character plans nor organizes his return: he is anything but an active agent—there is no doubt that the protagonist of **"Among the Ruins"** attains a deeper awareness and insight as the reward of his experience. At least his realization of each generation's variations on "donging the tower" presumably is going to have an appreciable effect upon his future relationships with his growing children. His discovery that the past does have meaning—". . . simply continuance, life repeating itself and surviving"—is in stark contrast to Joe Brennan's disheartening but only partially perceived notions of the mortality of life and the ephemeral nature of bricks and mortar and even prestigious wealth. But the main difference between the two disillusioned individuals is that Joe Brennan, much more than his counterpart, must fight to retain his childhood illusions in order to sustain himself. Neither man, of course, has a sympathetic or understanding wife: their husbands' boyhoods, in the final analysis, provide both women with some measure of amused contempt. What Joe has learned at Corradinna he will probably one day share with his children; certainly, it is beyond Margo's comprehension. Joe Brennan is more fortunate, if his nine unruly children fail to share his boyish awe of the Hogans in Foundry House, at least he is astute enough to conceal his disillusionments from his shrewish wife and at the same time honor his family's half-century of loyalty to the Hogan clan. Perhaps the saddest disillusionment and irony in both stories is Brian Friel's acute grasp of the gulf that exists between both pairs of husbands and wives and their inability to sit together at the close of the day to establish a bond of understanding of a pathetically shared experience that is common to so much of humanity.

Richard Kearney (essay date Autumn 1987)

SOURCE: "Friel and the Politics of Language Play," in *The Massachusetts Review,* Vol. 28, No. 3, Autumn 1987, pp. 510-15.

[*In the following essay, Kearney speculates on the political and social dimensions of language as text and subject matter in Friel's* Translations *and* The Communication Cord.]

Brian Friel's drama has sometimes been accused of engaging too directly in Irish nationalist politics. In a recent issue of the Belfast magazine, *Fortnight,* Brian McEvera offers a typical example of this accusation: "Friel's work is directly political in its implications," he charges, "and its 'awareness' is one-sided. The 'shape' observed is a nationalist one—and a limited partial view of nationalism at that." McEvera concludes with the hope that the "more overt political element will disappear from (Friel's) work."

Friel's overriding concern is to examine the contemporary crisis of language as a medium of communication and representation.
—Richard Kearney

Such charges of political propaganda are, I believe, quite mistaken. Several of Friel's later plays do indeed have a political content—in the sense that they address the nature of Irish nationalist ideology in both its historical and contemporary guises. But they do so in a way that is profoundly anti-propagandist. One of Friel's primary concerns in such recent plays as *Translations* and *The Communication Cord* is to explore the complex relationship between political ideology and the problematic nature of language itself. Like most artists influenced by the modernist movement, Friel is deeply preoccupied by the workings of language. And like most genuine artists he is aware that language does not exist in a timeless vacuum but operates in and from a specific historical situation. It is not surprising then that Friel should display a particular attentiveness to the ways in which different political ideologies—i.e. those of British colonialism and Irish nationalism in particular—have so often informed or deformed the communicative function of language. Those

who accuse Friel of propagandistically supporting the cause of political nationalism are grossly misconstruing his work. For they fail to appreciate that his overriding concern is to examine the contemporary crisis of language as a medium of communication and representation.

I will confine most of my remarks to Friel's most recent play, *The Communication Cord,* for it is here arguably that the rapport between language and nationalist politics is most critically explored. Friel has stated that *The Communication Cord* should be read in tandem with *Translations.* While the latter highlighted the way in which language was used by the British to exploit (both culturally and politically) an indigenous community in County Donegal, the former shows how language may be used by this same Irish community some hundred years later in order to exploit each other. But it should be pointed out that already in *Translations,* Friel was aware that a narrowly nationalistic attitude toward language could be invoked as a refusal to communicate with others. The callous murder of the British officer, Yolland, by the Donnelly Twins is represented as just such a refusal. And the Gaelic hedge-school master, Hugh, recognizes the necessity of translating from the old language into the new when he agrees to teach English to his pupil, Maire, or when he declares, "We like to think we endure around truths immemorially posited, but we remember that words are signals, counters. They are not immortal. And it can happen that a civilisation can be imprisoned in a linguistic contour which no longer matches the landscape of fact." Pointing to the Name Book of translations from Gaelic into English, Hugh concedes the need for historical change. "We must learn those new names," he soberly challenges, "we must learn to make them our own, we must make them our new home."

In *The Communication Cord* Friel satirizes the contemporary attitude of certain sentimental nationalists who seek to revive the old culture, which is now irretrievably lost, while at the same time employing the ad-man's language of opportunism and deceit.

If *Translations* set out to chart the transition of a language from the mythological past to the modern present, *The Communication Cord* operates in reverse order: it portrays the attempt to retrace language from its contemporary condition back to its pristine ancestry. Both plays conspire to present us with a fascinating genealogy of the process of human speech, the ways in which we use words to progress or regress in history, to find or lose ourselves, to confuse or to communicate. The fact that the former play is composed in *tragic* tones, while the latter is written as a *farce,* is in itself an indicator of Friel's tragic-comic realization that there is no going back in history; that the best that can be achieved is a playful deconstruction and reconstruction of words in the hope that new modes of communication might be made possible.

Both plays situate the conflict of language models in the specific context of Irish culture. *Translations* deals with pre-famine Ireland bracing itself for the final transplantation of Gaelic into English. *The Communication Cord* takes up the story more than a century later. It shows us modern Ireland taking stock of its linguistic identity and attempting to recover the ancient pieties of its prefamine heritage. While one play features the old language looking forward to its ominous future, the other features the new language looking back to its dispossessed origins.

The scene of the action in *The Communication Cord*—a restored thatched cottage in Ballybeg—is simply an inverted replica of the condemned school house in Baile Beag, The Donegal Village of *Translations.* In similar fashion, Tim Gallaher, the central character of the play—a university lecturer in linguistics preparing a Ph.D. on communication—serves as an inverted mirror-image of his ancestral prototype, Hugh.

The distinctively ersatz character of the restored cottage betokens the futility of any literal quest for the lost grail of our cultural past. Adorned with the antiquarian accoutrements of churn, creel, crook, hanging pot, thatched roof and open hearth, the cottage is described by Friel in a stage note as "false . . . too pat . . . *too* authentic." It is, short, an artificial reproduction, a holiday home of today counterfeiting the real home of yesterday.

> **At the . . . more fundamental level, language transcends its purely pragmatic function as a formal transmission of information and seeks a more profound sharing of one's existential experience. . . .**
> —*Richard Kearney*

This play about communication begins, significantly, with a failure of communication. Tim is saying that the door to the cottage is open, while Jack McNeilis, his friend, misunderstands him to say that it is locked. From the outset their language is at cross purposes. Jack is a successful, suave, and self-assured barrister from Dublin. He possesses all those qualities of the modern Irish bourgeoisie which Tim lacks—efficiency, sexual confidence and above all, since language remains the key, a remarkable felicity with conversational repartee.

Jack's *nouveau-riche* family bought the rickety cottage in Ballybeg and refurbished its rustic charms in order to experience the "soul and authenticity of the place." Jack's de-

scription of this romantic return to the land is presented as a saucy parody of Hugh's genuine *pietas.* "Everybody's grandmother was reared in a house like this," Jack quips, claiming it to be the "ancestral seat of the McNeilis dynasty, restored with love and dedication, absolutely authentic in every last detail. . . . This is where we all come from. This is our first cathedral. This shaped our souls. This determined our first pieties. Yes. Have reverence for this place." Jack's way of revering his "father's house" is, ironically, to recite a tedious inventory or "map" of all the objects contained in the cottage (fireplace, pot-iron, tongs, etc.) He employs naming according to the model of utilitarian representation in order to classify each thing as a use-item. For Jack, language is a filing cabinet of objects.

One of the central themes of the play is the conflict between Tim's view of communication as a genuine response cry expressing true feeling and Jack's view of communication as a commercial contract or sentimental nostalgia.

Friel has Tim expound his linguistic thesis in the opening act of the play, thereby establishing the conceptual coordinates for the subsequent unfolding of the plot. Tim argues that language operates on two levels—as *information* and as *conversation.* At the first and ultimately inferior level, words function as messengers transmitting information from a speaker to a listener. Language becomes a process of encoding and decoding messages. Where a common code exists messages can be exchanged, where not there is misunderstanding. Echoing the terms of [Claude] Lévi-Strauss, Tim explains that "all social-behaviour, the entire social order, depends on communicational structures, on words mutually agreed on and mutually understood. Without that agreement, without that shared code, you have chaos." It is surely no coincidence that the example that Tim chooses to illustrate his point is the absence of a common code of *translation* (when one person speaks only English and the other only German).

At the second but more fundamental level, language transcends its purely pragmatic function as a formal transmission of information and seeks a more profound sharing of one's existential experience: "You desire to share my experience—and because of that desire our exchange is immediately lifted out of the realm of mere exchange of basic messages and aspires to something higher, something much more important—*conversation* . . . a response cry!" Response cries forgo all linguistic strategies of willful manipulation and commerce. But the difficulty is how to discriminate between genuine response cries which speak straight from the heart and the mere pretense at such speech. How is language to escape from the insincerity of role-playing? Tim's inability to resolve this dilemma is not only the reason why he cannot complete his thesis or decide whom he truly loves; it is the very *raison d'être* for the play itself!

The real villain of the piece is Jack's father, Senator Donovan. He is cast as an "amateur antiquarian," a self-made man full of his own self-importance as both doctor and politician, who fatuously extolls the "absolute verity" of the cottage. Donovan is a caricature of all that is sentimental and sententious in Irish cultural nationalism. His speeches are reeled off like farcical travesties of Hugh's *desiderium nostrorum*—the sacramental longing for older, quieter things. Arriving in Ballybeg he pretentiously muses: "This silence, this peace, the restorative power of that landscape . . . this speaks to me, this whispers to me . . . And despite the market place, all the years of trafficking in politics and medicine, a small voice within me still knows the *responses* . . . This is the touchstone . . . the apotheosis."

Donovan, while exploiting to the full the conveniences of the modern multi-national society, still clings to the craven illusion that nothing has changed, that Romantic Ireland is alive and well in a restored Donegal cottage waiting to be purchased by the highest bidder. In other words, Donovan would have it both ways. He is hypocrisy incarnate, a symbol of the very *discontinuity* in Irish cultural history which he refuses to acknowledge. But Donovan's charade of assumed *pietas* is finally scotched when, invoking the mythic shibboleth of Ireland as the "woman with two cows," he actually chains himself to a restored cow harness in the cottage and is unable to extricate himself. The myth becomes literal. As his rantings become more desperate, the entire stage is plunged into darkness. All the characters lose their bearings and stagger about in farcical mimicry of the cultural-linguistic disorientation which has befallen them.

When the light returns the truth begins to dawn; the aliases and alibis are debunked and the artifices of the confounding language games exposed. This enlightenment of consciousness is nowhere more evident than in the concluding love scene between Tim and Claire. Their masks removed and their real feelings made plain, the lovers move towards the most authentic form of language—the response cry of silence. As Tim explains: "Maybe the units of communication don't matter that much . . . We're conversing now but we're not exchanging units . . . I'm not too sure what I'm saying . . . Maybe the message doesn't matter at all then . . . Maybe silence is the perfect language." The employment of language for the exchange of women and property between the different individuals or tribes in the play (Irish, German and French), does not produce either communication or community as Lévi-Strauss's theory would have us believe. The existential secrets of the heart cannot be disclosed through the verbal exchange of informational units, but only through the "reverberations" occasioned by a genuine "response" of human feelings. Responding to Claire's genuine response cry—"Kiss me"—Tim embraces her. As he does so, the lovers lean against the fragile upright beam of the cottage causing it to collapse around them in a flurry of apocalyptic chaos. The local tower of babel is demolished in one loving stroke. And even Jack, the consummate wizard of word-play is compelled to resort to a response cry—"O my God."

What does Friel's play tell us about the relationship between language and political propaganda? The conclusion to **The Communication Cord** is, equivocal. The hint of some salvation through silence is counteracted by the literal unleashing of darkness and destruction. While the abandonment of speech spells loving communion for Tim and Claire, it spells the collapse of the community as a whole. Silence is a double-edged sword heralding *both* the beginning of love *and* the end of society. While the departure from language may well lead to love, it may equally well lead to violence. So that Friel's existential optimism with regard to silence as the "perfect language" appears to go hand in glove with a pessimistic, or at least skeptical, appraisal of its socio-historical implications. The word "*cord*" itself conveys this double sense of a bond and an alarm signal.

Seen in conjunction with **Translations,** the ambiguity of Friel's conclusion becomes even more explicit. While the former attempted to show how language once operated in terms of a cultural rootedness and centeredness, the latter de-centers all easy assumptions about the retrieval of such lost, cultural origins. *The Communication Cord* affirms the irreversibility of *history* as an alienation from the natural prehistory of words; and this very affirmation exposes the impotence of language to save a community from the corrosive effects of time, from the mixed blessings of Modern Progress.

Seamus Deane, one of the directors of Friel's *Field Day Theatre Company,* states this dilemma with admirable concision in the preface to **The Communication Cord.** "Nostalgia for the lost native culture," writes Deane, "appears ludicrous and sham . . . Friel has presented us here with the vacuous world of a dying culture. The roof is coming in on our heads . . . There is little or no possibility of inwardness, of dwelling in rather than on history." Situating this crisis of language in the more specific context of Irish cultural and political history, Deane adds: "Irish discourse, especially literary discourse, is ready to invoke history but reluctant to come to terms with it . . . So we manage to think of our great writers as explorers of *nature,* as people who successfully fled the historical nightmare and reintroduced us to the daily nature we all share, yet this feeling is itself historically determined. A colony always wants to escape from history. It longs for its own authenticity, the element it had before history came to disfigure it."

By refusing to flee from history and from its complex rapport with language, Friel's drama is political, but in a sense radically opposed to political propaganda. Friel's art is political in a way which defends language against the abuses of political ideology.

Marilyn Throne (essay date September 1988)

SOURCE: "The Disintegration of Authority: A Study of the Fathers in Five Plays of Brian Friel," in *Colby Library Quarterly*, Vol. 24, No. 3, September 1988, pp. 162-72.

[*In the following essay, Throne studies the features of the fathers in Friel's plays, drawing conclusions about the social and political implications of the characters.*]

In his introduction to Brian Friel's *Selected Plays,* Seamus Deane observes that several of Friel's plays "have in common an interest in the disintegration of traditional authority. . . ." In particular, Deane is thinking of *Living Quarters* (1977) and *The Aristocrats* (1979) where that traditional authority is clearly lodged in the characters of the fathers. In *Living Quarters,* the father, Frank Butler, is also the commandant of the battalion stationed in Ballybeg, a recently returned hero who has carried nine wounded men to safety during U.N. service in the Middle East. The father of *The Aristocrats* is O'Donnell, district judge in Ballybeg. Butler has four adult children; O'Donnell, five. The authority examined in the plays is both familial and social. And in both plays we encounter disintegration in the authority roles: Frank Butler may be a hero and about to be promoted, but he has only cardboard authority at home where his son has had an affair with his second wife; similarly Judge O'Donnell is a stroke victim his children keep tabs on via a "baby tender."

If we look beyond these two plays, we find Friel commonly investigating this same disintegration by examining the role of the father. Furthermore, he invariably casts the father into some societal role that is also authoritarian. In the early play *Philadelphia, Here I Come!* (1965), S. B. O'Donnell—sometimes known as Screwballs—is a county councillor who owns a general shop. In *Faith Healer* (1979), Grace Hardy's father is a judge by name of O'Dwyer; and while Frank Hardy's father was really a storeman in a factory, Frank insists that he was a sergeant of the guards and imagines him always in the role and setting of a policeman. And finally, in *Translations* (1980), although the legal and civil authority is in the hands of the ignorant, ruthless, and English Captain Lancey, Hugh Mor O'Donnell has enormous social prestige within the Irish community of Baile Beag because he is the hedge-schoolmaster.

However, whatever titles and real or titular power Friel's fathers have, they also have a shared impotence. Two of these characters, Judge O'Dwyer of *Faith Healer* and Judge

O'Donnell of *The Aristocrats,* have suffered strokes. In *Living Quarters,* Frank Butler has been twice set aside by his wives in favor of his son Ben who stands beside his mother when Gerald Kelly arrives to date Helen and who has an affair with Anna, his father's second wife. And two of the fathers are made powerless by inarticulation: S. B. O'Donnell, a silent man, awed by his memory of the way his little boy once chattered, and Hugh Mor, articulate in the wrong languages, in Latin, Greek, and Irish, who can therefore hurl only classical epithets at an English solidiery too ill-educated to be insulted by them.

This combination in the fathers of a power or authority, which is sometimes crippling to their children, and an impotence in solving the problems of life in general and of Ireland in particular creates conflicts with and within those children. Such conflicts are the crises of the several dramas. "The sins of the fathers are visited unto the third and fourth generations"—or, in Friel's plays, at least unto the second. For it is significant that it is the fathers who play the authoritarian roles; the impact of the mothers is negligible in most of the plays. Only in *Living Quarters* is the mother a real force in her children's lives, trying to teach *noblesse oblige* to Helen who marries a mere batman and becoming the presence her son both loves and hates; but she is already six years dead when the play begins and the conflict arises not from her interaction with her offspring but with their versions of their father's ill treatment or lack of authority over her. Indeed, the mother is dead before any of the five plays begins. In *Translations,* she is barely a memory; in *Faith Healer,* though Frank Hardy says he went home for his mother's funeral, in fact he went home for his father's, and his only real memory of his mother is of her singing a hymn, "Yes, heaven, yes, heaven, yes, heaven is the prize." In the same play, Grace's mother is portrayed as living a half-mad and chaotic life.

> **It is . . . clear that in all of [Friel's] plays the children are presented as actually or psychologically crippled by their fathers.**
> **—Marilyn Throne**

The mother is a more vibrant memory in *Philadelphia* and *The Aristocrats,* but one we suspect has been created by her children. The O'Donnell brood in *The Aristocrats* cannot remember their mother as the actress suddenly wooed and won by their stern father judge, so they have concocted false memories of her playing "The Bedtime Waltz" and dancing with John McCormack. Similarly, in *Philadelphia,* Gar has had to construct in his mind a picture of the mother who died when he was only three days old; he keeps repeating the little he knows; that she came from "Bailtefree beyond the mountains; and her eyes were bright, and her hair was loose . . ."

and that "for many a night" S. B. "must have heard her crying herself to sleep . . ."

It is clear, then, that Friel is emphasizing not the parent's role, but rather the father's role. It is also clear that in all of the plays the children are presented as actually or psychologically crippled by their fathers.

In *Philadelphia,* Friel's treatment of Gar O'Donnell's psychological crippling is simply presented by dividing the character on stage into two roles played by separate actors, Public Gar and Private Gar. His dilemma is that he is twenty-five years old and still a virgin; his days are spent working in his father's store and his evenings with a group of young men equally frustrated by their equally limited prospects. Gar's only possible resolution is to escape to Philadelphia, and this self-imposed exile is made bitterer by the fact that he does not believe that his leaving will mean a great deal to his silent, uncommunicative father.

In the other plays, because the families are larger—or in the case of *Faith Healer,* because we deal with two separate single-child families—Friel has more scope to present the multiplicities of effects the fathers have on their children.

For instance, there are four offspring in *Living Quarters.* Tina, still a child at eighteen, is brought into sudden adulthood by her father's suicide. But before that event, her only employment was tending to household chores within her father's house which she has not yet left; we see her and the middle daughter, Miriam, getting Frank's uniform ready for the ceremonies in honor of his heroism. Miriam says: "The years may have passed but we're still Daddy's little beavers." Miriam herself, twenty-five years old and the mother of three children, is the plump practical wife of the local court clerk, Charlie Donnelly. Miriam has opted for an absolutely ordinary life with an absolutely ordinary husband, and Friel makes clear in little and big ways that she is an uncertain, narrow-minded woman. She holds her family, the Butlers, as superior to the people of Ballybeg: ". . . all the buckos from the village—the Morans and the Sharkeys and all that gang—all squinting and gleeking and not missing a bar;" she believes Anna is too young to have married her father; and she blames her father's refusal to accept a transfer away from Ballybeg, "this bloody wet hole," for her mother's ill health and death.

Frank Butler's eldest daughter, Helen, who married his batman, Gerald Kelly, is divorced and living in London. Her relationship with her father is special; it is she who plays at writing his after-dinner speech and who teases him. Frank promises to send her a copy of his report on his heroic rescue mission, she is supportive of his marriage with the young Anna, and Frank confides in this daughter: he wonders aloud if his rigid military discipline has carried over too much into his household and family; he analyzes his family and sees Anna's difference from them: "So unlike us: measured, watching, circling one another, peeping out, shying back." After her father's suicide, Helen seems to accept responsibility for Tina, but she is too much affected by the tragedy of her own life. She has told her brother, Ben, that she still loves her ex-husband: "I thought I'd squeezed every drop of him out of me. But now I know I haven't forgotten a second of him." And in London, after the denouement, she and Tina "seldom meet," and Sir, the narrator cum stage director, tells us "Helen has had to give up her office job because of an acute nervous breakdown."

Ben, the only son in the family, is hesitant and nervous; Miriam calls him a "mother's boy." The day his mother died, Ben called his father a murderer, and he tells his sister Helen he has "preserved" that hostility for the past six years "out of a sense of loyalty:"

> —which you do in a state of confusion, out of some vague residual passion that no longer fires you; hitting out, smashing back, not at what's there but at what you remember; and which you regret instantly—oh, yes, yes, yes, never underestimate the regret. But then it's too late, too late—

Sir informs us that Ben's father wanted him to go into the army, but his mother wanted him to be a doctor. He was in his first year as a medical student when his mother died, and he never went back to college; he lives in a caravan on the strand, and he has spent the time his father was being heroic in the Mid East having an affair with his father's new young wife. He says: "I don't give a damn about anyone or anything," but in fact that is not true. Ben treasures the memory of his father stroking his face on the childhood trip home when the boy got drunk and sick from sampling the wrong thermos. In impassioned speeches, he reveals to Sir, after his father's suicide, that his behavior has not been based on love for his mother and hatred for his father but just the opposite:

> And what I was going to say to him was that ever since I was a child I always loved him and always hated her—he was always my hero. And even though it wouldn't have been the truth, it wouldn't have been a lie either: no, no; no lie.

The four children of the Butler family of *Living Quarters* are each crippled psychologically: Tina is kept a child until she is forced into instant adulthood by Frank's suicide; Miriam is bigoted and narrow; Helen suffers a nervous breakdown; Ben, twice jailed after his father's death for being drunk and disorderly, is on his way to alcoholism. In *The Aristocrats,* the crippling is even more clearly seen. Here there are five children, Judith, Anna, Alice, Claire—the youngest daughter—and the only son, Casimir.

Although he is in his thirties and his father has been brought low by several strokes, Casimir still trembles at his father's voice. He was nine years old when his father told him that he was different, and when he discovered that large areas of human life were not "accessible" to him, that he must conduct himself with "circumspection." He has matriculated in law but not completed his studies nor joined the family judicial tradition. Instead, he works part time in a food factory in Germany; he is married to the very German Helga with whom he raises a family of three sons and a dachshund. The sons hardly speak English; Casimir hardly speaks German, despite the fact that mostly he is the *kinder mädchen,* or nanny, for his sons. Casimir is the O'Donnell child most engaged in recounting made-up memories of past glories for the visiting American researcher Tom Hoffnung; he tells the stories linking the furniture and knickknacks with past great people—the George Moore candlestick, the Yeats cushion, and the Daniel O'Connell chaise longue. And in the madness of Act II, it is Casimir who finds the holes of the old croquet court and begins the imaginary game with Claire.

This youngest sister is emotionally unstable. A talented pianist who had a scholarship to study in Paris, Claire was thwarted in her ambition by Father who didn't want her to become "an itinerant musician," and who therefore trapped her in Ballybeg Hall with himself, his silent brother, Uncle George, and her unmarried sister. Claire is oppressed by the situation in Ballybeg Hall, confiding "I don't know how Judith stands it. She's lucky to be so . . . so strong-minded. Sometimes I think it's driving me mad." And she plans to escape that situation by marrying a greengrocer who drives a "great white lorry with an enormous plastic banana on top of the cab," a fifty-three-year-old widower with children and a live-in sister.

The two middle sisters have found equally unsatisfactory means of escape from their father's house. Anna is Sister John Henry, a nun in St. Joseph's mission in Kuala in Zambia. From her Christmas tape we learn that she is really in an arrested childhood; she pictures the family unchanged by time; she teaches her African children Irish songs; and her violin playing is "*the playing of a child.*" Alice has escaped into alcoholism. She has married Eamon, who is from the village; a man whose grandmother was a maid at Ballybeg Hall and regaled the boy with stories of its glamour, Eamon has fallen in love with each of the O'Donnell sisters in turn and married Alice, one assumes, simply because she was the one who said yes. Her fights with Eamon descend into physical violence; she enters the play with a bruised cheek from a blow from him after she threw a book. At home in London, she spends her days drinking in their basement flat.

The oldest O'Donnell child, Judith, is paradoxically the child most tied to the father in practical ways and most free of the father in the ways of mind and spirit. On Judith has fallen the care of Father, Uncle George, and Ballybeg Hall, the once proud seat of a Lord Chief Justice, which is now, in fact, a ruin with a leaky roof, dryrotted floors, and inadequate heat. On the other hand, Judith is a political activist who once ran away from the house of her politically indifferent father to take part in the Battle of the Bogside, and she is the mother of an illegitimate child whom she intends to retrieve from Coventry and raise after her father dies. She survives as an independent spirit who maintains sanity in a servile condition through dedication to an exhausting routine of chores: "Maybe it's an unnatural existence. I don't know. But it's my existence-here-now. And there is no end in sight."

There is no doubt that the two central characters of **Faith Healer,** Frank Hardy and his sometimes acknowledged wife, Grace, are crippled, both in their relationship with each other and in their perceptions of themselves. Frank Hardy not only pursues oblivion by drinking, he also deliberately courts death by going out into the courtyard in Ballybeg, although, according to Frank's own testimony, he was both warned by the barman that he'd be killed if he failed to cure the cripple and knew that himself as a fact. He is incapable of staying with his wife in Kinlochbervie when she bears their child and cannot bring himself to ask Teddy about the dead child. Grace has once run away from Frank and back home where, in the past, she was the lawyer-daughter of a judge-father. But she returns to the husband who often introduces her as his mistress rather than as his wife; and after Frank's gruesome death, Grace herself commits suicide.

What is less clear in this play, simply because Frank and Grace are middle-aged, is the influence of their fathers. Still we have that chilling interview between Grace Hardy and her father, Judge O'Dwyer. The old man is stricken and at first does not recognize his daughter, but when he does, he pronounces sentence against her: "sentencing me to nine months in jail but suspending the sentence . . . threatening that if I ever appeared before him again he would have no option but to send me to jail and impose the maximum penalty . . ." And Frank Hardy is unable even to acknowledge his father's death; he says he went home from Kinlochbervie to attend his mother's funeral—though his mother died long before and Kinlochbervie is the site of his child's death (Grace tells us that in fact Frank went home to his father's funeral from Wales). He recounts his father's telling about her death "as if he were giving evidence;" his childhood memories include his father "watching me through the bars of the dayroom windows as I left for school . . ." and kowtowing to inspectors from Dublin, and showing rotten teeth when he laughed. And those memories of his father are at the root of Frank's need to return to Ireland to regain his faith-healing gift and of his suicidal keeping of the appointment with the young men and their crippled friend in the courtyard of the inn in Ballybeg.

Manus and Owen, the two sons of Hugh Mor O'Donnell, the hedgeschoolmaster in *Translations,* are again evidently crippled by their father. Both have been brought up in the erudite and intoxicating atmosphere of this Irish scholar. Manus, the older, has been actually crippled by Hugh Mor's falling drunk over his crib when he was a baby. Manus cares for his father, baking his bread, making his tea, and taking his classes when his father is absent or drunk, but he receives no pay for this last chore and therefore he cannot propose to Maire until he is offered the school at Inis Meadhon. Owen, the younger, has become a collaborator with the English; not only is he engaged in renaming the Irish places, he even for a while accepts the English name Roland in place of his own Irish name. And after Yolland disappears and Manus must flee Baile Beag, Owen takes his brother's place to care for Hugh Mor.

It is clear that in each of these plays we are observing men and women whose lives have been damaged because of or through their relationships with their fathers. And yet, paradoxically, we must also acknowledge that in each of these plays the relationships of the fathers and their children share intensity and love. And it is in the real or imagined characters of the fathers that we discover the motive for the intensity of the love of tne children, and the reason for the failure of the relationships.

S. B. O'Donnell, of *Philadelphia,* is a monumentally silent man, who loved the wild, barefoot girl from over the mountains in Bailtefree, when "She was nineteen and he was forty . . ." He does not remember what Gar does, the rainy afternoon fishing in the blue boat when he wrapped his coat around his son and sang "All Round My Hat I'll Wear A Green Coloured Ribbono," but he remembers Gar in a sailor suit even Madge has forgotten, and he remembers walking his son to school:

> . . . you tried to coax him to go to school, and not a move you could get out of him, and him as manly looking, and this wee sailor suit as smart on him, and—and—and at the heel of the hunt I had to go with him myself, the two of us, hand in hand, as happy as larks—we were that happy, Madge—and him dancing and chatting beside me—mind?—you couldn't get a word in edge-ways with all the chatting he used to go through . . . Maybe, Madge, maybe it's because I could have been his grandfather, eh?

Frank Butler of *Living Quarters* fears that perhaps he has brought too much military discipline into the house. Two of

his children, Alice and Ben, seem to blame him for their mother's death, because he wouldn't accept a transfer to another area, but Ben's betrayal of his father, through the affair with Anna, brings from Frank a plaintive protest that his life with his first wife has not been a happy one and that he has sought long delayed happiness in this late marriage. He says:

> But an injustice *has* been done to me, Sir, and a protest must be made. I don't claim that I have been blameless. Maybe my faults have been greater than most. But it does seem—well, spiteful that when a point is reached in my life, and late in my life, when certain modest ambitions are about to be realized, when certain happinesses that I never experienced are suddenly about to be attainable, it does seem spiteful that these fulfilments should be snatched away from me—and in a particularly wounding manner. Yes, I think that is unfair. Yes, that is unjust.

It is a mild protest, for his first wife has been shrewish and demanding as well as ill and unhappy with what she considers too low a station in life.

There is less room for forgiving Father Judge O'Donnell in *The Aristocrats,* or for understanding him, except that like S. B. he, too, has married a younger woman with a free nature, Friel thus suggesting a romanticism and a vulnerability, a possibility of dreams, in the man that once was. Mother was an actress, traveling with the Charles Doran Company:

> Spotted by the judge in the lounge of the Railway Hotel and within five days decently wed and ensconced in the Hall here. . . . And a raving beauty by all accounts.

And Willie remembers the judge dealing leniently when Willie was caught driving a car without license tags, insurance, or brakes:

> Let me off with a caution! He must have believed me. No, he didn't. Knew damn well I was a liar. He just pretended he believed me.

Still the ledger against Father Judge O'Donnell is long: his wife committed suicide; he informed his only son, then aged nine, that it was lucky he hadn't been born in the village where he'd have become the village idiot, but "Fortunately" in Ballybeg Hall where "we can absorb you;" he kept his daughter Claire from pursuing her music; Alice recalls that until this last visit when she saw him wasted with the strokes and impotent, she had never touched his face, ". . . is that possible never to have touched my father's face?" and he torments Judith, the daughter who tends to his needs, by seniley informing her that "Judith betrayed us," but ". . . Anna's praying for her."

Such simultaneous rigidity and impotence in the midst of an intense relationship is germane to *Faith Healer* as well. Grace's father, Judge O'Dwyer, calls Frank Hardy a mountebank who has implicated his child in a "career of chicanery;" he is symbolically represented by ". . . the long straight avenue" of his estate, "flanked with tall straight poplars, across the lawn, beyond the formal Japanese garden . . ." Frank's father, actually a "storeman in a factory in Limerick," is remembered as a policeman, but one without authority, whose son can slip his hands in and out of the locked bracelets of the handcuffs, who is servile to the inspectors from Dublin, and who exposes a mouthful of rotten teeth when he laughs—clearly a symbol of law which has no bite. And yet, impotent as this pair of fathers is, they draw their children back actually and in imagination to Ireland and they are intensely involved in their children's understanding of themselves.

In *Translations,* Hugh Mor O'Donnell, an alcoholic mocked by his students and crippling to his sons, is nevertheless vouchsafed by Friel the late-dawning comprehension that what he has prided himself on—the classical languages and literatures of Greece, Rome, and Ireland—is not sufficient to defeat the barbaric English who are conquering his land. When he sees his contemporary, the Infant Prodigy, Jimmy Jack, sliding out of reality into a realm where he believes he is going to marry the Greek goddess Athene and have family suppers with his father-in-law, Zeus, Hugh Mor capitulates to Maire's request to teach her English. He tells his remaining son, Owen, that they must learn the new names the English have imposed on their ancient land. And yet, though Friel gives Hugh Mor understanding and knowledge, he does not grant him the ability to do anything about the tragedies taking place around him: Manus is fleeing up the coast for the murder of Yolland, the Irish language and place names are being supplanted by English, Maire and others like her are determined to emigrate to a better life, and the English soldiery are plundering the town of Baile Beag.

And Hugh Mor's impotency, clear in the face of the conquering English, is echoed in each of the other plays. In every case, we are witness to the impotence of the father in passing along whatever heritage he represents to his offspring.

In *Living Quarters* and *The Aristocrats,* the families fall away after their fathers' deaths. "Things fall apart; the center cannot hold; / Mere anarchy is loosed upon the world . . ." Most of the children, we understand, are doomed to unhappiness and despair. Frank Butler's four, Tina, Miriam, Helen, and Ben, become respectively a waitress in an all-night cafe, a snobbish woman who thinks she is superior to her neighbors, a sufferer from a nervous breakdown and unable to work, and a man twice jailed for being drunk and disorderly. Father Judge O'Donnell's five are no more fortunate. Anna will remain a child immured in St. Joseph's mission in Africa; Claire will marry her greengrocer and care for his children while his sister runs the household; Alice will fight her alcoholism in the basement flat in London with silent Uncle George as her companion; Casimir will continue as nanny for his children, impressively not even passing his own language on to his sons; and Judith, the only one we can hope might find some happiness, will raise her illegitimate child alone because Willie, who loves her, will not accept the child.

In *Philadelphia, Faith Healer,* and *Translations,* our only hope is that the offspring will find their ways into new worlds, because the worlds of their fathers are either lost or doomed. Gar leaves the sterility of his father's world for Philadelphia. Owen is told by his father that he must make the transition into the Ireland being created by the English language and soldiery. And Frank Hardy's escape, if it can be called that, is into the mysticism of his profession; but as his art is arcane and he has no control over it, he must ultimately return defeated to Ireland and to his ritualized death for his failure to cure the incurable.

Policeman, city councillor, judge, commandant—no real or imagined authority can achieve the continuity of the culture, as Friel perceives it. Insofar as the fathers of these plays are loved—and truly they are all loved by their children—they affect their children's lives. But insofar as they are figures of authority, they do not affect their children's lives.

In *The Aristocrats,* Eamon, who has married into the family, says: "And this was always a house of reticence, of things unspoken, wasn't it?" He might well be speaking for all the houses in all the plays. Friel emphasizes that these fathers are good men and that there is something warm and loving about most of them. After all, both *The Aristocrats'* Judge O'Donnell and S. B. O'Donnell in *Philadelphia* have wooed and won young, vibrant wives, the judge an actress from Charles Doran's troop, and S. B. the girl from beyond the mountains. And not only has *Living Quarters'* Frank Butler also won and married a beautiful young woman, he has romantically told the wounded men he carried to safety in the Mid East all about her:

> Each time I crawled back to base with a man on my back—each trip took about half an hour—I told him about you—everything about you—your hair, your neck, your shoulders, the way you laugh—everything. Luckily most of them were too ill to listen. Not that that made any difference—I'd have told them anyway.

The fathers may have been warm, may have been loving, may even have lived a romantic hour or two in their lives, but, sadly, that humanness is not communicated to their children. Frank Hardy, in *Faith Healer,* has no loving memories of his father, nor has Frank's wife Grace, though somehow both those fathers are part of the lure of Ireland for their children. In *Translations,* Hugh Mor's wisdom is couched in the dead languages of Latin, Greek, and Irish. To his sons he and his world are a burden, if not as mad as the world of Jimmy Jack, at least comically alcoholic and pathetically impotent in the face of English modernism. Hugh Mor might well say with Manus that he has only "The wrong gesture in the wrong language.

Clearly Friel is almost obsessively investigating a familial catastrophe, and in his reiteration of it in play after play, he is exposing the failure of the Irish culture to communicate its heritage to its offspring. It is the relationship with the fathers that is presented time after time, the relationship with the parent traditionally associated with societal authority. And that authority is reinforced by giving the fathers the various roles of judge, councillor, policeman, commandant, and teacher. But juxtaposed against those titles and postures of authority is not only the impotence of these fathers, an impotence created by silence, cuckolding, illness and age, servility, or—in the case of Hugh Mor—the displacement of the culture, but also the startling repetition of the crippling effect they have on their children. Instead of leading their children toward productive, useful lives, the fathers leave only exile, alcoholism, nervous breakdowns, sterile marriages, and suicide.

Friel probes the Irish culture, examining the past (*Translations*) as well as the present in both the upper class (*Living Quarters* and *The Aristocrats*) and middle class (*Philadelphia* and *Faith Healer*). The problems within Irish society are severally examined. In *Translations,* Friel concentrates on the historical and cultural impact of the imposition of the English language. In *Philadelphia,* the frustrations of young Gar's life expose the limitations of a puritanical and closed society. *Faith Healer* balances the tatters of faith against the formulas of law. And in *Living Quarters* and *The Aristocrats* we search the ability of the younger generation to carry on, not an upper class role, but any sort of valuable social role at all. In each and every situation, Friel's conclusion is adamant: there is no help from one generation to the next.

Brian Friel is not the only Irish writer to be consumed with a need to define the father image for himself and his audience. James Joyce was similarly drawn to the theme, as were Frank O'Connor, Sean O'Faolain, and Sean O'Casey. In a national literature rife with powerful and beautiful images of good, strong women characters like Kathleen ni Houlihan and the Shan Van Vocht, like Synge's Maurya and O'Casey's Juno, it is significant to find Leopold Bloom and Yeats's Cuchulain, O'Faolain's Phil Crone and O'Casey's Paycock. Like his brother writers, Friel is confident in the creation of strong, loving females, Madge of *Philadelphia,* Crystal of *Crystal and the Fox,* Judith of *The Aristocrats,* and Maire of *Translations,* but when he searches for comparable male strength, he finds only delusion, frustration, silence, tyranny, and confusion.

For all a father means to any of us, he must also be our definition of our society, of its laws and its justice, of its artistry and its imagination. Perhaps the mother is too rapidly cast into symbolically spiritual—and therefore heroic—roles, and thus eludes the bitterness of reality. Or perhaps the Irish writers are consistent within their culture; for if a culture, like the Irish or the American black, is deprived of its sovereignty, then the societal role of the father as symbol and reality of authority must be eroded, and forever there can be no relationship between the father and his children except one of a frustration that ultimately exposes the impotence of the father and the crippling of the children.

Eric Binnie (essay date September 1988)

SOURCE: "Brecht and Friel: Some Irish Parallels," in *Modern Drama,* Vol. XXXI, No. 3, September 1988, pp. 365-70.

[*In the following essay, Binnie considers Friel's plays and his involvement with Field Day Theatre Company, drawing parallels to the work of Bertolt Brecht.*]

In the ancient and troubled frontier city of Derry, Brian Friel established the Field Day Theatre Company in 1980. He was joined in this bold endeavour by a number of other artists, including the actor Stephen Rea and the poet Seamus Heaney. All of the Board of Directors are Northerners. Their motives, in founding the new company, were to reappraise the political and cultural situation in Northern Ireland as it affects the whole of Ireland. They aim to examine and analyze the established opinions, slogans, myths and war-cries which have gone to the creation of the present troubles in Ireland. Like Brecht's Galileo in his final exchange with Andrea, perhaps like Brecht himself in his final years, on a not dissimilar frontier, Friel and his fellow directors clearly believe that there can, indeed, be a new age, despite all the evidence to the contrary.

The name Field Day has several implications—a day spent away from normal activities, a day spent outdoors, a sports day, a festival, a brawl, and, for example, in such popular usage, as "the critics had a field day," it suggests the chance to assert oneself to the fullest and most triumphant or pleasurable extent. In terms of famous paintings, one thinks of

Breughel's rustic holidays, the topsy-turvy world of periodic and necessary excess by which means rampant vitality is contained—a safety valve on the darker, less manageable energies of the people. Brian Friel has chosen the title Field Day wisely, having in mind most of the implications just listed. It is a theatre company which flourishes defiantly in the face of a grim, relentless, daily existence; festive, certainly, but also portentous.

Just as Brecht chose to create his ensemble company right on the border between East and West, in order fully to exploit each side's fears and suspicions of the other in ways which were, ultimately, uniquely creative, so Friel founded his company in the strife-torn city of Derry, right on the edge of British Ireland, artificially cut off from its hinterland of Donegal, now in the Republic (Southern Ireland). During his East Berlin years Brecht used the paradoxical invulnerability provided by the East/West dichotomy to create a theatrical system which now rightly bears his name. Brechtian theatre, or dialectical theatre, became a mature form during these frontier years. As yet, Brian Friel's plays are too diverse in form to be compared to Brecht's later works, yet they may be comparable, in terms of their similar origins on border locations, which are, by their very nature, dialectical.

The aims of Field Day Theatre Company are to create a shared context which might make possible communication across Ireland's border; to give all Irishmen an artistic "fifth province" rising above and covering the whole island, an hypothetical province which would neither accept the North/South division, nor ignore the separate traditional strengths of those on either side. Thus Field Day is located in the North (British Ireland) and works in both North and South, yet has strong reservations about both. The intention is to create an awareness, a sense of the whole country, North and South together, and to examine predominant attitudes to the island as a whole. Friel's artistic development since the formation of Field Day has moved steadily towards a closer integration of historical considerations and contemporary themes, achieved, for example, by examining the role of language as a reflection of national character. He expresses this concern for language in the statement, "We [Irish playwrights] are talking to ourselves as we must, and if we are overheard in America or England, so much the better.

Friel sees contemporary Ireland as being in a state of uneasy confusion, in which it is the dramatist's overwhelming duty to clarify, elucidate, and establish agreed codes, for purposes of communication and discussion. In explicating Friel's play *Translations,* Seamus Heaney points to the speechless character, Sarah, as a type of Kathleen ni Houlihan (a symbolic figure for Ireland itself), whose difficult struggle to pronounce her own name "constitutes a powerful therapy, a set of imaginative exercises that give her

[Ireland] a chance to know and say herself properly to herself again."

> **Friel sees contemporary Ireland as being in a state of uneasy confusion, in which it is the dramatist's overwhelming duty to clarify, elucidate, and establish agreed codes, for purposes of communication and discussion.**
>
> —*Eric Binnie*

The creation of Field Day has forced Friel into a more prominent public role, yet he shuns easy political labels or pat solutions. He sees his role as that of one who creates self-awareness through the critical examination of Irish beliefs, as these are expressed in the contours of everyday speech. For this reason his translation of Chekhov's *The Three Sisters* avoids the many fine English versions and attempts to make the play accessible to his audience by using identifiably Irish forms of English speech. Reaching his audience through adaptation to Irish speech should not be confused with any belated twitterings over a new Celtic Twilight. In his most recent play, **The Communication Cord,** Friel makes farcical use of the sentimentalism of artificial traditional. The stage directions read:

> *Every detail of the kitchen and its furnishings is accurate of its time (from 1900 to 1930) But one quickly senses something false about the place. It is too pat, too 'authentic'. It is in fact a restored house, a reproduction, an artefact of today making obeisance to a home of yesterday.*

His satire makes it clear that there is no going back, that uncritical restoration of the Irish past is no solution to the contemporary malaise. This latest play acts as a humorous corrective to any superficial impression wrongly created by the elegiac mood of the earlier play **Translations.**

To what extent can we call Friel a political writer? He is not committed to any particular party or faction. Yet his later plays, especially, are dependent upon the dialectical method to the extent that the spectator may feel that he is watching a particularly fine debate. Undoubtedly Friel himself would not describe himself as a Brechtian, yet the effect he and his company are having on audiences in contemporary Ireland is not far removed from the political excitement achieved by Brecht during his consciously ambivalent Berliner Ensemble years.

Perhaps a sense of the directors' intentions can be gathered from the series of pamphlets published by Field Day as a separate activity from that of play production. The aim of the pamphleteers is to re-examine those aspects of Irish life which have come to be accepted uncritically. Twelve pamphlets have so far been issued by Field Day, and the public response has been exciting. Naturally, many reviews have been polemical, but the over-all result has been to raise the level of critical debate about issues which have for far too long been shrouded in blind, partisan myth. Looking over the titles, or sub-titles, of these pamphlets one is reminded of nothing so much as of the theatre songs or scene captions from such Brecht plays as *The Measures Taken* or *The Mother.* Typical pamphlet headings are "An Open Letter," "Civilians and Barbarians," "Myth and Motherland," "Dynasties of Coercion," and "The Apparatus of Repression." It is characteristic of Field Day, that when the first half-dozen pamphlets were collected and published in one volume, this included, by invitation, an afterword by Denis Donoghue, whose comments were far from laudatory. This is a telling detail about the publishing aspect of the company. Clearly, as with the plays, the purpose of the pamphlets is to encourage discussion and to question mindless obedience to any one cause. Despite this intention, there has been a tendency to berate Field Day simply for raising such issues. One is reminded that it has taken a critic of the stature of John Willett something like thirty years to shake up popular notions about Brecht's hard-line adherence to one unique system of belief, by repeatedly drawing attention to Brecht's inbred scepticism and detachment. Let us hope that the detachment of the Field Day Company and its directors will be accepted more readily.

The theatrical function of Field Day is organised on lines more akin to the early productions of Planchon in Lyon, or even to the pre-war productions of Brecht, than to those of the Berliner Ensemble. Using tiny budgets, mostly raised from the Arts Councils of both Northern Ireland and the Republic, the company manages to commission one new play each year, to workshop this production extensively and to tour the play to every variety of make-shift venue, before audiences at every level of theatrical experience, holding diverse political or religious persuasions, and living on both sides of the border.

Friel is not the only playwright whose works are produced by Field Day. The directors have encouraged younger writers both in the creating of new works, such as Thomas Kilroy's *Double Cross,* and in the writing of Irish adaptations of foreign classics, such as Derek Mahon's *High Time*—a version of Moliere's *The School for Husbands.* The plays are first presented in the town hall, or Guildhall, of Derry, on an improvised stage which provides little more than Frank Fay's "two planks and a passion." After their initial run they go on tour. The latest production, Kilroy's *Double Cross,* transferred to the Royal Court Theatre, London, for a very successful run. The company has few constant elements: there is no permanent roster of actors or crew,

rather members are hired to meet the demands of each play. Nevertheless, Stephen Rea, one of the founders of Field Day, has either directed or acted in all of the plays produced so far, and a number of other actors re-appear fairly frequently. Clearly this does not constitute an ensemble in any sense that Brecht would have used the term, but, given the financial constraints of producing theatre in such seemingly unfavourable conditions, there is still a remarkable element of continuity. Friel and Rea are closely involved in all planning and selection. The plays produced so far demonstrate considerable variety of form, yet there appears to be a consistency of purpose—to challenge accepted notions, to counteract lethargy or despair, to make Irish men and women more aware of their own responsibilities and potentiality, to create open-ended speculation, and to do so with wit and style.

There can be few dramatists writing during the last thirty years who have not felt the impact of Brecht's theatrical innovations. Brian Friel is no exception. One need only think of the use of the double (or alter-ego) in *Philadelphia Here I Come,* the separate but interlocking monologues of *Faith Healer,* or the chorus of speaking corpses which ends *The Freedom of the City,* to recall Friel's attention to experimental form. While his more recent plays, *Translations* and *The Communication Cord,* depend upon more conventionally realistic settings, experimentation continues in the plays of younger writers within the group. With considerable success, Thomas Kilroy's *Double Cross* explores the complexity of the Irish/English relationship. One actor plays both the sycophantic Brendan Bracken (Churchill's Minister of Information) and the quisling, William Joyce (Lord Haw-Haw). The juxtaposition of these two Irish characters within the performance of a single actor, manifesting different aspects of the love-hate relationship between the Irish and the English, is a dramaturgical conceit worthy of Brecht, and in the tradition of Brecht's doubling of Shen Te and Shui Ta in the *Good Person of Setzuan.*

This fine new play by one of the younger Field Day writers has a unique structure and effectiveness. Thematically, it raises the same questions as Friel's best known play, *Translations.* Both plays present the effects of Irish emotionalism in face of the rationality of the more powerful and ponderous neighbour, England. While Kilroy's play examines this characteristic in terms of personality, Friel's treatment used historical incident as his starting point. The early nineteenth-century process of standardization which the central British government imposes upon the local inhabitants, in particular the systematic Anglicizing of Irish place-names, becomes a telling metaphor for the relationship of one country to the other. Friel presents the resultant loss of Irish self-confidence in socio-linguistic terms—briefly, language creates history; a people who do not keep faith with the historical names of their location lose their identity; a people without a sense of their own history become vulnerable for take-over. Vagueness about the past leads from a loss of self-confidence either to hopelessness or to violent crisis. Thus, without spelling it out, the relationship between the historic context and present Irish problems is relayed to the contemporary audience. Yet the structure of the play is complex, its subtle effects unfolding with reflection rather than immediately. Friel was concerned that the play should not be received as a simple lament for what is past, that it should make its political point quietly but clearly. His fears were unwarranted. The play became a new national classic almost immediately. Though the play is not Brechtian in structure or style, its theme reminds one of Brecht's warning "one must not build on the good old things, but on the bad new ones." Its historical setting does not detract from its relevance to the contemporary audience. Its immense popularity may owe something to its elegiac charm, but its gentle satire on Irish passivity has not been lost. If we try to evaluate the play in Brechtian terms, it must be through the Brecht of quiet subversion rather than the Brecht of chilling rationality and didacticism.

Each playwright, Brecht and Friel, has mastered the implication of his own frontier location, and has used it in his own way. Brecht's ambitions were greater—his concern was with global, rather than with local issues; though the larger questions can be seen, at least in part, as having arisen out of his specific situation. Each playwright has shown his genius in the individuality of his plays, but, also, in the important effect he has had on younger dramatists. Brecht's legacy is all about us; Friel's is best described by Thomas Kilroy, in the preface to his recently published text of *Double Cross:*

> This play could not have been written without Field Day. Some years ago Field Day asked me to write one of their *Pamphlets* and I completely failed to do so. It was round about that time that I decided to try and write a play for the company instead, addressing the kind of topics which Field Day has restored to serious debate in Ireland. For me, Field Day is the most important movement of its kind in Ireland since the beginning of this century. It has provided a platform for the life of the mind, of whatever persuasion, at a time when mindlessness threatens to engulf us all.

Richard Tillinghast (essay date October 1991)

SOURCE: "Brian Friel: Transcending the Irish National Pastime," in *The New Criterion,* Vol. 10, pp. 35-41.

[*In the following essay, Tillinghast discusses the function of* language in Friel's plays and its pertinence to issues of Irish society.]

> HUGH: Indeed, Lieutenant. A rich language. A rich literature. You'll find, sir, that certain cultures expend on their vocabularies and syntax acquisitive energies and ostentations entirely lacking in their material lives. I suppose you could call us a spiritual people.
>
> OWEN: (*Not unkindly; more out of embarrassment before the Lieutenant*) Will you stop that nonsense, Father?
>
> HUGH: Nonsense? What nonsense? . . . Yes, it is a rich language, Lieutenant, full of the mythologies of fantasy and hope and self-deception—a syntax opulent with tomorrows. It is our response to mud cabins and a diet of potatoes; our only method of replying to . . . inevitabilities. (*To* OWEN) Can you give me the loan of half-a-crown?

"How these people blather on!", the London *Sunday Times*'s drama critic, John Peter, wrote recently about a new production of Sean O'Casey's *Plough and the Stars.* Irish playwrights have, over the years, confirmed the nation's reputation for talk by mounting plays which live or die by their characters' ability to keep an audience enthralled by language. From *The School for Scandal* by Sheridan (one forgets he was Irish) to *The Importance of Being Earnest* by Wilde, to Beckett's *Waiting for Godot,* we remember the great Irish plays for their dialogue rather than for the inventiveness of their dramatic structure. One tends to think of Beckett as an international phenomenon rather than as an Irishman; but how quintessentially Irish he was to put his characters in trashcans or bury them up to their necks in sand so that, their movements severely restricted, they were free to spellbind with their talk! After eight hundred years of invasion, military occupation, economic plundering, and systematic attempts to eradicate their native religion and culture, what has been left to the Irish other than talk? Talk is the national pastime.

Among the myriad ironies of Irish history is that even after the colonizing British had virtually stamped out the Gaelic language, the Irish went to work on English itself and transformed it into the colorful hybrid that is spoken on the island today. This variety of English, though it largely uses standard vocabulary, has taken on the rhythms, syntax, intonations, and often even the grammar of Irish, which, though almost extinct, has managed while dying to inseminate another linguistic organism with its inventiveness, its evasions and qualifications, its elaborate and ambiguous courtesies.

Brian Friel, the foremost living Irish playwright, author of over twenty plays and a prolific short-story writer, has consistently created characters who have defined themselves through talk. While his focus on language places him firmly within Irish theatrical tradition, his insistence that language is a tool of oppression both from above and from within has put the politics of language at the center of his concerns. This emphasis is unprecedented on the Irish stage. Seamus Deane, in his book *Celtic Revivals* (1985), has made the point that Friel, who was born in Northern Ireland in 1929 and grew up in Derry, a Northern city plagued by chronic unemployment and sectarian tensions between the Protestant descendants of British colonists and the native Catholic Irish, grew up in a world where failure and frustration were a constant, and politics was a given. Friel, unlike writers from more comfortable backgrounds who "discover" politics and see it as a solution, regards politics as part of the problem, as basic as bad weather.

Despite modernization and the growth of a new spirit of optimism in Ireland following the economic boom of the Sixties and the country's entry into the European Community, the stereotype—amounting almost to a cultural icon—of the brilliant failure, the great talker who accomplishes nothing, still persists. No other Irish writer has been as forthright as Friel in identifying talk, not as a way to charm, but as a temperamental response to, and compensation for, failure—itself seen as resulting from centuries of defeat and suppression.

While Friel and the other writers who founded the Field Day Theatre Company in 1980, partially as a way of addressing the political crisis in the north, have made a point of writing especially for an Irish audience, his plays make clear to the non-Irish playgoer that oceans of sentimentality and prejudice keep us from seeing the Irish in their true complexity. The sentimentality is likely to be initiated by Irish-Americans who from a position of relative prosperity are free to romanticize The Ould Sod. The prejudice is more likely to come from the British who still, after all these hundreds of years, seem unable to admit how they crushed the Irish nation.

Beyond his political analysis of the national passion for talk, to which I shall return, Friel stands out among Irish playwrights by his deft touch with theatrical devices and dramatic structure. At a performance of *Philadelphia, Here I Come!* (1964), the audience may not at first realize—unless they have read the play, or unless they are serious types who arrive at the theater early and study the program before the house lights go down—that the two young men they see talking onstage are, as Friel's notes put it, "two views of the same man." What the audience apprehends are two characters unnervingly familiar with each other's thoughts and lives—or rather with that single life they constitute as private and public aspects of the same character. Considerable time passes before we notice that Gar (Private) is invisible to the other characters and that, in the words of the stage notes, Gar (Public) "never sees him and *never looks at him.* One cannot look at one's *alter ego.*"

Friel's employment of this and similar devices is both bold and simple. The confidence of his dramatic imagination is apparent in *Dancing at Lughnasa*—pronounced "*Loo*-nu-suh"—(1990) a triumph in its Abbey Theatre premiere and winner of the Olivier Theatre Award for Best Play of 1990 in London. [. . .] As the play opens, Michael stands downstage, reminiscing to the audience about his childhood, to one side of the set's rendering of an Irish country kitchen, where the family spends much of its time. The kitchen in the Abbey production was realistic but set at an angle to the audience, with its front and side walls removed so that the space outside the house was not blocked from the vision of either actors or audience. Gerard McSorley, who played Michael at the Abbey, wore a good but rumpled suit and the dark shirt and solid-colored tie of someone in the arts, journalism, advertising, etc. It was clear both from his dress and his accent that he had come some distance from his upbringing in Donegal, the remotest and "wildest" Irish country. As the action of the play begins, the child Michael is meant to be sitting on the ground outside the cottage, making kites, and his mother and aunts address him and respond to him, though the child is invisible and his remarks are assumed rather than heard.

More radical and more difficult, since the illusion must be carried off not visually but by dialogue alone, is the pretense that most of the characters in *Translations* (1981)—though of course the play is in English—speak Irish, which is their only language other than a smattering of Greek and Latin they learn from their "hedge" schoolmaster. Dialogue like the following is a bit disorienting:

> MAIRE: *Sum fatigatissima.*
>
> JIMMY: *Bene! Optime!*
>
> MAIRE: That's the height of my Latin. Fit me better if I had even that much English.
>
> JIMMY: English? I thought you had some English?
>
> MAIRE: Three words . . .

In *Living Quarters* (1978), using the non-naturalistic character Sir as an omniscient guide who stage-manages the Butler family through their shared catastrophe, Friel deconstructs plot as a device for revealing the truth. Such ploys, sometimes outlandish but very clear-cut once the audience has accepted the illusion, give Friel's plays a satisfying crispness on the stage, a reassuring sense that what we are witnessing is guided by a sure hand.

Faith Healer (1980) deserves mention here because it represents a crucial moment in Friel's development. In the Fifties his short stories appeared frequently in *The New Yorker,* and perhaps their popularity owed something to the American taste for the occasional glass of Irish sentimentality. In *Philadelphia,* the play that established Friel's reputation on the New York stage, Gar (Private)'s palaver smoothed over, in performance at least, dark truths about the desperate conspiracy in rural Ireland to strangle any attempt to rise above the stultifying influence of the Church, the schools, and a class structure that is all the more rigid for having such a short distance between its cellar and attic. But Friel later got himself branded as what in Ireland is called a Republican— i.e., an IRA supporter and exponent of violence—and he suffered at the box office as a result.

Faith Healer may be seen as a gesture of defiance by Friel as an artist. The play has no political surround. Nor has it a conventional dramatic structure. Instead it daringly structures itself around four monologues, delivered in turn by the play's three characters. Radical in construction, it is at the same time utterly traditional, utterly Irish one might say—because it depends completely on the Irish genius for captivating an audience, whether in a pub, in someone's kitchen, or in the theater, by telling a story. The easy approach to the leading role would be to play Frank Hardy, the faith healer of the title, as a charlatan. The problem is that Frank is not really a fake. He has the gift—on certain nights. I should think the actor would find the parallels to his own art a challenge, and more. James Mason played the role in its first production, at the Long-acre Theater in New York. I saw Donal McCann—whom moviegoers will remember as Gabriel in John Huston's film of Joyce's story "The Dead"—as Frank in the 1990 Abbey revival. What one could never forget about his performance was the stillness, the sense of nothingness almost, from which his rendering of the character sprang. As he stood motionless on the bare stage, risking the longest pauses I have ever heard and getting away with them, one glimpsed the abyss from which the human enterprise proceeds.

The sense that the play represented, for its author, not merely a comeback, but more than that—a definition of himself as an artist—is borne out in resemblances between the faith healer and the playwright or fictionalist. "It wasn't that he was simply a liar," his wife, Grace, says about Frank, "it was some compulsion he had to adjust, to refashion, to re-create everything around him. Even the people who came to him . . . yes, they were real enough, but not real as persons, real as fictions, his fictions, extensions of himself . . ."

The high-spirited banter of Gar (Private) in *Philadelphia* consists of asides audible only by stage convention: remarks Gar (Public) makes to himself. They delight the audience because they remind us of our own inner commentaries. For Gar O'Donnell himself, though, they serve a complex and ambivalent function. Interior dialogue is, first of all, a survival mechanism in this character who exists as his father's employee in the family grocery and dry-goods business in a small town in Ireland in the Fifties. On the other hand his rich inner life facilitates Gar's further isolation, because providing as it does an outlet for his humor, cynicism, idealism, ambition, and hostility, it prevents him from confronting openly his frustrations in the public arena.

While in performance the fine talker familiar from Irish life and literature has his way with the audience, who leave the theater under the spell of his charm, all that fine talk constitutes, Friel suggests, a kind of pathology—a character's means not only of surviving psychically through what Skinner in *Freedom of the City* (1974) calls "defensive flippancy" but of managing to keep any hard self-analysis from penetrating his defenses. In *Aristocrats* (1980) Casimir, a dotty fabulist, lives in a world of his own invention, wherein his ancestors rub elbows with the famous, as at the birthday party for Balzac in Vienna which he "remembers" his grandfather telling him about:

> Everybody was there: Liszt and George Sand and Turgenev and Mendelssohn and the young Wagner and Berlioz and Delacroix and Verdi—and of course Balzac. Everybody. It went on for days. God knows why Grandfather was there—probably gate-crashed.

A foil to this highly amusing blather is Tom Hoffnung, an American academic doing research on "recurring cultural, political and social modes in the upper strata of Roman Catholic society in rural Ireland since the act of Catholic Emancipation," as he puts it. To which Casimir, taken aback, replies, "Good heavens. Ha-ha." Tom, with the utmost tact, questions the veracity of Casimir's fables: "A few details, Casimir; perhaps you could help me with them?" Even when he catches Casimir out in all sorts of improbabilities and patent lies, he remains gentle and apologetic: "I make little mistakes like that all the time myself. My mother worked for the Bell Telephone Company and until I went to high school I thought she worked for a Mr. Bell who was my uncle for God's sake . . ." Casimir manages to fabulize even this, getting a huge laugh from the audience by saying a few minutes later, "I suspect he may be a very wealthy man: his uncle owns the Bell Telephone Company."

Friel characters often maintain fictions about themselves, using talk, of course, as a way of supporting these fictions. As in the classic English mystery novel of the Thirties, the action of these plays takes place within a closed community—usually adhering to the classical unities of time, place, and action. The friction of interaction between characters wears these fictions away, and the secret that lies behind the fiction is revealed. In *Translations* the action occurs in the classroom of an Irish "hedge" school of the 1830s; in *Freedom* in the Lord Mayor's parlor in the Guildhall, Derry; in *Faith Healer* on a stage that simulates the provincial hired halls where Frank Hardy failed or succeeded in working his healing magic. The three characters, Frank, Grace, and their cockney manager, Teddy, form a family of sorts.

An observer of Irish society might be tempted to identify the Church as the nation's most potent institution. But Tom, the family priest in *Living Quarters,* occupies (though not in his own view) a position only a step above Commandant Frank Butler's personal servant:

SIR: [*reading from a ledger in which he has written out the family's story*] "'Is Uncle Tom coming with us?' they'd say. And he did. Always. Everywhere. Himself and the batman—in attendance."

TOM: That's one way of—

SIR. "—and that pathetic dependence on the Butler family, together with his excessive drinking make him a cliché, a stereotype. He knows this himself—"

The Canon, played by Derry Power in the Second Age production of *Philadelphia* I saw in Dublin last winter, got a huge laugh at his first appearance onstage, his white hair and lobster-red face triggering an immediate shock of recognition, as Gar (Private) muttered "Bugger the Canon!" Like Uncle Tom in *Living Quarters,* this priest is a harmless old parasite whom no one takes seriously. Here he is arriving for his nightly game of draughts with S. B. O'Donnell:

CANON: She says I wait till the rosary's over and the kettle's on . . . hee-hee-hee.

S. B.: She's a sharp one, Madge.

CANON: "You wait," says she, "till the rosary's over and the kettle's on!"

The schoolmaster, another brick in the wall of the Irish village, gives Gar, as a going-away present, a book of his poems ("I had them printed privately last month. Some of them are a bit mawkish but you'll not notice any distinction") before touching him up for the loan of ten shillings on his way to the pub.

But the observer I invoked in the previous paragraph would be mistaken if he gave the Church pride of place among Irish institutions. The family, that prototype of the closed community, is the prime focus of Brian Friel's analytical dissection of Irish society. Why the family is an even mightier force in Ireland than elsewhere may be explained in part by the country's history. Though there were petty kings in Ireland as far back as its history can be traced, Ireland never had the centralized government of countries like England. Loyalty always meant loyalty to a clan. When Ireland was forced into the British Empire, the family provided one of the few available defenses against the redcoats and the landlord.

> **The family, that prototype of the closed community, is the prime focus of Brian Friel's analytical dissection of Irish society. Why the family is an even mightier force in Ireland than elsewhere may be explained in part by the country's history . . . Ireland never had the centralized government of countries like England.**
> **—*Richard Tillinghast***

I have mentioned how the three characters in *Faith Healer* form an impromptu family, and how Tom in *Living Quarters* clings pathetically to the Butler family. Likewise Madge, the housekeeper in *Philadelphia,* gives Gar the maternal love he never received from his mother, who died three days after giving birth to him. The play's central pathos, though, resides in Gar's and his father S. B.'s inability to connect. The moment that Gar remembers fondly from childhood involves a blue boat in which father and son once went fishing. When Gar finally brings himself to mention the boat, this is his father's response:

S. B.: (*Justly, reasonably*) There was a brown one belonging to the doctor, and before that there was a wee flat-bottom—but it was green—or was it white? I'll tell you, you wouldn't be thinking of a punt—it could have been blue—one that the curate had down at the pier last summer—

Once Gar has gone to bed on his last night at home before emigrating to America, his father tenderly relates to Madge some moments he recalls from Gar's childhood. But they can never say these things to each other. The bonds between parent and child are parodied in the play when Gar (Public) discusses with his friend Joe his decision to emigrate:

JOE: Lucky bloody man. I wish I was you.

PUBLIC: There's nothing stopping you, is there?

JOE: Only that the mammy planted sycamore trees last year, and she says I can't go till they're tall enough to shade the house.

PUBLIC: You're stuck for another couple of days, then.

To put broader political issues in a larger context, Friel's favorite ploy is to bring an "expert," like Tom Hoffnung in *Aristocrats,* onstage—or, in *Freedom,* Dr. Dodds, another American professor, who announces: "I'm a sociologist and my field of study is inherited poverty or the culture of poverty or more accurately the subculture of poverty." Dr. Dodd's ideas simplify the characters, but do not ultimately distort them. That the subculture of poverty provides the chronically poor with strategies for self-definition and survival will find little disagreement. But a balance of viewpoint is achieved by the presence and the dialogue of characters who actually come from "the subculture of poverty," and who are more likely to be talking about things like how their feet hurt, or whether the horses they bet on have won or lost. These characters—or some of them, at any rate—are not incapable of analyzing their own predicaments:

> SKINNER: If I'm sick, the entire wisdom of the health authority is at my service. And should I die, the welfare people would bury me in style. It's only when I'm alive and well that I'm a problem.

Friel's cultural explorations in his latest play, *Dancing at Lughnasa,* are both broader and more dramatic than anything he has attempted before. Early in the play the casual language of the characters establishes a framework or "civilized" Christian contempt for all that is "pagan," non-European, uncontrollable. The new wireless set, which Maggie, the joker of the family, at first wants to call "Lugh, after the old Celtic God of the Harvest" (this is the narrator Michael's voice), has thrown the household into disarray here in the summer of 1936. One of the sisters calls two of the others, who have hiked up their skirts and are dancing, "A right pair of pagans, the two of you." But the "voodoo" radio is not alone in disrupting this tightly controlled household. Living a short distance from the imaginary town of Ballybeg (where most of Friel's plays are set), the Mundys are "townies" who hold themselves above the country people—particularly the back-country folk who celebrate the druidic festival of Lughnasa. "Pagan" influences, though, seep irresistibly into the Mundys' lives.

Some of the play's funniest moments are provided by Michael's Uncle Jack, a priest who has been repatriated from Africa not, as we at first are told, because of poor health but because, during his years in mythical Ryanga, he has been converted to the wisdom of the "pagan" religion the natives follow. Jack often finds himself using the pronoun "we" when describing Ryangan customs: "That's what we do in Ryanga when we want to please the spirits—or to appease them: we kill a rooster or a young goat." Significantly, Jack has come to think in Swahili and is having a hard time

recovering his English: "When Europeans call, we speak English."

In answer to Maggie's having asked whether, if they went to Ryanga, Jack could find husbands for the four sisters, Jack replies: "I couldn't promise four men but I should be able to get one husband for all of you." Not a bad solution to the Mundy sisters' problems, since "the husband and his wives and his children make up a small commune where everybody helps everybody else and cares for them." The schoolteacher Kate's response brings the house down:

> KATE: It may be efficient and you may be in favor of it, Jack, but I don't think it's what Pope Pius XI considers to be the holy sacrament of matrimony. And it might be better for you if you paid just a bit more attention to our Holy Father and a bit less to the Great Goddess . . . Iggie.

A few moments later, Michael's errant father, Gerry, dancing with one of Michael's mother's sisters to the tune of "Anything Goes," hints that group marriage might suit him very well. Later we learn that he has another wife and family in Wales. So in this and other ways Jack may be correct in saying "In some respects [the Ryangans are] not unlike us."

Having identified the family as his characters' major frustration, Friel asks: as constricting, as repressive, as the family may be, where would we be without its support? Kate, head of the predominantly female family, puts it this way:

> You work hard at your job. You try to keep the home together. You perform your duties as best you can—because you believe in responsibilities and obligations and good order. And then suddenly, suddenly you realize that hair cracks are appearing everywhere; that control is slipping away; that the whole thing is so fragile it can't be held together much longer. It's all about to collapse, Maggie.

That provincial Irish life is hag-ridden by failure and small-mindedness, that the country still has a long mile to go before shaking off its post-colonial mentality, in no way diminishes the humor, good-heartedness, and courage of its people. Certainly it makes little sense to speak of Ireland as Ben, the Episcopalian from America, speaks of the United States: "It's just another place to live, Elise: Ireland—America—what's the difference?" On the one hand Ireland's best and brightest are constantly leaving, asking themselves, from Camden Town to South Boston and the Bronx to Sydney: "God, Boy, why do you have to leave? Why? Why?" Gar asks himself this question on the eve of his departure from Ballybeg, only to answer: "I don't know. I—I—I don't know." For the exiles in Friel's plays, according to Seamus Deane, "their ultimate perception is that fidelity to the native place is a lethal form of nostalgia." If emigration opens up a dream world of infinite possibility, home is where everything is known. Frank Hardy, returning to Ireland, sensing he will die there, concludes, "At long last I was renouncing chance."

And yet for all that, Friel sees in Ireland an authenticity of culture and personality, an integral society, unchanged in essence since the Middle Ages. In *Philadelphia,* Friel identifies Ireland—and he is only partly ironic here—with the *ancien régime,* having Gar O'Donnell recite as a recurrent motif Edmund Burke's paean to pre-Revolutionary France: "It is now sixteen or seventeen years since I saw the Queen of France, then the Dauphiness, at Versailles; and surely never lighted on this orb, which she hardly seemed to touch, a more delightful vision . . ."

A play is not a tissue of ideas, however, or even of words, but rather a spectacle, an experience. Leaving a Brian Friel play, looking for a taxi or hurrying to the pub before closing time, one is less likely to feel depressed by the puritanical repressiveness of small-town Ireland than heartened by an impression of the human spirit asserting itself in the face of impediments: Gar's mordant asides; the risky improvisations of Skinner, who, just before stepping outside into Guildhall Square in Derry, where he will be slaughtered by automatic weapons fire from British troops, signs himself in the visitors' book in the mayor's office: "Freeman of the city." And remembering *Lughnasa,* one smiles, thinking of the play's most celebrated (and, significantly, almost wordless) scene, where the Mundy sisters, inspired by music from their "voodoo" radio, break into spontaneous dance, a pure expression of defiance and transcendence.

Robert Tracy (review date Spring 1994)

SOURCE: "Work in Progress," in *Irish Literary Supplement,* Vol. 13, No. 1, Spring 1994, pp. 17-18.

[*In the following review, Tracy considers the Dionysian motifs in* Wonderful Tennessee *and in some of Friel's other work.*]

A Donegal pier fills the stage left to right, one of those long stone piers, walled on the seaward side, that are common all along the Irish coast. On this pier's two levels, Friel's six characters in search of a meaning pass the time, from late afternoon until 7:30 a.m., waiting to be ferried to the island they cannot see clearly: "Oileán Drafochta . . . Island of Otherness. Island of Mystery."

Stephen Dedalus defined a pier as a disappointed bridge.

Friel's play is about disappointment, non-fulfillment, both actual and symbolic. None of his characters reach the island. Each is a study in failure. Terry is a professional gambler who has lost his luck, and, near the play's end, literally loses his shirt. His wife Berna is a lawyer, now deeply depressed and usually confined to a nursing home. Frank is an unsuccessful writer, at work on a coffee-table book clearly destined for the remainder table. He is married to Berna's sister, Angela, a classics lecturer who dislikes her profession; she seems to be having a muted affair with Terry. George, failed classical musician, is dying of cancer. He can only whisper, but plays heartbreakingly cheerful songs: "I Want to be Happy," "Jolly Good Company." Trish, his wife, is Terry's sister. They are all therefore an extended family, supported, at least until now, by Terry.

We glean these biographical details gradually, and, as it were, incidentally. Tolstoy tells us that all happy families are alike, but each unhappy family is unhappy in its own way. These unhappy couples share a generic unhappiness that Friel wisely does not try to explain. He has eliminated most of the background information playwrights usually provide about each character's past. In *Living Quarters, Translations, Making History, Dancing at Lughnasa,* there is a kind of stage-manager/narrator who knows what happened, what is to happen. The characters in *Wonderful Tennessee* have to create and present themselves before our eyes, in their two acts/single night of existence, decking themselves with what scraps of background they have time for and consider absolutely essential.

This is partly dictated by the situation: they have all known each other for years, and can hardly exchange biographical information. But it is further dictated by the setting, between anywhere and a somewhere that may be nowhere. In the middle of life's journey they find themselves stranded. The bus has left, and they have missed the boat—or rather, the expected boatman, one Carlin, a thinly disguised Charon, fails to appear. Like Beckett's tramps they must pass the time, with songs, dances, telling stories.

Friel learned important lessons from Chekhov, but with *Dancing at Lughnasa,* and even more with *Wonderful Tennessee,* he is moving away from his mentor and reaching toward a new kind of play. *Dancing at Lughnasa* still retains some Chekhovian characteristics: five (not three) sisters trapped in a provincial backwater, an ineffective brother. Even the maenadic dancing of the Mundy sisters, at the play's most intensive moments, recalls the all-too-brief carnival night revels in *Three Sisters.* But Friel, as he distances himself from Field Day, seems also to be moving away from political drama, however implicit, and from his related—and Chekhovian—preoccupation with the use/misuse of language.

Much of *Wonderful Tennessee* depends on music and dance. George and his accordion replace Marconi, the intermittently working radio of *Dancing at Lughnasa.* George rarely speaks, but he constantly pours out music which interacts with the spoken dialogue and at times controls it: hymns, music hall songs, popular songs from the forties and fifties, even a bit from Beethoven's *Moonlight Sonata,* and of course the American minstrel show song which gives Friel his title:

> Down by the cane-brake, close by the mill
> There lived a blue-eyed girl by the name of Nancy Dill.
> I told her that I loved her, I loved her very long,
> I'm going to serenade her and this will be my song:
> (Chorus)
> Come, my love, come, my boat lies low,
> She lies high and dry on the O-hi-o.
> Come my love, come, and come along with me,
> And I'll take you back to Tennessee.

There is some slight revisionism at work here: in the original, Nancy is "a colored gal," and the goal may be the Tennessee River, not the State.

We are back near the origins of drama, which began in dances invoking Dionysus, himself a dancing god. The characters of *Wonderful Tennessee* perform an impromptu but frenzied Conga line, "heads rolling, arms flying—a hint of the maenadic." Angela tells a story about Dionysus, who later becomes Saint Dionysus. We hear of a youth torn to bits in a maenadic orgy which is bloodlessly reenacted. If this play has a prototype, mistily hidden and hinted at like the elusive Island of Mystery, it is Euripides's *Bacchae.*

In *Dancing at Lughnasa,* Uncle Jack, cashiered missionary priest converted to the religion of the African tribe he came to Christianize, directs us to the pagan elements in rural Irish Catholicism, and we learn of mysterious Lughnasa rites—orgies—celebrated in the back hills. That pagan underlay is more hauntingly presented in *Wonderful Tennessee,* merging sinisterly with Catholic ritual. The elusive island was once a monastic settlement, later a place of pilgrimage at Lughnasa. But in June 1932, seven young men and seven young women, just back from the Eucharistic Congress in Dublin, intoxicated by the splendors of the Congress, by perhaps too many references to the sacrifice of Christ's body and blood, and by *poitín,* tore one of their number, a young man, to pieces there.

The island is at once holy and dangerous, charged with the religious intensity of its ancient monks and the equal intensity of that 1932 sacrifice, at once pagan and Christian. No longer a place of pilgrimage, it has become unreachable, at least to the play's characters—the promised but perhaps unattainable Tennessee.

So far we are in a slightly more animated Beckett situation, where actors must perform to pass the time while they wait for an event that may never come. Something of Beckett's mistrust of language, of his yearning for a non-verbal drama, for silence, is already evident at the end of *Dancing at Lughnasa,* when Michael speaks of "Dancing as if language had surrendered to movement—as if this ritual, this wordless ceremony, was now the way to speak, to whisper private and sacred things, to be in touch with some otherness . . . Dancing as if language no longer existed because words were no longer necessary." In *Wonderful Tennessee* the island's mystery becomes, "Whatever it is we desire but can't express. What is beyond language. The inexpressible. The ineffable . . . Because there is no vocabulary for the experience. Because language stands baffled before all that . . . Or maybe [the old monks] did write it all down—without benefit of words! That's the only way it could be written . . . A book without words!"

Friel gives this speech to Frank, like himself a writer, a man of words. Friel does not yet have quite enough self-confidence to dispense—as Beckett dispenses—with symbols, to create the austere abstract drama he seems to crave, and to which both *Dancing at Lughnasa* and *Wonderful Tennessee* aspire. Here we are dazzled with symbols: blood sacrifice, a book about time, a voyage not taken, a cross, the invisible ferryman who controls access to that other place, the idea of pilgrimage. Berna talks about miracles and Angela gives a little lecture about the Eleusinian Mysteries. *Wonderful Tennessee* is, I suggest, a work in progress. By that I do not mean an incomplete work, though it is about an incomplete action. It represents a new direction in Friel's work. It anticipates, aspires toward some future play—perhaps his next, perhaps his next plus one—that will mark a new stage in Friel's development. We can only wait, and cheer him on.

A mystery cannot be put into words, as Angela reminds us in her Eleusinian lecture. But it can be acted—danced, performed, ritualized. Frank has his vision when he sees a dolphin dancing, "with a deliberate, controlled, exquisite abandon. Leaping, twisting, tumbling, gyrating in wild and intricate contortions . . . A performance so considered, so aware, that you knew it knew it was being witnessed, wanted to be witnessed. Thrilling; and wonderful; and at the same time . . . that manic, leering face . . . somehow very disturbing." It is at once the beauty and the terror that Dionysus embodied. The dolphin, Frank suggests, might be the spirit of the sacrificial victim, perhaps "searching for the other thirteen."

The play begins with the words, "Help! We're lost!" It ends

with ritual and song, in an act of affirmation. This time the ritual sacrifice is bloodless. The others surround Terry, force him to the ground, and tear off his shirt. They hang part of the shirt on the pier's cruciform life-preserver stand, which, with its half-decayed life-preserver, already resembles a Celtic cross. The traditional Irish pilgrimage to a sacred well or mountain involves leaving some token of oneself, a coin, a rag, at the sacred spot. Here each member of the group formally hangs some possession—a bracelet, a scarf, a hat—on the cross/life-preserver stand, which is at once a symbol of death and of life, salvation, resurrection. Each one in turn performs a little ceremony, placing a stone atop a cairn, circling it, adding a second stone, circling again, touching his or her "votive offering" on the cross, then finally leaving the stage. All the while, George is again playing "Down by the cane-brake" in his "'sacred' style." George, who is to die, makes no offering, performs no ritual. He will not be coming back, as the others vow to do. But Angela places her hat on cross "for both of us." They will return yearly to repeat the ritual, and George will be affirmed, attested, in a wordless celebration of life over death, affirmation over negation, a pilgrimage "To remember again—to be reminded . . . To be in touch again—to attest." They will come, "Not out of need—out of desire! Not in expectation—but to attest, to affirm, to acknowledge—to shout Yes, Yes, Yes!"

Helen Lojek (essay date Spring 1994)

SOURCE: "Brian Friel's Plays and George Steiner's Linguistics: Translating the Irish," in *Contemporary Literature,* Vol. 35, No. 1, Spring 1994, pp. 83-99.

[*In the following essay, Lojek establishes the concept of "translation" as a central metaphor for Friel's concerns as a playwright.*]

The tremendous success of Brian Friel's 1980 play *Translations*—and the vigorous discussion which it still elicits—is one sign of the deep resonances it struck in a country where, as Seamus Deane has noted, "The assertion of the existence of a cultural (and largely literary) tradition . . . depended to an extraordinary degree on a successful act of translation". That the play which many at the time saw as a "climax" to Friel's career served instead to usher in a vigorous new period in that career is one sign of the deep resonances it struck within Friel himself, who seems to have discovered in the concept of translation a metaphor for the central impulse of his life's work.

Now that more than a dozen years have passed and *The Communication Cord* (1982), *Making History* (1988), and *Dancing at Lughnasa* (1990) (as well as a number of dramatic "translations") have followed, the centrality of trans-

lation to understanding Friel's work is increasingly clear. In fact, the idea of translation, especially given Friel's understanding of it in the context of George Steiner's linguistic study *After Babel,* illuminates the entire body of his drama, casting light back on what came before 1980 and forward on what came after.

> **Friel . . . seems to have discovered in the concept of translation a metaphor for the central impulse of his life's work.**
> **—Helen Lojek**

Translation—a word whose full range of meaning includes *transformation, transmutation, interpretation, carrying over,* and even *removal from earth to heaven*—involves the desire to understand, to find meaning, to *make* meaning if that is necessary. And it is that desire which animates character after character in Friel's plays. Discovering meaning through translation often involves changing statements from one language to another. More often, it involves the process of interpretation which takes place within a single language. Most often, it involves an adaptation of use so that traditional (often outmoded) words and actions may gain new resonance. Underlying all of these kinds of translation is an unstated linkage of word and Word, so that the search for literal meaning often involves a search for spiritual meaning as well. In all of its senses, the term is central to Friel's work. Understanding that centrality begins most logically with *Translations,* the play which treats the issues most directly, but whose implications radiate outward to the other works.

By now surely every student of contemporary drama is aware of *Translations'* discussion of the connections between language and national culture. The nineteenth-century British ordinance team which anglicized the place names of Ireland was part of a deliberate effort to wipe out Irish culture (and therefore Irish cohesiveness and power) by wiping out the Irish language, and Friel's play demonstrates the connection between linguistic landscape and geographic landscape.

The absurdities and confusions which accompany the process of renaming local places in *Translations* are counterpointed by the naming ceremony of an off-stage christening and by confusion about whether the Irishman who helps the English is named Owen or Roland—or Rowen or Oland (a variation which approximates the name of his English colleague Yolland. Noting such absurdities of naming, Hugh (Friel's hedge schoolmaster whose authority is modified by his fondness for a drop) cautions against a simplified view of the consequences. It can happen, he observes, that "a civilization can be imprisoned in a linguistic contour which no longer matches the landscape of . . . fact. Like the process of translation itself, Hugh's warning about the inevitability of linguistic change and the dangers of linguistic rigidity resonates against the backdrop of the dead classical languages his students recite—and against the audience's awareness that the Gaelic Hugh speaks is now virtually as dead a language as Greek.

Hugh's remark is a direct quotation from George Steiner's 1975 study *After Babel: Aspects of Language and Translation,* which Friel has cited as an important text for the play's composition. For Steiner, as for Friel, "translation" involves more than movement from one language to another. The term also refers to interpretation within a single language, and ultimately to communication and the shaping of meaning in general. Even without noting the numerous times Friel puts Steiner's words in his characters' mouths, a reader of *After Babel* immediately senses connections between the authors.

Exchanges between Friel's lovers, for example, illustrate both Steiner's contention that simple repetition changes meaning and his discussion of the ways in which linguistic logic influences the logic of a culture's world view. Maire (understanding only Irish) and Yolland (understanding only English) are forced to communicate across the barriers of language. At one point, Maire says (in Irish): "The grass must be wet. My feet are soaking." And Yolland responds (in English): "Your feet must be wet. The grass is soaking. In a way, meaning is repeated in this exchange. But in addition to the altered meaning which derives simply from this—or any—repetition, the variation of word order reveals opposing deductive and inductive logics. Love, however, enables Maire and Yolland to communicate despite their inability to understand each other's words.

Or, to choose another example from *Translations* of what Steiner calls "metamorphic repetitions," at one point Maire (who understands nothing of what Yolland is saying) tells him, "Say anything at all. I love the sound of your speech." And moments later Yolland (who understands nothing of what Maire is saying) tells her, "say anything at all—I love the sound of your speech." The words are the same, but knowledge of the characters reveals the extent to which the meanings vary. Maire loves the sound of Yolland's voice, and the sound of the English which she is eager to learn in order to translate herself out of Ireland. Yolland loves the sound of Maire's voice, and the rhythms of her Irish language, which enchants him as much as the Irish landscape where he would like to be more at home. Nevertheless, this direct repetition suggests that the heart communicates without language and with a logic all its own, so that the lovers do indeed understand, despite the barrier of language. Here, as in the case of Sarah's learning to speak, it is clearly love which encourages communication and communion.

It is part of Steiner's thesis in *After Babel* that language exists not just to communicate, however, but also to conceal.

The thousands of tongues in the world resulted, Steiner suggests, not from some cosmic or divine accident or punishment, but from a deep human instinct for privacy and territory. Language serves not just to tell things, but to hide them from outsiders, to disguise them, even to change them. Such tactical linguistic concealments certainly occur in Friel's play. Hugh deliberately speaks Irish in order to flout English authority. And Owen deliberately mistranslates in order to obscure the military and tax purposes of the English. Both Steiner and Friel, however, recognize that the "saying of things which are not" need not be a social evil or even undesirable. In fact, Steiner argues, "planned counter-factuality" and the creation of alternative realities are "overwhelmingly positive and creative," allowing visions which motivate humans to continue in the face of despair and to work to improve reality. Steiner repeatedly cites Odysseus, the wily deceiver so admired by Athena for his creative fictions, and Friel's Jimmy also refers regularly to the Greek whose words transform reality and whose physical appearance is transformed by Athena—in both instances, with the goal of Odysseus's preservation from his enemies.

Friel's first major stage success, ***Philadelphia, Here I Come!*** (which opened in 1964 and thus predates *After Babel*), suggests similarly varied possibilities in the creation of alternative realities. On the one hand, Gar Private mockingly points out that once he moves to America his memory of Ireland will be "distilled of all its coarseness; and what's left is going to be precious, precious gold." Gar has good reason to suspect his (future) memory. He has heard Con and Lizzie remember different pasts, and he knows that he and his father—though they remember the same (or at least similar) fishing trips—somehow remember *different* trips. In these instances, memory's alternative reality seems somehow false and limiting. On the other hand, Gar's "planned counter-factuality" is also what enables him to move toward the future with hope. With Kate he plans a future with fourteen children. He will "'develop' the hardware lines" in his father's store, and she will "take charge of the 'drapery.'" Their seven girls will "all be gentle and frail and silly" like Kate, and their seven sons will be "thick bloody louts, sexy goats" like Gar. When Kate's marriage to another eliminates that alternative reality, Gar plans one in America: "I'll come home when I make my first million, driving a Cadillac and smoking cigars and taking movie-films." Neither planned counterfiction has much to do with reality, and the America scheme seems no more likely to succeed than did the Kate scheme. Nevertheless, such counterfictions are what make life bearable, and they help Gar move forward out of his present despair.

Counterfictions which are used not positively (to create hope) but negatively (to conceal), of course, frequently result from fear. People are afraid and seek a way of resisting translations which are too threatening. The ultimate protection of privacy, as Steiner has pointed out, is the lapsing into total silence. That is the course Sarah follows in *Translations.* The play opens with Manus teaching Sarah (whose speech defect is so serious that it has thus far rendered her dumb) to speak. Sarah, who is clearly in love with Manus, does learn to say her name, and then the name of her town. Later, however, it is Sarah's words which reveal to Manus a painful reality, and Sarah, her personal life in chaos and her town renamed by the English, lapses into the protection of total silence.

Sarah's choice of protective silence is reflected in choices made by other Friel characters: the extreme taciturnity of S. B. O'Donnell in *Philadelphia, Here I Come!*; the silence of *Aristocrats'* Uncle George, who speaks only at the very end; the stuttering, incomplete speech of Ben in *Living Quarters* and Eamon in *Aristocrats;* the deafness of Gran McGuire in *The Loves of Cass McGuire* and Papa in *Crystal and Fox,* which reduces other characters to effective silence. Characters in *Lovers, The Loves of Cass McGuire,* and *Faith Healer* deliver monologues which—however much they indicate an awareness of a listening theater audience—make no attempt to communicate with other individuals in their worlds. But if silence (in either its positive or its negative guises) is often protective or a bar to full communication, it is also often the reverse—an opportunity for fuller, deeper transfer of meaning. In *Translations* Maire and Yolland, who do not share a language, communicate beyond words. And in *Dancing at Lughnasa,* Michael's memory of his family's wordless dancing (reminiscent of the unity embodied by Yeats's dancer) provides one of Friel's most positive images of full communication and communion—expressed here, as so often in Friel, in the vocabulary of the sacred:

> Dancing with eyes half closed because to open them would break the spell. Dancing as if language had surrendered to movement—as if this ritual, this wordless ceremony, was now the way to speak, to whisper private and sacred things, to be in touch with some otherness. . . . Dancing as if language no longer existed because words were no longer necessary.

Richard Kearney discusses the silence of Friel's *The Communication Cord* in relation to Heidegger's "notion of a mystical 'tolling of silence' at the heart of language." Kearney notes Friel's quotation of Heidegger in the prefatory program notes for *Translations,* but as both F. C. McGrath and Richard Pine have pointed out, Steiner prefaces *After Babel* with this same Heidegger passage. [In a 1972 BBC self-interview Friel mocked the sententious tendancy of critics (and himself?) to link Heidegger to trends in contemporary drama.] Friel, who may not even be quoting Heidegger from the original, is probably more directly influenced by Steiner's powerful argument about the "true understanding" of silence. The Tower of Babel, Steiner postulates,

> did not mark the end of a blessed monism, of a universal-language situation. The bewildering prodigality of tongues had long existed, and had materially complicated the enterprise of men. In trying to build the tower, the nations stumbled on the great secret: that true understanding is possible only when there is silence. They built silently, and there lay the danger to God.

In Friel's *Dancing at Lughnasa,* dance is a repeated metaphor for the true understanding which is linked to silent communication. Dance is central to the ancient pagan Irish harvest festival at Lughnasa, to the Ugandan harvest festival Father Jack describes, to village courtship in general, and to the particular courtship of Michael's parents, Gerry and Chris. The word "ceremony" is applied to all of these dances, and their sacred, religious dimension is clearly felt—as is the depth of their wordless communication.

> GERRY: Do you know the words [of the song to which they are dancing]?
>
> CHRIS: I never know any words.
>
> GERRY: Neither do I. Doesn't matter. This is more important. . . .
>
> CHRIS: Don't talk any more; no more words.

The wordless communication of love here is obviously close to that between Maire and Yolland in *Translations.* Friel's awareness of the power of wordless communication is interestingly highlighted by his willingness to mock such communication in his farce *The Communication Cord.* In a section full of comic references to translation, understanding, and lies, the lascivious Senator Donovan ogles a beautiful house guest and observes: "When you're as young and beautiful as Madame Giroux, language doesn't matter does it? Words are superfluous, aren't they?"

In *Dancing at Lughnasa,* Father Jack's return after twenty-five years working in a leper colony in Uganda further illustrates the complex relation of language and meaning. Father Jack's years of speaking Swahili have left him uncertain in his English and a direct illustration of Steiner's observation that "neglect, the lying fallow, even of one's first language, . . . will cause a certain dimming, a recession of vocabulary and of grammatical nuance from immediate recall." What has happened to Father Jack's language has also happened to his religion. His Catholicism has undergone a "certain dimming" and is now inextricably intertwined with

African pagan ritual. The mixed ceremonies over which Father Jack presided in Uganda indicate that "interference effects" exist on ceremonial as well as on linguistic levels. Kate's conclusion that her brother is engaged in "his own distinctive spiritual search" is a comforting rationalization, but also a hint to us that perhaps the form of the ritual and its words are not so important as the quest it embodies.

Michael's description of his aunts' dance as "this ritual, this wordless ceremony" is a powerful conclusion for Friel's play. It encapsulates what we have heard in previous references to dance. It reiterates what we have seen in earlier dances by Gerry and Chris, by Father Jack, and by the aunts. It embodies Friel's central point about the true understanding of silent communication. And it clarifies the link between individual love (Chris and Gerry), family love (the aunts), communal love (Ireland, Uganda), and the sacred love which links all humans. One of the recurring painful ironies in Friel's work is that we often come closest to the Word when we abandon words.

Once language is no longer necessary, of course, all problems of translation and interpretation disappear—including the problem Hugh (echoing Steiner) wrestles with in *Translations,* the problem of how to "interpret between privacies."

If Steiner's linguistic model has clearly influenced Friel, then, it is his broader notion of translation as interpretation and the making of meaning which provides the most general and useful way of approaching not just one Friel play, but the whole body of Friel's works. Thinking about the range of meanings in the term "translations," for example, reveals important aspects of meaning in the play *Translations.* What happens when an Irish laborer *translates* the classics? When Athena *translates* Ulysses into an uncouth peasant? When English culture is *translated* across the Irish Sea? But the term "translations" also provides a useful metaphor for other Friel plays, and since some of Friel's plays predate *After Babel,* it seems likely that Steiner's work caught Friel's imagination in large part because it explored aspects of language and meaning that had concerned the playwright for some time.

A brief recapitulation of key aspects of other Friel plays indicates the extent to which the translation metaphor can lead us to develop fuller understandings. In *Philadelphia, Here I Come!* (1964), for example, Gar Private pleads with the Canon, "you could *translate* all this loneliness, this groping, this dreadful bloody buffoonery into Christian terms that will make life bearable for us all" (emphasis added). In *The Loves of Cass McGuire* (1966), Cass gives her life of spinsterish drudgery in New York shape and meaning by translating herself into "Catherine," whose late husband "General Cornelius Olsen . . . made quite a name for himself in the last war."

In *Aristocrats* (1979) the O'Donnells translate Yeats and G. K. Chesterton into old family friends. In *Faith Healer* (1979) characters offer varying explanations of how crooked fingers may be made straight. In *The Communication Cord* (1982), a sort of companion piece to *Translations,* an Irish peasant cottage is translated into a vacation cottage for the upper middle class, just as Gaelic is translated from a folk language into an amusement for the educated middle class.

> **Often, as in both *Volunteers* and *Living Quarters,* the concern with translation is directly linked to concern with discovering and recovering the past.**
> —*Helen Lojek*

In *The Freedom of the City* (1973), the death of three unarmed citizens during a Derry civil rights march results in a variety of "authoritative" interpretations or translations. British judicial hearings "prove" that these hapless citizens were armed and dangerous, killed only when a restrained British army found it had no choice. An American sociologist turns events into a depersonalized examination of the culture of poverty. An Irish balladeer simultaneously trivializes and celebrates the three dead citizens by transforming them into one hundred Irish patriots who died trying to free their country from British domination. An Irish priest begins by praising their willingness to die for their beliefs and ends by condemning them as part of an excessive fringe element. An Irish telecaster surrounds their funeral with the sticky sweetness of popular sentimentality. Each jargon-studded official voice attempts to confine individual experience within an accepted dogma—to translate these lives into meaningful experience—but Friel's play suggests that the truth, if there is a truth, hovers somewhere as far beyond the formulations of a playwright as it is beyond the formulations of priest, judge, or newsperson.

In *Volunteers* (1975), Irish political prisoners excavate a historical site to discover the past even as they make way for the future (in the form of a luxury hotel to be built there). Finding a skeleton with a hole in the skull and a noose around its neck, the prisoners christen it Leif and create explanatory stories. These stories explain the prisoners' experiences as well as Leif's. Each offers a specific, convincing reason for the hole in the skull and the noose around the neck. It hardly matters that the stories cannot all be true, since their major function is not to reveal reality, but to create explanations—to "translate" reality and make it bearable for us all. So great is the human need for such translations that even when people conceive a "final adjudicator" whose exact knowledge should clarify their past actions (Sir in *Living Quarters* [1977]), they cannot resist attempting to circumvent him, to translate "facts" into more acceptable visions.

Often, as in both *Volunteers* and *Living Quarters,* the concern with translation is directly linked to concern with discovering and recovering the past—a concern which in Ireland includes translation both in its narrow sense (translating Irish into English to make available the texts of the past) and in its broad sense (transmogrifying the past so that it is connected to and usable in the present). This translation of the past is the central focus of *Making History* (1988). In that play Hugh O'Neill, seeking to consolidate Irish forces and lead them against the English armies, is a skilled practicer of tactical linguistics, readily swearing and forswearing allegiance to Elizabeth I, using language itself to dupe the oppressor who seeks to rob him of language, power, and independence. When his English sister-in-law protests at this breaking of a "solemn oath" O'Neill asserts: "Nothing more than a token gesture is asked for—the English, unlike us, never drive principles to embarrassing conclusions . . . it means nothing, nothing. . . . I'm loyal today—disloyal tomorrow—you know how capricious we Gaels are."

Ironically, it is the oft-forsworn O'Neill who objects to the falsities of the biography of him being prepared by Archbishop Lombard. O'Neill insists over and over that Lombard tell the "truth," something which Lombard says can't be done: "I don't believe that a period of history . . . contains within it one 'true' interpretation . . . it may contain within it several possible narratives." At the end of the play, O'Neill protests the biography's description of him as "A dove in meekness." That, says O'Neill, is "a bloody lie." "Not a lie," replies Lombard. "Merely a convention." The difference between O'Neill's "token gesture" of a false oath and Lombard's "convention" of biographical distortion is at best blurry. Even the motives for the falsities (if that is what they are) are similar. O'Neill seeks to protect his position and buy time in which to unify the Irish, and Lombard argues that his falsehoods protect the Irish. This argument that lies are protective, of course, parallels one motivation for use of alternative realities pointed out by Steiner and epitomized by Athena and Odysseus.

In *Making History* Friel also allows his characters' language once again to reflect the religious dimension of the word/Word: "Now is the time for a hero. . . . And I'm offering them Hugh O'Neill as a national hero. . . . there are times when a hero can be as important to a people as a God." O'Neill's and Lombard's untruths are what Steiner would call "alternative realities," and he recognizes that such alternatives are often creative and beneficent. They are also examples of the extent to which all speech requires translation.

History, of course, may be the greatest translation of all, for

it seeks to translate deed into word. In *After Babel,* Steiner argues that translation is necessary not just horizontally (between languages, between cultures, between individuals), but also vertically (between time periods) and that all history is translation:

> By far the greatest mass of the past as we experience it is a verbal construct. History is a speech-act, a selective use of the past tense. . . . We have no total history, no history which could be defined as objectively real because it contained the literal sum of past life. To remember everything is a condition of madness. We remember culturally, as we do individually, by conventions of emphasis, foreshortening, and omission. . . .the reality of felt history in a community depend[s] on a never-ending, though very often unconscious, act of internal translation.

> All descriptions are partial. We speak less than the truth, we fragment in order to reconstruct desired alternatives, we select and elide. It is not 'the things which are' that we say, but those which might be, which we would bring about, which the eye and remembrance compose.

In *Translations* Hugh echoes Steiner: "it is not the literal past, the 'facts' of history, that shape us, but images of the past embodied in language." And in *Making History* Lombard echoes them both: history is "imposing a pattern on events that were mostly casual and haphazard and shaping them into a narrative that is logical and interesting. . . . I'm not sure that 'truth' is a primary ingredient. . . . Maybe when the time comes, imagination will be as important as information."

In a passage which may well have suggested the punning title of Friel's play, Steiner says:

> When we use past tenses, when we remember, *when the historian "makes history"* (for that is what he is actually doing), we rely on . . . *axiomatic fictions.*

> These may well be indispensable to the exercise of rational thought, of speech, of shared remembrance, without which there can be no culture. But their justification is comparable to that of the foundations of Euclidean geometry whereby we operate, with habitual comfort, in . . . mildly idealized space. (first emphasis added)

In his new study of Friel, Richard Pine suggests another influence on the final shaping of *Making History.* Pointing to Friel's tendency to adapt or dramatize core arguments and central facts of sources, Pine suggests (apparently on the basis of an interview with the playwright) that as a child Friel read Sean O'Faolain's biography of O'Neill and "was fascinated by O'Faolain's suggestion that 'a talented dramatist might write an informative, entertaining, ironical play on the theme of the living man helplessly watching his *translation* into a star in the face of all the facts that had reduced him to poverty, exile and defeat'" (emphasis added). If O'Faolain is indeed one source for Friel's play, there is a happy conjunction between his use of the word "translation" and the use Steiner makes of it.

Precisely because history is a process of translation, Friel's play illustrates not just what happened when Lombard translated a real life into the myth of a hero, but also what happens when Friel retranslates the same real life into a different myth. Lombard is interested in O'Neill as a national figure—a man of war, politics, national consciousness. Friel (no doubt influenced by current debates about history) is interested in O'Neill the private man—the newlywed, the husband suddenly bereft of wife and son, the helpless exile who must be abjectly grateful for pensions and who consoles himself with wine and women. The extent to which both myths are translations—shaped realities—is emphasized by Lombard's and O'Neill's disagreement about whether O'Neill's wife Mabel should be portrayed in Lombard's biography. O'Neill is insistent that she should be. Lombard, however, is convinced that O'Neill's wives "didn't contribute significantly to . . . the overall thing . . . I mean they didn't reroute the course of history." But Lombard also recognizes that his myth is not the only one which could be woven from the threads of O'Neill's life:

> In the big canvas of national events—in your exchanges with popes and kings and queens—is that where Mabel herself thought her value and her importance resided? Is that how she saw herself? But she had her own value, her own importance. And at some future time and in a mode we can't imagine now I have no doubt that story will be told fully and sympathetically. It will be a domestic story, Hugh; a love story; and a very beautiful love story it will be.

It is, of course, that domestic story, that love story, which Friel gives us in *Making History,* and he is quite conscious of the extent to which his own "O'Neill" involves a definite shaping of the facts:

> I have tried to be objective and faithful—after my artistic fashion—to the empirical method. But when there was tension between historical "fact" and the imperative of the fiction, I'm glad to say I kept faith with the narrative. . . . history and fiction are related and comparable forms of discourse and . . . an historical text is a kind of literary artifact.

> (*Making History*)

Friel's play thus both discusses and illustrates the extent to which to write history is indeed to *translate* the past, to *make* a story. It also illustrates Friel's agreement with Hugh in *Translations* that "we must never cease renewing those images [of the past embodied in language]; because once we do, we fossilise." In many ways, it is a recasting of Oscar Wilde's dictum, "The one duty we owe to history is to rewrite it."

These are not new concerns for Friel. The fact that O'Neill's life is susceptible to retranslation is parallel to the existence of various translations of events in *The Freedom of the City* and to the more private retranslations which are at the core of *Faith Healer*—and it is not far removed from the retranslations of life histories in *The Loves of Cass McGuire.* What Steiner's book seems to have provided for Friel is a theory of language and culture which reinforces his own and allows for a refocusing of attention on things which have concerned Friel for decades.

This recurring sense that the major task is interpreted, communicated, transformed meaning—and the recurring use of the word "translation" to describe that process—meshes naturally with bilingual, largely Catholic Ireland's acute sense that both language and being need translation. Frank O'Connor, for example, in a chapter of his autobiography which discusses the link between language and imagination, describes his felt need to transform his world in literature:

> All I could believe in was words, and I clung to them frantically. I would read some word like "unsophisticated" and at once I would want to know what the Irish equivalent was. In those days I didn't even ask to be a writer; a much simpler form of transmutation would have satisfied me. All I wanted was to *translate,* to feel the unfamiliar become familiar, the familiar take on all the mystery of some dark foreign face I had just glimpsed on the quays. (emphasis added)

The mixture of linguistic and religious terms in such a statement is also typical of the task of translation central to so many Friel works.

Richard Kearney for example, discusses *The Faith Healer* as a play about words (often words which "lie") as marvelous, miraculous instruments of faith—words which make possible the release of the faith healer's audience "from what they are into what they *might* be. . . . the fiction of a life transformed;" "Frank's 'performance' can only work when the healer and the healed come together in a ritual of magic communion—when they agree to play the language game of faith." Building on Friel's statement that *The Faith Healer* is "some kind of metaphor for the art, the craft of writing," Kearney goes on to remind us of the "origins of drama in primitivistic ritual," and to suggest that the play "teases out that subtle knot in which religious and aesthetic faith are intertwined."

Patrick Rafroidi similarly argues that Friel uses "an approach which, to a point, is a religious one," and that Friel's plays are "catholic" in their "deep, crippling sense of . . . original sin." Rafroidi reminds us that Tim in **The Communication Cord** refers to the restored cottage (closely associated with the effort to restore Gaelic) as the "first cathedral" of the Irish, a structure which "shaped all our souls."

Richard Pine suggests that Friel "almost inevitably" fulfills "a liminal, shamanistic role as he sets about his task of divining the elements of ritual and *translating* them into drama" (emphasis added). Indeed, Pine's book in general supports the thesis that translation is a crucial metaphor for consideration of all of Friel's work, for the word peppers his critical evaluation. Friel, Pine suggests, "translates" private psychology into public culture, "translates" real places into words and images, "translates . . . the mind into the world and the world into the mind; intellect into emotion and emotion into intellect;" "translates . . . the absolute into the particular;" "translates" tragedy into comedy; "translates" the facts of Hugh O'Neill into a consideration of life as myth.

Pine asserts that the dramatist who produced **Dancing at Lughnasa** is "the same man, *translated,* who began writing short stories in the 1950s" (emphasis added). And Pine returns over and over—directly and indirectly—to the notion that there is a religious dimension to Friel's translations, which—as "drama-ritual"—are "a special form of communal process" which *"translates* us from one state to another"* (emphasis added).

Earlier critics such as Ulf Dantanus were more likely to use words such as "interpret" or "transform" and to emphasize the importance of communication as a Friel theme. Once Friel used Steiner's discussion of translation as a basis for his play **Translations,** however, he pointed interpreters toward an inclusive, useful metaphor for approaching the body of his work. The term provides an entree to earlier Friel works, and it is equally applicable to much of what concerns the playwright in **Making History** and **Dancing at Lughnasa**—though the impact of Steiner on these works is nowhere nearly so direct as it was on **Translations.**

If translation is a useful concept for understanding individual Friel plays, it is equally useful in understanding Friel's place in Irish literature and culture. His plays embody an ancient and current debate in Ireland and provide images and vocabulary for discussing the connections between linguistic translation, historical understanding, colonialism and nationalism, and religion. As Friel's colleague Seamus Deane puts

it in the general introduction to *The Field Day Anthology of Irish Writing,*

> [Nationalism] too is an act of translation or even of retranslation. The assumption it shares with colonialism is the existence of an original condition that must be transmitted, restored, recuperated, and which must replace that fallen condition which at present obtains. It is not necessarily true that something always gets lost in translation. It is necessarily true that translation is founded on the idea of loss and recuperation; it might be understood as an action that takes place in the interval between these alternatives. This conception lies at the heart of much Irish writing, especially in the modern period, and has of course affinities with the modern theories of writing as a practice.

To notice such affinities between Friel and Irish writing in general is, of course, simply to come full circle in awareness of the extent to which the playwright is both product and shaper of his culture. But it is to come full circle translated to a realm of fuller understanding.

Martine Pelletier (essay date Autumn/Winter 1994)

SOURCE: "Telling Stories and Making History: Brian Friel and Field Day," in *Irish University Review,* Vol. 24, No. 2, Autumn/Winter 1994, pp. 186-97.

[*In the following essay on Friel's drama and his association with Field Day Theatre Company, Pelletier examines Friel's treatment of Irish history.*]

As a short-story writer and as a playwright Brian Friel has been busy telling his audience stories; but as co-founder of the Field Day Theatre Company in 1980 one could argue that he has also literally been 'making history'. Whereas the early plays tend to concentrate on the individual's need for consoling or enabling fictions and the role of the artist as story-teller, the more political plays written after 1972 address another key issue which he felt he could no longer ignore in the light of the tragic events taking place in Northern Ireland at the time and of the debate surrounding revisionism in the South: the role of that other very powerful story-teller, the historian. The realisation that the workings of the fictions in an individual mind could be repeated in the collective mind of a country to the extent that a civilisation could find itself "imprisoned in a [fictional] contour which no longer matches the landscape of . . . fact."

For Friel, this reflection culminated in the portrayal of Hugh O'Neill in **Making History** (1988), with the playwright deliberately manipulating myths the better to demonstrate the shaping power of personal, cultural and artistic fictions. For Field Day, a more theoretical and comprehensive approach to the problems of history and literature led to their five series of pamphlets, their book *Revising the Rising* and to their most ambitious and controversial venture so far, the *Field Day Anthology of Irish Writing* published in 1991.

The tension between the private realm of the individual story and that most public of realms, History with a capital H, has characterised Friel's work since the early days. Up to 1972 though, Friel was using history in a very free and unself-conscious manner as one can see in both *The Mundy Scheme* and *The Enemy Within.* In *The Mundy Scheme,* that play which many IASAIL members discovered or rediscovered at the Leiden conference, Friel was trying to accommodate more public concerns after his tetralogy of love plays and choosing the form of a violent satire of the political life in the Republic: "What happens when a small nation that has been manipulated and abused by a huge colonial power for hundreds of years wrests its freedom by blood and anguish? What happens to an emerging country after it has emerged?" Answer: while the Northern part of it is busy turning itself into a bloody battlefield, the rest agrees greedily to sell itself as a gigantic graveyard to America . . . A cynical and despondent view of Ireland in the late sixties. Friel never used that genre again and is very dismissive of the play today.

Before tackling politics, he had used history as a backdrop for the more private struggles of his main character, St Columba, in *The Enemy Within* (1962). Friel was careful to protect himself in the preface against potential attacks from the scholars, acknowledging that in portraying Columba, the inner man, he had taken some liberties with the historical facts known about the saint: "*The Enemy Within* is neither a history nor a biography but an imaginative account, told in dramatic form, of a short period in St Columba's thirty-four years of voluntary exile." That was 1962 and one senses that Friel did not feel particularly uneasy about his 'manipulation' of history. Neither did the critics. Twenty years later though, when the controversy surrounding *Translations* was raging, (*Translations* was attacked from various corners, partly for a lack of verisimilitude in its use of historical material: did the English sappers in 1833 have bayonets or not? Is it likely that British officers could not speak Latin and Greek at that time?) he had to reiterate more forcefully his belief in the need to recognise the freedom of imaginative literature:

> Writing an historical play may bestow certain advantages, but it also imposes certain responsibilities. The apparent advantages are the established historical facts, or at least the received historical ideas in which the work is rooted and which gives

it its apparent familiarity and accessibility. The concomitant responsibility is to acknowledge those facts or ideas but not to defer to them. Drama is first a fiction. With the authority of fiction. You don't go to *Macbeth* for history.

In this very balanced assessment can be found a lead into Friel's way of dealing with the problem of historical fiction. He craves and claims that freedom of imagination that any writer of fiction requires but over the years he has come to the realisation that when writing in Ireland and about history certain responsibilities could not be avoided.

A playwright of the private world, Friel has nevertheless 'strayed' into the public sphere too often and with too much talent for such plays as *The Freedom of the City, Volunteers, Translations* and *Making History* to be dismissed as unconvincing surrenders to the calls of the tribe or atypical concessions to the heat of the political moment. Differing assessments of Friel coexist, some seeing him as essentially a playwright of the family and the individual, others seeing in him the epitome of the committed writer, Ireland's leading "écrivain engagé" (Ulick O'Connor's pamphlet has to limit its corpus to three plays to try and make this point).

What confuses many is that Friel can be equally convincing in both these roles, (even if he may himself acknowledge a certain predilection for 'the personal, interior world of self-deception' he also knows that he is obsessed with the political) because he comes to history at an angle which allows him to see the interaction, the connections between the private mode of the story and the public mode of history. What he comes to realise as he looks into history is that the lure of fictionalisation which is so potent in the lives of individuals, also affects history as a form of storytelling. As a playwright, the stories he tells become coloured by larger public issues and politics in the wider sense of the word appear on Friel's stage, inaugurating a new and transitional phase in his writing in the seventies.

The Freedom of the City, widely acknowledged as a turning point, concentrated on immediate history and the distortions and oversimplifications people and events were subjected to when integrated into the wider pattern of history. The story of Michael, Lily and Skinner had to be shaped and altered to fit the differing versions of official or unofficial history depending on the mediators (the Army, the Judge, the balladeer, the RTE journalists, the Church . . .). In *Volunteers,* a step back was taken and history was used self-consciously as a point of comparison, setting Viking Ireland versus modern Ireland to try and understand how and why the stalemate in Northern Ireland had come about. The play offers little comfort: the official historian in charge of the archaeological site never appears on stage and seems to have precious little time for the hard work of digging into history. Soon a hotel will be built on the site (Wood Quay) and a part of history will be buried again, this time maybe for good. Again Friel emphasises the uncertainty of all 'historical truth', denying its objective claim to veracity the better to show its subjective, relative, imaginative wealth and relevance. "Certain truths [. . . may be] beyond [the historian's] kind of scrutiny" says one character in *Aristocrats.* Historical facts always depend for their ultimate meaning on interpreters, mediators who can or cannot be trusted: Keeney and Pyne offer various stories of Leif, the Viking skeleton, the value of which depends wholly on the relation the teller has to his story. Mimicking a schoolteacher on an educative outing with her pupils, Keeney declares:

> And as I keep insisting to my friends here, the more we learn about our ancestors, children, the more we discover about ourselves—isn't that so? So that what we are all engaged in here is really a thrilling voyage in *self*-discovery. [. . .] But the big question is: How many of us want to make *that* journey?

For Friel, history never ceases to be at least partly a personal issue, hence the trauma and the make-believe and the recurrence of those questions that haunt the individual mind. The struggle between the claims of history and those of fiction and Friel's growing fear that he might not be equal to his task are marvellously illustrated in his sporadic diary written at the time when he was working on *Translations:*

> 22 May. The thought occurred to me that what I was circling around was a political play and that thought panicked me. But it is a political play—how can that be avoided? If it is not political, what is it? Inaccurate history? Social drama?

> 6 July. One of the mistakes of the direction in which the play is presently pulling is the almost fully *public* concern of the theme. [. . .] The play must concern itself only with the exploration of the dark and private places of individual souls.

In the end Friel managed to merge the public and the private most satisfactorily in *Translations* but the play was heavily attacked precisely for the reasons he had foreseen: 'inaccurate history'. Hence his spirited defence of the need to recognise the specific 'truth' of fiction. A perfect illustration too of [George] Steiner's point in *After Babel,* the main subtext for *Translations:* "It is not the literal past that rules us. It is images of the past" applied by Friel to the localised context of Northern Ireland:

> In some ways the inherited images of 1916, or 1960, control and rule our lives more profoundly than the historical truth of what happened on those two occasions. [. . .] For example, is our understanding of

the Siege of Derry going to be determined by Macaulay's history of it, or is our understanding of Parnell going to be determined by Lyons's portrait of Parnell?

Here we come across the problem of the confusion of genres, an issue that has exercised many theoreticians and practitioners of both disciplines: what happens when a writer starts meddling with history? Is History's claim to objectivity to be taken seriously or is it just a delusion? Do historical facts matter more than or as much as their representations? If such issues are of particular relevance in Ireland today, they are also widespread concerns bearing witness to the need to question the nature of 'truth' and of 'fiction'.

Graham Swift, the English novelist, places the dispute between story and history at the centre of his powerful novel, *Waterland.* It is of particular interest to see a writer coming from the supposedly stable English tradition, (something that the Northern Irish minority feels it has been excluded from) being prey to the same unease about history and using in a work of literature a vocabulary and a rhetoric not alien to the Irish situation. The protagonist, Tom Crick, is a history teacher (again). Explaining how he came to his vocation he says:

> So I began to demand of history an Explanation. Only to uncover in this dedicated search more mysteries, more fantasticalities, more wonders and ground for astonishment than I started with, only to conclude forty years later—notwithstanding a devotion to the usefulness, to the educative power of my chosen discipline—that history is a yarn. And can I deny that what I wanted all along was not some golden nugget that history would at last yield up, but History itself, the Grand Narrative, the filler of vacuums, the dispeller of fears of the dark?

Ireland, caught between revisionism and nationalism, still seems to be wondering whether her history is a yarn or the Grand Narrative. Friel was clearly influenced by this state of affairs when writing *Translations* in 1980. It was also then that together with actor Stephen Rea he decided to found his own theatre company in Derry. Field Day, as it was called, was soon to turn into a controversial politico-intellectual venture, putting history and literature at the top of their agenda. In his introduction to the *Field Day Anthology of Irish Writing,* Seamus Deane, one of the directors, sums up his (and the company's?) conclusions, stressing that in Ireland, history had largely forfeited its rights to be accepted as objective:

> In a country like Ireland, where nationalism had to be politically opposed to the prevailing power-systems, there was a serious attempt to create a

counter-culture and to define it as authentic to the nation. In doing so, it used historical and archaeological scholarship in a tendentious and polemical fashion. For this, it was rebuked. It distorted the facts of history and reduced literature to propaganda. The rebuke came from groups equally anxious to assert some other position against nationalism—unionism, liberalism, internationalism. The political animus informing all these non-nationalist groups was concealed as much as possible, and the most frequently worn disguise was, in history, the pretence to 'objectivity' and in literature the claim to 'autonomy'. Both words had the magical appeal of not being polemical or political; both were against 'propaganda' which pretended to be either history or art.

Such a view is confirmed by Alan Harrison and Andrew Carpenter in their section on *Ireland and Her Past: Topographical and Historical Writing to 1690:*

> However impartial he claims to be, no historian writes of the past without being strongly influenced by the age in which he lives. During periods of change and conflict, objectivity is not only difficult for the historian but is sometimes deliberately rejected so that 'history' can be written specifically to further the cause of one political group or another.

They also stress the mixing of history and literature in medieval Irish culture:

> The Irish word for this traditional history, *seanchas* (ancient lore) embraces not only the formal recording of history—annals, regnal lists, genealogies and laws—but also much that, in later generations, would be considered literature—sagas, origin legends, hagiography, political propaganda, stories associated with place-names, and even romantic tales concerning mythical figures. The dividing line between 'history' and 'literature' was never clear or distinct in early and medieval Irish culture.

So much for history's claim to objectivity in this context at least: somebody's historical truth could be somebody else's grotesquely distorted or oversimplified fiction. Or, as Stewart Parker had it in *Northern Star:* "History's a whore. She rides the winners."

If *Translations* and the foundation of Field Day marked, temporarily, the culmination of the public strand in Friel's work, another play, dating from exactly the same period, followed on the more private vein, confirming the coexistence of these two domains and their interaction. The playwright's

most complex and convincing statement on the "gentle art of story-telling" is to be found in *Faith Healer.* In that play, three characters, each in isolation, present their version of the events leading to the death of Frank Hardy, Faith Healer, illustrating what Friel once said: "Perhaps the most important thing is not the accurate memory but the successful invention." The three accounts often differ and blatantly contradict one another, the facts just refuse to fall into place and in the very discrepancies is to be found the 'truth' of the play. A 'truth' that reflects on the role of the artist since Frank Hardy is clearly a metaphor for the writer and his power to create fictions. As Gerald Fitzgibbon remarked in his article entitled "Garnering the Facts: Unreliable Narrators in some Plays of Brian Friel":

> Observation of his characters suggests that the search for absolute 'fact and reason' is futile, that no individual narrator has access to 'the truth'. Within their systems of language, thought and feeling, and with varying degrees of integrity, the characters invent whatever versions of reality they can live with.

Or returning to [Graham] Swift and Tom Crick:

> Children, only animals live entirely in the Here and Now. Only nature knows neither memory nor history. But man—let me offer you a definition—is the story-telling animal. Wherever he goes he wants to leave behind not a chaotic wake, not an empty space, but the comforting marker-buoys and trail-signs of stories. He has to go on telling stories. He has to keep on making them up. As long as there's a story, it's all right. Even in his last moments, it's said, in the split second of a fatal fall—or when he's about to drown—he sees, passing rapidly before him, the story of his whole life.

Isn't that exactly what *Faith Healer* is all about? Isn't that exactly what Keeney and Pyne were doing in *Volunteers?* Interestingly enough Gerald Fitzgibbon's conclusion embraces both *The Freedom of the City* and *Faith Healer,* showing the links between two apparently very different works:

> In *Faith Healer* and *The Freedom of the City,* Brian Friel completely exposes to the audience the process by which they surrender their own judgment to characters in a fiction. He does not merely show us characters who survive by making fictions; he repeatedly reminds us that the author too survives in this way.

And looking at Friel's *Making History* (1988), one is tempted to add and so do nations and historians. The human craving for a history that would put an end to all squabbling by establishing its undisputed truth is part of that quest for a transcendental value but can also be hijacked: isn't the 'true history' merely the most satisfying one? This question is at the heart of Friel's *Making History* and represents an effort on the part of the playwright to free himself from the continuing grip of history on his work, to reclaim some freedom as an artist by demythologising the role of the historian.

The human craving for a history that would put an end to all squabbling by establishing its undisputed truth is part of that quest for a transcendental value but can also be hijacked: isn't the 'true history' merely the most satisfying one?
—Martine Pelletier

Making History could be seen as a very late companion piece to *The Enemy Within.* Another form of hagiography, with a difference . . . Its protagonist is none other than Hugh O'Neill, the last of the great Gaelic chiefs, whose biography by Sean O'Faolain Friel had read avidly many years earlier. In 1968 Tom Kilroy, a close friend of Friel's and also a director of Field Day, had written a play about this same historical figure who occupies a very prominent place in Irish nationalist history. Can Hugh O'Neill ever be anything but a public figure ensconced in a mythic image? As he had already done with St Columba, it is by turning away from the public image that Friel constructs his O'Neill, leaving a theatrical gap where the Battle of Kinsale should have been. Instead there is the death in childbirth of Mabel Bagenal, Hugh's English wife; and the replacement of a public event (a military disaster), by a private, intimate tragedy. The exiled O'Neill, a broken man, comes to the realisation that it was in his private life, in the person of Mabel that his salvation lay. The public myth turns into a private one, the flawless military hero is but a grieving husband. And thankfully, Friel is here to portray that other truth about Hugh O'Neill which Lombard will steadfastly refuse to acknowledge as relevant in his *The Life and Times of Hugh O'Neill:*

In Ireland, the period between the assumption of the lordship of Ireland by Henry VIII and the battle of the Boyne—a time of high tension between religious, racial and cultural factions—stands out for the polemic of its historians and for the bias of their histories.

Indubitably, Friel caught the spirit of the time in *Making History* in which he shows Archbishop Lombard busy putting the final touches to that "Grand Narrative" of the Gaelic world, the "dispeller of fears of the dark" that was about to engulf the native Irish in the wake of the Battle of Kinsale:

People think they just want to know the 'facts'; they think they believe in some sort of empirical truth, but what they really want is a story. And that's what this will be: the events of your life categorized and classified and then structured as you would structure any story. No, no, I'm not talking about falsifying, about lying, for heaven's sake. I'm simply talking about making a pattern. That's what I'm doing with all this stuff—offering a cohesion to that random catalogue of deliberate achievement and sheer accident that constitutes your life. And that cohesion will be a narrative that people will read and be satisfied by. And that narrative will be as true and as objective as I can make it—with the help of the Holy Spirit.

Disturbing echoes of Lombard's version of history can be heard in Desmond Fennell's pamphlet against revisionism, dating from 1989 in which he attacks 'revisionist' history on two grounds:

First because I believe that its moral interpretation is not correct; second, because such history does not serve the well-being of the nation. [. . .]

The modern Irish nation—the new Irish nation formed from the late eighteenth century onwards—was provided with such a[n enabling] history by scholars whose aim was, often explicitly, to supply it with such a history in place of the nationally useless and undermining histories or pseudo-histories of Ireland written by Englishmen. And this new Irish nation would not have formed [. . .] without that history-writing.

Obviously, I am talking about a science of history which is also an art: an art like that of those composers or musicians who, in successive generations, with meticulous dedication, and each differently than his contemporaries, rearrange an old tune or song. But this art comes easily, and without betrayal of self, but rather with affirmation and satisfaction of self, to those historians whose passion for factual truth, and for conscientious moral judgment, is equalled by their piety for their nation's pattern of historical meaning, and their regard for what their fellow-countrymen, and they themselves, need from their national history for their minds and hearts.

This last sentence takes up almost the same vocabulary as Lombard's argument against Hugh O'Neill's appeal for the truth to be told:

Think of this [*book*] as an act of *pietas.* Ireland is reduced as it has never been reduced before—we are talking about a colonized people on the brink of extinction. This isn't the time for a critical assessment of your 'ploys' and your 'disgraces' and your 'betrayal'—that's the stuff of another history for another time. Now is the time for a hero. Now is the time for a heroic literature. So I'm offering Gaelic Ireland two things. I'm offering them this narrative that has the elements of myth. And I'm offering them Hugh O'Neill as a national hero. A hero and the story of a hero.

While Friel apparently believed, with the revisionists, that Ireland was now ready to hear versions of the past that differed from the myth ("the received historical ideas"), Fennell rejects any history-writing that would alter Ireland's view of herself in any way, in the fear that the country has not yet grown out of its need for "the filler of vacuums" and suggesting that it might never do. I might add that Mr Fennell's interesting thesis is somewhat endangered by his resorting to the example of the former USSR's supposedly enabling history, a fiction that the dismantling of the communist empire has exposed for what it was.

Disturbingly enough, Seamus Deane seems to join in the attack against revisionism when he claims in a passage that corresponds exactly to the double time frame of *Making History:*

At times it seems that there is a link between the impulse to heroicize the past and the consciousness of present political weakness or defeat. Similarly, in those 'revisionist' periods, when the myths are dismantled and the concept of 'objectivity' rules, there is often an anxiety to preserve the status quo, to lower the political temperature and to offer the notion that historical processes are so complex that any attempt to achieve an overview cannot avoid the distortions and dogmatism of simple-minded orthodoxy. This is a powerful antidote against criticism and rebellion. Since rebellion is, of its nature, devoted to a simplified view of a complex situation, its proponents can be accused of indulging in historical fantasy, of intellectual narcosis and uneducated convictions.

Lombard would subscribe wholeheartedly to such a statement and claim that the time is not ripe for such a history . . . Deane continues:

There is a current of opinion that holds that we would mythologize less if we knew more. (That itself might be a myth.) But surely what is to be understood here is the felt need for mythologies,

heroic lineages, dreams of continuity; in short, the need, expressed by different generations, in individual ways, to colonize historical territory and repossess it.

Friel's position however is not so clear-cut. He senses in himself too that need to repossess what he called "claiming the disinheritance" and to remythologize; he does not deride it but he remains wary of the consequences, especially after what happened to *Translations,* the pieties that were offered to the play as a result of misunderstandings:

I have no nostalgia for that time [The Gaelic Ireland of Baile Beag]. I think one should look back on the process of history with some kind of coolness. The only merit in looking back is to understand, how you are and where you are at this moment. Several people commented that the opening scenes of the play were a portrait of some sort of idyllic, Forest of Arden life. But this is a complete illusion, since you have on stage the representatives of a certain community—one is dumb, one is lame and one is alcoholic, a physical maiming which is a public representation of their spiritual deprivation.

After *Making History* Friel returned to a more limited use of history as a setting for other stories, stories of heart and hearth in his beautifully moving and deservedly acclaimed play, *Dancing at Lughnasa.* Fintan O'Toole was probably correct when he described *Making History* as "a wiping clean of the slate in preparation for a new beginning" adding:

Just as a friend and colleague Seamus Heaney, a fellow director of Field Day, gave himself in his long poem, "Station Island", permission to be free of the burdens of history and the demands of the tribe, so Friel is doing in *Making History.* The play abjures history, undercuts all political hero-worship. By dealing with the impossibility of ever constructing a narrative which is more than an acceptable fiction, Friel frees himself from any perceived need to be a chronicler of his times.

Two separate conclusions then, for two personae which make up the complete man: on the one hand, *Dancing at Lughnasa, A Month in the Country* (after Turgenev), and in 1993 *Wonderful Tennessee* which, taken together, definitely suggest a return to the more traditional role of storyteller; on the other hand, the attempt to stage a "reprise" of *The Freedom of the City,* Friel's most overtly political play (the most controversial too), by Field Day at the Guildhall in Derry in September 1992, was vetoed by the local authorities although this could have been a major attraction for Irish playgoers who had shown a certain disaffection vis-à-vis the last two Field Day productions, Seamus Heaney's *The Cure at Troy* (1990) and Tom Kilroy's *The Madame MacAdam Travelling Theatre* (1991). The company did not tour in 1992-93 and has officially taken a sabbatical for a year to review their critical and theatrical activities while Seamus Deane, who had become their spokesman as editor of the long-awaited *Anthology,* is in the United States. Friel definitely seemed to have resumed a working relationship with the Abbey in Dublin and his official resignation from the board of Field Day (now under the leadership of Stephen Rea who is, it would seem, planning a tour for September 1994 with a McGuinness version of *Uncle Vanya*) on the 1st of February 1994 came only as half a surprise in the light of the recent redefinition of his artistic priorities and his desire for more freedom. Today, more than ever, it might be worth remembering what Friel said over ten years ago in an interview when asked about Field Day, political nationalism and the achievement of a united Ireland:

> I think they are serious issues and big issues, and they are issues that exercise us all, the six of us, very much. But you've also got to be very careful to retain some strong element of cynicism about the whole thing.

Could it be that, in Friel's eyes, Field Day had unfortunately proved it had come to lack that distance and cynicism? Or was it unavoidable that, at some point, Friel should feel that his artistic integrity was being threatened by the sheer (ideological/political) pressure that had accumulated within and around Field Day in recent times?

Richard Bonaccorso (essay date June 1996)

SOURCE: "Personal Devices: Two Representative Stories by Brian Friel," in *Colby Quarterly,* Vol. 32, No. 2, 1996, pp. 93-9.

[*In the following study of "The Flower of Kiltymore," and "The Saucer of Larks," Bonaccorso considers Friel's more private story-telling voice.*]

Between 1964 and 1967, with the productions of ***Philadelphia, Here I Come!*** in Dublin, London, and New York, Brian Friel began to commit his talents fully to drama. This was about ten years into his public career as a writer of short stories and radio plays and following a half-year of study at the Tyrone Guthrie Theatre in Minneapolis. In 1967, in an essay entitled **"The Theatre of Hope and Despair,"** Friel makes a distinction between the strategies of the playwright and those of the storywriter, between engaging a collective audience and a solitary reader. In doing so he reveals a de-

termination to maintain an artistic faith with himself that he had established in the writing of short fiction. Friel considers that the playwright must employ a kind of stealth in order to evoke a fresh response from the conventional and often complacent mentality of theatre audiences. But storywriters, he states, "function privately" as in "a personal conversation. Everything they write has the implicit preface, 'come here till I whisper in your ear'." This air of intimacy—a characteristic of the story tradition—is a condition toward which all of Friel's art aspires and tends. Friel's stories, however, provide a direct path to the writer's inner ground. They approach the reader as a co-conspirator, one who is invited to discover the real story existing beneath appearances, in the undercurrent of the writer's technique.

Mainly gathered in two collections published in the sixties, Friel's stories introduce the small-town social world of the plays and the inner orientations of Friel's dramatic characters; they also anticipate the subtle manner of the playwright, particularly in his well-noted reticence, spareness of direct commentary, and reliance on dialogue to carry implications. The stories also display Friel's special talent for the most intriguing dialogue of all, the silent interchange within the individual.

In Friel's tales technique is ultimately embodied in subtleties of characterization. With what seems a quiet inevitability, the Friel story progresses from considerations of outer roles to those of inner identities. Beneath ordinary concerns and routines, the hidden interchanges between individuals and their communities come to be seen as crucial encounters. Without pronouncement the story gradually arrives at the threshold of a profound individual consciousness. Through a protagonist captured at a point of personal reconsideration, a moral pressure is recognized among the old debris of experience and memory. Though not usually autobiographical projections, these characters and these situations represent the patterns of Friel's personal concerns. Like a Wordsworth in prose, Friel excels at elapsed time reflections, and his stories explore the modifications of identity that aging produces. With each modification come new mysteries and responsibilities. These are the personal equations hidden beneath the common contexts of community and family life. To answer the call of self in such circumstances, to overcome the inertia of static myths, one must rely upon personal devices.

Friel's people live in an Irish village culture that is fading into obsolescence, yet one which maintains its grip upon the psyches of its citizens and demands conformity to its questionable codes. His fictional small towns, such as Ballybeg, Beannafreaghan, and Coradinna, represent, as Mel Gussow observes, "the small towns around the world," their "emotional environments" becoming adjuncts of character. While casting a sometimes sardonic eye upon the community culture, Friel also acknowledges its significance in the lives of his people and, by implication, in the life of his own imagination. Speaking of the autobiographical aspect of his art, he has called himself "the miner and the mined." As in the work of Sean O'Faolain, Friel's flirtation with nostalgia becomes a creative strategy, a way of engaging the heart into what is essentially a critical assessment of the familial and cultural inheritance of his childhood in Tyrone and Donegal, where the stories are generally set.

The characteristic Friel tonality is comic-elegiac, wherein irony checks charm and bitterness underlies humor. Though humorous and nostalgic, these works seriously examine the costs of sentimentality, how it can falsify history and stall personal development. Seamus Deane has pointed out that since history has made Friel's provincial world "anachronistic," that world can also become "susceptible to sentimentality, self-pity, and, in the last stages, to a grotesque caricaturing of what it had once been." Though Friel's nostalgia genuinely evokes the charms of place and past, he also reveals how emotional passivity challenges the freedom of the character, the intellect of the writer, and the understanding of the reader. At the same time, genuine sensitivity to place and past is one measure of humanity and balanced discrimination. Feeling is part of understanding. While communal failures bear heavily upon Friel's characters, he does not define reality along deterministic lines. Deane states that Friel's "transactions" between character and community elicit "the recognition that the formal structures of social life are what we live by, not what we live for. Yet what we live for is clarified only by the insufficiency of what we live by." Place need not determine one's identity, but inevitably bears upon the self.

A good example of these dynamics between society and the individual is **"The Flower of Kiltymore,"** an ironically titled story from *The Gold in the Sea.* Friel begins this tale of a clownish, rural police sergeant named Burke with what seems a simple narrative. Nevertheless, it is a passage filled with defining nuance:

> The calm and peace that the death of Lily, his wife, brought to Sergeant Burke's life were an experience so new and so strange to him that the only explanation he could imagine was that he must be ill himself, the unnatural tranquility he had often heard about that frequently forebodes the end. And this knowledge was a vague comfort. Not that he wanted to die—he was, after all, only sixty-two, as strong as a bull, and within sight of retiring from the police force—but he felt guilty at having her lying all alone up there for the past four weeks in the new graveyard, the only grave in the cemetery, with not even a wall around it yet to keep the wandering sheep out.

In this subdued manner and with a language that mimics Burke's, Friel evokes a double view of the character's personality. Mundane, simple-minded responses accompany hints of emotional depth and individuality. This method of characterization, probing regions of exotic sensibility under unexceptional behavioral facades, is one of Friel's signatures. In this case, Burke himself does not understand his own feelings, and he reduces them to a kind of social problem—his dead wife's isolation in the graveyard.

Bungling and absent-minded, the sergeant is superfluous as a social being except as an object of community laughter. Even Lily had nagged and mocked him. Since her death, however, he has grown indifferent to his clownish reputation, preoccupied as he is with his sense of alienation from himself. Lily's lonesome resting place is hardly more removed from the community than is the sergeant's mood, and he goes off to consult with a doctor, leaving the incompetent and slyly dishonest Guard Finlan on duty at the police station. Though a ludicrous figure himself, Finlan, like many of the younger members of the community, likes to make fun of the sergeant. The Blue Boys, a group of young hooligans, devise false alarms to keep the sergeant in a perpetual state of foolish and meaningless activity. Since the death of Lily, however, they have been quiet. Significantly, Burke misses the self-renewing stoicism that their mockery inspires in him. When an actual emergency takes place, the mockers are themselves mocked by reality itself, and, ironically, by means of another of his outward blunders, Burke ascends to a higher level of inner freedom.

Finlan ignores what he considers to be a prank call—a warning that a mine has washed up on Kiltymore's beach. In fact the mine is real, and the Blue Boys, fooling with it as they have fooled with the sergeant, cause it to explode. Two are killed and several are maimed. The sergeant, who will be blamed for the disaster, belatedly arrives at the scene, heralded by a local madwoman: "The flower of Kiltymore!" she excitedly cries, "The flower of Kiltymore—all gone!" The mock-heroic aspect of her words anticipates the absurd public hysteria that is now turned against Sergeant Burke.

But the crisis has a happy effect upon him. As he prepares to face an inquiry by his superiors and whatever public disgrace that may follow, he senses an unexpected renewal within himself:

> They might dismiss him right away; or they might question him for hours, for days, and then dismiss him; or they might make a "case" of him, compile a file on him, keep him on tenter hooks for months, and then demote him, and send him to the back of beyond. It must be a terrible offence, he thought, that would bring the Commissioner all the way from Dublin tomorrow.

And yet, although he knew that his future was in the balance, he was neither afraid, nor even anxious. Because for the first time in four weeks he felt normal again. There was the fatigue, yes; but it was a healthy exhaustion. But the emptiness in his stomach had evaporated, and his head was clear, and his heart—his heart was gay, sure, vibrant.

It is interesting that this simple man should reach this emotional plateau without the aid of indignation against his accusers. He does not rebel against the injustice of his situation nor does he rail against the hypocrisy of the inquiry. As the comic butt of the community he had been alienated. He is therefore now able to find refuge within himself, when the community is accusing him of failure in his societal role. He also has another humble but unique satisfaction:

> But even more important, in a few days' time Lily would be alone no longer; she would have company in the new cemetery, the eternal company of the two Blue Boys, and that was a great relief to him. It might not have been the company she would have chosen, but they would have a lot in common, he felt. At last he had been instrumental in making her happy, even once.

Burke is not conscious of being subversive; he does not sense the air of retribution clinging to his considerations. His personality turns bitterness into atonement, and, without a trace of vainglory or deviousness, he finds personal solace in the public disaster.

Friel effects a complex of ironies here. By means of a satire on the community, Friel elevates the sergeant, not just despite his social blundering, but because of it, and the story evokes the inviolate aspect of his heretofore underrated individuality. Yet the sergeant remains a social being in his own mind. Having considered himself a failure as a husband, he finds satisfaction in his imagined usefulness to his dead wife, thinking as he does of the growing little community of the graveyard. While Friel exposes the hypocrisies of communal life, the story also acknowledges people's imaginative need for each other.

Small-town mentalities are not necessarily small mentalities. Rich implications can exist in unexceptional lives, simple situations, and ordinary consciousness. Friel adapts himself to the mentality of his characters, and his generally inarticulate and isolated protagonists have their moments of grace and eloquence. In these moments we sense that they speak for the artist, though the message is usually indirect or disguised. "It is through his self-effacement," comments George O'Brien of Friel, "that we become aware of him." Ultimately, as Seamus Heaney has pointed out, Friel is a writer engaged in a "quarrel with himself, between his heart and his

head. . . ." Like Turgenev's gentle provincials, Friel's country folk seem alternately silly and shrewd. Though they do not act the cosmopolitan, they are often more canny than naive, and they embody a complex dynamic with their surroundings.

The protagonist of **"The Saucer of Larks"** is another aging police sergeant. (Curiously, his assistant is named Burke, the sergeant's name in **"The Flower of Kiltymore."**) This tale's sergeant protagonist is also a man whose sensibility is belied by the gruff externals of looks, behavior, and speech (all typical trappings of his social status). He and Guard Burke escort two German officials of the War Graves Commission out to a lonely but beautiful Donegal valley, Glennafuiseog, a name which means "the valley of the larks." They go there to locate the grave of a German pilot who crashed near the spot during the war. A stout man with a pipe between his teeth, the sergeant comments with self-deprecating irony as they drive out into the country: "This is my kingdom as far as you can see." But in a way he means it, for he responds to the beauty of the place so intensely that he feels compelled to speak, albeit roughly, of his emotions:

> "Dammit, could you believe that there are places like this still in the world, eh? D'you know, there are men who would give fortunes for a place like this. Fortunes. And what would they do if they got it? What would they do?"
>
> "What, Sergeant?" asked Burke dutifully.
>
> "They would destroy it! That's what they would do! Dig it up and flatten it out and build houses on it and ring it round with cement. Kill it. That's what they would do. Kill it. Didn't I see them myself when I was stationed in Dublin years ago, making an arse of places like Malahide and Skerries and Bray. That's what I mean. Kill it! Slaughter it!"

His alienation from society's affairs deepens his private bond with this wild place. Indignant against the modern world, he is keen to escape from its obligations, some of which extend to him in his duties as a policeman. But as if to spite him, and in keeping with a questionable general policy, the German officials have come to exhume the body and take the remains to a mass grave in County Wicklow. Without fully realizing it, the sergeant has been made a grudging servant of blunt and narrow systemization. Nevertheless, his heart rebels within him as he surveys the surrounding beauty. On a moment's impulse, he turns to the German officials and makes an appeal that surprises them and, indeed, himself:

> "I'm going to ask you to do something." His breath came in short puffs and he spoke quickly. "Leave that young lad here. Don't dig him up."

Herr Grass stiffened.

"Let him lie here where he has all that's good in God's earth around about him. He has been here for the past eighteen years; he's part of the place by now. Leave him in it. Let him rest in peace."

These words might as well be a plea for the sergeant himself, for he has been in these same regions for many years (he was called in when the pilot crashed and was buried by local fishermen eighteen years ago), and his impulse comes out of his long-formed piety for the place.

But he senses that the Germans do not understand his feeling, for he hardly understands it himself. They go about their duties, exhume the remains of the body and effectively violate the connection that time and nature had established with the human remains. The sergeant seems to sag within his uniform, and, contrasting with his exultation of a few moments before over the soaring of a flock of larks (a "confirmation of his humanity," as George O'Brien puts it), he descends into his officer's manner:

"I think that is everything," said Herr Grass. "Now we are prepared."

"Right," said the Sergeant irritably. "We'll go then. This bloody place is like an oven. My shirt's sticking to my back."

The job is done, but it is certainly not "everything." The sergeant feels depressed in his isolation but also angry that he has been foolish enough to compromise it. When Guard Burke tries to draw him out later by criticizing the Germans, he shuns the overture and threatens Burke against speaking of the episode by the pilot's grave. The sergeant has gained a bitter wisdom. On another rare day his spirit may ascend with the larks again, but if it happens, no one else will know of it. Even as the larks fill up the untravelled valley, the sergeant, like all of us, fills his fated isolation with his own sensibility.

In Friel's stories, imposed values of social, historical, or ethical circumstance bear upon each human impulse, but not with a paralyzing inevitability. By depicting characters in situations that seem overpowering, Friel invests greater value upon those traces of autonomy that do arise, at least as a missed option. Typically, as these two stories illustrate, the Friel protagonist stops short of overtly subversive behavior, but, in a sense, Friel defines each character to the degree that the heart is not scripted and the mind is not programmed.

Maureen S. G. Hawkins (essay date Fall 1996)

SOURCE: "Schizophrenia and the Politics of Experience in Three Plays by Brian Friel," in *Modern Drama*, Vol. 39, No. 3, Fall 1996, pp. 465-74.

[*In the following essay, Hawkins establishes some characteristics of Schizophrenia and applies these to an analysis of the characters and situations in Friel's work.*]

In *Saints, Scholars, and Schizophrenics,* Nancy Scheper-Hughes states that the Irish and Northern Irish have the world's highest rates of hospitalization for schizophrenia, and, to establish that these rates do not merely reflect the availability of beds for treatment, she adds that Irish-Americans and Irish-Canadians are more frequently treated for schizophrenia than are members of other ethnic groups. The highest rate of schizophrenia in Ireland, she says, is in the West of Ireland in isolated rural areas dependent on peripheral agriculture and suffering from depopulation, and the most commonly afflicted are celibate males, suggesting that all of these factors are connected with Irish schizophrenia.

Scheper-Hughes's statistics about the Irish rate of schizophrenia suggest that the schizoid condition may be particularly characteristic of the Irish psyche, North and South—an opinion that dramatist Brian Friel, who has called both Northern Ireland and Dublin "schizophrenic," appears to share. Furthermore, suggesting that he sees this schizoid split embodied in his work, he speaks of the "projection of some kind of dual personality in a lot of [his] plays," which he thinks reflects an aspect of his self which stems from his membership in the Catholic minority in the divided community of Northern Ireland.

The most obvious example of this "dual personality" is the split character of Public Gar and Private Gar in *Philadelphia, Here I Come!* Gar dramatizes the schizoid state not only through his division into two "selves" but through their interactions with each other and with others, and he repeatedly emphasizes it by asserting that he and everyone else in Ballybeg has been, or will be, driven crazy.

Despite his desire for closeness with others, Public Gar strives for the indifference and withdrawal which characterize the schizoid individual. While he is not clinically hallucinated, his vivid reliving of past experiences, such as his last walk with Kate and his interviews with her father and with his Aunt Lizzie, as well as his ability to hear Private Gar, whom no one else hears, suggest hallucinatory states. Although he does not have delusions of persecution or omnipotence, his fantasies verge on both. Furthermore, Private Gar frequently adopts the role of internalized persecutor often found in schizoid individuals.

T. P. McKenna points out that "the divided mind of Gar epitomize[s] not only his own but a whole community's life."

Gar's community, whose dominant characteristics he embodies, well fits the pattern which Scheper-Hughes says is associated with schizophrenia in Ireland. Ballybeg is in the West and is connected with peripheral agriculture. Gar (like his motherless family and his friends) is male. Everyone, with the possible exception of Kate, is isolated and celibate, and Gar's impending emigration reflects the depopulation endemic to the region.

The schizophrenogenic effect of all of these factors can be traced in *Philadelphia, Here I Come!* (and in many of Friel's other plays). Given that Friel has described the Irish community as a family and that he repeatedly presents these psycho-social problems in the context of a (usually dysfunctional, often motherless) family unit suggests that an analysis of familial/communal interactions may provide clues to the origins of both Gar's schizoid condition and that of his community.

R. D. Laing, the Scots psychiatrist, was one of the first to argue that certain patterns of familial interaction can induce schizoid states. These patterns affect what he calls "experience," which he distinguishes from "behaviour." Experience is the way one perceives and comprehends the world, including one's self. Behaviour is the way one acts as a result of one's experience. Experience, in this sense, conditions and either supports or threatens one's sense of identity which he says, "requires recognition of oneself by others as well as the simple recognition one accords to oneself."

If what Laing calls "significant others"—usually parents, though any members of one's family and/or community who have a strong formative effect on the individual would fit this category—confirm one's experience, they confirm the validity of one's perception of oneself, of others, and of the world; by so doing, they validate one's self-recognized identity. They can, however, "disconfirm" one's experience—and so reject the validity of one's self-recognized identity—by denying that experience. They can also disconfirm it through "collusion"—that is, by validating a false experience in preference to an unacceptable true one, thus doubly denying the reality of the true experience. Through such denial or collusion, one's experience can be "destroyed"; as a result, the two dimensions which make up one's sense of identity are in disagreement, leaving one in doubt as to whose perceptions of reality to trust; one's own or those of the significant others. The result, Laing says, is that the schizoid individual experiences "a rent in his relation with his world and . . . a disruption of his relation with himself."

In *Philadelphia, Here I Come!,* we find precisely such destructions of experience by significant others. Gar perceives, or at least wishes to perceive, himself as a valued member of a family and a community which he loves and which will miss him after he emigrates. He repeatedly seeks validation of this status, but, one by one, others implicitly deny it, often by refusing to acknowledge even that he is leaving; thus, they deny him the confirmation of saying or showing that they will miss him, though it is apparent to the audience that each denial is a result of their fears of acknowledging how much they do love him and will miss him because they fear that Gar will deny their experience of their relationships to him. Everyone is caught in a schizophrenogenic "double-bind" situation.

Gar's father, S. B., apparently ignores Gar's impending departure, insisting that everything is "as usual. Not a thing happening." Gar seeks confirmation from his friends, but they, too, resolutely avoid the subject of his leaving, and the confirmation implied by their unexpected visit is apparently invalidated by Joe's revelation that Madge asked them to call.

Master Boyle's farewell visit seems to offer confirmation, not only of Gar's status in the community, but also of his desired role as a beloved "son"; Gar's dead mother, Maire, was courted by Boyle before she married S. B., and Gar imagines Boyle loving him as the son he never had by the woman he loved and lost. But the schoolmaster apparently denies kinship with Gar by stressing Gar's merely average intelligence and lack of poetic taste. He ends his visit by asking for a loan, leaving Gar convinced that Boyle views him as a soft touch rather than as a lost son.

Madge, the housekeeper, denies Gar's experience of himself as *her* surrogate son. Like S. B., she feigns indifference to his departure: "The clock'll be set," she says, "If you hear it well and good." When he urges her to visit her niece, she goes, implicitly rejecting him by confirming his fear that it is her niece's children whom she regards as her surrogate children, not him. Further, she denies Gar's desire to see himself as *someone's* loved son, the product of a loving relationship. When he asks whether Boyle became an alcoholic out of disappointment at losing Maire as his wife (and hence Gar as his son), she evades the question. Though she asserts that Maire married the better man, thus implying that the seemingly uncaring S. B. is the more appropriate father for Gar, she denies that Gar is the product of a love match or, implicitly, that Maire would have truly loved her son had she lived; Maire's love, Madge suggests, was indiscriminate and valueless: "she went with a dozen—that was the kind of her—she couldn't help herself."

Even Kate's farewell visit, which would appear to validate Gar's desired experience by confirming that someone whom he loves will miss him, actually denies that experience through collusion. Her urging Gar to present a false self to her father when they were courting, by telling him to tell the Senator that he has money saved and a good income, has convinced him that his true self is unacceptable to her—an experience confirmed by her father's praise of the socially-prominent doctor, Francis King, as a prospective son-in-law and by Kate's marriage to King after Gar, intimidated, fails to ask for her hand. Hoping to impress Kate with what she's lost by losing him, Public Gar spins boastful fantasies of how well he expects to do in America; when Kate agrees with his fantasies, she colludes with his false self to deny the worth and lovableness of his true self, thus denying his last hope that she might have loved him for himself rather than for the fantasy self he is trying to project.

The most damaging and explicit denial of Gar's experience, however, occurs when he finally works up the courage to ask his father to confirm his memory of an event which he has cherished for fifteen years as proof that S. B., though unable to say so, truly loves him: the day they went fishing in the blue boat. S. B., he remembers, symbolically expressed his love by putting his hat and jacket on Gar to protect him from the rain. "Between us," Private Gar says, ". . . there was this great happiness, this great joy—you must have felt it too—although nothing was being said—just the two of us . . . and then, then for no reason at all except that you were happy too, you began to sing: . . . All round my hat I'll wear a green coloured ribbono"—a song of love for one who "is far, far away," as Gar will be on the morrow. But, when Public Gar finally asks S. B. to confirm this memory, his father denies the existence of the blue boat and insists that he has never heard, much less sung, that song. Private Gar's bitter reaction vividly illustrates the destruction of his experience: "So now you know: it never happened!"

Gar's experience, however, is not the only one denied. Denial of experience is so ingrained a pattern of behaviour in his community that the majority of the characters habitually deny the experiences of others, as well as denying their own experiences to forestall others from doing so, behaviour which fits Laing's argument that "If our experience is destroyed, our behaviour will be destructive." Aunt Lizzie contradicts her husband's memories and denies their American benefactor's religious identity as an Episcopalian because it reinforces the identity she left Ireland to escape—that of a member of the socially—and economically—inferior Catholic community. Boyle rejects the possibility of kinship with Gar even as he asks for it. Madge denies her yearning for surrogate motherhood by feigning indifference both to Gar's departure and to her niece's failure to name the new baby after her. Kate and "the Boys" collude to validate false experiences in order to avoid acknowledging the true ones which they fear will be denied. And S. B. is afraid to ask Gar to validate his memory of shared love, not only with Gar as his son but with Gar as the product of a love match with the dead Maire, from whom Gar takes his middle name. Instead, S. B. turns to Madge, asking her if she remembers the day that Gar, dressed in his sailor suit, walked with him, "hand in hand," the two of them "as happy as larks"—but

Madge denies that Gar ever had a sailor suit, just as S. B. denied that there ever was a blue boat.

As a result, all display schizoid characteristics. Aunt Lizzie calls herself Elise and claims that Lizzie is dead. Kate and "the Boys" present "false" selves. Madge, S. B., and Gar feign indifference and withdraw. Gar's ambivalence is so marked that twice Private Gar recoils in terror from the love and offered kinship he so deeply desires: once when Boyle embraces him and once when Lizzie calls him "my son." That this deep, self-destructive division within the self and against the self is a familial (in both the nuclear and communal senses) characteristic is emphasized by Madge, who says of Gar and S. B.: "When the boss was [Gar's] age, he was the very same as him. . . . And when [Gar is] the age the boss is now, he'll turn out just the same. . . . That's people for you—they'd put you astray in the head if you thought long enough about them."

The Freedom of the City, an overtly political play, would seem a departure from the familial context characteristic of most of Friel's plays unless one remembers Friel's definition of the community as a family. Then it becomes apparent that Northern Ireland is, in fact, a metaphorical family whose composition echoes the British imperialist analogy of the Union between Britain and Ireland as a marriage between John Bull and Hibernia—two of the significant others whose destruction of the experience of their last children still living at home, the Northern Irish, results in extremely (self-)destructive behaviour. As such, it clearly fits Laing's contention that manipulating the experience of others is political behaviour, a violent exercise of "the power to define reality" commonly carried out to preserve the power structure within the family.

As in ***Philadelphia, Here I Come!,*** Friel dramatizes another schizoid condition which appears to be created by the destruction of experience; he splits Michael, Lily, and Skinner into two "selves" each: their live selves and their dead selves. Alive and subject to significant others' disconfirmation of their experiences, they are, to varying degrees, unable either to articulate completely or to validate their own experiences, and they behave destructively, denying each other's experiences. Only their dead selves can fully affirm and articulate the meanings of their lives.

In denying their own and each other's experiences, the three living protagonists internalize and replicate the destruction inflicted on them by their society's significant others: the British government, the republican nationalists, the Church, the middle-class academic establishment, and the Southern Irish. Each significant other defines the experiences of Michael, Lily, and Skinner in terms which, denying their realities, validate its own version of reality in order to consolidate its power. The British government defines them as dangerous terrorists, the republican nationalists as rebel heroes. The Church first defines them as martyrs for Catholic rights; then, fearing that some might construe those rights to include rights for the poor, which would jeopardize its capitalist power-base, it redefines them as unfortunate victims of "Godless communism."

Even Dodds, the American sociologist, rejects their experience by depersonalizing and de-nationalizing them to enhance the "objective" authority of middle-class academia. By portraying them as nameless representatives of the world's poor, he denies the effect of British imperialism on their reality. He justifies the destruction of their experience by attributing to them the compensation of having "a hell of a lot more fun than [the middle class] have," just as racists long justified discrimination against Blacks (yet another colonized people) by portraying them as happy, watermelon-eating, banjo-playing piccaninnies whose simple *joie-de-vivre* would be destroyed by equal opportunity. Finally, he denies the validity of the identity which their dead selves achieve by asserting that once "they acquire an objective view of their condition," they are no longer legitimate members of their "subculture" (III).

The RTE announcer endorses the British government's description of them as terrorists and uses their funeral to celebrate the ascendancy of the alliance between Southern Irish politicians and the Church. His misnaming Skinner "Fitzmaurice" rather than "Fitzgerald" and dropping his middle name, Casimir, has multiple functions. It denies Skinner's identity, but it also repudiates kinship between the dominantly Catholic Southern Irish state and the Northern Irish Catholic minority. Casimir was the name of Countess Markievicz's husband, who, like his revolutionary wife, supported pre-independence Irish nationalism, though (appropriately, given Skinner's level of political awareness) in a more dilettantish fashion, and who fought for Polish freedom during the First World War; dropping "Casimir" from Skinner's name denies him association with the Irish nationalist movement which established Éire and with other national liberation movements. Changing "Fitzgerald" to "Fitzmaurice" rejects any possible relationship between Skinner and Garret Fitzgerald, the leader of Fine Gael, historically Éire's pro-Treaty (and therefore pro-Partition) party. As Éire's official spokesman, the RTE announcer's deliberate distancing of himself from the three protagonists implies that, like many of Friel's other families, the Northern Irish "family" is motherless; Hibernia, having left the marriage, has, at best, abandoned her Northern Irish children to the untender mercies of John Bull.

On another level, the three central characters are three aspects of the same schizoid self, the Northern Irish community divided against itself, with Michael as the will, Lily as the body, and Skinner as the intellect. Skinner, the one most aware of the discrepancies between his experience and the false experience imposed on him, the one most alienated and, apparently, paranoid, is, significantly, the one whom Michael calls bad, and Lily, mad. But it is Skinner who confirms the experiences of the other two, preparing them and himself for the self-realization, self-validation, and final unity which their "family" will allow them only in death. He does this by refusing to collude with Michael, the false self who has most thoroughly internalized the authorities' disconfirmation of his experience and who most adamantly denies the experiences of the others, and by confirming Lily's self-denied experiences, including helping her to reject her husband's denigration of her experience as the false perception of a "bone stupid bitch," as well as his denial of her worth and that of their retarded son.

By inducing Michael to entertain the possibility that his paranoia is really metanoia, Skinner prepares him to question and reject the false experience that has been imposed on him. By confirming Lily's experience and articulating it for her, he prepares her to understand that her experience, unassessed and unarticulated, has not been validated. By taking her experience seriously, he prepares himself to dare for the first time to take his own experience seriously and validate it.

The three finally realize that, given their metaphorical "parents'" destructive behaviour, they are better off as self-validating "orphans." However, to become such "orphans" in life would require them to unite and kill their "parents" because their significant others would, and ultimately do, kill them rather than allow them to leave the "family." In *The Freedom of the City,* the "family" is not merely dysfunctional, schizoid, and schizophrenogenic—it is murderously/suicidally schizophrenic.

Having extended his examination of the schizophrenogenic effects of the destruction of experience from the post-colonial nuclear and communal "family" in *Philadelphia, Here I Come!* to the colonized national "family" in *The Freedom of the City,* in *Translations* Friel moves his examination backwards in time to the colonized communal "family" of nineteenth-century Ireland from which both the post-colonial South and the still-colonized North derive. By focusing on the schizophrenogenic effects of the destruction of the Irish language and the experience which it embodies, he elaborates Lily's perception that unarticulated experience cannot be validated. Destroying the linguistic tools with which one organizes and expresses experience destroys the experience itself.

As in *The Freedom of the City,* there is no doubt that the authorities' manipulation of experience through the manipulation of language is a politically motivated exercise of the power to define reality. Names equal identity, and the act of naming (or renaming) confers possession of and control over the person or object thus identified. Therefore renaming is a military action whose purpose, like that of previous British renamings of Ireland, is to effect what Lancey admits is the "forfeiture and violent transfer of property," including the most important "property" of all—the identity and experience of the colonized.

The process is first exemplified by the British renaming of Owen. The name which they attribute to him, "Roland," denies his experience, and therefore his identity, as "Owen Hugh Mor. From Baile Beag," an Irish locus of experience. A conflation of his own name with Yolland's, it not only denies him an individual identity, but renders his a subsidiary, derivative identity dependent for meaning, and even existence, on his British masters. Though he eventually comes to realize that Owen and Roland are not "the same me," his recognition comes too late to save his experience or that of his communal "family."

As the play proceeds, Owen colludes with the British to establish similar bastardized false identities for local place names, thus transferring control and possession of both the physical and psychological environment to the colonizers—a process which he vindicates by denying the local inhabitants' experience. They do not know, he asserts, why Tobair Vree is called Tobair Vree, nor does the name embody a valid experience because there is no longer a well (Ir. *tobair*) there. Because the experience embodied in the name is invalid, it is justifiable to redefine it by renaming it.

The schizophrenogenic result of renaming is most effectively exemplified by Owen's use of it to deny explicitly his father's experience. The priest does not, as Hugh thinks, live "at Lis na Muc" because, Owen asserts, "Lis na Muc, the Fort of the Pigs, has become Swinefort. . . . And to get to Swinefort you pass through Greencastle and Fair Head and Strandhill and Gort and Whiteplains. And the new school isn't at Poll na gCaorach—it's at Sheepsrock." His father, he insists, does not know the places because he does not know their names. Hugh apparently refuses to "hear" what Owen has said, but his oblique response suggests his recognition of the destruction of his experience through the destruction of his linguistic control over it. Irish, he replies (ostensibly speaking to Yolland), is a language "full of the mythologies of fantasy and hope and self-deception"—that is, it is the language of the schizoid condition.

That this renaming is destructive of the entire community's experience is later concretized by Lancey and Owen's litany of townlands to be levelled. As Lancey reads the Anglicized names, echoed by Owen's translation, each Irish place-name is obliterated, presaging the literal obliteration of the places themselves. Owen's enforced cooperation in this destruction, like the Donnelly twins' murder of Yolland, fits Laing's contention that destroyed experience results in destructive

behaviour, while the retributive levelling of the town-lands fits his argument that the use of power to define reality is, in fact, a violent, destructive, political act.

However, the psychological effects of non-military imperialism will, in the long run, more efficiently destroy the native Irish experience than the military destruction which is a metaphor for it. The inroads of cultural and economic imperialism, manifested by Maire's desire to learn English so that she can emigrate to America to escape Baile Beag's poverty, begin even before the cartographic expedition reaches the village and have already begun to divide the Irish community against itself, as O'Connell's collusion with the British to validate English over Irish demonstrates. The establishment of the national school, in which only English will be spoken, will complete the process of denying the Irish experience; every morning there, the students will sing a song thanking God that they are happy little *English* boys.

None the less, Friel is not politically or psychologically naive enough to subscribe to "Maud Gonne's catechism"—the nationalist formulation that the origin of all evil is England. That his early nineteenth-century Baile Beag, like its modern descendant, Gar's Ballybeg, is a schizoid community is not due solely to the effects of British imperialism. The motherless nuclear family which embodies the schizoid communal family is headed by an alcoholic father who retreats into fantasies of omnipotence to compensate for his inability to cope with reality and who requires his symbolically crippled son, Manus, to assume both paternal and maternal roles in order to keep the young man from leaving home. This western community, like the schizophrenogenic ones Scheper-Hughes describes, is already characterized by peripheral agriculture, depopulation, isolation, and celibacy; the males are either unmarried or widowed, while most of the eligible females are either emigrating, like Maire, or reduced to mute impotence, like Sarah.

The foremost exemplar of the schizophrenogenic destruction of the community's experience is the obviously schizophrenic Jimmy Jack. Though his condition, and that of Hugh, results at least partly from the defeat of Irish nationalist hopes in the crushing of the 1798 Rebellion, they carried another source and symptom of the destruction of their experience into battle with them then: the *Aeneid*. Even in 1798, both lived in a fantasy world; in Glenties, Hugh says, they "got homesick for Athens, just like Ulysses" and since their return, both have retreated further into their imagined Athens, compensating for their defeat by reliving the glories of dead civilizations. Just as the British deny the Irish experience of the present generation, their immersion in Classical Greek and Roman experience have denied and continued to deny, devalue, and destroy Hugh and Jimmy Jack's experience, and Hugh has perpetuated that denial by teaching his students Latin and Greek but not Irish. Hugh is a poet, not in Irish but in Latin. Jimmy Jack knows of Grania, but his schizophrenic hallucinatory fantasies are of Athene—and, though they mock him for them, all the others collude with him to validate those fantasies. Hugh's insistence on the superiority of Classical language and culture has already denied the validity of Irish experience, thus preparing the ground for the triumph of British cultural imperialism.

As a result of generations of denied experience, all of Ireland is, in the early-nineteenth as in the later-twentieth century, a divided, self-destructive "family" which, like the Carthage to which Hugh's last speech compares it, destroys its own children. Just as Aeneas's Roman descendants destroyed Carthage, his British "descendants" are destroying Ireland, and the Irish, overwhelmed by these significant others, are colluding with them in the denial and destruction of their own reality. "To remember everything," as Hugh says, "is a form of madness." Part of Ireland's problem is that, like Jimmy Jack, she can no longer discriminate between "the literal past . . . [and the] images of the past embodied in language," and she has failed to renew those images. Worse, however, she has accepted false images in which to "fossilize" herself. The result is the destructive and self-destructive "petrification" or "depersonalization" which Laing says that the schizoid fears from and perpetrates on others

and which Friel presents as resulting in the schizoid "privacies" which are now, as Hugh says, "all we have."

FURTHER READING

Criticism

Cullingford, Elizabeth. "British Romans and Irish Carthaginians: Anticolonial Metaphor in Heaney, Friel, and McGuiness." *Publications of the Modern Language Association of America* 111, No. 2 (March 1996): 222-239.
> Elaborates the "imaginative Irish resistance" to British colonialism found in the work of Friel and two prominent contemporaries.

Grene, Nicholas. "In a Dark Time." *Irish Literary Supplement* (Spring 1995): 25.
> A review of *Molly Sweeney* that compares the play to John Millington Synge's *The Well of the Saints.*

Peacock, Alan J., ed. *The Achievement of Brian Friel.* Gerrards Cross: Colin Smythe, 1993, 261 p.
> A book of essays covering several of Friel's works from varied perspectives.

Garrison Keillor
1942-

(Born Gary Edward Keillor) American novelist, essayist, scriptwriter, and short story writer.

The following entry presents an overview of Keillor's career through 1995. For more information on his life and works, see *CLC*, Volume 40.

INTRODUCTION

Garrison Keillor is best known for his creation of the fictional Minnesota town of Lake Wobegon, and for the trademark opening statement of his radio show, "It's been a quiet week in Lake Wobegon, my hometown." His stories from Lake Wobegon appeared on his syndicated radio show "A Prairie Home Companion" and in two collections of short stories. Keillor's down home humor and gentle satire have endeared him to listeners across America. His radio show evokes the feeling of family-oriented programs that were popular during the 1930s and 1940s, and his written work retains the qualities of oral storytelling found in his monologues.

Biographical Information

Keillor was born in Anoka, Minnesota, in 1942. After attending high school in his hometown, Keillor left to attend the University of Minnesota. In 1969 he began writing for *The New Yorker,* a publication he had always admired. In 1974 he was sent to cover a story about the Grand Ole Opry, and it inspired him to create a live variety show for radio. The result was Keillor's "A Prairie Home Companion," which ran from April 1974 to June 1987. The program steadily gained popularity and became nationally syndicated in 1980, making Keillor a celebrity. Keillor wrote his first book, *Lake Wobegon Days* (1985), a collection of short stories based on the monologues from his radio show. Keillor ceased production of the show in 1987 and moved with his wife to Copenhagen, Denmark, where they lived a short time before returning to America and settling in New York. Keillor once again worked for *The New Yorker* and continued to write stories about Lake Wobegon in *Leaving Home* (1987). He also published additional collections of short stories, essays, and a novel. After a change of editors, Keillor left *The New Yorker,* but continues to contribute pieces to *The New York Times* and *The Atlantic Monthly.* In 1990 Keillor resurrected his radio program as "American Radio Company," and in 1993 he changed the name back to "A Prairie Home Companion." In addition, Keillor hosts a poetry program, "The Writer's Almanac."

Major Works

Much of Keillor's written work derives from his radio show, "A Prairie Home Companion." The premise of the show, originally done for Minnesota Public Radio, is based on Keillor's fictional hometown of Lake Wobegon, Minnesota. The format of the show featured Keillor sharing news from the town interspersed with an eclectic variety of music. The stories are obtained from the town's fictional residents with whom Keillor ostensibly remains in touch. The show's authenticity extends to fictional sponsors from Lake Wobegon businesses such as the Chatterbox Cafe, Ralph's Grocery, and Bunsen Motors. The residents of Lake Wobegon resist change and technology and live a simple life. Keillor's narratives of town life are often rambling, unformed, and full of sensory detail, and he creates his imaginary world by adding layer upon layer of convincing detail. He typically uses a first-person central narrative voice. Keillor's descriptions of the town include a great deal of negativity, but he always reaffirms the town's values. The stories in both *Lake Wobegon Days* and *Leaving Home* are based on the monologues from the radio show. Keillor has attempted to extend his talent beyond the sphere of Lake Wobegon. His short-story collection *We Are Still Married* (1989) contains celebrations of life, love, and simple pleasures. His first novel, *WLT: A Radio Romance* (1991) is written in the form of radio segments and tells the story of life behind the scenes at a radio station. Keillor's *The Book of Guys* (1993) is a collection of stories about middle-class, middle-aged men struggling to survive in the contemporary world. The stories are filled with quips about domesticity, demanding women, and bodily functions.

Critical Reception

Reviewers often focus on the oral quality of Keillor's work, from his radio monologues to his written fiction. Michael Kline states that, "One of Keillor's greatest skills as a narrator is to use both oral and literate discourse features in complement, a practice which supports the view that there is no absolute dichotomy between written and spoken forms of language." Critics also note the folksy, down-home nature of his themes, which tend to celebrate and uphold the values of small-town America. However, some critics complain that Keillor represents an overly sentimental and nostalgic view of small-town life. Reviewers often compare Keillor to Mark Twain, Will Rogers, and James Thurber. Many discuss Keillor's use of humor, including his ability to laugh at himself. Philip Greasley states, "Aside from the interest factor, Keillor's humor functions regularly as a leavening, softening agent, easing the harshness of criticism and heightening audience acceptance of his social commentary." *WLT: A Radio Romance,* Keillor's his first novel, did not receive the approval that his shorter works garnered. Reviewers conclude that the structure of the book, based on radio segments, is too limiting to the create a full story. Elizabeth Beverly says, "[Keillor] is learning to work in a medium which, in this case, has resisted him."

PRINCIPAL WORKS

G. K. the D. J. (short stories) 1977
The Selected Verse of Margaret Haskins Durber (poetry) 1979
A Prairie Home Companion Anniversary Album (recording) 1980
The Family Radio (recording) 1982
Happy to Be Here (short stories) 1982
News from Lake Wobegon (recording) 1982
Prairie Home Companion Tourists (recording) 1983
Ten Years on the Prairie: A Prairie Home Companion 10th Anniversary (recording) 1984
Gospel Birds and Other Stories of Lake Wobegon (recording) 1985
Lake Wobegon Days (novel) 1985

A Prairie Home Companion: The Final Performance (recording) 1987
Leaving Home (short stories) 1987
We Are Still Married (short stories and letters) 1989
WLT: A Radio Romance (novel) 1991
The Book of Guys (short stories) 1993
Cat, You Better Come Home (children's literature) 1995
The Old Man Who Loved Cheese (children's literature) 1996
The Sandy Bottom Orchestra [with Jenny Lind Nilsson] (children's literature) 1997

CRITICISM

John E. Miller (essay date Fall 1987)

SOURCE: "The Distance Between Gopher Prairie and Lake Wobegon: Sinclair Lewis and Garrison Keillor on the Small Town Experience," in *Centenniel Review,* Vol. 31, Fall, 1987, pp. 432-46.

[*In the following essay, Miller compares and contrasts Keillor's and Sinclair Lewis's portrayal of small-town life.*]

When Garrison Keillor took stories and characters which he's been developing for a decade on his radio program, **"Prairie Home Companion,"** and expanded and reworked them into a book, the resulting ***Lake Wobegon Days*** quickly shot up to the top of the best seller lists and earned the tall (6'4"), lanky Minnesota humorist cover stories in such publications as *Time, Saturday Evening Post,* and *The New York Times Book Review.* Like another tall, skinny writer who came from a town just up the road a ways, Keillor has become an unmistakable presence on the American scene. At age thirty-five, Sinclair Lewis was eight years younger than Keillor when he burst on the literary scene in 1920 with *Main Street,* a novel that, more than any other literary work of its time, redefined the way in which Americans thought about their small towns. "*Main Street* broke into the literary atmosphere like an explosion, like something absolutely new and absolutely devastating, not only unlike anything Sinclair Lewis had done before but unlike anything that anyone had done before," according to Mark Schorer, one of his biographers.

Main Street launched a series of novels that were intended to provide a panoramic view of American society. Having been honed during his journalistic apprenticeship, Lewis's forte was a remarkable capacity for detailed observation and description. Joseph Wood Krutch admiringly observed in Lewis's novels "a completeness of documentation not less than amazing" and "a power of mimicry which, so far as I know, no living author can equal." Lewis resisted such appraisals, saying of himself: "He has only one illusion: that he is not a journalist and 'photographic realist' but a stylist whose chief concerns in writing are warmth and lucidity." But most critics agreed that his genius lay in limning the surface realities of life, not in probing character or in developing plot. It was the "amazing skill with which he reproduces his world" that impressed T. K. Whipple, who viewed the novels as "triumphant feats of memory and observation."

The memory of his home town—Sauk Centre, Minnesota—provided the basis for the writing of *Main Street,* but he drew on his observations of other towns as well, places like Melrose, Faribault, St. Cloud, Mankato, Rochester, and Fergus Falls. "It is extraordinary how deep is the impression made by the place of one's birth and rearing, and how lasting are its memories," Lewis wrote in "The Long Arm of the Small Town," an essay for the Sauk Centre high school yearbook in 1931. After being absent for more than a quarter of a century, except for a few visits lasting only several months' time, the town remained, he said, "as vivid to my mind as though I had left there yesterday."

Lewis called upon his marvelous powers of observation and memory to create perhaps the most celebrated fictional walk in American literature—Carol Kennicott's thirty-two minute stroll around Gopher Prairie's main business thoroughfare, which in the words of Lewis's preface, was "the continuation of Main Streets everywhere." On her walk through town, she saw places like the Minniemashie House, a "tall lean shabby structure" catering to traders and traveling salesmen"; Dyer's Drug Store, with its "greasy marble soda-fountain with an electric lamp of red and green and curdled-yellow mosaic shade"; the Rosebud Movie Palace, showing a film called "Fatty in Love"; Howland and Gould's Grocery, with Knights of Pythias, Macabees, Woodmen, and Masonic lodges in second floor rooms; Dahl and Oleson's Meat Market; a jewelry shop with "tinny looking" wrist watches; several saloons; a tobacco shop; a clothing store, its dummies like "corpses with painted cheeks"; The Bon Ton Store; Axel Egge's General Store; Sam Clark's Hardware Store; Chester Dashaway's House Furnishing Emporium; Billy's Lunch; a dairy; a produce warehouse; Ford and Buick garages; an agricultural implement dealer; a feed store; Ye Art Shoppe; a barber shop and pool room; Nat Hicks's Tailor Shop, on a side street off Main Street; the post office; the State Bank; the Farmers' National Bank; and a score of similar stores and businesses.

To Carol, they were drab, ugly, uninviting. But it wasn't the overwhelming ugliness that distressed her so much as "the planlessness, the flimsy temporariness of the buildings, their faded unpleasant colors." Only one building held any aesthetic appeal for Carol—the Ionic-styled Farmers' National Bank. Lewis's picture is almost unrelievedly squalid: storage tanks are "grim," train depots are "squat," lawns are

"parched," leaves are "sickly yellow," bay windows are "lugubrious," cars sound like they're "shaking to pieces," smells are "sour." Carol's impulse was to flee back to the security of the city. No wonder: "Oozing out from every drab wall, she felt a forbidding spirit which she could never conquer."

Measured in terms of physical distance, Garrison Keillor's Lake Wobegon can't be far from Gopher Prairie, but in terms of time and imagination it lies at great remove. Keillor provides plenty of clues about Lake Wobegon's location, indicating it is near St. Cloud, northwest of St. Cloud, and, more specifically, thirty-two miles from St. Cloud. That would put it almost exactly at Freeport, the town Keillor lived in when he started inventing stories about Lake Wobegon as a radio announcer for Minnesota Public Radio during the early 1970's. It could hardly be closer to Sauk Centre, which is just ten miles up Highway 52 from Freeport.

Lewis's strikingly detailed visual images capture one kind of reality; Keillor's carefully wrought word images evince another. The former's strength lies in visual description, photographic in its effect; Keillor's is aural, finely tuned to subtle tones and gestures. Lewis was not deaf to the sounds of the town. If Carol Kennicott's thirty-two minute walk is described almost entirely through visual images, the simultaneous tour of Bea Sorenson, a country girl come to town to work as a maid, climaxes with her bewilderment at all the noises around her: "The roar of the city began to frighten her. There were five automobuls [sic] on the street all at the same time—and one of 'em was a great big car that must of cost two thousand dollars—and the 'bus was starting for a train with five elegant-dressed fellows." Later in the book Lewis catalogs a series of sounds that impress upon Carol the tediousness of the street in front of her house, rendering it "a street beyond the end of the world, beyond the boundaries of hope." Now, at dusk, it was "meshed in silence. There was but the hum of motor tires crunching the road, the creak of a rocker on the Howlands' porch, the slap of a hand attacking a mosquito, a heat-weary conversation starting and dying, the precise rhythm of crickets, the thud of moths against the screen—sounds that were a distilled silence."

Like Lewis, Keillor catalogs the sounds heard in his town—the hum of an air conditioner on a sweltering August evening, the "memorable sound" of a rotten tomato splatting on the projecting rear of his older sister, the distant faint mutter of ancient combines operated by Norwegian bachelor farmers. Keillor's superior sensibility comes through in a passage describing his impressions of a cold snowy evening when he was sixteen: "So still on a cold night. I could hear his boots crunch in the snow, could hear a car not quite starting a long way away, and then the door slamming when the guy got out and him hitting the hood with his fist. The volume of the world was turned up so the air molecules hummed a deep bass note. If the fire siren went off it would knock a person into the middle of next week." Keillor excels not so much in straight description as in the evocation of mood. Usually he's describing people feeling or meditating or experiencing and not simply acting.

> **The authorial presence constantly weaves in and out of *Lake Wobegon Days* as Keillor varies stories about himself with those about other people in town. While Lewis kept his readers guessing about whether Carol Kennicott's view of the town was his own, Keillor begins with a straightforward description of his town as he knows it.**
> **—*John E. Miller***

The authorial presence constantly weaves in and out of *Lake Wobegon Days* as Keillor varies stories about himself with those about other people in town. While Lewis kept his readers guessing about whether Carol Kennicott's view of the town was his own, Keillor begins with a straightforward description of his town as he knows it. Now, approximately seventy years after Carol first viewed Main Street, Keillor guides us on a tour of a town about one-third the size of Gopher Prairie. Lewis calls his a "wheat-prairie town of something over three thousand people" while Keillor says his town contains "the homes of some nine hundred souls, most of them small white frame houses." It is significant that he refers to "souls," a term that the antireligious Lewis would have used only ironically or satirically. For Keillor, a backslidden member of the fundamentalist Plymouth Brethren who still values much in that heritage, "soul" carries a heavy burden of meaning.

Viewing people as more than mechanical toys, Keillor also perceives the structures they live in not simply as houses but as homes. Even granting that seven decades have wrought a revolutionary transformation in American material life, the contrasting visions of Lewis and Keillor are necessary to explain why the former (through his protagonist, Carol Kennicott) sees "huddled low wooden" houses on the plains, "prosaic frame" houses with "small parched" lawns, and "square smug brown" houses, "rather damp," while the latter observes "small white frame houses sitting forward on their lots and boasting large tidy vegetable gardens and modest lawns, many featuring cast-iron deer, small windmills, clothespoles and clotheslines, various plaster animals such as squirrels and lambs and small elephants, white painted rocks at the end of the driveway, a nice bed of petunias planted within a white tire, and some with a shrine in the rock garden, the Blessed Virgin standing, demure, her eyes averted, arms slightly extended, above the peonies and mari-

golds." Imagine what Lewis would have done with that statue and those elephants!

There isn't as much to see in Lake Wobegon as in Gopher Prairie. In his initial tour of the town, Keillor mentions only several business places—Ralph's Grocery, Bunsen Motors, and the Chatterbox Cafe. Interestingly, as we are taken from place to place it is with a child kicking an asphalt chunk down the street, and we are introduced to other people—the mayor, Clint Bunsen, peering out from a grease pit; his brother Clarence, wiping the showroom window; an old man sitting on Ralph's bench; and Ralph, leaning out of the back of the store to get a breath of fresh, meatless air.

The picture Keillor paints is much brighter and cheerier, while less distinct, than Lewis's, though it does not lack shades of gray and black. If Lewis is a master of shape and form, Keillor excels with color. Perhaps what distinguishes his portrait most from his predecessor's is its unpredictability. Lewis, who admitted that his own views were wrapped up in the persona of Carol Kennicott, also put much of himself into the disillusioned lawyer, Guy Pollock, who, at one stage of the novel's development, was going to be its major character. Their criticisms of the town were balanced by the positive viewpoints expressed by Will Kennicott, Bea Sorenson, and others. But if Lewis did create characters who represent opposing points of view about the town, their thoughts and actions are generally predictable. Carol's thought after first glimpsing Gopher Prairie is indicative of a lack of imagination: "The people—they'd be as drab as their houses, as flat as their fields."

Keillor, unlike Lewis, is willing to let his characters surprise him. Not that he is unaware of constraints operating on people's behavior, placed there by inheritance, conditioning, and habit. These are not wild, soaring, free spirits he is talking about but real human beings whose dreams and aspirations run head on into other people's desires and expectations, their own limitations, and the social bounds imposed by institutions and organizations. Still, one does not know what to expect from week to week from Pastor Ingqvist or Senator K. Thorvaldson or Johnny Tollefson. All have firmly rooted characters and habits; yet all are capable of surprise. Father Emil, for instance, may be a staunchly conservative priest dedicated to protecting his flock from the dangers of modernism, but who would predict his passion for bus tours of Civil War battlefields?

Keillor's ability to get inside of his characters is no trivial accomplishment. It betokens both a talent for listening and a faculty for imagining. Lewis's work suffers from deficiency of creative imagination; D. J. Dooley summarized the indictment by observing that "everything is lifelike, but nothing is real, especially the people." H. L. Mencken, who considered *Main Street* to be "good stuff," felt that the characters "often remain flat; . . . one seldom sees into them very deeply or feels with them very keenly."

Lewis, the Midwestern kid who went to Yale and spent most of his life gallavanting around the globe, viewed his own town through the lenses of the outsider and found it wanting. Keillor, the small town kid who went down the road to the University of Minnesota and returned home after failing to land a journalism job out East, remains more rooted. He looks at his home town and finds it wanting also, in some respects, but for him the defects lie in the human heart, not in some imagined "village virus" that condemns all small towns to narrow, twisted existences.

Lewis, in fact, undercuts much of the force of his indictment when, toward the end of *Main Street,* he has Carol ask herself why she rages at individuals so. Not individuals, but institutions, are the enemy: "They insinuate their tyranny under a hundred guises and pompous names, such as Polite Society, the Family, the Church, Sound Business, the Party, the Country, the Superior White Race; and the only defense against them, Carol beheld, is unembittered laughter." Such a sociological analysis can be defended, but by shifting the target from individuals to institutions, it undermines the force of the satire that has gone before.

Keillor grants no such pardon to Wobegonians. He holds them accountable for their actions. His view of human motivation is more complex than that of Lewis, whose inclination is to caricature people, which makes for good satire but not for empathic understanding. Keillor, at the age of forty-three, possesses a more mature acceptance of human foibles and inconsistencies than Lewis did when he published *Main Street* at the age of thirty-five.

Lewis's interests and thinking were wide-ranging, but just as he never found a place to settle down, he never seemed to find an intellectual resting place, flitting from a shallow socialism during his college days to the bourgeois satisfactions of job and family to a general cynical outlook that found many targets for satire but few, if any, objects to admire and identify with. To T. K. Whipple, Lewis possessed a multiple personality, being one who "shifts his point of view so often that finally we come to wonder whether he has any."

Garrison Keillor went east once too, looking for a writing job after college, but when none was forthcoming, he returned to live near the place where he grew up and has remained in the area ever since. Unlike Lewis, who was curiously unaware of himself, Keillor enters into his subject, sometimes in his own persona, sometimes partly hidden in the characters he invents. Being part of the story, he naturally experiences the same hurts and satisfactions, dilemmas and accommodations that his characters do. Therefore, he does not convert his characters into objects of scorn or satire in the way Lewis often did.

It is amazing in how many ways the two authors' lives overlap. Like Lewis, whose adoption of radical opinions at Yale gave his classmates a second reason to call him "Red," Keillor, if we believe *Lake Wobegon Days,* consciously redesigned himself in college. He, too, contested with a father "of the old regime." He, too, felt the sting of being ungainly and different as a kid growing up. If Lewis was laughed at as an amiable freak, friendless and isolated, stricken by an acne-ridden visage that, according to his second wife, would come to look like the "face of a man who had walked through flame throwers," Keillor, too, according to his book, felt rejected on the sandlots of youth, the "skinny kid with the glasses and the black shoes" who usually was chosen toward the end for pickup baseball games. Like Lewis, and probably like most of us who went through childhood, he wished he could be popular. Like Lewis, he had a rich fantasy life and is sometimes prone to delusions of grandeur, having crowned himself at the age of twelve "King of Altrusia," though at the age of fourteen his playmates sort of faltered in maintaining their play-act adoration. Now on his radio program, Keillor can at least in part fulfill his fantasy of being a singing star like Elvis Presley or George Beverly Shea. If Keillor still harbors over-inflated expectations of greatness, he is the first to prick the bubble, unlike Lewis, who lacked the ability to laugh at himself and others in the way that Keillor does.

If Keillor still harbors over-inflated expectations of greatness, he is the first to prick the bubble, unlike Lewis, who lacked the ability to laugh at himself and others in the way that Keillor does.
—*John E. Miller*

Lewis's childhood miseries derived to a large extent from his failure to live up to expectations of his respectable doctor father and to compete successfully with his older brother Claude, who also became a doctor. Keillor's frustrations obtained more from living in a family that was judged to be different—one that would get up and walk out of a restaurant whose prices exceeded expectations. "This is humiliating," Keillor has himself saying after one such episode, "I feel like a leper or something. Why do we always have to make such a big production out of everything? Why can't we be like regular people?" Unwilling to carry a bookbag festooned with a Biblical verse to school, young Gary was afraid he'd be "laughed off the face of the earth." At the same age, Lewis had no friends and no interest in sports, and, according to John Koblas, was always an outsider. Sensitivities heightened by their positions on the fringes, both authors were able to perceive things about their towns that other residents either overlooked or took for granted.

Lewis compensated for his insecurities by diverting his animosities against society and other people. Keillor, on the other hand, makes light of his shyness by laughing at it and continually reminding people of it on his radio program. He refuses to extract himself from his condition. Whatever pain Wobegonians suffer, whatever crimes they commit, he is implicated in them. His characters are his constellation of neighbors; they also embody his own contradictions. He savors the triumphs of his life: a perfect rendition of the Twenty-third Psalm at Memorial Day exercises, a sharp throw from third base to catch a baserunner by a stride, making time with an older girl from Minneapolis. Juxtaposed to this, however, is a frequent tone of wistfulness, large ambitions only partially realized or not at all, ambivalences unresolved.

The tragedy of Lewis's personal life, and the fatal flaw that marred his literary vision, was his failure to imagine a higher goal than unrestricted personal freedom. Freedom was his obsession, and with the publication of *Main Street* he possessed the wherewithal to realize it. Eventually he carried the passion to escape social, intellectual, and marital constraints to absurd lengths. He worked so hard at smashing traditional standards and beliefs that he paid little attention to attempting to reconstruct a positive social philosophy that went beyond vague platitudes regarding a wiser, juster social order. Lewis was a man caught in a trap of his own making. Condemned to view the world and its inhabitants with a cynical and world-weary eye, he lacked the capacity for true commitment to people, place, or social program. That he desperately desired friendship, roots, and love can be seen in his befriending of young authors, his affair with an actress forty years his junior, his periodic returns to Sauk Centre, and his desire to have his remains buried there. The title of his last novel published during his lifetime, *The God-Seeker,* mirrored his own search, not for a conventional God that his irreligious nature refused to accept, but for a secular god that was embodied in a search for truth and the realization of personal freedom and individual fulfillment.

What Keillor's ultimate values and personal demons are we can be much less sure of, because he avoids self-revelatory interviews and has not had his life subjected to the kind of detailed scrutiny given Lewis's by a host of scholars. There are clues, however, to be found in the radio monologues and published work and some of the articles that have been written about him. Profoundly influenced by his conservative religious upbringing, Keillor has not joined Lewis in waging a fierce campaign against religion but rather seeks to understand the meaning of religious values in a secular age. Aware of the hypocrisies and inconsistencies attending religious (as well as any other kind of) values, Keillor pokes

fun at them while maintaining his respect for the people who commit them. If a couple breaks a window while using a Bible for a missile during a domestic spat, Keillor treats it as just another episode in the lives of finite, fallen creatures. Though he is a backslidden church-goer, he integrates Christian insights into his value system. The Bible says, don't let the sun go down on your wrath, and that is good advice to follow. Living a good life is not an easy proposition. Reflecting upon his pleasure in hitting his sister with a ripe tomato, Keillor observes that "knowing right from wrong is the easy part. Knowing is not the problem." Life's inconsistencies do not become for him a target of stinging satire. Rather he tends to operate in the ironic mode. In high school football, it's kill or be killed, and the team needs some killers. "There is an animal in you and I intend to bring it out," the coach tells his players. "The new boys glance at each other—it isn't what they learned in Luther League."

In their own different ways the two authors, separated so far by time and mood, connected so closely in space and intent, teach us a great deal about the twentieth century small town. If Lewis is obsessed by a desire to smash the idols of tradition, complacency, prejudice, and provinciality, Keillor, living in the post-modern era, is searching for serviceable values and places of repose for people traumatized by culture in which all fixed principles and values are rendered problematical. Lewis, committed as he was to personal freedom, was not unaware of its elusiveness and the problems it entailed. Carol Kennicott's ambivalence reflected his own. Toward the end of the novel, as her train takes her away from Gopher Prairie toward Washington, she wants to run back to Will. "She had her freedom, and it was empty. The moment was not the highest of her life, but the lowest and most desolate, which was altogether excellent, for instead of slipping downward she began to climb." Lewis never managed to reconcile his desire for freedom and personal fulfillment with his wish to be part of community. His visit home in 1905 at the age of twenty persuaded him that neighborliness was a fake—that the "village virus" of prejudice, dull conformity, and hypocrisy ruled the small town, and while he did try to present both sides of the story in *Main Street,* the negative viewpoint clearly predominated his vision. Yet it oscillated with the one he expressed in the 1931 school annual that in no other place were people more friendly. "It was a good time," he said, "a good place, a good preparation for life."

What makes Keillor's approach more ultimately satisfying is that instead of wavering between diametrically opposed positions in his thinking about the small town, he integrates the light side with the dark side in his work as he goes along. Anyone who attributes to him a syrupy optimistic view of the small town need only refer to his "95 Theses 95," an unrestrained manifesto against the putative parents and neighbors of a former son of Lake Wobegon who still suffers from the results of his overly protective and repressive childhood. Nothing in Sinclair Lewis's work is more scathing.

The former Wobegonian who wrote these bitter recriminations is not the only resident who left or wanted to leave town: Fred Krebsbach up and left his family at thirty-four; Johnny Tollefson went off to college; two men at the Sidetrack itch to go away, if only for a moment, with two babes passing through from St. Cloud. Another escapee is Garrison Keillor, who at the end of the book is tooling down the road in a '56 Ford. A refugee whose heart never really left the town, Keillor brings an outsider's perspective to the subject and at the same time an intimate acquaintance with it. Unlike Brother Bob, the evangelist, he doesn't consider Lake Wobegon to be a Sodom or Gomorrah, although he might agree that "in our hearts we are guilty of every sin." Nor does he identify with the Norwegian bachelor farmers, whose behavior renders them outsiders in their own community because of their refusal to abide by society's rules and restrictions. They spit where and when they feel like it, blow their noses with one finger, let dirty dishes pile high on kitchen tables. "We are all crazy in their eyes. All the trouble we go to for nothing: ridiculous."

In their complete unwillingness to submit to societal norms, they resemble Sinclair Lewis. What he had that they don't have was enough money to allow him to take his freedom beyond the confines of the immediate area. Where Garrison Keillor differs from all of them is that he realizes that there is no escape. We all carry the burden of our history, our beliefs, our habits and customs. His stories are parables of patience rewarded, of adversity endured. These are the messages they teach: life is fraught with peril; doing without makes you appreciate things more; life is full of disappointments; it's good to wait; nothing should come easy, you'll appreciate it more if you work for it.

Life in Lake Wobegon is not perfect, but it is whole. It is within this community that a collectivity of individuals find meaning and freedom, not in escape nor in quixotic efforts to remake society, but in the day to day transactions, resolutions, and interactions that make an individual a social being.
—John E. Miller

Keillor considers the hopes and fears, the fantasies and dreams of people to be legitimate. He seldom judges but rather accepts and affirms. He recalls in the book when Brother Louie retired after thirty years as assistant cashier at the First Ingqvist State Bank. He had grown old and fat and bald sitting there every day, enjoying ritual conversa-

tions with the customers: "Good Morning. You certainly look well." "How's Lena doing? And Harold? What do you hear from Elsie?" He knew everybody by name. Keillor writes, "It never occurred to me until he retired that once Louie had wanted to make something of himself in the banking business." It's an important revelation for Keillor.

We can imagine with what scorn Lewis would have treated such a "petty" ambition. And therein lies the distance between Gopher Prairie and Lake Wobegon. They are almost contiguous geographically and are products of the same culture and people, two generations removed in time. But time does not constitute the greatest gulf between the two towns. Keillor notes how much continuity exists between himself and his predecessors; when he entered school in 1948, it was on the same day, in the same brick school house, with the same misty paintings of Washington and Lincoln that had gazed down on his father and grandfather before him. What separates Lake Wobegon most from Gopher Prairie is that Garrison Keillor considers these facts to be important and worthy of respect. Brother Louie's original aspiration and eventual accommodation are equally human, equally estimable. Life in Lake Wobegon is not perfect, but it is whole. It is within this community that a collectivity of individuals find meaning and freedom, not in escape nor in quixotic efforts to remake society, but in the day to day transactions, resolutions, and interactions that make an individual a social being.

Spalding Gray (review date 4 October 1987)

SOURCE: A review of *Leaving Home,* in *The New York Times Book Review,* October 4, 1987, p. 9.

[*In the following review, Gray states that, "At their best these stories are contemporary folk tales of American comic-karma . . . [a]t their worst many of these stories are like honey-coated breakfast cereal."*]

For years I have listened to National Public Radio's evening news program "All Things Considered," and often on Saturdays I would forget that it was cut from 90 to 60 minutes to make room for a show called **"A Prairie Home Companion."** Not being one to turn off my radio until I'm outright offended, I passively left it on, and that's how Garrison Keillor slowly crept into my life. He seemed if not a remedy to the news at least a soft escape, an alternative to a third martini. Like Mr. Keillor, I perform monologues myself for a living, so I would often force myself to stay tuned through all that tacky sexless music to try to find out why that golden voice was, if not better than, then at least more popular than mine.

To be both true to yourself and at the same time capture the American imagination was something for me both feared and desired. So after my second martini I would sit back in a proper receptive haze and begin to listen. But always somewhere at the beginning, just after Garrison Keillor got warmed up, my girlfriend, Renée, would charge into the room yelling, "Turn that garbage off! It makes me want to swear!" Then she'd threaten to throw my little KLH radio out the window and the whole broadcast would be wiped out by our great traditional Saturday night fight—me defending Garrison Keillor by saying things like, "But Renée, he's not all good. I hear he chain-smokes Camel regulars." By the time we thrashed it out, his monologue was over.

But all is not lost. Having missed the monologues on the radio, I've been able to catch up with them in book form and read them all with a flashlight under the sheets before Renée came to bed. In fact, I recommend that you read *Leaving Home* just that way because these are perfect bedtime stories. They are exactly the right length and mood to put you out at the end and not in the middle, so you can slip off with a well-rounded sense of joyful completion. Also, I was surprised to find that these little stories about the people of the mythical town of Lake Wobegon are not as much like milk toast as I had anticipated. They are primarily wholesome American images that often begin with a description of local weather and glide through a landscape of meat loaf, roasted wieners, homemade jam and unconditional love, all falling cozily into place like a Norman Rockwell painting. But they are also perversely peppered with such contrasting earthy items as the autoignition of flatulence, cutting the heads off chickens, cancer and 68 dead pigs all on their backs with their legs turned up toward the sun.

At their best these stories are contemporary folk tales of American comic-karma, always demonstrating that you reap what you sow. Each detail collapses onto another, and as with Rube Goldberg, Uncle Wiggily or James Thurber, the stories all fall together like a row of dominoes, leaving you more with a memory of motion than of content. When these tales work, as they often do, they are like American Zen, about "sweet single-minded people" who work when they work and eat when they sit down to eat. Many of these monologues echo Thoreau's idea of salvation through simplicity, that "we need pray for no higher heaven than the pure senses can furnish, a purely sensuous life."

At their worst many of these stories are like honey-coated breakfast cereal. They give you a sugar rush only to let you crash by midmorning. I realize they are pure fantasy, but that doesn't bother me so much as the style of the fantasy. They ring of a kind of apolitical false naïveté; they are a throwback to a time when America was genuinely innocent. In the face of America's contemporary complexities, the realities of Lake Wobegon seem stupefying, cloistering and overripe.

Somewhere under that overstuffed, hometown patchwork quilt I keep hearing someone screaming, "Help, I can't breathe! Let me out of here! Someone get me to the coast!" Everyone seems to be protected by living so far inland. America's worst traumas can be glimpsed only through the hazy mediation of their television tubes, a feeling poignantly expressed in **"Aprille,"** one of my favorite stories. It is a beautifully constructed piece that reads like a perfect little sermon, about a girl who is about to be confirmed in the local Lutheran church. Suddenly, "she turned on the TV and lost her faith. Men in khaki suits were beating people senseless, shooting them with machine guns, throwing the bodies out of helicopters. . . . And she thought, 'This could happen here.'"

As with all movements in the realm of nostalgia—the longing for the thing that never happened—a sort of whitewash occurs here. That kind of cover-up often provokes the unchosen to hurl their radios out the window. As I read these stories I can't help wanting to lift the rug to see the other truth underneath. Perhaps Mr. Keillor's art would have been enough if he hadn't written such a tantalizing introduction, which for me proved to be the most interesting part of the book.

It's in this introduction, **"A Letter From Copenhagen,"** that he expresses a more vital autobiographic truth and discusses his historic impulses as a storyteller, his disenchantment with Minneapolis and how he has rediscovered his sense of smell by giving up smoking after 24 years, along with details of his relocation in Copenhagen, another white homogeneous northern climate where, he tells us, eating corn is better than sex. I like Garrison Keillor when he talks about his "real" life. The only part I missed and wanted to hear more about was his personal reaction to what he calls "the collapse of an American career," and how he decided to walk away from so many years of a successful radio show.

There is an old saying, "Happy people don't make history." I have a feeling Mr. Keillor is more than happy, he's content. He has not left home but rather carries it with him in the form of a fertile imagination. I am sure he can't go home again. But I only wonder what he plans to do in Denmark. Whatever it is, it will have to be something new. There's no doubt in my mind that he has written one side of himself to completion. I'd love one day to read the other side, what he really feels about Copenhagen.

Leaving Home will most likely make Garrison Keillor's fans love him all the more. For you who don't like him or have not taken the time to shape an opinion, I recommend that you at least go to a bookstore and open the book to a story at random and read it while standing up. They're short enough to do that without getting tired. For some of you, they will make you remember the home you never had.

Dan Sullivan (review date 11 October 1987)

SOURCE: "Goodbye, Garrison," in *The Los Angeles Times Book Review,* October 11, 1987, pp. 1, 12.

[*In the following review, Sullivan discusses the picture of Lake Wobegon which emerges from Keillor's* Leaving Home, *and how one realizes in many of the stories that the place does not exist.*]

In his introduction, written from his new home in Copenhagen, Garrison Keillor recalls his monologues on the **"Prairie Home Companion"** radio show as "seances." Exactly, and there must have been some nervousness about committing them to print.

But the spell holds. Those who enjoyed hearing the news from Lake Wobegon, Minnesota—how Wally's pontoon boat sank with the 24 Lutheran ministers on board; how Florian Krebsbach absent-mindedly left his wife Myrtle behind at the truck stop, to the refreshment of their marriage; how Lyle Krebsbach, Florian's son, finally came to an understanding with himself about getting his roof fixed, although this would mean consulting his handy brother-in-law, Carl; how Clarence Bunsen found a new enlightenment after suffering a near-near-death experience (possibly) in the shower—will also enjoy reading about these adventures.

Keillor doesn't ramble as much in type as he did on the air. That won't bother everybody. But he still likes to head the story down a gravel turnoff and then, just when nothing at all looks familiar, hook up with the main highway. A little test of faith.

All that a devout Lake Wobegoner really needs to know about this book is that it's out. However a few words may be in order for non-believers.

The objection seems to be that Keillor is the Norman Rockwell of the 1980s. I don't see it. To begin with, there's nothing picturesque about Lake Wobegon. It is your basic squat Minnesota hamlet, with its one blinking-yellow traffic light. In winter the typical vista is "a cold gray street lined with miserable yards." In summer, the leading natural feature is the mosquitoes.

Also, Lake Wobegon people are a little depressed because "living in Minnesota takes it out of you." Not just because of the climate, but because in a town this size (fewer than 1,000), everybody knows your least little mistake. Try to hide it and you may have the town snickering all winter.

Lake Wobegon residents would do anything for a person if they figured that he really had a problem, but on the small issues they can be mean; and for Keillor it's the small issues where life is decided—the little kindnesses as well as the slaps. Unlike most small-town satirists, he doesn't attack the religiosity of his characters as hypocritical. He sees this as something absolutely called for, given our fallen natures.

Marriage also is a necessity, "because we can't get attractive every day on a regular basis," especially in winter. When a man really feels himself getting ugly, he goes and hunkers in the fish house, possibly with a bottle.

The Gospel According to Peanuts does not go on Lake Wobegon. "Shame," for example, is as strong a force here as it is in Japan. And while Keillor wishes that his characters weren't so prone to feeling guilty about themselves—especially the young people—he nevertheless prefers this to letting it all hang out. Better repression than tackiness.

Take the "expert" from the city who screwed up a fireplace job for Clarence Bunsen and then insisted on sharing his feelings on this disaster with Clarence over the phone, rather than coming back to fix the thing.

The guy turned out to be from L. A. Lake Wobegon people know all about Los Angeles (they are on cable), and they pity anybody who would have to live there, except during late March.

Keillor approves his characters' distrust of facile emotion—of facile *anything.* But he worries that they are too wrapped-up in doing the next thing to see the big picture. Like Emily in *Our Town,* he wants them to see how wonderful it all is, while there's time. This leads to some praise-to-the-morning finales that don't work as well in type as they did on the radio, the listener not having been softened up by an hour of bluegrass guitar and hymns.

But something else comes across better on the page: the realization that Lake Wobegon does not exist. This is not news when you think about it, but usually we haven't thought about it. There's been something very solid about the Sidetrack Tap and the Chatterbox Cafe.

Here, though, every now and then, the whole town starts to waver, like a mirage, and you see Keillor, the Maker, wondering whether to send a character into her house to discover the mess that her kids have made, or to let her take a walk around the block first. It's a responsible job, running a universe.

Michael Kline (essay date 1988)

SOURCE: "Narrative Strategies in Garrison Keillor's 'Lake

Wobegon' Stories," in *Studies in American Humor,* Vol. 6, 1988, pp. 129-41.

[In the following essay, Kline analyzes the different narrative approaches Keillor uses in his monologues about Lake Wobegon.]

Garrison Keillor's immensely popular Lake Wobegon episodes, recounted for thirteen years (1974-1987) on his **"A Prairie Home Companion"** radio show, constitute a comic soap opera masterfully crafted by an expert storyteller. Given its radio format, Keillor's humor is managed by the strategies of oral presentation, differentiating it from written versions of the tales in **Lake Wobegon Days,** or even the modified radio monologues of **Leaving Home,** since oral presentation entails different modalities of grammar and rhetoric, elements of style, and paralinguistic features such as voice quality. Yet, in our print-based, literate culture, so far removed from the artistic traditions of societies in which the oral mode predominates, it is unlikely that a story-teller would achieve popular success merely by adopting the techniques of the bard. Alongside oral narrative techniques there exist in Keillor's monologues narrative strategies that we usually associate with written texts by virtue of their complexities of voice and mode. One of Keillor's greatest skills as a narrator is to use both oral and literate discourse features in complement, a practice which supports the view that there is no absolute dichotomy between written and spoken forms of language. As Tannen has stated, "Both oral and literate strategies can be seen in spoken discourse. Written discourse is not decontextualized . . . it is possible to be both highly oral and highly literate."

While we would expect that in our literate society written strategies would influence oral form, it is also the fact that the features of literate style found in Keillor's oral narratives—sophisticated subordination, grammar dependency and a lexically complex relationship between ideas and expression—are frequently disturbed by oral structures that coexist with them incongruously, producing a discursive humor that is not totally dependent upon content. The Keillor monologues interlace oral and literate styles without homogenizing them to the point that they cease to retain their own character or fail to produce particular effect. The elements of oral and literate narration may be separated for purposes of contrast, but we should remember that they combine in the tales to form the complex strategies, developmental approach, and rich texturing of a composite narration which undergirds the deceptively simple humor of the town that "the decades cannot improve."

In listening to the Lake Wobegon monologues one is rapidly struck by the "additive rather than subordinative" elements of the discourse, a characteristic typical of oral narration. Many of the best passages marking typical Lake Wobegon predicaments are strung together by coordinate clauses linked by *and,* rather than by connectors that subordinate ideas, such as *so* or *because.* These two general types of relationships between clauses are either paratactic or hypotactic. Hypotaxis is the "relation between a dependent element and its dominant" while parataxis "is the relation between two like elements of equal status, one initiating and the other continuing." Because in parataxis no element depends on any other, there is no ordering other than the sequential. It is the narrator who chooses to coordinate elements by means of extension rather than subordination.

The reliance on the connective *and* in paratactic construction is the source of much narrative humor for Keillor, who builds long strings of coordinate clauses, allowing one clause to enhance the meaning of another by qualifying it. Overqualification, however, soon grows into hyperbole, exaggeration of insignificant detail, enumeration of obsessive tendencies, or incongruous contrast. Semantic relations between propositions are not always clearly delineated, such that the events recounted often collide in a connived discursive reciprocity. Some good examples of this paratactic humor are found in a series of Lake Wobegon episodes devoted to Lyle, Florian Krepsbach's inept son-in-law, a high-school science teacher:

> So as he was thinking about this *and* what a rewarding kind of life this would be compared to what he's doing now, he looked *and* he noticed *and* he was a little bit surprised to see between his index finger *and* his middle finger a cigarette that was there between his fingers. Which wasn't really surprising considering that it had come from a pack of cigarettes which was in his shirt pocket *and* he had taken it out *and* put it in his mouth, *and* lit it *and* yet he couldn't quite remember having lit it *and* as he looked at this thing between his fingers he thought to himself, "I don't need these any more" *and* took the pack of cigarettes out of his shirt pocket *and* threw it out the window *and* at the same time took his foot off the gas *and* coasted to a stop *and* turned around at the cross roads *and* came back to about the point where he thought he had tossed those. (Emphasis is mine in all quotations.)

Another case of accretive style reveals Lyle's estrangement from Wobegonian society (he is suspect because he teaches science and has only lived there for twelve years). Given his exclusion, Lyle is eager for recognition, and so he is easily taken in, as in this scene:

> . . . he got a letter in the mail in a beautiful creamy envelope *and* he opened it *and* it said, "Dear Fellow Teacher: Congratulations, you have been selected by our awards committee to be included in

the 1985 edition of 'Who's Who in Minnesota Secondary Education.'" *And* he was so thrilled, he sat down right away with this form you have to fill out with biographical information about yourself *and* didn't notice until later that the return address was in Escondido, California, *and* that this form for him to fill out with biographical information about himself was also an order blank for one copy of 'Who's Who in Minnesota Secondary Education' *and* that by signing it you agreed to pay $39.95 for a handsome leather-bound edition of this work. . . .

The consecutive clauses are all equal in importance, since there are no other rhetorical organizers like *firstly* or *moreover,* which is a style perfectly adapted to Lyle's inability to distinguish the authentic from the unauthentic. Coordinative style perfectly suggests the mimetic dimension of character here, as the first three instances of *and* are "inflationary," leading to the heights of vanity, while the second group of three serve the comic deflation of pretense.

Furthermore, Keillor marks *and* as a discourse coordinator in order to identify upcoming "idea units" that are coordinate in structure to prior units. Paratactic style thus clusters and maximizes detail, while helping listeners to stay attuned to the narration through the development of the story along slowly evolving parallel lines. However, as Schiffren notes, *and* does not provide information about what is being continued nor about what is being coordinated. This situation is a key to Keillor's humor, for if content is repetitive, and syntax changes little, then the accretion, repetition, and incremental parallelisms of coordinative style work to form hyperbolic metonymic chains where one thing leads to another, until situations lose their logic due to overbearing detail or break down under the weight of accumulated evidence.

Furthermore, facts, statistics, or other precise elements in oral narratives are relevant only to human activities, and particularly to those which are situational. Anne Amory Parry made the point in citing the epithet *amymon* applied by Homer to Aegisthus, which means not "blameless," as many had believed, but "beautiful-in-the-way-a-warrior-ready-to-fight-is-beautiful." We need but contrast Aegisthus to Lyle at the end of the story about guilt:

> And Lyle is full of pain, full of shame, full of guilt and still not smoking. . . . And when he feels at his worst then he goes out and he runs, which makes him feel even worse than that which makes him feel better in a way. He's not a runner, and if you see him out there on the roads you can tell that he's not. He's overweight, he's kind of flat-footed and he moves slowly when he runs. . . . But if you see him out there, if you see him out there on the road in

the dust, running down the road in his old grey warm-up pants and his old letter jacket from high school which doesn't fit anymore so that you can't zip it up but he's hoping to some day, and the two little bike reflectors on the heels of his sneakers, when you see him out there running down a gravel road, old Lyle, don't feel sorry for him, don't feel bad for him. He's in misery, he's suffering, he's in pain, but it's OK, he's just one of us, just one of us sinners, you know, trying to make his way home. . . .

Lyle, the underequipped warrior in life's struggles, is a man who jogs to expiate guilt, remembered as such by virtue of considerable vestmental detail. The notion of guilt and expiation is made palatable for the listener through the pathetically humorous vision of the overweight man paying his dues by the mile. Keillor arrives at his moral through the characters' situations, never in spite of them, and thereby keeps his monologues in the realm of humor, rather than permitting them to slide into sermonettes.

Keillor returns often to the most basic narrative level, that of the word, where redundancy is copious, creating a framework for humor by accretion, as action is driven to frenetic levels of pointless activity. The sound of language being derailed by its own mass and velocity is analogous to Bergson's notion of "mechanical inelasticity." While the man who slips on a banana peel becomes involuntarily objectified by circumstances, Keillor makes language the butt of a kind of discursive practical joke in which the narrator plays the role of Bergson's "mischievous wag" who intervenes to remove a chair just as the subject is sitting. Burdened by its own weight, and careening out of control, language has no other recourse than to collapse from the strain of sheer repetition. Thus, in the narrative referred to earlier, Lyle is found searching desperately for a cigarette. In the following passage, the combination of coordinate clauses and repetitions of the verb "look" not only measures the beat of Lyle's growing frustration, but transforms him into a comically maniacal creature of habit. Language and action fuse in the service of humor:

> . . . and he was *looking* around in the dirty clothes hamper, hauling clothes out of there hand over fist one after the other *looking* in pants pockets, shirt pockets, *looking* in the pocket of his bathrobe—anything. Even *looked* in the medicine cabinet, who knows, who could tell, there might be one in the medicine cabinet. He took everything out of the medicine cabinet, he *looked* behind everything, he didn't find anything, he *looked* around on the floor. . . .

This "redundant or copious" nature of oral style owes its existence to the "disappearance" of oral utterances as they are pronounced. Since the mind cannot return to a prior reference affixed to a printed page in order to check on the continuity of the narrative, it is important for the storyteller to move forward with caution, always keeping what has preceded in the narrative in the mind's eye of the listener. The result is not the linear progression identified with literate discourse, but a tale marked of necessity by redundancy and repetition, serving to position the listener periodically within the development of the story. Redundancy may therefore exist as a thematic marker, acting as a common thread for narrative development, but existing independently of story content. In one monologue, for example, the theme of guilt ties together five or six different events or commentaries. Thus, when Florian Krepsbach is knocked off his feet by the Deener boy on his bicycle, the old fellow is not really upset because he feels guilty for having left Myrtle at the truck stop (this incident is related to a prior story, but for Keillor's regular audiences the mere mention of it evokes laughter and ties it to the communality of experience among the reappearing characters). This situation leads to a comment by Keillor in the role of public narrator on the subject of the pleasant reaction of a woman into whose car he had just crashed, because apparently she was feeling guilty about something else. In turn, the Deeners are said to show too much guilt, since they thought the awful smell in the dining room was coming from themselves, rather than from the cat that had been plastered into a wall. In contrast, there follows a brief reference to egotistical "yuppie scum" who have not enough guilt, and, finally, the guilt theme circumscribes the narrative by dredging up none other than Lyle, who returns to suffer the guilt of having knocked his daughter Becky against the radiator during his desperate search for a smoke. Whereas purely oral societies find in story-telling a way to conserve knowledge, Garrison Keillor modifies the griot's role by both celebrating and mocking unbending tradition, in part by undermining the importance of narrative as the guardian of conceptualized knowledge. In the tales of Lake Wobegon, as it is in those of Balzat, Chelm, Mols, Schilda, and other communities of idiots, knowledge is incomplete, fossilized or irrelevant, such as the question of who remembers how to make *lutefisk* (it's Ralph), and, even more importantly, who is willing to eat it. Or, there is the case of Wendel, a high-school classmate of the narrator, who was sent to Venice as a Lutheran missionary. Poor Wendel had not had much luck proselytizing there. Some time later, he received a letter from the Lutheran Missionary Board informing him that they had meant to send him to Vienna! Not everyone in Lake Wobegon is an idiot, of course, but neither do the Wobegonians seem to advance much. The place is fixed as "the little town that time forgot and that the decades cannot improve," the motto of which is *sumus quod sumus.* Wobegonians have civic virtue and moral rectitude, and they persevere, so that "all the women are strong, the men are good-looking and the children are above average." These epithets are used for ironically comic effect, since in

spite of their virtues and talents, what Wobegonians know and what they do are often at odds, making them appear singular and not infrequently lunatic.

The humor of logically illogical characters as an operational mode of Keillor's style is carried over to another aspect of oral narrative, that which is "empathetic and participatory rather than objectively distanced." Since the nonlinear nature of oral narrative does not permit leisurely references to past events, causality, or justification for prior actions, narrator and audience must know where they stand in relation to each other at all times. Keillor practices a type of phatic communication which enables him to jog the listener frequently, as well as to bring him or her into the tale. If we look at the example of Lyle as comic Aegisthus with an eye toward the relationship between narrator and audience, we can count numerous references to the listener in the form of the pronoun *you.* This *you* is not synonymous with the general-reference pronoun *one,* for the listener is progressively drawn into the narrative, when, for example, the hypothetical "if you see him out there," repeated three times, changes to the indicative "*when* you see him out there," followed by an imperative. By maintaining contact with the tale, the listener is guaranteed (tongue in cheek) that the character's mimetic dimension will be assured. Moreover, the moral of the story, that Lyle is "just one of us, just one of us sinners, you know . . ." is inclusive of narrator, character and narratee, all adherents to the same non-exclusive club of guilt-burdened members. Thus, monologic and interactive discourse, usually thought of as opposing parameters, are brought into complement to bond the auditor of the tale to its speaker.

This intimacy is felt throughout Keillor's Lake Wobegon stories. One might think that such a close relationship to the audience would be impossible in a format which supposes broadcasting the news from Lake Wobegon. But Keillor is no objective reporter, as all listeners recognize, because the "news" from Lake Wobegon doesn't really have the characteristics of news. What comes from Lake Wobegon has little sensational value, nor does it have general interest beyond itself. After all, every week is a quiet week there, for time has forgotten the place. If there is no reason to narrate the news, of which there is none anyway, telling it makes the listener suspect the presence of another narrative strategy, this one having to do with the relationship between narrator and audience. The artifice of supposedly phoning a contact in Lake Wobegon weekly to catch up on the non-news is a means by which to maintain a close relationship with listeners. Keillor can participate in and narrate the tale at the same time, since as conduit for Lake Wobegon's events of the week he can relate them, but because he supposedly maintains contacts there he can also position himself within the story whenever he wishes. Since a characteristic of oral narrative is always some kind of coincidence between whatever posture the speaker adopts and the existence of the speaker as a biographical person, Keillor can play both roles simultaneously, telling the tale and acting in it when he desires. The listener is thus implicated at both levels of the narration.

If we refer to the continuing saga of Lyle, we find this example of the kind of narrative play by which Keillor assumes the role of both protagonist and witness in order to justify his participatory narrational stance. Here Keillor is validating the contention that friendship exists in Lake Wobegon, but that one has to have lived there far longer than Lyle's twelve years to recognize it:

> I was in the Side Track Tap one night this winter playing pinball. It was that old baseball machine which I've always liked, the old kind that doesn't beep, you know, it dings and it keeps score in the hundreds and the thousands and not in the hundreds of thousands. Kind of my speed, and I was standing there and doing pretty well at it and making it ring pretty well and getting it up to 9,000 and was on my bonus ball when suddenly a hole opened up out of nowhere and just ate this thing. And I looked at it and I felt a hand on my shoulder, on my right shoulder, and I turned to my right and there was Carl Krepsbach, who had been standing beside me and who put his arm around me and I tell you it may not sound like much but I just about burst into tears and sat down because I've known him, you see, just about all my life, and I know that he does not go around doing that. It was an amazing thing. I felt so grateful to him for it.

Keillor's autodiegetic participation, both internal and external to the spoken text is also a strategy that functions to confer upon him the authorization of the listener to tell the tale, given the diegetic authority which derives from the conceit of privileged purveyor of information from Lake Wobegon. This narrative ubiquity appears symbolically as a comic synecdoche in the perennial Keillor favorite, **"The Living Flag."** In that story, the Wobegonians form a living flag by wearing red, white or blue beanies and by positioning themselves properly in Main Street. Of course, when the flag is complete it is not possible to see it unless one breaks ranks and goes up to the roof of the Central Building to look at it, which, naturally, incites others to break ranks so as to take a peek. The living flag becomes a "sitting" and a "kneeling" flag, deformed by those defectors who wish to cease participating in order to observe. The narrational analogy to the problematic of the flag is well expressed by Jean-Paul Sartre's dictum in *Nausea*, ". . . il faut choisir: vivre ou raconter." In theory, one can't be authentically involved in life and have sufficient objective distance from it to tell about it at the same time. While it is impossible to assume the pos-

ture of grammatical first and third person narrative voice simultaneously, Keillor's strategy permits him to shift from the position of narrator to that of participant in order to create the illusion of being both outside the tale and within it. The external narration of Lake Wobegon activities, foibles, and secrets is maintained, while the internal narration establishes a homodiegetic presence among the Wobegonians, foci that link storyteller to audience from different perspectives. This dual point of view is a feature of contemporary literary practice, all the more remarkable when it is found in oral narration. It bridges both the oral and literate narrational features of the texts.

By the same measure that he assumes different types of focalizing perspectives as both external and internal narrator, Keillor works at different levels of narration through embedding stories within stories. The impression that his sub-tales seem to wander away from each other is only apparent. Successive narrations, even embedded ones, are held together thematically as well as by replication of content. They usually evolve organically, each succeeding narrative arising from the preceding one. The main theme is typically rejoined at the end of the story. Nevertheless, given the nonlinear nature of oral presentation, it is difficult to maintain contact with the listener using embedding, a strategy not unknown to oral narration, but more coherent in literate narration. The example of Father Emil's preretirement visit from the Bishop of Brainard illustrates how the primary humorous theme is maintained through a series of embedded stories, each funny by itself. The narrative begins when Mr. Odegaard's old Ford pickup won't start outside the Side Track Tap on the kind of cold day that only Minnesota knows. As Odegaard attempts to hitch a ride home, Mr. Bowser's green postal Chevy passes him by, for Bowser is deep in thought about organizing a cross-country riding-mower competition from New York to California. This story is then melded into another, which is provoked by a team of young evangelists from a bible college in Georgia who pass Mr. Odegaard by in their blue motor home. Finally, we arrive at the main tale, that of the Bishop, who arrives at the rectory to talk to Father Emil. He pulls up in a long, black limousine, it too passing Mr. Odegaard by, not once but twice, which prompts the old Norwegian bachelor farmer to hit it with a clod scooped from the side of the road.

Each of the stories contains separate content, but the unifying element is the series of vehicles, each one passing Odegaard, but not stopping for him. The vehicles themselves are not the main point of the story. They are a literate reprise, neither aggregative nor redundant, as in the oral mode. They are denotative signifiers of embedding in a tale which has many components and which of necessity needs to conform to the requirement of wrapping its successive layers into a circular pattern graspable by the listener as an Ariadne's thread. What is clever in this is the fact that although each of the successive stories has different content, they all function metonymically to create a framework for the main story, that of the bishop's visit to Father Emil. The layers of stories within the story serve the explicative function of embedding, which elucidates the punch line of the first narrative: why poor old Odegaard threw filth on the bishop's car. Thus, Keillor's strategy is to blend literate narrative formats with the demands of oral performance to form a narrative that is richly complex but easy to follow.

Narrators must convince their audience to give authorization for the mimetic process to a mimetic authority. Literate narration frequently shifts the burden for establishing mimetic authority to the character, often assigning the role of speaking and seeing to internal focalizers, characters who function as cameras or recorders and who adopt a point of view. Keillor does this too, but he often creates humorous effect by limiting, rather than sharpening, the focalizing capacities of a character. In the case of the bishop's visit, for example:

> Halfway into algebra, the long black car sat by the curb, its motor running, so that the children who went to the blackboard to work problems all looked out the window and down, watching that car, clouds of exhaust coming out, until sister Arvonne said, *"Don't look at it, don't think about it, I'm watching it, I'll let ya know if anything happens."* What happened, *though she didn't know this and still doesn't,* was that Father Emil had submitted his resignation as priest asking to be relieved of his duties—he's 74.

In this case, the comic effect is produced by a script switch in which the curious nun is left as much in the dark as her pupils. Sister Arvonne's limited knowledge causes her failure to perform as an effective focalizer. Her view of things is then transformed to direct discourse, which in turn serves as a stepping-stone for the external narrator to return in order to provide the needed information. That move in turn provides rationale for a "historical" explanation of the founding of Our Lady of Perpetual Responsibility Church, yet another embedded story.

Characters' point of view is usually associated with literate discourse, but it can find its way into oral narrative through techniques such as the narrator's mimicry of the characters' voices or their intonation. In this vein, characters often speak directly in the Lake Wobegon monologues. It is unusual, however, to find oral narratives that not only include the direct and indirect discourse of characters, but also the literary device of free indirect discourse, in which the focalizing function of the character is blended with the syntax of the narrator. Keillor uses free indirect discourse effectively as a focalizing mechanism and as a strategy to vary the level

of discourse from that of simple internal or external focalization. In this way, the narrator is not restricted only to what the character knows, or to what can be observed from outside, but a third dimension of focalization may be achieved, one that includes both perspective and level, in a melding of characters' discourse with narrator's point of view. The following example occurs in the episode known as "Tomato Butt," in which air conditioning has become a topic of some interest to Lake Wobegonians:

> It was when Mrs. Deener got an air conditioner that people started to talk. There was nothin' wrong with *her.* Who did she think she was? *She* said that she got it for her daughter because her daughter would break into a heat rash, but her daughter only came to visit for a couple of weeks during the summer, and she always came in June. So what did she need it for? Mrs. Deener said, "Well," she said, "as long as I've got to have it I might as well get the use of it. . . ." And I decided that air conditioning was something that I'd dearly love to have.

In this passage the external narrator's introduction leads into a discourse of gossip which is neither direct, as is Mrs. Deener's, nor indirect, in which case it would be introduced by the narrator, most commonly following a relative pronoun. In fact, the free indirect discourse contains within it indirect discourse as metanarrative ("*She* said that she got it . . ."). Moreover, the counterpoint of free indirect discourse and direct discourse then permits the shift to homodiegetic narration, in which the indirect discourse of the narrator as boy in Lake Wobegon is introduced, leading finally to the moral of the story and a laughter-provoking twist. The richness of this frame is based upon the tripartite view of the air-conditioning problem as seen in the three modalities of discourse.

Free indirect discourse is generally used by Keillor to evoke the presence of the character within the extradiegetic narration, thus affording a brief binocular vision as extradiegetic narration and intradiegetic narration fuse. In this example, Lyle has finally caught on that his insertion in "Who's Who" is merely a commercial venture, a vanity press seduction:

> He filled it out all the way down to the bottom and then he saw little boxes down there to be marked "Check enclosed" or "Visa" or "Master Card." *Oh,* [snort] *no wonder they mailed it to him at home, not at work. All the teachers in Minnesota probably got one, every single one. What a sucker!* He felt like such a sucker.

The first paragraph, focalized externally, yields to free indirect discourse in the second. The paralinguistic snort is a concession to the oral format, as well as a marker for the change to free indirect discourse, which then continues as it would in a literate text. Lyle's vanity is underscored by his brief appearance at the moment of his epiphany, his words grafted onto the extradiegetical narrator's syntax. Finally, the external narration pulls away from the eruption of the character onto the scene by another bow to orality, as the narrator reestablishes himself extradiegetically in the last sentence through a redundant statement that merely repeats from his perspective what Lyle has already told us. The sequence thus begins in the oral mode then moves into the literate mode, finally returning to the oral mode. These focalizing displacements emphasize the superiority of listener over narrated subject, which is the source of humor in this instance.

Finally, in the same way that redundancy must be built into the oral narrative to remind the narratee of the development of the tale, so do oral cultures avoid abstract analytic categories *per se,* those having no relationship to activities in the real world. Oral style is "close to the human lifeworld," since in oral cultures the elements of the tale are never remote from lived experience. The same may be said for Keillor's stories, for even in their most complex configurations, they remain rooted in life experiences. In the story about guilt, for example, Keillor opens his narrative with a temporal marker:

> Last Saturday, as a matter of fact, right about the time I was talking about him on the radio, last Saturday afternoon, Florian Krepsbach came out the door of the Side Track Tap in the early evening before supper, having gone in for a bump. . . .

The notion of time here is fairly abstract, since Keillor is using a "split screen" technique to create a spacio-temporal distance between himself as external narrator and the character, who is seen to have an authenticated past and autonomy of action, given Florian's "presence" in Lake Wobegon, his presence in the preceding week's monologue, and Keillor's double presence on the stage, that of last week and that of this week. Moreover, the charm of Keillor's narration in this instance derives from the interplay of the spatial and temporal facets of focalization. Keillor plays at being a narrator with a limited point of view who is able to describe what characters do only because he gets "news" of them weekly. His true optic is panoramic, which allows the simultaneous description of events separated in space. In the same way, focalization here is panchronic, where it is possible to perceive all temporal distances together. The listener understands that Keillor, as narrator, controls the complete range of temporal distance through the past, present, and even future of the character, but what is "assumed" by the narration is a limited focalization in time, one that is circumscribed by the present tense of the character. Thus, while Keillor talks about Florian in the past, another Florian, one whose autonomy is assumed by the narrator, circulates in his own present moment at the very instant his past is being recounted. The character is therefore free to develop in a natural way, integrated into the time and space of Lake Wobegon's rhythms. All of this takes place, however, within the context of a familiar Lake Wobegon haunt. Florian's verisimilitude as a character is linked not to an abstract, literate notion of time and space (which is nevertheless present), but to a "real-world" situation which defines him as an old-time Lake Wobegonian who likes his afternoon pick-me-up after a slow day at the Chevy agency. The old fellow's bump is yet another example of the interlacing of the oral and the literate, for it marks his place in the spacio-temporal matrix of stories whose organicism in the form of continuously evolving situations is never calcified by the fact of their sophisticated narration.

Alison Lurie (review date 24 November 1988)

SOURCE: "The Frog Prince," in *The New York Review of Books,* November 24, 1988, pp. 33-4.

[*In the following review, Lurie discusses Keillor's work as a humorist in his books and in articles for* The New Yorker.]

Over the last few years Lake Wobegon, Minnesota (population 942), has become the best-known town of its size in America. Millions of people are sentimentally familiar with its rival Lutheran and Catholic churches; its Chatterbox Cafe, where the specials are always meatloaf and tunafish hotdish; Bertha's Kitty Boutique ("for persons who care about cats"); and Ralph's Pretty Good Grocery ("If you can't get it at Ralph's, you can probably get along without it").

Lake Wobegon, of course, does not exist; it is the invention of Garrison Keillor, former radio variety-show host and occasional short-story writer. It is known to the world through his show, **"Prairie Home Companion,"** and the books that grew out of it, *Lake Wobegon Days* and *Leaving Home.* Keillor describes his imaginary home town with Balzacian energy and detail. Everyone and everything there interests and excites him, from Father Emil's hay fever to Irene Bunsen's attempts to grow the biggest tomato on record (twenty-five ounces). He knows so much about the town and is so eager to share it that *Lake Wobegon Days* keeps breaking out into long informative footnotes.

> A memorable council meeting was that of 5/16/62 to discuss a motion to hold a special election to vote on a bond issue to repair sidewalks and install new streetlights. It was the late Leo Mueller who suggested that with a little more inner light ("Thy Word is a lamp unto my feet"), fewer people would need

assistance walking home. He hinted that it was Lutherans who were walking into trees.

At first glance Lake Wobegon is an American pastoral in the comic tradition of Twain and Booth Tarkington, with an occasional slide into the romantic idealism of Thornton Wilder's *Our Town*. It is a dream of a vanishing America where life makes sense and neighbors know and care about each other, even if they aren't always speaking. They endure the freezing prairie winters and broiling summers with philosophical stoicism, and express themselves in highly characteristic speech and gesture:

> Mr. Berge said to Wally in the Sidetrack [the local bar], "Shees, it's bin cool out, don't you think. I thought dey said it was supposta warm up a little, fer crine out loud." Wally said, "It's almost October, Berge. It's going to be getting a lot cooler from here on out right through the end of the year and into the next. It's not going to warm up any time soon."

> It's easy for Wally to be a realist. He spends his days in the Sidetrack like a bear in a cave—a cave with green and orange and blue neon beer signs and a bevy of older bears leaning against the bar and belching beer breath.

One of Garrison Keillor's greatest gifts is his ability to modulate like this from realism to fantasy, or from low farce to high comedy. The range of Keillor's sympathy is wider than Twain's, however. It includes not only children and outsiders, but also the most conventional citizens of Lake Wobegon: people like the local Lutheran pastor, David Ingqvist, and his wife:

> Advent exhausted them—so much joy and great tidings proclaimed while inside they felt crummy—and before the candlelight service they stood in the vestibule, he in his vestments and she at the head of the children's choir, and they got in a fight and hissed at each other. "How could you say that to me?" she said.

> "I never said any such thing."

> "You certainly did."

> "Oh shut up."

> In this little town, as winter descends, we depend on marriage to get us through, because we can't be attractive every day on a regular basis, we need loyalty, money in the bank, and if it's the Church that stands behind marriage, then the Ingqvists' marriage

is crucial to everyone. So then they tried hard to be nice to each other, and that was almost worse. To treat your true love like they are a customer. "Good morning, how are you? What can I do for you today?" They needed to sit in the sun and hear birds cry, paradise birds, non-Lutheran birds, with their sharp cries. Lutheran birds wear brown wool plumage and murmur, "No thanks, none for me, I'm fine, you go ahead," but these paradise birds in their brilliant orange-and-green silks are all screaming, "MORE MORE MORE! I want MORE MORE MORE!"

Keillor's attitude toward his imaginary neighbors is affectionate but hardheaded. After a series of comic disasters, the Ingqvists do get away to Florida at the last minute, but their lives are not transformed. At the end of the chapter they are "at Château Suzanne, in the sunshine, listening to birds cry: MORE. But that's all there is."

Sometimes a darker chord is sounded. Characters and events appear that recall the grotesques of Sherwood Anderson's *Winesburg, Ohio*. People are obsessed by the fear of cancer and injured in freak accidents; they desert their wives and children. Plump, prim little Mr. Geske misses his dead mother so much that he goes to the cemetery and digs up her grave.

> They found her body on a chair in the kitchen. He had set a cup of coffee in front of her and a piece of lemon meringue pie. There was meringue on her lips.

Keillor, in an interview, has said that this incident is based on a true story he heard in North Dakota. "These stories are not common, but still they're not utterly strange, they happen sometimes. The perils of that little town on the prairie have to be set out: boredom, loneliness, alcohol, self-hatred, and madness."

Small-town religion, which Keillor usually treats with amused nostalgia, is sometimes shown to have a harsher side. He was brought up as a member of a splinter sect called the Sanctified Brethren, which he describes in terms that recall Samuel Butler and Edmund Gosse. ("We were 'exclusive' Brethren, a branch that believed in keeping itself pure of false doctrine by avoiding association with the impure.") *Lake Wobegon Days* contains a long, angry outpouring of rage: "95 Theses 95," which its author (described only as a Lutheran and a "former Wobegonian") originally intended to nail to the door of his church. The manifesto accuses his elders of having ruined his life with their teachings:

> 4. You have taught me to worship a god who is like you, who shares your thinking exactly, who is go-

ing to slap me one if I don't straighten out fast. I am very uneasy every Sunday, which is cloudy and deathly still and filled with silent accusing whispers.

5. You have taught me to feel shame and disgust about my own body, so that I am afraid to clear my throat or blow my nose. Even now I run water in the sink when I go to the bathroom. "Go to the bathroom" is a term you taught me to use. . . .

The task of the humorist is in its nature contradictory. He (or, less often in our history, she) both destroys and defuses. He can rail at and expose pretensions and lies so that they lose their power; or, by affectionately mocking our flaws; he can encourage us to smile and accept rather than change anything.

The greatest American humorists can be roughly located along this continuum from destroyer to defuser. But if they are to be widely popular they must avoid both extremes. When they become obsessed by the evils of the world, their mockery grows bitter and corrosive; middle-of-the-road audiences reject them as self-righteous moralists or spiteful scolds. Mark Twain in his later years and more recently Lenny Bruce were eventually sucked into the dark whirlpool of constant rage.

Humorists who have too much love for the smiling side of life, on the other hand, may grow lazy and soft. Their wit is blunted, and they begin to reassure their audiences rather than challenge them; they tell the sort of jokes that excuse rather than excoriate evil. Will Rogers, who "never met a man [he] didn't like" (including, presumably, Warren G. Harding and Benito Mussolini), sometimes seems to be drifting in the direction of these deceptive shallows. Many other lesser humorists have drowned there.

At the moment Garrison Keillor, too, seems nearer to the latter danger than to the former. Like Will Rogers, with whom he shares a rural frontier background, he began with a distrust of the rich and the conviction that most ordinary Americans are decent folks. Also, like Rogers, Keillor is most himself in front of an audience; he does not regard the role he plays on stage as an act, but as his true self.

Keillor, like Will Rogers, creates an immediate emotional relationship with his listeners:

You can get into a range of powerful feelings with an audience [he recently told an interviewer]: feelings that bring you up to the edge of your endurance, to where you are about to weep and be unable to continue. It's not pathos, it's loyalty to the audience and a sense that these people are the people

you're talking about. You must be true to them and true to their lives.

Will Rogers grew up before broadcasting, and always preferred performing on stage; but radio is Keillor's natural habitat:

A storyteller reaches something like critical mass, passing directly from solid to radio waves without going through the liquid or gaseous phase. You stand in the dark, you hear people leaning forward, you smell the spotlight, and you feel invisible. No scripts, no clock, only pictures in your mind.

By 1987 Lake Wobegon had made Keillor famous. He was no longer the gangling six-foot-five teen-ager of his reminiscences, a Frog Prince obsessed by acne and sexual guilt, but a media celebrity. He broke up with his long-time girlfriend, Margaret Moos, the producer of his show, and married the beautiful Danish exchange student he had admired when he was a shy, unathletic, self-confessed "dork." After the last broadcast of **"Prairie Home Companion"** he left Minneapolis and moved with his wife to Copenhagen. Three months later he was back in America—not in Minnesota, but in New York, and writing for *The New Yorker.*

It was in some ways a strange move, though Keillor has always had a fascination with the magazine, which he first read at the age of fourteen.

My people weren't much for literature, and they were dead set against conspicuous wealth, so a magazine in which classy paragraphs marched down the aisle between columns of diamond necklaces and French cognacs was not a magazine they welcomed into their home. I was more easily dazzled than they, and to me *The New Yorker* was a fabulous sight. . . . What I most admired was not the decor or the tone of the thing but rather the work of some writers.

When Keillor discovered *The New Yorker* in the Fifties its portrait of New York had considerable relation to reality. The magazine itself has not changed much, but now it presents a strange, skewed version of the city. To judge by its editorial pages, cartoons, and advertising, New York is still a kind of glorified small town, full of interesting and eccentric persons. Most of its citizens are decent people, its streets are safe, and the scenery is pretty. *The New Yorker* covers, with their views of Central Park, colorful flower and vegetable stalls, and commuters planting bulbs or raking leaves, underline the illusion.

Meanwhile the real New York is turning into one of the most dangerous, ugly, and corrupt urban centers in the world—

and one of the most expensive. It is no longer a place where most of its readers can afford to live; it belongs more and more to the very rich and destitute. The tense mood of New York in the Eighties seems better represented by *New York Magazine.*

As yet the change is not complete. There are still pockets of *The New Yorker's* city here and there; and Garrison Keillor has set out to find them. His essays in the magazine, and his pieces for its "Talk of the Town" section—unsigned, but recognizable from the down-home diction and wry self-mockery—maintain the fiction of New York as a glorified small town. In the same tone he used in describing Lake Wobegon, Keillor writes of messages left on a department store typewriter, of baseball games, of drives to the country on weekends. Like E. B. White he is a delicately accurate humorist and a brilliant but wholly unpretentious stylist; though he speaks as an educated country bumpkin rather than a New England gentleman of letters, it is White's place that he now seems to be filling at *The New Yorker.*

Though Keillor abandoned Lake Wobegon in June 1987, the town did not die: instead it became a popular tourist attraction. Replays of **"Prairie Home Companion"** are still broadcast every week on over two hundred stations to large audiences, and Minnesota Public Radio puts out a catalog from which Keillor's fans can order tapes of the entire show or of his monologues. The catalog also sells T-shirts with the emblem of Keillor's imaginary sponsor, Powdermilk Biscuits, and others advertising Bertha's Kitty Boutique (brilliant fuchsia with a picture showing four monumental cats carved into Mount Rushmore). *The Prairie Home Companion Folk Song Book,* (from **"Billy Boy"** to **"The Beer was Spilled on the Barroom Floor"**) will appear later this month with a foreword by Keillor.

One of the most discouraging things about America today is our tendency to simplify and commercialize whatever is most genuine in our art and literature. A writer who is widely known only as the source of a T-Shirt, or the celebrant of a city that no longer exists, is unlikely to attract serious readers. It would be a shame if Garrison Keillor's originality, his humor, and his understanding of American small-town life were overlooked because of his popularity. But of course Keillor's story is not over: he may return to Minnesota, or become a partisan political commentator like will Rogers; he may travel around the world and produce a new version of *Innocents Abroad;* or he may complete the downbeat novel he is currently working on, in which strangers—perhaps New Yorkers, he says—will invade Lake Wobegon, and there will be a real-estate boom.

> Money is there to be made, and the strangers will have all kinds of money to pay for bits of land that nobody thought was particularly valuable. They will

bring their lives with them, and the townspeople will also have that to deal with.

Maybe, after all, Garrison Keillor needs to live in New York for a while, as a spy in the camp of the invaders.

Stephen Wilbers (essay date Spring 1989)

SOURCE: "Lake Wobegon: Mythical Place and the American Imagination," in *American Studies,* Vol. 30, No. 1, Spring, 1989, pp. 5-20.

[*In the following excerpt, Wilbers traces the common features of a mythical place exhibited by Keillor's Lake Wobegon.*]

. . . At a time when live radio programs are an anomaly and there seems little time for all the things we busy Americans have to do, much less for listening to slow-moving tales of small-town life in rural America, the phenomenal popularity of Garrison Keillor's weekly radio program and the remarkable success of his best-selling books seem baffling. How can one account for this unexpected popularity? And what does America's enthusiastic response to Keillor's imaginary world tell us about ourselves as Americans?

When **"The Prairie Home Companion"** was broadcast live from the World Theater in St. Paul for the last time on June 13, 1987, it was the nation's most popular radio show. Two hundred seventy-nine United States public radio stations carried it, as did the Australian Broadcasting Corporation. According to estimates from Minnesota Public Radio, between 3 and 4 million of us were tuning in for our weekly dose of entertainment and companionship.

Lake Wobegon Days, Keillor's book comprised largely of vignettes and anecdotes from the show's monologues, won acclaim in its own right as a work of fiction. Considered "the publishing sleeper of the year," the hardcover edition was on the New York Times best-seller list for 48 weeks, making it the top selling hardcover fiction of 1985. The paperback edition appeared on the list for sixteen weeks. Altogether the book sold over 1.2 million copies. Its sequel, *Leaving Home,* appeared on the *Times* best-seller list for twenty weeks following its release in October, 1987.

Since he first got the idea to do a live radio show after traveling to Nashville in 1974 to write a piece for *The New Yorker* on the Grand Ole Opry, Garrison Keillor has become something of a national cult hero. He was featured in a cover profile in *Time* magazine, made TV appearances with David Letterman and Ted Koppel, led the singing of the national anthem at the 1988 Democratic national convention in Atlanta, and, to his only faintly disguised gratification, was designated as one of the ten sexiest men in America by *Playgirl* magazine.

Champion of the shy person and spokesperson for the small-town hick, Keillor has been described as exuding Minnesotan normalcy; yet beneath this folksy exterior one senses an unusually keen intellect and rare talent. In spinning his fanciful and gently satiric tales of life in Lake Wobegon, "the town that time forgot and the decades cannot improve," Keillor invites comparison with an earlier Midwesterner, James Thurber, and with the late E. B. White, whose stories evoke life in rural Maine so convincingly. Some find his spell-binding wit and humor reminiscent of Will Rogers. Others even compare him to America's greatest humorist, Mark Twain, a link that is perhaps invited by Keillor's propensity for wearing white suits.

> **Keillor's creation of a mythical place captivated the imagination of American audiences because it addressed a long-standing cultural need, one that has existed since the settling of the North American continent by western Europeans. That need is for a sense of community and belonging, for reassurance against social disruption and the threat of loss—the need, in short, for a sense of place.**
> —*Stephen Wilbers*

One might argue that **"The Prairie Home Companion"** was simply a product of a particular historical period, that it was popular because it captured and gave voice to the animating spirit of its time. A more interesting and finally more revealing approach, however, is to examine the show's remarkable popularity in a broader historical context, one that raises fundamental questions relating to national identity and the collective American experience. The argument presented in this article is that Keillor's creation of a mythical place captivated the imagination of American audiences because it addressed a long-standing cultural need, one that has existed since the settling of the North American continent by western Europeans. That need is for a sense of community and belonging, for reassurance against social disruption and the threat of loss—the need, in short, for a sense of place.

Myth and legend are, by their nature, timeless. In depicting the town "that time forgot and the decades cannot improve," Keillor plays with the notion of timelessness. This is especially apparent in his rendering of character. Like most writers, Keillor defines and delineates his characters in relation to place. But what sets Keillor apart is that his characters seem not to respond to time. A good example of an unchang-

ing character wedded to timeless place is Myrtle, who "is seventy but looks like a thirty-four-year-old who led a very hard life." She is

> Carl Krebsbach's mother . . . who, they say, enjoys two pink Daiquiris every Friday night and between the first and second hums "Tiptoe Through the Tulips" and does a turn that won her First Prize in a Knights of Columbus talent show in 1936 at the Alhambra Ballroom. It burned to the ground in 1955. "Myrtle has a natural talent, you know," people have always told her, she says. "She had a chance to go on to Minneapolis." Perhaps she is still considering the offer.

Not only do Keillor's characters live in a town "that time forgot," but also they themselves are timeless. On the one hand they are representations of unchanging human nature, which partly explains their appeal, and on the other they are more or less exempt from the vicissitudes of time, which partly explains why it feels comforting and secure to be around them. By their timelessness, they offer us a promise of permanence and an assurance against loss. It is the promise of never-never land that only a mythical place can offer.

Myrtle's husband Florian provides an even more striking example of Keillor's use of timelessness in rendering character:

> Her husband Florian pulls his '66 Chevy into a space between two pickups in front of the Clinic. To look at his car, you'd think it was 1966 now, not 1985; it's so new, especially the back seat, which looks as if nobody ever sat there unless they were gift-wrapped. He is coming to see Dr. DeHaven about stomach pains that he thinks could be cancer, which he believes he has a tendency toward. Still, though he may be dying, he takes a minute to get a clean rag out of the trunk, soak it with gasoline, lift the hood, and wipe off the engine. He says she runs cooler when she's clean, and it's better if you don't let the dirt get baked on. Nineteen years old, she has only 42,000 miles on her, as he will tell you if you admire how new she looks. "Got her in '66. Just 42,000 miles on her." It may be odd that a man should be so proud of having not gone far, but not so odd in this town. Under his Trojan Seed Corn cap pulled down tight on this head is the face of a boy, and when he talks his voice breaks, as if he hasn't talked enough to get over adolescence completely. He has lived here all his life, time hardly exists for him, and when he looks at this street and when he sees his wife, he sees them brand-new, like this car. Later, driving the four blocks home at about trolling speed, having forgot-

ten the misery of a rectal examination, he will notice a slight arrhythmic imperfection when the car idles, which he will spend an hour happily correcting.

What we have here is the ultimate statement of traditional values, those that don't change at all. For the Lake Wobegonian, time is simply not an issue.

Myth and legend are, by their nature, timeless. In depicting the town "that time forgot and the decades cannot improve," Keillor plays with the notion of timelessness. This is especially apparent in his rendering of character.
—Stephen Wilbers

This thinking is epitomized by the town's prevailing attitude toward progress and technology:

> Since arriving in the New World, the good people of Lake Wobegon have been skeptical of progress. When the first automobile chugged into town, driven by the Ingqvist twins, the crowd's interest was muted, less whole-hearted than if there had been a good fire. When the first strains of music wafted from a radio, people said, 'I don't know.' Of course, the skeptics gave in and got one themselves. But the truth is, we still don't know.

This same fundamental skepticism is wonderfully apparent in the townspeople's reaction to a visiting university professor who offers them a glimpse of the future:

> Every spring, the Thanatopsis Society sponsored a lecture in keeping with the will of the late Mrs. Bjornson, who founded the society as a *literary* society, and though they had long since evolved into a conversational society, the Thanatopsians were bound by the terms of her bequest to hire a lecturer once a year and listen. One year it was World Federalism (including a demonstration of conversational Esperanto), and then it was the benefits of a unicameral legislature, and in 1955, a man from the University came and gave us "The World of 1980" with slides of bubble-top houses, picture-phones, autogyro copter-cars, and floating factories harvesting tasty plankton from the sea. We sat and listened and clapped, but when the chairlady called for questions from the audience, what most of us wanted to know we didn't dare ask: "How much are you getting paid for this?"

The professor's futuristic vision of a world of technological wonder is clearly one that the townspeople do not believe or care to see. The reason for their aversion is that technology represents change, and change, as we all know, is unsettling. As Rip Van Winkle discovered upon waking from his twenty-year slumber, to confront a familiar place that has been transformed nearly beyond recognition is frightening. And as Leonard Lutwack and others have pointed out, Rip Van Winkle's experience has become a central metaphor of our time. Faced with change at an alarming and ever increasing pace, we are left with a sense of placelessness, "a peculiarly modern malaise" that the geographer Yi-Fu Tuan calls "spatial segmentation."

At its most rudimentary, myth-making is simply story-telling, and Keillor is a consummate story-teller. His technique is to construct an imagined milieu by building layer upon layer of convincing detail. As with William Faulkner and his mythical Yoknapatawpha County, Keillor coaxes his listeners into his created world by luring and hypnotizing them with the "authenticity and authority of experience" (to use Wendell Berry's phrase) and by presenting them with an array of characters who seem somehow truer than real life.

In the passage that follows, Keillor evokes a vivid sense of place by presenting a catalogue of objective visual detail, subjectively perceived. The narrator knows that most people think that tall or big is beautiful and that small or short is unremarkable. This awareness leads the narrator to present his home town to the outside world in terms of a comically absurd hierarchy of people and buildings based on relative height, as though height were tantamount to virtue or importance:

> A town with few scenic wonders such as towering pines or high mountains but with some fine people of whom some are over six feet tall, its highest point is the gold ball on the flagpole atop the Norge Co-op grain elevator south of town on the Great Northern spur, from which Mr. Tollefson can see all of Mist County when he climbs up to raise the flag on national holidays. . . . Next highest is the water tower, then the boulder on the hill, followed by the cross on the spire of Our Lady, then the spire of Lake Wobegon Lutheran (Christian Synod), the Central Building (three stories), the high school flagpole, the high school, the top row of bleachers at Wally ("Old Hard Hands") Bunsen Memorial Field, the First Ingqvist State Bank, Bunsen Motors, the Hjalmar Ingqvist home, etc.

It is the tension between the concreteness of the visual detail and the comic misapplication of someone else's notion of grandeur that generates a sense of recognizable place. Implicit in the narrator's description of his home town is a way of thinking, an inherent sense of inferiority that many have used to characterize small-town America.

In the act of myth-making, Keillor succeeds in making us feel a sense of belonging by calling on our shared experience. He does this in many ways, but perhaps the most important is his use of language. He appeals to our collective experience and our collective identity as Americans by expressing himself in a particular kind of language. Wendell Berry calls it "community speech," a certain "precision in the speech of people who share the same knowledge of place and history and work." It is a "precision of direct reference or designation . . . in which words live in the presence of their objects." Its effect is to force us "out of the confines of 'objective' thought and into action, out of solitude and into community." Taking its meaning and sources from locale and place, this particular language creates connections among people, land and community.

Similar to Berry's notion of "standing by words" is Jerome Bruner's concept of "the language of education," a value-laden language "revealing one's stance toward matters of human pith and substance." To use this language is to set aside the "so-called uncontaminated language of fact and 'objectivity'" and to invite reflection. To use language in this way, as Keillor knows so well, is to make certain connections that contribute to a sense of common identity and to the creation of culture. According to Tuan, this culture-creating is related to the concept of mythical space, which is rooted in "localized value" and used as a frame to interpret our day-to-day experience. The process of culture-creating is interactive, one in which speaker and listener alike become myth-makers.

This use of a particular language is evident in Keillor's brand of democratic humor. Like Mark Twain, he operates in the comic tradition of self-depreciation and false humility. Take for example the following scene, in which the thin veneer of sophistication affected by the narrator as a first-quarter university freshman is challenged by the traditional values of common sense and practical knowledge. Significantly, the humor comes at the narrator's expense:

> I went home for Christmas and gave books for presents, Mother got *Walden*, Dad got Dostoevsky. I smoked a cigarette in my bedroom, exhaling into an electric fan in the open window. I smoked another at the Chatterbox. I wore a corduroy sportcoat with leather patches on the elbows. Mr. Thorvaldson sat down by me. "So. What is it they teach you down there?" he said. I ticked off the courses I took that fall. "No, I mean what are you learning?" he said. "Now, 'Humanities in the Modern World,' for example? What's that about?" I said, "Well, it covers a lot of ground, I don't think I could explain it in a

couple of minutes." "That's okay," he said, "I got all afternoon."

I told him about work instead.

The language in this passage is a perfect example of Keillor's skillful and evocative use of "community speech." A whole lifestyle, for instance, is suggested by Mr. Thorvaldson's value-laden response. Although we in the audience may not "have all afternoon," we understand the language and feel a natural kinship toward someone who does.

What we have here and throughout Keillor's work is a leveling process and an attack on pretense. (Consider what the narrator likes about his dog Buster and what he dislikes about Minneapolis.) As revealed by the town's motto, *"Sumus quod sumus"* ("We are what we are"), Keillor's humor reflects a fundamentally democratic spirit. He invites us to laugh with him on equal terms.

In his vision of a mythical place, Keillor delights in walking that thin line between imagination and reality. These days when asked where he's from, he says, without hesitation, Lake Wobegon. When asked if Lake Wobegon exists, his usual response goes something like this:

> I don't mean to be cute when I say, "this is not an easy yes-or-no question." No, there is no town in Minnesota named Lake Wobegon that I could show you, at least I'm not aware of one. But I would also have a hard time showing you the Ninth Federal Reserve District, the Archdiocese of St. Paul and Minneapolis, the Big Ten, or the upper middle class. Most people deal very comfortably with abstractions much more far-fetched than Lake Wobegon, e.g. the Moral Majority, secular humanists, Hollywood, etc. Compared to any of those, Lake Wobegon is as real as my hands on this typewriter and sometimes more real than *that*.

In the same way, he seems to blur imagined and real space when he describes the mistake made by the Coleman Survey of 1866, a mistake "which omitted fifty square miles of central Minnesota (including Lake Wobegon)." This supposed error explains why no one today seems able to locate the town in real life, but it becomes more than a convenient fiction when he goes on to assert that the error "lives on in the F.A.A.'s Coleman Course Correction, a sudden lurch felt by airline passengers as they descend into Minnesota air space on flights from New York or Boston." Here the imagined intrudes on the real.

This blurring of imagined and real space makes it difficult to distinguish fantasy from reality, subjective perception from objective truth and mythical place from actual place.

In fact, this lack of clear boundaries, many have argued, is a fundamental characteristic of human experience.

In *Space and Place: The Perspective of Experience,* Yi-Fu Tuan addresses this phenomenon. Tuan identifies two principal kinds of mythical space. The first is "hazy" knowledge or "a fuzzy area of defective knowledge surrounding the empirically known," which "frames pragmatic space." The second is "the spatial component of a world view, a conception of localized values within which people carry on their practical activities." It is the second type of mythical space, the ordinary, day-to-day mythologizing that we all do in interpreting our daily experience, that Keillor exploits so effectively. He appeals, in this sense, to the Lake Wobegon within each of us. In rendering his mythical construct, Keillor brings into play all the tools of the regionalist: particular detail, sharply pronounced personality types, local manners, speech, folklore and history. In the process of mythologizing both his experience and ours, his subjective view of reality begins to take on literal truth and meaning. As Tuan defines it, mythical place is "a response of feeling and imagination to fundamental human needs." This makes it, as Keillor understands so well, as real as a real place, and in some ways more useful.

Mythical place as we have examined it, then, seems to possess the following attributes. It is timeless in the sense that it is not subject to the forces of change. This in turn makes it a comforting and reassuring place to be. It is subjective in the sense that it reflects the commonly held values and beliefs of a particular locale, as illustrated and embodied by "community speech." And it is real in the sense that it reflects the "inner truth" of reality. Because we believe that it exists, it does exist, and its existence influences our perception, our world view and our behavior.

There is at least one other important attribute of mythical place, however, and that is the prominent role given to chance and improbability. In the case of Garrison Keillor's Lake Wobegon, this is illustrated by the curious happenstance of the town's founding. Its first white settlers were Unitarian missionaries and Yankee promoters who named the area "New Albion," thinking it would become the Boston of the west. Next came Norwegian Lutherans "who straggled in from the west" and German Catholics "who, bound for Clay County, had stopped a little short, having misread their map, but refused to admit it." Like America's first white visitors, these settlers arrived at the new land under a misconception of where they were.

One wonders if Keillor isn't suggesting that we modern-day immigrants to the New World even now aren't too sure of where we are or how we got here—and that perhaps we too refuse to admit it. It could be that in attempting to help us mythologize our collective experience, Keillor, while poking fun, is seeking to help us deepen our relationship with the land, to help us feel more at home.

Whatever Keillor's intent, that the town was founded on a mapping error seems, in the mythical scheme of things, perfectly natural. That Lake Wobegon was established by settlers who came there by accident suggests a particular notion of history as something unpredictable, uncontrolled, and problematic—history as chance. The irony (no doubt intended by our gentle satirist) is that Lake Wobegon itself, the symbol of permanence in a world of change, is there only by accident, and that the people are permanent there only because their ancestors didn't know what they were doing.

With mythical place, we have entered the realm of the improbable and the unlikely. We are surprised by what we find there only because the bias of our Western (rationalistic and mechanistic) mind often prevents us from recognizing the obvious: chance happenings are, in fact, commonplace, in both real and imagined landscapes. Keillor's incorporation of chance into mythical place reminds us that chance and uncertainty are, to paraphrase William Beatty Warner, just as real as being and certitude.

While it may be too early to determine the ultimate significance of the Lake Wobegon phenomenon, one might begin an assessment with a few basic questions. One might ask, for example, whether Wobegon should be interpreted as an exploration of a regional phenomenon, and hence part of the discovery of subcultures that began in the 1960s and continued into the 1970s and the 1980s? Or, one might ask, should Keillor's creation of mythical place be interpreted as an effort to establish a framework that transcends subcultures and binds all Americans?

That **"The Prairie Home Companion"** was a product of a particular historical period is undeniable. To appreciate the extent to which the program was in keeping with the spirit of its time, one need only consider some of the important cultural trends of the last decade or so. The 1970s, for example, witnessed a search for roots and community, as evidenced by the mid-1970s genealogy boom and the enormous popularity of the TV miniseries, "Roots." The period was also characterized by a general hostility toward technology and science, by a revival of Jeffersonian simplicity, as promoted by Wendell Berry and others, and by a renewed interest in what David Shi calls "homesteading simplicity." The book that may best capture the spirit of the times was E. F. Schumacher's extremely popular *Small is Beautiful,* a treatise on simple living. Though it is doubtful that Keillor would approve, one might even compare the anti-pretense dimension of **"The Prairie Home Companion"** to the punk-rock movement's search for an authentic rock 'n' roll.

Be that as it may, it is important to recognize the program's significance in a historical context that goes far beyond what was happening in the 1970s. In *The Simple Life: Plain Living and High Thinking in American Culture,* David Shi chronicles "a rich tradition of enlightened material restraint in the American experience dating back to the colonial era." It is a tradition that takes its origins from two societies, the Puritans and the Quakers, both of which "promoted a 'Christianity writ plain.'" While this tradition of "plain living and high thinking" may no longer serve as "a dominant standard of behavior," Shi provides ample evidence to show that it has persisted "both as an attainable ideal on an individual basis and as a sustaining myth of national purpose."

Like many American writers before him, Garrison Keillor is taking part in the continuing formulation of America as an idea and an ideal. His creation of mythical place is tied to the creation and definition of the American experience.
—*Stephen Wilbers*

In other ways as well, Keillor's vision of the simple life in small-town, rural America isn't new. It is, in fact, the latest manifestation of a long and well established literary tradition that can be traced back to the ancient Greeks, whose bucolic poets often used Arcadia as a setting epitomizing rustic contentment and simplicity. As Leo Marx in *The Machine in the Garden* reminds us, American writers have used the pastoral ideal to define the meaning of our country "since the age of discovery." An early and prominent example is Washington Irving, who in 1820 described a "peaceful spot with all possible laud." Irving's words foreshadow a latter-day Sleepy Hollow that time likewise forgot:

> . . . for it is in such little retired . . . valleys . . . that population, manners, and customs, remain fixed; while the great torrent of migration and improvement, which is making such incessant change in other parts of this restless country, sweeps by them unobserved.

Here in these sleepy valleys rural peace and repose stand in sharp contrast to a "great torrent" of change, and this change implies dislocation, conflict and anxiety. Marx goes on to point out that "the theme of withdrawal from society into an idealized landscape is central to a remarkably large number of . . . the American books admired most." Citing Cooper, Thoreau, Melville, Faulkner, Frost and Hemingway, he argues that "the imagination of our most respected writers . . . has been set in motion by this impulse." Clearly, Garrison Keillor is solidly within this tradition. And in offering his own version of an idealized landscape, he is touching something deep within the American psyche.

There is still the question of whether the program appealed to minority cultures. There seems to be no evidence that it did. It should be noted, however, that the music on the program was often off-beat, ranging from the throaty blue grass songs of Greg Brown to the Scottish ballads of Jean Redpath. And whenever Keillor took the show on the road (as when he broadcast from Alaska and Hawaii), he took care to include songs and tales from the indigenous cultures. Still, Keillor's is a white middle-class vision of America depicting white middle-class concerns.

This is not to say, however, that Keillor lacks insight into the minority experience. As the following passage indicates, Keillor has a keen understanding of a very important dimension of the minority experience in America, and that is the immigrant experience:

> Homesickness hit the old-timers hard, even after so many years, and it was not unusual, Hjalmar says, to see old people weep openly for Norway or hear about old men so sad they took a bottle of whiskey up to the cemetery and lay down on the family grave and talked to the dead about home, the home in Norway, heavenly Norway.

> America was the land where they were old and sick, Norway where they were young and full of hopes—and much smarter, for you are never so smart again in a language learned in middle age nor so romantic or brave or kind. All the best of you is in the old tongue, but when you speak your best in America you become a yokel, a dumb Norskie, and when you speak English, an idiot. No wonder the old-timers loved the places where the mother tongue was spoken, the Evangelical Lutheran Church, the Sons of Knute lodge, the tavern, where they could talk and cry and sing to their hearts' content.

Clearly, Keillor knows what it means to find oneself outside the dominant culture.

Despite the phenomenal popularity of his show, Garrison Keillor is not, of course, without his critics. There are many people who simply could do without him. Some Minnesotans would have preferred a less folksy image for what became the major symbol of their state in the eyes of the outside world. One local newspaper reviewer noted that Keillor's work has been accused of "being for Americans what *All Creatures Great and Small* has been for the English: a sweet picture of small-town life, misty around the edges, that panders to the nostalgic and escapist yearnings of a society alienated from the present and aware that it is on the skids." Others are still more harsh. They are concerned that nostalgic yearning for a golden age might divert our attention and energies from addressing and solving today's real problems. They are repelled by the political implications of this sentimentality, which in their view supports the myth of "the good ol' days," a myth they claim has been used by conservatives to justify the do-nothing social policies of the Reagan administration.

> **By evoking a usable past and animating a recognizable common culture, Keillor invites his listeners to tell their own story, just as he invites them to speak when he reads their personal and usually humorous messages during his broadcast. This myth-making is a participative and interactive and dynamic process . . .**
> **—Stephen Wilbers**

But this last criticism allows political implications, probably unintended by Keillor, to overshadow the cultural significance of his accomplishment. It overlooks an important part of what Keillor is after as story-teller and myth-maker. His phenomenal popularity is surely more than an affirmation of fundamentally conservative values, just as his work is certainly more than the latest kitsch served up to exploit an untapped market.

Like many American writers before him, Garrison Keillor is taking part in the continuing formulation of America as an idea and an ideal. His creation of mythical place is tied to the creation and definition of the American experience. In the act of story-telling and myth-making, this "prairie home companion" offers security and solace to his fellow homesteaders. He invites them to explore with him and to create the legends of a new world. It is a world, both a real and imagined landscape, that evokes the conventional wisdom and traditional values that define the American experience and the American character, the values of perseverance and practicality and expedience. It is more than a nostalgic and sentimental look at the past, and it isn't exactly escapist.

By evoking a usable past and animating a recognizable common culture, Keillor invites his listeners to tell their own story, just as he invites them to speak when he reads their personal and usually humorous messages during his broadcast. This myth-making is a participative and interactive and dynamic process, one that, to use Jerome Bruner's word, calls on the "subjunctivizing" function of story or narrative art to elicit its many and various interpretations. The result is creation of culture and affirmation of community, a process that looks forward as much as backward. Though whimsical and often corny, Keillor's work is part of a serious and significant effort by Americans to come to grips with their physical and cultural landscape, to find a common thread in their increasingly fragmented experience and to put down roots in a shifting and ever changing society.

Bill Henderson (review date 9 April 1989)

SOURCE: "Ordinary Folks, Repulsive and Otherwise," in *The New York Times Book Review,* April 9, 1989, p. 13.

[*In the following review, Henderson states, "The worst I could probably say about the 11 poems and 61 prose pieces brought together in* We Are Still Married . . . *is that I liked some pieces better than others, but—and this is more than one can say for most such collections—I liked them all."*]

Garrison Keillor is the first author, poet, composer or singer to have ever caused me to drive off the road and stop the car in tears. A friend had sent me a tape that I played on the car stereo—a tape of Mr. Keillor singing a birthday song to his son, who had almost died at birth. It was a sentimental subject, but somehow the man captured it all—all the terror, the wonder, the joy of birth—and in that one brief song he turned me into a traffic menace.

Expect no distance or dispassion here. I admire Garrison Keillor. The worst I could probably say about the 11 poems and 61 prose pieces brought together in *We Are Still Married* (many previously published in *The New Yorker*) is that I liked some pieces better than others, but—and this is more than one can say for most such collections—I liked them all.

A few of my favorites: **"Laying on Our Backs Looking at the Stars"** is an essay about just that, a subject that in less capable hands might turn out sappy. Mr. Keillor brings it off, in passages like this: "Indoors, the news is second-hand, mostly bad, and even good people are drawn into a dreadful fascination with doom and demise . . . but here under heaven our spirits are immense, we are so blessed. The stars in the sky, my friends in the grass, my son asleep on my chest, his hands clutching my shirt."

"The Meaning of Life" might be the title of a C-minus sophomore work, but in two paragraphs this essay convinces, inspires and reminds us: "To know and to serve God, of course, is why we're here, a clear truth that, like the nose on your face, is near at hand and easily discernible but can make you dizzy if you try to focus on it hard. . . . Gentleness is everywhere in daily life, a sign that faith rules through ordinary things; through cooking, and small talk, through storytelling, making love, fishing . . ."

If you're searching for a more objective review of the author of this collection, look to his own **"Letters From Jack,"** a file of letters from the owner of Jack's Auto Repair, one of the first sponsors—all of them fictitious—of **"A Prairie Home Companion,"** Mr. Keillor's radio show. Here are a few of Jack's opinions: "I've advertised on the show for six years, and would have done better writing my phone number on barroom walls," he writes in one letter. And again, "You're honest (you never claimed to be good), and people listen to you thinking that if they get to know you real well, may be eventually they'll like you. Well, I've been listening for years and must admit that its appeal is sporadic." And, "Thirty minutes of a man speaking in a flat Midwestern voice about guilt, death, the Christian faith, and small-town life is not what people look for in a stage performance."

The fictions are typical Keillor, bittersweet tales of ordinary folks that remind us that nobody is ordinary. The title story chronicles the marital adventures of Willa and Earl, Minnesota residents who are invaded by a reporter for *People* magazine named Blair Hague. Blair lives with them and writes a piece convincing Willa that her marriage is a disaster and her husband "often personally repulsive." Willa becomes a celebrity. She does the talk show circuit, sells movie and book rights about the horrors of married life, is a New York cocktail party sensation—and returns home to Earl and her small town. No apologies asked, none given. Life resumes as before.

The other poems, opinions, stories, letters and whatnots in this collection ponder the meaning and nuance of yard sales, sneezes, Woodlawn Cemetery, the last surviving cigarette smokers, the solo sock, the old shower stall, the perils of celebrity, being nearsighted, growing up fundamentalist and traveling with teen-age children. And in these "ordinary things," the grace of Garrison Keillor shines through.

In his introduction, Mr. Keillor complains: "I grow old. Boys and girls in their thirties who compose essays on the majestic sorrows of aging—*give me a break.* I'm forty-six. Wait until you're forty-six and then tell me about it. I'll be sixty then. I grew up in a gentler, slower time. When Ike was President, Christmases were years apart, and now it's about five months from one to the next."

He can complain about that if he wants. But this reviewer (who is 47) hopes that Mr. Keillor is just entering the prime of his career, and is going to guide us through the perils and the foibles of the decades to come. The guy occupies the same place as Twain, Benchley and Thurber. I am glad he is with us.

Elizabeth Beverly (review date 10 April 1992)

SOURCE: "Static on the Page," in *Commonweal,* Vol. 119, April 10, 1992, pp. 26-7.

[*In the following review, Beverly asserts that Keillor's style is not successful in the novel form in his* WLT: A Radio Romance.]

On page 12 of Garrison Keillor's mocking and rowdy first novel **WLT: A Radio Romance,** which tells the story of the rise and fall of a radio "empire" in mid-century Minnesota, "Roy [pays] Leo La Valley $10 to tell a raw one on the 'Noontime Jubilee,' to get a rise out of Ray." Here's the joke: "So Knute told Inga he loved her so much he wanted to buy her a fancy new bed—he said, I want one with that big cloth thing up over it? She said, a canopy! He said, no, that's *under* the bed and we're going to *keep* it down there."

The book tempts me as critic to advise simply, "If you like this sort of joke, you'll like the book. Read it." And with that partial recommendation I could dismiss it. But I find Keillor's novel to represent such a troubling failure, one which raises so many fundamental questions not just about the art of writing, but also about the art of reading, that I want to linger with the joke, and the set-up, a little longer. Here we have it all: what is most intriguing, frustrating, tantalizing, and ultimately disheartening about this first novel.

What intrigues me is simple. Our eyes alone cannot get this joke. We must hear it. We know that Keillor, the well-known radio personality, understands this. Does such understanding mean that the novel will innovatively meet the challenge of revealing a primarily aural culture through the medium of print? Does Keillor wish to make a serious statement about competing technologies? Will philosophical or cultural ghosts haunt the novel? Will we be treated to jokes, plot, and thought, all at once?

My frustration originates in Keillor's one genuine technical innovation. He decides to tell the story in countless short sections that resemble nothing so much as segments of mid-century radio programming. Short installments that variously inch forward moment by moment or lurch forward through catastrophe. Train wrecks and bran muffins rate both the same space and the same pacing. These short sections may accommodate Keillor's snappy style, but they seriously hinder his ability to tell a story from the inside. There's not enough room to move, not enough time to fill in background information.

We readers have another problem: the device immediately reveals that we are in the absolute thrall of a petty tyrant of narrative. We know that we'll get what we're given and not a sentence more. Naturally, this truth underlies all fictions, but the greatest fiction writers conceal it, and allow their readers to imagine that they alone conspire and dream with the characters. Most readers never want to wonder just who is running the show. They just want the show to go on, and to include them perfectly.

Keillor's attachment to his device keeps his characters at a distance. There is no room for reflection; their plights simply drive the engine of plot, and resist the serious consideration we would give them were such events to happen in the lives of people who mattered to us. Is this the philosophical point of the novel: that the medium of print entraps as surely as that of radio waves? When finally, in chapter 14, Keillor indulges his philosophical ruminations about the role of radio as oral art, we don't know how to read his meanings. Is this straight parody? Or heartfelt intellectual yearning? Or simply a joke that we should get?

I'm tantalized by what this particular author thinks about this particular story. Garrison Keillor, the clever, appealing guru of folksy contemporary radio, wrote this novel and it concerns the life of radio. We cannot forget the promise inherent in the conjunction of author and subject. Yes, this is an extra-literary yearning, that we might learn something from a master, but even the text swells with the promise. Take the joke on page 12. If we simply tune into the program, we'll hear the joke and either get it or not. The book offers us the real story of what goes on behind the scenes. It suggest that we'll learn something about radio, something about human motivation, something about industry and spirit.

If this is the hope, the reader is bound to be disheartened, for the joke is a mild killer. The joke is a bad joke. I don't mean bad in the sense of "raw," although some readers might find it so. And I don't mean bad in the sense that puns are always bad; we get them and we laugh and then we feel stupid because we got them and wanted to laugh. No, I mean that this is a bad joke because the impulse that gives rise to laughter is a tiny meanness. We laugh at someone else's expense. Poor dumb Knute. A kind man, a loving man, and a man who can't tell a canopy from a piss-pot.

In just the way that the Inga-Knute Joke is a bad joke, so is **WLT: A Radio Romance** a bad novel. But it doesn't take its own temptation to be bad quite seriously enough. And this puts the reader in an odd position. Reading this book feels a lot like standing in the cloakroom of a Midwestern elementary school before the bell rings while a big guy in your class tells first the one about the fat lady who must use the freight elevator, then the one about the "old lecher named Wendell / Whose cock was indeed monumental. . . ," and then the one about a little boy whose father died in a boiler explosion on a train so that other kids in another school can gather around him and sing "Ashes in the overalls / From one little weiner and two black balls." What is the big guy getting at? Is this humor? Is this cynicism? Oral culture? Folk history? Maybe you laugh, and maybe you don't, but you've got to wonder why the big guy goes on and on. You've got to wonder what you'll say when he's through.

Oddly this book, in its good-natured refusal to embrace its own moral questioning, introduces the notion of sportsmanship into reading. Are you a good sport, finding the book an "endearing" portrait of a moment in America's life, or are you a goody-goody, someone who needs to lighten up? These are not issues that should occupy a reader. It is the author's job to understand his intentions. If he wants his readers to laugh at fat ladies and pity orphans, his writing will invisibly direct them to do so. If he wants them to worry about a culture in which some cruel people laugh at fat ladies, then such a worry will seem like the most sensible one in the world.

I think that Keillor the novelist doesn't know what he wants. He cannot hear what he wants. He is learning to work in a medium which, in this case, has resisted him. This novel is a failed venture, but bespeaks a great hope. Maybe Keillor is embittered, maybe he's lighthearted. In either case, Garrison Keillor can tell remarkable stories; he can drop one-liners and spin out endless yarns. He can make us laugh. Hard. What he needs is practice on the page, not just as a writer, but as a reader.

If he were my friend I'd send him right to the work of Eudora Welty, tell him to listen not with his ears, but with his eyes too. Look at the white space, the shape of paragraphs, the length and roominess of lines. Listen to tempo and cadence and mood. Learn that great fiction may sound harsh or may sound gentle, but it always dignifies its characters and their stories with seriousness, even as it laughs. When stories work on the page, we hear the warm voice of them rising in the print. They are sure and helpful, and invite us to read.

Lisa Zeidner (review date 12 December 1993)

SOURCE: "Why Is Marriage Like the Electoral College?" in *The New York Times Book Review,* December 12, 1993, p. 13.

[*In the following review, Zeidner calls Keillor's* The Book of Guys *"an endearingly acerbic collection of 22 stories about men with women trouble."*]

With his sixth book, Garrison Keillor spices up his act for those who might be tiring of the "Prairie Home Companion" routine that made him famous. **The Book of Guys** is an endearingly acerbic collection of 22 stories about men with women trouble. Though Mr. Keillor's woeful guys hail from an impressive range of times and places, from the Old West to ancient Rome, they're all middle-class, middle-aged and miserable.

"We're selling out our manhood, bit by bit," a speaker complains at the convention of a men's movement group called the Sons of Bernie. Don Giovanni, a two-bit piano player at a bar catering to hard hats on their lunch breaks, offers a similarly grim view. "A woman takes over a man's life and turns it to her own ends," the Don warns. "She heaps up his plate with stones, she fills his bed with anxiety, she destroys his peace so that he hardly remembers it."

Women are dour and demanding. They're bad cooks. They drag you to pretentious plays and strong-arm you into heavy talks about The Relationship. Even on a romantic cruise, the whiny wife in **"Marooned"** is hunched over a magazine quiz called **"How Lousy Is Your Marriage: A 10-Minute Quiz That Could Help You Improve It,"** whereas every sane man in the universe realizes that "marriage is like the Electoral College: it works O.K. if you don't think about it."

And this is marital bliss *before* the screaming kids! No wonder that Lonesome Shorty, a grumpy cowboy with a bad back, has so much trouble settling down. No wonder that the amiable radio show announcer in **"Roy Bradley, Boy Broadcaster"** defends his bachelorhood so vigilantly: "Everyone else in radio talks with the voice of marriage and duty. I speak with the voice of one who eats his dinner at an odd time out of white cardboard containers while standing at the kitchen counter and reading the sports page."

Mr. Keillor is hardly trying to copyright this view of the battle between the sexes. In fact, his comedy depends on the very silliness of the setup: "a boy's constant struggle to maintain his buoyancy" against his ball and chain. That domesticity is disappointing—at least in men's minds—is the given. Then Mr. Keillor begins to riff on the premise, stretching it to its absurd conclusion—as in **"The Mid-Life Crisis of Dionysus,"** wherein "the god of wine and whoopee," demoted at age 50 to chairman of wine by his dad, Zeus, waxes nostalgic for wild revelry ("He missed those nymphs, doggone it").

Many of the pieces in *The Book of Guys* are less stories than skits. The fable of the country mouse and the city mouse—in which a mild-mannered fellow abused by life in a major metropolis returns to, say, South Dakota—gets more air time than it can bear. Dependent as the slighter sketches are on Mr. Keillor's self-mocking voice, they're more effective in performance than on the page (buy the companion audiocassette, or see him live in a 17-city "Show of Guys Tour").

The most substantial tales aren't really about manhood at all, but about the arbitrariness and absurdity of modern success, especially in show business. In **"The Chuck Show of Television"** and **"Al Denny"**—at once the most autobiographically revealing stories and the most wildly imaginative ones—Mr. Keillor is at his subversive best. He drags his heroes through the mud of contemporary culture and teaches them the essential tongue-in-cheek Lake Wobegon lesson, as he formulated it in the book *We Are Still Married:* "not to imagine we *are* someone but to be content being who we are."

Once these Mr. Nice Guys get their comeuppance, they can relax and do the thing that guys like best—picking their noses and making jokes about it. *The Book of Guys* also contains a dozen-odd quips about flatulence, in all of its death-defying variety. Mr. Keillor may be performing a public service here, helping to pinpoint for sociologists the single major difference between men and women: the limit of their tolerance for witticisms about wind.

Judith Yaross Lee (essay date 1994)

SOURCE: "Five Ways of Looking at Aprille (with Apologies to Wallace Stevens): Analysis of Storytelling in the Twenty-First Century," in *Eye on the Future: Popular Culture Scholarship into the Twenty-First Century,* edited by Marilyn F. Motz, Bowling Green State University, 1994, pp. 91-106.

[*In the following essay, Yaross Lee uses Keillor's story "Aprille" to analyze the effect of medium on a story.*]

A slippery problem facing scholars of popular culture involves how to analyze examples that exist as multiple texts or performances rather than as a single stable artifact. Stable artifacts include the texts of popular fiction, tapes of radio or television broadcasts, and theatrical films or videotapes. The comic strip or book is somewhat less stable, since a scholar may have to grapple with the historical authority of the newspaper feature page versus the narrative authority of the anthology or comic book, but one can make a case for studying either version or both. A similar problem exists for some television series, which broadcast videotapes of live performances before a studio audience. *All in the Family* (1971-79), for instance, exists in two video forms: the master tapes of the live performances and the edited tapes of the broadcast series. Although the edited tapes captured most of the live performance's spontaneity—various pratfalls and glitches in performance became evidence of the taped show's authenticity—the cuts not only kept the show within necessary time limits, but also altered its substance: the off-color remark or gesture, long laughter from the audience. Still, a scholar can distinguish between the master and broadcast tapes in much the same way as between an author's manuscript and the published text. Despite the limitations of the broadcast tapes, which (among other things) obscure whether the audience laughed for 15, 30 or 55 seconds—they nonetheless are the authoritative texts for studying the work of producer Norman Lear and his cast. They represent commercial television, whereas the master tapes record only a studio performance.

By contrast with stable artifacts such as these, consider standup comedy and public storytelling. Both involve multiple performances that vary the material in many ways. Some variations are minor; others, substantive. Some represent a refinement; others, simply a variation with only subtle shifts in sense. Folklorists have made progress on but not really resolved the interpretive problems that result from multiple texts. Richard Bauman and Sandra K. D. Stahl have focused on the relation of each telling to its narrative context, for example, accounting for differences in the tellings in terms of the different narrative events. Contextual criticism thus downplays variations in phrasing and concentrates instead on theme, structure, and cultural significance. Seeing narrative details mainly as elements of a cultural message, however, gives the criticism a didactic thrust more appropriate to fairy tales than to the monologues of Johnny Carson or Spalding Gray. Under the circumstances, it is not surprising that even folklorists have found the thematic and structural approaches limiting. As Dell Hymes observed in his examination of a pair of transcriptions, "Each telling makes use of common ingredients, but it is precisely in the difference in the way they are deployed and shaped that the meaning of each is disclosed."

Variations matter even more in popular performances, which have become commodified as commercial art. Whereas the traditional folk narrator served as a medium of transmission, today's standup comedian or storyteller is the author of the material as well as its performer. The oral narratives of the standup comedian or public storyteller may sound like folklore, particularly the genre known as the personal experience narrative, and the anecdotes may in fact have originated in experience, yet the comedian and professional storyteller have no obligations to truthfulness. Audiences grant these performers the novelist's license to invent, and willingly suspend their disbelief. Variations from performance to performance are therefore more substantive than variations among performances of a folktale, even though traditional tellers commonly had their own, distinctive ways of telling a tale.

They are also more significant than variations in the performances of a scripted play. Whether introduced accidentally or deliberately by actors, director, crew, or performance space, variations on a script give different audiences different experiences of the play, but theoretically, at least, the performance remains somehow distinct from the play itself. Just as the musical performance is recognized as the approximate rendering of the ideas in the score (Dehnert), the dramatic performance is recognized as an approximate rendering of a definitive text. Such a text does not even exist for standup comedy and public storytelling, although we tend to behave as if it does. For a recent example of this phenomenon, con-

sider the efforts by Lenny Bruce's producer, Don Friedman, to recreate the comedian's 1961 Carnegie Hall performance in commemoration of what would have been Bruce's 67th birthday. The fifteen actors who auditioned in July 1992 based their impersonations not on Bruce's own monologues, which were of course ephemeral, nor even on Bruce's own recordings, which are more stable, but on the stable 1974 text of Dustin Hoffman's re-enactment of unstable routines in the film *Lenny*.

> **More important, the tale itself invites us to examine relations between oral and written storytelling, since Keillor structured "Aprille" around the ten-line opening of Chaucer's "Prologue," giving the oral story a thoroughly literary grounding.**
> *—Judith Yaross Lee*

As oral genres grounded in colloquial talk and tending toward improvisation, standup comedy and storytelling reverse the stage play's implied priority of written text over live performance. And not only is the performance more definitive than the written text: the various oral performances of a single story or routine vary in authority in relation to one another. Unlike the multiple video-texts of the television broadcast, one public performance will not have more authority than others, unless some are designated rehearsals or trials. Unlike the successive drafts of a manuscript, the most recent performance does not always stand as the artist's last word.

A particularly illuminating case in point is Garrison Keillor's 1986 story **"Aprille,"** which nearly defies classification. The story takes its inspiration from *The Canterbury Tales,* builds its theme on a passage from the New Testament, and blends his wife Ulla Skaerved's recollection of a childhood game on the bus with half a dozen fictional Lake Wobegon anecdotes—all the while purporting to tell his own experiences. So, **"Aprille"** is not folklore, not even "literary" folklore like the personal experience narrative, though it imitates folklore: the monologue is a professional performance presenting fictional personal experiences of narrator Garrison Keillor of Lake Wobegon, Minnesota (a fictional town)—all of these created by writer Garrison Keillor of Anoka. Nor is **"Aprille"** a short story, since it was composed primarily for oral performance, not for print. Nor is it television, since the Disney cameras that recorded the show (originally transmitted live via cable and later shown over public television) shot it from the vantage point of the studio audience—as a radio program being witnessed by an audience, not as a show that was meant to be telecast. But the monologue is not conventional radio, either, since the speaker engages in intimate conversation and lies instead of the public and factual material that make up normal radio talk. All these modes of storytelling contribute to the tale's humor by inviting and then frustrating our generic expectations.

More important, the tale itself invites us to examine relations between oral and written storytelling, since Keillor structured **"Aprille"** around the ten-line opening of Chaucer's "Prologue," giving the oral story a thoroughly literary grounding. The recitation not only reminds us that *The Canterbury Tales* itself presented purportedly oral stories as written texts, but also calls attention to the difference between the text-bound activity of memorization and the performance-based activity of improvisation in Keillor's own narration. In addition, as Chaucer's words set the springtime Minnesota scene for the main story—how Lois Tollerud, a young woman troubled by the existence of evil in the world, does not find her faith on Confirmation Day, yet nothing happens as a result—Keillor also establishes a series of thematic parallels among the three pilgrims of the tale. Lois, Keillor, and Chaucer all undertake spiritual journeys that turn into occasions for storytelling, and in **"Aprille"** as in *The Canterbury Tales,* the pilgrims' stories become more important than the religious goals inspiring them.

Despite the seriousness of its themes and structure, **"Aprille"** remains typical of Keillor's work: it is also a very amusing story. Narrator Keillor's own pilgrimage fails when he arrives in Lake Wobegon and finds that his whole family apparently ran out the back door, at which point his journey to see them devolves into a quest for a toilet. His goddaughter Lois is also on a quest (she's looking to regain her faith in God), but at first they find only each other. As one anticlimactic anecdote leads to another, the humor builds in a conversational, apparently unstructured way that belies Keillor's intense labor on it.

The monologue was the centerpiece of a performance celebrating the grand re-opening of St. Paul's World Theater on Friday, April 25, 1986, and it was broadcast live the following night during his regular Saturday evening radio show, **"A Prairie Home Companion"** (1974-87). Keillor's popularity in 1986, soon after he agreed to allow the Disney Channel to cablecast the weekly show, made the April 26 broadcast extremely important to him, and even after the opening "concert" (i.e., non-broadcast) performance on Friday evening he continued tinkering with the details and themes of the story all the way up to broadcast time on Saturday night. Before each oral performance, he worked at his word-processor, printed out a draft, and edited it by hand. The result of this process is five variants of the tale: the Friday computer printout with handwritten emendations (version 1, 4/25/86), the Friday evening broadcast (version 2, 4/25/86), the Saturday computer printout with handwritten emendations (version 3, 4/26/86), the Saturday evening broadcast (version 4, 4/26/86), and the published *Leaving Home* story (version 5).

The first text (version 1) contains all three of the main stories—Lois's lost faith, Einer Tingvold's lost binoculars, and young Gary's fear of being isolated from family and friends—along with a fourth anecdote about the Tolleruds' agnostic Uncle Gunnar, which remained in all three written versions but was never included in an oral rendition. But several crucial details in Lois's story changed after the first performance, and the ending of the narrative continued to evolve through the second performance (version 4). Several of the most significant changes in his second performance did not, however, find their way into the published version of **"Aprille,"** which appeared in *Leaving Home,* a collection of Lake Wobegon tales published shortly after **"A Prairie Home Companion"** went off the air. Although Keillor's introductory **"Letter from Copenhagen"** described *Leaving Home'*s stories as "written for performance on the radio," this fifth, published version of **"Aprille"** is neither a transcription nor a reworking of either oral performance, but rather a minor revision of the second printout (version 3).

Together the five variants of **"Aprille"** illustrate the problems inherent in analyzing the unstable texts of oral popular culture and point the way toward more systematic and sensitive analysis of storytelling in the twenty-first century. We need to find techniques appropriate to these texts and to understand the increasingly important roles of print, broadcasting, computers, and audio tape in defining them.

"Aprille" illustrates the fundamental difficulty of identifying exactly what is the story, since unlike the successive drafts of a manuscript the five variants of the tale do not exist in simple chronological relation to one another. Additions to the written text carry over thematically, if not always literally, into the next oral telling, yet improvisations in the oral tale are seldom incorporated into the next draft. The process thus underlines the greater importance of the oral versions, and their greater autonomy, and suggests that the final written version of the story (version 5) remains less significant than the second oral performance (version 4).

The first printout, for example, shows Keillor working to expand the description of springtime in Lake Wobegon at the beginning of **"Aprille."** Next to the typed remarks about trees and birds, he added a handwritten note in the margin: "The NBFs are washing their sheets, a sure sign" (version 1). In the first oral performance that same evening, he provided an even fuller description, saying, "this last week the Norwegian bachelor farmers washed their sheets, which is a sure sign that the cold weather, cold weather is over, and they're starting now to think about the danger of, the danger of infection" (version 2). The repetition of the phrases "cold weather" and "the danger of" work like "um" or "uh," as voiced pauses suggesting that Keillor invented the phrasing on the spot, and this implication of spontaneity asserts the authenticity of the storytelling event: the speaker hasn't prepared his remarks in advance. In this case the phrasing almost certainly was spontaneous, however, since none of the other variants repeats it exactly.

The next day, the second printout (version 3) shows Keillor integrating into his electronic text the marginal note from the first printout, but *not* the remark about "the danger of infection" from the previous night's oral performance. Instead, the text notes merely, "and now the Norwegian bachelor farmers are washing their sheets—" (version 3). The remark remains in that form in version 5, the version published in *Leaving Home* 15 months later. In the second oral performance (version 4), however, Keillor altered not only the phrasing of the item but also its placement and details. He postponed mentioning the Norwegian bachelor farmers until after he had described Lake Wobegon's springtime scenery in detail, finally noting, "the Norwegian bachelor farmers hung out their sheets, this last week, finally washing their sheets after those long winter months. Now it's finally safe to do em" (version 4).

These variations in such a simple matter demonstrate that Keillor's weekly monologue had more in common with a jazz performance than with an impromptu speech. That is, the monologue was a planned performance featuring spontaneous talk. The demands of live radio made this risky enterprise all the more precarious, since a live broadcast cannot be edited if the program runs too long. In all his years on this tightrope, Keillor fell only once, in Juneau, Alaska on July 12, 1986, when he just could not bring his monologue to a close, even though he had written a nine-page text for himself. Keillor worked out the components of **"Aprille"** carefully but nonetheless embellished and altered it in performance. His written drafts therefore represent prompts for the performance, suggesting the directions of his thoughts and his thematic intentions, but remaining subordinate as texts to the public performances.

For example, consider the different reasons that the bachelor farmers finally do their laundry. In the first telling they wash the sheets because it's warm enough for the bacteria in them to breed; in the second telling they wash them because it's finally warm enough to risk coming in contact with water. Keillor does not seem simply to have changed his mind here; the two jokes are equivalent. The point is the eccentric variation on the traditional obsession with spring cleaning. The exact rite is less important than the fact that a rite exists because the rite is more ritualistic than practical. In the case of the Norwegian bachelor farmers, spring cleaning accomplishes very little. Washing their sheets—for whatever reason—will not appreciably raise their level of hygiene. Perhaps more important for a theory of oral narra-

tive, equivalent variation is possible because oral tellings do not supplant one another in the same way that successive drafts do. Whereas interpretation of writing rests on the principle of final intention, in which the authoritative text is the last of successive written drafts, interpretation of oral storytelling requires a principle of simultaneous authority, in which each telling has equal validity.

If the substance of these differences matters very little, the fact that the differences exist matters very much, indeed. The anecdote is full in the oral performances and sketchy in the printouts, in a progression typical of oral retellings. Richard Baumann notes that stories tend to grow when retold, especially when the teller commands the attention of the audience without having to seize it from other parties present— the difference, for example, between yarn spinning around a campfire or in conversation and the full performance of a storytelling festival, in which the featured storyteller is expected to demonstrate virtuosity. But the relationship between Keillor's written texts and the next telling reflects the complexity of the hybrid genre within which he works. Although details become more elaborate in the retellings, episodes may be rearranged, truncated, or eliminated. For example, both oral performances of **"Aprille"** mention the day of a rainstorm, and in the second performance Keillor elaborates the detail by making a show of searching his memory for the exact day—"[I'm] thinking about an afternoon, like—well, Tuesday, or Wednesday aft—Wednesday afternoon, after that tremendous rain that we had in the morning" (version 4)—but none of the written versions, including the version published in *Leaving Home,* refers to a specific day of the week. By contrast, Keillor apparently considered Daryl's Uncle Gunnar important enough to devote about 250 words to his eccentricities in each of the written texts, including the *Leaving Home* version, but Uncle Gunnar does not make even a brief appearance in either oral performance. We cannot know whether Keillor dropped the anecdote to keep the monologue within the allotted time (one aspect of his virtuosity was surely his ability to work within the finely calibrated time intervals of live radio), or whether he lost interest in the material but failed to delete it from the computer file that ultimately became the text in *Leaving Home.* Any analysis of the story must take this inconsistency into account, but it points to the theoretical difficulty of assuming that versions in two media stand in strict chronological succession to one another.

Other differences, however, clearly show the artist changing his material and sharpening his vision of it. Apparently dissatisfied with the tale he told on Friday night, Keillor sat down on Saturday and made two major changes in the computer text that became version 3. He deleted three suspected miracles that inspired Lois to keep an open mind about her lost faith, and moved the anecdote about Einer Tingvold to follow rather than precede the tale of playing strangers on the bus. Integrating these changes led to others, resulting in very different themes and meanings between the Friday and Saturday versions, oral and written.

In Friday's versions 1 and 2, the possibility of miracles tempers Lois's crisis of faith. The hot water does not run out as usual on Saturday night, her mother manages to get a stain out of Lois's confirmation dress, and her father's arm does not burn when his new sweater catches fire from the candles on her cake. These events strike her as possible evidence that God does exist, and they allow **"Aprille"** to end with some optimism for Lois and for all the faithful. Removing them, on the other hand, diverts the tale from questions of God's existence to questions of human faith. It also allows Keillor to emphasize the parallels between Lois and himself: she becomes terrified when her prayers echo without response, just as he had been frightened as a child when another Lois, his aunt, pretended during their game of "Strangers" that she did not know him.

As deleting the miracles diminished the tale's optimism, so moving the Einer Tingvold anecdote altered the story's original theme. An example of faith sure-to-be-found in versions 1 and 2 became a warning about faith abandoned in versions 3 through 5. With the story of how Tingvold threw away the next day's breakfast eggs and his own beloved binoculars just because he was frustrated that an unruly group of Boy Scouts wouldn't learn semaphore signals, Keillor provides a highly comic parable on the dangers facing Lois in her doubts about God on the eve of her confirmation. The anecdote's new position after the story of playing "Strangers," a game in which a young Keillor and his aunt Lois pretend not to know one another until the boy feels frightened and lost, emphasizes the consequences of throwing away one's religious values in the heat of a moment's disappointment. At the same time, the binoculars need not symbolize faith or even integrity to provide a reason for telling Einer's tale, since its details offer the considerable pleasures of comic retribution. As a result, **"Aprille"** not only implies the orthodox conclusions that Lois's faith in God matters less than God's faith in her, and that neither God nor faith will abandon her if she does not throw them away or try to become someone she is not, but also insinuates the downright blasphemous notion that faith is irrelevant to a good story. In this context, the parallel between Lois's story and Einer's also intensifies relations among the three storytellers in **"Aprille"**: Keillor, Lois, and Chaucer.

Eliminating divine intervention (or the perception of it) also required changes to the ending of the monologue. In the first oral performance, he started with the simple conclusion of his written text—"For the fourteen year olds of this world, I'm glad to get old so they can grow up and we'll see what they do with themselves" (version 1)—and extended it into

a comment on how the world as a whole benefits from the courage of the young, "who having lost their faith could stand on the edge of darkness and wait for it to return" (version 2). By the next day, however, his written text proposed that loss of faith has less to do with God than with ourselves. People get caught up in games like "Strangers" and, after a time of playing at being someone else, forget who they really are. Nonetheless, God's grace remains as reliable as the signs of springtime: "the sweet breath, the tendre croppes, and the smale fowle maken melodye—God watches each one and knows when it falls, and so much more does He watch us all" (version 3). The power of Chaucer's poetry and Keillor's rhythmic line, a resolution to the question of evil, and the storyteller's virtuoso control over an apparently formless tale bring the third version of **"Aprille"** to a powerful close.

But although Keillor carried over this ending from version 3 to version 5, the text published in *Leaving Home,* he did not repeat it in version 4, his final oral performance. Apparently on inspiration in that Saturday night broadcast, he loosened the connection between spring and reborn faith. Instead, he proposed a more generalized power in "this world, and each other, and the people in it": "Well, I'm transformed by this world, the one that I look at. It's so beautiful. I believe that it has the power to make us brave, and to make us good. This world, and each other, and the people in it. It has the power to give us faith, the sweet breath of the wind and the tender crops, and the small fowles maken melodye that slepen all the nycht with open eye" (version 4). Whereas the written texts of versions 3 and 5 offer the traditional Christian insistence on faith in spite of doubt, the oral text of version 4 offers consolation through poetry, not doctrine.

My point is not simply that Keillor declined to revise the second written version to incorporate changes made in the second telling, or even (as I suspect), that at some level of consciousness he chose an orthodox conclusion for his stable written texts and a more ambiguous ending for his unstable oral texts. Rather, the issue is, what finally is "the story"? The lesson of **"Aprille"** is that scholars of storytelling need to answer that question on an individual basis for every tale and teller. For now we must conclude that the story is not, to borrow terms proposed by Barbara Herrnstein Smith, some "basic story" consisting of elements common to the five variants, nor a Platonic ideal of the tale constructed from bits and pieces of the variants. Moreover, a reliable analysis cannot look solely at the published text of an oral tale, no matter how much one would like to replace multiple unstable texts with a single stable one. Any reconstruction of "the story" must take into account sequential, substantive changes that amount to revisions, as well as accidental variations, like the bachelor farmers' laundry day, that represent what Erving Goffman calls "fresh talk."

"Aprille" is, therefore, a different story in each of the two media that its author worked in and in the different versions in each medium. The tale of faith lost and found clearly belongs to the stable world of print texts, as represented in *Leaving Home.* The more ambiguous quest for faith in the oral versions of "Aprille" remains, appropriately enough, unresolved in the unstable texts of the performances. We cannot really understand "Aprille" if we do not know whether the ending envisions a world made wonderful by God or by the people in it, whether the answer to the problem of evil in the world lies in religious faith or in awe over nature. Yet the nature of oral storytelling means that instead of choosing one ending, we must somehow—like Keillor himself—embrace both.

The discontinuity between the fourth and fifth versions—that is, between the second performance and the published version in *Leaving Home*—reminds us that every oral telling begins afresh, whereas successive printouts from a word processor reflect only changes wrought upon the electronic text. The five variants together illustrate the creative process of a single mind, but as texts the oral and written versions of "Aprille" stand somewhat independent of one another. Instead of looking at the five versions as a single series, then, we need to see a more complex relationship among the variants. The three written variants (versions 1, 3, 5) have an evolutionary relationship to one another, yet the second printout has a special significance. It incorporates ideas stimulated by the first oral telling and plots out the most important changes incorporated into the second telling. For similar reasons, the second telling has somewhat more authority than the first, since Keillor incorporates into the Saturday night version ideas first used in the Friday performance and the Saturday draft. On the other hand, Keillor's practice of improvising his narratives like jazz performances rather than memorizing his texts like scripts means that every oral telling is an authoritative text somewhat autonomous from the most recent written text. An oral telling has an evolutionary relationship to previous performances yet stands independent of them.

The different endings of different versions thus offer yet another contrast between the unstable texts of oral stories, and such stable texts as Chaucer's poetry and the Bible. Oral stories are unidirectional, unlike written texts, which allow a reader to flip back and forth among the pages. And whereas the intent listener concentrates on the last joke only at risk of missing the next gem, a reader has the leisure to explore implications between the lines. In the context of three subverted pilgrimages, the dominant theme of the written tale, whether God loves Lois seems not so much paradoxical (the implication of the oral story) as irrelevant. In the end, the "Aprille" of the written texts characterizes religion as the narrative means to a narrative end—a subject for tales and an excuse for storytelling. Perhaps the goal of the oral yarn was to encourage religious faith, perhaps not: the end at once promotes and suspects piety. But in the written tale, which acquires a different emphasis, religion itself has a goal, and that goal undoubtedly is storytelling itself.

> **In the oral performance of "Aprille," Keillor's memory not only sustains him through a long recitation in passable Middle English, but also enables him to embellish the prepared story on the spot. Without this display of memory, the story loses other crucial elements: our awe of the storyteller, apparently spinning this yarn just for us as we sit enchanted by his gift; and our delight in language, perhaps the most powerful oral gratification.**
> *—Judith Yaross Lee*

For this reason, transcription will never provide a satisfactory solution to the problems of studying oral performance. The process of transforming an oral text into a written one also gives the unstable oral text the appearance of a stable printed text. On that basis, audio tape is probably not the answer, either, though it represents a tremendous improvement over the inadequate transcript. Audio-visual CD-ROM technology, on the other hand, offers a superior means of storing, retrieving, and perhaps even quoting excerpts from oral narratives, since it can evade some problems of transcription by using the speakers already installed in personal computers (a sound board will improve the fidelity), and CD-ROM technology already in use makes it possible to search for specific phrases and hear them recited while the text also appears on the screen. With appropriate software, scholars could input their own material for such random access and analysis, which would offset the unidirectionality of live and conventionally recorded storytelling. Ideally, we could search not only for keywords but also for inflections, pauses, and mannerisms—all of them represented as digitized patterns—without the trouble of optical scanning or other forms of data entry. In this utopian scheme, the oral source will continue to be examined as an oral source, not as a visual representation of an oral source. Newer technologies may offer better alternatives.

While transcription therefore threatens any oral performance, it is particularly damaging to "Aprille," whose oral performances rely on devices for which no print-based equivalents exist. How can the printed page express the unselfconscious tone of voice, the appearance of artlessness and spontaneity, or the perfectly timed pause? Keillor's practice of plotting out his monologues but not scripting or memorizing them gave the tales elements of literary composition while fostering genuine improvisation in performance. When he structured **"Aprille"** around a ten-line passage from *The Canterbury Tales* and lengthy verse from the New Testament, he intensified this already risky game of memory and improvisation. A printed quotation cannot convey the least degree of artlessness or spontaneity. Nor can it demonstrate Keillor's remarkable memory, which produces these effects in the first place. By contrast, in the oral performance of **"Aprille,"** Keillor's memory not only sustains him through a long recitation in passable Middle English, but also enables him to embellish the prepared story on the spot. Without this display of memory, the story loses other crucial elements: our awe of the storyteller, apparently spinning this yarn just for us as we sit enchanted by his gift; and our delight in language, perhaps the most powerful oral gratification. Seven pages of reading cannot match the rhetorical impact of Keillor's 30-minute performance—he called it a séance—for the very medium of print inhibits, though of course it does not entirely obscure, the tale's celebration of words—Chaucer's, Keillor's, and the Bible's.

In the oral performance of **"Aprille,"** even *script*ure is oral. Several times the storyteller recites parts of Lois's confirmation verse, relishing its sounds, but he quotes the full text only once, when describing how Marilyn Tollerud inscribed all 31 words—"Be not conformed to this world: but be ye transformed by the renewing of your mind, that ye may prove what is that good, and acceptable, and perfect, will of God"—in blue frosting atop Lois's cake. One could hardly ask for a more oral use of a text than to turn it into food, and then to turn the food into a joke for oral performance. This gentle ridicule of the Tolleruds' celebration quite literally, and not so gently, reduces the Bible to a mouthful of words, of which Keillor's share on his square of cake reads "Con but for"—a hint at the humorist's con-game. The long recitation of the verse on the cake exploits the advantages of oral performance by demonstrating the teller's prodigious memory, all the more impressive at the end of the narrative when he reasserts his control over all his apparent digressions by reciting Chaucer's poetry.

But no moment of **"Aprille"** better illustrates the essence of oral yarn spinning, and Keillor's brilliance at it, than his modulations and pauses at a key point in mid-story. (The phrasing varies from version to version, but the episode exists in all five variants.) Slipping from his role of observing narrator, he adopts Lois's point of view to relate her thoughts on good and evil during a solitary walk in the woods after lunch, while her family eats the cake. He continues to tell the story from Lois's perspective as he describes her frantic efforts to run away from a man standing by the road, whom "she knew . . . was put there by an evil force . . . and that this was Evil roaming the world, and looking for whomever it may devour" (version 4, 4/26/86). Tension increases as she falls, begging him for mercy. "'Please, please,' she said, 'don't do it.'" Keillor's voice drops to a whisper in the ten-

sion. Then he pauses, raises the pitch, and in a slightly bewildered tone, adds unexpectedly, "Which surprised me. . . ." In the pause following this wrenching shift of perspective, we realize that our storyteller was the man standing there, that Lois made a mistake; the revelation rescues Lois and the tale comically as it evades the question of evil. Nonetheless, this exquisite moment from the oral performances, a rhetorical tour de force, does not appear in *Leaving Home.* In the printed version of **"Aprille,"** a new paragraph just under Lois's words begins simply and directly, "I hadn't seen her for five years." Whether or not he had added the remark about his surprise, Keillor might still have revised the written text to startle his readers as he had shocked his listeners—that is, to translate the oral-aural experience into a literary one. But he didn't. In place of the stunning oral performance, the printed text offers the aesthetic compensations of print, careful construction and themes worth reflection.

> **Seven pages of reading cannot match the rhetorical impact of Keillor's 30-minute performance—he called it a séance—for the very medium of print inhibits, though of course it does not entirely obscure, the tale's celebration of words—Chaucer's, Keillor's, and the Bible's.**
> —*Judith Yaross Lee*

The power of the monologues also derives from a number of non-narrative elements in their performance. Keillor's voice—intense, sincere, companionable—was a major factor in his stories' appeal, much enhanced by the intimacy of radio as a medium and his understanding of how to exploit it. The monologues portray one colloquial, confessional voice speaking directly to the individual radio listener—one companion chatting to another. The obviously live, unscripted performance added to the illusion of spontaneous conversation. So did the choice of "panned mono" technique for the stereo broadcasts, since this sound mix emulates live, directional, non-broadcast speech. But Keillor's genius lay in matching his message to the medium. As he worked out the Matter of Minnesota for oral storytelling, he borrowed techniques from oral narrative traditions. In these traditions, Walter Ong observes in "Writing is a Technology That Restructures Thought," oral stories link present and past, memory and orality, knower and known—all in the "simultaneous present" created by live narration. The fundamental orality of **"Aprille,"** despite its literary structure and literate story material, points to the source of the Lake Wobegon monologues' appeal: they mimic our most beloved kinds of folklore.

"Aprille" and Keillor's other apparently improvised monologues, like those of many standup comics and professional storytellers, are invented stories masquerading as personal experience narratives. That is, they are literary fictions imitating folk legends and artistic performances imitating unpremeditated talk. Autobiographical experience inspired many Lake Wobegon anecdotes, yet Keillor consistently subordinated facts to his narrative purpose, fully fictionalizing them. Similarly, interaction with his audience helped shape the narration of his oral stories even though the rules of professional storytelling performances allow a studio audience only the limited responses of laughter and applause. In conversational storytelling, by contrast, listeners may ask questions if they're interested, and seize the floor from the speaker if they're not. They may also cue the performer in any number of nonverbal ways to alter the pace of the tale. But just as his stories are not folklore, neither are they "radio talk," as Goffman terms it. Announcers are supposed to talk about real events of moment in the real world, not invented anti-climaxes in an imaginary town, and at least part of the monologues' humor from the very beginning stemmed from their violation of listeners' expectations. Radio storytelling separates teller and listener even further than the professional story performance. A radio audience has no active role to play during narration. Neither the performer nor anyone else notices if a listener falls asleep, walks away, or even turns off the set (commercial radio has a vested interest in identifying programs that cannot hold their listeners, but public radio, lacking sponsors, has no such audience research). Despite such odds against him, Keillor at the height of his popularity drew an estimated audience of some four million listeners to the weekly broadcast of **"A Prairie Home Companion,"** and they certainly were not passive. Each new story in the Lake Wobegon saga brought letters of commentary, suggestions for stories, and gifts to the storyteller.

Keillor's success as an oral storyteller came largely from his transformation of the personal narrative into a narrative genre appropriate for the electronic age.
—*Judith Yaross Lee*

Keillor's success as an oral storyteller came largely from his transformation of the personal narrative into a narrative genre appropriate for the electronic age. In that sense, he finally accomplished in the 1980s the return to tribal orality that Marshall McLuhan first predicted some 20 years earlier in *Understanding Media,* although it is his skill as a writer that makes this achievement possible. But of course Keillor's stories belong to the *electronic* hearth, and as a result they exemplify the ephemerality of communication in an electronic age. Radio stories leave no artifactual texts. Computers allow writers to write and overwrite the same text, bringing us many authoritative texts, even though some revisions will

remain invisible, existing only on a disk. In this sense, despite its origins in such canonical literature as the Bible and *The Canterbury Tales,* **"Aprille"** belongs to the world of post-modernism, in which instability, ambiguity, and multiplicity rule.

In its liminal position between the literate and the oral, **"Aprille"** challenges scholars to move beyond reductive transcriptions that put oral texts into print. Instead, we must interpret the artifacts of popular culture—print, broadcast, computer texts, audio and video tape—in the terms of whatever media they use. For broadcasts and other unstable artifacts, that means acknowledging simultaneous authority of multiple texts rather than seeking the stable meanings of a writer's last intention. The list of popular narrative media will surely grow in the twenty-first century, and our theory must be ready to meet them.

Robert M. Adams (review date 13 January 1994)

SOURCE: "Boys Will Be Boys," in *The New York Review of Books,* January 13, 1994, p. 19.

[*In the following review, Adams asserts that, "It's not likely that* [The Book of Guys] *will give rise to much prolonged reflection, but it can hardly fail to provoke a number of chuckles."*]

Though in colloquial usage it's become something else, a *guy* began as a dummy, something to kick around, and out of a number of such masculine boobies, Garrison Keillor has made a book. Keillor has done sketches of this nature for recital on television—he is best known as the laureate of Lake Wobegon—and many of these fantasies-satires-diatribes would not be out of place in the saga of that freshwater metropolis. One thing *The Book of Guys* is not is a comprehensive report on the state of guydom in America. Keillor's guys are a hen-pecked, downtrodden bunch, to be sure, not quite at the level of Dagwood Bumstead, but sheepish and oppressed and inarticulate after the fashion of George F. Babbitt. There was, if memory serves, quite a flurry in the earlier years of the century about the spiritual castration of the American male. Philip Wylie denounced the trend with Old Testament indignation, and James Thurber played on the theme, bringing to it, as one would expect, a delicate vein of irony. Keillor is a great deal closer to Thurber than to his other predecessors, but in either mode it is an interestingly persistent theme.

At the heart of guydom, whatever the particular form it takes, one can generally recognize a trace of little-boy nostalgia for freedom from manners and the respectable, generally maternal, disciplines they imply. The guy is generally an authentic little savage who refuses to wash his face, comb his hair, or put on a necktie, lest he be considered "sissy." Huck Finn is a guy of guys, and good as he is, we've had too many versions of him. Fortunately, Garrison Keillor has more strings to his bow than that one. Along with the multiple restraints of small-town domestic respectability, his guys are menaced by particularly voracious females mouthing the lingo of ill-digested psychoanalysis, and by the depressing debilitations of the mid-life crisis.

Consider, for example, the difficulties of Dionysus, the eternal party animal, who finds to his dismay that he has turned fifty, his immortality having been suspended for the sake of the satire, his existence being in thrall to a particularly dreary psychoanalyst, and for the first time in thousands of years he is experiencing a backache. (In passing, one cannot help thinking that advancing years are not a particularly guy problem, that Venus herself, subjected to the same life changes as Dionysus, would have much the same troubles adjusting.)

The piquancy of these occasional classical sketches is heightened by Keillor's splendid command of the lingo of modern pretension. His women are, naturally, particularly good at this gibberish. "Danny," says a wife to her husband, "in some way my love for you is a symptom of my denial of myself, an attempt to make myself invisible."

Or again, from the same female: "We need to change that love from something angry to a *mature* love. I can't use you as an instrument of my self-hatred."

Or there's a vagabond floozie who confesses to Buddy the Leper that she doesn't "have broad parameters when it comes to happiness." This is fine stuff. Despisers of George Bush will particularly relish the burlesque devoted to that unhappy man. It begins:

> The day the barbarians came, George Bush was out in a boat on the Potomac River with Willie Horton, fishing, and Willie said, "Mister Butch, how come you always be jigglin and tappin yo foot? Man, those fish ain't goin to come within a *mile* of us if you makin this racket. Let your foot be, man. Sit still."

> "Willie," said the President, "you know the—we're going to clean up here, get some fish, have a heck of a time. Not a vague hope. Talkin promise now. Serious fishing. Got you out of prison for the afternoon. Little favor. Don't mention it. Didn't bring you out here to get a tan, Willie. Came to do a little *fishin.*"

In all there are twenty-two of these skits; arranged on weekly television shows, doubtless they would be more effective one at a time than when crowded together in the form of a book. But nothing prevents the reader from nibbling on them at intervals as he chooses. It's not likely that the book will give rise to much prolonged reflection, but it can hardly fail to provoke a number of chuckles. I wouldn't predict for it a large feminine readership.

Sam Walker (review date 26 January 1994)

SOURCE: "Two Authors Grade the Inner Guy," in *The Christian Science Monitor,* Vol. 86, January 26, 1994, p. 14.

[*In the following excerpt, Walker praises Keillor's comic talents, but criticizes* The Book of Guys *for a lack of focus, consistency, and its vulgarity.*]

After years of quiet confusion, American men are telling their stories. Sometimes the result is invigorating. Other times it's like aiming a mirror at a group of angry gorillas. Nevertheless, the dialogue has made it out of the sweat lodge and into the mainstream.

The Book of Guys, by Garrison Keillor, and *Working Men,* by Michael Dorris, are the latest initiates into the fraternity of "male" literature. Both writers have men on their minds, but that's where the similarity ends.

Keillor, host of a weekly radio show and author of *Radio Days,* uses *The Book of Guys* to flex his funny muscles. Throughout the book, his talent for exposing societal absurdities shines, and one doesn't have to be a Midwesterner to appreciate his biting satire of the region. If you like to mark memorable passages by folding down corners, beware: Keillor can be funny on both sides of the page.

His best story is **"Lonesome Shorty,"** an account of a cowboy who gets fed up with life on the range and decides to settle down. **"That Old Picayune-Moon,"** the tale of a mayor harassed by a zealous newspaper editor, and the book's lengthy introduction also contain flashes of comic genius. And at times, Keillor's characters express real insights: **"Don Giovanni"** points up the difficulty many men have with competing desires for family and freedom. But behind the giggles, the reader can hear the unmistakable whir of an irritated guy grinding a few axes. Keillor uses *The Book of Guys* to take swings at everybody and perhaps to chop away at the cute, folksy image he cultivated in his most popular book, *Lake Wobegon Days.*

In **"Winthrop Thorpe Tortuga,"** Keillor tells the story of a man who balances a laissez faire attitude toward his family with a penchant for "random acts of cruelty." After counseling his wife about her adulterous affair and cooking breakfast for his teenage daughter's sleep-over boyfriend, Winthrop soothes himself by, among other things, calling in a bomb threat to a home for indigent actors.

Winthrop's behavior is amusing at first, but the novelty wanes as Keillor stirs in too many cruel, off-color jokes. Other stories lack focus. **"George Bush"** has a clever premise—the former president going fishing with Willie Horton—but quickly deteriorates into a pointless political satire. In the middle of **"Earl Grey"** and **"Roy Bradley, Boy Broadcaster,"** the reader can sense Keillor's concentration fading. **"The Chuck Show of Television"** barely rivals Howard Stern for sophistication. On the whole, Keillor's portrait of men is grim. His protagonists come in three categories: hapless and gentle, hapless and depressed, or hapless and cruel, in descending order of appeal. They have trouble with family life, traditional values, and societal conventions, and they appear to be content only in rare moments of glory.

In addition, female characters appear almost solely as bossy matrons or sex objects. **"Buddy the Leper"** is particularly difficult in this regard.

If you read this book, your level of pleasure may not surpass your threshold for vulgarity. . . .

So don't put these two books on the same shelf of your literary pantry. When the male gender gets you down, grab *The Book of Guys* as you would a box of Cheez-Its. But when you're ready for the earthy flavor of a baked potato, reach for *Working Men*. Either way, Dorris and Keillor can help to feed the hunger of a thinking guy.

Sonja K. and Karen A. Foss (essay date November 1994)

SOURCE: "The Construction of Feminine Spectatorship in Garrison Keillor's Radio Monologues," in *The Quarterly Journal of Speech,* Vol. 80, No. 4, November, 1994, pp. 410-26.

[*In the following essay, Sonja and Karen Foss delineate the ways in which Keillor's radio monologues uphold a feminist epistomology.*]

Interest in the role played by cultural texts in subject formation has contributed to the development of the notion of spectatorship, a preferred viewpoint from which to view the world of the text. A text, this notion suggests, constructs a position the spectator must occupy in order to participate in the pleasures and meaning of the text. This position requires a participatory cultural experience in order to make sense of the text and is the result of the structures of characters, meanings, aesthetic codes, attitudes, norms, and values the author projects into the text. Despite its origin in film theory, the notion of the spectator need not be confined to cinematic texts. Gledhill's term, *"textual spectator,"* suggests a position that may be held in regard to any kind of text. Mulvey also suggests that spectatorship occurs in various types of cultural material, both verbal and visual.

Most popular representations structure a masculine position for the spectator; they assume and construct a "male protagonist . . . free to command the stage . . . of spatial illusion in which he articulates the look and creates the action." Mulvey explains the results of this masculine spectatorship:

> As the spectator identifies with the main male protagonist, he projects his look onto that of his like, his screen surrogate, so that the power of the male protagonist as he controls events coincides with the active power of the erotic look, both giving a satisfying sense of omnipotence.

The female subject in such texts, in contrast, usually is positioned as the object rather than the subject of the gaze—displayed for the gaze and enjoyment of men. As a spectator, the woman positions herself either as a passive recipient of male desire or as a viewer of another woman who is a passive recipient of male desire. Visual pleasure in film, on television, in the press, and in most popular narratives "reproduces a structure of male looking/female-to-be-looked-at-ness" that "replicates the structure of unequal power relations between men and women."

As useful and insightful as analyses of masculine viewing patterns have been in explicating patriarchal ways of looking, "they offer largely negative accounts of female spectatorship, suggesting colonized, alienated, or masochistic positions of identification." Feminist theorists, particularly film critics, have begun to take up the challenge to move beyond a preoccupation with how women have been constructed as objects to answer questions such as: "Can we envision a female dominant position that would differ qualitatively from the male form of dominance?" "How have we come to understand cinematic pleasure . . . as pleasurable to the male viewer, but not the female?" Feminist scholars have sought to discover, in other words, the nature of women's presence in, rather than absence from, the viewing experience—the nature of feminine spectatorship.

The notion of feminine spectatorship is not meant to suggest that it is a vantage point that can be assumed only by women, that its characteristics are natural or essential attributes of femininity, or that women always see differently from men. The term suggests, instead, a repertoire of culturally constructed characteristics likely to be possessed by and/or ascribed to women under present cultural and political arrangements. Construction of a feminine vantage point in a text, then, is the structuring into the text of activities, experiences, and qualities more likely to characterize women's than men's lives.

But many feminist theorists seek larger goals than the identification and explication of the nature of feminine spectatorship. They want to change patriarchal relations of looking, seeking to discover how the patriarchal perspective can be shifted and a female gaze inscribed as an option into cultural life. As Gamman and Marshment suggest, because women and men are offered the culture's dominant definitions of themselves in popular culture, "[i]t would therefore seem crucial to explore the possibilities and pitfalls of intervention in popular forms in order to find ways of making feminist meanings a part of our pleasures." They aim to discover techniques and forms that could "be used by feminists to 'subvert' dominant meanings about women in popular culture and to create pleasure, surprise, and interest in feminism." Such is our intent in this essay. We are interested in discovering how a feminine reader or spectator is constructed rhetorically in a text and how that construction can be used to subvert dominant meanings about women in popular culture. We will explore this question in the radio monologues of Garrison Keillor and will suggest that he constructs in them a position of feminine spectatorship.

We long have suspected that gender plays a critical role in Keillor's monologues simply because of the line with which his monologues end, "And that's the news from Lake Wobegon, where all the women are strong and all the men are good looking," an obvious reversal of traditional gender roles. Not until we focused our attention on the gendered dimensions of his monologues, however, did we realize the full extent to which he creates a preferred spectator position that relies on traditionally feminine competences and is structured to correspond with women's lives.

Garrison Keillor's monologues are part of a weekly radio program, initially called **"A Prairie Home Companion,"** sponsored by Minnesota Public Radio. The program was broadcast from St. Paul, Minnesota, on Saturday nights from April, 1974, until June, 1987, when Keillor ended the show to pursue other projects. In 1990, he resurrected the program with a new name, **"American Radio Company";** this new version originally was broadcast from New York City but was moved back to St. Paul in 1993. At the start of the 1993-94 season, Keillor resumed use of the program's previous name, **"A Prairie Home Companion."** The two-hour program consists of music ranging from country and folk to jazz and hymns, interspersed with fictitious commercials for Powdermilk Biscuits, Guy's Shoes, and the Cafe Boeuf. The highlight of each program for most listeners—and the focus of our interest here—is Keillor's monologues about an imaginary town in Minnesota, Lake Wobegon, introduced with the line, "It's been a quiet week in Lake Wobegon, my home town."

To analyze Keillor's monologues, we drew on observations developed from regular listening to **"A Prairie Home Companion"** from 1982 through the conclusion of the show in 1987 and to **"American Radio Company"** from 1990 to the present. We specifically taped 25 monologues from **"A Prairie Home Companion"** and 10 from **"American Radio Company"** from which to draw for specific examples and illustrations. We also analyzed the six tapes in the *News from Lake Wobegon* and *Gospel Birds and Other Stories of Lake Wobegon* collections, recordings of monologues by Keillor that have been packaged and sold by Minnesota Public Radio. Keillor's book, *Lake Wobegon Days,* provided background information about the imaginary town and its inhabitants to supplement the monologues.

We turn now to an analysis of the rhetorical processes Keillor uses to create a feminine spectator stance. We will suggest that this construction occurs through Keillor's refusal to privilege sight, dismantling of the male gaze, creation of Lake Wobegon as a feminine setting, and feminine speaking style.

Keillor's choice of radio as his medium of communication is a strong indication of his rejection of sight as a dominant way of approaching the world. His eschewal of vision as a means of coming to knowledge and understanding does not falter even when the show has been videotaped for airing on PBS and the Disney Channel. The programs that are videotaped are "still a show for the ear, not the eye" in that they are unaltered for television viewing. The backdrop for the show is the red brick wall at the rear of the stage, and the performers make no accommodations to the television medium, as Keillor explains:

> Nobody ever told us, "Look to Camera 3 here when you're doing this song," or "Walk upstage to your right." There were no chalk marks for us to hit. It's a television show of a radio show. It's all done as a radio show, sort of absentmindedly, nearsightedly, bumbling around on stage.

In his lack of adaptation to the visual dimension of television, Keillor highlights the reliance on sound that both radio and television share. Altman claims that the intermittent spectatorship that characterizes television viewing requires that the sound track carry the significant information to be conveyed because it "alone remains in contact with the audience." Television's emphasis on the "message-carrying ability of the sound track" is consistent with Keillor's reliance on sound to communicate with his listeners, even when the medium is television. Although the medium offers the possibility of the privileging of sight, Keillor refuses to take advantage of the option.

By refusing to privilege vision, Keillor disrupts the modern notion that seeing is believing—that vision "goes without deliberation." In his rejection of the notion that what is presented visually constitutes good evidence and is sufficient for knowledge, Keillor also rejects the view that vision is superior to the other senses, a claim supported by vision's detachment from objects and the purely theoretical relationship it adopts to them. Such a view of vision suggests the possibility, although fictive, of an objective distance from the world and of access to an objective truth about the world.

Although Keillor creates the world of Lake Wobegon in part through visual references, he does not posit vision as a privileged means of access to knowledge; he encourages his listeners to experience Lake Wobegon in terms other than sight alone. In one monologue, he privileges smell as capturing the essence of a family:

> Every family, I think, has their characteristic smell. It's how we know each other, and it's a smell that puts us at ease and makes us comfortable. The smell that says to us, "You don't need to be smart in front of these people, they know you. You just be yourself." A wonderful smell that we wash off every morning when we take a shower so that we get nervous and can go to work.

In another monologue, the sense of touch is his focus as he describes the sensation of climbing into bed, of crawling "into your cool, clean envelope of sheets."

Because the senses other than sight cannot be reduced to the mere collection of information but involve a more direct experience of the environment, Keillor grounds his monologues in the materiality of the body and creates a nearness to the object or person he seeks to know and understand. He throws off his authority as an objective observer who remains distant and withdrawn from what he observes. He centers understanding instead in the subjective, individual experiences of his listeners and in their participatory involvement in the world through an array of senses—not just sight.

That vision is not a privileged route to knowledge is evident in Keillor's monologues in that sight often does not provide access to truth—it may not result in insight or understanding. Temporary blindness or a blockage of sight on the part of characters in his monologues frequently foils the advantages vision is presumed to bring to the observer. Sometimes, the residents of Lake Wobegon actually are prevented from physically seeing, as when the rain is "falling in the lake and mist out on the lake so that you can't see to the other side." Ella Anderson's efforts to gain knowledge through sight are blocked when "a mosquito landed right on her eyeball," and a group of men hunting bear at night find their vision limited: "They drove to the edge of the woods. They aimed their headlights in. They couldn't see very far in." On other occasions, the characters in Keillor's monologues are themselves responsible for obstructing their own sight, as when "the Luther Leaguers put their hands over their eyes" in embarrassment as they listen to their parents singing."

In other instances, characters in Keillor's monologues witness phenomena that are not physically real, suggesting that sight can deceive. When a boat carrying Lutheran ministers begins to sink in the lake so the ministers appear to be walking on water, "to the people standing on shore, it looked like a genuine miracle before their eyes." The Reverend Neeley also sees what is not present when he "fell down on the rocks, speaking in tongues and seeing visions." Vision as a path to knowledge is questioned, as well, by Daryl Tollerud, who cannot interpret or trust what he sees after a tractor accident: "He could see everything, but it looked strange. It looked as if it were not real. Nothing looked real to him, and he did not feel real."

A view of vision as objective and thus superior to other avenues of perception derives from the Cartesian model of vision. The Cartesian schema succeeded in becoming the reigning visual model of modernity because it best expresses the "natural" experience of sight established by the scientific world view. The Cartesian stance can be conceptualized as a lone eye looking through a peephole at the scene in front of it; the view is static, unblinking, and fixed. The Cartesian stance also requires, of course, the withdrawal of the observer from the object depicted.

But other scopic schemata have existed alongside the Cartesian. The one Keillor selects for the vantage point of his monologues is the Baroque, a mode that is dynamic, conveys the idea of space being progressively dilated, and produces indeterminacy of effect in its play of solid and void, light and dark. In his rejection of the Cartesian schema in favor of the Baroque, Keillor chooses the glance over the gaze. Whereas the act of viewing in the Cartesian model is that of the observer who gazes, arresting the flux of phenomena, the Baroque model

> never allows a privileged, definitive, frontal view; rather, it induces the spectator to shift his position continuously in order to see the work in constantly new aspects, as if it were in a state of perpetual transformation.

In the glance that characterizes Baroque vision, the viewer's looks are fleeting, dynamic, flickering, and mobile. Keillor's monologues follow such a pattern, consisting largely of fragments or units immediately linked with each other, suggestive of an eye shifting from one thing to another. In one monologue, for example, Keillor moves from discussing a cold night in June to tomato growing to Roger Hedland's daughter's new kitten to his self-pitying Aunt Marie. His eye traverses the scene, and the irregular, unpredictable, and intermittent path of movement means that only one area of the image is clarified at each moment. Each glance momentarily consumes Keillor as he focuses in minute detail on one seemingly mundane object or process after another.

Because various details capture Keillor's attention, the picture of Lake Wobegon emerges a bit at a time rather than as a coherent and complete landscape. Bryson describes this postponement of "the apprehension of the compositional order . . . until more information . . . will have been admitted" as a natural consequence of the glance. The larger picture emerges only as a result of repeated exposure to Keillor's monologues. One listener new to the show described the attention to seemingly disconnected details and the overall lack of coherence that is apparent to new listeners not yet used to Keillor's glance: "Yeah, well, this guy was talking about guilt and death, and he went on and on, . . . and then there was some music, people from Lapland or someplace singing about I guess it was reindeer milking."

In his rejection of the Cartesian scopic regime and, concomitantly, rejection of an objectifying gaze "that goes forward and masters," Keillor refuses the masculinity with which the Cartesian regime has been associated. The glance most closely approximates the female experience of and attention to detail, the accumulation of information through interaction, and the valuing of relationship over objective, static knowledge. The refusal to privilege vision creates a more comprehensive, subjective, and relational orientation to the text.

Unwilling to allow his listeners to assume a typical masculine position of spectatorship in terms of scopic schemata, Keillor further dismantles male spectatorship and replaces it with a feminine one by refusing to prescribe any one vantage position as the appropriate one. He deflects the single scrutinizing gaze and creates a multiple narrative structure in which the events of Lake Wobegon are recounted through the eyes of many different characters. He provides multiple options for spectatorship in a restlessness or instability of vantage point described by Mulvey as the mobile position of the female spectator. The place Keillor creates for the spectator of events elides typical divisions among narrator, characters, and audience and requires an ability to move among and acknowledge different viewpoints at once.

At times, Keillor takes the perspective of characters in his monologues, experiencing the world from those characters' points of view. In this mode, Keillor's listeners look out through the characters' eyes, feeling their feelings and thinking their thoughts. Listeners experience with Carl Krebsbach, for example, the sense of security that overtakes him as he walks home across the ice from his fish house in the middle of Lake Wobegon:

> It was dark—clear sky, billions of stars in the sky. The lake was white, shiny, and straight ahead; just above the line of dark trees, the lights of the town, like stars in the sky. And one of them was his house, where people were waiting for him and would be glad to see his face.

At other times, Keillor positions himself as a character in his monologues—as a resident of the imaginary Lake Wobegon—thus assuming a second vantage point. He presents himself as having grown up in Lake Wobegon, as someone who knows the people intimately, and who continues to visit the town and talk on the phone with its residents. Assumption of this viewing position was particularly evident when Keillor married in real life and told of his marriage in a monologue that involved Lake Wobegon residents' participation in the celebration. They supposedly mailed him a toaster for a wedding present, "addressed to a person formerly of Lake Wobegon who was getting married toward the end of December in Copenhagen." This vantage point of Keillor as a character sometimes has the added qualities of distance and reflection because it embodies Keillor as the sophisticated urban dweller who has left Lake Wobegon and now has a different view of the town from those who currently live there. Keillor acknowledges this outsider status explicitly in one monologue:

> I got kind of a cold silence when I called up there to talk to the folks here this last week, trying to get the news in town. Got hold of Elizabeth at the telephone exchange, of course, and once she recognized my voice, there was a long stillness and . . . she said, "All you're trying to do is get some dirty linen so you can go tell it to all your swell friends down there and make fun of us and make us the laughing stock."

Keillor sometimes tells his monologues from a third vantage point—that of the listener. He moves into this spectator position through the use of the second person pronoun, *you.* In the following example, he is describing his experience of sitting in a classroom as a boy in Lake Wobegon on a sunny Monday after a rainy weekend. In mid-sentence, Keillor moves from a description of his perspective to assumption of the vantage point of his listeners and their perspectives: "But it just is a matter of tremendous indifference to me as I get older and you learn to enjoy everything of life—the sun and the kind of elation that comes with it and excitement and you also learn to enjoy gloom and depression and grief." Keillor's description of the feeling of leaving the cool darkness of the Sidetrack Tap on a hot day also exemplifies this stance: "To open that door, the sunlight hits you like a two-by-four. And as you walk down the street, the beer in your brain begins to rise like a lump of bread dough inside its small, cardboard carrying case." Kacandes explains that "'*you*' implies an 'I/you' pair and concomitantly relationship and communication" because the presence of a *you* "cannot be conceived without an *I*." She suggests that such a use of *you* invites an identificatory response and that "we feel compelled to respond to the second person."

Not only does the construction of multiple perspectives prevent assumption of the conventional male spectator position, but it references a conventional feminine experience of self. In contrast to the masculine experience of self, rooted in a fundamental separation of other from self and characterized by objectivity and impartiality, the feminine experience is based on a blurring of boundaries between self and other. It is characterized by response and connectedness within a framework of relationships, which Keillor accomplishes by merging the narrator, his characters, and his audience into overlapping roles.

But Keillor's dismantling of the male gaze does not depend on multiple perspectives alone. He frequently gives women control over the gaze, thus actually reversing the expected roles of male viewer and female object of the gaze. In Keillor's monologues, women look at men, in contrast to the more common gazing by men at women. This observational stance is highlighted in the closing line of each monologue, where Keillor states that Lake Wobegon is a place where "all the men are good looking." Granted, the men who are the objects of women's desire in Keillor's monologues are not depicted as explicitly sexual—after all, this *is* Lake Wobegon, populated by reserved Norwegians—but men are subjected to visual scrutiny of various kinds. Keillor himself is the object of a woman's look when he recounts how, as an adolescent, he would ask his mother, "'Am I good looking?' 'You're nice enough looking,'" his mother would reply. Daryl Tollerud, in fact, knows he is alive (after a near-fatal tractor accident) by his wife's look: "And it was not until she looked out the window and saw him coming and ran out to meet him . . . that he knew he was alive."

In other instances, the look of women includes the pleasure and desire typically associated with the male gaze directed by men toward women. "Oh, you good-looking man. Oh, my goodness, are you handsome," says Arlene Bunsen to her husband, Clarence, upon his return from a trip to St. Cloud. "Let me feast my eyes on you." Mildred Winblad is similarly interested in looking. "Mister," she says when she first meets her future husband. "I'd like to get somewhere where I could get a closer look at your features."

When men do look at women in Keillor's monologues, they deliberately avoid looking at those parts of women's bodies that typically receive attention from men, or they first notice other features they apparently consider to be more important. When Matt McKinley meets Mildred for the first time, he "took one look at her and he said, 'Woman, you are the strongest woman I ever saw in my life.'" Women's strength, rather than their physical appearance, also is the focus of Keillor's closing line of his monologues, where he describes Lake Wobegon as a place "where all the women are strong. . . ." When the Norwegian bachelor farmers look at pictures of women in magazines, they reject the typical physical appeal of such women, contributing to Keillor's challenge to the male gaze:

> Old bachelor farmer sitting down in the barber shop, . . . looking at pictures of women in a magazine, saying, "You know, I wouldn't have a woman like that if she come beg me, if she come up to my front door on bended knees and begged me, I wouldn't have a woman like that—she just complicates your life."

Yet another way in which Keillor disrupts the traditional masculine spectator position is through his recognition of and empathy for the discomfort involved in being watched. Carl Krebsbach, for example, delights in harming a squirrel that was eating food he put out for the birds, but his glee changes to guilt and self-consciousness when he "realizes his daughter has seen the whole thing from the upstairs window." After he climbs a tree and is watching youngsters play below, Clarence Bunsen wonders: "What if they look up here, see a 55-year-old-man sitting in the tree?" The discomfort frequently felt by women subject to the male gaze is felt by Lake Wobegon residents, including Keillor. He shares his own uneasiness with being watched when he describes his feelings upon leaving the theater after his radio show—an uneasiness he associates with sneaking into movie theaters as an adolescent, hoping not to be seen because movies were forbidden by his religion: "Makes me nervous that as I go out the door, someone is going to see me come out."

Keillor also dismantles the male gaze in his depiction of individuals' assumption of both subject and object roles. The capacity to assume the roles of both spectator and object of the gaze is common to women's viewing within patriarchy. In the traditional construction of the gaze, men look at women, while women watch themselves being looked at. Thus, women turn themselves into objects of vision—a sight—and they survey themselves just as men survey them: "A woman must continually watch herself. She is almost continually accompanied by her own image of herself." The result, as Minh-Ha describes, is that the woman "necessarily looks in from the outside while also looking out from the inside."

With striking frequency in Keillor's monologues, he and his characters are simultaneously the subject (masculine) and the object (feminine) of beholding. On Flag Day, for example, the residents of the town don red, white, and blue caps to form a living flag and then one by one take turns going up to the top of the Central Building to look at it: "Then somebody got out from the living flag who had a red cap on—he was part of a stripe—and he ran up to the top of the Central Building 'cause he wanted to see it, and then, of course, everybody had to do it." In another monologue, Dale Eaker observes himself, seeing himself both as the subject and object of his own gaze. As "he walked down the stairs, he saw himself in the mirror. He didn't have a shirt on, and he was kinda admiring himself. He looked pretty good." The privileged position of the observer cannot be assumed by Keillor's characters because they are aware of themselves as "others" among others, as displaced from the observational center at the moment that they, themselves, become the objects of the gaze of others.

As a result of this subject-object spectator position, Keillor, his characters, and his listeners experience double vision, which develops from the need of subordinated groups to learn the language and ways of the dominant group while staying attuned to their own authentic perceptions. Such a position is in contrast to the vision of the master, the one in the privileged position, whose "vision is a one-way street; his privileged position hasn't allowed him to benefit from that double vision." But the dual position of insider turned outsider has disadvantages as well as advantages: "Not quite the Same, not quite the Other, she stands in that undetermined threshold place where she constantly drifts in and out. . . . [H]er intervention is necessarily that of both a deceptive insider and a deceptive outsider." This double vision, with its possibility for insight and deceit, is best illustrated in the town's name, Lake Wobegon, meaning both bedraggled in appearance and the disappearance of one's woes, as in "woe be gone."

The double vision that results from the assumption of multiple perspectives and, in particular, from adoption of a simultaneous subject-object position also can be seen in Keillor's refusal to see his own perspective as superior to others. The spectator who sees from multiple perspectives recognizes both the value in and limitations of those perspectives. "As we become aware that our . . . commitments slowly reveal themselves as postures," Gergen suggests, "we can . . . hardly advocate our own beliefs, reasons, and passions above all others, for the very effort attests to the hollowness of their bases." The result is an irony and a playfulness that come to characterize the spectatorship as Keillor appears to "play with the truths of the day, shake them about, try them on like funny hats." The irony that emerges as Keillor describes Lena Johnson's horror at her granddaughter's christening party, which her son and daughter-in-law have had catered, is typical:

Bunch of people standing around, eating food off tiny plates, holding beverages in their hands. My gosh! If Merlette didn't have room for all these people at her dining room table, the least she coulda done was bring out the TV trays and so people'd have a place to sit and eat!

The playfulness and irony that result from Keillor's multiple vantage points invite the audience to "join in the fun. Because no one is ultimately in control in this game, everyone can play."

The small-town setting of Lake Wobegon, Keillor's discursive site, also contributes to the creation of feminine spectatorship because Keillor suggests that, in many ways, it is a feminine place. Lake Wobegon is, literally and figuratively, a homeplace, the nostalgic place that continues to serve as the American ideal of home. In such a home, women traditionally have been relegated "the task of creating and sustaining a home environment . . . to construct domestic households as spaces of care and nurturance."

Part of the traditional image of home is that it is a private place; in fact, concern with the private sphere often is cited as a feature associated with the feminine gender. Lake Wobegon is presented as primarily a private world, focused on interior spaces and thoughts and on intimate details of personal lives, rarely do public issues of "political" importance intrude. Keillor tends to capture the residents of Lake Wobegon in moments of relationship with each other, an emphasis equated with a feminine orientation. The narrative suspense of his monologues is not built on the expectations of a significant event or a socially momentous act but rather on the contemplation and dissection of the nature of relationships among and between individuals.

The activities that characterize the lives of Lake Wobegon residents are limited to and oriented around the everyday and the minute, ranging from the worries of tomato growers "wondering if they ought to go out and cover them" to singing songs at the Sweetheart Supper "in dim light, with candles in the red polka-dot, cut-glass globes on the table" to "taking down all the decorations off the tree, and wrapping them individually in tissue paper." This concern for dailiness is another way of locating the feminine standpoint. Metzger suggests that dailiness forms a method by which to know about and gain access to the feminine realm: "Each day is a tapestry, threads of broccoli, promotion, couches, children, politics, shopping, building, planting, thinking interweave in intimate connection with insistent cycles of birth, existence, and death."

Keillor's focus on daily life demonstrates the feminine connections with process rather than product: dailiness, by definition, is a process best captured in the details; it is not a product to be arrived at quickly via a linear sequence. Keillor connects with the details that mark the forms of many women's everyday lives—whether family stories, quilts, gardens, poems, rituals, or songs—and creates in Lake Wobegon a world that looks very much like the ones with which women tend to be familiar. The monologues construct, as de Lauretis suggests about the film, *Jeanne Dielman,* "a picture of female experience, of duration, perception, events, relationships and silences, which feels immediately and unquestionably true."

The private world of Lake Wobegon is spatially limited, physically confining, and almost secluded in a way that approximates women's confinement to, or at least greater responsibility for, the home. As constricting as this world is, it is an ordered world in which one feels comfortable and safe; to leave this world is to encounter possible danger. The youngsters of Lake Wobegon are frequently told, "don't go off by yourself," a metaphoric suggestion not to leave Lake Wobegon. "See those people out there in the world today? Things like that don't happen to people here in Lake Wobegon," suggests Keillor. "I tell you, they never should have been out there. Stay with the others, stick with the group, don't go off by yourself." On another occasion, Keillor says he's going "back there" to Lake Wobegon because "I'm afraid that if I left I would lose my own story. It's kept back there. And when you lose your story, you've lost something that nobody should ever lose." When his characters ignore his advice and venture beyond the city limits of Lake Wobegon, they experience a variety of negative consequences, as does Clarence Bunsen when he goes to St. Cloud for a haircut. It was a disastrous cut that was "about right for a clown, kind of sticking up in strange ways around."

The fact that most residents of Lake Wobegon remain in Lake Wobegon and hesitate to leave it to reside elsewhere reinforces the perception of Lake Wobegon as a feminine setting. Wolff makes the point that "there is an *intrinsic* relationship between masculinity and travel. (By 'intrinsic', though, I do *not* mean 'essential'; rather my interest is in the centrality of travel/mobility to *constructed* masculine identity.)" Enloe concurs with Wolff's analysis, suggesting:

> In many societies being feminine has been defined as sticking close to home. Masculinity, by contrast, has been the passport for travel. Feminist geographers and ethnographers have been amassing evidence revealing that a principal difference between women and men in countless societies has been the license to travel away from a place thought of as "home."

That many of those reluctant to leave the "home" of Lake Wobegon are men only increases the underlying sense of femininity in Keillor's monologues. Florian Krebsbach wants to stay in Lake Wobegon, although his wife is agitating to move to a high rise in St. Cloud. Florian responds by building up his herd of ducks and collecting farm equipment in order to ensure his immobility.

Furthermore, Lake Wobegon is a feminine place in its eschewal of technology, usually thought of as a masculine invention and activity. In fact, one definition of *technology* is that "it consists of the devices, machinery and processes which men are interested in." Technology also is considered masculine in that it "is usually considered 'big world' talk, connected . . . with the 'public' sphere, men, mass media, machines, and market prices." The residents of Lake Wobegon reject even basic technologies such as air conditioners, with no optimism at all about the value of such devices:

> It was luxuries like A/C that brought down the Roman Empire. With A/C, their windows were shut, they couldn't hear the barbarians coming. . . . You get A/C and the next day Mom leaves the house in a skin-tight dress, holding a cigarette and a glass of gin, walking an ocelot on a leash.

Clarence Bunsen's lament about the coming of technology is representative of Lake Wobegon residents' attitudes toward technology as well:

> Like everything else nowadays, they got coffee without caffeine, they got soda pop without sugar in it. . . . They're developing new ways of cultivation. They won't use plows anymore, just kind of a low-frequency sonic boom will do it. Cultivate all of Minnesota in 15 seconds. They're breeding new dairy cows now, new dairy cows down by Chicago someplace—I don't know where, but they're breeding new dairy cows, without legs. Legs just get in the way. Interrupt things.

As Lake Wobegon residents reject technology, they also reject the wealth and power that accompany technological development. Lyotard succinctly describes the connection as "no technology without wealth, but no wealth without technology." Lake Wobegon residents' rejection of technology contributes to the town's femininity, then, not simply because women tend not to be associated with technology but because Lake Wobegon residents deliberately espouse a position of low wealth and thus low status and powerlessness—a rejection, of course, of masculine values and standards.

The feminine gender of Keillor's spectatorship is reinforced by the narrative style Keillor uses in presenting his monologues. The form and style of his narratives embody features that typically are associated with feminine patterns, including lack of closure, refusal to judge, and feminine speech forms.

Keillor ends many monologues without telling the outcome of the story. Monologues simply end, with the plot of the narrative unresolved, as when Mrs. Beeler struggles with whether or not to destroy the tickets to a rock concert her son stood in line all night to buy. She had read an article about the dangerous effects of rock concerts on youth and wondered: "What should a mother do? Shouldn't a mother tear them up into little tiny bits? And throw them away?. . . Doesn't she have an obligation to destroy those tickets? And to save her son?" The monologue ends here, with listeners left to wonder about the action Mrs. Beeler decided to take. In another monologue, Senator K. Thorvaldson finally gets up the courage to write to and declare his love for a woman he met while vacationing in Florida. The monologue ends when Thorvaldson receives a phone call; he responds to the caller, "Oh, you sweet lady, oh, you sweet woman. It's so good to hear your voice." Listeners can guess but cannot be certain that the woman responded positively to the letter, and how the relationship progressed from this point is left untold.

Keillor's incomplete monologues serve as allegories "of the impossibility of ever finishing in the sense of imposing a single, coherent meaning" on a text or activity. As with many of the tasks traditionally assumed by women—housework, child rearing, shopping—the process is perpetual and unfinished, and the focus becomes the process rather than its end result. Keillor's monologues, relying as they do on open-ended and continuous processes, embody the kind of rhythm women experience in their daily lives—a rhythm characterized by repetitiveness, interruption, and distraction. Although lack of closure does not provide the relief of an ending, it does contain an invitation to openness—to imaginative possibility—that is not possible when a story is finished. The criteria for interpretation remain open, albeit slippery and fragmentary. By failing to provide narrative closure, Keillor does not grant authority to any single standard of meaning to restrict, integrate, or totalize the monologues.

The feminine vantage point offered by Keillor in his monologues stands in contrast to the textual rhythm of commercials, sports and news programs as well as most other dramatic narratives presented through mass media that emphasize closure. Such texts construct disorder—disequilibrium, excitement, and suspense—for the purpose of providing the pleasures that come from its resolution. The disorder, in other words, is being brought under control (if only temporarily) by sorting out incoherence and containing contradiction (if only partially). This pleasure of closure is typically achieved at the expense of traditionally constructed femaleness—that which is brought into control often is the disruptiveness of female values or female sexuality.

Thus, this kind of rhythm codes the kinds of traits traditionally ascribed to masculinity—the ability to be rational and to have the power to control one's circumstances. Accordingly, the vantage point offered in a textual rhythm of closure implies if not a male viewer at least a traditionally valued masculine approach to the tensions and contradictions of experience.

In a narrative style in which process rather than closure is emphasized and the text is seen as offering the rhythms of daily life in which varied interpretations are possible, that Keillor does not make judgments about his characters and their actions is not surprising. Lyotard aptly describes the stance Keillor adopts in his monologues when he notes that the only rule that applies is the rule that says, "do not prejudge, suspend judgment, give the same attention to everything that happens as it happens."

Keillor's unconditional acceptance of any decision a character makes is exemplified in one monologue in which he describes the carpet in the Tolleruds' bedroom as purple, but he neither sneers at the color nor applauds its courage. Neither does he moralize about Pastor Ingqvist's lack of enthusiasm for the advent sermons he must preach each Christmas. Keillor allows listeners to make their own decisions about, and interpretations of, the events he reports, a stance suggested clearly when he describes the talk of groups of men in cafes when it's raining and the land is too soggy to work. He allows spectators to select their own interpretations of these conversations:

> Is it a sad conversation or is it funny or does it have a kind of secret elation of its own is really up to you and how you feel about it. To me, it's always been religious, this conversation; it's endless, even when people are silent. This murmur of talk goes on and on, back among my people, and it includes wisdom and useful advice and recollections of cars and trucks and large animals and farms and the people who lived on them and everything that they did.

Keillor's manner of speaking reinforces the feminine content of his monologues. Many of the features that are believed—accurately or not—to characterize women's speech distinguish Keillor's monologues. His frequent reiterations of words and phrases recall the lengthening of statements and indirectness that have been suggested as characteristic of women's speech. Such repetition is evident when he discusses a local brewery:

> A person thinks of this, a guy thinks of all this history when you sit in a dim bar on Tuesday evening and have a bottle of Wendy. You think about all this history of the Dimmers family and you think about

that St. Wendell's brewery out there in St. Wendell's, meant to look like a beautiful castle, a Bavarian castle, they intended it to look like and it is sort of a beautiful brick castle about the first two stories but then the brick layers got a little dizzy. . . .

In part, the repetitiveness of this style is typical of the storyteller who needs time to think about where to move the story. At the same time, however, it is a style that has been ascribed to and associated with women.

Keillor's speech contains adjectives and adverbs as qualifiers, a style also considered feminine. He sprinkles his monologues with words such as "kind of," "sort of," and "I think"—indirect speech forms that suggest the stance of someone not expected or allowed to have strong opinions or to make strong statements about the world. An example is Keillor's statement, "Through talk, I think, is how people are intimidating." This same hesitation surfaces throughout his monologues in phrases such as "a sort of strange kind of virtue"; "it's kind of a Lake Wobegon holiday"; and "I think he puts a toenail from his left foot into it or something, I don't know." His choice of adverbs and adjectives is similarly conventionally feminine: A classmate of Keillor's in the school choir sings "pretty good"; when describing Father Emil's reaction upon hearing that vacation time and IRAs have been implemented for priests, Keillor responds with, "My gosh," a particularly feminine exclamatory form. Just as Keillor structures a content that is associated with the feminine, he does so, too, in his narrative style.

We have suggested that Keillor's radio monologues create a feminine spectator position through his refusal to privilege sight, dismantling of the male gaze, creation of Lake Wobegon as a feminine setting, and feminine speaking style. By providing an example of how such a position looks and feels, Keillor is able "to ruin certain representations and to welcome a female spectator into the audience of men." But Keillor's presentation of feminine spectatorship goes beyond simply presenting a feminine world view to listeners. The monologues function to introduce listeners to a feminist epistemology—an epistemology that privileges feminine ways of coming to knowledge and understanding.

A nearness or closeness to objects of knowledge is one quality of this epistemology. The close-up perspective that results allows for the possibility of greater understanding of those objects. The refusal to privilege vision and the involvement of senses in addition to sight in the process of coming to know ground the epistemology of Keillor's monologues in materiality, in concrete particulars. Keillor moves away from the molar toward the molecular level, or from the deductive to the inductive, suggesting the specific detail as the gateway to understanding. When individuals consciously attend to information gathered from all of the senses, they have more detailed data on which to base interpretation, knowledge, and understanding.

The feminist epistemology that results from Keillor's feminine spectatorship also suggests a use of personal experiences—the details, processes, and contexts of everyday life—as data for knowing. Knowledge does not come only from external, objective, or authoritative sources but from direct contact with other people and their lives and from the specific experiences of one's own life. The epistemology of Keillor's monologues is rooted in relationship, in the consciousness that emerges from personal participation in events.

Because one experience cannot be judged superior to others, the epistemology offered in Keillor's monologues fosters an openness to multiple interpretations and an awareness of the limitations of one's own perspective, as Le Guin suggests: "How, after all, can one experience deny, negate, disprove, another experience? Even if I've had a lot more of it, *your* experience is your truth. How can one being prove another being wrong?" With the adoption of myriad perspectives, knowers are less likely to cling to one perspective and are more likely to be open to other possible viewpoints.

A legitimate and useful way of coming to knowledge, Keillor's monologues suggest, is that typically associated with the feminine—a way of knowing that moves the knower close to the object of inquiry to ground understanding in the particular, values personal experience as a means of knowing, and encourages an openness to multiple perspectives. Keillor legitimizes and accords value to this feminist epistemology in various ways. One is through his own modeling of the feminine spectator position that gives rise to a feminist epistemology. He accords the position credibility simply because he would not be expected to assume it given the other options available to him—he is, after all, a man of celebrity status with access to traditional sources of power and thus knowledge. He also supports a feminist epistemology by revealing it as nonthreatening, comfortable, and safe in his use of the nostalgic and familiar Lake Wobegon setting, his humor, and his relaxed speaking style.

Yet another way in which Keillor's monologues legitimize a feminist epistemology is that they do not simply present or depict the epistemology but instead enable listeners to experience it as enacted or embodied. As audience members position themselves in the feminine spectator stance suggested by the texts, they actually experience the concomitant feminist epistemology. They come to know through or from within a feminist perspective—they are able to try it on and to discover how it works and feels in their lives. Moreover, because their experience of the perspective is associated with pleasure, interest, and humor, listeners are likely to view the experience as a positive one; they are less likely to evaluate it as negative or to remain detached from and thus unaffected by it.

Keillor's monologues, characterized by feminine spectatorship and rooted in a feminist epistemology, thus provide a free space in which listeners may experience a feminist perspective in a safe, non-threatening, pleasurable environment—where they are able to discover for themselves the utility of such a perspective and the insights it offers. As such, Keillor's monologues constitute an emancipatory rhetoric that has the power to disrupt "the dour certainties of pictures, property, and power."

FURTHER READING

Criticism

Brennan, Geraldine. "Hung Up With the Strings." *The Times Educational Supplement* (4 July 1997): 7.
  Calls *The Sandy Bottom Orchestra,* by Keillor and his wife Jenny Lind Nilsson, "a rewarding study of what it means to live in a small community as the gifted only child of arty, liberal, eccentric parents."

Cooper, Ilene. "It's Not as Easy as It Looks." *Booklist* 92, No. 19 (1 and 15 June 1996): 1732.
  Asserts that authors of adult books often fail in their attempts at children's fiction, including Garrison Keillor in his *The Old Man Who Loved Cheese.*

Doan MacDougall, Ruth. Review of *Lake Wobegon Days,* by Garrison Keillor. *The Christian Science Monitor* 77 (6 September 1985): B4.
  Praises Keillor's *Lake Wobegon Days.*

Michelson, Bruce. "Keillor and Rolvaag and the Art of Telling the Truth." *American Studies* 30, No. 1 (Spring 1989): 21-34.
  Argues that Keillor "is engaged in an old, paradoxical art which no ideology has ever stamped out or explained away, the expression of cultural truth through the telling of tales, and the transformation of American mythology as the surest way of keeping it alive."

Narveson, Robert D. "Catholic-Lutheran Interaction in Keillor's *Lake Wobegon Days* and Hassler's *Grand Opening.*" In *Exploring the Midwestern Literary Imagination,* edited by Marcia Noe, pp. 180-91. Troy, New York: Whitston Publishing Co., 1993.
  Discusses the representation of sectarian relations in Keillor's *Lake Wobegon Days* and Jon Hassler's *Grand Opening,* and the reality of Catholic-Lutheran relations in small midwestern towns.

Ostrem, William. "Nietzsche, Keillor and the Religious Heritage of Lake Wobegon." *Midamerica* 18 (1991): 115-23.
  Analyzes the relationship between the philosophy of Friedrich Nietzsche and Keillor's *Lake Wobegon Days.*

Parrinder, Patrick. "Last in the Funhouse." *The London Review of Books* 8, No. 7 (17 April 1986): 18-9.
  Discusses the style of American fiction in the 1980s as seen in several novels, including Keillor's *Lake Wobegon Days.*

Sexton, David. "When Here is Nowhere." *The Times Literary Supplement,* No. 4327 (7 March 1986): 257.
  States that, "Half memoir, half fiction, [Keillor's] *Lake Wobegon Days* is wholly a success."

Wilson, Gahan. "Cats and Their Discontents." *The New York Times Book Review* (21 May 1995): 20.
  Discusses the Roaring Twenties mood of Keillor's *Cat, You Better Come Home.*

Milan Kundera

1929-

Czech-born French novelist, short story writer, dramatist, poet, critic, and essayist.

The following entry provides an overview of Kundera's career through 1996. For further information on his life and works, see *CLC*, Volumes 4, 9, 19, 32, and 68.

INTRODUCTION

Celebrated internationally as one of Europe's most outstanding contemporary novelists, Kundera has lived in exile in France since 1975, and much of his work was banned until recently in his native country, the former Czechoslovakia. He began his writing career as a poet and dramatist before he wrote the fiction that brought him international critical attention, most notably the novels *Le livre du rire et de l'oubli* (1979; *The Book of Laugher and Forgetting*) and *L'Insoutenable l'égèreté de l'être* (1984; *The Unbearable Lightness of Being*). Kundera's novels represent the psychological motivations, emotional complexes, and erotic impulses of vulnerable characters who question their various aspects of their identities when faced with political events and social values beyond their control. Kundera often infuses authorial commentary into his narratives, presents events in disjointed time frames and from multiple perspectives, and patterns his novels in a manner similar to musical compositions. Dismissing traditional novelistic structures, Kundera uses these narrative devices to illustrate his own aesthetic of the novel, which emphasizes parallel explorations of related themes, active philosophical contemplation, and the integration of dreams and fantasy with realistic analysis. Although some reviewers have considered his work in the context of exile literature or have labeled him a "dissident" writer despite his protests to the contrary, most critics have noted the complex structure of his novels, identifying that component as one of the integral aspects of his art.

Biographical Information

Born and raised in Brno, Czechoslovakia, Kundera is the son of Ludvik Kundera, a well-known pianist who collaborated with the famous Czech composer Leos Janácek. Although he once studied piano, Kundera decided at age nineteen that music was not his true vocation. In 1948 he left Brno to study scriptwriting and directing at the Film Faculty of the Prague Academy of Music and Dramatic Arts. At this time Kundera, like many other idealistic and progressive students who had witnessed the atrocities of World War II, joined the

Communist Party. In 1952 he began teaching cinematography at the Prague Academy, and the next year he published his first poetry collection, *Clovek, zahrada širá*, which was immediately condemned by the Communists for using surrealistic techniques and lacking universality. Kundera wrote two other volumes of poetry, *Poslední máj* (1955) and *Monology* (1957), while teaching at the academy, but he later renounced these works as adolescent and insignificant. During the early 1960s Kundera attained literary prominence in his homeland by serving on the Central Committee of the Czechoslovak Writers Union from 1963 to 1969 and on the editorial boards of the journals *Literarni noviny* and *Listy*. Meanwhile, he published a critical work about Czechoslovakian novelist Vladislava Vancury, *Unemí románu* (1961), and his first play, *Majitelé klícu* (1962; *The Owners of the Keys*) was staged in Czechoslovakia and abroad. Kundera then turned his attention to writing fiction. Despite his esteemed reputation, Kundera spent two years battling the censorship board before his first novel, *Zert* (1967; *The Joke*), was deemed acceptable for publication in its original form. In a 1967 speech opening the Fourth Czechoslovak Writers Congress, Kundera candidly admonished censorship and other repressive tactics used against writers. During the so-called "Prague Spring" of 1968, when the push for cultural freedom had reached its zenith, Kundera's novel enjoyed enormous popular success. However, when Russian military forces invaded Czechoslovakia later that year, Kundera was expelled from the Communist Party and released from his teaching position at the Prague Academy, and his works were removed from libraries and bookstores. He eventually fled his native country in 1975 after he was invited to teach comparative literature at the University of Rennes in France. In 1979, after the publication of *The Book of Laughter and Forgetting,* the Czechoslovak government revoked his citizenship. In 1980, Kundera accepted a professorship at the École des hautes études en sciénces sociales in Paris. Since garnering international praise for *The Unbearable Lightness of Being,* which was later adapted for film and produced in 1988, Kundera has written two additional books of literary criticism, *L'art du roman* (1986; *The Art of the Novel*) and *Les Testaments trahis* (1993; *Testaments Betrayed*), and three novels, *L'Immortalité* (1990; *Immortality*), *La Lenteur* (1995; *Slowness*), and *L'identité* (1997; *Identity.*

Major Works

Kundera's collection of short stories, *Laughable Loves,* addresses the illusory nature of love and the consequences of using sexuality to gain power and influence. In these stories, some characters use sexual encounters to exercise their personal power; others see them as a gauge of self-worth. One of his best-known stories, "The Hitchhiking Game," involves a young couple who engage in role-playing while on vacation, but the game ultimately reveals the painful implications of their relationship. In "Symposium" a doctor refuses a sexual encounter with a nurse as an assertion of independence. Many of Kundera's works are dominated by a form based on the number seven. *The Joke* focuses on Ludvik, a university student who firmly embraces Communist ideology. After Ludvik sends a postcard in which he playfully parodies Marxist slogans to his zealously political girlfriend, she shows it to Zamenek, a fervent, humorless Communist student-leader, who has Ludvik expelled from both the university and the party. Years later, after Ludvik has been drafted into the army and forced to work in a coal mine, he seeks revenge by seducing Zamenek's wife, who, unknown to Ludvik, has been separated from her husband for two years. *La vie est ailleurs* (1973; *Life Is Elsewhere*) is a satirical portrait of Jaromil, a young poet, who was bullied by his doting mother to develop an artistic temperament and runs away to write; this novel exposes the way poetry can contribute to the hysteria of revolution and presents Kundera's belief that youth is a "lyrical age" laced with neuroses, romantic illusions, and endless self-contemplation. *La valse aux adieux* (1976; *The Farewell Party*) concerns the destructive nature of sexual politics and self-deception. Set in a Czechoslovakian resort town famous for infertility treat-

ments, this novel chronicles the aftermath of a one-night stand that results in pregnancy and addresses such ethical issues as abortion, sperm-banking, and suicide. *The Book of Laughter and Forgetting* portrays numerous characters who are linked thematically yet never interact. Focusing on the repercussions of forgetting personal and cultural histories, the metaphysical implications of laughter, and how ideological doctrines often lead to deluded notions of good and evil, *The Book of Laughter and Forgetting* suggests that memory is a form of self-preservation in a world where history is usually distorted by cultural forces. *The Unbearable Lightness of Being* treats similar themes and centers on the connected lives of two couples—Tomas and Tereza, and Franz and Sabina. Set in Czechoslovakia around the time of the Russian invasion, this novel examines the hardships and limitations that can result from commitment yet also reveals the lack of meaning for life without such responsibility. In addition, each character represents a particular motif that is explored throughout the novel in various contexts, reminiscent of the variations in a musical composition. *Immortality* is spiked throughout by authorial intrusions commenting on the writing process of the narrative and is the first of Kundera's novels to be set in France. The book considers the way media manipulation, popular culture, and capitalist technocracy distort the perception of reality. Besides presenting a love triangle among its principal characters, *Immortality* also contains dialogues between such notable literary figures as Johann Wolfgang von Goethe and Ernest Hemingway. *Slowness,* Kundera's first novel originally written in French, is a fictional triptych that features the simultaneous stories of the narrator and his wife (Milan and Vera Kundera) en route to a French chateau; an eighteenth-century chevalier and his mistress engaged in a highly stylized sexual encounter at the same chateau; and a entomologist, an exiled woman ex-scientist, and her groupie who are attending a conference at the chateau on the day of the narrator's arrival. The action of the entire novel apparently takes place in a single location over the course of a single night through a telescoping of time, a device sometimes read as a parody of the classical rules of unity of action. Both *The Art of the Novel* and *Testaments Betrayed* discuss Kundera's ideas about the aesthetics of the novel, the former outlining in seven sections the formal development of the European novel and the latter suggesting in nine parts that critics of the novel form have betrayed the profound sense of humor that informs the novelistic tradition, particularly with respect to Russian novelist Franz Kafka.

Critical Reception

Throughout his career Kundera has received numerous literary awards, and his novels have earned him worldwide critical acclaim. Kundera has been consistently admired for juxtaposing fictitious and biographical elements in his novels and for simultaneously exploring recurrent themes. Many critics have focused on the political disillusionment that is perceived in Kundera's work, usually in consideration of his close involvement in Czechoslovakian political and cultural turmoils of the twentieth century. But Kundera has claimed that there has been too much emphasis on the politics of his novels, and that he especially dislikes being classified as a dissident writer. While some critics have castigated his narrative techniques as disorienting, usually citing his disjointed plotting, episodic characterizations, and authorial intrusions as principal distractions, a number of critics have appreciated Kundera's style, focusing on his use of humor and his sense of "play" in narration, particularly in terms of the vitality of his erotic themes. Richard Gaughan has observed that comedy and laughter "bring to the surface and make explicit the often hidden and always painful struggle between the equally necessary but mutually exclusive demands of freedom and belief—a struggle that Kundera sees as the characteristic condition of the modern European mind." Although he was recognized as an important literary figure in his homeland early in his career, critical attacks on his writings from Czech quarters "have been unceasing" since he left, according to Karen von Kunes, particularly for what has been perceived as his abandonment of his Czech heritage for the adulation of Western European and American readers and critics.

PRINCIPAL WORKS

Zert [*The Joke,* 1969; definitive English edition, 1992] (novel) 1967

*Smesne lasky [*Laughable Loves;* first English edition, 1974; definitive English edition, 1987] (short stories) 1970

***La vie est ailleurs* [*Life Is Elsewhere,* 1974; definitive English edition, 1986] (novel) 1973

***La valse aux adieux* [*The Farewell Party;* first English edition, 1976; new translation by Aaron Asher, based on Kundera's revised French text, published as *Farewell Waltz: A Novel,* 1998] (novel) 1976

***Le livre du rire et de l'oubli* [*The Book of Laughter and Forgetting,* 1980; new translation by Aaron Asher, 1996] (novel) 1979

***Jacques et son maître: Hommage a Denis Diderot* [*Jacques and His Master: An Homage to Diderot in Three Acts,* 1985] (drama) 1981

***L'insoutenable l'égèreté de l'être* [*The Unbearable Lightness of Being*] (novel) 1984

L'art du roman [*The Art of the Novel,* 1988] (essays) 1986

***L'immortalite* [*Immortality,* 1991] (novel) 1990

Les Testaments trahis [*Testaments Betrayed: An Essay in Nine Parts,* 1995] (essay) 1993

La Lenteur [*Slowness: A Novel,* 1996] (novel) 1995

L'identite [*Indentity: A Novel,* 1998] (novel) 1997

*Kundera collected the eight stories contained in the original Czech edition of this work from three notebooks of short stories: *Smesne lasky* ("Laughable Loves"), 1963, *Druhy sesit smesnych lasek* ("The Second Notebook of Laughable Loves"), 1965, and *Treti sesit smesnych lasek* ("The Third Notebook of Laughable Loves"), 1968; the original notebooks comprised ten stories; translated editions contain only seven stories.

**These works are French translations from the original Czech manuscripts *Zivot je jinde, Valcik na rozloucenou, Kniha smichu a zapomneni, Jakub a jeho pan, Nesnesitelna lehkost byti,* and *Nesmrtelnost,* respectively.

CRITICISM

Ronald de Feo (review date 3 January 1975)

SOURCE: A review of *Life Is Elsewhere* and *Laughable Loves,* in *Commonweal,* Vol. CI, No. 11, January 3, 1975, pp. 307-9.

[*In the following review, de Feo explores the role of eroticism in* Life Is Elsewhere *and* Laughable Loves.]

Many of the characters who populate these two volumes [*Life Is Elsewhere* and *Laughable Loves*] by the Czech writer Milan Kundera are deeply affected by the erotic element in their natures. Often their strong sexual instincts surprise them. They may play various games and adopt various roles to free themselves from their repressed skins. They find freedom and release, even creative inspiration, in sex. As they make an effort to explore erotic possibilities, they discover sides of their personalities that have previously remained hidden. For some the revelations result in confusion and pain—ugliness and desperation have been exposed. For others the revelations are cause for wonder and joy—a form of beauty has entered their lives.

Life Is Elsewhere is a comic novel that traces the life of a poet, Jaromil, from his birth to his death. Jaromil's mother, Maman, on whom the author focuses first, is a typical Kundera character. Ashamed and unsure of her body for years, she has an affair with an engineer and rapidly becomes aware of her sexual potential, learning "to savor the pleasures of physical existence." After recording this phase in the life of her body, the author notes the next important change—her pregnancy: "It [her body] ceased to be a mere object of someone else's eye, and became a living body . . ." Two beings then are born: Jaromil, literally, and Maman, figuratively. Kundera wonderfully describes the physical and emotional bond that exists between mother and child. We can understand why Maman later becomes an almost unbearably possessive mother and why Jaromil comes to regard her with so much reverence and fear.

We follow Jaromil's early creative attempts and the comic manner in which his art matures. Once again we have the link between mother and child—as a painter inspires Jaromil to develop his artistic talent, he inspires Maman to toss off any sexual inhibitions she may still have and to live freely. "If we cannot change the world," he tells her, "let's at least change our lives. . . . Let's reject everything that is not fresh and new." Jaromil eventually adopts this very philosophy ("the religion of The New"), but he does so, the author suggests, to disguise his longing for physical love. In this case at least, eroticism and art are closely related. Jaromil's sexual impulses find expression in his poetry. After spying on the family maid in the bath, Jaromil is inspired to record the stimulating experience, to give it a certain permanence. During the creative process, however, the concrete is transformed into the abstract, an intensely private experience is concealed by the veil of art. Jaromil is somewhat similar to many of the characters in *Laughable Loves* whose erotic urges cause them to adopt various roles. His sexual impulses lead him to assume the identity of a lyric poet. Later he even emulates a fictional character he himself has created, for that character possesses the freedom that Jaromil has not quite been able to attain.

At times the structure of *Life Is Elsewhere* grows too slack—particularly towards the end—and at other times the action is not quite convincing: Jaromil's political activities, for example, or the episode in which Maman works with a photographer who is making a film about Jaromil. But these are minor qualms when one considers Kundera's fine ability to dramatize ideas and to stimulate and entertain the reader in the process.

The characters in the short story collection, *Laughable Loves,* are a very dissatisfied group who long for some change in their everyday lives, anything that will enable them to achieve physical and psychological freedom. In the excellent story **"The Hitchhiking Game,"** a young man and his girl friend assume the roles of driver and hitchhiker to free themselves from their particular identities and to give vent to their hidden erotic impulses. As is often the case with Kundera's people, they allow the game to get out of hand. They attain their freedom, but they completely sacrifice their identities while doing so. The girl behaves like a whore and the young man begins to treat her accordingly. The game ends in mutual disgust. While sexual freedom is an admirable goal, it can sometimes have devastating results. The young couple failed to realize what a potentially dangerous and unpredictable game they were playing. And now that the game has ended and they have exposed highly unattractive sides of their personalities, what next? "There are still," Kundera reminds us, "thirteen days' vacation before them."

The couple in the equally superb **"Let the Old Dead Make Room for the New Dead"** also play an erotic game, though here the results are somewhat more satisfying. Meeting for the first time after fifteen years, the couple (a man and an older woman) try to recapture the passion of their first and only sexual encounter. Though they are moderately successful, there is more than a degree of desperation in their effort. They long for their youth, but a return to the past—perhaps an idealized past—is impossible. When Kundera notes that "This time the room was full of light," he is not only contrasting the old sexual encounter with the new one, but he is also suggesting that the couple now fully understand the implications of their act. They are too knowing to engage in blind passion. Their desperation haunts them.

The other stories in this volume are perceptive and quite delightful and they are well worth any reader's time, but I don't think that any of them really succeeds as well as the first two tales. For me at least, Kundera's stories work best when they are very tightly structured and narrowly focused. His stories exploring various Don Juan types, like Dr. Havel, are entertaining, but a little too casually developed, a bit too sketchlike. As a result, they lack the impact and intensity of the earlier tales.

The only other work of Kundera's that has appeared in English was his famous political novel, *The Joke* (which he made into a film). These two new books reveal a different side of the artist's sensibility and talent, and they are very welcome indeed. Though one may occasionally tire of the author's concern—perhaps *obsession* is a better word—with the erotic, Kundera's originality, intelligence and witty narrative voice are irresistible.

E. L. Doctorow (review date 29 April 1984)

SOURCE: "Four Characters under Two Tyrannies," in *New York Times Book Review,* April 29, 1984, p. 1.

[*In the review below, Doctorow examines Kundera's narrative style in* The Unbearable Lightness of Being, *describing the relation between the characters and themes of his book.*]

"I am bored by narrative," Virginia Woolf wrote in her diary in 1929, thus suggesting how the novel has been kept alive in our century by novelists' assaults on its conventions. Writers have chosen to write novels without plots or characters or the illusion of time passing. They have disdained to represent real life, as the painters did a half century before them. They have compacted their given languages, or invented their own, or revised the idea of composition entirely by assembling their books as collages.

Appearing noticeably in the United States 15 or 20 years ago was the disclaimed fiction in which the author deliberately broke the mimetic spell of his text and insisted that the reader should not take his story to heart or believe in the existence of his characters. Disclaiming had the theoretical advantage of breaking through to some approximation of the chaos and loss of structure in life. The subject of these fictions became the impossibility of maintaining them, and the author by his candor became the only character the reader could believe in. John Barth is one writer who comes to mind as having explored the possibilities of this strategy, and the distinguished Czech novelist Milan Kundera in his new book, *The Unbearable Lightness of Being,* continues to find it useful.

"And once more I see him the way he appeared to me at the very beginning of the novel," Mr. Kundera says of one of the characters, who is described standing at a window and staring across a courtyard at a blank wall. "This is the image from which he was born.... Characters are not born, like people, of woman; they are born of a situation, a sentence, a metaphor, containing in a nutshell a basic human possibility ... the characters in my novels are my own unrealized possibilities. That is why I am equally fond of them and equally horrified by them.... But enough. Let us return to Tomas."

The question may reasonably be asked if this convention too isn't ready for assault. May it not be too late to return to Tomas? Do we have to be told where he comes from any more than we have to be told where babies come from? There is a particular hazard to the author who intrudes on his text: He had better be as interesting as the characters he competes with and the story he subverts or we may find him self-indulgent or, worse, coy, like those animated cartoons where a hand draws a little animal and colors it in and pushes it along to its adventure down the road.

Even now, in our age, there is a sanctity to the story. Because it is supremely valuable to us—as valuable as science or religion—we feel all violence done to it must finally be in its service. Virginia Woolf's experiment in avoiding narrative, *Mrs. Dalloway,* discovered another way to construct it or, perhaps, another place in which it could occur. The idea has always been to make it beat with life's beating heart.

Let us return to Tomas. Mr. Kundera has made him a successful surgeon. In Prague, in the spring of 1968, when Alexander Dubcek is trying to make the Czech Communist Government more human, Tomas writes a letter to a newspaper to add his voice to a public debate. Thereafter, the Russians invade Prague, Dubcek is replaced, public debate ceases, and Tomas is asked by the authorities to sign a statement retracting the sentiments of his letter. But he knows that once he does, if he ever again speaks out the Government will publish his retraction and his name among his fellow Czechs will be ruined. So he refuses and for his intransigence is then asked to sign a letter avowing his love for the Soviet Union, a possibility so unthinkable that he quits medicine and becomes a window washer. He hopes that now that he is down at the bottom he will no longer matter to the authorities and they will let him alone. What he discovers is that he no longer matters to anyone. When he was supposed by his hospital colleagues to be thinking of signing the retraction in order to keep his job they turned up their noses at him. Now that he's been declassed for maintaining his integrity, he's become an untouchable.

> Tomas is one of four main characters born frankly of images in Mr. Kundera's mind. All of them to one extent or another enact the paradox of choices that are not choices, of courses of action that are indistinguishable in consequence from their opposite.
>
> —*E. L. Doctorow*

The first thing to note about this character's fate is that it is a gloss on Orwell: To destroy Tomas, Mr. Kundera is saying, the powerfully inertial police apparatus doesn't have to expend the energy required to torture him. It need only send around an affable plainclothesman with a letter to be signed. Once the policeman appears, no matter how Tomas responds his life is ruined.

The second thing to note is the idea of the exhaustion of meaningful choice. Tomas is one of four main characters born frankly of images in Mr. Kundera's mind. All of them to one extent or another enact the paradox of choices that are not choices, of courses of action that are indistinguishable in consequence from their opposite. He shows us Sabina, a painter, as she is deciding whether or not to keep her current lover, Franz, a university professor. Franz is physically strong. If he used his strength on her and ordered her about, Sabina knows she wouldn't put up with him for five minutes. But he is gentle, and because she believes physical love must be violent she finds Franz dull. Either way, whatever Franz does, she will have to leave him.

Mr. Kundera says Sabina lives by betrayal, abandoning family, lovers and, finally, country, in a way that condemns her to what he calls a "lightness of being," by which he means a life so lacking in commitment or fidelity or moral responsibility to anyone else as to be unattached to the real earth. By contrast, his fourth character, Tereza, the loyal wife of Tomas, suffers an unflagging love for her philandering husband that finally is responsible for his ruin, because it's her unwillingness to live in exile that brings him back to his fate in Czechoslovakia after he has set himself up nicely in a

Swiss hospital. Thus, Tereza, the exact opposite of Sabina in commitment and fidelity and rootedness to the real earth, sinks under an unbearable moral burden, weight and lightness, in the Kunderian physics, adding up to the same thing.

So there is a pattern in the subservience of his characters to Mr. Kundera's will. They all exemplify the central act of his imagination, which is to conceive of a paradox and express it elegantly. The paradox he is most fond of is the essential identity of opposites, and he plays with it over and over again, with minor characters as well as major ones and with little essays and one-line observations. For instance, he shows us a dissident Czech emigre in Paris in the act of reproaching his fellow emigres for their lack of anti-Communist fervor, and he finds in him the same bullying quality of mind as in the former head of state, Antonin Novotny, who ruled Czechoslovakia for 14 years. The elegance lies in the image Mr. Kundera uses to make the observation that both the emigre and the former ruler point their index fingers at whomever they address. In fact, people of this sort, Mr. Kundera tells us, have index fingers longer than their middle fingers.

Whether personal or political, all attitudes, stands, positions in the Kunderian vision come up short. He will kill off three of his quartet and allow the fourth to disappear from the book, presumably from a lightness of being; but his true story, the one to which he gives honest service, is the operation of his own mind as it formulates and finds images for the disastrous history of his country in his lifetime. The paradox of the essential identity of opposites describes an intractable world in which human beings are deprived of a proper context for their humanity. The author who ostentatiously intrudes in his characters' lives and tells them how to behave mimics, of course, the government that interferes deeply in its citizens' lives and tells them how to behave. Tomas and Sabina and Franz and Tereza were invented to live under two tyrannies, the tyranny of contemporary Czechoslovakia and the tyranny of Mr. Kundera's despair.

Readers of the author's celebrated novel **The Book of Laughter and Forgetting** will recognize here his structural use of leitmotif, the repertoire of phrases and fancies among which he circulates and recirculates. They will find the same ironic tone and brilliance of annotation of the fearful emptiness of Eastern European life under Communist management. Here too is the author's familiarity with music, his preoccupation with Don Juanism, his almost voyeuristic attention to the female body and its clothes. And the pointed, surreal image: Park benches from the city of Prague, colored red, yellow and blue, floating inexplicably on the Vltava River. Like Gabriel Garcia Marquez, Mr. Kundera knows how to get ahead of his story and circle back to it and run it through again with a different emphasis. But the prose is sparer here, and the Garcia Marquez levitations are not

events now, but ideas. There is less clutter in the prose, less of the stuff of life, as if the author had decided to send the myriad furnishings of novels, its particulars, down the Vltava, after the benches. This is a kind of conceptualist fiction, a generic-brand, no-frills fiction, at least in Michael Henry Heim's translation. Mr. Kundera is not inclined to dwell on the feel of human experience except as it prepares us for his thought.

And what is his thought? Asking this question leads to the novel on its own terms. Mr. Kundera is a good psychologist of the rutting male. His idea of love as the occupation by another person of one's own poetic memory is a sweet one. He adds to the meaning of the word kitsch by describing it, first, as an esthetic ideal that denies the existence of excrement and, second, as the inevitable adjunct of political power. "Whenever a single political movement corners power we find ourselves in the realm of *totalitarian kitsch*," he says. "Everything that infringes on kitsch must be banished for life . . . every display of individualism . . . every doubt . . . all irony." Thus, "the gulag is a septic tank used by totalitarian kitsch to dispose of its refuse."

> **The author who ostentatiously intrudes in his characters' lives and tells them how to behave mimics, of course, the government that interferes deeply in its citizens' lives and tells them how to behave.**
> **—*E. L. Doctorow***

It is a not unattractive philosophical bent that sends Mr. Kundera into his speculative exercises. He has a first-rate mind and, like Bernard Shaw, the capacity to argue both sides of a question and make each side seem reasonable in its turn. But every now and then a wryly argued proposition seems flawed, a weakness for literary idea rather than a strength of thought—that a concentration camp, for instance, is defined first and foremost by the complete absence of privacy; it might be argued that slave labor and starvation and mass graves are its primary characteristics. Or the idea, coming from Sabina's walk through New York City, that its beauty, unlike that of European cities, is unintentional, or "beauty by mistake, the final phase in the history of beauty." New York may indeed be unintentionally beautiful, but we are younger than Europe, and, whatever holocaust is in sight, beauty by mistake might just as easily be the first phase in the history of beauty as the last.

One recurrent theme in the book is that the ideal of social perfection is what inevitably causes the troubles of mankind, that the desire for utopia is the basis of the world's ills, there being no revolution and therefore no totalitarianism without it. This idea has currency among expatriate Eastern European intellectuals, and perhaps their bitter experience entitles them to it. But the history of revolutions begins, more likely, in the desire to eat or to breathe than in the thought that man must be perfected. And a revolutionary document like the American Constitution is filled with instructions and standards for civilized life under equitable law; and it is truly utopian, but its ideals are our saving grace and drive us to our best selves, not our worst.

It is not exactly self-indulgence or coyness that threatens *The Unbearable Lightness of Being.* The mind Mr. Kundera puts on display is truly formidable, and the subject of its concern is substantively alarming. But, given this subject, why are we forced to wonder, as we read, where his crisis of faith locates itself, in the world or in his art? The depiction of a universe in which all human choice wallows in irresolution, in which, as Yeats wrote, "The best lack all conviction, while the worst / Are full of passionate intensity," sometimes sets off the technique of this novel as an act of ego in excess of the sincere demands of despair. Mr. Kundera's master, the prophet Kafka, we can't help remembering, wrote a conceptualist no-frills fiction in which, however, he never appeared.

All this said, the work of reconceiving and redesigning the novel continues through the individual struggles of novelists all over the world, like an instinct of our breed. What is fine and valiant in Mr. Kundera is the enormous struggle not to be characterized as a writer by his exile and by his nation's disenfranchisement, even though they are the conditions his nose is rubbed in by Czechoslovak history. He works with cunning and wit and elegiac sadness to express "the trap the world has become," and this means he wants to reconceive not only narrative but the language and history of politicized life if he is to accord his experience the dimensions of its tragedy. This is in direct contrast to the problem of the American writer who must remember not to write of life as if it had no political content whatsoever. We can hope, with Milan Kundera, not to enact one of his elegant paradoxes in our separate choices and discover that either one leads to the same exhausted end.

John Bayley (review date 7-20 June 1984)

SOURCE: "Kundera and Kitsch," in *London Review of Books,* Vol. 6, No. 10, June 7-20, 1984, pp. 18-19.

[*Below, Bayley explains the meaning and use of "kitsch" in the context of* The Unbearable Lightness of Being.]

There is always comedy in the ways in which we are impressed by a novel. It can either impress us (if, that is, it is one of the very good ones) with the sort of truths that Nietzsche, Kafka and Dostoevsky tell us, or with the truths that Tolstoy and Trollope tell us. To the first kind we respond with amazement and delight, awe even. 'Of course that's it! Of *course* that's it!' The second kind of truths are more sober, more laboriously constructed, more ultimately reassuring. They are the truths necessary for fiction, and therefore necessary for life. The first kind contribute brilliantly not to life itself but to what seems an understanding of it. And that too is necessary for us, or at least desirable, and enjoyable.

Milan Kundera's latest novel is certainly one of the very good ones. It is in fact so amazingly better than anything he has written before that the reader can hardly believe it, is continually being lost in astonishment. In manner and technique it is not much different from his previous books, but the story here at last really compels us, and so do the hero and heroine. Kundera's great strength has always been his wit and intelligence, and his particular way with these assets. He was a Nietzschean truthteller rather than a Tolstoyan one. But this new novel [*The Unbearable Lightness of Being*] dissolves my distinction while at the same time drawing attention to it. Its impact is considerable. Whether it will last, whether one will want to read it again, are more difficult questions to answer.

Salman Rushdie described *The Book of Laughter and Forgetting,* which appeared in English in 1980, as 'a whirling dance of a book', and went on to bury it under all the chic epithets, sad, obscene, tender, wickedly funny, wonderfully wise, 'a masterpiece full of angels, terror, ostriches and love'. It was not as bad as that. But Kundera was like a man let loose among all the literary fashions of the West, grabbing this and that, intoxicated by the display patterns of freedom. On the publication of the book the Czech Government revoked his citizenship. Both this decision and the book itself followed logically from Kundera's early novels and stories, like *The Joke,* published in Prague during the Prague Spring. *The Book of Laughter and Forgetting* (the title is shorter in Czech and sounds better) used every device of French and American 'fictiveness', and its pornography, though cheerful, was so insistent in repudiating any shadow of Iron Curtain puritanism that it now seems as didactic and determined as the evolutions of Komsomol girls in red gymslips.

Unfair maybe, but circumstances made the book weightless, cosmopolitan. Despite its title, there is nothing weightless about *The Unbearable Lightness of Being.* In one sense, indeed, it satirises its predecessor. Nor could it possibly have been written by a Frenchman or an American. It is deeply, centrally European, both German and Slav, as Nietzsche himself was both Pole and German. Prague is the centre of this Europe, and with this book we are right back in Kafka's city, where neither Kafka nor Kundera can be published. None the less, Kundera's intelligence has quietly forsaken contemporary Western fashion and gone back to its deep roots, in

Europe's old repressions and nightmares, to a time and an art long before the cinema and the modern happening.

Both in Poland and in Czechoslovakia the cinema represented a method of escape into the modernity which the Communist system rejected and forbade. Kundera was a professor of film technology and his pupils produced the new wave in the Czech cinema. His work, even the present novel, has been influenced by film techniques, but they have here been thoroughly absorbed into the forms of traditional literature, and Kundera now seems positively old-fashioned in the way in which he combines the authorial presence with the 'story'. The author is the purveyor of Nietzschean truth, but the story is of the Tolstoyan kind. Lightness of being is associated with the author's voice, with the cinema and sex, with irresponsibility and definition, with politics. Weight or heaviness of being, on the other hand, is associated with love and fidelity, suffering, chance, fiction, form and content ('The sadness was form, the happiness content. Happiness filled the space of sadness'), death.

The story has weight, though it is lightly told. A Prague surgeon, an insatiable womaniser, visits a hospital in a small provincial town. He gives a kind smile to a waitress at the hotel, who falls in love with him. She follows him to Prague. She has weight (her whole background is described). They make love in order to sleep together afterwards (he has never been able to sleep with a woman before, only to make love to her). They are necessary to each other, but he cannot give up other girls. At night his hair smells of them, though he always remembers carefully to wash the rest of himself, and Tereza in her unbearable jealousy has nightmares, dreams that are part of the lightness of being. He marries her to make up for it.

He gets a good job in Zurich, but his habits continue, and Tereza leaves him, goes back to Prague. Realising he cannot live without her, he goes back too, just in time for the Russian invasion. He loses his job, becomes a window-washer, then a driver on a collective farm. With their dog Karenin he and Tereza remain together. Fate is a story; fate is Beethoven's *Es muss sein.* Karenin dies of cancer, a moving episode—for animals, being powerless, have all the weight lacking in human consciousness. We learn that Tomas and Tereza die in a car accident, but the novel goes on, leaving them at a moment of settled happiness not unlike the tranquil ending of a traditional novel, on what is presumably their last night on earth. Tomas might have been a successful surgeon in Zurich; he might have emigrated to America, as one of his weightless mistresses, Sabina, has done, and lived in the permanent limbo of non-fiction. But his destiny is the Tolstoyan story and Tereza, who could never 'learn lightness'.

In one sense, then, Kundera's novel neatly turns the tables on today's theorists about the novel. It is, after all, ironical that we are now told all the time how totally fictive fiction is, while the writers who hold this view do not in practice make much effort to render their novels thoroughly fictive— that is, convincingly *real.* When the novel begins to insist that it is all made up, it tends to strike the reader as not made up at all. Kundera's aim is to emphasise that the novel is, or was, true to one aspect of human life, while the free play of thought and consciousness is true to another.

What then shall we choose? Weight or lightness?

Parmenides posed this very question in the sixth century before Christ. He saw the world divided into pairs of opposites . . . Which one is positive, weight or lightness?

Parmenides responded: lightness is positive, weight negative.

Was he correct or not? That is the question. The only certainty is: the lightness/weight opposition is the most mysterious, most ambiguous of all.

Kundera thus ingeniously suggests that the aspects of life that constitute a novel about it, a determined story, are as authentic as the sense of consciousness, the lightness of being. To understand either we require both. Tomas stands for lightness, Teresa for weight. This sounds as if they were not 'real' characters: but they are, because of the opposition between them.

It would be senseless for author to try to convince reader that his characters had actually lived. They were not born of a mother's womb; they were born of a stimulating phrase or two or from a basic situation. Tomas was born of the saying '*Einmal ist keinmal.*' Tereza was born of the rumbling of a stomach.

Tereza was overcome with shame because her stomach rumbled when Tomas first kissed and possessed her. It was empty from the strain of her travelling and she could do nothing about it. Not being able to do anything about it is the sense in which we live as if we were being controlled by the plot of a novel. Tomas is a personified symbol of the German saying, of the idea that nothing ever happens to us because it can only happen once. Because nothing ever happens we can control it—it becomes as light as feathers, like history. 'Because they deal with something that will not return, the bloody years of the French Revolution have turned into mere words, theories and discussions, frightening no one.' We also read this:

Not long ago I caught myself experiencing a most

incredible sensation. Leafing through a book on Hitler, I was touched by some of his portraits: they reminded me of my childhood. I grew up during the war; several members of my family perished in Hitler's concentration camps; but what were their deaths compared with the memories of a lost period of my life, a period that would never return?

This reconciliation with Hitler reveals the profound moral perversity of a world that rests essentially on the nonexistence of return, for in this world everything is pardoned in advance and therefore everything cynically permitted.

Well, it doesn't follow. Nietzschean discoveries, however sensational, in practice leave common sense and common morality much as they were. One such reconciliation with Hitler does not alter the general sense of things, or even that of the man who has made this discovery. Much more important from the point of view of the novel is Kundera's manipulation of two sorts of awareness of things: the light and the heavy, the perpetual and the fictional. It is as if he had decided to write a novel—and perhaps he did—which would acquire its reality by contrasting two theoretical views of how the novel presents it: Virginia Woolf's idea of the perpetual transparent envelope of consciousness, helplessly receiving impressions, and the 'row of giglamps', the sequential and determined tale told by a novelist like Arnold Bennett.

The transparent, envelope of promiscuous Tomas is dragged down to earth by the determined—in all senses—weight of the faithful Tereza. He is compelled against his nature to become a character in a novel, the character that she by nature is. Their relation is both funny and moving, dominating the book and giving it the dignity of fiction and its weight. (Kundera reminds us that the rise of the novel is both the expression of ever-increasing self-consciousness, and its antidote. By representing ourselves in fictions we escape from the unbearable insubstantiality of awareness. In Cartesian formula: we create the Archers, therefore we exist.)

Kundera has always been a flashy writer, his chief interest in sexual discussion and gossip. This is of course so common now as to be standard practice, at least for writers in the West, and it always involves a degree of self-indulgence. His flashiness here becomes an asset, however, blending nicely with his fictive strategy, which is to separate the splendid and various experience of sex—the area of lightness and the will, conquest, curiosity and enterprise—from the heavy, fated and involuntary area of love. Love shapes the novel, sex provides the commentary: a facile arrangement, perhaps, but effective. Like Stendhal, Kundera categorises with engaging relish the different sorts of womaniser, notably those whose obsession is *lyrical,* founded on a romantic ideal

which is continually disappointed and, continually reborn, and the *epic* womaniser, 'whose inability to be disappointed has something scandalous about it. The obsession of the epic womaniser strikes people as lacking in redemption (redemption by disappointment).'

Tomas belongs to the second category. Being a surgeon he could not, with his mistresses, 'ever quite put down the imaginary scalpel. Since he longed to take possession of something deep inside them, he needed to slit them open.' Sabina, Tomas's female counterpart, is similarly questing and capricious. For her love is a kind of kitsch, a breaking of faith and truth, spoiling an honest relationship. As an epic-style female Don Juan she is the ruin of her lover Franz, whose obsession with her is of the lyric variety.

All this schematisation is fairly glib: in his miniature play *The Stone Guest* Pushkin handles the theme of the light-hearted mistress, and the seducer endlessly fascinated by feminine diversity, with a true depth of art, and it seems likely that Kundera has recalled what Pushkin termed a 'dramatic investigation', and made it diagrammatic and explicit. More compellingly original is the political aspect of lightness, and the fact that, as Kundera perceives, it forms the normal social atmosphere of a Communist state. No one believes any more in the false weightiness of the ideology of such a state, and since that ideology has replaced old-fashioned and instinctive morality the citizens' personal lives are left in a condition of weightlessness.

Sabina associates the kitsch of love with the overwhelming kitsch of the Communist regime, seeing any long-term personal fidelity or integrity as if it were an analogy of that apotheosis of kitsch, the 'Grand March' towards the gleaming heights of socialism. This Kundera suggests is the vilest outcome of the totalitarian kitsch of our time: that it negates any natural and individual pattern of responsibility and weight in private life. Indeed, in a Communist regime there is no private life, but only bottomless cynicism on the one side and measureless kitsch on the other. Sabina had been trained as a painter in the Socialist Realist manner and she soon learnt to practise a subterfuge which in the end became her own highly original and personal style, and makes her rich and successful when she gets away to the West and then to America. She paints a nicely intelligible socialist reality, but with the aid of a few random drops of red paint, or something of the kind, she conjures up an unintelligible reality beneath it, an evocation of meaningless, and therefore to her saving and liberating, lightness of being. She is filled with repulsion when her admirers in the West mount an exhibition, after she has got out, showing her name and a blurb against a tasteful background of barbed wire and other symbols of oppression conquered by the human spirit. This is the same old kitsch by other means, and Sabina, who has a fastidious taste in such things, protests it is not Communism she is rejecting and getting away from, but kitsch itself. 'Kitsch,' observes Kundera, 'is the aesthetic ideal of all politicians and all political parties and movements . . . The brotherhood of man on earth will only be possible on a basis of kitsch.'

It is unfortunately typical of Kundera to run a good idea into the ground, to become increasingly entranced in the development of a lively perception until it spreads too easily. It is thus with kitsch, the concept he opposes to lightness of being, and which he deals with in a lyrical analysis in the penultimate section of the novel. The point of this is that though kitsch opposes itself to lightness of being, the true antithesis to kitsch is the weight of love and death in Tereza, the weight with which she envelops Tomas. Kitsch has no answer to death ('kitsch is a folding screen set up to curtain off death'), just as it has no relation to the true necessities of power and love. Sabina is wholly accurate in her perception of the relation between kitsch and Communism: what she loathes and fears is not Communist 'reality'—persecution, meat queues, overcrowding, everlasting suspicion and shabbiness, all of which is quite honest and tolerable—but Soviet idealism. 'In the world of Communist ideal made real', the world of Communist films and 'grinning idiots', 'she would have nothing to say, she would die of horror within a week.'

The term 'kitsch', as used by Kundera, oversimplifies the whole question of the mechanism by which we accept life and open our arms to its basic situations. All good writers, from Homer to Hemingway, have their own versions of it. If we accept his definition, all art would be as full of kitsch— the stereotyped formula of gracious living—as any Hollywood or Soviet film. What matters, surely, as he also recognises, is the purpose behind kitsch today, the ways in which commercial and political interests have taken over and control a basic human need. Kitsch—the word and its meaning—arrived in the 19th century as a substitute for the other kinds of human illusion, religious and chiliastic, which were withering away. 'What makes a leftist is the kitsch of the Grand March.' Yes, but what makes living endurable is the kitsch of life itself. Here Kundera, it must be said, makes a nice distinction.

> Kitsch causes two tears to flow in quick succession. The first tear says: How nice to see children running on the grass!

> The second tear says: How nice to be moved, together with all mankind, by children running on the grass!

> It is the second tear that makes kitsch kitsch.

Even Sabina comforts herself sometimes with the image of

herself as part of 'a happy family living behind two shining windows', but 'as soon as the kitsch is recognised for the lie it is, it moves into the context of non-kitsch, thus losing its authoritarian power and becoming as touching as any other human weakness.' By always recognising kitsch, Sabina shows herself incapable of those deep involuntary movements of the soul experienced by Tereza, and by Tomas-with-Tereza. Sabina can only know the unbearable lightness of being.

These are old platitudes dressed up in new styles? Inevitably so, to some extent, and like all Nietzschean demonstrators, Kundera cannot afford to admit the relative aspect of things. Kitsch does not define an absolute concept; it only suggests tendency and style. Kundera has a Continental passion for getting things defined, as when he gives us Tereza's dream vision of her death and Tomas's:

> Horror is a shock, a time of utter blindness. Horror lacks every hint of beauty . . . Sadness, on the other hand, assumes we are in the know. Tomas and Tereza knew what was awaiting them. The light of horror thus lost its harshness, and the world was bathed in a gentle bluish light that actually beautified it.

In spite of this, his ending is imaginative and very moving, as moving as the end of Kafka's *The Trial*. Indeed Kundera could be said to have written a kind of *explication* of Kafka's novel, shedding light on its basic allegory and at the same time making use of it for the structure of a new work. Kafka's title is a deep pun. The German word for trial—*Prozess*—could also refer to the process of living, and it is living which is impossible for Kafka's hero, because all life has been sentenced to death. The strangest moment in *The Trial* is when the hero, about to suffer execution, sees a light go on in a nearby house and someone lean out of the window. That someone is unaware of his fate, or indifferent to it, as the process of living is unaware of death. Kundera the novelist is exceptionally aware, as Kafka was, of the difference between that process and the state of consciousness, of what he calls the unbearable lightness of being. But whereas living for Kafka was not a feasible process, for Kundera it is extremely so. And for him the real enemies of life are not Death and the Law but kitsch and the politician.

Italo Calvino (essay date 5 May 1985)

SOURCE: "On Kundera," in *Review of Contemporary Fiction*, Vol. 9, No. 2, Summer, 1989, pp. 53-7.

[*In the essay below, originally published in the periodical* La Repubblica *on May 5, 1985, Calvino discusses the sig-*

nificance of digressive elements of Kundera's narrative style in The Unbearable Lightness of Being.]

> *When he was twelve, she suddenly found herself alone, abandoned by Franz's father. The boy suspected something serious had happened, but his mother muted the drama with mild, insipid words so as not to upset him. The day his father left, Franz and his mother went into town together, and as they left home Franz noticed that she was wearing a different shoe on each foot. He was in a quandary: he wanted to point out her mistake, but was afraid he would hurt her. So during the two hours they spent walking through the city together he kept his eyes fixed on her feet. It was then that he had his first inkling of what it means to suffer.*

This passage from ***The Unbearable Lightness of Being*** illustrates well Milan Kundera's art of storytelling—its concreteness, its finesse—and brings us closer to understanding the secret due to which, in his last novel, the pleasure of reading is continuously rekindled. Among so many writers of novels, Kundera is a true novelist in the sense that the characters' stories are his first interest: private stories, stories, above all, of couples, in their singularity and unpredictability. His manner of storytelling progresses by successive waves (most of the action develops within the first thirty pages; the conclusion is already announced halfway through; every story is completed and illuminated layer by layer) and by means of digressions and remarks that transform the private problem into a universal problem and, thereby, one that is ours. But this overall development, rather than increasing the seriousness of the situation, functions as an ironic filter lightening its pathos. Among Kundera's readers, there will be those taken more with the goings-on and those (I, for example) more with the digressions. But even these become the tale. Like his eighteenth-century masters Sterne and Diderot, Kundera makes of his extemporaneous reflections almost a diary of his thoughts and moods.

The universal-existential problematic also involves that which, given that we are dealing with Czechoslovakia, cannot be forgotten even for a minute: that ensemble of shame and folly that once was called history and that now can only be called the cursed misfortune of being born in one country rather than another. But Kundera, making of this not "the problem" but merely one more complication of life's inconveniences, eliminates that dutiful, distancing respect that every literature of the oppressed rouses within us, the undeserving privileged, thereby involving us in the daily despair of Communist regimes much more than if he were to appeal to pathos.

The nucleus of the book resides in a truth as simple as it is ineludible: It is impossible to act according to experience because every situation we face is unique and presents itself to us for the first time. "Any schoolboy can do experiments in the physics laboratory to test various scientific hypotheses. But man, because he has only one life to live, cannot conduct experiments to test whether to follow his passion (compassion) or not."

Kundera links this fundamental axiom with corollaries not as solid: the lightness of living for him resides in the fact that things only happen once, fleetingly, and it is therefore as if they had not happened. Weight, instead, is to be found in the "eternal recurrence" hypothesized by Nietzsche: every fact becomes dreadful if we know that it will repeat itself infinitely. But (I would object) if the "eternal recurrence"—the possible meaning of which has never been agreed upon—is the return of the same, a unique and unrepeatable life is precisely equal to a life infinitely repeated: every act is irrevocable, non-modifiable for eternity. If the "eternal recurrence" is, instead, a repetition of rhythms, patterns, structures, hieroglyphics of fate that leave room for infinite little variants in detail, then one could consider the possible as an ensemble of statistical fluctuations in which every event would not exclude better or worse alternatives and the finality of every gesture would end up lightened.

Lightness of living, for Kundera, is that which is opposed to irrevocability, to exclusive univocity: as much in love (the Prague doctor Tomas likes to practice only "erotic friendships" avoiding passionate involvements and conjugal cohabitation) as in politics (this is not explicitly said, but the tongue hits where the tooth hurts, and the tooth is, naturally, the impossibility of Eastern Europe's changing—or at least alleviating—a destiny it never dreamed of choosing).

But Tomas ends up taking in and marrying Tereza, a waitress in a country restaurant, out of "compassion." Not just that: after the Russian invasion of '68, Tomas succeeds in escaping from Prague and emigrating to Switzerland with Tereza who, after a few months, is overcome by a nostalgia that manifests itself as a vertigo of weakness over the weakness of her country without hope, and she returns. Here it is then that Tomas, who would have every reason, ideal and practical, to remain in Zurich, also decides to return to Prague, despite an awareness that he is entrapping himself, and to face persecutions and humiliations (he will no longer be able to practice medicine and will end up a window washer).

Why does he do it? Because, despite his professing the ideal of the lightness of living, and despite the practical example of his relationship with his friend, the painter Sabina, he has always suspected that truth lies in the opposing idea, in weight, in necessity. "Es muss sein!" / "It must be" says the last movement of Beethoven's last quartet. And Tereza, love nourished by compassion, love not chosen but imposed by fate, assumes in his eyes the meaning of this burden of the ineluctable, of the "Es muss sein!"

We come to know a little later (and here is how the digressions form almost a parallel novel) that the pretext that led Beethoven to write "Es muss sein!" was in no way sublime, but a banal story of loaned money to be repaid, just as the fate that had brought Tereza into Tomas's life was only a series of fortuitous coincidences.

In reality, this novel dedicated to lightness speaks to us above all of constraint: the web of public and private constraints that envelops people, that exercises its weight over every human relationship (and does not even spare those that Tomas would consider passing *couchages*). Even the Don Juanism, on which Kundera gives us a page of original definitions, has entirely other than "light" motivations: whether it be when it answers to a "lyrical obsession," which is to say it seeks among many women the unique and ideal woman, or when it is motivated by an "epic obsession," which is to say it seeks a universal knowledge in diversity.

Among the parallel stories, the most notable is that of Sabina and Franz. Sabina, as the representative of lightness and the bearer of the meanings of the book, is more persuasive than the character with whom she is contrasted, that is, Tereza. (I would say that Tereza does not succeed in having the "weight" necessary to justify a decision as self-destructive as that of Tomas.) It is through Sabina that lightness is shown to be a "semantic river," that is to say, a web of associations and images and words on which is based her amorous agreement with Tomas, a complicity that Tomas cannot find again with Tereza, or Sabina with Franz. Franz, the Swiss scientist, is the Western progressive intellectual, as can be seen by he who, from Eastern Europe, considers him with the impassive objectivity of the ethnologist studying the customs of an inhabitant of the antipodes. The vertigo of indetermination that has sustained the leftist passions of the last twenty years is indicated by Kundera with the maximum of precision compatible with so elusive an object: "The dictatorship of the proletariat or democracy? Rejection of the consumer society or demands for increased productivity? The guillotine or an end to the death penalty? It is all beside the point." What characterizes the Western left, according to Kundera, is what he calls the Grand March, which develops with the same vagueness of purpose and emotion:

> . . . yesterday against the American occupation of Vietnam, today against the Vietnamese occupation of Cambodia; yesterday for Israel, today for the Palestinians; yesterday for Cuba, tomorrow against Cuba—and always against America; at times against massacres and at times in support of other massacres; Europe marches on, and to keep up with events, to leave none of them out, its pace grows

faster and faster, until finally the Grand March is a procession of rushing, galloping people and the platform is shrinking and shrinking until one day it will be reduced to a mere dimensionless dot.

In accordance with the agonized imperatives of Franz's sense of duty, Kundera brings us to the threshold of the most monstrous hell generated by ideological abstractions become reality, Cambodia, and describes an international humanitarian march in pages that are a masterpiece of political satire.

At the opposite extreme of Franz, his temporary partner Sabina, by virtue of her lucid mind, acts as the author's mouthpiece, establishing comparisons and contrasts and parallels between the experience of the Communist society in which she grew up and the Western experience. One of the pivotal bases for these comparisons is the category of kitsch. Kundera explores kitsch in the sense of edulcorated, edifying, "Victorian" representation, and he thinks naturally of "socialist realism" and of political propaganda, the hypocritical mask of all horrors. Sabina, who, having established herself in the United States, loves New York for what there is there of "non-intentional beauty," "beauty by error," is upset when she sees American kitsch, Coca-Cola-like publicity, surface to remind her of the radiant images of virtue and health in which she grew up. But Kundera justly specifies:

> Kitsch is the aesthetic idea of all politicians and all political parties and movements.
>
> Those of us who live in a society where various political tendencies exist side by side and competing influences cancel or limit one another can manage more or less to escape the kitsch inquisition. . . . But whenever a single political movement corners power, we find ourselves in the realm of *totalitarian kitsch.*

The step that remains to be taken is to free oneself of the fear of kitsch, once having saved oneself from its totalitarianism, and to be able to see it as an element among others, an image that quickly loses its own mystifying power to conserve only the color of passing time, evidence of mediocrity or of yesterday's naïveté. This is what seems to me to happen to Sabina, in whose story we can recognize a spiritual itinerary of reconciliation with the world. At the sight, typical of the American idyll, of windows lit in a white clapboard house on a lawn, Sabina is surprised by an emotional realization. And nothing remains but for her to conclude: "No matter how we scorn it, kitsch is an integral part of the human condition."

A much sadder conclusion is that of the story of Tereza and Tomas; but here, through the death of a dog, and the obliteration of their own selves in a lost site in the country, there is almost an absorption into the cycle of nature, into an idea of the world that not only does not have man at its center, but that is absolutely not made for man.

My objections to Kundera are twofold: one terminological and one metaphysical. The terminological concerns the category of kitsch within which Kundera takes into consideration only one among many meanings. But the kitsch that claims to represent the most audacious and "cursed" broadmindedness with facile and banal effects is also part of the bad taste of mass culture. Indeed, it is less dangerous than the other, but it must be taken into account to avoid our believing it an antidote. For example, to see the absolute contrast with kitsch in the image of a naked woman wearing a man's bowler hat does not seem to me totally convincing.

The metaphysical objection takes us farther. It regards the "categorical agreement with being," an attitude that, for Kundera, is the basis of kitsch as an aesthetic ideal. "The line separating those who doubt being as it is granted to man (no matter how or by whom) from those who accept it without reservation" resides in the fact that adherence imposes the illusion of a world in which defecation does not exist because, according to Kundera, shit is absolute metaphysical negativity. I would object that for pantheists and for the constipated (I belong to one of these two categories, though I will not specify which) defecation is one of the greatest proofs of the generosity of the universe (of nature or providence or necessity or what have you). That shit is to be considered of value and not worthless is for me a matter of principle.

From this some fundamental consequences derive. In order not to fall either into vague sentiments of a universal redemption that end up by producing monstrous police states or into generalized and temperamental pseudo-rebellions that are resolved in sheepish obedience, it is necessary to recognize how things are, whether we like them or not, both within the realm of the great, against which it is useless to struggle, and that of the small, which can be modified by our will. I believe then that a certain degree of agreement with the existent (shit included) is necessary precisely because it is incompatible with the kitsch that Kundera justly detests.

Terry Eagleton (essay date Winter 1987)

SOURCE: "Estrangement and Irony," in *Salmagundi*, No. 73, Winter, 1987, pp. 25-32.

[*In the following essay, Eagleton considers the various ideological conflicts that inform Kundera's fiction.*]

Milan Kundera tells the story in *The Book of Laughter and*

Forgetting of a Czech being sick in the middle of Prague, not long after the Soviet invasion of the country. Another Czech wanders up to him, shakes his head and says: "I know exactly what you mean".

The joke here, of course, is that the second Czech reads as *significant* what is in fact just a random event. In the post-capitalist bureaucracies, even vomiting is made to assume some kind of instant symbolic meaning. Nothing in Eastern Europe can happen by accident. The logical extreme of this attitude is paranoia, a condition in which reality becomes so pervasively, oppressively meaningful that its slightest fragments operate as minatory signs in some utterly coherent text. Once the political state extends its empire over the whole of civil society, social reality becomes so densely systematized and rigorously coded that one is always being caught out in a kind of pathological 'overreading', a compulsive semiosis which eradicates all contingency. "No symbol where none intended", Samuel Beckett once remarked; but in 'totalitarian' societies, monolithic structures of meaning, one can never be quite certain what's intended and what isn't—whether there is ominous meaning or not in the delayed arrival of your spouse, the boss's failure to say good morning, that car which has been behind your own for the past ten miles. Tereza in *The Unbearable Lightness of Being* makes love with an engineer in his flat, but later she will wonder about the drabness of the place compared to his elegance, that edition of Sophocles on the shelf, the few moments he was away making the coffee. Is it the abandoned apartment of an imprisoned intellectual? Is the engineer a police agent, and was he turning on the ciné camera while supposedly making the coffee?

Survival in Eastern Europe demands an awareness of this possible sub-text, a daily hermeneutics of suspicion; but then how, in behaving with such vigilance, is one to avoid becoming collusive with a power for which no event can be accidental, no gesture innocent? How to read without overreading, avoid a naive empiricism without falling prey to semiological paranoia? The most celebrated of all modern Czech writers, Franz Kafka, suspends his readers between narrative and sub-text, the bald appearance of events and the ceaselessly elusive truth of which they might just be dimly allegorical. Such truth is never totalisable, shifting its ground each time one approaches it; there is, perhaps, a metanarrative which rigorously determines the slightest detail of quotidian life but which is always elsewhere. If this is an allegory of the disappeared God, it is also one of the post-capitalist state, a paradoxical condition in which everything is at once compulsively legible, locking smoothly into some univocal story, and yet where history is awash with secrets, whispered treacheries, tell-tale traces. In this drably positivist world, everything lies on the one hand drearily open to view, tediously repetitive and flatly two-dimensional, the mysterious depths of subjectivity drained off from a world which becomes brutely self-identical. On the other hand, nothing is ever quite what it seems; so that a 'postmodernist' eradication of depth, mystery, subjectivity co-exists strangely with a persistent 'modernist' impulse to decipher and decode, a sense of concealment and duplicity.

Kundera's fiction opposes to the sealed-off metanarrative of post-capitalist bureaucracy a set of notably dislocated texts, although not at all in the manner of some sophisticated Western deconstruction. The structural subversiveness of his novels lies simply in the loose capaciousness whereby they encompass *different stories,* sometimes to the point of appearing like a set of *nouvelles* within the same covers. This is not the modernist undermining of narrative realism of a Beckett, for whom one arbitrary story generates another equally gratuitous and that another, until the whole text becomes no more than a machine for pumping out tall groundless tales in an honorable Irish tradition. Each of Kundera's stories has a 'sense' to it, and interacts with the others; but it must be allowed to exist in its own narrative space free from metanarrational closure, absolved from the authoritarianism of the 'closed book'. Kundera constantly interrupts himself in order to give the slip to the totalitarian drive of literary fiction, breaking off the narrative to deliver his latest ontological musings, inserting a sheaf of brief philosophical reflections between episodes, airily abandoning the fictional pretence in the interests of historical documentation. All of this is done casually, apparently spontaneously, without modernist outrage or obtrusiveness, utterly bereft of any intense aesthetic self-consciousness or portentous experimentalism. There is no sense of shock or rupture in his texts, no heavily calculated violations of plausibility or deftly engineered incongruities, no calculated cacophony of discourses. For this to happen would suggest that one was still in thrall to some literary orthodoxy one was grimly or scandalously intent on discrediting, whereas Kundera conveys the rather more shocking sense of *unconcern,* a writer who has, so to speak, just not been told that you shouldn't hold up the narrative with metaphysical speculations about angels and devils, and who would not understand what you were talking about if you were to tell him so. He treats the novel as a place where you can write anything you like, anything, as it were, that has just come into your head, as a *genre* released from constraint rather in the manner of a diary. No doubt, psychobiographically speaking, this artlessness is the effect of a finely conscious art, but his writing bears none of its traces and communicates instead a quite astonishing 'naturalness', a stunning off-handedness and laid-back companionability which forces the reader genuinely to doubt whether it is in the least aware of its own brilliance. Nothing could be more suspect for the *avant-garde* West than this spurious naturalisation of the sign, this cavalier lucidity and apparently effortless transparency, which could only for us be yet another craftily contrived style, a cultural sign every

bit as eloquent and flamboyant as the laboriously constructed 'degree zero' writing of a Camus or a Hemingway. But our own suspicion of the natural springs from the conditions of a late bourgeois society in which ideology has had several centuries to disseminate itself into the textures of lived experience, crystallizing its devious impulses as the self-evident or commonsensical; in this sense we suspect the 'natural' exactly because ideology has succeeded in its historic task, requiring a violent demystification in fictions which ironise their every proposition. This is not the situation in Eastern Europe, whose political hegemony was only recently installed, moreover, from the outside, and which has therefore had little time or opportunity to flesh itself into a full-blooded phenomenology of everyday life. In such societies, given the grotesque discrepancy between material hardship and the idealising claims of the state, it is ideology which is transparently fictional, portentously self-conscious, the very reverse of spontaneous or self-evident; and the 'naturalness' of the Kundera style, its easy, intimate relation with the experiential, is thus as politically significant as is its conversion of the novel into a space of free-floating discourses in a rigorously codified society. Kundera's relaxed, unfussy lucidity is post-modernist in a genuine sense of the word, an art which becomes possible only when all the heart-burnings and agonisings of modernism proper, its heady transgressions and self-important experiments, can now at last be taken for granted, put quietly to use once shorn of their portentousness. For it is exactly that portentousness which links them, in sensibility if not in doctrine, with the histrionic posturings of the ideological.

"The only thing we *can* do", comments one of Kundera's characters about the writing of fiction, "is to give an account of our own selves. Anything else is an abuse of power. Anything else is a lie". The paradox of such liberalism for Kundera is that it keels over inexorably into a kind of totalitarianism. The narrative of just one individual becomes a closed book, a sealed, autonomous world every bit as absolute and author-itarian as the absolutist state. Such solipsism is the mere flipside of Stalinism, sucking reality into its own self-regulating logic with all the imperiousness of the central committee. Difference and uniqueness are no salvation in themselves from the dreary self-identity of the post-capitalist state; the unique has an unbearable lightness and frailty about it, as though anything which happens only once might as well not have happened at all. *Einmal ist keinmal.* If history can be dissolved into pure difference, then the result is a massive haemorrhage of meaning; because past events only happen once they fail to take firm root and can be expunged from memory, having about them the ineradicable aura of pure accident. The past thus perpetually threatens to dissolve beneath the heel of the present, and this plays straight into the hands of the absolutist state, devoted as it is to airbrushing disgraced politicians out of ceremonial photographs. What imbues persons and events with unique value, then, is precisely what renders them insubstantial, and Kundera's writing is deeply gripped by this sickening ontological precariousness. Pure difference cannot be valuable, for value is a relational term; but repetition is an enemy of value too, because the more something is repeated the more its meaning tends to fade. Kundera's fiction, both formally and thematically, is given over to examining this contradiction: it must keep different stories structurally separate, exploring the distinctiveness of particular relationships and identities, but always with a profoundly ironic sense of what they share in common, a suspicion that they are in some covert way variations upon a single theme.

The point where difference and identity undecidably converge for Kundera is above all sexuality, linking as it does the unrepeatable quality of a particular love-relationship with the ceaselessly repetitive, tediously predictable character of the bodily drives. What might be thought to be most deviant, stimulating, shockingly unconventional—a sexual orgy—turns out to be hilariously comic in its endless mechanical repetitions, the supposed singularity of erotic love uproariously repeated in a wilderness of mirrors, each individuated body mockingly mimicking the next. Kundera recognizes the profound comedy of repetition, which is one reason why sex is usually the funniest part of his novels: his laughter is that release of libidinal energy which comes from momentarily decathecting the utterly self-identical love-object, the magnificent *non-pareil,* in the moment of wry recognition that we all share a common biology. The traditional name of this moment is, of course, the carnivalesque, that aggressive onslaught on the fetishism of difference which ruthlessly, liberatingly reduces back all such metaphysical singularity to the solidarities of the flesh. *The Farewell Party* in particular centres upon fertility, child-bearing, procreation, and like several of Kundera's texts is particularly interested in animals.

The political problem of all this is apparent: how is one to use the fleshly solidarity of the human species as a powerfully demystifying force while avoiding that brutal erasure of differences which is Stalinist uniformity? Kundera's anti-Stalinism is interesting precisely because it refuses to fall back upon an unquestioning romantic idealism of the individual; indeed its carnivalesque impulse presses any such romantic idealism to the point of absurdity. The problem is how to stay faithful to that recognition without lapsing into biologistic cynicism, or, as Kundera might himself put it, crossing over that hairthin border which distinguishes 'angelic' meaning from the demonic cackle of meaninglessness. Reproduction, in every sense of the word, may be a source of emancipatory humor, which is one thing Marx meant by suggesting that all tragic events repeated themselves as farce; but the farce in question is destructive as well as redemptive, which was another of Marx's meanings. The bureaucratic state is itself a contradictory amalgam of romantic

idealism and cynical materialism: its discourse is the undiluted *kitsch* of high-sounding sentiment, whereas its practice renders individual bodies and events indifferently exchangeable. It is difficult, then, to subvert its romantic idealism without lapsing into a version of its own lethal leveling. The image of ungainly naked bodies crowded into a single space stirs Kundera to debunking laughter, but it is also for him the image of the concentration camp.

Every time something is repeated, it loses part of its meaning; the unique, however, is a romantic illusion. This is the contradiction within which Kundera struggles, which can be rephrased as an unrelaxable tension between too much meaning and too little. An order in which everything is oppressively meaningful buckles under its own weight: this is the realm of what Kundera names the 'angelic', which the demonic exists to puncture. The demonic is the laughter which arises from things being suddenly deprived of their familiar meanings, a kind of estrangement effect akin to Heidegger's broken hammer, and which a monstrous proliferation of the supposedly singular can bring about. Meaninglessness can be a blessed moment of release, a lost innocent domain for which we are all nostalgic, a temporary respite from the world's tyrannical legibility in which we slip into the abyss of silence. The demonic is thus closely associated in Kundera's fiction with the death drive, a spasm of deconstructive mockery which, like carnival, is never far from the cemetery. It is a dangerous force, by no means to be euphorically, unqualifiedly celebrated as in the naiveties of some Western deconstruction: it has a malicious, implacable violence about it, the pure negativity of a Satanic cynicism. It is therefore, as Kundera well sees, a tempting lure for the opponents of angelic-authoritarian order, who will be led by it to their doom. The savage irony of the demonic is that it finally dismantles the antithesis of the angels only to conflate the whole of reality indifferently together in a leveling not far from the angels' own. Bodies are interchangeable for both Stalinism and carnival, transgression prized by both revolutionary and cynic. Just as we are precariously positioned by our very bodiliness on an indeterminate frontier between sameness and difference, biology and history, so we must seek to situate ourselves on some almost invisible border between meaning and meaninglessness, embracing all that the angels reject ('shit' is the blunt term Kundera gives to the angelically unacceptable) without settling for that shitlike amorphousness which is Stalinism or nihilism. Happiness is the yearning for repetition, but repetition is what erodes it; the male sexual drive, rather like the authoritarian state, is cripplingly divided between a romantic idealism of the particular (the wife, the permanent mistress) and a promiscuous exchangeability of bodies. The novel records these truths, but is itself an image of them: to write is to cross a border where one's own ego ends, creating characters who are neither imaginary self-identifications nor opaquely alien, but who repeat the self with a difference.

The novel has its inward necessity, its specific structural logic, but it is also a place where the contingency of existence, the unbearable lightness of being, can be reinvented and to some degree redeemed. When Beethoven, as Kundera reminds us, based a quartet on the words *Es muss sein,* he weaved an idea of destiny out of what had in fact been a casual joke between himself and a friend. Metaphysical truth was born of playfulness; as in Kundera's *The Joke* a whole metaphysical politics is set in motion by a piece of wit. Human beings, unable to tolerate the frail contingency of their being, must for Kundera rewrite their chance histories as necessity; and this, precisely, is what the novel itself continually does, endowing the accidental with a determinate form. But it is also the characteristic strategy of Stalinism, for which nothing is allowed to escape into pure randomness; and Kundera must therefore write *lightly* as well as lucidly, bathing what is in the aura of what might not have been. It is for this reason, perhaps, that his narratives are as spare and uncluttered as they are, eschewing the ponderousness of the metaphysical. His cavalier way with them reminds us of their frailness as fictional inventions; and when he speaks in his own voice, the philosophical wisdom he communicates is more the auratic, Benjaminesque 'experience' of the traditional tale-teller than the speculations of a theoretically-minded modernist. What intensities there are in Kundera's work belong, as it were, to the subject-matter rather than to the mode of conveying it, hedged round continually with an irony which represents the borderline between too much meaning and too little, the portentous solemnity of the ideological and the bland dissociation of the cynic.

The dissonance in Kundera between a conventionally romantic subject-matter and a decidedly non-romantic handling of it has itself a political root. For if on the one hand his astonishingly subtle explorations of personal relationships redeems that which Stalinism expels, the ironic pathos with which such relationships are invested is just the reverse of that triumphalistic sentimentality which is Stalinism's ideological stock-in-trade. 'Kitsch' is the name Kundera gives to all such 'shitless' discourse, all such idealising disavowal of the unacceptable; and in the realm of kitsch, the dictatorship of the heart reigns supreme. Totalitarian *kitsch* is that discourse which banishes all doubt and irony, but it is not a grim-faced, life-denying speech: on the contrary, it is all smiles and cheers, beaming and euphoric, marching merrily onwards to the future shouting 'Long live life!' The Gulag, as Kundera comments, is the septic tank used by *kitsch* to dispose of its refuse. If Stalinism cannot be opposed by romanticism it is precisely because it has a monopoly of it; and this is one reason why Kundera's own critique is bent inevitably towards the materialism of the body, whose joyous affirmations must always be radically double-edged, which knows shit and ecstasy together. Carnival generates a collective imagery which can undermine ideological *kitsch*; but in the end Kundera is unable to accept this, precisely because he comes to define kitsch as any *collective* imagery whatsoever. His critique of oppressive ideologies is at root curiously formalistic: what seems wrong with *kitsch* is finally not this or that enunciation or emotion, but the bare fact that it must be a commonly shareable discourse. This is not simply individualist dissent, of a familiarly Eastern European kind: it is that Kundera seems genuinely unable to imagine any universally shared emotion which would not, by definition, be intolerably banal. It is this which leads him to write that "The brotherhood of man on earth will be possible only on a base of kitsch". The best response to this is not to produce the kinds of political argument with which Kundera is doubtless all too familiar; it is simply to point out that any such formulation is untrue to the power of his own fiction. For it is exactly from the irresolvable conflict between the unique and the necessarily repeatable, the fragility of the particular and the comedy of the collective, that his fiction draws part of its formidable strength. To collapse that tension on either side is the real banality; and if Kundera's writing is valuable, it is among other reasons because he makes any such erasure of conflict harder to effect.

Perry Meisel (review date 10 April 1988)

SOURCE: "Beautifying Lies and Polyphonic Wisdom," in *New York Times Book Review,* April 10, 1988, p. 13.

[*In the following review of* The Art of the Novel, *Meisel focuses on Kundera's treatment of formal devices of the novel genre.*]

Milan Kundera has charmed the world with his sonorous fictions—five novels, a play and a volume of stories-although it is formalist rigor as much as charm that distinguishes his first book of nonfiction, *The Art of the Novel.* A collection of five essays and two dialogues published over the last decade, *The Art of the Novel* recommends self-effacement as a precept of writing and dooms purveyors of dogma in either literature or criticism. Whatever moral arrangements the Czechoslovak subjects of his narratives might suggest to us, Mr. Kundera as critic is little inclined to dwell upon them. Instead, he dispassionately explains—and with singular instructiveness, as he ranges from Cervantes and Richardson to Kafka, Joyce and Hermann Broch—how novels are made and why; how the novel and its history constitute a specific form of knowledge not to be confused with philosophy, politics or psychology; and why novels are and should be written at all. Linda Asher's translation from the French deftly conveys the lucidity of Mr. Kundera's prose.

The emphasis on the formal aspects of fiction in *The Art of the Novel* is accompanied by an overt disavowal of any political agenda. Disingenuous as such a claim may sound coming from an Eastern European writer living in exile in Paris, it is nonetheless the first of three working principles in *The Art of the Novel.* Mr. Kundera bases it on his belief in "the radical autonomy of the novel" as a form, as he puts it in his essay on Kafka, **"Somewhere Behind."**

The second principle is derived from the first, and it is the rejection of kitsch. Not simply bad or laughable art, kitsch is, in Mr. Kundera's definition from **"Sixty-three Words"** (his dictionary of the terms and categories that organize his imagination), "the need to gaze into the mirror of the beautifying lie and to be moved to tears of gratification at one's own reflection."

Mr. Kundera's most recent novel, *The Unbearable Lightness of Being,* gives us examples of Communist kitsch, American kitsch, fascist kitsch, feminist kitsch—even artistic kitsch. The **"Jerusalem Address"** in *The Art of the Novel* bluntly describes the last as "the translation of the stupidity of received ideas into the language of beauty and feeling." The "either-or" mentality of kitsch, as Mr. Kundera phrases it in **"The Depreciated Legacy of Cervantes,"** is, in the final analysis, the result of "an inability to tolerate the essential relativity of things human, an inability to look squarely at the absence of the Supreme Judge."

Hence the novel's distinctive value as a form. Good novels are not kitsch because they do not take sides in the situations they imagine. The point is perfectly documented in Mr. Kundera's own fiction, and especially in his frequent satirizing of the well-intentioned delusions of Communists and Western individualists alike.

One antidote to kitsch is to write novels according to Mr. Kundera's third principle—what he refers to throughout *The Art of the Novel* as "novelistic counterpoint" or "polyphony." "Counterpoint," or "polyphony," is, strictly speaking, the play among different kinds of writing—essay, dream, narrative—in a single text. Mr. Kundera's own version of counterpoint, however, has a temporal dimension, in contrast to some of his relatively static models, such as Broch's neglected masterpiece of 1930-32, *The Sleepwalkers.* The technique also has its roots deep in the history of the novel. With Cervantes, Mr. Kundera argues, the novel discovered multiple perspective; with Richardson, he argues again in **"Dialogue on the Art of the Novel,"** it discovered the "interior life." To these formal discoveries, Mr. Kundera has himself added "chronologic displacement," a term he coins in the book's richest piece, **"Dialogue on the Art of Composition."**

By means of "chronologic displacement," the novelist can tell crossing or intersecting stories, not only from the alternating perspectives of the relevant characters, but in staggered chronology as well. The yield of this technical innovation is emotionally astonishing. It enlarges the reader's vision by producing resonances and relations among a series of lives that no one individual is in a position to apprehend. Mr. Kundera's polyphonic novels provide this mode of seeing, what he calls a "suprapersonal wisdom."

The Joke, Mr. Kundera's first novel, is a polyphonic tour de farce, although the last two sections of *The Unbearable Lightness of Being* are probably the most remarkable illustration of polyphony in his work. There the deaths of Tomas and Tereza are mentioned in passing in the novel's sixth section, which is told from the point of view of the novel's other lovers, Franz and Sabina; the seventh section goes back in time to tell the story of Tomas and Tereza's happy retreat to the Bohemian countryside, stopping just short of the accident that takes their lives. Our foreknowledge of their end—and the novel's refusal to allow us to witness it—is unashamedly compelling.

Mr. Kundera's polyphonic novels are, among other things, nothing less than strategies for surmounting one's sense of entrapment in events outside one's control or even awareness—thus the enormous importance he places on Kafka in **"Somewhere Behind"** and **"Notes Inspired by *The Sleepwalkers.*"** The quality of the "Kafkan," as Mr. Kundera calls it, is the best precedent for understanding his own fictional world, since it provides an uncannily elegant rehearsal of life as it has recently become in Kafka's very own Prague—that is, Mr. Kundera's.

While it is traditional to view Kafka as an absurdist, for Mr. Kundera such a view is mistaken. To him, Kafka does not represent the breakdown of writing, but a possibility of real existence on which the novel can draw. The Kafkan is an acute sense of "the trap the world has become." It even pressures Mr. Kundera's prose into epigrammatic concision, as though, like Kafka's Joseph K., he were running out of time: "The world according to Kafka: the bureaucratized universe. The office not merely as one kind of social phenomenon among many but as the essence of the world." In fact, Mr. Kundera implies the Kafkan is the characteristic state of the West as well as the East. Unlike the obvious coerciveness of the "police apparatus," however, Western bureaucratization uses milder, more covert ideological instruments such as "the mass media apparatus."

To see Mr. Kundera in the light of this reading of Kafka makes it clear why his essays promise a future for the novel. Instead of tracing novelistic invention by way of the exhausted legacy of Joyce (or "establishment modernism"), Mr. Kundera, through his heightened sense of the Kafkan, suggests that the novel still has unlimited sources of inquiry in the "bureaucratic"; it also has great power, by virtue of the formal devices available to it, over the sense of confinement bureaucracies and kitsch engender. Mr. Kundera transforms the Kafkan by locating its vision in decidedly realist settings, and by imagining a means of "suprapersonal" escape from the claustrophobic universe common to East and West alike.

Richard T. Gaughan (essay date Winter 1992)

SOURCE: "'Man Thinks; God Laughs': Kundera's 'Nobody Will Laugh,'" in *Studies in Short Fiction,* Vol. 29, No. 1, Winter, 1992, pp. 1-10.

[*Below, Gaughan discusses the purpose of laughter and comedy in "Nobody Will Laugh," especially as they relate to the individual and society.*]

Comedy and laughter are often important thematic concerns, as well as prominent qualities, of Milan Kundera's novels and stories. At first glance, this seems to be because comedy and laughter are good ways of resisting oppressive codes of conduct and ways of thinking, especially those enforced and imposed by public authorities. But, while comedy and laughter are undoubtedly ways of negating or ameliorating the effects of various kinds of belief, they also do something more. They bring to the surface and make explicit the often hidden and always painful struggle between the equally necessary but mutually exclusive demands of freedom and belief—a struggle that Kundera sees as the characteristic condition of the modern European mind. Comedy and laughter, in other words, are not just corrective responses or antidotes to the imposition of someone else's idea of moral and social order; they are expressions of the mind's attempt to understand itself and its world when the imperatives of beliefs about how life should be are suspended. For this reason, comedy and laughter do not by themselves resolve the dilemmas of Kundera's characters (who are neither entirely free nor entirely defined by beliefs, whether their own or those they are forced to accept), any more than the abstract formulas of order imposed on them do. They are, instead, the conditions under which these characters can experience and explore what freedom is and, at the limits of freedom, the suffering they share with each other.

In *Laughable Loves,* many of the characters use whimsy, practical jokes, or their imaginative agility to rebel against a grim and monotonous social world and tedious private lives. But the freedom they gain from their ironic detachment and their willingness to view both themselves and others as a comic spectacle also entail a loss of meaning and an isolation that is often as empty as it is sometimes blissful. Their rebellion is mostly negative and leaves them without any firm footing they can use to gain a deeper understanding of themselves or others. This understanding

takes place, when it does take place, on the other side of the disorder laughter creates where the shared suffering of being human momentarily appears between the seductive consolations of uncaring freedom and unreflective belief. Of these stories, **"Nobody Will Laugh"** provides one of the best examples of how comedy and laughter help resist the deadening effects of enforced beliefs, not to achieve some ultimate and satisfying freedom, but to reveal a vanishing common ground where understanding and solidarity are, at least, possible, if only for a time.

Late in **"Nobody Will Laugh,"** Klima, the story's major character and narrator, while trying to explain to his department chairman that the terrible fix he has gotten himself into is simply the result of some misunderstood practical jokes, says, "I shall explain before everyone the things that took place. If people are human they will have to laugh at it." The sage department chairman, however, is less sanguine than Klima and tells him, "As you like. But you'll learn either that people aren't human or that you don't know what humans are like. They will not laugh."

That people will, if they are human, laugh is Klima's last hope and, in some respects, his last illusion. He seems to have good reason to believe that people will laugh, since what has happened to him is certainly the stuff of comedy. Klima, a brash young intellectual, is asked by a stolid and unremarkable schoolteacher, Mr. Zaturetsky, to write a review of an article he has worked on for three years so that the prestigious *Visual Arts Journal* will publish it. Klima, impulsively and somewhat recklessly, decides not to write the review after he determines that the article is nothing more than a rehash of what others have already said on the subject, but he does not refuse to write the review either. Klima is flattered by the high esteem in which he is held by Zaturetsky and does not want to lose an admirer. He also resents being asked to do the dirty work that the editors of the journal should do. When Zaturetsky presses the issue, Klima begins a prolonged game of hide-and-seek with the persistent and terribly earnest Zaturetsky. Naturally, neither Zaturetsky nor his equally implacable and determined wife is amused, and Klima eventually finds himself hauled before a grim and humorless local committee to explain his actions and give up the name of the woman with whom he has secretly been living. Worse still, Klima's pranks and the trouble they have caused give his faculty colleagues the reason they need to dump such an unorthodox and irreverent (not to mention popular) young teacher. The joke is now on the joker as the very events Klima thought he was controlling turn against him. His only hope is that people will see that everything was just a joke and will laugh. That they do not suggests that Klima may not, in fact, know what humans are like or, more likely and more disturbingly, that something has caused laughter, and with it a part of humanity, to vanish from Klima's world.

Laughter, of course, is not at all easy to explain. One major difficulty is the fact that laughter always has at least two sides. On the one hand, laughter is a way of liberating ourselves from the oppressiveness of our ideas and beliefs. We laugh, as Bergson points out, when we see the fluidity of life outstrip some rigid definition or idea of how life should be. We laugh, in other words, because anything mechanical in character, events, or even words reminds us that life is never quite what we want it to be and that our ideas and beliefs must remain supple and adaptable if our understanding of ourselves and our world is to continue to grow. On the other hand, because it subverts our certainty that things are the way we want them to be, laughter is also discomfiting and nihilistic. For, while it is true that if things were always what they seem to be, there would be no freedom, no room for growth, it is equally true that if things are never what they seem and there is no order or certainty, life would quickly become unbearable.

Laughter's volatile and hazardous nature is one reason why comedy and tragedy are always dangerously close to each other. When all the unforeseen mishaps and misunderstandings that make up comedy do not liberate a character from some narrow conception of himself and his world but instead simply destroy his world, comic misadventure can become something very like a tragic fate. (It works the other way around as well, as any poorly written or poorly played tragedy will readily prove.) Klima's own obviously comic story bears this out. If seen from a slightly different angle, Klima's predicament is not at all unlike the predicament of Oedipus, who also believes that he can control events through his rational understanding and ends up being shunned by his society.

To further complicate matters, laughter, as Bergson shows, is essentially a form of social discipline and renewal. It is society's way of punishing any individual who shows too much of an inclination to withdraw from society into private ideas, habits, or obsessions. The reasons for withdrawing from society do not matter. Even virtue can be a target of laughter if it is deemed excessive or not sociable. Society, for Bergson, is an organism that, like all organisms, does what it must to keep itself alive, and laughter is an almost biological tool to assure the continued growth and development of the social group against all tendencies to inertia, especially the inertia of substituting fixed ideas for the dynamic flow of thought and life itself. This view of laughter makes perfect sense and is very likely entirely true, but it depends on one crucial condition: that society, like its individual members, be responsive to the changing requirements of human needs. But, just as liberation can turn into anarchy and comedy can easily turn into tragedy, the role of laughter in a society, when the society is not an organic outgrowth of its members, can be usurped by institutional force, thereby making the devices of comic correction of individual excesses into the machinery of coercion.

It is just this kind of social world that Kundera constructs for Klima, and this complicates and changes what laughter is and what it can mean. When Klima plays his practical jokes he must rely, like all jokers, on the understanding of those around him, but this is exactly what he cannot find. True, his treatment of Zaturetsky may be a little cruel, irresponsible, and insensitive, and Klima may well deserve to be chastised for his hubristic belief that he can saddle and control events for his pleasure, but this is not what happens. Instead, Klima is isolated, hunted down and punished as if he were a criminal or worse. His real sin, in the eyes of his society, is not that he has been cruel, insensitive, irresponsible, or even arrogant, but that he has not acted according to the rules, that he has expressed exactly the kind of quick intelligence and adaptability that Bergson associates with social health. So what has gone wrong? Why is laughter not, as Bergson argues, a means of social rejuvenation?

Part of the answer is that what society means to Bergson is no longer what it can mean to Kundera. The largely philosophical idea Bergson had in mind has been inverted in Kundera's story. The social needs of human life are here subordinated to rigid formulas embodied in a pervasive bureaucracy that is accountable only to itself. In fact in this story, it is society that has all the qualities Bergson associates with the comic automaton, but, because it also has all the power, no one dares laugh at it. The creation and imposition of social norms is not, as it was for Bergson, an organic and uniquely human process, one that is an extension of the ways individuals are forever creating symbolic forms to make sense of themselves and their world. The norms in Klima's world have become abstract ideas imposed by force as *the* way experience, both social and personal, is to be ordered and understood.

It would not be too much of an exaggeration to say that society, as it is understood by Bergson, does not really exist in Klima's world. What Ortega y Gasset calls society, spontaneous social effort and historical action, and what he calls the state, the machinery constructed for public order and administration, have been virtually equated. Society, insofar as it exists at all, exists only as a fugitive shadow on the periphery of the State. What is called society is little more than a rigid and rule-bound abstraction imposed from above. Community has been replaced by more or less random collections of people who have only arbitrary connections to each other and, consequently, no initial way to understand or sympathize with each other. In the absence of understanding and sympathy, rules, not needs or affiliation, define how people will live together and obedience replaces cooperation as the basis of social life. Adaptability and spontaneity, the very qualities Bergson believes the comic fosters, have become the deadly enemies of the state and must be identified and crushed by the kind of social violence that, under other circumstances, is an essential part of the comic.

This change in society, however, is not enough by itself to explain why Bergson's ideas about the purpose of laughter and the comic are turned so completely around. Society, after all, is just one form that human thought takes. To understand why laughter and the comic are no longer welcome, why no one will laugh, it is necessary to understand that in Kundera's story the comic spirit, in the person of Klima, is up against a way of thinking as well as a particular social and political system.

In his **"Jerusalem Address,"** Kundera expresses this conflict in terms of the Jewish proverb, "Man thinks, God laughs." God laughs because as man thinks and takes his thinking seriously, the truth of things slowly slips away from him. Eventually, thinking, and believing that what is thought is true, creates a kind of person Kundera calls, after Rabelais, the *agelaste,* those who will not laugh. This type of person, Kundera claims, is the mortal enemy of the novelist:

> No peace is possible between the novelist and the *agelaste.* Never having heard God's laughter, the *agelastes* are convinced that the truth is obvious, that all men necessarily think the same thing, and that they themselves are exactly what they think they are. But it is precisely in losing the certainty of truth and the unanimous agreement of others that man becomes an individual. (*Art of the Novel*)

What is true of the novelist is equally true of the storyteller, and Klima is, if nothing else, a compulsive storyteller. He relies heavily on his ability to invent stories to seduce his girlfriend Klara, to play practical jokes on Zaturetsky, to fend off the intrusive inquiries of the local committee—in short, to live in his world. Klima, in other words, not only disregards the rules, a dangerous enough thing to do in both his and our world, he goes further and refuses to accept the certainty about life and what life means that is implicit in the rules he is supposed to live by. Klima's sense of humor, as cruel and puerile as it sometimes seems, is nonetheless his way of breaking with the "unanimous agreement of others" so that he can preserve his individuality and freedom in a world that demands both as a sacrifice for an abstract and narrowly defined social order. The only blame that Klima justly bears for what happens to him is his belief that he can saddle and control events. This is a belief that he, albeit unconsciously, shares with the very society he is trying to resist and is really the only guilt that Klima needs to expiate.

That Klima's opposition to his society and its way of thinking is not just political but is, in fact, philosophical, is made clear when he defends his lies and jokes to Klara, who has asked him why he will not lie just once more and write the good review for Zaturetsky that will solve all of their problems:

> "You see, Klara," I said, "you think that a lie is a lie and it would seem that you're right. But you aren't. I can invent anything, make a fool of someone, carry out hoaxes and practical jokes—and I don't feel like a liar and I don't have a bad conscience. These lies, if you want to call them that, represent myself as I really am. With such lies I'm not simulating anything, with such lies I am in fact speaking the truth. But there are things I cannot lie about. There are things I've penetrated, whose meaning I've grasped, which I love and take seriously. I can't joke about these things. If I did I would humiliate myself. It's impossible, don't ask me to do it, I can't."

Here, in this seemingly paradoxical explanation, Klima is defending not only himself but also the storytelling imagination. Stories, like Klima's lies, are expressions of truth, even though this truth cannot be fixed in abstract categories. Klima's problem is that his defense of his lies relies on a conception of truth that is diametrically opposed to the conception of truth that underlies and controls his society. For Klima, truth is ambiguous. It takes many forms, even the form of untruth, and, although it is to be taken seriously, it cannot be taken seriously without play and laughter. For Klima to tell the lie Klara wishes him to tell would mean accepting the rules of his society as the truth they pretend to be. It would mean, in other words, that he would have to accept a lie as truth rather than finding the truth even in lies. To do so would not only be personally humiliating, it would be an abdication of what we have come to regard as a quintessential human freedom: the freedom to investigate, without restraint, the kind of world we live in.

Ironically, or perhaps not so ironically, Klima's belief in the truthfulness of lies is what enables him, and him alone, to develop in the course of the story, to discover his own solitude and powerlessness and to recognize the pain and alienation of others. This deepening of Klima's understanding of himself is especially evident when, to bring matters to a head, he arranges a meeting with Mrs. Zaturetsky, the woman he has come to regard as his nemesis. While she is sitting in his office, the nearly blind Mrs. Zaturetsky, like a latter day Tiresias, brings Klima the unexpected knowledge that he has entirely misunderstood the meaning of his own actions:

> The connection between her and the incident, in which we'd both played a sad role, suddenly seemed vague, arbitrary, accidental, and not our fault. All at once I understood that it had only been my illusion that we ourselves saddle events and control their course; the truth is that they aren't *our* stories at all, that they are foisted upon us from somewhere *outside*; that in no way do they represent us; that we are not to blame for the queer path that they fol-

low; they carry us away, since they are controlled by some *alien* forces.

Klima is here brought face to face with the fact that, although he can create stories at will, he cannot control how they unfold and what they will mean. He realizes at last that meaning cannot be determined in advance but can only be discovered as a result of already lived experience, that his comic and critical intelligence must eventually come to roost in the fuller human context of limitation and suffering. Ironically, this apparent loss of freedom is also the realization that frees Klima to act in a way that is contrary to the values of his world and not just in defiance of them: he can incorporate suffering, both his own and that of others, into his playful search for what is true.

This is why Klima, while discovering that he does not have the freedom he thought he had, also comes to see Mrs. Zaturetsky as a faithful and devoted soldier and comes to understand the sacrifices both Zaturetskys have made in this desperate attempt by Mr. Zaturetsky to salvage something unique out of an otherwise drab and anonymous life. The series of comic events of the story coalesce into a kind of tragic fate in which the muted pain of the Zaturetskys and Klima's playful intelligence are laid waste by a society that requires not loyalty or reasoned assent, but only the degrading obedience of the slave.

> **Just as Klima begins with a comic certainty about himself and ends in tragic doubt about the meaning of the events that affect him so dearly but are not truly his, Kundera makes his story appear alternately comic and tragic so that the comic implications of tragedy and the tragic implications of comedy negate any certainty about which the story is.**
> —*Richard T. Gaughan*

At this point it would seem that comedy has slipped imperceptibly into tragedy. Klima has lost everything he values and faces the bleak future of being a *persona non grata* in the workers' paradise. Mr. and Mrs. Zaturetsky, although they have succeeded in bringing to bear the force of the state on Klima, still do not have what they want to have. And yet, Klima does not accept a tragic interpretation of his story. After Klara leaves him, presumably for the editor who set Zaturetsky on Klima's trail in the first place, Klima ends his story with this surprising remark:

> Only after a while did it occur to me (in spite of the chilly silence which surrounded me) that my

story was not of the tragic sort, but rather of the comic variety.

That afforded me some comfort.

To understand why Klima chooses a comic rather than a tragic view of his own story, it is helpful to keep in mind an old Central European tale that Timothy Garton Ash relates. In this tale, a German general says to his Austrian ally, "The situation is serious but not tragic," to which the Austrian general responds, "No, Mein Lieber, it is tragic but not serious." Like the Austrian general, Klima has come to understand a tragedy, the tragedy of the individual in the modern bureaucratized state (a tragedy not limited to any particular political system), but he cannot regard this tragedy as serious. Tragedy, after all, requires that some value be accorded the individual and his suffering, and this is exactly what is missing from Klima's world. Comedy, on the other hand, being essentially negative, does not require this value and can laugh even at its own demise.

Klima understands, in other words, that the last resource of comedy is to laugh at itself. He himself, as an individual, has become laughable in a world where only force and obedience matter, and this is a new truth to which Klima must now remain faithful. Still, like that "fascinating imaginative realm where no one owns the truth and everyone has the right to be understood" (*Art of the Novel*) that Kundera believes the novel is, Klima, for all his faults, in fact because of all his faults, becomes the imaginative realm in this story where no one, including Klima, owns the truth and where everyone, including the Zaturetskys, has the right to be understood.

What gives Klima's story its tragic coloring is that his laughter at himself cannot find its necessary echo. Without some response from others, laughter must turn in on itself and this destroys the traditionally affirmative and liberating qualities of comedy. For Kundera, laughter is not the Archimedean point from which the world can be criticized and changed that it is for Bergson. It is as historically conditioned as the world it responds to and can be nothing but a final futile gesture of human freedom in the midst of the chilly silence of fear and conformity.

Nevertheless, this overlapping of tragedy and comedy serves an important purpose in the story. It is the formal equivalent or correlative of Klima's ambiguous experiences and his uncertainly about what the truth is and how it can be expressed. Just as Klima begins with a comic certainty about himself and ends in tragic doubt about the meaning of the events that affect him so dearly but are not truly his, Kundera makes his story appear alternately comic and tragic so that the comic implications of tragedy and the tragic implications of comedy negate any certainty about which the story is. This suspension of the story between formal categories is the story's own comic subversion of the kind of categories of thought that menace not only Klima but, through him, the story itself. This moment of uncertainty, like Descartes's moment of doubt, is the brief moment of the human mind breaking with any kind of consensus of belief and living the only truth it can be sure of—the truth that it cannot really know anything, that all it can do is play and wonder.

> **This moment of uncertainty, like Descartes's moment of doubt, is the brief moment of the human mind breaking with any kind of consensus of belief and living the only truth it can be sure of—the truth that it cannot really know anything, that all it can do is play and wonder.**
> —*Richard T. Gaughan*

This doubting and uncertain consciousness, the modern mind itself, however, is doomed to fail and disappear. Doubt based on the conviction that truth is forever changing its face and its meaning renders the free individual consciousness unable to replace lost certainties with certainties of its own, thereby making the free individual powerless against any form of belief, especially absolute belief. Lost somewhere between God and History, the radically individual consciousness rejects the blandishments of imperial truth in any of its forms solely for the sake of a mystery it cannot even hope to solve, but nonetheless wishes to explore fully and live out to the end. Pushed to the last extremity, as Klima is, the free individual consciousness has one last recourse; it can contemplate and play with the conditions and circumstances of its own inevitable extinction. This may be, in some respects, tragic, but it is certainly not serious, since this is also a moment of truth in a world controlled by lies, a moment when laughter can at least laugh at itself for laughing.

James S. Hans (essay date Spring 1992)

SOURCE: "Kundera's Laws of Beauty," in *Essays in Literature,* Vol. XIX, No. 1, Spring, 1992, pp. 144-58.

[*In the following essay, Hans analyzes Kundera's conception of beauty and shame in* The Unbearable Lightness of Being.]

Milan Kundera's novel *The Unbearable Lightness of Being* provides a serious revision of our conceptions of the nature of beauty, and in so doing it forces us to reconsider the relationship between the aesthetic and our daily lives. At the same time, the novel itself reflects the changes Kundera has brought about via his Nietzschean assessment of forms. Part traditional fiction, part essay, part lyrical exclamation, *The Unbearable Lightness of Being* is a decidedly impure form, one that celebrates its mixed heritage even as it establishes an essential relationship between shame and beauty. In addressing the linkages between the beautiful and the shameful, the novel also registers the ways in which our attitude toward these most fundamental regions of human existence affect our political disposition as well, for Kundera demonstrates throughout the book that even as all human relationships have something to do with questions of power, so too do the manifestations of power reflect the individual's attitude toward his or her sense of beauty and shame. The ultimate effect of all these revisions of the basic categories of human experience is to raise again the question that Nietzsche first posed for us, to ask us once more what it means to be wholly human, what it would mean if we were finally capable of accepting existence on the terms through which it presents itself to us.

Kundera's most striking appraisal of beauty occurs early in the novel when he is discussing the relationship between coincidences in life and in fiction. He has established that his two main characters, Tomas and Tereza, have met through a series of rather mundane fortuities and thereby irrevocably changed their lives, and this prompts him to discuss the great importance of chance on the outcome of our individual fates:

> Much more than the card he slipped her at the last minute, it was the call of all those fortuities (the book, Beethoven, the number six, the yellow park bench) which gave her [Tereza] the courage to leave home and change her fate. It may well be those few fortuities (quite modest, by the way, even drab, just what one would expect from so lackluster a town) which set her love in motion and provided her with a source of energy she had not yet exhausted at the end of her days.

> Our day-to-day life is bombarded with fortuities, or, to be more precise, with the accidental meetings of people and events we call coincidences. "Coincidence" means that two events unexpectedly happen at the same time, they meet: Tomas appears in the hotel restaurant at the same time the radio is playing Beethoven. We do not even notice the great majority of such coincidences. If the seat Tomas occupied had been occupied instead by the local butcher, Tereza never would have noticed that the radio was playing Beethoven (though the meeting of Beethoven and the butcher would also have been an interesting coincidence). But her nascent love inflamed her sense of beauty, and she would never forget that music. Whenever she heard it, she would

be touched. Everything going on around her at that moment would be haloed by the music and take on its beauty.

According to our traditional ways of thinking, the kinds of fortuities that prompt Tereza to take an interest in Tomas—and those that prompt him to be interested in her—are not to be taken seriously. We all know how seemingly unrelated things can come together during the initial moments of important relationships, and we tend to denigrate their importance. These coincidences may enhance the memory of first meetings and the like a bit, but they are not to be taken seriously precisely because of their idiosyncratic nature. Tereza would be most foolish to assert that her love for Tomas was important *because* it was linked from the beginning with the music of Beethoven, or the number six, or books, or park benches. Yet that is precisely what Kundera argues here.

The initial meeting between Tereza and Tomas prompts us to pay more attention to the fortuities in our own lives, for if Kundera can assert that the small coincidences in Tereza's life may well have "set her love in motion and provided her with a source of energy she had not yet exhausted at the end of her days," we must assume that such events can have great power both to transform and to sustain our lives. Why, then, do we tend to disregard them so much? Why act as though these coincidences are largely unrelated to the outcomes of our lives? And why do we in turn expect our writers of narrative fiction to keep the fortuities in their stories to a minimum? Without directly explaining why, Kundera tells us what we are missing when we ignore them:

> Early in the novel that Tereza clutched under her arm when she went to visit Tomas, Anna meets Vronsky in curious circumstances: they are at the railway station when someone is run over by a train. At the end of the novel, Anna throws herself under a train. This symmetrical composition—the same motif appears at the beginning and at the end—may seem quite "novelistic" to you, and I am willing to agree, but only on condition that you refrain from reading such notions as "fictive," "fabricated," and "untrue to life" into the word "novelistic." Because human lives are composed in precisely such a fashion.
>
> They are composed like music. Guided by his sense of beauty, an individual transforms a fortuitous occurrence (Beethoven's music, death under a train) into a motif, which then assumes a permanent place in the composition of the individual's life. Anna could have chosen another way to take her life. But the motif of death and the railway station, unforgettably bound to the birth of love, enticed her in her hour of despair with its dark beauty. Without

realizing it, the individual composes his life according to the laws of beauty even in times of greatest distress.

> It is wrong, then, to chide the novel for being fascinated by mysterious coincidences (like the meeting of Anna, Vronsky, the railway station, and death or the meeting of Beethoven, Tomas, Tereza, and the cognac), but it is right to chide man for being blind to such coincidences in his daily life. For he thereby deprives his life of a dimension of beauty.

Turning the tables on us, Kundera argues that instead of criticizing him for building a relationship between his characters out of such flimsy coincidences, we ourselves are to be faulted for failing to recognize the ways in which similar fortuities shape our own lives.

More importantly, Kundera establishes the fundamental premise of the novel by asserting: "Without realizing it, the individual composes his life according to the laws of beauty even in times of greatest distress." Instead of creating our lives out of a series of rational considerations about what we should be doing that would be based on various considerations for the future, here we are told that instead we compose our lives according to the laws of beauty. And we do this *without realizing* it. First and foremost, Kundera has shifted the control of our lives away from any self-aware context and moved it to another location that does its work without any necessary reflection on our part. Unlike Freud's unconscious, though, this location construes our lives in terms of the laws of beauty, a phrase that marks out a considerably different space from one like "libidinal urges" or "the pleasure principle." The motifs in Tereza's life—Beethoven's music, reading books, the number six—have nothing to do with sexual energy per se any more than they concentrate exclusively on the pursuit of pleasure. These are ordering processes that differ precisely because they are self-centered, because they reflect only the interests of the libido or the unconscious forces that urge us into one mode of pleasure-seeking or another. The laws of beauty would by definition be something beyond mere self-interest, something that adds another dimension to our lives rather than something that reduces them to the endless expression of libidinal energies.

Not that Tomas and Tereza don't have active libidos, for they most surely do. Nor is the implication of "the laws of beauty" that sexual and bodily activity in general take a subordinate place to "higher" forms of human expression. On the contrary, the laws of beauty work themselves out most pertinently in sexual and bodily contexts, situations that are not to be separated from Beethoven's music or Tolstoy's novels. If body and soul are not always in accord—as Tereza's rumbling stomach emphasizes—the laws according to which they both operate remain the same, even if we fail too often to recognize this to be so.

Nevertheless, when one considers the fortuities that brought Tereza and Tomas together, "laws of beauty" seems a rather excessive term to apply to them. It is not just that they are fortuities but that they are such slight and meaningless ones. Even Kundera emphasizes their drabness, and their highly idiosyncratic nature seems to deny any linkage to a law, even if in some respects they might have some connection to beauty. The logic of Tereza's interest in Beethoven, for example, is skewed from the beginning, for there is no indication that she properly appreciates the value of the music itself. Instead, she values Beethoven because he symbolizes something "higher" to her, and yet this "higher" sensibility comes not from what others might have suggested about the greatness of his work but rather from the fact that his music was associated with a context that had nothing to do with the music per se. Tereza

> had known his music from the time a string quartet from Prague had visited their town. Tereza (who, as we know, yearned for "something higher") went to the concert. The hall was nearly empty. The only other people in the audience were the local pharmacist and his wife. And although the quartet of musicians on stage faced only a trio of spectators down below, they were kind enough not to cancel the concert, and gave a private performance of the last three Beethoven quartets.

> Then the pharmacist invited the musicians to dinner and asked the girl in the audience to come along with them. From then on, Beethoven became her image of the world on the other side, the world she yearned for.

If there is beauty here, it has little to do with an aesthetic appreciation of Beethoven's last quartets. Beethoven himself may rightly symbolize in some fashion "something higher," but just what that "something higher" is remains located instead in the special privilege of the private performance of the musicians and the invitation to the pharmacist's house, hardly the sort of things that have to do with beauty.

It is worth noting that as a result of Tereza's interest in Beethoven, Tomas too attends to his music, and consequently Tomas himself establishes one of his own motifs on the basis of "the difficult resolution" to be found in the "*Es muss sein*" motif in Beethoven's last quartet; it is thus possible for the patterns one establishes on the basis of pure idiosyncrasy to bear resemblance finally to their original source. Likewise, it is "co-incidental" in this way that Tereza's rather frivolous use of Beethoven's music becomes more serious when it is connected to Tomas's difficult deci-

sion to return to Prague and Tereza, for, as Kundera tells us, the same thing originally happened to the "*Es muss sein*" formula for Beethoven, which was once part of a humorous anecdote concerning a debt that was owed to Beethoven but was in the end turned into the weighty resolution of the last quartet. These fortuities suggest something beyond mere coincidence, or at the very least offer the possibility that one grows into the full consequences of the coincidences that give shape to one's life.

If we are to take the laws of beauty seriously, though, we have to assume that it doesn't matter that Teresa doesn't understand fully the beauty of Beethoven's music. The laws of beauty as they manifest themselves in her life don't necessarily have anything at all to do with the music, even if the music itself symbolizes "something higher." This is made clear by the complete frivolity of some of the other coincidences connected to Tereza's first meeting with Tomas, particularly the yellow park bench and the number six. Neither the bench nor the number six has anything that intrinsically connects it to beauty; the linkage is a purely idiosyncratic one based on Tereza's life, derived from the emerging motifs that have been established in her past. She herself has conferred special values on these things, and when they turn up again in contexts that may well have further significance for her, their value is increased yet again. The individual items in the motif are, we might say, *totally arbitrary*. There is nothing in the number six that gives it special value; its value comes only from its place within the lived experience that Tereza places it in, derives from its coincidental connection in her mind with something important in her life. But the *pattern* that is established on the basis of these arbitrary linkages reflects the *laws* of beauty and demonstrates the way patterns and motifs are inevitably developed in *any* domain, regardless of their idiosyncratic origins.

The "*Es muss sein*" of Beethoven reflects this process very well, for the original context, we could say, is totally idiosyncratic. Beethoven is owed some money, he needs the money and therefore asks the debtor if he can give it to him, and the man asks "*Muss es sein?*" To which, Kundera tells us, "Beethoven replied, with a hearty laugh, '*Es muss sein!*' and immediately jotted down these words and their melody." But the melody is hardly the serious one of the last quartet: "On this realistic motif he then composed a canon for four voices: three voices sing '*Es muss sein, es muss sein, ja, ja, ja!*' (It must be, it must be, yes, yes, yes, yes!), and the fourth voice chimes in with '*Heraus mit dem Beutel!*' (Out with the purse!)."

This jocular request for money is far from the difficult resolution of the last quartet, and yet there is no reason why the phrase "*Es muss sein*" should not take on another cast later in Beethoven's life and become a heavier motif about weighty decisions. The phrase itself first has significance only because Beethoven chooses to note it and turn it back on its originator, thereby making fun of the rather serious response to a minor request, and in this way it has no more weight than any other phrase one might pick out of another's conversation to play with. But that idiosyncratic beginning establishes the phrase as a musical motif in Beethoven's life, to which he can return at a later date and translate into a more serious musical enterprise.

Kundera suggests through these characters' lives that our existence is fundamentally aesthetic in nature, even if we fail to recognize this, even if we assume that we are always in rational control of the direction of our lives.
—*James S. Hans*

Tereza's and Tomas's lives, then, are composed according to the laws of beauty, which means that the coincidental things their own particular situation prompts them to attend to become motifs that reflect the general patterns of beauty and the motifs out of which all aesthetic aspects of the world are constructed. There are *laws* to their behavior, even if those laws coincide with the purely gratuitous elements of their lives that fate throws in their paths, and those laws give their lives all the beauty they will ever have. Kundera suggests through these characters' lives that our existence is fundamentally aesthetic in nature, even if we fail to recognize this, even if we assume that we are always in rational control of the direction of our lives. Again, he emphasizes that "the individual composes his life according to the laws of beauty *even in times of greatest distress*", when beauty would be the last thing one would likely think about. And again, Kundera does *not* say that we compose our lives according to the pleasure principle, or on the basis of libidinal flows or the desire for the other or anything like that; he says we compose our lives according to the laws of beauty, establishing *that* as the fundamental principle out of which the other flows of our lives emerge in turn. Our lives are first and foremost constructed on aesthetic principles, and the patterns we develop reflect laws that go beyond any subjective response to the world.

If existence is fundamentally aesthetic, though, one must ask why humans have resisted this knowledge for so long. After all, if Kundera is forced to assert that he will agree that coincidences are "novelistic" only as long as we do not interpret "novelistic" to mean "fictive," "fabricated" or "untrue to life," we must obviously have a heritage that suggests otherwise. We are normally inclined to do precisely what Kundera suspects: we will look at the coincidences of Tereza's and Tomas's life and belittle them because of their arbitrariness. Their lives look too contrived, we think, for

in reality people don't fall in or out of love on the basis of such minor things as the number six or the music playing on the radio. Actually, we probably do know that people fall in love on the basis of such things, but we go along with Aristotle, who preferred his fictions to have probable improbabilities rather than improbable probabilities. And it is precisely that distinction which Kundera is attacking in his novel through the coincidences on which it is based.

Kundera is something of an experimental novelist in the sense that *The Unbearable Lightness of Being* is reflexive and regularly reminds us that it is a *fiction,* but as we have just seen, this distinction means something to Kundera that it doesn't ordinarily mean to us. If he has asserted that in some fundamental ways our very lives are fictional, if not in the way we think, it follows in turn that fictions are in some ways as real as our lives are, if not in the way we think. If an American writer like John Barth can humorously exploit the divide between fiction and life that engenders paralyzing self-consciousness because of one's awareness of how fictional (hence *unreal*) one's life really is in some respects and how real (hence *fictional*) one's fictions have become, Kundera locates the unreality of fictions elsewhere and is not concerned that his "unreal" characters might have nothing to do with the "reality" of our lives.

The characters are "unreal," to be sure. We are reminded of that again and again, most specifically with Tomas, who, we are told, was born of an image and of the saying "*Einmal ist keinmal.*" Yet in spite of this "unreal" birth, Tomas's "life" in the novel takes on as much "reality," that is, "plausibility" and "richness" and "representational accuracy," as any character in a more traditional novel. Kundera does not call attention to the fictional nature of Tomas and Tereza to make us suspicious of the "reality" of their lives any more than he wants us to question in turn the fictionality of our own lives, at least when it comes to the compositions we create on the basis of the laws of beauty. Kundera is denying the value of the distinction "fictive, unreal" as it applies to both novels and lives, at least as it has developed over the past few hundred years.

The border between real and unreal is not something to be demarcated so easily by distinctions between "literature" and "life," and if there are useful and necessary discriminations to be made between the two, they certainly get lost in the endless babble about the unreality of our artificial linguistic and cultural artifacts and the artificiality of the lives we build on the basis of the constructs our culture presents us with. The crucial markers to be established disappear in this chaffering, Kundera would have us think, and we need therefore to return to a consideration of the notion that our lives are first and foremost aesthetic in nature, that we compose our lives according to the laws of beauty.

We compose our lives according to the laws of beauty, *but. . . .* There has to be a *but* in this utterance somewhere, for otherwise we would not have gotten into the trap that suggests "fiction" means "unreal." In some respects this too may only be a coincidence of our culture, but it is a coincidence we have built into a major motif by now, and if we did so, there must be a *but* that follows after the assertion that we compose our lives according to the laws of beauty. In *The Unbearable Lightness of Being,* that *but* is to be found in Kundera's discussion of kitsch, that phenomenon that truly does intersect the realm of the fictive and the unreal. And in his essayistic fashion, Kundera is quite straightforward in his exposition of our commitment to kitsch:

> Behind all the European faiths, religious and political, we find the first chapter of Genesis, which tells us that the world was created properly, that human existence is good, and that we are therefore entitled to multiply. Let us call this basic faith a *categorical agreement with being.*

> The fact that until recently the word "shit" appeared in print as s——- has nothing to do with moral considerations. You can't claim that shit is immoral, after all! The objection to shit is a metaphysical one. The daily defecation session is daily proof of the unacceptability of Creation. Either/or: either shit is acceptable (in which case don't lock yourself in the bathroom!) or we are created in an unacceptable manner.

> It follows, then, that the aesthetic ideal of the categorical agreement with being is a world in which shit is denied and everyone acts as though it did not exist. This aesthetic ideal is called *kitsch.*

> "Kitsch" is a German word born in the middle of the sentimental nineteenth century, and from German it entered all Western languages. Repeated use, however, has obliterated its original metaphysical meaning: kitsch is the absolute denial of shit, in both the literal and the figurative senses of the word; kitsch excludes everything from its purview which is essentially unacceptable in human existence.

If Kundera's assertions about the place of the laws of beauty in our lives are in striking contrast to our own vision of things, that is because we have adopted a different aesthetic framework in order to convince ourselves that we have a categorical agreement with being. Inasmuch as we are unable to face certain aspects of our existence, expressed here by Kundera under the rubric of "shit," the only way we can bring ourselves to declare the creation good is to live in "a world in which shit is denied and everyone acts as though it did not exist." This is the world of kitsch.

Kitsch "excludes everything from its purview which is essentially unacceptable in human existence," which means that it is an aesthetic based on *unreal* depictions of the way things are in order to establish a vision in which the world seems at least potentially a pleasing place to us. This view of the aesthetic, of course, is the one best expressed in Nietzsche's famous phrase that "We possess *art* lest we *perish of the truth,*" and at base such a sentiment reflects a refusal to accept the nature of things at any level. More pertinently still, Kundera elaborates on the nature of the "shit" we deny when he tells us that "kitsch is a folding screen set up to curtain off death." In some respects "the daily defecation session" is no more than a reminder of our bodily natures and hence a demonstration of our mortality, that against which we so strenuously fight. So our world is based on the Bible and on Genesis, on the declaration of the world as essentially good, yet we don't really find it to be so and thus establish an aesthetic of denial rather than acceptance.

It is worth remembering that in contrast to the more famous statement quoted above, Nietzsche was finally devoted to a contrary thesis, one based on "Saying Yes to life even in its strangest and hardest problems," and this is certainly the sentiment of Kundera as well. Likewise, we need to recognize that although Kundera does finally associate kitsch with a fear of death, he begins with "shit," and not only because it is a more graphic depiction of our distaste for life but rather because it reflects something deeper than mere anxiety in the face of death: it manifests our *shame.* If Genesis asserts that the world is good and urges us to accede to this categorical agreement with being, it also makes clear that the first thing that Adam and Eve feel after they eat the apple is shame. Indeed, as a description of their prelapsarian state we are told in Genesis 2:25, "And they were both naked, the man and his wife, and were not ashamed," a statement suggesting that the distinguishing feature of life after the fall is shame. "Shit" symbolizes that shame, and the consequent revulsion at being human—and the inevitable *denial* of the categorical agreement with being—that the aesthetic of the West has been based on as far back as Plato's *Republic.*

The Unbearable Lightness of Being, then, establishes two kinds of aesthetic, the traditional one of kitsch, that aesthetic which begins by removing from our purview everything we find unpalatable about the world, and that aesthetic which is based on the attempt to say Yes to life even in its most difficult problems. Both conceptions of beauty are finally based on the essential relationship between beauty and shame, but the one begins by repressing that knowledge while the other embraces it as a necessary aspect of the overall whole. The one creates fictions that are deliberately "unreal," artifacts that are constructed in order to keep us from seeing what is real, and the other creates fictions that, while "artificial," nevertheless approach both the real *and* a categorical agreement with being.

The laws of beauty operate within both of these visions of the aesthetic, though one is more aware of the fact that the laws of beauty determine the motifs of one's life in the Kunderian perspective, and that is precisely the problem, for when the laws of beauty lose their essential connection to that which we construe as the shameful elements of life, they become disengaged from that which would be a sufficient measure of their "reality." If the real has been put out of play from the outset in the denial of shit, there is no way that the truth value of the aesthetic can be measured, for it has no linkage to the real in the first place. The only way to determine its reality quotient is to look for that which it represses, for when that is found, the aesthetic can be seen as one that is based on kitsch. Likewise, a life that is based on the laws of beauty and on a denial of shit at the same time will inevitably become an *unreal* life, one that establishes its sense of reality on the basis of kitsch.

If these two kinds of aesthetic were only relevant to the productions of the artistic world, the problem of shit and kitsch would be a relatively meaningless one; they would simply be the standard through which one could establish the validity of a work of art. The problem is that our vision of beauty is not restricted to such a localized environment. Kundera has already told us: "Behind all the European faiths, religious and political, we find the first chapter of Genesis, which tells us that the world was created properly, that human existence is good," and if we don't believe this to be the case, the religious and political faiths through which we construct our societies will reflect our refusal to agree with the conditions of being as they are established. This in turn means that our faiths will be based on an aesthetic of kitsch rather than on one that seriously seeks to address the shameful aspects of life: "Kitsch is the aesthetic ideal of all politicians and all political parties and movements." In this respect, the fictions with the highest unreality quotient are inevitably *political,* and they are so because the political system always appeals to our tendencies to want to deny that which is shameful.

Political kitsch is so dangerous because of the mechanisms through which it asserts its power. This is most obviously the case in the realm of what Kundera calls "totalitarian kitsch" because in such a world "everything that infringes on kitsch must be banished for life: every display of individualism (because a deviation from the collective is a spit in the eye of the smiling brotherhood); every doubt (because anyone who starts doubting details will end by doubting life itself); all irony (because in the realm of kitsch everything must be taken quite seriously)." And whereas we live in more or less pluralistic societies and thus in some respects manage to escape totalitarian kitsch, it is still the case that *all* political parties and movements depend on kitsch, and life is increasingly overwhelmed by the notion that society is *nothing but* political parties and movements.

The aesthetic of political kitsch is so dangerous precisely because it seems to saturate virtually every domain in the present world, from the domestic scene to the political movements we all recognize on the evening news. More importantly, the repression of shame that kitsch requires inevitably leads to problems of resentment and the need for victims when the world regularly turns out not to conform to the images of it that one's kitsch presents one with. Kundera gives us examples of the local expression of these problems throughout the novel. In Tereza's case, the embodiment of totalitarian kitsch is her mother, a woman who is determined to find someone to blame for a life gone wrong: "When [Tereza's mother] realized she had lost everything, she initiated a search for the culprit. Anyone would do: her first husband, manly and unloved, who had failed to heed her whispered warning; her second husband, unmanly and much loved, who had dragged her away from Prague to a small town and kept her in a state of permanent jealousy by going through one woman after another. But she was powerless against either. The only person who belonged to her and had no means of escape, the hostage who could do penance for all the culprits, was Tereza." Resentful over the outcome of her life, the product largely of her own choices and the aging process in general, Tereza's mother needs someone to blame for the unfortunate way things have gone and can find only Tereza for a victim. It doesn't matter that the mother's fate is not the fault of the daughter; what matters is that the mother herself find a way of placing the blame for the inevitabilities of her own life onto somebody else.

Curiously, though, Tereza's mother makes another gesture as well, one that would seem to deny the world of kitsch rather than uphold it: "Tereza's mother blew her nose noisily, talked to people in public about her sex life, and enjoyed demonstrating her false teeth. She was remarkably skillful at loosening them with her tongue, and in the midst of a broad smile would cause the uppers to drop down over the lowers in such a way as to give her face a sinister expression." Far from feeling shame in the face of her body and its decaying presence, the mother seems to revel in the most shameless of behavior and even ridicules Tereza when she tries to run from such actions. Rather than reflecting an acceptance of her lot, though, "Her behavior was but a single grand gesture, a casting off of youth and beauty. In the days when she had nine suitors kneeling round her in a circle, she guarded her nakedness apprehensively, as though trying to express the value of her body in terms of the modesty she accorded to it. Now she had not only lost that modesty, she had radically broken with it, ceremoniously using her new immodesty to draw a dividing line through her life and proclaim that youth and beauty were overrated and worthless."

These are hardly the acts of an individual who has put kitsch behind her; Tereza's mother has merely erected her own form of kitsch in order to deny her relationship to death and decay and to attempt to drag others down with her into a utopian community of non-difference: "Tereza's mother demanded justice. She wanted to see the culprit penalized. That is why she insisted her daughter remain with her in the world of immodesty, where youth and beauty mean nothing, where the world is nothing but a vast concentration camp of bodies, one like the next, with souls invisible." If all political images of kitsch are based on the ideal of a universal brotherhood—as Kundera phrases it, "The brotherhood of man on earth will be possible only on a base of kitsch"— Tereza's mother makes use of the same kitsch here, simply arriving at the universal brotherhood by a more ruthless way of stripping away the differences among people.

Tereza's mother is a terrorist, a totalitarian who seeks to impose her own kitschy image of reality onto others out of resentment and denial of who she herself really is, and in this she resembles all too much a great many political movements based on resentment and denial as well. Kundera provides an example from his own country to flesh out the seriousness of the problem:

> The first years following the Russian invasion could not yet be characterized as a reign of terror. Because practically no one in the entire nation agreed with the occupation regime, the Russians had to ferret out the few exceptions and push them into power. But where could they look? All faith in Communism and love for Russia was dead. So they sought people who wished to get back at life for something, people with revenge on the brain. Then they had to focus, cultivate, and maintain those people's aggressiveness, give them a temporary substitute to practice on. The substitute they lit upon was animals.
>
> All at once the papers started coming out with cycles of features and organized letters-to-the-editor campaigns demanding, for example, the extermination of all pigeons within city limits. And the pigeons would be exterminated. But the major drive was directed against dogs. People were still disconsolate over the catastrophe of the occupation, but radio, television, and the press went on and on about dogs: how they soil our streets and parks, endanger our children's health, fulfill no useful function, yet must be fed. . . . Only after a year did the accumulated malice (which until then had been vented, for the sake of training, on animals) find its true goal: people. People started being removed from

their jobs, arrested, put on trial. At last the animals could breathe freely.

If the occupying forces are to be able to maintain the fiction that the Russian invasion *saved* Czechoslovakia from certain ruin, *someone* must be blamed for the horrors the people had to go through. Moving from pigeons to dogs to people who are presumably inimical to the regime allows the Czech people to accommodate themselves to the victims they need, yet cannot admit to. After all, those who come to be victimized aren't really responsible for the fate of the nation, but, as with Tereza's mother, when one cannot fight back against those who are truly responsible—in this case the Russians—one must find someone else to blame or else seemingly die of shame.

In turn it is not an accident that the regime uses shame as its most masterful weapon, tape-recording conversations among the dissidents in order to discredit them by revealing their all-too-human pettinesses, by coercing individuals like Tomas into silence by way of demands for letters that explain their mistaken opposition to the occupying forces, and by making full use of the normal human tendency to buckle under in order to save one's own position in life. Tomas is forced to confront precisely this kind of shame and recognize its dual nature:

> Tomas was considered the best surgeon in the hospital. Rumor had it that the chief surgeon, who was getting on towards retirement age, would soon ask him to take over. When that rumor was supplemented by the rumor that the authorities had requested a statement of self-criticism from him, no one doubted he would comply.
>
> That was the first thing that struck him: although he had never given people cause to doubt his integrity, they were ready to bet on his dishonesty rather than on his virtue.
>
> The second thing that struck him was their reaction to the position they attributed to him. I might divide it into two basic types:
>
> The first type of reaction came from people who themselves (they or their intimates) had retracted something, who had themselves been forced to make public peace with the occupation regime or were prepared to do so (unwillingly, of course—no one wanted to do it). . . .
>
> The second type of reaction came from people who themselves (they or their intimates) had been persecuted, who had refused to compromise with the occupation powers or were convinced they would

refuse to compromise (to sign a statement) even though no one requested it of them. . . .

> And suddenly Tomas grasped a strange fact: *everyone* was smiling at him, *everyone* wanted him to write the retraction; it would make *everyone* happy! The people with the first type of reaction would be happy because by inflating cowardice, he would make their actions seem commonplace and thereby give them back their lost honor. The people with the second type of reaction, who had come to consider their honor a special privilege never to be yielded, nurtured a secret love for the cowards, for without them their courage would soon erode into a trivial, monotonous grind admired by no one.

Both those who have been shamed and those who have had to demonstrate (or think they would demonstrate) courage want Tomas to sign a retraction in order to keep their fictions about themselves more comfortably in place. Those who are already shamed will be able to feel that their act was a normal one simply because Tomas, a man of considerable integrity, gave way under the force of the pressure too, and those who have resisted the pressures need to keep their grandiose vision of their courageous acts in place through repeated acts of humiliation on the part of others. Either way, shame is avoided as an essential aspect of the human condition, and either way the kitsch of the world increases.

What Kundera has given us, then, is a novel in which the characters explore the relationship between the aesthetic possibilities of the human condition and their connection to the political world of which they are also always a part. The book is based on the assumption that we invariably compose our lives according to the laws of beauty, but it also shows that those laws of beauty can move in two directions, in accord with the conventions of kitsch that dominate our social and political lives through their perpetual denial of the shit of life and the shame that is an inevitable part of it, or in line with an aesthetic that assumes a necessary relationship to the shame that came about in the moment that Adam and Eve ate the apple and that will never disappear from human existence. The latter vision is admittedly an "impure" one precisely to the extent that, like ***The Unbearable Lightness of Being,*** it reflects the ways in which the shit and the beauty of life are intermingled, but it is also an aesthetic that is devoted to the depiction of what is rather than to a repression of that which we should prefer to avoid in this world. And inasmuch as the novel demonstrates again and again the pernicious effects of a sociopolitical system that is based on the illusions of kitsch, the greater value of the impure form of beauty that Kundera presents us with is made manifest throughout the novel.

The direction of Kundera's aesthetic is reflected in his re-marks on the value of heaviness, a commentary that embraces both the weighty decision of Beethoven's "*Es muss sein*" and the heavy burdens that Nietzsche envisioned through his conceptions of the eternal return and the overman. As the appropriate measure of our relation to heaviness, Kundera calls us to account for the relationship we have established with the animals, a relationship that is totally scandalous in all too many respects. This relationship too derives from our understanding of the first books of Genesis, so it is only fitting that Kundera should return there for his elaboration of our treatment of animals:

> The very beginning of Genesis tells us that God created man in order to give him dominion over fish and fowl and all creatures. Of course, Genesis was written by a man, not a horse. There is no certainty that God actually did grant man dominion over other creatures. What seems more likely, in fact, is that man invented God to sanctify the dominion that he had usurped for himself over the cow and the horse. Yes, the right to kill a deer or a cow is the only thing all of mankind can agree upon, even during the bloodiest of wars.

If we asserted dominion over the other animals on the planet for ourselves and invented a God to justify that hubristic act, we know now that our reasons for doing so concerned our need for hierarchical priority, our desire to escape from the shame that would quickly follow in the Bible and from which we ourselves would never be able to escape. To one who is self-conscious, the killing of another animal has to be the most shameful of acts, far more horrifying than the mere recognition of one's own bodily nature and private parts. The endless parade of sacrifice that surrounds the killing of herds for food and the like testifies to our great need to escape from this shame and our thorough inability ever to do so.

But we tried, and when the dominion that the Bible gave to us was not sufficient to help us overcome our shame, we worked on other strategies, reflected most pertinently in Descartes and his attitude toward the animal world:

> Even though Genesis says that God gave man dominion over all animals, we can also construe it to mean that He merely entrusted them to man's care. Man was not the planet's master, merely its administrator, and therefore eventually responsible for his administration. Descartes took a decisive step forward: he made man "*maître et propriétaire de la nature.*" And surely there is a deep connection between that step and the fact that he was also the one who point-blank denied animals a soul. Man is master and proprietor, says Descartes, whereas the beast is merely an automaton, an animated machine, a *machine animata.*

In order finally to escape from the degradation involved in our own bodily condition and that which stemmed from it— the need to devour other species—we had to take one more step and deny that animals had souls, thereby turning them into mere "automatons" that could be dispensed with as we saw fit, surely the way we continue to view them to this very day. In order, that is, to escape from our own degradation, we had to degrade completely all the rest of the species on the planet, the equivalent mode within the animal kingdom that we already saw at work in the political regimes represented by Tereza's mother and the occupying forces within Czechoslovakia.

For Kundera the degradation of animals reflects the larger human shame put on display throughout the novel: "True human goodness, in all its purity and freedom, can come to the fore only when its recipient has no power. Mankind's true moral test, its fundamental test (which lies deeply buried from view), consists of its attitude towards those who are at its mercy: animals. And in this respect mankind has suffered a fundamental debacle, a debacle so fundamental that all others stem from it." The kitsch through which we have framed our world—that sociopolitical aesthetic that is nothing more than "a folding screen set up to curtain off death"—has repeatedly attempted to escape from the scandal of its own hypocrisy, yet our need to deny our position in the world has prompted us again and again to degrade ourselves still further in the guise of a higher and purer vision to be found in the kitsch we so desperately want to believe in. There can be no doubt that we have devastated the species on the planet as a result of these urges, and thus one can only conclude that the aesthetic vision upon which our sense of the world has been based has been a complete failure and has shown itself to be morally bankrupt at the core.

The alternative aesthetic imagined by Kundera reflects a break with this tradition even as it acknowledges the chief originator of that break: Nietzsche. Kundera reflects on the moment when Nietzsche's madness overtook him and relates it to the human relationship with animals in order to establish the full difference between the Nietzschean view of things and the kitsch to which it was opposed:

> Seeing a horse and a coachman beating it with a whip, Nietzsche went up to the horse and, before the coachman's very eyes, put his arms around the horse's neck and burst into tears.

> That took place in 1889, when Nietzsche, too, had removed himself from the world of people. In other words, it was at the time when his mental illness had just erupted. But for that very reason I feel his gesture has broad implications: Nietzsche was trying to apologize to the horse for Descartes. His lunacy (that is, his final break with mankind) began at the very moment he burst into tears over the horse.

> And that is the Nietzsche I love, just as I love Tereza with the mortally ill dog resting his head in her lap. I see them one next to the other: both stepping down from the road along which mankind, "the master and proprietor of nature," marches onward.

Our tendency may be to want to quibble with this particular interpretation of the onset of Nietzsche's madness, arguing that Kundera is making far too much of it by suggesting that at this moment Nietzsche both apologizes to the horse for Descartes and steps down from the road on which our civilization continues to march, but given the full weight of existence and the necessary acceptance of it that Nietzsche was devoted to trying to embrace and affirm, there is every reason to think that this is not merely a "poetic"—and hence "fictive" and "unreal"—rendition of the stakes of this touching action on Nietzsche's part.

Like Kundera, Nietzsche was committed to a fundamentally aesthetic view of human existence, one that was both based on the laws of beauty and established through those laws the richness of life in the midst of its most shameful aspects, and if it took Kundera to recognize that the best measure of this new aesthetic was to be found in our relationship to the rest of the animals on the planet, he would be the first to admit that this insight is to be found at the very center of Nietzsche's work and is best represented by his final break with mankind over the shameless treatment of an animal that should not have had to bear our own shame for all these millennia. And if the image of Nietzsche in his madness hugging the horse is a most sobering gauge of the distance between an aesthetic of kitsch and one that embraces life in all of its beauty and shame, it should not deter us from questioning with continuing persistence another possible road for our own species to march on, nor should it keep us from realizing the degree to which our lives continue to be composed according to the laws of beauty even when we least expect it.

Ellen Pifer (essay date Spring 1992)

SOURCE: "*The Book of Laughter and Forgetting:* Kundera's Narration against Narration," in *Journal of Narrative Technique,* Vol. 22, No. 2, Spring, 1992, pp. 84-96.

[*In the essay below, Pifer examines the way that Kundera's notion of the novel informs his narrative methods and practice, focusing mainly on* The Book of Laughter and Forgetting.]

In Milan Kundera's novel, ***The Book of Laughter and Forgetting,*** the narrator diagnoses the disease of "graphomania." "An obsession with writing books," graphomania has, he says, overtaken contemporary mass society and reached "epidemic" proportions. While graphomaniacs attempt to write their way out of the isolation induced by an advanced state of "social atomization," their obsession with self-expression paradoxically reinforces and perpetuates the sense of "general isolation" that is symptomatic of the disease. Kundera's narrator thus concludes his diagnosis: "The invention of printing originally promoted mutual understanding. In the era of graphomania the writing of books has the opposite effect: everyone surrounds himself with his own writings as with a wall of mirrors cutting off all voices from without."

Diagnosing within his own book the disease of book-writing, Kundera does more than parody the conditions under which his texts are generated and produced. Through his novel approach to novel-writing—most particularly, through the ironic voice of his narrator—he identifies, in order to subvert, some of those linguistic and cultural processes by which the writer isolates himself from others. The "wall of mirrors," cutting the writer's voice off from those "voices from without," makes obvious reference to the solipsistic tendencies of aesthetic creation and self-reflection. It recalls most directly the literary premises and practices of modernism. The monumental narratives of Proust, Woolf, Joyce, Faulkner and others tend to dissolve the world of material and social phenomena in the medium of consciousness. Depriving Paris, Dublin or Jefferson County of any reality beyond the prisms of a character's isolated consciousness, the avatars of modernism declared the victory of imagination over the chaos of history and the ruins of time.

To those living in a less heroic literary age, Kundera's "wall of mirrors" further suggests our contemporary sense of the limitations of language and of the literary enterprise as a whole. We are reminded of what poststructuralist critics have to say about the isolation of text from world, the confinement of all writing to the "prison house of language." In contrast to the poststructuralist critic, however, this Czech novelist regards the estrangement of language, a world of signs, from the world of things as a historical rather than necessary condition. It is a condition, in Kundera's view, that the writer must vigilantly oppose, even if his resistance to these solipsistic tendencies may never wholly succeed. In his own fiction Kundera strives to create a kind of writing that, unlike the graphomaniac's, forces open a window to the world of referents beyond language and its system of signs.

The extent to which any work of narrative fiction or history can reflect actual events taking place in a world beyond language is a matter of ongoing critical debate—and I have no intention of entering this theoretical quagmire in the discussion at hand. My interest lies, rather, in the way that

Kundera's vision of the novelistic enterprise, and of the novelist's obligations to a world of referents beyond the self and language, governs his narrative methods and practice. This is not to say, however, that Kundera's view of language is nostalgic or naive. Breaking through the "wall of mirrors"—unlocking the circle of the self—exposes both the writer and his readers to uncertainty. To admit the world is to admit ambiguity, contingency, irony—above all, to question. As Kundera has said on more than one occasion, the novel's task is not to answer questions but to raise them. Scrupulously practicing what he preaches, this novelist disrupts conventional narrative structure and sabotages the writer's authority in order to interrogate the text. Sprinkling his narration with rhetorical questions, countering an "obvious explanation" with one he finds "more convincing," the author's narrating persona exposes both the characters and their author to skeptical scrutiny.

In the opening section of ***The Book of Laughter and Forgetting,*** for example, the narrator confronts his readers with a question: why, he asks, is Mirek, an intellectual whose history is being recounted here, so ashamed of an affair he had, twenty-five years ago, with an "ugly" woman named Zdena? The narrator offers an "obvious explanation" that he immediately retracts, because he doesn't "find it convincing enough." Reluctantly he admits the more convincing explanation, which also proves less flattering to the male ego: cowardly and insecure in his youth, Mirek had "taken an ugly mistress because he didn't dare go after beautiful women."

In his subsequent attempt to remove all traces, all record of his (now humiliating) three-year affair with Zdena, Mirek has, the narrator points out, set himself up as an author—claiming the rights of any novelist over his material. "One of a novelist's inalienable rights," the narrator states, "is to be able to rework his novel. If he takes a dislike to the beginning, he can rewrite it or cross it out entirely." Unfortunately, when Zdena reappears on the scene, Mirek is forced to confront the discomfiting fact that this woman is *not* his own invention. Kundera's narrator slyly comments: "But Zdena's existence deprived Mirek of his prerogative as an author. Zdena insisted on remaining part of the opening pages of the novel. She refused to be crossed out." While Mirek remains the focus of Kundera's satire here, the author is not above satirizing his own enterprise as well. Novelists will always claim the right to "rework" their novels for the sake of style, structure and effect. Still, the writer's efforts to provide a seamless work of art—ironing out the unsightly wrinkles caused by human nature and history—may implicate him in the same criticism levelled at Mirek. Foregrounding the processes by which the novelist rewrites and revises his material, Kundera undermines the illusion that his text is either timeless or impersonal. As Ann Banfield observes in her study, *Unspeakable Sentences,* "Only in writing [as opposed to speaking] may the process of revision, which is part of the process of composition, vanish in the finished piece, the 'clean copy,' leaving no sign of what the first or any intervening versions may have looked like." By calling attention to the erasure of those telling "signs" of revision, Kundera undermines the effects by which the written text appears to transcend the ephemeral and contingent conditions of its own production.

"*Écriture*," Banfield explains in another study, "is the name for the coming to language of a knowledge, whether objective or subjective, which is not personal." Resisting the notion of writing's impersonality—a notion that, as Banfield points out, French writers from Flaubert to Foucault have sought to emphasize—Kundera flagrantly inserts his personal biography into the narrative. Enlisting his narrating persona as guide, goad and *agent provocateur,* Kundera draws attention not only to the author behind the text but to the way that personal experience motivates the act of writing. "Why is Tamina on a children's island?" asks the narrator of *The Book of Laughter and Forgetting.* "Why is that where I imagine her?" His answer characteristically fails to provide a definite answer. "I don't know," he admits, adding: "Maybe it's because on the day my father died the air was full of joyful songs sung by children's voices."

Undermining the illusion of "knowledge" that *écriture* creates, Kundera would open his text to uncertainty as well as the personal. Interspersing what Gerald Prince calls "signs of the 'you'" throughout the novel, Kundera's narrator repeatedly addresses and queries the narratee—the "you" implicitly or explicitly being addressed. In this way he opens the text not only to question but, in Prince's phrase, to "another world" outside the novel and its characters, which is "known to both the narrator and the narratee." Enlisting a narrating persona who shares this "other world" and all its problematic conditions with the reader, Kundera abandons the covert operations of an omniscient creator for the overt strategies of a self-conscious narrator.

By inserting his personal background and history into the text, Kundera is not building a "wall of mirrors" around himself as writing subject. Instead, he employs the biographical persona, like the other narrative devices characteristic of his art, to open a window (both literally and figuratively) on the political history of Czechoslovakia and on the invented history of his characters. In *The Book of Laughter and Forgetting,* for example, the narrator identifies the "joyful" tune sung by "children's voices" on the day Kundera's father died as the "Internationale": "Everywhere east of the Elbe," he explains, "children are banded together in what are called Pioneer organizations" that teach them to become good communists. On the day that Kundera's father died, Gustav Husak—installed by the Russians in 1969 as the seventh president of Czechoslovakia—received an award from these

children's groups. At "a festive ceremony in Prague Castle," the narrator tells us, Husak, "*the president of forgetting,*" is "being named an Honorary Pioneer." At the end of the ceremony, the President's words, amplified over the loudspeaker, drift in through the very window of the room where Kundera's father lies dying: "Children! You are the future!" Husak proclaims. "Children! Never look back!" (italics Kundera's).

Here the author's personal loss, the death of his beloved father, serves as yet another variation on the theme of "forgetting" that informs each section of the novel. The erosion of memory that constitutes Tamina's personal tragedy is identified with the author's personal tragedy and, on a larger scale, with the tragedy of Czechoslovakia under totalitarian rule. In Kundera's unsentimental vision, moreover, children serve as emblems of the mindless "infantocracy" overtaking contemporary culture in both East and West. In the oblivious consciousness of childhood, devoid of past and memory, the author perceives the dire future of postindustrial society. Because, as the narrator later points out, children "have no past whatsoever," they bear no "burden of memory"; hence "childhood is the image of the future." In Western technocracy's enslavement to the blandishments of mass media as well as in Eastern Europe's seventy-year subjugation to totalitarian rule, Kundera detects the same mindless faith in the future. Wooed by the urge to escape history and its burdens, contemporary culture risks losing not only its collective memory but the very source of individual identity.

Calling attention to the biographical author, his history, and the temporal processes that help to erode as well as create written artifacts, Kundera stresses the connection not only between author and text, but between language and identity. The reliance of human and cultural identity upon language, and of language upon memory, is a central theme in *The Book of Laughter and Forgetting*—a theme succinctly dramatized by the ten-year illness that proves fatal for Kundera's father. One major symptom of this disease is the gradual erosion of memory, which causes his father to lose "the power of speech" and ultimately the ability to write a coherent text. "At first," the narrator says, his father "simply had trouble calling up certain words or would say similar words instead and then immediately laugh at himself. In the end he had only a handful of words left. . . . Things lost their names and merged into a single, undifferentiated reality. I was the only one who by talking to him could temporarily transform that nameless infinity into the world of clearly named entities." In the end, the father's "memory lapses" become so fierce that the dying man has to abandon his "study of Beethoven's sonatas"; "no one," the narrator explains, "could understand the text." The father's writing, like his speech, becomes an incomprehensible jumble: an impersonal void or "nameless infinity" of "undifferentiated" language.

It is through language, Kundera reminds us, that we name or identify not only things but ourselves. Identity, like meaning in a text, arises from difference; and the ability to differentiate one word from another—or one thing, one event, one person, one author, one culture from another—depends on memory. Memory of the past, recorded as history, keeps alive our sense of differentiation and identity; it prevents us from slipping into the "nameless infinity" of "undifferentiated reality." As the novelist's character Tamina comes to realize, "the sum total of her being is no more than what she sees in the distance, behind her. And as her past begins to shrink, disappear, fall apart, Tamina begins shrinking and blurring" as well.

Such "shrinking and blurring," Kundera suggests, befalls each of us as we age, lose our faculties and slowly surrender to oblivion. Not only does the aging Mother, in Part Two of *The Book of Laughter and Forgetting,* begin to lose her sight—she loses her memory and with it her experience of history:

> One night, for example, the tanks of a huge neighboring country [as Kundera's narrator puts it] came and occupied their country. The shock was so great, so terrible, that for a long time no one could think about anything else. It was August, and the pears in their garden were nearly ripe. The week before, Mother had invited the local pharmacist to come and pick them. He never came, never apologized. The fact that Mother refused to forgive him drove [her son] Karel and [his wife] Marketa crazy. Everybody's thinking about tanks, and all you can think about is pears, they yelled.

Karel's old Mother, the narrator suggests, has "moved on to the different world" of a second childhood. She has joined "a different order of creature: smaller, lighter, more easily blown away."

Whereas an old woman's second childhood appears natural and even comic, notwithstanding the announcement of death that it brings, Tamina's fate is truly tragic. A young woman exiled from her country and all that she loves, Tamina slides into premature death when she is brought to an island "wilderness" populated by children. There, surrounded by these tiny beings who have no past, no memory, no history, she is consigned to oblivion. On this remote "children's island," Tamina confronts a world hostile to privacy, individuation or difference. "We're all children here!" the youthful inhabitants gleefully shout. Held captive like Gulliver among the Lilliputians, Tamina tries but fails to escape. Making a run for the shore, she spies the children dancing together in a clearing and takes refuge "behind the thick trunk of a plane tree." From this hiding place she watches the children jerk and gyrate to the rhythms of rock music, the din of amplified guitars blaring from a tape recorder set down in the middle of the clearing. "The lewdness of the motions superimposed on their children's bodies," Kundera's narrator observes, "destroys the dichotomy between obscenity and innocence, purity and corruption. Sensuality loses all its meaning, innocence loses all its meaning, words fall apart." Once again taking language as his paradigm, Kundera links the forces of forgetting with the death of difference.

Pitting memory against oblivion, Kundera's novels celebrate difference at every level—starting with the systematic polarities by which language operates to create meaning. Each of these novels, moreover, typically incorporates a variety of types or modes of discourse within its narrative. Interspersing the fictional histories of his characters with passages devoted to philosophical speculation, historical commentary, and even quotations from other published and unpublished texts, Kundera makes contrast or difference both a structural and a thematic principle. The overall effect of this counterpoint is to dispel the intensity of any single, or single-voiced, narration. By disrupting the seamless effects of narration, Kundera wakens his readers from the "spell" cast by art and confronts them with the burden of history. "We who remember," his narrator tells us in *Life Is Elsewhere,* "must bear witness."

Just as Flaubert employed the devices of realism to undercut Emma Bovary's romantic reveries—and created, in the process, a novel about the dangers of reading novels—so Kundera, at a later stage of the novel's development, employs the self-conscious devices of postmodernist narrative to subvert the lyric spell of his own narration. "Lyrical poetry," he has said, "is a realm in which any statement immediately becomes truth. Yesterday the poet said *life is a vale of tears*; today he said *life is a land of smiles*; and he was right both times. There is no inconsistency. The lyrical poet does not have to prove anything. The only proof is the intensity of his own emotions." The novelist, on the other hand, must assume the burden of history and, therefore, of "proof." The distinction Kundera draws between novels and lyric poetry further suggests why so much of his own writing is devoted to speculation and argument. And while the novelist endeavors, through his narrating persona, to present certain conclusions, as well as questions, with vigor and force, this persona also reminds Kundera's readers that the author is no prophet or visionary. Declining the role of omniscient creator, he is simply another limited mortal caught in "the trap" of history. As such, he enlists in his narrative not only the voice of his biographical persona but the timely voices of the author's friends and family, of Czech officials and world leaders, of current dogmas and classic works of literature.

The devices of narrative reflexivity are, paradoxically, the means by which Kundera lays siege to the graphomaniac's self-absorbed, self-reflecting "wall of mirrors." It is in the "mirrored house of poetry," moreover, that Kundera locates this "wall of mirrors" and its isolating effects. Drawing a distinction between novels and poetry that recalls Bakhtin's theory of discourse in *The Dialogic Imagination,* Kundera celebrates the novel's hybrid language and structure—contrasting the formal freedoms of this genre with the strictures of poetry and its compulsively "lyric attitude." But with freedom comes responsibility; the novel, unlike the poem, is answerable to history. What Kundera's narrator says of his character Tamina, who makes a scrupulous record of her past in order to oppose the forces of forgetting, may also be said of her author: "She has no desire to turn the past into poetry, she wants to give the past back its lost body. She is not compelled by a desire for beauty, she is compelled by a desire for life."

This distinction between poetry and life, beauty and history, informs all of Kundera's fiction. In *The Book of Laughter and Forgetting,* Tamina's efforts to retrieve, with all its ugliness, the past's "lost body" are contrasted with Karel's preference for poetic oblivion. Earlier in the novel, Karel rhapsodically muses over the stages of his bygone youth. Rather than strive "to give the past back its lost body," he begins to manipulate—and even to dismember—that elusive body for his own gratification. As Karel projects his desire upon the past, conjuring an "idyllic landscape" that never existed, his author likens him to "a collage artist, cutting out part of one engraving and pasting it over another." Taking delight in his finished creation, Karel gratefully contemplates the transcendent power of art: "Beauty," he reflects, "is a clean sweep of chronology, a rebellion against time."

Not only in this passage but throughout the novel Kundera invites us to contemplate the difference between the operation of historical memory—our urgent efforts to retrieve and preserve what has transpired in our experience, no matter how painful or daunting the task—and the immemorial desire of human beings "to turn the past into poetry." "History," as his narrator later remarks, "is a succession of ephemeral changes. Eternal values exist outside history. They are immutable and have no need of memory." Human memory—in contrast to Apollo's lyre—is a mortal rather than divine attribute; and those who exercise it must serve time. Those of us who seek to remember, to "bear witness," must acknowledge contingency in the very act of giving "the past back its lost body." Invoking "chronology" and the ephemeral at every turn, Kundera's skeptical, antimodernist version of narrative undermines the quest for transcendence. Precisely because they are so time-laden, his novels announce "the unbearable lightness of being."

While Kundera's distinction between poetry and prose, art and life sheds light on his enterprise as a novelist, it would be misleading to regard the distinction he draws as absolute.

In the preface to his novel, *Life Is Elsewhere,* the author identifies the relationship of poetry to his own works of prose. In composing this novel, Kundera says, he wanted "to solve an esthetic problem: how to write a novel which would be a 'critique of poetry' and yet at the same time would itself be poetry"—would, that is, "transmit poetic intensity and imagination." Only by "catching [an] image" in the depths of its own linguistic "mirrors," he later suggests, can a novel be said to reflect or represent reality. Like most novelists since Cervantes, Kundera registers a fertile ambivalence about his obligations to art, on the one hand, and to history or actuality on the other. What merits particular attention in his case is the way that his narrative isolates and foregrounds its aesthetic or "lyric" impulse in order to undermine the spell that it casts.

It was Edmund Wilson, writing over half a century ago in *Axel's Castle,* who first cautioned readers about the tendency of modernist writers to abandon the novelist's traditional, and salutary, ambivalence toward the seductive power of imagination. Expressing admiration for Proust's formidable accomplishments in *A la recherché du temps perdu,* Wilson nonetheless offers a critical reservation: "The fascination of Proust's novel is so great that, while we are reading it, we tend to accept it *in toto.* In convincing us of the reality of his creations, Proust infects us with his point of view, even where his point of view has falsified his picture of life" (italics Wilson's). Now, to charge a work of fiction with "falsification" may strike some readers—particularly if they are students of narrative theory—as paradoxical, if not confused. The difference between novels and history, Banfield maintains in *Unspeakable Sentences,* "is that the fictional narrative statement is immune to judgments of truth or falsity; in fiction, they are suspended. Rather, it [fiction] creates by fiat a fictional reality which can only be taken as fictionally true."

Nevertheless, as Wilson's comment on Proust's "falsification" makes clear, even the most sophisticated readers of narrative fiction may implicitly acknowledge the novelist's traditional obligations to truth or history. Thomas Leitch, in a theoretical study entitled *What Stories Are,* is more willing to acknowledge the blurred border between fictional and nonfictional narrative, allowing that it is "a difference in emphasis." The "success or failure of a work of history," says Leitch, clearly depends on the status of the implicated propositions" it makes. By contrast, novels—even those that "may propose implicated explanations of historical events"—do not display the same degree of "this commitment." That is why, we might add, Edmund Wilson can both admire Proust's novel and find it guilty of "falsification." Wilson would certainly employ more stringent criteria, or "judgments of truth," when assessing the work of a French historian of the same period.

Still, as Banfield herself points out, the fiction writer's power to create a world "by fiat" can be viewed as a liability by novelists seeking to uphold their obligations to history. The fiction writer, Banfield says, can neither "tell the truth" nor "write a sentence of narration which is false"—which, in other words, "can be taken by readers of novels as false. His or hers is the midas touch which turns all fiction, that is, to fictional truth, and thereby abolishes all distinctions between the true and the false." By insisting, stylistically and thematically, upon the novel's burden of "proof," Kundera would deliver his readers from the "midas touch" of narrative art. By interrogating his text—inviting the reader to question and debate the narrator's assertions—he overtly appeals to those "distinctions between the true and the false" of which Banfield judges the novel incapable. To distinguish a statement of truth from a "lie," Banfield says, there must be "a communication to an interlocutor." Perhaps that is why Kundera insists that his readers adopt the role of interlocutor. He would guard against the hypnotic spell of narrative—the power of Proust's novel to transform, midas-like, the false into the true—and offer, instead, a critique of that power to which all novels, including his own, nonetheless aspire. By curbing the degree of "infection" that "poetic intensity and imagination" visit upon the novel's readers, Kundera would lift the quarantine that seals contemporary writing in a "wall of mirrors" and denies the novelist healthy exposure to history and its "judgments of truth."

The liberties Kundera takes with the categories of fiction and nonfiction, narrative and essay—the way he flagrantly juxtaposes historical reportage and documentary with the symbolic landscape of fantasy and fable—signals his commitment to the political as well as formal freedoms he perceives in the novel-genre. This is hardly surprising for a writer who regards the aesthetic and political processes as springing from a common source and operating according to the same human laws. "The metaphysics of man," he maintains, "is the same in the private sphere as in the public one."

In the "lyric attitude" of the poet Kundera identifies the same totalizing urge, the same desire to create or transform reality *in toto,* that fosters human faith in a cosmic order or in sundry ideologies promising paradise on earth. The same impulse that compels the poet or writer to seek immortality in song, perfection in art, leads to the creation of larger allied and alloyed structures, including grandiose political schemes. When society allows itself to be carried away by "the lyric attitude," constructing an ideal or "idyll" of absolute order and harmony, for example, the quest ends in collective disaster. That is why Kundera refers to Czechoslovakia's era of communist repression—an "era of political trials, persecutions, forbidden books, and legalized murder"—as "not only an epoch of terror, but also an epoch of lyricism, ruled hand in hand by the hangman and the poet." Desire for absolute order in the social sphere, like in-

sistence upon absolute truth or meaning in the linguistic, leads to repression. "The impulse to totalization," as Hazard Adams and Leroy Searle summarize Derrida's argument, is linked to "the *totalitarian.* . . . The desire for closure, as guarantor of meaning and intelligibility, becomes the instrumentality of repression" (italics theirs).

Observing a similar connection between the totalizing and totalitarian impulse but developing its implications well beyond the linguistic, Kundera tells an interviewer: "Totalitarianism is not only hell, but also the dream of paradise—the age-old dream of a world where everybody would live in harmony, united by a single common will and faith. . . . The whole period of Stalinist terror was a period of collective lyrical delirium." He adds, "hell is already contained in the dream of paradise and if we wish to understand the essence of hell we must examine the essence of the paradise from which it originated. It is extremely easy to condemn gulags, but to reject the totalitarian poesy which leads to the gulag by way of paradise is as difficult as ever." When the "lyric attitude" spills over from art to life, Kundera suggests, it may take disastrous social and political forms. Fleeing from contingency, desiring to escape the burden of memory and history, the utopian dreamer embraces a nonexistent future, attempting to realize paradise—a perfect world of order, harmony and "eternal values"—on earth.

The consequences, Kundera warns, are dangerous if not fatal: "Once the dream of paradise starts to turn into reality, however, here and there people begin to crop up who stand in its way, and so the rulers of paradise must build a little gulag on the side of Eden. In the course of time this gulag grows ever bigger and more perfect, while the adjoining paradise gets ever smaller and poorer." The structure is maintained through violence; elements that cannot or will not join the happy circle must be cast out, consigned to the prisons and torture chambers devised by those in charge. The totalitarian hell gradually subsumes its putative heaven.

The implications of Kundera's secular version of heaven and hell are grim. But the dire nature of these observations belies their bracing comic effect in the novels, tricked out as they are by the narrator's characteristic lightness of delivery. Nowhere is this combination of deft narration and dark inference more apparent, and effective, than in the final scene of ***The Book of Laughter and Forgetting.*** The novel draws to a close on the private beach of "an abandoned island" somewhere on the Adriatic, where a small resort hotel caters to vacationers. The island and its shoreline offer a kind of realistic counterpoint to that symbolic wilderness, the "children's island," from which Tamina, earlier in the novel, tries to escape. On the latter island, the symbolic circle of identical children is supplanted by a population of vacationing nudists equally uniform in their nakedness: "They went naked down the steps to the beach, where other naked people were sitting in groups, taking walks, and swimming—naked mothers and naked children, naked grandmothers and naked grandchildren, the naked young and the naked elderly."

Surrounded by this anonymous population, Kundera's protagonists, a young man named Jan and his girlfriend Edwige, make friends with a smaller "group of naked people," all of whom have come to this "natural paradise" seeking to rid themselves of "the hypocrisy of a society that cripples body and soul." By casting off their clothing, the group collectively embraces the ideal of natural freedom, of living "at one with nature." A theory advanced by one member of the group, "a man with an extraordinary paunch," formulates their collective ideal and goal: to "be freed once and for all from the bonds of Judeo-Christian thought." The idyll of "perfect harmony," perfect freedom, "perfect solidarity" requires that the accumulated legacy of the past—the traditions, norms, structures and systems of a civilization, the cultural language by which its members have identified themselves to one another and themselves—be not altered but erased. "Eternal values," as Kundera's narrator has already observed, "exist outside history."

In the nudists' shared dream of a "natural paradise" we detect the "collective lyrical delirium" that in Kundera's view governs all utopian heavens, giving rise in turn to the hell latent in each artificial paradise. As Jan gazes at the mass of naked bodies scattered along the shore, he has a dark inkling of the connection between earthly notions of heaven and the various forms of hell to which they lead. Made "melancholy" by the spectacle of so much undifferentiated, "meaningless" flesh, Jan is suddenly "overwhelmed by a strange feeling of affliction, and from that haze of affliction came an even stranger thought: that the Jews had filed into Hitler's gas chambers naked and en masse." Jan is led to consider the possibility that "nudity" is itself a kind of "uniform." Here Kundera's language evokes a suggestive connection between the Jews' uniform nakedness and the uniforms of their Nazi exterminators. Unable to bear "the sight of all those naked bodies on the beach," Jan suddenly arrives at the startling notion "that nudity is a shroud."

Bewitched by a particularly virulent strain of "totalitarian poesy," the German nature participated in the dream of an Aryan paradise—and stoked the hellish fires of the gas chambers. Genocide, the attempt to erase a people and their history from the face of the earth, is one outgrowth of that totalizing impulse, or "collective lyrical delirium," which makes the nude bathers so eager to free themselves of the fetters of the past. To erase the memory of an admittedly troubled and imperfect history leads not to a brave new world, however, but to the loss of human differentiation and identity. Mass murder, mass extinction, Kundera suggests, is simply the dark fulfillment of mankind's oblivious dream of utopia.

The sunlight that shines on the closing scene of *The Book of Laughter and Forgetting* is tinged with dark irony. The small circle of nudists standing together on the sand look harmless enough as they congratulate themselves on their temporary freedom from the "civilization" that "imprisons" them. But then the man whose single distinguishing feature is that "extraordinary paunch" begins to extol the future and its promised liberation from the strictures of the past. As the group attends to what the paunchy man is saying, Kundera draws this scene and his novel to a close: "On and on the man talked. The others listened with interest, their naked genitals staring dully, sadly, listlessly at the yellow sand." More eloquent than any words the nudists can muster is the limp expression of their exposed genitals. Like domestic pets suddenly turned loose from their leashes, these naked organs appear bewildered by their abrupt and unexpected release from bondage; something more than mere clothing appears to have been discarded. Exposed to the harsh glare of daylight, the nudists' bodies inadvertently register the oblivion into which they have been cast: the hell of "undifferentiated reality." The pride of their once private parts has mysteriously vanished with the clothing that constrained them. The body's sudden liberation from social "bonds," from all the trappings of civilization, consigns these sad appendages to the same flaccid existence that, Kundera wittily suggests, the mind's longed-for deliverance from a binding system of difference, linguistic and cultural, would entail.

Sustaining a polyphony of light and dark themes, personal and public voices, Kundera takes full advantage of what he calls the "synthetic power of the novel." By coming at his "subject from all sides," as he puts it, the novelist combines "ironic essay, novelistic narrative, autobiographical fragment, historic fact, flight of fantasy." The culminating effect is not of closure but of equilibrium, like the contrapuntal harmony created by "the voices of polyphonic music." The musical analogy is one that Kundera consistently favors. In *The Book of Laughter and Forgetting,* his narrator draws an instructive parallel between the novel's structure and the "journey of the variation form" in music. "This entire book," he announces, "is a novel in the form of variations." Likening his narrative to the voyage of discovery Beethoven undertook, Kundera hints at the special attraction that this mode of exploration holds for a novelist attempting to cure himself of the disease of graphomania. "What Beethoven discovered in his variations," the novel's narrator points out, "was another space and direction"—"the infinity of internal variety concealed in all things."

Structuring his novel on a set of stylistic and thematic variations, Kundera, like Beethoven, seeks "another space and direction." It is *an other* space and direction not only because the territory is new but because it lies beyond the isolated self, outside the "wall of mirrors" enclosing the writer in endless self-reflections. The writer liberates himself by liberating his readers: he does not carry us away in the mesmerizing flow of narrated events or in a lyric flight so compelling that it cannot be examined and resisted. Instead of cutting off *our* "voices from without," he opens up the text to query and debate. To clear this ground or mental "space" for the reader, Kundera develops his narration, structurally and thematically, as an ongoing process of interrogation, differentiation and contrast. Differentiation discovers a virtually endless variety of entities and identities, of contrasting forms, patterns and poles of meaning. The "polyphonic" text disrupts the flow of narration, cancels its lyric impetus, by juxtaposing unlike elements that insistently retain their discrete and contrary identities. Juxtaposing these contrasting elements—interrogating one tone, stance, concept or style with another as the narrative swerves between sexual highjinks and high seriousness—Kundera's text resists the solipsistic forces that drive its production. Turning the art of narration against itself, the author creates a novel that is at once an artful manifestation of "graphomania" and his bracing attempt at a cure.

John O'Brien (essay date Fall 1992)

SOURCE: "Milan Kundera: Meaning, Play, and the Role of the Author," in *Critique,* Vol. XXXIV, No. 1, Fall, 1992, pp. 3-18.

[*Below, O'Brien analyzes "play," intrusive authorship, and the significance of history in Kundera's fiction, particularly in* The Book of Laughter and Forgetting, The Unbearable Lightness of Being, *and, in a brief postscript,* Immortality.]

In the world of books, the author is dead and has been for quite a while—as has the traditionally axiomatic idea that the author has some say in what is being said. Yet outside the discussions of authorship taking place within the academic circle, Milan Kundera has experienced first-hand some very real implications of being an author and writing a "dangerous" text. Because of the works he authored before the Russian invasion, Kundera was fired from his teaching post, his books were removed from libraries and universally banned, and he was denied the means to support himself. Until recently, his novels have been read in dozens of languages with the ironic exception of the language in which the novels were written.

The challenge to the common effacement of the author is more appropriately found, however, in Kundera's texts themselves. Kundera's novels give voice to a powerful intrusive author identifying himself bluntly as none other than Milan Kundera. Enriched by the more radical narrative examples of Sterne and Diderot, Kundera weaves an author-figure into his texts with stark autobiographical intrusions that threaten

the provocative flippancy with which Roland Barthes announced/pronounced the demise of the author in his famous essay.

Still, on closer analysis, what Barthes says and Kundera does are not as diametrically opposed as one might assume. The focus of this analysis of Kundera and his authorship will be to examine these issues, appropriately concentrating on the degree to which Barthes (the author's executioner) provides a valuable theoretical tool for the exploration of Kundera's authorial stance and for the kind of *play* that characterizes his novels. Barthes's general sense of authorship and the erotic potential of texts are strikingly close to the kind of reading Kundera's texts invite. Contrary to the position of Nina Pelikan Straus—against which much of what follows can be read—I contend that the intrusive author-figure does not work to demand a strict adherence to historical or political context. In fact, I argue that the opposite is true.

In an insightful discussion of *The Book of Laughter and Forgetting,* Nina Pelikan Straus furthers her claim that the novel is intended to be bound inextricably to Czechoslovak history, depending on the understanding that the intrusive author-figure is autobiographical in nature, not a dispersed extension or modality of the writing subject. [Straus, "Erasing History and Deconstructing the Text: Milan Kundera's *The Book of Laughter and Forgetting,*" in *Critique,* Vol. 28, No. 2, pp. 69-85]. She argues that the novel consistently parodies the over-theorization of criticism to the degree that all context is lost in the rush to reveal the chaotic indeterminacy of the text. Most polemical in her attack of deconstruction, she goes so far as to claim that in the novel Kundera is speaking out directly against even the belief that no single interpretation is "right" or should be preferred over another. Straus sees deconstruction as an attempt to turn the more "obvious intentions" of *The Book* upside down, and she argues that the novel's structure and technique (including the intrusive author) are directly related to the content—the recurring, simple motif that history tends to get lost or erased by others. When she contends that the strong authorial voice functions as protection against "inhuman theories" that would insist on plural meanings, she bluntly denies Barthes in the process:

> This is not to say that the anti-deconstructionist critic has no "fun," but that his [or her] fun must be qualified by the awareness that history, and the language which ties us to history, can never quite be "jouissant"—a mere game and plaything for the mind—in the sense that Roland Barthes describes it. The dehumanization of the text into a game without reference to the facts of history is, for Kundera, simply painful.

In claiming that Kundera intends to defend against—and

even to satirize—such a critical practice, Straus later argues that his texts support this agenda with his use of "authorial commentary and self-exposure":

> Inscribing himself as witness and critic of his own book, Kundera cannot but remind the reader . . . [that] no reading, *except what the author intends,* is quite legitimate in his terms; and the facts pertinent to that reading must forever be given priority. (emphasis added)

The voice of the intrusive author, according to Straus, is an intentional narrative device employed to make the text indeconstructible, closed to interpretations that stray from the author's intended agenda.

My analysis is largely propelled by an interest in the question of whether Kundera's use of the intrusive author in his novels challenges the critical assumptions of "The Death of the Author" and related essays. Barthes's most direct statements on authorship correspond in broad terms to the three areas relevant in this analysis: (1) the distinction between the author (the scriptor, the writing subject) and the institutional handling of the term, (2) the author as means of foreclosing on the possibility of *play,* and (3) the erotic potential of writing. Looking beyond the obvious provocation, one finds in Barthes's work not so much the corpse of the writer, as the "body" reassembled/disassembled in the text itself, though with no algebraic symmetry or recognizable coherence. This "author" is not to be confused with the institutional use of the term, such as Foucault's Author-Function or any "biographical hero" (see also *The Pleasure of the Text*). The author, as Barthes uses the term, is the subject as "dispersed" in the Text, which is itself the "destroyer of all subject." The "presence" of the "author" is tolerated only insomuch as it promotes *play.*

The questions suggested, if Barthes is to offer a productive means of approaching Kundera's novels, are twofold: Does Kundera actually appear in the guise of direct autobiography? If he does, does the appearance act to solidify some larger meaning antithetical to Barthes's pluralism? Kundera manages to introduce to the text an author-figure far less "dispersed" than the one suggested by Barthes, while at the same time he uses the opportunity to facilitate (if not demand) *play.* In this way, Kundera forces a reconsideration of Barthes's theoretical stance or at least calls into question the mutual exclusivity of the bliss of indeterminacy and the existence of a strong authorial voice.

However, in direct opposition to Straus's idea that Kundera uses the author-figure to make his novels resistant to anything but interpretation firmly located in history, it is much more arguable that these intrusions add a sense of *play* by admitting that characters are not real, questioning motiva-

tions, digressing, telling stories, and so on. Although some stories are historically placed, that fact does not mean that they or the author-figure are immovable or in any way privileged. The clearest aim is not to provide answers but to question, and this view is most consistently reflected in the novels' treatment of characterization and theme. Where Straus concludes it must be "painful" for Milan Kundera to see his work taken out of what she sees as its proper context, the interview reprinted immediately after the text of *The Book of Laughter and Forgetting* (the "Afterword") addresses this kind of reading, locating whatever pain he might experience elsewhere: "The stupidity of the world comes from having an answer for everything. The wisdom of the novel comes from having a question for everything."

In this light, Milan Kundera must be seen as an advocate, not for historical context, but for the kind of interrogation underscored repeatedly by his novels and his polemical statements made in interviews. In particular, the intrusive and inimitable voice of Kundera as author stirs up the text. Take out this intrusive dynamic, and the text is far less radical because it is precisely this "I" that rips away the facade of verisimilitude, that questions the possibility of meaning, and that carries through a recognizable disgust for any system that refuses free play with codes—whether political (Communist or Western), linguistic, or literary. Literature that only provides answers would be as totalitarian as the regime Kundera left behind, and Barthes, too, stresses this capability of writing:

> Writing is the art of asking questions, not of answering or resolving them. Only writing can ask a question, and because writing has this power, it can afford to leave questions in abeyance. . . . When a work is successful, it asks its question with ambiguity and, in that way, becomes poetic.

> *(The Grain)*

It may be that the political events around and after 1968 provide a convenient and concrete historical framework that is meaningful, but to translate Kundera's use of historical reference points as a maneuver of closure is simply a more refined way of saying that a text can be read in one way only.

To some extent, the question of the necessity of looking outside the text for historical context is a moot point. The texts provide such reference points internally. Kundera discusses the problem and his use of history in his preface to *Life Is Elsewhere:*

> Even though the story of Jaromil and his mother takes place in a specific historic period which is portrayed truthfully (without the slightest satiric intent), it was not my aim to describe a period. . . .

In other words: for a novelist, a given historic situation is an *anthropologic laboratory* in which he explores his basic question: *What is human existence?* In the case of this novel, several related questions also presented themselves.... The novel, of course, does not answer any of these questions.

So, one must question the appropriateness of Straus's characterization of Kundera's pain or her own general sense of urgency, her fear that somehow history is going to be airbrushed out of existence as in the falsified photos mentioned in the vignette opening **The Book of Laughter and Forgetting.**

Actually, there is reason to believe that, of all the interesting and viable implications of the intrusive author, an emphasis on historical context—which must occur at the expense of *play*—is neither a sufficient explanation of the author-figure's function in the text nor (for what it's worth) close to the agenda of the Kundera who wrote the novels. Such historical placement of the characters amounts to little more than the equivalent of a minimal backdrop or collection of props to stage a drama, and Kundera concludes that the novel that merely illustrates a historical situation is severely limited. Contrary to Straus's contention that the "text is nothing but an effort to recoup literature from its modern self-enclosure and to tie it as closely as possible to physically experienced history," historical context is "secondary matter" to what Kundera calls the problems of existence that he repeatedly stresses are his only interest.

As one might expect of any writer, Kundera repeatedly resists pigeonholing or what he calls "the termites of reduction," and, in comment after comment, he posits the writer as far outside the field of commitment as Barthes did the writers of the New Novel. Perhaps Kundera is even more provocative:

> If you cannot view the art that comes to you from Prague, Budapest, or Warsaw in any other way than by means of this wretched political code, you murder it, no less brutally than the worst of the Stalinist dogmatists. And you are quite unable to hear its true voice. The importance of this art does not lie in the fact that it pillories this or that political regime but that, on the strength of social and human experience of a kind people here in the West cannot even imagine, it offers a new testimony about mankind.

In numerous theoretical discussions, Kundera speaks of the need to revitalize the novel in what amounts to the direction of noncommitment, arguing that the "voice of the novel" is hard to hear over the temptation to find any or especially a single truth. The result is a plea to indeterminacy:

> A novel does not assert anything; a novel searches and poses questions. I don't know whether my nation will perish and I don't know which of my characters is right. I invent stories, confront one with another, and by this means I ask questions ... The novelist teaches the reader to comprehend the world as a question ... In a world built on sacrosanct certainties the novel is dead. The totalitarian world, whether founded on Marx, Islam, or anything else, is a world of answers rather than questions. There, the novel has no place.

History is important, but only inasmuch as it facilitates insights into self-consciously imagined characters.

Therefore, Kundera's vision of the literary possibilities coincides with Barthes's understanding that the text should enjoy a displacement from social responsibility, *play* instead of commitment, and eventually (ideally) the bliss of complete hedonistic detachment. Kundera's works share the emphasis of text over context and do so unapologetically at the expense of meaning. Kimball's basic observations in his analysis of ambiguity in Kundera's writing are accurate ["The Ambiguities of Milan Kundera," *New Criterion,* Vol.4, No. 5, January, 1986, pp. 5-13]. Though he later accuses the author of "transcendental buffoonery" in his aloofness regarding his writing from any "definite commitment," he correctly highlights the problematic nature of the "terminal paradox" that Kundera embraces: "[Kundera wants] to have it both ways: he wants both the freedom of fiction and the authority of historical fact." Yet the problem begs the question that is fairly resolved when one is reminded that when Kundera talks about the novel in general and his novels in particular, he speaks similarly of his writing not as a "rebus to be decoded" but as a game, sounding all the while unmistakably like one of Barthes's reveries on the pleasure of the text when he says a novel is "a game with invented characters ... [that gives you] the joy of imagination, of narration, the joy provided by a game. That is how I see a novel—as a game."

Kundera's penchant for asking questions instead of answering them, combined with an episodic structure and lack of temporal coherence, assures ellipses and ambiguity; this much is self-evident. The effect of the intrusive author-figure, however, is more complicated. Does this author/ narrator, as one would expect (and Straus demands), work to pull the disparate fragments together? However philosophically difficult the notion of one demonstrable self may be, it must be admitted that the authorial voice is a relatively stable feature of a narrative strategy that constantly changes almost everything else. Yet when that voice digresses or asks broad metaphysical questions, the voice of the author-figure works to prevent prefigured answers to a text of questions:

Why is Tamina on a children's island? Why is that where I imagine her?

I don't know.

Kundera exploits this technique repeatedly to assert his aesthetics of ambiguity. The same chapter/fragment that tells of the death of Tereza's dog is interwoven with essayistic authorial commentary, including a story of Nietzsche's stopping the beating of a horse with a tearful embrace. To some extent, the authorial digressions and intrusions add to a certain thematic unity, but only in that they sometimes share a tangential connection; they do not contribute to an understanding as much as they are inconclusive in comparably similar ways. Lodge agrees in "Milan Kundera and the Idea of the Author in Modern Criticism," when he mentions that "paradoxically, this overt appearance of the author in the text does not make it easier, but harder, to determine what it 'means'" [*Critical Quarterly,* Vol. 26, Nos. 1-2, 1984, pp. 105-21].

Finally, there is in Kundera's work also a decidedly self-conscious effort toward elaborate linguistic *play,* an acknowledgment on the level of content and presentation that language is itself indeterminate. Room for plural interpretation and erotic bliss is cleared away in the unpredictable space between the shifting allegiances of signifier and signified. Just as the questions that the novels pose offer myriad possible answers (or none), there is a kind of unsettling recognition in the language of the texts and their parenthetical clarifications of the arbitrary nature of language. The most obvious display of this modern/postmodern notion is in *The Unbearable Lightness of Being,* especially in the linguistic problems in the relationship of Franz and Sabina.

The unforgettable feature of the time Sabina and Franz share together is the frequency of their inability to understand each other, and that misunderstanding has everything to do with semiotics: "If [people] meet when they are older, like Franz and Sabina, the [musical compositions of their lives] are more or less complete, and every motif, every object, every word means something different to each of them." And elsewhere: "Although they had a clear understanding of the logical meaning of the words they exchanged, they failed to hear the semantic susurrus of the river flowing through them." Kundera generates an ironically lengthy *Short Dictionary of Misunderstood Words* to take up systematically the topic of their drastically mismatched systems of codes. Indeed, the novel goes further to include discussion of images as signs, pointing out that the meaning of a particular sign—the bowler hat in particular—not only means different things to different people, but also different things at different times to the same person:

Each time the same object would give rise to a new

meaning, though all former meanings would resonate (like an echo, like a parade of echoes) together with a new one. Each new experience would resound, each time enriching the harmony.

The same phenomenon is found in *The Book of Laughter and Forgetting,* for example, in the parodic section "The Angels," where two American students are giving an oral report for their favorite teacher on Ionesco's *Rhinoceros.* In their conversation, the two girls stumble on the arbitrary nature of semiotics:

"I'm not so sure I understand what all those people turning into rhinoceroses is supposed to mean," said Gabrielle.

"Think of it as a symbol," Michelle told her.

"True," said Gabrielle, "literature is a system of signs."

"And the rhinoceros is first and foremost a sign," said Michelle.

"Yes, but even if we accept the fact they turn into signs instead of rhinoceroses, how do they choose what signs to turn into?"

"Yes, well, that's a problem," said Michelle sadly. They were on their way back to the dormitory and walked awhile in silence.

It is a problem that is never clarified, and the story of two girls trying to figure out what it all means finally, after repeated interruption, reaches a dramatic conclusion, but even that is inconclusive. The girls give their report wearing cardboard rhino horns, but, the author-figure volunteers, it is as embarrassing as if a man had stood up in front of the class and shown off his amputated arm. Still, the girls accept the laughter of their teacher as a sign of encouragement. Next, a girl in the class who hates the two Americans calmly walks to the front of the class and kicks them one at a time, then returns to her seat. The girls read *her* sign clearly enough (*you are making fools of yourself,* and *I hate you*), but the teacher, assuming the kick is a planned part of the presentation, laughs all the more. A surrealist finale of semiotic confusion builds and concludes the story. The kick is the crux of the scene. It promptly recalls the girls' realization that language is no longer working (the class missed their point that the play was comic and instead thought the girls were embarrassingly ludicrous). Without the kick, the miscommunication is ironic, but with it the irony is amplified to a tragic comedy on the failure of language.

Always there is an inherent contradiction in these kinds of

critical analyses that take pages upon pages to argue that a novel does not mean anything. So, if only to validate the critical act that Straus so powerfully denies, it is tempting to qualify somewhat—even though Barthes would see no need to justify the text that creates bliss. If Kundera calls into question the ability of his texts to reflect any single truth, interpretation, or historical/political context, many less-Epicurean readers will start to wonder: (1) If the novelist is not only "nobody's spokesman," but—according to Kundera— "not even the spokesman for his own ideas," why should we bother to read the author's books? (2) Is such a maneuver an attempt to shrug off responsibility for what the novel might seem to mean or promote, such as the over-worn and even offensive sexual stereotypes that Kundera's novels seem to perpetuate?

The texts, though fragmented and drastically nonlinear, are hardly complete anarchy. So when the author-figure speaks in **The Book of Laughter and Forgetting** of an equilibrium of power between "too much uncontested meaning on earth" and the world if it "loses all its meaning," an accurate schematic of the tensions of Kundera's writing might be drawn. An analysis of the sexual politics of his work can function both as an attempt to justify reading novels that question the ability to communicate in a systematically productive way and as an attempt to suggest that his merciless contesting of meaning works to overturn other points where the texts may offer more-or-less misogynist representations.

Initially, however, one way to understand more exactly the way in which Barthes's aesthetics of bliss lives within this apparent contradiction is to look at the traditional approach to literary aesthetics, such as that described in Ames's *Aesthetics of the Novel* (1928), where a distinction is drawn between the sensuality of the plastic arts and the primarily social value of literature: "If the test of sensuous art is in its effect upon the physical self, the test of literature must be in its effect upon the social self." Consequently a "beautiful book" is one that evokes a deep social response, which "ministers better to the modern self than any art"; such a book suggests "harmonies unheard." Ames suggests that modern art employs sensuality in language, but in the Machiavellian style of Shaw or Brecht, in order to lure the reader/audience into becoming receptive to the social message. Consequently, "the weakness of much modern art lies in its lack of purpose beyond giving a sensuous impression, which by itself cannot possibly absorb a social being."

Barthes and Kundera present an opposite aesthetic understanding that savors the fact that a text is beyond any such social responsibility. Bliss thrives on contradiction, including the admitted cohabitation within the text of both the revolutionary and the asocial. In fact, for Barthes, this edge defines the "site of bliss" itself. When Kimball claims that Kundera "wants it both ways," he focuses on the novels'

ambiguity, identifying an erotic surface blasphemously inscribed with distractions and abrasions—what Barthes calls the seam where meaning is lost and everything clashes. This fault line in Kundera's novels is underscored by the intrusive author, who repeatedly strips away false simplicity to reveal not a smooth, codified continuity but a clash of codes and cliché much in the spirit of Sabina's maxim: "On the surface, an intelligible lie; underneath, the unintelligible truth."

Literal eroticism (here in the physical sense) is central to Kundera's novels. In part, the unrestrained sexual honesty is responsible for his success, but it also creates problems when the texts seem guilty of propagating sexist stereotypes as readers' sensitivity to matters of gender continues to improve. However, a reading of the novels, combined with an understanding of the kind of *play* elaborated upon here, suggests that the handling of gender roles and sexual stereotypes in the novels can arguably work to up-end sexist foundations—a specific example of *play* at work, inverting instead of affirming codes and stereotypes. Just as his novels resist the dissident stereotype in their refusal to accept the good guy/bad guy (Western/Communist) hierarchy that many readers never move beyond, the seeming weak woman/strong man (Tereza/Tomas, Marketa/Karel) misogynist surface of the texts is more likely just that, a surface smooth only from a distance.

With its moment of dislocation and hedonistic incoherence, the sexual act is, in Kundera's novels, a crucial point for precisely the reasons Barthes draws on this metaphor for his articulation of bliss. In an ironic gesture of conjugation, all semiotic systems fall apart in dislocating sexual bliss, leaving contradictions both revealed and reveled in. Appropriately, Kundera describes his erotic scenes as generating an "extremely sharp light which suddenly reveals the essence of characters" and goes on to cite the example of Tamina's making love to Hugo while she thinks about "lost vacations with her dead husband." He repeats the theme in **The Unbearable Lightness of Being** when Tereza makes loveless love to the engineer; here, too, there is no joining or communication beyond the physical coupling, and this event is simply a representation of what happens throughout the novels on levels more subtle than this obvious example of two people making love for not only different but contradictory reasons. Kundera, therefore, resists the use of stereotypes, as discussed by Barthes in *The Pleasure of the Text,* where he recognizes "the bliss repressed beneath the stereotype."

It stands to reason that if, as earlier discussed in relation to the *Short Dictionary of Misunderstood Words,* language fails, the cultural and sexual codes and stereotypes constructed from/in language must fail, too. A naive reading of a Kundera text "as though it were natural" (Barthes's definition of the stereotype) abounds with the type of sexual cliché exemplified by Kael's review of the film:

> But the young Binoche [Tereza] gives the role a sweet gaucheness and then a red-cheeked desperation.... She verges on peasant-madonna darlingness, but that's what the conception requires [*New Yorker*, February 8, 1988, pp. 67-70].

Allowing the termites of reduction to go to work will produce a weak character in Tereza and a Don Juan in Tomas, but clearly beneath the surface of such a reading lies the kind of complex contradiction and "terminal paradox" that Edmund White enjoys when he writes that "Kundera's heroes may be Don Juans, but they are shy, apologetic ones; his women are intensely physical beings, but they are also as quirkily intelligent and stubbornly independent as his men." Following the social script, Tereza also sees herself as weak and Tomas strong, but her epiphany, pages before the end of the novel, betrays the inadequacy of the signifiers "weak" and "strong" to explain the complexity of the apparently simple roles. And it is the intrusive author again who brings the reader to examine the issue directly:

> We all have a tendency to consider strength the culprit and weakness the innocent victim. But now Tereza realized that in her case the opposite was true! Even her dreams, as if aware of the single weakness in a man otherwise strong, made a display of her suffering to him, thereby forcing him to retreat. Her weakness was aggressive and kept forcing him to capitulate until eventually he lost his strength and was transformed into the rabbit in her arms.

Furthermore, weakness in the texts is hardly gender specific. It is, after all, Sabina who is the epitome of "lightness," with her chronology of betrayals. In Franz is found the inversion of the stereotype suggested by Tereza. Defining love as the expectation of rejection and the renunciation of strength, Franz ultimately is abandoned by both mistress (Sabina) and wife:

> [For Franz, love] meant a longing to put himself at the mercy of his partner. He who gives himself up like a prisoner of war must give up his weapons as well. And deprived in advance of defense against a possible blow, he cannot help wondering when the blow will fall. That is why I can say that for Franz, love meant the constant expectation of a blow.

Straus claims that Kundera wishes to "insure that his own discourse will not be deconstructed or its meaning erased." Although the assertion may be primarily motivated by a desire to refute deconstruction (for whatever reason), the intrusive author presents codes and roles in what amount to an *already-deconstructed* form.

This play, especially in matters as grave as gender-based oppression and exploitation, is necessarily not always *playful* in a humorous sense. However, that which results from the breakdown of semiotic systems is central to the comic/ironic perspective of all Kundera's works as far back as his first collection of short stories tellingly titled ***Laughable Loves,*** where a cynical comic vision hinges on the stereotype or the cliché. As Barthes is interested in innocent language being twisted out of proportion and into bliss, Kundera's comedy resides in the condition of characters who live codes and gender roles as if they were Truth ("as if they were natural"). His short story **"The Hitchhiking Game"** is an ideal example in the way it begins with a much-abused erotic cliché (picking up the pretty hitchhiker) but ends with a tragic misunderstanding. They are actually lovers on vacation playing a role-change game during a long drive, the girl pretending to be a promiscuous hitchhiker when she is really "old-fashioned." The power of codes is, in these texts, most forcefully revealed when the codes are split open by a realization as dramatic as the already-mentioned kick.

It is fair to say that in writing that is interested in depicting sexuality in an honest way, clichés, restrictive gender roles, and stereotypes that set one's teeth on edge will most likely be included among the props. But if Kundera doesn't slip from them by openly divulging their contradictions, it might be in part a result of the infestation of archaic codes in language, for they are shown consistently to be inverted and subverted just below the surface of the texts themselves.

One final point at which the erotic textual qualities come in contact with the actual erotic themes of the novels is in the repeated associations with the terms "weight" and "lightness." It is possible to interpret these two opposites (among, of course, the infinite possibilities) as alluding to the "weight" of uncontested meaning and eternal return and the "lightness" of a world or a text without meaning. Thus, it is possible to equate Tomas's infidelity and numerous erotic friendships as a rejection of the temptation to believe in a single interpretation of truth. Furthermore, the vacillation of Tomas between lightness and weight could simply represent an extension of humanity's attempt to reach an equilibrium between these diametrically opposed but equally unbearable epistemological attitudes. In contrast to the lightness of the signifier's "instant, not consistent, relationships," Barthes, too, associates weight with stabilized meaning. When Kimball, then, notices that if Kundera's work is a game it is deprived of "authority and weight," it is easy to see that this fact, along with his choice of metaphors, may be exactly what Kundera (not to mention Barthes) would be happy to hear.

Surely it should not be assumed that to grant the obvious, that the author-figure in these texts is a more dynamic, self-acknowledged "author," is somehow to elevate the author to status beyond that of what Barthes calls the "paper character," especially when that figure repeatedly reasserts a textual *play*ground on various levels (linguistic play and play with the semiotic structures that form the foundations of culture). What Kundera calls the joy of a game and Barthes calls bliss is that which flies in the face of meaning and the expectation of meaning—that which condemns mere consumption and promotes nothing but its own indeterminacy.

In a way, the figure of the author substitutes for traditional historical context, but this author-figure in the texts does not "bring things together." He is not functioning in a way as to reinstitute "man-and-his-work criticism" or to resurrect Herder's view of reading as "divination into the soul of the creator." True, much apparently autobiographical matter is presented, but these events are treated, as are the historical ones, as points for questions. At every turn, like the narrator in *Tristram Shandy,* the author-figure digresses, interrupts, tells stories, meditates, extrapolates, and interpolates—encouraging the same relationship with his text as that of a reader of a text of bliss: "What I enjoy in a narrative is not directly its content or even its structure, but rather the abrasions I impose upon the fine surface: I read on, I skip, I look up, I dip in again." And if the resulting questions, contradictions, and lack of clear context deprive the reader of recognizable reference points, this also serves to discourage thoughtless consumption. The resulting ambiguity and lack of commitment are not, after all, what consumers expect.

If, however, the analogy is valid and the author-figure in the text acts as a kind of preacher of indeterminacy, it should be mentioned that the texts more correctly preach against the imposition of meaning rather than the entire possibility that some stabilization of meaning might take place. They are not as much nihilist as they are deferring to the reader, paralleling the changing of the guard that concludes "The Death of the Author." It is not surprising that this kind of move would anger those with very specific interpretive agendas—like Podhoretz who scolds Kundera's for his political aloofness, which he maintains is nothing short of "cooperating with your own kidnappers." In fact, by winding the reader through a vertiginous array of perspectives and questions, the urgency to find an answer is itself lost, as is the necessity to divide existence into binary oppositions. Finally, Barthes would undoubtedly see this very representative maneuver as the kind of "violence that enables [the text] to *exceed* the laws that a society, an ideology, a philosophy establish for themselves in order to agree among themselves in a fine surge of historical intelligibility. This excess is called: writing."

Postscript: Kundera's *Immortality*

This analysis of *play,* intrusive authorship, and the significance of history in Kundera's fiction has focused considerably on **The Book of Laughter and Forgetting** and **The Unbearable Lightness of Being,** but Kundera's novels develop contrapuntal patterns and motifs both within and between his particular texts. For example, one could hardly manage a comprehensive analysis of history without discussing **The Joke** at length, where, "the joke" *is* History. Similarly, questions about Kundera's intrusive stance in his fiction would need to look to his latest effort, **Immortality.** Here, the intrusive author is not only named "Milan Kundera" but compares characters in this book to characters in earlier books and lends a copy of **Life Is Elsewhere** to another character (who never reads it). **Immortality** is also Kundera's most extended attempt to discuss directly the significance of the author in interpretation. In particular, the novel strongly argues against the idea that interpretation should be constrained by historical or biographical contexts.

Hemingway laments to Goethe how "instead of reading my books, they're writing books about me," with specific disgust aimed at the "army of university professors all over America . . . busy classifying, analyzing, and shoveling everything into articles and books." And Goethe answers by retelling his nightmare of theater fans that come to see a puppet show of his *Faust:*

> I turned around and I was aghast: I expected them out front, and instead they were at the back of the stage, gazing at me with wide-open, inquisitive eyes. As soon as my glance met theirs, they began to applaud. And I realized that my *Faust* didn't interest them all and that the show they wished to see was not the puppets I was leading around the stage, but me myself! Not *Faust,* but Goethe. . . . I realized that I would never get rid of them, never, never, never.

As if finally to underscore his assertion that actual authors who produce texts should not be confused with whatever/whoever appears in those texts, Goethe aggressively argues the point even further than Hemingway:

> "Forget for a moment that you're an American and exercise your brain: he who doesn't exist cannot be present. Is that so complicated? The instant I died I vanished from everywhere, totally. I even vanished from my books. Those books exist in the world without me. Nobody will ever find me in them. . . . Don't make a fool of yourself, Ernest," said Goethe. "You know perfectly well that at this moment we are but the frivolous fantasy of a novelist who lets us say things we would probably never say on our own."

If the surreal conversation of two dead, distant authors is not concrete enough to make clear what is "painful" in the eyes of "Milan Kundera," Paul's long, drunken speech near the end of the novel is an exaggerated characterization of biographical reading:

> We started to talk about all sorts of things. Avenarius referred a few more times to my novels, which he had not read, and so provoked Paul to make a remark whose rudeness astonished me: "I don't read novels. Memoirs are much more amusing and instructive for me. Or biographies. Recently I've been reading books about Salinger, Rodin, and the loves of Franz Kafka. And a marvelous biography of Hemingway. What a fraud. What a liar. What a megalomaniac." Paul laughed happily. "What an impotent. What a sadist. What a macho. What an erotomaniac. What a misogynist."

Immortality, then, argues forcefully both against privileging contextual interpretation and for a playful irresponsibility in the relationship between the author and the authored text. It is not historical context itself that runs contrary to the kind of interpretation I think Kundera's texts invite, but interpretation that exclusively privileges the prop or backdrop at the expense of the questions that resonate beyond both history and authorship.

Tom Wilhelmus (review date Spring 1993)

SOURCE: "Time and Distance," in *Hudson Review,* Vol. XLVI, No. 1, Spring, 1993, pp. 247-55.

[*In the following excerpt, Wilhelmus evaluates "the new 'definitive' version" of* The Joke *in relation to contemporary history.*]

In *Thus Spoke Zarathustra,* the animals say to Nietzsche's philosopher-mystic:

> "Look, we know what you teach: that all things return forever, and we along with them, and that we have already been here an infinite number of times, and all things along with us."

According to Milan Kundera, this "mad myth" is Nietzsche's means of forcing us to contemplate the horror as well as the beauty and sublimity of life's events in a way which prevents our overlooking them because they are so fleeting. Without some such concept—that an event may return again and again to haunt us—"We would need take no more note of it than of a war between two African kingdoms in the fourteenth century, a war that altered nothing in the destiny of the world, even if a hundred thousand blacks perished in excruciating torment" (*The Unbearable Lightness of Being*). Repetition, recurrence, the myth of eternal return show the weight of history and create the awareness that life has significance and depth. In some fashion, this fact is illustrated in each of the works which follow. Each is concerned with time, and each creates perspective and distance. Each also deals with recurrence, without which time itself is only duration.

. . . . .

[When] it originally came out—in Czechoslovakia in 1965—the publication of Kundera's *The Joke,* must have seemed like a miracle, though with the crackdown following the Prague Spring three years later, it was one of the first works suppressed and its author banned. In the space remaining, I cannot treat the details that have made the new "definitive" version of *The Joke* necessary. But since the recent events in Eastern Europe and the Soviet Union, it may be time to re-read the novel anyway, for in the interim, history has played an even greater joke on Communism itself, and Kundera's reflections may provide a hint as to why it occurred.

The novel begins as its principal character Ludvik stands at a crossroads in a small Moravian village where he grew up on the day before a festival celebrating the traditional Ride of the Kings, a folk ritual from the remote past. Ludvik, however, has come home primarily to carry out a private act of revenge against someone who had played an important role in the most significant event of his life—his expulsion from the university and from the Party for playing a stupid, adolescent joke. The joke had consisted of sending a postcard with some anti-Party slogans on it to a girl he was courting, and Ludvik means to cuckold the party official who had an opportunity to prevent Ludvik's expulsion but who had engineered it instead. In the town he also sees people from his youth whom he had left when as a student he went to Prague.

Actually, three types of history are present in Ludvik's situation: personal, political, and Moravian. The latter includes the folk traditions inherent in the Ride of the Kings as well as comments about folk music and Christianity later in the novel. Each type of history represents a form of recurrence that Ludvik would rather be without. The desire to lay the blame for all his failures on a single absurd event in the past, always before his eyes, has led him to pursue a needless act of revenge. Communism, "official history," has meant that once out of the Party he has no place in history. And the nostalgic belief in "origins" seems like mindless obedience to a set of rituals repeated aimlessly from the past. During a moment of revelation late in the novel, Ludvik says:

> Yes, suddenly I saw it clearly: most people deceive

themselves with a pair of faiths: they believe in *eternal memory* (of people, things, deeds, nations) and in *redressibility* (of deeds, mistakes, sins, wrongs). . . . [Whereas] In reality the opposite is true: everything will be forgotten and nothing will be redressed.

And, in fact, Ludvik's revenge fails, even at the moment of his success. No longer a serious threat, Communism too becomes irrelevant to his personal life. And the Ride of the Kings will always contain a message which "will never be decoded, not only because there is no key to it, but also because people have no patience to listen."

Yet as in most of his novels since *The Joke* this vision of the quixotic unreliability of history is as liberating as it is a source of despair. Long before the current breakup of the Eastern bloc, the Hungarian Gyorgy Konrad's classic *Anti-Politics* argued that Russian-style, "official" Communism would increasingly become irrelevant because people would find the means to create spontaneous unofficial social, political, and economic organizations within the official state. And just as a country cannot do without some kind of organization it cannot eliminate history either.

History, recurrence, creates weight and depth and perspective. Painful as such knowledge may be, it provides us with identity and community, two things we will always need. Nonetheless, like Ludvik, we might prefer a version of history which is more humane, essentially private, contingent, semi-official, made up on the run. Perhaps that is what Eastern Europe is learning now, though it is a view of things which, like Nietzsche's myth of eternal return, may essentially be mad.

Vicki Adams (essay date 1993)

SOURCE: "Milan Kundera: The Search for Self in a Post-Modern World," in *Imagination, Emblems and Expressions: Essays on Latin American, Caribbean, and Continental Culture and Identity,* edited by Helen Ryan-Ranson, Bowling Green State University Popular Press, 1993, pp. 233-46.

[*In the following essay, Adams highlights the way Kundera's folk heritage informs his concept of identity in both his theoretical writings and his fiction, suggesting reasons for his international appeal.*]

Carlos Fuentes has said that the most urgent poles of contemporary narrative are found in Latin America and in Central Europe, and the modern reader automatically thinks of Gabriel García Márquez and Milan Kundera. This paper will look at one of these well-known authors, Milan Kundera, in terms of the Slavic soul representing its geographic stand-

ing between East (the land of orthodoxy or ideology), and West (the land of nihilism). Kundera is interesting in this connection because he resists either camp: what he calls the angelic laughter of certainty, of truth, of ideology, and the demonic laughter of infinite relativism, cynicism, and nihilism we have heard so much about in Western philosophy.

Milan Kundera, the Czech writer who has been living in Paris for more than twenty years, and writing for a foreign audience because his books were banned in his own land, does lean toward the abyss (nihilism), does favor what R. B. Gill has called "epicurean accommodation," does opt for the novel of relative truths, but somehow has managed to keep a foothold on the cliff overhanging the modern abyss of nothingness. His particular foothold seems to be a rediscovery of his folk culture, as the comforts found in his early Moravian roots offer him touchstones of identity perhaps not available to other contemporary writers. His philosophical novels offer a compromise between memory and forgetting, between irony and commitment. What might be so fetching about this writer is that, instead of arriving at the modern conclusion that life has less and less meaning in a post-Derridian world, he celebrates those very weaknesses that make us human (angst, confusion, hopelessness, uncertainty, and especially, man's simplicity) as synonymous with beauty. Thus, he turns the modern philosophical world topsy-turvy, because aesthetics has a way of turning to ethics in his post modern fiction . . . his post-structuralist worldview emphasizes the beauty of the uncertainty. Unlike other modern spokesmen of a bleak and dreary reality, his acceptance of relative truths seems to be a manifestation of a wry Kunderian accommodation to man's powerlessness in post-Stalinist Central Europe.

The goal of this paper is to underscore the role of Kundera's folk heritage in the formation of his world view in his search for self and, in doing that, to consider the source of his international appeal. The investigation will first of all consider Kundera as firmly in the post-modernist camp and then look at some of Kundera's own theoretical statements on fiction and the novel (including revelatory excerpts from six of his novels). Attempting to show how his chosen form of expression—the novel—is the only one capable of expressing his concept of identity in a post-modern world, a transition will then be made from the seemingly value-free post-modern viewpoint to Kundera's other side—where his individual characters are called upon to make choices, and where the destinies of "Der Volk" matter intensely. The transition will use some very recent ideas of Derrida and Lyotard to pose the obvious question: How can a novelist, clearly so post-modern in his techniques and philosophical thrust, be at the same time a heralder of the beauty in a life chock full of irony and chaos?

Jacques Derrida offers a justification for deconstructionist thought in our world that Kundera will echo in both his novels and his own critical writings. If the truth of reason is really our own experience of it, it is relative anyway. So, we need new kinds of "knowledge" to deal with this relative world, new unheard of thoughts, "qui se cherchent à travers la memoire des vieux signes" [sought from the memories of old signs]. This is precisely what Kundera will discover in his folk culture—memories of old signs—which will offer the possibility of an identity, a spiritual or psychological homeland waiting to be repossessed by him.

In terms of history (and Kundera is mainly concerned with man's relationship to the past, to history), his theory was already introduced by Foucault's deconstructionist views that it is just possible that history is made up of interpretation, not fact; that any sign/event is already an interpretation of another sign/event. The goal of history has always been the triumph of meaning, annihilation of the negative, the presence of a truth; but, when this happens, according to the deconstructionists, there is nothing left to do, nothing more to learn. Kundera's view of history has more to do with disorder than triumph of meaning. While his sentimental side yearns for a safe, unchanging, constantly returning, idyllic past, his skepticism tells us that Foucault's view was right: alternative accounts are possible when authorities in Czechoslovakia tear down the old heroic monuments, give the streets new Russian names, and fabricate in the schools a tidy and sentimental account of Czech history. Kundera writes his fiction to awaken doubts or skepticism as an alternative. He insists that the novel is the form to express this doubt, or contradiction. The novel teaches us to comprehend other peoples' truths and the limitations of our own truth, so the novel should be deeply non-ideological: "it is as essential to our insanely ideological world as is bread" ["Interview," *Le Monde,* Vol. 23, January, 1976]. In another article, **"Man Thinks, God Laughs,"** he says that the novel's wisdom is different from that of philosophy—it is born of the spirit of humor. The novel contradicts ideological certitudes: "Like Penelope, it undoes each night the tapestry that . . . philosophy and learned men wove the day before." Life is seen rationally, as a:

> glowing trajectory of causes and effects, failures, and successes, and man, setting his impatient gaze on the causal chain of his actions, accelerates further his mad race toward death.

Kundera sees human existence (its beauty) located "where the bridge between a cause and an effect is ruptured." At this juncture, there is liberty, digression, the incalculable, a lack of reason, the opposite of eighteenth-century rationalism and Liebniz. So the art born of God's laughter—the novel—is the "art that has managed to create the . . . imaginative realm where no one is the possessor of the truth, and there everyone has the right to be understood." Clearly,

Foucault's view of history as interpretation, or as "alternative accounts" is manifested in this 1985 essay by Kundera [*New York Review of Books,* June 13, 1985; reprinted in *The Art of the Novel*].

In Kundera's own fiction, one strongly senses a deconstructionist view of the modern world and an example of Kundera's attempt to deal with the concept of identity in this deconstructed world of his novels. In his 1973 ***Life Is Elsewhere,*** the theme is that the poetic viewpoint should not dominate one's life because it is incapable of irony; its only goal is beauty. Because lyricism is never ironic, it risks being totalitarian. In this novel, Jaromil, the young poet, cannot draw human faces, giving the reader a metaphor for an ideology—where only causes, and not individuals, exist, where nuance and irony are absent. At one point the narrator says of Jaromil:

> The raw simplicity of the statement made him happy because it placed him in the ranks of those direct and simple men who laughed at nuances and whose wisdom lies in their understanding of the ridiculously simple essentials of life.

Speaking later in the novel of the "adult world" of relativity, Kundera compares it with poetic form:

> In rhyme and rhythm reside a certain magical power. An amorphous world becomes at once orderly, lucid and clear, and beautiful when squeezed into regular meters. Death is chaotic, but if it is in rhyme, it is orderly.

He goes on later to say: "The adult world knows perfectly well that the absolute is an illusion, that nothing human is either great or eternal."

In ***Laughable Loves*** (1974) Kundera portrays love as a meaningless game, but one area of life where we are convinced we have some control, one area (along with religion) where we try to find our essence, our peculiar identity. Man has little control over most spheres of life, but in love, there is a sense of relative freedom, and that being so, women became, for one of his characters, the "one legitimate criterion of his life's destiny." Women became, for the protagonist, a way of choosing his identity in a society where he was, in every other way, powerless to express himself. Later in the same story, however, the same character complains:

> All at once I understood that it had only been my illusion that we ourselves saddle events, and are able to control their course. The truth is that they aren't our stories at all, that they are foisted upon us from somewhere outside, that we are not to blame for the queer path they follow.

The interesting, diverse group of characters in *The Fare-well Party* (1976) try to control their destinies in a fertility clinic where sex is used to trick destiny. They gather to say good-bye to a comrade who has gotten permission to emigrate, and the themes are similar to those in his other novels. One character says: "We really had no choices," after he had carried with him what he thought was a suicide pill for years, feeling that at least in the end, if things turned bad, he could decide his own life or death. The doctor who gave him the pill explains: ". . . the fake pill allowed him to turn his life into a noble myth," the myth of some control over his destiny. Kundera has also created characters in his novels who equate order with identity, who need to have the authorities establish their identities. An outspoken, and very ideological nurse at the clinic dislikes the emigré's face because it looks "ironic" to her, and she hates irony. All irony was, for her, "like an armed watchman guarding the portal to her future, disdainfully refusing her admittance." Admittance to what? To Kundera's adulthood of irony, or uncertainty, to real life? Kundera asks, "What motivates people to totalitarianism? The longing for order, the desire to turn the human world into an inorganic one?" This kind of Kunderian character needs her identity established for her; she fears that in freedom, in the chaos of uncertainty, she will not know who she is. For Kundera, real life is disorder, chaos, while a willfully imposed order is akin to death.

Kundera's two most successful novels are *The Book of Laughter and Forgetting,* published in 1978, and *The Unbearable Lightness of Being,* published in 1984. Both texts are concerned with man's relationship to history and both texts resist a single reading. Both texts need to be considered in any discussion of problems of identity because Kundera himself has equated the absurd chaos in historical events with an individual's life. The two novels keep insisting that understanding the absurdity, the lack of a rational structure in historical events is just one more way to understand his concept of individual identity. Both are inaccessible to our human understanding. The structuralists' view of history is just as mistaken as the poetic view of individual identity: rational cause and effect in history is just as illusory as is the absolute (he would say, childish) concept of apprehending one's individual identity, of knowing who we really are. Control over history and individual identity is a fiction. Both novels place their protagonists in a world where the border is warped between reality and art, or between history and the fantastic, between memory and forgetting. *The Book of Laughter and Forgetting* is called by David Lodge, "a masterpiece of post-modernist fiction." The novel offers several separate stories, some having the same characters which flow (or, as Lodge puts it, "leak") into each other. Themes, motifs and author's comments are repeated. It is a novel in the form of variations, which is not so much manipulation of chronology or point of view as it is a disruption between author and narrator. Milan Kundera keeps

leaping over his narrator to appear overtly in the stories. It is in *Laughter and Forgetting* that Kundera moves back and forth from the historical to the fantastic, where previously introduced motifs and fantastic events are brought together with real facts. (We think of Marquez's magical realism here, and the broader connection between Central Europe and Latin American literature in our era.) As Lodge has said: "The outrages of modern history in those regimes are of such a scale that only the 'overt lie' of the fantastic and the grotesque can represent them."

It is in both *The Book of Laughter and Forgetting* and *The Unbearable Lightness of Being* that Kundera clearly portrays history as a narrated story, and shows the fabrication of what is called the truth, or shows history as an interpretation. In the more recent novel, Kundera's most philosophical novel to date, he considers such questions as individual responsibility, Nietzsche's 'eternal return,' and chance and coincidence in life. Again, familiar motifs are here: erotic trickery in order to outwit fate, self deception, the limits of human lucidity, and the games of history. The now-familiar technique of mixing history and the fantastic is rampant in this story. The characters have a goal of making decisions, but, since Kundera rejects Nietzsche's eternal return, his characters cannot learn from repeated events, and thus, decisions or actions cannot weigh heavily on them. We are, like his characters, relieved of that responsibility of learning from history. Robert interprets Kundera's sense of "lightness of being" in this way: "If reality were like clockwork, history would have been infinitely organized. Any accident would have affected the whole: there would have to be individual responsibility in history." If individuals are as light and meaningless as historical events, if individuals have no responsibility for these events (as Kundera's narrator suspects in this novel) then how can we determine who we are, where we fit into the scheme of society's fate, its progress, its demise? Kundera jumps into his novel to tell us that history is as light as an individual's life. In fact, as early as 1958, Kundera would write [in "Quelque part la derriere," *Le debat,* Vol 8, January, 1981, pp. 50-63]:

> . . . les mécanismes psychologiques qui fonctionnent dans les grands événements historiques (apparemment incroyables et inhumains) sont les mêmes qui régissent les situations intimes (tout à fait banales et humaines.).

> [. . . the psychological mechanisms which function in the grand (and apparently inhuman and unbelievable) historic events are the same which rule intimate (and completely banal and human) situations.].

Whether readers understand the novel's quartet of Tereza, Tomas, Sabina and Franz as representing weightiness or lightness, (or probably, as structures or variations on a theme), it is clear that Kundera's fictional mode is now more philosophical than political. He uses Nietzsche as an introduction to Tomas's philosophical quandary between weightiness and lightness, and the reader is led through the philosophical maze of questions concerning individual identity in this world either devoid of individual responsibility or filled to overflowing with personal responsibility. Tomas keeps fluctuating between the negation of both social and personal responsibility, and accepting the burden of Teresa's ponderous love, his country's shame, and his medical work (where he, as a surgeon, claims to be able to find another's identity with the act of cutting open another's body). Tomas finally chooses the responsibility of another's life (weightiness), marries Teresa and moves to a farm commune, and thus has his identity given to him by his circumstances. By Kundera's ironic slight of hand, however, Tomas has also managed to choose lightness of being: he has moved from city to simple country life; he has given up a very controlled medical profession (the weightiness of his beloved work); and, he is now free and away from authorities, living a simpler, rather idyllic life of limited responsibility, freer to define who he is. Kundera has ended his novel ironically; the reader may choose the philosophical stance he prefers as he finishes the novel. Has the protagonist found an identity, or given up the search?

After having looked at Kundera's oeuvre in terms of his being solidly based in the post-modern intellectual camp, it would be beneficial to digress briefly for the purpose of coming at a conclusion from another angle. The original question of this investigation was: How does Milan Kundera, who is solidly post-modern in his theoretical stance and in his fiction, who espouses a modernist (some say, nihilistic or anti-humanist) credo of lack of certainties in life, lack of high tragedy in human events, how does this very modern writer manage to convey the bittersweet beauty inherent in the sometimes absurd, often meaningless lives in his books? How does he successfully shun, as R. C. Porter claims he does, both the literature of incoherence and the literature of absolute ideas? The following brief digression is meant to put his seemingly janus-faced contribution into an historical context.

First of all, intellectuals from Central Europe have always been engaged, have always had an ethical motivation for their theoretical output. The charges of an "arid formalism or political escapism" which members of literature departments level against post-modern theoreticians are just not applicable to Slavic writers. "In the Slavic world, structuralism is seen not as the cerebral play of a few armchair theoreticians, but as a clear-cut political stance. . . ." For Kundera, whose nostalgia yearns for the Bohemia of pre-history, who sees his whole oeuvre [in "Un occident kidnappé," *Le debat,* Vol. 27, November, 1983, pp. 3-22], "comme une longue méditation sur le fin possible de l'humanité

européene" [as a long meditation on the possible end of European civilization], literary theory must be attached to the ethical; and, in fact, the importance of this art (modern literature from Prague, Budapest or Warsaw) does not lie in the fact that it criticizes this or that political regime, but "that it offers new testimony about mankind in a social or political setting which people here in the West cannot even imagine" [Kundera, "Comedy Is Everywhere," *Index on Censorship,* Vol. 6, November/December, 1977].

Secondly, even Jacques Derrida admits to an ethical, even political thrust of modern literary theory when he writes in *Ecriture et la différence* that the only way to do battle with Western metaphysical absolutism is through stratagem or strategy. Sounding particularly political, he suggests playing a "double game" or double agent, "serving two sides" or feigning obedience to a system of rule while simultaneously trying to undermine its rule by posing unsolvable problems. He continues: "The question here is to pretend to speak the master's language in order to kill him." This sounds like the strategy of any minority, and defeated group (i.e., Kundera's citizens in post-1969 occupied Czechoslovakia). The key to keeping one's identity intact is that "arriére pensée," a mental reservation, held back so that one does not buy into the ideology completely. Kundera calls it a moment of pause before we give an arbitrary significance to a word. So, Derrida concludes, modern theories need not be so alienated from ethical concerns; they can be, on the contrary, "active interventions." An artist need not be enclosed in some "prison house of language," but rather engaged in very political, ethical pursuits. Milan Kundera elegantly makes that bridge or crossover from aesthetics to ethics, and his motivation is clear in this borrowed quote from a 1983 article: "Only in opposing history can you oppose today's history." By questioning an individual's responsibility in historical events, the individual can better define his responsibility and his essence in contemporary events.

Francois Lyotard, author of *The Post-Modern Condition* and several other texts considering that state of contemporary knowledge, has said that post-modern knowledge refines our sensitivity to differences and reinforces our ability to tolerate the incommensurable. Milan Kundera's work is a product of this post-scientific era, an era, according to Lyotard, in which narrative knowledge will be more valuable to us than scientific knowledge. Since, according to most post-modern theorists, language is no longer a system of signs, but "tricks or games," or, to quote Jameson's forward to this text, "a conflictual relationship between tricksters," Kundera's themes of linguistic and historical trickery of sleight of hand are definitely post-modern. But also, Kundera shares with these new theorists the goal of generating new ideas, new kinds of knowledge, and ultimately, a new way of looking at man. Kundera's art offers a way of seeking one's identity in this post-modern world of extremes. He suggests, in his novels, another alternative—beyond those of nihilism or absolute truth.

Each age has its dominant way of the sign, and the things they signify, says Foucault in *The Archeology of Knowledge.* Lyotard, in *The Post-Modern Condition,* claims that there are scientific periods of history, but now, there is a revival of the narrative view of truth. He insists that scientific knowledge is based on narrative truth anyway, that theories are just disguised narratives, that philosophy too was just a seductive tale. He gives as examples Plato's "Myth of the Cave," a non-scientific narrative used to inaugurate science, or Descartes resorting to what he calls the "story of the mind" in his *Discourses* or even Aristotle suggesting that scientific knowledge is composed only of arguments (i.e., dialectics). For Lyotard, narrative is not just a new field of research, but a mode of thinking, fully as legitimate as that of abstract logic.

Another urgent level of Lyotard's text proposes that the narrative must generate the illusion of an imaginary resolution of real contradictions. It is on this level that a real correspondence between Kundera and Lyotard can be made: using as his backdrop real contradictions, (social, political and historical), Kundera creates illusions (a fiction) of imaginary resolutions, or he emphasizes the imaginary aspects of his resolutions. That, then, is another function of mixing the fantastic with the real in these novels. The very idea of "idyll" on which Kundera relies so often, is his "illusion of a resolution." Carlos Fuentes calls Kundera's notion of idyll, "a Communist offering to forget the past, a false remembering." His characters are desperately looking back (into prehistory?), through the memory of "old signs" to find themselves. It is this concept of idyll that will be exploited to suggest a dreamy, almost mythic, remembering of early Moravian folk culture as sedative to the barrage of absurdities in the postmodern world. Kundera defines idyll this way in *The Unbearable Lightness of Being:* ". . . an image . . . like a memory of Paradise" or ". . . a looking back to Paradise." But, Kundera's ultimate message is that the good old days cannot return because there never was an original, or a model to imitate. The concept of an original is only a disabled metaphor. The narrative, or history, had always already begun, and it changed a little each time in the telling, so now history is a story that never ends. What is myth, but a collection of stories endlessly retold, and Lyotard would add that all discourse is narrative, so really we live in an age when reason or truth is transformed into *mythos* (myth) and thus all history is myth.

Many of Kundera's contemporaries in Czechoslovakia see him portraying Central Europe as "a Europe raped by Asia . . . a spiritual graveyard maintained by governments of forgetting," and his idea of history as an "inexhaustible store of cruel jokes." For [Vaclav] Havel, Kundera's history is a

"deity capable of deceiving and destroying us, playing tricks on us," and thus real life is elsewhere, outside of history. Real life, for Kundera as well as for other post-modern theorists like Lyotard, is in myth, or in narration, or in interpretation.

In 1964, Kundera wrote *The Joke,* a cult book for the intelligentsia in Czechoslovakia, and the book that resulted in his expulsion from his homeland and emigration to France. This early novel seems to embody his later themes of history as myth and, at the same time, to provide the rationale for proclaiming Kundera as a modern humanist. The novel deals with folk culture and prehistory in an absurd environment. Ludvic, a clever university student, sends a post-card to his girlfriend (a passionate Stalinist), and as a joke says, "optimism is the opium of the people . . . long live Trotsky." The result is his expulsion from the university and the Party, and years of labor in the mines. Years later, after a completely unsatisfactory life as a result of that one joke, he is in his hometown, and witnesses the legendary "Ride of the Kings," a folk tradition that will illustrate to him "our world of ever-accelerating forgetting." He writes:

> Suddenly I saw it all clearly. People willingly deceive themselves with a double false faith. They believe in eternal memory (of men, deeds, things) . . . and in rectification (of deeds, errors, sins, injustice). Both are shams. The truth lies at the opposite end of the scale: everything will be forgotten, and nothing will be rectified. All rectification will be taken over by oblivion. No one will rectify wrongs; all wrongs will be forgotten.

While watching the "Ride of the Kings," however, Kundera's narrator (whose son was chosen to be this year's King in the parade) reflects on the origin of the legend of the King's Ride:

> Where did it come from and what does it mean? Does it perhaps date back to pagan times . . . The "Ride of the Kings" is a mysterious rite; no one knows what it signifies, what its message is . . . perhaps the Ride of Kings is beautiful to us at least partly because the message it was meant to communicate has long been lost, leaving the gestures, colors, and words to stand out all the more clearly.

It is in Moravia, Kundera's ancestral land, where he:

> had the sensation of hearing verse in the most primitive sense of the word, the kind of verse I could never hear on the radio or on TV . . . it was a sublime and polyphonic music—each of the heralds declaimed his verse in a monotone, but each on his

own individual note, so the voices combined willy-nilly into chords.

This music of variation describes also Kundera's technique of theme building already noted.

Kundera's sense of myth (of history as myth), which his protagonist seems to find in his folk culture, is the key to his love of humanity. Perhaps he believes it is futile to seek to shape the future, or to recapture the past, but it is in these rare moments when his characters fall back beyond history into myth, that Kundera reveals his own nostalgia for human solidarity, some common past which is an amalgam of truth and legend. The narrator's thoughts, while playing the final folk concert after the "Ride of the Kings" is played out, are moving. He says, "I felt a long-forgotten sense of companionship come over me." He and three friends are playing in a noisy cafe filling up with a young, boisterous audience; but, says the narrator:

> We managed to forget what was going on around us and create a magic circle of music; it was like being walled off from the drunks in a glass cabin at the bottom of the sea . . . I felt happy inside of the songs . . . where sorrow wasn't playful, laughter wasn't mocking, love wasn't laughable . . . where love is still love, pain, pain and values free from devastation.

This a rare instance, among all of Kundera's novels, where the author describes a freedom from irony, where the author feels no irony, and this instance is in myth, in Kundera's rediscovery of his folk culture. This is Kundera's nostalgia, his own kitsch, his own way of forgetting history—through folk tradition, legend or myth. Predictably, however, he immediately counters with:

> I was equally aware that my home was not of this world . . . that everything we sang and played was only a memory, a monument, a recreation in images of something that no longer was, and I felt the firm ground of my homeland sinking under my feet, felt myself falling . . . into the depths where love is love and pain, pain, and I said to myself that my only real home was this descent, this searching eager fall, and I gave myself up to it, savoring the sensuous vertigo.

Here is Kundera, the master of "epicurean accommodation"; he has chosen accommodation to an absurd world, not denial or revolt, and he is instantly a post-modern writer. For an instant, I think, we see what is the core of his attraction for modern readers, why he is not a nihilist, why he is not an ideologue. It is his method of accommodation to modern angst.

In his choice of accommodation, Kundera leaves room for the importance of the individual; while institutions and political systems may be absurd, individuals are not. In *The Unbearable Lightness of Being,* Kundera is constantly studying individual life, how concrete it is, how varied it is, how beautiful it can be. Most of his characters in this novel have no outside system of reference, so they must constantly make decisions. Human life is celebrated in this novel in all its chaotic progress, and, as Robert has described it, in all its existential contingency. The protagonist's life turns on coincidences; the very beauty of life, however, is in these coincidences.

The characters in this novel live in a non-tragic mode of fiction, in their own brand of twentieth-century folk culture. Kundera sees his characters as central European, representing the flip-side of European history, its outsiders, its victims. It is this historical disenchantment which is the source of their non-tragic character which "se moque de la grandeur et de la gloire" [mocks grandeur and glory]. In Kundera's post-Stalinist Central Europe there are few of the elements of high tragedy like grandeur, high status, or fatal flaw, so it is understandable that what is left is a sense of humor, a sense of humor which allows one to see other points of view, and to seek a measure of values on a human scale. But Kundera also finds beauty in man's sense of discomfort in the modern ideological world. Fuentes explains that while "Central Europe took care to demonstrate that a man need not be an insect in order to be treated as such," there is, when one reads Kundera, a change in Kafka's scenario: "The cockroach no longer thinks he knows; now he knows he thinks." He suggests that even if the future has already taken place and it stinks, maybe the answer for Kundera is "an internal utopia," a real space of untouchable life. Herein may lie the core of his constant preoccupation with sex and love. Kundera wrote in *The Book of Laughter and Forgetting:*

> The symphony is a musical epic. We might compare it to a journey leading through the boundless reaches of the external world, on and on, farther and farther. Variations also constitute a journey, but not through the external world. You recall Pascal's pensee about how man lives between the abyss of the infinitely large and the infinitely small. The journey of the variation form leads to that second infinity, the infinity of internal variety concealed in all things.

While there is nothing new in this approach to modern life, Kundera is fresh in his ability to see beauty in our very postmodern condition: the common folk, be he comrade, poet, peasant or professor, swimming in a disconnected world, uncertain of its past, of what is its real present, wallowing sometimes in irony, reveling in coincidence. It is Kafka sans insects, with flesh and blood characters in a modern communist society, striving for some sense of joy and vitality. His is neither the literature of incoherence, nor the fiction of ideology. He is capable of satirizing loss of memory, but still offering unlimited possibilities of choices to his characters. He talks about the "semantic hoax" by which the same word can be endowed with the opposite meaning, or with a meaning just a little off, the same successive approximations which he and Lyotard and Derrida use to describe communication in general. I suppose we are talking here about a metonymic and not a metaphoric relation (an associational and not an exact correspondence), and that it applies to Kundera's treatment of historic truth, meaning in language, and possibilities of knowing. Kundera's very ethical goal [according to Carlos Fuentes] seems to be to "discover the yet unknown avenues that depart from history and lead us to realities we had hardly suspected." What is pleasing about this goal is that it celebrates our very post-modern condition; instead of wallowing in the hopelessness of it all, it celebrates our very lack of connection to external codes, to institutions, and heralds the yet unknown possibilities for men—unconnected, demystified, and deconstructed. Kundera's (and Derrida's and Lyotard's) contribution might be as simple as the suggestion that the invariable is only one way of looking at things, that others do exist. Perhaps Kundera's folk culture offers not a collision with these post-modern forces, but an instance of beautiful accommodation.

Karen von Kunes (review date Winter 1995)

SOURCE: A review of *Les testaments trahis,* in *World Literature Today,* Vol. 69, No. 1, Winter, 1995, pp. 96-7.

[*In the following review of* Testaments Betrayed, *von Kunes focuses on Kundera's views on the arts of Kafka and Janácek.*]

Milan Kundera continues his discussion on the art of the novel in his new collection of essays **Les testaments trahis** (The Betrayed Testaments), published seven years after *L'art du roman* (Eng. **The Art of the Novel**) by the same house, Gallimard. Breaking his traditional structure of seven parts, Kundera examines writers from Rabelais, Hemingway, and Kafka to Kundera himself, and musicians from Stravinsky to Janácek, this time in nine parts, each independent yet—like a novel—united by the theme of betrayed art. He advances his thesis of "the art of the novel being born from humor, i.e. laughing at God," arguing that humor—dispersed in a novel's ambiguity—is the most difficult aspect of art to understand. As in his previous essays, Kundera treats music as an aggressive, mysterious force that has influenced the history and development of the art of the novel.

The central figure of the author's discussions is Kafka, in particular his two works *The Castle* and *The Trial.* Examining word by word a passage on the sexual encounter of K. and Frieda, Kundera proves the translators' betrayals: their liberty in adapting Kafka's situations to their own world and epoch or, even more, in replacing Kafka's repetitions by a range of synonyms because of their feeling of being ashamed of his inadequate language. In Kundera's eyes, Kafka remains a misunderstood artist. The "dryness" of his German style, which has been considered a kind of unestheticism—"his indifference toward beauty"—is in fact, Kundera claims, Kafka's esthetic intention and one of the most distinctive signs of beauty in Kafka's prose.

It is not only history that betrays art; it is also the position that a nation holds within nations; whereas a small nation may enjoy the richness of its cultural life, it suffers from an inaccessibility (in terms of its language, history, and culture) in the world arena. Janácek, the composer and musician from Moravia, used a technique of destroying the unimportant in his compositions: only a musical note that conveys something should remain; everything else (variations, transitions) should be left out. This is the very same literary approach that Kundera has adopted for his prose writing. He proudly acknowledges Janácek to be the greatest artist that Czechoslovakia, his own country of origin, has ever had. However, the smallness of his country did not allow recognition of Janácek's genius, just as the provincialism of Prague did not allow Kafka to be recognized as a leading writer of his own time.

Josef K.'s trial takes place on two levels: in the novel and in the criticism of the novel. As critics search for reasons for Josef K.'s guilt, they come up with a spectrum of accusations, another sort of trial, another *force qui juge.* Is not Kundera himself, however, an additional "power that accuses"? Accusing Max Brod of betraying Kafka (it is solely because of Brod that Kafka's letter to his father is known to the public, in fact to everyone except Kafka's father), or accusing Ansermet of betraying Stravinsky (for suggesting to Stravinsky that he edit one of his symphonies), Kundera accuses too, and he does so in his typically flamboyant, original, and witty way.

Mark Hutchinson (review date 22 October 1995)

SOURCE: "In Defense of Fiction," in *New York Times Book Review,* October 22, 1995, p. 30.

[*In the review below, Hutchinson addresses the main themes of* Testaments Betrayed.]

In 1979, while interviewing Milan Kundera for *Corriere della Serra,* the essayist Alain Finkielkraut remarked on how

Mr. Kundera's style—"flowery, baroque"—in his first novel, *The Joke,* had become spare and limpid in his later books. Flowery? Baroque? On examining the French edition of *The Joke,* Mr. Kundera discovered that his translator had sown the book with metaphors. "The sky was blue"? No: "A periwinkle October sky hoisted its sumptuous colors on the masthead." This outlandish piece of literary embroidery was then used as the source text for the Argentine edition, among others. Nor did the book fare any better with Mr. Kundera's original English publisher, who helpfully edited out all the reflexive passages, along with the chapters on musicology, and then changed the order of the various parts. Few writers can have been quite so unfortunate in their appointed go-betweens. But Mr. Kundera had learned his lesson: as a note tells us at the end of the revised French translation of *The Joke,* he now devotes almost as much time to overseeing foreign editions of his work as he does to writing.

A writer's work can be betrayed in many ways. The French edition of Nadezhda Mandelstam's memoirs rearranges her furious, rambling prose into three tidy volumes according to theme, utterly destroying the mnemonic logic that binds the narrative together. Auden, who removed a whole article of "verbose rubbish" from his version of Goethe's *Italian Journey* on the grounds that it did not represent Goethe's views, has himself come back to life as the author of a pamphlet of love poems for adolescents. The preface to a new edition of *Ulysses* tries to turn Joyce, the most internationally minded of writers, whose alter ego coined one of the most damning remarks ever made about history, into a kind of closet Irish nationalist. The greater the work, the greater the wealth of connotation; to simplify is always to betray.

An essay in nine parts, **Testaments Betrayed** is in many respects a continuation of **The Art of the Novel** and, like all of Mr. Kundera's books, is organized along musical lines, each section being both a variation on the title theme and an essay that is itself composed of variations of its own. Many of the themes taken up in the earlier work are here fleshed out in further detail: the art of narrative, the novel as the outrider of modernity, the morality of irony, the confusions of an age obsessed by ideas and indifferent to work and, of course, to the hazards of translation (his own translator here, Linda Asher, has nothing to fear). The book ranges widely, with a cast that includes both writers and musicians—Rabelais, Rushdie, Mann, Musil, Broch, Bach, Janacek, Stravinsky, Kafka and Mr. Kundera himself. It is a defense of fiction and a lesson in the art of reading.

About Rabelais and the invention of humor: humor, says Mr. Kundera, quoting Octavio Paz, is the great invention of the modern spirit, a species of the comic that renders ambiguous everything it touches. The source of that humor is the novel, and the ambiguity it breeds, its refusal to pass judgment, is the novel's morality. The Rights of Man? Prior to

the novel, the individual in the modern sense simply didn't exist. The arts had first of all to invent him. For Mr. Kundera, this is of the essence: from Rabelais and Cervantes on, the rise of the novel and the rise of modern society are one, and failure to grasp this reduces the novel to a form of polite entertainment or, what is just as bad, to an ideological skeleton hung with the author's rags.

All of Mr. Kundera's novels are carnivals of misunderstanding, and there is hardly a character in his fiction who doesn't at some stage betray someone or something—husband, wife, family, colleagues, country, ideals. The thematic overlap with the essays is striking, yet there is an important difference: the kind of misrepresentations and betrayals Mr. Kundera explores in his novels are part of the human predicament, a category of existence the author sees as inseparable from modern society—lacking the finished text for our lives, having no certain knowledge as to what the "right" decision might be, we can only take our esthetic instinct for a guide and improvise. But in the testaments he examines in his essays, it is man's works, not his days, that are at stake, and here we do indeed have the finished text, the musical score.

The writer whose work best embodies the thrust of Mr. Kundera's argument is Kafka, whose work, he suggests, has been betrayed on several fronts. His French translators, for example, have destroyed the rhythm of his prose by punctuating his long sentences with semicolons and chopping his paragraphs up into a whole host of shorter ones. (In manuscript the third chapter of *The Castle* consists of just two long paragraphs; in Max Brod's edition there are four, in one French translation a mind-boggling ninety-five, and Mr. Kundera devotes a whole section to comparing three translations of a long sentence in *The Castle* before providing his own.) Next come those publishers who, despite Kafka's insistence that his books be printed in large type, chose typefaces so small they must have ruined the eyes of more than one reader. Above all, there are critics who, rather than address the novels' particular achievement within the larger context of European fiction, prefer to immerse themselves in hagiography and speculations about the author's private life. Mr. Kundera is particularly severe on Brod, whom he holds responsible for Kafka's disastrous metamorphosis from novelist into saint; to illustrate this collapse of critical priorities, he cites an essay taken "at random" in which the letters are quoted fifty-four times, the diaries forty-five, the Janouch *Conversations* thirty-five, the stories twenty, *The Trial* five, *The Castle* four and *Amerika* not once.

Inevitably, this book has its weak moments. There are times when he seems to want to read Kafka for erotic comedy alone, and some of his arguments about the relations between politics and art are shaky. (Blaming the Romantic tradition and all things "lyrical" for the horrors of totalitarianism is as much of a simplification as the kind of reasoning he denounces in the debate surrounding Heidegger's involvement with the Nazi Party.) And though I understand his despair at the sheer volume of noise surrounding our lives, he should avoid writing about rock music, which, as readers of his novels will have noticed, invariably brings out some of his worst prose.

But these are quibbles. Mr. Kundera's essays should be placed alongside those of that other great emigre, Joseph Brodsky, the one performing for fiction what the other has done for poetry and both men sharing a now-unfashionable belief in the importance of esthetics to ethics. Mr. Kundera, for whom our passion for passing judgment before we have even begun to understand is a sure sign of our depravity, feels that art, by leading us into the labyrinth, can lead us out. He thinks that if we could come to terms with this the world would be a better place. He may well be right.

Robert Tashman (review date 6 May 1996)

SOURCE: A review of *Slowness* and *Testaments Betrayed,* in *Nation,* Vol. 262, No. 18, May 6, 1996, pp. 58-60.

[*Below, Tashman faults the structure and characterization of* Slowness, *then complains about various arguments presented in* Testaments Betrayed, *finding them "without merit but worth countering."*]

In reading **Slowness,** I did not feel the need, as one does with a strong piece of writing, to establish a distance from it and allow it to work indirectly, and to put it down for a time; and having put it down anyway, I was not eager to pick it up again and resume reading. I disliked the first twenty pages of this novel, which seemed random and directionless; then, in a crazed and rushing confluence of unexplained references and abruptly introduced characters, it caught my interest. Unfortunately, my engagement did not continue; my expectations, at first high because the book is by Kundera, then lowered, and then suddenly raised, were in the end excessive. I have admired Kundera for showing, in some of his other books, a vein of the rarest mineral in contemporary fiction: honesty regarding the state of the novel form. He has offered, elsewhere, constructive efforts out of a retrenched and unpromising aesthetic that draws from film, the bad influences of television and commercial culture, and impersonal developments in the history of the novel. He has also tried to avoid a blurb-encompassing style that currently predominates—even, in England and America, among the highly proficient elite of novelists. In execution and conception, **Slowness** seems well below standard for him.

Like an old man, Kundera complains strenuously about the modern world. Patience, romance, discretion and memory are the qualities of premodern life he values; today, when all is fast and physical, people are forgetful and brutish. His characters are educated wretches who speculate, worry and exploit others; and they unknowingly repeat one another's words and phrases. Kundera seems to want to establish a connection between the impossible political choices forced by glaring publicity, and the choices that occur in seduction. The action of the novel is slight: an entomologist in contemporary France has a brief affair; the plot of an eighteenth-century French novel, concerning a brief affair, is summarized; the entomologist and the protagonist of that novel meet at the end. I do not understand why the contemporary protagonist is an entomologist; since he could have been in another profession, he should have been. The novel also contains the story of Kundera's writing it. I am tired of books within books; they should be seen, not read.

The rupturing of the unity of time, in the meeting between Kundera's eighteenth- and twentieth-century men, is achieved by strict adherence to unity of place. The contemporary affair, the affair in the eighteenth-century novel, and the writing of Kundera's novel occur in the same chateau, once a residence and now a hotel. The meeting across centuries does not seem to result from the characters' occupying an eternal dimension, as Hemingway and Goethe do in their meetings in **Immortality,** Kundera's preceding novel. His characters can inhabit the same time, Kundera suggests, because they inhabit the same space. The device may be intended as a metaphor for television and other instantaneous media, which can bring together on a screen events and details from different times; or, more mundanely, it may result from the characters' being products of the author's imagination.

Kundera, as a character in the book, sees one of his characters sitting on a motorcycle. This subjective prerogative, which is perceptual insofar as it operates in thought and fancy, exceeds anything allowed by Bishop Berkeley. The great models, in literary narrative, for overcoming the unity of time are the accounts of the underworld in the eleventh book of the *Odyssey* and sixth of the *Aeneid;* Virgil, in following Homer, is even more audacious in including inhabitants of the future as well as the past. In film, where vast transitions can be achieved gracefully, the collapsing of time in a scenic unit can be avoided: as in D. W. Griffith's *Intolerance,* which establishes a beautiful parallel between divided epochs and separated lovers. In the modern novel it has been done successfully in satire—in Twain's *A Connecticut Yankee in King Arthur's Court.* There is too much emphasis, in the meeting between characters in **Slowness,** on the incongruity in their apparel.

Unlike Kundera's other novels, **Slowness** is written in the present tense. The present tense in fiction is like a fly buzzing in one's ear. It is the first novel Kundera has written in

French, but it contains passages that would be infelicitous in any language. At times enthusiasm overtakes him: "It is as if she had put a grenade of euphoria into his hand"; "the Asshole is the miraculous focal point for all the nuclear energy of nakedness." Elsewhere an indicative clumsiness obtrudes: "The entomologists are strange boors"; "the place beside him in bed is vacant." The humor in the book is effortful and feeble as well as pervasive. Kundera is a brisk observer—he is particularly good on manipulations of argument in the human rights movement—but in extended discussion he falters. His many digressions have the quality of a dialogue between himself and a gagged auditor; the story seems to interrupt the exposition of opinions, rather than the reverse. An unkind critic might observe that the book's structure resembles that of the Communist bureaucracy formerly in place in Kundera's native Czechoslovakia: The digressions, resembling political speeches, become expositions; the living narrative is demoted to an illustration of general truths; the speaking personages are not characters but functionaries. Kundera's impulse in writing this book seems to have been didactic rather than imaginative.

Kundera's **Testaments Betrayed** is a stimulating critical entertainment: Intelligent and energetically written, it contains arguments that are without merit but worth countering. It is less diffuse and more carefully organized than his **The Art of the Novel** (1986); throughout, topics recur like themes in a narrative. Kundera organizes **Testaments Betrayed** after Nietzsche's books, with each of its nine parts divided into small sections and the presentation of ideas furtive and associational rather than closely or even distantly argued. Kundera is no Nietzsche, but his book is refreshing when compared with academic and nonacademic literary criticism as currently practiced in America. Literary criticism outside universities, in magazines and newspapers, has grown closer to advertising and promotional writing, and because of commercial imperatives is directed mainly to work in which the gap between actual and purported value is greatest. Academic criticism, on the other hand, has discounted immediate response and aims to produce elaborate demonstrations, and it has become a poor stepchild of philosophy; it has also developed its own mannerisms, above all a weird propriety and hesitancy in argument, alternating with brute assertion. In **Testaments Betrayed** Kundera states his views and writes well—an unusual combination.

Kundera's claims about the history of the novel are fanciful and easily corrected. He confuses the status of the novel in European culture with the distinctiveness of the modern European novel compared with other novelistic traditions. He describes the novel as "that most European of the arts"; I do not see why it is more European than the symphony or the self-portrait, which do not have an equivalent in Japan and China, where the *Tale of Genji* and *Dream of the Red Chamber* appeared. Kundera adopts something of the pious tone of poets writing on poetry when he designates as unique to the novel qualities that are attributable to other forms as well. He states that "humor is an invention bound up with the birth of the novel." But the irreverent comic attitude that he views as a modern creation, and as emerging from the novel, is manifest in Aristophanes and Chaucer. He seems to claim that the picaresque novel is exclusively European. But the originator of the picaresque, as best can be determined, was Apuleius, a Roman North African; in Europe the form is distinctively Spanish, but Spain was an Arab and Muslim outpost: The picaresque of Cervantes, while obviously drawing on and satirizing chivalric romance, has qualities reminiscent of the tales in the *Arabian Nights.* Kundera may be a better writer on music than on literary history; the most instructive portion of the book is his discussion of Janacek's operas, which he champions.

The title of the book refers to its main theme and argument. Kundera is an advocate for writers and other artists who through death or unfavorable circumstances are unable to defend themselves against well-meaning but insensitive editors, publicists and executors who disregard their stated intentions regarding the presentation of their work. He cites several examples of such "betrayed testaments"; his main one is Max Brod's well-intentioned betrayal of his friend Kafka (Brod was also an advocate of Janacek's work). Brod not only disregarded Kafka's written instructions concerning which of his works could be published after his death but also, like a voyeuristic literary biographer, published those instructions. Some of Kundera's other comments along these lines are overheated. He criticizes German publishers of *The Castle* for printing, in an appendix, passages deleted by Kafka. Since the excised material did not appear in the body of the printed text, I do not see the grounds for complaint. But Kundera is more measured on Brod's sort of activity, which he regards as more common and more complacently accepted today than previously, and as posing a danger to artistic independence. He feels that writers' prerogatives should be defended and their intentions respected.

There are two problems with Kundera's argument. The first—which he acknowledges at the end of the book—is that writers may be poor judges of their own work. The argument that a writer's intentions—if these have been specified and if the writer is a master—should in all cases be respected seems unreasonable, for it assumes that the writer will always be right. The best and truest judges of finished work are readers, not writers. The other and more compelling objection is that posterity, whether it is capricious or validating, is all one can depend on; one cannot master it or bargain with it. There is a limit to the amount of control that any writer or artist has over the dissemination of his work, and when he attempts to overcome it he will appear petulant and peevish. This can be stated in another way: There is a limit to how far readers can determine the intentions of writers, especially deceased writers. If editors and publishers were to follow Kundera strictly, minor writers would benefit; more frequently than superior ones, they announce their intentions to the world. Of course, there are instances of challengeable editing, but in many of these—as in some of the decisions on punctuation in the new Oxford Shakespeare—the issue is not infidelity to the writer's explicit or imputed intentions but taste and literary judgment. Kundera confuses a writer's control over his work's presentation in his lifetime—which is usually, though not always, a reasonable expectation—with control over its reception after he is gone, which is unreasonable. Indeed, over time, as a writer and his contemporaries die, a work's presentation becomes one form of its reception. Writers who follow Kundera's exhortations, and expend energy in battling circumstances they cannot control, will probably not write well.

Angeline Goreau (review date 7 July 1996)

SOURCE: "Speed," in *New York Times Book Review,* July 7, 1996, p. 5.

[*In the following review, Goreau outlines the plot of* Slowness, *admiring its complexity of themes despite its brevity.*]

Metaphysical speculation was once happily married to the novel, practiced to great effect by masters like Voltaire and Diderot. Since the end of the Enlightenment, however, the philosophical novel—as opposed to the novel of ideas or the novel of social protest—has become a rarity. Milan Kundera, who has more or less single-handedly reinvented the form for his own use, is careful to point out that his novels are not engaged in the translation of philosophy into fiction. His modus operandi is to bring ideas into play—floating hypotheses, improvising, interrogating.

In roomy, expansive novels like *The Unbearable Lightness of Being, The Book of Laughter and Forgetting* and, most recently, *Immortality,* he uses an astonishing spectrum of instruments to get at meaning. Cutting rapidly from one story to another, interleaving different historical periods, he shifts from anecdote to satire, biography to autobiography, dramatization to historical narrative, ontological meditation to criticism—given voice by narrators who range from omniscient to personal, including an invented "I" whose name happens to be Milan.

But this richness is anything but disparate: Mr. Kundera, who began his artistic life as a musician, creates remarkable unity by sounding a theme, then circling and returning to it again and again with a great breadth of variations. The next theme he introduces might seem at first unconnected, but as he spins it out, the deep affinities gradually surface.

Slowness, Mr. Kundera's new novel, now translated by Linda Asher, appears to depart from what we have come to expect from him. It is, to begin with, the first novel he has written in French. It is also surprisingly short, less than half the number of pages of his last novel. The action occurs in a single place and, through the novel's witty telescoping of time, over a single night—a sort of parody of the classical unities.

The novel opens with Vera and Milan Kundera driving out from Paris to a chateau in the country to spend the night. A motorcyclist, bent on passing, appears behind them and prompts a banal observation by Vera that people are utterly without fear when they get behind the wheel. At this, the novel's central subject is announced, in a lyrical meditation on speed and time, technology and the body, escape and engagement, memory and forgetting: "The man hunched over his motorcycle can focus only on the present instant of his flight; he is caught in a fragment of time cut off from both the past and the future; he is wrenched from the continuity of time . . . in other words, he is in a state of ecstasy; in that state he is unaware of his age, his wife, his children, his worries, and so he has no fear, because the source of fear is in the future, and a person freed of the future has nothing to fear." Speed is the form of ecstasy technology has given us, the novel proposes. It then asks, "Why has the pleasure of slowness disappeared?"

At the end of this opening, a parallel journey begins, one recounted in a novella Milan has been reading entitled *Point de Lendemain* ("No Tomorrow"), by Vivant Denon, an 18th-century libertine who chose to remain anonymous. In it, a young chevalier travels by coach to the same chateau 200 years earlier to keep an assignation with the chatelaine. Their lovemaking, drawn out over a whole night, is informed by the elaborate rules of conduct their century affected. Denon's novel, known only to a small circle in its own time and republished in 1992, has come to represent, the narrator tells us, "the art and the spirit of the 18th century."

The young man on the motorcycle, Vincent, the chevalier's modern counterpart, is the protagonist of the third part of Mr. Kundera's fictional triptych. He has arrived at the chateau for a conference on entomology, also attended by a pretty typist named Julie, a Czech scientist whose career was fatally interrupted by the 1968 Russian invasion, a famous leftist intellectual named Berck (in French, "berck" is a colloquial expression of disgust), a would-be camp follower who is gainfully employed as a television producer and her devoted slave of a cameraman. The complications that entangle them multiply in the course of the evening with increasing frenzy until what looks like comedy turns to farce, ending in a howlingly funny failed orgy.

Taking the ontological temperature of today and of the pre-revolutionary 18th century, Mr. Kundera finds that the speed we love has beggared us of pleasure. Vincent and Julie's rush to make love in public view leads to a rather entertaining misunderstanding with the former's penis, whose eloquent— it makes a speech—but stubborn refusal to cooperate confirms the novel's earlier assertion that in delegating speed to a machine (the motorcycle) we leave the body "outside the process."

Through an accumulating tissue of action and metaphor, the novel is proposing that perhaps real freedom doesn't lie in the jettisoning of all restraint. The 18th century framed its lovemaking in high formality, while we celebrate spontaneity. But look here, *Slowness* says, the chevalier and his mistress are sexier than their frenetic modern counterparts: "Everything is composed, confected, artificial, everything is staged, nothing is straightforward, or in other words, everything is art; in this case: the art of prolonging the suspense, better yet: the art of staying as long as possible in a state of arousal."

Cutting back and forth between Denon's novel and the chateau's unzipped entomology conference, *Slowness* floats another hypothesis: that the nature of fame has undergone a profound alteration since the invention of the camera, one that alters the foundation of what Mr. Kundera elsewhere calls our "map of existence." Vivant Denon never claimed authorship of his novel. "Not that he rejected fame," the narrator speculates, "but fame meant something different in his time; I imagine the audience that he cared about, that he hoped to beguile, was not the mass of strangers today's writer covets but the little company of people he might know personally and respect."

The modern part of the novel's triptych lays out the proposition that no one now—in the age of television—can act in the world without imagining a large and invisible audience. The novel then carries this proposition to its absurd conclusion, in a dark burlesque not unlike the one Voltaire used to prove that all is most emphatically not for the best in this best of all possible worlds.

As all of Milan Kundera's other novels do, *Slowness* deals with the issue of how the novel defines itself—how does the audience novelists write for change the way the writing takes shape? And, like the novel's arrogant intellectual, Pontevin, who chooses to spin ideas for his own pleasure only, do writers risk turning themselves into monsters of selfishness if they choose to remain silent? Since one suggestion here is that form may well be more freeing than its opposite, and that form is inseparable from content, it seems unfair to accuse the novel of overschematizing. Clearly Mr. Kundera is playing with the idea of writing a novel whose form itself recalls the 18th century. And the speeding up to farce at the end of the book is inextricably part of the point he is making. But, for all its audacity, wit and sheer brilliance, I miss

here the expansive feel of the earlier novels. There are parts of *Slowness* that feel uncharacteristically heavy-handed.

Vera says that Milan might be writing a novel without a single serious word, *A Big Piece of Nonsense.* But Mr. Kundera's attack on the idea of progress in *Slowness* is very much in earnest, echoed in his most recent long essay, *Testaments Betrayed:* "History is not necessarily a path climbing upward," he wrote, adding that "the demands of art may be counter to the demands of the moment (of this or that modernity)." Modernism, he said, was once synonymous with experiment, but since the invention of mass media, it has embraced "received ideas" with an enthusiasm for conformity that borders on the totalitarian.

Mr. Kundera comes closer to polemic here than in his other fiction, but he is fiercely defending the "spirit of complexity" that the novel embodies. The novel's business, he wrote in *The Art of the Novel,* is to say to us, "Things are not as simple as you think." So it seems almost churlish to point out shortcomings in a writer of his spirit of play, breadth of reach and perspicacity—all admirably at work once again in *Slowness.* Much can be forgiven a writer who fearlessly takes on impossible questions like "What does it mean to be modern?"

FURTHER READING

Criticism

Bayley, John. "Fictive Lightness, Fictive Weight." *Salmagundi,* Vol. 73 (Winter 1987): 84-92.
> Discusses the dialectic organization of *The Unbearable Lightness of Being* in relation to the development of the modern novel.

Bold, Alan. "Half Love, Half Joke." *Times Literary Supplement,* No. 4114 (5 February 1982): 131.
> Reviews *The Book of Laughter and Forgetting,* emphasizing its expression of the problem of existential identity.

Caldwell, Ann Stewart. "The Intrusive Narrative Voice of Milan Kundera." *Review of Contemporary Fiction* 9, No. 2 (Summer 1989): 46-52.
> Overview of the function of the narrator's voice in Kundera's fiction.

Cooke, Michael. "Milan Kundera, Cultural Arrogance and Sexual Tyranny." *Critical Survey* 4, No. 1 (1992): 79-84.
> Contests Kundera's conception of the novel genre in several theoretical articles as the embodiment of "the European spirit," identifying its flaws and limitations.

Gray, Paul. "Broken Circles." *Time* 116, No. 24 (15 December 1980): 89.

Review of *The Book of Laughter and Forgetting,* focusing on the characters's psychological motivations.

Gunn, Dan. "The Book of Betrayals." *Times Literary Supplement,* No. 4854 (12 April 1996): 21-2.

Concentrates on the effects of misreading and mistranslation in both *Testaments Betrayed* and *Slowness.*

Lodge, David. "From Don Juan to Tristan." *Times Literary Supplement,* No. 4234 (25 May 1984): 567-68.

Evaluates *The Unbearable Lightness of Being* in the context of Kundera's fictional and theoretical oeuvre.

O'Rear, Joseph Allen. A review of *Slowness* by Milan Kundera. *Review of Contemporary Literature* 16, No. 3 (Fall 1996): 182.

Praises the "laughing, dancing story" of *Slowness,* finding its conclusion "as evocative of the Marx Brothers as it is of Rabelais."

Petro, Peter. "Apropos Dostoevsky: Brodsky, Kundera and the Definition of Europe." In *Literature and Politics in Central Europe: Studies in Honour of Markéta Goetz-Stankiewicz,* edited by Leslie Miller, Klaus Petersen, Peter Stenberg, and Karl Zaenker, pp. 76-90. Columbia, SC: Camden House, 1993.

Analyzes the public debate between Joseph Brodsky and Kundera over the interpretation of Dostoevski's literary vision in relation to the problem of defining Europe.

Pochoda, Elizabeth. "The Mysteries of the Status Quo." *Nation* 223, No. 8 (18 September 1976): 245-47.

Examines the personalities of the characters in *Laughable Loves.*

Ricard, François. "The Fallen Idyll: A Rereading of Milan Kundera." *Review of Contemporary Fiction* 9, No. 2 (Summer 1989): 17-26.

Meditates on the representation of the idyll and of beauty in Kundera's fiction.

Rosenblatt, Roger. "The Only Game in Town." *New Republic* 173, No. 10 (6 September 1975): 29-30.

Explains the playful but paradoxical propensities of the stories in *Laughable Loves.*

Schubert, P. Z. Review of *The Farewell Party* by Milan Kundera. *World Literature Today* 52, No. 4 (Autumn 1978): 663.

Brief review of *The Farewell Party,* describing it as "a fine blend of politics, sex and humor."

Sosa, Michael. Review of *The Art of the Novel* by Milan Kundera. *World Literature Today* 62, No. 4 (Autumn 1988): 685.

Summarizes the predominant theme of *The Art of the Novel.*

Stavans, Ilan. "*Jacques and His Master:* Kundera and His Precursors." *Review of Contemporary Fiction* 9, No. 2 (Summer 1989): 88-96.

Traces the influence of Cervantes, Sterne, and Diderot on Kundera's writings with respect to the circumstances surrounding the creation of *Jacques and His Master.*

"Behind the Masks." *Times Literary Supplement,* No. 3527 (2 October 1969): 1122.

Outlines the structure and main themes of *The Joke.*

von Kunes, Karen. "The National Paradox: Czech Literature and the Gentle Revolution." *World Literature Today* 65, No. 2 (Spring 1991): 237-40.

Comparative study of the collective and individual impact of Havel, Hrabal, and Kundera on Czech literature before the fall of communism.

Wall, Stephen. "Nuvvles." *London Review of Books* 11, No. 6 (16 March 1989): 24-5.

Details Kundera's methodology in *The Art of the Novel.*

Bharati Mukherjee
1940-

Indian-born American novelist, short story writer, nonfiction writer and journalist.

The following entry presents an overview of Mukherjee's career through 1997. For further information on her life and works, see *CLC,* Volume 53.

INTRODUCTION

Bharati Mukherjee has spent most of her career portraying the humiliation and pain often associated with Third World peoples adapting to North American culture. She has developed an understated prose style and tells her story from many different cultural perspectives. Her protagonists are usually sensitive, lack a stable sense of personal and cultural identity, and are victimized by racism, sexism, or other forms of social oppression. Several critics have compared her studies of cultural clashes to the works of V. S. Naipaul, while others have noted the influence of Bernard Malamud on her portrayal of minority individuals who have difficulty adapting to their new surroundings.

Biographical Information

Mukherjee was born in Calcutta, India, in 1940 to an upper-middle-class Bengali Brahmin family. Her father was the head of a pharmaceutical firm. Her early childhood was spent in the few years before India's independence in August of 1947. She attended schools in both Britain and Switzerland, and then returned to India to attend the Loretto School run by Irish nuns. She was taught to devalue the Bengali culture, and it was not until later that she reconnected with her Hindu heritage. Mukherjee received a B.A. in English at the University of Calcutta in 1959 and an M.A. in English and ancient Indian culture from the University of Calcutta in 1961. Also in 1961 Mukherjee came to the United States to study at the Iowa Writers' Workshop. There she met and married Canadian writer Clark Blaise, with whom she later collaborated on two nonfiction works. Mukherjee's marriage to someone outside her culture changed her life and writing dramatically. She moved with her husband to his native Canada and encountered racism and alienation. She quickly became a vocal civil rights activist and the nature of her fiction changed irrevocably. In 1980 she decided that she could not survive as an outsider in Canada and moved with her family to the United States. She became an American citizen in 1988. Mukherjee has been a professor of English and creative writing at various

universities in both Canada and the United States, including Columbia University in New York and the University of California at Berkeley. In 1988 she won the National Book Critics Circle Award for *The Middleman and Other Stories.*

Major Works

Mukherjee's fiction portrays the delicate place of Indian and other Third World immigrants in North American culture. *The Tiger's Daughter* (1972) provides a satiric look at Indian society from the point of view of a young expatriate, Tara Banerjee Cartwright. Cartwright is caught between an American culture to which she is not yet accustomed and the culture of her native land from whose morals and values she is estranged. *Wife* (1975) tells the story of, Dimple, who moves to the United States with her husband and becomes torn between Indian and American cultures. *Days and Nights in Calcutta* (1977), written with her husband Clark Blaise, is a journal of the couple's 1973 visit to India. Mukherjee also collaborated with Blaise on *The Sorrow and the Terror* (1987) which tells the story of the bombing of an Air India flight that killed over 300 people. Mukherjee's short story collection *The Middleman and Other Stories* (1988) traces the lives of Third World immigrants and their adjustment to becoming Americans. The protagonists struggle to survive economically while facing alienation and racism. The stories celebrate "differentness" and express the value of maintaining distinction in the face of becoming American. In the novel *Jasmine* (1989) based on Mukherjee's short story by the same name, the title character is widowed, which in her native Punjab means a life of sorrow and loneliness. She rejects this fate and leaves for America, where she undergoes a series of transformations. Her travels eventually lead her to a new identity as Jane with a common-law husband and child in the farm country of Iowa. The novel ends with the protagonist abandoning her life again for a new existence in California. The novel is a celebration of the American freedom to develop an individual identity, a freedom characterized by both pain and excitement. *The Holder of the World* (1993) traces the story of two women, in two different time periods. A diamond called the Tear Drop connects Beigh Masters to a 19th-century Puritan, Hannah Easton. Most of the novel takes up Beigh's narration of Hannah's story, which includes growing up in Massachusetts and eventually ending up in India as the lover of the Raja. When she returns to New England pregnant with the Raja's child, the reader learns that Hannah is actually Hester Prynne, the protagonist of Nathaniel Hawthorne's *The Scarlet Letter*. *Leave It to Me* (1997) traces the search of Debbie DiMartino to find her origins and identity.

Critical Reception

Some critics insist that Mukherjee is exploiting a fad of postcolonial literature, but many reviewers find her work valuable. Critics often point out the violence in Mukherjee's fiction arising from the clashing of old and new worlds. However, most reviewers do not find Mukherjee's vision as without hope. Victoria Carchidi says, "Mukherjee insists that when such multiple worlds meet, the result *can be* a glorious freeing of the leaves of the kaleidoscope, that completely intermix and produce a new pattern." Though Mukherjee has never been noted for the plausibility of her plots, some critics had the most trouble with *Leave It to Me*. Michiko Kakutani says, "Certainly, plausibility has never been Ms. Mukherjee's strong suit, but in earlier books, her crazy-quilt plots not only possessed a fable-like power but also remained grounded in meticulously observed descriptions and edgy, pointillist prose." Mukherjee has been recognized for developing her own style and message that has relevance in American literature. As Gary Boire states, "Mukherjee's is a revisionary, appropriative technique, one that 'channels' deeply . . . into an existent literary landscape in order to excavate her own highly deserved space."

PRINCIPAL WORKS

The Tiger's Daughter (novel) 1972
Wife (novel) 1975
Days and Nights in Calcutta [with Clark Blaise] (nonfiction) 1977
Darkness (short stories) 1985
The Sorrow and the Terror: The Haunting Legacy of the Air India Tragedy [with Blaise] (nonfiction) 1987
The Middleman and Other Stories (short stories) 1988
Jasmine (novel) 1989
Political Culture and Leadership in India (nonfiction) 1991
Regionalism in Indian Perspective (nonfiction) 1992
The Holder of the World (novel) 1993
Leave It to Me (novel) 1997

CRITICISM

Carol Ascher (review date September 1989)

SOURCE: "After the Raj," in *Women's Review of Books*, Vol. VI, No. 12, September, 1989, p. 17-19.

[*In the following excerpt, Ascher praises Mukherjee's* The Middleman and Other Stories *and states that "one of the great joys, for me, of reading* The Middleman *is experiencing a world that generally remains just at the edge of my consciousness."*]

. . . In *The Middleman and Other Stories* Bharati Mukherjee leaves the zenana far behind as she writes with the rushed, rootless, naively cynical voices of Third World newcomers and those who get involved with them. The eleven stories in this swift-moving collection are about the immigrants filling US cities and campuses: they come from India, Iraq, Afghanistan, Trinidad, Uganda, the Philippines, Sri Lanka, Vietnam, and they are all busy creating new ties and scrambling for a living, often in the shadier niches of the economy. As the narrator of **"Danny's Girls,"** a Ugandan living in Flushing, says of his neighbor and idol, Danny, a northern Indian,

> He started out with bets and scalping tickets for Lata Mangeshkar or Mithun Chakravorty concerts at Madison Square Garden. Later he fixed beauty contests and then discovered the marriage racket.

> Danny took out ads in papers in India promising "guaranteed Permanent Resident status in the U.S." to grooms willing to proxy-marry American girls of Indian origin. He arranged quite a few. The brides

and grooms didn't have to live with each other, or even meet or see each other. Sometimes the "brides" were smooth-skinned boys from the neighborhood.

Jasmine, in the story by her name, is a Trinidadian who's come over to Detroit from Canada hidden in the back of a truck. Without a Green Card, she finds a job at the Plantation Motel, run by a family of Trinidad Indians. "The Daboos were nobodies back home. They were lucky, that's all. They'd gotten here before the rush and bought up a motel and an ice-cream parlor." For her room and a few dollars, Jasmine does the book-keeping and cleaning up, as well as working on Mr. Daboo's match-up marriage service on Sundays.

It's "life in the procurement belt," as a white Vietnam vet says in **"Loose Ends,"** his cold rage building at the fact that native Miami-ites like him are becoming "coolie labor" to foreigners.

> So I keep two things in mind nowadays. First, Florida was built for your pappy and grammie. I remember them, I was a kid here. . . . The second is this: Florida is run by locusts and behind them are sharks and even pythons and they've pretty well chewed up your mom and pop and all the other lawn bowlers and blue-haired ladies.

As enraging as it may be to the "natives" that Mukherjee's immigrants are so adept at finding ways to stay afloat economically, their piecemeal assimilation is also a source of wonder. "I envy her her freedom, her Green Card politics. It's love, not justice, that powers her," says Jeff of his Filipino girlfriend, Blanquita, in **"Fighting for the Rebound."** Although these newcomers may insist that they're ignored, misunderstood, or even despised, and that "Here, everything mixed up. Is helluva confusion, no?" they rapidly get the local lingo, and they are voracious consumers of microwave ovens, sweatsuits, VCRs, Press-On Nails, Cuisinart machines. In fact, if Bobbie Ann Mason has made being a hick chic, as Diane Johnston once said, then Bharati Mukherjee may be at the forefront of immigrant chic. Her prose has the flat deadpan that is very much in style, and she has an unerring eye for the detritus of shopping malls that draws these lonely newcomers.

As if in a covert lesson on the power of rootlessness to sever the author's own loyalties to gender as much as to homeland, Mukherjee's collection contains as many stories with male as with female narrators. Yet I found two stories about Indian women particularly poignant. This may be because the two women are also academics, and more thoughtful and torn about their experiences than are the others whose dog-eat-dog world offers them little time for reflection.

In **"A Wife's Story,"** Mrs. Bhatt has come to New York to take a two-year course in Special Ed at Teachers College. Freed from the strict roles of Indian society, she has even become friends with a Hungarian man with whom she goes to the theatre. When her husband comes for a short visit, he seems an unlikely stranger. Still, she puts on her sari, gets tickets for a depressing package tour of the city, and obligingly takes him shopping at the discount stores.

In **"The Tenant,"** Maya Sanyal of Calcutta is in Cedar Falls, Iowa, where she has come to teach Comparative Literature. Afraid of her bachelor landlord, Maya answers the "India Abroad" personals from Indian men, and puts on her best sari to go to tea at the home of the other Indian professor on campus, a Dr. Chatterji. There everything remains traditional, the old "virtues made physical." Yet something has snapped for Dr. Chatterji—as it has for Maya. Both experience their loneliness and anomie as erotic craving.

Although Mukherjee's characters only participate in public life to advance their narrow private interests, in total they *are* the great social transformation affecting North America. Finishing the collection, one senses that the strategy of short stories has served her well. Whether or not one might add other characters to the mosaic to form a truer, more complete picture, there is no other writer documenting these largely unseen immigrants; one of the great joys, for me, of reading *The Middleman* is experiencing a world that generally remains just at the edge of my consciousness.

Michael Gorra (review date 10 September 1989)

SOURCE: "Call It Exile, Call It Immigration," in *The New York Times Book Review*, September 10, 1989, p. 9.

[*In the following review, Gorra discusses Mukherjee's expansion of her short story "Jasmine" into a novel and asserts "she's done so without losing a short story's virtues, above all its sense of speed and compression, its sense of a life distilled into its essence."*]

Bharati Mukherjee's third novel carries the same title as one of the best stories in her prize-winning collection of last year, *The Middleman and Other Stories.* That earlier **"Jasmine"** told of an Indian girl from Trinidad who "came to Detroit . . . by way of Canada . . . [crossing] the border at Windsor in the back of a gray van loaded with mattresses and box springs." Jasmine works first in an Indian-owned motel, then as an au pair. And by the end of the story she's learned to see herself, as she makes love to the man whose child she takes care of, as "a bright pretty girl with no visa, no papers, and no birth certificate. No nothing other than what she wanted to invent and tell . . . a girl rushing wildly in the future," an American with an American's freedom to shape her own destiny.

For the rich novel that's grown from that story, Ms. Mukherjee has shifted the narrative into the first person and placed her heroine's origins in the Punjab rather than Trinidad, where the added weight of tradition makes the character's love affair with the possibilities of America all the more exhilarating. "Lifetimes ago," the novel begins, "under a banyan tree in the village of Hasnapur, an astrologer cupped his ears—his satellite dish to the stars—and foretold my widowhood and exile." But the 7-year-old Jyoti—not yet Jasmine, still less the Jane she'll become when she invents a new life in Iowa—rejects the fate he assigns her. Which of them is right?

Widowhood is certainly hers. At 14 she marries Prakash-Vijh, "a modern man. . . . He wanted me to call him by his first name," instead of the pronouns village women use to address their husbands. And he calls her "Jasmine," a new name as a way to "break off the past." But this is the Punjab in the 1980's, and as he's preparing to go study in America, Prakash falls victim to a Sikh terrorist bomb. With Prakash dead, Jasmine wants only to burn herself alive, like a good Hindu wife of old, on the Florida campus he had so badly wanted to reach. Ms. Mukherjee's handling of Jasmine's illegal immigration into the United States provides some of the novel's best pages. "The longest line between two points is the least detected," Jasmine thinks, as she moves through the world of "refugees and mercenaries and guest workers; you see us sleeping in airport lounges . . . taking out for the hundredth time an aerogram promising a job or space to sleep. . . . dressed in shreds of national costumes . . . the wilted plumage of intercontinental vagabondage." She finally reaches Florida on a shrimper out of Suriname. But once landed, the ship's captain rapes her, and in taking her revenge, Jasmine discovers she wants to live.

From Florida to the stiflingly old-world Indian community in Flushing; then work as an au pair on the Upper West Side, where she falls in love with a WASP world of "careless confidence and graceful self-absorption," with the pleasures of being unconsciously American. And on to Iowa. From Jasmine Vijh to Jane Ripplemeyer—though remembering the astrologer keeps her from marrying the middle-aged Iowan banker whose name she takes and whose child she bears—and whom she leaves at the end of the novel, moving on to California "greedy with wants and reckless from hope," in love with the "adventure, risk, transformation" through which she has redefined herself as an American. Reading Ms. Mukherjee's short stories about immigrants, I've often thought of the Irish writer Frank O'Connor's argument that while the novel deals with the structure of society, the short story tends to concentrate on what he calls "the lonely voice," on "outlawed figures wandering about" on that

society's fringes. In expanding that sense of marginality into the material of a novel, Ms. Mukherjee has made her heroine emblematic of this nation of outsiders as a whole, but she's done so without losing a short story's virtues, above all its sense of speed and compression, its sense of a life distilled into its essence.

Jasmine is so tightly made one wants to read it in a sitting. Yet, paradoxically, that's also the novel's chief weakness. Its other characters, however vivid, remain too firmly subordinated to Jasmine. Their stories matter only insofar as they affect hers, in a way that not only suggests the novel's origins as a short story, but that troubles me precisely because those characters are so vivid. It's not easy, as Jasmine lights out for the territories once more, to view her abandonment of Jane Ripplemeyer's responsibilities with the complacency the novel seems to call for. Yet perhaps that uneasiness is intended; perhaps *Jasmine* is as much an implicit criticism of the self-absorption of American life as it is a celebration of its inventive openness.

What does seem clear is that Ms. Mukherjee wants the question posed by the astrologer's prediction to remain an open one. Jasmine may in some ways be in control of her own destiny, but she is also a widow and in exile. Or rather in an exile that she chooses to redefine as immigration—as the Indian-born Ms. Mukherjee herself has recently done in choosing to become an American citizen. As a young writer, Ms. Mukherjee has said, she dreamed of updating *A Passage to India;* now, she writes, it's Henry Roth's immigrant classic *Call It Sleep. Jasmine* stands as one of the most suggestive novels we have about what it is to become an American.

Uma Parameswaran (review date Spring 1990)

SOURCE: A review of *The Middleman and Other Stories,* in *World Literature Today,* Vol. 64, No. 2, Spring, 1990, p. 363.

[*In the following review, Parameswaran discusses the stories in Mukherjee's* The Middleman and Other Stories.]

Bharati Mukherjee's second volume of short fiction consists of eleven stories that are wide-ranging in both settings and themes. Following her self-proclaimed American identity stated in her first volume of stories, *Darkness,* she explores the American experience through various personae or protagonists, four of whom are white American males and six of whom are females (only three of the women are of Indian origin). The result is a curious mix of voices and experiences that go to make up the celebration of being American (as she states in *Darkness*) as opposed to being Canadian.

Mukherjee's explorations of male attitudes and diction are interesting as experiments. Alfred Judah, the protagonist of the title story, is a macho operator in the rough-and-tumble world of smugglers: "Me? I make a living from things that fall. The big fat belly of Clovis T. Ransome bobs above me like whale shit at high tide." This image from the Florida scenery seems to have impressed her deeply, for in the next story we find "python turds, dozens of turds, light as cork and thick as a tree, riding high in the water." One is led to see a metaphorical streak that runs through the volume: these characters may be full-blooded Americans racing with both hands grabbing at all that life has to offer, but what they grasp is rather obnoxious all the way. More disturbing is the fact that Mukherjee's control of language is as devastating as ever, but now geared to a kind of cynicism that was absent in her earlier works. The characters who appear in the American stories, especially those from India, are stark caricatures of individuals: motel owners who use underpaid fellow Indians whenever possible; highly educated professionals whose linguistic idiosyncrasies are laughed at; a Vietnam veteran who brings home his daughter Eng and "rescues" her from "our enemies," the doctor and the hospital that terrify her; a ruffian who, we are asked to believe, is driven to auto theft and rape by his feeling of betrayal by some larger entity, the state.

The final story in the collection is **"The Management of Grief."** It has clearly come out of Mukherjee's scintillating and controversial documentary *The Sorrow and the Terror* (co-authored with Clark Blaise), on the crash of Air India flight 182 on 23 June 1985, which killed 329 passengers, most of whom were Canadians of Indian origin. There are minor questions that come to the reader's mind. Would the Stanley Cup have been played so late in June? Would the two young Sikhs have left for India within a month of having brought over their parents, who did not know the language and had no other family members? However, the story is very poignant and improves on E. M. Forster's idea of the failure of disparate cultures to connect. Though the families of the victims manage their grief in their own ways, the Canadian government finds itself in a quandary of communication, trying ineffectually to get paperwork done through translators. Shaila, who has lost her husband and two sons in the crash, is a volunteer interpreter; when the government agent Judith takes Shaila to the old Sikh couple who had been in Canada only a month before losing both their sons, we see their intractability clashing with Judith's impatience. No amount of explanation will persuade them to accept aid, because such acceptance might "end the company's or the country's obligations to them." Or, as Judith perceptively concludes, "They think signing a paper is signing their sons' death warrants." As Judith and Shaila leave, Judith talks about the next woman, "who is a real mess." At this, Shaila asks Judith to stop the car, gets out, and slams the door, leaving Judith to ask plaintively, "Is there anything I said? Any-

thing I did . . . Shaila? Let's talk about it." The story would have been more effective if it had ended here, but Mukherjee follows her more traditional storytelling form of tying up loose ends.

The title of the volume goes beyond the title story to imply that many of Mukherjee's personae are middlemen, moving between cultures or events that pull others or themselves in opposite directions.

Arvindra Sant-Wade and Karen Marguerite Radell (essay date Winter 1992)

SOURCE: "Refashioning the Self: Immigrant Women in Bharati Mukherjee's New World," in *Studies in Short Fiction,* Vol. 29, No. 1, Winter, 1992, pp. 11-17.

[*In the following essay, Sant-Wade and Radell discuss the ways in which immigrant characters adapt to American culture in Mukherjee's* The Middleman and Other Stories.]

The female protagonist in one of Bharati Mukherjee's prize-winning short stories, from the collection titled *The Middleman and Other Stories,* is shocked when her landlord lover refers to the two of them as "two wounded people," and thinks to herself that "She knows she is strange, and lonely, but being Indian is not the same, she would have thought, as being a freak." The Indian woman, Maya Sanyal, who is the central figure of the story, **"The Tenant,"** recognizes her strangeness in America and her appalling loneliness, but she resists being recognized as a "freak." No doubt this term occurs to her when her current lover, Fred, a man without arms, refers to them both as wounded. She does not see herself as being as freakish as Fred, as bereft as Fred, though certainly the story makes clear that she has been wounded emotionally and spiritually by the struggle to come to terms with her new life in America. In one sense, Fred's assessment is accurate, for as the author indicates in all the stories in this collection, it is impossible to adapt to life in the New World without sustaining some kind of wound to one's spirit.

It is apparently a deeper wound for the women of the Third World, who are engaged in the struggle to fashion a new identity for themselves in an alien culture. Perhaps this struggle results from their sudden freedom from the bonds of superstition and chauvinism that held them fast in their old, familiar cultures, freedom that seems to leave them floating, unbalanced, in the complex, sometimes treacherous air of this new and unfamiliar culture. The irony is that this refashioning of the self is both painful and exhilarating; hence, the terrible ambivalence of the women toward their own freedom—the freedom to *become*—an ambivalence expressed by these women in the midst of arduous change, in the powerful act of rejecting the past and moving energetically toward an unknown future.

In a *Massachusetts Review* interview, Mukherjee asserts that

> we immigrants have fascinating tales to relate. Many of us have lived in newly independent or emerging countries which are plagued by civil and religious conflicts. We have experienced rapid changes in the history of the nations in which we lived. When we uproot ourselves from those countries and come here, either by choice or out of necessity, we suddenly must absorb 200 years of American history and learn to adapt to American society. Our lives are remarkable, often heroic.

Mukherjee goes on to say that she attempts to illustrate this remarkable, often heroic quality in her novels and short stories. Her characters, she asserts, "are filled with a hustlerish kind of energy" and, more importantly,

> they take risks they wouldn't have taken in their old, comfortable worlds to solve their problems. As they change citizenship, they are reborn.

Mukherjee's choice of metaphor is especially apt with reference to the women in her fiction, for the act of rebirth, like birth itself, is both painful, and, after a certain point, inevitable. It is both terrible and wonderful, and an act or process impossible to judge while one is in the midst of it. So the women in Mukherjee's stories are seen deep in this process of being reborn, of refashioning themselves, so deep that they can neither extricate themselves nor reverse the process, nor, once it has begun, would they wish to. There is a part of themselves, however, that is able to stand back a little and observe their own reaction to the process, their own ambivalence. We know this because Mukherjee weaves contradiction into the very fabric of the stories: positive assertions in interior monologues are undermined by negative visual images; the liberation of change is undermined by confusion or loss of identity; beauty is undermined by sadness.

A close look at three stories from *The Middleman and Other Stories,* each with a female protagonist from the Third World, illustrates the author's technique and her success in conveying this theme of rebirth or refashioning of the self by immigrant women. The stories are **"The Tenant," "Jasmine,"** and **"A Wife's Story,"** and in each of them, we encounter a different woman at a different stage in the subtle, complex, and traumatic process of becoming a new woman, one who is at home in the sometimes terrifying freedom of the new American culture. In each story, the exhilarating sense of possibility clashes with the debilitating sense of loss, yet the exuberant determination of the women attracts us to them and denies the power of pity.

Perhaps this attraction without pity derives from the women's avoidance of self-pity. In **"The Tenant,"** we first meet the protagonist, Maya, sitting over a glass of bourbon (the first one of her life) with a new colleague from her new job in the English Department at the University of Northern Iowa. The American colleague, Fran, is on the Hiring, Tenure, and Reappointment Committee, and is partly responsible for bringing Maya to the school. While Fran chats about her own life and gossips a little about Maya's landlord, Maya contemplates the immensity of her isolation and loneliness. And although she longs to be able to confide in someone, Fran even, she realizes that Fran is unable to receive these confidences because Fran cannot see that Maya is a woman caught in the mingled web of two very different cultures. To Fran, "a utopian and feminist," Maya is a bold adventurer who has made a clean break with her Indian past, but Maya understands, as the reader does, that there is no such thing as a "clean" break.

When Maya is invited to Sunday afternoon tea by another Bengali, Dr. Rabindra Chatterji, a professor of physics at her new university, she accepts with somewhat mixed feelings but dresses carefully in one of her best and loveliest saris. Once inside the Chatterji's house, in a raw suburban development that seems full of other Third World nationalities, Maya allows the familiar sights and smells of Indian high tea to take her back to that other world of "Brahminness":

> The coffee table is already laid with platters of mutton croquettes, fish chops, onion pakoras, ghugni with puris, samosas, chutneys. Mrs. Chatterji has gone to too much trouble. Maya counts four kinds of sweetmeats in Corning casseroles on an end table. She looks into a see-through lid; spongy, white dumplings float in rosewater syrup. Planets contained, mysteries made visible.

Maya's hostess begins to ask questions about Maya's distinguished family in Calcutta, and Maya thinks to herself that "nothing in Calcutta is ever lost." She worries that the husband and wife may retreat to the kitchen, leaving her alone, so that they may exchange "whispered conferences about their guest's misadventures in America." Apparently the story of her "indiscretions" with various men, her marriage and divorce to an American, is known to the entire Bengali community in North America, which may be one of the reasons Dr. Chatterji both speaks and acts suggestively (he has one hand in his jockey shorts) when he drives her home that evening. Maya has been marked as a "loose" woman and as a divorcée, and therefore cannot ever hope to remarry respectably in the Indian (at least not the Brahmin) community: she is both in it and out of it, forever.

She occupies the same ambiguous position in the American community; although she has become an American citizen, she does not fully belong there either. She longs for a real sense of belonging, for the true companionship and love she dares to want, and eventually brings herself to answer an ad in the matrimonial column of *India Abroad,* the newspaper for expatriates. She answers the ad that declares:

> Hello! Hi! Yes, you *are* the one I'm looking for. You are the new emancipated Indo-American woman. You have a zest for life. You are at ease in USA and yet your ethics are rooted in Indian tradition. . . . I adore idealism, poetry, beauty. I abhor smugness, passivity, caste system. Write with recent photo. Better still, call!!!

Maya does call the man who placed the ad, Ashoke Mehta, and arranges a meeting at Chicago's O'Hare airport, "a neutral zone" they both prefer for this emotionally risky encounter. Until she meets Mehta, another immigrant who lives a life that bridges two worlds, she feels she lives in a "dead space" that she cannot articulate properly, even to herself. At the end of the story, after their courtship has entered its final phase, and she has decided to go to Connecticut to be with him, we know she will finally be able to repudiate her own accusations that her life is grim and perverse, that "she has changed her citizenship, but she hasn't broken through into the light, the vigor, the *bustle* of the New World." At the end, she does bustle off to meet the man who will make her whole again (and whom she will make whole) in this new life.

The next story, **"Jasmine,"** also explores some of the more appalling, perhaps even "violent and grotesque aspects of [the] cultural collisions" Mukherjee writes about. In this story, the protagonist is a young Trinidadian woman named Jasmine who has been smuggled illegally into the US, all paid for by her father ("Girl, is opportunity come only once"), and goes to work first in the motel of the Indian family who helped her get there, and later as a "mother's helper . . . Americans were good with words to cover their shame" for an American family. When her new American employers ask about her family and her home, Jasmine recognizes the need to deceive them:

> There was nothing to tell about her hometown that wouldn't shame her in front of nice white American folk like the Moffitts. The place was shabby, the people were grasping and cheating and lying and life was full of despair and drink and wanting. But by the time she finished, the island sounded romantic.

Jasmine must construct a suitable, tolerable narrative of her past and her roots, in the same way that she is attempting to construct a positive narrative of her life in the New World. She seems precariously balanced between what she once was and what she hopes to become. She is like other Mukherjee characters, who

> remind one of circus performers, a combination of tightrope walkers and trapeze artists, as they search for secure, even familiar, places they can claim as their home. . . . They try to transcend the isolation of being a foreigner not only in another country but also in their own cultures.

Jasmine tries hard to cut all ties with "anything too islandy" as she struggles to refashion herself in America. Though she cleans, cooks, and irons for the Moffitts, she never stops giving thanks for having found such "a small, clean, friendly family . . . to build her new life around." She is constantly thanking Jesus for her good luck. The irony is that through all the exuberance and energy we see how terribly she is exploited by the Moffitts, and how unaware she often is of this exploitation, though it is not something she could recognize, even if it were pointed out.

At Christmas time, Jasmine is taken by Bill Moffitt to see her only "relatives" in the country, the Daboos, the Indian family she had originally worked for. In her original interview, she had told Bill and Lara Moffitt that Mr. Daboo was her mother's first cousin because

> she had thought it shameful in those days to have no papers, no family, no roots. Now Loretta and Viola in tight, bright pants seemed trashy like girls at Two-Johnny Bissoondath's Bar back home. She was stuck with the story of the Daboos being family. Village bumpkins, ha! She would break out. Soon.

We never do get to see Jasmine "break out," but the sense that she is a survivor emanates from the story even when she weeps with homesickness on Christmas Day. However, Mukherjee undercuts Jasmine's enthralled sense of unlimited possibility with a poignant moment of epiphany at the end of the story. In the last scene, she is half-willingly seduced by Bill Moffitt:

> She felt so good she was dizzy. She'd never felt this good on the island where men did this all the time, and girls went along with it always for favors. You couldn't feel really good in a nothing place. . . . She was a bright, pretty girl with no visa, no papers, and no birth certificate. No, nothing other than what she wanted to invent and tell. She was a girl rushing wildly into the future. . . . it [the love-making] felt so good, so right that she forgot all the dreariness of her new life and gave herself up to it.

In **"A Wife's Story,"** another immigrant woman has had her share of dreariness, loneliness, confusion, and anger in the effort to reshape her life in the land of opportunity. She too is weighed down by the burdens of two cultures and the hardship of trying to balance parts of her old life with the best of the new. The wife is a woman who has left her husband temporarily to pursue a graduate degree in New York, to break the cycle begun hundreds of years before. The narration is first person this time:

> Memories of Indian destitutes mix with the hordes of New York street people, and they float free, like astronauts, inside my head. I've made it. I'm making something of my life. I've left home, my husband, to get a Ph.D. in special ed. I have a multiple-entry visa and a small scholarship for two years. After that, we'll see. My mother was beaten by her mother-in-law, my grandmother, when she registered for French lessons at the Alliance Française. My grandmother, the eldest daughter of a rich zamindar, was illiterate.

This woman has even gone so far as to befriend another lonely immigrant, a Hungarian named Imre, who also has a spouse and family back home in the old country. Their friendship, so necessary to her survival in New York, would be unthinkable in her own country; in India, married women are not friends with men married to someone else. But Imre helps her to survive assaults on her dignity and the hopelessness of not truly belonging. He comforts her after a David Mamet play (*Glengarry Glen Ross*) in which she must endure terrible lines about Indians, such as, "Their women . . . they look like they've just been fucked by a dead cat." She feels angry enough and strong enough to write a letter of protest to the playwright, or at least to write it in her head.

The Americanized but still Indian wife surprises herself occasionally by literally breaking out in very un-Indian behavior (like the time she impulsively hugs Imre on the street), and when her husband arrives for a visit, she realizes how many of the changes in her own behavior she now takes for granted. She dresses in a beautiful sari and her heavy, ornate wedding jewelery to greet him at JFK Airport, but underneath the familiar costume she is not the same woman at all. She is not even sure whether she is unhappy about it, though she can tell her husband is disconcerted.

The end of the story encapsulates both the strength of her spirited struggle to refashion herself and the difficulty of achieving wholeness when one is stretched between two cultures. On her way to bed with her husband, she stops to look at herself:

> In the mirror that hangs on the bathroom door, I watch my naked body turn, the breasts, the thighs glow. The body's beauty amazes. I stand here

shameless, in ways he has never seen me. I am free, afloat, watching somebody else.

This sense of floating is the key to the immigrant woman's experience, whether it is the English professor in **"The Tenant,"** the Indian girl from the Caribbean in **"Jasmine,"** or the PhD candidate in **"A Wife's Story."** Like Bernard Malamud, with whom Mukherjee compares herself in *The Massachusetts Review* interview, and other American writers of immigrant experiences, Mukherjee writes powerfully "about a minority community which escapes the ghetto and adapts itself to the patterns of the dominant American culture," and in her own words, her work "seems to find quite naturally a moral center." This moral center she speaks of comes quite naturally to her because she is attempting the nearly sacred task of making mysteries visible, to paraphrase an expression from **"The Tenant."**

Gary Boire (review date Spring 1992)

SOURCE: "Eyre and Anglos," in *Canadian Literature*, No. 132, Spring, 1992, pp. 160-61.

[*In the following review, Boire asserts that Mukherjee's "Jasmine is a tremendously interesting work, not simply because it foregrounds characters and situations and nationalities so often disguised or dismissed in the western/American tradition, but primarily because of Mukherjee's ironic nuance and sinewy revisionism."*]

Jasmine is Bharati Mukherjee's first novel in fourteen years; like her stories, it is highly crafted, impeccably understated, and virtually seamless in its unfolding. It is also, like many of her public statements and much of her writing, controversial. Like Atwood, Mukherjee has attracted a network of hecklers who pay more attention to her biography than her texts, and who delight in gainsaying as self-promotional Mukherjee's many observations about exclusionary racism and the Canadian literary scene. In this "word of mouth" category *Jasmine* has already gathered clusters of disagreeing admirers and critics. What for one reader is a startlingly intense "de-Europeanization" of the western/American novel (a hybrid mixture of romance, murder, and travel genres), is for another an opportunistic ride on the currently faddish postcolonial bandwagon. Just another novel about emigration, cultural difference, language, and racism. I mention this kind of extraneous networking because it is, to my mind, precisely the kind of detrimental gossip that would distort and ultimately disguise what I think is a very impressive and very important novel. *Jasmine* is a deceptively simple allegory which deliberately sabotages through rewriting. Consider.

On the simplest of levels this is a story about a young Indian woman who lights out for the new territories (which Mukherjee appropriates from her American sources with enviable skill). In sparse, symbolically condensed prose, amidst a series of time disjunctions and memory shifts, Mukherjee tells the life of Jyoti whose husband, Prakash, is murdered in India by a terrorist bomb during the partition riots. In rapid succession Jyoti smuggles herself to the Florida coast, emigrates to New York where she becomes a governess, and then to Iowa where she conceives a child with a banker who is confined to a wheelchair. Here she ultimately faces a moral choice of profound complexity. Along the way she becomes the adoptive mother of a Vietnamese refugee, changes her name from Jyoti to Jasmine to Jase to Jane, and witnesses first-hand the dereliction of the American Dream: the book is crammed with the violence of murder, rape, suicide, starvation and assassination.

In one sense, this story tells *the* paradigmatic "postcolonial" narrative; it is *the* story that "tells" Euro- and Americo-centricity back into itself by reversing readerly (read Anglo-American) expectations, by including all that is usually excluded, by bringing inside what is usually left outside. Mukherjee's crippled American banker who falls in love with a Punjabi woman and who then adopts a Vietnamese son (both of whom, interestingly, leave him to "rebirth" elsewhere and with others) develops into a resistant allegory that deconstructs the allure of American mythology. Horatio Alger may whisper from the wings, but he never steals the show. In fact, he is banished in short order.

But *Jasmine* is a "retelling" of considerably greater sophistication than this mere plot summary would indicate. Mukherjee writes with an almost surgical sense of irony (and indeed there is relatively little back-thumping humour to be found), an irony that subtly dismantles/unravels a history of oppressive positionings. I am thinking at this point of two comments by two very different writers: (1) Frederic Jameson, who so aptly remarks in *The Political Unconscious,*

> In its emergent strong form a genre is essentially a socio-symbolic message, or, in other terms, that form is immanently and intrinsically an ideology in its own right. When such forms are reappropriated and refashioned in quite different social and cultural contexts, this message persists and must be functionally reckoned into the new form . . . the ideology of the form itself, thus sedimented, persists into the latter, more complex structure, as a generic message which coexists—either as a contradiction or, on the other hand, as a mediatory or harmonizing mechanism—with elements from later stages.

And (2) Margery Fee, who recently commented, "radical writing, by definition, is writing that is struggling . . . to re-

write the dominant ideology from within, to produce a different version of reality." A strategy of reclamation and disclosure, this peculiar type of ironic recuperation is a means by which anti-colonialists might reappropriate the language so as to liberate both the worlds and roles suppressed by its official ideologues.

Significantly, Bharati Mukherjee writes in precisely this kind of ironically allusive/appropriative mode that sets up coexistent contradictions; for example, Jyoti recalls her childhood reading: "The British books were thick, with more long words per page. I remember *Great Expectations* and *Jane Eyre,* both of which I was forced to abandon because they were too difficult." The importance here is that Mukherjee also "abandons" both these Empire icons, not because of difficulty but because of her own need to "re-write" past literary and political wrongs. Both books (but especially *Jane Eyre*) echo and re-echo throughout ***Jasmine*** until Jane wearily and ruefully remarks, "I think maybe I am Jane with my very own Mr Rochester, and maybe it'll be okay for us to go to Missouri where the rules are looser and yield to the impulse in a drive-in chapel." Mukherjee not only echoes and then rejects the *Jane Eyre* scenario (Jane does *not* stay with her Rochester), but Mukherjee then replays Bronte's strategy of dividing the male lead into two distinct characters: the crippled Bud Ripplemeyer/Rochester and the professorial Taylor/St. John Rivers; ironically Mukherjee's Jane opts for the one learning Hindustani (but in a highly rewritten way!)

Jasmine is a tremendously interesting work, not simply because it foregrounds characters and situations and nationalities so often disguised or dismissed in the western/American tradition, but primarily because of Mukherjee's ironic nuance and sinewy revisionism. This is an important book not only for what it says, but also for how it says it. Mukherjee's is a revisionary, appropriative technique, one that "channels" deeply (to borrow from one of her rare comic scenes) into an existent literary landscape in order to excavate her own highly deserved space.

K. Anthony Appiah (review date 10 October 1993)

SOURCE: "Giving Up the Perfect Diamond," in *The New York Times Book Review,* October 10, 1993, p. 7.

[*In the following review, Appiah lauds Mukherjee's* The Holder of the World *stating, "Ms. Mukherjee draws us with vigor and scrupulous attention to detail across time . . . and space . . . into the footsteps of not one but two extraordinary women."*]

We live in a time of bad news for relations among communities. From Sri Lanka to Bosnia, from South Africa to Kashmir (and, dare I add, from Paris to Los Angeles), men and women live and die within the shifting alliances and antagonisms of constantly reshaping identities. The passions of these conflicts seem to call for the martial virtues: courage, strength, honor. It is tempting, in such a time, for those of us who favor the more peaceable virtues—gentleness, mercy, the compassion that the King James Bible calls loving kindness—to treat any novel that demonstrates how richly rewarding are the places between cultures as a moralizing allegory. In a world where a Bosnian Serb can murder a Muslim in-law, whose language he knows, whose table he has shared, we can find solace in even the fictional idea of a love that transcends more substantial cultural differences.

Bharati Mukherjee constantly reminds us of the interconnections among cultures that have made our modern world. And she records the brutalities and the squalor of these dealings between peoples, as well as the passions that yoke us together.
—K. Anthony Appiah

I report this temptation because Bharati Mukherjee's newest novel has taught me to resist it: it is one of the many values of *The Holder of the World* that it celebrates the borderlands without any such sentimentality. Ms. Mukherjee draws us with vigor and scrupulous attention to detail across time—from the present to the 17th and early 18th centuries—and space—from Salem, Mass., to the coast of Coromandel, in India—into the footsteps of not one but two extraordinary women.

The first woman, our contemporary, and one of the novel's two voices, is Beigh ("looks like 'Bee,' sounds like 'Bay-a'") Masters, who does "assets research"—high-toned snooping for antiques and art treasures. She has impeccable Puritan antecedents, descended from "one Charles Jonathan Samuel Muster, born in Morpeth, Northumberland," who "stowed away to Salem" in 1632 "in a ship heavy with cows, horses, goats, glass and iron."

The second woman is Hannah Easton. "In the remotest of ways," Beigh tells us, "Hannah Easton is a relative of mine." Hannah grew up in Salem, in the latter part of the 17th century. Her life comes to matter professionally to Beigh. In the tumultuous course of it, after her widowed mother's disappearance, Hannah was raised by another family and taught needlework. She later married, went to England, was widowed, remarried, traveled sometime around 1695 to Mogul India and held in her hands (for a moment, around 1700) the Emperor's Tear, "the world's most perfect diamond," an

"asset" Beigh is currently researching for an acquisitive client. The ruler in question was Aurangzeb, the last great Mogul emperor; the jewel, it seems, was taken from him during his victorious battle against Raja Jadav Singh, who happens to have been the love of Hannah Easton's life.

If it seems implausible, without the scaffolding of the whole tale, that a Puritan girl from Salem—still less a devout one—should, as a woman, become the concupiscent lover of a Gentoo prince, I can only say that Ms. Mukherjee knows how to make the tale work. Each of these women is written eloquently into full being. And the lines that connect them across time entwine them as surely as Hannah's life embraces Salem and the Coromandel coast.

Beigh traces the life of her almost-ancestress through texts and paintings, through museums in Massachusetts, graveyards in India and auctions in Bangkok, and, in the end, through a computer simulation, made by her lover, Venn, a contemporary Indian computer scientist. (In love, too, Hannah and Beigh have something in common.) But Beigh's passion to discover the truth of Hannah's life becomes more than professional: it consumes her. In the extraordinary climax of this extraordinary novel, Venn's technical time-tripping skills allow Beigh to experience Hannah's escape from the battle between Aurangzeb and Jadav Singh—and so to solve the mystery of the jewel.

Yet once she "finds" the jewel, Beigh tells us only where "I think the world's most perfect diamond lies." She doesn't need to dig it up; she has already uncovered the greater treasure, Hannah's amazing life.

Bharati Mukherjee constantly reminds us of the interconnections among cultures that have made our modern world. And she records the brutalities and the squalor of these dealings between peoples, as well as the passions that yoke us together. What she offers as a model of cultural cross-pollination—alas, one cannot forever resist the temptations of allegory—is not a gentle melding but a more vigorous, and a more bitter, fusion.

In this celebration of a life lived three centuries ago across cultures, Ms. Mukherjee discovers for us in Hannah a woman whose triumph is one of courage, of unyielding passion, of the obstinate will to survive. There is no place here for mawkish talk of tolerance and understanding. In Ms. Mukherjee's world, in the real world, we understand as much through butting heads as through shaking hands.

Hannah Easton survives both her English adventurer husband and her Hindu warrior lover and returns to Salem and to her mother, whom she remembers only as the woman who staged her own murder to run off with her American Indian lover. Her mother has come back to the white world with her five half-Nipmuc children, and after the custom of the time must wear an I, the badge of an "Indian lover." Mother and daughter live together in Salem with Hannah's child, the daughter of Jadav Singh, her "badge," the mark of her Indian love. Black Pearl, the gossips of Salem call the child; Hannah, the mother, they name White Pearl.

To sketch the plot of a book like *The Holder of the World* is to disfigure drama into melodrama. The truth is in the details, brilliantly conceived, finely written, sustained from the first to the last page. And when, at the end, Bharati Mukherjee has the hubris, the chutzpah, the sheer unmitigated gall, to connect her book, in Beigh's voice, with Hawthorne's novel *The Scarlet Letter,* which "many call our greatest work," it is, I think, a connection she has earned. Nathaniel Hawthorne is a relative of hers. And, like Hannah Easton, she has every right to claim her kinship across the centuries.

"When my writing is going well, I know that I'm writing out of my personal obsessions," says Bharati Mukherjee.

The obsession behind *The Holder of the World* appeared to her in 1989 at a pre-auction viewing at Sotheby's in New York—in the form of a 17th-century Indian miniature, a woman in ornate Mogul court dress holding a lotus blossom. The woman was Caucasian and blond.

"I thought, 'Who is this very confident-looking 17th-century woman, who sailed in some clumsy wooden boat across dangerous seas and then stayed there?'" Ms. Mukherjee said by telephone from her home in San Francisco. "She had transplanted herself in what must have been a traumatically different culture. How did she survive?" These questions prompted the novel.

Ms. Mukherjee's travels approximate, roughly in reverse, those of her 17th-century heroine, Hannah Easton. She was born in Calcutta in 1940, has lived in England and Canada, and first came to the United States in 1961 to study at the Iowa Writers' Workshop. She became an American citizen in 1988 and is now an English professor at the University of California, Berkeley.

Ms. Mukherjee researched her novel in the logbooks of European trading companies, in memoirs from colonial Massachusetts and in 17th-century travelers' accounts.

"I don't want to write that 500-page conventional historical novel, because that's a mimicry of a form," she said. "I want to bring the world into the 300-page novel without losing the complexity. What novelists have the power to do is imagine the inner life of people who acted out the facts of history. And do it with sympathy for every side."

Vivian Gornick (review date December 1993)

SOURCE: "Playing Games with History," in *The Women's Review of Books,* Vol. XI, No. 3, December, 1993, p. 15.

[*In the following review, Gornick complains that in Mukherjee's* The Holder of the World, *the "boisterous Hannah does in no way suggest the brooding Hester Prynne, and what Mukherjee has to say about repressed Westerners and sensual Indians is painfully familiar, not at all passionate or clarifying."*]

When a writer of serious purpose chooses to make imaginative use of genre writing—the historical romance, the science fiction novel, the mystery story—the reader feels compelled to ask: why? What is going to get said here, in this way, that would not otherwise have gotten said? How is this piece of artifice integral to the story that is actually being told? What internal urgency does the formal restriction serve? These are not rhetorical questions. The reader really wants an answer.

Bharati Mukherjee is the Calcutta-born author of seven novels and collections of essays. The situation in the novels, almost always, is that of the undocumented Indian immigrant in America. Mukherjee is one of the writers who has helped put the word "illegals" on the map of American literature. Because of her stories I have an ineradicable image in my head: that of an army of people in Queens living out their lives "in a room with tightly drawn curtains watching TV till [they're] glassy-eyed, hiding at every unexpected sound."

The narrating voice in these novels and stories is invariably intelligent, detached, savvy, benumbed. Humiliation is its middle name, humiliation permanent and historic, begun in India and only continued on in America; the deep buried-alive humiliation of people who have been "illegal" from the day they were born. In these stories Mukherjee is not psychologically inclined, but the mass of detail with which the characters present themselves is alive to the touch: painful in its authority, persuasive in its concreteness. The situation feels inevitable, and that often makes the narrator seem unavoidable.

The Holder of the World, Mukherjee's new novel, is a historical romance framed in a science fiction staple (time-travel), and it purports, in a surprise ending, to be relating the "true" history of a famous character in American literature. Let me summarize as best I can.

Beigh Masters, a thirty-year-old woman descended from the Puritans, lives in Cambridge (Mass.) with Venn Iyer, an Indian computer scientist at the Massachusetts Institute of Technology. She is an asset investigator (that is, a tracer of lost or hidden possessions); he "animates" information. Together, they are about to penetrate time. At his computer, Venn is trying to recreate a day in the past so perfectly that someone who is now alive will be able to step into it, if only for a few seconds. Beigh, meanwhile, has in the course of her investigations stumbled on the record of a distant relative, Hannah Easton, a woman born three hundred years ago in New England. Hannah survived a famous Indian massacre (in which her mother presumably perished), was then adopted and raised in Salem, married an Englishman, went to India with him, and in time became the mistress of a Raja. In 1700, Beigh concludes, Hannah Easton returned to Salem, pregnant with the Raja's baby, to become . . . Hester Prynne.

Venn and Beigh are both absorbed to the point of obsession by their twin projects: his to amass as much information as possible on his chosen day, hers to discover all there is to know about Hannah. The idea, for both of them, is that "with sufficient passion and intelligence, we can deconstruct the barriers of time and geography." And indeed: when Venn's technology is perfected Beigh is transported for a few seconds (in "virtual reality") back into Hannah's last violent days in India, where she (Beigh) solves a minor mystery that has been hanging down from the story like a loose end.

The Hannah Easton whom Beigh is investigating (ninety percent of the novel is Beigh's report on Hannah's imagined experience) is a woman who supposedly breaks the mold of Puritan repression. She has a sensual nature, inherited from her mother who apparently faked her own death to run off with an Indian lover. In the course of her life in India, as that nature is gradually revealed to her, Hannah discovers that she has the courage to act. What this finally comes down to is an extravagant passion for the Raja: her own hot-blooded Indian.

The background to Hannah's self-discovery is her life with Gabriel. Legge, the English husband who works for the plundering East India Company. Gabriel is intelligent, civil, ruthless. Hannah would have been happy to have had a passion for her own husband. The problem was that Gabriel, too, needed his hot-blooded Indian.

And so, of course, does Beigh Presumably this three-ring circus has been put into motion so that Beigh and Venn, a pair of abstract moderns, will become "interactive" with the (historically) buried stirrings of their own blood. Yes? No? It pains me to say this, but your guess is as good as mine. There is so much plot here and so little exploration of inner life that Beigh and Venn themselves remain shadowy: puppeteers jerking the strings of standup figures dancing around on a makeshift stage while they luck behind the curtain. As for Hannah, she seems a highly arbitrary explanation for one of the most mysterious figures in American literature. She might

just as easily have turned out to be the governess in *Anna and the King of Siam* as Hester Prynne.

Reading this novel I found myself thinking of *Wide Sargasso Sea.* That book also operates inside a piece of literary artifice; it, too, makes central use of the repressed English in the overheated tropics; and it, as well, takes as its subject the emotional accounting for a fictional character. But in *Wide Sargasso Sea* every sentence is penetrated with an innerliness of thought and feeling that makes the narrator seem inevitable, the story unavoidable. Jean Rhys once wrote that she had read *Jane Eyre* and thought to herself, "She [Bronte] doesn't know that woman. *I* know her." From the first sentence of Rhys's novel the reader accepts without equivocation the writer's need to work from inside the character of Mrs. Rochester. Reimagining Bertha was vital to the project; there was no other way for Rhys to say what she had to say.

The key words here are "inevitable" and "unavoidable." Need justifies the artifice. When a writer decides to enter the inner life of a fictional character created in another time and place the reader must be persuaded that the character is, for this writer, revelatory; psychologically compelling; necessary to the working out of some elusive but haunting insight. This sense of urgency is missing from ***The Holder of the World.*** It is hard to see what Mukherjee is really getting at. The boisterous Hannah does in no way suggest the brooding Hester Prynne, and what Mukherjee has to say about repressed Westerners and sensual Indians is painfully familiar, not at all passionate or clarifying. Inside the complicated apparatus of science-meta-fiction Mukherjee is, if anything, even less psychologically persuasive than in her tales of undocumented Indians.

This novel feels as though it was put in place by the requirements of literary fashion. When that happens the reader is being cheated. Mukherjee owes us one.

Kristin Carter-Sanborn (essay date September 1994)

SOURCE: "'We Murder Who We Were': *Jasmine* and the Violence of Identity," in *American Literature,* Vol. 66, No. 3, September, 1994, pp. 573-93.

[*In the following essay, Carter-Sanborn discusses the place of identity and violence in Mukherjee's* Jasmine.]

The narrator of Bharati Mukherjee's ***Jasmine*** implicitly positions herself early in her own text in terms of narratives already abandoned. At age seven, Jyoti is the star pupil of Masterji, "the oldest and sourest teacher in our school": "I was whiz in Punjabi and Urdu, and the first likely female candidate for English instruction he'd ever had. He had a pile of English books, some from the British Council Library, some with USIS stickers.... The British books were thick, with more long words per page. I remember *Great Expectations* and *Jane Eyre,* both of which I was forced to abandon because they were too difficult." By thus locating her novel in the space circumscribed by two classic texts of Victorian education and identity, Mukherjee signals to the reader the generic continuity between her *bildungsroman* and these earlier narratives. Like Jane's and Pip's stories, Jyoti's is told retrospectively, this time from the point of view of a young woman about to light out for the territory, having already experienced a whirlwind series of transformative events. After witnessing her mentor Masterji's death at the hands of Sikh militants, who will later murder her husband, Jyoti flees her native Punjab, "phantom[s her] way through three continents," and arrives with forged papers on the Gulf Coast of Florida. From there she travels to Queens, Manhattan, and then to a small town in Iowa, metamorphosing on the way into Jasmine, Jazzy, Jase, and Jane. The America she encounters is, in its endemic violence, not unlike the Punjab she left behind. Indeed, the latest influx of immigrants to the United States has transformed it into an "archipelago of ghettos seething with aliens"; or, as one reviewer put it, a "new Third World."

The contemporary complexities of "first" and "third" world relations foregrounded by *Jasmine* return us to *Great Expectations* and *Jane Eyre,* the mention of which must also invoke for us the Victorian imperial project in which their production was situated. Both of these earlier novels are indeed "thick" with the voice of an ostensibly progressive colonial authority addressing issues of gender and class formation. The fact that Jyoti abandons the deciphering of that voice as "too difficult" will signal to us that, as Homi Bhabha suggests, the site of that authority is vexed, compromised, "agonistic."

Although the literary voice of colonial authority hardly gets a hearing in Jyoti's Punjab village, the very dismissal of Brontë's book is coincident with its introduction as a structuring "presence" in *Jasmine.* I would like to use this framing presence as a starting point for my discussion of the postcolonial concerns of *Jasmine,* even as I too eventually abandon it in favor of a more general examination of the dynamics of subjectivity in Mukherjee's novel.

Jyoti's rejection of *Jane Eyre* only begins to suggest the complex relationship between the colonialist subtext of Brontë's novel and the "multicultural" implications of *Jasmine's* narrative. Jyoti leaves off reading *Jane Eyre* in Hasnapur only to take the Christian name of that novel's protagonist once she reaches Iowa; her character's development also echoes and revises Jane Eyre's in other ways, as we will see. And

just as we must consider whether Jane Eyre, in her search for a new female domestic identity, is implicated in the violent repression of colonial subjectivity as figured by Bertha Mason, we also need to ask whether Jyoti-Jasmine-Jane's "discovery" of an American selfhood covers up a similar complicity in the elision of the "third world" woman Mukherjee's narrator purportedly speaks as and for. More generally, we must question whether *Jasmine* is implicated in the neo-imperialist demands of the Western reader as they are described by Trinh in the epigraph to this essay—demands for "what we can't have," for an exotic diversion from the "monotony of sameness."

This question is especially critical in light of the novel's mainstream and academic popularity—it was received with acclaim in nearly every major review publication and has been increasingly taught since then in women's studies, ethnic studies, and contemporary American literature courses. I would argue that the novel's appeal can be traced in part to its readers' complicated investment in the racial and cultural otherness of the narrator (and, of course, her author). Beginning with Richard Eder's laudatory notice in the *Los Angeles Times Book Review,* the arrangement and selection of popular reviews on the back of the Fawcett Crest paperback edition foreground a simultaneous interest in both Jasmine's alterity and her suitability for naturalization to an "American" way of life:

> ARTFUL AND ARRESTING ... BREATHTAKING ... A Hindu woman flees her family's poverty, and the Sikh terrorism that bloodies her village.... After a time in New York—*only a foreign eye could fix the world of the Upper West Side with such hilarious and revealing estrangement*—she moves to a small town in Iowa. In corn and hog country—now prey to farm foreclosures and despair—she marks with unsparing brilliance the symptoms of a new Third World.

Subsequent blurbs reproduce the fascination with the estranged "foreign eye" of Eder's assessment (a fascination less evident, it should be noted, in sections of the review not quoted by the publisher). Helping us (that is, mainstream U.S. readers) to see "ourselves as others see us," the "uncanny third eye of the artist [that] forces us to see our country anew" reveals itself to be the uncanny eye of the third *world* artist for these reviewers. But at the same time it embodies the mystical insight of the Other, Jasmine's "third eye" represents a way of seeing that is ultimately transformed, in the mini-narrative of the book blurb, from the myopia of a backward "Indian village girl, whose grandmother wants to marry her off at 11," into the enlightened vision of "an American woman who finally thinks for herself." The book's selling power seems, then, to stem from its simultaneous exoticism and domesticability, its existence as a sort of pop multiculturalist prop not much different from the one envisioned by Trinh. This observation is not to suggest that *Jasmine* has no place on our course reading lists. On the contrary, its difficulties may provide us with more paths than obstacles to understanding the exigencies of representing "third world experience." I offer this critique of the novel in the hope that it may help us and our students reexamine our expectations regarding textual authenticity and ethnicity in the literature classroom.

We might consider these expectations in light of Trinh's assessment of the ends and means of the anthropological "dialogue." Essentially a "conversation of 'us' with 'us' about 'them,'" "the conversation [the anthropologist-nativist] aspires to turns out to be rather intimate: a chatty talk, which, under cover of cross-cultural communication, simply superposes one system of signs over another." Gayatri C. Spivak further complicates this conversational dynamic. Commenting on her own discussion of the suicide of a young Indian woman, Bhuvaneswari Bhaduri, in Calcutta in 1926 she remarks,

> What I was doing with the young woman who had killed herself was really trying to analyze and represent her text. She wasn't particularly trying to speak to me. I was representing her, I was re-inscribing her. To an extent, I was writing her to be read, and I certainly was not claiming to give her a voice. So if I'm read as giving her a voice, there again this is a sort of transaction of the positionality between the Western feminist listener who listens to me, and myself, signified as a Third World informant.

In the context of the "transaction" detailed in Spivak's and Trinh's descriptions, certain questions about Mukherjee's novel arise. Does the text in fact ask to be read as speaking the "subaltern" voice through Jasmine's first-person narrative? Or is such an assumption merely a function of the misguided expectations of what Spivak calls "cardcarrying listeners"?

The expectations of others—readers, listeners, lovers, and entire communities—do in fact provide one of the most important structural matrices on which *Jasmine* is plotted. When he first glimpses Jasmine, Bud Ripplemeyer tells her, *"It felt as if I was a child again, back in the Saturday-afternoon movies. You were glamour, something unattainable"* (author's emphasis). By renaming her Jane, her lover has something much more exotic and erotic in mind than the "Plain Jane" the narrator and her Victorian namesake would more readily identify with. "Me Bud, you Jane. I didn't get it at first," she reflects. "He kids. Calamity Jane. Jane as in Jane Russell." Her "genuine foreignness" frightens the relatively staid Midwestern banker, however, and as Jane to his

crippled Rochester-Tarzan, the narrator can assuage Bud's fears only by settling into the role of domesticated exotic. Earlier, having abandoned the village of her father for her "city man" husband Prakash Vijh, she even more readily settled into the "small and sweet and heady" role of "Jasmine," Vijh's modern wife and business partner—a "new kind of city woman" whom he can show off to friends. And between Jasmine and Jane, she becomes "Jase," exoticized domestic and au pair to Manhattan professionals Wylie and Taylor Hayes. The narrator's ability to "shuttle . . . between identities," to accept another's interpolation with little difficulty, is explicated in the text as a symptom of the liminality of the "third world" subject. The quick-changes she accomplishes reflect Jasmine's self-imposed mandate, expressed early in the novel, to "murder who we were so we can rebirth ourselves in the images of dreams."

The "images of dreams" . . . but of whose dreams? This ambiguous phrase, central to our understanding of Mukherjee's project, opens up a number of possible readings, all of which compete for primacy in the text. We might compare Jasmine's "suicides" and "rebirths" to the revolutionary process of decolonization as described by Frantz Fanon in *The Wretched of the Earth:* "National liberation, national renaissance, the restoration of nationhood to the people, commonwealth: whatever may be the headings used or the new formulas introduced, decolonization is always a violent phenomenon. . . . Without any period of transition, there is a total, complete, and absolute substitution."

Jasmine's violent substitution of self, then, could be recognized as a move constituting part of the ethnic nationalist repertoire, a liberatory gesture which achieves "that kind of *tabula rasa* which characterizes at the outset all decolonization," and which institutes a "new language and a new humanity." In this context the significance of "rebirth . . . in the images of dreams" is that "it is willed, called for, demanded"—the dream is a conscious hope, an aspiration or goal, an object of rational desire that determines anticipatory behavior. Most important, the dream and the program which follows from it are acts of agency, and in fact grant agency: "[T]he 'thing' which had been colonized becomes man during the same process by which it frees itself." Jasmine's agenda could offer a counterdiscourse or model of resistance to those who would name and thus control her. She is a "tornado, a rubble-maker, arising from nowhere and disappearing into a cloud," destroying all in her path as she chooses, including her old selves; her dream is a will to power.

But in the context of Mukherjee's representation of certain Hindu beliefs, the "images of dreams" take on a more spiritual dimension. With those dreams she may mean to invoke some kind of cataclysmic return of the repressed, in which consciousness or agency is subjected to an actor's own intuitive (and uncontrollable) dream-knowledge of who she "essentially" and unconsciously is. This "regression" may seem counter to the notion of rebirth. But the constellation of beliefs surrounding the birth-death cycle that the narrator invokes early in the novel, in addition to Jasmine's own "theoretical" belief in reincarnation and reliance on other traditional Hindu cultural forms, obliges us at least to investigate this particular shading of "dreams."

Reincarnation is figured in Jasmine's narrative as the shattering of fleshly vessels that had given only temporary shape to an essentially ephemeral spirit. Recounting the story of Vimla, a young woman who douses herself with kerosene and sets herself on fire after the death of her husband, Jasmine recalls that "[t]he villagers say when a clay pitcher breaks, you see that the air inside it is the same as outside." Vimla commits *sati* "because she had broken her pitcher; she saw there were no insides and outsides. We are just shells of the same Absolute. In Hasnapur," she adds, "Vimla's isn't a sad story." In fact, it is a triumphant one, guaranteeing for her as it does liberation from the cycle of transmigration and a return to an originary "Absolute." Anthropologist Michael M. J. Fischer has tried to articulate the "absoluteness" of ethnicity itself in language strikingly similar to that of the villagers, reading the "epiphanic" moments of ethnic autobiography as "revelations of traditions, re-collections of disseminated identities and of the divine sparks from the breaking of the vessels." Here an ethnic absolute or essence functions (quite problematically, I believe) like a neurosis "that manifests itself through repetition of behavioral patterns and that cannot be articulated in rational language but can only be acted out," fearfully and anxiously, through the mechanism of transference or "the return of the repressed in new forms." This inarticulate "acting out" of ethno-spiritual essence seems to have affinities with both Vimla's act of self-violence and Jasmine's generalization about the compulsive and metaphorically murderous process of "shuttl[ing] between identities."

At various points the novel asks to be read according to one of these glosses. It seems to me, however, that the first—decolonizing, ethnic nationalist—insufficiently explains what is going on in the text as a whole; the second—reincarnation—may in fact disguise the imperial subject dreaming of and violently remaking its "third world" Others to fit those dreams. In other words, it may disguise the dynamic of what Edward Said calls "Orientalism" (one form of which is manifested in Trinh's "conversation of 'us' with 'us' about 'them'"): "Orientalism is the discipline by which the Orient was (and is) approached systematically, as a topic of learning, discovery, and practice. But in addition I have been using the word to designate that collection of dreams, images, and vocabularies available to anyone who has tried to talk about what lies east of the dividing line. These two aspects of Orientalism are not incongruent, since by use of them both

Europe could advance securely and unmetaphorically upon the Orient." Bud, Taylor, and even her first husband Prakash, whom Jasmine characterizes as a type of Professor Higgins, call upon these vocabularies in order to speak the narrator's name and thus remake her in the shape of their own fantasies. And, as we will see, these fantasies are sometimes very unmetaphorically acted out on Jasmine's body. When Jasmine reflects that "there are no harmless, compassionate ways to remake oneself," then, she may actually be invoking a process in which change is predicated on pain wrought from without. Although one might expect Mukherjee to demonstrate some ironic distance on this construction of the transformative process, the author's own emphatic "yes," when asked by interviewers if she indeed saw violence as necessary to the metamorphosis of character reveals this not to be the case: "And I can see that in my own case it's been psychic violence. In my character Jasmine's case it's been physical violence because she's from a poor farming family." This response (the theoretical implications of which I will take up later) further confounds our efforts to locate agency in Jasmine's model of self-transformation.

To move closer to an understanding of this model, I would like to explore the ways in which Mukherjee has herself addressed key questions of agency and subjectivity in other essays, where those seem to be topics of some concern. In an early autobiographical collaboration with her husband Clark Blaise, Mukherjee has described herself as "a late-blooming colonial who writes in a borrowed language (English), lives permanently in an alien country [Canada at the time], and publishes in and is read, when read at all, in another alien country, the United States. My Indianness is fragile; it has to be professed and fought for, even though I look so unmistakably Indian. Language transforms our ways of apprehending the world; I fear that my decades-long use of English as a first language has cut me off from my *desh*." Here the author describes a consciousness that is characterized mainly by its liminality and sense of exile in a field where borders of identity are repositioned and fixed by language itself. In later work, however, Mukherjee seems to abandon the idea that in her current milieu she is somehow exiled or cut off from her "Indianness." Writing now as a recently naturalized U.S. citizen, she exhorts her fellow immigrant writers to "cash . . . in on the other legacy of the colonial writer, and that is his or her duality. From childhood, we learned how to be two things simultaneously; to be the dispossessed as well as the dispossessor. . . . History forced us to see ourselves as both the 'we' and the 'other.'"

Such a split subjectivity, Mukherjee asserts, can and must be brought to bear on the literary production of minority and immigrant writers. The "fluid set of identities" thus made available to the artist can broaden her range of materials and the perspectives that she may represent in her fiction. Her training as a "third-world" subject gives the artist the ability "to 'enter' lives, fictionally, that are manifestly not [her] own. . . . over and across the country, and up and down the social ladder," without sacrificing authenticity. In interviews, Mukherjee has schematized this fluidity in terms of psychological transformation, self-reinvention, or, as in *Jasmine,* murder and rebirth—a "shuttling" and shuffling of selves. Such reinvention, as I noted before, is always violent and, it seems, imperative in the context of emigration, particularly for women. The Asian man, Mukherjee argues, "comes for economic transformation, and he brings a wife who winds up being psychologically changed. . . . The men have a sense of accomplishment. They have no idea of staying here. The idea is saving money and going. But they don't realize the women have been transformed." Here the man transforms, the woman is transformed, and as positive as her transformation might be, it results from the opposition of violence to agency, of active force to passive object. The male postcolonial nurtures his American dream; with that dream he wields the power that will violently "rebirth" the wife.

On a purely theoretical level, Mukherjee's idea of the gendered colonial "ethnic" subject has easily recognizable affinities with the critique of colonial discourse elaborated in the work of Fanon and, more recently, of Homi Bhabha and Gayatri Spivak, although I would argue that the theoretical positions of the latter two ultimately undermine Mukherjee's argument. Obvious parallels can be found between Mukherjee's manipulation of the concept of cultural dualism or "simultaneity" and Bhabha's more labored articulation of the "hybridization" enacted at the site of native oppression. For Bhabha, hybridity represents "that ambivalent 'turn' of the discriminated subject into the terrifying, exorbitant object of paranoid classification—a disturbing questioning of the images and presences of authority." The ambivalence thus revealed "turns the discursive conditions of dominance into the grounds of intervention": the discriminated subject, incompletely contained by the power and paranoid knowledge invested in its constitution, participates in, confronts, and unsettles that very power.

Jasmine does take as one of its main subjects the authoritative "ambivalence" or uncertain promise of U.S. cultural space, itself described by the narrator as a "third world" or postcolonial field barely distinguishable, in its tortured and violent landscape, from Mexico, from Haiti, or from Jasmine's own Punjab. The lost promise of this place is at once a disappointment, a force of oppression, and a field of opportunity for the immigrant. "In America," the narrator muses, "[N]othing lasts. I can say that now and it doesn't shock me, but I think it was the hardest lesson of all for me to learn. We arrive so eager to learn, to adjust, to participate, only to find the monuments are plastic, agreements are annulled. *Nothing is forever, nothing is so terrible, or so*

wonderful, that it won't disintegrate" (my emphasis). The author would have her immigrant characters negotiate this hard lesson using the resources of "simultaneity" they have already learned at home; ideally, Mukherjee's protagonists would be able to tap into what Gloria Anzaldúa has called the "*mestiza* consciousness," a "tolerance for contradictions, a tolerance for ambiguity" like that demonstrated by Jane's adopted son Du, a young refugee who has established a "delicate thread of . . . hyphenization." The balance he has struck prevents his identity as a Vietnamese from being effaced by the dominant culture.

But in fact, for Gayatri Spivak the duality of which Mukherjee speaks is evidence of the colonial project's success in effacing the female subaltern subject. In the argument over the status of *sati,* or widow immolation, in modern Indian culture, an exchange emblematic of the collusion between elite nativist and colonial interests, "the figure of the woman disappears, not into a pristine nothingness, but into a violent shuttling which is the displaced figuration of the 'third-world woman' caught between tradition and modernization." Rather than speaking as both the woman-in-patriarchy and the woman-in-imperialism, Spivak asserts, she can speak as neither, precisely because she is constituted as both, and therefore subject to a "violent shuttling" that enacts a steady erasure of being, rather than a series of progressively triumphant rebirths.

I would argue, then, that Mukherjee's theorization of the gendered postcolonial self most closely follows the colonialist fantasy itself, described here by Fanon: "[I]t is implicit that to speak is to exist absolutely for the other. The black man has two dimensions. One with his fellows, the other with the white man. . . . That this self-division is a direct result of colonialist subjugation is beyond question. . . . The colonized is elevated above his jungle status in proportion to his adoption of the mother country's cultural standards. He becomes whiter as he renounces his blackness, his jungle." Implicit in Fanon's description is the assumption that the settler's fantasy (elsewhere outlined by Said) has in fact determined reality, enacting a "Manichean" world of "them or us." But this Manichean logic ultimately "leaves the native unshaken," for as we have already seen, he "has practically stated the problem of his liberation in identical terms. . . . For the native, [the violence of the settlers] represents the absolute line of [liberationist] action." The "simultaneity" which Mukherjee celebrates in essays and interviews is proposed but ultimately dismantled in her novelistic work: fluidity in *Jasmine* is theorized not as hybridity but as a perpetual gesture toward absolute otherness. The trajectory of Jasmine's meteoric transformation traces that of Fanon's theory of change in form only, which is to say that it ends up tracing a fairly traditional colonial itinerary, not without important consequences for the postcolonial "ethnic" gendered subject.

To act, for Jasmine, is to become entirely other. In an interesting inversion of the colonial project sketched by Bhabha, Jasmine can authoritatively impute the idea of "multiplicity" to her own character only retrospectively (again we are reminded of Jane Eyre's own retrospective identity-building), from the perspective of a woman with an all-seeing "third eye." She can look back and reflexively assert her difference from herself as the narrator of the text: "Jyoti of Hasnapur was not Jasmine, Duff's day mummy and Taylor and Wylie's *au pair* in Manhattan; *that* Jasmine isn't *this* Jane Ripplemeyer having lunch with Mary Webb at the University Club today. And which of us is the undetected murderer of a half-faced monster, which of us has held a dying husband, which of us was raped and raped and raped in boats and cars and motel rooms?" (author's emphasis). In cataloging her selves Jasmine is able to conjoin them in the overarching "multiple" consciousness of the narrative. But in the very construction of that consciousness there is no "simultaneity" or even continuity to be found. The narrator is not the widow *and* the *au pair;* the Iowa wife *and* the undetected murderer. The continuity between one of these states and any other is either obscured or destroyed, her implicit argument goes, by the violence of the transformative moment. She abandons agency in this moment to her theoretical Other, and it is this Other who determines and delivers her into new forms. Far from maintaining a "critical difference from [her]self," an ambivalent and non-unified, hybrid subjectivity, Jasmine's self-making insists on fixing "the differences made *between* entities comprehended as absolute presences." Having rejected the demands of a patriarchal nativism which (in the person of her father and the Sikh terrorist group, the Khalsa Lions) violently seeks to limit her cultural mobility, she turns to America and picks up the colonial "text" we thought she had set aside for good. Her flirtation with "multiplicity" ironically resolves itself into a domestic and domesticated fantasy, a classic American dream of assimilation. Disguised as a call for a revolution in our very understanding of the processes of identity in contemporary America, the narrative's lessons reveal a desire to invest American identity itself with presence and authority. Thus the novel may more than anything demonstrate the very impossibility of an integrated subjecthood in the framework of Western notions of independence and individual accomplishment.

At the time of its publication, Mukherjee said of *Jasmine,* "[I]t's not a realistic novel. It's meant to be a fable." The imaginative license Mukherjee thus allows herself enables her to elaborate a plot in which questions of gender, racial, and cultural identity are skirted through recourse to cultural icons and stereotypes (both Indian and American) and a broad indulgence in fictional extremes. In her novel, as in the Victorian dream of the "Orient" described by Said, the Punjab and even the U.S. itself become places "of romance, exotic beings, haunting memories and landscapes, remark-

able experiences." In this charmed landscape, selfhood and identity are mystified. Many of these mystifications are quite powerful, and indeed might be said to participate in the cultural work of myth-building. I will not attempt to argue against the liberating potential of mythification in general terms; however, I do believe that the specific instances of exoticism in *Jasmine* serve to reify subaltern identity rather than to liberate it.

> Disguised as a call for a revolution in our very understanding of the processes of identity in contemporary America, the narrative's lessons reveal a desire to invest American identity itself with presence and authority. Thus the novel may more than anything demonstrate the very impossibility of an integrated subjecthood in the framework of Western notions of independence and individual accomplishment.
> —*Kristen Carter-Sanborn*

This reification is accomplished in the context of a particular notion of rebirth or transformation that is, as we have seen, metaphorically if not literally violent. The ways in which *Jasmine* moves between the metaphorical violence of identity transformation, the notion of representation itself as violence, and the fact of empirical violence raise a number of theoretical and methodological difficulties. If we indulge too fully the Derridean play between the "violence of the letter" and violence in the social field, or if we define as violent the very forces of psychic transformation, we obviously run the risk of derogating material violence—the physical violation of living bodies—and any political motivation one might have for wanting to represent it textually. This happens when Mukherjee herself starts making comparisons, with little apparent irony, between the "psychic violence" she experienced as the daughter of a wealthy factory owner growing up in Calcutta and the actual physical violence someone like Jasmine might face: "I had to personally experience a great deal of labor violence and unrest. There were many times when I went to school with what we used to call 'flying squads.' Military policemen in vans in front, special policemen in vans in back, our car, with chauffeur and bodyguard in between so we could, the three sisters, take part as pretty maidens in . . . Gilbert and Sullivan light operas." While certainly the fear and psychic trauma associated with the threat of violence must have had very real effects on the young Mukherjee, there is obviously an incommensurable difference between the anxiety felt by a girl cradled in a "flying squad" and the kind of bodily oppression "labor" was experiencing at the same time, a difference Mukherjee only partially acknowledges.

As Spivak has noted, "The narrow epistemic violence of imperialism gives us an imperfect allegory of the general violence that is the possibility of an episteme." Imperfect but not arbitrary—it is imperative that we understand violence in its discursive articulation if we *are* to detail the real effects of material violence beyond the physical. These effects might include a community's or individual's self-description as circumscribed, limited, and defined in daily life by violence, for instance, which may in turn result in nonviolent interventionary practice in the realm of legal or social discourse. In any case, I am aware of the many difficulties involved in any negotiation of "literal" and "metaphoric" social practice. I will try to acknowledge carefully those difficulties as I explore the ways in which Mukherjee's text does in fact "allegorize" psychological violence and the representation of male and female empirical violence, as each extends, comments on, ironizes, and complicates the other.

In *Jasmine,* "textual" or metaphoric violence is generalized from the postcolonial experience to the immigrant and "minority" experience in the United States. More significantly, Mukherjee makes it contiguous with the very constitution of American identity, broadly construed to include dominant as well as "ethnic" cultural forms. As Edward Said has acknowledged, there is nothing "especially controversial or reprehensible" about the *fact* that "cultures impose corrections upon raw reality," including encounters with other cultures, in order to make sense of them; but the *way* those "corrections" are imposed can obviously have serious implications and consequences. Mukherjee's move to represent mainstream American culture in terms of "third world" identity must stand in problematic relation to a feminist or "third world" politics of difference. This becomes apparent when we examine the ways in which Jasmine adapts traditional Hindu doctrine, which argues for the contiguity of the human soul with an eternal *atman,* and which has historically been used to maintain a rigid caste system. Jasmine attempts to transplant this hierarchical doctrine onto the modern American idiom of class mobility and individual opportunity. It is as if she travels to America in order to radically, violently accelerate the evolution of her soul:

> What if the human soul is eternal—the swamis say
> of it, fires cannot burn it, water cannot drown it,
> winds cannot bend it—what if it is like a giant long-
> playing record with millions of tracks, each of them
> a complete circle with only one diamond-sharp mi-
> croscopic link to the next life, and the next, and only
> God to hear it all?

> I do believe that. And I do believe that extraordi-
> nary events can jar the needle arm, rip across in-
> carnations, and deposit a life into a groove that was
> not prepared to receive it.

Here, "Fate" still maintains its hold on Jasmine's understanding, and as an idea, if not an actual force, it does in fact determine her plot. A confluence of "extraordinary events" replaces the inexorable propulsion of human life along a predetermined track, and as we shall see, Jasmine's syncretic adaptation of sacred Hindu and secular American beliefs collapses under the weight of what it must support: an impossible negotiation between destiny and opportunity, between unwilled necessity and the willed, private revolution of the "self-made man." As in the debate over *sati* detailed by Spivak, the figure of the subaltern woman is erased in a proliferation of arguments over her place within feudal patriarchy on the one hand and capitalist patriarchy on the other, both of which posit an evanescent equality of opportunity.

The impossibility of Jasmine's project is not readily apparent in the opening pages of the novel. As a seven-year-old girl, she is foretold of her widowhood and exile by an astrologer and refuses vehemently to believe in her "fate." "'Suit yourself,' the astrologer cackled. 'What is to happen will happen.' Then he chucked me hard on the head," upon which the young girl falls down and a sharp stick punctures a hole in her forehead. This act of violence seems to inaugurate in Jyoti's life what Spivak has called a "discursive displacement"—a shift of perspective which can "only be operated by the force of a crisis," political or social. Such a shift or "functional change in sign-systems" can make the objects of historiography into the subjects of their own history, as in the work of the Subaltern Studies group about which Spivak writes. This collection of scholars has tried to demonstrate how the "criminality" of a rebellious subaltern group is transformed by them into "insurgency," the label of "bondsman" traded in for the radically charged category of "worker." Brought to crisis by the astrologer's prediction, Jyoti can thus assert to her family that her wound is in fact a "third eye," and she, a newly-born sage. A new way of seeing provides her with an intuitive rubric for knowing "what I don't want to become."

Later, on her morning trip to the outhouses with the other women of the village, Jyoti must confront a mad dog which she somehow knows "had come for me, not for the other women. It had picked me as its enemy." However, even as she recognizes "fate" in the terrifying form of the rabid jackal she resists that doom: "I wasn't ready to die." On the way to the outhouse she had picked up a thorny staff cast off by one of the Khalsa Lions and felt a "buzz of power" as her hand closed on it; this "buzz" now translates to action, and she kills the dog in mid-leap with the club. Jyoti's grandmother attempts to defuse Jyoti's moment of triumph over fate—"All it means is that God doesn't think you're ready for salvation. Individual effort counts for nothing"—but it seems in fact that against the violent forces of Sikh gangs, crazy astrologers, and mad dogs, individual effort is all, and holiness without significance.

Mukherjee describes the landscape of contemporary America in similarly violent terms, painting a picture of a state in economic, social, and political crisis: "Last week in Dalton County, a farmer dug a trench all around his banker's house with stolen backhoe equipment. On TV he said, 'Call it a moat of hate.' Over by Osage a man beat his wife with a spade, then hanged himself in his machine shed." Stable bonds of family and community seem to have dissolved, leaving behind only "Monster Truck Madness"; televised INS raids; farmers shooting bankers who foreclose on them; and the constant threat and reality of rape which first Jyoti, then Jasmine, then Jane and other immigrant women must constantly negotiate. As Jasmine muses, "Something's gotten out of hand in the heartland." The vertiginous violence of change in the American landscape unsettles and even nauseates the narrator: "I feel at times like a stone hurtling through diaphanous mist," she tells us, "unable to grab hold, unable to slow myself, yet unwilling to abandon the ride I'm on. Down and down I go, where I'll stop, God knows."

Between this moment and the one in which Jyoti describes the "buzz of power" she feels as she handles the thorned club, the text of *Jasmine* has accomplished a subtle displacement of agency. Jyoti has gone from being the subject to being the object of transformation, and it is violence itself which has displaced her on that positional continuum. Exactly at that instant when Jasmine desires to break the "diamond sharp links" from one state of being to another, she allows her own (not so peculiar) notion of female subjectivity to confirm her position as it stands, even as she is repositioned in terms of plot. The mysteriously accomplished shift recalls Mukherjee's description, in the interview excerpted earlier, of the passive "transformation" of the Indian women who trail after ambitious husbands seeking economic and educational riches here in the States. And indeed, even the language Jyoti uses to describe her confrontation with the mad dog is strangely passive: "I took aim and waited for it to leap on me. The staff crushed the dog's snout while it was still in mid-leap. Spiny twigs hooked deep into its nostrils and split them open. I saw all this as I lay on the winter-hard ground." It is as if the staff has leaped out of Jyoti's hands and done its work alone; she describes the scene from the point of view of prone and helpless observer.

A similar displacement of agency occurs as the narrator confronts another attacker, after she arrives on U.S. shores. Jasmine's killing of the rapist Half-Face constitutes a defining moment in the complex articulation of violence and gendered subjectivity that I have begun to sketch. In this moment Jasmine clearly reveals her complicity in an assimilative imperial and patriarchal practice, the primal scene of which, ironically, is the scene of Othering. The narrator's

complicity is crystallized not in her act of violence, but in her figuration of that violence—the way in which the act is discursively deployed. Thus I am emphatically *not* making the argument that any material act of violence implicates its executor in the perpetuation of imperialism or patriarchy. Rather, it is the way in which the narrator makes the act of violence intelligible to herself and to her witness, the reader, that is significant. The framework in which she enacts violence is one in which that act is seen only as a symptom of the greater epistemic violence of modern subjectivity, "first world" as well as "third world." Jasmine reinforces the colonizer's project by figuring her activity as assimilation or commutation to her Other—the "duality" she (and, implicitly, Mukherjee) has figured as power resolving itself into assimilation.

When Half-Face takes Jasmine to his motel room, several levels of violence—epistemic, metaphoric, and literal—are collapsed. Even as he drags her into the room she observes that "[h]is leg flew waist-high in a show-offy kick and the door thumped closed"—that is, his violence is stylized, it has meaning, and thus operates at the level of discourse. He forces himself on her and she, not surprisingly, refuses his advance. But Half-Face is surprised. "I thought you'd be different from the others. A spark, you know?" Something about her categorical difference, her "Indianness" has intrigued him. "You don't like white men, that it?" he asks. Jasmine here represents to Half-Face the inaccessible "exotic"—not in terms of her sexual availability, which he easily enforces, but in terms of her "inscrutability," her unknowability, her otherness. Angered by her suggestion that her life in India was not that much different from his life in the motel room—she looks at his television and notes that her husband had been a whiz repairman of such objects—Half-face must recapitulate epistemic violence at the literal level. "Don't tell me you ever *seen* a television set. Don't lie to me about no husbands and no television and we'll get along real good" (author's emphasis), he yells, even as he slams her head over and over into the set. His violence enacts his dream of the Other, in which he will be the one to painfully introduce the native to the requirements and perquisites of culture, assuming as he does that culture itself is unknown to her: "I got things I can do for you and you got something you can do for me, and I got lots of other things I can do *to* you, understand?" (author's emphasis).

Once he has raped her, Jyoti, in turn, enacts her own "dream" of violence, destroying in the same instant both Half-Face and her former self. Significantly, she plans to kill herself in order to purify her soul after the rape—she asserts, in fact, that she has already left her earthly body and would soon be joining her father's and husband's souls, even before she puts her knife to her own throat. As she hides in the motel bathroom, the "murkiness of the mirror" into which she looks "and a sudden sense of mission" stay her literal suicide. At the very moment, in other words, that she loses sight of her "self," she is subjected to a mandate spoken by an authority from *elsewhere*. Jyoti implicitly acknowledges this splitting of her subjectivity by symbolically slicing her tongue with the knife she will then use to slit Half-Face's throat. In doing so she becomes Kali of the bloody tongue, the destroyer goddess, "walking death. Death incarnate." Only in this dissociative state can she do what she has to do. It is important to note that even as Mukherjee figures the act as one of agency rather than reactive self-defense—after all, Jasmine leaves Half-Face and *upon reflection* returns to murder him—she makes the murderer not Jasmine, but Kali. Where before she had stood before him a naked, vulnerable young girl, she would now return to stand over him with her "mouth open, pouring blood, [her] red tongue out," in the classic pose of the vengeful goddess. When it is over, the narrator still feels that her "body was merely the shell, soon to be discarded"; in the wake of this violent birth into America, she can only look forward to future rebirths, a perpetual "revolution" of the soul which begs the question of its own existence.

As Mukherjee represents her, the "third world" woman cannot be violent without recourse to some original mythic, mystic "presence" (in this instance, the Bengali Hindu goddess Kali) that ironically blocks access to agency. As I stated earlier, the invocation of cultural heroes is not automatically disempowering—it can be a valuable tool for amassing spiritual strength and focus. But in Jasmine's case, Kali's presence overcomes and effaces Jasmine and the personal history which has brought her to this point. Kali, the "Goddess *ex machina*" appears and positions herself as a kind of midwife in the "rebirthing" process, an intermediary between one Jasmine and another. (The flesh-and-blood Lillian Gordon and Mother Ripplemeyer serve the same function in other instances. They each arrive on the scene just in time to pluck her from a dangerous situation and arrange for her a new "position.") Rebirth is a violent event, then, but this violence does not secure agency, as it does for Fanon. Rather, Jasmine's "act" of violence is an "act" of de-selfing, much like *sati* itself. Literal violence, in this case, murder, stands in for, even numbs, the pain of individual transformation. This violence of identity in turn replaces or masks the discursive violence Jasmine is subjected to as a "third world" gendered subject objectified by the "first world," represented here by her own author, Bharati Mukherjee.

The central problematic for any radical theory of change, according to Spivak, is that "the possibility of action lies in the dynamics of the disruption of the [continuous sign-chain constituting the socius], the breaking and relinking of the [semiotic] chain. This line of argument does not set consciousness over against the socius, but sees it as itself also constituted as and on a semiotic chain. It is thus an instrument of study which participates in the nature of the object of study. *To see consciousness thus is to place the historian in a position of irreducible compromise.*" The tangle of metaphorical and empirical violence itself has brought Jasmine to this same "irreducible" position, never interrogated and always abandoned, only to make its violent return again and again.

As the novel ends, we find Jane, pregnant with her Rochester's child, facing once again the "promise" of America and preparing herself for the next transformation. This time around it is at the hands of Taylor, once her employer and now her lover. "I realize I have already stopped thinking of myself as Jane," she tells us. "'Ready?' Taylor grins. I cry into Taylor's shoulder, cry through all the lives I've given birth to, cry for all my dead." In these few minutes, she seems finally to begin acknowledging the strength of her former "attachments"—but the mourning period is brief, and "then there is nothing I can do." In the final moments of the book, then, the narrator abdicates agency once again, scrambling forward to meet a fate and a frontier already "pushing indoors," she hopes, to embrace and assimilate her.

Suzanne Kehde (essay date 1995)

SOURCE: "Colonial Discourse and Female Identity: Bharati Mukherjee's *Jasmine*," in *International Women's Writing: New Landscapes of Identity*, edited by Anne E. Brown and Marjanne E. Goozé, Greenwood Press, 1995, pp. 70-7.

[*In the following essay, Kehde analyzes Mukherjee's focus on the myth of America as Eden and Jasmine's identification first and foremost as a woman in Mukherjee's* Jasmine.]

For Jasmine, Mukherjee's eponymous protagonist, the kind of liberty she enjoys is a consequence of, rather than the reason for, her coming to the New World. An illegal immigrant from Punjab, who "phantom[s her] way through three continents" on unscheduled flights landing on the disused airfields of the shadow world, she finally crosses the Atlantic in a sea voyage as horrifying as any suffered by the Mayflower pilgrims. Her first sight of America is no more attractive than Plymouth Rock was to them:

> The first thing I saw were the two cones of a nuclear plant, and smoke spreading from them in complicated but seemingly purposeful patterns, edges lit by the rising sun, like a gray, intricate map of an unexplored island continent, against the pale unscratched blue of the sky. I waded through Eden's waste: plastic bottles, floating oranges, boards, sodden boxes, white and green plastic sacks tied shut but picked open by birds and pulled apart by crabs.

The "unexplored island continent" is not what Spivak calls "uninscribed earth"; it is aggressively inscribed with the signs of contemporary American culture. This passage, however, is not as simply ironic as it may appear in isolation. As throughout the novel, the relationship between the myth of Eden and the narrative trajectory is not that of parodic inversion. For example, nuclear plants may be dangerous, but they signal a country where hot water is taken for granted: "a miracle, that even here in a place that looked deserted . . . the tiles and porcelain should be clean, without smells, without bugs."

Invoking the myth of America as Eden, Mukherjee brings colonial discourse into play. The image of Paradise has informed representations of America since the news of Columbus's discovery reached Europe at the beginning of the mercantile period. The Genesis account of Eden justifies a "natural" hierarchy based on gender and control of the natural world enforced by language. Man is the focus of power. All the resources of the earth exist for his welfare and pleasure. His right to rule legitimated by the Heavenly Father, Adam is the first patriarch; naming the animals while he is the sole human being, he establishes language as a function of domination. Eve is born into a preexistent hierarchy with only a father, thus entering an already constituted discourse with no one to speak for her as a woman; flesh of Adam's flesh, her identity is forever subordinated to his. This model provides the justification for the "natural" subordination of women to men and, by extension, the appropriation of the land, goods, and labor of the colonial subject, whose feminization is a condition of his subjugation.

As Doris Lessing's *Golden Notebook* and Angela Carter's *Passion of New Eve* suggest, the exploitative opportunities implicit in the myth are not available to women in the same configurations as to men because the myth constitutes women as already colonized subjects. This is not to imply that women cannot be colonizers, exploiters, or oppressors, only that their relationship to colonial discourse is more problematic. In Jasmine's case, her relationships to people she meets are defined by colonial discourse; that is, they attempt to construct her by the mechanisms of difference, resemblance, and desire. She may resist these constructions in some cases, acquiesce in others. Half-Face, the owner of the boat bringing her to Florida—whose injuries sustained in Vietnam might perhaps have suggested to him that colonizers do not necessarily escape unscathed—reads Jasmine as "one prime little piece" who is so afraid of the Immigration and Naturalization Service that he can rape her with impunity, so docile he falls asleep while she is in the shower. When he sees her above him naked with her mouth open and blood pouring from her tongue, he is so startled he cannot prevent her from slitting one of his carotid arteries. Lillian Gordon, for whom "the world's misery was a challenge to her ingenuity," scrutinizes Jasmine for marks of difference

that must be erased lest they betray her to the Immigration and Naturalization Service: her jeweled sandals, her inability to manage escalators and revolving doors, her un-American gait. The Vadheras, earlier (legal) immigrants who give her shelter in New York, emphasize resemblance, trying to pressure her into the "modesty of appearance and attitude" proper to a Hindu widow. Educated people are interested in differences because "they are always out to improve themselves"—in this case, by learning from her experience, which is perhaps democratic, as Jasmine sees it, but is also a kind of exploitation. The farmers she meets in Iowa, on the other hand, familiarize her because "alien knowledge means intelligence." Rapists, sympathizers, intellectuals, and farmers read her according to their own desires.

In some cases, Jasmine uses her Otherness to construct herself according to the colonizer's desires. This behavior began with her marriage in Punjab (as a girl, she strenuously resisted the traditional Hindu engenderment of *woman*.) Taken in as an au pair, she wishes to become what Taylor and Wylie imagine her to be: "humorous, intelligent, refined, affectionate. Not illegal, not murderer, not widowed, destitute, fearful." An Iowa farm banker falls in love with her "because I am alien. I am darkness, mystery, inscrutability." Here is an example of what Homi Bhabha calls "the repeated hesitancy that afflicts the colonialist discourse when it contemplates its discriminated subjects—the *inscrutability* of the Chinese, the *unspeakable* rites of the Indians, the *indescribable* habits of the Hottentots"; however, it is colonial discourse used by the colonial subject to describe herself as she believes she appears to the colonizer. Once more, Mukherjee's use of colonial discourse is problematized. When a distraught farmer shoots and cripples Bud Ripplemeyer, Jasmine becomes what he needs—nurse, inventive sex partner, adoptive parent, expectant mother. Because she accepts them consciously, these identities provide sites of resistance for her. She never internalizes any one role—refusing to settle into being, she is always becoming. She draws attention to her multiplicity of identities: "I have had a husband for each of the women I have been. Prakash for Jasmine, Taylor for Jase, Bud for Jane, Half-Face for Kali." Although she consciously adapts to these proffered roles, her exploitation is not cynical. She is not hypocritical in the sense that she pretends to be someone she is not while clinging to another image of her "real" self. Rather, she has never conceived of herself as a unified, single, transcendental subject, but as a contingent being—a position of considerable strength. Her fluidity of personality not only allows her to survive multiple trauma but also makes room for hope.

The myth of America as Eden disrupts an earlier mythology. Jyoti/Jasmine's earliest memory, with which the novel opens, is of a Hindu astrologer's prediction of her widowhood and exile. This the seven year old resists by asserting her own claim to wisdom, through which resistance she accidentally acquires her "third eye." This star-shaped scar on her forehead (in the spot where Hindu women traditionally wear a *tika*) is thus an emblem of both her self-assertion and her power of foresight, forever throbbing with "pain and hope, hope and pain." In the same way, as a twelve-year-old she resists her father's essentialist construction—"the thing is that bright ladies are bearing bright sons, that is nature's design"—with a demand to be educated as a physician. Jasmine does not abandon Hindu mythology: she carries with her a small Ganpati (a version of Ganesha, the elephant god of knowledge); she makes frequent references to Lord Yama, the god of death, and others to Brahma, Vishnu, and Shiva. The myth of America as Eden begins to appear even before Jasmine/Jyoti thinks of coming to America. Her most desired characteristic in a prospective husband is his ability to speak English: "To want English was to want more than you had been given at birth, it was to want the world." Prakash, who attempts to remake Jyoti into Jasmine, a new woman, yearns for America, where his fellow graduates live in houses with electricity twenty-four hours a day and hot running water, which becomes for Jasmine the enduring paradisal attribute. But the myth of America never displaces Hindu mythology. In America, Jasmine seems to embrace the idea of reincarnation: "[T]he Lord lends us a body, gives us an assignment, and sends us down. When we get the job done, the Lord calls us home again for the next assignment." Though astonished by "the American need . . . to *possess* a vision so privately," she responds to an anthropologist's claim to out-of-body experiences by saying, "[T]heoretically, I believe in reincarnation"—a belief that underlies her ability to assume different identities. The colonial discourse of the American myth and the metaphysical discourse of Hinduism disrupt each other continually.

Juxtaposed to both these discourses is Jasmine's personal story of origin. Wishing to spare her fifth daughter both the pain of a dowryless bride and the exclusion from heaven of an unmarried woman, Jasmine's mother tried to strangle her at birth. Jasmine understands this attempted murder as an act of love. The act propels her into a new identity: "My grandmother may have named me Jyoti/Light, but in surviving I was already Jane, a fighter and adapter." This personal myth of intertwined ends and beginnings helps Jyoti/Jasmine/ Jane negotiate the American and Hindu myths without allowing either one to define her. Consequently, she can maintain the fluid personality necessary for survival in a contingent world.

For Jasmine, events that appear as ends may, in fact, be beginnings—her widowhood at eighteen, for example, which in India would have mandated a life of mourning as a companion to her mother in her native village. Instead, Jasmine takes Prakash's new suit to the campus of the Florida college where he had been accepted, there to burn it and with the intention to commit *sati* in the blaze. This sense of a divinely appointed mission supports her through all the difficulties of her journey—one example of the way elements from all her myth systems provide support at critical moments. America turns out to be a site of new beginnings for Jasmine in spite of her intention to make it the site of her end. Throughout, beginnings and ends are woven inextricably together, and both are steeped in violence. Jasmine sees new beginnings as the assumptions of new identities rather than as the simpler assumption of a new way of life: "There are no harmless, compassionate ways to remake oneself. We murder who we were so we can rebirth ourselves in the images of dreams." These self-murders are the inner corollary of exterior violence, psychological suicides necessitated by the shift in power position attendant upon murder and rape. Jasmine does not see her rape by Half-Face as a satiric comment on America as Eden. The world is generally violent: her mother's murder attempt, and her husband's death at the hands of a Sikh fanatic both took place in India. Each of these acts of violence propels her into a new identity.

In spite of the realist surface of her fiction, Mukherjee sees identity as constituted by discourse rather than as a stable attribute of the transcendent, unified individual of the realist novel. The flexibility necessary for survival in a changing world comes from the understanding—either conscious or unconscious—of the discursive basis of identity and the willingness to negotiate the discourse(s). Jasmine's well-honed ability to survive depends on her resistance to definition by any one discourse. This is emphasized by the trajectory of Darrel Lutz's story. He is conflicted by two identities constructed from incompatible myths. The first is the myth of the midwest family farm he grew up with, the second of a more nebulous idea of getting off the land. Jasmine succinctly describes these two identities: "Crazy, Darrel wants an Indian princess and a Radio Shack franchise in Santa Fe. . . . Sane, he wants to baby-sit three hundred hogs and reinvent the fertilizer/pesticide wheel." What provokes Jasmine to label these alternatives *crazy* and *sane* is unclear; they are, however, obviously incompatible. Needing to constitute himself as a single, unified personality, Darrel cannot live in this split condition. Suicide—a solution to difficult situations that Jasmine repeatedly entertains, then resists— is the only way he can imagine to resolve his conflict.

Jasmine/Jane's ruminations on Darrel's situation as the site of irreconcilable discourses provide a foil for her own colonized condition, which is augmented by her analysis of the subjectivity of Du, her adopted son. He is split in a much more complex way than Darrel Lutz, who is merely caught in a conflict generated by a single culture. Du, a Vietnamese orphan, is already split before coming to the United States. A "Saigon sophisticate" whose family owned technological appliances like television, he was presumably displaced by the United States withdrawal from Saigon in 1975, which made him a refugee (once more, presumably, Mukherjee shows the consequences of his history rather than furnishing that history itself) in another country, most probably Thailand, where the Vietnamese are alien outcasts, herded into camps, surviving on "live worms and lizards and crabs so [they] wouldn't starve to death." In Iowa, he tries to assimilate as quickly as possible. Seeing as Jasmine does that America is "a place where the language you speak is what you are," he refuses to talk if he doesn't know the right English phrases. He rejects the role of colonial subject his teacher attempts to impose: "Yogi's [a nickname bestowed by his classmates] in a hurry to become all-American, isn't he?. . . They were like that, the kids who hung around us in Saigon. . . . I tried a little Vietnamese on him . . . and he just froze up." In order to define the context of these comments, Mukherjee has Jasmine (silently) gloss them: "How *dare* you? What must [Du] have thought? His history teacher in Baden, Iowa, just happens to know a little street Vietnamese? Now where would he have picked it up?" The benevolent teacher reminds the refugee of his own role as colonial aggressor—the representative of the most recent of a long line of colonizers, including the Chinese and the French—by equating Du with the beggar orphans Jasmine knows he would have despised. Barely veiled, American imperialism controls student-teacher relations in a high school in America, where in the cinemas and in the home innumerable movies show rivers full of corpses and tracts of leafless "jungle" while Vietnamese teenagers write of the beautiful forests and the white, sandy river beaches they do not expect to see ever again.

Mr. Skola's representative attempt to constitute Du as a colonial subject provides for Du a site of resistance and for Jasmine an opportunity to scrutinize an especially overt manifestation of the mechanisms by which the colonial subject is constituted. Through Jasmine, Mukherjee forwards an analysis of the constitution of the (male) colonial subject so complex and subtle that, in contrast to the way in which Jasmine's situation is generally presented, it needs to be articulated rather than implied. When Jasmine discovers that, although she has never before heard Du speak Vietnamese, he has "made a life for himself among the Vietnamese in Baden," she realizes that he is "a hybrid." Here Mukherjee seems to use Bhabha's formulation of hybridization:

> Produced through the strategy of disavowal, the *reference* of discrimination is always to a process of splitting as the condition of subjection; a discrimination between the Mother culture and its bastards, the self and its doubles, where the trace of what is disavowed is not repressed, but repeated as something *different*—a mutation, a hybrid. . . . [Hybridity] unsettles the mimetic or narcissistic demands of colonial power, but re-implicates its identifications in strategies of subversion that turn the gaze

of the discriminated back upon the eye of power. For the colonial hybrid is the articulation of the ambivalent space where the rite of power is enacted on the site of desire.

Bhabha's formulation explains Du's apparent attempt to become the all-American boy as mimicry rather than emulation, a site of resistance rather than acquiescence. Caught between two languages (and at least two discourses), Du establishes a position that not only enables him to deal with the conflict but empowers him to constitute that conflict as an opportunity for self definition. Jasmine sees him as hyphenated: "Du (Yogi) Ripplemeyer, a Vietnamese-American." Although Du's hyphenation allows him to move between two cultures taking advantage of select features of each, his split condition precludes the desirable power position of the transcendent (male) individual—a position that male postcolonial theorists like Bhabha seem to want to reclaim for Third World men.

Jasmine, comparing her own state with Du's hyphenation, remarks that her "transformation has been genetic." She apparently does not regard this transformation—so thorough as to require a biological metaphor—as a capitulation to the colonizer's demands; she does not constitute herself as hybrid or hyphenated Indian American. Her relationship to nationality cannot be the same as Du's not only because of their countries' different colonial histories, not only because the construction of *nationality* itself is specific to each nation, but also because of the difference of gender. Du has more to gain by maintaining his cultural and national identity. According to the Edenic myth that served as a blueprint for the depredations of the Old World, woman is the primary colonial subject; further, contemporary psychoanalytic theory holds that the sense of self depends upon differentiation from the Other, for signs of which the colonizer scrutinizes the colonized, just as gender categories are typically reinforced by policing the boundaries. Thus a male from a Third World country oppressed by a thousand years of successive colonial masters is inevitably constructed as a feminized Other by the imperial power. However, if he maintains ties with his native community, he may be able to retain at least a simulacrum of his position in his accustomed hierarchy. He will always outrank a woman or a Hmong peasant, for example. Jyoti/Jasmine/Jane has no comparable reason for remaining in touch with an Indian community, a vivid emblem of which is provided by the Vadheras in New York, for whom Jasmine was completely constituted by her marital history. She rejects the past they represent just as she rejects the nostalgia of the grade B Bombay movies they rent daily from the video store. She understands the attraction of clinging to the safety of a sanitized, burnished past but refuses it for herself: "To bunker herself inside nostalgia, to sheathe the heart in a bullet-proof vest, was to be a coward."

America allows for a greater range of positive and negative freedoms—admittedly, the latter are constrained by the threat of (male) violence, but, as Jasmine remarks, in the Indian district where she was born "bad luck dogged dowryless wives, rebellious wives, barren wives. They fell into wells, they got run over by trains, they burned to death heating milk on kerosene stoves." Even young, unmarried girls evacuating their bowels in a field before dawn may be attacked by mad dogs. As women have less to gain from ideologies of nationality, so they may be less invested in them. In both India and America, Jasmine's primary identification is as a woman, which she constitutes as a site of flexibility.

Thus, through her appropriation of the myth of America as Eden, Mukherjee brings colonial discourse into play; analyzing the construction of the colonial subject, she engages in a postcolonial critique of that discourse. Eschewing simple inversion, her critique of the myth, neither ironic nor parodic, takes the form of disruption: just as Jasmine's identity is disrupted, so are the various discourses that Mukherjee uses. The novel ends without closure. Jasmine sets off on a new life—or, rather, on a new version of a previous life when Taylor drives up and urges her to accompany him to California. Pregnant with Bud's child, and "caught between the promise of America and old-world dutifulness," she nonetheless chooses "adventure, risk, transformation." She bounds out the door to the car "greedy with wants and reckless from hope." There is no criticism of Jasmine (no longer thinking of herself as Jane) for her refusal to be pinned down to the past. Certainly, her acceptance of family configurations and caretaking roles (even of unorthodox ones) may be construed as a manifestation of the essentialist sense of self preached by her father, but it also suggests a willingness to recognize opportunity in unlikely situations. There is no reason to suppose that Jasmine, at twenty-four, still in the process of becoming, will be forever trapped in domestic preoccupations. Rather, Mukherjee endorses the fluid personality as a site of possibility, particularly for a woman, for whom in this novel the operant discourses are always restrictive, always forcing Jasmine back into the paternal essentialism, always (re)constructing her as the primary colonial subject. In this examination of the construction of national identity and gender identity, Mukherjee recommends not an ideology of female resistance but an ad hoc selection of useful features from whatever discourse is at hand—a resistance to ossification of identity, a resiliency articulated toward survival.

Victoria Carchidi (essay date Winter 1995)

SOURCE: "'Orbiting': Bharati Mukherjee's Kaleidoscope Vision," in *MELUS,* Vol. 20, No. 4, Winter, 1995, pp. 91-101.

[*In the following essay, Carchidi asserts that Mukherjee's short story "'Orbiting' . . . evokes an image of the interweaving of diverse points of view to create a new perspective that is neither wholly like nor wholly different from the elements that make it up, an image well-suited to Bharati Mukherjee's vision of America.*"]

"Orbiting," the story I discuss here, is included in a collection entitled *Braided Lives.* This title evokes an image of the interweaving of diverse points of view to create a new perspective that is neither wholly like nor wholly different from the elements that make it up, an image well-suited to Bharati Mukherjee's vision of America. Peter Nazareth writes that when Mukherjee claims to be a North American writer, she is affiliating herself with the "America that embraces all the peoples of the world both because America is involved with the whole world and because the whole world is in America." In this perspective, we—whoever we may be—are not outside the multitude of cultures in the United States, but are a part of the fabric that is being woven. An example of constantly changing, vibrant, and dynamic elements that come together is offered us by Bharati Mukherjee in **"Orbiting."**

The story's plot is quickly told and seems almost insignificant: a young woman's family comes over to her apartment for Thanksgiving dinner and meets her new lover. The protagonist Renata herself acknowledges the mundanity of this situation in the story: "All over the country, I tell myself, women are towing new lovers home to meet their families." Such a story, one might think, offers mainstream America for our examination. One might even be disappointed; from an Asian writer, we encounter a family of Americans. Renata is not an immigrant, nor is her father; although proud of his North Italian heritage, he is the son of a man who was "a fifteenweek old fetus when his mother planted her feet on Ellis Island." They live in New Jersey; they talk about sports, a child listens to her Walkman; these certainly are American characters. But what it means to be American is precisely the focus of this story, as it has been of Mukherjee's life as well. **"Orbiting"** is the culmination of a journey that has taken a lifetime, in multiple ways: the time necessary for Mukherjee to mature into a writer able to express this vision and the experiences of her youth in India and her subsequent transformation into a North American that give depth to her characters' emotions.

Mukherjee was born, in 1940, into the most élite caste level of Indian society; she was a Bengali Brahmin. Along with the Indian heritage that gave her such privilege, however, came the colonized identity of all of India, subordinate to the British Raj. Mukherjee was educated as a proper Indian girl of good family: she spoke Bengali her first three years, then entered English schools in Britain and Switzerland and, when she returned to India, the Loretto School run by Irish nuns, at which she was taught to devalue all things Bengali. Not until she was in graduate school did Mukherjee recover knowledge of the Hindu culture she had known as a child.

In 1961, Mukherjee found herself at the University of Iowa Writing Workshop, where she met and married Clark Blaise, instead of accepting the Indian nuclear physicist her family was arranging for her. Mukherjee notes that had she chosen otherwise, she would still have written—but "elegant, ironic, wise stories . . . marked by detachment." Marriage outside her culture took Mukherjee beyond the safe enclave of certainty in which she had been raised, offered new possibilities for her to explore.

That awareness of different cultures was further developed when Blaise decided to embrace his Canadian heritage. For Mukherjee, Canada "was like going to England, a step backward to an old world, a hierarchical society." While her husband was regaining a sense of his ancestral identity, Mukherjee had already decided she "wanted to get away from that sense of belonging. I didn't want anyone to know where I fit in, so I could be whoever I wanted to be." Canada was a step backward, in terms of this flexible identity. She was labeled a "dirty Paki" there and over the next fourteen years saw and experienced tremendous racism that colored her writing and can still be sensed in Mukherjee's sharp memories: "if one hadn't played in snow and grown up eating oatmeal one didn't have anything relevant to say to Canadian readers."

Feeling beleaguered in Canada, Mukherjee became, as she described herself, a "shrill" civil rights activist. Despite her affection for the West, Mukherjee clearly felt the need to claim her identity as different in a powerful way as a means of warding off the racial slurs to which she was subjected. These tensions emerge in *The Tiger's Daughter,* a novel about a woman's claustrophobic entanglement with family and friends, and in *Wife,* in which the main character kills her husband after the couple have emigrated to the United States and the wife has been so torn between cultures that she begins to lose her sanity. The writing of this period shows characters defining their identity only with violent difficulty.

In 1973 Mukherjee and her husband went to India for a year; *Days and Nights in Calcutta* details their different responses to the country. This trip helped Mukherjee see that despite "all the trouble I was going through in Canada, it was still the new world that I wanted to live in, and that the old world was dead for me." She had cast her lot with the West and needed to remake her identity in a way that no longer clung to an outmoded vision from her past.

In 1980 Mukherjee resigned her post at McGill University and brought her family back to the United States. She felt, she says, terrible about so disrupting their lives, but "it was a question of self-preservation." Since that time, Mukherjee and Blaise have produced an investigative report on the bombing of an Air India plane that killed over 300 people, *The Sorrow and the Terror;* and Mukherjee has written *Darkness; The Middleman and Other Stories,* which won the National Book Critics Circle Award and from which **"Orbiting"** is taken, in 1988; and most recently, *Jasmine.* This last novel illustrates how far Mukherjee has come from her early pessimistic vision; although violence still plagues the protagonist's world, she is less controlled by it. Jasmine's husband is killed by a terrorist bomb which his wife feels is intended for her; she vows to commit *suttee,* to kill herself in honor of his death, in Florida, where they had been planning to move. Instead, she kills the man who takes advantage of her illegal alien status and youth to rape her. With the help of several strong women, she finds a new life for herself, and at end of the novel has acquired a family whose connections are nontraditional in the extreme; pregnant by the man she has decided to leave, she heads west for California to find his adopted Vietnamese son; she is accompanied by the man whom she met and loved while working as his illegal *au-pair* and his adopted daughter.

The novel *Jasmine* is a culmination of Mukherjee's characters: although a young Asian woman is the protagonist, she has changed from being a victim or passive agent to someone willing to make hard choices in pursuit of an identity not offered by the easy, pre-existing patterns from which she can choose: to be the burnt widow of her first husband; to be the victim of the man who raped her; to settle into a "Little India" enclave, isolated from America; or to be the caregiver of an older man. Instead, she and the motley recipients of her love have remade themselves into an atypical—and therefore more truly American—family unit.

This summary illustrates how far and through how much turmoil Mukherjee herself had to come to find herself able to write as an American. A major concern she had to negotiate was her own identity: in her introduction to *Darkness,* Mukherjee described immigrants as "pathetic lost souls," in contrast to the expatriate, who with irony and detachment drifts aloof from his or her new world. Undergoing a metamorphosis from her early work and experiences in Canada, Mukherjee has rejected élitist detachment and joined herself to "the underclass of semi-assimilated Indians": "instead of seeing my Indianness as a fragile identity to be preserved against obliteration . . . I see it now as a set of fluid identities to be celebrated. Indianness is now a metaphor, a particular way of partially comprehending the world." Couple this statement with her claim, after the writing of *The Middleman and Other Stories,* that to be American "is a quality of mind and desire. It means that you can be yourself, not what you were fated to be . . . you can try to shape your fate yourself," and one begins to see the braiding of perspectives that renders **"Orbiting"** so rich.

"Orbiting" shows how powerful this emotional development has been for Mukherjee as a writer, and how it has broadened her vision. In *The Middleman and Other Stories,* Mukherjee speaks for those not recognizably tied to her own history. Renata's family is Italian-American; other characters in this collection are Vietnamese, Filipino, Afghan. Mukherjee feels free to speak for other nationalities and backgrounds because they are her natural subject as an American writer, and these many colored strands of people's lives are the quintessentially American experience. We are not Indian, Italian, Jewish, fighting to retain our identity against a monolithically other America; America is made up of all our strands.

Despite its seemingly trivial plot and setting, **"Orbiting"** encapsulates the breadth of Mukherjee's vision of and for America. Tightly crafted, the story opens with an exposition, setting the stereotypically American scene and family relationships. Then it broadens a bit to allow entry of the immigrant figure, Roashan, referred to elsewhere by Mukherjee as the "unhoused"; his reception by the "housed" DeMarcos launches a comedy of manners worthy of Jane Austen, whom Mukherjee has acknowledged as an influence on her work. We see misunderstandings, and correct understandings, where least expected as the characters enact in miniature the ballet of complementary moves that is America.

> **Despite its seemingly trivial plot and setting, "Orbiting" encapsulates the breadth of Mukherjee's vision of and for America.**
> *—Victoria Carchidi*

Let me pause here for a moment and consider what it means to be American. All people living in the United States, with the possible exception of Native Americans, came to this country—willingly or not—at some point; and without exception we have been shaped by the intermingling of cultures that makes up what has been called the United States's melting pot. This admixture or mélange, in contrast to the Canadian metaphor of a mosaic with its invocation of flat, discrete units in juxtaposition, is what fascinates Mukherjee. She encourages her readers to look more closely at the layers that have been compressed to make this country's texture. Despite the distance from their ethnic homeland, being Italian is part of the DeMarcos's cultural inheritance. And more recent immigrants do figure in the story: Renata's mother grew up in Calabria, and "Before Mom began to find herself," she would recount tales of privation from her girlhood. Even more centrally, Renata's new lover, Ro, is a very

recent immigrant, from Afghanistan; his clothing is an odd mixture of his old world's elegance and a recent discount store purchase. He holds himself differently from the other men in the room; Renata thinks in exasperation, "even his headshake is foreign." But this amalgam, for Mukherjee, *is* America.

As the story opens, Mukherjee details with precision the ways people who are familiar interact: as Renata's father brings over the turkey for dinner, he and his daughter communicate less through language than through expected attitudes and preconceptions. When her father tells Renata that her mother thawed the turkey, saying "You wouldn't have room in your Frigidaire," Renata interprets the statement otherwise: "You mean Mom said [I] shouldn't be living in a dump, right?" When her father explains why he brought the turkey over instead of letting Renata pick it up, again Renata interprets: "I know what he's saying. He saying he's retired and *he* should be able to stay in bed till noon if he wants to, but he can't. . . ." This running commentary of what is being meant, counterpoised against what is being said, is inescapable in the first several pages. Renata explains, "Let's talk about me means: What do you think of Mom? I'll take over the turkey means: When will Rindy settle down?" Yet against these "comfortingly rigid" expectations of family are Renata's memories in the story's first paragraph of Vic, the lover who had been with her through last Thanksgiving. Vic had made cranberry sauce, "which Dad had interpreted as a sign of permanence in my life. . . . Dad cannot imagine cooking as self-expression. . . . Vic's sauce was a sign of his permanent isolation, if you really want to know." Renata's father is limited to the only interpretations he can think of; these were not appropriate in Vic's case, so his readings were misreadings. Even Renata, close as she was to Vic, misread him: "I should have listened," she thinks. "I mean really listened. I thought he was talking about us, but I know now he was only talking incessantly about himself. I put too much faith in mail-order nightgowns and bras." Putting such responsibility on oneself for failing to "really listen" leaves aside the possibility that deception is occurring—as it does when Renata evades her father's question when he asks if her mother has mentioned that he's acting funny. "'No, Dad, she hasn't said anything about you acting funny.' What she *has* said is do we think she ought to call Doc. . . ." To save her father pain, or to avoid a painful subject, Renata has chosen to withhold the truth, an option she doesn't allow Vic. Such inbred patterns of communication, such a desire to see into the heads of others and blaming oneself for any failure to do so may be what drives Vic to leave so abruptly, leaving behind Renata and their ritual of looking through the real estate want ads as if they were different people.

That ritual indicates the desire to break out of the enclosed security of family myths, to shape oneself rather than simply to be shaped. Renata and her sister feel the desire to establish their own identities early on: "Renata and Carla are what we were christened. We changed to Rindy and Cindi in junior high," Renata tells us. The sign that Cindi's husband Brent, son of an Amish farmer in Iowa, "is a rebel" is a similar self-recreation. "He was born Schwartzendruber, but changed his name to Schwartz. Now no one believes Brent, either. They call him Bernie on the street and it makes everyone more comfortable." The touch of comfort, however, Mukherjee suggests, is not what such recreation should be about. Brent is no longer plausible in his original guise; in addition to changing his name, he sports "the obvious hairpiece and a gold chain." There has been no amalgamation of his Amish upbringing and the Italian family he has married into; he has simply been absorbed.

Into this tightly-knit, almost claustrophobic community, steps Ro, Renata's lover from Kabul—now for something completely different. And Ro is a new kind of different. Where Brent has been absorbed, Vic had offered a kind of difference to Renata—"he talked of feminism and holism and macrobiotics. Then he opened up on cinema and literature, and I was very impressed, as who wouldn't be?" But Vic's identity is only the flip side of Brent's; he identifies himself through separation. He talks only of himself, he is caught in the exile's self-constructed world that cherishes its opposition to the culture being resisted: "He was macrobiotic in lots of things, including relationships. Yin and yang, hot and sour." Vic offers opposition rather than revision.

Ro's presence in Renata's life offers differences that enrich: "I can tell one Afghan tribe from another now, even by looking at them or by their names. I can make out some Pashto words," Renata tells us. A name no longer signals individuality, but community. When Ro tells Renata about a cousin named Abdul, she thinks that all his cousins "are named Abdul something. When I think of Abdul, I think of a giant black man . . . running down a court." Her stereotyped identification of the name with a basketball star has begun to change; and despite the multiplicity of Abduls, she knows about this Abdul's difficulty with immigration papers. The name is not what matters, but the connection. When Ro introduces himself by his full name, Roashan, to Renata's parents, her father is stumped: "'Come again?' he says, baffled. I cringe as [Ro] spells his name. My parents are so parochial. With each letter he does a graceful dip and bow. "Try it syllable by syllable, sir. Then it is not so hard." Again Ro is broadening the horizons of the established, or "housed" figure; but equally important is Mr. DeMarco's willingness to try to grasp the difference. Both parties here are trying, and that effort gets them beyond Renata's mother's first reaction—which is to scream for the police when Ro enters unannounced.

Mukherjee seems to suggest that marriage can be the best way to enrich one's culture, wedding one as it does to an-

other world; such marriages have created the multifaceted variety of Renata's family, augmenting its cultural myths through literal intermarriage with other exotics. Renata's father's "one big adventure" was marrying her mother, a "Calabrian peasant"; this marriage has the nineteenth-century touch Mukherjee acknowledges in her writing—"He married down, she married well. That's the family story"—a Cinderella story. Brent, although more assimilated than offering alternatives, also brings his daughter Franny into the family; Carla must deal with the next generation's mixed response to the family. And that marriage opens the way to greater tolerance: Renata thinks about her father's reaction to Ro's religious prohibitions against drinking, "Carla didn't marry a Catholic, so he has no right to be upset about Ro, about us." Diversity also brings an odd kind of harmony; although Brent's efforts to assimilate the stranger among them as "Roy" and engage him in talk of sports fail—since, as Ro points out, "I have not familiarized myself with these practices"—Franny is intrigued by him as she is by no one else. Her interest is so great she takes off her headphones and even chooses to sit beside him at dinner.

Mukherjee gives us, in this story, the collision of compressed lives. Each of us lives in a community, a culture, a background we have built up out of ethnic, religious, regional, or other affiliations. We carry with us prejudices, connections, defenses, that are idiosyncratic and impenetrable to all except those closest to us. Yet Mukherjee insists that when such multiple worlds meet, the result *can be* a glorious freeing of the leaves of the kaleidoscope, that complexly intermix and produce a new pattern. Renata believes she is the "middleman" in a collision between two mutually incomprehensible worlds. When Ro says this is his first thanksgiving, Renata explains he's from Afghanistan. "But Dad gets continents wrong. He says, 'We saw your famine camps on TV.'" Ethiopia, Afghanistan, it's all foreign to him. Renata wants to tell her family about Ro's background, wants to unpack who he is: "I want to tell Brent that Ro's skied in St. Moritz. . . . He's sophisticated, he could make monkeys out of us all, but they think he's a retard." However, he is not totally incomprehensible to her family. At other times Renata wants to buffer the true understanding. When Ro says New York flowers have no smell, Renata intervenes: "His father had a garden estate outside Kabul." I don't want Mom to think he's putting down American flowers, though in fact he is. Along with American fruits, meats, and vegetables." A middleman is only necessary between opposed camps; Mukherjee describes her earlier work as a bridge. She has gotten past the detached judgment; now she always sees the pageant as ongoing. The confusions, understandings and miscomprehensions between Ro and the DeMarcos echo the earlier misreadings of Vic; the difference is that understanding Vic offered nothing new to the world. Ro is already changing this family through the discomfort he gives Mr. DeMarco in having to learn of his religious prohibitions, in the interest he affords Franny, and most centrally in the opportunity to grow that he offers Renata. Deeper understandings are possible through the effort to assimilate someone who seems different.

This increased understanding operates on both the characters' and the readers' levels. Renata sees some of her true feelings; more significantly, however, her interventions allow the *reader* to see into both Ro's and Renata's worlds in a way that the characters cannot. Renata clearly understands her father's discomfort with Ro's prohibition against drinking alcohol: "In my father's world, grown men bowl in leagues and drink the best whiskey they can afford"; faced with a conflicting world view, he whistles a Frank Sinatra song—"He must be under stress. That's his usual self-therapy." She has less insight into a similar conflict between her expectations and Ro's odd desire to watch her get picked up by men who think she is by herself at a bar: "Ro likes to swagger out of a dark booth as soon as someone buys me a drink, I go along. He comes from a macho culture." Renata thinks she is compromising, because she understands his need to see how she is valued by her culture. Yet her thoughts on this topic reveal that she shares the same attitudes: "In a few more months he'll know I'm something of a catch in my culture. . . . Even Brent Schwartzendruber has begged me to see him alone." Renata, too, values her physical attractions as a sign of her being a "good catch." And just as Ro likes to see her attractiveness through other men's eyes, Renata realizes she will marry Ro if he asks only after she kisses him in front of her parents, a kiss she makes deliberately sexy so they will know the two are lovers. Although one may argue with these attitudes that might seem to stereotype Italian and Afghanistan cultures—the one values women for physical voluptuousness and the other is a "macho" culture of pain—Mukherjee's point maintains that even widely different cultures value social decisions.

To become truly free, in Mukherjee's worlds, is not to escape from other people: Renata pictures Vic in a new kitchen making his sauce and explaining his philosophies. We are all caught in a dense and inescapable tissue of human connections. All we can do is choose whether that fabric will be all of a piece or shot through with brilliant strands from other cultures, unevenly woven by changing circumstance and growth. Renata's freedom is not an alternative to her family; it is a part of her. Instead, freedom leads to enriched ways of viewing, a broader sense of connection to the world, and greater flexibility of actions.

Mukherjee has encountered some resistance, particularly from what she sees as the "imperialism" of western feminism that requires women to act in their own self-interest rather than being willing to please others. This attribute in some of her female characters—what I would call an internalization of attitudes that value women as somehow less

complete or accessory human beings, rather than people in their own rights—is a trait that has disturbed me in some of her work. Yet to resolve this seeming difficulty, one need only look at Mukherjee's willingness to let her characters—and readers—learn from their experiences. She is not forcing her characters to enact a didactic or stereotypically oppressed position. The growth in her characters illustrates that rejecting dogma from whatever direction allows one to develop in accordance with one's own set of values, and this would accord with my understanding of a feminist agenda—that a woman be free to work out her own choices in life in accordance with her own priorities. In other words, although at a given moment a character may seem to acquiesce in a restrictive assumption, Mukherjee's unwillingness to allow any one position the final word allows such restrictions to crash and break up against each other like ice floes in a thawing river.

This fluid approach to the world is also what marks Mukherjee as different from the stereotype of contemporary conventional American literature, novels and tales about domestic crisis and angst in white, middle-class suburbia. To write about that world, one must have faith in its stability, and that faith is denied those who have gone through great change in their lives. Mukherjee is such a one; she accepts the contrast between her privileged childhood and her frequently impoverished adult life. This, and the breadth of her background, gives her a broader perspective, less of a reliance on a given approach as right or best or even constant, than more mainstream American writers. For Mukherjee, "a social and political vision is an integral part of writing a novel. . . . Whereas for contemporary American writers, fictions exist only in a vacuum of personal relationships." Comparing Mukherjee to John Updike, Adam Hochschild notes how much more ambitious Mukherjee is in the range of her subjects. Polly Shulman points out that Mukherjee's message may be that "everyone is living in a new world, even those who never left home."

This global awareness adds richness: Celia McGee writes that the depth of the stories in ***Middleman*** "comes from the sudden interference of history and tragedy, and the exigencies of politics and war"; certainly such an intersection is what gives **"Orbiting"** its powerful core. From the concern Renata's family—and Renata—feels about Ro's name, clothing, speech, or looks, the story suddenly plunges into the particular history of the man—a history that includes torture, jail, and escape, a history that forces the DeMarco family to reexamine its own rituals at the same time that it alleviates any fear we may have that Ro will be assimilated as Brent has been.

At story's end, Renata elides Ro with America in her mind: "Ro is Clint Eastwood, scarred hero and survivor." But the story allows us to see the limits of Renata's facile equation of a man's personal history with a celluloid Hollywood survivor: Ro becomes America in a far more tangible way, as he makes the DeMarcos see through the cellophane to the content of America's shared heritage. Mukherjee believes in reincarnation in the sense that we remake our lives as we kill our old ones; Ro has left behind his "culture of pain"; he is embarrassed to speak of it because he does not treasure the scars of difference. He has come to America, to a land that celebrates Thanksgiving, but he will not lose his core as he integrates himself into his new land; instead, he will invest its rituals with new meaning; he brings a new dimension to the family meal. As Ro talks about his torture, even Franny takes off her earphones and listens. The communal gathering hears graphic stories of "electrodes, canes, freezing tanks. He leaves nothing out." As the family looks sick, Renata thinks, "The meaning of Thanksgiving should not be so explicit." But why not? Eleanor Wachtel writes that for Mukherjee the conflict of societies "is not simply a culture gap; the immigrant changes the way Americans see themselves." Ro's incorporation changes the DeMarcos, as he revitalizes what had become simply a ritual of food.

I presented a version of this essay in November, 1992—on the day George Bush or Bill Clinton was to be elected president and close to Thanksgiving; the timing brought to mind another aspect of America. During a discussion of politics, a friend said to me, "It's an amazing American spectacle, whoever wins: 250 million people choosing their president, and the decision will be accepted by all, whatever it is." That is something to give thanks for; and it is through our knowledge of other cultures in which that freedom, that responsibility to vote is not exerciseable or is not respected, that we can better see what it means to be American. We are all part of the multicultured fabric Mukherjee celebrates; we ignore the inextricable, many-colored threads of our plurality at our own cost.

Abha Prakash Leard (review date Winter 1997)

SOURCE: "Mukherjee's *Jasmine*," in *The Explicator,* Vol. 55, No. 2, Winter, 1997, pp. 114-17.

[*In the following review, Leard states that, "With the connotations of both dislocation and progress within the tangled framework of the narrator's personal history, journey as metaphor in* [Jasmine] *stands for the ever-moving, regenerating process of life itself."*]

Despite postcolonial readings of Bharati Mukherjee's novel *Jasmine,* Western critics have not placed in context the pivotal play of migrations, forced and voluntary, literal and figurative, found in the plural female subjectivity of the novel. With the connotations of both dislocation and progress

within the tangled framework of the narrator's personal history, journey as metaphor in the novel stands for the ever-moving, regenerating process of life itself. In presenting a woman capable of birthing more than one self during the course of her lifetime, Mukherjee invests her novel with the unique form of a Hindu bildungsroman, where the body is merely the shell for the inner being's journey toward a more enlightened and empowered subjectivity.

But the material self exists and is the site of oppression and transformation. Cognizant of the formidable interventions of gender, class, religion, and historical circumstances, Mukherjee shapes her heroine as a "fighter and adapter," who is perpetually in the process of remaking her self and her destiny. Set in the seventies and eighties when the violent separatist demands of the militant Sikhs forced many Hindus to migrate from Punjab, *Jasmine* centers around the experiences of Jyoti, a teenage Hindu widow, who travels all the way from Hasnapur, India, her feudalistic village, to America. These experiences are told in first person by a woman who identifies herself as Jane Ripplemeyer, the pregnant, twenty-four-year-old, live-in girlfriend of Bud Ripplemeyer, a Jewish banker in Baden, Iowa. But the "I" in the past and present fragments of this first-person narrative belongs to a woman who sees herself as more than one person. Officially known as Jyoti Vijh in India, the narrator, in America, is a many-named immigrant with a fake passport and forged residency papers. By giving her protagonist more than one name, usually through the character of a husband/lover, Mukherjee subverts the notion of a fixed, uniform subject. Simultaneously, the narrator's plurality of names—Jasmine, Jazzy, Jase, Jane (which successively became more Westernized)—helps to mask her ethnic difference and enable her to survive in a hostile, alien land.

Jasmine's decision to leave her homeland coincides with her desire to escape the confines of her cultural identity. This desire, articulated in the dramatic recollection of the opening chapter, is a subtext that continually spurs the narrative's critique of the patriarchal underpinnings of Hindu culture and its social fabric. The little girl's refusal to accept the astrologer's prophecy translates into the adult narrator's unwillingness to imprison herself within traditional, predetermined codes of femininity. As Jyoti matures into a young woman, her resistance against a determinate existence continues in her unconventional marriage to Prakash, a "modern man," who wants them to leave the backwardness of India for a more satisfying life in America. Within a cultural context that privileges arranged marriages, Jyoti's romance, that she has engineered, can indeed be seen not only as nontraditional but also as a subversive tactic against the established cultural norm. Her marriage is not only liberating but transforming as well. Comparing her husband to Professor Higgins, the benevolent patriarch of *Pygmalion,* the narrator recollects the early days of her marriage when Prakash, in an attempt to make her a "new kind of city woman," changes her name to Jasmine. Although "shutt[ling] between identities," the narrator is eager to transcend the name/identity of her child self in the hope of escaping the doomed prophecy lurking in her future. To leave the country of her birth would mean new beginnings, "new fates, new stars." But before the seventeen-year-old bride can embark on a new life with her husband, he is killed in a terrorist bombing.

The motif of the broken pitcher in *Jasmine* epitomizes not only the temporality of one life journey within the ongoing Hindu cycle of rebirth, but also the fragility of constructed boundaries, whether of the self, the family, or the nation. The author parallels the violence of the Khalistan movement that is responsible for Jasmine's widowhood and her subsequent displacement and exile to the bloody communal riots between the Hindus and Muslims at the time of India's independence in 1947. Despite her distance from this historical event, which rendered millions of people homeless and destitute overnight, the narrator can still empathize with her parents' anguished memories of the Partition that forced them to leave their ancestral home in Lahore and flee to Punjab. The fragmentation of the nation and the family as well as the haunting journey from terror to refuge have seeped into Jasmine's subconscious—"the loss survives in the instant replay of family story: forever Lahore smokes, forever my parents flee."

Directly or indirectly, historical conflicts (sparked by religious intolerance) within India determine the problematic constitution of Jasmine's shifting individuality. Her "illegal" migrant life in America is an extension of an existence that began in the shadow of political refuge and later, with her husband's death, almost ended in her widowed status. Within the enclosures of the Hindu culture, a widow must atone the death of her husband for the rest of her life. Jasmine's widowhood cancels her right to material fulfillment. It entails a life of isolation in the "widow's dark hut," on the margins of Hasnapur society. For Jasmine, to live the life of a widow is to live a fate worse than death.

Jasmine's difficult "odyssey" to America and her initial experiences in an alien society parallel the emergence of a new selfhood despite the vulnerability of her youth and material circumstances. Her brutal rape at the hands of Half-face, a man who represents the worst of America in his racist and inhuman treatment of the Asian and black refugees aboard his trawler, is a climactic moment in the text which signals the sudden awakening of Jasmine's "sense of mission." Refusing to "balance [her] defilement with [her] death," a traditional ending for most rape victims in orthodox Indian society, Jasmine, infused with the destructive energy of the goddess Kali, murders the man who symbolizes the "underworld of evil" and begins a new "journey, traveling light."

Given a world where violence and bloodshed, exploitation and persecution are constants, Jasmine's plurality of selves is her only strategy for survival. Knowing only too well that there are "no harmless, compassionate ways to remake oneself," Jasmine views her multiple selves with a detachment that has been forged in pain. But beneath this carefully maintained distance is the terrible agony of a woman who cannot free herself from the collective memory of her haunting past:

> Jyoti of Hasnapur was not Jasmine, Duff's day mummy and Taylor and Wylie's *au pair* in Manhattan; *that* Jasmine isn't *this* Jane Ripplemeyer. . . . And which of us is the undetected murderer of a half-faced monster, which of us has held a dying husband, and which of us was raped and raped and raped in boats and cars and motel rooms?

Having lived through "hideous times," Jasmine, in her arduous journey of survival, has accomplished the rare mission of transcending the boundaries of a unitary self and identifying with all the nameless victims of gender, culture, class, and imperialism. The narrative ends on a note of optimism where Jasmine, "cocooning a cosmos" in her pregnant belly, and about to "re-position her stars" again, is ready to plunge into another life and another journey of transformation.

Michiko Kakutani (review date 24 June 1997)

SOURCE: "A Madcap Search for Bio-Mom," in *The New York Times,* June 24, 1997, p. C18.

[*In the following review, Kakutani complains that Mukherjee's* Leave It to Me *is "a book in which her favorite themes have warped into didactic obsessions, and her stylistic idiosyncrasies have slipped perilously close to mannerism."*]

Leave It to Me, Bharati Mukherjee's latest novel, has all her trademark preoccupations: exiles, émigrés and outsiders tirelessly reinventing themselves, as they shed old lives, old lovers, old selves; and an America reeling from violence and nonstop change, a country in which freedom has translated into rootlessness, possibility into dislocation. It has a heroine who's addicted to change, a supporting cast of eccentrics and a wildly manic plot.

The problem is *Leave It to Me* reads less like a Bharati Mukherjee novel than a parody of a Bharati Mukherjee novel. It's a book in which her favorite themes have warped into didactic obsessions, and her stylistic idiosyncrasies have slipped perilously close to mannerism. There are still glimpses, here and there, of her Seinfeldian eye for the odd and her Beattiesque ear for the clever, but they are overwhelmed, in the end, by erratic writing and the pompous absurdity of her story.

Like so many earlier Mukherjee characters, the narrator of *Leave It to Me* is a woman with multiple lives—a self-proclaimed chameleon who talks vaguely of fulfilling her fate. When we first meet her, she's Debby DiMartino, the adopted daughter of a nice Italian-American family in the Hudson Valley. Her birth mother, she learns, was a hippie who called herself Clear Water Iris-Daughter; her father was simply identified in the adoption papers as an Asian National. Debby determines to find them: she says she is sick of thinking of herself as a dog who was adopted at the pound.

Debby has an affair with a Chinese immigrant named Frankie Fong, who shares her taste for self-invention. In a previous life; Frankie was the star-director-producer of dozens of kick-boxing movies; more recently he's become an American con man. When Frankie betrays her, Debby casually torches his house, then takes off for California to look for her birth mother. On the way there, she has an epiphany and changes her name to Devi Dee—a name reminiscent of the Indian goddess, "the eight-armed, flame-bright, lion-riding dispenser of Divine Justice."

Debby—er, Devi—winds up in San Francisco's Haight-Ashbury district, where she meets Ham, a former counter-culture type turned movie maker; Larry, a paranoid Vietnam veteran who's got an arsenal of weapons in his apartment; and Jess, one of Ham's former hippie girlfriends, who has opened a successful business devoted to the care and feeding of famous writers on book tours.

Ms. Mukherjee's California sums up all that she finds distressing about American life: it's a place where people can discard the past and begin again, a place where trendy life styles and belief systems are picked up and discarded at whim. In this novel, we aren't shown glimpses of the bright promise of the American dream, just its sordid betrayal.

Devi, of course, is one of these reinvented people herself, but she harbors an almost cosmic anger against her birth mother and against members of her mother's generation. She even draws self-important analogies, between her mother's abandonment of her and the American invasion of—and subsequent withdrawal from—Vietnam.

A private detective whom Devi has hired tells her that her father was "one of the most notorious serial murderers in modern history"—"a sex-guru serial killer" named Romeo Haq, who kept a harem of hippie girls that included Devi's birth mother. "Bio-Mom," it seems, eventually turned Romeo into the police, accusing him of having strangled some 17 women and men.

These lurid revelations echo Devi's own plans to wreak vengeance on Bio-Mom for abandoning her and for betraying her father. While searching for Bio-Mom (who may or may not be Devi's new employer, Jess), Devi thinks nothing of mowing down innocent bystanders whose only sin has been to belong to her mother's generation. Hearing that funeral arrangements have been made for two people who have been violently killed, Devi says: "In private, I celebrated. The dead women were the same age as Jess. Two stand-ins for Mother down. I was closing in."

None of this, needless to say, is remotely believable—nor is the apocalyptic ending that reunites the demented Devi with her alleged birth parents. Certainly, plausibility has never been Ms. Mukherjee's strong suit, but in earlier books, her crazy-quilt plots not only possessed a fable-like power but also remained grounded in meticulously observed descriptions and edgy, pointillist prose.

In *Leave It to Me,* Ms. Mukherjee's highly tuned radar for language seems to have gone on the blink. While there are some wonderfully satiric asides shoehorned into the story, the main narrative bogs down in prose that vacillates between the willfully trendy ("Go for bliss") and the self-consciously portentous ("Some nights destiny puts up detour signs"). Characters say things like "Destruction is creation's necessary prelude" or "He made me wanton."

No doubt the increasingly disturbing events that transpire in *Leave It to Me* are supposed to underscore Ms. Mukherjee's dark view of an America on the brink of the millennium. Unfortunately, the reader doesn't buy it. Instead of believing that a blood-dimmed tide of random violence has been unleashed upon the land, one simply finishes the book convinced that randomness has infected Ms. Mukherjee's writing and her story.

Lorna Sage (review date 20 July 1997)

SOURCE: "Wrath of the Goddess," in *The New York Times Book Review,* July 20, 1997, p. 33.

[*In the following review, Sage asserts that "Devi [from* Leave It to Me] *is a brilliant creation—hilarious, horribly knowing and even more horribly oblivious—through whom Bharati Mukherjee, with characteristic and shameless ingenuity, is laying claim to speak for an America that isn't 'other' at all."*]

Bharati Mukherjee is a writer who likes to ventriloquize. She lives inside her characters' first-person voices, so they always seem driven, a touch paranoid, a little too creative in their dealings with the Brave New World. The heroine of *Leave It to Me,* Debby DiMartino, is no exception. Indeed, once she comes of age she jettisons with scorn the ready-made life she inhabits—as a fun-loving college girl from Schenectady, N.Y., with a great future in telemarketing—to search for her true identity. It turns out that Debby was only adopted by the DiMartinos, these plump, pleasant, disappointingly ordinary people with their ordinary genes. Her unknown but reportedly Californian mother dumped her in rural India on the hippie trail; her father was either a Eurasian guru or a serial killer, or both. But if Debby hadn't been a foundling, she'd have invented a new past anyway. The DiMartinos are probably lucky she didn't need to do away with them to prove that she was special.

But that's to anticipate. Savagely impatient as she is to claim her psychic inheritance, Debby has to start somewhere. She gives us a brisk resume of her formative years: the English teacher who spotted her gift with words, the shoplifting, the social worker who fell for her exotic heritage, the job selling exercise equipment over the telephone—which introduced her to the power of her voice. "My callers were romantics. They believed in me, not in salvation through Elastonomics. They begged, If I call back, how do I know I'll get you? I made them effortless promises. Just ask for me, Helena. Or depending on the mood of the day, Staci, Traci, Eva, Magda, Desiree. Some nights I tried out 30 personas. My lies paid off."

So spectacular is her sales record that the owner of Elastonomics, Frankie Fong, himself a Hong Kong salad of racial genes, seeks her out and becomes her lover and first real mentor in the art of identity politics. Frankie (who was named after Frank Sinatra by a show-biz father who toured the clubs of the Chinese diaspora singing "One for My Baby") is the former star and former director of a string of kick-boxing epics. He's rich, streetwise, greedy, clever and (most important) a spellbinding storyteller: "I loved his made-up childhoods. . . . He reminisced. Of pariah dogs and flying foxes, floating bodies, ancient ruins, temple bells, Muslim calls, diesel fumes, painted 'lorries.' . . . Fevers, drugs, backroom-behind-the-beaded-curtain Asia." Frankie (in short, and he doesn't last long) gives her lost legacy substance. He's just about old enough to be her father, and that's an added frisson: "When you inherit nothing, you are entitled to everything." Having learned her lesson all too well, and pausing only to set fire to his mansion in Saratoga Springs (was there a rival girlfriend inside? *Tant pis*), Debby sets out for California, where the real action is.

On the state border she acquires a new Indian goddess name—Devi—from the bumper sticker of a blonde who cuts in on her, and becomes Devi Dee (Dee from DiMartino, but there's nothing much left of their baby now). Once in the Bay Area, she merges fearlessly with the human flotsam and jetsam—"a kind of outlaw, on the side of other outlaws. . . . It seemed totally natural to identify with dropouts." In another context, this would be one of the pieties of multiculturalism, but you can't trust Devi with words like "natural" and "identify." When she identifies with people, she steals their life stories, or at least the bits she wants. She's a psychic scavenger. In this, of course, she's also quite traditional—in the tradition of cosmopolitan street life. The beggars that Henry Mayhew interviewed on the streets of Victorian London, who inspired Dickens (and were probably inspired by him, since there's no secure boundary between fact and fiction in the soft city), all said that they stole one another's stories routinely. I've been a lace maker from Nottingham, they'd say, and a shipwrecked sailor, just depends on the mood of the day. Devi finds plenty of source material in San Francisco: "All my neighbors had come home to the Beulah rooming house from somewhere else. Vanuatu Man wasn't the only refugee, and Loco Larry wasn't the only war-maimed. Everything was flow, a spontaneous web without compartments. Somalia, Vanuatu, Vietnam, Belgium, India-Schenectady." As Devi closes in on her mother's world, she gathers to herself the accumulated grief and outrage of all these others.

You can get a rough idea of the bloody scenario in prospect from the strength of want and envy in Devi's style—all that use of "I," all those lists. Repeating the Frankie move, she becomes the lover of a 1960's survivor named Ham and the furious rival of his longtime girlfriend, Jess, who may or may not be her mother but deserves to pay anyway—for being there and being in the way. It's Jess who gives Devi her motto, "Leave It to Me"—a pun on the name of her Media Escort agency, through which Devi's Devil Dad himself tracks them down, having escaped like a genie out of a bottle from an Indian jail.

Jess, Ham and their Berkeley gang "marched for peace, for civil rights, for women, gays, migrants"; now "they also drove big cars, lived large lives." Devi is filled with resentment: "But what about us, Vietnam's war-bastards and democracy's love children? We're still coping with what they did." She's at her most lethal when she says "we": Devi, the eight-armed agent of divine justice, a fraction Pakistani, another fraction Chinese, another French Vietnamese and at least half Californian—but who's counting?

Leave It to Me is wittily billed as "the Electra story . . . reimagined for our time," and it's true that it's a tale of murderous female jealousy between generations. But that's only the beginning. Some readers will see in it visionary vengeance on American hubris, a triumph of alien genes, Devi as a force of nature. Yet it also seems to contain a mocking attack on the very notion of speaking for outsiders. Devi suffers from multiple personality disorder—and what's more Western than that? Backing up this reading is the extraordinary appearance of Dad in full drag and silver high-heeled slippers. Devi is a brilliant creation—hilarious, horribly knowing and even more horribly oblivious—through whom Bharati Mukherjee, with characteristic and shameless ingenuity, is laying claim to speak for an America that isn't "other" at all.

FURTHER READING

Criticism

Birch, Dinah. "Other People." *London Review of Books* 11, No. 13 (6 July 1989): 18-9.
> Lauds Mukherjee's *The Middleman and Other Stories* as an "uncompromising collection [which] presents a razor-sharp reflection of a world which is disconnected, but not without hope."

Brandmark, Wendy. "Looking for Devi Dee." *Times Literary Supplement,* No. 4920 (18 July 1997): 22.
> Complains that in Mukherjee's *Leave It to Me,* "The writing loses its vitality after the first few chapters and descends into a rather irritating mixture of computer jargon and West-Coast slang."

R. J. C. "Tiger's Daughter as a Kitten." *Christian Science Monitor* (27 January 1972): 10.
> Praises Mukherjee's *The Tiger's Daughter* and states that "It is a pleasure to read her delicate responses to coming of age between the two polarities of Calcutta and America."

Chua, C. L. "Passages from India: Migrating to America in the Fiction of V. S. Naipaul and Bharati Mukherjee." In *Reworlding: The Literature of the Indian Diaspora,* edited by Emmanuel S. Nelson, pp. 51-61. New York: Greenwood Press, 1992.
> Discusses the way in which Mukherjee and V. S. Naipaul portray the immigration of Indians into North America, and their difficulty in participating in the American Dream.

Drolet, Gilbert. Review of *The Sorrow and the Terror,* by Clark Blaise and Bharati Mukherjee. *Canadian Literature,* No. 121 (Summer 1989): 166-68.
> Complains about the shallow research and unnecessary elaboration of certain details in *The Sorrow and the Terror* by Mukherjee and Clark Blaise, while commending the intentions of its authors.

Harishankar, Bharathi. "See(k)ing Differences: Constructions of Gender and Culture in the Short Texts of Bharati Mukherjee." In *Intersexions: Issues of Race and Gender in Canadian Women's Writing,* edited by Coomi S. Vevaina and Barbara Godard, pp. 164-78. New Delhi: Creative Books, 1996.
> Analyzes the role of culture and gender differences in Mukherjee's short works and asserts that "By playing up the differences at all levels, Mukherjee questions the accepted social norms and also provides a holistic approach to gender and ethnicity."

Iyer, Nalini. "American/Indian: Metaphors of the Self in Bharati Mukherjee's 'The Holder of the World.'" *Ariel* 27, No. 4 (October 1996): 29-44.
> Analyzes the use of narrative and location in Mukherjee's *The Holder of the World.*

Kanaganayakam, Chelva. "Indias of the Mind." *Canadian Literature,* No. 148 (Spring 1996): 157-60.
> Lauds Mukherjee's *The Holder of the World* as a major contemporary work.

Klass, Rosanne. "Indian Wife Lives Soap-Opera Life." *Ms.* IV, No. 4 (October 1975): 83-8.
> Criticizes Mukherjee's *Wife* for being "carelessly written, erratic, disjointed, often ludicrously improbable, and ultimately pointless."

Koshy, Susan. Review of *The Holder of the World,* by Bharati Mukherjee. *Amerasia Journal* 20, No. 1 (1994): 188-90.
> Argues that Mukherjee's *The Holder of the World* shows that "As a writer, Mukherjee has yet to arrive at a keen sense of the complicities within which post-colonial and minority writing takes place."

Levin, Martin. Review of *Wife,* by Bharati Mukherjee. *The New York Times Book Review* (8 June 1975): 17, 20.
> Discusses Dimple, the main character of Mukherjee's novel *Wife.*

Messud, Claire. "The Emperor's Tear." *The Times Literary Supplement,* No. 4728 (12 November 1993): 23.
> Asserts that Mukherjee's *The Holder of the World* "takes itself so seriously that it risks becoming more interesting to think about than to read."

Mitra, Indrani. "'Luminous Brahmin Children Must Be Saved': Imperialist Ideologies, 'Postcolonial' Histories in Bharati Mukherjee's *The Tiger's Daughter.*" In *Between the Lines: South Asians and Postcoloniality,* edited by Deepika Bahri and Mary Vasudeva, pp. 284-97. Philadelphia: Temple University Press, 1996.
> Discusses the implications of studying Mukherjee's *The Tiger's Daughter* in terms of "postcolonial" literature.

Ricks, Christopher. "Youth and Asia." *The New York Review of Books* XVIII, No. 4 (9 March 1972): 23-5.

    Discusses Mukherjee's portrayal of India in her *The Tiger's Daughter.*

Additional coverage of Mukherjee's life and career is contained in the following sources published by Gale: *Bestsellers,* **Vol. 89:2;** *Contemporary Authors,* **Vol. 107;** *Contemporary Authors New Revision Series,* **Vol. 45;** *Dictionary of Literary Biography,* **Vol. 60;** *DISCovering Authors Modules: Novelists;* **and** *Major Twentieth-Century Writers.*

☐ Contemporary Literary Criticism

Indexes

Literary Criticism Series
Cumulative Author Index
Cumulative Topic Index
Cumulative Nationality Index
Title Index, Volume 115

How to Use This Index

The main references

Camus, Albert
1913-1960 . . . . . . .CLC 1, 2, 4, 9, 11,
14, 32, 69; DA; DAB; DAC; DAM
DRAM, MST, NOV; DC2; SSC 9;
WLC

list all author entries in the following Gale Literary Criticism series:

BLC = *Black Literature Criticism*
BLCS = *Black Literature Criticism Supplement*
CLC = *Contemporary Literary Criticism*
CLR = *Children's Literature Review*
CMLC = *Classical and Medieval Literature Criticism*
DA = *DISCovering Authors*
DAB = *DISCovering Authors: British*
DAC = *DISCovering Authors: Canadian*
DAM = *DISCovering Authors Modules*
  DRAM = *dramatists;* *MST* = *most-studied*
  authors; *MULT* = *multicultural authors;* *NOV* =
  novelists; *POET* = *poets;* *POP* = *popular/genre*
  writers; *DC* = *Drama Criticism*
HLC = *Hispanic Literature Criticism*
LC = *Literature Criticism from 1400 to 1800*
NCLC = *Nineteenth-Century Literature Criticism*
PC = *Poetry Criticism*
SSC = *Short Story Criticism*
TCLC = *Twentieth-Century Literary Criticism*
WLC = *World Literature Criticism, 1500 to the Present*
WLCS = *World Literature Criticism Supplement*

The cross-references

See also CA 89-92; DLB 72; MTCW

list all author entries in the following Gale biographical and literary sources:

AAYA = *Authors & Artists for Young Adults*
AITN = *Authors in the News*
BEST = *Bestsellers*
BW = *Black Writers*
CA = *Contemporary Authors*
CAAS = *Contemporary Authors Autobiography Series*
CABS = *Contemporary Authors Bibliographical Series*
CANR = *Contemporary Authors New Revision Series*
CAP = *Contemporary Authors Permanent Series*
CDALB = *Concise Dictionary of American Literary Biography*
CDBLB = *Concise Dictionary of British Literary Biography*

DLB = *Dictionary of Literary Biography*
DLBD = *Dictionary of Literary Biography Documentary Series*
DLBY = *Dictionary of Literary Biography Yearbook*
HW = *Hispanic Writers*
JRDA = *Junior DISCovering Authors*
MAICYA = *Major Authors and Illustrators for Children and Young Adults*
MTCW = *Major 20th-Century Writers*
NNAL = *Native North American Literature*
SAAS = *Something about the Author Autobiography Series*
SATA = *Something about the Author*
YABC = *Yesterday's Authors of Books for Children*

Literary Criticism Series
Cumulative Author Index

MAICYA; SATA 100; YABC 1
Aldanov, M. A.
See Aldanov. Mark (Alexandrovich)
Aldanov, Mark (Alexandrovich) 1886(?)-1957
TCLC 23
See also CA 118
Aldington, Richard 1892-1962 .... **CLC 49**
See also CA 85-88; CANR 45; DLB 20, 36, 100,
149
Aldiss, Brian W(ilson) 1925- . **CLC 5, 14, 40;
DAM NOV**
See also CA 5-8R; CAAS 2; CANR 5, 28, 64;
DLB 14; MTCW 1; SATA 34
Alegria, Claribel 1924-**CLC 75; DAM MULT**
See also CA 131; CAAS 15; CANR 66; DLB
145; HW
Alegria, Fernando 1918-................. **CLC 57**
See also CA 9-12R; CANR 5, 32, 72; HW
Aleichem, Sholom .... **TCLC 1, 35**
See also Rabinovitch, Sholem
Aleixandre, Vicente 1898-1984 ... **CLC 9, 36;
DAM POET; PC 15**
See also CA 85-88; 114; CANR 26; DLB 108;
HW; MTCW 1
Alepoudelis, Odysseus
See Elytis, Odysseus
Aleshkovsky, Joseph 1929-
See Aleshkovsky, Yuz
See also CA 121; 128
Aleshkovsky, Yuz .... **CLC 44**
See also Aleshkovsky, Joseph
Alexander, Lloyd (Chudley) 1924- .. **CLC 35**
See also AAYA 1, 27; CA 1-4R; CANR 1, 24,
38, 55; CLR 1, 5, 48; DLB 52; JRDA;
MAICYA; MTCW 1; SAAS 19; SATA 3, 49,
81
Alexander, Samuel 1859 1938 .... **TCLC 77**
Alexie, Sherman (Joseph, Jr.) 1966- **CLC 96;
DAM MULT**
See also CA 138; CANR 65; DLB 175; NNAL
Alfau, Felipe 1902-............................ **CLC 66**
See also CA 137
Alger, Horatio, Jr. 1832-1899 .... **NCLC 8**
See also DLB 42; SATA 16
Algren, Nelson 1909-1981 .... **CLC 4, 10, 33**
See also CA 13-16R; 103; CANR 20, 61;
CDALB 1941-1968; DLB 9; DLBY 81, 82;
MTCW 1
Ali, Ahmed 1910-............................... **CLC 69**
See also CA 25-28R; CANR 15, 34
Alighieri, Dante
See Dante
Allan, John B.
See Westlake, Donald E(dwin)
Allan, Sidney
See Hartmann, Sadakichi
Allan, Sydney
See Hartmann, Sadakichi
Allen, Edward 1948-........................ **CLC 59**
Allen, Paula Gunn 1939- .... **CLC 84; DAM
MULT**
See also CA 112; 143; CANR 63; DLB 175;
NNAL
Allen, Roland
See Ayckbourn, Alan
Allen, Sarah A.
See Hopkins, Pauline Elizabeth
Allen, Sidney H.
See Hartmann, Sadakichi
Allen, Woody 1935- **CLC 16, 52; DAM POP**
See also AAYA 10; CA 33-36R; CANR 27, 38,
63; DLB 44; MTCW 1
Allende, Isabel 1942-. **CLC 39, 57, 97; DAM**

MULT, NOV; HLC; WLCS
See also AAYA 18; CA 125; 130; CANR 51;
DLB 145; HW; INT 130; MTCW 1
Alleyn, Ellen
See Rossetti. Christina (Georgina)
Allingham, Margery (Louise) 1904-1966**CLC
19**
See also CA 5-8R; 25-28R; CANR 4, 58; DLB
77; MTCW 1
Allingham, William 1824-1889 ...... **NCLC 25**
See also DLB 35
Allison, Dorothy E. 1949-................. **CLC 78**
See also CA 140; CANR 66
Allston, Washington 1779-1843 .... **NCLC 2**
See also DLB 1
Almedingen, E. M. ....**CLC 12**
See also Almedingen, Martha Edith von
See also SATA 3
Almedingen, Martha Edith von 1898-1971
See Almedingen, E. M.
See also CA 1-4R; CANR 1
Almodovar, Pedro 1949(?)-.............. **CLC 114**
See also CA 133; CANR 72
Almqvist, Carl Jonas Love 1793-1866 **N C L C
42**
Alonso, Damaso 1898-1990 .... **CLC 14**
See also CA 110; 131; 130; CANR 72; DLB
108; HW
Alov
See Gogol, Nikolai (Vasilyevich)
Alta 1942-...**CLC 19**
See also CA 57-60
Alter, Robert B(ernard) 1935- ....**CLC 34**
See also CA 49-52; CANR 1, 47
Alther, Lisa 1944- .... **CLC 7, 41**
See also CA 65-68; CAAS 30; CANR 12, 30,
51; MTCW 1
Althusser, L.
See Althusser, Louis
Althusser, Louis 1918-1990 .... **CLC 106**
See also CA 131; 132
Altman, Robert 1925-........................ **CLC 16**
See also CA 73-76; CANR 43
Alvarez, A(lfred) 1929- .... **CLC 5, 13**
See also CA 1-4R; CANR 3, 33, 63; DLB 14,
40
Alvarez, Alejandro Rodriguez 1903-1965
See Casona, Alejandro
See also CA 131; 93-96; HW
Alvarez, Julia 1950-............................**CLC 93**
See also AAYA 25; CA 147; CANR 69
Alvaro, Corrado 1896-1956............ **TCLC 60**
See also CA 163
Amado, Jorge 1912- **CLC 13, 40, 106; DAM
MULT, NOV; HLC**
See also CA 77-80; CANR 35; DLB 113;
MTCW 1
Ambler, Eric 1909- .... **CLC 4, 6, 9**
See also CA 9-12R; CANR 7, 38; DLB 77;
MTCW 1
Amichai, Yehuda 1924- .... **CLC 9, 22, 57**
See also CA 85-88; CANR 46, 60; MTCW 1
Amichai, Yehudah
See Amichai, Yehuda
Amiel, Henri Frederic 1821-1881 .... **NCLC 4**
Amis, Kingsley (William) 1922-1995**CLC 1, 2,
3, 5, 8, 13, 40, 44; DA; DAB; DAC; DAM
MST, NOV**
See also AITN 2; CA 9-12R; 150; CANR 8, 28,
54; CDBLB 1945-1960; DLB 15, 27, 100,
139; DLBY 96; INT CANR-8; MTCW 1
Amis, Martin (Louis) 1949-**CLC 4, 9, 38, 62,
101**

See also BEST 90:3; CA 65-68; CANR 8, 27,
54; DLB 14, 194; INT CANR-27
Ammons, A(rchie) R(andolph) 1926-**CLC 2, 3,
5, 8, 9, 25, 57, 108; DAM POET; PC 16**
See also AITN 1; CA 9-12R; CANR 6, 36, 51;
DLB 5, 165; MTCW 1
Amo, Tauraatua i
See Adams, Henry (Brooks)
Anand, Mulk Raj 1905- .. **CLC 23, 93; DAM
NOV**
See also CA 65-68; CANR 32, 64; MTCW 1
Anatol
See Schnitzler, Arthur
Anaximander c. 610B.C.-c. 546B.C.**CMLC 22**
Anaya, Rudolfo A(lfonso) 1937- ..... **CLC 23;
DAM MULT, NOV; HLC**
See also AAYA 20; CA 45-48; CAAS 4; CANR
1, 32, 51; DLB 82; HW 1; MTCW 1
Andersen, Hans Christian 1805-1875**NCLC 7;
DA; DAB; DAC; DAM MST, POP; SSC
6; WLC**
See also CLR 6; MAICYA; SATA 100; YABC
1
Anderson, C. Farley
See Mencken, H(enry) L(ouis); Nathan, George
Jean
Anderson, Jessica (Margaret) Queale 1916-
CLC 37
See also CA 9-12R; CANR 4, 62
Anderson, Jon (Victor) 1940-.. **CLC 9; DAM
POET**
See also CA 25-28R; CANR 20
Anderson, Lindsay (Gordon) 1923-1994**C L C
20**
See also CA 125; 128; 146
Anderson, Maxwell 1888-1959**TCLC 2; DAM
DRAM**
See also CA 105; 152; DLB 7
Anderson, Poul (William) 1926- ...... **CLC 15**
See also AAYA 5; CA 1-4R; CAAS 2; CANR
2, 15, 34, 64; DLB 8; INT CANR-15; MTCW
1; SATA 90; SATA-Brief 39
Anderson, Robert (Woodruff) 1917-**CLC 23;
DAM DRAM**
See also AITN 1; CA 21-24R; CANR 32; DLB
7
Anderson, Sherwood 1876-1941 **TCLC 1, 10,
24; DA; DAB; DAC; DAM MST, NOV;
SSC 1; WLC**
See also CA 104; 121; CANR 61; CDALB
1917-1929; DLB 4, 9, 86; DLBD 1; MTCW
1
Andier, Pierre
See Desnos, Robert
Andouard
See Giraudoux, (Hippolyte) Jean
Andrade, Carlos Drummond de .... **CLC 18**
See also Drummond de Andrade, Carlos
Andrade, Mario de 1893-1945 .... **TCLC 43**
Andreae, Johann V(alentin) 1586-1654**LC 32**
See also DLB 164
Andreas-Salome, Lou 1861-1937 ... **TCLC 56**
See also DLB 66
Andress, Lesley
See Sanders, Lawrence
Andrewes, Lancelot 1555-1626 .... **LC 5**
See also DLB 151, 172
Andrews, Cicily Fairfield
See West, Rebecca
Andrews, Elton V.
See Pohl, Frederik
Andreyev, Leonid (Nikolaevich) 1871-1919
TCLC 3

See also CA 104
Andric, Ivo 1892-1975 ....CLC 8
  See also CA 81-84; 57-60; CANR 43, 60; DLB 147; MTCW 1
Androvar
  See Prado (Calvo), Pedro
Angelique, Pierre
  See Bataille, Georges
Angell, Roger 1920- .... CLC 26
  See also CA 57-60; CANR 13, 44, 70; DLB 171, 185
Angelou, Maya 1928-CLC 12, 35, 64, 77; BLC 1; DA; DAB; DAC; DAM MST, MULT, POET, POP; WLCS
  See also Johnson, Marguerite (Annie)
  See also AAYA 7, 20; BW 2; CA 65-68; CANR 19, 42, 65; CLR 53; DLB 38; MTCW 1; SATA 49
Anna Comnena 1083-1153 .... CMLC 25
Annensky, Innokenty (Fyodorovich) 1856-1909 TCLC 14
  See also CA 110; 155
Annunzio, Gabriele d'
  See D'Annunzio, Gabriele
Anodos
  See Coleridge, Mary E(lizabeth)
Anon, Charles Robert
  See Pessoa, Fernando (Antonio Nogueira)
Anouilh, Jean (Marie Lucien Pierre) 1910-1987 CLC 1, 3, 8, 13, 40, 50; DAM DRAM; DC 8
  See also CA 17-20R; 123; CANR 32; MTCW 1
Anthony, Florence
  See Ai
Anthony, John
  See Ciardi, John (Anthony)
Anthony, Peter
  See Shaffer, Anthony (Joshua); Shaffer, Peter (Levin)
Anthony, Piers 1934- ..... CLC 35; DAM POP
  See also AAYA 11; CA 21-24R; CANR 28, 56; DLB 8; MTCW 1; SAAS 22; SATA 84
Anthony, Susan B(rownell) 1916-1991 T C L C 84
  See also CA 89-92; 134
Antoine, Marc
  See Proust. (Valentin-Louis-George-Eugene-) Marcel
Antoninus, Brother
  See Everson, William (Oliver)
Antonioni, Michelangelo 1912- .... CLC 20
  See also CA 73-76; CANR 45
Antschel, Paul 1920-1970
  See Celan, Paul
  See also CA 85-88; CANR 33, 61; MTCW 1
Anwar, Chairil 1922-1949 .... TCLC 22
  See also CA 121
Apess, William 1798-1839(?)NCLC 73; DAM MULT
  See also DLB 175; NNAL
Apollinaire, Guillaume 1880-1918TCLC 3, 8, 51; DAM POET; PC 7
  See also Kostrowitzki, Wilhelm Apollinaris de
  See also CA 152
Appelfeld, Aharon 1932- .... CLC 23, 47
  See also CA 112; 133
Apple, Max (Isaac) 1941-.............. CLC 9, 33
  See also CA 81-84; CANR 19, 54; DLB 130
Appleman, Philip (Dean) 1926-........ CLC 51
  See also CA 13-16R; CAAS 18; CANR 6, 29, 56
Appleton, Lawrence
  See Lovecraft, H(oward) P(hillips)

Apteryx
  See Eliot, T(homas) S(tearns)
Apuleius, (Lucius Madaurensis) 125(?)-175(?) CMLC 1
Aquin, Hubert 1929-1977 ....CLC 15
  See also CA 105; DLB 53
Aragon, Louis 1897-1982 ..CLC 3, 22; DAM NOV, POET
  See also CA 69-72; 108; CANR 28, 71; DLB 72; MTCW 1
Arany, Janos 1817-1882 .... NCLC 34
Arbuthnot, John 1667-1735 .... LC 1
  See also DLB 101
Archer, Herbert Winslow
  See Mencken, H(enry) L(ouis)
Archer, Jeffrey (Howard) 1940- ..... CLC 28; DAM POP
  See also AAYA 16; BEST 89:3; CA 77-80; CANR 22, 52; INT CANR-22
Archer, Jules 1915-............................CLC 12
  See also CA 9-12R; CANR 6, 69; SAAS 5; SATA 4, 85
Archer, Lee
  See Ellison, Harlan (Jay)
Arden, John 1930-CLC 6, 13, 15; DAM DRAM
  See also CA 13-16R; CAAS 4; CANR 31, 65, 67; DLB 13; MTCW 1
Arenas, Reinaldo 1943-1990 .CLC 41; DAM MULT; HLC
  See also CA 124; 128; 133; DLB 145; HW
Arendt, Hannah 1906-1975 .... CLC 66, 98
  See also CA 17-20R; 61-64; CANR 26, 60; MTCW 1
Aretino, Pietro 1492-1556 .... LC 12
Arghezi, Tudor 1880-1967 ....CLC 80
  See also Theodorescu, Ion N.
  See also CA 167
Arguedas, Jose Maria 1911-1969 CLC 10, 18
  See also CA 89-92; DLB 113; HW
Argueta, Manlio 1936- ....CLC 31
  See also CA 131; DLB 145; HW
Ariosto, Ludovico 1474-1533 .... LC 6
Aristides
  See Epstein, Joseph
Aristophanes 450B.C.-385B.C.CMLC 4; DA; DAB; DAC; DAM DRAM, MST; DC 2; WLCS
  See also DLB 176
Arlt, Roberto (Godofredo Christophersen) 1900-1942TCLC 29; DAM MULT; HLC
  See also CA 123; 131; CANR 67; HW
Armah, Ayi Kwei 1939- . CLC 5, 33; BLC 1; DAM MULT, POET
  See also BW 1; CA 61-64; CANR 21, 64; DLB 117; MTCW 1
Armatrading, Joan 1950- ....CLC 17
  See also CA 114
Arnette, Robert
  See Silverberg, Robert
Arnim, Achim von (Ludwig Joachim von Arnim) 1781-1831 ...... NCLC 5; SSC 29
  See also DLB 90
Arnim, Bettina von 1785-1859 ....NCLC 38
  See also DLB 90
Arnold, Matthew 1822-1888NCLC 6, 29; DA; DAB; DAC; DAM MST, POET; PC 5; WLC
  See also CDBLB 1832-1890; DLB 32, 57
Arnold, Thomas 1795-1842 ....NCLC 18
  See also DLB 55
Arnow, Harriette (Louisa) Simpson 1908-1986 CLC 2, 7, 18
  See also CA 9-12R; 118; CANR 14; DLB 6;

MTCW 1; SATA 42; SATA-Obit 47
Arouet, Francois-Marie
  See Voltaire
Arp, Hans
  See Arp, Jean
Arp, Jean 1887-1966 ....CLC 5
  See also CA 81-84; 25-28R; CANR 42
Arrabal
  See Arrabal, Fernando
Arrabal, Fernando 1932-.... CLC 2, 9, 18, 58
  See also CA 9-12R; CANR 15
Arrick, Fran ....CLC 30
  See also Gaberman, Judie Angell
Artaud, Antonin (Marie Joseph) 1896-1948 TCLC 3, 36; DAM DRAM
  See also CA 104; 149
Arthur, Ruth M(abel) 1905-1979 ......CLC 12
  See also CA 9-12R; 85-88; CANR 4; SATA 7, 26
Artsybashev, Mikhail (Petrovich) 1878-1927 TCLC 31
Arundel, Honor (Morfydd) 1919-1973CLC 17
  See also CA 21-22; 41-44R; CAP 2; CLR 35; SATA 4; SATA-Obit 24
Arzner, Dorothy 1897-1979 ....CLC 98
Asch, Sholem 1880-1957 .... TCLC 3
  See also CA 105
Ash, Shalom
  See Asch, Sholem
Ashbery, John (Lawrence) 1927-CLC 2, 3, 4, 6, 9, 13, 15, 25, 41, 77; DAM POET
  See also CA 5-8R; CANR 9, 37, 66; DLB 5, 165; DLBY 81; INT CANR-9; MTCW 1
Ashdown, Clifford
  See Freeman, R(ichard) Austin
Ashe, Gordon
  See Creasey, John
Ashton-Warner, Sylvia (Constance) 1908-1984 CLC 19
  See also CA 69-72; 112; CANR 29; MTCW 1
Asimov, Isaac 1920-1992 CLC 1, 3, 9, 19, 26, 76, 92; DAM POP
  See also AAYA 13; BEST 90:2; CA 1-4R; 137; CANR 2, 19, 36, 60; CLR 12; DLB 8; DLBY 92; INT CANR-19; JRDA; MAICYA; MTCW 1; SATA 1, 26, 74
Assis, Joaquim Maria Machado de
  See Machado de Assis, Joaquim Maria
Astley, Thea (Beatrice May) 1925- ...CLC 41
  See also CA 65-68; CANR 11, 43
Aston, James
  See White, T(erence) H(anbury)
Asturias, Miguel Angel 1899-1974 CLC 3, 8, 13; DAM MULT, NOV; HLC
  See also CA 25-28; 49-52; CANR 32; CAP 2; DLB 113; HW; MTCW 1
Atares, Carlos Saura
  See Saura (Atares), Carlos
Atheling, William
  See Pound, Ezra (Weston Loomis)
Atheling, William, Jr.
  See Blish, James (Benjamin)
Atherton, Gertrude (Franklin Horn) 1857-1948 TCLC 2
  See also CA 104; 155; DLB 9, 78, 186
Atherton, Lucius
  See Masters, Edgar Lee
Atkins, Jack
  See Harris, Mark
Atkinson, Kate ....CLC 99
  See also CA 166
Attaway, William (Alexander) 1911-1986 CLC 92; BLC 1; DAM MULT

See also BW 2; CA 143; DLB 76

Atticus
See Fleming, Ian (Lancaster); Wilson, (Thomas) Woodrow

Atwood, Margaret (Eleanor) 1939-CLC 2, 3, 4, 8, 13, 15, 25, 44, 84; DA; DAB; DAC; DAM MST, NOV, POET; PC 8; SSC 2; WLC
See also AAYA 12; BEST 89:2; CA 49-52; CANR 3, 24, 33, 59; DLB 53; INT CANR-24; MTCW 1; SATA 50

Aubigny, Pierre d'
See Mencken, H(enry) L(ouis)

Aubin, Penelope 1685-1731(?) .... LC 9
See also DLB 39

Auchincloss, Louis (Stanton) 1917-CLC 4, 6, 9, 18, 45; DAM NOV; SSC 22
See also CA 1-4R; CANR 6, 29, 55; DLB 2; DLBY 80; INT CANR-29; MTCW 1

Auden, W(ystan) H(ugh) 1907-1973CLC 1, 2, 3, 4, 6, 9, 11, 14, 43; DA; DAB; DAC; DAM DRAM, MST, POET; PC 1; WLC
See also AAYA 18; CA 9-12R; 45-48; CANR 5, 61; CDBLB 1914-1945; DLB 10, 20; MTCW 1

Audiberti, Jacques 1900-1965CLC 38; DAM DRAM
See also CA 25-28R

Audubon, John James 1785-1851 ..NCLC 47

Auel, Jean M(arie) 1936-CLC 31, 107; DAM POP
See also AAYA 7; BEST 90:4; CA 103; CANR 21, 64; INT CANR-21; SATA 91

Auerbach, Erich 1892-1957 .... TCLC 43
See also CA 118; 155

Augier, Emile 1820-1889 .... NCLC 31
See also DLB 192

August, John
See De Voto, Bernard (Augustine)

Augustine, St. 354-430 .... CMLC 6; DAB

Aurelius
See Bourne, Randolph S(illiman)

Aurobindo, Sri
See Ghose, Aurabinda

Austen, Jane 1775-1817 NCLC 1, 13, 19, 33, 51; DA; DAB; DAC; DAM MST, NOV; WLC
See also AAYA 19; CDBLB 1789-1832; DLB 116

Auster, Paul 1947- .... CLC 47
See also CA 69-72; CANR 23, 52

Austin, Frank
See Faust, Frederick (Schiller)

Austin, Mary (Hunter) 1868-1934 . TCLC 25
See also CA 109; DLB 9, 78

Autran Dourado, Waldomiro
See Dourado, (Waldomiro Freitas) Autran

Averroes 1126-1198 .... CMLC 7
See also DLB 115

Avicenna 980-1037 .... CMLC 16
See also DLB 115

Avison, Margaret 1918- CLC 2, 4, 97; DAC; DAM POET
See also CA 17-20R; DLB 53; MTCW 1

Axton, David
See Koontz, Dean R(ay)

Ayckbourn, Alan 1939- CLC 5, 8, 18, 33, 74; DAB; DAM DRAM
See also CA 21-24R; CANR 31, 59; DLB 13; MTCW 1

Aydy, Catherine
See Tennant, Emma (Christina)

Ayme, Marcel (Andre) 1902-1967 ..... CLC 11

See also CA 89-92; CANR 67; CLR 25; DLB 72; SATA 91

Ayrton, Michael 1921-1975 .... CLC 7
See also CA 5-8R; 61-64; CANR 9, 21

Azorin .... CLC 11
See also Martinez Ruiz, Jose

Azuela, Mariano 1873-1952 . TCLC 3; DAM MULT; HLC
See also CA 104; 131; HW; MTCW 1

Baastad, Babbis Friis
See Friis-Baastad, Babbis Ellinor

Bab
See Gilbert, W(illiam) S(chwenck)

Babbis, Eleanor
See Friis-Baastad, Babbis Ellinor

Babel, Isaac
See Babel, Isaak (Emmanuilovich)

Babel, Isaak (Emmanuilovich) 1894-1941(?) TCLC 2, 13; SSC 16
See also CA 104; 155

Babits, Mihaly 1883-1941 .... TCLC 14
See also CA 114

Babur 1483-1530 .... LC 18

Bacchelli, Riccardo 1891-1985 .... CLC 19
See also CA 29-32R; 117

Bach, Richard (David) 1936- CLC 14; DAM NOV, POP
See also AITN 1; BEST 89:2; CA 9-12R; CANR 18; MTCW 1; SATA 13

Bachman, Richard
See King, Stephen (Edwin)

Bachmann, Ingeborg 1926-1973 .... CLC 69
See also CA 93-96; 45-48; CANR 69; DLB 85

Bacon, Francis 1561-1626 .... LC 18, 32
See also CDBLB Before 1660; DLB 151

Bacon, Roger 1214(?)-1292 .... CMLC 14
See also DLB 115

Bacovia, George .... TCLC 24
See also Vasiliu, Gheorghe

Badanes, Jerome 1937- .... CLC 59

Bagehot, Walter 1826-1877 .... NCLC 10
See also DLB 55

Bagnold, Enid 1889-1981 ...... CLC 25; DAM DRAM
See also CA 5-8R; 103; CANR 5, 40; DLB 13, 160, 191; MAICYA; SATA 1, 25

Bagritsky, Eduard 1895-1934 .... TCLC 60

Bagrjana, Elisaveta
See Belcheva, Elisaveta

Bagryana, Elisaveta .... CLC 10
See also Belcheva, Elisaveta
See also DLB 147

Bailey, Paul 1937- .... CLC 45
See also CA 21-24R; CANR 16, 62; DLB 14

Baillie, Joanna 1762-1851 .... NCLC 71
See also DLB 93

Bainbridge, Beryl (Margaret) 1933-CLC 4, 5, 8, 10, 14, 18, 22, 62; DAM NOV
See also CA 21-24R; CANR 24, 55; DLB 14; MTCW 1

Baker, Elliott 1922- .... CLC 8
See also CA 45-48; CANR 2, 63

Baker, Jean H. .... TCLC 3, 10
See also Russell, George William

Baker, Nicholson 1957- . CLC 61; DAM POP
See also CA 135; CANR 63

Baker, Ray Stannard 1870-1946 .... TCLC 47
See also CA 118

Baker, Russell (Wayne) 1925- .... CLC 31
See also BEST 89:4; CA 57-60; CANR 11, 41, 59; MTCW 1

Bakhtin, M.
See Bakhtin, Mikhail Mikhailovich

Bakhtin, M. M.
See Bakhtin, Mikhail Mikhailovich

Bakhtin, Mikhail
See Bakhtin, Mikhail Mikhailovich

Bakhtin, Mikhail Mikhailovich 1895-1975 CLC 83
See also CA 128; 113

Bakshi, Ralph 1938(?)- .... CLC 26
See also CA 112; 138

Bakunin, Mikhail (Alexandrovich) 1814-1876 NCLC 25, 58

Baldwin, James (Arthur) 1924-1987CLC 1, 2, 3, 4, 5, 8, 13, 15, 17, 42, 50, 67, 90; BLC 1; DA; DAB; DAC; DAM MST, MULT, NOV, POP; DC 1; SSC 10; WLC
See also AAYA 4; BW 1; CA 1-4R; 124; CABS 1; CANR 3, 24; CDALB 1941-1968; DLB 2, 7, 33; DLBY 87; MTCW 1; SATA 9; SATA-Obit 54

Ballard, J(ames) G(raham) 1930-CLC 3, 6, 14, 36; DAM NOV, POP; SSC 1
See also AAYA 3; CA 5-8R; CANR 15, 39, 65; DLB 14; MTCW 1; SATA 93

Balmont, Konstantin (Dmitriyevich) 1867-1943 TCLC 11
See also CA 109; 155

Balzac, Honore de 1799-1850NCLC 5, 35, 53; DA; DAB; DAC; DAM MST, NOV; SSC 5; WLC
See also DLB 119

Bambara, Toni Cade 1939-1995 CLC 19, 88; BLC 1; DA; DAC; DAM MST, MULT; WLCS
See also AAYA 5; BW 2; CA 29-32R; 150; CANR 24, 49; DLB 38; MTCW 1

Bamdad, A.
See Shamlu, Ahmad

Banat, D. R.
See Bradbury, Ray (Douglas)

Bancroft, Laura
See Baum, L(yman) Frank

Banim, John 1798-1842 .... NCLC 13
See also DLB 116, 158, 159

Banim, Michael 1796-1874 .... NCLC 13
See also DLB 158, 159

Banjo, The
See Paterson, A(ndrew) B(arton)

Banks, Iain
See Banks, Iain M(enzies)

Banks, Iain M(enzies) 1954- .... CLC 34
See also CA 123; 128; CANR 61; DLB 194; INT 128

Banks, Lynne Reid .... CLC 23
See also Reid Banks, Lynne
See also AAYA 6

Banks, Russell 1940- .... CLC 37, 72
See also CA 65-68; CAAS 15; CANR 19, 52; DLB 130

Banville, John 1945- .... CLC 46
See also CA 117; 128; DLB 14; INT 128

Banville, Theodore (Faullain) de 1832-1891 NCLC 9

Baraka, Amiri 1934-CLC 1, 2, 3, 5, 10, 14, 33, 115; BLC 1; DA; DAC; DAM MST, MULT, POET, POP; DC 6; PC 4; WLCS
See also Jones, LeRoi
See also BW 2; CA 21-24R; CABS 3; CANR 27, 38, 61; CDALB 1941-1968; DLB 5, 7, 16, 38; DLBD 8; MTCW 1

Barbauld, Anna Laetitia 1743-1825NCLC 50
See also DLB 107, 109, 142, 158

Barbellion, W. N. P. .... TCLC 24
See also Cummings, Bruce F(rederick)

Barbera, Jack (Vincent) 1945- .... **CLC 44**
See also CA 110; CANR 45

Barbey d'Aurevilly, Jules Amedee 1808-1889
NCLC 1; SSC 17
See also DLB 119

Barbusse, Henri 1873-1935 .... **TCLC 5**
See also CA 105; 154; DLB 65

Barclay, Bill
See Moorcock, Michael (John)

Barclay, William Ewert
See Moorcock, Michael (John)

Barea, Arturo 1897-1957 .... **TCLC 14**
See also CA 111

Barfoot, Joan 1946- .... **CLC 18**
See also CA 105

Baring, Maurice 1874-1945 .... **TCLC 8**
See also CA 105; 168; DLB 34

Barker, Clive 1952- .... **CLC 52; DAM POP**
See also AAYA 10; BEST 90:3; CA 121; 129;
CANR 71; INT 129; MTCW 1

Barker, George Granville 1913-1991 **CLC 8,
48; DAM POET**
See also CA 9-12R; 135; CANR 7, 38; DLB
20; MTCW 1

Barker, Harley Granville
See Granville-Barker, Harley
See also DLB 10

Barker, Howard 1946- .... **CLC 37**
See also CA 102; DLB 13

Barker, Pat(ricia) 1943- .... **CLC 32, 94**
See also CA 117; 122; CANR 50; INT 122

Barlach, Ernst 1870-1938 .... **TCLC 84**
See also DLB 56, 118

Barlow, Joel 1754-1812 .... **NCLC 23**
See also DLB 37

Barnard, Mary (Ethel) 1909- .... **CLC 48**
See also CA 21-22; CAP 2

Barnes, Djuna 1892-1982 **CLC 3, 4, 8, 11, 29;
SSC 3**
See also CA 9-12R; 107; CANR 16, 55; DLB
4, 9, 45; MTCW 1

Barnes, Julian (Patrick) 1946- **CLC 42; DAB**
See also CA 102; CANR 19, 54; DLB 194;
DLBY 93

Barnes, Peter 1931- .... **CLC 5, 56**
See also CA 65-68; CAAS 12; CANR 33, 34,
64; DLB 13; MTCW 1

Baroja (y Nessi), Pio 1872-1956 **TCLC 8; HLC**
See also CA 104

Baron, David
See Pinter, Harold

Baron Corvo
See Rolfe, Frederick (William Serafino Austin
Lewis Mary)

Barondess, Sue K(aufman) 1926-1977 **CLC 8**
See also Kaufman, Sue
See also CA 1-4R; 69-72; CANR 1

Baron de Teive
See Pessoa, Fernando (Antonio Nogueira)

Baroness Von S.
See Zangwill, Israel

Barres, (Auguste-) Maurice 1862-1923 **T C L C
47**
See also CA 164; DLB 123

Barreto, Afonso Henrique de Lima
See Lima Barreto, Afonso Henrique de

Barrett, (Roger) Syd 1946- .... **CLC 35**

Barrett, William (Christopher) 1913-1992
CLC 27
See also CA 13-16R; 139; CANR 11, 67; INT
CANR-11

Barrie, J(ames) M(atthew) 1860-1937 **T C L C
2; DAB; DAM DRAM**

See also CA 104; 136; CDBLB 1890-1914;
CLR 16; DLB 10, 141, 156; MAICYA; SATA
100; YABC 1

Barrington, Michael
See Moorcock, Michael (John)

Barrol, Grady
See Bograd, Larry

Barry, Mike
See Malzberg, Barry N(athaniel)

Barry, Philip 1896-1949 .... **TCLC 11**
See also CA 109; DLB 7

Bart, Andre Schwarz
See Schwarz-Bart, Andre

Barth, John (Simmons) 1930- **CLC 1, 2, 3, 5, 7,
9, 10, 14, 27, 51, 89; DAM NOV; SSC 10**
See also AITN 1, 2; CA 1-4R; CABS 1; CANR
5, 23, 49, 64; DLB 2; MTCW 1

Barthelme, Donald 1931-1989 **CLC 1, 2, 3, 5, 6,
8, 13, 23, 46, 59, 115; DAM NOV; SSC 2**
See also CA 21-24R; 129; CANR 20, 58; DLB
2; DLBY 80, 89; MTCW 1; SATA 7; SATA-
Obit 62

Barthelme, Frederick 1943- .... **CLC 36**
See also CA 114; 122; DLBY 85; INT 122

Barthes, Roland (Gerard) 1915-1980 **CLC 24,
83**
See also CA 130; 97-100; CANR 66; MTCW 1

Barzun, Jacques (Martin) 1907- .... **CLC 51**
See also CA 61-64; CANR 22

Bashevis, Isaac
See Singer, Isaac Bashevis

Bashkirtseff, Marie 1859-1884 .... **NCLC 27**

Basho
See Matsuo Basho

Bass, Kingsley B., Jr.
See Bullins, Ed

Bass, Rick 1958- .... **CLC 79**
See also CA 126; CANR 53

Bassani, Giorgio 1916- .... **CLC 9**
See also CA 65-68; CANR 33; DLB 128, 177;
MTCW 1

Bastos, Augusto (Antonio) Roa
See Roa Bastos, Augusto (Antonio)

Bataille, Georges 1897-1962 .... **CLC 29**
See also CA 101; 89-92

Bates, H(erbert) E(rnest) 1905-1974 **CLC 46;
DAB; DAM POP; SSC 10**
See also CA 93-96; 45-48; CANR 34; DLB 162,
191; MTCW 1

Bauchart
See Camus, Albert

Baudelaire, Charles 1821-1867 **NCLC 6, 29,
55; DA; DAB; DAC; DAM MST, POET;
PC 1; SSC 18; WLC**

Baudrillard, Jean 1929- .... **CLC 60**

Baum, L(yman) Frank 1856-1919 ... **TCLC 7**
See also CA 108; 133; CLR 15; DLB 22; JRDA;
MAICYA; MTCW 1; SATA 18, 100

Baum, Louis F.
See Baum, L(yman) Frank

Baumbach, Jonathan 1933- .... **CLC 6, 23**
See also CA 13-16R; CAAS 5; CANR 12, 66;
DLBY 80; INT CANR-12; MTCW 1

Bausch, Richard (Carl) 1945- .... **CLC 51**
See also CA 101; CAAS 14; CANR 43, 61; DLB
130

Baxter, Charles (Morley) 1947- **CLC 45, 78;
DAM POP**
See also CA 57-60; CANR 40, 64; DLB 130

Baxter, George Owen
See Faust, Frederick (Schiller)

Baxter, James K(eir) 1926-1972 .... **CLC 14**
See also CA 77-80

Baxter, John
See Hunt, E(verette) Howard, (Jr.)

Bayer, Sylvia
See Glassco, John

Baynton, Barbara 1857-1929 .... **TCLC 57**

Beagle, Peter S(oyer) 1939- .... **CLC 7, 104**
See also CA 9-12R; CANR 4, 51; DLBY 80;
INT CANR-4; SATA 60

Bean, Normal
See Burroughs, Edgar Rice

Beard, Charles A(ustin) 1874-1948 **TCLC 15**
See also CA 115; DLB 17; SATA 18

Beardsley, Aubrey 1872-1898 .... **NCLC 6**

Beattie, Ann 1947- **CLC 8, 13, 18, 40, 63; DAM
NOV, POP; SSC 11**
See also BEST 90:2; CA 81-84; CANR 53;
DLBY 82; MTCW 1

Beattie, James 1735-1803 .... **NCLC 25**
See also DLB 109

Beauchamp, Kathleen Mansfield 1888-1923
See Mansfield, Katherine
See also CA 104; 134; DA; DAC; DAM MST

Beaumarchais, Pierre-Augustin Caron de 1732-
1799 .... **DC 4**
See also DAM DRAM

Beaumont, Francis 1584(?)-1616 **LC 33; DC 6**
See also CDBLB Before 1660; DLB 58, 121

Beauvoir, Simone (Lucie Ernestine Marie
Bertrand) de 1908-1986 **CLC 1, 2, 4, 8,
14, 31, 44, 50, 71; DA; DAB; DAC; DAM
MST, NOV; WLC**
See also CA 9-12R; 118; CANR 28, 61; DLB
72; DLBY 86; MTCW 1

Becker, Carl (Lotus) 1873-1945 ..... **TCLC 63**
See also CA 157; DLB 17

Becker, Jurek 1937-1997 .... **CLC 7, 19**
See also CA 85-88; 157; CANR 60; DLB 75

Becker, Walter 1950- .... **CLC 26**

Beckett, Samuel (Barclay) 1906-1989 **CLC 1,
2, 3, 4, 6, 9, 10, 11, 14, 18, 29, 57, 59, 83;
DA; DAB; DAC; DAM DRAM, MST,
NOV; SSC 16; WLC**
See also CA 5-8R; 130; CANR 33, 61; CDBLB
1945-1960; DLB 13, 15; DLBY 90; MTCW
1

Beckford, William 1760-1844 .... **NCLC 16**
See also DLB 39

Beckman, Gunnel 1910- .... **CLC 26**
See also CA 33-36R; CANR 15; CLR 25;
MAICYA; SAAS 9; SATA 6

Becque, Henri 1837-1899 .... **NCLC 3**
See also DLB 192

Beddoes, Thomas Lovell 1803-1849 **NCLC 3**
See also DLB 96

Bede c. 673-735 .... **CMLC 20**
See also DLB 146

Bedford, Donald F.
See Fearing, Kenneth (Flexner)

Beecher, Catharine Esther 1800-1878 **N C L C
30**
See also DLB 1

Beecher, John 1904-1980 .... **CLC 6**
See also AITN 1; CA 5-8R; 105; CANR 8

Beer, Johann 1655-1700 .... **LC 5**
See also DLB 168

Beer, Patricia 1924- .... **CLC 58**
See also CA 61-64; CANR 13, 46; DLB 40

Beerbohm, Max
See Beerbohm, (Henry) Max(imilian)

Beerbohm, (Henry) Max(imilian) 1872-1956
TCLC 1, 24
See also CA 104; 154; DLB 34, 100

Beer-Hofmann, Richard 1866-1945 **TCLC 60**

See also CA 160; DLB 81

Begiebing, Robert J(ohn) 1946- .... **CLC 70**
See also CA 122; CANR 40

Behan, Brendan 1923-1964 **CLC 1, 8, 11, 15, 79; DAM DRAM**
See also CA 73-76; CANR 33; CDBLB 1945-1960; DLB 13; MTCW 1

Behn, Aphra 1640(?)-1689 **LC 1, 30; DA; DAB; DAC; DAM DRAM, MST, NOV, POET; DC 4; PC 13; WLC**
See also DLB 39, 80, 131

Behrman, S(amuel) N(athaniel) 1893-1973 **CLC 40**
See also CA 13-16; 45-48; CAP 1; DLB 7, 44

Belasco, David 1853-1931 .... **TCLC 3**
See also CA 104; 168; DLB 7

Belcheva, Elisaveta 1893- .... **CLC 10**
See also Bagryana, Elisaveta

Beldone, Phil "Cheech"
See Ellison, Harlan (Jay)

Beleno
See Azuela, Mariano

Belinski, Vissarion Grigoryevich 1811-1848 **NCLC 5**
See also DLB 198

Belitt, Ben 1911- .... **CLC 22**
See also CA 13-16R; CAAS 4; CANR 7; DLB 5

Bell, Gertrude (Margaret Lowthian) 1868-1926 **TCLC 67**
See also CA 167; DLB 174

Bell, J. Freeman
See Zangwill, Israel

Bell, James Madison 1826-1902 ... **TCLC 43; BLC 1; DAM MULT**
See also BW 1; CA 122; 124; DLB 50

Bell, Madison Smartt 1957- ..... **CLC 41, 102**
See also CA 111; CANR 28, 54

Bell, Marvin (Hartley) 1937- **CLC 8, 31; DAM POET**
See also CA 21-24R; CAAS 14; CANR 59; DLB 5; MTCW 1

Bell, W. L. D.
See Mencken, H(enry) L(ouis)

Bellamy, Atwood C.
See Mencken, H(enry) L(ouis)

Bellamy, Edward 1850-1898 .... **NCLC 4**
See also DLB 12

Bellin, Edward J.
See Kuttner, Henry

Belloc, (Joseph) Hilaire (Pierre Sebastien Rene Swanton) 1870-1953 **TCLC 7, 18; DAM POET; PC 24**
See also CA 106; 152; DLB 19, 100, 141, 174; YABC 1

Belloc, Joseph Peter Rene Hilaire
See Belloc, (Joseph) Hilaire (Pierre Sebastien Rene Swanton)

Belloc, Joseph Pierre Hilaire
See Belloc, (Joseph) Hilaire (Pierre Sebastien Rene Swanton)

Belloc, M. A.
See Lowndes, Marie Adelaide (Belloc)

Bellow, Saul 1915- **CLC 1, 2, 3, 6, 8, 10, 13, 15, 25, 33, 34, 63, 79; DA; DAB; DAC; DAM MST, NOV, POP; SSC 14; WLC**
See also AITN 2; BEST 89:3; CA 5-8R; CABS 1; CANR 29, 53; CDALB 1941-1968; DLB 2, 28; DLBD 3; DLBY 82; MTCW 1

Belser, Reimond Karel Maria de 1929-
See Ruyslinck, Ward
See also CA 152

Bely, Andrey .... **TCLC 7; PC 11**

See also Bugayev, Boris Nikolayevich

Belyi, Andrei
See Bugayev, Boris Nikolayevich

Benary, Margot
See Benary-Isbert, Margot

Benary-Isbert, Margot 1889-1979 .... **CLC 12**
See also CA 5-8R; 89-92; CANR 4, 72; CLR 12; MAICYA; SATA 2; SATA-Obit 21

Benavente (y Martinez), Jacinto 1866-1954 **TCLC 3; DAM DRAM, MULT**
See also CA 106; 131; HW; MTCW 1

Benchley, Peter (Bradford) 1940- . **CLC 4, 8; DAM NOV, POP**
See also AAYA 14; AITN 2; CA 17-20R; CANR 12, 35, 66; MTCW 1; SATA 3, 89

Benchley, Robert (Charles) 1889-1945 **TCLC 1, 55**
See also CA 105; 153; DLB 11

Benda, Julien 1867-1956 .... **TCLC 60**
See also CA 120; 154

Benedict, Ruth (Fulton) 1887-1948 **TCLC 60**
See also CA 158

Benedict, Saint c. 480-c. 547 .... **CMLC 29**

Benedikt, Michael 1935- .... **CLC 4, 14**
See also CA 13-16R; CANR 7; DLB 5

Benet, Juan 1927- .... **CLC 28**
See also CA 143

Benet, Stephen Vincent 1898-1943 . **TCLC 7; DAM POET; SSC 10**
See also CA 104; 152; DLB 4, 48, 102; DLBY 97; YABC 1

Benet, William Rose 1886-1950 ... **TCLC 28; DAM POET**
See also CA 118; 152; DLB 45

Benford, Gregory (Albert) 1941- ...... **CLC 52**
See also CA 69-72; CAAS 27; CANR 12, 24, 49; DLBY 82

Bengtsson, Frans (Gunnar) 1894-1954 **TCLC 48**

Benjamin, David
See Slavitt, David R(ytman)

Benjamin, Lois
See Gould, Lois

Benjamin, Walter 1892-1940 .... **TCLC 39**
See also CA 164

Benn, Gottfried 1886-1956 .... **TCLC 3**
See also CA 106; 153; DLB 56

Bennett, Alan 1934- **CLC 45, 77; DAB; DAM MST**
See also CA 103; CANR 35, 55; MTCW 1

Bennett, (Enoch) Arnold 1867-1931 **TCLC 5, 20**
See also CA 106; 155; CDBLB 1890-1914; DLB 10, 34, 98, 135

Bennett, Elizabeth
See Mitchell, Margaret (Munnerlyn)

Bennett, George Harold 1930-
See Bennett, Hal
See also BW 1; CA 97-100

Bennett, Hal .... **CLC 5**
See also Bennett, George Harold
See also DLB 33

Bennett, Jay 1912- .... **CLC 35**
See also AAYA 10; CA 69-72; CANR 11, 42; JRDA; SAAS 4; SATA 41, 87; SATA-Brief 27

Bennett, Louise (Simone) 1919- **CLC 28; BLC 1; DAM MULT**
See also BW 2; CA 151; DLB 117

Benson, E(dward) F(rederic) 1867-1940 **TCLC 27**
See also CA 114; 157; DLB 135, 153

Benson, Jackson J. 1930- .... **CLC 34**

See also CA 25-28R; DLB 111

Benson, Sally 1900-1972 .... **CLC 17**
See also CA 19-20; 37-40R; CAP 1; SATA 1, 35; SATA-Obit 27

Benson, Stella 1892-1933 .... **TCLC 17**
See also CA 117; 155; DLB 36, 162

Bentham, Jeremy 1748-1832 .... **NCLC 38**
See also DLB 107, 158

Bentley, E(dmund) C(lerihew) 1875-1956 **TCLC 12**
See also CA 108; DLB 70

Bentley, Eric (Russell) 1916- .... **CLC 24**
See also CA 5-8R; CANR 6, 67; INT CANR-6

Beranger, Pierre Jean de 1780-1857 **NCLC 34**

Berdyaev, Nicolas
See Berdyaev, Nikolai (Aleksandrovich)

Berdyaev, Nikolai (Aleksandrovich) 1874-1948 **TCLC 67**
See also CA 120; 157

Berdyayev, Nikolai (Aleksandrovich)
See Berdyaev, Nikolai (Aleksandrovich)

Berendt, John (Lawrence) 1939- ..... **CLC 86**
See also CA 146

Beresford, J(ohn) D(avys) 1873-1947 . **TCLC 81**
See also CA 112; 155; DLB 162, 178, 197

Bergelson, David 1884-1952 .... **TCLC 81**

Berger, Colonel
See Malraux, (Georges-)Andre

Berger, John (Peter) 1926- .... **CLC 2, 19**
See also CA 81-84; CANR 51; DLB 14

Berger, Melvin H. 1927- .... **CLC 12**
See also CA 5-8R; CANR 4; CLR 32; SAAS 2; SATA 5, 88

Berger, Thomas (Louis) 1924- **CLC 3, 5, 8, 11, 18, 38; DAM NOV**
See also CA 1-4R; CANR 5, 28, 51; DLB 2; DLBY 80; INT CANR-28; MTCW 1

Bergman, (Ernst) Ingmar 1918- **CLC 16, 72**
See also CA 81-84; CANR 33, 70

Bergson, Henri(-Louis) 1859-1941 **TCLC 32**
See also CA 164

Bergstein, Eleanor 1938- .... **CLC 4**
See also CA 53-56; CANR 5

Berkoff, Steven 1937- .... **CLC 56**
See also CA 104; CANR 72

Bermant, Chaim (Icyk) 1929- .... **CLC 40**
See also CA 57-60; CANR 6, 31, 57

Bern, Victoria
See Fisher, M(ary) F(rances) K(ennedy)

Bernanos, (Paul Louis) Georges 1888-1948 **TCLC 3**
See also CA 104; 130; DLB 72

Bernard, April 1956- .... **CLC 59**
See also CA 131

Berne, Victoria
See Fisher, M(ary) F(rances) K(ennedy)

Bernhard, Thomas 1931-1989 **CLC 3, 32, 61**
See also CA 85-88; 127; CANR 32, 57; DLB 85, 124; MTCW 1

Bernhardt, Sarah (Henriette Rosine) 1844-1923 **TCLC 75**
See also CA 157

Berriault, Gina 1926- . **CLC 54, 109; SSC 30**
See also CA 116; 129; CANR 66; DLB 130

Berrigan, Daniel 1921- .... **CLC 4**
See also CA 33-36R; CAAS 1; CANR 11, 43; DLB 5

Berrigan, Edmund Joseph Michael, Jr. 1934-1983
See Berrigan, Ted
See also CA 61-64; 110; CANR 14

Berrigan, Ted .... **CLC 37**

See also Berrigan. Edmund Joseph Michael, Jr.
See also DLB 5. 169
Berry, Charles Edward Anderson 1931-
See Berry, Chuck
See also CA 115
Berry, Chuck .... **CLC 17**
See also Berry. Charles Edward Anderson
Berry, Jonas
See Ashbery. John (Lawrence)
Berry, Wendell (Erdman) 1934- **CLC 4, 6, 8,**
27, 46; DAM POET
See also AITN 1; CA 73-76; CANR 50; DLB 5,
6
Berryman, John 1914-1972 **CLC 1, 2, 3, 4, 6, 8,**
10, 13, 25, 62; DAM POET
See also CA 13-16; 33-36R; CABS 2; CANR
35; CAP 1; CDALB 1941-1968; DLB 48;
MTCW 1
Bertolucci, Bernardo 1940- .... **CLC 16**
See also CA 106
Berton, Pierre (Francis Demarigny) 1920-
CLC 104
See also CA 1-4R; CANR 2, 56; DLB 68; SATA
99
Bertrand, Aloysius 1807-1841 .... **NCLC 31**
Bertran de Born c. 1140-1215 .... **CMLC 5**
Beruni, al 973-1048(?) .... **CMLC 28**
Besant, Annie (Wood) 1847-1933 ..... **TCLC 9**
See also CA 105
Bessie, Alvah 1904-1985 .... **CLC 23**
See also CA 5-8R; 116; CANR 2; DLB 26
Bethlen, T. D.
See Silverberg, Robert
Beti, Mongo ... **CLC 27; BLC 1; DAM MULT**
See also Biyidi, Alexandre
Betjeman, John 1906-1984 **CLC 2, 6, 10, 34,**
43; DAB; DAM MST, POET
See also CA 9-12R; 112; CANR 33, 56; CDBLB
1945-1960; DLB 20; DLBY 84; MTCW 1
Bettelheim, Bruno 1903-1990 .... **CLC 79**
See also CA 81-84; 131; CANR 23, 61; MTCW
1
Betti, Ugo 1892-1953 .... **TCLC 5**
See also CA 104; 155
Betts, Doris (Waugh) 1932- ...... **CLC 3, 6, 28**
See also CA 13-16R; CANR 9, 66; DLBY 82;
INT CANR-9
Bevan, Alistair
See Roberts. Keith (John Kingston)
Bey, Pilaff
See Douglas. (George) Norman
Bialik, Chaim Nachman 1873-1934 **TCLC 25**
Bickerstaff, Isaac
See Swift, Jonathan
Bidart, Frank 1939- .... **CLC 33**
See also CA 140
Bienek, Horst 1930- .... **CLC 7, 11**
See also CA 73-76; DLB 75
Bierce, Ambrose (Gwinett) 1842-1914(?)
TCLC 1, 7, 44; DA; DAC; DAM MST; SSC
9; WLC
See also CA 104; 139; CDALB 1865-1917;
DLB 11, 12, 23, 71, 74. 186
Biggers, Earl Derr 1884-1933 .... **TCLC 65**
See also CA 108; 153
Billings, Josh
See Shaw, Henry Wheeler
Billington, (Lady) Rachel (Mary) 1942- **C L C**
43
See also AITN 2; CA 33-36R; CANR 44
Binyon, T(imothy) J(ohn) 1936- ...... **CLC 34**
See also CA 111; CANR 28
Bioy Casares, Adolfo 1914-1984 **CLC 4, 8, 13,**
88; DAM MULT; HLC; SSC 17
See also CA 29-32R; CANR 19, 43. 66; DLB
113; HW; MTCW 1
Bird, Cordwainer
See Ellison, Harlan (Jay)
Bird, Robert Montgomery 1806-1854 **NCLC 1**
See also DLB 202
Birney, (Alfred) Earle 1904-1995 **CLC 1, 4, 6,**
11; DAC; DAM MST, POET
See also CA 1-4R; CANR 5. 20; DLB 88;
MTCW 1
Bishop, Elizabeth 1911-1979 **CLC 1, 4, 9, 13,**
15, 32; DA; DAC; DAM MST, POET; PC
3
See also CA 5-8R; 89-92; CABS 2; CANR 26,
61; CDALB 1968-1988; DLB 5. 169;
MTCW 1; SATA-Obit 24
Bishop, John 1935- .... **CLC 10**
See also CA 105
Bissett, Bill 1939- .... **CLC 18; PC 14**
See also CA 69-72; CAAS 19; CANR 15; DLB
53; MTCW 1
Bitov, Andrei (Georgievich) 1937- .... **CLC 57**
See also CA 142
Biyidi, Alexandre 1932-
See Beti, Mongo
See also BW 1; CA 114; 124; MTCW 1
Bjarme, Brynjolf
See Ibsen. Henrik (Johan)
Bjoernson, Bjoernstjerne (Martinius) 1832-
1910 .... **TCLC 7, 37**
See also CA 104
Black, Robert
See Holdstock, Robert P.
Blackburn, Paul 1926-1971 .... **CLC 9, 43**
See also CA 81-84; 33-36R; CANR 34; DLB
16; DLBY 81
Black Elk 1863-1950 **TCLC 33; DAM MULT**
See also CA 144; NNAL
Black Hobart
See Sanders. (James) Ed(ward)
Blacklin, Malcolm
See Chambers, Aidan
Blackmore, R(ichard) D(oddridge) 1825-1900
TCLC 27
See also CA 120; DLB 18
Blackmur, R(ichard) P(almer) 1904-1965
CLC 2, 24
See also CA 11-12; 25-28R; CANR 71; CAP 1;
DLB 63
Black Tarantula
See Acker, Kathy
Blackwood, Algernon (Henry) 1869-1951
TCLC 5
See also CA 105; 150; DLB 153, 156, 178
Blackwood, Caroline 1931-1996 **CLC 6, 9, 100**
See also CA 85-88; 151; CANR 32, 61, 65; DLB
14; MTCW 1
Blade, Alexander
See Hamilton, Edmond; Silverberg, Robert
Blaga, Lucian 1895-1961 .... **CLC 75**
See also CA 157
Blair, Eric (Arthur) 1903-1950
See Orwell, George
See also CA 104; 132; DA; DAB; DAC; DAM
MST, NOV; MTCW 1; SATA 29
Blais, Marie-Claire 1939- **CLC 2, 4, 6, 13, 22;**
DAC; DAM MST
See also CA 21-24R; CAAS 4; CANR 38; DLB
53; MTCW 1
Blaise, Clark 1940- .... **CLC 29**
See also AITN 2; CA 53-56; CAAS 3; CANR
5, 66; DLB 53

Blake, Fairley
See De Voto, Bernard (Augustine)
Blake, Nicholas
See Day Lewis, C(ecil)
See also DLB 77
Blake, William 1757-1827 . **NCLC 13, 37, 57;**
DA; DAB; DAC; DAM MST, POET; PC
12; WLC
See also CDBLB 1789-1832; CLR 52; DLB 93,
163; MAICYA; SATA 30
Blasco Ibanez, Vicente 1867-1928 **TCLC 12;**
DAM NOV
See also CA 110; 131; HW; MTCW 1
Blatty, William Peter 1928- **CLC 2; DAM POP**
See also CA 5-8R; CANR 9
Bleeck, Oliver
See Thomas, Ross (Elmore)
Blessing, Lee 1949- .... **CLC 54**
Blish, James (Benjamin) 1921-1975 . **CLC 14**
See also CA 1-4R; 57-60; CANR 3; DLB 8;
MTCW 1; SATA 66
Bliss, Reginald
See Wells, H(erbert) G(eorge)
Blixen, Karen (Christentze Dinesen) 1885-1962
See Dinesen, Isak
See also CA 25-28; CANR 22, 50; CAP 2;
MTCW 1; SATA 44
Bloch, Robert (Albert) 1917-1994 .... **CLC 33**
See also CA 5-8R; 146; CAAS 20; CANR 5;
DLB 44; INT CANR-5; SATA 12; SATA-Obit
82
Blok, Alexander (Alexandrovich) 1880-1921
TCLC 5; PC 21
See also CA 104
Blom, Jan
See Breytenbach, Breyten
Bloom, Harold 1930- .... **CLC 24, 103**
See also CA 13-16R; CANR 39; DLB 67
Bloomfield, Aurelius
See Bourne, Randolph S(illiman)
Blount, Roy (Alton), Jr. 1941- .... **CLC 38**
See also CA 53-56; CANR 10, 28, 61; INT
CANR-28; MTCW 1
Bloy, Leon 1846-1917 .... **TCLC 22**
See also CA 121; DLB 123
Blume, Judy (Sussman) 1938- ... **CLC 12, 30;**
DAM NOV, POP
See also AAYA 3, 26; CA 29-32R; CANR 13,
37, 66; CLR 2, 15; DLB 52; JRDA;
MAICYA; MTCW 1; SATA 2, 31, 79
Blunden, Edmund (Charles) 1896-1974 **C L C**
2, 56
See also CA 17-18; 45-48; CANR 54; CAP 2;
DLB 20, 100, 155; MTCW 1
Bly, Robert (Elwood) 1926- **CLC 1, 2, 5, 10, 15,**
38; DAM POET
See also CA 5-8R; CANR 41; DLB 5; MTCW
1
Boas, Franz 1858-1942 .... **TCLC 56**
See also CA 115
Bobette
See Simenon, Georges (Jacques Christian)
Boccaccio, Giovanni 1313-1375 .. **CMLC 13;**
SSC 10
Bochco, Steven 1943- .... **CLC 35**
See also AAYA 11; CA 124; 138
Bodel, Jean 1167(?)-1210 .... **CMLC 28**
Bodenheim, Maxwell 1892-1954 .... **TCLC 44**
See also CA 110; DLB 9, 45
Bodker, Cecil 1927- .... **CLC 21**
See also CA 73-76; CANR 13, 44; CLR 23;
MAICYA; SATA 14
Boell, Heinrich (Theodor) 1917-1985 **CLC 2,**

3, 6, 9, 11, 15, 27, 32, 72; DA; DAB; DAC; DAM MST, NOV; SSC 23; WLC
See also CA 21-24R; 116; CANR 24; DLB 69; DLBY 85; MTCW 1
Boerne, Alfred
See Doeblin, Alfred
Boethius 480(?)-524(?) .... **CMLC 15**
See also DLB 115
Bogan, Louise 1897-1970 . **CLC 4, 39, 46, 93; DAM POET; PC 12**
See also CA 73-76; 25-28R; CANR 33; DLB 45, 169; MTCW 1
Bogarde, Dirk .... **CLC 19**
See also Van Den Bogarde, Derek Jules Gaspard Ulric Niven
See also DLB 14
Bogosian, Eric 1953- .... **CLC 45**
See also CA 138
Bograd, Larry 1953- .... **CLC 35**
See also CA 93-96; CANR 57; SAAS 21; SATA 33, 89
Boiardo, Matteo Maria 1441-1494 ...... **LC 6**
Boileau-Despreaux, Nicolas 1636-1711 **LC 3**
Bojer, Johan 1872-1959 .... **TCLC 64**
Boland, Eavan (Aisling) 1944- .. **CLC 40, 67, 113; DAM POET**
See also CA 143; CANR 61; DLB 40
Boll, Heinrich
See Boell, Heinrich (Theodor)
Bolt, Lee
See Faust, Frederick (Schiller)
Bolt, Robert (Oxton) 1924-1995 ..... **CLC 14; DAM DRAM**
See also CA 17-20R; 147; CANR 35, 67; DLB 13; MTCW 1
Bombet, Louis-Alexandre-Cesar
See Stendhal
Bomkauf
See Kaufman, Bob (Garnell)
Bonaventura .... **NCLC 35**
See also DLB 90
Bond, Edward 1934- **CLC 4, 6, 13, 23; DAM DRAM**
See also CA 25-28R; CANR 38, 67; DLB 13; MTCW 1
Bonham, Frank 1914-1989 .... **CLC 12**
See also AAYA 1; CA 9-12R; CANR 4, 36; JRDA; MAICYA; SAAS 3; SATA 1, 49; SATA-Obit 62
Bonnefoy, Yves 1923- .. **CLC 9, 15, 58; DAM MST, POET**
See also CA 85-88; CANR 33; MTCW 1
Bontemps, Arna(ud Wendell) 1902-1973 **C L C 1, 18; BLC 1; DAM MULT, NOV, POET**
See also BW 1; CA 1-4R; 41-44R; CANR 4, 35; CLR 6; DLB 48, 51; JRDA; MAICYA; MTCW 1; SATA 2, 44; SATA-Obit 24
Booth, Martin 1944- .... **CLC 13**
See also CA 93-96; CAAS 2
Booth, Philip 1925- .... **CLC 23**
See also CA 5-8R; CANR 5; DLBY 82
Booth, Wayne C(layson) 1921- .... **CLC 24**
See also CA 1-4R; CAAS 5; CANR 3, 43; DLB 67
Borchert, Wolfgang 1921-1947 .... **TCLC 5**
See also CA 104; DLB 69, 124
Borel, Petrus 1809-1859 .... **NCLC 41**
Borges, Jorge Luis 1899-1986 **CLC 1, 2, 3, 4, 6, 8, 9, 10, 13, 19, 44, 48, 83; DA; DAB; DAC; DAM MST, MULT; HLC; PC 22; SSC 4; WLC**
See also AAYA 26; CA 21-24R; CANR 19, 33; DLB 113; DLBY 86; HW; MTCW 1

Borowski, Tadeusz 1922-1951 .... **TCLC 9**
See also CA 106; 154
Borrow, George (Henry) 1803-1881 **NCLC 9**
See also DLB 21, 55, 166
Bosman, Herman Charles 1905-1951 . **T C L C 49**
See also Malan, Herman
See also CA 160
Bosschere, Jean de 1878(?)-1953 ... **TCLC 19**
See also CA 115
Boswell, James 1740-1795 . **LC 4; DA; DAB; DAC; DAM MST; WLC**
See also CDBLB 1660-1789; DLB 104, 142
Bottoms, David 1949- .... **CLC 53**
See also CA 105; CANR 22; DLB 120; DLBY 83
Boucicault, Dion 1820-1890 .... **NCLC 41**
Boucolon, Maryse 1937(?)-
See Conde, Maryse
See also CA 110; CANR 30, 53
Bourget, Paul (Charles Joseph) 1852-1935 **TCLC 12**
See also CA 107; DLB 123
Bourjaily, Vance (Nye) 1922- .... **CLC 8, 62**
See also CA 1-4R; CAAS 1; CANR 2, 72; DLB 2, 143
Bourne, Randolph S(illiman) 1886-1918 **TCLC 16**
See also CA 117; 155; DLB 63
Bova, Ben(jamin William) 1932- ...... **CLC 45**
See also AAYA 16; CA 5-8R; CAAS 18; CANR 11, 56; CLR 3; DLBY 81; INT CANR-11; MAICYA; MTCW 1; SATA 6, 68
Bowen, Elizabeth (Dorothea Cole) 1899-1973 **CLC 1, 3, 6, 11, 15, 22; DAM NOV; SSC 3, 28**
See also CA 17-18; 41-44R; CANR 35; CAP 2; CDBLB 1945-1960; DLB 15, 162; MTCW 1
Bowering, George 1935- .... **CLC 15, 47**
See also CA 21-24R; CAAS 16; CANR 10; DLB 53
Bowering, Marilyn R(uthe) 1949- .... **CLC 32**
See also CA 101; CANR 49
Bowers, Edgar 1924- .... **CLC 9**
See also CA 5-8R; CANR 24; DLB 5
Bowie, David .... **CLC 17**
See also Jones, David Robert
Bowles, Jane (Sydney) 1917-1973 **CLC 3, 68**
See also CA 19-20; 41-44R; CAP 2
Bowles, Paul (Frederick) 1910-1986 **CLC 1, 2, 19, 53; SSC 3**
See also CA 1-4R; CAAS 1; CANR 1, 19, 50; DLB 5, 6; MTCW 1
Box, Edgar
See Vidal, Gore
Boyd, Nancy
See Millay, Edna St. Vincent
Boyd, William 1952- .... **CLC 28, 53, 70**
See also CA 114; 120; CANR 51, 71
Boyle, Kay 1902-1992 **CLC 1, 5, 19, 58; SSC 5**
See also CA 13-16R; 140; CAAS 1; CANR 29, 61; DLB 4, 9, 48, 86; DLBY 93; MTCW 1
Boyle, Mark
See Kienzle, William X(avier)
Boyle, Patrick 1905-1982 .... **CLC 19**
See also CA 127
Boyle, T. C. 1948-
See Boyle, T(homas) Coraghessan
Boyle, T(homas) Coraghessan 1948- **CLC 36, 55, 90; DAM POP; SSC 16**
See also BEST 90:4; CA 120; CANR 44; DLBY 86

Boz
See Dickens, Charles (John Huffam)
Brackenridge, Hugh Henry 1748-1816 **N C L C 7**
See also DLB 11, 37
Bradbury, Edward P.
See Moorcock, Michael (John)
Bradbury, Malcolm (Stanley) 1932- **CLC 32, 61; DAM NOV**
See also CA 1-4R; CANR 1, 33; DLB 14; MTCW 1
Bradbury, Ray (Douglas) 1920- **CLC 1, 3, 10, 15, 42, 98; DA; DAB; DAC; DAM MST, NOV, POP; SSC 29; WLC**
See also AAYA 15; AITN 1, 2; CA 1-4R; CANR 2, 30; CDALB 1968-1988; DLB 2, 8; MTCW 1; SATA 11, 64
Bradford, Gamaliel 1863-1932 ...... **TCLC 36**
See also CA 160; DLB 17
Bradley, David (Henry, Jr.) 1950- .. **CLC 23; BLC 1; DAM MULT**
See also BW 1; CA 104; CANR 26; DLB 33
Bradley, John Ed(mund, Jr.) 1958- . **CLC 55**
See also CA 139
Bradley, Marion Zimmer 1930- **CLC 30; DAM POP**
See also AAYA 9; CA 57-60; CAAS 10; CANR 7, 31, 51; DLB 8; MTCW 1; SATA 90
Bradstreet, Anne 1612(?)-1672 **LC 4, 30; DA; DAC; DAM MST, POET; PC 10**
See also CDALB 1640-1865; DLB 24
Brady, Joan 1939- .... **CLC 86**
See also CA 141
Bragg, Melvyn 1939- .... **CLC 10**
See also BEST 89:3; CA 57-60; CANR 10, 48; DLB 14
Brahe, Tycho 1546-1601 .... **LC 45**
Braine, John (Gerard) 1922-1986 **CLC 1, 3, 41**
See also CA 1-4R; 120; CANR 1, 33; CDBLB 1945-1960; DLB 15; DLBY 86; MTCW 1
Bramah, Ernest 1868-1942 .... **TCLC 72**
See also CA 156; DLB 70
Brammer, William 1930(?)-1978 ...... **CLC 31**
See also CA 77-80
Brancati, Vitaliano 1907-1954 .... **TCLC 12**
See also CA 109
Brancato, Robin F(idler) 1936- .... **CLC 35**
See also AAYA 9; CA 69-72; CANR 11, 45; CLR 32; JRDA; SAAS 9; SATA 97
Brand, Max
See Faust, Frederick (Schiller)
Brand, Millen 1906-1980 .... **CLC 7**
See also CA 21-24R; 97-100; CANR 72
Branden, Barbara .... **CLC 44**
See also CA 148
Brandes, Georg (Morris Cohen) 1842-1927 **TCLC 10**
See also CA 105
Brandys, Kazimierz 1916- .... **CLC 62**
Branley, Franklyn M(ansfield) 1915- **CLC 21**
See also CA 33-36R; CANR 14, 39; CLR 13; MAICYA; SAAS 16; SATA 4, 68
Brathwaite, Edward Kamau 1930- **CLC 11; BLCS; DAM POET**
See also BW 2; CA 25-28R; CANR 11, 26, 47; DLB 125
Brautigan, Richard (Gary) 1935-1984 **CLC 1, 3, 5, 9, 12, 34, 42; DAM NOV**
See also CA 53-56; 113; CANR 34; DLB 2, 5; DLBY 80, 84; MTCW 1; SATA 56
Brave Bird, Mary 1953-
See Crow Dog, Mary (Ellen)
See also NNAL

Bruccoli, Matthew J(oseph) 1931-... **CLC 34**
See also CA 9-12R; CANR 7; DLB 103
Bruce, Lenny .... **CLC 21**
See also Schneider, Leonard Alfred
Bruin, John
See Brutus, Dennis
Brulard, Henri
See Stendhal
Brulls, Christian
See Simenon, Georges (Jacques Christian)
Brunner, John (Kilian Houston) 1934-1995
CLC 8, 10; DAM POP
See also CA 1-4R; 149; CAAS 8; CANR 2, 37;
MTCW 1
Bruno, Giordano 1548-1600 .... **LC 27**
Brutus, Dennis 1924- **CLC 43; BLC 1; DAM
MULT, POET; PC 24**
See also BW 2; CA 49-52; CAAS 14; CANR 2,
27, 42; DLB 117
Bryan, C(ourtlandt) D(ixon) B(arnes) 1936-
CLC 29
See also CA 73-76; CANR 13, 68; DLB 185;
INT CANR-13
Bryan, Michael
See Moore, Brian
Bryant, William Cullen 1794-1878 . **NCLC 6,
46; DA; DAB; DAC; DAM MST, POET;
PC 20**
See also CDALB 1640-1865; DLB 3, 43, 59,
189
Bryusov, Valery Yakovlevich 1873-1924
TCLC 10
See also CA 107; 155
Buchan, John 1875-1940 .... **TCLC 41; DAB;
DAM POP**
See also CA 108; 145; DLB 34, 70, 156; YABC
2
Buchanan, George 1506-1582 .... **LC 4**
See also DLB 152
Buchheim, Lothar-Guenther 1918-....**CLC 6**
See also CA 85-88
Buchner, (Karl) Georg 1813-1837 . **NCLC 26**
Buchwald, Art(hur) 1925- .... **CLC 33**
See also AITN 1; CA 5-8R; CANR 21, 67;
MTCW 1; SATA 10
Buck, Pearl S(ydenstricker) 1892-1973**CLC 7,
11, 18; DA; DAB; DAC; DAM MST, NOV**
See also AITN 1; CA 1-4R; 41-44R; CANR 1,
34; DLB 9, 102; MTCW 1; SATA 1, 25
Buckler, Ernest 1908-1984.... **CLC 13; DAC;
DAM MST**
See also CA 11-12; 114; CAP 1; DLB 68; SATA
47
Buckley, Vincent (Thomas) 1925-1988**CLC 57**
See also CA 101
Buckley, William F(rank), Jr. 1925-**CLC 7, 18,
37; DAM POP**
See also AITN 1; CA 1-4R; CANR 1, 24, 53;
DLB 137; DLBY 80; INT CANR-24; MTCW
1
Buechner, (Carl) Frederick 1926-**CLC 2, 4, 6,
9; DAM NOV**
See also CA 13-16R; CANR 11, 39, 64; DLBY
80; INT CANR-11; MTCW 1
Buell, John (Edward) 1927- .... **CLC 10**
See also CA 1-4R; CANR 71; DLB 53
Buero Vallejo, Antonio 1916- ..... **CLC 15, 46**
See also CA 106; CANR 24, 49; HW; MTCW
1
Bufalino, Gesualdo 1920(?)- .... **CLC 74**
See also DLB 196
Bugayev, Boris Nikolayevich 1880-1934
TCLC 7; PC 11

See also Bely, Andrey
See also CA 104; 165
Bukowski, Charles 1920-1994**CLC 2, 5, 9, 41,
82, 108; DAM NOV, POET; PC 18**
See also CA 17-20R; 144; CANR 40, 62; DLB
5, 130, 169; MTCW 1
Bulgakov, Mikhail (Afanas'evich) 1891-1940
TCLC 2, 16; DAM DRAM, NOV; SSC 18
See also CA 105; 152
Bulgya, Alexander Alexandrovich 1901-1956
TCLC 53
See also Fadeyev, Alexander
See also CA 117
Bullins, Ed 1935- **CLC 1, 5, 7; BLC 1; DAM
DRAM, MULT; DC 6**
See also BW 2; CA 49-52; CAAS 16; CANR
24, 46; DLB 7, 38; MTCW 1
Bulwer-Lytton, Edward (George Earle Lytton)
1803-1873 ....**NCLC 1, 45**
See also DLB 21
Bunin, Ivan Alexeyevich 1870-1953 **TCLC 6;
SSC 5**
See also CA 104
Bunting, Basil 1900-1985 ..... **CLC 10, 39, 47;
DAM POET**
See also CA 53-56; 115; CANR 7; DLB 20
Bunuel, Luis 1900-1983 .. **CLC 16, 80; DAM
MULT; HLC**
See also CA 101; 110; CANR 32; HW
Bunyan, John 1628-1688 ... **LC 4; DA; DAB;
DAC; DAM MST; WLC**
See also CDBLB 1660-1789; DLB 39
Burckhardt, Jacob (Christoph) 1818-1897
NCLC 49
Burford, Eleanor
See Hibbert, Eleanor Alice Burford
Burgess, AnthonyCLC 1, 2, 4, 5, 8, 10, 13, 15,
22, 40, 62, 81, 94; DAB**
See also Wilson, John (Anthony) Burgess
See also AAYA 25; AITN 1; CDBLB 1960 to
Present; DLB 14, 194
Burke, Edmund 1729(?)-1797 **LC 7, 36; DA;
DAB; DAC; DAM MST; WLC**
See also DLB 104
Burke, Kenneth (Duva) 1897-1993**CLC 2, 24**
See also CA 5-8R; 143; CANR 39; DLB 45,
63; MTCW 1
Burke, Leda
See Garnett, David
Burke, Ralph
See Silverberg, Robert
Burke, Thomas 1886-1945 .... **TCLC 63**
See also CA 113; 155; DLB 197
Burney, Fanny 1752-1840 .... **NCLC 12, 54**
See also DLB 39
Burns, Robert 1759-1796 .... **PC 6**
See also CDBLB 1789-1832; DA; DAB; DAC;
DAM MST, POET; DLB 109; WLC
Burns, Tex
See L'Amour, Louis (Dearborn)
Burnshaw, Stanley 1906- .... **CLC 3, 13, 44**
See also CA 9-12R; DLB 48; DLBY 97
Burr, Anne 1937- .... **CLC 6**
See also CA 25-28R
Burroughs, Edgar Rice 1875-1950 . **TCLC 2,
32; DAM NOV**
See also AAYA 11; CA 104; 132; DLB 8;
MTCW 1; SATA 41
Burroughs, William S(eward) 1914-1997**CLC
1, 2, 5, 15, 22, 42, 75, 109; DA; DAB; DAC;
DAM MST, NOV, POP; WLC**
See also AITN 2; CA 9-12R; 160; CANR 20,
52; DLB 2, 8, 16, 152; DLBY 81, 97; MTCW

1
Burton, Richard F. 1821-1890 ....**NCLC 42**
See also DLB 55, 184
Busch, Frederick 1941- ..... **CLC 7, 10, 18, 47**
See also CA 33-36R; CAAS 1; CANR 45; DLB
6
Bush, Ronald 1946- .... **CLC 34**
See also CA 136
Bustos, F(rancisco)
See Borges, Jorge Luis
Bustos Domecq, H(onorio)
See Bioy Casares, Adolfo; Borges, Jorge Luis
Butler, Octavia E(stelle) 1947-**CLC 38; BLCS;
DAM MULT, POP**
See also AAYA 18; BW 2; CA 73-76; CANR
12, 24, 38; DLB 33; MTCW 1; SATA 84
Butler, Robert Olen (Jr.) 1945-**CLC 81; DAM
POP**
See also CA 112; CANR 66; DLB 173; INT 112
Butler, Samuel 1612-1680 .... **LC 16, 43**
See also DLB 101, 126
Butler, Samuel 1835-1902 . **TCLC 1, 33; DA;
DAB; DAC; DAM MST, NOV; WLC**
See also CA 143; CDBLB 1890-1914; DLB 18,
57, 174
Butler, Walter C.
See Faust, Frederick (Schiller)
Butor, Michel (Marie Francois) 1926-**CLC 1,
3, 8, 11, 15**
See also CA 9-12R; CANR 33, 66; DLB 83;
MTCW 1
Butts, Mary 1892(?)-1937 .... **TCLC 77**
See also CA 148
Buzo, Alexander (John) 1944- .... **CLC 61**
See also CA 97-100; CANR 17, 39, 69
Buzzati, Dino 1906-1972 .... **CLC 36**
See also CA 160; 33-36R; DLB 177
Byars, Betsy (Cromer) 1928- .... **CLC 35**
See also AAYA 19; CA 33-36R; CANR 18, 36,
57; CLR 1, 16; DLB 52; INT CANR-18;
JRDA; MAICYA; MTCW 1; SAAS 1; SATA
4, 46, 80
Byatt, A(ntonia) S(usan Drabble) 1936-**C L C
19, 65; DAM NOV, POP**
See also CA 13-16R; CANR 13, 33, 50; DLB
14, 194; MTCW 1
Byrne, David 1952- .... **CLC 26**
See also CA 127
Byrne, John Keyes 1926-
See Leonard, Hugh
See also CA 102; INT 102
Byron, George Gordon (Noel) 1788-1824
**NCLC 2, 12; DA; DAB; DAC; DAM MST,
POET; PC 16; WLC**
See also CDBLB 1789-1832; DLB 96, 110
Byron, Robert 1905-1941 .... **TCLC 67**
See also CA 160; DLB 195
C. 3. 3.
See Wilde, Oscar (Fingal O'Flahertie Wills)
Caballero, Fernan 1796-1877 ....**NCLC 10**
Cabell, Branch
See Cabell, James Branch
Cabell, James Branch 1879-1958 .... **TCLC 6**
See also CA 105; 152; DLB 9, 78
Cable, George Washington 1844-1925 **T C L C
4; SSC 4**
See also CA 104; 155; DLB 12, 74; DLBD 13
Cabral de Melo Neto, Joao 1920- ... **CLC 76;
DAM MULT**
See also CA 151
Cabrera Infante, G(uillermo) 1929- ..**CLC 5,
25, 45; DAM MULT; HLC**
See also CA 85-88; CANR 29, 65; DLB 113;

HW; MTCW 1

Cade, Toni
   See Bambara. Toni Cade
Cadmus and Harmonia
   See Buchan. John
Caedmon fl. 658-680 .... CMLC 7
   See also DLB 146
Caeiro, Alberto
   See Pessoa, Fernando (Antonio Nogueira)
Cage, John (Milton, Jr.) 1912-1992 . CLC 41
   See also CA 13-16R; CANR 9; DLB 193; INT
   CANR-9
Cahan, Abraham 1860-1951 .... TCLC 71
   See also CA 108; 154; DLB 9, 25, 28
Cain, G.
   See Cabrera Infante. G(uillermo)
Cain, Guillermo
   See Cabrera Infante. G(uillermo)
Cain, James M(allahan) 1892-1977CLC 3, 11,
   28
   See also AITN 1; CA 17-20R; 73-76; CANR 8.
   34. 61; MTCW 1
Caine, Mark
   See Raphael. Frederic (Michael)
Calasso, Roberto 1941- .... CLC 81
   See also CA 143
Calderon de la Barca, Pedro 1600-1681 . L C
   23; DC 3
Caldwell, Erskine (Preston) 1903-1987CLC 1,
   8, 14, 50, 60; DAM NOV; SSC 19
   See also AITN 1; CA 1-4R; 121; CAAS 1;
   CANR 2, 33; DLB 9, 86; MTCW 1
Caldwell, (Janet Miriam) Taylor (Holland)
   1900-1985CLC 2, 28, 39; DAM NOV, POP
   See also CA 5-8R; 116; CANR 5; DLBD 17
Calhoun, John Caldwell 1782-1850NCLC 15
   See also DLB 3
Calisher, Hortense 1911-CLC 2, 4, 8, 38; DAM
   NOV; SSC 15
   See also CA 1-4R; CANR 1, 22, 67; DLB 2;
   INT CANR-22; MTCW 1
Callaghan, Morley Edward 1903-1990CLC 3,
   14, 41, 65; DAC; DAM MST
   See also CA 9-12R; 132; CANR 33; DLB 68;
   MTCW 1
Callimachus c. 305B.C.-c. 240B.C. CMLC 18
   See also DLB 176
Calvin, John 1509-1564 .... LC 37
Calvino, Italo 1923-1985CLC 5, 8, 11, 22, 33,
   39, 73; DAM NOV; SSC 3
   See also CA 85-88; 116; CANR 23, 61; DLB
   196; MTCW 1
Cameron, Carey 1952- .... CLC 59
   See also CA 135
Cameron, Peter 1959- .... CLC 44
   See also CA 125; CANR 50
Campana, Dino 1885-1932 .... TCLC 20
   See also CA 117; DLB 114
Campanella, Tommaso 1568-1639 ...... LC 32
Campbell, John W(ood, Jr.) 1910-1971 C L C
   32
   See also CA 21-22; 29-32R; CANR 34; CAP 2;
   DLB 8; MTCW 1
Campbell, Joseph 1904-1987 .... CLC 69
   See also AAYA 3; BEST 89:2; CA 1-4R; 124;
   CANR 3, 28, 61; MTCW 1
Campbell, Maria 1940- .... CLC 85; DAC
   See also CA 102; CANR 54; NNAL
Campbell, (John) Ramsey 1946-CLC 42; SSC
   19
   See also CA 57-60; CANR 7; INT CANR-7
Campbell, (Ignatius) Roy (Dunnachie) 1901-
   1957 .... TCLC 5

See also CA 104; 155; DLB 20
Campbell, Thomas 1777-1844 .... NCLC 19
   See also DLB 93; 144
Campbell, Wilfred .... TCLC 9
   See also Campbell. William
Campbell, William 1858(?)-1918
   See Campbell. Wilfred
   See also CA 106; DLB 92
Campion, Jane .... CLC 95
   See also CA 138
Campos, Alvaro de
   See Pessoa. Fernando (Antonio Nogueira)
Camus, Albert 1913-1960CLC 1, 2, 4, 9, 11, 14,
   32, 63, 69; DA; DAB; DAC; DAM DRAM,
   MST, NOV; DC 2; SSC 9; WLC
   See also CA 89-92; DLB 72; MTCW 1
Canby, Vincent 1924- .... CLC 13
   See also CA 81-84
Cancale
   See Desnos. Robert
Canetti, Elias 1905-1994CLC 3, 14, 25, 75, 86
   See also CA 21-24R; 146; CANR 23, 61; DLB
   85. 124; MTCW 1
Canin, Ethan 1960- .... CLC 55
   See also CA 131; 135
Cannon, Curt
   See Hunter. Evan
Cao, Lan 1961- .... CLC 109
   See also CA 165
Cape, Judith
   See Page. P(atricia) K(athleen)
Capek, Karel 1890-1938 ... TCLC 6, 37; DA;
   DAB; DAC; DAM DRAM, MST, NOV; DC
   1; WLC
   See also CA 104; 140
Capote, Truman 1924-1984CLC 1, 3, 8, 13, 19,
   34, 38, 58; DA; DAB; DAC; DAM MST,
   NOV, POP; SSC 2; WLC
   See also CA 5-8R; 113; CANR 18, 62; CDALB
   1941-1968; DLB 2. 185; DLBY 80, 84;
   MTCW 1; SATA 91
Capra, Frank 1897-1991 .... CLC 16
   See also CA 61-64; 135
Caputo, Philip 1941- .... CLC 32
   See also CA 73-76; CANR 40
Caragiale, Ion Luca 1852-1912 ...... TCLC 76
   See also CA 157
Card, Orson Scott 1951-CLC 44, 47, 50; DAM
   POP
   See also AAYA 11; CA 102; CANR 27, 47; INT
   CANR-27; MTCW 1; SATA 83
Cardenal, Ernesto 1925- .... CLC 31; DAM
   MULT, POET; HLC; PC 22
   See also CA 49-52; CANR 2. 32, 66; HW;
   MTCW 1
Cardozo, Benjamin N(athan) 1870-1938
   TCLC 65
   See also CA 117; 164
Carducci, Giosue (Alessandro Giuseppe) 1835-
   1907 .... TCLC 32
   See also CA 163
Carew, Thomas 1595(?)-1640 .... LC 13
   See also DLB 126
Carey, Ernestine Gilbreth 1908- .... CLC 17
   See also CA 5-8R; CANR 71; SATA 2
Carey, Peter 1943- .... CLC 40, 55, 96
   See also CA 123; 127; CANR 53; INT 127;
   MTCW 1; SATA 94
Carleton, William 1794-1869 .... NCLC 3
   See also DLB 159
Carlisle, Henry (Coffin) 1926- .... CLC 33
   See also CA 13-16R; CANR 15
Carlsen, Chris

See Holdstock. Robert P.
Carlson, Ron(ald F.) 1947- .... CLC 54
   See also CA 105; CANR 27
Carlyle, Thomas 1795-1881 . NCLC 70; DA;
   DAB; DAC; DAM MST
   See also CDBLB 1789-1832; DLB 55; 144
Carman, (William) Bliss 1861-1929 TCLC 7;
   DAC
   See also CA 104; 152; DLB 92
Carnegie, Dale 1888-1955 .... TCLC 53
Carossa, Hans 1878-1956 .... TCLC 48
   See also DLB 66
Carpenter, Don(ald Richard) 1931-1995C L C
   41
   See also CA 45-48; 149; CANR 1. 71
Carpentier (y Valmont), Alejo 1904-1980CLC
   8, 11, 38, 110; DAM MULT; HLC
   See also CA 65-68; 97-100; CANR 11. 70; DLB
   113; HW
Carr, Caleb 1955(?)- .... CLC 86
   See also CA 147
Carr, Emily 1871-1945 .... TCLC 32
   See also CA 159; DLB 68
Carr, John Dickson 1906-1977 .... CLC 3
   See also Fairbairn. Roger
   See also CA 49-52; 69-72; CANR 3. 33. 60;
   MTCW 1
Carr, Philippa
   See Hibbert. Eleanor Alice Burford
Carr, Virginia Spencer 1929- ....CLC 34
   See also CA 61-64; DLB 111
Carrere, Emmanuel 1957- ....CLC 89
Carrier, Roch 1937-CLC 13, 78; DAC; DAM
   MST
   See also CA 130; CANR 61; DLB 53
Carroll, James P. 1943(?)- .... CLC 38
   See also CA 81-84
Carroll, Jim 1951- .... CLC 35
   See also AAYA 17; CA 45-48; CANR 42
Carroll, Lewis ...... NCLC 2, 53; PC 18; WLC
   See also Dodgson. Charles Lutwidge
   See also CDBLB 1832-1890; CLR 2. 18; DLB
   18. 163. 178; JRDA
Carroll, Paul Vincent 1900-1968 ...... CLC 10
   See also CA 9-12R; 25-28R; DLB 10
Carruth, Hayden 1921- CLC 4, 7, 10, 18, 84;
   PC 10
   See also CA 9-12R; CANR 4. 38. 59; DLB 5.
   165; INT CANR-4; MTCW 1; SATA 47
Carson, Rachel Louise 1907-1964 .. CLC 71;
   DAM POP
   See also CA 77-80; CANR 35; MTCW 1; SATA
   23
Carter, Angela (Olive) 1940-1992 CLC 5, 41,
   76; SSC 13
   See also CA 53-56; 136; CANR 12, 36, 61; DLB
   14; MTCW 1; SATA 66; SATA-Obit 70
Carter, Nick
   See Smith. Martin Cruz
Carver, Raymond 1938-1988 CLC 22, 36, 53,
   55; DAM NOV; SSC 8
   See also CA 33-36R; 126; CANR 17, 34. 61;
   DLB 130; DLBY 84, 88; MTCW 1
Cary, Elizabeth, Lady Falkland 1585-1639
   LC 30
Cary, (Arthur) Joyce (Lunel) 1888-1957
   TCLC 1, 29
   See also CA 104; 164; CDBLB 1914-1945;
   DLB 15, 100
Casanova de Seingalt, Giovanni Jacopo 1725-
   1798 .... LC 13
Casares, Adolfo Bioy
   See Bioy Casares. Adolfo

Casely-Hayford, J(oseph) E(phraim) 1866-1930 **TCLC 24; BLC 1; DAM MULT**
See also BW 2; CA 123; 152

Casey, John (Dudley) 1939- .... **CLC 59**
See also BEST 90:2; CA 69-72; CANR 23

Casey, Michael 1947- .... **CLC 2**
See also CA 65-68; DLB 5

Casey, Patrick
See Thurman. Wallace (Henry)

Casey, Warren (Peter) 1935-1988 .... **CLC 12**
See also CA 101; 127; INT 101

Casona, Alejandro .... **CLC 49**
See also Alvarez. Alejandro Rodriguez

Cassavetes, John 1929-1989 .... **CLC 20**
See also CA 85-88; 127

Cassian, Nina 1924- .... **PC 17**

Cassill, R(onald) V(erlin) 1919- ... **CLC 4, 23**
See also CA 9-12R; CAAS 1; CANR 7, 45; DLB 6

Cassirer, Ernst 1874-1945 .... **TCLC 61**
See also CA 157

Cassity, (Allen) Turner 1929- .... **CLC 6, 42**
See also CA 17-20R; CAAS 8; CANR 11; DLB 105

Castaneda, Carlos 1931(?)- .... **CLC 12**
See also CA 25-28R; CANR 32. 66; HW; MTCW 1

Castedo, Elena 1937- .... **CLC 65**
See also CA 132

Castedo-Ellerman, Elena
See Castedo. Elena

Castellanos, Rosario 1925-1974 **CLC 66; DAM MULT; HLC**
See also CA 131; 53-56; CANR 58; DLB 113; HW

Castelvetro, Lodovico 1505-1571 .... **LC 12**

Castiglione, Baldassare 1478-1529 ..... **LC 12**

Castle, Robert
See Hamilton. Edmond

Castro, Guillen de 1569-1631 .... **LC 19**

Castro, Rosalia de 1837-1885 **NCLC 3; DAM MULT**

Cather, Willa
See Cather. Willa Sibert

Cather, Willa Sibert 1873-1947. **TCLC 1, 11, 31; DA; DAB; DAC; DAM MST, NOV; SSC 2; WLC**
See also AAYA 24; CA 104; 128; CDALB 1865-1917; DLB 9. 54. 78; DLBD 1; MTCW 1; SATA 30

Catherine, Saint 1347-1380 .... **CMLC 27**

Cato, Marcus Porcius 234B.C.-149B.C. **CMLC 21**

Catton, (Charles) Bruce 1899-1978 . **CLC 35**
See also AITN 1; CA 5-8R; 81-84; CANR 7; DLB 17; SATA 2; SATA-Obit 24

Catullus c. 84B.C.-c. 54B.C. .... **CMLC 18**

Cauldwell, Frank
See King. Francis (Henry)

Caunitz, William J. 1933-1996 .... **CLC 34**
See also BEST 89:3; CA 125; 130; 152; INT 130

Causley, Charles (Stanley) 1917- .... **CLC 7**
See also CA 9-12R; CANR 5, 35; CLR 30; DLB 27; MTCW 1; SATA 3, 66

Caute, (John) David 1936- ..... **CLC 29; DAM NOV**
See also CA 1-4R; CAAS 4; CANR 1, 33, 64; DLB 14

Cavafy, C(onstantine) P(eter) 1863-1933 **TCLC 2, 7; DAM POET**
See also Kavafis. Konstantinos Petrou
See also CA 148

Cavallo, Evelyn
See Spark. Muriel (Sarah)

Cavanna, Betty .... **CLC 12**
See also Harrison. Elizabeth Cavanna
See also JRDA; MAICYA; SAAS 4; SATA 1. 30

Cavendish, Margaret Lucas 1623-1673 **LC 30**
See also DLB 131

Caxton, William 1421(?)-1491(?) .... **LC 17**
See also DLB 170

Cayer, D. M.
See Duffy. Maureen

Cayrol, Jean 1911- .... **CLC 11**
See also CA 89-92; DLB 83

Cela, Camilo Jose 1916- **CLC 4, 13, 59; DAM MULT; HLC**
See also BEST 90:2; CA 21-24R; CAAS 10; CANR 21, 32; DLBY 89; HW; MTCW 1

Celan, Paul .... **CLC 10, 19, 53, 82; PC 10**
See also Antschel. Paul
See also DLB 69

Celine, Louis-Ferdinand **CLC 1, 3, 4, 7, 9, 15, 47**
See also Destouches. Louis-Ferdinand
See also DLB 72

Cellini, Benvenuto 1500-1571 .... **LC 7**

Cendrars, Blaise 1887-1961 ..... **CLC 18, 106**
See also Sauser-Hall. Frederic

Cernuda (y Bidon), Luis 1902-1963 **CLC 54; DAM POET**
See also CA 131; 89-92; DLB 134; HW

Cervantes (Saavedra), Miguel de 1547-1616 **LC 6, 23; DA; DAB; DAC; DAM MST, NOV; SSC 12; WLC**

Cesaire, Aime (Fernand) 1913- . **CLC 19, 32, 112; BLC 1; DAM MULT, POET**
See also BW 2; CA 65-68; CANR 24, 43; MTCW 1

Chabon, Michael 1963- .... **CLC 55**
See also CA 139; CANR 57

Chabrol, Claude 1930- .... **CLC 16**
See also CA 110

Challans, Mary 1905-1983
See Renault, Mary
See also CA 81-84; 111; SATA 23; SATA-Obit 36

Challis, George
See Faust. Frederick (Schiller)

Chambers, Aidan 1934- .... **CLC 35**
See also AAYA 27; CA 25-28R; CANR 12, 31. 58; JRDA; MAICYA; SAAS 12; SATA 1, 69

Chambers, James 1948-
See Cliff. Jimmy
See also CA 124

Chambers, Jessie
See Lawrence. D(avid) H(erbert Richards)

Chambers, Robert W(illiam) 1865-1933 **TCLC 41**
See also CA 165; DLB 202

Chandler, Raymond (Thornton) 1888-1959 **TCLC 1, 7; SSC 23**
See also AAYA 25; CA 104; 129; CANR 60; CDALB 1929-1941; DLBD 6; MTCW 1

Chang, Eileen 1920-1995 .... **SSC 28**
See also CA 166

Chang, Jung 1952- .... **CLC 71**
See also CA 142

Chang Ai-Ling
See Chang. Eileen

Channing, William Ellery 1780-1842 . **NCLC 17**
See also DLB 1. 59

Chaplin, Charles Spencer 1889-1977 **CLC 16**
See also Chaplin. Charlie
See also CA 81-84; 73-76

Chaplin, Charlie
See Chaplin. Charles Spencer
See also DLB 44

Chapman, George 1559(?)-1634 **LC 22; DAM DRAM**
See also DLB 62. 121

Chapman, Graham 1941-1989 .... **CLC 21**
See also Monty Python
See also CA 116; 129; CANR 35

Chapman, John Jay 1862-1933 .... **TCLC 7**
See also CA 104

Chapman, Lee
See Bradley. Marion Zimmer

Chapman, Walker
See Silverberg. Robert

Chappell, Fred (Davis) 1936- ..... **CLC 40, 78**
See also CA 5-8R; CAAS 4; CANR 8, 33. 67; DLB 6, 105

Char, Rene(-Emile) 1907-1988 **CLC 9, 11, 14, 55; DAM POET**
See also CA 13-16R; 124; CANR 32; MTCW 1

Charby, Jay
See Ellison. Harlan (Jay)

Chardin, Pierre Teilhard de
See Teilhard de Chardin. (Marie Joseph) Pierre

Charles I 1600-1649 .... **LC 13**

Charriere, Isabelle de 1740-1805 ... **NCLC 66**

Charyn, Jerome 1937- .... **CLC 5, 8, 18**
See also CA 5-8R; CAAS 1; CANR 7. 61; DLBY 83; MTCW 1

Chase, Mary (Coyle) 1907-1981 .... **DC 1**
See also CA 77-80; 105; SATA 17; SATA-Obit 29

Chase, Mary Ellen 1887-1973 .... **CLC 2**
See also CA 13-16; 41-44R; CAP 1; SATA 10

Chase, Nicholas
See Hyde. Anthony

Chateaubriand, Francois Rene de 1768-1848 **NCLC 3**
See also DLB 119

Chatterje, Sarat Chandra 1876-1936(?)
See Chatterji. Saratchandra
See also CA 109

Chatterji, Bankim Chandra 1838-1894 **NCLC 19**

Chatterji, Saratchandra .... **TCLC 13**
See also Chatterje. Sarat Chandra

Chatterton, Thomas 1752-1770 . **LC 3; DAM POET**
See also DLB 109

Chatwin, (Charles) Bruce 1940-1989 **CLC 28, 57, 59; DAM POP**
See also AAYA 4; BEST 90:1; CA 85-88; 127; DLB 194

Chaucer, Daniel
See Ford. Ford Madox

Chaucer, Geoffrey 1340(?)-1400 **LC 17; DA; DAB; DAC; DAM MST, POET; PC 19; WLCS**
See also CDBLB Before 1660; DLB 146

Chaviaras, Strates 1935-
See Haviaras, Stratis
See also CA 105

Chayefsky, Paddy .... **CLC 23**
See also Chayefsky, Sidney
See also DLB 7, 44; DLBY 81

Chayefsky, Sidney 1923-1981
See Chayefsky, Paddy
See also CA 9-12R; 104; CANR 18; DAM DRAM

Chedid, Andree 1920- .... **CLC 47**

Coppola, Francis Ford 1939- .... **CLC 16**
See also CA 77-80; CANR 40; DLB 44
Corbiere, Tristan 1845-1875 .... **NCLC 43**
Corcoran, Barbara 1911- .... **CLC 17**
See also AAYA 14; CA 21-24R; CAAS 2;
CANR 11, 28, 48; CLR 50; DLB 52; JRDA;
SAAS 20; SATA 3, 77
Cordelier, Maurice
See Giraudoux, (Hippolyte) Jean
Corelli, Marie 1855-1924 .... **TCLC 51**
See also Mackay, Mary
See also DLB 34, 156
Corman, Cid 1924- .... **CLC 9**
See also Corman, Sidney
See also CAAS 2; DLB 5, 193
Corman, Sidney 1924-
See Corman, Cid
See also CA 85-88; CANR 44; DAM POET
Cormier, Robert (Edmund) 1925- **CLC 12, 30;**
DA; DAB; DAC; DAM MST, NOV
See also AAYA 3, 19; CA 1-4R; CANR 5, 23;
CDALB 1968-1988; CLR 12; DLB 52; INT
CANR-23; JRDA; MAICYA; MTCW 1;
SATA 10, 45, 83
Corn, Alfred (DeWitt III) 1943- ...... **CLC 33**
See also CA 104; CAAS 25; CANR 44; DLB
120; DLBY 80
Corneille, Pierre 1606-1684 .... **LC 28; DAB;**
DAM MST
Cornwell, David (John Moore) 1931- **CLC 9,**
15; DAM POP
See also le Carre, John
See also CA 5-8R; CANR 13, 33, 59; MTCW 1
Corso, (Nunzio) Gregory 1930- .... **CLC 1, 11**
See also CA 5-8R; CANR 41; DLB 5, 16;
MTCW 1
Cortazar, Julio 1914-1984 **CLC 2, 3, 5, 10, 13,**
15, 33, 34, 92; DAM MULT, NOV; HLC;
SSC 7
See also CA 21-24R; CANR 12, 32; DLB 113;
HW; MTCW 1
CORTES, HERNAN 1484-1547 .... **LC 31**
Corvinus, Jakob
See Raabe, Wilhelm (Karl)
Corwin, Cecil
See Kornbluth, C(yril) M.
Cosic, Dobrica 1921- .... **CLC 14**
See also CA 122; 138; DLB 181
Costain, Thomas B(ertram) 1885-1965 . **C L C**
30
See also CA 5-8R; 25-28R; DLB 9
Costantini, Humberto 1924(?)-1987 **CLC 49**
See also CA 131; 122; HW
Costello, Elvis 1955- .... **CLC 21**
Cotes, Cecil V.
See Duncan, Sara Jeannette
Cotter, Joseph Seamon Sr. 1861-1949 **T C L C**
28; BLC 1; DAM MULT
See also BW 1; CA 124; DLB 50
Couch, Arthur Thomas Quiller
See Quiller-Couch, SirArthur (Thomas)
Coulton, James
See Hansen, Joseph
Couperus, Louis (Marie Anne) 1863-1923
TCLC 15
See also CA 115
Coupland, Douglas 1961- **CLC 85; DAC; DAM**
POP
See also CA 142; CANR 57
Court, Wesli
See Turco, Lewis (Putnam)
Courtenay, Bryce 1933- .... **CLC 59**
See also CA 138

Courtney, Robert
See Ellison, Harlan (Jay)
Cousteau, Jacques-Yves 1910-1997 ..**CLC 30**
See also CA 65-68; 159; CANR 15, 67; MTCW
1; SATA 38, 98
Cowan, Peter (Walkinshaw) 1914- ....**SSC 28**
See also CA 21-24R; CANR 9, 25, 50
Coward, Noel (Peirce) 1899-1973 **CLC 1, 9, 29,**
51; DAM DRAM
See also AITN 1; CA 17-18; 41-44R; CANR
35; CAP 2; CDBLB 1914-1945; DLB 10;
MTCW 1
Cowley, Abraham 1618-1667 .... **LC 43**
See also DLB 131, 151
Cowley, Malcolm 1898-1989 .... **CLC 39**
See also CA 5-8R; 128; CANR 3, 55; DLB 4,
48; DLBY 81, 89; MTCW 1
Cowper, William 1731-1800 . **NCLC 8; DAM**
POET
See also DLB 104, 109
Cox, William Trevor 1928- .... **CLC 9, 14, 71;**
DAM NOV
See also Trevor, William
See also CA 9-12R; CANR 4, 37, 55; DLB 14;
INT CANR-37; MTCW 1
Coyne, P. J.
See Masters, Hilary
Cozzens, James Gould 1903-1978 **CLC 1, 4, 11,**
92
See also CA 9-12R; 81-84; CANR 19; CDALB
1941-1968; DLB 9; DLBD 2; DLBY 84, 97;
MTCW 1
Crabbe, George 1754-1832 .... **NCLC 26**
See also DLB 93
Craddock, Charles Egbert
See Murfree, Mary Noailles
Craig, A. A.
See Anderson, Poul (William)
Craik, Dinah Maria (Mulock) 1826-1887
NCLC 38
See also DLB 35. 163; MAICYA; SATA 34
Cram, Ralph Adams 1863-1942 ..... **TCLC 45**
See also CA 160
Crane, (Harold) Hart 1899-1932 **TCLC 2, 5,**
80; DA; DAB; DAC; DAM MST, POET;
PC 3; WLC
See also CA 104; 127; CDALB 1917-1929;
DLB 4, 48; MTCW 1
Crane, R(onald) S(almon) 1886-1967 **CLC 27**
See also CA 85-88; DLB 63
Crane, Stephen (Townley) 1871-1900 **T C L C**
11, 17, 32; DA; DAB; DAC; DAM MST,
NOV, POET; SSC 7; WLC
See also AAYA 21; CA 109; 140; CDALB 1865-
1917; DLB 12, 54, 78; YABC 2
Crase, Douglas 1944- .... **CLC 58**
See also CA 106
Crashaw, Richard 1612(?)-1649 .... **LC 24**
See also DLB 126
Craven, Margaret 1901-1980 . **CLC 17; DAC**
See also CA 103
Crawford, F(rancis) Marion 1854-1909 **TCLC**
10
See also CA 107; 168; DLB 71
Crawford, Isabella Valancy 1850-1887 **N C L C**
12
See also DLB 92
Crayon, Geoffrey
See Irving, Washington
Creasey, John 1908-1973 .... **CLC 11**
See also CA 5-8R; 41-44R; CANR 8, 59; DLB
77; MTCW 1
Crebillon, Claude Prosper Jolyot de (fils) 1707-

1777 .... **LC 28**
Credo
See Creasey, John
Credo, Alvaro J. de
See Prado (Calvo), Pedro
Creeley, Robert (White) 1926- **CLC 1, 2, 4, 8,**
11, 15, 36, 78; DAM POET
See also CA 1-4R; CAAS 10; CANR 23, 43;
DLB 5, 16, 169; DLBD 17; MTCW 1
Crews, Harry (Eugene) 1935- **CLC 6, 23, 49**
See also AITN 1; CA 25-28R; CANR 20, 57;
DLB 6, 143, 185; MTCW 1
Crichton, (John) Michael 1942- **CLC 2, 6, 54,**
90; DAM NOV, POP
See also AAYA 10; AITN 2; CA 25-28R; CANR
13, 40, 54; DLBY 81; INT CANR-13; JRDA;
MTCW 1; SATA 9, 88
Crispin, Edmund .... **CLC 22**
See also Montgomery, (Robert) Bruce
See also DLB 87
Cristofer, Michael 1945(?)- .... **CLC 28; DAM**
DRAM
See also CA 110; 152; DLB 7
Croce, Benedetto 1866-1952 .... **TCLC 37**
See also CA 120; 155
Crockett, David 1786-1836 .... **NCLC 8**
See also DLB 3, 11
Crockett, Davy
See Crockett, David
Crofts, Freeman Wills 1879-1957 .. **TCLC 55**
See also CA 115; DLB 77
Croker, John Wilson 1780-1857 ..... **NCLC 10**
See also DLB 110
Crommelynck, Fernand 1885-1970 ..**CLC 75**
See also CA 89-92
Cromwell, Oliver 1599-1658 .... **LC 43**
Cronin, A(rchibald) J(oseph) 1896-1981 **C L C**
32
See also CA 1-4R; 102; CANR 5; DLB 191;
SATA 47; SATA-Obit 25
Cross, Amanda
See Heilbrun, Carolyn G(old)
Crothers, Rachel 1878(?)-1958 ...... **TCLC 19**
See also CA 113; DLB 7
Croves, Hal
See Traven, B.
Crow Dog, Mary (Ellen) (?)- .... **CLC 93**
See also Brave Bird, Mary
See also CA 154
Crowfield, Christopher
See Stowe, Harriet (Elizabeth) Beecher
Crowley, Aleister .... **TCLC 7**
See also Crowley, Edward Alexander
Crowley, Edward Alexander 1875-1947
See Crowley, Aleister
See also CA 104
Crowley, John 1942- .... **CLC 57**
See also CA 61-64; CANR 43; DLBY 82; SATA
65
Crud
See Crumb, R(obert)
Crumarums
See Crumb, R(obert)
Crumb, R(obert) 1943- .... **CLC 17**
See also CA 106
Crumbum
See Crumb, R(obert)
Crumski
See Crumb, R(obert)
Crum the Bum
See Crumb, R(obert)
Crunk
See Crumb, R(obert)

Deer, Sandra 1940- .... **CLC 45**

De Ferrari, Gabriella 1941- .... **CLC 65**
    See also CA 146

Defoe, Daniel 1660(?)-1731 **LC 1; DA; DAB; DAC; DAM MST, NOV; WLC**
    See also AAYA 27; CDBLB 1660-1789; DLB 39, 95, 101; JRDA; MAICYA; SATA 22

de Gourmont, Remy(-Marie-Charles)
    See Gourmont. Remy (-Marie-Charles) de

de Hartog, Jan 1914- .... **CLC 19**
    See also CA 1-4R; CANR 1

de Hostos, E. M.
    See Hostos (y Bonilla). Eugenio Maria de

de Hostos, Eugenio M.
    See Hostos (y Bonilla). Eugenio Maria de

Deighton, Len .... **CLC 4, 7, 22, 46**
    See also Deighton, Leonard Cyril
    See also AAYA 6; BEST 89:2; CDBLB 1960 to Present; DLB 87

Deighton, Leonard Cyril 1929-
    See Deighton. Len
    See also CA 9-12R; CANR 19, 33, 68; DAM NOV, POP; MTCW 1

Dekker, Thomas 1572(?)-1632 .. **LC 22; DAM DRAM**
    See also CDBLB Before 1660; DLB 62, 172

Delafield, E. M. 1890-1943 .... **TCLC 61**
    See also Dashwood. Edmee Elizabeth Monica de la Pasture
    See also DLB 34

de la Mare, Walter (John) 1873-1956 **TCLC 4, 53; DAB; DAC; DAM MST, POET; SSC 14; WLC**
    See also CA 163; CDBLB 1914-1945; CLR 23; DLB 162; SATA 16

Delaney, Franey
    See O'Hara. John (Henry)

Delaney, Shelagh 1939- **CLC 29; DAM DRAM**
    See also CA 17-20R; CANR 30, 67; CDBLB 1960 to Present; DLB 13; MTCW 1

Delany, Mary (Granville Pendarves) 1700-1788 **LC 12**

Delany, Samuel R(ay, Jr.) 1942- **CLC 8, 14, 38; BLC 1; DAM MULT**
    See also AAYA 24; BW 2; CA 81-84; CANR 27, 43; DLB 8, 33; MTCW 1

De La Ramee, (Marie) Louise 1839-1908
    See Ouida
    See also SATA 20

de la Roche, Mazo 1879-1961 .... **CLC 14**
    See also CA 85-88; CANR 30; DLB 68; SATA 64

De La Salle, Innocent
    See Hartmann, Sadakichi

Delbanco, Nicholas (Franklin) 1942- **CLC 6, 13**
    See also CA 17-20R; CAAS 2; CANR 29, 55; DLB 6

del Castillo, Michel 1933- .... **CLC 38**
    See also CA 109

Deledda, Grazia (Cosima) 1875(?)-1936 **TCLC 23**
    See also CA 123

Delibes, Miguel .... **CLC 8, 18**
    See also Delibes Setien, Miguel

Delibes Setien, Miguel 1920-
    See Delibes, Miguel
    See also CA 45-48; CANR 1, 32; HW; MTCW 1

DeLillo, Don 1936- **CLC 8, 10, 13, 27, 39, 54, 76; DAM NOV, POP**
    See also BEST 89:1; CA 81-84; CANR 21; DLB 6, 173; MTCW 1

de Lisser, H. G.
    See De Lisser. H(erbert) G(eorge)
    See also DLB 117

De Lisser, H(erbert) G(eorge) 1878-1944 **TCLC 12**
    See also de Lisser. H. G.
    See also BW 2; CA 109; 152

Deloney, Thomas (?)-1600 .... **LC 41**
    See also DLB 167

Deloria, Vine (Victor), Jr. 1933- ..... **CLC 21; DAM MULT**
    See also CA 53-56; CANR 5, 20, 48; DLB 175; MTCW 1; NNAL; SATA 21

Del Vecchio, John M(ichael) 1947- ... **CLC 29**
    See also CA 110; DLBD 9

de Man, Paul (Adolph Michel) 1919-1983 **CLC 55**
    See also CA 128; 111; CANR 61; DLB 67; MTCW 1

De Marinis, Rick 1934- .... **CLC 54**
    See also CA 57-60; CAAS 24; CANR 9, 25, 50

Dembry, R. Emmet
    See Murfree. Mary Noailles

Demby, William 1922- **CLC 53; BLC 1; DAM MULT**
    See also BW 1; CA 81-84; DLB 33

de Menton, Francisco
    See Chin. Frank (Chew. Jr.)

Demijohn, Thom
    See Disch. Thomas M(ichael)

de Montherlant, Henry (Milon)
    See Montherlant, Henry (Milon) de

Demosthenes 384B.C.-322B.C. ...... **CMLC 13**
    See also DLB 176

de Natale, Francine
    See Malzberg. Barry N(athaniel)

Denby, Edwin (Orr) 1903-1983 .... **CLC 48**
    See also CA 138; 110

Denis, Julio
    See Cortazar. Julio

Denmark, Harrison
    See Zelazny. Roger (Joseph)

Dennis, John 1658-1734 .... **LC 11**
    See also DLB 101

Dennis, Nigel (Forbes) 1912-1989 .... **CLC 8**
    See also CA 25-28R; 129; DLB 13, 15; MTCW 1

Dent, Lester 1904(?)-1959 .... **TCLC 72**
    See also CA 112; 161

De Palma, Brian (Russell) 1940- .... **CLC 20**
    See also CA 109

De Quincey, Thomas 1785-1859 .... **NCLC 4**
    See also CDBLB 1789-1832; DLB 110; 144

Deren, Eleanora 1908(?)-1961
    See Deren. Maya
    See also CA 111

Deren, Maya 1917-1961 .... **CLC 16, 102**
    See also Deren, Eleanora

Derleth, August (William) 1909-1971 **CLC 31**
    See also CA 1-4R; 29-32R; CANR 4; DLB 9; DLBD 17; SATA 5

Der Nister 1884-1950 .... **TCLC 56**

de Routisie, Albert
    See Aragon. Louis

Derrida, Jacques 1930- .... **CLC 24, 87**
    See also CA 124; 127

Derry Down Derry
    See Lear. Edward

Dersonnes, Jacques
    See Simenon. Georges (Jacques Christian)

Desai, Anita 1937- **CLC 19, 37, 97; DAB; DAM NOV**
    See also CA 81-84; CANR 33, 53; MTCW 1;
    SATA 63

de Saint-Luc, Jean
    See Glassco. John

de Saint Roman, Arnaud
    See Aragon. Louis

Descartes, Rene 1596-1650 .... **LC 20, 35**

De Sica, Vittorio 1901(?)-1974 .... **CLC 20**
    See also CA 117

Desnos, Robert 1900-1945 .... **TCLC 22**
    See also CA 121; 151

Destouches, Louis-Ferdinand 1894-1961 **CLC 9, 15**
    See also Celine. Louis-Ferdinand
    See also CA 85-88; CANR 28; MTCW 1

de Tolignac, Gaston
    See Griffith, D(avid Lewelyn) W(ark)

Deutsch, Babette 1895-1982 .... **CLC 18**
    See also CA 1-4R; 108; CANR 4; DLB 45; SATA 1; SATA-Obit 33

Devenant, William 1606-1649 .... **LC 13**

Devkota, Laxmiprasad 1909-1959 . **TCLC 23**
    See also CA 123

De Voto, Bernard (Augustine) 1897-1955 **TCLC 29**
    See also CA 113; 160; DLB 9

De Vries, Peter 1910-1993 **CLC 1, 2, 3, 7, 10, 28, 46; DAM NOV**
    See also CA 17-20R; 142; CANR 41; DLB 6; DLBY 82; MTCW 1

Dexter, John
    See Bradley. Marion Zimmer

Dexter, Martin
    See Faust. Frederick (Schiller)

Dexter, Pete 1943- ... **CLC 34, 55; DAM POP**
    See also BEST 89:2; CA 127; 131; INT 131; MTCW 1

Diamano, Silmang
    See Senghor. Leopold Sedar

Diamond, Neil 1941- .... **CLC 30**
    See also CA 108

Diaz del Castillo, Bernal 1496-1584 ... **LC 31**

di Bassetto, Corno
    See Shaw. George Bernard

Dick, Philip K(indred) 1928-1982 **CLC 10, 30, 72; DAM NOV, POP**
    See also AAYA 24; CA 49-52; 106; CANR 2, 16; DLB 8; MTCW 1

Dickens, Charles (John Huffam) 1812-1870 **NCLC 3, 8, 18, 26, 37, 50; DA; DAB; DAC; DAM MST, NOV; SSC 17; WLC**
    See also AAYA 23; CDBLB 1832-1890; DLB 21, 55, 70, 159, 166; JRDA; MAICYA; SATA 15

Dickey, James (Lafayette) 1923-1997 **CLC 1, 2, 4, 7, 10, 15, 47, 109; DAM NOV, POET, POP**
    See also AITN 1, 2; CA 9-12R; 156; CABS 2; CANR 10, 48, 61; CDALB 1968-1988; DLB 5, 193; DLBD 7; DLBY 82, 93, 96, 97; INT CANR-10; MTCW 1

Dickey, William 1928-1994 .... **CLC 3, 28**
    See also CA 9-12R; 145; CANR 24; DLB 5

Dickinson, Charles 1951- .... **CLC 49**
    See also CA 128

Dickinson, Emily (Elizabeth) 1830-1886 **NCLC 21; DA; DAB; DAC; DAM MST, POET; PC 1; WLC**
    See also AAYA 22; CDALB 1865-1917; DLB 1; SATA 29

Dickinson, Peter (Malcolm) 1927- **CLC 12, 35**
    See also AAYA 9; CA 41-44R; CANR 31, 58; CLR 29; DLB 87, 161; JRDA; MAICYA; SATA 5, 62, 95

Dickson, Carr
See Carr, John Dickson
Dickson, Carter
See Carr, John Dickson
Diderot, Denis 1713-1784 .... **LC 26**
Didion, Joan 1934-**CLC 1, 3, 8, 14, 32; DAM NOV**
See also AITN 1; CA 5-8R; CANR 14, 52; CDALB 1968-1988; DLB 2, 173, 185; DLBY 81, 86; MTCW 1
Dietrich, Robert
See Hunt, E(verette) Howard, (Jr.)
Difusa, Pati
See Almodovar, Pedro
Dillard, Annie 1945- .. **CLC 9, 60, 115; DAM NOV**
See also AAYA 6; CA 49-52; CANR 3, 43, 62; DLBY 80; MTCW 1; SATA 10
Dillard, R(ichard) H(enry) W(ilde) 1937-**CLC 5**
See also CA 21-24R; CAAS 7; CANR 10; DLB 5
Dillon, Eilis 1920-1994 .... **CLC 17**
See also CA 9-12R; 147; CAAS 3; CANR 4, 38; CLR 26; MAICYA; SATA 2, 74; SATA-Obit 83
Dimont, Penelope
See Mortimer, Penelope (Ruth)
Dinesen, Isak .... **CLC 10, 29, 95; SSC 7**
See also Blixen, Karen (Christentze Dinesen)
Ding Ling .... **CLC 68**
See also Chiang, Pin-chin
Disch, Thomas M(ichael) 1940- ... **CLC 7, 36**
See also AAYA 17; CA 21-24R; CAAS 4; CANR 17, 36, 54; CLR 18; DLB 8; MAICYA; MTCW 1; SAAS 15; SATA 92
Disch, Tom
See Disch, Thomas M(ichael)
d'Isly, Georges
See Simenon, Georges (Jacques Christian)
Disraeli, Benjamin 1804-1881 .... **NCLC 2, 39**
See also DLB 21, 55
Ditcum, Steve
See Crumb, R(obert)
Dixon, Paige
See Corcoran, Barbara
Dixon, Stephen 1936- .... **CLC 52; SSC 16**
See also CA 89-92; CANR 17, 40, 54; DLB 130
Doak, Annie
See Dillard, Annie
Dobell, Sydney Thompson 1824-1874 **N C L C 43**
See also DLB 32
Doblin, Alfred .... **TCLC 13**
See also Doeblin, Alfred
Dobrolyubov, Nikolai Alexandrovich 1836-1861
NCLC 5
Dobson, Austin 1840-1921 .... **TCLC 79**
See also DLB 35; 144
Dobyns, Stephen 1941- .... **CLC 37**
See also CA 45-48; CANR 2, 18
Doctorow, E(dgar) L(aurence) 1931- **CLC 6, 11, 15, 18, 37, 44, 65, 113; DAM NOV, POP**
See also AAYA 22; AITN 2; BEST 89:3; CA 45-48; CANR 2, 33, 51; CDALB 1968-1988; DLB 2, 28, 173; DLBY 80; MTCW 1
Dodgson, Charles Lutwidge 1832-1898
See Carroll, Lewis
See also CLR 2; DA; DAB; DAC; DAM MST, NOV, POET; MAICYA; SATA 100; YABC 2
Dodson, Owen (Vincent) 1914-1983 **CLC 79; BLC 1; DAM MULT**
See also BW 1; CA 65-68; 110; CANR 24; DLB

76
Doeblin, Alfred 1878-1957 .... **TCLC 13**
See also Doblin, Alfred
See also CA 110; 141; DLB 66
Doerr, Harriet 1910- .... **CLC 34**
See also CA 117; 122; CANR 47; INT 122
Domecq, H(onorio) Bustos
See Bioy Casares, Adolfo; Borges, Jorge Luis
Domini, Rey
See Lorde, Audre (Geraldine)
Dominique
See Proust, (Valentin-Louis-George-Eugene-) Marcel
Don, A
See Stephen, SirLeslie
Donaldson, Stephen R. 1947- **CLC 46; DAM POP**
See also CA 89-92; CANR 13, 55; INT CANR-13
Donleavy, J(ames) P(atrick) 1926-**CLC 1, 4, 6, 10, 45**
See also AITN 2; CA 9-12R; CANR 24, 49, 62; DLB 6, 173; INT CANR-24; MTCW 1
Donne, John 1572-1631**LC 10, 24; DA; DAB; DAC; DAM MST, POET; PC 1**
See also CDBLB Before 1660; DLB 121, 151
Donnell, David 1939(?)- .... **CLC 34**
Donoghue, P. S.
See Hunt, E(verette) Howard, (Jr.)
Donoso (Yanez), Jose 1924-1996**CLC 4, 8, 11, 32, 99; DAM MULT; HLC**
See also CA 81-84; 155; CANR 32; DLB 113; HW; MTCW 1
Donovan, John 1928-1992 .... **CLC 35**
See also AAYA 20; CA 97-100; 137; CLR 3; MAICYA; SATA 72; SATA-Brief 29
Don Roberto
See Cunninghame Graham, R(obert) B(ontine)
Doolittle, Hilda 1886-1961**CLC 3, 8, 14, 31, 34, 73; DA; DAC; DAM MST, POET; PC 5; WLC**
See also H. D.
See also CA 97-100; CANR 35; DLB 4, 45; MTCW 1
Dorfman, Ariel 1942- ...... **CLC 48, 77; DAM MULT; HLC**
See also CA 124; 130; CANR 67, 70; HW; INT 130
Dorn, Edward (Merton) 1929- ... **CLC 10, 18**
See also CA 93-96; CANR 42; DLB 5; INT 93-96
Dorris, Michael (Anthony) 1945-1997 ..**C L C 109; DAM MULT, NOV**
See also AAYA 20; BEST 90:1; CA 102; 157; CANR 19, 46; DLB 175; NNAL; SATA 75; SATA-Obit 94
Dorris, Michael A.
See Dorris, Michael (Anthony)
Dorsan, Luc
See Simenon, Georges (Jacques Christian)
Dorsange, Jean
See Simenon, Georges (Jacques Christian)
Dos Passos, John (Roderigo) 1896-1970 **C L C 1, 4, 8, 11, 15, 25, 34, 82; DA; DAB; DAC; DAM MST, NOV; WLC**
See also CA 1-4R; 29-32R; CANR 3; CDALB 1929-1941; DLB 4, 9; DLBD 1, 15; DLBY 96; MTCW 1
Dossage, Jean
See Simenon, Georges (Jacques Christian)
Dostoevsky, Fedor Mikhailovich 1821-1881
NCLC 2, 7, 21, 33, 43; DA; DAB; DAC; DAM MST, NOV; SSC 2; WLC

Doughty, Charles M(ontagu) 1843-1926
TCLC 27
See also CA 115; DLB 19, 57, 174
Douglas, Ellen .... **CLC 73**
See also Haxton, Josephine Ayres; Williamson, Ellen Douglas
Douglas, Gavin 1475(?)-1522 .... **LC 20**
See also DLB 132
Douglas, George
See Brown, George Douglas
Douglas, Keith (Castellain) 1920-1944**T C L C 40**
See also CA 160; DLB 27
Douglas, Leonard
See Bradbury, Ray (Douglas)
Douglas, Michael
See Crichton, (John) Michael
Douglas, (George) Norman 1868-1952**T C L C 68**
See also CA 119; 157; DLB 34, 195
Douglas, William
See Brown, George Douglas
Douglass, Frederick 1817(?)-1895**NCLC 7, 55; BLC 1; DA; DAC; DAM MST, MULT; WLC**
See also CDALB 1640-1865; DLB 1, 43, 50, 79; SATA 29
Dourado, (Waldomiro Freitas) Autran 1926-
CLC 23, 60
See also CA 25-28R; CANR 34
Dourado, Waldomiro Autran
See Dourado, (Waldomiro Freitas) Autran
Dove, Rita (Frances) 1952-**CLC 50, 81; BLCS; DAM MULT, POET; PC 6**
See also BW 2; CA 109; CAAS 19; CANR 27, 42, 68; DLB 120
Doveglion
See Villa, Jose Garcia
Dowell, Coleman 1925-1985 .... **CLC 60**
See also CA 25-28R; 117; CANR 10; DLB 130
Dowson, Ernest (Christopher) 1867-1900
TCLC 4
See also CA 105; 150; DLB 19, 135
Doyle, A. Conan
See Doyle, Arthur Conan
Doyle, Arthur Conan 1859-1930**TCLC 7; DA; DAB; DAC; DAM MST, NOV; SSC 12; WLC**
See also AAYA 14; CA 104; 122; CDBLB 1890-1914; DLB 18, 70, 156, 178; MTCW 1; SATA 24
Doyle, Conan
See Doyle, Arthur Conan
Doyle, John
See Graves, Robert (von Ranke)
Doyle, Roddy 1958(?)- .... **CLC 81**
See also AAYA 14; CA 143; DLB 194
Doyle, Sir A. Conan
See Doyle, Arthur Conan
Doyle, Sir Arthur Conan
See Doyle, Arthur Conan
Dr. A
See Asimov, Isaac; Silverstein, Alvin
Drabble, Margaret 1939-**CLC 2, 3, 5, 8, 10, 22, 53; DAB; DAC; DAM MST, NOV, POP**
See also CA 13-16R; CANR 18, 35, 63; CDBLB 1960 to Present; DLB 14, 155; MTCW 1; SATA 48
Drapier, M. B.
See Swift, Jonathan
Drayham, James
See Mencken, H(enry) L(ouis)
Drayton, Michael 1563-1631 ...... **LC 8; DAM**

55; DLB 196; MTCW 1

Eddison, E(ric) R(ucker) 1882-1945 **TCLC 15**
See also CA 109; 156

Eddy, Mary (Morse) Baker 1821-1910 **T C L C 71**
See also CA 113

Edel, (Joseph) Leon 1907-1997 .. **CLC 29, 34**
See also CA 1-4R; 161; CANR 1, 22; DLB 103;
INT CANR-22

Eden, Emily 1797-1869 .... **NCLC 10**

Edgar, David 1948- ... **CLC 42; DAM DRAM**
See also CA 57-60; CANR 12, 61; DLB 13;
MTCW 1

Edgerton, Clyde (Carlyle) 1944- ..... **CLC 39**
See also AAYA 17; CA 118; 134; CANR 64;
INT 134

Edgeworth, Maria 1768-1849 .... **NCLC 1, 51**
See also DLB 116, 159, 163; SATA 21

Edmonds, Paul
See Kuttner, Henry

Edmonds, Walter D(umaux) 1903-1998 **C L C 35**
See also CA 5-8R; CANR 2; DLB 9; MAICYA;
SAAS 4; SATA 1, 27; SATA-Obit 99

Edmondson, Wallace
See Ellison, Harlan (Jay)

Edson, Russell .... **CLC 13**
See also CA 33-36R

Edwards, Bronwen Elizabeth
See Rose, Wendy

Edwards, G(erald) B(asil) 1899-1976 **CLC 25**
See also CA 110

Edwards, Gus 1939- .... **CLC 43**
See also CA 108; INT 108

Edwards, Jonathan 1703-1758 ..... **LC 7; DA; DAC; DAM MST**
See also DLB 24

Efron, Marina Ivanovna Tsvetaeva
See Tsvetaeva (Efron), Marina (Ivanovna)

Ehle, John (Marsden, Jr.) 1925- ...... **CLC 27**
See also CA 9-12R

Ehrenbourg, Ilya (Grigoryevich)
See Ehrenburg, Ilya (Grigoryevich)

Ehrenburg, Ilya (Grigoryevich) 1891-1967
CLC 18, 34, 62
See also CA 102; 25-28R

Ehrenburg, Ilyo (Grigoryevich)
See Ehrenburg, Ilya (Grigoryevich)

Ehrenreich, Barbara 1941- .... **CLC 110**
See also BEST 90:4; CA 73-76; CANR 16, 37,
62; MTCW 1

Eich, Guenter 1907-1972 .... **CLC 15**
See also CA 111; 93-96; DLB 69, 124

Eichendorff, Joseph Freiherr von 1788-1857
NCLC 8
See also DLB 90

Eigner, Larry .... **CLC 9**
See also Eigner, Laurence (Joel)
See also CAAS 23; DLB 5

Eigner, Laurence (Joel) 1927-1996
See Eigner, Larry
See also CA 9-12R; 151; CANR 6; DLB 193

Einstein, Albert 1879-1955 .... **TCLC 65**
See also CA 121; 133; MTCW 1

Eiseley, Loren Corey 1907-1977 .... **CLC 7**
See also AAYA 5; CA 1-4R; 73-76; CANR 6;
DLBD 17

Eisenstadt, Jill 1963- .... **CLC 50**
See also CA 140

Eisenstein, Sergei (Mikhailovich) 1898-1948
TCLC 57
See also CA 114; 149

Eisner, Simon
See Kornbluth, C(yril) M.

Ekeloef, (Bengt) Gunnar 1907-1968 **CLC 27; DAM POET; PC 23**
See also CA 123; 25-28R

Ekelof, (Bengt) Gunnar
See Ekeloef, (Bengt) Gunnar

Ekelund, Vilhelm 1880-1949 .... **TCLC 75**

Ekwensi, C. O. D.
See Ekwensi, Cyprian (Odiatu Duaka)

Ekwensi, Cyprian (Odiatu Duaka) 1921- **CLC 4; BLC 1; DAM MULT**
See also BW 2; CA 29-32R; CANR 18, 42; DLB
117; MTCW 1; SATA 66

Elaine .... **TCLC 18**
See also Leverson, Ada

El Crummo
See Crumb, R(obert)

Elder, Lonne III 1931-1996 .... **DC 8**
See also BLC 1; BW 1; CA 81-84; 152; CANR
25; DAM MULT; DLB 7, 38, 44

Elia
See Lamb, Charles

Eliade, Mircea 1907-1986 .... **CLC 19**
See also CA 65-68; 119; CANR 30, 62; MTCW
1

Eliot, A. D.
See Jewett, (Theodora) Sarah Orne

Eliot, Alice
See Jewett, (Theodora) Sarah Orne

Eliot, Dan
See Silverberg, Robert

Eliot, George 1819-1880 **NCLC 4, 13, 23, 41, 49; DA; DAB; DAC; DAM MST, NOV; PC 20; WLC**
See also CDBLB 1832-1890; DLB 21, 35, 55

Eliot, John 1604-1690 .... **LC 5**
See also DLB 24

Eliot, T(homas) S(tearns) 1888-1965 **CLC 1, 2, 3, 6, 9, 10, 13, 15, 24, 34, 41, 55, 57, 113; DA; DAB; DAC; DAM DRAM, MST, POET; PC 5; WLC**
See also CA 5-8R; 25-28R; CANR 41; CDALB
1929-1941; DLB 7, 10, 45, 63; DLBY 88;
MTCW 1

Elizabeth 1866-1941 .... **TCLC 41**

Elkin, Stanley L(awrence) 1930-1995 **CLC 4, 6, 9, 14, 27, 51, 91; DAM NOV, POP; SSC 12**
See also CA 9-12R; 148; CANR 8, 46; DLB 2,
28; DLBY 80; INT CANR-8; MTCW 1

Elledge, Scott .... **CLC 34**

Elliot, Don
See Silverberg, Robert

Elliott, Don
See Silverberg, Robert

Elliott, George P(aul) 1918-1980 .... **CLC 2**
See also CA 1-4R; 97-100; CANR 2

Elliott, Janice 1931- .... **CLC 47**
See also CA 13-16R; CANR 8, 29; DLB 14

Elliott, Sumner Locke 1917-1991 ..... **CLC 38**
See also CA 5-8R; 134; CANR 2, 21

Elliott, William
See Bradbury, Ray (Douglas)

Ellis, A. E. .... **CLC 7**

Ellis, Alice Thomas .... **CLC 40**
See also Haycraft, Anna
See also DLB 194

Ellis, Bret Easton 1964- .. **CLC 39, 71; DAM POP**
See also AAYA 2; CA 118; 123; CANR 51; INT
123

Ellis, (Henry) Havelock 1859-1939 **TCLC 14**
See also CA 109; DLB 190

Ellis, Landon
See Ellison, Harlan (Jay)

Ellis, Trey 1962- .... **CLC 55**
See also CA 146

Ellison, Harlan (Jay) 1934- ... **CLC 1, 13, 42; DAM POP; SSC 14**
See also CA 5-8R; CANR 5, 46; DLB 8; INT
CANR-5; MTCW 1

Ellison, Ralph (Waldo) 1914-1994 **CLC 1, 3, 11, 54, 86, 114; BLC 1; DA; DAB; DAC; DAM MST, MULT, NOV; SSC 26; WLC**
See also AAYA 19; BW 1; CA 9-12R; 145;
CANR 24, 53; CDALB 1941-1968; DLB 2,
76; DLBY 94; MTCW 1

Ellmann, Lucy (Elizabeth) 1956- ..... **CLC 61**
See also CA 128

Ellmann, Richard (David) 1918-1987 **CLC 50**
See also BEST 89:2; CA 1-4R; 122; CANR 2,
28, 61; DLB 103; DLBY 87; MTCW 1

Elman, Richard (Martin) 1934-1997 **CLC 19**
See also CA 17-20R; 163; CAAS 3; CANR 47

Elron
See Hubbard, L(afayette) Ron(ald)

Eluard, Paul .... **TCLC 7, 41**
See also Grindel, Eugene

Elyot, Sir Thomas 1490(?)-1546 .... **LC 11**

Elytis, Odysseus 1911-1996 **CLC 15, 49, 100; DAM POET; PC 21**
See also CA 102; 151; MTCW 1

Emecheta, (Florence Onye) Buchi 1944- **C L C 14, 48; BLC 2; DAM MULT**
See also BW 2; CA 81-84; CANR 27; DLB 117;
MTCW 1; SATA 66

Emerson, Mary Moody 1774-1863 **NCLC 66**

Emerson, Ralph Waldo 1803-1882 . **NCLC 1, 38; DA; DAB; DAC; DAM MST, POET; PC 18; WLC**
See also CDALB 1640-1865; DLB 1, 59, 73

Eminescu, Mihail 1850-1889 .... **NCLC 33**

Empson, William 1906-1984 **CLC 3, 8, 19, 33, 34**
See also CA 17-20R; 112; CANR 31, 61; DLB
20; MTCW 1

Enchi, Fumiko (Ueda) 1905-1986 .... **CLC 31**
See also CA 129; 121

Ende, Michael (Andreas Helmuth) 1929-1995
CLC 31
See also CA 118; 124; 149; CANR 36; CLR
14; DLB 75; MAICYA; SATA 61; SATA-
Brief 42; SATA-Obit 86

Endo, Shusaku 1923-1996 **CLC 7, 14, 19, 54, 99; DAM NOV**
See also CA 29-32R; 153; CANR 21, 54; DLB
182; MTCW 1

Engel, Marian 1933-1985 .... **CLC 36**
See also CA 25-28R; CANR 12; DLB 53; INT
CANR-12

Engelhardt, Frederick
See Hubbard, L(afayette) Ron(ald)

Enright, D(ennis) J(oseph) 1920- **CLC 4, 8, 31**
See also CA 1-4R; CANR 1, 42; DLB 27; SATA
25

Enzensberger, Hans Magnus 1929- . **CLC 43**
See also CA 116; 119

Ephron, Nora 1941- .... **CLC 17, 31**
See also AITN 2; CA 65-68; CANR 12, 39

Epicurus 341B.C.-270B.C. .... **CMLC 21**
See also DLB 176

Epsilon
See Betjeman, John

Epstein, Daniel Mark 1948- .... **CLC 7**
See also CA 49-52; CANR 2, 53

Epstein, Jacob 1956- .... **CLC 19**

Ghosh, Amitav 1956- .... CLC 44
See also CA 147

Giacosa, Giuseppe 1847-1906 .... TCLC 7
See also CA 104

Gibb, Lee
See Waterhouse, Keith (Spencer)

Gibbon, Lewis Grassic .... TCLC 4
See also Mitchell, James Leslie

Gibbons, Kaye 1960-CLC 50, 88; DAM POP
See also CA 151

Gibran, Kahlil 1883-1931 . TCLC 1, 9; DAM
POET, POP; PC 9
See also CA 104; 150

Gibran, Khalil
See Gibran, Kahlil

Gibson, William 1914- .. CLC 23; DA; DAB;
DAC; DAM DRAM, MST
See also CA 9-12R; CANR 9, 42; DLB 7; SATA
66

Gibson, William (Ford) 1948- ... CLC 39, 63;
DAM POP
See also AAYA 12; CA 126; 133; CANR 52

Gide, Andre (Paul Guillaume) 1869-1951
TCLC 5, 12, 36; DA; DAB; DAC; DAM
MST, NOV; SSC 13; WLC
See also CA 104; 124; DLB 65; MTCW 1

Gifford, Barry (Colby) 1946- .... CLC 34
See also CA 65-68; CANR 9, 30, 40

Gilbert, Frank
See De Voto, Bernard (Augustine)

Gilbert, W(illiam) S(chwenck) 1836-1911
TCLC 3; DAM DRAM, POET
See also CA 104; SATA 36

Gilbreth, Frank B., Jr. 1911- .... CLC 17
See also CA 9-12R; SATA 2

Gilchrist, Ellen 1935-CLC 34, 48; DAM POP;
SSC 14
See also CA 113; 116; CANR 41, 61; DLB 130;
MTCW 1

Giles, Molly 1942- .... CLC 39
See also CA 126

Gill, Eric 1882-1940 .... TCLC 85

Gill, Patrick
See Creasey, John

Gilliam, Terry (Vance) 1940- .... CLC 21
See also Monty Python
See also AAYA 19; CA 108; 113; CANR 35;
INT 113

Gillian, Jerry
See Gilliam, Terry (Vance)

Gilliatt, Penelope (Ann Douglass) 1932-1993
CLC 2, 10, 13, 53
See also AITN 2; CA 13-16R; 141; CANR 49;
DLB 14

Gilman, Charlotte (Anna) Perkins (Stetson)
1860-1935 .... TCLC 9, 37; SSC 13
See also CA 106; 150

Gilmour, David 1949- .... CLC 35
See also CA 138, 147

Gilpin, William 1724-1804 .... NCLC 30

Gilray, J. D.
See Mencken, H(enry) L(ouis)

Gilroy, Frank D(aniel) 1925- .... CLC 2
See also CA 81-84; CANR 32, 64; DLB 7

Gilstrap, John 1957(?)- .... CLC 99
See also CA 160

Ginsberg, Allen 1926-1997CLC 1, 2, 3, 4, 6, 13,
36, 69, 109; DA; DAB; DAC; DAM MST,
POET; PC 4; WLC 3
See also AITN 1; CA 1-4R; 157; CANR 2, 41,
63; CDALB 1941-1968; DLB 5, 16, 169;
MTCW 1

Ginzburg, Natalia 1916-1991CLC 5, 11, 54, 70

See also CA 85-88; 135; CANR 33; DLB 177;
MTCW 1

Giono, Jean 1895-1970 ....CLC 4, 11
See also CA 45-48; 29-32R; CANR 2, 35; DLB
72; MTCW 1

Giovanni, Nikki 1943-CLC 2, 4, 19, 64; BLC
2; DA; DAB; DAC; DAM MST, MULT,
POET; PC 19; WLCS
See also AAYA 22; AITN 1; BW 2; CA 29-32R;
CAAS 6; CANR 18, 41, 60; CLR 6; DLB 5.
41; INT CANR-18; MAICYA; MTCW 1;
SATA 24

Giovene, Andrea 1904- .... CLC 7
See also CA 85-88

Gippius, Zinaida (Nikolayevna) 1869-1945
See Hippius, Zinaida
See also CA 106

Giraudoux, (Hippolyte) Jean 1882-1944
TCLC 2, 7; DAM DRAM
See also CA 104; DLB 65

Gironella, Jose Maria 1917- .... CLC 11
See also CA 101

Gissing, George (Robert) 1857-1903TCLC 3,
24, 47
See also CA 105; 167; DLB 18, 135, 184

Giurlani, Aldo
See Palazzeschi, Aldo

Gladkov, Fyodor (Vasilyevich) 1883-1958
TCLC 27

Glanville, Brian (Lester) 1931- ....CLC 6
See also CA 5-8R; CAAS 9; CANR 3, 70; DLB
15, 139; SATA 42

Glasgow, Ellen (Anderson Gholson) 1873-1945
TCLC 2, 7
See also CA 104; 164; DLB 9, 12

Glaspell, Susan 1882(?)-1948 .... TCLC 55
See also CA 110; 154; DLB 7, 9, 78; YABC 2

Glassco, John 1909-1981 .... CLC 9
See also CA 13-16R; 102; CANR 15; DLB 68

Glasscock, Amnesia
See Steinbeck, John (Ernst)

Glasser, Ronald J. 1940(?)- .... CLC 37

Glassman, Joyce
See Johnson, Joyce

Glendinning, Victoria 1937- ....CLC 50
See also CA 120; 127; CANR 59; DLB 155

Glissant, Edouard 1928- .. CLC 10, 68; DAM
MULT
See also CA 153

Gloag, Julian 1930- ....CLC 40
See also AITN 1; CA 65-68; CANR 10, 70

Glowacki, Aleksander
See Prus, Boleslaw

Gluck, Louise (Elisabeth) 1943-CLC 7, 22, 44,
81; DAM POET; PC 16
See also CA 33-36R; CANR 40, 69; DLB 5

Glyn, Elinor 1864-1943 .... TCLC 72
See also DLB 153

Gobineau, Joseph Arthur (Comte) de 1816-
1882 ....NCLC 17
See also DLB 123

Godard, Jean-Luc 1930- ....CLC 20
See also CA 93-96

Godden, (Margaret) Rumer 1907-....CLC 53
See also AAYA 6; CA 5-8R; CANR 4, 27, 36,
55; CLR 20; DLB 161; MAICYA; SAAS 12;
SATA 3, 36

Godoy Alcayaga, Lucila 1889-1957
See Mistral, Gabriela
See also BW 2; CA 104; 131; DAM MULT;
HW; MTCW 1

Godwin, Gail (Kathleen) 1937- CLC 5, 8, 22,
31, 69; DAM POP

See also CA 29-32R; CANR 15, 43, 69; DLB
6; INT CANR-15; MTCW 1

Godwin, William 1756-1836 ....NCLC 14
See also CDBLB 1789-1832; DLB 39, 104, 142,
158, 163

Goebbels, Josef
See Goebbels, (Paul) Joseph

Goebbels, (Paul) Joseph 1897-1945TCLC 68
See also CA 115; 148

Goebbels, Joseph Paul
See Goebbels, (Paul) Joseph

Goethe, Johann Wolfgang von 1749-1832
NCLC 4, 22, 34; DA; DAB; DAC; DAM
DRAM, MST, POET; PC 5; WLC 3
See also DLB 94

Gogarty, Oliver St. John 1878-1957TCLC 15
See also CA 109; 150; DLB 15, 19

Gogol, Nikolai (Vasilyevich) 1809-1852NCLC
5, 15, 31; DA; DAB; DAC; DAM DRAM,
MST; DC 1; SSC 4, 29; WLC
See also DLB 198

Goines, Donald 1937(?)-1974CLC 80; BLC 2;
DAM MULT, POP
See also AITN 1; BW 1; CA 124; 114; DLB 33

Gold, Herbert 1924- .... CLC 4, 7, 14, 42
See also CA 9-12R; CANR 17, 45; DLB 2;
DLBY 81

Goldbarth, Albert 1948- .... CLC 5, 38
See also CA 53-56; CANR 6, 40; DLB 120

Goldberg, Anatol 1910-1982 .... CLC 34
See also CA 131; 117

Goldemberg, Isaac 1945- ....CLC 52
See also CA 69-72; CAAS 12; CANR 11. 32;
HW

Golding, William (Gerald) 1911-1993CLC 1,
2, 3, 8, 10, 17, 27, 58, 81; DA; DAB; DAC;
DAM MST, NOV; WLC
See also AAYA 5; CA 5-8R; 141; CANR 13,
33, 54; CDBLB 1945-1960; DLB 15, 100;
MTCW 1

Goldman, Emma 1869-1940 .... TCLC 13
See also CA 110; 150

Goldman, Francisco 1954- ....CLC 76
See also CA 162

Goldman, William (W.) 1931- ...... CLC 1, 48
See also CA 9-12R; CANR 29, 69; DLB 44

Goldmann, Lucien 1913-1970 ....CLC 24
See also CA 25-28; CAP 2

Goldoni, Carlo 1707-1793LC 4; DAM DRAM

Goldsberry, Steven 1949- ....CLC 34
See also CA 131

Goldsmith, Oliver 1728-1774LC 2; DA; DAB;
DAC; DAM DRAM, MST, NOV, POET;
DC 8; WLC
See also CDBLB 1660-1789; DLB 39, 89. 104,
109, 142; SATA 26

Goldsmith, Peter
See Priestley, J(ohn) B(oynton)

Gombrowicz, Witold 1904-1969CLC 4, 7, 11,
49; DAM DRAM
See also CA 19-20; 25-28R; CAP 2

Gomez de la Serna, Ramon 1888-1963CLC 9
See also CA 153; 116; HW

Goncharov, Ivan Alexandrovich 1812-1891
NCLC 1, 63

Goncourt, Edmond (Louis Antoine Huot) de
1822-1896 .... NCLC 7
See also DLB 123

Goncourt, Jules (Alfred Huot) de 1830-1870
NCLC 7
See also DLB 123

Gontier, Fernande 19(?)- ....CLC 50

Gonzalez Martinez, Enrique 1871-1952

Grenville, Pelham
See Wodehouse, P(elham) G(renville)
Greve, Felix Paul (Berthold Friedrich) 1879-
1948
See Grove, Frederick Philip
See also CA 104; 141; DAC; DAM MST
Grey, Zane 1872-1939 .. **TCLC 6; DAM POP**
See also CA 104; 132; DLB 9; MTCW 1
Grieg, (Johan) Nordahl (Brun) 1902-1943
TCLC 10
See also CA 107
Grieve, C(hristopher) M(urray) 1892-1978
CLC 11, 19; DAM POET
See also MacDiarmid, Hugh; Pteleon
See also CA 5-8R; 85-88; CANR 33; MTCW 1
Griffin, Gerald 1803-1840 .... **NCLC 7**
See also DLB 159
Griffin, John Howard 1920-1980 .... **CLC 68**
See also AITN 1; CA 1-4R; 101; CANR 2
Griffin, Peter 1942- .... **CLC 39**
See also CA 136
Griffith, D(avid Lewelyn) W(ark) 1875(?)-1948
TCLC 68
See also CA 119; 150
Griffith, Lawrence
See Griffith, D(avid Lewelyn) W(ark)
Griffiths, Trevor 1935- .... **CLC 13, 52**
See also CA 97-100; CANR 45; DLB 13
Griggs, Sutton Elbert 1872-1930(?)**TCLC 77**
See also CA 123; DLB 50
Grigson, Geoffrey (Edward Harvey) 1905-1985
CLC 7, 39
See also CA 25-28R; 118; CANR 20, 33; DLB
27; MTCW 1
Grillparzer, Franz 1791-1872 .... **NCLC 1**
See also DLB 133
Grimble, Reverend Charles James
See Eliot, T(homas) S(tearns)
Grimke, Charlotte L(ottie) Forten 1837(?)-1914
See Forten, Charlotte L.
See also BW 1; CA 117; 124; DAM MULT,
POET
Grimm, Jacob Ludwig Karl 1785-1863**NCLC
3**
See also DLB 90; MAICYA; SATA 22
Grimm, Wilhelm Karl 1786-1859 ...... **NCLC 3**
See also DLB 90; MAICYA; SATA 22
Grimmelshausen, Johann Jakob Christoffel von
1621-1676 .... **LC 6**
See also DLB 168
Grindel, Eugene 1895-1952
See Eluard, Paul
See also CA 104
Grisham, John 1955- ..... **CLC 84; DAM POP**
See also AAYA 14; CA 138; CANR 47, 69
Grossman, David 1954- .... **CLC 67**
See also CA 138
Grossman, Vasily (Semenovich) 1905-1964
CLC 41
See also CA 124; 130; MTCW 1
Grove, Frederick Philip .... **TCLC 4**
See also Greve, Felix Paul (Berthold Friedrich)
See also DLB 92
Grubb
See Crumb, R(obert)
Grumbach, Doris (Isaac) 1918-**CLC 13, 22, 64**
See also CA 5-8R; CAAS 2; CANR 9, 42, 70;
INT CANR-9
Grundtvig, Nicolai Frederik Severin 1783-1872
NCLC 1
Grunge
See Crumb, R(obert)
Grunwald, Lisa 1959- .... **CLC 44**

See also CA 120
Guare, John 1938- . **CLC 8, 14, 29, 67; DAM
DRAM**
See also CA 73-76; CANR 21, 69; DLB 7;
MTCW 1
Gudjonsson, Halldor Kiljan 1902-1998
See Laxness, Halldor
See also CA 103; 164
Guenter, Erich
See Eich, Guenter
Guest, Barbara 1920- .... **CLC 34**
See also CA 25-28R; CANR 11, 44; DLB 5,
193
Guest, Judith (Ann) 1936- . **CLC 8, 30; DAM
NOV, POP**
See also AAYA 7; CA 77-80; CANR 15; INT
CANR-15; MTCW 1
Guevara, Che .... **CLC 87; HLC**
See also Guevara (Serna), Ernesto
Guevara (Serna), Ernesto 1928-1967
See Guevara, Che
See also CA 127; 111; CANR 56; DAM MULT;
HW
Guild, Nicholas M. 1944- .... **CLC 33**
See also CA 93-96
Guillemin, Jacques
See Sartre, Jean-Paul
Guillen, Jorge 1893-1984 .... **CLC 11; DAM
MULT, POET**
See also CA 89-92; 112; DLB 108; HW
Guillen, Nicolas (Cristobal) 1902-1989 . **C L C
48, 79; BLC 2; DAM MST, MULT, POET;
HLC; PC 23**
See also BW 2; CA 116; 125; 129; HW
Guillevic, (Eugene) 1907- .... **CLC 33**
See also CA 93-96
Guillois
See Desnos, Robert
Guillois, Valentin
See Desnos, Robert
Guiney, Louise Imogen 1861-1920 **TCLC 41**
See also CA 160; DLB 54
Guiraldes, Ricardo (Guillermo) 1886-1927
TCLC 39
See also CA 131; HW; MTCW 1
Gumilev, Nikolai (Stepanovich) 1886-1921
TCLC 60
See also CA 165
Gunesekera, Romesh 1954- .... **CLC 91**
See also CA 159
Gunn, Bill .... **CLC 5**
See also Gunn, William Harrison
See also DLB 38
Gunn, Thom(son William) 1929-**CLC 3, 6, 18,
32, 81; DAM POET**
See also CA 17-20R; CANR 9, 33; CDBLB
1960 to Present; DLB 27; INT CANR-33;
MTCW 1
Gunn, William Harrison 1934(?)-1989
See Gunn, Bill
See also AITN 1; BW 1; CA 13-16R; 128;
CANR 12, 25
Gunnars, Kristjana 1948- .... **CLC 69**
See also CA 113; DLB 60
Gurdjieff, G(eorgei) I(vanovich) 1877(?)-1949
TCLC 71
See also CA 157
Gurganus, Allan 1947- ... **CLC 70; DAM POP**
See also BEST 90:1; CA 135
Gurney, A(lbert) R(amsdell), Jr. 1930- . **C L C
32, 50, 54; DAM DRAM**
See also CA 77-80; CANR 32, 64
Gurney, Ivor (Bertie) 1890-1937 ... **TCLC 33**

See also CA 167
Gurney, Peter
See Gurney, A(lbert) R(amsdell), Jr.
Guro, Elena 1877-1913 .... **TCLC 56**
Gustafson, James M(oody) 1925- .. **CLC 100**
See also CA 25-28R; CANR 37
Gustafson, Ralph (Barker) 1909- ..... **CLC 36**
See also CA 21-24R; CANR 8, 45; DLB 88
Gut, Gom
See Simenon, Georges (Jacques Christian)
Guterson, David 1956- .... **CLC 91**
See also CA 132
Guthrie, A(lfred) B(ertram), Jr. 1901-1991
CLC 23
See also CA 57-60; 134; CANR 24; DLB 6;
SATA 62; SATA-Obit 67
Guthrie, Isobel
See Grieve, C(hristopher) M(urray)
Guthrie, Woodrow Wilson 1912-1967
See Guthrie, Woody
See also CA 113; 93-96
Guthrie, Woody .... **CLC 35**
See also Guthrie, Woodrow Wilson
Guy, Rosa (Cuthbert) 1928- .... **CLC 26**
See also AAYA 4; BW 2; CA 17-20R; CANR
14, 34; CLR 13; DLB 33; JRDA; MAICYA;
SATA 14, 62
Gwendolyn
See Bennett, (Enoch) Arnold
H. D. .... **CLC 3, 8, 14, 31, 34, 73; PC 5**
See also Doolittle, Hilda
H. de V.
See Buchan, John
Haavikko, Paavo Juhani 1931- .. **CLC 18, 34**
See also CA 106
Habbema, Koos
See Heijermans, Herman
Habermas, Juergen 1929- .... **CLC 104**
See also CA 109
Habermas, Jurgen
See Habermas, Juergen
Hacker, Marilyn 1942- . **CLC 5, 9, 23, 72, 91;
DAM POET**
See also CA 77-80; CANR 68; DLB 120
Haeckel, Ernst Heinrich (Philipp August) 1834-
1919 .... **TCLC 83**
See also CA 157
Haggard, H(enry) Rider 1856-1925**TCLC 11**
See also CA 108; 148; DLB 70, 156, 174, 178;
SATA 16
Hagiosy, L.
See Larbaud, Valery (Nicolas)
Hagiwara Sakutaro 1886-1942**TCLC 60; PC
18**
Haig, Fenil
See Ford, Ford Madox
Haig-Brown, Roderick (Langmere) 1908-1976
CLC 21
See also CA 5-8R; 69-72; CANR 4, 38; CLR
31; DLB 88; MAICYA; SATA 12
Hailey, Arthur 1920-**CLC 5; DAM NOV, POP**
See also AITN 2; BEST 90:3; CA 1-4R; CANR
2, 36; DLB 88; DLBY 82; MTCW 1
Hailey, Elizabeth Forsythe 1938- ..... **CLC 40**
See also CA 93-96; CAAS 1; CANR 15, 48;
INT CANR-15
Haines, John (Meade) 1924- .... **CLC 58**
See also CA 17-20R; CANR 13, 34; DLB 5
Hakluyt, Richard 1552-1616 .... **LC 31**
Haldeman, Joe (William) 1943- .... **CLC 61**
See also CA 53-56; CAAS 25; CANR 6, 70,
72; DLB 8; INT CANR-6
Haley, Alex(ander Murray Palmer) 1921-1992

Herlihy, James Leo 1927-1993 .... CLC 6
    See also CA 1-4R; 143; CANR 2
Hermogenes fl. c. 175- .... CMLC 6
Hernandez, Jose 1834-1886 .... NCLC 17
Herodotus c. 484B.C.-429B.C. .... CMLC 17
    See also DLB 176
Herrick, Robert 1591-1674LC 13; DA; DAB;
        DAC; DAM MST, POP; PC 9
    See also DLB 126
Herring, Guilles
    See Somerville, Edith
Herriot, James 1916-1995CLC 12; DAM POP
    See also Wight, James Alfred
    See also AAYA 1; CA 148; CANR 40; SATA
        86
Herrmann, Dorothy 1941- .... CLC 44
    See also CA 107
Herrmann, Taffy
    See Herrmann, Dorothy
Hersey, John (Richard) 1914-1993CLC 1, 2, 7,
        9, 40, 81, 97; DAM POP
    See also CA 17-20R; 140; CANR 33; DLB 6,
        185; MTCW 1; SATA 25; SATA-Obit 76
Herzen, Aleksandr Ivanovich 1812-1870
        NCLC 10, 61
Herzl, Theodor 1860-1904 .... TCLC 36
    See also CA 168
Herzog, Werner 1942- .... CLC 16
    See also CA 89-92
Hesiod c. 8th cent. B.C.- .... CMLC 5
    See also DLB 176
Hesse, Hermann 1877-1962CLC 1, 2, 3, 6, 11,
        17, 25, 69; DA; DAB; DAC; DAM MST,
        NOV; SSC 9; WLC
    See also CA 17-18; CAP 2; DLB 66; MTCW 1;
        SATA 50
Hewes, Cady
    See De Voto, Bernard (Augustine)
Heyen, William 1940- .... CLC 13, 18
    See also CA 33-36R; CAAS 9; DLB 5
Heyerdahl, Thor 1914- .... CLC 26
    See also CA 5-8R; CANR 5, 22, 66; MTCW 1;
        SATA 2, 52
Heym, Georg (Theodor Franz Arthur) 1887-
        1912 .... TCLC 9
    See also CA 106
Heym, Stefan 1913- .... CLC 41
    See also CA 9-12R; CANR 4; DLB 69
Heyse, Paul (Johann Ludwig von) 1830-1914
        TCLC 8
    See also CA 104; DLB 129
Heyward, (Edwin) DuBose 1885-1940 T C L C
        59
    See also CA 108; 157; DLB 7, 9, 45; SATA 21
Hibbert, Eleanor Alice Burford 1906-1993
        CLC 7; DAM POP
    See also BEST 90:4; CA 17-20R; 140; CANR
        9, 28, 59; SATA 2; SATA-Obit 74
Hichens, Robert (Smythe) 1864-1950 . T C L C
        64
    See also CA 162; DLB 153
Higgins, George V(incent) 1939-CLC 4, 7, 10,
        18
    See also CA 77-80; CAAS 5; CANR 17, 51;
        DLB 2; DLBY 81; INT CANR-17; MTCW
        1
Higginson, Thomas Wentworth 1823-1911
        TCLC 36
    See also CA 162; DLB 1, 64
Highet, Helen
    See MacInnes, Helen (Clark)
Highsmith, (Mary) Patricia 1921-1995CLC 2,
        4, 14, 42, 102; DAM NOV, POP

    See also CA 1-4R; 147; CANR 1, 20, 48, 62;
        MTCW 1
Highwater, Jamake (Mamake) 1942(?)- C L C
        12
    See also AAYA 7; CA 65-68; CAAS 7; CANR
        10, 34; CLR 17; DLB 52; DLBY 85; JRDA;
        MAICYA; SATA 32, 69; SATA-Brief 30
Highway, Tomson 1951-CLC 92; DAC; DAM
        MULT
    See also CA 151; NNAL
Higuchi, Ichiyo 1872-1896 .... NCLC 49
Hijuelos, Oscar 1951-CLC 65; DAM MULT,
        POP; HLC
    See also AAYA 25; BEST 90:1; CA 123; CANR
        50; DLB 145; HW
Hikmet, Nazim 1902(?)-1963 .... CLC 40
    See also CA 141; 93-96
Hildegard von Bingen 1098-1179 . CMLC 20
    See also DLB 148
Hildesheimer, Wolfgang 1916-1991 ..CLC 49
    See also CA 101; 135; DLB 69, 124
Hill, Geoffrey (William) 1932- CLC 5, 8, 18,
        45; DAM POET
    See also CA 81-84; CANR 21; CDBLB 1960
        to Present; DLB 40; MTCW 1
Hill, George Roy 1921- .... CLC 26
    See also CA 110; 122
Hill, John
    See Koontz, Dean R(ay)
Hill, Susan (Elizabeth) 1942- .... CLC 4, 113;
        DAB; DAM MST, NOV
    See also CA 33-36R; CANR 29, 69; DLB 14,
        139; MTCW 1
Hillerman, Tony 1925- ..CLC 62; DAM POP
    See also AAYA 6; BEST 89:1; CA 29-32R;
        CANR 21, 42, 65; SATA 6
Hillesum, Etty 1914-1943 .... TCLC 49
    See also CA 137
Hilliard, Noel (Harvey) 1929- .... CLC 15
    See also CA 9-12R; CANR 7, 69
Hillis, Rick 1956- .... CLC 66
    See also CA 134
Hilton, James 1900-1954 .... TCLC 21
    See also CA 108; DLB 34, 77; SATA 34
Himes, Chester (Bomar) 1909-1984CLC 2, 4,
        7, 18, 58, 108; BLC 2; DAM MULT
    See also BW 2; CA 25-28R; 114; CANR 22;
        DLB 2, 76, 143; MTCW 1
Hinde, Thomas .... CLC 6, 11
    See also Chitty, Thomas Willes
Hindin, Nathan
    See Bloch, Robert (Albert)
Hine, (William) Daryl 1936- .... CLC 15
    See also CA 1-4R; CAAS 15; CANR 1, 20; DLB
        60
Hinkson, Katharine Tynan
    See Tynan, Katharine
Hinton, S(usan) E(loise) 1950- CLC 30, 111;
        DA; DAB; DAC; DAM MST, NOV
    See also AAYA 2; CA 81-84; CANR 32, 62;
        CLR 3, 23; JRDA; MAICYA; MTCW 1;
        SATA 19, 58
Hippius, Zinaida .... TCLC 9
    See also Gippius, Zinaida (Nikolayevna)
Hiraoka, Kimitake 1925-1970
    See Mishima, Yukio
    See also CA 97-100; 29-32R; DAM DRAM;
        MTCW 1
Hirsch, E(ric) D(onald), Jr. 1928- ..... CLC 79
    See also CA 25-28R; CANR 27, 51; DLB 67;
        INT CANR-27; MTCW 1
Hirsch, Edward 1950- .... CLC 31, 50
    See also CA 104; CANR 20, 42; DLB 120

Hitchcock, Alfred (Joseph) 1899-1980CLC 16
    See also AAYA 22; CA 159; 97-100; SATA 27;
        SATA-Obit 24
Hitler, Adolf 1889-1945 .... TCLC 53
    See also CA 117; 147
Hoagland, Edward 1932- .... CLC 28
    See also CA 1-4R; CANR 2, 31, 57; DLB 6;
        SATA 51
Hoban, Russell (Conwell) 1925- . CLC 7, 25;
        DAM NOV
    See also CA 5-8R; CANR 23, 37, 66; CLR 3;
        DLB 52; MAICYA; MTCW 1; SATA 1, 40,
        78
Hobbes, Thomas 1588-1679 .... LC 36
    See also DLB 151
Hobbs, Perry
    See Blackmur, R(ichard) P(almer)
Hobson, Laura Z(ametkin) 1900-1986CLC 7,
        25
    See also CA 17-20R; 118; CANR 55; DLB 28;
        SATA 52
Hochhuth, Rolf 1931-...CLC 4, 11, 18; DAM
        DRAM
    See also CA 5-8R; CANR 33; DLB 124; MTCW
        1
Hochman, Sandra 1936- .... CLC 3, 8
    See also CA 5-8R; DLB 5
Hochwaelder, Fritz 1911-1986CLC 36; DAM
        DRAM
    See also CA 29-32R; 120; CANR 42; MTCW 1
Hochwalder, Fritz
    See Hochwaelder, Fritz
Hocking, Mary (Eunice) 1921- .... CLC 13
    See also CA 101; CANR 18, 40
Hodgins, Jack 1938- .... CLC 23
    See also CA 93-96; DLB 60
Hodgson, William Hope 1877(?)-1918 T C L C
        13
    See also CA 111; 164; DLB 70, 153, 156, 178
Hoeg, Peter 1957- .... CLC 95
    See also CA 151
Hoffman, Alice 1952- ... CLC 51; DAM NOV
    See also CA 77-80; CANR 34, 66; MTCW 1
Hoffman, Daniel (Gerard) 1923-CLC 6, 13, 23
    See also CA 1-4R; CANR 4; DLB 5
Hoffman, Stanley 1944- .... CLC 5
    See also CA 77-80
Hoffman, William M(oses) 1939- ..... CLC 40
    See also CA 57-60; CANR 11, 71
Hoffmann, E(rnst) T(heodor) A(madeus) 1776-
        1822 .... NCLC 2; SSC 13
    See also DLB 90; SATA 27
Hofmann, Gert 1931- .... CLC 54
    See also CA 128
Hofmannsthal, Hugo von 1874-1929TCLC 11;
        DAM DRAM; DC 4
    See also CA 106; 153; DLB 81, 118
Hogan, Linda 1947-... CLC 73; DAM MULT
    See also CA 120; CANR 45; DLB 175; NNAL
Hogarth, Charles
    See Creasey, John
Hogarth, Emmett
    See Polonsky, Abraham (Lincoln)
Hogg, James 1770-1835 .... NCLC 4
    See also DLB 93, 116, 159
Holbach, Paul Henri Thiry Baron 1723-1789
        LC 14
Holberg, Ludvig 1684-1754 .... LC 6
Holden, Ursula 1921- .... CLC 18
    See also CA 101; CAAS 8; CANR 22
Holderlin, (Johann Christian) Friedrich 1770-
        1843 .... NCLC 16; PC 4
Holdstock, Robert

See Holdstock, Robert P.
Holdstock, Robert P. 1948- .... **CLC 39**
See also CA 131
Holland, Isabelle 1920- .... **CLC 21**
See also AAYA 11; CA 21-24R; CANR 10, 25,
47; JRDA; MAICYA; SATA 8, 70
Holland, Marcus
See Caldwell, (Janet Miriam) Taylor (Holland)
Hollander, John 1929- .... **CLC 2, 5, 8, 14**
See also CA 1-4R; CANR 1, 52; DLB 5; SATA
13
Hollander, Paul
See Silverberg, Robert
Holleran, Andrew 1943(?)- .... **CLC 38**
See also CA 144
Hollinghurst, Alan 1954- .... **CLC 55, 91**
See also CA 114
Hollis, Jim
See Summers, Hollis (Spurgeon, Jr.)
Holly, Buddy 1936-1959 .... **TCLC 65**
Holmes, Gordon
See Shiel, M(atthew) P(hipps)
Holmes, John
See Souster, (Holmes) Raymond
Holmes, John Clellon 1926-1988 ..... **CLC 56**
See also CA 9-12R; 125; CANR 4; DLB 16
Holmes, Oliver Wendell, Jr. 1841-1935**T C L C
77**
See also CA 114
Holmes, Oliver Wendell 1809-1894 **NCLC 14**
See also CDALB 1640-1865; DLB 1, 189;
SATA 34
Holmes, Raymond
See Souster, (Holmes) Raymond
Holt, Victoria
See Hibbert, Eleanor Alice Burford
Holub, Miroslav 1923- .... **CLC 4**
See also CA 21-24R; CANR 10
Homer c. 8th cent. B.C.- ... **CMLC 1, 16; DA;
DAB; DAC; DAM MST, POET; PC 23;
WLCS**
See also DLB 176
Hongo, Garrett Kaoru 1951- .... **PC 23**
See also CA 133; CAAS 22; DLB 120
Honig, Edwin 1919- .... **CLC 33**
See also CA 5-8R; CAAS 8; CANR 4, 45; DLB
5
Hood, Hugh (John Blagdon) 1928-**CLC 15, 28**
See also CA 49-52; CAAS 17; CANR 1, 33;
DLB 53
Hood, Thomas 1799-1845 .... **NCLC 16**
See also DLB 96
Hooker, (Peter) Jeremy 1941- .... **CLC 43**
See also CA 77-80; CANR 22; DLB 40
hooks, bell .... **CLC 94; BLCS**
See also Watkins, Gloria
Hope, A(lec) D(erwent) 1907- ...... **CLC 3, 51**
See also CA 21-24R; CANR 33; MTCW 1
Hope, Anthony 1863-1933 .... **TCLC 83**
See also CA 157; DLB 153, 156
Hope, Brian
See Creasey, John
Hope, Christopher (David Tully) 1944- **C L C
52**
See also CA 106; CANR 47; SATA 62
Hopkins, Gerard Manley 1844-1889 .. **N C L C
17; DA; DAB; DAC; DAM MST, POET;
PC 15; WLC**
See also CDBLB 1890-1914; DLB 35, 57
Hopkins, John (Richard) 1931- .... **CLC 4**
See also CA 85-88
Hopkins, Pauline Elizabeth 1859-1930**T C L C
28; BLC 2; DAM MULT**

See also BW 2; CA 141; DLB 50
Hopkinson, Francis 1737-1791 .... **LC 25**
See also DLB 31
Hopley-Woolrich, Cornell George 1903-1968
See Woolrich, Cornell
See also CA 13-14; CANR 58; CAP 1
Horatio
See Proust, (Valentin-Louis-George-Eugene-)
Marcel
Horgan, Paul (George Vincent O'Shaughnessy)
1903-1995 .... **CLC 9, 53; DAM NOV**
See also CA 13-16R; 147; CANR 9, 35; DLB
102; DLBY 85; INT CANR-9; MTCW 1;
SATA 13; SATA-Obit 84
Horn, Peter
See Kuttner, Henry
Hornem, Horace Esq.
See Byron, George Gordon (Noel)
**Horney, Karen (Clementine Theodore
Danielsen)** 1885-1952 .... **TCLC 71**
See also CA 114; 165
Hornung, E(rnest) W(illiam) 1866-1921
TCLC 59
See also CA 108; 160; DLB 70
Horovitz, Israel (Arthur) 1939-**CLC 56; DAM
DRAM**
See also CA 33-36R; CANR 46, 59; DLB 7
Horvath, Odon von
See Horvath, Oedoen von
See also DLB 85, 124
Horvath, Oedoen von 1901-1938 ... **TCLC 45**
See also Horvath, Odon von
See also CA 118
Horwitz, Julius 1920-1986 .... **CLC 14**
See also CA 9-12R; 119; CANR 12
Hospital, Janette Turner 1942- .... **CLC 42**
See also CA 108; CANR 48
Hostos, E. M. de
See Hostos (y Bonilla), Eugenio Maria de
Hostos, Eugenio M. de
See Hostos (y Bonilla), Eugenio Maria de
Hostos, Eugenio Maria
See Hostos (y Bonilla), Eugenio Maria de
Hostos (y Bonilla), Eugenio Maria de 1839-1903
TCLC 24
See also CA 123; 131; HW
Houdini
See Lovecraft, H(oward) P(hillips)
Hougan, Carolyn 1943-...................... **CLC 34**
See also CA 139
Household, Geoffrey (Edward West) 1900-1988
CLC 11
See also CA 77-80; 126; CANR 58; DLB 87;
SATA 14; SATA-Obit 59
Housman, A(lfred) E(dward) 1859-1936
**TCLC 1, 10; DA; DAB; DAC; DAM MST,
POET; PC 2; WLCS**
See also CA 104; 125; DLB 19; MTCW 1
Housman, Laurence 1865-1959 .... **TCLC 7**
See also CA 106; 155; DLB 10; SATA 25
Howard, Elizabeth Jane 1923-..... **CLC 7, 29**
See also CA 5-8R; CANR 8, 62
Howard, Maureen 1930-......... **CLC 5, 14, 46**
See also CA 53-56; CANR 31; DLBY 83; INT
CANR-31; MTCW 1
Howard, Richard 1929- .... **CLC 7, 10, 47**
See also AITN 1; CA 85-88; CANR 25; DLB 5;
INT CANR-25
Howard, Robert E(rvin) 1906-1936 **TCLC 8**
See also CA 105; 157
Howard, Warren F.
See Pohl, Frederik
Howe, Fanny (Quincy) 1940- .... **CLC 47**

See also CA 117; CAAS 27; CANR 70; SATA-
Brief 52
Howe, Irving 1920-1993 .... **CLC 85**
See also CA 9-12R; 141; CANR 21, 50; DLB
67; MTCW 1
Howe, Julia Ward 1819-1910 .... **TCLC 21**
See also CA 117; DLB 1, 189
Howe, Susan 1937- .... **CLC 72**
See also CA 160; DLB 120
Howe, Tina 1937- .... **CLC 48**
See also CA 109
Howell, James 1594(?)-1666 .... **LC 13**
See also DLB 151
Howells, W. D.
See Howells, William Dean
Howells, William D.
See Howells, William Dean
Howells, William Dean 1837-1920**TCLC 7, 17,
41**
See also CA 104; 134; CDALB 1865-1917;
DLB 12, 64, 74, 79, 189
Howes, Barbara 1914-1996 .... **CLC 15**
See also CA 9-12R; 151; CAAS 3; CANR 53;
SATA 5
Hrabal, Bohumil 1914-1997 .... **CLC 13, 67**
See also CA 106; 156; CAAS 12; CANR 57
Hroswitha of Gandersheim c. 935-c. 1002
CMLC 29
See also DLB 148
Hsun, Lu
See Lu Hsun
Hubbard, L(afayette) Ron(ald) 1911-1986
CLC 43; DAM POP
See also CA 77-80; 118; CANR 52
Huch, Ricarda (Octavia) 1864-1947**TCLC 13**
See also CA 111; DLB 66
Huddle, David 1942- .... **CLC 49**
See also CA 57-60; CAAS 20; DLB 130
Hudson, Jeffrey
See Crichton, (John) Michael
Hudson, W(illiam) H(enry) 1841-1922**T C L C
29**
See also CA 115; DLB 98, 153, 174; SATA 35
Hueffer, Ford Madox
See Ford, Ford Madox
Hughart, Barry 1934- .... **CLC 39**
See also CA 137
Hughes, Colin
See Creasey, John
Hughes, David (John) 1930- .... **CLC 48**
See also CA 116; 129; DLB 14
Hughes, Edward James
See Hughes, Ted
See also DAM MST, POET
Hughes, (James) Langston 1902-1967**CLC 1,
5, 10, 15, 35, 44, 108; BLC 2; DA; DAB;
DAC; DAM DRAM, MST, MULT, POET;
DC 3; PC 1; SSC 6; WLC**
See also AAYA 12; BW 1; CA 1-4R; 25-28R;
CANR 1, 34; CDALB 1929-1941; CLR 17;
DLB 4, 7, 48, 51, 86; JRDA; MAICYA;
MTCW 1; SATA 4, 33
Hughes, Richard (Arthur Warren) 1900-1976
CLC 1, 11; DAM NOV
See also CA 5-8R; 65-68; CANR 4; DLB 15,
161; MTCW 1; SATA 8; SATA-Obit 25
Hughes, Ted 1930-**CLC 2, 4, 9, 14, 37; DAB;
DAC; PC 7**
See also Hughes, Edward James
See also CA 1-4R; CANR 1, 33, 66; CLR 3;
DLB 40, 161; MAICYA; MTCW 1; SATA
49; SATA-Brief 27
Hugo, Richard F(ranklin) 1923-1982 **CLC 6,**

33; MTCW 1

Jones, James 1921-1977 ...... CLC 1, 3, 10, 39
See also AITN 1, 2; CA 1-4R; 69-72; CANR 6;
DLB 2, 143; DLBD 17; MTCW 1

Jones, John J.
See Lovecraft, H(oward) P(hillips)

Jones, LeRoi .... CLC 1, 2, 3, 5, 10, 14
See also Baraka, Amiri

Jones, Louis B. .... CLC 65
See also CA 141

Jones, Madison (Percy, Jr.) 1925- .... CLC 4
See also CA 13-16R; CAAS 11; CANR 7, 54;
DLB 152

Jones, Mervyn 1922- .... CLC 10, 52
See also CA 45-48; CAAS 5; CANR 1; MTCW
1

Jones, Mick 1956(?)- .... CLC 30

Jones, Nettie (Pearl) 1941- .... CLC 34
See also BW 2; CA 137; CAAS 20

Jones, Preston 1936-1979 .... CLC 10
See also CA 73-76; 89-92; DLB 7

Jones, Robert F(rancis) 1934- .... CLC 7
See also CA 49-52; CANR 2, 61

Jones, Rod 1953- .... CLC 50
See also CA 128

Jones, Terence Graham Parry 1942- CLC 21
See also Jones, Terry; Monty Python
See also CA 112; 116; CANR 35; INT 116

Jones, Terry
See Jones, Terence Graham Parry
See also SATA 67; SATA-Brief 51

Jones, Thom 1945(?)- .... CLC 81
See also CA 157

Jong, Erica 1942- CLC 4, 6, 8, 18, 83; DAM
NOV, POP
See also AITN 1; BEST 90:2; CA 73-76; CANR
26, 52; DLB 2, 5, 28, 152; INT CANR-26;
MTCW 1

Jonson, Ben(jamin) 1572(?)-1637 .. LC 6, 33;
DA; DAB; DAC; DAM DRAM, MST,
POET; DC 4; PC 17; WLC
See also CDBLB Before 1660; DLB 62, 121

Jordan, June 1936-CLC 5, 11, 23, 114; BLCS;
DAM MULT, POET
See also AAYA 2; BW 2; CA 33-36R; CANR
25, 70; CLR 10; DLB 38; MAICYA; MTCW
1; SATA 4

Jordan, Neil (Patrick) 1950- .... CLC 110
See also CA 124; 130; CANR 54; INT 130

Jordan, Pat(rick M.) 1941- .... CLC 37
See also CA 33-36R

Jorgensen, Ivar
See Ellison, Harlan (Jay)

Jorgenson, Ivar
See Silverberg, Robert

Josephus, Flavius c. 37-100 .... CMLC 13

Josipovici, Gabriel 1940- .... CLC 6, 43
See also CA 37-40R; CAAS 8; CANR 47; DLB
14

Joubert, Joseph 1754-1824 .... NCLC 9

Jouve, Pierre Jean 1887-1976 .... CLC 47
See also CA 65-68

Jovine, Francesco 1902-1950 .... TCLC 79

Joyce, James (Augustine Aloysius) 1882-1941
TCLC 3, 8, 16, 35, 52; DA; DAB; DAC;
DAM MST, NOV, POET; PC 22; SSC 3,
26; WLC
See also CA 104; 126; CDBLB 1914-1945;
DLB 10, 19, 36, 162; MTCW 1

Jozsef, Attila 1905-1937 .... TCLC 22
See also CA 116

Juana Ines de la Cruz 1651(?)-1695LC 5; PC
24

Judd, Cyril
See Kornbluth, C(yril) M.; Pohl, Frederik

Julian of Norwich 1342(?)-1416(?) .... LC 6
See also DLB 146

Junger, Sebastian 1962- .... CLC 109
See also CA 165

Juniper, Alex
See Hospital, Janette Turner

Junius
See Luxemburg, Rosa

Just, Ward (Swift) 1935- .... CLC 4, 27
See also CA 25-28R; CANR 32; INT CANR-
32

Justice, Donald (Rodney) 1925- .. CLC 6, 19,
102; DAM POET
See also CA 5-8R; CANR 26, 54; DLBY 83;
INT CANR-26

Juvenal .... CMLC 8
See also Juvenalis, Decimus Junius

Juvenalis, Decimus Junius 55(?)-c. 127(?)
See Juvenal

Juvenis
See Bourne, Randolph S(illiman)

Kacew, Romain 1914-1980
See Gary, Romain
See also CA 108; 102

Kadare, Ismail 1936- .... CLC 52
See also CA 161

Kadohata, Cynthia ...,......................... CLC 59
See also CA 140

Kafka, Franz 1883-1924TCLC 2, 6, 13, 29, 47,
53; DA; DAB; DAC; DAM MST, NOV;
SSC 5, 29; WLC
See also CA 105; 126; DLB 81; MTCW 1

Kahanovitsch, Pinkhes
See Der Nister

Kahn, Roger 1927- .... CLC 30
See also CA 25-28R; CANR 44, 69; DLB 171;
SATA 37

Kain, Saul
See Sassoon, Siegfried (Lorraine)

Kaiser, Georg 1878-1945 .... TCLC 9
See also CA 106; DLB 124

Kaletski, Alexander 1946- .... CLC 39
See also CA 118; 143

Kalidasa fl. c. 400- .... CMLC 9; PC 22

Kallman, Chester (Simon) 1921-1975 CLC 2
See also CA 45-48; 53-56; CANR 3

Kaminsky, Melvin 1926-
See Brooks, Mel
See also CA 65-68; CANR 16

Kaminsky, Stuart M(elvin) 1934- ..... CLC 59
See also CA 73-76; CANR 29, 53

Kane, Francis
See Robbins, Harold

Kane, Paul
See Simon, Paul (Frederick)

Kane, Wilson
See Bloch, Robert (Albert)

Kanin, Garson 1912- .... CLC 22
See also AITN 1; CA 5-8R; CANR 7; DLB 7

Kaniuk, Yoram 1930- .... CLC 19
See also CA 134

Kant, Immanuel 1724-1804 ..... NCLC 27, 67
See also DLB 94

Kantor, MacKinlay 1904-1977 .... CLC 7
See also CA 61-64; 73-76; CANR 60, 63; DLB
9, 102

Kaplan, David Michael 1946- .... CLC 50

Kaplan, James 1951- .... CLC 59
See also CA 135

Karageorge, Michael
See Anderson, Poul (William)

Karamzin, Nikolai Mikhailovich 1766-1826
NCLC 3
See also DLB 150

Karapanou, Margarita 1946- .... CLC 13
See also CA 101

Karinthy, Frigyes 1887-1938 .... TCLC 47

Karl, Frederick R(obert) 1927- .... CLC 34
See also CA 5-8R; CANR 3, 44

Kastel, Warren
See Silverberg, Robert

Kataev, Evgeny Petrovich 1903-1942
See Petrov, Evgeny
See also CA 120

Kataphusin
See Ruskin, John

Katz, Steve 1935- .... CLC 47
See also CA 25-28R; CAAS 14, 64; CANR 12;
DLBY 83

Kauffman, Janet 1945- .... CLC 42
See also CA 117; CANR 43; DLBY 86

Kaufman, Bob (Garnell) 1925-1986 CLC 49
See also BW 1; CA 41-44R; 118; CANR 22;
DLB 16, 41

Kaufman, George S. 1889-1961CLC 38; DAM
DRAM
See also CA 108; 93-96; DLB 7; INT 108

Kaufman, Sue .... CLC 3, 8
See also Barondess, Sue K(aufman)

Kavafis, Konstantinos Petrou 1863-1933
See Cavafy, C(onstantine) P(eter)
See also CA 104

Kavan, Anna 1901-1968 .... CLC 5, 13, 82
See also CA 5-8R; CANR 6, 57; MTCW 1

Kavanagh, Dan
See Barnes, Julian (Patrick)

Kavanagh, Patrick (Joseph) 1904-1967 C L C
22
See also CA 123; 25-28R; DLB 15, 20; MTCW
1

Kawabata, Yasunari 1899-1972 CLC 2, 5, 9,
18, 107; DAM MULT; SSC 17
See also CA 93-96; 33-36R; DLB 180

Kaye, M(ary) M(argaret) 1909- .... CLC 28
See also CA 89-92; CANR 24, 60; MTCW 1;
SATA 62

Kaye, Mollie
See Kaye, M(ary) M(argaret)

Kaye-Smith, Sheila 1887-1956 .... TCLC 20
See also CA 118; DLB 36

Kaymor, Patrice Maguilene
See Senghor, Leopold Sedar

Kazan, Elia 1909- .... CLC 6, 16, 63
See also CA 21-24R; CANR 32

Kazantzakis, Nikos 1883(?)-1957 TCLC 2, 5,
33
See also CA 105; 132; MTCW 1

Kazin, Alfred 1915- .... CLC 34, 38
See also CA 1-4R; CAAS 7; CANR 1, 45; DLB
67

Keane, Mary Nesta (Skrine) 1904-1996
See Keane, Molly
See also CA 108; 114; 151

Keane, Molly .... CLC 31
See also Keane, Mary Nesta (Skrine)
See also INT 114

Keates, Jonathan 1946(?)- .... CLC 34
See also CA 163

Keaton, Buster 1895-1966 .... CLC 20

Keats, John 1795-1821NCLC 8, 73; DA; DAB;
DAC; DAM MST, POET; PC 1; WLC
See also CDBLB 1789-1832; DLB 96, 110

Keene, Donald 1922- .... CLC 34
See also CA 1-4R; CANR 5

See also CA 33-36R; DLB 5

Klein, A(braham) M(oses) 1909-1972 CLC 19;
DAB; DAC; DAM MST
See also CA 101; 37-40R; DLB 68

Klein, Norma 1938-1989 .... CLC 30
See also AAYA 2; CA 41-44R; 128; CANR 15,
37; CLR 2, 19; INT CANR-15; JRDA;
MAICYA; SAAS 1; SATA 7, 57

Klein, T(heodore) E(ibon) D(onald) 1947-
CLC 34
See also CA 119; CANR 44

Kleist, Heinrich von 1777-1811 NCLC 2, 37;
DAM DRAM; SSC 22
See also DLB 90

Klima, Ivan 1931- .... CLC 56; DAM NOV
See also CA 25-28R; CANR 17, 50

Klimentov, Andrei Platonovich 1899-1951
See Platonov, Andrei
See also CA 108

Klinger, Friedrich Maximilian von 1752-1831
NCLC 1
See also DLB 94

Klingsor the Magician
See Hartmann, Sadakichi

Klopstock, Friedrich Gottlieb 1724-1803
NCLC 11
See also DLB 97

Knapp, Caroline 1959- .... CLC 99
See also CA 154

Knebel, Fletcher 1911-1993 .... CLC 14
See also AITN 1; CA 1-4R; 140; CAAS 3;
CANR 1, 36; SATA 36; SATA-Obit 75

Knickerbocker, Diedrich
See Irving, Washington

Knight, Etheridge 1931-1991 CLC 40; BLC 2;
DAM POET; PC 14
See also BW 1, CA 21-24R; 133; CANR 23;
DLB 41

Knight, Sarah Kemble 1666-1727 .... LC 7
See also DLB 24, 200

Knister, Raymond 1899-1932 .... TCLC 56
See also DLB 68

Knowles, John 1926- .. CLC 1, 4, 10, 26; DA;
DAC; DAM MST, NOV
See also AAYA 10; CA 17-20R; CANR 40;
CDALB 1968-1988; DLB 6; MTCW 1;
SATA 8, 89

Knox, Calvin M.
See Silverberg, Robert

Knox, John c. 1505-1572 .... LC 37
See also DLB 132

Knye, Cassandra
See Disch, Thomas M(ichael)

Koch, C(hristopher) J(ohn) 1932- ... CLC 42
See also CA 127

Koch, Christopher
See Koch, C(hristopher) J(ohn)

Koch, Kenneth 1925- .... CLC 5, 8, 44; DAM
POET
See also CA 1-4R; CANR 6, 36, 57; DLB 5;
INT CANR-36; SATA 65

Kochanowski, Jan 1530-1584 .... LC 10

Kock, Charles Paul de 1794-1871 .. NCLC 16

Koda Shigeyuki 1867-1947
See Rohan, Koda
See also CA 121

Koestler, Arthur 1905-1983 CLC 1, 3, 6, 8, 15,
33
See also CA 1-4R; 109; CANR 1, 33; CDBLB
1945-1960; DLBY 83; MTCW 1

Kogawa, Joy Nozomi 1935- .. CLC 78; DAC;
DAM MST, MULT
See also CA 101; CANR 19, 62; SATA 99

Kohout, Pavel 1928- .... CLC 13
See also CA 45-48; CANR 3

Koizumi, Yakumo
See Hearn, (Patricio) Lafcadio (Tessima Carlos)

Kolmar, Gertrud 1894-1943 .... TCLC 40
See also CA 167

Komunyakaa, Yusef 1947- CLC 86, 94; BLCS
See also CA 147; DLB 120

Konrad, George
See Konrad, Gyoergy

Konrad, Gyoergy 1933- .... CLC 4, 10, 73
See also CA 85-88

Konwicki, Tadeusz 1926- .... CLC 8, 28, 54
See also CA 101; CAAS 9; CANR 39, 59;
MTCW 1

Koontz, Dean R(ay) 1945- ..... CLC 78; DAM
NOV, POP
See also AAYA 9; BEST 89:3, 90:2; CA 108;
CANR 19, 36, 52; MTCW 1; SATA 92

Kopernik, Mikolaj
See Copernicus, Nicolaus

Kopit, Arthur (Lee) 1937- CLC 1, 18, 33; DAM
DRAM
See also AITN 1; CA 81-84; CABS 3; DLB 7;
MTCW 1

Kops, Bernard 1926- .... CLC 4
See also CA 5-8R; DLB 13

Kornbluth, C(yril) M. 1923-1958 .... TCLC 8
See also CA 105; 160; DLB 8

Korolenko, V. G.
See Korolenko, Vladimir Galaktionovich

Korolenko, Vladimir
See Korolenko, Vladimir Galaktionovich

Korolenko, Vladimir G.
See Korolenko, Vladimir Galaktionovich

Korolenko, Vladimir Galaktionovich 1853-
1921 .... TCLC 22
See also CA 121

Korzybski, Alfred (Habdank Skarbek) 1879-
1950 .... TCLC 61
See also CA 123; 160

Kosinski, Jerzy (Nikodem) 1933-1991 CLC 1,
2, 3, 6, 10, 15, 53, 70; DAM NOV
See also CA 17-20R; 134; CANR 9, 46; DLB
2; DLBY 82; MTCW 1

Kostelanetz, Richard (Cory) 1940- ... CLC 28
See also CA 13-16R; CAAS 8; CANR 38

Kostrowitzki, Wilhelm Apollinaris de 1880-
1918
See Apollinaire, Guillaume
See also CA 104

Kotlowitz, Robert 1924- .... CLC 4
See also CA 33-36R; CANR 36

Kotzebue, August (Friedrich Ferdinand) von
1761-1819 .... NCLC 25
See also DLB 94

Kotzwinkle, William 1938- ..... CLC 5, 14, 35
See also CA 45-48; CANR 3, 44; CLR 6; DLB
173; MAICYA; SATA 24, 70

Kowna, Stancy
See Szymborska, Wislawa

Kozol, Jonathan 1936- .... CLC 17
See also CA 61-64; CANR 16, 45

Kozoll, Michael 1940(?)- .... CLC 35

Kramer, Kathryn 19(?)- .... CLC 34

Kramer, Larry 1935- CLC 42; DAM POP; DC
8
See also CA 124; 126, CANR 60

Krasicki, Ignacy 1735-1801 .... NCLC 8

Krasinski, Zygmunt 1812-1859 .... NCLC 4

Kraus, Karl 1874-1936 .... TCLC 5
See also CA 104; DLB 118

Kreve (Mickevicius), Vincas 1882-1954 TCLC
27

Kristeva, Julia 1941- .... CLC 77
See also CA 154

Kristofferson, Kris 1936- .... CLC 26
See also CA 104

Krizanc, John 1956- .... CLC 57

Krleza, Miroslav 1893-1981 .... CLC 8, 114
See also CA 97-100; 105; CANR 50; DLB 147

Kroetsch, Robert 1927- CLC 5, 23, 57; DAC;
DAM POET
See also CA 17-20R; CANR 8, 38; DLB 53;
MTCW 1

Kroetz, Franz
See Kroetz, Franz Xaver

Kroetz, Franz Xaver 1946- .... CLC 41
See also CA 130

Kroker, Arthur (W.) 1945- .... CLC 77
See also CA 161

Kropotkin, Peter (Aleksieevich) 1842-1921
TCLC 36
See also CA 119

Krotkov, Yuri 1917- .... CLC 19
See also CA 102

Krumb
See Crumb, R(obert)

Krumgold, Joseph (Quincy) 1908-1980 C L C
12
See also CA 9-12R; 101; CANR 7; MAICYA;
SATA 1, 48; SATA-Obit 23

Krumwitz
See Crumb, R(obert)

Krutch, Joseph Wood 1893-1970 ..... CLC 24
See also CA 1-4R; 25-28R; CANR 4; DLB 63

Krutzch, Gus
See Eliot, T(homas) S(tearns)

Krylov, Ivan Andreevich 1768(?)-1844 N C L C
1
See also DLB 150

Kubin, Alfred (Leopold Isidor) 1877-1959
TCLC 23
See also CA 112; 149; DLB 81

Kubrick, Stanley 1928- .... CLC 16
See also CA 81-84; CANR 33; DLB 26

Kumin, Maxine (Winokur) 1925- CLC 5, 13,
28; DAM POET; PC 15
See also AITN 2; CA 1-4R; CAAS 8; CANR 1,
21, 69; DLB 5; MTCW 1; SATA 12

Kundera, Milan 1929- .. CLC 4, 9, 19, 32, 68,
115; DAM NOV; SSC 24
See also AAYA 2; CA 85-88; CANR 19, 52;
MTCW 1

Kunene, Mazisi (Raymond) 1930- ... CLC 85
See also BW 1; CA 125; DLB 117

Kunitz, Stanley (Jasspon) 1905- CLC 6, 11, 14;
PC 19
See also CA 41-44R; CANR 26, 57; DLB 48;
INT CANR-26; MTCW 1

Kunze, Reiner 1933- .... CLC 10
See also CA 93-96; DLB 75

Kuprin, Aleksandr Ivanovich 1870-1938
TCLC 5
See also CA 104

Kureishi, Hanif 1954(?)- .... CLC 64
See also CA 139; DLB 194

Kurosawa, Akira 1910- CLC 16; DAM MULT
See also AAYA 11; CA 101; CANR 46

Kushner, Tony 1957(?)- CLC 81; DAM DRAM
See also CA 144

Kuttner, Henry 1915-1958 .... TCLC 10
See also Vance, Jack
See also CA 107; 157; DLB 8

Kuzma, Greg 1944- .... CLC 7
See also CA 33-36R; CANR 70

Kuzmin, Mikhail 1872(?)-1936 ...... **TCLC 40**

Kyd, Thomas 1558-1594LC 22; **DAM DRAM;
DC 3**
See also DLB 62

Kyprianos, Iossif
See Samarakis. Antonis

La Bruyere, Jean de 1645-1696 .... **LC 17**

Lacan, Jacques (Marie Emile) 1901-1981
CLC 75
See also CA 121: 104

Laclos, Pierre Ambroise Francois Choderlos de
1741-1803 .... **NCLC 4**

Lacolere, Francois
See Aragon. Louis

La Colere, Francois
See Aragon. Louis

La Deshabilleuse
See Simenon. Georges (Jacques Christian)

Lady Gregory
See Gregory. Isabella Augusta (Persse)

Lady of Quality, A
See Bagnold. Enid

La Fayette, Marie (Madelaine Pioche de la
Vergne Comtes 1634-1693 .... **LC 2**

Lafayette, Rene
See Hubbard. L(afayette) Ron(ald)

Laforgue, Jules 1860-1887NCLC 5, 53; PC 14;
SSC 20

Lagerkvist, Paer (Fabian) 1891-1974 CLC 7,
10, 13, 54; **DAM DRAM, NOV**
See also Lagerkvist, Par
See also CA 85-88; 49-52; MTCW 1

Lagerkvist, Par .... **SSC 12**
See also Lagerkvist. Paer (Fabian)

Lagerloef, Selma (Ottiliana Lovisa) 1858-1940
TCLC 4, 36
See also Lagerlof, Selma (Ottiliana Lovisa)
See also CA 108; SATA 15

Lagerlof, Selma (Ottiliana Lovisa)
See Lagerloef. Selma (Ottiliana Lovisa)
See also CLR 7; SATA 15

La Guma, (Justin) Alex(ander) 1925-1985
CLC 19; BLCS; DAM NOV
See also BW 1; CA 49-52; 118; CANR 25; DLB
117; MTCW 1

Laidlaw, A. K.
See Grieve. C(hristopher) M(urray)

Lainez, Manuel Mujica
See Mujica Lainez, Manuel
See also HW

Laing, R(onald) D(avid) 1927-1989 . CLC 95
See also CA 107; 129; CANR 34; MTCW 1

Lamartine, Alphonse (Marie Louis Prat) de
1790-1869NCLC 11; **DAM POET; PC 16**

Lamb, Charles 1775-1834..... NCLC 10; DA;
DAB; DAC; DAM MST; WLC
See also CDBLB 1789-1832; DLB 93. 107, 163;
SATA 17

Lamb, Lady Caroline 1785-1828 ... NCLC 38
See also DLB 116

Lamming, George (William) 1927- CLC 2, 4,
66; **BLC 2; DAM MULT**
See also BW 2; CA 85-88; CANR 26; DLB 125;
MTCW 1

L'Amour, Louis (Dearborn) 1908-1988 . C L C
25, 55; **DAM NOV, POP**
See also AAYA 16; AITN 2; BEST 89:2; CA 1-
4R; 125; CANR 3. 25. 40; DLBY 80; MTCW
1

Lampedusa, Giuseppe (Tomasi) di 1896-1957
TCLC 13
See also Tomasi di Lampedusa, Giuseppe
See also CA 164; DLB 177

Lampman, Archibald 1861-1899 ... **NCLC 25**
See also DLB 92

Lancaster, Bruce 1896-1963 .... **CLC 36**
See also CA 9-10; CANR 70; CAP 1; SATA 9

Lanchester, John .... **CLC 99**

Landau, Mark Alexandrovich
See Aldanov. Mark (Alexandrovich)

Landau-Aldanov, Mark Alexandrovich
See Aldanov. Mark (Alexandrovich)

Landis, Jerry
See Simon, Paul (Frederick)

Landis, John 1950- .... **CLC 26**
See also CA 112; 122

Landolfi, Tommaso 1908-1979 .... **CLC 11, 49**
See also CA 127; 117; DLB 177

Landon, Letitia Elizabeth 1802-1838 . N C L C
15
See also DLB 96

Landor, Walter Savage 1775-1864 **NCLC 14**
See also DLB 93, 107

Landwirth, Heinz 1927-
See Lind. Jakov
See also CA 9-12R; CANR 7

Lane, Patrick 1939- .... CLC 25; **DAM POET**
See also CA 97-100; CANR 54; DLB 53; INT
97-100

Lang, Andrew 1844-1912 .... **TCLC 16**
See also CA 114; 137; DLB 98. 141, 184;
MAICYA; SATA 16

Lang, Fritz 1890-1976 .... **CLC 20, 103**
See also CA 77-80; 69-72; CANR 30

Lange, John
See Crichton. (John) Michael

Langer, Elinor 1939- .... **CLC 34**
See also CA 121

Langland, William 1330(?)-1400(?) ... LC 19;
DA; DAB; DAC; DAM MST, POET
See also DLB 146

Langstaff, Launcelot
See Irving. Washington

Lanier, Sidney 1842-1881 ..... NCLC 6; **DAM
POET**
See also DLB 64; DLBD 13; MAICYA; SATA
18

Lanyer, Aemilia 1569-1645 .... **LC 10, 30**
See also DLB 121

Lao-Tzu
See Lao Tzu

Lao Tzu fl. 6th cent. B.C.- .... **CMLC 7**

Lapine, James (Elliot) 1949- .... **CLC 39**
See also CA 123; 130; CANR 54; INT 130

Larbaud, Valery (Nicolas) 1881-1957**TCLC 9**
See also CA 106; 152

Lardner, Ring
See Lardner. Ring(gold) W(ilmer)

Lardner, Ring W., Jr.
See Lardner. Ring(gold) W(ilmer)

Lardner, Ring(gold) W(ilmer) 1885-1933
TCLC 2, 14; SSC 32
See also CA 104; 131; CDALB 1917-1929;
DLB 11, 25. 86; DLBD 16; MTCW 1

Laredo, Betty
See Codrescu. Andrei

Larkin, Maia
See Wojciechowska. Maia (Teresa)

Larkin, Philip (Arthur) 1922-1985CLC 3, 5, 8,
9, 13, 18, 33, 39, 64; **DAB; DAM MST,
POET; PC 21**
See also CA 5-8R; 117; CANR 24, 62; CDBLB
1960 to Present; DLB 27; MTCW 1

Larra (y Sanchez de Castro), Mariano Jose de
1809-1837 .... **NCLC 17**

Larsen, Eric 1941- .... **CLC 55**

See also CA 132

Larsen, Nella 1891-1964 .... CLC 37; BLC 2;
DAM MULT
See also BW 1; CA 125; DLB 51

Larson, Charles R(aymond) 1938- ... **CLC 31**
See also CA 53-56; CANR 4

Larson, Jonathan 1961-1996 .... **CLC 99**
See also CA 156

Las Casas, Bartolome de 1474-1566... **LC 31**

Lasch, Christopher 1932-1994 .... **CLC 102**
See also CA 73-76; 144; CANR 25; MTCW 1

Lasker-Schueler, Else 1869-1945 ... **TCLC 57**
See also DLB 66. 124

Laski, Harold 1893-1950 .... **TCLC 79**

Latham, Jean Lee 1902-1995 .... **CLC 12**
See also AITN 1; CA 5-8R; CANR 7; CLR 50;
MAICYA; SATA 2, 68

Latham, Mavis
See Clark. Mavis Thorpe

Lathen, Emma .... **CLC 2**
See also Hennissart, Martha; Latsis, Mary J(ane)

Lathrop, Francis
See Leiber. Fritz (Reuter. Jr.)

Latsis, Mary J(ane) 1927(?)-1997
See Lathen. Emma
See also CA 85-88; 162

Lattimore, Richmond (Alexander) 1906-1984
CLC 3
See also CA 1-4R; 112; CANR 1

Laughlin, James 1914-1997 .... **CLC 49**
See also CA 21-24R; 162; CAAS 22; CANR 9,
47; DLB 48; DLBY 96, 97

Laurence, (Jean) Margaret (Wemyss) 1926-
1987 .. CLC 3, 6, 13, 50, 62; **DAC; DAM
MST; SSC 7**
See also CA 5-8R; 121; CANR 33; DLB 53;
MTCW 1; SATA-Obit 50

Laurent, Antoine 1952-..................... **CLC 50**

Lauscher, Hermann
See Hesse. Hermann

Lautreamont, Comte de 1846-1870NCLC 12;
SSC 14

Laverty, Donald
See Blish. James (Benjamin)

Lavin, Mary 1912-1996CLC 4, 18, 99; **SSC 4**
See also CA 9-12R; 151; CANR 33; DLB 15;
MTCW 1

Lavond, Paul Dennis
See Kornbluth, C(yril) M.; Pohl, Frederik

Lawler, Raymond Evenor 1922- .... **CLC 58**
See also CA 103

Lawrence, D(avid) H(erbert Richards) 1885-
1930TCLC 2, 9, 16, 33, 48, 61; **DA; DAB;
DAC; DAM MST, NOV, POET; SSC 4, 19;
WLC**
See also CA 104; 121; CDBLB 1914-1945;
DLB 10, 19, 36, 98, 162. 195; MTCW 1

Lawrence, T(homas) E(dward) 1888-1935
TCLC 18
See also Dale, Colin
See also CA 115; 167; DLB 195

Lawrence of Arabia
See Lawrence. T(homas) E(dward)

Lawson, Henry (Archibald Hertzberg) 1867-
1922 .... **TCLC 27; SSC 18**
See also CA 120

Lawton, Dennis
See Faust. Frederick (Schiller)

Laxness, Halldor .... **CLC 25**
See also Gudjonsson, Halldor Kiljan

Layamon fl. c. 1200-..................... **CMLC 10**
See also DLB 146

Laye, Camara 1928-1980 CLC 4, 38; **BLC 2;**

DAM MULT
See also BW 1; CA 85-88; 97-100; CANR 25;
MTCW 1
Layton, Irving (Peter) 1912-CLC 2, 15; DAC;
DAM MST, POET
See also CA 1-4R; CANR 2. 33, 43. 66; DLB
88; MTCW 1
Lazarus, Emma 1849-1887 .... NCLC 8
Lazarus, Felix
See Cable, George Washington
Lazarus, Henry
See Slavitt, David R(ytman)
Lea, Joan
See Neufeld, John (Arthur)
Leacock, Stephen (Butler) 1869-1944TCLC 2;
DAC; DAM MST
See also CA 104; 141; DLB 92
Lear, Edward 1812-1888 .... NCLC 3
See also CLR 1; DLB 32, 163. 166; MAICYA;
SATA 18, 100
Lear, Norman (Milton) 1922- .... CLC 12
See also CA 73-76
Leautaud, Paul 1872-1956 .... TCLC 83
See also DLB 65
Leavis, F(rank) R(aymond) 1895-1978CLC 24
See also CA 21-24R; 77-80; CANR 44; MTCW
1
Leavitt, David 1961- ...... CLC 34; DAM POP
See also CA 116; 122; CANR 50. 62; DLB 130;
INT 122
Leblanc, Maurice (Marie Emile) 1864-1941
TCLC 49
See also CA 110
Lebowitz, Fran(ces Ann) 1951(?)-CLC 11, 36
See also CA 81-84; CANR 14, 60, 70; INT
CANR-14; MTCW 1
Lebrecht, Peter
See Tieck, (Johann) Ludwig
le Carre, John .... CLC 3, 5, 9, 15, 28
See also Cornwell, David (John Moore)
See also BEST 89:4; CDBLB 1960 to Present;
DLB 87
Le Clezio, J(ean) M(arie) G(ustave) 1940-
CLC 31
See also CA 116; 128; DLB 83
Leconte de Lisle, Charles-Marie-Rene 1818-
1894 .... NCLC 29
Le Coq, Monsieur
See Simenon, Georges (Jacques Christian)
Leduc, Violette 1907-1972 .... CLC 22
See also CA 13-14; 33-36R; CANR 69; CAP 1
Ledwidge, Francis 1887(?)-1917 .... TCLC 23
See also CA 123; DLB 20
Lee, Andrea 1953- .... CLC 36; BLC 2; DAM
MULT
See also BW 1; CA 125
Lee, Andrew
See Auchincloss, Louis (Stanton)
Lee, Chang-rae 1965- .... CLC 91
See also CA 148
Lee, Don L. .... CLC 2
See also Madhubuti, Haki R.
Lee, George W(ashington) 1894-1976CLC 52;
BLC 2; DAM MULT
See also BW 1; CA 125; DLB 51
Lee, (Nelle) Harper 1926- .. CLC 12, 60; DA;
DAB; DAC; DAM MST, NOV; WLC
See also AAYA 13; CA 13-16R; CANR 51;
CDALB 1941-1968; DLB 6; MTCW 1;
SATA 11
Lee, Helen Elaine 1959(?)- .... CLC 86
See also CA 148
Lee, Julian

See Latham, Jean Lee
Lee, Larry
See Lee, Lawrence
Lee, Laurie 1914-1997 CLC 90; DAB; DAM
POP
See also CA 77-80; 158; CANR 33; DLB 27;
MTCW 1
Lee, Lawrence 1941-1990 .... CLC 34
See also CA 131; CANR 43
Lee, Li-Young 1957- .... PC 24
See also CA 153; DLB 165
Lee, Manfred B(ennington) 1905-1971CLC 11
See also Queen. Ellery
See also CA 1-4R; 29-32R; CANR 2; DLB 137
Lee, Shelton Jackson 1957(?)- .... CLC 105;
BLCS; DAM MULT
See also Lee. Spike
See also BW 2; CA 125; CANR 42
Lee, Spike
See Lee. Shelton Jackson
See also AAYA 4
Lee, Stan 1922- .... CLC 17
See also AAYA 5; CA 108; 111; INT 111
Lee, Tanith 1947- .... CLC 46
See also AAYA 15; CA 37-40R; CANR 53;
SATA 8. 88
Lee, Vernon .... TCLC 5
See also Paget, Violet
See also DLB 57, 153. 156, 174, 178
Lee, William
See Burroughs, William S(eward)
Lee, Willy
See Burroughs. William S(eward)
Lee-Hamilton, Eugene (Jacob) 1845-1907
TCLC 22
See also CA 117
Leet, Judith 1935- .... CLC 11
Le Fanu, Joseph Sheridan 1814-1873NCLC 9,
58; DAM POP; SSC 14
See also DLB 21, 70, 159, 178
Leffland, Ella 1931- .... CLC 19
See also CA 29-32R; CANR 35; DLBY 84; INT
CANR-35; SATA 65
Leger, Alexis
See Leger. (Marie-Rene Auguste) Alexis Saint-
Leger
Leger, (Marie-Rene Auguste) Alexis Saint-
Leger 1887-1975 ..CLC 4, 11, 46; DAM
POET; PC 23
See also CA 13-16R; 61-64; CANR 43; MTCW
1
Leger, Saintleger
See Leger. (Marie-Rene Auguste) Alexis Saint-
Leger
Le Guin, Ursula K(roeber) 1929- CLC 8, 13,
22, 45, 71; DAB; DAC; DAM MST, POP;
SSC 12
See also AAYA 9, 27; AITN 1; CA 21-24R;
CANR 9, 32, 52; CDALB 1968-1988; CLR
3, 28; DLB 8, 52; INT CANR-32; JRDA;
MAICYA; MTCW 1; SATA 4, 52, 99
Lehmann, Rosamond (Nina) 1901-1990CLC 5
See also CA 77-80; 131; CANR 8; DLB 15
Leiber, Fritz (Reuter, Jr.) 1910-1992 CLC 25
See also CA 45-48; 139; CANR 2, 40; DLB 8;
MTCW 1; SATA 45; SATA-Obit 73
Leibniz, Gottfried Wilhelm von 1646-1716LC
35
See also DLB 168
Leimbach, Martha 1963-
See Leimbach, Marti
See also CA 130
Leimbach, Marti .... CLC 65

See also Leimbach. Martha
Leino, Eino .... TCLC 24
See also Loennbohm. Armas Eino Leopold
Leiris, Michel (Julien) 1901-1990 .... CLC 61
See also CA 119; 128; 132
Leithauser, Brad 1953- .... CLC 27
See also CA 107; CANR 27; DLB 120
Lelchuk, Alan 1938- .... CLC 5
See also CA 45-48; CAAS 20; CANR 1, 70
Lem, Stanislaw 1921- .... CLC 8, 15, 40
See also CA 105; CAAS 1; CANR 32; MTCW
1
Lemann, Nancy 1956- .... CLC 39
See also CA 118; 136
Lemonnier, (Antoine Louis) Camille 1844-1913
TCLC 22
See also CA 121
Lenau, Nikolaus 1802-1850 .... NCLC 16
L'Engle, Madeleine (Camp Franklin) 1918-
CLC 12; DAM POP
See also AAYA 1; AITN 2; CA 1-4R; CANR 3,
21, 39, 66; CLR 1, 14; DLB 52; JRDA;
MAICYA; MTCW 1; SAAS 15; SATA 1, 27,
75
Lengyel, Jozsef 1896-1975 .... CLC 7
See also CA 85-88; 57-60; CANR 71
Lenin 1870-1924
See Lenin, V. I.
See also CA 121; 168
Lenin, V. I. .... TCLC 67
See also Lenin
Lennon, John (Ono) 1940-1980 . CLC 12, 35
See also CA 102
Lennox, Charlotte Ramsay 1729(?)-1804
NCLC 23
See also DLB 39
Lentricchia, Frank (Jr.) 1940- .... CLC 34
See also CA 25-28R; CANR 19
Lenz, Siegfried 1926- .... CLC 27
See also CA 89-92; DLB 75
Leonard, Elmore (John, Jr.) 1925-CLC 28, 34,
71; DAM POP
See also AAYA 22; AITN 1; BEST 89:1, 90:4;
CA 81-84; CANR 12, 28, 53; DLB 173; INT
CANR-28; MTCW 1
Leonard, Hugh .... CLC 19
See also Byrne. John Keyes
See also DLB 13
Leonov, Leonid (Maximovich) 1899-1994
CLC 92; DAM NOV
See also CA 129; MTCW 1
Leopardi, (Conte) Giacomo 1798-1837NCLC
22
Le Reveler
See Artaud, Antonin (Marie Joseph)
Lerman, Eleanor 1952- .... CLC 9
See also CA 85-88; CANR 69
Lerman, Rhoda 1936- .... CLC 56
See also CA 49-52; CANR 70
Lermontov, Mikhail Yuryevich 1814-1841
NCLC 47; PC 18
Leroux, Gaston 1868-1927 .... TCLC 25
See also CA 108; 136; CANR 69; SATA 65
Lesage, Alain-Rene 1668-1747 .... LC 28
Leskov, Nikolai (Semyonovich) 1831-1895
NCLC 25
Lessing, Doris (May) 1919-CLC 1, 2, 3, 6, 10,
15, 22, 40, 94; DA; DAB; DAC; DAM MST,
NOV; SSC 6; WLCS
See also CA 9-12R; CAAS 14; CANR 33, 54;
CDBLB 1960 to Present; DLB 15, 139;
DLBY 85; MTCW 1
Lessing, Gotthold Ephraim 1729-1781 LC 8

See also DLBD 6
MacDougal, John
See Blish, James (Benjamin)
MacEwen, Gwendolyn (Margaret) 1941-1987
CLC 13, 55
See also CA 9-12R; 124; CANR 7, 22; DLB 53; SATA 50; SATA-Obit 55
Macha, Karel Hynek 1810-1846 .... **NCLC 46**
Machado (y Ruiz), Antonio 1875-1939 **T C L C 3**
See also CA 104; DLB 108
Machado de Assis, Joaquim Maria 1839-1908
TCLC 10; BLC 2; SSC 24
See also CA 107; 153
Machen, Arthur .... **TCLC 4; SSC 20**
See also Jones, Arthur Llewellyn
See also DLB 36, 156, 178
Machiavelli, Niccolo 1469-1527 **LC 8, 36; DA; DAB; DAC; DAM MST; WLCS**
MacInnes, Colin 1914-1976 .... **CLC 4, 23**
See also CA 69-72; 65-68; CANR 21; DLB 14; MTCW 1
MacInnes, Helen (Clark) 1907-1985 **CLC 27, 39; DAM POP**
See also CA 1-4R; 117; CANR 1, 28, 58; DLB 87; MTCW 1; SATA 22; SATA-Obit 44
Mackay, Mary 1855-1924
See Corelli, Marie
See also CA 118
Mackenzie, Compton (Edward Montague) 1883-1972 .... **CLC 18**
See also CA 21-22; 37-40R; CAP 2; DLB 34, 100
Mackenzie, Henry 1745-1831 .... **NCLC 41**
See also DLB 39
Mackintosh, Elizabeth 1896(?)-1952
See Tey, Josephine
See also CA 110
MacLaren, James
See Grieve, C(hristopher) M(urray)
Mac Laverty, Bernard 1942- .... **CLC 31**
See also CA 116; 118; CANR 43; INT 118
MacLean, Alistair (Stuart) 1922(?)-1987 **C L C 3, 13, 50, 63; DAM POP**
See also CA 57-60; 121; CANR 28, 61; MTCW 1; SATA 23; SATA-Obit 50
Maclean, Norman (Fitzroy) 1902-1990 . **C L C 78; DAM POP; SSC 13**
See also CA 102; 132; CANR 49
MacLeish, Archibald 1892-1982 **CLC 3, 8, 14, 68; DAM POET**
See also CA 9-12R; 106; CANR 33, 63; DLB 4, 7, 45; DLBY 82; MTCW 1
MacLennan, (John) Hugh 1907-1990 **CLC 2, 14, 92; DAC; DAM MST**
See also CA 5-8R; 142; CANR 33; DLB 68; MTCW 1
MacLeod, Alistair 1936- **CLC 56; DAC; DAM MST**
See also CA 123; DLB 60
Macleod, Fiona
See Sharp, William
MacNeice, (Frederick) Louis 1907-1963 **C L C 1, 4, 10, 53; DAB; DAM POET**
See also CA 85-88; CANR 61; DLB 10, 20; MTCW 1
MacNeill, Dand
See Fraser, George MacDonald
Macpherson, James 1736-1796 .... **LC 29**
See also Ossian
See also DLB 109
Macpherson, (Jean) Jay 1931- .... **CLC 14**
See also CA 5-8R; DLB 53

MacShane, Frank 1927- .... **CLC 39**
See also CA 9-12R; CANR 3, 33; DLB 111
Macumber, Mari
See Sandoz, Mari(e Susette)
Madach, Imre 1823-1864 .... **NCLC 19**
Madden, (Jerry) David 1933- .... **CLC 5, 15**
See also CA 1-4R; CAAS 3; CANR 4, 45; DLB 6; MTCW 1
Maddern, Al(an)
See Ellison, Harlan (Jay)
Madhubuti, Haki R. 1942- **CLC 6, 73; BLC 2; DAM MULT, POET; PC 5**
See also Lee, Don L.
See also BW 2; CA 73-76; CANR 24, 51; DLB 5, 41; DLBD 8
Maepenn, Hugh
See Kuttner, Henry
Maepenn, K. H.
See Kuttner, Henry
Maeterlinck, Maurice 1862-1949 .... **TCLC 3; DAM DRAM**
See also CA 104; 136; DLB 192; SATA 66
Maginn, William 1794-1842 .... **NCLC 8**
See also DLB 110, 159
Mahapatra, Jayanta 1928- .... **CLC 33; DAM MULT**
See also CA 73-76; CAAS 9; CANR 15, 33, 66
Mahfouz, Naguib (Abdel Aziz Al-Sabilgi) 1911(?)-
See Mahfuz, Najib
See also BEST 89:2; CA 128; CANR 55; DAM NOV; MTCW 1
Mahfuz, Najib .... **CLC 52, 55**
See also Mahfouz, Naguib (Abdel Aziz Al-Sabilgi)
See also DLBY 88
Mahon, Derek 1941- .... **CLC 27**
See also CA 113; 128; DLB 40
Mailer, Norman 1923- **CLC 1, 2, 3, 4, 5, 8, 11, 14, 28, 39, 74, 111; DA; DAB; DAC; DAM MST, NOV, POP**
See also AITN 2; CA 9-12R; CABS 1; CANR 28; CDALB 1968-1988; DLB 2, 16, 28, 185; DLBD 3; DLBY 80, 83; MTCW 1
Maillet, Antonine 1929- .... **CLC 54; DAC**
See also CA 115; 120; CANR 46; DLB 60; INT 120
Mais, Roger 1905-1955 .... **TCLC 8**
See also BW 1; CA 105; 124; DLB 125; MTCW 1
Maistre, Joseph de 1753-1821 .... **NCLC 37**
Maitland, Frederic 1850-1906 .... **TCLC 65**
Maitland, Sara (Louise) 1950- .... **CLC 49**
See also CA 69-72; CANR 13, 59
Major, Clarence 1936- **CLC 3, 19, 48; BLC 2; DAM MULT**
See also BW 2; CA 21-24R; CAAS 6; CANR 13, 25, 53; DLB 33
Major, Kevin (Gerald) 1949- .. **CLC 26; DAC**
See also AAYA 16; CA 97-100; CANR 21, 38; CLR 11; DLB 60; INT CANR-21; JRDA; MAICYA; SATA 32, 82
Maki, James
See Ozu, Yasujiro
Malabaila, Damiano
See Levi, Primo
Malamud, Bernard 1914-1986 **CLC 1, 2, 3, 5, 8, 9, 11, 18, 27, 44, 78, 85; DA; DAB; DAC; DAM MST, NOV, POP; SSC 15; WLC**
See also AAYA 16; CA 5-8R; 118; CABS 1; CANR 28, 62; CDALB 1941-1968; DLB 2, 28, 152; DLBY 80, 86; MTCW 1
Malan, Herman

See Bosman, Herman Charles; Bosman, Herman Charles
Malaparte, Curzio 1898-1957 .... **TCLC 52**
Malcolm, Dan
See Silverberg, Robert
Malcolm X .... **CLC 82; BLC 2; WLCS**
See also Little, Malcolm
Malherbe, Francois de 1555-1628 .... **LC 5**
Mallarme, Stephane 1842-1898 **NCLC 4, 41; DAM POET; PC 4**
Mallet-Joris, Francoise 1930- .... **CLC 11**
See also CA 65-68; CANR 17; DLB 83
Malley, Ern
See McAuley, James Phillip
Mallowan, Agatha Christie
See Christie, Agatha (Mary Clarissa)
Maloff, Saul 1922- .... **CLC 5**
See also CA 33-36R
Malone, Louis
See MacNeice, (Frederick) Louis
Malone, Michael (Christopher) 1942- **CLC 43**
See also CA 77-80; CANR 14, 32, 57
Malory, (Sir) Thomas 1410(?)-1471(?) **LC 11; DA; DAB; DAC; DAM MST; WLCS**
See also CDBLB Before 1660; DLB 146; SATA 59; SATA-Brief 33
Malouf, (George Joseph) David 1934- **CLC 28, 86**
See also CA 124; CANR 50
Malraux, (Georges-)Andre 1901-1976 **CLC 1, 4, 9, 13, 15, 57; DAM NOV**
See also CA 21-22; 69-72; CANR 34, 58; CAP 2; DLB 72; MTCW 1
Malzberg, Barry N(athaniel) 1939- .... **CLC 7**
See also CA 61-64; CAAS 4; CANR 16; DLB 8
Mamet, David (Alan) 1947- **CLC 9, 15, 34, 46, 91; DAM DRAM; DC 4**
See also AAYA 3; CA 81-84; CABS 3; CANR 15, 41, 67, 72; DLB 7; MTCW 1
Mamoulian, Rouben (Zachary) 1897-1987 **CLC 16**
See also CA 25-28R; 124
Mandelstam, Osip (Emilievich) 1891(?)-1938(?) **TCLC 2, 6; PC 14**
See also CA 104; 150
Mander, (Mary) Jane 1877-1949 ... **TCLC 31**
See also CA 162
Mandeville, John fl. 1350- .... **CMLC 19**
See also DLB 146
Mandiargues, Andre Pieyre de .... **CLC 41**
See also Pieyre de Mandiargues, Andre
See also DLB 83
Mandrake, Ethel Belle
See Thurman, Wallace (Henry)
Mangan, James Clarence 1803-1849 **NCLC 27**
Maniere, J.-E.
See Giraudoux, (Hippolyte) Jean
Mankiewicz, Herman (Jacob) 1897-1953 **TCLC 85**
See also CA 120; DLB 26
Manley, (Mary) Delariviere 1672(?)-1724 **L C 1**
See also DLB 39, 80
Mann, Abel
See Creasey, John
Mann, Emily 1952- .... **DC 7**
See also CA 130; CANR 55
Mann, (Luiz) Heinrich 1871-1950 ... **TCLC 9**
See also CA 106; 164; DLB 66
Mann, (Paul) Thomas 1875-1955 **TCLC 2, 8, 14, 21, 35, 44, 60; DA; DAB; DAC; DAM MST, NOV; SSC 5; WLC**

See also CA 29-32R; 162; CAAS 18; CANR 12, 57; DLB 5

Matthias, John (Edward) 1941- .... **CLC 9**
See also CA 33-36R; CANR 56

Matthiessen, Peter 1927-**CLC 5, 7, 11, 32, 64; DAM NOV**
See also AAYA 6; BEST 90:4; CA 9-12R; CANR 21, 50; DLB 6, 173; MTCW 1; SATA 27

Maturin, Charles Robert 1780(?)-1824**NCLC 6**
See also DLB 178

Matute (Ausejo), Ana Maria 1925- .. **CLC 11**
See also CA 89-92; MTCW 1

Maugham, W. S.
See Maugham, W(illiam) Somerset

Maugham, W(illiam) Somerset 1874-1965 **CLC 1, 11, 15, 67, 93; DA; DAB; DAC; DAM DRAM, MST, NOV; SSC 8; WLC**
See also CA 5-8R; 25-28R; CANR 40; CDBLB 1914-1945; DLB 10, 36, 77, 100, 162, 195; MTCW 1; SATA 54

Maugham, William Somerset
See Maugham, W(illiam) Somerset

Maupassant, (Henri Rene Albert) Guy de 1850-1893**NCLC 1, 42; DA; DAB; DAC; DAM MST; SSC 1; WLC**
See also DLB 123

Maupin, Armistead 1944-**CLC 95; DAM POP**
See also CA 125; 130; CANR 58; INT 130

Maurhut, Richard
See Traven, B.

Mauriac, Claude 1914-1996 .... **CLC 9**
See also CA 89-92; 152; DLB 83

Mauriac, Francois (Charles) 1885-1970 **C L C 4, 9, 56; SSC 24**
See also CA 25-28; CAP 2; DLB 65; MTCW 1

Mavor, Osborne Henry 1888-1951
See Bridie, James
See also CA 104

Maxwell, William (Keepers, Jr.) 1908-**CLC 19**
See also CA 93-96; CANR 54; DLBY 80; INT 93-96

May, Elaine 1932-.............................. **CLC 16**
See also CA 124; 142; DLB 44

Mayakovski, Vladimir (Vladimirovich) 1893-1930 .... **TCLC 4, 18**
See also CA 104; 158

Mayhew, Henry 1812-1887 .... **NCLC 31**
See also DLB 18, 55, 190

Mayle, Peter 1939(?)- .... **CLC 89**
See also CA 139; CANR 64

Maynard, Joyce 1953- .... **CLC 23**
See also CA 111; 129; CANR 64

Mayne, William (James Carter) 1928-**CLC 12**
See also AAYA 20; CA 9-12R; CANR 37; CLR 25; JRDA; MAICYA; SAAS 11; SATA 6, 68

Mayo, Jim
See L'Amour, Louis (Dearborn)

Maysles, Albert 1926- .... **CLC 16**
See also CA 29-32R

Maysles, David 1932- .... **CLC 16**

Mazer, Norma Fox 1931- .... **CLC 26**
See also AAYA 5; CA 69-72; CANR 12, 32, 66; CLR 23; JRDA; MAICYA; SAAS 1; SATA 24, 67

Mazzini, Guiseppe 1805-1872 .... **NCLC 34**

McAuley, James Phillip 1917-1976 . **CLC 45**
See also CA 97-100

McBain, Ed
See Hunter, Evan

McBrien, William Augustine 1930- . **CLC 44**
See also CA 107

McCaffrey, Anne (Inez) 1926-**CLC 17; DAM NOV, POP**
See also AAYA 6; AITN 2; BEST 89:2; CA 25-28R; CANR 15, 35, 55; CLR 49; DLB 8; JRDA; MAICYA; MTCW 1; SAAS 11; SATA 8, 70

McCall, Nathan 1955(?)- .... **CLC 86**
See also CA 146

McCann, Arthur
See Campbell, John W(ood, Jr.)

McCann, Edson
See Pohl, Frederik

McCarthy, Charles, Jr. 1933-
See McCarthy, Cormac
See also CANR 42, 69; DAM POP

McCarthy, Cormac 1933- **CLC 4, 57, 59, 101**
See also McCarthy, Charles, Jr.
See also DLB 6, 143

McCarthy, Mary (Therese) 1912-1989**CLC 1, 3, 5, 14, 24, 39, 59; SSC 24**
See also CA 5-8R; 129; CANR 16, 50, 64; DLB 2; DLBY 81; INT CANR-16; MTCW 1

McCartney, (James) Paul 1942- . **CLC 12, 35**
See also CA 146

McCauley, Stephen (D.) 1955- .... **CLC 50**
See also CA 141

McClure, Michael (Thomas) 1932-**CLC 6, 10**
See also CA 21-24R; CANR 17, 46; DLB 16

McCorkle, Jill (Collins) 1958-........... **CLC 51**
See also CA 121; DLBY 87

McCourt, Frank 1930- .... **CLC 109**
See also CA 157

McCourt, James 1941- .... **CLC 5**
See also CA 57-60

McCoy, Horace (Stanley) 1897-1955**TCLC 28**
See also CA 108; 155; DLB 9

McCrae, John 1872-1918 .... **TCLC 12**
See also CA 109; DLB 92

McCreigh, James
See Pohl, Frederik

McCullers, (Lula) Carson (Smith) 1917-1967 **CLC 1, 4, 10, 12, 48, 100; DA; DAB; DAC; DAM MST, NOV; SSC 9, 24; WLC**
See also AAYA 21; CA 5-8R; 25-28R; CABS 1, 3; CANR 18; CDALB 1941-1968; DLB 2, 7, 173; MTCW 1; SATA 27

McCulloch, John Tyler
See Burroughs, Edgar Rice

McCullough, Colleen 1938(?)- **CLC 27, 107; DAM NOV, POP**
See also CA 81-84; CANR 17, 46, 67; MTCW 1

McDermott, Alice 1953-..................... **CLC 90**
See also CA 109; CANR 40

McElroy, Joseph 1930- .... **CLC 5, 47**
See also CA 17-20R

McEwan, Ian (Russell) 1948- .... **CLC 13, 66; DAM NOV**
See also BEST 90:4; CA 61-64; CANR 14, 41, 69; DLB 14, 194; MTCW 1

McFadden, David 1940-....................**CLC 48**
See also CA 104; DLB 60; INT 104

McFarland, Dennis 1950- .... **CLC 65**
See also CA 165

McGahern, John 1934-**CLC 5, 9, 48; SSC 17**
See also CA 17-20R; CANR 29, 68; DLB 14; MTCW 1

McGinley, Patrick (Anthony) 1937- .**CLC 41**
See also CA 120; 127; CANR 56; INT 127

McGinley, Phyllis 1905-1978.............**CLC 14**
See also CA 9-12R; 77-80; CANR 19; DLB 11, 48; SATA 2, 44; SATA-Obit 24

McGinniss, Joe 1942- .... **CLC 32**

See also AITN 2; BEST 89:2; CA 25-28R; CANR 26, 70; DLB 185; INT CANR-26

McGivern, Maureen Daly
See Daly, Maureen

McGrath, Patrick 1950-..................... **CLC 55**
See also CA 136; CANR 65

McGrath, Thomas (Matthew) 1916-1990**CLC 28, 59; DAM POET**
See also CA 9-12R; 132; CANR 6, 33; MTCW 1; SATA 41; SATA-Obit 66

McGuane, Thomas (Francis III) 1939-**CLC 3, 7, 18, 45**
See also AITN 2; CA 49-52; CANR 5, 24, 49; DLB 2; DLBY 80; INT CANR-24; MTCW 1

McGuckian, Medbh 1950- ..... **CLC 48; DAM POET**
See also CA 143; DLB 40

McHale, Tom 1942(?)-1982 .... **CLC 3, 5**
See also AITN 1; CA 77-80; 106

McIlvanney, William 1936- .... **CLC 42**
See also CA 25-28R; CANR 61; DLB 14

McIlwraith, Maureen Mollie Hunter
See Hunter, Mollie
See also SATA 2

McInerney, Jay 1955-**CLC 34, 112; DAM POP**
See also AAYA 18; CA 116; 123; CANR 45, 68; INT 123

McIntyre, Vonda N(eel) 1948-........... **CLC 18**
See also CA 81-84; CANR 17, 34, 69; MTCW 1

McKay, Claude**TCLC 7, 41; BLC 3; DAB; PC 2**
See also McKay, Festus Claudius
See also DLB 4, 45, 51, 117

McKay, Festus Claudius 1889-1948
See McKay, Claude
See also BW 1; CA 104; 124; DA; DAC; DAM MST, MULT, NOV, POET; MTCW 1; WLC

McKuen, Rod 1933- .... **CLC 1, 3**
See also AITN 1; CA 41-44R; CANR 40

McLoughlin, R. B.
See Mencken, H(enry) L(ouis)

McLuhan, (Herbert) Marshall 1911-1980 **CLC 37, 83**
See also CA 9-12R; 102; CANR 12, 34, 61; DLB 88; INT CANR-12; MTCW 1

McMillan, Terry (L.) 1951-**CLC 50, 61, 112; BLCS; DAM MULT, NOV, POP**
See also AAYA 21; BW 2; CA 140; CANR 60

McMurtry, Larry (Jeff) 1936-**CLC 2, 3, 7, 11, 27, 44; DAM NOV, POP**
See also AAYA 15; AITN 2; BEST 89:2; CA 5-8R; CANR 19, 43, 64; CDALB 1968-1988; DLB 2, 143; DLBY 80, 87; MTCW 1

McNally, T. M. 1961-...........................**CLC 82**

McNally, Terrence 1939- ... **CLC 4, 7, 41, 91; DAM DRAM**
See also CA 45-48; CANR 2, 56; DLB 7

McNamer, Deirdre 1950- .... **CLC 70**

McNeile, Herman Cyril 1888-1937
See Sapper
See also DLB 77

McNickle, (William) D'Arcy 1904-1977 **C L C 89; DAM MULT**
See also CA 9-12R; 85-88; CANR 5, 45; DLB 175; NNAL; SATA-Obit 22

McPhee, John (Angus) 1931- .... **CLC 36**
See also BEST 90:1; CA 65-68; CANR 20, 46, 64, 69; DLB 185; MTCW 1

McPherson, James Alan 1943-.. **CLC 19, 77; BLCS**
See also BW 1; CA 25-28R; CAAS 17; CANR

24; DLB 38; MTCW 1

McPherson, William (Alexander) 1933- **C L C 34**
See also CA 69-72; CANR 28; INT CANR-28

Mead, Margaret 1901-1978 .... **CLC 37**
See also AITN 1; CA 1-4R; 81-84; CANR 4;
MTCW 1; SATA-Obit 20

Meaker, Marijane (Agnes) 1927-
See Kerr, M. E.
See also CA 107; CANR 37, 63; INT 107;
JRDA; MAICYA; MTCW 1; SATA 20, 61.
99

Medoff, Mark (Howard) 1940- ... **CLC 6, 23; DAM DRAM**
See also AITN 1; CA 53-56; CANR 5; DLB 7;
INT CANR-5

Medvedev, P. N.
See Bakhtin, Mikhail Mikhailovich

Meged, Aharon
See Megged. Aharon

Meged, Aron
See Megged. Aharon

Megged, Aharon 1920- .... **CLC 9**
See also CA 49-52; CAAS 13; CANR 1

Mehta, Ved (Parkash) 1934- .... **CLC 37**
See also CA 1-4R; CANR 2, 23, 69; MTCW 1

Melanter
See Blackmore. R(ichard) D(oddridge)

Melies, Georges 1861-1938 .... **TCLC 81**

Melikow, Loris
See Hofmannsthal, Hugo von

Melmoth, Sebastian
See Wilde, Oscar (Fingal O'Flahertie Wills)

Meltzer, Milton 1915- .... **CLC 26**
See also AAYA 8; CA 13-16R; CANR 38; CLR
13; DLB 61; JRDA; MAICYA; SAAS 1;
SATA 1, 50, 80

Melville, Herman 1819-1891 **NCLC 3, 12, 29, 45, 49; DA; DAB; DAC; DAM MST, NOV; SSC 1, 17; WLC**
See also AAYA 25; CDALB 1640-1865; DLB
3, 74; SATA 59

Menander c. 342B.C.-c. 292B.C. .... **CMLC 9; DAM DRAM; DC 3**
See also DLB 176

Mencken, H(enry) L(ouis) 1880-1956 **T C L C 13**
See also CA 105; 125; CDALB 1917-1929;
DLB 11, 29, 63, 137; MTCW 1

Mendelsohn, Jane 1965(?)- .... **CLC 99**
See also CA 154

Mercer, David 1928-1980 **CLC 5; DAM DRAM**
See also CA 9-12R; 102; CANR 23; DLB 13;
MTCW 1

Merchant, Paul
See Ellison, Harlan (Jay)

Meredith, George 1828-1909 .. **TCLC 17, 43; DAM POET**
See also CA 117; 153; CDBLB 1832-1890;
DLB 18, 35, 57, 159

Meredith, William (Morris) 1919- **CLC 4, 13, 22, 55; DAM POET**
See also CA 9-12R; CAAS 14; CANR 6, 40;
DLB 5

Merezhkovsky, Dmitry Sergeyevich 1865-1941
TCLC 29

Merimee, Prosper 1803-1870 **NCLC 6, 65; SSC 7**
See also DLB 119, 192

Merkin, Daphne 1954- .... **CLC 44**
See also CA 123

Merlin, Arthur
See Blish, James (Benjamin)

Merrill, James (Ingram) 1926-1995 **CLC 2, 3, 6, 8, 13, 18, 34, 91; DAM POET**
See also CA 13-16R; 147; CANR 10, 49, 63;
DLB 5. 165; DLBY 85; INT CANR-10;
MTCW 1

Merriman, Alex
See Silverberg. Robert

Merriman, Brian 1747-1805 .... **NCLC 70**

Merritt, E. B.
See Waddington. Miriam

Merton, Thomas 1915-1968 **CLC 1, 3, 11, 34, 83; PC 10**
See also CA 5-8R; 25-28R; CANR 22, 53; DLB
48; DLBY 81; MTCW 1

Merwin, W(illiam) S(tanley) 1927- **CLC 1, 2, 3, 5, 8, 13, 18, 45, 88; DAM POET**
See also CA 13-16R; CANR 15, 51; DLB 5.
169; INT CANR-15; MTCW 1

Metcalf, John 1938- .... **CLC 37**
See also CA 113; DLB 60

Metcalf, Suzanne
See Baum. L(yman) Frank

Mew, Charlotte (Mary) 1870-1928 .. **TCLC 8**
See also CA 105; DLB 19, 135

Mewshaw, Michael 1943- .... **CLC 9**
See also CA 53-56; CANR 7, 47; DLBY 80

Meyer, June
See Jordan. June

Meyer, Lynn
See Slavitt. David R(ytman)

Meyer-Meyrink, Gustav 1868-1932
See Meyrink. Gustav
See also CA 117

Meyers, Jeffrey 1939- .... **CLC 39**
See also CA 73-76; CANR 54; DLB 111

Meynell, Alice (Christina Gertrude Thompson)
1847-1922 .... **TCLC 6**
See also CA 104; DLB 19. 98

Meyrink, Gustav .... **TCLC 21**
See also Meyer-Meyrink, Gustav
See also DLB 81

Michaels, Leonard 1933- **CLC 6, 25; SSC 16**
See also CA 61-64; CANR 21, 62; DLB 130;
MTCW 1

Michaux, Henri 1899-1984 .... **CLC 8, 19**
See also CA 85-88; 114

Micheaux, Oscar 1884-1951 .... **TCLC 76**
See also DLB 50

Michelangelo 1475-1564 .... **LC 12**

Michelet, Jules 1798-1874 .... **NCLC 31**

Michener, James A(lbert) 1907(?)-1997 **C L C 1, 5, 11, 29, 60, 109; DAM NOV, POP**
See also AAYA 27; AITN 1; BEST 90:1; CA 5-
8R; 161; CANR 21, 45, 68; DLB 6; MTCW
1

Mickiewicz, Adam 1798-1855 .... **NCLC 3**

Middleton, Christopher 1926- .... **CLC 13**
See also CA 13-16R; CANR 29, 54; DLB 40

Middleton, Richard (Barham) 1882-1911
TCLC 56
See also DLB 156

Middleton, Stanley 1919- .... **CLC 7, 38**
See also CA 25-28R; CAAS 23; CANR 21, 46;
DLB 14

Middleton, Thomas 1580-1627 **LC 33; DAM DRAM, MST; DC 5**
See also DLB 58

Migueis, Jose Rodrigues 1901- .... **CLC 10**

Mikszath, Kalman 1847-1910 .... **TCLC 31**

Miles, Jack .... **CLC 100**

Miles, Josephine (Louise) 1911-1985 **CLC 1, 2, 14, 34, 39; DAM POET**
See also CA 1-4R; 116; CANR 2, 55; DLB 48

Militant
See Sandburg, Carl (August)

Mill, John Stuart 1806-1873 .... **NCLC 11, 58**
See also CDBLB 1832-1890; DLB 55, 190

Millar, Kenneth 1915-1983 ....**CLC 14; DAM POP**
See also Macdonald. Ross
See also CA 9-12R; 110; CANR 16, 63; DLB
2; DLBD 6; DLBY 83; MTCW 1

Millay, E. Vincent
See Millay. Edna St. Vincent

Millay, Edna St. Vincent 1892-1950 **TCLC 4, 49; DA; DAB; DAC; DAM MST, POET; PC 6; WLCS**
See also CA 104; 130; CDALB 1917-1929;
DLB 45; MTCW 1

Miller, Arthur 1915- **CLC 1, 2, 6, 10, 15, 26, 47, 78; DA; DAB; DAC; DAM DRAM, MST; DC 1; WLC**
See also AAYA 15; AITN 1; CA 1-4R; CABS
3; CANR 2, 30, 54; CDALB 1941-1968;
DLB 7; MTCW 1

Miller, Henry (Valentine) 1891-1980 **CLC 1, 2, 4, 9, 14, 43, 84; DA; DAB; DAC; DAM MST, NOV; WLC**
See also CA 9-12R; 97-100; CANR 33, 64;
CDALB 1929-1941; DLB 4, 9; DLBY 80;
MTCW 1

Miller, Jason 1939(?)- .... **CLC 2**
See also AITN 1; CA 73-76; DLB 7

Miller, Sue 1943- .... **CLC 44; DAM POP**
See also BEST 90:3; CA 139; CANR 59; DLB
143

Miller, Walter M(ichael, Jr.) 1923- **CLC 4, 30**
See also CA 85-88; DLB 8

Millett, Kate 1934- .... **CLC 67**
See also AITN 1; CA 73-76; CANR 32, 53;
MTCW 1

Millhauser, Steven (Lewis) 1943- **CLC 21, 54, 109**
See also CA 110; 111; CANR 63; DLB 2; INT
111

Millin, Sarah Gertrude 1889-1968 .. **CLC 49**
See also CA 102; 93-96

Milne, A(lan) A(lexander) 1882-1956 **TCLC 6; DAB; DAC; DAM MST**
See also CA 104; 133; CLR 1. 26; DLB 10. 77.
100, 160; MAICYA; MTCW 1; SATA 100;
YABC 1

Milner, Ron(ald) 1938- **CLC 56; BLC 3; DAM MULT**
See also AITN 1; BW 1; CA 73-76; CANR 24;
DLB 38; MTCW 1

Milnes, Richard Monckton 1809-1885 **N C L C 61**
See also DLB 32, 184

Milosz, Czeslaw 1911- **CLC 5, 11, 22, 31, 56, 82; DAM MST, POET; PC 8; WLCS**
See also CA 81-84; CANR 23, 51; MTCW 1

Milton, John 1608-1674 **LC 9, 43; DA; DAB; DAC; DAM MST, POET; PC 19; WLC**
See also CDBLB 1660-1789; DLB 131, 151

Min, Anchee 1957- .... **CLC 86**
See also CA 146

Minehaha, Cornelius
See Wedekind, (Benjamin) Frank(lin)

Miner, Valerie 1947- .... **CLC 40**
See also CA 97-100; CANR 59

Minimo, Duca
See D'Annunzio, Gabriele

Minot, Susan 1956- .... **CLC 44**
See also CA 134

Minus, Ed 1938- .... **CLC 39**

See Wonder, Stevie
See also CA 111

Morris, William 1834-1896 .... **NCLC 4**
See also CDBLB 1832-1890; DLB 18, 35, 57, 156, 178, 184

Morris, Wright 1910-1998 **CLC 1, 3, 7, 18, 37**
See also CA 9-12R; 167; CANR 21; DLB 2; DLBY 81; MTCW 1

Morrison, Arthur 1863-1945 .... **TCLC 72**
See also CA 120; 157; DLB 70, 135, 197

Morrison, Chloe Anthony Wofford
See Morrison, Toni

Morrison, James Douglas 1943-1971
See Morrison, Jim
See also CA 73-76; CANR 40

Morrison, Jim .... **CLC 17**
See also Morrison, James Douglas

Morrison, Toni 1931- **CLC 4, 10, 22, 55, 81, 87; BLC 3; DA; DAB; DAC; DAM MST, MULT, NOV, POP**
See also AAYA 1, 22; BW 2; CA 29-32R; CANR 27, 42, 67; CDALB 1968-1988; DLB 6, 33, 143; DLBY 81; MTCW 1; SATA 57

Morrison, Van 1945- .... **CLC 21**
See also CA 116; 168

Morrissy, Mary 1958- .... **CLC 99**

Mortimer, John (Clifford) 1923- **CLC 28, 43; DAM DRAM, POP**
See also CA 13-16R; CANR 21, 69; CDBLB 1960 to Present; DLB 13; INT CANR-21; MTCW 1

Mortimer, Penelope (Ruth) 1918- .... **CLC 5**
See also CA 57-60; CANR 45

Morton, Anthony
See Creasey, John

Mosca, Gaetano 1858-1941 .... **TCLC 75**

Mosher, Howard Frank 1943- .... **CLC 62**
See also CA 139; CANR 65

Mosley, Nicholas 1923- .... **CLC 43, 70**
See also CA 69-72; CANR 41, 60; DLB 14

Mosley, Walter 1952- **CLC 97; BLCS; DAM MULT, POP**
See also AAYA 17; BW 2; CA 142; CANR 57

Moss, Howard 1922-1987 **CLC 7, 14, 45, 50; DAM POET**
See also CA 1-4R; 123; CANR 1, 44; DLB 5

Mossgiel, Rab
See Burns, Robert

Motion, Andrew (Peter) 1952- .... **CLC 47**
See also CA 146; DLB 40

Motley, Willard (Francis) 1909-1965 **CLC 18**
See also BW 1; CA 117; 106; DLB 76, 143

Motoori, Norinaga 1730-1801 .... **NCLC 45**

Mott, Michael (Charles Alston) 1930- **CLC 15, 34**
See also CA 5-8R; CAAS 7; CANR 7, 29

Mountain Wolf Woman 1884-1960 .. **CLC 92**
See also CA 144; NNAL

Moure, Erin 1955- .... **CLC 88**
See also CA 113; DLB 60

Mowat, Farley (McGill) 1921- **CLC 26; DAC; DAM MST**
See also AAYA 1; CA 1-4R; CANR 4, 24, 42, 68; CLR 20; DLB 68; INT CANAR-24; JRDA; MAICYA; MTCW 1; SATA 3, 55

Moyers, Bill 1934- .... **CLC 74**
See also AITN 2; CA 61-64; CANR 31, 52

Mphahlele, Es'kia
See Mphahlele, Ezekiel
See also DLB 125

Mphahlele, Ezekiel 1919-1983 **CLC 25; BLC 3; DAM MULT**
See also Mphahlele, Es'kia

See also BW 2; CA 81-84; CANR 26

Mqhayi, S(amuel) E(dward) K(rune Loliwe) 1875-1945 **TCLC 25; BLC 3; DAM MULT**
See also CA 153

Mrozek, Slawomir 1930- .... **CLC 3, 13**
See also CA 13-16R; CAAS 10; CANR 29; MTCW 1

Mrs. Belloc-Lowndes
See Lowndes, Marie Adelaide (Belloc)

Mtwa, Percy (?)- .... **CLC 47**

Mueller, Lisel 1924- .... **CLC 13, 51**
See also CA 93-96; DLB 105

Muir, Edwin 1887-1959 .... **TCLC 2**
See also CA 104; DLB 20, 100, 191

Muir, John 1838-1914 .... **TCLC 28**
See also CA 165; DLB 186

Mujica Lainez, Manuel 1910-1984 ... **CLC 31**
See also Lainez, Manuel Mujica
See also CA 81-84; 112; CANR 32; HW

Mukherjee, Bharati 1940- **CLC 53, 115; DAM NOV**
See also BEST 89:2; CA 107; CANR 45, 72; DLB 60; MTCW 1

Muldoon, Paul 1951- **CLC 32, 72; DAM POET**
See also CA 113; 129; CANR 52; DLB 40; INT 129

Mulisch, Harry 1927- .... **CLC 42**
See also CA 9-12R; CANR 6, 26, 56

Mull, Martin 1943- .... **CLC 17**
See also CA 105

Muller, Wilhem 1794-1827 .... **NCLC 73**

Mulock, Dinah Maria
See Craik, Dinah Maria (Mulock)

Munford, Robert 1737(?)-1783 .... **LC 5**
See also DLB 31

Mungo, Raymond 1946- .... **CLC 72**
See also CA 49-52; CANR 2

Munro, Alice 1931- .... **CLC 6, 10, 19, 50, 95; DAC; DAM MST, NOV; SSC 3; WLCS**
See also AITN 2; CA 33-36R; CANR 33, 53; DLB 53; MTCW 1; SATA 29

Munro, H(ector) H(ugh) 1870-1916
See Saki
See also CA 104; 130; CDBLB 1890-1914; DA; DAB; DAC; DAM MST, NOV; DLB 34, 162; MTCW 1; WLC

Murasaki, Lady .... **CMLC 1**

Murdoch, (Jean) Iris 1919- **CLC 1, 2, 3, 4, 6, 8, 11, 15, 22, 31, 51; DAB; DAC; DAM MST, NOV**
See also CA 13-16R; CANR 8, 43, 68; CDBLB 1960 to Present; DLB 14, 194; INT CANR-8; MTCW 1

Murfree, Mary Noailles 1850-1922 ... **SSC 22**
See also CA 122; DLB 12, 74

Murnau, Friedrich Wilhelm
See Plumpe, Friedrich Wilhelm

Murphy, Richard 1927- .... **CLC 41**
See also CA 29-32R; DLB 40

Murphy, Sylvia 1937- .... **CLC 34**
See also CA 121

Murphy, Thomas (Bernard) 1935- ... **CLC 51**
See also CA 101

Murray, Albert L. 1916- .... **CLC 73**
See also BW 2; CA 49-52; CANR 26, 52; DLB 38

Murray, Judith Sargent 1751-1820 **NCLC 63**
See also DLB 37, 200

Murray, Les(lie) A(llan) 1938- **CLC 40; DAM POET**
See also CA 21-24R; CANR 11, 27, 56

Murry, J. Middleton
See Murry, John Middleton

Murry, John Middleton 1889-1957 **TCLC 16**
See also CA 118; DLB 149

Musgrave, Susan 1951- .... **CLC 13, 54**
See also CA 69-72; CANR 45

Musil, Robert (Edler von) 1880-1942. **TCLC 12, 68; SSC 18**
See also CA 109; CANR 55; DLB 81, 124

Muske, Carol 1945- .... **CLC 90**
See also Muske-Dukes, Carol (Anne)

Muske-Dukes, Carol (Anne) 1945-
See Muske, Carol
See also CA 65-68; CANR 32, 70

Musset, (Louis Charles) Alfred de 1810-1857 **NCLC 7**
See also DLB 192

My Brother's Brother
See Chekhov, Anton (Pavlovich)

Myers, L(eopold) H(amilton) 1881-1944 **TCLC 59**
See also CA 157; DLB 15

Myers, Walter Dean 1937- . **CLC 35; BLC 3; DAM MULT, NOV**
See also AAYA 4, 23; BW 2; CA 33-36R; CANR 20, 42, 67; CLR 4, 16, 35; DLB 33; INT CANR-20; JRDA; MAICYA; SAAS 2; SATA 41, 71; SATA-Brief 27

Myers, Walter M.
See Myers, Walter Dean

Myles, Symon
See Follett, Ken(neth Martin)

Nabokov, Vladimir (Vladimirovich) 1899-1977 **CLC 1, 2, 3, 6, 8, 11, 15, 23, 44, 46, 64; DA; DAB; DAC; DAM MST, NOV; SSC 11; WLC**
See also CA 5-8R; 69-72; CANR 20; CDALB 1941-1968; DLB 2; DLBD 3; DLBY 80, 91; MTCW 1

Nagai Kafu 1879-1959 .... **TCLC 51**
See also Nagai Sokichi
See also DLB 180

Nagai Sokichi 1879-1959
See Nagai Kafu
See also CA 117

Nagy, Laszlo 1925-1978 .... **CLC 7**
See also CA 129; 112

Naidu, Sarojini 1879-1943 .... **TCLC 80**

Naipaul, Shiva(dhar Srinivasa) 1945-1985 **CLC 32, 39; DAM NOV**
See also CA 110; 112; 116; CANR 33; DLB 157; DLBY 85; MTCW 1

Naipaul, V(idiadhar) S(urajprasad) 1932- **CLC 4, 7, 9, 13, 18, 37, 105; DAB; DAC; DAM MST, NOV**
See also CA 1-4R; CANR 1, 33, 51; CDBLB 1960 to Present; DLB 125; DLBY 85; MTCW 1

Nakos, Lilika 1899(?)- .... **CLC 29**

Narayan, R(asipuram) K(rishnaswami) 1906- **CLC 7, 28, 47; DAM NOV; SSC 25**
See also CA 81-84; CANR 33, 61; MTCW 1; SATA 62

Nash, (Frediric) Ogden 1902-1971 . **CLC 23; DAM POET; PC 21**
See also CA 13-14; 29-32R; CANR 34, 61; CAP 1; DLB 11; MAICYA; MTCW 1; SATA 2, 46

Nashe, Thomas 1567-1601(?) .... **LC 41**
See also DLB 167

Nashe, Thomas 1567-1601 .... **LC 41**

Nathan, Daniel
See Dannay, Frederic

Nathan, George Jean 1882-1958 .... **TCLC 18**
See also Hatteras, Owen

15, 19, 33, 52, 108; DA; DAB; DAC; DAM MST, NOV, POP; SSC 6; WLC
See also AAYA 15; AITN 1; BEST 89:2; CA 5-8R; CANR 25, 45; CDALB 1968-1988; DLB 2, 5, 130; DLBY 81; INT CANR-25; MTCW 1

O'Brien, Darcy 1939-1998 .... **CLC 11**
See also CA 21-24R; 167; CANR 8, 59

O'Brien, E. G.
See Clarke, Arthur C(harles)

O'Brien, Edna 1936- **CLC 3, 5, 8, 13, 36, 65; DAM NOV; SSC 10**
See also CA 1-4R; CANR 6, 41, 65; CDBLB 1960 to Present; DLB 14; MTCW 1

O'Brien, Fitz-James 1828-1862 ..... **NCLC 21**
See also DLB 74

O'Brien, Flann .... **CLC 1, 4, 5, 7, 10, 47**
See also O Nuallain, Brian

O'Brien, Richard 1942- .... **CLC 17**
See also CA 124

O'Brien, (William) Tim(othy) 1946- **CLC 7, 19, 40, 103; DAM POP**
See also AAYA 16; CA 85-88; CANR 40, 58; DLB 152; DLBD 9; DLBY 80

Obstfelder, Sigbjoern 1866-1900 ... **TCLC 23**
See also CA 123

O'Casey, Sean 1880-1964 **CLC 1, 5, 9, 11, 15, 88; DAB; DAC; DAM DRAM, MST; WLCS**
See also CA 89-92; CANR 62; CDBLB 1914-1945; DLB 10; MTCW 1

O'Cathasaigh, Sean
See O'Casey, Sean

Ochs, Phil 1940-1976 .... **CLC 17**
See also CA 65-68

O'Connor, Edwin (Greene) 1918-1968 **CLC 14**
See also CA 93-96; 25-28R

O'Connor, (Mary) Flannery 1925-1964 **C L C 1, 2, 3, 6, 10, 13, 15, 21, 66, 104; DA; DAB; DAC; DAM MST, NOV; SSC 1, 23; WLC**
See also AAYA 7; CA 1-4R; CANR 3, 41; CDALB 1941-1968; DLB 2, 152; DLBD 12; DLBY 80; MTCW 1

O'Connor, Frank .... **CLC 23; SSC 5**
See also O'Donovan, Michael John
See also DLB 162

O'Dell, Scott 1898-1989 .... **CLC 30**
See also AAYA 3; CA 61-64; 129; CANR 12, 30; CLR 1, 16; DLB 52; JRDA; MAICYA; SATA 12, 60

Odets, Clifford 1906-1963 **CLC 2, 28, 98; DAM DRAM; DC 6**
See also CA 85-88; CANR 62; DLB 7, 26; MTCW 1

O'Doherty, Brian 1934- .... **CLC 76**
See also CA 105

O'Donnell, K. M.
See Malzberg, Barry N(athaniel)

O'Donnell, Lawrence
See Kuttner, Henry

O'Donovan, Michael John 1903-1966 **CLC 14**
See also O'Connor, Frank
See also CA 93-96

Oe, Kenzaburo 1935- **CLC 10, 36, 86; DAM NOV; SSC 20**
See also CA 97-100; CANR 36, 50; DLB 182; DLBY 94; MTCW 1

O'Faolain, Julia 1932- .... **CLC 6, 19, 47, 108**
See also CA 81-84; CAAS 2; CANR 12, 61; DLB 14; MTCW 1

O'Faolain, Sean 1900-1991 **CLC 1, 7, 14, 32, 70; SSC 13**
See also CA 61-64; 134; CANR 12, 66; DLB

15, 162; MTCW 1

O'Flaherty, Liam 1896-1984 **CLC 5, 34; SSC 6**
See also CA 101; 113; CANR 35; DLB 36, 162; DLBY 84; MTCW 1

Ogilvy, Gavin
See Barrie, J(ames) M(atthew)

O'Grady, Standish (James) 1846-1928 **T C L C 5**
See also CA 104; 157

O'Grady, Timothy 1951- .... **CLC 59**
See also CA 138

O'Hara, Frank 1926-1966 . **CLC 2, 5, 13, 78; DAM POET**
See also CA 9-12R; 25-28R; CANR 33; DLB 5, 16, 193; MTCW 1

O'Hara, John (Henry) 1905-1970 **CLC 1, 2, 3, 6, 11, 42; DAM NOV; SSC 15**
See also CA 5-8R; 25-28R; CANR 31, 60; CDALB 1929-1941; DLB 9, 86; DLBD 2; MTCW 1

O Hehir, Diana 1922- .... **CLC 41**
See also CA 93-96

Okigbo, Christopher (Ifenayichukwu) 1932-1967 **CLC 25, 84; BLC 3; DAM MULT, POET; PC 7**
See also BW 1; CA 77-80; DLB 125; MTCW 1

Okri, Ben 1959- .... **CLC 87**
See also BW 2; CA 130; 138; CANR 65; DLB 157; INT 138

Olds, Sharon 1942- .... **CLC 32, 39, 85; DAM POET; PC 22**
See also CA 101; CANR 18, 41, 66; DLB 120

Oldstyle, Jonathan
See Irving, Washington

Olesha, Yuri (Karlovich) 1899-1960 ... **CLC 8**
See also CA 85-88

Oliphant, Laurence 1829(?)-1888 .. **NCLC 47**
See also DLB 18, 166

Oliphant, Margaret (Oliphant Wilson) 1828-1897 .... **NCLC 11, 61; SSC 25**
See also DLB 18, 159, 190

Oliver, Mary 1935- .... **CLC 19, 34, 98**
See also CA 21-24R; CANR 9, 43; DLB 5, 193

Olivier, Laurence (Kerr) 1907-1989 . **CLC 20**
See also CA 111; 150; 129

Olsen, Tillie 1913- **CLC 4, 13, 114; DA; DAB; DAC; DAM MST; SSC 11**
See also CA 1-4R; CANR 1, 43; DLB 28; DLBY 80; MTCW 1

Olson, Charles (John) 1910-1970 **CLC 1, 2, 5, 6, 9, 11, 29; DAM POET; PC 19**
See also CA 13-16; 25-28R; CABS 2; CANR 35, 61; CAP 1; DLB 5, 16, 193; MTCW 1

Olson, Toby 1937- .... **CLC 28**
See also CA 65-68; CANR 9, 31

Olyesha, Yuri
See Olesha, Yuri (Karlovich)

Ondaatje, (Philip) Michael 1943- **CLC 14, 29, 51, 76; DAB; DAC; DAM MST**
See also CA 77-80; CANR 42; DLB 60

Oneal, Elizabeth 1934-
See Oneal, Zibby
See also CA 106; CANR 28; MAICYA; SATA 30, 82

Oneal, Zibby .... **CLC 30**
See also Oneal, Elizabeth
See also AAYA 5; CLR 13; JRDA

O'Neill, Eugene (Gladstone) 1888-1953 **TCLC 1, 6, 27, 49; DA; DAB; DAC; DAM DRAM, MST; WLC**
See also AITN 1; CA 110; 132; CDALB 1929-1941; DLB 7; MTCW 1

Onetti, Juan Carlos 1909-1994 ... **CLC 7, 10;**

DAM MULT, NOV; SSC 23
See also CA 85-88; 145; CANR 32, 63; DLB 113; HW; MTCW 1

O Nuallain, Brian 1911-1966
See O'Brien, Flann
See also CA 21-22; 25-28R; CAP 2

Ophuls, Max 1902-1957 .... **TCLC 79**
See also CA 113

Opie, Amelia 1769-1853 .... **NCLC 65**
See also DLB 116, 159

Oppen, George 1908-1984 ...... **CLC 7, 13, 34**
See also CA 13-16R; 113; CANR 8; DLB 5, 165

Oppenheim, E(dward) Phillips 1866-1946 **TCLC 45**
See also CA 111; DLB 70

Opuls, Max
See Ophuls, Max

Origen c. 185-c. 254 .... **CMLC 19**

Orlovitz, Gil 1918-1973 .... **CLC 22**
See also CA 77-80; 45-48; DLB 2, 5

Orris
See Ingelow, Jean

Ortega y Gasset, Jose 1883-1955 .... **TCLC 9; DAM MULT; HLC**
See also CA 106; 130; HW; MTCW 1

Ortese, Anna Maria 1914- .... **CLC 89**
See also DLB 177

Ortiz, Simon J(oseph) 1941- .. **CLC 45; DAM MULT, POET; PC 17**
See also CA 134; CANR 69; DLB 120, 175; NNAL

Orton, Joe .... **CLC 4, 13, 43; DC 3**
See also Orton, John Kingsley
See also CDBLB 1960 to Present; DLB 13

Orton, John Kingsley 1933-1967
See Orton, Joe
See also CA 85-88; CANR 35, 66; DAM DRAM; MTCW 1

Orwell, George **TCLC 2, 6, 15, 31, 51; DAB; WLC**
See also Blair, Eric (Arthur)
See also CDBLB 1945-1960; DLB 15, 98, 195

Osborne, David
See Silverberg, Robert

Osborne, George
See Silverberg, Robert

Osborne, John (James) 1929-1994 **CLC 1, 2, 5, 11, 45; DA; DAB; DAC; DAM DRAM, MST; WLC**
See also CA 13-16R; 147; CANR 21, 56; CDBLB 1945-1960; DLB 13; MTCW 1

Osborne, Lawrence 1958- .... **CLC 50**

Oshima, Nagisa 1932- .... **CLC 20**
See also CA 116; 121

Oskison, John Milton 1874-1947 . **TCLC 35; DAM MULT**
See also CA 144; DLB 175; NNAL

Ossian c. 3rd cent. - .... **CMLC 28**
See also Macpherson, James

Ossoli, Sarah Margaret (Fuller marchesa d') 1810-1850
See Fuller, Margaret
See also SATA 25

Ostrovsky, Alexander 1823-1886 **NCLC 30, 57**

Otero, Blas de 1916-1979 .... **CLC 11**
See also CA 89-92; DLB 134

Otto, Rudolf 1869-1937 .... **TCLC 85**

Otto, Whitney 1955- .... **CLC 70**
See also CA 140

Ouida .... **TCLC 43**
See also De La Ramee, (Marie) Louise
See also DLB 18, 156

Ousmane, Sembene 1923- .... **CLC 66; BLC 3**
See also BW 1; CA 117; 125; MTCW 1

Ovid 43B.C.-18(?)**CMLC 7; DAM POET; PC 2**

Owen, Hugh
See Faust, Frederick (Schiller)

Owen, Wilfred (Edward Salter) 1893-1918 **TCLC 5, 27; DA; DAB; DAC; DAM MST, POET; PC 19; WLC**
See also CA 104; 141; CDBLB 1914-1945; DLB 20

Owens, Rochelle 1936- .... **CLC 8**
See also CA 17-20R; CAAS 2; CANR 39

Oz, Amos 1939-**CLC 5, 8, 11, 27, 33, 54; DAM NOV**
See also CA 53-56; CANR 27, 47, 65; MTCW 1

Ozick, Cynthia 1928-**CLC 3, 7, 28, 62; DAM NOV, POP; SSC 15**
See also BEST 90:1; CA 17-20R; CANR 23, 58; DLB 28, 152; DLBY 82; INT CANR-23; MTCW 1

Ozu, Yasujiro 1903-1963 .... **CLC 16**
See also CA 112

Pacheco, C.
See Pessoa, Fernando (Antonio Nogueira)

Pa Chin .... **CLC 18**
See also Li Fei-kan

Pack, Robert 1929- .... **CLC 13**
See also CA 1-4R; CANR 3, 44; DLB 5

Padgett, Lewis
See Kuttner, Henry

Padilla (Lorenzo), Heberto 1932- .... **CLC 38**
See also AITN 1; CA 123; 131; HW

Page, Jimmy 1944- .... **CLC 12**

Page, Louise 1955-............................ **CLC 40**
See also CA 140

Page, P(atricia) K(athleen) 1916- **CLC 7, 18; DAC; DAM MST; PC 12**
See also CA 53-56; CANR 4, 22, 65; DLB 68; MTCW 1

Page, Thomas Nelson 1853-1922 .... **SSC 23**
See also CA 118; DLB 12, 78; DLBD 13

Pagels, Elaine Hiesey 1943-............. **CLC 104**
See also CA 45-48; CANR 2, 24, 51

Paget, Violet 1856-1935
See Lee, Vernon
See also CA 104; 166

Paget-Lowe, Henry
See Lovecraft, H(oward) P(hillips)

Paglia, Camille (Anna) 1947- .... **CLC 68**
See also CA 140; CANR 72

Paige, Richard
See Koontz, Dean R(ay)

Paine, Thomas 1737-1809 .... **NCLC 62**
See also CDALB 1640-1865; DLB 31, 43, 73, 158

Pakenham, Antonia
See Fraser, (Lady) Antonia (Pakenham)

Palamas, Kostes 1859-1943 .... **TCLC 5**
See also CA 105

Palazzeschi, Aldo 1885-1974 .... **CLC 11**
See also CA 89-92; 53-56; DLB 114

Paley, Grace 1922-**CLC 4, 6, 37; DAM POP; SSC 8**
See also CA 25-28R; CANR 13, 46; DLB 28; INT CANR-13; MTCW 1

Palin, Michael (Edward) 1943- ,....... **CLC 21**
See also Monty Python
See also CA 107; CANR 35; SATA 67

Palliser, Charles 1947- .... **CLC 65**
See also CA 136

Palma, Ricardo 1833-1919 .... **TCLC 29**

See also CA 168

Pancake, Breece Dexter 1952-1979
See Pancake, Breece D'J
See also CA 123; 109

Pancake, Breece D'J .... **CLC 29**
See also Pancake, Breece Dexter
See also DLB 130

Panko, Rudy
See Gogol, Nikolai (Vasilyevich)

Papadiamantis, Alexandros 1851-1911**T C L C 29**
See also CA 168

Papadiamantopoulos, Johannes 1856-1910
See Moreas, Jean
See also CA 117

Papini, Giovanni 1881-1956 .... **TCLC 22**
See also CA 121

Paracelsus 1493-1541 .... **LC 14**
See also DLB 179

Parasol, Peter
See Stevens, Wallace

Pardo Bazan, Emilia 1851-1921 .... **SSC 30**

Pareto, Vilfredo 1848-1923 .... **TCLC 69**

Parfenie, Maria
See Codrescu, Andrei

Parini, Jay (Lee) 1948- .... **CLC 54**
See also CA 97-100; CAAS 16; CANR 32

Park, Jordan
See Kornbluth, C(yril) M.; Pohl, Frederik

Park, Robert E(zra) 1864-1944 ...... **TCLC 73**
See also CA 122; 165

Parker, Bert
See Ellison, Harlan (Jay)

Parker, Dorothy (Rothschild) 1893-1967**C L C 15, 68; DAM POET; SSC 2**
See also CA 19-20; 25-28R; CAP 2; DLB 11, 45, 86; MTCW 1

Parker, Robert B(rown) 1932-**CLC 27; DAM NOV, POP**
See also BEST 89:4; CA 49-52; CANR 1, 26, 52; INT CANR-26; MTCW 1

Parkin, Frank 1940- .... **CLC 43**
See also CA 147

Parkman, Francis, Jr. 1823-1893 ... **NCLC 12**
See also DLB 1, 30, 186

Parks, Gordon (Alexander Buchanan) 1912- **CLC 1, 16; BLC 3; DAM MULT**
See also AITN 2; BW 2; CA 41-44R; CANR 26, 66; DLB 33; SATA 8

Parmenides c. 515B.C.-c. 450B.C. **CMLC 22**
See also DLB 176

Parnell, Thomas 1679-1718 .... **LC 3**
See also DLB 94

Parra, Nicanor 1914- .... **CLC 2, 102; DAM MULT; HLC**
See also CA 85-88; CANR 32; HW; MTCW 1

Parrish, Mary Frances
See Fisher, M(ary) F(rances) K(ennedy)

Parson
See Coleridge, Samuel Taylor

Parson Lot
See Kingsley, Charles

Partridge, Anthony
See Oppenheim, E(dward) Phillips

Pascal, Blaise 1623-1662 .... **LC 35**

Pascoli, Giovanni 1855-1912 .... **TCLC 45**

Pasolini, Pier Paolo 1922-1975 . **CLC 20, 37, 106; PC 17**
See also CA 93-96; 61-64; CANR 63; DLB 128, 177; MTCW 1

Pasquini
See Silone, Ignazio

Pastan, Linda (Olenik) 1932- **CLC 27; DAM POET**
See also CA 61-64; CANR 18, 40, 61; DLB 5

Pasternak, Boris (Leonidovich) 1890-1960 **CLC 7, 10, 18, 63; DA; DAB; DAC; DAM MST, NOV, POET; PC 6; SSC 31; WLC**
See also CA 127; 116; MTCW 1

Patchen, Kenneth 1911-1972 ... **CLC 1, 2, 18; DAM POET**
See also CA 1-4R; 33-36R; CANR 3, 35; DLB 16, 48; MTCW 1

Pater, Walter (Horatio) 1839-1894 .. **NCLC 7**
See also CDBLB 1832-1890; DLB 57, 156

Paterson, A(ndrew) B(arton) 1864-1941 **TCLC 32**
See also CA 155; SATA 97

Paterson, Katherine (Womeldorf) 1932-**C L C 12, 30**
See also AAYA 1; CA 21-24R; CANR 28, 59; CLR 7, 50; DLB 52; JRDA; MAICYA; MTCW 1; SATA 13, 53, 92

Patmore, Coventry Kersey Dighton 1823-1896 **NCLC 9**
See also DLB 35, 98

Paton, Alan (Stewart) 1903-1988 **CLC 4, 10, 25, 55, 106; DA; DAB; DAC; DAM MST, NOV; WLC**
See also AAYA 26; CA 13-16; 125; CANR 22; CAP 1; DLBD 17; MTCW 1; SATA 11; SATA-Obit 56

Paton Walsh, Gillian 1937-
See Walsh, Jill Paton
See also CANR 38; JRDA; MAICYA; SAAS 3; SATA 4, 72

Patton, George S. 1885-1945 .... **TCLC 79**

Paulding, James Kirke 1778-1860 ... **NCLC 2**
See also DLB 3, 59, 74

Paulin, Thomas Neilson 1949-
See Paulin, Tom
See also CA 123; 128

Paulin, Tom .... **CLC 37**
See also Paulin, Thomas Neilson
See also DLB 40

Paustovsky, Konstantin (Georgievich) 1892-1968 .... **CLC 40**
See also CA 93-96; 25-28R

Pavese, Cesare 1908-1950 ... **TCLC 3; PC 13; SSC 19**
See also CA 104; DLB 128, 177

Pavic, Milorad 1929- .... **CLC 60**
See also CA 136; DLB 181

Payne, Alan
See Jakes, John (William)

Paz, Gil
See Lugones, Leopoldo

Paz, Octavio 1914-1998**CLC 3, 4, 6, 10, 19, 51, 65; DA; DAB; DAC; DAM MST, MULT, POET; HLC; PC 1; WLC**
See also CA 73-76; 165; CANR 32, 65; DLBY 90; HW; MTCW 1

p'Bitek, Okot 1931-1982 .... **CLC 96; BLC 3; DAM MULT**
See also BW 2; CA 124; 107; DLB 125; MTCW 1

Peacock, Molly 1947- ....**CLC 60**
See also CA 103; CAAS 21; CANR 52; DLB 120

Peacock, Thomas Love 1785-1866 . **NCLC 22**
See also DLB 96, 116

Peake, Mervyn 1911-1968............. **CLC 7, 54**
See also CA 5-8R; 25-28R; CANR 3; DLB 15, 160; MTCW 1; SATA 23

Pearce, Philippa ....**CLC 21**
See also Christie, (Ann) Philippa

See also CA 37-40R; CANR 12. 36. 58; DLBY
    83; INT CANR-12; MTCW 1
Plath, Sylvia 1932-1963 **CLC 1, 2, 3, 5, 9, 11,
    14, 17, 50, 51, 62, 111; DA; DAB; DAC;
    DAM MST, POET; PC 1; WLC**
    See also AAYA 13; CA 19-20; CANR 34; CAP
    2; CDALB 1941-1968; DLB 5. 6. 152;
    MTCW 1; SATA 96
Plato 428(?)B.C.-348(?)B.C. ... **CMLC 8; DA;
    DAB; DAC; DAM MST; WLCS**
    See also DLB 176
Platonov, Andrei .... **TCLC 14**
    See also Klimentov. Andrei Platonovich
Platt, Kin 1911- .... **CLC 26**
    See also AAYA 11; CA 17-20R; CANR 11;
    JRDA; SAAS 17; SATA 21. 86
Plautus c. 251B.C.-184B.C. .. **CMLC 24; DC 6**
Plick et Plock
    See Simenon. Georges (Jacques Christian)
Plimpton, George (Ames) 1927- .... **CLC 36**
    See also AITN 1; CA 21-24R; CANR 32. 70;
    DLB 185; MTCW 1; SATA 10
Pliny the Elder c. 23-79 .... **CMLC 23**
Plomer, William Charles Franklin 1903-1973
    CLC 4, 8
    See also CA 21-22; CANR 34; CAP 2; DLB
    20. 162. 191; MTCW 1; SATA 24
Plowman, Piers
    See Kavanagh. Patrick (Joseph)
Plum, J.
    See Wodehouse. P(elham) G(renville)
Plumly, Stanley (Ross) 1939- .... **CLC 33**
    See also CA 108; 110; DLB 5. 193; INT 110
Plumpe, Friedrich Wilhelm 1888-1931**T C L C
    53**
    See also CA 112
Po Chu-i 772-846 .... **CMLC 24**
Poe, Edgar Allan 1809-1849**NCLC 1, 16, 55;
    DA; DAB; DAC; DAM MST, POET; PC
    1; SSC 1, 22; WLC**
    See also AAYA 14; CDALB 1640-1865; DLB
    3. 59. 73. 74; SATA 23
Poet of Titchfield Street, The
    See Pound. Ezra (Weston Loomis)
Pohl, Frederik 1919- .... **CLC 18; SSC 25**
    See also AAYA 24; CA 61-64; CAAS 1; CANR
    11. 37; DLB 8; INT CANR-11; MTCW 1;
    SATA 24
Poirier, Louis 1910-
    See Gracq. Julien
    See also CA 122; 126
Poitier, Sidney 1927- .... **CLC 26**
    See also BW 1; CA 117
Polanski, Roman 1933- .... **CLC 16**
    See also CA 77-80
Poliakoff, Stephen 1952-................... **CLC 38**
    See also CA 106; DLB 13
Police, The
    See Copeland. Stewart (Armstrong); Summers.
    Andrew James; Sumner. Gordon Matthew
Polidori, John William 1795-1821 . **NCLC 51**
    See also DLB 116
Pollitt, Katha 1949- .... **CLC 28**
    See also CA 120; 122; CANR 66; MTCW 1
Pollock, (Mary) Sharon 1936-**CLC 50; DAC;
    DAM DRAM, MST**
    See also CA 141; DLB 60
Polo, Marco 1254-1324 .... **CMLC 15**
Polonsky, Abraham (Lincoln) 1910- **CLC 92**
    See also CA 104; DLB 26; INT 104
Polybius c. 200B.C.-c. 118B.C. ...... **CMLC 17**
    See also DLB 176
Pomerance, Bernard 1940- .... **CLC 13; DAM**

DRAM
    See also CA 101; CANR 49
Ponge, Francis (Jean Gaston Alfred) 1899-1988
    CLC 6, 18; DAM POET
    See also CA 85-88; 126; CANR 40
Pontoppidan, Henrik 1857-1943 .... **TCLC 29**
Poole, Josephine ....**CLC 17**
    See also Helyar. Jane Penelope Josephine
    See also SAAS 2; SATA 5
Popa, Vasko 1922-1991 .... **CLC 19**
    See also CA 112; 148; DLB 181
Pope, Alexander 1688-1744 **LC 3; DA; DAB;
    DAC; DAM MST, POET; WLC**
    See also CDBLB 1660-1789; DLB 95. 101
Porter, Connie (Rose) 1959(?)- ....**CLC 70**
    See also BW 2; CA 142; SATA 81
Porter, Gene(va Grace) Stratton 1863(?)-1924
    TCLC 21
    See also CA 112
Porter, Katherine Anne 1890-1980**CLC 1, 3, 7,
    10, 13, 15, 27, 101; DA; DAB; DAC; DAM
    MST, NOV; SSC 4, 31**
    See also AITN 2; CA 1-4R; 101; CANR 1. 65;
    DLB 4. 9. 102; DLBD 12; DLBY 80; MTCW
    1; SATA 39; SATA-Obit 23
Porter, Peter (Neville Frederick) 1929-**CLC 5,
    13, 33**
    See also CA 85-88; DLB 40
Porter, William Sydney 1862-1910
    See Henry. O.
    See also CA 104; 131; CDALB 1865-1917; DA;
    DAB; DAC; DAM MST; DLB 12. 78. 79;
    MTCW 1; YABC 2
Portillo (y Pacheco), Jose Lopez
    See Lopez Portillo (y Pacheco). Jose
Post, Melville Davisson 1869-1930 **TCLC 39**
    See also CA 110
Potok, Chaim 1929- .... **CLC 2, 7, 14, 26, 112;
    DAM NOV**
    See also AAYA 15; AITN 1. 2; CA 17-20R;
    CANR 19. 35. 64; DLB 28. 152; INT CANR-
    19; MTCW 1; SATA 33
Potter, (Helen) Beatrix 1866-1943
    See Webb. (Martha) Beatrice (Potter)
    See also MAICYA
Potter, Dennis (Christopher George) 1935-1994
    CLC 58, 86
    See also CA 107; 145; CANR 33. 61; MTCW 1
Pound, Ezra (Weston Loomis) 1885-1972**CLC
    1, 2, 3, 4, 5, 7, 10, 13, 18, 34, 48, 50, 112;
    DA; DAB; DAC; DAM MST, POET; PC
    4; WLC**
    See also CA 5-8R; 37-40R; CANR 40; CDALB
    1917-1929; DLB 4. 45. 63; DLBD 15;
    MTCW 1
Povod, Reinaldo 1959-1994 .... **CLC 44**
    See also CA 136; 146
Powell, Adam Clayton, Jr. 1908-1972**CLC 89;
    BLC 3; DAM MULT**
    See also BW 1; CA 102; 33-36R
Powell, Anthony (Dymoke) 1905-**CLC 1, 3, 7,
    9, 10, 31**
    See also CA 1-4R; CANR 1. 32. 62; CDBLB
    1945-1960; DLB 15; MTCW 1
Powell, Dawn 1897-1965 .... **CLC 66**
    See also CA 5-8R; DLBY 97
Powell, Padgett 1952-........................**CLC 34**
    See also CA 126; CANR 63
Power, Susan 1961- .... **CLC 91**
Powers, J(ames) F(arl) 1917-**CLC 1, 4, 8, 57;
    SSC 4**
    See also CA 1-4R; CANR 2. 61; DLB 130;
    MTCW 1

Powers, John J(ames) 1945-
    See Powers. John R.
    See also CA 69-72
Powers, John R. ....**CLC 66**
    See also Powers. John J(ames)
Powers, Richard (S.) 1957-................ **CLC 93**
    See also CA 148
Pownall, David 1938- .... **CLC 10**
    See also CA 89-92; CAAS 18; CANR 49; DLB
    14
Powys, John Cowper 1872-1963**CLC 7, 9, 15,
    46**
    See also CA 85-88; DLB 15; MTCW 1
Powys, T(heodore) F(rancis) 1875-1953
    TCLC 9
    See also CA 106; DLB 36. 162
Prado (Calvo), Pedro 1886-1952 .... **TCLC 75**
    See also CA 131; HW
Prager, Emily 1952- .... **CLC 56**
Pratt, E(dwin) J(ohn) 1883(?)-1964 **CLC 19;
    DAC; DAM POET**
    See also CA 141; 93-96; DLB 92
Premchand .... **TCLC 21**
    See also Srivastava. Dhanpat Rai
Preussler, Otfried 1923-..................... **CLC 17**
    See also CA 77-80; SATA 24
Prevert, Jacques (Henri Marie) 1900-1977
    CLC 15
    See also CA 77-80; 69-72; CANR 29. 61;
    MTCW 1; SATA-Obit 30
Prevost, Abbe (Antoine Francois) 1697-1763
    LC 1
Price, (Edward) Reynolds 1933-**CLC 3, 6, 13,
    43, 50, 63; DAM NOV; SSC 22**
    See also CA 1-4R; CANR 1. 37. 57; DLB 2;
    INT CANR-37
Price, Richard 1949- .... **CLC 6, 12**
    See also CA 49-52; CANR 3; DLBY 81
Prichard, Katharine Susannah 1883-1969
    CLC 46
    See also CA 11-12; CANR 33; CAP 1; MTCW
    1; SATA 66
Priestley, J(ohn) B(oynton) 1894-1984**CLC 2,
    5, 9, 34; DAM DRAM, NOV**
    See also CA 9-12R; 113; CANR 33; CDBLB
    1914-1945; DLB 10. 34. 77. 100. 139; DLBY
    84; MTCW 1
Prince 1958(?)-..................................**CLC 35**
Prince, F(rank) T(empleton) 1912-...**CLC 22**
    See also CA 101; CANR 43; DLB 20
Prince Kropotkin
    See Kropotkin. Peter (Aleksieevich)
Prior, Matthew 1664-1721 .... **LC 4**
    See also DLB 95
Prishvin, Mikhail 1873-1954 .... **TCLC 75**
Pritchard, William H(arrison) 1932-**CLC 34**
    See also CA 65-68; CANR 23; DLB 111
Pritchett, V(ictor) S(awdon) 1900-1997 **C L C
    5, 13, 15, 41; DAM NOV; SSC 14**
    See also CA 61-64; 157; CANR 31. 63; DLB
    15. 139; MTCW 1
Private 19022
    See Manning. Frederic
Probst, Mark 1925- ....**CLC 59**
    See also CA 130
Prokosch, Frederic 1908-1989 ..... **CLC 4, 48**
    See also CA 73-76; 128; DLB 48
Prophet, The
    See Dreiser. Theodore (Herman Albert)
Prose, Francine 1947- .... **CLC 45**
    See also CA 109; 112; CANR 46; SATA 101
Proudhon
    See Cunha. Euclides (Rodrigues Pimenta) da

Proulx, Annie
  See Proulx, E(dna) Annie
Proulx, E(dna) Annie 1935- ... CLC 81; DAM
  POP
  See also CA 145; CANR 65
Proust, (Valentin-Louis-George-Eugene-)
  Marcel 1871-1922 TCLC 7, 13, 33; DA;
  DAB; DAC; DAM MST, NOV; WLC
  See also CA 104; 120; DLB 65; MTCW 1
Prowler, Harley
  See Masters, Edgar Lee
Prus, Boleslaw 1845-1912 .... TCLC 48
Pryor, Richard (Franklin Lenox Thomas) 1940-
  CLC 26
  See also CA 122
Przybyszewski, Stanislaw 1868-1927TCLC 36
  See also CA 160; DLB 66
Pteleon
  See Grieve, C(hristopher) M(urray)
  See also DAM POET
Puckett, Lute
  See Masters, Edgar Lee
Puig, Manuel 1932-1990CLC 3, 5, 10, 28, 65;
  DAM MULT; HLC
  See also CA 45-48; CANR 2, 32, 63; DLB 113;
  HW; MTCW 1
Pulitzer, Joseph 1847-1911 .... TCLC 76
  See also CA 114; DLB 23
Purdy, A(lfred) W(ellington) 1918-CLC 3, 6,
  14, 50; DAC; DAM MST, POET
  See also CA 81-84; CAAS 17; CANR 42, 66;
  DLB 88
Purdy, James (Amos) 1923-CLC 2, 4, 10, 28,
  52
  See also CA 33-36R; CAAS 1; CANR 19, 51;
  DLB 2; INT CANR-19; MTCW 1
Pure, Simon
  See Swinnerton, Frank Arthur
Pushkin, Alexander (Sergeyevich) 1799-1837
  NCLC 3, 27; DA; DAB; DAC; DAM
  DRAM, MST, POET; PC 10; SSC 27;
  WLC
  See also SATA 61
P'u Sung-ling 1640-1715 .... LC 3; SSC 31
Putnam, Arthur Lee
  See Alger, Horatio, Jr.
Puzo, Mario 1920-CLC 1, 2, 6, 36, 107; DAM
  NOV, POP
  See also CA 65-68; CANR 4, 42, 65; DLB 6;
  MTCW 1
Pygge, Edward
  See Barnes, Julian (Patrick)
Pyle, Ernest Taylor 1900-1945
  See Pyle, Ernie
  See also CA 115; 160
Pyle, Ernie 1900-1945 .... TCLC 75
  See also Pyle, Ernest Taylor
  See also DLB 29
Pyle, Howard 1853-1911 .... TCLC 81
  See also CA 109; 137; CLR 22; DLB 42, 188;
  DLBD 13; MAICYA; SATA 16, 100
Pym, Barbara (Mary Crampton) 1913-1980
  CLC 13, 19, 37, 111
  See also CA 13-14; 97-100; CANR 13, 34; CAP
  1; DLB 14; DLBY 87; MTCW 1
Pynchon, Thomas (Ruggles, Jr.) 1937-CLC 2,
  3, 6, 9, 11, 18, 33, 62, 72; DA; DAB; DAC;
  DAM MST, NOV, POP; SSC 14; WLC
  See also BEST 90:2; CA 17-20R; CANR 22,
  46; DLB 2, 173; MTCW 1
Pythagoras c. 570B.C.-c. 500B.C. . CMLC 22
  See also DLB 176
Q

See Quiller-Couch, SirArthur (Thomas)
Qian Zhongshu
  See Ch'ien Chung-shu
Qroll
  See Dagerman, Stig (Halvard)
Quarrington, Paul (Lewis) 1953- ...... CLC 65
  See also CA 129; CANR 62
Quasimodo, Salvatore 1901-1968 ..... CLC 10
  See also CA 13-16; 25-28R; CAP 1; DLB 114;
  MTCW 1
Quay, Stephen 1947- .... CLC 95
Quay, Timothy 1947- .... CLC 95
Queen, Ellery .... CLC 3, 11
  See also Dannay, Frederic; Davidson, Avram;
  Lee, Manfred B(ennington); Marlowe,
  Stephen; Sturgeon, Theodore (Hamilton);
  Vance, John Holbrook
Queen, Ellery, Jr.
  See Dannay, Frederic; Lee, Manfred
  B(ennington)
Queneau, Raymond 1903-1976 CLC 2, 5, 10,
  42
  See also CA 77-80; 69-72; CANR 32; DLB 72;
  MTCW 1
Quevedo, Francisco de 1580-1645 ...... LC 23
Quiller-Couch, SirArthur (Thomas) 1863-1944
  TCLC 53
  See also CA 118; 166; DLB 135, 153, 190
Quin, Ann (Marie) 1936-1973 .... CLC 6
  See also CA 9-12R; 45-48; DLB 14
Quinn, Martin
  See Smith, Martin Cruz
Quinn, Peter 1947- .... CLC 91
Quinn, Simon
  See Smith, Martin Cruz
Quiroga, Horacio (Sylvestre) 1878-1937
  TCLC 20; DAM MULT; HLC
  See also CA 117; 131; HW; MTCW 1
Quoirez, Francoise 1935- .... CLC 9
  See also Sagan, Francoise
  See also CA 49-52; CANR 6, 39; MTCW 1
Raabe, Wilhelm (Karl) 1831-1910 . TCLC 45
  See also CA 167; DLB 129
Rabe, David (William) 1940- ... CLC 4, 8, 33;
  DAM DRAM
  See also CA 85-88; CABS 3; CANR 59; DLB 7
Rabelais, Francois 1483-1553LC 5; DA; DAB;
  DAC; DAM MST; WLC
Rabinovitch, Sholem 1859-1916
  See Aleichem, Sholom
  See also CA 104
Rachilde 1860-1953 .... TCLC 67
  See also DLB 123, 192
Racine, Jean 1639-1699 . LC 28; DAB; DAM
  MST
Radcliffe, Ann (Ward) 1764-1823NCLC 6, 55
  See also DLB 39, 178
Radiguet, Raymond 1903-1923 ...... TCLC 29
  See also CA 162; DLB 65
Radnoti, Miklos 1909-1944 .... TCLC 16
  See also CA 118
Rado, James 1939- .... CLC 17
  See also CA 105
Radvanyi, Netty 1900-1983
  See Seghers, Anna
  See also CA 85-88; 110
Rae, Ben
  See Griffiths, Trevor
Raeburn, John (Hay) 1941- .... CLC 34
  See also CA 57-60
Ragni, Gerome 1942-1991 .... CLC 17
  See also CA 105; 134
Rahv, Philip 1908-1973 .... CLC 24

See also Greenberg, Ivan
  See also DLB 137
Raimund, Ferdinand Jakob 1790-1836NCLC
  69
  See also DLB 90
Raine, Craig 1944- .... CLC 32, 103
  See also CA 108; CANR 29, 51; DLB 40
Raine, Kathleen (Jessie) 1908- ...... CLC 7, 45
  See also CA 85-88; CANR 46; DLB 20; MTCW
  1
Rainis, Janis 1865-1929 .... TCLC 29
Rakosi, Carl 1903- .... CLC 47
  See also Rawley, Callman
  See also CAAS 5; DLB 193
Raleigh, Richard
  See Lovecraft, H(oward) P(hillips)
Raleigh, Sir Walter 1554(?)-1618 . LC 31, 39
  See also CDBLB Before 1660; DLB 172
Rallentando, H. P.
  See Sayers, Dorothy L(eigh)
Ramal, Walter
  See de la Mare, Walter (John)
Ramana Maharshi 1879-1950 .... TCLC 84
Ramon, Juan
  See Jimenez (Mantecon), Juan Ramon
Ramos, Graciliano 1892-1953 .... TCLC 32
  See also CA 167
Rampersad, Arnold 1941- .... CLC 44
  See also BW 2; CA 127; 133; DLB 111; INT
  133
Rampling, Anne
  See Rice, Anne
Ramsay, Allan 1684(?)-1758 .... LC 29
  See also DLB 95
Ramuz, Charles-Ferdinand 1878-1947T C L C
  33
  See also CA 165
Rand, Ayn 1905-1982CLC 3, 30, 44, 79; DA;
  DAC; DAM MST, NOV, POP; WLC
  See also AAYA 10; CA 13-16R; 105; CANR
  27; MTCW 1
Randall, Dudley (Felker) 1914-CLC 1; BLC 3;
  DAM MULT
  See also BW 1; CA 25-28R; CANR 23; DLB
  41
Randall, Robert
  See Silverberg, Robert
Ranger, Ken
  See Creasey, John
Ransom, John Crowe 1888-1974CLC 2, 4, 5,
  11, 24; DAM POET
  See also CA 5-8R; 49-52; CANR 6, 34; DLB
  45, 63; MTCW 1
Rao, Raja 1909- ...... CLC 25, 56; DAM NOV
  See also CA 73-76; CANR 51; MTCW 1
Raphael, Frederic (Michael) 1931-CLC 2, 14
  See also CA 1-4R; CANR 1; DLB 14
Ratcliffe, James P.
  See Mencken, H(enry) L(ouis)
Rathbone, Julian 1935- .... CLC 41
  See also CA 101; CANR 34
Rattigan, Terence (Mervyn) 1911-1977CLC 7;
  DAM DRAM
  See also CA 85-88; 73-76; CDBLB 1945-1960;
  DLB 13; MTCW 1
Ratushinskaya, Irina 1954- .... CLC 54
  See also CA 129; CANR 68
Raven, Simon (Arthur Noel) 1927- ... CLC 14
  See also CA 81-84
Ravenna, Michael
  See Welty, Eudora
Rawley, Callman 1903-
  See Rakosi, Carl

Roth, Philip (Milton) 1933-CLC **1, 2, 3, 4, 6, 9, 15, 22, 31, 47, 66, 86; DA; DAB; DAC; DAM MST, NOV, POP; SSC 26; WLC**
See also BEST 90:3; CA 1-4R; CANR 1, 22, 36, 55; CDALB 1968-1988; DLB 2, 28, 173; DLBY 82; MTCW 1

Rothenberg, Jerome 1931- .... CLC **6, 57**
See also CA 45-48; CANR 1; DLB 5, 193

Roumain, Jacques (Jean Baptiste) 1907-1944 **TCLC 19; BLC 3; DAM MULT**
See also BW 1; CA 117; 125

Rourke, Constance (Mayfield) 1885-1941 **TCLC 12**
See also CA 107; YABC 1

Rousseau, Jean-Baptiste 1671-1741 ..... LC **9**

Rousseau, Jean-Jacques 1712-1778LC **14, 36; DA; DAB; DAC; DAM MST; WLC**

Roussel, Raymond 1877-1933 .... TCLC **20**
See also CA 117

Rovit, Earl (Herbert) 1927- .... CLC **7**
See also CA 5-8R; CANR 12

Rowe, Elizabeth Singer 1674-1737 ..... LC **44**
See also DLB 39, 95

Rowe, Nicholas 1674-1718 .... LC **8**
See also DLB 84

Rowley, Ames Dorrance
See Lovecraft, H(oward) P(hillips)

Rowson, Susanna Haswell 1762(?)-1824 **NCLC 5, 69**
See also DLB 37, 200

Roy, Arundhati 1960(?)- .... CLC **109**
See also CA 163; DLBY 97

Roy, Gabrielle 1909-1983 CLC **10, 14; DAB; DAC; DAM MST**
See also CA 53-56; 110; CANR 5, 61; DLB 68; MTCW 1

Royko, Mike 1932-1997 .... CLC **109**
See also CA 89-92; 157; CANR 26

Rozewicz, Tadeusz 1921- ...CLC **9, 23; DAM POET**
See also CA 108; CANR 36, 66; MTCW 1

Ruark, Gibbons 1941- .... CLC **3**
See also CA 33-36R; CAAS 23; CANR 14, 31, 57; DLB 120

Rubens, Bernice (Ruth) 1923- .... CLC **19, 31**
See also CA 25-28R; CANR 33, 65; DLB 14; MTCW 1

Rubin, Harold
See Robbins, Harold

Rudkin, (James) David 1936- .... CLC **14**
See also CA 89-92; DLB 13

Rudnik, Raphael 1933- .... CLC **7**
See also CA 29-32R

Ruffian, M.
See Hasek, Jaroslav (Matej Frantisek)

Ruiz, Jose Martinez .... CLC **11**
See also Martinez Ruiz, Jose

Rukeyser, Muriel 1913-1980CLC **6, 10, 15, 27; DAM POET; PC 12**
See also CA 5-8R; 93-96; CANR 26, 60; DLB 48; MTCW 1; SATA-Obit 22

Rule, Jane (Vance) 1931- .... CLC **27**
See also CA 25-28R; CAAS 18; CANR 12; DLB 60

Rulfo, Juan 1918-1986 ....CLC **8, 80; DAM MULT; HLC; SSC 25**
See also CA 85-88; 118; CANR 26; DLB 113; HW; MTCW 1

Rumi, Jalal al-Din 1297-1373 .... CMLC **20**

Runeberg, Johan 1804-1877........... NCLC **41**

Runyon, (Alfred) Damon 1884(?)-1946T C L C **10**
See also CA 107; 165; DLB 11, 86, 171

Rush, Norman 1933- .... CLC **44**
See also CA 121; 126; INT 126

Rushdie, (Ahmed) Salman 1947-CLC **23, 31, 55, 100; DAB; DAC; DAM MST, NOV, POP; WLCS**
See also BEST 89:3; CA 108; 111; CANR 33, 56; DLB 194; INT 111; MTCW 1

Rushforth, Peter (Scott) 1945- .... CLC **19**
See also CA 101

Ruskin, John 1819-1900 .... TCLC **63**
See also CA 114; 129; CDBLB 1832-1890; DLB 55, 163, 190; SATA 24

Russ, Joanna 1937-............................ CLC **15**
See also CANR 11, 31, 65; DLB 8; MTCW 1

Russell, George William 1867-1935
See Baker, Jean H.
See also CA 104; 153; CDBLB 1890-1914; DAM POET

Russell, (Henry) Ken(neth Alfred) 1927-C L C **16**
See also CA 105

Russell, William Martin 1947- .... CLC **60**
See also CA 164

Rutherford, Mark .... TCLC **25**
See also White, William Hale
See also DLB 18

Ruyslinck, Ward 1929- .... CLC **14**
See also Belser, Reimond Karel Maria de

Ryan, Cornelius (John) 1920-1974 ..... CLC **7**
See also CA 69-72; 53-56; CANR 38

Ryan, Michael 1946- .... CLC **65**
See also CA 49-52; DLBY 82

Ryan, Tim
See Dent, Lester

Rybakov, Anatoli (Naumovich) 1911-CLC **23, 53**
See also CA 126; 135; SATA 79

Ryder, Jonathan
See Ludlum, Robert

Ryga, George 1932-1987CLC **14; DAC; DAM MST**
See also CA 101; 124; CANR 43; DLB 60

S. H.
See Hartmann, Sadakichi

S. S.
See Sassoon, Siegfried (Lorraine)

Saba, Umberto 1883-1957 .... TCLC **33**
See also CA 144; DLB 114

Sabatini, Rafael 1875-1950 .... TCLC **47**
See also CA 162

Sabato, Ernesto (R.) 1911-CLC **10, 23; DAM MULT; HLC**
See also CA 97-100; CANR 32, 65; DLB 145; HW; MTCW 1

Sa-Carniero, Mario de 1890-1916 . TCLC **83**

Sacastru, Martin
See Bioy Casares, Adolfo

Sacher-Masoch, Leopold von 1836(?)-1895 **NCLC 31**

Sachs, Marilyn (Stickle) 1927- .... CLC **35**
See also AAYA 2; CA 17-20R; CANR 13, 47; CLR 2; JRDA; MAICYA; SAAS 2; SATA 3, 68

Sachs, Nelly 1891-1970 .... CLC **14, 98**
See also CA 17-18; 25-28R; CAP 2

Sackler, Howard (Oliver) 1929-1982 CLC **14**
See also CA 61-64; 108; CANR 30; DLB 7

Sacks, Oliver (Wolf) 1933-................. CLC **67**
See also CA 53-56; CANR 28, 50; INT CANR-28; MTCW 1

Sadakichi
See Hartmann, Sadakichi

Sade, Donatien Alphonse Francois, Comte de
1740-1814 .... NCLC **47**

Sadoff, Ira 1945- .... CLC **9**
See also CA 53-56; CANR 5, 21; DLB 120

Saetone
See Camus, Albert

Safire, William 1929- .... CLC **10**
See also CA 17-20R; CANR 31, 54

Sagan, Carl (Edward) 1934-1996CLC **30, 112**
See also AAYA 2; CA 25-28R; 155; CANR 11, 36; MTCW 1; SATA 58; SATA-Obit 94

Sagan, Francoise .... CLC **3, 6, 9, 17, 36**
See also Quoirez, Francoise
See also DLB 83

Sahgal, Nayantara (Pandit) 1927- .... CLC **41**
See also CA 9-12R; CANR 11

Saint, H(arry) F. 1941- .... CLC **50**
See also CA 127

St. Aubin de Teran, Lisa 1953-
See Teran, Lisa St. Aubin de
See also CA 118; 126; INT 126

Saint Birgitta of Sweden c. 1303-1373CM L C **24**

Sainte-Beuve, Charles Augustin 1804-1869 **NCLC 5**

Saint-Exupery, Antoine (Jean Baptiste Marie Roger) de 1900-1944 ....
TCLC 2, 56; DAM NOV; WLC
See also CA 108; 132; CLR 10; DLB 72; MAICYA; MTCW 1; SATA 20

St. John, David
See Hunt, E(verette) Howard, (Jr.)

Saint-John Perse
See Leger, (Marie-Rene Auguste) Alexis Saint-Leger

Saintsbury, George (Edward Bateman) 1845-1933 .... TCLC **31**
See also CA 160; DLB 57, 149

Sait Faik .... TCLC **23**
See also Abasiyanik, Sait Faik

Saki .... TCLC **3; SSC 12**
See also Munro, H(ector) H(ugh)

Sala, George Augustus .... NCLC **46**

Salama, Hannu 1936-......................... CLC **18**

Salamanca, J(ack) R(ichard) 1922-CLC **4, 15**
See also CA 25-28R

Sale, J. Kirkpatrick
See Sale, Kirkpatrick

Sale, Kirkpatrick 1937- .... CLC **68**
See also CA 13-16R; CANR 10

Salinas, Luis Omar 1937- ...... CLC **90; DAM MULT; HLC**
See also CA 131; DLB 82; HW

Salinas (y Serrano), Pedro 1891(?)-1951 **TCLC 17**
See also CA 117; DLB 134

Salinger, J(erome) D(avid) 1919-CLC **1, 3, 8, 12, 55, 56; DA; DAB; DAC; DAM MST, NOV, POP; SSC 2, 28; WLC**
See also AAYA 2; CA 5-8R; CANR 39; CDALB 1941-1968; CLR 18; DLB 2, 102, 173; MAICYA; MTCW 1; SATA 67

Salisbury, John
See Caute, (John) David

Salter, James 1925-................. CLC **7, 52, 59**
See also CA 73-76; DLB 130

Saltus, Edgar (Everton) 1855-1921 . TCLC **8**
See also CA 105; DLB 202

Saltykov, Mikhail Evgrafovich 1826-1889 **NCLC 16**

Samarakis, Antonis 1919-................... CLC **5**
See also CA 25-28R; CAAS 16; CANR 36

Sanchez, Florencio 1875-1910 .... TCLC **37**
See also CA 153; HW

Singer, Isaac Bashevis 1904-1991 **CLC 1, 3, 6, 9, 11, 15, 23, 38, 69, 111; DA; DAB; DAC; DAM MST, NOV; SSC 3; WLC**
See also AITN 1, 2; CA 1-4R; 134; CANR 1, 39; CDALB 1941-1968; CLR 1; DLB 6, 28, 52; DLBY 91; JRDA; MAICYA; MTCW 1; SATA 3, 27; SATA-Obit 68

Singer, Israel Joshua 1893-1944 .... **TCLC 33**

Singh, Khushwant 1915- .... **CLC 11**
See also CA 9-12R; CAAS 9; CANR 6

Singleton, Ann
See Benedict, Ruth (Fulton)

Sinjohn, John
See Galsworthy, John

Sinyavsky, Andrei (Donatevich) 1925-1997 **CLC 8**
See also CA 85-88; 159

Sirin, V.
See Nabokov, Vladimir (Vladimirovich)

Sissman, L(ouis) E(dward) 1928-1976 **CLC 9, 18**
See also CA 21-24R; 65-68; CANR 13; DLB 5

Sisson, C(harles) H(ubert) 1914- .... **CLC 8**
See also CA 1-4R; CAAS 3; CANR 3, 48; DLB 27

Sitwell, Dame Edith 1887-1964 **CLC 2, 9, 67; DAM POET; PC 3**
See also CA 9-12R; CANR 35; CDBLB 1945-1960; DLB 20; MTCW 1

Siwaarmill, H. P.
See Sharp, William

Sjoewall, Maj 1935- .... **CLC 7**
See also CA 65-68

Sjowall, Maj
See Sjoewall, Maj

Skelton, Robin 1925-1997 .... **CLC 13**
See also AITN 2; CA 5-8R; 160; CAAS 5; CANR 28; DLB 27, 53

Skolimowski, Jerzy 1938- .... **CLC 20**
See also CA 128

Skram, Amalie (Bertha) 1847-1905 **TCLC 25**
See also CA 165

Skvorecky, Josef (Vaclav) 1924- **CLC 15, 39, 69; DAC; DAM NOV**
See also CA 61-64; CAAS 1; CANR 10, 34, 63; MTCW 1

Slade, Bernard .... **CLC 11, 46**
See also Newbound, Bernard Slade
See also CAAS 9; DLB 53

Slaughter, Carolyn 1946- .... **CLC 56**
See also CA 85-88

Slaughter, Frank G(ill) 1908- .... **CLC 29**
See also AITN 2; CA 5-8R; CANR 5; INT CANR-5

Slavitt, David R(ytman) 1935- ..... **CLC 5, 14**
See also CA 21-24R; CAAS 3; CANR 41; DLB 5, 6

Slesinger, Tess 1905-1945 .... **TCLC 10**
See also CA 107; DLB 102

Slessor, Kenneth 1901-1971 .... **CLC 14**
See also CA 102; 89-92

Slowacki, Juliusz 1809-1849 .... **NCLC 15**

Smart, Christopher 1722-1771 ... **LC 3; DAM POET; PC 13**
See also DLB 109

Smart, Elizabeth 1913-1986 .... **CLC 54**
See also CA 81-84; 118; DLB 88

Smiley, Jane (Graves) 1949- **CLC 53, 76; DAM POP**
See also CA 104; CANR 30, 50; INT CANR-30

Smith, A(rthur) J(ames) M(arshall) 1902-1980 **CLC 15; DAC**

See also CA 1-4R; 102; CANR 4; DLB 88

Smith, Adam 1723-1790 .... **LC 36**
See also DLB 104

Smith, Alexander 1829-1867 .... **NCLC 59**
See also DLB 32, 55

Smith, Anna Deavere 1950- .... **CLC 86**
See also CA 133

Smith, Betty (Wehner) 1896-1972 ..... **CLC 19**
See also CA 5-8R; 33-36R; DLBY 82; SATA 6

Smith, Charlotte (Turner) 1749-1806 **NCLC 23**
See also DLB 39, 109

Smith, Clark Ashton 1893-1961 .... **CLC 43**
See also CA 143

Smith, Dave .... **CLC 22, 42**
See also Smith, David (Jeddie)
See also CAAS 7; DLB 5

Smith, David (Jeddie) 1942-
See Smith, Dave
See also CA 49-52; CANR 1, 59; DAM POET

Smith, Florence Margaret 1902-1971
See Smith, Stevie
See also CA 17-18; 29-32R; CANR 35; CAP 2; DAM POET; MTCW 1

Smith, Iain Crichton 1928- .... **CLC 64**
See also CA 21-24R; DLB 40, 139

Smith, John 1580(?)-1631 .... **LC 9**
See also DLB 24, 30

Smith, Johnston
See Crane, Stephen (Townley)

Smith, Joseph, Jr. 1805-1844 .... **NCLC 53**

Smith, Lee 1944- .... **CLC 25, 73**
See also CA 114; 119; CANR 46; DLB 143; DLBY 83; INT 119

Smith, Martin
See Smith, Martin Cruz

Smith, Martin Cruz 1942- ..... **CLC 25; DAM MULT, POP**
See also BEST 89:4; CA 85-88; CANR 6, 23, 43, 65; INT CANR-23; NNAL

Smith, Mary-Ann Tirone 1944- .... **CLC 39**
See also CA 118; 136

Smith, Patti 1946- .... **CLC 12**
See also CA 93-96; CANR 63

Smith, Pauline (Urmson) 1882-1959 **TCLC 25**

Smith, Rosamond
See Oates, Joyce Carol

Smith, Sheila Kaye
See Kaye-Smith, Sheila

Smith, Stevie .... **CLC 3, 8, 25, 44; PC 12**
See also Smith, Florence Margaret
See also DLB 20

Smith, Wilbur (Addison) 1933- .... **CLC 33**
See also CA 13-16R; CANR 7, 46, 66; MTCW 1

Smith, William Jay 1918- .... **CLC 6**
See also CA 5-8R; CANR 44; DLB 5; MAICYA; SAAS 22; SATA 2, 68

Smith, Woodrow Wilson
See Kuttner, Henry

Smolenskin, Peretz 1842-1885 .... **NCLC 30**

Smollett, Tobias (George) 1721-1771 ... **LC 2**
See also CDBLB 1660-1789; DLB 39, 104

Snodgrass, W(illiam) D(e Witt) 1926- **CLC 2, 6, 10, 18, 68; DAM POET**
See also CA 1-4R; CANR 6, 36, 65; DLB 5; MTCW 1

Snow, C(harles) P(ercy) 1905-1980 **CLC 1, 4, 6, 9, 13, 19; DAM NOV**
See also CA 5-8R; 101; CANR 28; CDBLB 1945-1960; DLB 15, 77; DLBD 17; MTCW 1

Snow, Frances Compton

See Adams, Henry (Brooks)

Snyder, Gary (Sherman) 1930- **CLC 1, 2, 5, 9, 32; DAM POET; PC 21**
See also CA 17-20R; CANR 30, 60; DLB 5, 16, 165

Snyder, Zilpha Keatley 1927- .... **CLC 17**
See also AAYA 15; CA 9-12R; CANR 38; CLR 31; JRDA; MAICYA; SAAS 2; SATA 1, 28, 75

Soares, Bernardo
See Pessoa, Fernando (Antonio Nogueira)

Sobh, A.
See Shamlu, Ahmad

Sobol, Joshua .... **CLC 60**

Socrates 469B.C.-399B.C. .... **CMLC 27**

Soderberg, Hjalmar 1869-1941 ..... **TCLC 39**

Sodergran, Edith (Irene)
See Soedergran, Edith (Irene)

Soedergran, Edith (Irene) 1892-1923 . **TCLC 31**

Softly, Edgar
See Lovecraft, H(oward) P(hillips)

Softly, Edward
See Lovecraft, H(oward) P(hillips)

Sokolov, Raymond 1941- .... **CLC 7**
See also CA 85-88

Solo, Jay
See Ellison, Harlan (Jay)

Sologub, Fyodor .... **TCLC 9**
See also Teternikov, Fyodor Kuzmich

Solomons, Ikey Esquir
See Thackeray, William Makepeace

Solomos, Dionysios 1798-1857 .... **NCLC 15**

Solwoska, Mara
See French, Marilyn

Solzhenitsyn, Aleksandr I(sayevich) 1918- **CLC 1, 2, 4, 7, 9, 10, 18, 26, 34, 78; DA; DAB; DAC; DAM MST, NOV; SSC 32; WLC**
See also AITN 1; CA 69-72; CANR 40, 65; MTCW 1

Somers, Jane
See Lessing, Doris (May)

Somerville, Edith 1858-1949 .... **TCLC 51**
See also DLB 135

Somerville & Ross
See Martin, Violet Florence; Somerville, Edith

Sommer, Scott 1951- .... **CLC 25**
See also CA 106

Sondheim, Stephen (Joshua) 1930-. **CLC 30, 39; DAM DRAM**
See also AAYA 11; CA 103; CANR 47, 68

Song, Cathy 1955- .... **PC 21**
See also CA 154; DLB 169

Sontag, Susan 1933- **CLC 1, 2, 10, 13, 31, 105; DAM POP**
See also CA 17-20R; CANR 25, 51; DLB 2, 67; MTCW 1

Sophocles 496(?)B.C.-406(?)B.C. .... **CMLC 2; DA; DAB; DAC; DAM DRAM, MST; DC 1; WLCS**
See also DLB 176

Sordello 1189-1269 .... **CMLC 15**

Sorel, Julia
See Drexler, Rosalyn

Sorrentino, Gilbert 1929- **CLC 3, 7, 14, 22, 40**
See also CA 77-80; CANR 14, 33; DLB 5, 173; DLBY 80; INT CANR-14

Soto, Gary 1952-. **CLC 32, 80; DAM MULT; HLC**
See also AAYA 10; CA 119; 125; CANR 50; CLR 38; DLB 82; HW; INT 125; JRDA; SATA 80

Swift, Augustus
  See Lovecraft. H(oward) P(hillips)
Swift, Graham (Colin) 1949- ...... **CLC 41, 88**
  See also CA 117; 122; CANR 46, 71; DLB 194
Swift, Jonathan 1667-1745 **LC 1; DA; DAB;
    DAC; DAM MST, NOV, POET; PC 9;
    WLC**
  See also CDBLB 1660-1789; CLR 53; DLB 39,
    95, 101; SATA 19
Swinburne, Algernon Charles 1837-1909
    **TCLC 8, 36; DA; DAB; DAC; DAM MST,
    POET; PC 24; WLC**
  See also CA 105; 140; CDBLB 1832-1890;
    DLB 35, 57
Swinfen, Ann .... **CLC 34**
Swinnerton, Frank Arthur 1884-1982**CLC 31**
  See also CA 108; DLB 34
Swithen, John
  See King. Stephen (Edwin)
Sylvia
  See Ashton-Warner. Sylvia (Constance)
Symmes, Robert Edward
  See Duncan, Robert (Edward)
Symonds, John Addington 1840-1893 **N C L C
    34**
  See also DLB 57, 144
Symons, Arthur 1865-1945 .... **TCLC 11**
  See also CA 107; DLB 19, 57, 149
Symons, Julian (Gustave) 1912-1994 **CLC 2,
    14, 32**
  See also CA 49-52; 147; CAAS 3; CANR 3,
    33, 59; DLB 87, 155; DLBY 92; MTCW 1
Synge, (Edmund) J(ohn) M(illington) 1871-
    1909 .. **TCLC 6, 37; DAM DRAM; DC 2**
  See also CA 104; 141; CDBLB 1890-1914;
    DLB 10, 19
Syruc, J.
  See Milosz, Czeslaw
Szirtes, George 1948- .... **CLC 46**
  See also CA 109; CANR 27, 61
Szymborska, Wislawa 1923- .... **CLC 99**
  See also CA 154; DLBY 96
T. O., Nik
  See Annensky, Innokenty (Fyodorovich)
Tabori, George 1914- .... **CLC 19**
  See also CA 49-52; CANR 4, 69
Tagore, Rabindranath 1861-1941**TCLC 3, 53;
    DAM DRAM, POET; PC 8**
  See also CA 104; 120; MTCW 1
Taine, Hippolyte Adolphe 1828-1893 . **N C L C
    15**
Talese, Gay 1932- .... **CLC 37**
  See also AITN 1; CA 1-4R; CANR 9, 58; DLB
    185; INT CANR-9; MTCW 1
Tallent, Elizabeth (Ann) 1954- .... **CLC 45**
  See also CA 117; CANR 72; DLB 130
Tally, Ted 1952-................................. **CLC 42**
  See also CA 120; 124; INT 124
Tamayo y Baus, Manuel 1829-1898 . **NCLC 1**
Tammsaare, A(nton) H(ansen) 1878-1940
    TCLC 27
  See also CA 164
Tam'si, Tchicaya U
  See Tchicaya, Gerald Felix
Tan, Amy (Ruth) 1952-**CLC 59; DAM MULT,
    NOV, POP**
  See also AAYA 9; BEST 89:3; CA 136; CANR
    54; DLB 173; SATA 75
Tandem, Felix
  See Spitteler, Carl (Friedrich Georg)
Tanizaki, Jun'ichiro 1886-1965**CLC 8, 14, 28;
    SSC 21**
  See also CA 93-96; 25-28R; DLB 180

Tanner, William
  See Amis, Kingsley (William)
Tao Lao
  See Storni, Alfonsina
Tarassoff, Lev
  See Troyat. Henri
Tarbell, Ida M(inerva) 1857-1944 . **TCLC 40**
  See also CA 122; DLB 47
Tarkington, (Newton) Booth 1869-1946**TCLC
    9**
  See also CA 110; 143; DLB 9, 102; SATA 17
Tarkovsky, Andrei (Arsenyevich) 1932-1986
    CLC 75
  See also CA 127
Tartt, Donna 1964(?)- ....**CLC 76**
  See also CA 142
Tasso, Torquato 1544-1595 .... **LC 5**
Tate, (John Orley) Allen 1899-1979**CLC 2, 4,
    6, 9, 11, 14, 24**
  See also CA 5-8R; 85-88; CANR 32; DLB 4,
    45, 63; DLBD 17; MTCW 1
Tate, Ellalice
  See Hibbert, Eleanor Alice Burford
Tate, James (Vincent) 1943- ..... **CLC 2, 6, 25**
  See also CA 21-24R; CANR 29, 57; DLB 5,
    169
Tavel, Ronald 1940- ....**CLC 6**
  See also CA 21-24R; CANR 33
Taylor, C(ecil) P(hilip) 1929-1981 .....**CLC 27**
  See also CA 25-28R; 105; CANR 47
Taylor, Edward 1642(?)-1729 ..... **LC 11; DA;
    DAB; DAC; DAM MST, POET**
  See also DLB 24
Taylor, Eleanor Ross 1920- ....**CLC 5**
  See also CA 81-84; CANR 70
Taylor, Elizabeth 1912-1975 ..... **CLC 2, 4, 29**
  See also CA 13-16R; CANR 9, 70; DLB 139;
    MTCW 1; SATA 13
Taylor, Frederick Winslow 1856-1915 **T C L C
    76**
Taylor, Henry (Splawn) 1942- ....**CLC 44**
  See also CA 33-36R; CAAS 7; CANR 31; DLB
    5
Taylor, Kamala (Purnaiya) 1924-
  See Markandaya, Kamala
  See also CA 77-80
Taylor, Mildred D. ....**CLC 21**
  See also AAYA 10; BW 1; CA 85-88; CANR
    25; CLR 9; DLB 52; JRDA; MAICYA; SAAS
    5; SATA 15, 70
Taylor, Peter (Hillsman) 1917-1994**CLC 1, 4,
    18, 37, 44, 50, 71; SSC 10**
  See also CA 13-16R; 147; CANR 9, 50; DLBY
    81, 94; INT CANR-9; MTCW 1
Taylor, Robert Lewis 1912- ....**CLC 14**
  See also CA 1-4R; CANR 3, 64; SATA 10
Tchekhov, Anton
  See Chekhov, Anton (Pavlovich)
Tchicaya, Gerald Felix 1931-1988 . **CLC 101**
  See also CA 129; 125
Tchicaya U Tam'si
  See Tchicaya, Gerald Felix
Teasdale, Sara 1884-1933 .... **TCLC 4**
  See also CA 104; 163; DLB 45; SATA 32
Tegner, Esaias 1782-1846 .... **NCLC 2**
Teilhard de Chardin, (Marie Joseph) Pierre
    1881-1955 .... **TCLC 9**
  See also CA 105
Temple, Ann
  See Mortimer, Penelope (Ruth)
Tennant, Emma (Christina) 1937-**CLC 13, 52**
  See also CA 65-68; CAAS 9; CANR 10, 38,
    59; DLB 14

Tenneshaw, S. M.
  See Silverberg, Robert
Tennyson, Alfred 1809-1892 ... **NCLC 30, 65;
    DA; DAB; DAC; DAM MST, POET; PC
    6; WLC**
  See also CDBLB 1832-1890; DLB 32
Teran, Lisa St. Aubin de .... **CLC 36**
  See also St. Aubin de Teran, Lisa
Terence 195(?)B.C.-159B.C. **CMLC 14; DC 7**
Teresa de Jesus, St. 1515-1582 .... **LC 18**
Terkel, Louis 1912-
  See Terkel, Studs
  See also CA 57-60; CANR 18, 45, 67; MTCW
    1
Terkel, Studs .... **CLC 38**
  See also Terkel, Louis
  See also AITN 1
Terry, C. V.
  See Slaughter, Frank G(ill)
Terry, Megan 1932- .... **CLC 19**
  See also CA 77-80; CABS 3; CANR 43; DLB 7
Tertullian c. 155-c. 245 .... **CMLC 29**
Tertz, Abram
  See Sinyavsky, Andrei (Donatevich)
Tesich, Steve 1943(?)-1996 .... **CLC 40, 69**
  See also CA 105; 152; DLBY 83
Teternikov, Fyodor Kuzmich 1863-1927
  See Sologub, Fyodor
  See also CA 104
Tevis, Walter 1928-1984 .... **CLC 42**
  See also CA 113
Tey, Josephine .... **TCLC 14**
  See also Mackintosh, Elizabeth
  See also DLB 77
Thackeray, William Makepeace 1811-1863
    **NCLC 5, 14, 22, 43; DA; DAB; DAC; DAM
    MST, NOV; WLC**
  See also CDBLB 1832-1890; DLB 21, 55, 159,
    163; SATA 23
Thakura, Ravindranatha
  See Tagore, Rabindranath
Tharoor, Shashi 1956- .... **CLC 70**
  See also CA 141
Thelwell, Michael Miles 1939- .... **CLC 22**
  See also BW 2; CA 101
Theobald, Lewis, Jr.
  See Lovecraft. H(oward) P(hillips)
Theodorescu, Ion N. 1880-1967
  See Arghezi, Tudor
  See also CA 116
Theriault, Yves 1915-1983 .... **CLC 79; DAC;
    DAM MST**
  See also CA 102; DLB 88
Theroux, Alexander (Louis) 1939-**CLC 2, 25**
  See also CA 85-88; CANR 20, 63
Theroux, Paul (Edward) 1941- **CLC 5, 8, 11,
    15, 28, 46; DAM POP**
  See also BEST 89:4; CA 33-36R; CANR 20,
    45; DLB 2; MTCW 1; SATA 44
Thesen, Sharon 1946-........................ **CLC 56**
  See also CA 163
Thevenin, Denis
  See Duhamel, Georges
Thibault, Jacques Anatole Francois 1844-1924
  See France. Anatole
  See also CA 106; 127; DAM NOV; MTCW 1
Thiele, Colin (Milton) 1920-............. **CLC 17**
  See also CA 29-32R; CANR 12, 28, 53; CLR
    27; MAICYA; SAAS 2; SATA 14, 72
Thomas, Audrey (Callahan) 1935-**CLC 7, 13,
    37, 107; SSC 20**
  See also AITN 2; CA 21-24R; CAAS 19; CANR
    36, 58; DLB 60; MTCW 1

Thomas, D(onald) M(ichael) 1935- . **CLC 13, 22, 31**
See also CA 61-64; CAAS 11; CANR 17. 45; CDBLB 1960 to Present; DLB 40; INT CANR-17; MTCW 1

Thomas, Dylan (Marlais) 1914-1953 **TCLC 1, 8, 45; DA; DAB; DAC; DAM DRAM, MST, POET; PC 2; SSC 3; WLC**
See also CA 104; 120; CANR 65; CDBLB 1945-1960; DLB 13, 20, 139; MTCW 1; SATA 60

Thomas, (Philip) Edward 1878-1917 . **T C L C 10; DAM POET**
See also CA 106; 153; DLB 19

Thomas, Joyce Carol 1938- .... **CLC 35**
See also AAYA 12; BW 2; CA 113; 116; CANR 48; CLR 19; DLB 33; INT 116; JRDA; MAICYA; MTCW 1; SAAS 7; SATA 40, 78

Thomas, Lewis 1913-1993 .... **CLC 35**
See also CA 85-88; 143; CANR 38, 60; MTCW 1

Thomas, Paul
See Mann, (Paul) Thomas

Thomas, Piri 1928- .... **CLC 17**
See also CA 73-76; HW

Thomas, R(onald) S(tuart) 1913- **CLC 6, 13, 48; DAB; DAM POET**
See also CA 89-92; CAAS 4; CANR 30; CDBLB 1960 to Present; DLB 27; MTCW 1

Thomas, Ross (Elmore) 1926-1995 .. **CLC 39**
See also CA 33-36R; 150; CANR 22, 63

Thompson, Francis Clegg
See Mencken, H(enry) L(ouis)

Thompson, Francis Joseph 1859-1907 **TCLC 4**
See also CA 104; CDBLB 1890-1914; DLB 19

Thompson, Hunter S(tockton) 1939- . **CLC 9, 17, 40, 104; DAM POP**
See also BEST 89:1; CA 17-20R; CANR 23, 46; DLB 185; MTCW 1

Thompson, James Myers
See Thompson, Jim (Myers)

Thompson, Jim (Myers) 1906-1977(?) **CLC 69**
See also CA 140

Thompson, Judith .... **CLC 39**

Thomson, James 1700-1748 .... **LC 16, 29, 40; DAM POET**
See also DLB 95

Thomson, James 1834-1882 **NCLC 18; DAM POET**
See also DLB 35

Thoreau, Henry David 1817-1862 **NCLC 7, 21, 61; DA; DAB; DAC; DAM MST; WLC**
See also CDALB 1640-1865; DLB 1

Thornton, Hall
See Silverberg, Robert

Thucydides c. 455B.C.-399B.C. ...... **CMLC 17**
See also DLB 176

Thurber, James (Grover) 1894-1961 . **CLC 5, 11, 25; DA; DAB; DAC; DAM DRAM, MST, NOV; SSC 1**
See also CA 73-76; CANR 17, 39; CDALB 1929-1941; DLB 4, 11, 22, 102; MAICYA; MTCW 1; SATA 13

Thurman, Wallace (Henry) 1902-1934 **T C L C 6; BLC 3; DAM MULT**
See also BW 1; CA 104; 124; DLB 51

Ticheburn, Cheviot
See Ainsworth, William Harrison

Tieck, (Johann) Ludwig 1773-1853 **NCLC 5, 46; SSC 31**
See also DLB 90

Tiger, Derry
See Ellison, Harlan (Jay)

Tilghman, Christopher 1948(?)- .... **CLC 65**
See also CA 159

Tillinghast, Richard (Williford) 1940- **CLC 29**
See also CA 29-32R; CAAS 23; CANR 26, 51

Timrod, Henry 1828-1867 .... **NCLC 25**
See also DLB 3

Tindall, Gillian (Elizabeth) 1938- .... **CLC 7**
See also CA 21-24R; CANR 11, 65

Tiptree, James, Jr. .... **CLC 48, 50**
See also Sheldon, Alice Hastings Bradley
See also DLB 8

Titmarsh, Michael Angelo
See Thackeray, William Makepeace

Tocqueville, Alexis (Charles Henri Maurice Clerel Comte) 1805-1859 ...**NCLC 7, 63**

Tolkien, J(ohn) R(onald) R(euel) 1892-1973 **CLC 1, 2, 3, 8, 12, 38; DA; DAB; DAC; DAM MST, NOV, POP; WLC**
See also AAYA 10; AITN 1; CA 17-18; 45-48; CANR 36; CAP 2; CDBLB 1914-1945; DLB 15, 160; JRDA; MAICYA; MTCW 1; SATA 2, 32, 100; SATA-Obit 24

Toller, Ernst 1893-1939 .... **TCLC 10**
See also CA 107; DLB 124

Tolson, M. B.
See Tolson, Melvin B(eaunorus)

Tolson, Melvin B(eaunorus) 1898(?)-1966 **CLC 36, 105; BLC 3; DAM MULT, POET**
See also BW 1; CA 124; 89-92; DLB 48, 76

Tolstoi, Aleksei Nikolaevich
See Tolstoy, Alexey Nikolaevich

Tolstoy, Alexey Nikolaevich 1882-1945 **T C L C 18**
See also CA 107; 158

Tolstoy, Count Leo
See Tolstoy, Leo (Nikolaevich)

Tolstoy, Leo (Nikolaevich) 1828-1910 **TCLC 4, 11, 17, 28, 44, 79; DA; DAB; DAC; DAM MST, NOV; SSC 9, 30; WLC**
See also CA 104; 123; SATA 26

Tomasi di Lampedusa, Giuseppe 1896-1957
See Lampedusa, Giuseppe (Tomasi) di
See also CA 111

Tomlin, Lily ....**CLC 17**
See also Tomlin, Mary Jean

Tomlin, Mary Jean 1939(?)-
See Tomlin, Lily
See also CA 117

Tomlinson, (Alfred) Charles 1927- **CLC 2, 4, 6, 13, 45; DAM POET; PC 17**
See also CA 5-8R; CANR 33; DLB 40

Tomlinson, H(enry) M(ajor) 1873-1958 **TCLC 71**
See also CA 118; 161; DLB 36, 100, 195

Tonson, Jacob
See Bennett, (Enoch) Arnold

Toole, John Kennedy 1937-1969 **CLC 19, 64**
See also CA 104; DLBY 81

Toomer, Jean 1894-1967 **CLC 1, 4, 13, 22; BLC 3; DAM MULT; PC 7; SSC 1; WLCS**
See also BW 1; CA 85-88; CDALB 1917-1929; DLB 45, 51; MTCW 1

Torley, Luke
See Blish, James (Benjamin)

Tornimparte, Alessandra
See Ginzburg, Natalia

Torre, Raoul della
See Mencken, H(enry) L(ouis)

Torrey, E(dwin) Fuller 1937- .... **CLC 34**
See also CA 119; CANR 71

Torsvan, Ben Traven
See Traven, B.

Torsvan, Benno Traven

See Traven, B.

Torsvan, Berick Traven
See Traven, B.

Torsvan, Berwick Traven
See Traven, B.

Torsvan, Bruno Traven
See Traven, B.

Torsvan, Traven
See Traven, B.

Tournier, Michel (Edouard) 1924- **CLC 6, 23, 36, 95**
See also CA 49-52; CANR 3, 36; DLB 83; MTCW 1; SATA 23

Tournimparte, Alessandra
See Ginzburg, Natalia

Towers, Ivar
See Kornbluth, C(yril) M.

Towne, Robert (Burton) 1936(?)- .... **CLC 87**
See also CA 108; DLB 44

Townsend, Sue .... **CLC 61**
See also Townsend, Susan Elaine
See also SATA 55, 93; SATA-Brief 48

Townsend, Susan Elaine 1946-
See Townsend, Sue
See also CA 119; 127; CANR 65; DAB; DAC; DAM MST

Townshend, Peter (Dennis Blandford) 1945- **CLC 17, 42**
See also CA 107

Tozzi, Federigo 1883-1920 .... **TCLC 31**
See also CA 160

Traill, Catharine Parr 1802-1899 .. **NCLC 31**
See also DLB 99

Trakl, Georg 1887-1914 .... **TCLC 5; PC 20**
See also CA 104; 165

Transtroemer, Tomas (Goesta) 1931- **CLC 52, 65; DAM POET**
See also CA 117; 129; CAAS 17

Transtromer, Tomas Gosta
See Transtroemer, Tomas (Goesta)

Traven, B. (?)-1969 .... **CLC 8, 11**
See also CA 19-20; 25-28R; CAP 2; DLB 9, 56; MTCW 1

Treitel, Jonathan 1959- .... **CLC 70**

Tremain, Rose 1943- .... **CLC 42**
See also CA 97-100; CANR 44; DLB 14

Tremblay, Michel 1942- **CLC 29, 102; DAC; DAM MST**
See also CA 116; 128; DLB 60; MTCW 1

Trevanian .... **CLC 29**
See also Whitaker, Rod(ney)

Trevor, Glen
See Hilton, James

Trevor, William 1928- .. **CLC 7, 9, 14, 25, 71; SSC 21**
See also Cox, William Trevor
See also DLB 14, 139

Trifonov, Yuri (Valentinovich) 1925-1981 **CLC 45**
See also CA 126; 103; MTCW 1

Trilling, Lionel 1905-1975 ...... **CLC 9, 11, 24**
See also CA 9-12R; 61-64; CANR 10; DLB 28, 63; INT CANR-10; MTCW 1

Trimball, W. H.
See Mencken, H(enry) L(ouis)

Tristan
See Gomez de la Serna, Ramon

Tristram
See Housman, A(lfred) E(dward)

Trogdon, William (Lewis) 1939-
See Heat-Moon, William Least
See also CA 115; 119; CANR 47; INT 119

Trollope, Anthony 1815-1882 **NCLC 6, 33; DA;**

Van Druten, John (William) 1901-1957 TCLC 2
    See also CA 104; 161; DLB 10
Van Duyn, Mona (Jane) 1921- CLC 3, 7, 63; DAM POET
    See also CA 9-12R; CANR 7, 38, 60; DLB 5
Van Dyne, Edith
    See Baum, L(yman) Frank
van Itallie, Jean-Claude 1936- .... CLC 3
    See also CA 45-48; CAAS 2; CANR 1, 48; DLB 7
van Ostaijen, Paul 1896-1928 .... TCLC 33
    See also CA 163
Van Peebles, Melvin 1932- . CLC 2, 20; DAM MULT
    See also BW 2; CA 85-88; CANR 27, 67
Vansittart, Peter 1920- .... CLC 42
    See also CA 1-4R; CANR 3, 49
Van Vechten, Carl 1880-1964 .... CLC 33
    See also CA 89-92; DLB 4, 9, 51
Van Vogt, A(lfred) E(lton) 1912- .... CLC 1
    See also CA 21-24R; CANR 28; DLB 8; SATA 14
Varda, Agnes 1928- .... CLC 16
    See also CA 116; 122
Vargas Llosa, (Jorge) Mario (Pedro) 1936- CLC 3, 6, 9, 10, 15, 31, 42, 85; DA; DAB; DAC; DAM MST, MULT, NOV; HLC
    See also CA 73-76; CANR 18, 32, 42, 67; DLB 145; HW; MTCW 1
Vasiliu, Gheorghe 1881-1957
    See Bacovia, George
    See also CA 123
Vassa, Gustavus
    See Equiano, Olaudah
Vassilikos, Vassilis 1933- .... CLC 4, 8
    See also CA 81-84
Vaughan, Henry 1621-1695 .... LC 27
    See also DLB 131
Vaughn, Stephanie .... CLC 62
Vazov, Ivan (Minchov) 1850-1921 . TCLC 25
    See also CA 121; 167; DLB 147
Veblen, Thorstein B(unde) 1857-1929 T C L C 31
    See also CA 115; 165
Vega, Lope de 1562-1635 .... LC 23
Venison, Alfred
    See Pound, Ezra (Weston Loomis)
Verdi, Marie de
    See Mencken, H(enry) L(ouis)
Verdu, Matilde
    See Cela, Camilo Jose
Verga, Giovanni (Carmelo) 1840-1922 T C L C 3; SSC 21
    See also CA 104; 123
Vergil 70B.C.-19B.C. .... CMLC 9; DA; DAB; DAC; DAM MST, POET; PC 12; WLCS
Verhaeren, Emile (Adolphe Gustave) 1855-1916 TCLC 12
    See also CA 109
Verlaine, Paul (Marie) 1844-1896 NCLC 2, 51; DAM POET; PC 2
Verne, Jules (Gabriel) 1828-1905 TCLC 6, 52
    See also AAYA 16; CA 110; 131; DLB 123; JRDA; MAICYA; SATA 21
Very, Jones 1813-1880 .... NCLC 9
    See also DLB 1
Vesaas, Tarjei 1897-1970 .... CLC 48
    See also CA 29-32R
Vialis, Gaston
    See Simenon, Georges (Jacques Christian)
Vian, Boris 1920-1959 .... TCLC 9
    See also CA 106; 164; DLB 72

Viaud, (Louis Marie) Julien 1850-1923
    See Loti, Pierre
    See also CA 107
Vicar, Henry
    See Felsen, Henry Gregor
Vicker, Angus
    See Felsen, Henry Gregor
Vidal, Gore 1925- CLC 2, 4, 6, 8, 10, 22, 33, 72; DAM NOV, POP
    See also AITN 1; BEST 90:2; CA 5-8R; CANR 13, 45, 65; DLB 6, 152; INT CANR-13; MTCW 1
Viereck, Peter (Robert Edwin) 1916- . CLC 4
    See also CA 1-4R; CANR 1, 47; DLB 5
Vigny, Alfred (Victor) de 1797-1863 NCLC 7; DAM POET
    See also DLB 119, 192
Vilakazi, Benedict Wallet 1906-1947 TCLC 37
    See also CA 168
Villa, Jose Garcia 1904-1997 .... PC 22
    See also CA 25-28R; CANR 12
Villaurrutia, Xavier 1903-1950 ...... TCLC 80
    See also HW
Villiers de l'Isle Adam, Jean Marie Mathias Philippe Auguste, Comte de 1838-1889 NCLC 3; SSC 14
    See also DLB 123
Villon, Francois 1431-1463(?) .... PC 13
Vinci, Leonardo da 1452-1519 .... LC 12
Vine, Barbara .... CLC 50
    See also Rendell, Ruth (Barbara)
    See also BEST 90:4
Vinge, Joan (Carol) D(ennison) 1948- CLC 30; SSC 24
    See also CA 93-96; CANR 72; SATA 36
Violis, G.
    See Simenon, Georges (Jacques Christian)
Virgil
    See Vergil
Visconti, Luchino 1906-1976 .... CLC 16
    See also CA 81-84; 65-68; CANR 39
Vittorini, Elio 1908-1966 .... CLC 6, 9, 14
    See also CA 133; 25-28R
Vizenor, Gerald Robert 1934- CLC 103; DAM MULT
    See also CA 13-16R; CAAS 22; CANR 5, 21, 44, 67; DLB 175; NNAL
Vizinczey, Stephen 1933- .... CLC 40
    See also CA 128; INT 128
Vliet, R(ussell) G(ordon) 1929-1984 . CLC 22
    See also CA 37-40R; 112; CANR 18
Vogau, Boris Andreyevich 1894-1937(?)
    See Pilnyak, Boris
    See also CA 123
Vogel, Paula A(nne) 1951- .... CLC 76
    See also CA 108
Voigt, Cynthia 1942- .... CLC 30
    See also AAYA 3; CA 106; CANR 18, 37, 40; CLR 13, 48; INT CANR-18; JRDA; MAICYA; SATA 48, 79; SATA-Brief 33
Voigt, Ellen Bryant 1943- .... CLC 54
    See also CA 69-72; CANR 11, 29, 55; DLB 120
Voinovich, Vladimir (Nikolaevich) 1932- CLC 10, 49
    See also CA 81-84; CAAS 12; CANR 33, 67; MTCW 1
Vollmann, William T. 1959- ... CLC 89; DAM NOV, POP
    See also CA 134; CANR 67
Voloshinov, V. N.
    See Bakhtin, Mikhail Mikhailovich
Voltaire 1694-1778 LC 14; DA; DAB; DAC; DAM DRAM, MST; SSC 12; WLC

von Daeniken, Erich 1935- .... CLC 30
    See also AITN 1; CA 37-40R; CANR 17, 44
von Daniken, Erich
    See von Daeniken, Erich
von Heidenstam, (Carl Gustaf) Verner
    See Heidenstam, (Carl Gustaf) Verner von
von Heyse, Paul (Johann Ludwig)
    See Heyse, Paul (Johann Ludwig von)
von Hofmannsthal, Hugo
    See Hofmannsthal, Hugo von
von Horvath, Odon
    See Horvath, Oedoen von
von Horvath, Oedoen
    See Horvath, Oedoen von
von Liliencron, (Friedrich Adolf Axel) Detlev
    See Liliencron, (Friedrich Adolf Axel) Detlev von
Vonnegut, Kurt, Jr. 1922- CLC 1, 2, 3, 4, 5, 8, 12, 22, 40, 60, 111; DA; DAB; DAC; DAM MST, NOV, POP; SSC 8; WLC
    See also AAYA 6; AITN 1; BEST 90:4; CA 1-4R; CANR 1, 25, 49; CDALB 1968-1988; DLB 2, 8, 152; DLBD 3; DLBY 80; MTCW 1
Von Rachen, Kurt
    See Hubbard, L(afayette) Ron(ald)
von Rezzori (d'Arezzo), Gregor
    See Rezzori (d'Arezzo), Gregor von
von Sternberg, Josef
    See Sternberg, Josef von
Vorster, Gordon 1924- .... CLC 34
    See also CA 133
Vosce, Trudie
    See Ozick, Cynthia
Voznesensky, Andrei (Andreievich) 1933- CLC 1, 15, 57; DAM POET
    See also CA 89-92; CANR 37; MTCW 1
Waddington, Miriam 1917- .... CLC 28
    See also CA 21-24R; CANR 12, 30; DLB 68
Wagman, Fredrica 1937- .... CLC 7
    See also CA 97-100; INT 97-100
Wagner, Linda W.
    See Wagner-Martin, Linda (C.)
Wagner, Linda Welshimer
    See Wagner-Martin, Linda (C.)
Wagner, Richard 1813-1883 .... NCLC 9
    See also DLB 129
Wagner-Martin, Linda (C.) 1936- .... CLC 50
    See also CA 159
Wagoner, David (Russell) 1926- CLC 3, 5, 15
    See also CA 1-4R; CAAS 3; CANR 2, 71; DLB 5; SATA 14
Wah, Fred(erick James) 1939- .... CLC 44
    See also CA 107; 141; DLB 60
Wahloo, Per 1926-1975 .... CLC 7
    See also CA 61-64
Wahloo, Peter
    See Wahloo, Per
Wain, John (Barrington) 1925-1994 . CLC 2, 11, 15, 46
    See also CA 5-8R; 145; CAAS 4; CANR 23, 54; CDBLB 1960 to Present; DLB 15, 27, 139, 155; MTCW 1
Wajda, Andrzej 1926- .... CLC 16
    See also CA 102
Wakefield, Dan 1932- .... CLC 7
    See also CA 21-24R; CAAS 7
Wakoski, Diane 1937- . CLC 2, 4, 7, 9, 11, 40; DAM POET; PC 15
    See also CA 13-16R; CAAS 1; CANR 9, 60; DLB 5; INT CANR-9
Wakoski-Sherbell, Diane
    See Wakoski, Diane

Literary Criticism Series
Cumulative Topic Index

This index lists all topic entries in Gale's *Classical and Medieval Literature Criticism, Contemporary Literary Criticism, Literature Criticism from 1400 to 1800, Nineteenth-Century Literature Criticism,* and *Twentieth-Century Literary Criticism.*

Topic Index

Contemporary Literary Criticism
Cumulative Nationality Index

Nationality Index

Nationality Index

Nationality Index

Nationality Index

CLC-115 Title Index

Title Index